CRIME AND CRIMINOLOGY

CRIME AND CRIMINOLOGY

THIRTEENTH EDITION

SUE TITUS REID, JD, PhD

FLORIDA STATE UNIVERSITY

*To Steve,
With my appreciation
for your kindness and
courtesy — Sue July 2011*

New York   Oxford

OXFORD UNIVERSITY PRESS

Oxford University Press, Inc., publishes works that further Oxford University's objective of excellence in research, scholarship, and education.

Oxford New York
Auckland   Cape Town   Dar es Salaam   Hong Kong   Karachi
Kuala Lumpur   Madrid   Melbourne   Mexico City   Nairobi
New Delhi   Shanghai   Taipei   Toronto

With offices in
Argentina   Austria   Brazil   Chile   Czech Republic   France   Greece
Guatemala   Hungary   Italy   Japan   Poland   Portugal   Singapore
South Korea   Switzerland   Thailand   Turkey   Ukraine   Vietnam

For titles covered by Section 112 of the U.S. Higher Education Opportunity
Act, please visit www.oup.com/us.he for the latest information about
pricing and alternate formats.

Published by Oxford University Press, Inc.
198 Madison Avenue, New York, New York 10016
http://www.oup.com

Library of Congress Cataloging-in-Publication Data
Reid, Sue Titus.
Crime and criminology / by Sue Titus Reid.—13th ed.
    p. cm.
Includes bibliographical references and index.
ISBN 978-0-19-978318-2
1. Criminology.   2. Crime—United States.   3. Criminal justice,
Administration of—United States.
I. Title.
HV6025.R515 2012
364.973—dc22   2011003692

9 8 7 6 5 4 3 2 1

Printed in the United States of America
on acid-free paper

To Gay Blosser, my cousin and dear friend.
And to the memory of our mothers and grandmother.

About the Author

Sue Titus Reid, a professor in the Reubin O'Donovan Askew School of Public Administration and Policy at Florida State University, Tallahassee, has taught law students, graduate students, and undergraduate students in many states. She has served on the board of the Midwest Sociological Society and the executive staff of the American Sociological Association. She has served as chairperson, associate dean, and dean. In 1985, she held the prestigious George Beto Chair in criminal justice at the Criminal Justice Center, Sam Houston State University, Huntsville, Texas. In 1976–1977, she served as a visiting distinguished professor at the University of Tulsa College of Law and then joined the faculty as a professor and later as an associate dean. In 1979, Dr. Reid received the Distinguished Alumna Award from Texas Woman's University, and in 2000, she received a university award "for excellence in teaching" at Florida State University.

Dr. Reid's formal training in criminology began in graduate school, but her interest in the field dates back to her early childhood. She was strongly influenced in her career by her father, who was born in the jail where his father, the undersheriff of a small east Texas county, lived with his family. As a child, she helped her father in his grocery store and was quite disturbed when, on three separate occasions, he was victimized by criminals, one an armed robber. In each instance, the offender took all the cash and checks; no one was ever apprehended.

Dr. Reid graduated with honors from Texas Woman's University in 1960 and received graduate degrees in sociology (MA in 1962 and PhD in 1965) from the University of Missouri–Columbia. In 1972, she graduated with distinction from the University of Iowa College of Law. She was admitted to the Iowa Bar that year and later to the District of Columbia Court of Appeals. She has also been admitted to practice before the U.S. Supreme Court.

Dr. Reid is unique among authors in the criminal justice field because of her distinguished qualifications in both law and the social sciences. She launched her text publishing career with *Crime and Criminology* in 1976, and that text, now in its thirteenth edition, has been widely adopted throughout the United States and in foreign countries. Dr. Reid's other titles include *The Correctional System: An Introduction; Criminal Law: The Essentials; Criminal Law*, 8th edition; and *Criminal Justice*, 8th edition. She has contributed articles to the *Encyclopedia of Crime and Justice* and the *Encyclopedia of American Prisons*, as well as to other books, in addition to publishing scholarly articles in both law and sociology.

Dr. Reid's contributions to her profession have been widely recognized nationally and abroad. In 1982, the American Society of Criminology elected her a fellow "for outstanding contributions to the field of Criminology." Other national honors include the following: Who's Who Among Women; Who's Who in America; Who's Who in American Education; Who's Who in Criminal Law; 2,000 Notable Women (Hall of Fame for Outstanding Contributions to Criminal Law, 1990); Personalities of America; and Most Admired Woman of the Decade, 1992.

Her international honors include numerous recognitions from the International Biographical Centre (IBC), Cambridge, England, including the prestigious International Order of Merit. The IBC named Dr. Reid an inaugural member as one of the Top 100 Educators—2008, an honor limited by the IBC "to those individuals who, in our belief, have made a significant enough contribution in their field to engender influence on a local, national or international basis." Among the other international honors received by Dr. Reid are the following: International Woman of the Year, 1991–1992; International Who's Who of Intellectuals; International Who's Who of Professionals; International Who's Who of Professional and Business Women; International Order of Merit, 1993; Who's Who in the World; International Biographical Centre, England, Marquis Who's Who in the World; and the Manchester Who's Who Among Executive and Professional Women.

Dr. Reid has traveled extensively to widen her knowledge of criminal justice systems in the United States and in other countries. In 1982, she was a member of the Eisenhower Foundation sponsored People-to-People Crime Prevention delegation to the People's Republic of China. Her international travels included a three-month study and lecture tour of 10 European countries in 1985.

In August 2010, the Commission on Physical and Mental Disabilities of the 400,000-member American Bar Association featured Dr. Reid in its monthly spotlight on lawyers and judges who, despite disabilities, have made significant contributions to the legal profession.

BRIEF CONTENTS

CONTENTS

CHAPTER 6

Sociological Theories of Criminal Behavior II: The Social-Process Approach   152

■ **Chapter Outline**   ■ **Key Terms**   ■ **Introduction**

PART IV

Criminal Justice Systems   356

CHAPTER 11

U.S. Criminal Justice Systems   358

■ Chapter Outline   ■ Key Terms   ■ Introduction

CHAPTER 12

Police   400

■ Chapter Outline   ■ Key Terms   ■ Introduction

FOCUS BOXES

PREFACE

As a discipline, criminology is concerned with the causes of crime—the traditional emphasis of sociologists—as well as with criminal justice and correctional systems. The exploration of these areas in this text features the integration of law with pertinent social science theories and empirical studies. This integrated approach is the result of my years of teaching criminology to undergraduates, my background as a law professor and legal consultant, and my experiences as a social scientist. In teaching undergraduates, I have been impressed with their eagerness to learn how law relates to the traditional topics covered in criminology and criminal justice courses, even to the point that they enjoy reading and briefing court cases. For this reason, I have included within the text some excerpts from appellate opinions to illustrate decisions and legal thinking and to demonstrate the role of courts in criminal justice systems.

The responses to the 12 previous editions of this text confirm that students and faculty find the integration of law and social science an interesting and effective approach to the study of criminal behavior. No less important to users of earlier editions has been the text's assessment of society's response to criminal behavior. Therefore, I have retained the text's integrated approach but have made some significant revisions and numerous updates, the most important of which are detailed later in the section entitled "New to the Thirteenth Edition."

As a social scientist, I want to ensure that the text discusses the results of recent sociological research on criminal justice systems and does so in the context of sociological theory. Summaries and critiques of classic works in criminology, analyses of recent social science research, and attention to major social science theorists who have contributed significantly to the study of crime are greatly expanded in this edition, which also features the utilization of these contributions in the practical world of policy.

Features

As in the previous editions, I have included learning aids to help students comprehend the text's wealth of material.

The book has been designed not only to have visual appeal but also to better draw students into the text material. Each chapter of the thirteenth edition begins with a brief introduction, an outline, and a list of key terms—which serve as a student's road map to the chapter. As an aid to students' mastery of the vast array of legal and social science vocabulary terms, the key terms are identified in boldface within the text. They are also collected in a comprehensive glossary at the end of the text for easy reference later. Each chapter closes with a built-in study guide consisting of a chapter summary, plentiful review questions, brief essay assignments, and Internet activities.

Numerous exhibits, tables, and figures support the book's integration of social science research and law. These features provide insights and background information on current events, legal decisions, and other topics of interest; charts, graphs, and tables present the most recent crime and victimization data. Court case excerpts illustrate how legal decisions affect criminal justice systems. All legal citations have been checked to determine whether any changes were made on appeal; all statutes have been updated to the latest possible time during the production process of this text; all Internet sources were accurate as of the accession dates.

The three previous editions contained Media Focus boxes, which have been retained and updated or changed in this edition. These boxes illustrate how media treatment of a crime can distort or enhance our views of it. For example, Media Focus 2.1 contains reference to a 2010 article about a study by criminologists who obtained information from hundreds of former high-ranking police administrators, some of whom disclosed that pressures to report decreased crime rates led to data misrepresentation. But the media can also enhance our understanding of an event or issue. Media Focus 7.1, "Media Impact on Rape Prosecutions," which focuses on the rape allegations against basketball player Kobe Bryant, notes the impact that media coverage might have on the willingness of future rape victims to report the crime. Media Focus 14.1, "The Crisis in Recruiting Correctional Officers," explores the need to find ways to attract individuals to this profession.

The thirteenth edition also retains the Global Focus boxes, emphasizing the belief that a complete understanding of criminology and criminal justice systems requires knowledge of the research, policies, and laws of other countries. Thus, although a comparative analysis of all areas covered in this text is not reasonable, the text includes a Global Focus box in each chapter to illustrate one or more areas of coverage on the international front. This feature begins in Chapter 1 with Global Focus 1.1, "The Necessity and Value of Transnational Comparative Study," which emphasizes the importance of global study. Global Focus 2.1, "Violence in Japan," informs us that the United States is not the only country that has experienced school and neighborhood violence. Japan, traditionally a low-crime country, has recently confronted serious violent crimes within its schools, and this edition updates the discussion with a 2008 neighborhood shooting spree. Global Focus 3.2 includes an analysis of deterrence policies in Northern Ireland. The 2007 shooting rampage in a Finnish high school presented in Global Focus 6.1 raises the issue of a theory of criminal behavior discussed in Chapter 6: the theory of imitation. Global Focus 11.1 concentrates on the widespread existence of illegal sex trafficking throughout the world.

Appendix A contains the amendments to the U.S. Constitution for easy reference and to facilitate those who wish to read a full amendment as it is mentioned in the text. Appendix B discusses how to read a case citation. The indexes are divided by cases, names, and general subject topics.

New to the Thirteenth Edition

Significant content changes have been made in this edition. Although the text retains its 15-chapter format for ease of use in both semester- and quarter-length courses, changes have been made to the outlines within some chapters, and many new topics have been added along with current research on topics covered in previous editions. Many of these changes are indicated in the following paragraphs.

■ Part I, "Introduction to the Study of Crime and Criminology," introduces the study of criminology and criminal law. Chapter 1, "Crime, Criminal Law, and Criminology," explains and analyzes the concept of crime. Its discussion of the concept of law covers the nature and purpose as well as the limits of law, looking in particular at law as a method of social control. This chapter demonstrates the text's goal of integrating social science theory and the law. To illustrate the extent to which the criminal law should cover behavior such as consensual sexual behavior between adults in private, the chapter features the U.S. Supreme Court case *Lawrence v. Texas*, which struck down the statute criminalizing sex between members of the same gender. The chapter also presents the case of the Georgia teen who was sentenced to prison for 10 years for having sex as a 17-year-old with a consensual 15-year-old. This raises the question of how extensive criminal law should be in its efforts

to protect minors. The resolution of that case is noted. The chapter also explores the current issue of whether the use of marijuana for medicinal purposes should be legal. A discussion of the role of criminology in public policy completes the chapter.

■ Chapter 2, "The Measurement of Crime and Its Impact," focuses on the compilation of crime data through official and unofficial methods, utilizing the most recent official data available, those from 2009. The chapter features charts and graphs of crime and victimization data. It expands the information on characteristics (age, race and ethnicity, and gender) of offenders and victims, with particular attention to juvenile crime and disproportionate minority contacts in criminal justice systems. This chapter features a new section on victims with disabilities.

■ Part II, "Explanations of Criminal Behavior," contains four theory chapters. Chapter 3, "Early Explanations of Criminal Behavior and Their Modern Counterparts," begins with a section on the historical background of punishment and criminal law and proceeds to an examination of the contributions of Cesare Beccaria, Jeremy Bentham, and others in the classical school. That school is contrasted with the neoclassical and positivist schools of thought, followed by a discussion of punishment philosophies. The sections on rehabilitation and deterrence were significantly modified and updated, and the section on deterrence now features policy implications. Chapter 3, like the following three theory chapters, contains exhibits that present features or summarize the contributions of the major criminological theorists discussed in that chapter.

■ Chapter 4, "Biological and Psychological Theories of Criminal Behavior," recognizes the increasing attention given to factors such as chemical imbalance, substance abuse, psychological problems, and intelligence because they may be related to criminal behavior, especially violence. A complete discussion of criminology cannot ignore these issues even though they remain controversial. The exhibit on the Human Genome Project was updated with critical information through June 2010. More research has been added on families, twins, adoptees, and the function of the brain in explaining criminal behavior. Mental illness, a critical topic in criminal justice systems today, is discussed in several chapters; this chapter sets the stage for that attention. Figure 4.1 graphs the adolescent brain and development, which is presented in connection with the 2010 U.S. Supreme Court decision holding that life without parole for a crime other than homicide committed as a juvenile is cruel and unusual punishment.

■ Part II concludes with two chapters on sociological explanations of criminal behavior. Chapter 5, "Sociological Theories of Criminal Behavior I: The Social-Structural Approach," focuses on the relationship between social structure and criminal behavior. The chapter notes the recent crimes of juveniles, such as the killing of Elizabeth Kay Olten, 9, allegedly by her 15-year-old neighbor and the two murders committed by 9-year-old Christian Romero. The chapter adds several new topics, such as Cullen's social support theory; race and ethnicity and gangs; and in the discussion of female crime, a new focus includes sections on liberation theory, opportunity theory, economic marginalization hypothesis, power-control theory, and a critique of women's liberation theory. A new exhibit (5.5) focuses on school crime and safety.

- Chapter 6, "Sociological Theories of Criminal Behavior II: The Social-Process Approach," focuses on the processes by which criminal behavior may be acquired. The chapter contains significant additions to learning theory and control theory. It cites new research on the use of social control theory to predict outcomes in other areas of the criminal justice system (e.g., lower self-control persons are more likely to be convicted) and new research on the link between opportunity theory and low self-control with delinquency. The discussion of life-course theory is updated as are other integrated theories. Significant additions were made to the policy discussion.

- Part III, "Types of Crime," begins with Chapter 7, "Violent Crimes," which introduces the study of criminology typologies. This chapter contains the latest available official data on both offenders and victims. There is an updated and enhanced discussion of statutory rape, elder abuse, and domestic violence, including an extended presentation of intimate partner violence (IPV). Its expanded exploration of hate crime notes the application of social disorganization theory to this crime and discusses a bill passed by the House of Representatives in 2007 adding sexual orientation and gender identity to the federal hate crime statute. Data on stalking are updated. The section on terrorism includes the Christmas Eve 2009 attempt to blow up an airplane. The Elder Justice Act, which is part of the 2010 health care reform statute, is noted. A section on kidnapping features coverage of victims such as Jaycee Lee Dugard, Elizabeth Smart, Ben Ownby, and Shawn Hornbeck. Discussions on pornography are updated with legal cases and social science research. The explanation of the PROTECT Act notes the 2008 *Williams* case, in which the U.S. Supreme Court upheld the act. Chapter 7's presentation on gun control and the 2007 decision of *Parker v. District of Columbia* are enhanced with a discussion of the holding and implications of the June 2010 gun control decision by the U.S. Supreme Court, *McDonald v. Chicago*.

- Chapter 8, "Property Crimes," includes expanded and updated information on the four serious property crimes—burglary, larceny-theft, motor vehicle theft, and arson—as well as some property crimes considered lesser offenses, such as check and credit card fraud. Increased coverage of identity theft, one of the fastest-growing property crimes, adds the Identity Theft Enforcement and Restitution Act (ITERA) of 2008, which targets spam, phishing, and identity theft. The discussion of computer crimes is updated and includes the 2004 CAN-SPAM Act regarding the placing of sexually explicit material on the Internet. The first conviction under this act is noted; the information on computer hackers is updated through 2010. Cybercrimes are detailed (noting that we now have a cybercrime czar!), and bully crimes are featured, including the prosecution of Lori Drew, who posed as a boy and posted false and cruel information on the Internet aimed at a young girl who subsequently committed suicide. The chapter's final section on professional and career criminals is highlighted with a discussion of recent U.S. Supreme Court cases.

- Chapter 9, "Business- and Government-Related Crimes," features the U.S. Department of Justice's (DOJ) strategic plan for 2007–2012, which shows that combating corporate crime is much lower on the DOJ's list of priorities than was previously the case. This reflects the current focus of most government agencies on combating terrorism, now the department's top priority. This chapter contains the cases of numerous offenders, all of which have been updated concerning their trials and sentences. New information on health care fraud, another rapidly growing crime, is included. This chapter presents updated examples (Congressman William Jefferson; Enron's Jeffrey Skilling, and the 2010 U.S. Supreme Court case involving him) and adds new ones (Bernie Madoff and his former employees; Mickey Sherman, a lawyer who pleaded guilty to income tax evasion; Joran van der Sloot, from Aruba, charged with extortion in the Natalee Holloway case and murder in a Peruvian case). This chapter includes much more information on Medicare fraud.

- Chapter 9's section on workplace violations features a discussion of the federal OSHA statute and recent California prosecutions as well as the criminal convictions and prison terms of the Derderian brothers due to their role in the Rhode Island nightclub fire in 2003. The June 2010 U.S. Supreme Court decision concerning the constitutionality of the Sarbanes-Oxley Act (SOX) is presented. A new section on mortgage fraud is included. Finally, the chapter raises the issue of whether BP could be criminally prosecuted for the Gulf oil spill of 2010.

- Chapter 10, "Drug Abuse, Drug Trafficking, and Organized Crime," notes the latest available data on substance abuse, including the effects on users of such drugs as Ecstasy and marijuana. Fetal abuse caused by pregnant women ingesting illegal drugs has been updated with a 2010 Kentucky case by the U.S. Supreme Court, *Cochran v. Commonwealth*. All data, for example, the $414 billion spent annually for illegal drug abuse, are updated. The National Drug Control Policy's 2011 budget is noted along with the current administration's position on drug control. The chapter contains a new section on the decriminalization of marijuana for personal use and the latest on medical marijuana.

- Chapter 10 also gives attention to the legal implications of drug abuse. Sentencing practices that are alleged to discriminate against minorities are introduced; they are discussed in more detail in Chapter 13. State approaches to drug abuse include the recent changes in New York's Rockefeller laws, the most stringent drug laws in the nation. Treatment rather than punishment of nonviolent drug abusers is considered along with drug courts and drug testing. Information on drug trafficking is updated and features Mexican cartels operating in the United States. The final focus of Chapter 10 is organized crime, featuring the history of the subject as well as a look at some of the modern players. The infiltration of organized crime into legitimate businesses such as health care, food, construction, and garbage carting is updated along with attempts to control organized crime.

- Part IV, "Criminal Justice Systems," includes three chapters. The outline of Chapter 11, "U.S. Criminal Justice Systems," contains an overview of the processes of the adversary systems characteristic of the United States. Exhibit 11.1, on wrongful convictions, is updated with 2010 examples. All of the stages in U.S. criminal justice systems are listed and briefly explained.

- The chapter focuses on selected constitutional rights of defendants. It covers search and seizure of vehicles, homes, and persons, the right not to testify against oneself, the right to counsel, and the right to trial by jury. All of these involve significant legal cases, including the following: *United States v. Grubbs* (upholding anticipatory search warrants); *Brendlin v. California* (passengers have the same rights as drivers to challenge a vehicle stop); *Hudson v. Michigan* (police are permitted to violate the knock-and-announce rule and to execute a search warrant in a home—for drugs and guns); *Yarborough v. Alvarado* (applied *Miranda* decision to juveniles); *Georgia v. Randolph* (search of a home without a warrant is invalid if one present party does not consent); *United States v. Gonzalez-Lopez* (right to counsel involves the right to one's choice of retained counsel); and *Uttecht v. Brown* (appellate courts must give deference to trial courts in their decisions regarding whether potential jurors can reasonably consider imposing the death penalty). Several 2009 and 2010 cases were added: *Maryland v. Shatzer* (*Miranda* warning); *Berghuis v. Thompkins* (*Miranda* warning); *Porter v. McCollum* (death penalty and right to counsel); *Bobby v. van Hook* (death penalty and counsel); *Montejo v. Louisiana* and *Florida v. Powell* (both regarding the *Miranda* warning). A new exhibit on the *Miranda* rule is available in Exhibit 11.3. A new case concerning aid to terrorists, *Holder v. Humanitarian Law Project*, is discussed. A new exhibit (11.5) presents the California Penal Code's Rights of Victims and Witnesses of Crimes.

- Chapter 12, "Police," explores the emergence of policing in Europe and the United States, contains a global focus on modern policing in England and Wales (updated in this edition), and expands the discussion of public policing to include security at U.S. borders, shopping malls, and college and university campuses. The chapter elaborates on two 2006 immigration cases as well as the Secure Fence Act of 2006. The new Arizona immigration statute and reactions to it are presented. A new case concerning deportation is noted, *Carachuri-Rosendo v. Holder*, decided in June 2010. The chapter discusses the investigation into the November 2009 shooting at Fort Hood, Texas. It gives attention to changes in the Federal Bureau of Investigation (FBI), including an exhibit on the FBI's drug policy for employees. Recent salary and other pertinent data regarding policing are provided. The updated discussion of the COPS program includes data from the 2010 budget.

- More attention is paid to campus security, with the investigation into the Virginia Tech shootings noted. There is a discussion on block grants along with significant updates on racial profiling. Controlling policing now includes the DOJ and its role in New Orleans. Information on the Los Angeles Police Department and Atlanta Police Department is updated. Significantly more material is presented on the exclusionary rule, including the 2009 U.S. Supreme Court decision in *Herring v. United States*. The section on private security contains information on private forces hired by the U.S. government to protect its employees, especially in Iraq. The section focuses on the largest of these contractors, Blackwater, including its renaming. Police intervention in domestic violence cases is expanded. Finally, the chapter notes the changes in policing necessitated by modern terrorism and the need for intelligence led policing (ILP).

- Chapter 13, "Court Systems," provides an overview of the criminal justice processes that occur in the courts from pretrial to posttrial. It includes coverage of specialized courts: juvenile, domestic violence, drug, and mental health courts (new research is discussed in Exhibit 13.4). The section on the role of lawyers includes the actions of Mike Nifong, the prosecutor in the Duke University case involving false rape allegations against four lacrosse players. Much of the updating in Chapter 13 focuses on issues surrounding the sentencing process. An important feature in this edition is Exhibit 13.2, which excerpts the U.S. Supreme Court case decided in May 2010, *Graham v. Florida*, holding that life without parole for a crime other than murder committed by one who was a juvenile at the time constitutes cruel and unusual punishment. Indigent defense systems are covered in detail, citing current cases in which appellants are challenging their convictions based on allegations of inadequate defense counsel.

- The long discourse over the 100-to-1, crack to powder cocaine sentencing issue is noted in the discussion of the Fair Sentencing Act of 2010, which was signed by President Barack Obama on 3 August 2010 and took effect 1 November 2010. The chapter notes two important cases the U.S. Supreme Court will hear in its 2010–2011 term. Both concern the death penalty. The section on the death penalty is enlarged and updated. The federal sentencing guidelines, which have generated considerable controversy, are seen in the new light of two 2007 cases combined for decision by the U.S. Supreme Court: *Gall v. United States* and *Kimbrough v. United States*. The chapter presents excerpts from *Kimbrough*. Finally, Chapter 13 contains additional coverage on the impact of gender, race, and ethnicity in sentencing decisions.

- Part V, "Social Reaction to Crime: Corrections," consists of two chapters. Chapter 14, "The Confinement of Offenders," includes a brief historical account of the emergence of prisons and jails for punishment, discusses U.S. contributions to this movement, and distinguishes among community corrections, jails, and prisons. Jail and prison overcrowding is one focus of this chapter; the review analyzes the attempted solutions to this serious problem. All data are as recent as available. The discussion of prisons includes four topics. The first distinguishes prison security levels. The second contains a focus on supermax prisons, with an analysis of the reasons for these institutions and a critique of them. The recent U.S. Supreme Court decision, *Austin v. Wilkinson*, is included. Federal and state prisons are distinguished, followed by an analysis of private jails and prisons. The chapter contains more information on mentally challenged inmates in prisons and jails as well as new studies of the particular needs of elderly and physically challenged inmates. The issue of juveniles in prison and jails includes a discussion of the rehabilitation philosophy and public support for it.

- The prison problems in California are detailed, complete with an introduction to the federal monitorship and its implications. The case of *Coleman v. California* is discussed. The chapter also notes that some prisons, for example, in New York, have been closed. The chapter's focus is on the changes necessitated by severe budget cuts in many states. Considerable attention is given to inmate parents and the problems faced by their children, with the citation of new programs, including one for dads and their children. Substance abuse and other forms of treatment programs provided for inmates, both juvenile and adults, are considered. Chapter 14 presents more material on the problems prisons face with regard to elderly inmates. Prison violence is highlighted with prison rape data released in June 2010, a 2009 riot in California, and 2009 escapes from Texas prisons. The unique health issues of female inmates are explored in the context of a 2009 federal appeals court case concerning shackling pregnant women during labor. A new media focus (14.2) on jailhouse lawyers explains how competent and clever one of them was.

- Chapter 15, "Corrections in the Community," contains a discussion of the types of community correctional facilities and programs. The chapter begins with a U.S. Senate bill proposed in 2007 and reintroduced in 2010, and featured in Exhibit 15.1, which contains a statement of the purpose of the bill: The Prevention Resources for Eliminating Criminal Activity Using Tailored Interventions in Our Neighborhoods, or PRECAUTION

Act. This legislation calls for a national commission of experts to compile information regarding successful treatment and intervention programs. Exhibit 15.2 excerpts the Second Chance Act of 2007, which became law on 10 April 2008. The exhibit states the purpose of this act, which is designed to assist inmates in their reentry back into society. With the increased interest on diversion and treatment, it is logical that there is much updated information to include in a chapter on community corrections. Every topic has been updated when possible. The section on boot camps includes the latest research on their effectiveness (or lack thereof) and the lawsuits involving problems within them. Updates are also included on electronic monitoring and global positioning systems. The most recent data on probation and parole are included, and special attention is given to medical probation and medical parole. The latter is a big issue, for example, in California, with its enormous prison populations, many of whom are elderly with significantly higher medical costs than other inmates. The section entitled "Reentry: The Challenge" was significantly updated with information for preparing inmates for reentry back into society, for development programs, and for evaluating the effects of those programs. It includes a discussion on the work of Alfred Blumstein and others at Carnegie Mellon University concluding that it is possible to develop a "hazard rate" to predict the time it is reasonable to assume that an ex-offender will not reoffend.

- Megan's Law, which requires the registration of sex offenders released into the community, continues to attract widespread attention and is viewed historically and in light of recent statutory and judicial changes. California's and Florida's efforts to enact even stricter sex offender registration laws are noted. Critics of such legislation, such as Human Rights Watch, are considered. The June 2010 U.S. Supreme Court decision in *Carr v. United States* is presented as is the Court's opinion *United States v. Comstock*, a May 2010 decision concerning the constitutionality of sex offender civil commitment provisions. The Keeping the Internet Devoid of Sexual Predators (KIDS) Act, a bill noted in the previous edition of this text, became law in 2008 and is discussed. A commission report criticizing the California sex registration system is highlighted. The failure of that state's system is illustrated by the case of Jaycee Dugard, kidnapped and held captive for 18 years, allegedly by a sex offender.

- Chapter 15 closes the text with a discussion of the future of corrections. This analysis includes such topics as an evaluation of community corrections, juvenile justice, and evidence-based practices. This new edition emphasizes the importance of both theory and policy. It details the impact of state budget cuts, and it illustrates changes with two states: California and South Carolina. The latter boasts a revised criminal code; the former is under a federal monitor and in deep trouble. The proposed National Criminal Justice Commission on crime prevention is noted, along with its passage in the U.S. House of Representatives on 27 July 2010.

Supplements Package

As a full-service publisher of quality educational products, Oxford University Press does much more than just sell textbooks. The company creates and publishes an extensive array of print, video, and digital supplements for students and instructors. This edition of *Crime and Criminology* is accompanied by the following valuable supplements:

Instructor's Manual/Test Bank Chapter outlines, key terms, overviews, lecture notes, discussion questions, a complete test bank, and more.

Computerized Test Bank Easy-to-use computerized testing program for both Macintosh and Windows computers.

These supplements are provided free of charge to students and instructors. Orders of new (versus used) textbooks help us defray the cost of developing such supplements, which is substantial. Please contact your local Oxford University Press representative for more information on any of these supplements.

Acknowledgments

The writing and production of a text require the assistance and cooperation of many people. To all of them, I give my appreciation and thanks.

First, my appreciation goes to my family, who have for years supported my writing efforts. Thanks, Jill and Roger Pickett, Stephanie and Clint Pickett, John and Rhonda Santoyo, and my cousin Gay Blosser, to whom this book is dedicated. Special thanks to all the charming and entertaining conversations and experiences I shared with "the little princess," my great-niece, Cherith Pickett. The sixth birthday English tea party was special; the trip to San Diego to explore Sea World and the famous San Diego Zoo, along with the side trip to Disney Land, were highlights of your fifth year that I will always remember. And who could forget not one but two ballet recitals; you were delightful.

My job at Florida State University is a bit distant from my home in New Hampshire, and on those weekly flights, I am encouraged and supported by airline employees, many of whom have become personal friends over my numerous years of travel. Special thanks to Kimberly Haggert, manager of customer relations for Atlantic Southeast Airlines, and her replacement, Rachelle Anderton, who were always available to retrieve my much-needed bulkhead seat assignment when it disappeared into the computer after yet one more Delta Airlines schedule change, along with the

following Atlanta-based Delta Airlines employees: Jeffery P. Penzkowski, Libby and Tom Hunt, Bruce Moniz, Michele Patrick, Norm Pawloski, Stan Strong, Tara Zinsmaster, and Steve Garrett.

As always, Mike Wescott had the car warm and clean and picked me up when I returned weekly from Florida to the Portland JetPort on my way home. He and the Delta employees and skycaps at Portland as well as those in Tallahassee, Florida, eased the travel burdens when I most needed help. Even the TSA agents got into the help act from time to time, lifting the heavy bags onto the conveyor belt for me.

John Kraniou, JD and a PhD candidate in the Askew School of Public Administration and Policy at Florida State University, was my teaching assistant while I was on medical leave and my research assistant during the rest of the year. Thanks, John, for your sense of humor, your sense of detail, and your hard work. My thanks also to Dr. Robert Eger, Professor and PhD Director of the Askew School, for your support, especially in assigning John to work with me.

Three of my colleagues and friends who have supported this text for a combination of over almost 100 years are Professors H. H. A. Cooper, JD, David Fabianic, PhD, and Marlyn Mather, PhD. You have all always been there, encouraging me in my teaching and writing experiences, and to you I owe a big debt for your professional assistance and your personal friendship. The frequent email support of my college roommate, Heidi Trept van Hulst, my friend Chris Morales (whom I met on a Delta flight in 1990), my friend and former student, Delta Airlines flight attendant, Kerri L. Murray, and my high school friend who resurfaced last year, Uelaine Lengefeld, sustained me even on the most difficult days.

My New Hampshire friends assisted in many ways during my absence as well as during my brief weekends at home. To the cat nanny, Sandy Louis, Ashley and I say thanks for feeding, watering, combing, and playing with "the kid" when the writer was unable to do so. Thanks also, Sandy, for checking on the house and pouring those heavy bags of salt tablets into the water filter container!

A critical area of work on a text involves the computer, and I could not have completed this work without the expert assistance of Jerry Jacobson, who taught me that burning CDs would not activate my home's fire alarm system. Jerry, thanks for installing the new printer and security systems and answering a lot of dumb questions. Jerry, the general manager of Jackson's historic Eagle Mountain House, and his delightful staff, saved newspapers for me daily and provided delicious food and social life at Sunday brunches, where I was frequently seen proofing this manuscript. As with previous editions, Robin Reid was always willing to help by phone or email with computer issues.

The writing and production of a text revision require the expertise, hard work, and in my case, patience and understanding of the publisher's employees. To my editor and friend, Sherith Pankratz, thanks for always being there, checking on progress at your end, and providing me with encouragement and assistance on the little as well as the big issues. Her assistant, Taylor Pilkington, answered my questions quickly and efficiently when Sherith was away from the office. Prior to the publication of this book, both Sherith and Taylor moved into another division of the Oxford University Press, and they are missed. I welcome my new editor, Sarah Calabi, and look forward to many more editions with her. My copy editor, Frank Hubert, found mistakes I was certain I had avoided, and his attention to the details of fact as well as technique improved the quality of the book. Linda Sykes secured all of my photo suggestions and submitted them to me in a manner that facilitated my work on them. Keith Faivre guided this text through all of the production phases with speed, efficiency, and consistency so that I would not be overwhelmed with too much work at once. To all of you and your behind-the-scenes colleagues, I am grateful for your assistance, your professionalism, and your concern for my schedule and my limitations. You made it possible!

As always, I am grateful to my students, who are inspiring and rewarding as they show their enthusiasm for many

of the topics discussed in this text. Many of them keep in touch after they complete the course, and I delight in hearing about their studies, jobs, and personal lives.

This edition has also benefited from the suggestions of reviewers. All were anonymous to me during the review process, but now your names emerge from the publisher, and I have an opportunity to thank you for your suggestions: Tony A. Barringer, Florida Gulf Coast University; Dennis R. Brewster, Southeastern Oklahoma State University; James F. Kenny, Fairleigh Dickinson University; M. Michaux Parker, North Carolina Central University; Donald J. Shoemaker, Virginia Polytechnic Institute and State University; Katherine L. Bass, Eastern Illinois University.

Finally, my thanks to my local police chief, Karl F. Meyers, Corporal Sean Cowland, and Officer Douglas Jetti, for keeping me in contact with the "real" world.

Sue Titus Reid, JD, PhD
Professor, Askew School of Public
Administration and Policy
Florida State University

CRIME AND CRIMINOLOGY

PART ONE

Introduction to the Study of Crime and Criminology

The study of crime and criminology is a complex but fascinating venture. It should begin with an understanding of the basic concepts of crime, criminal law, and criminology, and those are the focus of the first chapter of Part I. The chapter explores the meaning of these concepts in the context of which behaviors should be covered by the criminal law and whether the discipline of criminology should focus on a broader range of behaviors.

CHAPTER **1** Crime, Criminal Law, and Criminology

CHAPTER **2** The Measurement of Crime and Its Impact

Chapter 2 concludes the introductory material with a focus on how crime is measured. It looks at the collection and analysis of crime and victimization data, the characteristics of offenders and victims, and the treatment of victims in criminal justice systems. The discussions pay close attention to gender, race and ethnicity, and age, and this edition features data on physically challenged victims. The chapter also considers research in criminology.

CHAPTER 1

Crime, Criminal Law, and Criminology

Criminal acts are often complicated, irrational, and difficult to explain. They may also involve danger to others and to law enforcement officers, who in this photo are attempting to capture a suspect, who was threatening to blow up the van, located one block from the White House in Washington, D.C. The suspect's alleged purpose was to regain the legal custody of his child in a domestic dispute.

CHAPTER OUTLINE

KEY TERMS

administrative law
case law
causation
civil law
crime
criminal law
criminology
culpability
custom
defense
felony
forfeit
intent
jurisdiction
jury nullification
legal duty
lesser included offenses
mala in se
mala prohibita
mens rea
misdemeanor
Prohibition
sanctions
social control
stare decisis
status quo
statutory law

INTRODUCTION

This first chapter provides an introduction to the study of crime and the criminal. The concept of crime is explored, followed by an analysis of the concept of law and the distinction between civil law and criminal law. Criminal law as an agent of social control is discussed in relation to which behaviors should be included within the reach of criminal law. In its final section, the chapter discusses criminology and the study of crime.

She was a beautiful, petite, bright young woman who was studying for a PhD in pharmacy. On the day in September 2009 when she was to be married, her body was found stuffed behind a basement wall in an animal research lab at Yale University. Raymond Clark III was arrested and charged with the strangulation of Annie Le in a crime that stunned her co-workers, saddened her family and friends, and captured media attention for weeks. Clark, who was held on $3 million bail, was a lab technician described as a control freak, whose motive may have been a dispute over how the mouse cages were attended.

He was only 16, an innocent bystander in a fight between rival gang members on a Chicago street. Derrion Albert was beaten to death as he walked home from school in September 2009. He was not a member of either group, just a bystander in the wrong place at the wrong time. Four youths were arrested for his slaying in a city where actress Jennifer Hudson lost three relatives to murder in October 2008.

These and other recent crimes, such as the 9/11 terrorist attacks, the 1995 bombing of the federal building in Oklahoma City, the sending of mail bombs by the Unabomber, and the shootings by teenagers in schools in several U.S. cities, have led many to ask why people engage in violent acts. The senseless and unexplainable violence of these acts is frightening and baffling. But violent crimes are not the only concerns. In addition to the traditional serious property crimes of burglary, larceny-theft, auto theft, and arson, the numerous allegations of fraud and related crimes against corporate executives and others, such as Bernard Madoff, who was a highly successful financial trader later convicted in a multibillion dollar fraud scheme, have resulted in the erosion of confidence in corporate America and the loss of billions of dollars to investors and employees.

Such crimes lead us to examine theories of crime **causation** and prevention and to question how to process offenders. Attempts to explain and control criminal behavior involve many disciplines. Although other disciplines are mentioned, this text focuses on the social sciences and their interaction with criminal law, the legal mechanism by which society reacts to crime and through which it attempts to prevent criminal behavior. But the social sciences do not tell the full story of the country's interest in crime. In fact, probably few read the scientific reports of the scholars who study criminal behavior. Rather, public attention is captured by the media, as Media Focus 1.1 notes.

The study of crime should begin with an analysis of that concept.

The Concept of Crime

The concept of **crime** formulates the basis for a study of criminal behavior. The word is difficult to explain, for not all agree on how it should be defined. This text uses the legal approach because that is the basis for permitting the state to take action against persons accused of crimes. But before we dissect the definition of the word *crime*, it is important to understand that approaches other than the legal are also important.

Social scientists argue that if we are interested in knowing why people engage in behavior that is detrimental to society, we should go beyond the legal definition of crime and include behavior that is defined as criminal but for which no arrests were made. We should include accused persons who are not prosecuted because of legal technicalities. The focus is on behavior: Why do people do what they do? This approach claims that the legal technicalities of arrest and conviction are not relevant to a study of criminal behavior.

In addition, some social scientists argue that *deviant behavior*, which is different from that of the generally held social norms but not normally covered by criminal law, should also be studied. Still others argue that criminology should explore why certain people who engage in specific acts are labeled criminal or deviant while others who engage in those same acts are not labeled.

Yale University pharmacology PhD graduate student Annie Le disappeared just days before her wedding day in September 2009. Le's body was discovered inside a wall in the building, which housed the animal research center lab where Le worked and was last seen. Raymond J. Clark III, one of the lab's technicians, was arrested and charged with murder and felony murder. Clark's trial is pending and a motive is not known, but it was suggested that it may have been a work dispute.

1.1 Crime in the Media

Television, movies, newspapers, and news magazines carry a recurrent theme of crime, especially violence. A *New York Times* article entitled "On TV, Crime Will Pay" enumerated the popular crime-focused television shows and concluded:

> New York may have many fancy addresses, but where prime-time television is concerned, the most impressive is One Police Plaza. So many New York badges glisten in the lights of the cameras these days, it might behoove the police brass to think about recruiting from the drama schools.[1]

In addition to providing entertainment by focusing on crime, the media provide an important news function in times of crisis, such as during and after the tragic terrorist acts of 11 September 2001, when hijacked planes flew into the Twin Towers of the World Trade Center, demolishing those buildings and some surrounding ones, while another plane was flown into the Pentagon in Washington, D.C. A fourth hijacked plane crashed in Pennsylvania, apparently after passengers fought with the hijackers. Presumably, the hijackers on that aircraft were headed for Washington, D.C., as well. This most severe of all terrorist attacks on American soil changed a nation and its people.

The media also play a role in relaying criminal trials and appeals to the public. Criminal trials are televised in some courts (although others, along with the U.S. Supreme Court, refuse to permit this practice). Another crime-related role assumed by the media is to present information on unsolved crimes. In some cases, this has resulted in incorrect media "convictions," such as that of handyman Richard Albert Ricci, prime suspect in the abduction of Elizabeth Smart of Salt Lake City. Some television pundits proclaimed that he was the likely perpetrator of the crime, citing circumstantial evidence to boost their claims. Ricci died in prison; subsequently, Smart was located and two persons were charged with her kidnapping: Brian D. Mitchell, who was convicted in December 2010, and his wife, Wanda Barzee, who entered a guilty plea in the fall of 2009. Although one might reasonably question the rush to judgment of lawyers who should have

known better, it is likely that the intense media coverage in the Smart case led to the success in locating her after a nine-month search.

In the case of Kobe Bryant, famed basketball star accused of raping a young woman in Colorado, some believe that the intense media publicity given to the case, including the allegations regarding the alleged victim's sexual experiences with other men before and after she had sex with Bryant (who admitted they had sex but said it was consensual), along with death threats, resulted in the alleged victim's decision that she did not wish to go forward with the prosecution. The criminal charges against Bryant were dropped; the civil lawsuit brought against him by the alleged victim was settled out of court, and the terms were not disclosed.

Research indicates that media portrayal of crimes is not always adequate and may be sensationalized. Criminologists have called on their colleagues to assume a more active role in working with the media to give more accurate pictures of crime and to direct their research "toward better understanding the connections between media, public opinion, and policy formation."[2]

In addition to concerns with media accuracy, we must consider that intense media coverage of crimes raises the issues of whether the media render it impossible for defendants to get a fair trial; actually assist well-liked defendants; or possibly even contribute to future criminal acts by providing a forum for those who seek attention, even if in a socially unapproved manner. The delicate balance between the public's right to know, the media's right to report, and the defendant's right to a fair trial must be preserved, and it is the duty of criminal justice systems to ensure that the balance remains.

---

1. "On TV, Crime Will Pay," *New York Times* (11 May 2001), p. 1B.

2. Richard Tewksbury et al., "The Media and Criminologists: Interactions and Satisfaction," *Journal of Criminal Justice Education* 17, no. 2 (October 2006): 241.

All these positions and approaches are important in the analysis of why people do what they do and why society reacts as it does. This text contains four chapters (in Part II, "Explanations of Criminal Behavior") that explore social science theories of criminal and deviant behavior, and those chapters are important to an understanding of the *why* of criminal behavior. But in U.S. criminal justice systems, only those persons who have actually been convicted of crimes are considered criminal, and thus, it is important to focus on that approach for purposes of official data.

Crime is an act defined by law. Unless the elements specified by criminal law are present and the accused has entered a guilty plea or been found guilty in a court of law, that individual is technically not a criminal. The following legal definition of *crime* serves as our reference point:

> Crime is an intentional act or omission in violation of criminal law (statutory and case law), committed without defense or justification and sanctioned by the state as a felony or misdemeanor.[1]

An Act or Omission

The first part of the definition of *crime* embodies philosophies central to U.S. legal systems. A person may not be punished for his or her thoughts; crimes must involve actions. Under U.S. legal systems, an individual cannot be punished for thinking about committing a crime if no elements are put into action toward the commission of that crime. To consider murdering a spouse but to do nothing toward the commission of that act is not a crime; hiring someone to murder a spouse is a crime.

There is one important exception to the act requirement: In some cases, a *failure to act* may be criminal, but that is true only when there is a **legal duty** to act. Moral duty does not suffice. For example, a Michigan judge dismissed murder charges against a female defendant who did not give assistance to a woman locked in a car trunk and crying for help. The victim died of dehydration. The female defendant was a passenger in the car, but there was no evidence that she was involved in (or even knew about) the crimes for which the driver was charged. The judge dismissed the charges against her because he could not find a law that required her to aid the victim "even if she knew or suspected someone was locked in the trunk."[2]

In general, we do not have affirmative duties to prevent people from being injured or killed. We may watch (and take no action) while people are brutalized by others or while a child is drowning. Unless there is a legal duty to aid, the law may not be invoked even though it would have been easy for us to prevent the injury or death in these situations. We may be moral monsters, but we have not violated the civil or criminal law. A legal duty may exist, however, if we are the parent, spouse, or other close relative or if we have assumed a duty through a contractual relationship, such as operating a licensed day care center. Legal duties may also be imposed in other special relationships.

To be criminal, acts or omissions must be voluntary, and the actor must have control over his or her actions. If a person has a heart attack while driving a car and kills another human being, he or she should not be charged with a crime if the heart attack was an involuntary act over which the person had no control. The case might be different, however, if the individual had already experienced a series of heart attacks and therefore knew it might be dangerous to drive an automobile.

The Intent Requirement and Its Exceptions

An act or the omission of an act is not sufficient to constitute a crime. Generally, the law requires **intent**, or *mens rea*—the mental element—to establish criminal **culpability**. In many cases, intent is the critical factor in determining whether an act was or was not a crime. In addition, intent may determine the *degree* of crime committed (e.g., whether a killing is first- or second-degree murder or a lesser included offense, such as manslaughter). Despite the importance of *mens rea*, historically the term has not been defined clearly or developed thoroughly.

The Texas Penal Code provides an example of a frequently used approach to defining criminal intent. Texas divides legal culpability into four mental states: intentional, knowing, reckless, and criminal negligence. Each of these mental states is defined in Exhibit 1.1. The interpretation of these four tiers of culpability has been the subject of considerable dispute. It is clear, however, that a person may be held criminally responsible for the unintended consequences of an intended act. In addition, a person may be held criminally responsible for injury or death to a victim other than the intended victim or for a more serious degree of harm than that intended. Consider the following hypotheticals.

In the first case, Jones shot at Anders with the intent of killing him; but being a bad shot, he missed Anders and killed Williams. Jones can be charged with Williams's death. In the second case, an unhappy husband wanted to scare his wife to convince her that they should move to another neighborhood. The husband hired a man to fire several shots into the air while his wife was walking the dog, but he was a bad shot and killed the woman. Even though there was no specific intent to kill the woman, both men could be charged with murder. They both plotted, and one carried out an act that a reasonable person should have known could result in serious injury or death. It is possible that the charge would be reduced, but the point is that both men could be charged with murder.

There are exceptions to the requirement of a criminal intent. In some situations, employers may be liable for acts of their employees even if the employers do not know their employees are committing the acts. For example, the president of a drug company was found guilty of violating a provision of the Pure Food and Drug Act, which requires proper labeling of drugs. He did not know that the drugs had been mislabeled by his employees, who were responsible for repackaging and labeling the drugs received from the manufacturer, but the U.S. Supreme Court upheld the conviction.[3]

Violation of the Elements of Criminal Law

To be convicted of a crime, a person must violate **criminal law**. Criminal law comes from three sources: federal and state constitutions, statutes (and local ordinances), and court decisions. Statutes enacted by state legislatures and the U.S. Congress constitute **statutory law**. In contrast, **case law** is the term applied to law that develops from judicial decisions.

Another source of criminal law is **administrative law**. State legislatures and the U.S. Congress may delegate to administrative agencies—the Federal Trade Commission,

EXHIBIT 1.1

General Requirements of Culpability

Texas Penal Code, Chapter 6 (2010)

■ **Section 6.02. Requirement of Culpability.**

(a) Except as provided in Subsection (b), a person does not commit an offense unless he intentionally, knowingly, recklessly, or with criminal negligence engages in conduct as the definition of the offense requires.

(b) If the definition of an offense does not prescribe a culpable mental state, a culpable mental state is nevertheless required unless the definition plainly dispenses with any mental element. . . .

■ **Section 6.03. Definitions of Culpable Mental States.**

(a) A person acts intentionally, or with intent, with respect to the nature of his conduct or to a result of his conduct when it is his conscious objective or desire to engage in the conduct or cause the result.

(b) A person acts knowingly, or with knowledge, with respect to the nature of his conduct or to circumstances surrounding his conduct when he is aware of the nature of his conduct or that the circumstances exist. A person acts knowingly, or with knowledge, with respect to a result of his conduct when he is aware that his conduct is reasonably certain to cause the result.

(c) A person acts recklessly, or is reckless, with respect to circumstances surrounding his conduct or the result of his conduct when he is aware of but consciously disregards a substantial and unjustifiable risk that the circumstances exist or the result will occur. The risk must be of such a nature and degree that its disregard constitutes a gross deviation from the standard of care that an ordinary person would exercise under all the circumstances as viewed from the actor's standpoint.

(d) A person acts with criminal negligence, or is criminally negligent, with respect to circumstances surrounding his conduct or the result of his conduct when he ought to be aware of a substantial and unjustifiable risk that the circumstances exist or the result will occur. The risk must be of such a nature and degree that the failure to perceive it constitutes a gross deviation from the standard of care that an ordinary person would exercise under all the circumstances as viewed from the actor's standpoint.

---

the Internal Revenue Service, public universities, human rights commissions, and others—the power to make rules, interpret those rules, and process violations. The rule-making procedures must follow specified guidelines. These rules and the decisions concerning them constitute administrative law, which is civil law, although a violation of administrative law may result in a criminal penalty if it becomes necessary to petition a criminal court to enforce the administrative decision. Even in that case, however, society normally does not look upon the individual in the same negative light as it does upon those who are convicted in criminal courts.

This text focuses on criminal law rather than **civil law** because criminal law provides the framework for the government's **jurisdiction** over crime. There is considerable overlap between criminal and civil law, but there are also important distinctions. When a criminal wrong has been committed, the state (or federal government) initiates action against the person accused of the crime. The state becomes involved because a crime is considered a serious threat to the welfare of the entire society as well as to the alleged victim.

In contrast, a noncriminal, or civil, wrong is considered a wrong against a particular individual. In such cases, the person wronged may initiate legal action against the accused. Noncriminal law refers primarily to laws (such as those governing divorce, property, or contracts) that regulate the legal rights of private parties, organizations, corporations, and so on.

Civil wrongs and crimes may be tried in different courts, although that is not always the case. Different procedural rules apply, with criminal cases involving more extensive legal safeguards because of the potentially more serious results for those found guilty of crimes. In a civil case, the party at fault may be required to pay financial damages to the injured party or told to stop engaging in specified activities, but in a criminal case, the government may impose penalties that restrict the liberty of the individual, such as a sentence to be served in a correctional facility. The government may also impose fines and numerous other conditions in criminal cases and, in some jurisdictions, the government may take the life of the convicted person.

Without Justification or Defense

Individuals are not always held responsible for acts that cause harm or injury to others; the law recognizes some extenuating circumstances. An act or omission of an act is not a crime if the individual has a legally recognized justification or **defense** for the act. For example, a person faced with the possibility of being killed might use the defense of justifiable homicide. A police officer in pursuit of an armed robbery suspect who fires at the officer may be justified in killing that suspect. People may be excused from criminal liability for inflicting serious bodily harm (or even death) on others if they are in danger of being injured by those persons, but they may use only the force necessary.

Some acts may constitute violations of both the civil and the criminal law. In this scene, New York City police are investigating a hit-and-run accident in which at least seven people were injured. In most cases, a vehicle accident that results in injury raises only civil actions for personal injuries and wrongful death or property damage, but leaving the scene of an accident that results in injury or death may also constitute a criminal act. Driving while impaired may also raise both civil and criminal actions.

An individual charged with a crime may offer evidence to defeat the criminal charge. A variety of defenses are recognized; the extent and complexity of legal defenses are beyond the scope of this text, but Chapter 4 mentions the insanity defense, one of the more publicized—although infrequently used and seldom successful—defenses.[4]

Felony or Misdemeanor

Historically, the primary distinction between a **felony** and a **misdemeanor** was that a person could be required to **forfeit** all property upon conviction of a felony but not upon conviction of a misdemeanor. In addition, during some time periods, most, if not all, felonies were capital (death penalty) offenses. Today, the two crime categories are distinguished primarily in terms of the sentences that may be imposed. Usually, a *felony* is a crime for which a person may be sentenced to a long prison term or capital punishment, while a *misdemeanor* is a less serious offense for which a short jail term (less than a year), a fine, a period of probation, or some other alternative to incarceration may be imposed. Some of these lessor penalties may also be imposed on persons convicted of felonies. In some jurisdictions, felonies and misdemeanors are tried in separate courts.

The Judge or Jury as Final Decision Maker

A *crime* is defined as an act or an omission of an act that violates criminal statutory or case law and for which the state has provided a penalty. Not all acts that meet these criteria result in convictions. In cases that are tried before a jury, jurors may refuse to return a guilty verdict even when the facts point to the defendant's guilt, a process known as **jury nullification**. In cases tried without a jury, the judge may do the same. In other cases, the defendant may be convicted of a crime by the jury, but the judge may grant the defendant's motion for acquittal because he or she does not think the evidence was sufficient to support a conviction. Alternatively, the judge may allow the conviction to stand but reduce the sentence.

The Concept of Law

A study of crime, the criminal, and criminal law should rest on an understanding of the concept of law. Law is important because it touches virtually every area of human interaction. Law is used to protect ownership, to define the parameters of private and public property, to regulate business, to raise revenue, and to provide compensation when agreements are broken. Laws define the nature of institutions, such as the family. Laws regulate marriage and divorce or dissolution, adoption, the handling of dependent and neglected children, and the inheritance of property.

Laws are designed to protect legal and political systems. Laws organize power relationships. They establish who is superordinate and who is subordinate. Laws maintain the **status quo** while permitting flexibility when times change. Laws, particularly criminal laws, are designed to preserve order as well as to protect private and public interests. Society determines that some interests are so important that a formal system of control is necessary to preserve them; therefore, laws must be enacted to give the state enforcement power. Law is a formal system that may be exercised when other forms of **social control** are not effective. A closer look at the social control function of law distinguishes it from other social control efforts.

Law as Social Control

Prior to the emergence of law, social control was achieved in less formal ways. Most people took care of their own needs and lived at a subsistence level. They grew or captured their own food and made their own clothing and housing; they had no need for exchanging goods and services. Submission to **custom** controlled most of their behavior, and laws were not necessary. Those who deviated from the norms of the group were spotted easily; the community could react with nonlegal **sanctions**. These informal sanctions, which can be more effective than laws, could include a disapproving glance, an embarrassed silence, a smile, a nod, a frown, a social invitation, or social ostracism. The threat of being banished from society (or a smaller group) can be a serious deterrent to deviant behavior. These informal methods of social control are most successful when the group is closely knit, making it relatively easy to know the norms and the general will of the group and to identify transgressors.[5]

Although there are similarities between law and other methods of social control, there are also significant differences. At least in theory, law is more specific than less formal methods of social control. In criminal law, the law defines the nature of the offense and the punishment (or range of types of punishments) to be imposed for conviction of that offense. Laws cannot define every possible situation that would constitute a violation, but in the United States, they may be declared unconstitutional if they are vague. Laws must be clear enough to give adequate notice to potential transgressors that they are in danger of violating these laws. Exhibit 1.2 provides an example of a city ordinance that was declared void for vagueness.

A second distinction between law and other forms of social control is that law arises from a more rational procedure. It is a formal enactment by a legislative body or a court that, presumably, is the product of discussion and reflection. The law is applicable to all who transgress its provisions unless there are justifications or defenses for the otherwise illegal acts. Law specifies sanctions, and only those sanctions may be applied. Law differs from other types of social control in that its sanctions are applied exclusively by organized political agencies. Physical force may be involved in enforcing the sanctions, although this is limited to reasonable action applied by an official party.

Law is characterized by regularity, but that does not mean absolute certainty. It adheres to the principle of *stare decisis*, which means to abide by or adhere to rulings in previously settled cases. Law is based on the assumption that predictability and certainty are important. Decided cases establish precedent for the future, but courts may overrule prior decisions in the light of new facts, reasoning, or changing social conditions.

Unlike other social controls, law does not reward conforming behavior; it is concerned primarily with nega-tive sanctions. Another difference between other social controls and law is that, in most cases, the legal system provides a right of appeal, whereas most other social controls do not.

The Extent of Criminal Law

We should not expect to control all social behavior by criminal law. Criminal law should provide some standards, goals, and guidelines—a statement of what conduct is so important that it must be sanctioned by the state (or federal government). It should provide some moral guidance as well, but controversy arises over the extent to which the law should be used to regulate behavior.

In determining the acts to include within criminal law, it is helpful to distinguish between acts that are criminal within themselves and those that are criminal because they are defined as such. *Mala in se* crimes are evil in themselves, such as rape, murder, robbery, arson, aggravated assault, and serious property crimes, such as larceny-theft and burglary. There is general agreement that these acts are criminal. In contrast, *mala prohibita* crimes, such as public drunkenness, are considered evil because they are forbidden.

Historically, there was little difference between *mala in se* and *mala prohibita* crimes because most primitive societies did not distinguish morality, sin, and law. Today, the situation is quite different, and many acts that were previously covered by criminal law have been removed from its reach.

The serious impact of the criminal law should lead us to question what kinds of behavior ought to be covered by its reach. For example, some people question the use of criminal law to enforce wearing helmets while riding bicycles or motorcycles or wearing seat belts and shoulder straps in automobiles. In the case of seat belts and shoulder straps, some jurisdictions permit arrest only if a moving violation occurs. But in 2001, the U.S. Supreme Court upheld the right of police to make a full custodial arrest even when a motorist is committing only a minor infraction, such as violating the seat belt requirement.[6]

This case and many others raise the question of how extensive criminal law should be. Requiring motorists to wear seat belts may be a worthwhile cause, especially now that research data show a strong correlation between the lack of seat belt use and deaths from automobile accidents among teens (compared with very few deaths of children; all states require that children be in proper restraints while cars are in motion, and many parents comply with these laws).[7] But should we use criminal law to achieve this purpose? Would civil sanctions suffice?

Criminal Law and Sex Crimes

One area in which criminal law was used historically as a form of social control is that of consensual sexual acts between adults in private. Although in recent years many

EXHIBIT 1.2

Statutes Will Be Declared Void if They Are Vague: The Case of *State v. Metzger*

[The case involves Douglas E. Metzger, who was convicted of violating a city code that provided in part, "It shall be unlawful for any person within the City of Lincoln . . . to commit any indecent, immodest or filthy act in the presence of any person, or in such a situation that persons passing might ordinarily see the same."]

"According to the evidence, Metzger lived in a garden-level apartment located in Lincoln, Nebraska. A large window in the apartment faces a parking lot which is situated on the north side of the apartment building. At about 7:45 AM on April 30, 1981, another resident of the apartment, while parking his automobile in a space directly in front of Metzger's apartment window, observed Metzger standing naked with his arms at his sides in his apartment window for a period of five seconds.

The resident testified that he saw Metzger's body from his thighs on up. The resident called the police department and two officers arrived at the apartment at about 8 AM. The officers testified that they observed Metzger standing in front of the window eating a bowl of cereal. They testified that Metzger was standing within a foot of the window and his nude body, from the mid-thigh on up, was visible. . . .

The more basic issue presented to us by this appeal is whether the ordinance, as drafted, is so vague as to be unconstitutional. We believe that it is. There is no argument that a violation of the municipal ordinance in question is a criminal act. Since the ordinance in question is criminal in nature, it is a fundamental requirement of due process of law that such criminal ordinance be reasonably clear and definite.

Moreover, a crime must be defined with sufficient definiteness and there must be ascertainable standards of guilt to inform those subject thereto as to what conduct will render them liable to punishment thereunder. The dividing line between what is lawful and unlawful cannot be left to conjecture. A citizen cannot be held to answer charges based upon penal statutes whose mandates are so uncertain that they will reasonably admit of different constructions. A criminal statute cannot rest upon an uncertain foundation. The crime and the elements constituting it must be so clearly expressed that the ordinary person can intelligently choose in advance what course it is lawful for him to pursue. Penal statutes prohibiting the doing of certain things and providing a punishment for their violation should not admit of such a double meaning that the citizen may act upon one conception of its requirements and the courts upon another. A statute which forbids the doing of an act in terms so vague that men of common intelligence must necessarily guess as to its meaning and differ as to its application violates the first essential elements of due process of law. It is not permissible to enact a law which in effect spreads an all-inclusive net for the feet of everybody upon the chance that, while the innocent will surely be entangled in its meshes, some wrongdoers may also be caught.

The ordinance in question makes it unlawful for anyone to commit any "indecent, immodest or filthy act." We know of no way in which the standards required of a criminal act can be met in those broad, general terms. There may be those few who believe persons of opposite sex holding hands in public are immodest, and certainly more who might believe that kissing in public is immodest. Such acts cannot constitute a crime. Certainly one could find many who would conclude that today's swimming attire found on many beaches or beside many pools is immodest. Yet, the fact that it is immodest does not thereby make it illegal, absent some requirement related to the health, safety, or welfare of the community. The dividing line between what is lawful and what is unlawful in terms of "indecent," "immodest," or "filthy" is simply too broad to satisfy the constitutional requirements of due process. Both lawful and unlawful acts can be embraced within such broad definitions. That cannot be permitted. One is not able to determine in advance what is lawful and what is unlawful." . . .

Boslaugh, Justice, dissenting.

"The ordinance in question prohibits indecent acts, immodest acts, *or* filthy acts in the presence of any person. . . . The exhibition of his genitals under the circumstances of this case was, clearly, an indecent act."

Source: State v. Metzger, 319 N.W.2d 459, 460–463 (Neb. 1982), citations omitted.

---

states have revised their criminal codes and decriminalized these acts, some remain on the statute books. In 2003, the U.S. Supreme Court held a Texas statute unconstitutional because it criminalized sexual behavior between same-gender persons that was permitted between heterosexual persons. As the excerpt from this case reproduced in Exhibit 1.3 notes, in so doing the Court reversed a prior decision in which it had upheld a similar statute. Despite this decision, however, some states still have statutes that criminalize some sex acts between consenting adults in private, although a constitutional challenge to these statutes will probably be successful.

In 2007, consensual sex again became an issue of concern, but this case involved juveniles. Genarlow Wilson, who engaged in consensual oral sex with another teenager, was sentenced to 10 years in prison after his conviction

EXHIBIT

1.3

The U.S. Supreme Court Rules on Same-Gender Sex:
Lawrence v. Texas[1]

"Liberty protects the person from unwarranted government intrusions into a dwelling or other private places. In our tradition the state is not omnipresent in the home. And there are other spheres of our lives and existence, outside the home, where the state should not be a dominant presence. Freedom extends beyond spatial bounds. Liberty presumes an autonomy of self that includes freedom of thought, belief, expression, and certain intimate conduct. . . .

The question before the Court is the validity of a Texas statute making it a crime for two persons of the same sex to engage in certain intimate sexual conduct.

In Houston, Texas, officers of the Harris County Police Department were dispatched to a private residence in response to a reported weapons disturbance. They entered an apartment where one of the petitioners, John Geddes Lawrence, resided. The right of the police to enter does not seem to have been questioned. The officers observed Lawrence and another man, Tyron Garner, engaging in a sexual act. The two petitioners were arrested, held in custody overnight, and charged and convicted before a Justice of the Peace.

The complaints described their crime as deviate sexual intercourse, namely anal sex, with a member of the same sex (man). . . . The petitioners exercised their right to a trial *de novo* [a new trial] in Harris County Criminal Court. They challenged the statute as a violation of the Equal Protection Clause of the Fourteenth Amendment and of a like provision of the Texas Constitution. Those contentions were rejected. The petitioners, having entered a plea of *nolo contendere*, were each fined $200 and assessed court costs of $141.25. . . .

[The constitutional challenges were rejected, and the convictions were affirmed by the Court of Appeals for the Texas Fourteenth District.]

We granted certiorari to consider three questions:

1. Whether petitioners' criminal convictions under the Texas Homosexual Conduct law which criminalizes sexual intimacy by same-sex couples, but not identical behavior by different-sex couples violates the Fourteenth Amendment guarantee of equal protection of laws?

2. Whether petitioners' criminal convictions for adult consensual sexually intimacy in the home violate their vital interests in liberty and privacy protected by the Due Process Clause of the Fourteenth Amendment?

3. Whether *Bowers v. Hardwick*[2] should be overruled?

The petitioners were adults at the time of the alleged offense. Their conduct was in private and consensual. . . .

[The U.S. Supreme Court ruled in the affirmative on all issues and, among others statements, made the following:]

The central holding of *Bowers* has been brought into question by this case, and it should be addressed. Its continuance as precedent demeans the lives of homosexual persons. . . .

Bowers was not correct when it was decided, and it is not correct today. It ought not to remain binding precedent. *Bowers v. Hardwick* should be and now is overruled. . . .

The Texas statute furthers no legitimate state interest which can justify its intrusion into the personal and private life of the individual.

Had those who drew and ratified the Due Process Clauses of the Fifth Amendment or the Fourteenth Amendment known the components of liberty in its manifold possibilities, they might have been more specific. They did not presume to have this insight. They knew times can blind us to certain truths and later generations can see that laws once thought necessary and proper in fact serve only to oppress. As the Constitution endures, persons in every generation can invoke its principles in their own search for greater freedom."

[In 2005 the Virginia Supreme Court, citing *Lawrence*, ruled that Virginia's fornication statute was unconstitutional. The court stated, "We find no relevant distinction between the circumstances in *Lawrence* and the circumstances in the present case." *Martin v. Ziherl* involved a female plaintiff who had sued her former lover, alleging that he gave her a sexually transmitted disease. The lower court had dismissed the lawsuit on the basis of a former Virginia case, which held that a plaintiff who engaged in an illegal act could not recover in a civil lawsuit. The plaintiff and her lover were not married and thus, by engaging in sex, violated the state's statute prohibiting fornication.][3]

---

1. *Lawrence v. Texas*, 539 U.S. 558 (2003), citations omitted.
2. In *Bowers v. Hardwick*, 478 U.S. 186 (1986), the U.S. Supreme Court upheld a similar statute in Georgia.
3. *Martin v. Ziherl*, 607 S.E.2d 367 (Va. 2005). The statute at issue is Va. Code Ann., 18.2-344 (2010), "Fornication," which provides as follows: "Any person, not being married, who voluntarily shall have sexual intercourse with any other person, shall be guilty of fornication, punishable as a Class 4 misdemeanor."

---

for aggravated child molestation. Wilson was 17 and the girl was 15, which was below the state statute for consent; thus, she could not legally consent to the act. A national and international outcry about the unfairness of the mandatory minimum sentence provided by the state for the offense resulted in a legislative change in the state's statute the year that Wilson was convicted. Now, the Georgia aggravated child molestation statute contains an exception. If the victim is at least 14 but less than 16 and the accused offender is 18 or younger and no more than four years older than the victim, the offense is a misdemeanor and carries no more than one year in prison.[8] The legislature did not apply the law retroactively, however. Wilson was finally released in 2007, at the age of 21, after the Georgia Supreme Court ruled 4-to-3 that the sentence was disproportionate to the crime and thus unconstitutional as it constituted cruel and unusual punishment. Wilson had already served two years in prison.[9]

Another type of criminal law coverage that some question is that of the manufacture, prescription, and sale of marijuana for medicinal purposes.

Legalizing Marijuana for Medicinal Purposes

Subsequent discussions in the text consider including drug abuse within criminal law, but the focus here is solely on whether marijuana should be legalized for medicinal purposes. In the federal system, marijuana is a Schedule I drug, meaning it is one of the drugs that cannot be prescribed by doctors for any reason.[10] Schedule I drugs are permitted only when approved by the federal government for research purposes. In California and 15 other jurisdictions (Alaska, Arizona, Colorado, District of Columbia, Hawaii, Maine, Michigan, Montana, Nevada, New Jersey, New Mexico, Oregon, Rhode Island, Vermont, Washington), it is legal under *state* law to use marijuana for medical reasons with a prescription from a physician.[11] The drug relieves pain and other symptoms of some diseases and is tolerated by some patients who do not respond well to other drugs.

Federal authorities take the position that the prescription of marijuana for medical reasons violates federal law and have focused on prosecuting those in California who violate these laws, along with those who, for medicinal purposes, prescribe or grow marijuana. They have had some success, with the U.S. Supreme Court upholding the right of Congress to enact federal laws that regulate the sale of drugs. The Court has also rejected the defense that a medical necessity justifies using marijuana.[12]

Some defendants have been charged in California with violation of the *federal* criminal controlled substances statute. In 2003, Ed Rosenthal was convicted of three charges (manufacturing marijuana, conspiracy to manufacture marijuana, and maintaining a place for the manufacture of marijuana)[13] by a jury that was not given evidence during the trial that Rosenthal had permission from Oakland, California, officials to grow marijuana for medicinal purposes. The jury was not permitted to hear that evidence because it was not relevant in a federal prosecution, as federal law does not include a medical use exception. After the jury verdict and when jurors heard this information, some of them demanded that Rosenthal be retried. The judge refused, but at the sentencing hearing, Rosenthal, who had faced up to 100 years in prison and a fine of $4.5 million, was sentenced to only one day in prison and three years of court supervision. He appealed so he would not have a record of a felony conviction; the government appealed

Ed Rosenthal, who had permission from local authorities to grow marijuana for medicinal purposes in California, where it is legal under state law, was convicted of violating the federal statute, which prohibits any usage of marijuana except for approved research. Rosenthal, who faced up to 100 years in prison and a $4.5 million fine, was sentenced to only one day in prison and three years of court supervision. His conviction was reversed on appeal for technical reasons; he was again convicted. At his second sentencing in 2007, Rosenthal lectured the judge for not permitting the jury to hear evidence that he grew marijuana for medicinal reasons. The judge informed Rosenthal that he could take his complaints to the appeals court. He did and lost! Rosenthal, pictured here with three of the books he authored, continues to fight for the legalization of marijuana.

the one-day sentence. The case was reversed solely on the grounds of jury tampering (a juror sought the advice of an attorney on the eve of the jury's decision).

Rosenthal was retried and again convicted in 2007 of similar charges. Although he had served his one day in jail, he appealed in an effort to clear his name of felony convictions, again arguing that he should have been permitted to introduce evidence that he was acting in good faith in his belief that he was aiding the jurisdiction in implementing California's law, which recognizes the medical use of marijuana. In 2009, a three-judge panel of the Ninth Circuit

Court of Appeals rejected that argument. According to the panel, "The evidence of Rosenthal's belief in the legality of his actions was irrelevant." A conviction under federal law requires only that the defendant knew that he was growing marijuana.[14]

The lack of support for the federal government's position regarding the use of marijuana for medicinal purposes is highlighted by the increasing number of state statutes permitting such use. In June 2007, Rhode Island legislators overrode their governor's veto and voted to make permanent that state's temporary statute permitting the medical use of marijuana. The temporary statute was scheduled to expire at the end of that month. In 2009, the Rhode Island legislature took steps to develop the rules and regulations concerning the administration of marijuana for medicinal use.[15] In November 2010, Arizona legalized the medicinal use of marijuana. The issue of legalizing marijuana for medicinal purposes is given greater attention in Chapter 10, along with an analysis of other substance abuse issues.[16]

This discussion of the use of criminal law to regulate the consensual, private sexual behavior of adults and, in some cases, of juveniles, and the use of marijuana for medicinal purposes with a doctor's prescription raises the question of whether law is the best method of social control in certain areas of behavior. Whether the law serves its purpose of deterrence is a controversial issue (see Chapter 3). Whether the law serves as an adequate symbol of morality can be questioned when the law is enforced infrequently and is not widely supported. Whether the law is used to discriminate against particular groups—such as poor people, minorities, foreigners, or persons with a same-gender sexual orientation—is also an important issue that will be noted throughout the text.

Attempts to legislate morality have not been successful when the laws lacked substantial support by the American people, as illustrated by the widespread violation of **Prohibition** (laws prohibiting the manufacture, sale, and use of alcohol) in the 1920s and of some laws prohibiting other drugs today. The state does, however, have an interest in preserving the morals of its people. The law must be concerned with some moral principles and cannot permit people to abuse one another; it should provide moral guidance. But can that happen if people disrespect the law because it is applied unfairly or because it is difficult or impossible to enforce? Some laws—those regulating sexual behavior, for example—cannot be enforced without violating one or more of our basic freedoms, such as the right to privacy. Therefore, in many cases, no attempt is made to enforce such laws, and this creates disrespect for the law. If these criminal laws do not deter the behavior at which they are aimed, do they serve any positive function in society?

To some extent, laws regulating moral behavior are functional. Sociologists suggest that attaching the label of *deviant* or *criminal* to some persons who violate these laws may serve a positive function for the conformists in that the process may increase their group cohesion.[17] But selective enforcement of the laws also serves to preserve the power of the majority—keeping the weaker minority members of society in their places. In that sense, unequal administration of the law is functional because it keeps the status arrangements of society from being disrupted. For example, when drunks appear in public, police may react differently depending on the offenders' social status. Lower-class offenders may have a greater probability of being arrested. Upper- or middle-class offenders, in contrast, may just be driven home by police or permitted to call someone else to drive them.

Laws regulating morality may serve the function of making the majority feel that something is being done to preserve the morals of society. That is, these laws may create the impression that certain questionable behavior is disapproved of officially. It is argued that repealing these laws would condone the behavior and would not be a wise move for politicians. However, some of the statutes that regulate such crimes may have negative repercussions. Violation of privacy to obtain evidence of criminal conduct may drive demanded services underground. Laws may give the impression that something is being done when actually this is not the case.

The final section of this chapter overviews the study of criminal behavior.

Criminology and the Study of Crime

The study of crime, criminals, and criminal law is of ancient origin, although the development of **criminology** as a discipline took place in the 1900s, with the first textbooks in the field published in the 1920s. But earlier attempts should be recognized. Chapter 3 of this text discusses some pertinent historical developments in criminal law. Other developments are also important. In June 1909, the American Institute of Criminal Law and Criminology was organized at the National Conference of Criminal Law and Criminology held at Northwestern University in Chicago. A resolution was passed that allowed the president to appoint a committee of five persons to select criminological treatises that should be translated into English. An early writer on criminology noted: "For the community at large, it is important to recognize that criminal science is a larger thing than criminal law. The legal profession in particular has a duty to familiarize itself with the principles of that science, as the sole means for intelligent and systematic improvement of the criminal law."[18] Despite this step, the legal profession and policy makers have, until recently, remained generally aloof from the developments in the field of criminology, and even now, the recognition is not significant.

Today, however, most colleges and universities teach criminology and criminal justice courses; many offer graduate degrees in one or both areas. Regional professional organizations exist throughout the country. Professional journals in the field include one that focuses on education, the *Journal of Criminal Justice Education*, published by the Academy of Criminal Justice Sciences (ACJS). In addition to the ACJS, the field boasts another national and highly recognized professional association, the American Society of Criminology (ASC).

Of particular interest among professional journals in criminology and criminal justice is that of *Criminology & Public Policy*, first published in 2001 in an attempt to reduce the gap between social science research and policy decisions. Two scholars associated with the journal wrote in the first volume, "The gap between policy and knowledge appears to widen, even as the scope and depth of knowledge about crime and justice increases [*sic*] steadily." The journal, published by the American Society of Criminology, signaled "a timely recognition of the vitality of scholarship on crime and justice policy."[19] Six years later, those two scholars proclaimed that "in academic circles," the journal "is widely recognized as a notable success," citing a study that ranked *Crime & Public Policy* as number 7 out of 69 journals in the field.[20] This increased emphasis on public policy will be noted throughout the text.

Along with an increased emphasis on public policy has come greater diversion in the educational backgrounds of professionals in criminology and criminal justice. Most early teachers of criminology and related subjects were educated in sociology, psychology, political science, or some other related discipline or were practitioners in various fields of criminal justice. Today, many professors in the field have PhDs in criminal justice or criminology, law degrees, or both. It could be argued, however, that a criminologist needs training in sociology, law, medicine, psychiatry, psychology, history, anthropology, chemistry, biology, architecture, systems engineering, political science, social work, public administration, business, communications, economics, and perhaps other disciplines.

Significant progress has been made since the introduction of criminology textbooks in the 1920s. Today, the discipline of criminology is characterized by an interdisciplinary approach, sophisticated research methods, and a strong emphasis on empirical research. Many departments emphasize the interrelationship of theory and practice, and student demand for courses has increased significantly on many campuses.

Modern criminologists have moved away from the discipline's historically limited focus on explaining the behavior of criminals. The causes of crime are explored through discussions of biological, psychological, economic, and sociological theories, as the subsequent the-

Although this text focuses on U.S. criminal justice systems and research, attention is given to work in other countries by including a global focus box in each chapter.

1.1   The Necessity and Value of Transnational Comparative Study

GLOBAL FOCUS

In the November 2006 issue of *Criminology & Public Policy*, the Vollmer Award Address given before the American Society of Criminology by Franklin E. Zimring was published. Zimring, a noted criminologist and law professor and an author of numerous significant contributions to both fields, holds a named professorship and chairs the Criminal Justice Research Program at the University of California, Berkeley.[1]

Zimring noted that for years, transnational studies were not considered important in what he described as "the large and self-obsessed United States." To some extent, that has changed in recent years, as many of us have come to realize that we really cannot know our system's uniqueness without comparing it to other countries. Thus, each chapter in this text includes at least one Global Focus box. Most of these boxes focus on the subjects of the respective chapters, although that may not always be the case. Some reference countries with issues and programs similar to those of the United States, whereas others look primarily at contrasting systems and programs.

Zimring referred to his effort to study the decline in crime that began in the United States in 1991 and which has been attributed by some to tougher sentences and by others to larger and improved police forces. Zimring compared the crime rates of Canada during that same period, noted the similar decline of crime in that country, but pointed out that the country did not have higher rates of imprisonment than prior to the decline; it did not hire more police per capita; and its economic boom was not even close to that of the United States. "When the joint crime trends are considered in light of the divergent trends in the economy, imprisonment, and policing, it generates doubt that these three American changes were major causes of declines in crime in the United States." However, in both countries, similar demographic changes occurred, with the percentage of the population under age 29 declining significantly, and that is the age group that commits most of the crime.

These and other comparisons led Zimring to emphasize that no longer should criminal justice research in the United States focus only on this country. "We are all comparativists now, and this carries real promise for the quality of both research and theory in the study of crime."

1. Franklin E. Zimring, "The Necessity and Value of Transnational Comparative Study: Some Preaching from a Recent Convert," *Criminology & Public Policy* 5, no. 4 (November 2006): 615–622.

ory chapters of this text illustrate. But the modern study of crime involves more than an attempt to understand why people violate the law. The discipline of criminology includes the sociology of law, which analyzes why some acts and not others are defined as crimes, and a study of the social responses to crime, which examines why some people are processed through the system while others who commit the same acts are not. These areas of focus are not always separable (there is considerable overlap), and there is no agreement on which areas should re-

ceive research priorities. This text includes information on all three areas—law, criminology, and sociology—in addition to materials from other disciplines where pertinent.

This text contains focus boxes on the impact of the media on the study and understanding of crime (see again Media Focus 1.1) and, in an attempt to emphasize the international nature of understanding, focus boxes on global issues (see Global Focus 1.1), along with its enhanced discussions of public policy.

Summary

This chapter explored the meaning of crime and the nature and purpose of criminal law. Because criminal law defines criminal behavior, thus formulating the basis for the kinds of behavior on which this study of criminology focuses, the discussion is important in setting the stage for this text. Many of the questions raised throughout the text are related to the central issue of this chapter—the purpose of criminal law and the kinds of behavior that should be included within its reach. The answers to these questions determine who is and who is not a criminal and therefore who does and who does not constitute a basis for the study of criminology.

The inclusion or exclusion of morality within the reach of the criminal law affects all elements of criminal justice systems, including defendants' rights, victims' rights, and society's right to be protected from criminal behavior. Central to the entire discussion is the underlying theme of law as social control. A basic question is whether imposing sanctions discourages people from engaging in the proscribed behavior. Sociological contributions to our understanding of whether or not laws deter are crucial in the analysis of this issue.

This chapter began with an analysis of the concept of crime, exploring the elements required to establish that a crime has been committed. It then analyzed the concept of law and looked at law as a method of social control, comparing it with other social controls. The chapter then turned to a discussion of the use of criminal law to control behavior that many people do not consider criminal, such as consensual sexual behavior between adults and the use of marijuana for medicinal purposes. The chapter closed with a look at criminology and the study of crime.

In conclusion, it has been argued that the main purpose of criminal law is to protect persons and property from abuse, but according to two authorities in the field, "When the criminal law invades the spheres of private morality ... it exceeds its proper limits at the cost of neglecting its primary tasks. This unwarranted extension is expensive, ineffective, and criminogenic."[21]

What should be included within the province of criminal law? Certainly, criminal law should be used to protect individuals from being forced to engage in certain behaviors. For example, no person, adult or juvenile, should be forced to engage in a sexual act. Criminal law should penalize those who participate in sexual acts with persons under the age of consent; that is, immature persons should be protected from sexual exploitation. Also, consensual sex between adults should be restricted to where it is reasonable to expect privacy so that others are not forced to view it.

The law, however, cannot control the behavior of all people in a complex society. The law should provide some standards, goals, and guidelines—a statement that defines which conduct is so important that it must be sanctioned formally. The law should provide some moral guidance, but it should not be used to regulate behavior that could be regulated more effectively and more appropriately by other agencies or by individuals.

Nor should the law interfere with privacy rights. As one expert noted, "Any attempt to criminalize all wrongful conduct would involve intolerable intrusions into citizens' lives and choices. Much wrongdoing in people's private and working lives should not be legally punishable because it involves areas of behavior which a free society should keep clear of the drastic intervention of the criminal law."[22]

Finally, law is social. Sociological perspectives and inquiries are necessary if we are to appreciate the social nature of law.[23]

These and numerous other questions can be answered only when society has a thorough understanding of the causes and consequences of crime and the subsequent criminal law designed to deal with crime. This text is an effort to provide that understanding.

Study Questions

1. What is meant by the concept of crime?

2. Give a legal definition of *crime*, and explain the meaning of the terms within that definition.

3. Explain what is meant by a *legal duty* to act.

4. Discuss the meaning and importance of *mens rea* and the exceptions to this concept.

5. Distinguish statutory law, case law, constitutional law, and administrative law.

6. Distinguish between criminal law and civil law.

7. What is a *defense*?

8. Distinguish between a felony and a misdemeanor.

9. Why should a jury be permitted to determine guilt or innocence?

10. What is *jury nullification*?

11. How is law used to control people, and how does law differ from other forms of social control?

12. What are the major sources of criminal law?

13. Why does law adhere to the principle *of stare decisis?*

14. Distinguish *mala in se* and *mala prohibita* crimes, and discuss the relationship of these terms to criminal law.

15. Detail the facts of *Lawrence v. Texas*, and explain what the U.S. Supreme Court held and why.

16. Should any private, consensual sexual behavior be covered by criminal law? Discuss.

17. What is the legal status of using marijuana for medicinal purposes?

18. What is involved in the study of criminology?

Brief Essay Assignments

1. Why is law an important discipline to study?

2. What types of acts should the criminal law cover and why?

3. What should be the role of criminal law with regard to regulating private, consensual sexual behavior among adults? Among juveniles?

4. Should states be permitted to establish their own statutes with regard to the use of marijuana for medicinal purposes?

Internet Activities

1. Considerable debate surrounds the criminalization of acts such as drug use, consensual sex by adults in public, gambling, and prostitution, thought by some to be *victimless crimes*. For information concerning the issue of prostitution, check out the website for the organization Coalition Against Trafficking in Women, http://www.catwinternational.org, accessed 5 July 2010. This website includes facts, statistics, and issues on prostitution from several countries plus a number of articles on sex trafficking.

2. Search for information about cases that involve the prosecution of defendants with HIV/AIDS. Under what conditions were these cases prosecuted? (That is, what type of crime was involved?) What has been the outcome of these cases? Do you think the rulings were fair? Sites such as http://www.crimelibrary.com and http://www.crimelynx.com, accessed 5 July 2010, are good places to start.

Notes

1. Paul W. Tappan, *Crime, Justice and Correction* (New York: McGraw–Hill, 1960), p. 10.
2. "Cries Ignored, Charges Dropped," *Tampa Tribune* (20 July 1991), p. 3.
3. *United States v. Dotterweich*, 320 U.S. 277 (1943).
4. For a discussion of defenses, see Sue Titus Reid, Criminal Law, 8th ed. (New York: Oxford University Press, 2010), pp. 82–137.
5. See, for example, Richard D. Schwartz, "Social Factors in the Development of Legal Control: A Case Study of Two Israeli Settlements," *Yale Law Journal* 63 (February 1954): 471–491.
6. *Atwater v. City of Lago Vista*, 532 U.S. 318 (2001).
7. "Low Seat Belt Use Linked to Teenage Death Rates," *New York Times* (21 May 2001), p. 12, referring to a report released that day by the National Safety Council.
8. Ga. Code Annotated, Section 16-6-4 (2010).
9. *Humphrey v. Wilson*, 652 S.E.2d 501(Ga. 2007).
10. See U.S. Code, Title 21, Section 812(c) (2010).
11. See, for example, the California statute, the Compassionate Use Act, Cal. Health and Safety Code, Section 1136.25 (2010).
12. *United States v. Oakland Cannabis Buyers' Cooperative*, 532 U.S. 483 (2001), *injunction granted sub nom.*, 2002 U.S. Dist. LEXIS 10660 (N.D.Cal. 2002); *Gonzales v. Raich*, 545 U.S. 1 (2005).
13. The statutes are U.S. Code, Title 21, Sections 841(a)(1); 846; and 856(a)(1) (2010).
14. *United States v. Rosenthal*, 2009 U.S. App. LEXIS 12571 (9th Cir. 2009).
15. "Rhode Island: Legislature Approves Medical Marijuana Distribution Centers," National Organization for the Reform of Marijuana Laws, http://norml.org/index.cfm?Group_ID=7883, accessed 5 December 2010.
16. For a discussion of the medical uses of marijuana, along with the states that permit it, see the website of the National Organization for the Reform of Marijuana Laws, http://norml.org/index.cfm?Group_ID=2002, accessed 5 December 2010.
17. Edwin M. Schur, *Crimes Without Victims: Deviant Behavior and Public Policy* (Englewood Cliffs, NJ: Prentice-Hall, 1965), p. 4.
18. Willem A. Bonger, *Criminality and Economic Conditions*, trans. Henry P. Horton (Boston: Little, Brown, 1916), p. xi.
19. Todd R. Clear and Natasha A. Frost, "*Criminology & Public Policy*: A New Journal of the American Society of Criminology," *Criminology and Public Policy* 1, no. 1 (November 2001): 1–3; quotation is on p. 1.
20. Todd R. Clear and Natasha A. Frost, "Informing Public Policy," *Criminology and Public Policy* 6, no. 4 (November 2007): 633–640; quotation is on p. 635. The referenced study was conducted by Jon Sorensen et al., "An Assessment of Criminal Justice and Criminology Journal Prestige," *Journal of Criminal Justice Education* 17 (2006): 297–322, with specific reference to p. 314.
21. Norval Morris and Gordon P. Hawkins, *The Honest Politician's Guide to Crime Control* (Chicago: University of Chicago Press, 1969), p. 2.
22. Andrew von Hirsch, "Desert and Previous Convictions in Sentencing," *Minnesota Law Review* 65 (April 1981): 607.
23. Edwin M. Schur, *Law and Society: A Sociological View* (New York: Random House, 1968).

CHAPTER 2

The Measurement of Crime and Its Impact

Jennifer Ford visits the grave of her daughter Victoria McBryde, 24, in Northampton, England, in October 2009. McBryde was killed in an auto accident in 2007 when struck by a passing motorist as she stood by her impaired vehicle on the roadside waiting for service. Phillipa Curtis, 22, was sentenced to 21 months in a high security prison for "death by dangerous driving," a new provision in British law to cover texting while driving.

KEY TERMS

Bureau of Justice Statistics (BJS)
Crime Classification System (CCS)
crime rate
crimes known to the police
dualistic fallacy
ex post facto method
index offenses
National Crime Victimization Survey (NCVS)
National Criminal History Improvement Program (NCHIP)
National Incident-Based Reporting System (NIBRS)
National Youth Survey (NYS)
posttraumatic stress disorder
property crimes
self-report data (SRD)
Uniform Crime Reports (*UCR*)
victim compensation programs
victimology
victim precipitation
violent crimes

INTRODUCTION

This chapter focuses on crime data. It examines the official and unofficial ways data on crimes, criminals, and crime victims are collected. Variables affecting the accuracy of crime data collection include police discretion, reporting methods, victims' cooperation or refusal to cooperate, and administrative and bureaucratic changes. Following this background on the problems of collecting data, the chapter looks at the most recent data on offenders and victims with regard to the factors of age, race and ethnicity, and gender. It examines issues regarding victims in criminal justice systems. After an analysis of crime data collection, the chapter concludes with a look at research in criminology.

In its September 2010 publication regarding 2009 crime data, the Federal Bureau of Investigation (FBI) warned that the data the agency publishes yearly are used by various organizations for a variety of purposes. One example is to rank areas for tourism purposes. This and other purposes, warned the FBI, are "merely a quick choice made by the data user; they provide no insight into the many variables that mold the crime in a particular . . . jurisdiction." The FBI warned that uses such as this may result in misleading conclusions and should be viewed carefully.[1]

This warning is significant, but the FBI data can be viewed historically as long as we do so with caution. In October 2000, the FBI released crime data for 1999, and for the eighth consecutive year, serious crimes reported to police declined, this time by 7 percent. This was the longest consecutive period of decreases during the period the FBI had kept records.[2] These figures were encouraging, and even more encouraging was the fact that there was little change in serious crimes in 2000.[3] In 2001, crime data showed the first increase in serious crime in a decade, rising by 2.1 percent, but in 2002, crime data showed little change over the previous year, with serious crime dropping only 1.1 percent (0.2 percent for violent crimes and 0.9 percent for property crimes).[4]

In 2003, violent crimes decreased 3 percent from 2002, and property crimes decreased 0.2 percent. In 2004, the murder rate declined nationally for the first time since 2000, falling to its lowest level in 40 years.[5] In 2005, violent crimes increased by 2.3 percent, although property crimes decreased by 1.5 percent.[6] However, when the FBI released its official 2006 data on 24 September 2007, the agency stated as follows:

> For the second consecutive year, the estimated number of violent crimes in the nation increased, and for the fourth year in a row, the estimated number of property crimes decreased.[7]

Serious violent crimes decreased in 2007, 2008, and again in 2009, as we note later in the chapter. However, the point here is that crime data must be analyzed carefully in the light of changing demographics and other factors, and the collection of crime data is not as precise as some would have us believe. Not all crimes are reported to the police. Not all reported crimes are cleared by arrest; fewer still are cleared by conviction. This means that no data source is complete in its measure of criminal activity. Additional problems exist when comparisons are made among jurisdictions.

Despite the impossibility of detecting all criminal activity or prosecuting and convicting all guilty parties who are detected, crime data serve an important function. They are needed by official agencies to determine policies and budgets. They are utilized by police officials, who must decide the best use of their officers and their resources. Crime data are used by some individuals to decide where they wish to live, go to school, establish businesses, travel, and so on.

Crime data may be used by official agencies and by private citizens who are determined to make their communities safer for all who live there. Social scientists who study criminal behavior use crime data, both official and unofficial, in their analyses of why and under what circumstances people commit criminal acts. Crime data might also be used for political reasons in an effort to convince voters of the success or failure of crime prevention efforts.

The point is not to dismiss crime data because of problems with inaccuracy but rather to analyze carefully the various sources of data and to determine which are best for a particular purpose. This chapter examines and analyzes the most common sources of crime data. The chapter contains an overview of the amount and types of crime and offenders as determined by official data as well as by data collected from victimization studies. It also notes the relationships between victims and offenders and looks at how criminal justice systems treat crime victims. After an analysis of crime data collection methods, the chapter closes with a discussion of research in criminology, preparing the way for an understanding of the theory chapters that follow.

The importance of this discussion on crime data cannot be overemphasized. The reader should realize that, in many respects, all other discussions of crime hinge on data, as they influence the causation theories we advance and affect resource allocations in criminal justice systems.

Sources of Crime Data

Measurement of crime today is more sophisticated and more extensive than in earlier times, but serious disagreement remains over how crime should be measured. Even official crime data vary according to their sources, and unofficial sources differ from official sources. As we look at crime data, we must keep in mind that data collection methods differ and that they are not always comparable. Furthermore, conclusions about how much crime exists, what kinds of crimes are committed, who commits them, and who is victimized differ according to the measurement methods used. As noted in Media Focus 2.1 and discussed later in the text, there is some evidence that data may be used to distort crime for the benefit of those reporting the data.

Most media reports and most analyses of crime data are based on official data. The major sources of official data are the *Uniform Crime Reports* (*UCR*) and the National Crime Victimization Survey (NCVS). Official compilers are government agencies that collect crime data for a variety of different purposes. The most common source is agency reports. At the state level, data about criminal justice systems are updated routinely, but the systems differ in scope, definition, and quality. As a result, state-by-state comparisons of crime data are difficult.

2.1 Media Headlines Concerning Crime Data

MEDIA FOCUS

Information on crime makes headlines, and periodic reports of crime data are no exceptions. A few headlines from the media illustrate the impact the written news media might have on perceptions.

In May 2000, the *New York Times* carried this headline: "Serious Crimes Fall for 8th Consecutive Year." The article, based on the preliminary *UCR* data for 1999, stated that the decline in serious crimes had been continuous since 1992, although it did note that murders increased in some cities, such as New York City.[1]

Three months later, in August 2000, the same paper published an article with the headline "New York's Murder Rate, After Upturn, Starts to Slide Down." This article noted that, by the end of 1999, the number of murders in New York City had surpassed that of the previous year by 6 percent, and by the end of March 2000, the number was up 13 percent over the same period in 1999. However, the number of murders in the city was down 1 percent for the first seven months of the year 2000 compared with the same period in 1999. Police and politicians claimed credit for this decrease, but they had difficulty explaining why some of the efforts they said were responsible for the overall decrease did not lead to a decline in murders in the Bronx.[2]

Even so, it would be reasonable for New Yorkers to have concluded in August 2000 that, once again, murder was becoming less of a threat in their city. However, by the end of the year, another *New York Times* article, entitled "Data Hint Crime Plunge May Be Leveling Off," pointed out that although the nationwide murder rate during the first six months of 2000 fell by 1.8 percent, murders increased in New York City, Los Angeles, Dallas, and New Orleans "for the first time since the early 1990's."[3]

Such news can be very confusing to the public—that is, if anyone is reading the articles carefully. The end-of-year article stated that the number of murders in New York City increased in 2000 for the first time in years, yet the two articles that appeared earlier in the year claimed that murders in New York City had increased in 1999. So, what is the public to believe?

In June 2003, a news article quoted New York City Police Commissioner Raymond W. Kelly as acknowledging that in one precinct, police officials improperly reduced over 200 felonies to misdemeanors, thereby falsely cutting that area's crime rate to a 7.42 percent reduction rather than a 15.7 percent increase.[4]

A short-term downward movement in crime data does not present a reason to proclaim victory over crime. Nevertheless, in the spring of 2007, New York City's police commissioner announced that 2006 was "a very good year" despite the 10 percent increase in homicides. According to Commissioner Kelly, the number of murders in 2006 was significantly smaller than in 1990. Kelly also noted that in 2006, the city's other violent crimes decreased. Kelly emphasized that the overall decrease in the city's violent crimes in 2006 contrasted to the overall increase in violent crimes nationwide, and he credited his city's success, in part, to improved policing.[5]

By February 2010, however, the *New York Times* was reporting on a study by criminologists suggesting that New York City's crime data may have been distorted. The city's mayor, Michael R. Bloomberg, a staunch believer in and defender of the city's data on all issues, proudly proclaimed his motto: "In God we trust. . . . All others bring data." Still, data may be misrepresented or even purposely skewed by those who are using it to prove a point. The criminologists, who questioned hundreds of police who retired from the high ranks of the department, reported that pressures to report declining crime led some police administrators to misrepresent the reporting of crime data. The mayor denied such allegations.[6]

---

1. "Serious Crimes Fall for 8th Consecutive Year," *New York Times* (8 May 2000), p. 21.
2. "New York's Murder Rate, After Upturn, Starts to Slide Down," *New York Times* (8 August 2000), p. 8.
3. "Data Hint Crime Plunge May Be Leveling Off," *New York Times* (19 December 2000), p. 18.
4. "Precinct Altered Statistics: Kelly Admits Felonies Downgraded by Cops" (New York) *Newsday* (21 June 2003), p. 6.
5. "Homicides Up in New York; Other Crimes Keep Falling," *New York Times* (1 January 2007), p. 1.
6. "Crime Survey Raises Questions About Data-Driven Policy," *New York Times* (9 February 2010), p. 20.

The situation is not much better at the federal level. Many agencies have independent data systems; the usefulness of the data is reduced because of different definitions, reporting periods, and classification schemes. The sources of federal crime data include many agencies, such as the FBI, the National Criminal Justice Information and Statistics Service, the Drug Enforcement Administration, the National Institute on Drug Abuse, and many others.

Partly as a response to this fragmentation, in 1981 Congress authorized the creation of the **Bureau of Justice Statistics (BJS)**. This agency's main goal is to furnish an objective, independent, and competent source of police-relevant data to the government and to criminal justice and academic communities. Goals of the BJS are the unification of data, development of a program to follow an offender from the time of entering the criminal justice process until release from the correctional system, and provision of services to states and local communities to aid in comprehensive data gathering. The bureau is not involved in policy decisions. Although BJS data are useful, the most frequently cited and most comprehensive source of crime data is the ***Uniform Crime Reports (UCR)***, which falls under the jurisdiction of the FBI.

The Uniform Crime Reports (UCR)

In the 1920s, the International Association of Chiefs of Police (IACP) appointed a committee to develop a system for securing crime data on a national scale. By 1929, the committee had developed a plan that became the basis for the *UCR*. A 1930 law requires the U.S. attorney general to report annually on the amount of crime in the United States. Also in 1930, the FBI began issuing its publication on national crime data, the *Uniform Crime Reports*. At first, the *UCR* was issued monthly, then quarterly, then semiannually, and then annually. Today, the *UCR* is available on the Internet. The data for a particular year are generally published in September of the following year, with preliminary data published earlier.

Standardized definitions were drafted for all included offenses to provide uniformity in reporting data. Local agencies compile data and submit them through state *UCR* agencies. Although the FBI is responsible for administering the *UCR* program, it has no authority to *compel* reporting by state and local jurisdictions. Even though it is voluntary, the national *UCR* program covers approximately 98 percent of the U.S. population.

Originally, seven crimes (because of their seriousness and frequency) were selected to constitute Part I of the *UCR*; arson, the eighth, was added in 1978. The eight crimes are known as Part I offenses. They are the serious **violent crimes**—murder and nonnegligent manslaughter, forcible rape, robbery, and aggravated assault—and the serious **property crimes**—burglary, larceny-theft, motor vehicle theft, and arson. Each month, law enforcement agencies report the number of **crimes known to the police**, the number of Part I offenses verified by police investigation. The number of actual Part I crimes is reported whether or not there is any further action in the case; that is, a crime known to the police is counted even if no suspect is arrested and prosecution does not occur.

If a criminal act involves several different crimes, only the most serious is recorded as a crime. For example, if a victim is raped, robbed, and murdered, only the murder is counted in the *UCR*. In addition to reporting crimes known to the police, the *UCR* reports a **crime rate**, which is calculated by dividing the number of reported crimes by the number of people in the country. The result is expressed as a rate of crime per 100,000 people. In addition, the *UCR* reports trends in offenses and crime rates.

Prior to 2004, the FBI reported crimes using the term **index offenses**. Index offenses included the four serious violent crimes (murder and nonnegligent manslaughter, rape, robbery, and aggravated assault) and the four serious property crimes (burglary, larceny-theft, auto theft, and arson). In June 2004, the FBI ceased using the term *index offense*, stating that the index was misleading. For example, larceny-theft, the most frequently committed of all serious crimes (about 60 percent of the total) could increase significantly in a jurisdiction, driving up its overall index offenses.[8]

The number of Part I offenses that are cleared is also reported. Offenses are reported as cleared (1) when a suspect is arrested, charged, and turned over to the judicial system for prosecution and (2) by circumstances beyond the control of the police. For example, normally, the death of a suspect or a victim's refusal to press charges ends police involvement. In the first case, crimes are considered cleared whether or not the person arrested is convicted.

Several persons may be arrested and one crime cleared, or one person may be arrested and many crimes cleared. The *clearance rate* is the number of crimes solved expressed as a percentage of the total number of crimes reported to the police. The clearance rate is critical in policy decisions because it is one measure used to evaluate police departments. The higher the number of crimes solved by arrest, the better the police force looks in the eyes of the public. The clearance rate is higher for violent than for property crimes. Crimes may also be cleared by *exceptional means*, as, for example, when elements beyond the control of law enforcement (the alleged offender is now dead) prevent an arrest. In 2009, 47.1 percent of violent crimes and 18.6 percent of property crimes were cleared. Murder had the highest clearance rate (66.6 percent) among serious violent crimes, and larceny-theft had the highest rate (21.5 percent) among serious property crimes.[9]

The *UCR* records and publishes arrest data for Part II offenses, the less serious crimes, as well as for Part I offenses. The *UCR* lists the number of arrests made during one year for each offense per 100,000 population. The *UCR* does not report the number of persons arrested each year because some individuals are arrested more than once during the year. The actual number of persons arrested is likely to be smaller than the number of arrests.[10]

Official reports have been criticized for excluding some crimes. The *UCR* does not include federal offenses. It does not include computer crime, organized crime, and white-collar crime (all discussed in subsequent chapters). Some of these offenses, although they are violations of criminal law, are handled by administrative agencies rather than by criminal courts. Since these crimes, which are more often committed by people in the middle and upper classes, are not included in the *UCR*'s most serious crimes, by looking only at official data, we can conclude erroneously that there is a correlation between crime and socioeconomic status, with the greatest proportion of crimes committed by persons in the lowest socioeconomic classes.

In addition to the exclusion of some serious crimes, the *UCR* has several other limitations. First, the use of "crimes known to the police" as a measure of crime may result in a serious underestimation of actual crime because police departments do not use uniform procedures for coding a complaint. For example, a sexual offense may be coded as rape, indecent assault, sexual battery, assault with intent to harm, or some other offense.

Another variable that may limit crime data accuracy is police discretion in deciding whether a complaint is a crime. Several factors may influence police decision making. Police may decide not to file a complaint in cases involving close relationships, although that is changing as departments have altered their arrest policies in domestic violence cases. Police may decide not to file when the complainant does not want charges pressed. They may decide not to file if the alleged offenders show proper deference when apprehended. Socioeconomic status, race and ethnicity, gender, or other extralegal factors might also be influential. And as noted in Media Focus 2.1, police may manipulate data to show a lower crime rate.

A third factor affecting the measurement of crime is victims' cooperation. The BJS reports that only about one-half (47 percent) of violent crimes and 40 percent of property crimes are reported to police. Among violent crimes, rape and other sexual assaults are reported in only 41 percent of cases; robbery is reported by 61 percent of victims and aggravated assault by 62 percent. Among property crimes, the most frequently reported crime is motor vehicle theft at 80 percent. Female violent crime victims are slightly more likely than male violent crime victims to report the crimes to the police, and black females are more likely to report than white females.[11]

There are many reasons victims may not report crimes. Some believe nothing will happen, so why report? Some think they may be blamed for the crime. Some think others will report the incident or that it was a private matter and not important enough to report to police. Some victims may have had prior negative experiences with police or courts and thus do not report.[12]

The BJS has examined the issue of reporting domestic violence crimes to the police. In recent years, reporting such crimes has increased for both males and females, with females remaining more likely to report. The reporting of victimizations for nonfatal intimate partner violence showed that reporting was

- "higher for black females than white females.
- higher for black females than black males.
- about the same for black and white males. . . .
- about the same for Hispanic and non-Hispanic females.
- higher for male Hispanic victims than non-Hispanic males."

The most frequent reason for not reporting these crimes was that they were considered a personal or private mat-

ter, cited by almost 40 percent of males and 22 percent of females.[13]

A recent study of youths in high-crime neighborhoods reported that most of the respondents expressed negative views of police and that fewer than 10 percent would report a teen crime to them. These views were based primarily on previous negative experiences with police, yet these same young people responded that more police activity is needed for crime control in their communities, thus suggesting that if ways are found to improve attitudes toward police, more crimes will be reported.[14]

A fourth factor that may influence official crime data is a change in the administration or organization of police departments. A reduction in the size or location of police forces may affect data; methods of reporting may be changed, resulting in an apparent increase or decrease in the data.

A fifth factor that may influence crime data collection is the method of counting crimes. Crime data may be affected by decisions such as whether a series of criminal acts by one perpetrator is counted as one crime or as several. If an individual appears before a group of people, pulls a gun, and demands money from each person, has the suspect committed one act of armed robbery or several? If a perpetrator twice engages in sexual intercourse with force and without the consent of the alleged victim, have two rapes been committed or only one?

The one-operation, one-crime rule is followed in the United States. Official reports record crimes as single events, but victim surveys may record each victim separately. The two sources of crime data are not comparable in this regard. Further, the *UCR*'s method of counting crimes does not take into account the differing degrees of seriousness of crimes that have the same legal label. Even serious crimes such as rape or robbery differ in circumstances and severity. Some investigators measure crime by using an index that takes into account the components of the criminal act and the aggravating factors accompanying it. For example, greater weight is given to a rape aggravated by the use of a dangerous weapon than to one in which no weapon is used.

A sixth factor that may affect the reporting of crime rates, as noted earlier in Media Focus 2.1, is the desire of reporting authorities (e.g., high-level police administrators) to portray their jurisdictions in a positive light.

The FBI lists the following variables that might affect the data:

- "Population density and degree of urbanization.
- Variations in composition of the population, particularly youth concentration.
- Stability of the population with respect to residents' mobility, commuting patterns, and transient factors.
- Modes of transportation and highway system.
- Economic conditions, including median income, poverty level, and job availability.

- Cultural factors and educational, recreational, and religious characteristics.
- Family conditions with respect to divorce and family cohesiveness.
- Climate.
- Effective strength of law enforcement agencies.
- Administrative and investigative emphases of law enforcement.
- Policies of other components of the criminal justice system (i.e., prosecutorial, judicial, correctional, and probational).
- Citizens' attitudes toward crime.
- Crime reporting practices of the citizenry."[15]

The National Incident-Based Reporting System (NIBRS)

Because of the deficiencies in the *UCR*'s traditional methods of collecting crime data, the FBI approved a new collection method. The **National Incident-Based Reporting System (NIBRS)** categorizes crimes and collects data according to numerous elements. The NIBRS views a crime, along with all its components, as an incident and recognizes that the data constituting those components should be collected and organized for purposes of analysis. The FBI refers to *elements* of crimes, among which are the following:

- Alcohol and other drug influence
- Specified location of the crime
- Type of criminal activity involved
- Type of weapon used
- Type of victim
- Relationship of victim to offender
- Residence of victim and arrestee

The NIBRS collects data on additional crime categories beyond the 8 included as Part I offenses and the 21 included as Part II offenses in the *UCR*.

According to the BJS, the NIBRS increases our knowledge of crime in the following ways:

- "Expansion of the number of offense categories included.
- Detail on individual crime incidents (offenses, offenders, victims, property, and arrests).
- Linkage between arrests and clearances to specific incidents or offenses.
- Inclusion of all offenses in an incident rather than only the most serious offense.
- The ability to distinguish between attempted and completed crimes.
- Linkages between offense, offender, victim, property, and arrestee variables which permit examination of interrelationships."[16]

Exhibit 2.1 contrasts the *UCR* and NIBRS approaches.

The National Crime Victimization Survey (NCVS)

Victimization surveys were developed in response to criticisms of the FBI's *UCR*, which, as already noted, does not account for all crimes. One purpose of victimization surveys is to determine how many crimes are not reported and why. The major source of victimization data is the **National Crime Victimization Survey (NCVS)**, which comes from the BJS. The NCVS is based on the results of interviews conducted each six months with persons age 12 and older in about 50,000 households (the previous sample size of 60,000 has been cut because of costs). Respondents are questioned about whether they have been the victims of rape, robbery, assault, household burglary, personal and household larceny, and motor vehicle theft. As Exhibit 2.2 shows, two crimes included in the eight serious offenses of the *UCR* are omitted: murder and arson. Murder cannot be measured by this survey because the victim is dead. Arson is excluded because of the difficulty of determining whether the property owner was the perpetrator of the crime.

The NCVS should be considered a valuable addition to, not a substitute for, the *UCR*. Several scholars have compared crime data provided by the two sources, but they arrived at different conclusions. Some argue that the two sources "have tracked each other quite closely, at least for the serious crime types of burglary and robbery," but others disagree.[17]

One limitation common to both the NCVS and the *UCR* is that neither can estimate the extent to which a few offenders are responsible for large numbers of crimes. These reports tell us how many crimes were reported (not how many can be traced to the same offenders) and how many arrests were made (not how many times a particular person was arrested).

Self-Report Data (SRD)

Official crime data report the number of crimes that come to the attention of law enforcement officials. Victimization surveys report the number of crimes that occur regardless of whether they are reported to the police. Another way to measure crime is to survey people about their own criminal activity, resulting in the collection of **self-report data (SRD)**. The systematic use of the self-report method of measuring delinquency was introduced by James F. Short and F. Ivan Nye in 1957 and since that time has been improved upon and used extensively.[18] Self-report data are secured through interviews or anonymous questionnaires. Although the SRD approach originally was used primarily with juveniles, the method is employed today to measure adult criminality as well.

The use of the self-report method reveals that many people who have not been arrested for criminal or delinquent behavior report anonymously that they have engaged in such behavior, leading one researcher to

EXHIBIT 2.1

Contrasts Between the *Uniform Crime Reports* and the National Incident-Based Reporting System

Summary *UCR*

- Consists of monthly aggregate crime counts for eight index crimes
- Records one offense per incident as determined by *hierarchy rule*
- *Hierarchy rule* suppresses counts of lesser offenses in multiple-offense incidents
- Does not distinguish between attempted and completed crimes
- Applies *hotel rule* to burglary
- Records rape of females only
- Collects weapon information for murder, robbery, and aggravated assault
- Provides counts on arrests for the 8 index crimes and 21 other offenses

NIBRS

- Consists of individual incident records for the 8 index crimes and 38 other offenses with details on—
  - Offense
  - Victim
  - Offender
  - Property
- Records each offense occurring in incident
- Distinguishes between attempted and completed crimes
- Expands burglary *hotel rule* to include rental storage facilities
- Records rape of males and females
- Restructures definition of assault
- Collects weapon information for all violent offenses
- Provides details on arrests for the 8 index crimes and 49 other offenses

Source: Ramona R. Rantala, Bureau of Justice Statistics, *Effects of NIBRS on Crime Statistics* (Washington, D.C.: U.S. Department of Justice, July 2000, revised 23 February 2001), p. 1, http://bjs.ojp.usdoj.gov/content/pub/pdf/encs.pdf, accessed 20 September 2010.

---

conclude that criminal behavior is only a matter of degree "rather than an attribute that we either possess or lack."[19] Much criminal activity is simply not reported to law enforcement officials, with as many as 99 percent of upper-income persons in one study reporting that they had committed one or more acts for which they could have been arrested.[20]

Self-report studies comparing college students and institutionalized delinquents show that, although probably with less frequency of commission, college students admitted to having engaged in delinquent and criminal acts as serious as those for which delinquents had been adjudicated. Some of these students were honors students and leaders of school organizations.[21]

Several studies by the Rand Corporation, which conducts extensive research in many areas of criminal justice, have relied on the SRD approach to obtain data on the past criminal behavior of incarcerated persons. These studies reveal interesting facts about career criminals, those few who commit most of the crimes. They also disclose that individuals serving time after conviction of a crime were not arrested for most of the crimes they reported having committed.[22]

The SRD method has been criticized because of the possibility that respondents may purposely overreport or underreport their criminal activities, and others may forget prior criminal acts. The method has also been criticized for including too few African Americans in the surveyed samples.[23] Despite these criticisms, self-reporting is still utilized in some studies, especially those measuring drug use among young people. One of those studies (reported by the U.S. Department of Justice and published in 2008) concluded that, according to SRD, girls are not, as arrest data show, committing more crimes than previously. They are arrested in greater numbers, but according to this report (the Girls Study Group by researchers Margaret A. Zahn and Stephanie R. Hawkins of the RTI International research group), those arrests are based on changes in law and policy rather than a change in the behavior of young girls. For example, girls might be arrested for the crime of simple assault for engaging in behavior that previously would have been considered a status offense and processed, if at all, through the juvenile court.[24]

The National Youth Survey (NYS)

The **National Youth Survey (NYS)** is based on interviews conducted with adolescents over a five-year period and includes all *UCR* offenses except homicide and records crimes that are likely to be relevant to a delinquent lifestyle or culture, such as gang fights, sexual activity, and misdemeanors. The NYS may be more useful for comparison because it measures criminal activity from Christmas to Christmas. This period is close to the *UCR* calendar period and coincides with the more recent victimization surveys. The NYS allows researchers to pinpoint many types and levels of delinquent behavior and shows promise for gathering more accurate data.[25]

EXHIBIT 2.2

Comparison of the *Uniform Crime Reports* and the National Crime Victimization Survey

	Uniform Crime Reports	National Crime Victimization Survey
Offenses measured	Homicide Rape Robbery (personal and commercial) Assault (aggravated) Burglary (commercial and household) Larceny (commercial and household) Motor vehicle theft Arson	Rape Robbery (personal) Assault (aggravated and simple) Household burglary Larceny (commercial and household) Motor vehicle theft
Scope	Crimes reported to the police in most jurisdictions; considerable flexibility in developing small-area data	Crimes both reported and not reported to police; all data are available for a few large geographic areas
Collection method	Police department reports to FBI or to centralized state agencies that then report to FBI	Survey interviews; periodically measures the total number of crimes committed by asking a national sample of 49,000 households encompassing 101,000 persons age 12 and over about their experiences as victims of crime during a specified period
Kinds of information	In addition to offense counts, provides information on crime clearances, persons arrested, persons charged, law enforcement officers killed and assaulted, and characteristics of homicide victims	Provides details about victims (such as age, race, sex, education, income, and whether the victim and offender were related to each other) and about crimes (such as time and place of occurrence, whether or not reported to police, use of weapons, occurrence of injury, and economic consequences)
Sponsor	Department of Justice Federal Bureau of Investigation	Department of Justice Bureau of Justice Statistics

Source: Bureau of Justice Statistics, *Report to the Nation on Crime and Justice: The Data,* 2d ed. (Washington, D.C.: U.S. Department of Justice, 1988), p. 11.

The Crime Classification System (CCS)

Another approach that is utilized as an alternative to the *UCR* and the NCVS is the **Crime Classification System (CCS)**. The focus of the CCS is the harm suffered by the victim and the context in which the criminal activity occurs. Unlike the *UCR*, the CCS has the capacity to measure the degree of severity, giving more refined measures of the harm suffered by victims and the type of circumstances in which that harm occurred. This system might provide a more useful database for criminal justice agencies and a better understanding of victimization risk.

The National Criminal History Improvement Program (NCHIP)

The **National Criminal History Improvement Program (NCHIP)** began in 1995 and awards direct funding and technical assistance to states to assist them in improving the quality and timeliness of the criminal history and other records of crime suspects. The organization is administered by the Bureau of Justice Statistics, Office of Justice Programs, located within the Department of Justice. According to the BJS, the program objective is to ensure "accurate, timely, and complete history information" that will permit States to identify the following:

- ineligible firearm purchasers
- persons ineligible to hold positions involving children, the elderly, or the disabled
- persons subject to protection orders or wanted, arrested, or convicted of stalking and/or domestic violence
- persons ineligible to be employed or hold licenses for specified positions
- persons potentially presenting threats to public safety

The NCHIP system also provides technical assistance to states, which is designed to "improve the quality, timeliness, and immediate accessibility of criminal history records and related information."[26]

Crime in the United States: An Overview

The preceding discussion of sources should be kept in mind as we look at crime data throughout the rest of this text. When analyzing data, we must consider the source and the time period covered. For example, the media may report what appear to be conflicting crime data, but the conflict comes from reporting two sources that cover different time periods. Some examples of this problem are provided in the following discussion, which contains a brief look at the most recent official crime data as reported by the BJS and the FBI's *UCR*. Data on specific crimes are analyzed more carefully in later chapters as we discuss the nature and elements of those crimes.

National Crime Victimization Survey (NCVS) Data

The property and violent crimes for 2009, as measured by the National Crime Victimization Survey, were "near their lowest levels in over three decades." Figure 2.1 graphs the data for violent crime rates; Figure 2.2 shows the rates for property crimes. Methodological changes were made in the data collection in 2006; thus, rates for that year are omitted from these figures.

The NCVS data are similar to the findings from the *UCR* for the same period, and throughout the existence of the NCVS, the two measures have generally shown the

Figure 2.1

Violent Crime Rates Overall Fell by 39 Percent from 2000 to 2009

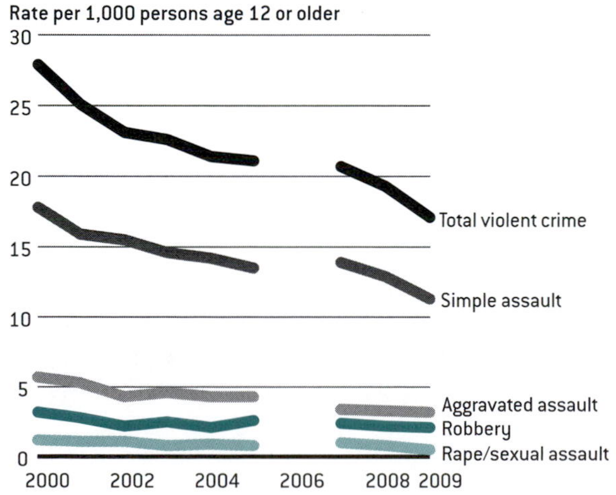

Rate per 1,000 persons age 12 or older

Note: Data for 2006 were omitted due to methodological changes in data collection that year.

Source: Jennifer L. Truman and Michael R. Rand, Bureau of Justice Statistics, Office of Justice Programs, National Crime Victimization Survey, *Criminal Victimization, 2009* (October 2010), p. 2, http://bjs.ojp.usdoj.gov/content/pub/pdf/cv09.pdf, accessed 20 October 2010.

Figure 2.2

Property Crime Rates Overall Fell by 29 Percent from 2000 to 2009

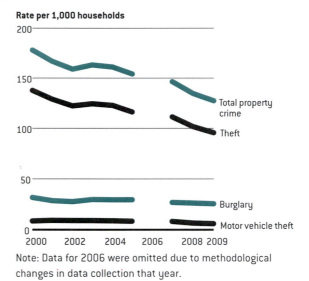

Note: Data for 2006 were omitted due to methodological changes in data collection that year.

Source: Jennifer L. Truman and Michael R. Rand, Bureau of Justice Statistics, Office of Justice Programs, National Crime Victimization Survey, *Criminal Victimization, 2009* (October 2010), p. 3, http://bjs.ojp.usdoj.gov/content/pub/pdf/cv09.pdf, accessed 20 October 2010.

same directions in crime trends,[27] although as Figure 2.3 shows, the number of offenses may differ by the measure used. Figure 2.3 graphs four measures and defines each.

Uniform Crime Reports (UCR) Data

In the foreword to the *UCR* for 1982, the FBI director announced with cautious optimism that the rate of serious offenses was down 3 percent from 1981. The cautiousness of his optimism stemmed from the fact that in the 1970s, crime rates dropped twice, only to turn upward again shortly thereafter.[28]

Both the number of offenses and the rate per 100,000 inhabitants continued their downward trends in 1983 and 1984 but started back up in 1985. Although the 1985 figures were below those of 1981, there was cause for concern after three consecutive years of declines in serious offenses. In reaction to these crime data, the FBI director emphasized that data must be analyzed over time and that although declines in crime data are welcome, "their accuracy is often questionable and certainly controversial." With regard to the increases in 1985, the director commented, "There are few social statements more tragic than these."[29]

The upward trend in the overall crime data continued through 1991,[30] but in 1992, the crime data began to decline again and continued to decline for eight years before leveling off in 2000. Figures 2.4 and 2.5 depict the fluctuations in the number of violent offenses (Figure 2.4) and property offenses (Figure 2.5) between 2005 and 2009, noting the continued declines in property offenses but the

Figure 2.3

Four Measures of Serious Violent Crime

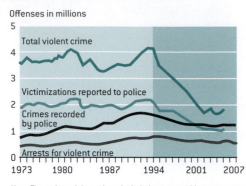

Offenses in millions

Note: The serious violent crimes included are rape, robbery, aggravated assault, and homicide. The National Crime Victimization Survey redesign was implemented in 1993; the area with the lighter shading is before the redesign and the darker area after the redesign. The data before 1993 are adjusted to make the comparable with data collected since the redesign.

The measures are:

Total serious violent crime
The estimated number of homicides of persons age 12 and older recorded by police plus the number of rapes, robberies, and aggravated assaults from the victimization survey whether or not they were reported to the police.

Victimizations reported to the police
The estimated number of homicides of persons age 12 and older recorded by police plus the number of rapes, robberies and aggravated assaults from the victimization survey that victims said were reported to police.

Crimes recorded by the police
The number of homicides, forcible rapes, robberies, and aggravated assaults included in the Uniform Crime Reports of the FBI excluding commercial robberies and crimes that involved victims under age 12.

Arrests for violent crimes
The number of persons arrested for homicide, forcible rape, robbery or aggravated assault as reported by law enforcement agencies to the FBI.

Source: Bureau of Justice Statistics, "Key Facts at a Glance," http://bjs.ojp.usdoj.gov/content/glance/cv2.cfm, accessed 20 September 2010. The data are from the National Crime Victimization Survey (NCVS) and the *Uniform Crime Reports (UCR)*.

rise in violent offenses between 2005 and 2006, with a decline after that year.[31]

Subsequent chapters discuss violent crimes (Chapter 7) and property crimes (Chapter 8) in detail, including data for the crimes included within each category.

Characteristics of Offenders

A thorough study of crime includes not only an analysis of the number and type of crimes but also information on the characteristics of those who commit crimes. The FBI data on crime offenders come from arrest records.

Figure 2.4

Trends in U.S. Violent Crimes, 2005–2009

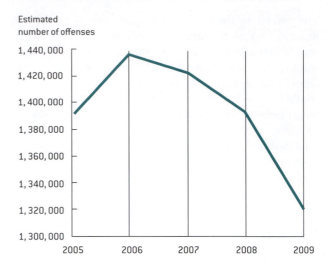

Source: Federal Bureau of Investigation, *Crime in the United States, Uniform Crime Reports 2009*, http://www2.fbi.gov/ucr/cius2008/offenses/violent_crime/index.html, accessed 20 September 2010.

Figure 2.5

Trends in U.S. Property Crimes, 2005–2009

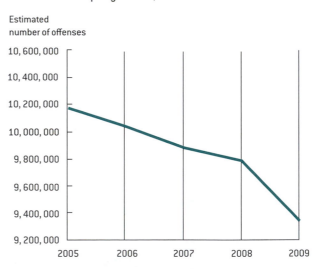

Source: Federal Bureau of Investigation, *Crime in the United States, Uniform Crime Reports 2009*, http://www2.fbi.gov/ucr/cius2009/offenses/property_crime/index.html, accessed 20 September 2010.

In 2009, law enforcement officials throughout the United States reported that they made an estimated 13,687,241 arrests (excluding traffic infractions). Of these arrests, 1,728,285 were for serious property crimes, representing a 1.6 percent increase over 2008; 581,765 arrests were for serious violent crimes, representing a 2.3 percent decrease over 2008 arrests. The offense for which the largest number of arrests was made was drug abuse violations, accounting for 1,663,582.[32]

Data on offenders are discussed by age, race and ethnicity, and gender.

Age

Age is the variable most often associated with crimes, most of which are committed by young people (ages 18–25). In 2009, 43.6 percent of all arrests were of persons under 25, 28.6 percent were of persons under 21, 14.1 percent were of persons under 18, and 3.8 percent were of individuals under 15. For serious violent crimes, 44.7 percent of arrestees were under 25, and 29.3 percent were under 21. For serious property crimes, 55.8 percent of arrested persons were under 25, 42.5 percent were under 21, and 24.4 percent were under 18. Persons under 25 accounted for 64.3 percent of all arson arrests, 65.2 percent of all robbery arrests, and 60.3 percent of all burglary arrests.[33]

In December 2009, the Office of Juvenile Justice and Delinquency Prevention (OJJDP) published an analysis of the arrest data for juveniles (defined as youths under age 18). A summary of that report is as follows:

- "Juveniles accounted for 16% of all violent crime arrests and 26% of all property crime arrests in 2008. . . .
- In 2008, although black youth accounted for just 16% of the youth population ages 10–17, they were in-

volved in 52% of juvenile Violent Crime Index arrests and 33% of juvenile Property Crime Index arrests.
- The 2008 arrest rates for . . . [serious violent crimes] were substantially lower than the rates in the 1994 peak year for every age group younger than 40."[34]

In December 2009, the OJJDP also published an analysis of juvenile sex offenses against other juveniles, noting that 35.6 percent of the sex crimes known by police to have been committed against juveniles were committed by other juveniles, with some offenders (one of eight) younger than 12. Seven percent of the juvenile sex offenders were females.[35]

Race and Ethnicity

Before the collection of self-report data, most studies of criminals were based on the *UCR* data, which revealed that a higher percentage of the arrestees were young African Americans from the lower socioeconomic class. Many people concluded that persons with these characteristics were more likely to commit crimes, whereas others argued that the data represented discrimination against these individuals.[36]

There is no general agreement on the impact of race or ethnicity on crime, an issue that is noted frequently throughout this text. Most arrestees are white (69.1 percent in 2009). Whites constituted 67.6 percent of property crime arrests and 58.7 percent of all violent crime arrests. Among serious violent crimes, blacks were arrested more frequently than whites for only two crimes: murder and nonnegligent manslaughter, 49.3 percent, and robbery,

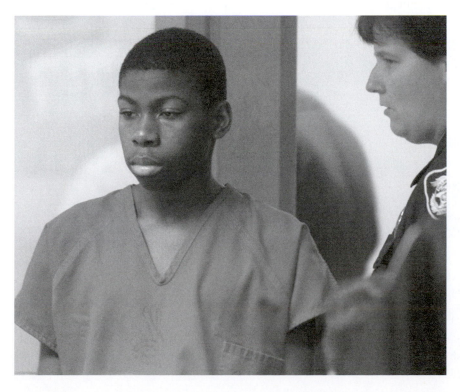

Nathaniel Brazill was 13 when he was accused of the shooting death of his favorite teacher, Barry Grunow, who refused him permission to enter the classroom and speak with two girls. Brazill was tried as an adult when he was 14. He was convicted of second-degree murder and faced a 25-years-to-life sentence. He was sentenced to 28 years in prison, and his sentence was affirmed on appeal. While in prison, Brazill has attained his GED and law clerk and paralegal certifications.

55.5 percent. For arson, 74.8 percent of arrestees were white compared to 22.8 percent black.[37]

These data should be analyzed in light of population data. African Americans constitute only approximately 11 percent of the total population, and the argument is made by many that African Americans are less likely than whites to receive justice at all levels of criminal justice system activity.[38]

Race and ethnicity data should also be analyzed in the context of age. As the OJJDP report just summarized indicated, black youths were disproportionately represented in 2008 arrests. Under federal legislation enacted in 2002, the OJJDP may withhold 20 percent of the formula grant allocation for any given year from a state that fails to address the issue of disproportionate minority contact (DMC) in juvenile justice systems.

It is also important to consider how the media report crimes by juveniles. Refer back to Media Focus 2.1 concerning the general issue of how the media report crime. An analysis of media reporting of crime emphasized the problems by age and race, stating the following:

> Overall, the studies taken together indicate that depictions of crime in the media are not reflective of the rate of crime generally, the proportion of crime which is violent, the proportion of crime committed by people of color, or the proportion of crime committed by young people.

In quoting that conclusion, the OJJDP was not questioning the accuracy of any individual media report on crime. Rather, it concluded that the problem is the "cumulative effect of what is included in the news—and what is not included," which causes it to appear "as though crime is more frequent and more severe than is actually the case."[39]

Gender

A third demographic factor associated with crime is gender. Historically, crime rates for men have been significantly higher than those for women with the exception of crimes that by definition are committed predominantly by women, such as prostitution. In 2009, men accounted for 74.7 percent of all arrests (81.2 percent of arrests for serious violent crimes and 62.6 percent of arrests for serious property crimes). However, in 2009 the number of female arrests increased by 11.4 percent over 2000, whereas those of males decreased by 4.9 percent. For that 9-year period, arrests of women for violent crimes increased only 0.1 percent (compared to an 8.1 percent decrease for men), but arrests for property crimes increased by 33.2 percent (compared to a decrease of 3.9 percent for men).[40]

When compared to 2008, arrests for men in 2009 were down 3.2 percent, but arrests for women increased by 0.2 percent. Larceny-theft was the only serious crime for which arrests increased (up 10.3 percent for women and 0.4 percent for men). Arrests for serious property crimes increased by 8.6 percent for women and decreased by 2.2 percent for men. Arrests for serious violent crimes decreased 2.7 percent for men and 0.4 percent for women. The largest decreases in arrests for serious crimes were for motor vehicle theft (down 17.5 percent for men and 14.1 percent for women) and arson (down 16.0 percent for men and 9.9 percent for women).[41]

In terms of juveniles (under 18) and gender, in 2009, arrests for males decreased 9.5 percent compared to a 7.5

American student Amanda Knox (far right) of Seattle, Washington, and her former Italian boyfriend, Raffaele Sollecito, were convicted of killing Knox's roommate, British student Meridith Kercher (middle), after sexually abusing her in the apartment the two women shared in the university town of Umbria, Italy. Knox is appealing her 26-year prison sentence.

Female inmates have been increasing in number, and some prisons are taking advantage of their presence. These women are part of a shackled work gang, picking up trash in Hamilton, Ohio.

percent decrease for females. Arrests for serious property crimes decreased by 7.3 percent for male juveniles and 0.2 percent for females.[42]

Characteristics of Crime Victims

Historically, the study of victims was not an important focus among social scientists. This has changed, and today, research attention is given to the characteristics and problems of victims as well as to improving the responses of criminal justice systems to victims' needs. Professional societies such as the National Organization for Victim Assistance (NOVA) have been instrumental in passing federal and state legislation concerning victims. NOVA has provided assistance to thousands of victims and works directly with local organizations to improve services at that level. Workshops on **victimology** have increased our knowledge and understanding of the problems of victims.

This text makes numerous references to victims discussed in the context of particular crimes (e.g., interpersonal violence against women, child abuse, elder abuse, and so on). This section presents general information about the characteristics of crime victims.

Concern with victims' needs has led to national legislation on their behalf. In response to the federal Victim and Witness Protection Act of 1982,[43] the U.S. attorney general's office issued detailed guidelines concerning the treatment of crime victims and witnesses by prosecutors and investigators in the Department of Justice. These guidelines are designed to protect the privacy of victims and witnesses and to provide medical, social, and counseling services. Notification of court proceedings, restitution, and other programs available for the assistance of victims and witnesses are also

provided. Some states have gone beyond the federal provisions and have enacted additional legislation to aid victims. In addition, in the 1994 federal crime bill, Congress included some provisions to enhance victims' rights, with a major focus on domestic violence victims.[44] Chapter 11 provides additional information on victims and especially victims' rights.

Recent programs do not, however, solve all of the problems of victims. Many of the programs are not adequately funded and thus do not provide enough money to satisfy reasonable claims. Sufficient prosecutors are not available to implement the programs or to supervise restitution orders.[45] Finally, many of the state laws are not written clearly or are not enforced widely.[46]

The NCVS provides data on the demographic characteristics of crime victims. Young people, men (except for rape and sexual assault), African Americans, Hispanics, divorced or separated people, the unemployed, the poor, and residents of central cities are the most frequent violent crime victims. The next sections look more closely at age, race and ethnicity, and gender. A new section on physically and mentally challenged victims is also included.

Age

Of all age groups, those 12 to 24 are the most frequent victims; the lowest rates of victimization are among those who are 50 or older.[47] The elderly (over 65) are the least frequently victimized, and most of the crimes against the elderly are property crimes. Approximately nine in ten crimes against the elderly are property crimes compared to four in ten crimes against the age group 12 to 24.[48]

The incidence of crimes against the elderly may not be as important, however, as the elderly's *perception* of the probability of becoming crime victims. Their fears may be

2.1 Violence in Japan

Japan, traditionally one of the countries with a low rate of violent crime, was the scene of a mass killing in June 2001, when a deranged man entered an elementary school of gifted students in Ikeda (10 miles from Osaka) armed with a kitchen knife and began a rampage. Eight children were killed; thirteen other students and two teachers were injured. The attacker was restrained by teachers and turned over to the police. He was identified as Mamoru Takuma, a 37-year-old drifter, who was said to have a grudge against children of affluent parents. Takuma was executed in 2004.[1]

Violent attacks had increased in Japan, but this mass killing was shocking and unusual. One U.S. news media referred to the shattering of Japan's "image as a haven of safety and order." Officials said the accused, who had been diagnosed with schizophrenia, had overdosed on medication.[2]

In June 2007, several of the students who witnessed that attack in 2001 were still suffering from serious mental problems, specifically, **posttraumatic stress disorder (PTSD)**, a disorder suffered by a person who has endured a severe trauma, such as rape, witnessing a crime, war, and so on. The survivors with PTSD become excessively frightened at the sound of loud noises or the sight of blood; they worry ex-cessively if doors and windows are not locked. Some avoid watching news reports on crimes against children.[3]

Seven years to the day later Tomohiro Kato, 25, went on a killing spree in a Tokyo neighborhood, killing seven people and injuring ten others. Kato, who stated he was just "tired of living," said he did not care whom he killed. He swerved his truck into a crowd of pedestrians and then hopped out and started knifing strangers. Kato was described as a sincere, hard-working man whose behavior shocked those who knew him. He graduated from one of Japan's top secondary schools and could have gone on to a university.[4]

1. "Knife-Wielding Man Kills 8 Children at Japanese School," *New York Times* (9 June 2007), p. 3; "Recent Major Campus Killings," *Asia Intelligence Wire* (18 April 2007), n.p.
2. "Shaken Japan Tries to Face Aftermath of School Attack," *New York Times* (10 June 2001), p. 14.
3. "Osaka School Kids Still Stressed Out from 2001 Stabbing Rampage," *Japan Economic Newswire* (7 June 2007), n.p.
4. "Tokyo Knife Rampage Kills Six," *The Australian* (9 June 2008), p. 13.

unrealistic, but the impact is dramatic. Many older people change their lifestyles in an effort to avoid becoming crime victims, even relocating if possible. Others become prisoners in their own dwellings, afraid to venture out even during the daylight hours. A purse snatching can have a far more serious impact on an elderly person than it might have on a younger victim. The elderly are more likely to be injured seriously if there is an altercation between the assailant and the victim, and the direct contact may be much more frightening. The loss of money may be more harmful, too, because many elderly people live on fixed incomes.

Just as the elderly may be peculiarly susceptible to some kinds of crime because they are so defenseless, the very young may also be easy prey. In addition, many young people are victimized by the apparent growing incidence of violence in schools, with some of the most shocking and tragic examples having occurred in recent years.[49] More attention is given to these issues in Chapter 7.

In some countries, children are rarely crime victims. There are exceptions, as Global Focus 2.1 demonstrates.

Race and Ethnicity

Victimization data show that African Americans suffer higher rates of violent and household crimes than whites, and generally, violent crimes against African Americans are more serious than those committed against whites. Of-fenders who victimize African Americans are more likely to use weapons; violent crimes against African Americans involve a gun in twice as many cases compared with whites. African American victims are more likely than whites to be attacked physically during the crime's commission.[50]

The BJS reported that in 2008,

- "The rate of violent victimization against blacks was 26 per 1,000 persons age 12 or older; for whites 18 per 1,000 and for persons of other races, 15 per 1,000.
- Blacks were victims of rape/sexual assault, robbery and aggravated assault at rates higher than those for whites."[51]

Blacks constitute only 13 percent of the total U.S. population, yet they constitute almost one-half of all homicide victims. According to the 2008 data, blacks have higher victimization rates than whites for all violent crimes that the NCVS measures with the exception of simple assault. The violent crime victimization rates of blacks are also generally higher than those of other racial groups, although there are some differences for Hispanics. In general, non-Hispanics have higher violent crime rates than Hispanics, primarily because they have a higher rate of simple assaults. Hispanics are more likely than non-Hispanics to be robbery victims.[52]

Violent crime rates of victimization by blacks and whites for the years 1973–2007 are graphed in Figure 2.6.

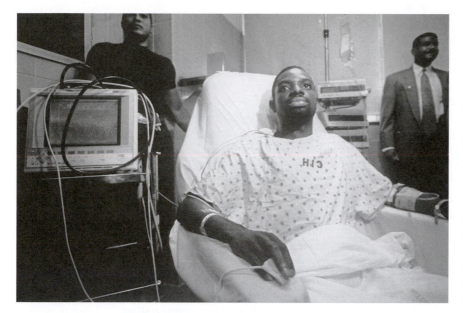

Abner Louima, a Haitian immigrant who alleged that he was sodomized and beaten by New York City police officers in 1997, talks to the press from his hospital bed. After the trial of five officers began, Justin A. Volpe entered a guilty plea; the jury found officer Charles Schwarz guilty of aiding in the attack; three other officers were acquitted. In 2001, Louima settled with New York City for $8.7 million. In March 2002, an appellate court overturned on technical grounds the conspiracy to obstruct justice conviction of Charles Schwarz, and the prosecutors chose not to retry him.

Figure 2.6

Violent Crime Rates by Race of Victim, 1973–2007

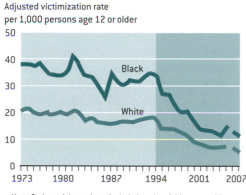

Note: Serious violent crimes included are homicide, rape, robbery, and aggravated assault. The National Crime Victimization Survey redesign was implemented in 1993; the area with the lighter shading is before the redesign and the darker area after the redesign. The data before 1993 are adjusted to make them comparable with data collected since the redesign.

Source: Bureau of Justice Statistics, "Key Facts at a Glance," http://bjs.ojp.usdoj.gov/content/glance/race.cfm, accessed 20 September 2010.

Gender

Overall, men are more likely than women to be victimized by crime, especially violent crime, although trend data show that the rates are getting closer. Women have higher violent crime victimization rates than men in only one category: forcible rape and other types of sexual assault. Men are far more likely to be murder victims, constituting 79 percent of that category. Men are also more likely to be carjacking victims. However, victimization rates for both women and men decreased between 1993 and 2008.[53] Violent crime rates by gender of victim for that time frame are graphed in Figure 2.7.

Men are more likely than women to be violent crime victims at the hands of strangers, with 44 percent of the violent crimes against men committed by strangers. For women, 27 percent of violent crimes are committed by strangers and 70 percent are committed by nonstrangers (18 percent by persons with whom the woman has or has had an intimate relationship, 3 percent by another relative, and 42 percent by a friend or acquaintance).[54] The victimization of men and women by their own intimates is discussed in more detail in Chapter 7.

Figure 2.7

Violent Crime Rates by Gender of Victim, 1973–2008

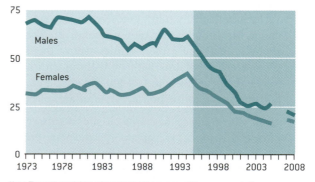

Note: The serious violent crimes included are rape, robbery, aggravated assault, and homicide. The National Crime Victimization Survey redesign was implemented in 1993; the area with the lighter shading is before the redesign and the darker area after the redesign. The data before 1993 are adjusted to make the comparable with data collected since the redesign.

Source: Bureau of Justice Statistics, "Key Facts at a Glance," http://bjs.ojp.usdoj.gov/content/glance/vsx2.cfm, accessed 20 September 2010.

Even though men are much more likely than women to be violent crime victims, research discloses that the fear of violent crime is greater among women, mainly because of the fear of forcible rape.[55]

Disabilities

On 1 October 2009, the Department of Justice released the data from the first national study by the Bureau of Justice Statistics (BJS) on persons with disabilities who were victimized by crimes, relying on 2007 data. The collection of such data is mandated by the Crime Victims with Disabilities Awareness Act.[56] Six types of disabilities were identified:

- Sensory
- Physical
- Cognitive functioning
- Self-care
- Go-outside-the home
- Employment

The BJS defined *disability* as "a long-standing (six months or more) sensory, physical, mental or emotional condition that makes it difficult for a person to perform daily living activities."[57]

Among other findings were the following:

- "Females with a disability had a higher victimization rate than males with a disability; males had a higher rate than females among those without a disability.
- Persons with a cognitive functioning disability had a higher risk of violent victimization than persons with any other type of disability.
- Persons with more than one type of disability accounted for about 56 percent of all violent crime victimizations against those with any disability.
- Nearly 1 in 5 violent crime victims with a disability believed that they became a victim because of their disability.
- Victims with a disability perceived offenders to be under the influence of either alcohol or drugs in about a third of all violent crimes against them.
- Violent crime victims with or without a disability were equally as likely to face an armed offender, report the crime to the police, or suffer an injury."[58]

Persons with some of the characteristics discussed may be (or perceive they are) at a greater disadvantage because of the reaction (or lack thereof) of criminal justice systems to them. It is therefore important to look at how criminal justice systems process alleged crime victims.

Criminal Justice Systems and Crime Victims

Research in the 1980s and 1990s provided information on how victims react to crime. Findings of this research led to significant changes in criminal justice systems. It has not been an easy journey for crime victims, and all of their problems have not been solved. Victim reaction, however, has been a key factor in these changes.

In 1982, President Ronald Reagan established the President's Task Force on Victims, which was followed in 1984 by the Attorney General's Task Force on Family Violence. Both commissions interviewed crime victims and others. Most of the victims spoke negatively about their treatment in criminal justice systems.

The criminal justice system's reaction to some crime victims means that they are victimized twice: once by the criminal and again by the system in a variety of ways. First, the victim may be blamed for the crime. Particularly in the case of sexual assault, the response of the system may be that the victim asked for it by being in a questionable place such as a bar, by hitchhiking, or by having a questionable reputation or wearing provocative clothing. This is referred to as **victim precipitation**.

In addition to being blamed for the crime, victims may perceive that police and others will not be sympathetic to crimes committed by persons known to the alleged victim and that they view those actions as domestic problems, not violence. Some rape victims have complained about the reactions of police and prosecutors, alleging that they have not tried to understand the problems suffered by the victims.

Third, some victims (and others) complain that U.S. criminal justice systems favor defendants over victims. This response should be analyzed in the light of later discussions of defendants' rights, but basically, the position is that criminal justice systems have gone too far in protecting defendants to the exclusion of victims.

Some changes designed to benefit victims have been made within criminal justice systems. Many departments now train police and prosecutors to be sensitive to the needs of adult rape and domestic violence victims, as well as young children who are abused in any way by their family, friends, or strangers. Other departments have special units of officers designated to handle allegations by these or other types of alleged victims.

Police departments have changed their arrest policies in response to persons who have complained that police often do not arrest offenders, and if they do, some prosecutors will not file charges. In an attempt to remove the responsibility (and thus increase the chances of retaliation by the accused) from alleged victims, some police departments have instituted a policy of mandatory arrests in domestic battery cases. Mandatory arrests remove from police the discretion to avoid the situation, mediate, or recommend civil action only. If called to the scene of a domestic battering, police must arrest if they have probable cause to believe that battering has occurred.

There have also been legislative and administrative changes in the roles of prosecutors and judges. Training programs for prosecutors have given them greater understanding of the unique problems suffered by forcible rape, domestic abuse, or child abuse victims. The provision of counseling services for victims; court-ordered counseling for those found guilty of forcible rape, domestic violence, or child abuse; greater restrictions on pretrial release of suspects; and many other changes have occurred.

A final area in which some criminal justice systems have responded to victims' needs is the development of **victim compensation programs**. Beginning in 1965 with California, the first state to adopt a victim compensation program, the trend toward adoption of such programs moved quickly. The provisions of state victim compensation programs vary considerably. The state plans also differ in the methods of application, eligibility requirements, and minimum and maximum awards. Unfortunately, many states have not provided adequate funding, leaving victims with an illusion that they will receive financial aid, medical care, counseling, and other assistance for the injuries and losses they have suffered as the result of crime.

Despite their popularity, victim compensation programs have been criticized. The passage of legislation in this area gives the impression that something is being done for victims. But for many reasons, many crime victims are not compensated adequately, if at all. Also, it is not clear that the programs meet other goals, such as increased crime reporting.

Some jurisdictions have enacted legislation to benefit witnesses as well as crime victims. Congress passed a victim compensation bill that applies to victims and witnesses involved in federal crimes, the Victim and Witness Protection Act of 1982 (VWPA), which has been amended subsequently. The act contains various provisions designed to prevent harassment of victims and witnesses. It establishes guidelines for fair treatment of crime victims and witnesses in criminal justice systems. It requires victim impact statements at sentencing, contains more stringent bail requirements, and provides that the sentencing judge must order defendants to pay restitution to victims or state reasons for not doing so.[59]

Congress also passed the Comprehensive Crime Control Act and the Victims of Crime Act of 1984 (VOCA), which authorizes the distribution of federal funds by the Office of Justice Programs through its Office for Victims of Crime and Bureau of Justice Statistics for state victim compensation and assistance programs. The funds are distributed to local agencies and have been used for hiring counselors to work with victims, for compensating victims, and even for acquiring technology, such as computers, that is used to assist victims.[60]

Although a proposed constitutional amendment on victims' rights was withdrawn by its sponsoring senators, who said they realized it would not get the necessary two-thirds vote to pass, a federal law establishing protections for victims was enacted in 2004 and is discussed in Chapter 11.

Analysis of Crime Data Collection

Crime data collection is critical to an understanding of crime and criminal justice systems. This chapter notes that data from official and unofficial sources do not always agree and considers the pros and cons of using the different methods of measuring crime. In the final analysis, the debate has been over which method is most accurate—that is, which minimizes the dark figures of unreported crime most successfully.

Keith Bottomley concluded that in the attempt to understand crime data, the important concern is not the accuracy with which data describe the extent of criminal behavior or illuminate the dark figures of unreported crime. Instead, the main concern is the way the data reflect the complex relationship between society and criminal behavior, providing a barometer of society's attitudes toward deviant behavior.[61] John I. Kitsuse and Aaron V. Cicourel emphasized that official crime data are the product of decisions to classify some behavior as criminal, and therefore, crime rates "can be viewed as indices of organizational processes rather than as indices of the incidence of certain forms of behavior."[62] According to Cicourel, the official data represent decisions by those in authority, and the decision to detain is based on a whole network of social action.[63]

These and other positions have led some social scientists, such as Kitsuse and Cicourel, to argue that new approaches should be taken toward official crime data. Instead of being criticized for not including all crimes, the data should be recognized for what they are—data concerning the social control of crime. They should be considered an end in themselves rather than a means to an end. Crime data are phenomena that are part of the social system, and therefore, they cannot be evaluated as inaccurate or unreliable. As an aspect of social organization and from a sociological point of view, crime data cannot be wrong.[64] Thus, official crime data may be viewed as indications of socially recognized deviant behavior. Any social system has acts of deviance that are not socially or officially recognized, but deviance should be regarded in terms of the reaction of legal and social control systems.

It is sociologically relevant to determine from the official data what behaviors are defined as deviant and how society organizes, classifies, and treats those forms of behavior. Official data indicate that deviants are distinguished from nondeviants. It is relevant sociologically to analyze the difference between a convicted person and one whose crime stops at the "crimes known to the police" stage. That both persons may have committed the same deviant act is as important sociologically as is the fact that officially they have been treated differently. Thus, as Kitsuse and Cicourel explain, official crime data may be viewed as the structural response to crime rather than as indicators of the actual incidence of crime.[65] In addition, such data provide important information about crime victims, changing policies of the courts (increases or decreases in the number of offenders placed on probation or fined), or trends in the length of sentencing; that is, they can be viewed as an *index of official action*.

Sociologist Stanton Wheeler suggested that the concept of crime data should be reformulated and considered as the interrelationship of three elements: (1) the person who commits the crime, (2) the victim or other citizens who may report the crime, and (3) the official agents of the state who are charged with controlling crime. Wheeler recommended this reformulation because of the increasing recognition that deviance depends on a social definition. Therefore, any analysis of crime data should recognize not only those who commit crimes but also those who define the behavior as criminal. Wheeler compared crime data with data on admission to and release from mental hospitals, arguing that neither could be understood by referring only to the characteristics of the subjects. Patients referred to child guidance clinics by doctors are admitted more quickly than are those referred by members of their own families; people with a higher socioeconomic status can get their family members into mental hospitals more quickly than people from lower classes can. In these cases, the reaction of others is important in determining who is labeled deviant.[66]

Wheeler discussed three practical consequences of this reformulation. First, police forces could be analyzed; perhaps the crime rates are high because the police are efficient. The police organizations of high-rate and low-rate areas could be compared; for example, the crime rates might reflect the relationship of the number of police cars to the number of people in an area. Differences among individual police officers could also be analyzed.

A second consequence would be an improved understanding of citizens and social control. Citizens who observe crimes being committed or who are victims affect the crime rate by their decisions on whether to report the crimes. Third, Wheeler's approach would lead to the development of consumer-oriented crime data. Crime data classify criminals by variables such as age, gender, race and ethnicity, disability, and so on. But more relevant to consumers is the *probability* that a crime will be committed against them. It is important to know that the crime rate went up because of an increase of people in the age bracket that commit most crimes, but it is more important for citizens to know the increase or decrease in their chances of being victimized. Empirical data could be used to describe crime victims as well as crime perpetrators.

Wheeler concluded that the result of this approach would be an improved understanding of criminals and criminal acts. Currently, comparisons of crime rates of one community with those of another have little meaning because of all the variables that make such comparisons of data unreliable. But within a community, crime could be better understood if the relevant variables were examined. Wheeler suggested that his new orientation toward crime data begin with the collection of data on (1) the complaining witnesses, (2) the social characteristics of the community, (3) the reporting or arresting officer, and (4) the nature of the police system as a whole.

Wheeler made these suggestions in 1967, and we have subsequently made some progress in our collection of crime data. Clearly, more needs to be done. In addition, it is important to take a brief look at how research is conducted in criminology.

Research in Criminology

Research in criminology is conducted to understand criminal behavior. If we can understand criminal behavior, we will have a better chance of predicting it and thus will be able to take policy steps to control, eliminate, or prevent it. All these purposes—control, elimination, and prevention—are, however, controversial.

Basing Policy Decisions on Research

Although it might seem obvious to the casual observer that the purpose of research in criminology is to control human behavior, traditionally, there has been disagreement within the social sciences over the role of the social scientist in a society's decision-making processes. In a provocative book entitled *Can Science Save Us?* sociologist George A. Lundberg stated the problem succinctly: "If we want results in improved human relations we must direct our research to the solution of these problems."[67] Early sociologists were interested in social reform; later sociologists argued that they should not be involved in making decisions based on their research results because scientists should be value-free. They should conduct their research rigorously but leave policy making to others.

Some scholars maintain that criminal justice systems are political and that they are used to discriminate against people who are not in positions of power (e.g., minorities). More recently, because of the widespread belief that nothing works in criminal justice, there has been a tendency to disregard research findings and to use common sense in setting policy. Sociologist Daniel Glaser contended in the late 1970s that public officials and many criminologists had abandoned crime causation theories. But, said Glaser, "explanatory theory cannot disappear, for it is inherent in human thinking, even in that of persons who disavow it." Glaser emphasized that any time we explain, we theorize, "and we theorize scientifically whenever we offer explanations that observation could prove erroneous." It is important to recognize these processes, for unless "it is made explicit, it cannot have cumulative growth and improvement." Most important, claimed Glaser, "the foundations of any science are the basic statements of its theory—its principles."[68]

One final statement regarding theory is important, and that is the need to relate those theories to practice. In their excellent theory text, Ronald L. Akers and Christine S. Sellers stated as their goals the following: (1) to state each theory concisely and clearly, (2) to evaluate each theory, and (3) to show the usefulness of each theory by offering examples of its application. Their work is a significant contribution to criminology in all these areas.[69] It is referenced frequently in the following theory chapters. This text also attempts to state practical applications of theories and concepts as well as to include recent examples of crimes and cases to bring criminology to life.

The Search for Explanations

The need for adequate research on criminal behavior has long been emphasized by social scientists; in the 1980s, this need gained the attention of the President's Task Force on Violent Crime. In its preliminary report in 1981, the task force stated, "It is imperative that we discover what works—what does not."[70] If we are to discover the answer to that question of what works, we must conduct scientific research. The discussion in this chapter is limited to analyzing the pitfalls and problems that we need to consider as we review the results of empirical research throughout this text.

Many different types of errors may occur in scientific research in the physical and social sciences. Some may be avoidable, but others may be due to the nature of the material being studied. Social scientists study human beings, who are capable of thinking, reflecting, forgetting, misrepresenting, and refusing to tell the truth. Given this practical reality, no criminal behavior research is without problems for the social scientist.

Selection of a Research Method

There are several methods to gather data. We have already looked at official data collected and published by the FBI, by the BJS, and by social scientists using SRD. Data may be secured by asking agencies to report data from their files, by asking individuals to complete questionnaires about their own behavior or the behavior of others, or by interviewing people about their involvement in crime or their perceptions of others' behavior.

There are advantages and disadvantages to selecting a particular method of securing data. Before selecting a method, the researcher should consider the nature of the study to be conducted. For example, although an in-depth study or a case study of a few inmates convicted of murder may give detailed information on the history of those criminals, that information would not be sufficient to permit generalizations about all murderers. Case studies are very helpful, however, in identifying variables that might be studied in larger populations. Depending on our purposes, it might be more valuable to survey a large number of murderers even though we would not find out as much about each murderer as we would if we conducted intensive individual case studies.

Research might take place over a period of time during which multiple sets of data are gathered. For example, if we wanted to know whether persons released from prison commit further crimes, we might decide to gather information six months or a year after their release. We could continue the research further into the future as well. If we did not want to consider the time variable, we might select samples of subjects (e.g., male inmates and female inmates) at the same time and collect data for comparative purposes. The method of gathering data depends on the nature of the study and the cost of the project. Following a sample over a period of years is expensive, and research funds for studies of this type are limited. Selecting a large sample for an in-depth study is costly, particularly if the subjects are located in different cities and numerous researchers are needed to conduct the study.

In some cases, the activities the researcher wishes to study have already taken place and cannot be repeated. In these cases, an ***ex post facto* method** is appropriate (the Latin phrase *ex post facto* means "after the fact"). A sample of people already convicted of murder might be selected and studied to find out whether any of their past events or characteristics could explain why they murdered. In contrast, when researchers want to study ongoing activities, they might go into the field to study behavior as it occurs. But they must be careful not to get so involved in the behavior under study that they lose their objectivity.[71]

Errors in Interpreting Data

Social scientists must take care in analyzing empirical data because the meaning of most facts is not obvious. Facts must be interpreted. Researchers must be careful not to go beyond the data—that is, not to use it to explain something that was not measured or to generalize the findings beyond the scope of the study. For example, if all members of a given sample are men, we cannot conclude that the research findings also apply to women because gender might be an important variable in explaining the delinquent or criminal behavior under study.

One of the most common errors in interpreting crime data is the **dualistic fallacy**, the assumption that there is necessarily a distinct difference between two groups: criminals and noncriminals. The assumption is that each group is homogeneous and that studies can compare the two groups on a given trait and conclude that the findings represent the differences between them—that is, criminals violate the law and noncriminals do not. As noted earlier, research shows that this assumption is not correct. The dualistic fallacy is so serious that all empirical studies of criminal behavior involving the error must be assumed to have limited scientific validity in distinguishing between those who commit crimes and those who do not.

Science assumes that a phenomenon can be measured empirically with valid and reliable tools and distinguished from something that is similar but not of the same classification. Even if the phenomenon cannot be measured with the senses, science presumes that it has consistent indicators of its existence that can be measured.

When these assumptions are applied to the study of crime, the critical issue is what phenomenon is assumed to exist. Is there something called *crime* that is unique behavior? Can it be distinguished from all other behavior? The answer to both questions must be no. There is nothing intrinsically unique or distinguishable about crime. A crime is defined not in terms of the properties or attributes of an act but in terms of the social situation in which it occurs. For example, sexual intercourse may be a lawful relationship between a husband and a wife; it is a physical act that can be described. In different circumstances, however, sexual intercourse may be incest, adultery, rape, statutory rape, or fornication, all of which are crimes in some jurisdictions. Furthermore, even though certain acts are defined as crimes, many violators are not prosecuted, in which case they should not be considered criminals as the term is defined legally.

Crime is a definitional term. It exists because certain acts are defined as such. But those acts cannot be distinguished clearly from similar acts, or even from identical acts, except by social reaction because intrinsically crime is just like noncrime. A given behavior may be a crime when committed by some people in some situations and not a crime when committed by others in different situations. In trying to understand criminal behavior, we must understand not only why people commit acts that are defined as crimes—the approach taken by many sociological theorists—but also the *process* by which some, but not all, people who engage in the acts are labeled criminal.

We could conclude from the discussion in this section that social science research is inherently suspect and that it never will be free of methodological problems to the extent that it can be used to explain crime. But many of the problems can be resolved with adequate planning. As methodologist George A. Lundberg observed, "Many of the fruits of science . . . can be used to advantage while still in the process of development. Science is at best a growth, not a sudden revelation." Research in the social sciences can be used "imperfectly and in part while it is developing."[72]

We have come a long way from the writings and thinking of the people whose ideas dominated the nineteenth and twentieth centuries, but those ideas were important in establishing the foundation for our current knowledge, and attention should be given to their contributions. That is the purpose of Chapter 3.

Summary

This chapter examined the official and unofficial sources of data on criminal activity. It focused on the collection and interpretation of crime data. The two major official sources of crime and victimization data, the *Uniform Crime Reports (UCR)* and the National Crime Victimization Survey (NCVS), were examined.

The official source of crime data, the *UCR*, was examined in terms of its coverage and its limitations. The source reports the most serious crimes, those referred to as Part I offenses, by two major categories: violent crimes and property crimes. The total number of crimes known to the police are reported. In addition, the *UCR* reports crime rates, clearance rates, and arrests for serious offenses. For less serious offenses, the *UCR* reports only arrest data.

After describing what the *UCR* does, the chapter turned to an analysis of the limitations of this source. Data may be influenced by police discretion in determining whether a crime has been committed, in deciding whether to report the crime, or even by policy changes within police departments. Victims may refuse to cooperate with police or refuse to report crimes. Administrative and bureaucratic changes within police departments, such as a change in the size of the police force, may affect crime data. Changes in personnel may be influential.

The way crimes are counted also influences crime data. Another factor is the method of categorizing an event. For example, forcible rape might be categorized either as rape or as a lesser offense, such as simple assault, and the decision will influence the number of crimes in each of those categories.

Another limitation of the *UCR* is that it excludes some crimes, such as computer crimes, organized crime, and white-collar crimes, which may occur frequently but do not fall within any of the categories in the *UCR*.

Recognition of these and other limitations of the *UCR* led the FBI to develop and implement the National Incident-Based Reporting System (NIBRS), which includes such elements of crimes as the relationship between the offender and the victim and the type of weapon used. Another reaction to the limitations of the *UCR* has been to utilize data from victimization surveys such as the Bureau of Justice Statistics' National Crime Victimization Survey (NCVS). These reports are based on the responses of alleged crime victims. Comparisons of data from the NCVS and the *UCR* must be made carefully and in light of the differences between the databases of the two sources.

Another source of crime and victimization data is self-report data (SRD), which are secured through anonymous questionnaires or interviews. This method is limited by factors such as nonresponsiveness or inaccurate reporting by the sample. Some of the methodological problems of SRD may be overcome by the National Youth Survey (NYS), which involves interviews with young people over a five-year period. A discussion of the Crime Classification System (CCS), which focuses on the harm suffered by victims and the context in which the crime occurs, was followed by a look at the National Criminal History Improvement Program (NCHIP).

From a discussion of methods of collecting data, the chapter turned to a focus on the actual data. Crime and victimization data were discussed in terms of trends as well as the demographic characteristics of criminals and their victims. The age, race and ethnicity, and gender of offenders and of victims were discussed. A new edition to this text was the discussion of victims who have disabilities. These analyses indicated the necessity of carefully examining the crime and victimization data as well as the variables associated with those data. At relevant points throughout the text, attention is given to age, race and ethnicity, and gender as factors that influence decision making in criminal justice systems. This chapter established the background on which those discussions are based.

In the final section regarding victims, the chapter also analyzed the ways criminal justice systems react to victims.

The next focus of the chapter was the position taken some years ago by a prominent sociologist, Stanton Wheeler, who proposed an expanded view of crime data collection. Wheeler's suggestion that crime is a social phenomenon is shared by others, some of whose views are represented throughout the text. It is important to view crime in the context in which it occurs, but it is also important to keep in mind the restrictions the law places on the use of the terms *crime* and *criminal*, as discussed in Chapter 1.

The chapter's final section contained a brief overview of the importance of research and a glance at the methods of social science research and its problems. This background is necessary for understanding the modern empirical studies on which subsequent chapters are based.

It is easy to become discouraged by the problems of data collection. We should not conclude that because no one source is accurate the situation is hopeless. The secret nature of crime, the shame and fear with which some victims react, and many other factors may contribute to the inaccuracy of crime data, but our sources are better today than they were in the past, and they continue to improve.

Study Questions

1. What is the function of the Bureau of Justice Statistics (BJS)?
2. Describe the *Uniform Crime Reports* (*UCR*).
3. Define *Part I offenses* of the *UCR*.
4. What changes has the FBI made in the use of index offenses for reporting crime data?
5. How does the FBI report data on crimes other than the eight serious offenses?
6. Explain the National Incident-Based Reporting System (NIBRS).
7. What is the National Crime Victimization Survey (NCVS)?
8. Do self-report data (SRD) shed any light on crime?

9. What contributions do the National Youth Survey (NYS) and the Crime Classification System (CCS) make to crime data collection?
10. Describe the National Criminal History Improvement Program (NCHIP).
11. Has the crime rate been going up or down in recent years? Discuss.
12. How important are the factors of age, race and ethnicity, and gender on crime and victimization?
13. Describe the recent addition of data on victims with disabilities. What is your assessment of this addition?
14. Discuss the meaning and importance of victim compensation programs.
15. Evaluate crime data in view of Stanton Wheeler's position.
16. What is the importance of the research methods used by those who study criminal behavior?
17. What is an *ex post facto* study?
18. Explain what is meant by the dualistic fallacy.

Brief Essay Assignments

1. Distinguish between the *UCR* and the NCVS as sources of crime data, and discuss the primary limitations of each.
2. Analyze the problems associated with crime reporting, and suggest ways to solve them.
3. Discuss the implications of age, race and ethnicity, and gender on crime and on victimization.
4. Discuss the potential impact of the addition of persons with disabilities to crime victimization data.
5. Crime data, no matter how they are collected and analyzed, are never accurate. Discuss the implications of this statement.

Internet Activities

1. Search the Internet to find information on campus security. You might begin with the Bureau of Justice Statistics site, http://bjs.ojp.usdoj.gov/. Select Law Enforcement and then Campus Law Enforcement for an overview of policing and security on college and university campuses. The website for Security on Campus, http://www.securityoncampus.org, also has campus crime data and is currently offering internships for college students. See what you can find about crime on your college campus. What is your college doing to make the campus safer? What has been the most frequently reported crime? How many serious violent and property crimes have been reported? (Sites accessed 20 September 2010.)
2. To find more information on victimization by age, race and ethnicity, gender, and disability, go to the Bureau of Justice Statistics website's home page, http://bjs.ojp.usdoj.gov/, accessed 20 September 2010. Select Victims, which has seven subheads. Select any of these headings to obtain more information on victims.

You might also want to check the Federal Bureau of Investigation's most recent *Uniform Crime Reports*, located at http://www2.fbi.gov/ucr/cius2009/, accessed 20 September 2010.

Notes

1. Federal Bureau of Investigation, *Crime in the United States: Uniform Crime Reports, 2009* (13 September 2010), http://www2.fbi.gov/ucr/cius2009/about/variables_affecting_crime.html, accessed 6 December 2010.
2. Federal Bureau of Investigation, *Crime in the United States: Uniform Crime Reports 1999* (Washington, D.C.: U.S. Government Printing Office, 2000), pp. 6–50.
3. "Crime in the United States, 2000," news release, Federal Bureau of Investigation (22 October 2001), p. 1.
4. "The Nation: Crime Falls Slightly in 2002, FBI Reports," *Los Angeles Times* (17 June 2003), p. 25; "FBI Reports 0.2 Percent Drop in Crime," United Press International Press Release (16 June 2003); FBI press release (28 October 2003).
5. Federal Bureau of Investigation, *Crime in the United States: Uniform Crime Reports 2003* (Washington, D.C.: U.S. Government Printing Office, 2004), pp. 11, 41; Federal Bureau of Investigation, *Crime in the United States: Uniform Crime Reports 2004* (Washington, D.C.: U.S. Government Printing Office, 2005), p. 11.
6. Federal Bureau of Investigation, *Crime in the United States: Uniform Crime Reports 2005*, http:// www2.fbi.gov/ucr/05cius/, accessed 9 December 2010.
7. Federal Bureau of Investigation Press Release (24 September 2007), http://www.fbi.gov/pressrel/pressre107/cius092407.htm, accessed 24 September 2007.
8. Federal Bureau of Investigation, *Uniform Crime Reports 2003*, p. 5.
9. Federal Bureau of Investigation, *Crime in the United States: Uniform Crime Reports 2009*, "Clearances," http://www2.fbi.gov/ucr/cius2009/offenses/clearances/index.html, accessed 13 September 2010.
10. *Uniform Crime Reports 2009*, "Arrests," http://www2.fbi.gov/ucr/cius2009/arrests/index.html, accessed 9 December 2010.
11. Michael R. Rand, National Crime Victimization Survey, Bureau of Justice Statistics, *Criminal Victimization, 2008* (September 2009), p. 6, http://bjs.ojp.usdoj.gov/content/pub/pdf/cv08.pdf, accessed 20 September 2010.
12. Timothy C. Hart and Callie Rennison, Bureau of Justice Statistics, *Reporting Crime to the Police, 1992–2000* (Washington, D.C.: U.S. Department of Justice, March 2003), p. 1.
13. Shannan Catalano, Bureau of Justice Statistics, *Intimate Partner Violence in the U.S.: Reporting to the Police,* http://bjs.ojp.usdoj.gov/content/intimate/report.cfm, accessed 20 September 2010.
14. Patrick J. Carr et al., "We Never Call the Cops and Here Is Why," *Criminology* 45, no. 2 (May 2007): 445–480.
15. "Variables Affecting Crimes," Federal Bureau of Investigation, *Crime in the United States 2009*, http://www2.fbi.gov/ucr/cius2009/about/variables_affecting_crime.html, accessed 18 September 2010.
16. Bureau of Justice Statistics, U.S. Department of Justice, Office of Justice Programs, "Incident-Based Statistics," www.ojp.usdoj.gov/bjs/ibrs.htm, accessed 8 August 2007.
17. See, for example, Alfred Blumstein et al., "Trend and Deviation in Crime Rates: A Comparison of UCR and NCS Data for Burglary and Robbery," *Criminology* 29 (May 1991): 237–263; Scott Menard, "Residual Gains, Reliability, and the UCR-NCS Relationship: A Comment on Blumstein, Cohen, and Rosenfeld," *Criminology* 30 (February 1992): 105–113; and Blumstein et al., "The UCR-NCS Relationship Revisited: A Reply to Menard," *Criminology* 30 (February 1992): 115–124.
18. James F. Short and F. Ivan Nye, "Extent of Unrecorded Juvenile Delinquency: Tentative Conclusions," *Journal of Criminal Law, Criminology, and Police Science* 49 (November/December 1957): 296–302. For an analysis, see Michael J. Hindelang, Travis Hirschi, and Joseph G. Weis, *Measuring Delinquency* (Beverly Hills, CA: Sage, 1981).
19. Thomas Gabor, *Everybody Does It! Crime by the Public* (Toronto: University of Toronto Press, 1994), p. xiii.
20. James S. Wallerstein and C. J. Wyle, "Our Law Abiding Lawbreakers," *Probation* 25 (April 1947): 107–112.
21. See Austin Porterfield, "Delinquency and Its Outcome in Courts and College," *American Journal of Sociology* 49 (November 1943): 199–208; Maynard L. Erikson and Lamar T. Empey, "Court Records, Undetected Delinquency, and Decision Making," *Journal of Criminal Law, Criminology, and Police Science* 54 (December 1963): 456–469; and Jay R. Williams and Martin Gold, "From Delinquent Behavior to Official Delinquency," *Social Problems* 20 (Fall 1962): 209–213.
22. See "Career Criminals and Criminal Careers," *Criminal Justice Research at Rand* (Santa Monica, CA: Rand, 1985), pp. 3–7. See also John D. Hewitt et al., "Self Reported and Observed Rule Breaking in Prison: A Look at Disciplinary Responses," *Justice Quarterly* 1, no. 3 (March 1983): 437–447.
23. See, for example, Michael J. Hindelang et al., "Correlates of Delinquency: The Illusion of Discrepancy Between Self-Report and Official Measures," *American Sociological Review* 44 (December 1979): 995–1014.
24. "Study Says Surge in Girls' Arrests Is Due to Changes in Policy and Law," *Criminal Justice Newsletter* (1 December 2008), pp. 4–6, referring to the Girls Study Group, a study sponsored by the Office of Juvenile Justice and Delinquency Prevention (OJJDP) of the U.S. Department of Justice and conducted by Margaret A. Zahn and Stephanie R. Hawkins.
25. See Delbert S. Elliott, David Huizinga, and Suzanne S. Ageton, *Explaining Delinquency and Drug Use* (Newbury Park, CA: Sage, 1985).
26. Gerald F. Ranker, Bureau of Justice Statistics, U.S. Department of Justice, Office of Justice Programs, "Improving Criminal History Records for Background Checks 2005" (July 2006), http://bjs.ojp.usdoj.gov/content/pub/pdf/ichrbc05.pdf, accessed 20 September 2010.
27. Jennifer Truman and Michael R. Rand, Bureau of Justice Statistics, *Criminal Victimization, 2009*, p. 1, http://bjs.ojp.usdoj.gov/content/pub/pdf/cn09.pdf, accessed 20 October 2010.
28. Federal Bureau of Investigation, *Crime in the United States, Uniform Crime Reports 1982* (Washington, D.C.: U.S. Government Printing Office, 1983), p. iii.
29. Federal Bureau of Investigation, *Crime in the United States, Uniform Crime Reports 1985* (Washington, D.C.: U.S. Government Printing Office, 1986), p. iii.
30. Federal Bureau of Investigation, *Crime in the United States, Uniform Crime Reports 1991* (Washington, D.C.: U.S. Government Printing Office, 1992), p. 6.

31. *Uniform Crime Reports 2009.*

32. Federal Bureau of Investigation, *Crime in the United States, Uniform Crime Reports 2009,* "Arrests."

33. Federal Bureau of Investigation, *Crime in the United States, Uniform Crime Reports 2009,* http://www2.fbi.gov/ucr/cius2009/data/table_41.html, accessed 20 September 2010.

34. Charles Puzzanchera, *Juvenile Arrests 2008,* Office of Juvenile Justice and Delinquency Prevention, U.S. Department of Justice (December 2009), http://www.ncjrs.gov/app/publications/abstract.aspx?ID=250498, accessed 9 December 2010.

35. David Finkelhor et al., *Juveniles Who Commit Sex Offenses Against Minors,* Office of Juvenile Justice and Delinquency Prevention, U.S. Department of Justice (December 2009), http://www.ncjrs.gov/pdffiles1/ojjdp/227763.pdf, accessed 3 March 2010.

36. See, for example, William Wilbanks, *The Myth of a Racist Criminal Justice System* (Monterey, CA: Brooks/Cole, 1987); Joan Petersilia et al., *Racial Equity in Sentencing* (Santa Monica, CA: Rand, 1988).

37. Federal Bureau of Investigation, *Crime in the United States, Uniform Crime Reports 2009,* http://www2.fbi.gov/ucr/cius2009/data/table_43.html, accessed 20 September 2010.

38. See, for example, Coramae Richey Mann et al., *Images of Color, Images of Crime,* 3rd ed. (Los Angeles: Roxbury, 2006).

39. Mark Soler and Lisa M. Garry, *Reducing Disproportionate Minority Contact: Preparation at the Local Level,"* Office of Juvenile Justice and Delinquency Prevention, U.S. Department of Justice (September 2009), p. 2, http://www.ncjrs.gov/pdffiles1/ojjdp/218861.pdf, accessed 9 December 2010.

40. Federal Bureau of Investigation, *Crime in the United States, Uniform Crime Reports 2009,* http://www2.fbi.gov/ucr/cius2009/data/table_33.html, accessed 20 September 2010.

41. Federal Bureau of Investigation, *Crime in the United States, Uniform Crime Reports 2009,* http://www2.fbi.gov/ucr/cius2009/data/table_37.html, accessed 20 September 2010.

42. Ibid.

43. U.S. Code, Title 18, Section 3663 (2010).

44. See, for example, Title 4, Violence Against Women, of the Violent Crime Control and Law Enforcement Act of 1994, Public Law 103-322 (13 September 1994).

45. "Victim Rights Impose Burdens on Prosecutors, Study Shows," *Criminal Justice Newsletter* 32, no. 10 (5 June 2002): 3.

46. "States Closing Loopholes in Victim Restitution Laws," *Criminal Justice Newsletter* (16 January 2003), p. 4.

47. Rand, *Criminal Victimization, 2009* , p. 4.

48. Bureau of Justice Statistics, Office of Justice Programs, U.S. Department of Justice, "Victim Characteristics," http://bjs.ojp.usdoj.gov/index.cfm?ty=tp&tid=92, accessed 20 September 2010.

49. For recent data on violence in schools, see Katrina Baum et al., *Indicators of School Crime and Safety: 2009,* Bureau of Justice Statistics, U.S. Department of Justice (December 2009), http://bjs.ojp.usdoj.gov/index.cfm?ty=pbdetail&iid=1762, accessed 20 September 2010.

50. Erika Harrell, Bureau of Justice Statistics, "Black Victims of Violent Crime," (August 2007), p. 1, http://bjs.ojp.usdoj.gov/content/pub/pdf/bvvc.pdf, accessed 20 September 2010.

51. Bureau of Justice Statistics, "Victim Characteristics."

52. Harrell, "Black Victims of Violent Crime."

53. Bureau of Justice Statistics, "Victim Characteristics."

54. Truman and Rand, *Criminal Victimization, 2009,* p. 5.

55. See, for example, Bonnie S. Fisher and John J. Sloan III, "Unraveling Fear of Victimization Among College Women: Is the 'Shadow of Sexual Assault Hypothesis' Supported?" *Justice Quarterly* 20, no. 3 (September 2003): 633–659.

56. Crime Victims with Disabilities Awareness Act, Public Law 105-301 (1998).

57. U.S. Department of Justice, Office of Justice Programs, Bureau of Justice Statistics, "First National Study on Crime Against Persons with Disabilities," Press release (1 October 2009), http://bjs.ojp.usdoj.gov/, accessed 20 September 2010.

58. Michael R. Rand and Erika Harrell, U.S. Department of Justice, Office of Justice Programs, Bureau of Justice Statistics, National Crime Victimization Survey, *Crime Against People with Disabilities, 2007* (October 2009), p. 1, http://bjs.ojp.usdoj.gov/content/pub/pdf/capd07.pdf, accessed 20 September 2010. The data were similar for 2009. See Harrell and Rand, *Crime Against People with Disabilities, 2008* (December 2010), http://bjs.ojp.usdoj.gov/content/pub/pdf/capd08.pdf, accessed 9 December 2010.

59. U.S. Code, Title 18, Section 3663 (2010).

60. U.S. Code, Title 42, Section 10601 et seq. (2010).

61. Keith Bottomley, *Decisions in the Penal Process* (South Hackensack, NJ: Rothman, 1973), p. 21.

62. John I. Kitsuse and Aaron V. Cicourel, "A Note on the Uses of Official Statistics," *Social Problems* 11 (Fall 1963): 137.

63. Aaron V. Cicourel, *The Social Organization of Juvenile Justice* (New York: Wiley, 1968), p. 37.

64. See Kitsuse and Cicourel, "A Note on the Uses of Official Statistics," pp. 131–139.

65. Ibid., p. 137.

66. Stanton Wheeler, "Criminal Statistics: A Reformulation of the Problem," *Journal of Criminal Law, Criminology and Police Science* 58 (September 1967): 317–324. All of the references here to Wheeler are from this article.

67. George A. Lundberg, *Can Science Save Us?* (New York: Longman, 1961), p. 134.

68. Daniel Glaser, "A Review of Crime Causation Theory and Its Application," in *Crime and Justice: An Annual Review of Research,* Vol. 1, ed. Norval Morris and Michael Tonry (Chicago: University of Chicago Press, 1979), pp. 204–205.

69. See Ronald L. Akers and Christine S. Sellers, *Criminological Theories: Introduction, Evaluation, and Application,* 5th ed. (New York: Oxford University Press, 2009), p. xii.

70. Attorney General William French Smith, "Federal, State, and Local Law Enforcement Must Cooperate to Fight Crime in America," *Justice Assistance News* (August 1981), p. 2.

71. See Hans Toch, "Cast the First Stone: Ethics as a Weapon," *Criminology* 19 (August 1981): 185–194; Marvin E. Wolfgang, "Confidentiality in Criminological Research and Other Ethical Issues," *Journal of Criminal Law and Criminology* 71 (Spring 1981): 345–361.

72. Lundberg, *Can Science Save Us?* pp. 143–144.

PART TWO

Explanations of Criminal Behavior

Part II covers the major concepts and theories utilized in attempts to explain criminal behavior. **Chapter 3** opens the discussion with a look at the historical background of punishment in Europe and an analysis of the early explanations of criminal behavior. The chapter compares those explanations with their modern counterparts by looking at punishment philosophies.

Chapter 4 covers biological and psychological theories. Both areas are gaining recognition among some scholars in criminology, although both remain controversial. Sociological theories, which constitute the major focus of criminological explanations of behavior, are divided into two chapters. **Chapter 5** analyzes theories that focus on society's structure and its impact, and **Chapter 6** is composed of social-process approaches.

CHAPTER 3

Early Explanations of Criminal Behavior and Their Modern Counterparts

This tribute to the 15 victims, including the student perpetrators, in the 1999 violent shootings at Columbine High School in Littleton, Colorado, raises the ultimate question that we have yet to answer: WHY?

CHAPTER OUTLINE

KEY TERMS

castration
classical theorists
constitutional approach
cruel and unusual punishment
determinism
deterrence
free will
general deterrence
hedonism
incapacitation
individual (or specific) deterrence
just deserts
justice model
neoclassical school
positivist school
punishment
rehabilitation
retribution
social contract
theory
utilitarianism

INTRODUCTION

This chapter begins with a look at the historical background of punishment and criminal law in Europe before proceeding to an analysis of the contributions of the classical, neoclassical, and positivist schools to the development of the study of crime. It examines the impact of these schools on modern punishment philosophies. The classical position of "let the punishment fit the crime," with its emphasis on the beliefs that we are rational in our thoughts and that we make rational choices to seek pleasure and avoid pain, argues that sufficient punishment is a deterrent to criminal behavior. If the punishment is a little worse than the pleasure of committing the crime, individuals will not commit the crimes. The chapter analyzes empirical research on this issue and contrasts the current emphasis on deterrence and retribution, or in the more palatable terms of today, just deserts, with the former emphasis on the need to reform or rehabilitate the criminal.

Chapter 2 discussed the measurement of crime and considered some of the factors, such as age, race and ethnicity, and gender, that are related to crime data. It also covered methods of studying crime. Collecting data on crime is the first step toward the goals of punishing, controlling, and preventing criminal behavior. To achieve one or more of these goals, we must develop ways to evaluate the data. Why are crime rates higher among men than among women? What are the reasons? The explanations? If we can understand why people engage in criminal behavior, we may be able to predict and control that behavior.

Simple facts are not sufficient; for example, it is not very helpful to know only that there are more arrests of men than of women. We need to know what the patterns and the variables are that might explain these differences. To come up with such explanations, social scientists, like physical scientists, engage in research to develop and test their theories. A **theory** is part of an explanation, an attempt to relate two or more variables in ways that can be tested. If properly constructed and tested, a theory can be supported, shown to be incorrect, or at least questioned. Thus, a theory is more than an assumption. It involves efforts to test the reality of thoughts or explanations about how variables (such as gender) are related to phenomena (such as criminal behavior). Research that involves empirical testing of theories can be, and usually is, very complex and therefore beyond the scope of this text. The text does, however, summarize research findings pertinent to the discussed topics.

Research findings may influence the decisions that are made regarding the processing of offenders. For example, if we believe that stiff penalties are more effective than light ones in deterring criminal activity, we will probably institute harsher penalties. Unfortunately, too often, we make such decisions on the basis of intuition or "common sense" without any reference to existing social science findings or any attempt to conduct research if none is available. This chapter sets the stage for subsequent chapters on social science research and theories that have been developed to explain criminal behavior.

The Historical Background of Punishment and Criminal Law

Ideas and philosophies do not exist within a vacuum; they must be understood in light of the social context in which they appear. To understand the significant contributions to modern criminology made by eighteenth-century writers, we must know something about the social conditions that existed at the time they wrote.

The eighteenth-century writers were rebelling against an arbitrary and corrupt system of law in which judges held an absolute and almost tyrannical power over those who came before them. Laws were often vague, and judges took it upon themselves to interpret the spirit of the law if the vagueness did not suit their purposes. Such widespread personal interpretation of the law led to a lack of consistency and impartiality. Accusations were often secret, and trials were often a farce. The law was applied unequally to citizens, and corruption was rampant. Confessions were obtained by the use of torture, and the death penalty was used for many offenses. Due process of law and equality before the law were unknown concepts. Brief comments on the conditions in two European countries, France and England, are illustrative.

During the Middle Ages in France, decisions regarding sentencing of the accused were made in secret; judges

Severe corporal punishments, such as the use of the rack, pictured here, are not permitted in the United States today, but criminals are incapacitated in other ways, such as imprisonment.

could make decisions without any restrictions. The sentences were usually severe, with the defendant having no right of defense at the trial. Punishments were decided by secret tribunals, and defendants were punished "according to the authority of the secret bench." Methods of torture differed from province to province within France, but most were severe, with some leading to death.[1]

At the beginning of the eighteenth century, one philosophical school advocated uniformity of laws, but the judges were opposed. They said the customs differed from province to province, and therefore, the laws must differ.[2] Philosophers were not successful in changing the barbarous punishments of the Middle Ages in France, and most of those laws remained until the eve of the French Revolution.

In England during the eighteenth century, laws were weak, and punishments were severe. Criminal laws relied on deterrence, not surveillance or detection. Capital punishment was provided for more than 200 offenses. In fact, the English Code of the eighteenth century, often called the *bloody code*, was one of the severest in history. It barred some forms of severe torture (such as cutting noses and ears), but it permitted others and provided for capital punishment for such offenses as cutting down trees in an avenue or a park, setting fire to a cornfield, taking part in a riot, shooting a rabbit, demolishing a turnpike gate, and escaping from jail. When the sentence was flogging at the end of a cart drawn through town, spectators would often pay the executioner to whip more vigorously.[3]

Although the European conditions provided the basis for the reform movement of the classical philosophers discussed later, many of these severe forms of punishment were also utilized in the American colonies. It was against the background of these severe punishments and harsh laws that the classical school emerged.

The Classical Beginnings

The development of formal criminology as a discipline is recent, but the ideas of people who might be called early criminologists can be traced historically. Most of these people were lawyers, doctors, philosophers, or social scientists whose primary interest was in reforming the criminal law, not in creating a science of criminal behavior. Nevertheless, the contributions of the **classical theorists** to criminology are immense and are seen in this chapter's subsequent discussions of deterrence and rational choice theory. Some familiarity with these early approaches is essential to an adequate understanding of current criminological theories. The number of contributors to the classical school of thinking was immense, but criminologists generally select two of them to illustrate the approach. These two are chosen because, in their writings, they directly targeted criminal law and the criminal justice system in contrast to others, who covered broader social philosophy.

Cesare Beccaria

The leader of the classical school was Cesare Beccaria, born in Milan, Italy, on 15 March 1738. Before his death in 1794, Beccaria published only one major book, a slim volume entitled *An Essay on Crime and Punishments*. It was not entirely original, for many of Beccaria's ideas were syntheses of those already expressed by others, but it was well received because many people in Europe were ready to hear about and implement the kinds of changes Beccaria proposed.[4] The 1963 translator of Beccaria's essay summarized his view of the writer's contributions in Global Focus 3.1, which also contains several brief excerpts from Beccaria's essay.

As you concentrate on Beccaria's words in Global Focus 3.1, consider how influential he has been on U.S. criminal justice systems. According to criminologist Stephen Schafer, Beccaria's short essay contained the basis for almost all modern penal reforms, but its greatest contribution is "the foundation it laid for subsequent changes in criminal legislation."[5]

This statue of Cesare Beccaria (1738–1794) in Milan, Italy, where he was born, pays tribute to the leader of the classical school of criminology. Beccaria is best known for his philosophy that the punishment should fit the crime rather than be individualized for the criminal. He is a controversial figure among modern criminologists. (Photo by Richard Kania.)

3.1   The Contributions of Cesare Beccaria

In his 1963 introduction to his translation of Cesare Beccaria's *On Crimes and Punishments*, Henry Paolucci began with the following:

> Historians of criminal law agree, almost without exception, that the "glory of having expelled the use of torture from every tribunal throughout Christendom" belongs primarily to Cesare Beccaria. His treatise . . . is generally acknowledged to have had "more practical effect than any other treatise ever written in the long campaign against barbarism in criminal law and procedure."[1]

In the beginning of his book, *On Crimes and Punishments*, Beccaria stated the premise for which he became so well known:

> If we glance at the pages of history, we will find that laws, which surely are, or ought to be, compacts of free men, have been, for the most part, a mere tool of the passions of some, or have arisen from an accidental and temporary need. Never have they been dictated by a dispassionate student of human nature who might, by bringing the actions of a multitude of men into focus, consider them from this single point of view: the *greatest happiness shared by the greatest number*.[2]

Beccaria expressed his knowledge of the magnitude of his undertaking in writing this little essay with these words:

> But very few persons have studied and fought against the cruelty of punishments and the irregularities of criminal procedures, a part of legislation that is as fundamental as it is widely neglected in almost all of Europe. Very few persons have undertaken to demolish the accumulated errors of centuries by rising to general principles, curbing, at least, with the sole force that acknowledged truths possess, the unbounded course of ill-directed power which has continually produced a long and authorized example of the most cold-blooded barbarity.[3]

Beccaria acknowledged the influence of another great philosopher of his time in this passage, as he stated his hopes for his own work.

> The immortal Montesquieu has cursorily touched upon this subject. Truth, which is one and indivisible, has obliged me to follow the illustrious steps of that great man, but the thoughtful men for whom I write will easily distinguish my traces from his. I shall deem myself happy if I can obtain, as he did, the secret thanks of the unknown and peace-loving disciples of reason, and if I can inspire that tender thrill with which persons of sensibility respond to one who upholds the interests of humanity.[4]

The last paragraph in Beccaria's short essay is as follows:

> From what has thus far been demonstrated, one may deduce a general theorem of considerable utility, though hardly conformable with custom, the usual legislator of nations; it is this: *In order for punishment not to be, in every instance, an act of violence of one or of many against a private citizen, it must be essentially public, prompt, necessary, the least possible in the given circumstances, proportionate to the crimes, dictated by the laws.*[5]

---

1. Henry Paolucci, "Introduction" to his translation of *On Crimes and Punishments* by Cesare Beccaria (Indianapolis, IN: Library of Liberal Arts, published by Bobbs-Merrill, 1963; originally published 1764), p. ix.

2. Ibid., p. 8.

3. Ibid., p. 9.

4. Ibid.

5. Ibid., p. 99. Emphasis in the translation, followed by this footnote: See Article VIII of the 'Declaration of the Rights of Man and of the Citizen,' passed by the revolutionary National Assembly of France, on August 26, 1789: "The law ought to impose no other penalties but such as are absolutely and evidently necessary; and no one ought to be punished, but in virtue of a law promulgated before the offense, and legally applied."

At the time Beccaria wrote, many philosophers and intellectuals were speaking about the **social contract**. This concept held that an individual is bound to society only by his or her consent, and therefore, society is responsible to the individual as well as vice versa. Beccaria believed in the concept of the social contract and felt that each individual surrenders only enough liberty to the state to make the society viable. Thus, laws should merely be the necessary conditions of the social contract, and punishments should exist only to defend the total sacrificed liberties against the usurpation of those liberties by other individuals. Beccaria also believed that the basic principle that should guide legislation was that of the greatest happiness to be shared by the greatest number of people.[6]

Another philosophy that influenced Beccaria was that of **free will**. He maintained that behavior is purposive and is based on **hedonism**, the pleasure–pain principle: Human beings choose those actions that give pleasure and avoid those that bring pain. Therefore, punishment should be assigned to each crime in a degree that results in more pain than pleasure for those who commit the forbidden acts. The punishment should fit the crime. This hedonistic view of conduct implies that laws must be written clearly and not be open to judicial interpretation. Only the legislature can specify punishment. Laws must be applied equally to all citizens; no defenses for criminal acts are permitted. The issue in court is whether an accused committed the act; if so, the particular penalty prescribed by law for that act must be imposed. Under this system, the law is rigid, structured, and impartial.[7]

Beccaria has been praised for helping make the law impartial. Contemporary American philosophy holds that all people should be equal under the law and that all cases must be weighed on an impartial scale of justice. Although that ideal has never been implemented fully, Beccaria should be recognized for his contributions to the concept of impartial justice.

Some modern scholars are critical of Beccaria, maintaining that his attacks on the criminal justice systems of his day were misplaced. Criminologist Graeme Newman referred to Beccaria as a "pampered intellectual who had no firsthand knowledge of the criminal justice system."[8] In a later publication, Newman and Pietro Marongiu reviewed the praise that social scientists and others had bestowed on Beccaria and concluded that it was misplaced. They took the position that "the majority of reforms that occurred during and soon after Beccaria's treatise can as easily be ascribed to prevailing social and political conditions as to Beccaria or his tract."[9]

The major weaknesses of Beccaria's ideas were the rigidity of his concepts and his lack of provision for justifiable criminal acts. These problems were acknowledged by the neoclassical school, discussed later, after a brief look at another classicist, Jeremy Bentham.

Jeremy Bentham

Jeremy Bentham, born in 1748 and thus a contemporary of Beccaria, was a British philosopher trained in law. He died in 1832. Bentham's legal thinking was described by one scholar as original, enormous, and many sided, with universal influence and far-reaching practical results. The scholar concluded that he was tempted to proclaim Bentham the "greatest legal philosopher and reformer the world has ever seen."[10]

Among Bentham's contributions was his belief that the greatest good must go to the greatest number. Bentham assumed that people are rational creatures who will consciously choose pleasure and avoid pain. Therefore, punishment should be assigned to each crime so that the pain resulting from the act would outweigh any pleasure of committing it. Like Beccaria, Bentham believed that the punishment should fit the crime. Bentham referred to his philosophy of social control as **utilitarianism**, a philosophy that makes the happiness of the individual or society the main goal and the criterion for determining what is morally good and right.

Criminologist Gilbert Geis summed up his opinion of Bentham by stating, "He deserves considerable credit . . . for his adherence to a theory of social (i.e., pleasure pursuit) causation of crime rather than a concept of biological, climatic or other non-social causation."[11]

Other Influential Scholars

All of the writers of the eighteenth century who emphasized the importance of human rights were important in establishing a framework in which the ideas of criminal reform would flourish. Voltaire (whose real name was François-Marie Arouet; Voltaire was his pen name) contributed both indirectly and directly to the success of Beccaria's reform measures. According to one scholar, "By fighting religious intolerance and fanaticism, he [Voltaire] contributed, more than any other, to the building of a more reasonable and humane society in which there was no longer any place for a criminal law based on superstition and cruelty."[12] Without Voltaire's work, criminal reform would have been significantly delayed. Beccaria's essay on crime and punishment probably would not have appeared. Voltaire contributed directly to the success of penal reform by publicizing Beccaria's work.[13]

Other influential writers of this period were Montesquieu and Rousseau. Charles-Louis de Secondat Montesquieu had considerable influence primarily by "stimulating the crusading zeal of . . . Beccaria."[14] Philosopher Jean-Jacques Rousseau's writings on the social contract influenced the classical school in its philosophy of crime and punishment.

The philosophy of the classical school was reflected in the changes in French penal codes, with the French Code of 1795 completing the process of replacing the arbitrary power of judges with fixed, determinate penalties. These

Among the eighteenth-century writers who influenced the nature and type of punishment was Voltaire, who emphasized the importance of human rights in punishment.

penalties were harsh, however, and in many cases, juries would not convict defendants, who, as a result, avoided all penalties. This situation led to the development of the neoclassical school.

The Neoclassical School

The writers in the **neoclassical school** of criminology, most of whom were British, flourished during the nineteenth century and had the same philosophical basis as the classical school—a belief in free will. However, the neoclassical criminologists viewed the penalties that resulted from the classical doctrine as too severe and all-encompassing for the humanitarian spirit of the time. The neoclassical school emphasized the need for an individualized reaction to offenders. Under the influence of the neoclassicists, criminal codes permitted more judicial discretion.

Another contrast between the neoclassical and the classical schools related to the age of offenders. The early nineteenth century's harsh penal codes did not provide for the separate treatment of children. One of the changes of the neoclassical period was that children under 7 years of age were exempt from the law because they were presumably unable to understand the difference between right and wrong.

Mental disease also became a reason to exempt a suspect from conviction, as it was seen as a sufficient cause of impaired responsibility. Any situation or circumstance that made it impossible to exercise free will was seen as reason to exempt a person from legal responsibility for what otherwise might be a criminal act. In short, the neoclassical school marked the beginning of the shift of society's interest in reforming the *system* to reforming the *offender*. This was the beginning of an ongoing struggle to address both; it continues today, as can be seen throughout this text.

Although the neoclassical school was not a scientific school of criminology, its writers did begin to explore the causation issue. They made exceptions to the law and recognized multiple causes of criminal behavior. The doctrine of free will could no longer stand alone as an explanation for criminal behavior. Even today, much modern law is based on the neoclassical philosophy of free will tempered by exceptions.

Before a science of criminology could emerge, however, it was necessary to gather and analyze empirical data on crime and criminals. The use of data to explain criminal behavior is characteristic of the positivist school of thought.

The Positivist School

The **positivist school** of criminology was composed of several Italians whose approaches differed to some extent but who all agreed that the study of crime should emphasize the scientific treatment of the criminal, not the penalties imposed after conviction.

The classical school, defining crime in legal terms, emphasized the concept of free will and the position that punishment gauged to fit the crime would deter criminal acts. The positivists rejected the harsh legalism of the classical school and substituted the doctrine of **determinism** for that of free will. They focused on the **constitutional approach** to crime, claiming that the structure or physical characteristics of an individual determine that person's behavior. Noting that these characteristics are not uniform, the positivists emphasized a philosophy of individualized, scientific treatment of criminals based on the findings of the physical and social sciences. According to theorist Stephen Schafer, the emergence of the positivists "symbolized clearly that the era of faith was over and the scientific age had begun."[15]

Cesare Lombroso

Cesare Lombroso (1835–1909), the leader of the positivist school, has been called "the father of modern criminology."[16] Lombroso rejected the classical doctrine of free will but was influenced by the positivist writings of early sociologists. He was best known for his biological theory of crime, which is discussed in Chapter 4, but he did not, as some critics have argued, neglect the sociological causes.

Lombroso described himself as a slave to facts, and he should be recognized for his emphasis on careful mea-

Cesare Lombroso (1835–1909), Italian leader of the positivist school of criminology, was criticized for his methodology and his attention to the biological characteristics of offenders, but his emphasis on the need to study offenders scientifically earned him the title "father of modern criminology."

surement in securing data. Despite his conscientiousness, Lombroso may be criticized for his failure to interpret the data in the light of his theory. It was his belief that the data, even if they appeared unrelated at the moment, would evolve subsequently into a theory of universal applicability. His method was to draw conclusions primarily from analogy and anecdote.

The reactions to Lombroso range from severe criticism to high praise, with criminologist Marvin E. Wolfgang stating that "Lombroso served to redirect emphasis from the crime to the criminal, not from social to individual factors."[17] Although Wolfgang acknowledged the serious methodological problems in Lombroso's research, as evaluated by modern techniques and knowledge, he believed that Lombroso "also manifested imaginative insight, good intuitive judgment, intellectual honesty, awareness of some of his limitations, attempts to use control groups and a desire to have his theories tested impartially."[18]

Raffaele Garofalo

Baron Raffaele Garofalo (1852–1934) was born in Naples, Italy. He studied law, was interested in criminal law reform, and served as a professor of criminal law and procedure during part of his career. Garofalo's major work was *Criminology*, first published in 1885, with a second edition in 1891. The book was translated into English in 1914. Garofalo was a member of the positivist, or Italian, school of thought. He rejected most of the classical school philosophies. He saw the need for empirical research to establish theories of criminal behavior. Although Garofalo embraced some of Lombroso's ideas, he was critical of others.

Garofalo and Lombroso differed in the emphasis they placed on the physical abnormality of the criminal. Garofalo agreed that criminals were abnormal, that they were lacking in the degree of "sentiments" held by others in society and exhibited "certain repugnances." But Garofalo thought that the question of whether this abnormality was caused by physiological factors must remain unanswered. He did note some physical differences between criminals and noncriminals, but he was cautious in his analysis of this phenomenon because he did not think the scientific evidence existed to substantiate the theories. Garofalo spoke of psychic anomalies and moral degeneracy, admitting that environmental factors *might* play a role in some crimes. But he also believed that the instincts of the true criminal had one element that was congenital, inherited, or somehow acquired in early infancy, which became inseparable from the criminal's psychic organism. Garofalo disagreed with the classification of criminals used by Lombroso and by Ferri (discussed in the next section), basing his own classification on the degree of moral inferiority of criminal types.[19]

Enrico Ferri

Enrico Ferri (1856–1929), the son of a poor shopkeeper, had already published some of his main ideas and become a positivist before he spent a year studying with Lombroso. Ferri, a professor of criminal law, published *Criminal Sociology*, in which he rejected the doctrine of free will, believing instead that it was not the criminal who willed to act but the situation that influenced the criminal's actions. Ferri believed that crime was produced primarily by the type of society from which the criminal came. He postulated the *law of criminal saturation*, which stated that "in a given social environment with definite individual and physical conditions, a fixed number of [crimes], no more and no less, can be committed."[20] Thus, crime could be corrected only by making changes in society.

Contributions of the Positivist School

The positivists made significant contributions to the development of a scientific approach to the study of criminal behavior and to the reform of criminal law. They emphasized the importance of empirical research. They believed that punishment should fit the criminal, not the crime (in contrast to the approach of the classical school). They developed the doctrine of determinism, some arguing that the cause of crime was physical, others that it was psychological, social, or economic, thus introducing the concept of environment into the study of crime.

The research of the positivists can be criticized for serious methodological errors. Their samples were not selected scientifically, and their subjects usually came from institutionalized populations. They made little use of follow-up studies; the concepts they measured were not clearly defined. The positivists did not use sophisticated statistical analyses because those had not yet been developed. Despite these and other criticisms, the positivist school had an important impact on the emergence and development of criminology.

The contributions of the positivists were only the *beginning* of the development of a scientific approach to the understanding of human behavior. Their influence is important but not definitive, and modern researchers have continued the march toward a scientific understanding of humans in the areas not only of physical characteristics or traits but also of mental illness and all types of behavior, including criminal.

The Classical and Positivist Schools Compared

The positivist and the classical schools had an important impact on the emergence and development of criminology. The basic differences between these schools of thought are

EXHIBIT

3.1 Major Contributors to Early Criminology

The Classical School

1. **Cesare Beccaria**—Wrote *On Crimes and Punishments*; believed that the punishment should fit the crime.
2. **Jeremy Bentham**—Developed the doctrine of free will, arguing that behavior is purposive and is based on hedonism, or the pleasure–pain principle.
3. **François-Marie Voltaire**—Laid the foundation for the Enlightenment; publicized Beccaria's contributions.
4. **Charles de Secondat Montesquieu**—Stimulated the reform crusade of Beccaria.
5. **Jean-Jacques Rousseau**—Influenced the classical school through his writings on the social contract.

The Positivist School

1. **Cesare Lombroso**—Rejected the classical doctrine of free will and advocated determinism, both biological and environmental; emphasized empirical research.
2. **Raffaele Garofalo**—Placed less emphasis than Lombroso on the biological and more on the psychic or environmental causes of crime.
3. **Enrico Ferri**—Rejected free will, believing that it is not the criminal who wills to act but the situation that determines the criminal's actions.

listed here. The premises on which our policies of punishment, treatment, and sentencing have been based subsequently may be traced to these schools of thought.

Classical School	Positivist School
1. Legal definition of crime	1. Rejection of legal definition
2. Let the punishment fit the crime	2. Let the punishment fit the criminal
3. Doctrine of free will	3. Doctrine of determinism
4. Death penalty for some offenses	4. Abolition of the death penalty
5. Anecdotal method—no empirical research	5. Empirical research, inductive method
6. Definite sentence	6. Indeterminate sentence

Exhibit 3.1 contains a summary of the contributions of the various individuals of the two schools.

Punishment Philosophies

The nineteenth-century explanations of criminal behavior and those that preceded them by thousands of years were attempts to explain behavior in a way that would justify **punishment**. In criminal law, *punishment* refers to penalties that are inflicted by the power of the state—that is, the authority of law after a court has found a defendant guilty of a crime. The question is not whether the state should punish offenders but under what circumstances, to what extent, and in what manner.

Punishments within U.S. criminal justice systems vary, and states are free to experiment in their laws as long as they do not violate the federal Constitution. The Eighth Amendment of the U.S. Constitution (see Appendix A) prohibits the imposition of **cruel and unusual punishment**, which has been interpreted to include any punishment that amounts to barbarity or torture or punishments that are not proportionate to the offense committed.

Punishments rest on one or more philosophical purposes.

Incapacitation

One purpose of punishment is that of **incapacitation**, which means to make it impossible for a person to commit a crime. Historically, in some countries, the government used physical means to prevent further crimes. Examples were cutting the hands off thieves, branding persons with the initials of their crimes, or subjecting offenders to capital punishment. Today, incarceration is used to prevent offenders from committing crimes against society, but it is unreasonable, if not impossible, to incarcerate all offenders; thus, a policy of *selective incapacitation* is employed.

Some recent attempts to incapacitate offenders target sex offenders. Efforts to incapacitate sex offenders through **castration** are utilized in a few states, but this approach is controversial. Compulsory, surgical castration is not permitted in the United States, although some state statutes, such as in Texas, provide for voluntary surgical castration under restricted circumstances. The Texas Penal Code also provides for a 10-year study of the repeat offenses committed by castrated sex offenders after their release from incarceration. These data are compared with the repeat offenses of released sex offenders who have not had the surgery, and this information is reported to the legislature. The Texas law also requires that sex offenders who are subjects of the study shall, during the 10 years they are studied, be provided with periodic monitoring and medical evaluation of their male hormone levels, along with psychiatric evaluations.[21]

Some jurisdictions permit the voluntary *chemical* castration of convicted sex offenders. This procedure involves treatment with a drug that reduces but does not eliminate the male sex drive. The normal sex drive is restored when the drug is discontinued. An example of a statute that permits chemical treatment of sex offenders is that of Montana, which provides that, in addition to other punishments, a sex offender may be required to undergo a medically safe drug treatment "that reduces sexual fantasies, sex drive, or both." A sex offender who is not sentenced to such treatment but who chooses to undergo it must be treated at the expense of the state's department of corrections. Inmates must be fully informed concerning the procedures, and no correctional employee who objects may be forced to administer such treatment.[22] Examples of sex offenders who have requested chemical or physical castration are discussed in Exhibit 3.2.

Recent incapacitation efforts with regard to sex offenders involve the involuntary civil commitment of these offenders after they finish their prison terms. In most jurisdictions, sex offenders are required to register where they are living once they are released from incarceration, and they are punished for failure to do so. These processes are discussed in Chapter 15.

Retribution

Historically, victims (or their families) were permitted to take measures to avenge crime, and at times, they were permitted to inflict upon the offender the same type of punishment suffered by the victim. The classical thinkers, however, did not accept the extreme forms of this eye-for-an-eye punishment philosophy. They rejected punishments that were too harsh, believing that criminal law should not be used as vengeance against offenders. As noted earlier, the classical thinkers believed that punishment should fit the crime. Beccaria, for example, insisted that the state has no right to impose a punishment greater than is necessary to deter further crime. One scholar explained Beccaria's view as follows: "Any law or punishment in excess of this

3.2 EXHIBIT — Incapacitation as Punishment: How Far Can We Go?

In 1991, Steven Allen Butler, a Houston, Texas, sex offender, raped a 13-year-old repeatedly while on probation for molesting a 7-year-old. Butler's attorney proposed a plea bargain to the judge, who had spoken publicly about castrating rapists. Butler would agree to undergo castration if he could be freed at once and placed on probation. The judge agreed to castration and a 10-year probationary term. Critics responded that castration (in which the testicles are removed) reduces but does not eliminate the ability to have an erection. Furthermore, many sex crimes are about power, not sex, and castration would not eliminate the hostility a sex offender has toward potential victims. Among other problems in this case was that officials could not find a physician who would castrate the offender. There was also opposition by civil liberties groups as well as allegations of racism.[1]

The issue of castration, but not of race, arose again in Texas in 1996. Larry Don McQuay, a 32-year-old offender who had almost completed his prison sentence for child molesting, stated that he had molested at least 240 children and that he would do so again unless he was castrated. McQuay was sentenced to eight years for having oral sex with a 6-year-old boy. He had served six years. With his good-time credits, he was ready for mandatory release to supervised parole, which meant that he would live under supervision in a halfway house. The state had no legal authority to keep McQuay in prison. Although he was indicted for aggravated sexual assault, through a plea bargain he pleaded guilty to indecency. Under the statute in effect when McQuay was sentenced, early release was permitted for indecency although not for aggravated sexual assault. (Subsequently, the statute was changed to include indecency as an offense for which early release is not permitted.)

McQuay was castrated in Texas, the first state to permit this practice, where it is voluntary. Some authorities on the treatment of sex offenders insist that castration will not change the sexual habits of pedophiles. McQuay was released from prison and moved to a work-release facility in May 2005. He was required to wear a monitoring device, and he could not leave the facility without being accompanied by a parole officer. In 2008, he was found to be in possession of sexually explicit materials that were contraband. The parole board ordered McQuay to spend 60 to 180 days in an intermediate sanction facility.[2]

In March 2004, an inmate described as the most notorious child molester in Dallas, Texas, voluntarily had himself castrated shortly before he was to leave prison and return home. The head of the Texas Department of Criminal Justice's sex offender treatment program stated that David Wayne Jones, only the second Texas inmate to undergo physical castration, had "matured quite nicely" since his incarceration in 1991 and that he had successfully undergone counseling (required in Texas). A psychiatrist who examined Jones concluded that Jones had been successfully treated with the drug Lupron, which creates a condition of chemical castration. The drug does not eliminate the pedophile's desire for sex with children, but it dramatically reduces "the incidence and intensity of the urges."[3] Jones is serving a life sentence.

1. "Court Abandons Castration Plan in a Rape Case," *New York Times* (17 March 1992), p. 6.
2. "Expert: Castration No Cure for Pedophilia; Drugs, Surgery May Temper Drive, but Sexual Interest Won't 'Normalize,'" *Houston Chronicle* (10 May 2005), p. 1. Metfront; "Is It Tarot or Porno? Offender in Trouble," *San Antonio Express-News* (9 October 2008), p. 1A; "Board Rules Offender Violated Parole with Sexy Tarot Cards," *San Antonio Express-News* (18 October 2008), p. 10B.
3. "Dallas Child Molester Undergoes Castration," *Dallas Morning News* (3 March 2004), p. 1.

limit is an abuse of power, not justice, and no unjust punishment may be tolerated, however useful it seems."[23]

Today, our justice systems refer to the punishment philosophy of **retribution**, which focuses on the conduct of the wrongdoer. Retribution was recognized in 1972 by the U.S. Supreme Court as an appropriate reason for capital punishment.[24] In a 1976 opinion, the Supreme Court discussed retribution as a justification for capital punishment. The Court stated that although retribution is no longer the dominant philosophy,

> neither is it a forbidden objective nor one inconsistent with our respect for the dignity of men. . . . Indeed, the decision that capital punishment may be the appropriate sanction in extreme cases is an expression of the community's belief that certain crimes are themselves so grievous an affront to humanity that the only adequate response may be the penalty of death.[25]

The U.S. Supreme Court suggested that the instinct for retribution is a part of human nature and that if the courts do not handle these situations, private individuals might take the law into their own hands.[26]

Another current justification for retribution is that it serves the important social function of legitimizing punishment. The argument, according to Ernest van den Haag, is that society desires to see crime punished because "the criminal has pursued his interests, or gratified his desires, by means noncriminals have restrained themselves from using for the sake of the law and in fear of its punishments." Therefore, the offender's act must be punished to justify the self-restraint of noncriminals. Finally, society punishes because it feels it wants to or it ought to; the sole purpose of retribution is to express moral outrage.[27]

Just Deserts

Retribution provides the rationale for the modern punishment and sentencing approach known as the **justice model**, or **just deserts**. This approach is illustrated by the writings of Andrew von Hirsch, representing the position of the Committee for the Study of Incarceration, in his book *Doing Justice: The Choice of Punishments*. Articulating their basic mistrust of the state's power, the committee members rejected rehabilitation and turned to deterrence (discussed later) and just deserts as reasons for punishment. The committee advocated shorter sentences and the limited use of incarceration.[28]

The justice model was supported by David Fogel in his book *We Are the Living Proof: The Justice Model for Corrections*. Fogel argued that punishment is necessary to implement criminal law, a law based on the belief that people act as a result of their own free will and must be held responsible for their actions. Inmates should be considered and treated as "responsible, volitional and aspiring human beings." All the processes of the agencies of criminal justice systems should be carried out "in a milieu of justice." Discretion cannot be eliminated, but according to the justice model, it can be controlled, narrowed, and subjected to review.[29]

Under Fogel's justice model, inmates should be allowed to choose whether or not to participate in rehabilitation programs. The purpose of the prison is to confine for a specified period of time, not to rehabilitate the criminal.

The influence of the classical school may be seen in the just deserts approach, which is related to Bentham's and Beccaria's argument that the punishment should fit the crime. The just and humane approach is to punish the criminal for what he or she has done, not to follow the treatment-rehabilitation approach.

The justice model, with its emphasis on retribution and just deserts, sounds fair and simple. Offenders get the punishment they deserve—no more, no less. The problem is to determine what is fair and just punishment for a particular offense.

Rehabilitation

Retribution and deterrence were the philosophies of the classical and neoclassical schools, with their emphasis on letting the punishment fit the crime. The positivist school emphasized the importance of letting the punishment fit the criminal; the individual criminal, not the crime, was the focal point. Positivists believed that, to prevent crime, changes must be made in the social environment. They favored sentences tailored to meet the needs of individual criminals. They set the stage for further development of the philosophy of **rehabilitation**, a philosophy that dominated U.S. criminal justice systems until recently and appears to be making a comeback.

The Rehabilitative Ideal

The rehabilitation philosophy became the modern philosophy of incarceration in the 1900s. It was described by legal scholar Francis A. Allen as the *rehabilitative ideal*, based on the premise that human behavior is the result of factors that may be known by objective analysis and that permit scientific control. The assumption was that the offender should be *treated*, not punished.[29]

The rehabilitative ideal is based on the belief that, although we cannot predict in advance how long rehabilitation will take in a given case, we can predict when offenders have been rehabilitated and are ready for release from prison or to a treatment program. Many social scientists endorsed the rehabilitative ideal and developed treatment programs for institutionalized inmates. The ideal was incorporated into statutes, proclaimed by courts, and supported by presidential commissions. It involved judicial discretion in sentencing and administrative discretion in releasing offenders.

In the 1970s, social scientists began to question the rehabilitation philosophy. It was alleged that treatment did not work.[31] Acceptance of the rehabilitative ideal also declined in the judicial system. In 1977, Judge David L. Bazelon, a strong supporter of using social science research findings in reaching court decisions, concluded: "The guiding faith of corrections—rehabilitation—has been declared a false god." Judge Bazelon argued that the problem with rehabilitation as a justification for punishment was that it "should never have been sold on the promise that it would reduce crime. Recidivism rates cannot be the only measure of what is valuable in corrections. Simple decency must count too."[32]

Perhaps an even stronger criticism of the rehabilitative ideal as a basis for punishment was the allegation of administrative abuse of the power to release. Another criticism was that offenders never knew when they would be released, and this created psychological problems.

Still another problem was the lack of guidelines, rules, or standards for release. This, along with the general unwillingness of appellate courts to review trial judges' sentencing decisions, led to attacks on the rehabilitative ideal approach. It was alleged that indeterminate sentencing was unjust and that the rehabilitative ideal removed the concept of just deserts. In effect, critics said, the criminal got more than he or she deserved. The foundation for this position was raised in the early 1950s by British theologian C. S. Lewis, who advocated a return to the philosophy of retribution. In analyzing the treatment-rehabilitation approach, Lewis said:

> Merciful though it appears, [this approach] really means that each one of us, from the moment he breaks the law, is deprived of the rights of a human being. . . . [W]hen we cease to consider what the criminal deserves and consider only what will cure him or deter others, we have tacitly removed him from the sphere of justice altogether; instead of a person, a subject of rights, we now have a mere object, a patient, a case.[33]

The belief that criminals should be processed in accordance with their acts, not with their rehabilitation, was supported in the 1970s by recognized social science and legal scholars.[34] Increasing dissatisfaction with the rehabilitative ideal and concern about the extent of crime, especially violent crime, led many to favor a get-tough sentencing policy. The argument was this: Treatment does not work, so let us try incarceration for longer periods of time. As stated in a 1982 news article, "Lock 'em up and throw away the key! Crudely put, that increasingly is the rallying cry in an America fed up with violent crime."[35]

By the late 1970s and early 1980s, many states had revised their sentencing statutes to include definite and longer sentences, along with stricter methods of release from prison. Even Congress expressed its position that rehabilitation was no longer the goal of sentencing and enacted sentencing legislation that referred to "the inappropriateness of imposing a sentence to a term of imprisonment for the purpose of *rehabilitating* the defendant or providing the defendant with needed educational or vocational training, medical care, or other correctional treatment."[36]

In 1989, in reference to federal sentencing reform, the U.S. Supreme Court stated that the new sentencing act revised former sentencing processes in several ways, including its rejection of "imprisonment as means of promoting *rehabilitation*, and it states that punishment should serve retributive, educational, deterrent, and incapacitative goals."[37] The federal sentencing guidelines, along with recent changes in their provisions and court decisions concerning their constitutionality, are discussed in detail in Chapter 13.

A Return to Rehabilitation?

Not all social scientists agreed with the position that "nothing works," and some scholars encouraged a return to rehabilitation as a viable reason for punishment. In 1982, Francis T. Cullen and Karen E. Gilbert published a book entitled *Reaffirming Rehabilitation*. According to Cullen and Gilbert, we should be careful in attributing all the problems of criminal justice systems to the rehabilitative ideal. Cullen spoke before a 1990 conference on rehabilitation and stated his belief that American people "have not given up on rehabilitation"; they want the correctional system to do more than "punish and cage."[38]

In a later article based on a nationwide study, Cullen and his collaborators reported that prison wardens were committed to rehabilitation as well as to custody and security.[39] In his 2004 address as president of the American Society of Criminology, Cullen declared that "the wind has begun to shift" back toward rehabilitation. Cullen credited the research efforts of 12 criminologists with the return to an emphasis on rehabilitation in U.S. criminal justice systems. These scholars are skilled in both theory and research, stated Cullen, and they effectively created a network "that was responsible for fighting back the ideas that offenders were beyond redemption and that corrections was a uniformly and inherently bankrupt enterprise."[40]

In a 2007 publication, Cullen summarized his efforts, declared that the "punishment paradigm has reached the point of exhaustion," and again called for a return to the philosophy of rehabilitation. Cullen gave the following reasons to support his position:

- "Rejecting rehabilitation was a mistake.
- Punishment does not work.
- Rehabilitation does work.
- The public likes rehabilitation . . . even if it is a liberal idea.
- Rehabilitation is the moral thing to do."[41]

Cullen explained each of these reasons and concluded that, although no one approach is perfect, rehabilitation has more merits than the punishment approach, and to continue the former "would be an unpardonable mistake."[42]

Social scientists are not the only ones to reaffirm rehabilitation. A significant move toward rehabilitation occurred in the fall of 2000, when 61 percent of voting Californians passed Proposition 36. The change provides *treatment* for offenders convicted of specified nonviolent drug offenses. That state's prison system was overcrowded primarily by drug offenders, who represented almost one of three of California's inmates. The new approach (discussed in more detail later in the text) views drug use as a health issue, not a matter of concern for the criminal law.[43]

In 2002, an opinion poll on public attitudes toward sentencing and punishment reported that the public was more in favor of nonpunitive approaches to criminal offenders than long, and especially mandatory, sentences. According to the report, 65 percent of respondents favored an approach that would assess the root causes of crime, and 32 percent favored a strict sentencing approach to criminal offenders. The 65 percent compared with the results of a Gallup poll taken in 1994, which reported that only 42 percent of the respondents favored the more treatment–oriented approach. Specifically, in 2002, 56 percent of adults favored a return to greater judicial discretion in sentencing and the removal of long, mandatory sentences.[44]

A 2006 study published findings that the public supported less punitive measures and a greater emphasis on rehabilitation in the processing of juvenile offenders.[45] In response to these findings, Cullen re-emphasized his position that rehabilitation should be reaffirmed. His reasons:

the public supports it, it works, and it is cost effective. . . . [I]t is time for criminologists—and others— to embrace a coherent and politically viable vision for an alternative system to save children and correct adults.[45]

Another scholar, in reacting to the 2006 study mentioned earlier, noted that the recent expansion of specialized treatment–oriented courts (such as drug courts, family courts, and mental health courts, along with the traditional juvenile courts, all addressed in this text in Chapter 13) was another indication of the increased enthusiasm for rehabilitation.[47]

In an analysis of studies on public opinion and crime, especially punishment and sentencing, The Sentencing Project, which promotes sentencing reforms, concluded the following:

- "The public is generally misinformed on crime and criminal justice policy.
- Public opinion is more complex than policymakers assume.
- Politicians misjudge public attitudes.
- Public opinion shifts in relation to political initiatives.
- Public opposition to rehabilitation and prevention is exaggerated.
- Public embraces alternative sentencing options when offered."[48]

Despite this resurgence of rehabilitation as one of the stated primary purposes of punishment, however, deterrence retains a prominent place in U.S. punishment philosophies and policies.

Deterrence

In addition to emphasizing a philosophy of punishment based on what the criminal deserves, the classical thinkers believed that a major purpose of punishment is **deterrence**. **Individual** (or **specific**) **deterrence** refers to the effect of punishment in preventing a particular individual from committing additional crimes. **General deterrence** is based on the assumption that punishing individuals convicted of crimes provides an example to potential violators, who, being rational persons and wishing to avoid pain, will not violate the law. Again, we see the influence of the classical thinkers' emphasis on free will and rational choice.

Deterrence theory is based on the assumption that appropriate punishments deter criminal activity because rational humans will not choose behavior that brings more pain than pleasure. Thus, punishment deters. The following discussion looks at some of the issues concerning deterrence as well as some empirical evidence on this punishment goal.

Deterrence of Types of Crime and Types of People

It is suggested that deterrence research should be more focused. For example, the research should be narrowed to types of crime and types of people. Perhaps punishment (or the threat of punishment) is effective in deterring people from shoplifting but not from killing their spouses. Perhaps certain types of people are deterred by laws, but other types are not. Or perhaps punishment perceptions may have a deterrent effect on some but not all persons. Research should also focus on what types of people need stiff penalties and what types are more likely to be deterred by publicity or lesser penalties. For an executive who must drive to conduct business and to entertain clients, the revocation of a driver's license and publication of a DUI might be sufficient deterrence. This sanction might also be sufficient to deter other professionals from driving while intoxicated. But even if those sanctions are sufficient deterrents, the effect may be short–lived and may be lost if people *perceive* that they will not be caught or that, if they are caught, the probability of punishment is slim.

Perceived Deterrence

Some researchers take the position that the key is *perceived deterrence*—what people think will happen determines whether they are deterred. The perception of the certainty and severity of punishment may be the major factor in explaining deterrence. It is also argued that the *actual* certainty of punishment influences people's perceptions of certainty. If they believe punishment is certain, they will be afraid to violate the law. The relationship between the actual certainty and the perceived certainty of punishment is difficult to test empirically, although there have been some suggestions of ways the test might be conducted. One study reported the results of a test of the hypothesis that a person's perception of the severity of legal punishments will increase when that person has an experience with the sanction, suggesting

> that more severe legal sanctions are more successful than less severe sanctions in achieving the first goal of deterrence, namely, raising perceptions of severity of formal legal sanctions and transmitting the message that legal sanctions are costly.[49]

Perceived deterrence may involve more variables than perceived legal punishment. A study of the deterrent effect of three variables—moral commitment (internalization of legal norms), fear of social disapproval, and fear of legal punishment—revealed that all three forms of social control were important as inhibitors of illegal behavior. The researchers noted that, according to some deterrence theorists, many people who internalize norms behave in legal ways not because they fear punishment but because they believe this is the proper way to behave. For these people, internalization of norms is a more effective form of social control than is fear of legal apprehension and punishment.[50]

The relationship between people's perceptions of what will happen if they violate a law and whether they decide to take that course may be far more complex than the classical thinkers envisioned when they argued that all behavior is rational and that people will choose to avoid behavior that might result in pain. For example, there is some evidence that persons in high–risk groups for receiving criminal sanctions (e.g., drug addicts) are not deterred significantly from criminal acts because of their perception of the risk of being caught and punished. They may, however, be influenced by their perceptions of their opportunities to commit crime and by their respect for criminal activities.[51]

Empirical Evidence Regarding Deterrence

Many reactions to the question of whether punishment deters crime are based on conjecture, faith, or emotion, with little or no empirical data. That advocates simply "know" that punishment does or does not deter is the case particularly in the death penalty debate, the focus of many deterrence studies. Despite the emphasis on deterrence theory from the classical criminologists on, empirical research in this area is relatively recent.

Sociologist Jack P. Gibbs addressed the issue of deterrence in 1975 in his insightful and provocative book that reviewed the empirical findings on punishment and deterrence. Noting that much of the initial sociological research on deterrence was concerned solely with the relationship of crime rates and the statutory existence of the death penalty, Gibbs pointed out that more recently, sociologists had turned to an "examination of the relation between actual legal punishments (imprisonment in particular) and crime rates." According to Gibbs, the findings of the earlier studies cannot be generalized to other types of punishment. They are also limited in their application to our understanding of the deterrent effect of capital punishment because most researchers did not measure the impact of the *certainty* of execution. Consider, for example, the impact that televised executions might have on potential criminal activity, such as murder. Media Focus 3.1 contains some questions you might ponder in your analysis. Gibbs argued that studies of the deterrent effect of punishment must allow for the differences between general and individual deterrence and take into account properties of punishment such as the perceived certainty that one would suffer a punishment. If a potential criminal thinks the law will not be enforced, he or she might not be deterred from criminal activity simply because the law provides a severe penalty for violation.[52]

Some social scientists have agreed that we cannot test deterrence until we can refine our research models and specify the variables determining whether or not

---

MEDIA FOCUS

3.1 Will Television Deter Crime?

When the execution of a well-known criminal is scheduled, it is not uncommon to hear requests for television coverage. Thus far, U.S. judges have refused to permit such coverage, although the U.S. attorney general did make arrangements for closed-circuit television of the 2001 execution of Timothy McVeigh, convicted in the 1995 bombing of the federal building in Oklahoma City. Due to space limitations, only a small number of persons were permitted to view the actual execution, which was conducted at the federal prison in Terre Haute, Indiana. The attorney general permitted victims' family members to view the execution by satellite at a designated facility in Oklahoma City as a means of allowing them to bring closure to the crime that killed their relatives.

Do you believe that if executions are shown on television, the event would serve as a deterrent to persons who might be inclined to commit murder? Would the type of murder under consideration be significant? For example, would televised executions be more likely to deter murders that occur within a domestic relationship or those that are the result of terrorist acts? Would age be a factor? Perhaps the viewing might deter older but not younger people. Would televised executions have any harmful effects on society?

Or is it possible that television may influence the commission of crime? The issue of imitation is discussed in Chapter 6 of this text.

punishment deters.[52] For example, there is evidence that punishment may have a quick but not a long-term deterrent effect.[54]

Some studies suggest that the deterrent effect of certainty is greater than that of severity, but few studies have been conducted on the swiftness of punishment. One criminologist reported that his research suggested the traditional statement of the greater deterrent effect of certainty compared with severity has been overstated. Undergraduate students enrolled in a large urban public university were asked to consider a hypothetical situation in which they had been drinking at a bar (and thought they might be impaired as a result) and had to decide whether to drive home. They were to assume that they had to be at work at 8 AM the following day; they could have someone drive them home, but if they did, they would have to return early the next morning to get their cars.[55]

The respondents were asked to note, on a scale of 0 to 100, the certainty that if they drove home under the conditions stated in the hypothetical situation, they would be apprehended and subsequently convicted of driving while impaired. The respondents were assigned randomly to groups, with one group told the penalty would be a 1-month driver's license suspension and the other told it would be a 12-month suspension. These penalties represent the minimum and maximum provided for first offenses in some states. The students were then asked to indicate, on a scale of 0 to 100, the likelihood that they would drive drunk under the stated circumstances. Finally, they were asked to consider whether they were certain that if they drove home under the stated circumstances, they would not be arrested. With all of this taken into account, how likely was it that they would drive?

On the basis of their answers to these questions, the respondents were placed in one of three categories:

- *Acute conformists* (persons who would not drive drunk even if there was no threat of punishment)
- *Deterrable respondents* (those who could be deterred by punishment), and
- *Incorrigible respondents* (those who paid no attention to the threat of punishment and were more likely than not to drive under the hypothetical conditions).

Respondents were also categorized by the degree to which they acted impulsively (this was based on their answers to six questions). They were asked how often they had driven when they thought they were under the influence of alcohol; whether they had ever been arrested for drunk driving; and whether they, a relative, or a close friend had been involved in a drunk-driving accident. Finally, the respondents were categorized by scores on questions designed to elicit measures of self- and social disapproval.

According to this study, 38 percent of college students "appeared to be unresponsive to threatened criminal sanctions for drunk driving." The respondents categorized as *acute conformists* conformed because of extralegal factors; that is, they were more influenced by self- and social disapproval, especially self-disapproval. Among those categorized as *deterrable respondents*, the severity of the sanction was a greater deterrent than the certainty of sanction, thus questioning the traditional findings concerning certainty and severity.[56]

Other research provides evidence that the threat of incarceration is a very strong incentive for probationers to pay court-ordered fines,[57] but we have to question whether we really want to use such a drastic measure as incarceration in these circumstances, and it is unlikely that sentencing policies will be changed to permit the use of fines rather than incarceration. It is suggested that the debate over whether sanctions deter "is as much ideological as it is empirical," depending on whether one is listening to economists, who argue that punishment deters, or criminologists, who are more likely to argue that it does not.

> Just like medications for treatment of disease have no single effect across type of medication and disease, we cannot expect that all sanctions will be equally effective. Indeed, some sanctions could be criminogenic, and others could have large deterrent effects.[58]

Another issue is that social scientists do not agree on the meaning of crime rates and the effect of deterrence. For example, of those who studied the effect of more severe penalties imposed in California in 1982, some concluded that the penalties had been effective in reducing crime rates,[59] but others claimed that conclusion was inaccurate.[60] Such disagreements are usually based on differences of opinion regarding the appropriate methods to be used in the research and its analysis. This can be very confusing to students as well as to politicians who might wish to base policy considerations on established research. Perhaps the most accurate conclusion is that of the researchers who stated:

> The reality, however, is that we will never conduct the one study that proves that the threat of more prison time deters individuals from committing crime. In the meantime, policy makers will continue to implement major interventions like Proposition 8 [the California policy referred to earlier].[61]

This discussion on deterrence began by distinguishing individual from general deterrence, and although some researchers approach the study as if those concepts represent two types of criminals, others advocate that people cannot be divided into groups influenced by general deterrence and those influenced by individual deterrence. Rather, some people are influenced by both types of deterrence, and research should attempt to measure a person's *indirect* experience with legal punishment and avoiding that punishment as well as the individual's *direct* experience with legal punishment and avoiding that punishment.[62]

Deterrence and Rational Choice Theories

A final issue with regard to deterrence is the development in the 1980s of *rational choice theory*. This approach, like deterrence, is based on the eighteenth-century utilitarian philosophies of Beccaria, Bentham, and others. People make decisions regarding their behavior based on minimizing the pain or costs and enhancing the pleasure or benefits; that is, the choice will be rational and based on a careful analysis of the expected results. Rational choice theory was applied to the study of crime primarily by economists.

Two proponents of rational choice theory, Ronald V. Clarke and Derek B. Cornish, stated the purpose of the theory and its relationship to classical writers by noting that it refers to rational offenders who calculate the behaviors that are in their own best interests. Clarke and Cornish, however, did not advocate that all criminal behavior is rational; rather, the behavior exhibits "a measure of rationality, albeit constrained by limits of time and ability and the availability of relevant information."[63] Clarke and Cornish listed six basic principles of rational choice theory enumerated in Exhibit 3.3.

According to Clarke and Cornish, rational choice theory (unlike many other theories discussed in subsequent chapters of this text) can explain all kinds of criminal behavior, not just a specific kind (e.g., theft). "In short, there is no kind of crime for which choice and purpose play an unimportant part."[64]

Although some have viewed rational choice theory as merely an extension of deterrence theory, according to Ronald L. Akers and Christine S. Sellers, "[R]ational choice theorists claim much more than just an expansion of deterrence theory. The theory is proposed as a general, all-inclusive explanation of both the decision to commit a specific crime and the development of, or desistance from, a criminal career."[65]

Modern rational choice theory is relatively new, but there is some empirical research on it. The research seems to suggest what we would expect from what we know about ourselves: Not all (if any) behavior is purely rational. We do think about the rewards; we do think about punishments; but most of us do not take into account all of the objectively determined costs and benefits of any given action. A study of repeat property offenders found, for example, that although the offenders thought they would gain money from their efforts, they either thought that they would not get caught, or if they did get caught, they would not be convicted, or if convicted, they would not serve a lengthy prison term. Thus, it was "worth it" to commit the crimes. In that sense, perhaps, these offenders made rational choices, but their perceptions of what might happen were actually irrational. "They were unable to make reasonable assessments of the risk of arrest, did little planning for the crime, and were uninformed about the legal penalties in the state where their crimes were committed." In addition, the property offenders reported that they did not think about the negative consequences; they focused on what they planned to achieve—that is, the positive results of their criminal acts. "They simply believed that they would not be caught and refused to think beyond that point."[66]

A study of burglars also failed to support a "completely rational model of decision making in residential burglary." Rather, the study showed that the decision to commit this crime was only partially rational. The researchers concluded, "[R]esearch reporting that a high percentage of burglars make carefully planned, highly rational decisions based upon a detailed evaluation of environmental cues may be in error."[67]

Another example of rational choice theory research involved a study of street robbers, who reported that they made rational decisions to rob for the purpose of obtaining

3.3 | **Fundamentals of Rational Choice Theory**

Ronald V. Clarke and Derek B. Cornish stated six fundamentals of rational choice theory as follows:

- "Crimes are purposive and deliberate acts, committed with the intention of benefitting the offender.
- In seeking to benefit themselves, offenders do not always succeed in making the best decisions because of the risks and uncertainty involved.
- Offender decision making varies considerably with the nature of the crime.
- Decisions about becoming involved in particular kinds of crime (involvement decisions) are quite different from those relating to the commission of a specific criminal act (event decisions).
- Involvement decisions can be divided into three stages—becoming involved for the first time (initia-

tion), continued involvement (habituation), and ceasing to offend (desistance)—that must be separately studied because they are so influenced by quite different sets of variables.
- Event decisions include a sequence of choices made at each stage of the criminal act (e.g., preparation, target selection, commission of the act, escape, and aftermath)."

Source: Ronald V. Clarke and Derek B. Cornish, "Rational Choice," in *Explaining Criminals and Crime: Essays in Contemporary Criminological Theory*, ed. Raymond Paternoster and Ronet Bachman (Los Angeles: Roxbury, 2001), p. 24.

money but had other and equally important nonrational motivations, such as emotional release, tension relief, impulsiveness, desperation, and moral ambiguity.[68]

In conclusion, rational choice theorists do not usually state their approach in pure terms, but as they broaden their theories, they become indistinguishable from other criminology theories in the level of rationality used to explain behavior.[69]

Policy Implications of Deterrence Theory

Deterrence theory is based on the assumption that legal punishments will deter crime, and this theory lends itself to significant policy implications. But what kind of laws should be enacted for the greatest deterrent benefit? One position is that, rather than drafting general laws to control behavior and prevent crime, it is important to be specific because "sanctions tend to work best when the goals of the sanctions are modest." In addition, research

demonstrates how *particular* types of sanction threats (the threat of incarceration) can bring about a *particular* type of prosocial behavior (paying fines) for a *particular* segment of the population (probationers).[70]

Unfortunately, policy makers do not think in such particular terms and are much more likely to espouse a general approach—for example, that people are rational and will not commit crimes if the punishment is severe. To the contrary, it may be argued that the get-tough sentencing approach has not worked, as illustrated by the results of the three-strikes legislation discussed later in this text.

Indeed, the most methodologically rigorous available research demonstrates that policies such as "three-strikes" laws and enhanced sentences, which bloat the prison population even more, as well as the policy of sticking a higher proportion of juvenile offenders into adult facilities have little to no appreciable impact on crime rates.[71]

Throughout this text, we will see examples of the results of get-tough policies in the United States, which have resulted in the highest incarceration rate in the world, overcrowded prisons, and numerous other negative effects of imposing longer sentences in an effort to deter crime.

Global Focus 3.2 explores the results of deterrence policy in another country: Northern Ireland.

GLOBAL FOCUS

3.2   An Analysis of Deterrence Policies in Northern Ireland

Three criminologists at the University of Maryland analyzed the effect that government reaction to terrorism in Northern Ireland had on the deterrence of violence in that country. The investigators introduced the findings of their research by emphasizing that government policies designed to deter may have the effect of accomplishing that goal or of creating a *negative backlash*, resulting in an increase in the behavior the policies were designed to deter.[1] The authors defined *terrorist attacks* as

the threatened or actual use of illegal force and violence by a non state actor to attain a political, economic, religious or social goal through fear, coercion or intimidation.[2]

The researchers measured deterrence by the "net decreases in the prevalence, incidence, or seriousness of future terrorist attacks in a given political location." They measured backlash by "the net increases in these attacks."[3]

After a review of the literature both in Northern Ireland and in the United States, the researchers concluded that the results regarding the effects of deterrence measures on terrorist activities were mixed, with some showing deterrence and some showing backlash. The authors traced the evolution of terrorist acts in Northern Ireland and identified six efforts made by the government to reduce violence in that

country. They found that, overall, "three of the six interventions produced backlash effects," resulting in an increase in terrorist attacks, but only one of the measures resulted in significantly reducing terrorist acts. The researchers concluded that, just as some empirical evidence had shown in other countries, harsh penalties designed to deter violent terrorist acts may actually result in the increase in such acts.[4]

These briefly summarized results lead to the question of why governments continue to impose harsh punishments for terrorist acts. One reason is that such events create pressure on governments to react and to do so quickly. Perhaps the lesson is that we need to look at the overall systems effect of government reactions, especially when we hope to deter future criminal acts.

1. Gary LaFree et al., "The Impact of British Counterterrorist Strategies on Political Violence in Northern Ireland: Comparing Deterrence and Backlash Models," *Criminology* 47, no. 1 (February 2009): 17–46.

2. Ibid., pp. 19–20.

3. Ibid., p. 20.

4. Ibid., pp. 37–38.

Punishment: An Analysis

Where does the preceding discussion leave us? The classical thinkers argued that the punishment should fit the crime; some modern thinkers take that statement to mean that criminals should get the punishment they deserve. Others interpret classical thinking in terms of its utilitarian principle of deterrence—that people behave rationally, seeking pleasure and avoiding pain. Therefore, for the criminal law to deter, it must be swift and sure. It must provide penalties that are perceived as just a little worse than the pleasure that would be gained from engaging in the criminal behavior. Others argue that people do not always behave rationally and may choose criminal behavior even when they know the chances of getting caught are high and that the penalty is severe.

Other problems arise from the justice model based on the classical position. If we assume that criminals should get what they deserve but that punishment should be severe enough to deter others from committing crimes, what do we do when these two goals are in conflict? Let us assume that the degree of punishment deserved by a particular criminal is not sufficient to deter others. Under the justice model, a criminal must not be punished more than he or she deserves; that would be as unfair as too little punishment. Thus, if this criminal gets what is deserved, the result may be punishment that has little or no deterrent effect on others.

What might happen if the only punishment that is a sufficient deterrent is one considered unfair or unjust? How do the principles of just deserts, utilitarianism, and deterrence apply to the punishment of corporate offenders? Should the corporation be punished by fine or by a withdrawal of its charter, or should its individual executives be punished? If so, how? Would it ever be just to punish a corporate executive for the criminal behavior of his or her employees? Would it be just to punish the employees if they were acting as directed? Which approach would create the best deterrent?

Although many questions about individual and general deterrence remain, one result is obvious: As subsequent discussions note, many U.S. jails and prisons are overcrowded. This overcrowding is caused primarily by the increased and extended penalties imposed on nonviolent drug offenders as well as by mandatory minimum sentences. This is not to suggest that we should retreat from our attempts to control drug-related offenses, but it does mean that policy makers should consider the *total* effect of any action before implementing a proposed reform.

The controversy over reasons for punishment can be expected to continue; it can also be expected that some people will argue that criminal law is the most appropriate mechanism for social control, whereas others will approach the issues by calling for removing some behaviors from the scope of criminal law and reducing the impact of the law's punishments in other cases.

Summary

This chapter began with a look at the relationship between the modern views of punishment and sentencing and the views of the thinkers of the classical, neoclassical, and positivist periods. It discussed the debate over how much punishment there should be to deter criminal behavior.

Because the classical, neoclassical, and positivist thinkers had an impact on the development of punishment philosophies, their views were examined and critiqued in this chapter. That discussion was followed by a more intensive analysis of the major punishment philosophies: incapacitation, retribution, just deserts, and rehabilitation. The previous emphasis on rehabilitation as the primary reason for punishment was examined in the light of historical developments that led to its partial demise, as legislators and others became convinced that tougher and more definite sentences were needed to deter crime.

The rehabilitation philosophy did not die, however, and the chapter noted its reemergence in recent years as a viable punishment philosophy. It is obvious, though, that deterrence theory is very important in explaining recent sentence reform. Deterrence theory was examined in terms of individual and general deterrence, with an analysis of some of the recent empirical studies. The chapter emphasized that deterrence is difficult to determine and that the issues must be broken down into relevant factors, such as deterrence of specific types of crime or persons and the relationship between deterrence and perception of the reality and severity of punishment. Considerable attention was given to recent developments in the area of rational choice theory. Attention was paid to the policy implications of deterrence theory. The final section of the chapter assessed the impact of punishment.

A reassessment of punishment philosophies is in order. Was it a mistake to abandon the rehabilitative ideal during the return to retribution, deterrence, and just deserts as the dominant reasons for punishment? Some who approved the demise of the rehabilitative ideal as the primary purpose of punishment have emphasized the importance of maintaining the *opportunity* for treatment. For example, David Fogel's justice model does not preclude treatment; it merely precludes *coercive* treatment.

The late Norval Morris, a noted authority on criminal justice and a professor and former dean of the University of Chicago College of Law, posed an argument for salvaging something of the rehabilitative ideal: "Rehabilitative programs in prisons have been characterized more by false rhetoric than by solid achievement. They have been corrupted to punitive purposes. But it does not follow that they should be discarded." According to Morris, we should not send people to prison *for* treatment. We should keep treatment programs but distinguish between the purposes of incarceration and the opportunities that might be provided for the incarcerated person. "Rehabilitation can be given only to a volunteer."[72]

Study Questions

1. What impact, if any, do you think the punishments in other countries had on the development of punishment in the United States? Discuss the general tenor of eighteenth-century punishment and criminal law.

2. Discuss the contributions of Cesare Beccaria and Jeremy Bentham to our understanding of criminal behavior.

3. Analyze the contributions of Cesare Lombroso and Enrico Ferri.

4. What do you think the phrase *cruel and unusual punishment* should mean?

5. Discuss castration as a means of punishment.

6. Distinguish *general* and *individual* deterrence.

7. How effective do you think deterrence is in preventing criminal behavior? Does the type of behavior matter? Does the severity or the certainty of punishment matter?

8. Which punishment philosophy do you think should form the basis of sentencing? Why?

9. What is rational choice theory? Do recent researchers add anything to classical contributions?

10. What are the policy implications of deterrence theory?

Brief Essay Assignments

1. Explain and contrast the approaches of the classical, neoclassical, and the positivist schools of thought.

2. Define, compare, and give examples of the major punishment philosophies.

3. Discuss the evidence of a recent return to rehabilitation.

4. Summarize the recent evidence on deterrence theory.

5. Assess the importance of rational choice theory in explaining why some people engage in criminal behavior.

Internet Activities

1. Check the website http://www.sentencingproject.org, accessed 10 December 2010. What can you find out about the long-term effects of sentencing, looking specifically at prison overcrowding? What can you discern about imprisoning juveniles, especially for long periods of time? Do any of the articles inform you regarding types of sentences or sentences for types of crime (such as drug offenses)? Is there any information concerning race relations and sentencing?

2. Access the Death Penalty Information Center at http://www.deathpenaltyinfo.org, accessed 10 December 2010, and see whether you can find any information on the possible deterrent effect of the death penalty. Is there any information concerning death penalty appeals? Can you secure information on the constitutionality of the death penalty?

Notes

1. Paul Lacroix, *France in the Middle Ages* (New York: Ungar, 1963), p. 394.
2. Paul Lacroix, *France in the Eighteenth Century* (New York: Ungar, 1963), p. 291
3. Will Durant and Auiel Durant, *The Story of Civilization*, Vol. 7, *The Age of Reason Begins* (New York: Simon & Schuster, 1961), p. 54 et seq.
4. Eliott Monochese, "Cesare Beccaria," in *Pioneers in Criminology*, ed. Herman Mannheim (Montclair, NJ: Patterson Smith, 1973), p. 48. Beccaria's book is *An Essay on Crime and Punishments* [originally published anonymously in 1764 as *Dei deletti e delle pene*, trans. Henry Paolucci] (Indianapolis, IN: Bobbs-Merrill, 1963).
5. Stephen Schafer, *Theories in Criminology* (New York: Random House, 1969), p. 106.
6. Beccaria, *An Essay on Crime and Punishments,* pp. 11–13.
7. For an article questioning Beccaria's contributions to the free will philosophy of crime, see Piers Beirne, "Inventing Criminology: The 'Science of Man' in Cesare Beccaria's *Dei delitti e delle pene* (1764)," *Criminology* 29 (November 1991): 777–820.
8. Graeme Newman, *Just and Painful: A Case for the Corporal Punishment of Criminals* (New York: Free Press, 1983), p. 71.
9. Graeme Newman and Pietro Marongiu, "Penological Reform and the Myth of Beccaria," *Criminology* 28, no. 2 (May 1990): 326.
10. Coleman Phillipson, *Three Criminal Law Reformers: Beccaria, Bentham, and Romilly* (New York: Dutton, 1923), p. 234.
11. Gilbert Geis, "Jeremy Bentham," in *Pioneers in Criminology*, ed. Mannheim, pp. 54, 57.
12. M. T. Maestro, *Voltaire and Beccaria as Reformers of the Criminal Law* (New York: Columbia University Press, 1942), p. 152.
13. Ibid., pp. 152–157.
14. Harry Elmer Barnes and Negley K. Teeters, *New Horizons in Criminology* (Englewood Cliffs, NJ: Prentice-Hall, 1959), p. 322.
15. Schafer, *Theories in Criminology,* p. 123.
16. Marvin E. Wolfgang, "Cesare Lombroso," in *Pioneers in Criminology,* ed. Mannheim, pp. 232–291. See also Cesare Lombroso, *Crime, Its Causes and Remedies*, trans. H. P. Horton (Boston: Little, Brown, 1911), p. 33.
17. Wolfgang, "Cesare Lombroso," p. 288.
18. Ibid., p. 271.
19. Raffaele Garofalo, *Criminology*, trans. Robert W. Millar (Boston: Little, Brown, 1914), pp. 95, 96.
20. Enrico Ferri, *Criminal Sociology*, trans. Joseph Killey and John Lisle (Boston: Little, Brown, 1917), p. 209.
21. Texas Penal Code, Sections 501.061 and 501.062 (2010).
22. Mont. Code Anno., Title 45, Section 45–5–512 (2010).
23. Francis Edward Devine, "Cesare Beccaria and the Theoretical Foundation of Modern Penal Jurisprudence," *New England Journal of Prison Law 7* (Winter 1981): 13.
24. *Furman v. Georgia*, 408 U.S. 238 (1972).
25. *Gregg v. Georgia*, 428 U.S. 153, 184–185 (1976).
26. *Gregg v. Georgia*, 428 U.S. 153, 183 (1976).
27. Ernest van den Haag, "Punishment as a Device for Controlling the Crime Rate," *Rutgers Law Review* 33 (Spring 1981): 719–730.
28. Andrew von Hirsch, *Doing Justice: The Choice of Punishments* (New York: Hill & Wang, 1976).
29. David Fogel, *We Are the Living Proof: The Justice Model for Corrections*, 2d ed. (Cincinnati, OH: Anderson, 1979), pp. 183–184.
30. Francis A. Allen, "Criminal Justice, Legal Values and the Rehabilitative Ideal," *Journal of Criminal Law, Criminology, and Police Science* 50 (September/October 1959): 226–232.
31. Robert Martinson, "What Works? Questions and Answers About Prison Reform," *The Public Interest* 35 (Spring 1974): 22–54. The complete work is published in Douglas Lipton, Robert Martinson, and Judith Wilks, *The Effectiveness of Correctional Treatment: A Survey of Treatment Education Studies* (New York: Holt, Rinehart & Winston, 1975).
32. David L. Bazelon, "Street Crime and Correctional Potholes," *Federal Probation* 42 (March 1977): 3.

33. C. S. Lewis, "The Humanitarian Theory of Punishment," *Res Judicatae* 6 (June 1953): 224–225.

34. See, for example, Norval Morris, *The Future of Imprisonment* (Chicago: University of Chicago Press, 1974); von Hirsch, *Doing Justice.*

35. "'What Are Prisons For,' No Longer Rehabilitation, but to Punish—and to Lock the Worst Away," *Time* (13 September 1982), p. 38.

36. USCS, Title 28, Section 994(k) (2010), emphasis added.

37. *Mistretta v. United States*, 488 U.S. 361 (1989).

38. "Believers in Prison Rehabilitation Told at Confab to 'Hang on to Hope,'" *Miami Herald* (24 June 1990), p. 5. See also Francis T. Cullen et al., "Is Rehabilitation Dead? The Myth of the Punitive Public," *Journal of Criminal Justice* 16, no. 4 (1988): 303–317; Francis T. Cullen and Karen E. Gilbert, *Reaffirming Rehabilitation* (Cincinnati, OH: Anderson, 1982).

39. Francis T. Cullen et al., "The Correctional Orientation of Prison Wardens: Is the Rehabilitative Ideal Supported?" *Criminology* 31 (February 1993): 69–92.

40. Francis T. Cullen, "The Twelve People Who Saved Rehabilitation: How the Science of Criminology Made a Difference," The American Society of Criminology 2004 Presidential Address, *Criminology* 43, no. 1 (February 2005): 1–42; quotations are on pp. 3, 4.

41. Francis T. Cullen, "Make Rehabilitation Corrections' Guiding Paradigm," *Criminology and Public Policy* 6, no. 4 (November 2007): 717–728; citations are on pp. 719–721.

42. Ibid., p. 722.

43. "California Gets Set to Shift on Sentencing Drug Users," *New York Times* (10 November 2000), p. 18.

44. "Public Opinion on Crime Is Shifting, Survey Shows," *Criminal Justice Newsletter* 32, no. 4 (12 March 2002): 3.

45. Daniel S. Nagin et al., "Public Preferences for Rehabilitation Versus Incarceration of Juvenile Offenders: Evidence from a Contingent Valuation Survey," *Criminology and Public Policy* 5, no. 4 (November 2006): 627–652.

46. Francis T. Cullen, "It's Time to Reaffirm Rehabilitation," *Criminology and Public Policy* 5, no. 4 (November 2006): 665–672; quotation is on p. 669.

47. Donna M. Bishop, "Public Opinion and Juvenile Justice Policy: Myths and Misconceptions," *Criminology and Public Policy* 5, no. 4 (November 2006): 653–664.

48. The Sentencing Project, "Crime, Punishment and Public Opinion: A Summary of Recent Studies and Their Implications for Sentencing Policy," http://www.sentencingproject.org, accessed 10 March 2010.

49. Eleni Apospori and Geoffrey Alpert, "Research Note: The Role of Differential Experience with the Criminal Justice System in Changes in Perceptions of Severity of Legal Sanctions over Time," *Crime & Delinquency* 39 (April 1993): 184–194; quotation is on p. 192.

50. Harold G. Grasmick and Donald E. Green, "Deterrence and the Morally Committed," *Sociological Quarterly* 22 (Winter 1981): 2, 13; Grasmick and Green, "Legal Punishment, Social Disapproval and Internalization as Inhibitors of Illegal Behavior," *Journal of Criminal Law and Criminology* 71 (Fall 1980): 325–335.

51. Irving Piliavin et al., "Crime, Deterrence, and Rational Choice," *American Sociological Review* 51 (February 1986): 101–119.

52. Jack P. Gibbs, *Crime, Punishment and Deterrence* (New York: Elsevier, 1975), pp. ix, 11.

53. See Robert F. Meier, "Correlates of Deterrence: Problems of Theory and Method," *Journal of Criminal Justice* 7 (Spring 1979): 18–19.

54. See Robert F. Meier et al., "Sanctions, Peers, and Deviance: Preliminary Models of a Social Control Process," *Sociological Quarterly* 25 (Winter 1984): 67–82; Robert F. Meier, "Perspectives on the Concept of Social Control," *Annual Review of Sociology* 8 (1982): 35–55.

55. Greg Pogarsky, "Identifying 'Deterrable' Offenders: Implications for Research on Deterrence," *Justice Quarterly* 19, no. 3 (September 2002): 431–452.

56. Ibid., p. 448. See also Greg Pogarsky et al., "Perceptual Change in the National Youth Survey: Lessons for Deterrence Theory and Offender Decision-Making," *Justice Quarterly* 22, no. 1 (March 2005): 1–29. For a more recent analysis of the concepts discussed in these articles, see Bruce A. Jacobs, "Deterrence and Deterrability," *Criminology* 48, no. 2 (May 2010): 417–442.

57. David Weisburd et al., "The Miracle of the Cells: An Experimental Study of Interventions to Increase Payment of Court-Ordered Financial Obligations," *Criminology and Public Policy* 7, no. 1 (February 2008): 9–36.

58. Daniel S. Nagin, "Thoughts on the Broader Implications of the 'Miracle of the Cells,'" *Criminology and Public Policy* 7, no. 1 (February 2008): 39–40.

59. Daniel Kessler and Steven D. Levitt, "Using Sentence Enhancements to Distinguish Between Deterrence and Incapacitation," *Journal of Law and Economics* 42 (1999): 343–363.

60. Cheryl Marie Webster et al., "Proposition 8 and Crime Rates in California: The Case of the Disappearing Deterrent," *Crime and Public Policy* 5, no. 3 (August 2006): 417–448.

61. Shawn D. Bushway and David McDowall, "Here We Go Again—Can We Learn Anything from Aggregate-Level Studies of Policy Interventions?" *Crime and Public Policy* 5, no. 3 (August 2006): 461–470; quotation is on p. 467.

62. Mark C. Stafford and Mark Warr, "Reconceptualizing Deterrence Theory," in *Criminological Theory: Past to Present: Essential Readings*, ed. Francis T. Cullen and Robert Agnew, 4th ed. (New York: Oxford University Press, 2011), pp. 394–399.

63. Derek B. Cornish and Ronald V. Clarke, *The Reasoning Criminal* (New York: Springer-Verlag, 1986), p. 1.

64. Ronald V. Clarke and Derek B. Cornish, "Rational Choice," in *Explaining Criminals and Crime: Essays in Contemporary Criminological Theory*, ed. Raymond Paternoster and Ronet Bachman (Los Angeles: Roxbury, 2001), pp. 33–34.

65. Ronald L. Akers and Christine S. Sellers, *Criminological Theories: Introduction, Evaluation, and Application*, 5th ed. (New York: Oxford University Press, 2009), p. 27.

66. Kenneth D. Tunnell, "Choosing Crime: Close Your Eyes and Take Your Chances," *Justice Quarterly* 7 (1990): 673–690; quotations are on pp. 680–681; as quoted in Akers and Sellers, *Criminological Theories,* 5th ed., p. 28.

67. Paul F. Cromwell et al., *Breaking and Entering: An Ethnographic Analysis of Burglary* (Newbury Park, CA: Sage, 1991), pp. 42, 43;

as quoted in Akers and Sellers, *Criminological Theories*, 5th ed., pp. 28, 29.

68. Willem DeHaan and Jaco Vos, "A Crying Shame: The Over–Rationalized Conception of Man in the Rational Choice Perspective," *Theoretical Criminology* 7 (2003): 29–54; as quoted in Akers and Sellers, *Criminological Theories*, 5th ed., p. 29.

69. Akers and Sellers, *Criminological Theories*, 5th ed., p. 30.

70. Travis C. Pratt, "Rational Choice Theory, Crime–Control Policy, and Criminological Relevance," *Criminology and Public Policy* 7, no. 1 (February 2008): 43–52; quotation is on p. 43.

71. Ibid., p. 44.

72. Norval Morris, *The Future of Imprisonment* (Chicago: University of Chicago Press, 1974), pp. 13, 15, 27.

Biological and Psychological Theories of Criminal Behavior

The United States Supreme Court has held that defendants may not be executed for murders they commit as juveniles, nor can juveniles be sentenced to life without parole for committing a nonhomicide crime. This sketch was made during oral arguments before the Court in the case of Graham v. Florida, which involved the issue of life without parole. In that case (decided in May 2010) and in an earlier one, Roper v. Simmons (2005), the Court acknowledged that juveniles are different from adults in many ways, including the lack of development of their brains and their maturity. Since this sketch, the composition of the Court has changed, with Associate Justice Elena Kagan replacing Associate Judge John Paul Stevens, who retired at the end of the Court's 2009–2010 term.

CHAPTER OUTLINE

KEY TERMS

attention-deficit hyperactivity disorder (ADHD)

Baby Moses laws

behavior genetics

behavior theory

biocriminology

cognitive development theory

demonology

forensic psychiatry

guilty but mentally ill

insanity defense

learning theory

phrenology

postpartum depression (PPD) syndrome

psychiatry

psychoanalysis

sociobiology

INTRODUCTION

This chapter covers a variety of approaches to understanding criminal behavior, many of which were popular in the past, lost favor, and have been revived but with more sophisticated research. The recent developments in biological and psychological theories are discussed against the background of the earlier contributions of the positivist school and those who studied the relationship between body type and crime. The chapter considers the importance of genetic, obstetric, neurological, and psychological factors to criminal behavior. It concludes with an analysis of the practical and legal implications of recent developments in biological and psychological approaches.

Fashions and fads in human thought affect many fields, and criminology is no exception. Chapter 3 noted that in the eighteenth century, the major emphasis regarding criminals was on a punishment philosophy that lost favor in the following century. During the nineteenth century, the concept of the influence of biology on criminal behavior was strong, stemming from the theory of evolution of Charles Darwin, whose 1859 publication, *On the Origin of Species by Means of Natural Selection,* is ranked by some as one of the most important books ever written and criticized bitterly by others.

In criminology, biological and psychological explanations of behavior have been out of style for some time. David P. Farrington, in his foreword to a book that is referred to often in this text (David C. Rowe's *Biology and Crime*), noted that in the leading criminology text from the 1920s until the 1970s, the authors, Edwin H. Sutherland and Donald R. Cressey, "clearly rejected the importance of biological factors" in explaining criminal behavior. Farrington pointed out that this has changed, and he welcomed Rowe's book "as a concise but superb, well-researched and up-to-date presentation of research in this field." Farrington, a professor of psychological criminology at Cambridge University, described Rowe as "one of the most brilliant and gifted researchers in this field."[1]

In recent years, there has been a resurgence of interest in studying the relationship of biology and psychology to criminal behavior. This chapter presents some of the classic and recent research on how the body and the mind may affect behavior. Taken together, studies of the impact of biology and psychology on criminal behavior leave no doubt that these variables are important to our understanding of the origins of antisocial behavior.

Biological Factors and Crime

Although the major biological theories of criminal behavior were developed in the nineteenth century, their origins can be found much earlier. The belief that personality is determined by the shape of the skull has been traced back to Aristotle (born in 384 BC). Belief in a relationship between criminal behavior and body type can be traced back to the 1500s, and the study of facial features and their relationship to crime goes back to the 1700s.

In the latter part of the 1700s, **phrenology** emerged as a discipline. Its development is associated mainly with the work of Franz Joseph Gall (1758–1828), who investigated the bumps and other irregularities of the skulls of those confined in penal and mental institutions. In addition, Gall studied the heads and head casts of persons who were not institutionalized and compared those findings with data on criminals. Phrenology is based on several propositions: that the exterior of the skull corresponds to the interior and to the brain's conformation, that the brain can be divided into functions or faculties that are related to the shape of the skull, and that by measuring the shape of the skull we can measure behavior.

In modern times, biologist David C. Rowe has looked at biology and crime from two perspectives, that of **sociobiology** (discussed next) and **behavior genetics**, which he described as "the study of genetic and environmental influences on individual differences in traits in humans and nonhuman animals." Rowe traced the development of behavior genetics to an Englishman, Francis Galton, who published *Hereditary Genius* in 1869. In that book, Galton traced families with members who were outstanding intellectually in an effort to determine the influence of genetics on that ability. Galton also studied behavior using samples of twins and adopted persons, an approach discussed later in this chapter. Behavior genetics looks at the individual differences in human beings, delving into their individual *phenotypes*, or measurable traits. Those might include intelligence or foot size.[2]

The term *sociobiology* was coined and developed by Edward O. Wilson in 1975. Wilson defined sociobiology as "the systematic study of the biological basis of all social behavior."[3] He wrote a book about behavior genetics in animal species and applied his evolutionary theory to human behavior. Wilson's sociobiological theory was controversial for several reasons, one of which was that he visualized it as enveloping social sciences. Some scientists denounced sociobiology as just another deterministic approach,[4] but others viewed the work of Wilson and his colleagues as a framework for the future unification of the social and natural sciences.[5] According to Rowe, in recent years, sociobiology "has come to be called *evolutionary psychology*, with a greater emphasis on how adaptation shapes thought and emotion rather than on social behaviors."[6]

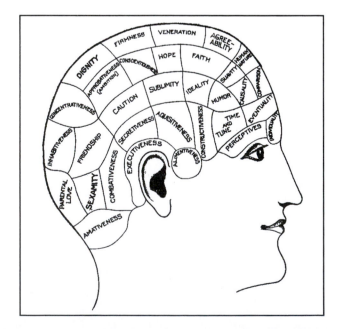

The association of brain functions with configurations of the brain was a concept espoused by early thinkers such as Franz Joseph Gall (1758–1828). Gall and others believed that the functions corresponded to bumps or irregularities on the head. (Bob McCoy)

Lombroso and the Positivists

If the study of phrenology is considered applicable, we are placing the beginning of scientific criminology about 70 years before the contributions of Cesare Lombroso and other positivists. With historical perspective, this may become a more commonly accepted conclusion, but today, most criminology scholars begin that study with Lombroso and his colleagues.

According to theorist Stephen Schafer, Lombroso (1835–1909) is "rarely discussed in a neutral tone; he is either adulated or condemned." Schafer quoted criminologist Marvin Wolfgang, "In the history of criminology probably no name has been eulogized or attacked so much as that of Cesare Lombroso."[7] Lombroso developed several categories of criminals, but he was best known for his concept of the biological, or born, criminal. He called such a person an *atavism*, a throwback or a reversion to prehuman creatures. Lombroso believed that he saw in criminals some of the characteristics of savages.[8]

Evolution theorists during Lombroso's time argued that, as humans evolved, their physical constitution changed, becoming more complex as it developed to a higher stage. Lombroso used these theories to support his belief that criminals were not merely physically different from noncriminals but also physically inferior to them; criminals had not evolved as far as noncriminals had. Lombroso also claimed that he had found biological characteristics that distinguished criminals according to the *kind* of crime they committed. He compared criminals to wild animals; both must be restrained to keep them from endangering others. But reforming the guilty is almost always an exception, claimed Lombroso. Most inmates are not rehabilitated in prison; many are worse for the experience. The state incarcerates offenders, and after they have served their sentences, they are released. This increases the danger to society because "the criminal always becomes more depraved in the promiscuity of the prison, and goes out more irritated and better armed against society."[9]

Besides the biological criminal, Lombroso recognized two other types: the criminaloid and the insane criminal. He defined the *criminaloid* as a person motivated by passion or some other emotional characteristic that, coupled with various factors, leads to criminal behavior. The *insane criminal* is one who is epileptic or psychotic and who, along with the idiot and the imbecile, is unfit for society.

Despite his development of the concepts of the insane criminal and the criminaloid, Lombroso's concept of the born criminal remained central to his analysis and was viewed by some criminologists as his main focus, which became "the dominant perspective on crime and triggered an onslaught of biological theorizing about crime."[10]

Lombroso and the other positivists generated heated responses ranging from high praise to scathing criticism. Sociologist Thorsten Sellin proclaimed that Lombroso's "ideas proved so challenging that they gave an unprecedented impetus to the study of the offender. Any scholar . . . whose ideas after half a century possess vitality, merits an honorable place in the history of thought."[11]

Considerable criticism has also been hurled at the positivists, especially at Lombroso, because of an *overemphasis* on biological causes of criminal behavior to the neglect of environmental factors.[12] Marvin Wolfgang responded to such criticisms with these words:

> The fears of these critics that Lombroso diverted attention from social to individual phenomena reveal their basic misunderstanding of his work and its effect. . . . Lombroso served to redirect emphasis from the crime to the criminal, not from social to individual factors.[13]

Even greater importance to Lombroso was given by Nicole Rafter, who insisted that this early writer called for real facts about crime and criminals, along with inductive reasoning regarding those facts, even though he did not always accomplish that task himself. Rafter noted that some of Lombroso's concepts contributed to recent theories (discussed in the next chapter); that he "anticipated genetic explanations of crime" as well as evolutionary criminology; that he had "one of the most fertile minds" of his time; and that he "produced a body of work seldom equaled for its variety, richness, and influence." According to Rafter, we are just now beginning to appreciate the full contributions of Lombroso along with other positivists.[14]

Lombroso and the other positivists of his time are important because they laid the foundation for a scientific and biological analysis of criminal behavior. In addition, some of the writers foresaw the need for changing the social structure and environment to ensure the effectiveness of crime prevention.

Physique and Crime

The constitutional (or physical) approach to the study of human behavior rests on the assumption that function is determined by structure. Applied to crime, constitutional approaches maintain that behavior is determined by the body's build, which may be the body type, the endocrine system, or some other physical or mental characteristic. The belief that criminal behavior is related to body type can be traced back to a 1926 translation of a book by Ernst Kretschmer.[15] However, the first significant development of this approach began in the 1940s with the work of William H. Sheldon, who measured physique and compared body type with temperament. Sheldon defined three body types: ectomorph, endomorph, and mesomorph. An *ectomorph* has a tall, skinny body; an *endomorph* has a short, fat body; and a *mesomorph* has an athletic body. Sheldon identified three types of temperament that he claimed were associated with the three body types. His purpose was to lay a foundation for a systematic study of human behavior and human personality.[16]

Sheldon has been criticized for his method of selecting samples for his research, the implication being that he selected only persons who would support his theory,[17] and for failure to define the three body types precisely enough so that they could be distinguished and measured.[18] He was also alleged to have overemphasized constitutional factors to the exclusion of environmental causes of crime. Sheldon reacted to the latter criticism by saying that he was not excluding environmental factors but only emphasizing constitutional factors because their importance had been neglected previously.

Two other researchers who focused on body type were Sheldon Glueck and Eleanor Glueck. They conducted studies on the relationship of body type and criminal behavior, although most of their research focused on juvenile delinquents. The Gluecks were two of the most prolific and most controversial writers in the field of constitutional criminology. They claimed that their research was of high quality, skillfully utilizing the precision control of samples of 500 delinquents and 500 nondelinquents matched on age, general intelligence, ethnic/racial origins, and residence in underprivileged neighborhoods. Physicians, psychiatrists, anthropologists, and others were involved in gathering the data from the samples. They found delinquency to be associated with the mesomorphic body type.[19]

Some critics point out that the Gluecks' findings were not surprising, as many delinquent activities require a strong body build. After examining the researchers' data, others have concluded that the information was complicated and not significant because there was no specific combination of character, physique, and temperament that would permit a prediction about whether or not a young person would become delinquent.[20] Critics have also argued that since the delinquent sample was taken from "persistently delinquent" boys, the data could not be generalized to the total population of delinquents. Another criticism is that the Gluecks' concepts and measuring techniques were vague.[21]

Criticisms of the body-type studies of Sheldon and the Gluecks led many to discredit the entire approach of explaining crime in terms of physique. But Juan B. Cortés and others thought the approach had merit. In 1972, Cortés published the results of 10 years of research in which he reported finding a high correlation between mesomorphy and delinquency. Cortés warned, however, that his research did not show that body type *causes* delinquency, only that the two often occur together.[22]

Cortés's work has been criticized because it was based on small samples that were not selected properly. In addition, he did not define measurement terms precisely and neglected the importance of the environment. His work is important, however, in establishing the *foundation* for a return to concern with the genetic factor in criminal behavior. Cortés emphasized that *constitution* (which he said was a term used almost synonymously with *physique* and *body build*) was not fixed and unalterable but was a result of genetics and environment: "It is not, therefore,

and should not be, heredity or environment, nor heredity versus environment nor heredity under or over environment, but only and always heredity *and* environment."[23] Therefore, it is necessary to look at heredity and examine what, if any, role genetic factors play in human behavior.

Genetic Factors

Perhaps it was not too difficult for some of the early students of criminal behavior to conclude that the differences between criminals and noncriminals *caused* the criminal behavior and that these differences are inherited. The criminal was seen as one who was predisposed or predetermined by biological factors to commit crimes. The next step was to look at family background to see whether the family had a history of criminal behavior. If so, it was assumed that criminality must be inherited.

Studies of Families

Most of the early studies of family histories were conducted in an effort to show the relationship between heredity and crime as well as other forms of deviant behavior (e.g., feeblemindedness occurring in several generations was assumed to be caused by genetics). These studies were discredited as lacking sufficient methodological sophistication to permit significant conclusions. Despite this, the studies were influential in legal decisions regarding defendants. Exhibit 4.1 introduces two of the best known of the early studies.

The Gluecks included family histories in their comparisons of delinquents and nondelinquents. They found that more delinquent than nondelinquent boys came from families characterized by a history of delinquency and crime, with the criminality of the father as the best predictor.[24]

In his pursuit of evidence to disprove Lombroso's theory of the born criminal, Charles Goring used statistical techniques to measure the degree of correlation, or resemblance, of members within a family line. He compared brothers as well as fathers and sons, attempting to show that the correlations for general criminality, as measured by imprisonment, were as high as for two other categories he measured: (1) ordinary physical traits and features and (2) inherited defects, insanity, and mental disease. He attempted to show that the correlations were the result of heredity, not environment. He used several arguments to support his position, such as the discovery that boys who were taken out of the home early in life became criminals as frequently as did those who remained longer in the home with their fathers. Also, he found the correlations as high for sex crimes (in which the fathers presumably would try to conceal their activities) as for stealing (in which the fathers might set an example for their sons).[25]

Goring's findings may be criticized on several grounds. He did not measure environmental influences adequately (indeed, it is questionable whether all environmental

4.1

The Jukes and the Kallikaks: A Look at History

Earlier studies of families provided the background for today's approach to the study of genetics. The most famous of the nineteenth-century studies were those of the Jukes and the Kallikaks.

In 1877, Richard Dugdale published his study of the Jukes family. From a hard-drinking but jolly and companionable person, hunter, and fisherman, Dugdale traced 540 descendants related by blood and 169 related by marriage or cohabitation, a total of 709 persons of the 1,200 who probably descended from the Juke line. Dugdale, who said his book was an inquiry into the largest family of criminals and paupers ever studied, emphasized the importance of environment as well as of heredity.[1]

Sociologist Franklin Giddings said that when the first edition of Dugdale's book was published, it was probably "the best example of scientific method applied to a sociological investigation." Giddings emphasized the empirical work conducted by Dugdale, which contrasted to the predominantly philosophical approach of his contemporaries. In addition, Dugdale should be remembered for his recognition of the factor of environment and the role it could play in intelligence.[2]

A second family study that gained considerable attention was that of Henry Goddard, who traced the Kallikak family, beginning with Martin Kallikak Sr., who fathered a son, Martin Kallikak Jr., by a barmaid. The elder Kallikak then married a so-called good girl and through that union produced a different type of offspring. From the first son, however, Goddard traced 480 descendants, many of whom were moral degenerates, including illegitimate children, prostitutes, alcoholics, epileptics, criminals, and keepers of houses of prostitution. These descendants married into other families "generally of about the same type, so that we now have on record and charted eleven hundred and forty-six individuals." Of that group, said Goddard, "we have discovered that two hundred and sixty-two were feebleminded, while one hundred and ninety-seven are considered normal, the remaining . . . still undetermined."[3]

The relationship between feeblemindedness and crime was seriously questioned when intelligence tests were used on Army recruits during World War I, and as many as 47.3 percent were found to be below the mental age of 13 and 30.3 percent below the mental age of 12.[4] Later studies comparing criminals with Army recruits found no significant difference in the intelligence of the two groups, and one study found the criminals to be superior.[5]

Subsequent research has improved our understanding of intelligence and crime (discussed later in this chapter), but in *Buck v. Bell*, the U.S. Supreme Court upheld sterilization orders on 18-year-old, white, feebleminded Carrie Buck, who was the daughter of a feebleminded woman. Justice Oliver Wendell Holmes, who wrote the opinion, stated the following:

It is better for all the world, if instead of waiting to execute degenerate offspring for crime, or to let them starve for their imbecility, society can prevent those who are manifestly unfit from continuing their kind. The principle that sustains compulsory vaccination is broad enough to cover cutting the Fallopian tubes [citation omitted]. Three generations of imbeciles are enough.[6]

1. Richard L. Dugdale, *The Jukes: A Study in Crime, Pauperism, Disease, and Heredity*, 4th ed. (New York: Putnam, 1942), p. 113.

2. Ibid., p. iii.

3. Henry H. Goddard, *The Kallikak Family: A Study in Heredity of Feeblemindedness* (New York: Macmillan, 1925), p. 19.

4. L. D. Zeleny, "Feeblemindedness and Criminal Conduct," *American Journal of Sociology* 38 (January 1933): 569.

5. Carl Murchison, *Criminal Intelligence* (Worcester, MA.: Clark University Press, 1926), chap. 4.

6. *Buck v. Bell*, 274 U.S. 200 (1927).

factors can be isolated), and he did not consider criminality among sisters. He offered no proof of his assumption that mental ability is inherited. He assumed that removing a boy from his criminal father's home and placing him in some other environment at an early age was putting him into a noncriminal environment.

Although the early studies of families have been criticized severely, they influenced some policy decisions. The belief that criminality was inherited led to the passage of laws that permitted compulsory sterilization of persons thought to be capable of passing on to their children genes that would result in criminal behavior; as noted in Exhibit 4.1, the U.S. Supreme Court upheld one of the statutes. Although we no longer sterilize people for mental reasons, Media Focus 4.1 details a current example in which some argued that genes may explain the behavior of a son who was accused of killing in ways similar to those of his father.

More recent studies have examined the behavior of children within the family structure and concluded that behavior, like disease, can be the result of contagion. A pattern of behavior is defined as contagious "if the risk to a given individual increases when someone in that person's vicinity, family, or social group becomes affected." For example, a younger sister is more likely to become pregnant out of wedlock if an older sister has done so. Other

4.1 Families and Crime

In previous times, criminologists and others concluded that violence in generations of families might be genetic. Today, criminologists recognize that, although a child might experience one or more factors conducive to becoming violent, not all children who experience those factors do become violent. Rather, it is the *interaction* of biological, social, and cultural factors that is used to explain the violence of families over time.

But this point of view is not always the one presented to the public. For example, consider a series of news articles on the Weaver family. The first family member, Ward Francis Weaver Jr., resides on death row in California's San Quentin prison. He has been there since 1981, when he was convicted of murdering a young woman and her fiancé and burying her body under a concrete slab in his backyard. The second family member is Ward Francis Weaver III, who was accused of sexually assaulting and murdering two teenagers in 1986. In 2002, investigators found a body sunk in concrete in the backyard of the younger Weaver. The body

was identified as Ashley Pond, age 12. Authorities also found the body of Miranda Gaddis, age 13, in a shed in Weaver's backyard. Weaver entered guilty pleas and was sentenced to life in prison without the possibility of parole.

Several media articles on the Weaver family raised the issue of whether genetics or learning explained these crimes. In addition to the similarities of the crimes, the *Los Angeles Times*, in an article entitled "Behavior May Leave a Mark on Genes," cited the following similarities between father and son:

- "Both are nicknamed Pete.
- Both were abused as children and were themselves abusive, according to court records and interviews with family members. Both were accused, never charged, of raping relatives. Both have been accused, never charged, of torturing animals.
- Both have been outdoorsmen and hunters. Both went into military service.
- Both married and divorced twice. Both have five children.
- Both have a record of violence against women."[1]

The article continued with specifics of the violent acts of the father and son, stating that scientists believe "genes influence behavior" and raising the issue of whether there are criminal genes. "Can homicidal behavior pass, like an heirloom, from one generation to the next?" But the article also pointed out there is evidence that "life experiences can alter the biochemistry of many genes."

Other facts that make this family's crimes intriguing are that Ward III had little contact with his father, who virtually abandoned the family when the young Weaver was only 4 years old. The younger Weaver could have read or heard about his father's burying his victims in concrete, but the similarities between the father and the son are far more extensive. Consider these facts:

Both sprung from relentless violence. . . . Both were driven by explosive tempers, but targeted violence only on the weak or the vulnerable. And both have been described as strangely detached during some of their attacks.

Not long after the younger Weaver assaulted the Ordona sisters, he told a probation officer he had no control of his temper. At times during such violent outbursts he felt as though someone was controlling him. And he felt as if that someone might just be his dad.[2]

The first article concluded: "The enigma of the two Ward Weavers goes beyond legal riddles of guilt and innocence. It taps into the wellspring of human violence, where the sins of the father may link to the sins of the son."[3]

Ward Francis Weaver III is escorted into the Clackamas County courtroom in Oregon City, Oregon, for sentencing on 22 September 2004. Weaver, who was accused of killing two of his daughter's friends and hiding their bodies on his property, pleaded guilty to those murders. His crimes were similar to those committed by his father, Ward Francis Weaver Jr., who was convicted and sentenced to death. Weaver III was sentenced to two consecutive life sentences in prison.

4.1

MEDIA FOCUS continued

An article on the Weavers was on the front page of *USA Today* with this headline: "A Town Wonders: Does Crime Run in Families?" This article went beyond suggesting that crime may run in families to including prediction and prevention with this statement:

Now, many in this city of 25,000 at the end of the Oregon Trail are wondering whether violence runs in the Weaver family. They're also wondering whether investigators, knowing the family history, could have pursued Weaver more aggressively and perhaps even saved the life of one of the girls.[4]

In 2009, a media article reported that Ward Weaver III appeared to be attempting to sell lurid drawings of dead women for $75 each.[5]

1. "Behavior May Leave a Mark on Genes; A Father Is on Death Row, His Son Is Accused of an Eerily Similar Crime. Scientists Are Exploring the Biochemistry Behind Violent Actions," *Los Angeles Times* (28 June 2003), p. 1.
2. "Violent Past Foreshadows Charges Against Weaver," *Sunday Oregonian* (6 October 2002), p. 1.
3. "Behavior May Leave a Mark on Genes," p. 1.
4. "A Town Wonders: Does Crime Run in Families?" *USA Today* (5 September 2002), p. 1.
5. "Online Market: Opponents Urge a Federal Law to Stop Booming Trade in Items from Violent Criminals," *The Oregonian* (Portland), (24 June 2009), Local news, n.p.

reports of antisocial behavior among siblings have been attributed to contagion rather than to social class, parental rearing system, parental substance abuse, or other factors, although not all of the studies control for the influence of genetics.[26]

The basic problem with these family studies was that they could not control for the environment. The parents who produced the children, thereby determining their genetic background, also socialized them; thus, genetics and environment were inseparable. This problem led to two other methods of studying genetic factors and criminality: the study of twins and adoptees, discussed next. It also led to the development of environmental and learning theories of behavior to explain generations of deviance and violence within families.[27]

Studies of Twins

If behavior is inherited, we would expect to find the same behavior among people with identical genes. Thus, identical twins should behave alike. Fraternal twins (nonidentical) of the same gender have about 50 percent identical genes; they should engage in similar behaviors.

Early studies of twins led researchers to conclude that heredity plays a major role in explaining behavior, but most of these studies were based on small samples. Until recently, the most recognized studies of twins were those conducted by Karl O. Christiansen, who avoided many of the sampling problems of the earlier studies. Christiansen studied the incidence of criminal behavior among 3,586 twins in one region of Denmark between 1881 and 1910. He reported that if one twin engaged in criminal behavior, the probability that his or her identical twin also would do so was 35 percent compared with only 12 percent if the twins were not identical.[28]

Sarnoff A. Mednick and his associates updated the Christiansen study and concluded "that genetic factors account for some of the variables associated with anti-social behavior."[29] The twin studies of Mednick and others have been criticized on methodological grounds. Despite the methodological errors, there is evidence of a correlation between genetic factors and criminality,

but the large number of methodological flaws and limitations in the research should make one cautious in drawing any causal inferences at this point in time. Our review leads us to the inevitable conclusion that current genetic research on crime has been poorly designed, ambiguously reported, and exceedingly inadequate in addressing the relevant issues. . . . [T]hese studies have muddied the already turbid waters of genetic research on crime.[30]

Mednick and one of his graduate students responded to this critique by alleging that the criticisms were too general and amounted to little more than name-calling. They claim that the article denigrates "the work of the many serious and honest researchers in this field."[31]

Among other critics of the Danish twins studies are Michael Gottfredson and Travis Hirschi, whose extensive criticism has "raised doubts as to how much [each study] validates the theory of inherited criminal potential."[32]

Studies of Adoptees

Concern with the problem of separating the influence of environment and of heredity, even in the study of twins, has led some researchers to study adoptees, most of whom are placed at birth.

Mednick and his associates conducted adoption studies using a sample of about 72,000 from Denmark's adoption

American parents pose with their newly adopted Korean children. Although many children are adopted at birth, an increasing number of foreign-born children are being adopted as infants or even toddlers by American couples. Social scientists study these and other adoptions in their efforts to determine the influence of genetics and environment on human behavior.

register. They found that criminal behavior was higher among adoptees who had only criminal biological parents in comparison with adoptees with only criminal adoptive parents, but the highest incidences of criminality were among adoptees who had both biological and adoptive parents who engaged in criminal behavior.[33] See Global Focus 4.1 for more details.

Mednick's studies have come under fire, and even he and his associates raised some pertinent questions about the research. In Denmark, efforts are made to place adoptable children in homogeneous environments, and the evidence shows that this approach is successful. For example, most babies born to lower-class parents are placed with

lower-class parents. Despite these and other factors suggesting that environment may play a part in criminal behavior, Mednick and his associates remained firm in their belief that there is also some association between genetic factors and criminal behavior. Critics are not so sure, with crinimologists Michael Gottfredson and Travis Hirschi estimating that the correlation between the criminality of biological fathers and their sons is very low.[34]

After discussing some unpublished, personal correspondence in which Mednick reacted to the criticisms of Gottfredson and Hirschi, David C. Rowe said, "I distrust Gottfredson and Hirschi's conclusion that genetic influences on criminal behavior were absent in adoptive

---

4.1   **Mednick's Classic Adoptions Study of Crime**

GLOBAL FOCUS

"Denmark is a small nation nestled against the cold and harsh North Sea. Eighty-six percent of Danes live in urban areas. The country is renowned for the fairy tales of Hans Christian Andersen and, at least to adoption researchers, for its system of excellent population records. In the 1950s, Sarnoff Mednick capitalized on this fact to locate the criminal records of adoptive children (then adults), their adoptive parents, and their biological parents. His question was simple: Do criminal records for a biological parent increase the likelihood of crime in his or her adopted-away offspring?

"Mednick and his colleagues' results on 14,487 adoptive children were published in *Science* in 1984. He found an increase in the rate of crime in the adopted-away offspring of criminal biological parents:

If neither the biological nor the adoptive parents are convicted, 13.5 percent of the sons are convicted. If

the adoptive parents are convicted and the biological parents are not, this figures [sic] rises only to 14.7 percent. However, if the adoptive parents are not convicted and the biological parents are, 20.0 percent of the sons are convicted. If the adoptive parents as well as the biological parents are convicted, then 24.5 percent of the sons are convicted. These data favor the assumption of a partial genetic etiology."[1]

1. David C. Rowe, *Biology and Crime* (Los Angeles: Roxbury, 2002), quoting Sarnoff A. Medick et al., "Genetic Influences in Criminal Convictions: Evidence from an Adoption Cohort," *Science* 224 (1997): 891–894; quotation is on p. 892.

children in the rural areas of Denmark. Other adoptive studies done in Sweden and in the United States also support a genetic transmission of criminal disposition." Rowe did acknowledge, however, that Gottfredson and Hirschi raised the interesting point that parental and other actions could affect heritability and even deter criminal behavior.[35]

In a 2002 publication, psychologist Adrian Raine emphasized that, in the previous 15 years, significant progress had been made in empirical research in the recognition of biological, psychological, and social factors associated with antisocial and violent behavior. Although little research had been conducted on the interrelationship of these factors, "There is now clear evidence from twin studies, adoption studies, twins reared apart, and molecular genetic studies to support the notion that there are genetic influences on antisocial and aggressive behavior." Studies of twins show stronger evidence than do studies of adoptees, but the real challenge now is to determine "if and how genetic processes interact with environmental processes in predisposing to antisocial behavior." Raine pointed out that "genetic processes need an environment in which to become expressed. As such, environmental changes will turn these genetic influences on and off across the lifespan."[36]

Genetics and Behavior: A Modern View

The early criminologists did not have modern research tools; most of their studies were based on small samples, and their data analyses were simplistic. In the past century or so, with the development of modern tools of analysis and the increased sophistication of the study of genetics, the conclusions of the early studies have been questioned and, in many cases, rejected. In recent decades, little attention has been paid to genetic explanations of criminal behavior; many criminologists have thought it unnecessary to tell their students about these earlier approaches.

Studies that have explored the relationship between heredity and behavior are controversial, but they are gaining more attention, and scholars are trying to improve our understanding of the relationship between biology and behavior. Some of these studies, for example, suggest that both sexual orientation and alcoholism are linked to heredity, that the ability to learn grammar may be controlled by genes, and that body fat may be controlled by heredity. Despite this renewed interest in the relationship between genetics and behavior, the research findings draw the skepticism of many, and the studies should be interpreted carefully.

There was hope this would change with the development of scientific knowledge about human genomes, discussed in Exhibit 4.2. In her presidential address to the American Society of Criminology at its 1998 annual meeting, sociologist Margaret A. Zahn spoke directly to the potentially rich source of data contained in an application of genomic sciences to the understanding of human behavior.

"It is important, if not imperative, that we become aware of the biological and biochemical bases for behavior and incorporate them, *where relevant*, into our theories about violent crime and its consequences."[37]

Anthony Walsh, who was challenged by Zahn's appeal, suggested that "it is time for mainstream criminology to at least pull back its blinders and peek at what behavior genetics has to offer." Walsh attempted to show how behavior genetics could enhance our understanding of criminal behavior through anomie/strain theory, which is discussed in Chapter 5. Walsh emphasized that behavior genetics is not a *biological* perspective of human behavior but, rather, a *biosocial perspective* "that takes seriously the proposition that all human traits, abilities, and behaviors are the result of the interplay of genetics and environments, and it is the only perspective with the research tools to untangle their effects." Walsh concluded:

> The question is no longer if genes affect human behavior, but how and under what circumstances they do. When we are able to dispassionately explore the individual correlates of criminal behavior, we will be in a much better position to develop theories that are vertically integrated with propositions from the more fundamental sciences. The history of science tells us that cross-disciplinary fertilization by a more mature science has, without exception, proven to be of immense value to the immature science. Criminology will be no exception.[38]

As Exhibit 4.2 notes, however, the scientific development of our understanding of genomes has not progressed as had been hoped.

Some scholars express optimism for the future study of the importance of biology in explaining crime, with one of them concluding, "Biological explanations shaped criminology at its inception, and today they are reemerging with fresh vigor and increased potential."[39]

The study of biology and especially genetic theories of evolution are difficult to test, but as David Rowe emphasized, we cannot fully understand human behavior without examining evolution. Therefore, we must continue to look for ways to increase our understanding of evolution and how it applies to behavior, particularly criminal behavior.[40]

One criminologist, however, was quite critical of the progress made in his field, stating in 2004: "The biological sciences have made more progress in understanding crime in the last 10 years than the social sciences have in the last 50."[41]

Support for such a statement comes from a recent disclosure that graduate students working toward their PhDs in criminal justice and criminology had little exposure to "contemporary biological and genetic findings associated with aggression and violence." In fact, the relationship between biology and crime was not a significant part of most graduate programs.[42]

EXHIBIT **4.2**

The Human Genome Project

Humans are more closely related to dogs than to mice reported some of the professional research teams attending a genome conference in Cold Spring Harbor, New York, in May 2001. The *genome*, first deciphered in 2000, maps or "spells" all our genes. The Human Genome Project (HGP), completed in 2003, had as one of its goals identifying all of the human genes. The result was a reduction of the estimated number of genes from 35,000 to only 20,000 to 25,000. In reporting these findings in 2004, the HGP proclaimed: "The availability of the highly accurate human genome sequence in free public databases enables researchers around the world to conduct even more precise studies of our genetic instruction book and how it influences health and disease."[1]

It was thought that these discoveries would enable geneticists to identify the causes of diseases such as cancer, arthritis, and diabetes, as well as to ascertain what causes hair and eye color. The implications for analyzing human behavior, including criminal behavior, were exciting. President Bill Clinton expressed his unequivocal enthusiasm in these words:

> We'll go from knowing almost nothing about how our genes work to enlisting genes in the struggle to prevent and cure illness. This will be the scientific breakthrough of the century, perhaps of all time.[2]

On 14 April 2003, the heads of government of six countries issued the following proclamation regarding the completion of the human genome sequence:

> We, the Heads of Government of the United States of America, the United Kingdom, Japan, France, Germany, and China, are proud to announce that scientists from our six countries have completed the essential sequence of three billion base pairs of DNA of the human genome, the molecular instruction book of human life.
>
> Remarkable advances in genetic science and technology have been made in the five decades since the landmark discovery of the double-helix structure of DNA in April 1953. Now, in the very month and year of the 50th anniversary of that important discovery by Watson and Crick, the International Human Genome Sequencing Consortium has completed decoding all the chapters of the instruction book of human life. This information is now freely available to the world without constraints via public databases on the World Wide Web.

> This genetic sequence provides us with the fundamental platform for understanding ourselves, from which revolutionary progress will be made in biomedical sciences and in the health and welfare of humankind. Thus, we take today an important step toward establishing a healthier future for all the peoples of the globe, for whom the human genome serves as a common inheritance.
>
> We congratulate all the people who participated in this project on their creativity and dedication. Their outstanding work will be noted in the history of science and technology, and as well in the history of humankind, as a landmark achievement.
>
> We encourage the world to celebrate the scientific achievement of completing the Human Genome Project, and we exhort the scientific and medical communities to rededicate themselves to the utilization of these new discoveries to reduce human suffering.[3]

In June 2010, however, the predictions had not come true, and we still did not know the causes of the diseases we thought we would be understanding. A British professor of molecular genetics declared with regard to the Human Genome Project,

> The project that promised so much has, so far, delivered very little. Very few genes have been found that account for more than 1 percent of the risk of any of those common diseases. And even the most significant intelligence gene yet found is responsible for variation in individual intelligence equivalent to less than one IQ point. The scientists who went in search of whoppers netted only a host of minnows.[4]

---

1. "International Human Genome Sequencing Consortium Describes Finished Human Genome Sequence," Human Genome Project, http://www.ornl.gov/sci/techresources/Human_Genome/project/20to 25K.shtml, accessed 3 January 2010.

2. Johnjoe McFadden, "Comment: Genes? It's Complicated: The Advance Heralded a Decade Ago in Mapping Human DNA Is Yet to Lead to the Answers We Craved," *The Guardian* (London) (24 June 2010), p. 32.

3. "Joint Proclamation by the Heads of Government of Six Countries Regarding the Completion of the Human Genome Sequence," *Weekly Compilation of Presidential Documents* 39, no. 16 (21 April 2003): n.p.

4. McFadden, "Comment: Genes?"

Obstetric Factors

According to Adrian Raine, who reviewed 39 empirical examples of biosocial interaction effects for antisocial behavior, "Of all the subfields of biological research on antisocial behavior, obstetric influences show the most compelling evidence for biosocial interactions." Raine divided the studies into three categories: minor physical anomalies, prenatal nicotine exposure, and birth complications. The first category, minor physical anomalies (MPAs), refers to pregnancy disorders that are thought to be markers for neural maldevelopment and that occur within the first three months of pregnancy. The studies found a relationship between MPAs and subsequent violent crimes but not to property crimes without violence. But when the subjects were divided into those from unstable, nonintact homes and those from stable homes, the results showed a possible relationship between social and biological factors in influencing antisocial behavior in that MPAs were predictive of violence only in the subjects from unstable homes.[43]

The second category of obstetric factors and crime is nicotine exposure. Raine emphasized that we have long known about a relationship between fetal exposure to alcohol and future behavior problems, "but recently a spate of studies has established beyond reasonable doubt a significant link between smoking during pregnancy and later conduct disorder and violent offending." Raine stated that smoking during pregnancy "may be an important contributory factor to the brain deficits that have been found in adult offenders."

Raine concluded that babies who endure complications at birth are more likely to become involved in conduct disorder and delinquency and to commit impulsive and violent crimes as adults.

Raine and others studied more than 4,000 Danish babies and concluded that many of the babies who suffered birth complications became criminals, but perhaps it was because they were rejected by their mothers. Raine emphasized the need to consider the *interaction* of birth complications with early maternal rejection.[44]

Another area of biology that some believe is associated with criminal behavior is that of the nervous system, which may also be connected to birth complications.

Neurological Factors

All of the nervous systems enclosed within the skull and spine are part of the *central nervous system* (CNS). Complex sensory information is processed in the CNS, which also controls voluntary muscle movement. One basic test of the CNS's functioning is the electroencephalogram (EEG), which creates graphic images of the brain's activities.[45] The EEG has been the most common tool for research on the relationship between the CNS and criminal behavior, with some findings that "incarcerated individuals tend to have higher proportions of abnormal EEGs than do individuals in the general population."[46]

A second way to examine the CNS's functioning is through neuropsychological tests, which combine psychological observation with neurological evidence from the nervous system. These tests include X-rays; *computerized axial tomography* (CAT), which takes X-rays of the brain; *magnetic resonance imaging* (MRI), which permits viewing detailed images of the brain or other parts of the body; and spinal taps, which determine whether the brain has been damaged. The results may be used to analyze the relationship between brain damage and criminal behavior. "Results of neuropsychological tests administered to criminals suggest that violent, impulsive individuals suffer from damage to specific brain areas," which may occur before birth or at delivery. Studies show, too, that criminals suffer injury with resulting unconsciousness earlier in life than noncriminals do.[47]

The MRI, the CAT, and X-rays show the anataomy of the brain, but another method of studying the neurological system and its relationship to behavior, *positron emission tomography* (PET), shows how the brain is working. The PET was described in 1999 by researchers at the Mayo Clinic in Rochester (Minnesota) as "the most sophisticated nuclear imaging tool to date."[48] PET scanning monitors the brain's radioactive substances, showing which areas of the brain are working hardest when the individual is engaged in a particular thought process. It has been used to determine differences between the thought processes and emotions of men and women as well as to differentiate between murderers and nonviolent criminals. It has been used to reveal the underlying causes of psychiatric illness and mental diseases of aging and to identify the risk of panic attacks.[49] It is also used to determine the progression of active cancerous tumors as well as to pinpoint the areas of the brain that are causing seizures. The PET is also used to understand traumatic brain injury, a condition common to many inmates, most of whom will be released back into society at some point. It is therefore important to understand and treat those brain injuries.

According to an article in the *Journal of the American Medical Association*:

> CAT and PET scans and MRI are powerful tools that . . . may help us solve some of biology's greatest remaining mysteries, such as how the brain establishes connections, how experiences alter development, [and] how the tremendous changes that occur in the brain during the first year or two of a child's life are related to the profound changes that occur in his or her behavior.[50]

Neuroendocrinology

Neuroendocrinologists have attributed criminal behavior to an imbalance of the body's chemicals. Much of the research distinguishes between men and women.

Premenstrual syndrome (PMS) among women, for example, has been studied in relationship to behavioral problems, including crime. PMS is associated with the imbalance of the two female hormones, estrogen and progesterone. More than 150 symptoms of PMS have been identified; most are not associated with criminal behavior, but those that might be are as follows:

- Depression
- Irritability
- Temporary psychosis

Medical treatment, consisting primarily of hormone therapy, is required in severe cases of PMS. Researchers insist that the effects of PMS are real and serious. The diagnosis is now included among depressive disorders in the American Psychiatric Association's *Diagnostic and Statistical Manual*, although the listing of PMS as a *possible disorder* rather than a disorder might limit its acceptability as a medical condition that affects behavior.[51]

Another hormone-related diagnosis among women is the **postpartum depression (PPD) syndrome**. PPD gained national attention in the events leading up to the 2002 conviction of Andrea Yates, a Houston, Texas, mother who drowned her five young children in the family bathtub and then called police. Yates was convicted of capital murders and sentenced to life in prison. Although both the defense and the prosecution in the *Yates* case agreed that the defendant had mental problems, even delusions, they did not agree on the extent, and the jury did not accept her insanity plea. In 2005, Yates's convictions were reversed. She was retried, and her insanity plea was successful. She is currently confined to a mental institution for treatment.[52]

Although it is reported that approximately three-fourths of all women suffer "baby blues" after giving birth, most recover in a few days. The American Psychiatric Association reports that between 10 and 20 percent of women suffer depression after giving birth, but only approximately 1 or 2 of every 1,000 of these women experience PPD as seriously as Andrea Yates. Still, an assistant professor of psychiatry and obstetrics at Duke University referred to PPD as "the most under-recognized, under-diagnosed, and under-treated obstetrical complication in America."[53]

In another case, a young Chicago mother, Melanie Stokes, who suffered from PPD, jumped off a twelfth-floor window ledge in 2001, just three months after she gave birth to a baby girl. Her case was remembered in 2009 when the new Illinois governor commuted to time served (24 years) the sentence of Debra Lynn Gindorf, who was sentenced to more than 20 years in prison for killing her two children. Gindorf also attempted suicide by the same method she used to kill her children (sleeping pills) but she awakened. After trying again and failing in kill herself, Gindorf turned herself in to authorities. One of the persons who worked for years for Gindorf's release was Carol Blocker, mother of Melanie Stokes. Blocker praised the governor for fighting for an understanding of postpartum depression, which she referred to as the "hidden illness."[54]

In a scholarly analysis of PPD and its medical and legal implications, one expert emphasized that the disorder is serious but that the medical community has been slow to recognize this. The legal community has been inconsistent in its reaction to crimes that are committed by women suffering from PPD.[55]

Some jurisdictions have recently enacted **Baby Moses laws**, which stipulate safe places (e.g., fire stations or hospitals) where women who give birth (or other persons who have custody of newborns they do not wish to raise) may leave the infants anonymously without any questions asked or any attempts to prosecute.

Research shows that women are more prone to depression after giving birth than at any other time in their lives and that, in general, women are twice as likely as men to suffer from depression. Among women, postpartum depression can lead to postpartum psychosis, which occurs in from 1 to 4 women of every 1,000 who give birth. "This devastating illness is characterized by a loss of contact with reality for an extended period of time and includes hallucinations, delusions, hearing voices and rapid mood swings," which may lead to violence. And even when the infants are not physically harmed, they may suffer psychologically and emotionally as a result.[56]

There is also evidence that hormonal imbalance is associated with the behavior of men. The male hormone testosterone is associated with aggressive, antisocial, and criminal behavior. Researchers have also studied the hormone in relation to sexual behavior, smoking, and substance abuse. A review of the research on the relationship between testosterone and criminality reported that "the association between testosterone and aggression was more consistent for adults than for adolescents, possibly because of the profound influence of puberty on hormone levels."[57]

One study of the relationship between testosterone and aggression concluded that there is "convincing evidence from a wide number of behavioral studies for a link between high testosterone and increased aggressive and violent behavior," but it found that the relationship might be weak or even absent with respect to the aggression levels of children. These studies point to the effects of socialization and other environmental factors on testosterone levels.[58]

After reviewing the research in this area, two criminologists concluded that "except for the unsurprising finding that testosterone level is associated with increased sexual activity," the relationship between the hormone and behavior is weak. And researchers have not suggested that the hormone *causes* deviant behavior but only that it *facilitates* such behavior.[59]

Neurochemistry

Scientists are also looking at a possible relationship between criminal behavior and diet. In October 1983, the National Conference on Nutrition and Behavior focused on an issue of growing recognition—the effects of nutrition (or its lack), chemicals, food additives, or preservatives on human behavior. Also in 1983, findings relating body chemistry and behavior, based on an analysis of hair samples from 24 pairs of brothers ranging in age from 6 to 18, were published. Each pair in the sample consisted of one child who was terrific and one who was always in trouble. The researcher found that the violent children were of two types. The brothers who were always violent had low amounts of copper, whereas those who engaged only in episodic violent acts were high in copper. The nonviolent brothers did not fit either of these patterns. The researcher then tested an additional 192 males, some of whom were on death row and others who had violent characteristics. One-half of the 192 were not violent. The researchers concluded that behavior is a combination of a deprived background and a poor living environment, along with a chemical imbalance. But the research showed that "some bodies are so aberrant, all the love and counseling in the world won't help. . . . Others are so strong that, even if they're brought up in an awful background, they're terrific from the very beginning." It was concluded that, in their efforts to help violent children become nonviolent, researchers were treating the children with a series of vitamins to change their chemical balance and, although it was too early to draw conclusions, the results looked promising.[60]

Other researchers began a 1988 report on the complex relationship between behavior and diet and its implications for understanding criminal behavior with a brief review of the study of **biocriminology**, which is the introduction of biological variables into criminology. After a literature review, the investigators concluded that the evidence was not yet sufficient to support a causal relationship between diet and criminal behavior. "Nevertheless . . . we do feel that current findings justify further attention to the possibility of a diet/behavior link that is relevant to the criminal justice system."[61]

By 1998, researchers were linking the influence of food or nutrients to such problems as hyperactivity, learning disabilities, mental illness, aggressive behavior, and antisocial behavior.[62]

In 2000, researchers reported that violence in numerous juvenile correctional institutions had been reduced by almost 50 percent "after implementing nutrient-dense diets that are consistent with the World Health Organization's guidelines for fats, sugar, starches, and protein ratios." In one study, some of the youths were given supplements, while others were not, in an effort to determine whether changes in behavior were influenced by the supplements or by psychological (or other) factors. The researchers concluded as follows:

> Poor nutritional habits in children lead to low concentrations of water-soluble vitamins in blood, impair brain function and subsequently cause violence and other serious antisocial behavior. Correction of nutrient intake, either through a well-balanced diet

or low-dose vitamin-mineral supplementation, corrects the low concentrations of vitamins in blood, improves brain function and subsequently lowers institutional violence and antisocial behavior by almost half.[63]

A similar study was conducted in English and Scottish prisons and is discussed in Global Focus 4.2.

There are, however, challenges to the belief that diet has an effect on behavior and thus may explain some criminal behavior. The National Council Against Health Fraud (NCAHF) publishes on its website its earlier conclusion that there is insufficient evidence to conclude that diet is "an important element" in aggressive or criminal behavior.[64]

Autonomic Nervous System Studies

Another area of biological study involves the autonomic nervous system (ANS), that part of the central nervous system that automatically controls vital life functions, such as heart rate. Researchers have found that persons who exhibit antisocial and criminal behavior, compared with those who do not exhibit such behavior, have slower than normal resting heart rates. Their autonomic nervous systems do not react as quickly to stimuli; thus, they may have to engage in more intense activities (e.g., crime) to get the level of stimulation they need.

Adrian Raine and his colleagues found evidence that young people whose autonomic nervous systems exhibited a higher rate of responsiveness were less likely to engage in criminal behavior. One reason might be the fact that a higher rate of responsiveness is accompanied by a higher level of fearfulness, which might lead the individuals to think about the consequences of criminal behavior and, in so doing, not engage in that behavior.[65]

Consider a simple example. To learn not to steal, a child must be taught—socialized—that it is wrong to take the property of others without their permission. Usually, this socialization occurs within the family, which acts as a censuring agent, and the appropriate fear response is developed. Children learn to fear punishment if they steal, and that fear enables them to inhibit their stealing impulses. Antisocial children do not learn adequate initial fear responses; thus, they may not anticipate negative reactions if they steal. The fear inhibitor does not work to repress their stealing impulses.

How does this factor relate to the ANS? The ANS is the primary control of the fear response. If children have quick ANS responses, they learn to react to stimuli with fear, and generally, that fear inhibits their desire to steal. Children who have slow ANS responses learn slowly to inhibit stealing, if at all. A number of studies suggest that those who exhibit criminal behavior tend to have slower than average ANS responses.[66]

Raine emphasized that children who are aggressive or antisocial may simply be relatively fearless youngsters who are seeking stimulation. Also, infants and very young

4.2	**Nutrition and Criminal Behavior: The British Investigate**

In 2002, the authors of a study of incarcerated young adults in Britain came to this conclusion:

> Antisocial behaviour in prisons, including violence, are [*sic*] reduced by vitamins, minerals and essential fatty acids with similar implications for those eating poor diets in the community.[1]

Subsequently, it was announced that "chips, pies and sweets" would be removed from the diets of inmates in three British prisons in an effort to determine whether this change in diet had any measurable effect on behavior.[2]

The British studies were highlighted on *CBS News* on 27 April 2004, when Charles Osgood hosted Bernard Gesch, who, with his team of colleagues, conducted the British research. According to Gesch, "Improving nutrition appears to be cheap, humane and highly effective at reducing violence in a prison. . . . The increase in nutrient intake caused the change in behavior [35 percent drop in disciplinary behavior]. It's the only explanation from a scientific perspective." Gesch concluded: "If it worked in a prison, it should work in the community."[3]

In a 2008 article in Britain, the success of the 2002 study was noted, emphasizing that according to Oxford University scientists, the positive impact of nutrition on behavior has not been sufficiently recognized. Consequently, the Wellcome Trust funded a three-year study of inmates consisting of 1,000 males ages 16 to 21 from three prisons in England and Scotland. For one year, some of these inmates were to receive dietary supplements while the others served as a control group. The dietary supplements consisted of 100 percent of the daily amount of 30 recommended vitamins

plus three fish oil tablets. The researchers noted that although the prisons served nutritional food, some inmates made poor choices; thus, the supplements were needed. It was argued that when the brain is deprived of essential nutrients, "especially omega-3 fatty acids, which are a central building block of brain neurons," it loses its flexibility. The result can be an undermining of self-control and the reduction of one's attention span. According to Professor Gesch,

> We are trying to rehabilitate the brain to criminal justice. The law assumes crime is a matter of free will. But you can't exercise free will without involving your brain and the brain can't function properly without an adequate nutrient supply. It may have an important influence on behaviour.
>
> This is a positive approach to preventing the problems of antisocial and criminal behaviour. It is simple, it seems to be highly effective and the only "risk" from a better diet is better health. It is a rare win-win situation in criminal justice.[4]

1. Bernard C. Gesch et al., "Influence of Supplementary Vitamins, Minerals and Essential Fatty Acids on the Antisocial Behaviour of Young Adult Prisoners," *British Journal of Psychiatry* 181 (2002): 22–28.
2. "Junk Food to Be Taken Off Prison Menus," *The Daily Telegraph* (London) (2 March 2003), p. 7.
3. "Study on Nutrition and Prison Violence," *CBS News Transcripts* (27 April 2004).
4. "Prison Study to Investigate Link Between Junk Food and Violence," *The Independent* (London) (29 January 2008), p. 4.

children with disinhibited temperaments, thought to predispose them to future delinquent behavior, are characterized by autonomic underarousal.[67]

In later research, Raine found support for the association between low arousal and low fear conditioning along with a lack of conscience and decision-making deficits, all characteristics found in antisocial, psychotic behavior. The respondents with low ANS responses were also likely to have structural brain deficits resulting from discernible brain trauma.[68]

Attention-Deficit Hyperactivity Disorder (ADHD)

The most commonly diagnosed psychiatric condition among U.S. children and teens today is **attention-deficit hyperactivity disorder (ADHD)**. The disorder has also been referred to as *minimal brain dysfunction, hyperactivity, hyperkinesis,* or simply *attention-deficit disorder* (ADD).

In 2010, the Centers for Disease Control and Prevention provided the following pertinent information about data and other significant issues concerning ADHD:

- "Approximately 9.5 percent or 5.4 million children 4–17 years of age have ever been diagnosed with ADHD as of 2007.
- The percentage of children with a parent-reported ADHD diagnosis increased by 22 percent between 2003 and 2007.
- Rates of ADHD diagnosis increased an average of 3 percent per year from 1997 to 2006 and an average of 5.5 percent per year from 2003 to 2007.
- Boys (13.2 percent) were more likely than girls (5.6 percent) to have been diagnosed with ADHD.
- Rates of ADHD diagnosis increased at a greater rate among older teens as compared to younger children.
- The highest rates of parent-reported ADHD diagnosis were noted among children covered by Medicaid and multiracial children.

■ Prevalence of parent-reported ADHD diagnosis varied substantially by state, from a low of 5.6 percent in Nevada to a high of 15.6 percent in North Carolina."[69]

This report on 2007 data included children aged 4–17 in contrast to 5–17 for 2006, which may account for some of the increase in the estimated number of children with ADHD (5.4 million compared to 4.5 million) and the increase in diagnosis of male children from 9.5 percent to 13.2 percent. The high percentage by state increased from 11.1 percent in 2006 (in Alabama) to the 2007 figure of 15.6 percent in North Carolina.

ADHD is also diagnosed in approximately 4.1 percent of adults.[70] It is manifested by inattentiveness, difficulty stifling inconvenient impulses, and daydreaming, as well as by not finishing projects, repeatedly making careless mistakes, switching haphazardly from one activity to another, and having problems obeying instructions. These and other behaviors inhibit school, work, and social relationships. Some of the symptoms are common in many people, but in ADHD children, the characteristics reach such a critical level that the children are diagnosed as having the psychiatric disorder.[71]

It is difficult to diagnose ADHD because the symptoms are not consistent. The disorder may result in a child's disruptive behavior in the classroom and difficulty on the playground. Or the child might be unruly in the classroom one day and show no symptoms of ADHD on another day. There is a lack of agreement concerning when to determine that a child's behavior constitutes a psychiatric disorder. Scholars have described children with ADHD as follows:

> Many of these children are . . . impulsive . . . irritable and impatient, unable to tolerate delay or frustration. They act before thinking and do not wait their turn. In conversation they interrupt, talk too much, too loud, and too fast, and blurt out whatever comes to mind. They seem to be constantly pestering parents, teachers, and other children. They cannot keep their hands to themselves, and often appear to be reckless, clumsy, and accident-prone.[72]

The association of ADHD with other disorders in children is a cause of concern for those studying delinquent and criminal behavior. Children with ADHD are more likely to suffer from "atypical depression, anxiety disorders, impaired speech or hearing, mild retardation, and traumatic stress reactions." One-third to one-half of these children develop major depression or anxiety disorders. Many are "easily angered and provoked to aggression, or seemingly callous, manipulative, and egocentric. They intimidate other children, start fights, and throw tantrums." In addition to these types of conduct disorders, many ADHD children suffer from learning disabilities.[73]

At one time or another, ADHD has been attributed to allergies, vitamin deficiencies, radiation, lead, sugar, and fluorescent lights. All of these alleged causes are rejected today. Although there is no agreement on the precise cause of ADHD, "[m]ost experts agree that ADHD is a brain disorder with a biological basis."[74]

Experts do not agree on the extent to which children diagnosed with ADHD should be medicated, if at all. Nor do they agree on the medications to prescribe. It does appear, however, that ADHD children can be diagnosed and treated, although both are expensive. The diagnostic process may involve numerous medical tests as well as examinations of intelligence and academic achievement; interviews with parents, siblings, teachers, and others who work with the children; and discussions with the children themselves.[75]

An analysis of the legal and social implications of ADHD, authored by a physician writing in a legal/medical journal, noted that between 52 and 72 percent of institutionalized juvenile delinquents (compared with approximately 7 to 22 percent of the general population of the same ages) exhibit characteristics qualifying them for a diagnosis of one or more psychiatric disorders, including ADHD. ADHD "truly is a distinct brain disorder. Inattention, lack of inhibition, motor disorganization, and working memory deficits are thought to be fundamental to the disorder," which can be described as "the management system of the brain gone awry." Although ADHD may increase the chances of behavior disorder, "studies have shown that it is the combination of ADHD and conduct disorder, rather than hyperactivity by itself, that leads to antisocial behaviors." And although research has not shown a definitive causal relationship between ADHD and delinquency or ADHD and substance abuse, the majority of the studies conclude that delinquency is associated with both ADHD and substance abuse. But according to the physician, with effective treatment, the impact of ADHD on future juvenile delinquent behavior can be significantly reduced.[76]

Psychological Theories of Criminal Behavior

Biologists and chemists are not the only professionals to link behavior to physical characteristics. Psychologists have done so, too. Early psychologists attempted to explain criminal behavior by means of *intelligence*, which they assumed to be inherited. Family studies were their sources of data. As the researchers traced criminality through generations of the same family, they concluded that inherited mental retardation was the *cause* of crime. Earlier in the chapter, we noted some of the problems with these studies, which were preceded by other problematic attempts to explain criminal behavior in terms of the mind or spirit. Later in this chapter, we look at the relationship between intelligence and crime. But first, the discussion takes a quick look at the overall picture of mental illness.

Mental Illness: A Brief Look

In May 2004, the preliminary results of the largest survey of mental illness in the world (90-minute interviews with 60,643 respondents in 14 countries) were published, noting that one in five persons in most of the countries surveyed had a serious mental illness, while 9 to 17 percent had some mental illness within the previous year. The United States led all countries, with 26 percent of its surveyed population having some mental illness (18 percent had anxiety disorders). Mental illness caused more lost workdays than any physical illnesses, including cancer and back pain. Not surprisingly, the researchers reported that wealthy people with minor mental illnesses receive better medical treatment than poor people with severe mental illnesses.[77]

In 2010, the National Institute of Mental Health (NIMH) posted on its website that in any given year in the United States, 26.2 percent of persons aged 18 and older suffer from a diagnosable mental disorder, with 1 in 17 persons suffering from *serious* mental illness. According to the NIMH, "mental illness, including suicide, accounts for over 15 percent of the burden of disease. . . . This is more than the disease burden caused by all cancers."[78]

Mental health issues are of serious concern in prisons and jails as will be noted in subsequent chapters. In a recent study, a group of sheriffs and jail administrators, asked to give funding advice to the federal government, recommended additional money for treating inmates with mental health problems. The group emphasized that jail inmates have more serious and costly mental health problems than previously. The report, published by the Center for Innovative Public Policies, concluded as follows:

> [I]nmate mental health care has become such a pervasive dilemma that serious consideration was given by some participants to determining how jails could obtain certification as mental health hospitals in order to officially recognize their responsibility . . . [for treating inmates with mental problems], and accomplish more effectively what they are now attempting to do unofficially in the absence of community support.[79]

The Bureau of Justice Statistics (BJS) published an analysis of data from prisons and jails, reporting that at midyear 2005 over one-half of all state and federal inmates had a mental health problem. In its latest information, posted in 2010, the BJS reported the following percentages of inmates who had mental health problems in state and federal prisons:

- State prisons: 73 percent of female inmates compared to 55 percent of male inmates.
- Federal prisons: 61 percent of female inmates compared to 44 percent of male inmates.
- Local jails: 75 percent of female inmates compared to 63 percent of male inmates.[80]

A study of inmates released from prisons in Ohio and Texas found that approximately four of every ten men and six of every ten women had a combination of mental illness, medical illness, and substance abuse conditions. A significant number reported mental health issues (such as difficulty controlling violent behavior and hallucinations) that could affect public safety.[81]

Throughout this text, we will see references to mental illness and its possible relationship to criminal behavior. Mental illness is often raised in cases involving mass murders. For example, the possible connection between mental illness and violence arose as experts and laypersons tried to understand the actions of Steve P. Kazmierczak, who entered a classroom dressed in black, carrying a shotgun and three handguns, opened fire, killed five students, and wounded many others at Northern Illinois University in DeKalb before killing himself. Kazmierczak, a graduate student focusing on sociology and criminal justice at another university, returned to the school he had once attended and, with no apparent motive and no comment, began his shooting rampage. He was known as a good student who was accepted and admired; no one apparently saw any problems that could predict his violent behavior.

The issue of whether mental illness is associated with victimization has also been raised. There is some evidence that mentally ill persons are more likely to become crime victims. One investigator reported that "mentally disordered people were more likely than were nonmentally disordered people to be victimized by violence," and this was particularly the case when illegal drug use was involved. However, when the factors of illegal drug use and conflicted social relationships were controlled, mentally disordered people were not more likely to become violent crime victims. Other investigators suggest that if violence is viewed as an informal social control method for those trying to change the behavior of others or to secure "justice," as the violent person defines that term, it may be reasonable to conclude that mentally disordered people might be introducing into their social interactions negative stimuli that trigger the violence in others who are trying to correct that behavior.[82]

Whatever view we take of offenders or victims, clearly, mental illness is a serious problem for criminal justice systems and for society in general. Further attention is given to mental illness in discussions of jail and prison inmates in later chapters as well as of capital punishment later in this chapter.

A quick look at the history of how mental illness has been treated historically is enlightening. One of the most popular early explanations of criminal behavior was **demonology**. Individuals were thought to be possessed by spirits that caused good or evil behavior. In medieval times, people believed that deviant behavior could not be changed unless the bad spirits were banished. One method of treating criminal behavior was to use a crude stone to cut a hole in the skull of a person thought to be possessed by devils. The process, called *trephining*, supposedly permitted the evil spirits to escape. There is evidence that some people survived the surgery. But the usual treatment for evil spirits was *exorcism*, which included having the "possessed" person drink horrible concoctions, pray, and make strange noises. Later, it was assumed that the only way to drive out the devils was to insult them or to make the body an unpleasant place for them to inhabit; sufferers underwent flogging and other forms of corporal punishment. During the latter part of the fifteenth century, the belief arose that some possessed people were actively and deliberately working with the devil of their own free will. Society reacted to this alleged witchcraft by imposing the death penalty.

In the eighteenth century, scholars began developing knowledge about human anatomy, physiology, neurology, general medicine, and chemistry. The discovery of an organic basis for many physical illnesses led to similar applications for some mental illnesses. These findings replaced the demonological theory of causation and dominated the fields of psychology and psychiatry until 1915. By the beginning of the twentieth century, a new viewpoint in psychiatry had been created with the argument that psychological problems could *cause* mental illness.

Psychiatric Approach

The field of medicine that specializes in the understanding, diagnosis, treatment, and prevention of mental illness is **psychiatry**. **Psychoanalysis** is a branch of psychiatry based on the theories of Sigmund Freud and generally involves the treatment method known as the *case study*. Psychiatry views each individual as a unique personality who can be understood only by a thorough case analysis.

The use of the case study in psychiatry characterized the work of William Healy, who is credited with shifting the positivists' emphasis from anatomical characteristics to psychological and social elements. Healy and his colleagues believed that the only way to find the roots or causes of delinquent behavior was to delve deeply into the individual's background, especially his or her emotional development. These researchers also measured personality disorders and environmental pathologies. They maintained that delinquency is purposive behavior that results when children are frustrated in their attempts to fulfill some of their basic needs. Healy and his associates found that delinquents had a higher frequency of personality defects and disorders than did nondelinquents.[83]

Despite their popularization of the case study method, Healy and his colleagues may be criticized for basing their studies on vaguely defined terms, giving little information on how they measured the concepts and characteristics, and using samples too small to permit generalization to the total population of delinquents.

Sigmund Freud (1856–1939), who is credited with having made the greatest contribution to the development of

The works of Sigmund Freud (1856–1939), an Austrian neurologist and the founder of psychoanalysis, have been influential in the development of psychological theories of human behavior for over a century.

early psychoanalytic theory, did not advance a theory of criminality per se. Freud's theories attempted to explain all behavior; thus, they have implications for criminology. Freud's contribution was not so much in terms of new ideas and concepts as in a synthesis of existing ideas and concepts. The organic base of mental illness had already been discovered. But by the turn of the twentieth century, Freud and others began to argue that psychological problems could cause mental illness, and a new viewpoint in psychiatry developed. The psychoanalytic theories of Freud and his colleagues introduced the concept of the *unconscious,* along with techniques for probing that element of the personality, and emphasized that all human behavior is motivated and purposive.

According to Freud, humans have mental conflicts because of desires and energies that are repressed into the unconscious. These urges, ideas, desires, and instincts are basic, but they are repressed because of society's morality. People frequently try to express these natural drives in some ways, often indirect, to avoid the reactions of others. Dreams are one example of indirect expression.

Freud saw original human nature as assertive and aggressive. Aggression is not learned but is rooted deeply in early childhood experiences. We all have criminal tendencies, but during the socialization process, most of us learn to control those tendencies by developing strong and effective inner controls. The improperly socialized child does not develop an ability to control impulses and, instead, either acts them out or projects them inward. In the latter case, the child may become neurotic; in the former case, delinquent.[84]

Let us examine this process. The infant begins to want things and cries until it is satisfied or exhausted. As the child grows older, it begins to realize that not all of its needs and desires can be gratified because, among other reasons, they may come into conflict with the needs and desires of other people. The child learns that there are limits to the desires that can be fulfilled. It will develop ambivalence toward its parents; although they are the ones who supply the child's needs for comfort, love, food, and protection, they are also the first socializing agents of society with whom the child comes into contact. They are the first to deny the child's fulfilling of some of its desires.

Freud stated that the personality consists of three elements. The *id* is the reservoir of urges, desires, drives, and instincts. The *superego*, developed by society's moral pressures, is the conscience of the individual and is constantly trying to suppress the id. The *ego* is constantly trying to achieve an acceptable balance between the id and the superego. The id and the superego are basically unconscious, while the ego is the conscious part of the personality.

Freud saw the personality in terms of the conflict between creativity and destruction. Creativity is represented by the natural instinctual drives of humans, mainly sexual expression and affectional love, and destruction is represented by society's urge to punish those who do not conform. The healthy personality achieves a balance between the two forms; without that balance, personality disorders develop. A healthy balance is achieved through proper socialization in which the child learns to defer some desires in return for other pleasures, such as the satisfaction and approval of its parents or other significant persons.

The child later learns to defer immediate desires to prepare for a career and a home. The process is fairly easy if the parents and other socializing agents are mature and do not make more demands on the child than it can handle at a given time. But if the parents are too demanding, unfair, arbitrary, punitive, or inconsistent, the child becomes confused and traumatized, resulting in the development of neurosis or psychosis. If the child has internalized the social norms, it may blame itself for its rebellious and delinquent behavior; if such internalization has not taken place, the child may blame others for its problems. But in either case, the child may not understand or recognize the causes of the problems. Psychoanalysis is a technique for probing into the unconscious and revealing these causes.

How did Freud discover the unconscious? He used hypnosis on some of his patients, encouraging them to talk freely. He discovered that patients would talk rather freely, which was a therapeutic release for them (a process Freud called *catharsis*), and also that they would reveal underlying situations that might be seen by the therapist (but not by the patient) as causes of the problems. He later discovered that he could achieve the same results without hypnosis by encouraging patients to talk freely, a process he called *free association*; he called the method *psychoanalysis*. Under psychoanalysis, the therapist would assist the patient to understand the meaning of what had been freely associated.

Others also contributed to the development of psychoanalysis. Alfred Adler (1870–1937) developed the concept of the *inferiority complex*. This might be an explanation of crime because the commission of a criminal act is one of the best ways to get attention, and the attention may help compensate for a person's sense of inferiority. Adler also mentioned the lack of cooperation in the criminal, which he traced to early childhood experiences—for example, the resentment the firstborn has about the birth of a subsequent sibling because of the time devoted to the new infant by the parents. But Adler placed too much emphasis on the rational side of behavior, and his work contained too much oversimplification and generalization.[85]

Carl Gustav Jung (1875–1960) developed and popularized (although he did not invent) the concepts of *extrovert* (outgoing) and *introvert* (shy). These concepts have been utilized in the modern research of psychoanalysis, especially with reference to recidivism and psychopathy.[86]

Before we leave the discussion of psychiatry, it is important to note an important and growing field of interest, even at the undergraduate level: **forensic psychiatry**. This branch of psychiatry deals with disorders of the mind as they relate to legal issues. It is not limited to a study of the criminal mind but includes issues in civil as well as criminal law. Forensic psychiatry is crucial to criminal law and criminology because criminal justice systems face the issues of whether mentally disordered persons should be held legally responsible for their criminal acts.

The psychiatric approach may be criticized for several reasons. The terms are vague, no operational definitions for most concepts are given, and most of the data are open to the analyst's subjective interpretation. Moreover, the research has been based on small samples that are selected primarily from psychiatric patients, many of whom are institutionalized. The use of control groups has not been adequate. The individual is the focus of the psychiatric approach, and this focus does not permit generalizations of behavior *patterns*. The emphasis on early childhood experiences has been questioned by social scientists, who deemphasize the deterministic nature of these experiences, arguing that their impact can be decreased or even eliminated through proper training.[87] In short, today's criminologists do not pay much attention to psychoanalytic theory.[88]

Personality Theory

In contrast to the emphasis psychoanalytic theory places on the subconscious is the approach of personality theory. The term *personality* is defined as the "sum total of the physical, mental, emotional, and social characteristics of an individual; it is the organized pattern of behavioral characteristics" of that person.[89] Personality theory looks at the behavioral characteristics that are ingrained in a person's being and that define the uniqueness of the person. Various tests have been developed in an attempt to measure personality characteristics,[90] especially those considered maladaptive, leading to such diagnoses as that of antisocial personality disorder (APD). APD is defined by the American Psychiatric Association as "a pervasive pattern of disregard for, and violation of, the rights of others that begins in childhood or early adolescence and comes into adulthood." A diagnosis of APD is appropriate when one's personality involves a combination of such actions as repeated violations of the law, frequent lying, repeated violence, failure to maintain consistent work behavior, and so on.[91]

Many criminals have APD characteristics, especially habitual offenders, leading some theorists to conclude that such deviations *cause* criminal behavior. But the critical questions are whether these factors distinguish criminals from law-abiding persons and, if so, whether the traits *cause* the illegal behavior. A number of early researchers found such differences,[92] but others found evidence that questioned the relationship between personality traits and criminal behavior.[93]

The earlier studies emphasized the frequency of an association between personality characteristics and crime. The belief that these characteristics *caused* criminal behavior led to confinement of the mentally ill in jails and prisons rather than in public hospitals. A 1984 report from the National Institute of Justice pointed out that, although mental disorders were found more often among criminals than among noncriminals, the explanation was not that mental disorders *caused* crime but that mental disorders and crime were both *associated with* some of the same demographic factors, such as age, gender, and race.[94]

One approach that is controversial among some experts and supported by others is the proposition that there is a *criminal personality*. The works of Stanton E. Samenow and Samuel Yochelson are often cited in this area. In a brief essay published in 2006, Samenow reviewed their work. Yochelson, a psychiatrist and psychologist, established the Program for the Investigation of Criminal Behavior at St. Elizabeths Hospital in Washington, D.C. This hospital is perhaps best known for its patient John Hinckley, who attempted to assassinate President Ronald Reagan. Yochelson began his program with the intent of understanding the criminal mind and developing techniques and programs for assisting criminals to become law-abiding persons. Samenow collaborated with Yochelson for 17 years and continued the work after Yochelson died. After the work of these two researchers and practitioners was reported on CBS News's *60 Minutes*, according to Samenow, their approach was widely disseminated and bitterly criticized.[95]

According to Samenow, the Yochelson/Samenow approach was resisted because it challenged the traditional deterministic view that criminal behavior is influenced by such factors as poverty, peer pressure, abusive parents,

divorce, and so on. But Yochelson and Samenow were advancing the position that "criminals, not the environment, cause crime, that there are patterns of thinking common to all hardcore criminals regardless of their backgrounds." Further, they stated that their programs were successful, and in some cases, criminals gave up their deviant actions and became responsible people. The approach was criticized as based on conjecture rather than science. The authors were merely stating their own opinions, and they had no control groups.[96] The family seems to have no effect on many criminals, who begin at early ages making decisions to engage in self-destructive patterns of antisocial behavior. These persons engage in *thinking errors*, which are thoughts people exhibit when they engage in irresponsible behavior. Examples are anger, lying, power playing, redefining a situation, and so on. Thinking errors are characteristic of all people at times, but for the criminal, one or more of these errors is taken to the extreme. In the words of Samenow, criminals "pursue excitement by doing the forbidden" and building themselves up "at the expense of others."

> Human relationships are seen by these people as avenues for conquest and triumph. Any means to self-serving ends, including deception, intimidation, and brute force, are employed without considering the impact on others.[97]

The thinking errors have been adapted and used in therapeutic work with juvenile and adult criminals.

In his more recent work, Samenow maintained that we already know enough to treat youngsters before they become involved in delinquent and criminal behavior and that we should intervene rather than merely label youths and take them out of society.[98]

Not everyone agrees, however, and the debate continues, especially among criminologists, many of whom remain wedded to the belief that personality factors are not sufficient explanations for criminal behavior. To illustrate, after reviewing the literature on personality and crime, sociologists Ronald L. Akers and Christine S. Sellers stated:

> The research using personality inventories and other methods of measuring personality characteristics [has] not been able to produce findings to support personality variables as major causes of criminal and delinquent behavior.[99]

Intelligence and Crime

Closely associated with the mental disorder approach is the linking of crime and intelligence. It is argued that low intelligence causes crime. This approach has long historical roots. As already discussed, early studies of family histories that found many people of lower intelligence in a family line of criminals concluded that the criminal behavior was *caused* by low intelligence, often referred to as *feeblemindedness*. These studies were discredited when researchers found few differences between the intelligence of criminals and that of World War I Army draftees. In the 1960s, however, attention turned to intelligence and crime once again. Intelligence testing began with the work of Alfred Binet (1857–1911), who later developed a test with Théodore Simon, referred to as the *Simon-Binet Scale of Intelligence*. The test first appeared in 1905 and was revised in 1908 when the measure of *mental age* was added. Before his death in 1911, Binet expressed concern that the test, which was designed to identify students who needed help in school, was being used to label children as slow, unteachable, superior, and so on. Binet did not believe that intelligence is innate, fixed, and cannot be changed.[100]

The idea that crime and intelligence are related got a boost with the 1985 publication of *Crime and Human Nature*, whose authors, Harvard professors James Q. Wilson (political scientist) and Richard J. Herrnstein (psychologist), stated that there is a "clear and consistent link between criminality and low intelligence"; they criticized criminology textbook authors for ignoring the research in this area.[101] Critics argued that Wilson and Herrnstein showed only that low intelligence and crime *appear* together frequently in the same groups; they did not demonstrate that low intelligence is the *cause* of crime.

Shortly after Herrnstein's death in 1994, his book *The Bell Curve: Intelligence and Class Structure in American Life*, coauthored with Charles Murray, was published. Herrnstein and Murray argued that success in life is dictated and influenced by intelligence, which is also linked to criminal behavior, dependence on welfare, and economic success. They further argued that the link is inherited and thus cannot be changed by environment.[102]

Critics take the position that environment is a *factor* in determining intelligence and in the effect intelligence has on behavior. For example, several studies show a correlation between low intelligence and delinquency; the higher the intelligence, the less likelihood there is of delinquent behavior. Furthermore, there is some evidence that this correlation remains even when researchers control for other variables associated with delinquency, such as social class, family interaction, and race. Critics argue that it is unreasonable to assume that intelligence is *determined* solely by biology and that therefore it cannot be altered.

In a study released in November 2001, Dr. Paul M. Thompson and his colleagues mapped brain structures using magnetic resonance imaging (MRI) and concluded that the size of certain regions of the human brain is controlled by genetics and that the larger these areas, the more intelligent the individual. These researchers utilized a sample of twins in Finland and discovered that the parts of the brain controlled by genetics differ only slightly in identical twins but differ considerably among fraternal twins and significantly among unrelated persons. According to Dr.

Thompson, these findings are "the first maps of the degree to which the genes control brain structure." Although the sample consisted of only 40 subjects, Dr. Thompson believed the results give "enough statistical power to identify the key brain systems."[103] A study published in 2004 by Dr. Thompson and his colleagues reported an association between structural deficits in the human brain and the chronic abuse of the drug methamphetamine.[104]

Criminologists have reacted by concluding that research shows a "weak to moderate negative correlation between IQ . . . and delinquent behavior, even when class, race, and others factors are controlled." Other factors, such as parental discipline, exposure to peers, and religions upbringing, are more predictive of future behavior.[105]

In a study of the relationship between crime and intelligence, however, it is important to understand that some criminals have very high intelligence, just as some manifest no evidence of mental disorders. It may also be important to consider the *type* of crime committed. Another factor to consider may be that persons with less intelligence (and certainly, those with less money) are more likely to be arrested, charged, and convicted.

Cognitive Development Theory

Another type of psychological theory that has been used to explain criminal behavior is **cognitive development theory**. This approach is based on the belief that the way people organize their thoughts about rules and laws results in either criminal or noncriminal behavior. Psychologists refer to this organization of thoughts as *moral reasoning*. When that reasoning is applied to law, it is termed *legal reasoning*, although that term has a different meaning to persons trained in law. The approach stems from the early works of Swiss psychologist Jean Piaget (1896–1980), who believed that there are two stages in the development of moral reasoning: (1) the belief that rules are sacred and immutable and (2) the belief that rules are the products of humans. According to Piaget, we leave the first stage at about the age of 13, and the second stage leads to more moral behavior than the first.[106]

In 1958, psychologist Lawrence Kohlberg (1927–1987) made some changes in the cognitive development approach. He called the first stage *preconventional* and the second *conventional*. He added a third and higher stage, *postconventional reasoning*. According to Kohlberg, between the ages of 10 and 13, most people move from preconventional to conventional reasoning or thinking; those who do not make this transition may be considered arrested in their development of moral reasoning, and they may become delinquent.[107] Kohlberg and others refined this position with a development of stages of moral judgment that are applicable to all kinds of behavior. The progression to higher stages should preclude criminal behavior, but most criminals do not progress beyond the earlier stages.[108]

Other modern scholars, such as Glenn D. Walters and Thomas W. White, developed the thesis that both criminal and noncriminal behavior are related to cognitive development and that people choose the behavior in which they wish to engage, just like the classical writers proclaimed in the eighteenth century. Walters and White, working at the U.S. penitentiary at Leavenworth, Kansas, emphasized that although environmental factors such as family background, peer relationships, and poverty may *limit* a person's choices, they do not *determine* those choices. They concluded: "The root causes of crime . . . are thought and choice."[109] Criminal behavior exists because of the way people think and the choices they make. Criminality is a lifestyle, and criminals must either be confined forever or be taught how to change their ways of thinking and acting.

Behavior Theory

Originating in the late 1800s, **behavior theory** gained attention in the twentieth century through the works of psychologist B. F. Skinner.[110] Behavior theory is the basis for behavior modification, one treatment approach used in institutionalized and noninstitutionalized settings for changing behavior. The primary thesis is that all behavior is learned and can be unlearned. The approach is concerned with observable behavior in contrast to the traditional psychoanalytic emphasis on deep, underlying personality problems that must be uncovered and treated.

Behavior theory is based on the belief that what is important is not the unconscious but, rather, behavior that can be observed and manipulated. It is assumed that neurotic symptoms and some deviant behaviors are acquired through an unfortunate quirk of learning and that they are rewarding to the patient. The undesirable behavior can be eliminated, modified, or replaced by taking away the reward value or by rewarding a more appropriate behavior that is incompatible with the deviant one. It is argued that behavior is controlled by its consequences. In dealing directly with behaviors that are undesirable, behavioral therapy attempts to change a person's long-established patterns of response to himself or herself and to others.

Learning Theory

Another psychological theory, **learning theory**, acknowledges that individuals have physiological mechanisms that permit them to behave aggressively, but whether or not they will do so is learned, as is the nature of their aggressive behavior. This theory may be contrasted with behavior theory in that the latter emphasizes performance and reinforcement, whereas learning theory emphasizes that learning may be accomplished by using other people as models. It is not necessary to engage in all the behavior that we learn; we engage in the behavior only if we have incentives and motivations to do so. Motivations may come from biological factors or from mental factors, the latter giving us the ability to imagine the behavior's consequences. (For a detailed discussion of social learning theory, see Chapter 6.)

Learning theorists view consequences as the factors that influence behavior. The three types of consequences are (1) *external reinforcement*, such as goods, money, social status, and punishment (effective in restraining behavior); (2) *vicarious reinforcement*, such as noting the status of others whom one observes being reinforced for their behavior; and (3) *self-regulatory mechanisms*, such as responding to one's own actions in ways that bring self-rewards or self-punishment. Learning theorists focus on the importance of the family, the subculture, and the media.

Learning theories have been combined with biological approaches to explain criminal behavior. English scholar and psychologist Hans J. Eysenck stressed the interrelationship between psychology and biology in explaining how humans learn to behave. He related his approach directly to criminal behavior.[111]

Eysenck's approach was based on the principle of *conditioning*. We learn appropriate and inappropriate behavior through a process of training that involves rewards for appropriate behavior, punishment for inappropriate behavior, and the establishment of models of appropriate behavior. Through these processes, we learn moral preferences as well as behavior. The process is slow and subtle. Often, we do not realize how we obtained our moral preferences, but in the process of learning, most of us develop a conscience. This conscience provides us with feelings of responsibility and duty and of shame and guilt as well as the need to do the right thing. If we do the wrong thing, we feel guilty, assuming, of course, that our conscience incorporates the moral preferences that define that activity as wrong.[112]

The process of training uses three tools: classical conditioning, operant conditioning, and modeling. Most of us have heard about classical conditioning in terms of Pavlov's dogs, which began to salivate when a bell rang because they knew from conditioning that the bell meant they would be fed. *Classical conditioning* is a learned response to a stimulus.

Operant conditioning is based on a reaction after we have acted. It is argued that this is the most powerful form of training. We are rewarded, or reinforced, when we behave appropriately, and we are punished when we misbehave. We learn by *models*, too; social learning occurs through the observation of others and from the media. In many languages, the verb *to teach* is synonymous with the verb *to show*.[113]

Eysenck's approach, based almost entirely on classical conditioning, took the position that "criminality can be understood in terms of conditioning principles." Criminals do not condition adequately to stimuli that society deems should be incorporated in a conscience.[114]

EXHIBIT 4.3

Summary of Major Biological and Psychological Theories

Biological Theories

- **Lombroso and the Positivists**—Believed in the theory of born criminals, who have specified physical characteristics that distinguish them from noncriminals. Lombroso also recognized the criminaloid and the insane criminal. Lombroso and other early positivists began the emphasis on the use of the scientific method in the study of crime and criminals.

- **Physique and Crime**—Constitutional approaches rested on the assumption that function is determined by structure. The primary early proponent was **William H. Sheldon**, who categorized body types as the ectomorph (tall, skinny), the endomorph (short, fat), and the mesomorph (athletic build), with a temperament type identified for each. Researchers **Sheldon and Eleanor Glueck** focused on juveniles and found most were mesomorphic types. Their findings were later supported by **Juan Cortés**.

- **Genetic Factors**—Early proponents viewed criminality associated with inherited family traits. **Charles Goring** conducted research that was severely criticized. Studies of twins by **Karl O. Christiansen** and **Sarnoff A. Mednick** and his colleagues found associations between heredity and crime. Subsequent studies of adoptions were conducted.

- **Genetics and Behavior Today**—Some scholars argue for increased attention to genetics and behavior, with an emphasis today on genomic research.

- **Obstetric Factors**—There is evidence that some factors at birth may be associated with aggressive behavior. Minor physical anomalies, nicotine exposure, and birth complications may be related to future behavior.

- **Neurological Factors**—Some scientists view crime as related to the body's nervous system, stating that aggressive or violent behavior is, at least in part, explained by the brain.

- **Neuroendocrinology**—Behavior is related, at least in part, to an imbalance of the body's chemicals. Aggressive men may have lower levels of certain hormones, and among women, problems such as postpartum depression may affect behavior.

- **Neurochemistry**—Looks at the possibility that nutrition, chemicals, food additives, or preservatives may affect behavior.

- **Autonomic Nervous System**—Changes in this system, such as in blood pressure, may affect behavior.

- **Attention-Deficit Hyperactivity Disorder (ADHD)**—This is the most commonly diagnosed psychiatric condition among U.S. children today. It causes inattentiveness, daydreaming, and many other characteristics and may be associated with behavioral patterns such as anxiety disorders, traumatic stress reactions, or atypical depression.

Eysenck believed that conditioning depends on the sensitivity of the inherited autonomic nervous system as well as the quality of conditioning that is received during the socialization process. In the third edition of his book, he emphasized that his original plan in 1964 was to outline a theory of antisocial behavior, relate that theory to personality, "and indicate some of the biological factors underlying both personality and criminality." Biological and psychological approaches were not given much credit at the time, but in 1977, Eysenck argued that we had much more evidence of the relationship between genetic factors and criminality, more evidence that personality traits are strongly determined by genetic factors, and much more empirical work "on the biological causes of personality differences, and by implication, of psychopathic and criminal conduct." Eysenck took the position that some of the sociological theories that previously had overshadowed biological and psychological theories were now less acceptable in explaining criminal behavior. He cited the variables of poverty, poor housing, and social inequality. Eysenck has been criticized for his overemphasis on classical conditioning to the exclusion of operant conditioning and modeling.[115]

The various theories and approaches discussed thus far are summarized in Exhibit 4.3.

Implications of Biological and Psychological Theories

The thesis of our discussion thus far is that the social, physical, and psychological sciences should be integrated in our attempt to understand criminal behavior.

Increased attention to biological and psychological explanations of human behavior and their implications for studying crime was fueled in 1985 by Wilson and Herrnstein's *Crime and Human Nature*, mentioned earlier. This book, replete with pages of summaries of criminological

4.3

EXHIBIT continued

Psychological Theories

- **Mental Illness**—Extensive in the United States and throughout the world; it may be associated with behavior and has legal implications regarding capital punishment.
- **Psychiatric Approach**—Field of medicine that specializes in the understanding, diagnosis, treatment, and prevention of mental problems. One of its branches, **psychoanalysis**, based on **Sigmund Freud's** concept of the unconscious, looks at the unique personality of each person by conducting case studies. Such studies were also typical of the work of **William Healy**, who saw the roots of delinquency as embedded deeply in a child's background. Freud viewed behavior as deeply rooted in early childhood experiences and believed original human nature was assertive and aggressive.
- **Personality Theory**—Looks at emotional conflict and personality deviations to explain behavior, with the early studies looking primarily at mental disorders and crime. Some proponents believe there is a *criminal personality*.
- **Intelligence and Crime**—Views crime as associated with low intelligence, with the early studies focusing on family histories. More recent advocates have been **James Q. Wilson** and **Richard J. Herrnstein**, who believed there was a clear and consistent link between low intelligence and crime.

- **Cognitive Development Theory**—Based on the belief that the way people organize their thoughts about rules and laws results in either criminal or noncriminal behavior, a process called *moral reasoning*. **Lawrence Kohlberg** listed three stages of moral reasoning: preconventional, conventional, and postconventional.
- **Behavior Theory**—The basis for behavior modification; based on the belief that all behavior is learned and can be unlearned. Primary proponent was **B. F. Skinner**.
- **Learning Theory**—Accepts that persons have physiological mechanisms that permit them to behave aggressively, but whether or not they do so is learned behavior. Three categories of consequences influence learning: *external reinforcement*, such as goods, money, or social status; *vicarious reinforcement*, such as noting the status of others whose behavior is reinforced; and *self-regulatory mechanisms*, such as responding to one's own actions in ways that bring self-rewards or self-punishment. **Hans J. Eysenck** based his learning theory approach on the principle of conditioning and discussed three types: *classical* (e.g., Pavlov's dogs' response to stimuli), *operant* (learned response to a stimuli), and *modeling* (reaction based on what we see in others' behaviors).

literature, received national attention through television talk shows, popular magazines, and newspapers. The authors, who refocused attention on genetic and biological components of criminal behavior, were well received by some but criticized by others. One sociologist warned that colleagues "who suffer from high blood pressure should be cautious in reading it."[116]

In contrast, biologist Sarnoff Mednick and his associates (writing a few years before Wilson and Herrnstein) concluded:

A half century of research and common sense leaves no doubt that social and cultural factors play a considerable role in the etiology of crime. The biological factors . . . must be seen as another set of variables involved in the etiology of crime. Both social and biological variables *and their interactions* are important for our complete understanding of the origins of antisocial behavior.[117]

The key word in this statement is *interactions*. Today, many scholars argue that the issue is not nature *or* nurture but nature *and* nurture. It is not a question of whether human behavior is the result of biology *or* environment but of what effect each has on the other.

Many scholars are writing about the interaction of biology (and other physical sciences) and the social sciences in an effort to explain criminal behavior. Diana Fishbein, who has worked extensively in the area of neurobiological research, emphasized the need for interdisciplinary research in biology and criminology to provide needed services to persons who have "compelling biological and genetic disadvantages." Fishbein noted that the research conclusions might also enable more people to understand that these individuals in question are not always in total control of their actions. She concluded:

Instead of waiting until a vulnerable child becomes old enough to be incarcerated, perhaps early assistance will enable us to avoid the personal and financial expense of criminal justice involvement. There is little evidence that present tactics are effective; thus, we need to move forward into an era of early intervention and compassionate treatment that neurobiological research may help to advance.[118]

In particular, Fishbein has explored the relationship between psychobiology and female aggression. She concluded that "pre- or postnatal biological experiences, combined with a socially disadvantageous environment, predispose certain women to antisocial behavior."[119]

Thomas J. Bernard has analyzed aggressive behavior among the "truly disadvantaged" members of our society. He pointed out that research on violent behavior, especially homicides, shows that many of the violent acts occur after relatively insignificant or trivial incidents, such as an insult. Why, among some people, do these incidents escalate into violent behavior? Bernard looked at three social-structural variables: urban environment, low social position, and racial and ethnic discrimination, which he believes explain why some people react violently to the incidents while others do not. He stressed that although the arousal of aggressive feelings occurs through the autonomic nervous system, there is evidence that individual cognition determines the level and type of that arousal. Some people are able to cope; others are not. Bernard maintained that the difference is in the variation of the social factors (low social position, racial and ethnic discrimination, and urban environment), not the biological factors. Thus, social variables operate with biological reactions to influence behavior.[120]

Adrian Raine, whose works were cited earlier in this chapter, published an article in 2002 that documented and summarized "39 empirical examples of biosocial interaction effects for antisocial behavior from the areas of genetics, psychophysiology, obstetrics, brain imaging, neuropsychology, neurology, hormones, neurotransmitters, and environmental toxins." Raine concluded:

Clearly there is recent, growing evidence that social and biological processes do interact in predisposing to antisocial behavior. To date, the best-replicated biosocial effect appears to consist of birth complications interacting with negative home environments in predisposing to adult violence, and there is also evidence that this effect particularly characterizes life-course persistent antisocial behavior.[121]

The policy implications of the biological and psychological approaches to explaining human behavior are extremely important in the social sciences, but the interdisciplinary research also has implications for criminal law. U.S. legal systems are based on the premise that people are responsible legally only for those criminal acts over which they have control; they are not responsible if they cannot control their behavior. Thus, if someone forces you

to shoot at another person, you may have a duress defense. A defense may mitigate the criminal act or eliminate criminal responsibility entirely.

Criminal defenses may (and often do) rest on the decisions we make concerning the relationship that biology and psychology have to the law. This may be illustrated by one of the best-known but least frequently used defenses, the **insanity defense**. A defendant who is judged by the jury to be insane may be totally excused from criminal liability; that is, he or she is found not guilty by reason of insanity. Various insanity tests are used, but there is little agreement on these tests or, for that matter, whether the insanity defense should be permitted. Some jurisdictions have abolished the defense.

The all-or-nothing aspect of "not guilty by reason of insanity" has led some jurisdictions to provide for a defense of **guilty but mentally ill**, under which the defendant may be found guilty of the offense charged and mentally ill but not insane at the time it was committed. He or she may be incarcerated but also provided with psychiatric treatment.[122]

These and other defenses have been criticized as removing responsibility from criminal defendants who should be liable for their behavior.[123] The debate is particularly critical when it involves capital punishment, as noted by the discussion of the U.S. Supreme Court's position regarding mental impairment and capital punishment as summarized in Exhibit 4.4.

More recently, the U.S. Supreme Court has emphasized the importance of psychological stress in explaining behavior. In December 2009, the Court returned a case for resentencing based on the failure of the defendant's trial attorney to introduce evidence of posttraumatic stress caused by fighting in a war. George Porter Jr., a decorated and wounded soldier, who was convicted in 1987 of killing his former girlfriend and her boyfriend, represented himself at his trial but had a court-appointed attorney for his sentencing hearing. The attorney called only one witness, Porter's ex-wife, and did not present any evidence based on Porter's schooling or his military or medical records. Porter had fought in two of the most horrific battles of the Korean War. In one of those battles, he lost one-half of his colleagues. After he was discharged, Porter suffered severe nightmares reliving some of his war experiences. The Court ruled that such evidence would show that Porter "served honorably under extreme hardship and gruesome conditions," which might have led the jury to mitigate his sentence rather than give him the death penalty.[124]

Finally, the impact of the relationship between biology and behavior has been emphasized by the U.S. Supreme Court in recent decisions involving the punishment of juveniles. The decisions of *Roper v. Simmons*, *Graham v. Florida*, and *Sullivan v. Florida* are discussed in Chapter 13 because they all involve sentencing, but it is important to note here that strong evidence of the relationship between

4.4   EXHIBIT

Mental Capacity and Capital Punishment

The U.S. Supreme Court has considered the relationship between intelligence (including mental illness and mental retardation) and capital punishment. In 1986, in *Ford v. Wainwright,* the Court held that it is unconstitutional to execute an insane person or "someone who is unaware of the punishment they are about to suffer and why they are to suffer it."[1] In 1989, in *Penry v. Lynaugh,* the Supreme Court held that a mildly retarded person may be executed. Johnny Paul Penry, a Texas death-row inmate, has the IQ of a 7-year-old, but the jury at his trial found that he "knew that his conduct was wrong and was capable of conforming his conduct to the requirement of the law." In refusing to reverse Penry's conviction, the U.S. Supreme Court stated as follows:

> In light of the diverse capacities and life experiences of mentally retarded persons, it cannot be said on the record before us today that all mentally retarded people, by definition, can never act with the level of culpability associated with the death penalty.[2]

In June 2001, the U.S. Supreme Court reversed the death sentence of Penry, who came within three hours of execution on 16 November 2000. The 2001 decision was based on narrow procedural grounds involving jury instructions and did not reach the issue of whether it is unconstitutional to execute mentally retarded persons.[3]

In 2003, in *Atkins v. Virginia,* the U.S. Supreme Court held that it is unconstitutional to execute a mentally retarded (but not necessarily a mentally ill) person. Daryl R. Atkins, who was sentenced to death for a murder he committed when he was 18, has an IQ of 59. In deciding the *Atkins* case, the Supreme Court left it to the states to determine when a person is mentally retarded and did not provide much guidance for making that determination.[4]

In March 2003, Texas executed James Colburn, who had been diagnosed as paranoid schizophrenic since he was 14. Colburn had made approximately 15 suicide attempts, claiming that voices in his head told him to take his own life. But there was also evidence that Colburn knew what was happening to him, understood the criminal justice process,

and even apologized to the victim's family before he was executed.[5]

In May 2004, Texas executed another mentally ill inmate. Kelsey Patterson, 50, who was diagnosed with schizophrenia, was executed after the state's governor refused to approve a rare plea from the state pardons board, which had ruled 5-to-1 to recommend clemency or a stay of execution. Patterson was under a death sentence for killing two persons in 1992. During his trial, Patterson was frequently removed from the courtroom because he was shouting claims that his behavior was controlled by remote devices and implants.[6]

On 3 December 2009, Texas executed Bobby Wayne Woods, 44, who had an IQ between 68 and 86. Woods's lawyer was unsuccessful in his argument that his client's IQ "hovers around 70, the magical cutoff point for determining whether someone is mentally retarded."[7]

In January 2010, the U.S. Supreme Court upheld the death sentence of a man whose inexperienced attorney did not pursue the argument that his client was mentally retarded despite evidence that the man's IQ was lower than 70. The Court held that no error occurred when defense counsel made a strategic decision not to call an expert witness to testify concerning the defendant's borderline mental retardation. There was no evidence that the decision prejudiced the defense. Holly Wood remains on Alabama's death row for the 1993 killing of his girlfriend.[8]

---

1. *Ford v. Wainwright*, 477 U.S. 399 (1986).

2. *Penry v. Lynaugh*, 492 U.S. 302 (1989).

3. *Penry v. Johnson*, 532 U.S. 782 (2001).

4. *Atkins v. Virginia*, 536 U.S. 304 (2002).

5. "A Mentally Ill Killer Is Executed in Texas," *New York Times* (27 March 2003), p. 12.

6. "National Briefing Southwest: Texas: Schizophrenic Is Executed," *New York Times* (19 May 2004), p. 21.

7. "Killer with Low I.Q. Is Executed in Texas," *New York Times* (4 December 2009), p. 19.

8. *Wood v. Allen*, 130 S.Ct. 841 (2010).

---

behavior and psychosocial development was before the Court in those cases. In *Roper*, the Court held that capital punishment of a person who committed murder while a teen would be cruel and unusual punishment in violation of the Eighth Amendment (see Appendix A). In both *Graham* and *Sullivan*, the Court held that life without parole for a juvenile who committed a nonhomicide as a teen would also be cruel and unusual. In all of these cases, the evidence showed that "kids are different." Figure 4.1 graphs the issue: The adolescent brain is not fully developed.

Commenting on the scientific evidence, Justice Anthony Kennedy, who wrote the decision in *Roper*, concluded:

These differences render suspect any conclusion that a juvenile falls among the worst offenders [for whom capital punishment is reserved]. . . . The susceptibility of juveniles to immature and irresponsible behavior means "their irresponsible conduct is not as morally reprehensible as that of an adult."[125]

The debate over the relationship of biology, psychology, and human behavior will continue, but to criminologists, the major focus is on the discipline of sociology. The next two chapters are devoted to sociological theories of criminal behavior.

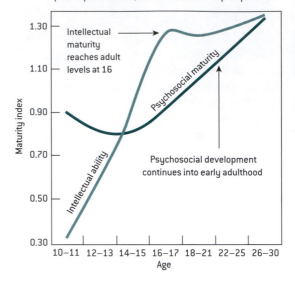

As psychosocial development lags behind intellectual maturity, juveniles make shortsighted decisions, show poor impulse control, and are vunerable to peer pressure.

Figure 4.1

The Immaturity Gap of Juveniles

Source: Mark Hansen, "What's the Matter with Kids Today," *ABA Journal* (posted 1 July 2010), http://www.abajournal.com, accessed 2 July 2010, reprinted with the permission of the American Bar Association.

Summary

This chapter continued the inquiry into the explanations of criminal behavior by concentrating on the contributions of biologists and psychologists. Once again, we saw the impact of the positivist school and how its constitutional approach to criminal behavior influenced the body-type theories of Sheldon and the Gluecks. These researchers, along with Cortés, saw the importance of environmental factors.

But this chapter went further in looking at the possible impact of biological, psychological, and psychiatric factors on human behavior. It considered David C. Rowe's work on biology and crime, noting his distinction between *sociobiology* and *behavior genetics*.

Following a discussion of genetic factors, including studies of families, studies of twins and adoptees, and a modern view of genetics, the chapter looked at obstetric factors and crime. It then considered neurological factors, looking at neuroendocrinology, neurochemistry, and the autonomic nervous system. The chapter featured a discussion of attention-deficit hyperactivity disorder (ADHD), which bridges the discussions of biology and psychology. ADHD is the most commonly diagnosed psychiatric problem among U.S. children, but it is believed to have a biological basis.

Psychiatry and psychology were discussed in the context of what appears to be increasing problems with mental health issues. Particular attention was given to the psychiatric approach and to personality theory. Intelligence and crime, cognitive development theory, behavior theory, and learning theory were also discussed. The implications of current research in biology and psychology, as well as the impact of these findings on criminology, enhance our understanding of criminal behavior. But they also raise significant legal issues, such as whether mentally impaired persons should be executed. Legal defenses to criminal behavior, such as insanity, were noted. The chapter closed with a glance at U.S. Supreme Court cases (discussed in subsequent chapters) in which the Court has based its decisions, at least in part, on our understanding of the influence of biology and psychology on behavior, at least in juveniles.

Perhaps the biological and psychological implications of criminal behavior will have a greater impact in the courtroom than in social science journals. To date, however, social science theories of criminal behavior continue to dominate the literature; the next two chapters are devoted to their explanations and analyses.

Study Questions

1. Distinguish between sociobiology and behavior genetics.

2. Evaluate Lombroso's criminal types.

3. What did Sheldon and the Gluecks contribute to criminology?

4. What might the relationship be between family and crime? Illustrate with a discussion of the Jukes and the Kallikacks.

5. What do studies of twins and adoptees tell us about criminal behavior?

6. What is a genome? What are the recent developments in the field? What are the implications of genome research for studying crime?

7. Contrast the uses of neuroendocrinology and neurochemistry in explaining crime.

8. Discuss the possible impact of obstetric factors on crime.

9. What, if any, relationship does postpartum depression have to criminal behavior? What, if any, effect does the hormone testosterone have?

10. Has the study of the autonomic nervous system shown any promise in explaining criminal behavior?

11. What is attention-deficit hyperactivity disorder (ADHD)? How do you think it might relate to delinquent or criminal behavior?

12. How important is the study of mental illness to crime? Discuss the nature and extent of mental illness in the United States.

13. Do you think posttraumatic stress sustained while fighting in a war should be introduced as evidence in a murder trial? In mitigation of a sentence?

14. What is the role of psychiatry in explaining criminal behavior?

15. What is meant by *thinking errors*, and what is the relationship, if any, to criminal behavior?

16. Does low intelligence *cause* crime? Explain.

17. Explain cognitive development theory.

18. What is behavior theory?

19. What is the importance of attempting to integrate biology, psychology, and the social sciences in explaining delinquent and criminal behavior?

20. What influence, if any, should biology and psychology have on criminal defenses? What, if anything, has the U.S. Supreme Court ruled on this topic?

Brief Essay Assignments

1. Explore the contributions of Lombroso and other positivists to our understanding of criminal behavior today.

2. Is there a relationship between physique and crime?

3. Discuss the statement that heredity *causes* crime.

4. Explain why researchers study twins and adoptees to learn about crime.

5. Contrast the importance of neurological factors and psychological approaches to the study of crime.

6. Discuss the extent of mental illness in the world, and evaluate its potential impact on criminal behavior.

7. What effect should biology and psychology have on policy decisions in criminal justice?

Internet Activities

1. Find out more about the study and applicability of genetics research in the criminal justice system by logging on to the Human Genome Project's website at http://www.ornl.gov/sci/techresources/Human_Genome/courts/courts.shtml, accessed 2 October 2010. Read the article by Mark A. Rothstein entitled "The Impact of Behavioral Genetics on the Law and the Courts." What future implications do you think the study of genetics on behavior will have on the law and criminal justice systems? What other systems/institutions might this type of research affect?

2. Go to the Mayo Clinic website, http://www.mayoclinic.com, accessed 2 October 2010. What can you find about postpartum depression? Mental health and mental disorders? Cognitive behavioral therapy?

Notes

1. David P. Farrington, "Foreword" to David C. Rowe, *Biology and Crime* (Los Angeles: Roxbury, 2002), p. ix.
2. Rowe, *Biology and Crime*, p. 7.
3. Edward O. Wilson, *Sociobiology: The New Synthesis* (Cambridge, MA: Harvard University Press, 1975), p. 4. See also Wilson, *On Human Nature* (Cambridge, MA: Harvard University Press, 1978).
4. See, for example, Sociobiology Study Group of Science for the People, "Sociobiology—Another Biological Determinism," in *The Sociobiology Debate: Readings on the Ethical and Scientific Issues Concerning Sociobiology*, ed. Arthur L. Caplan (New York: Harper & Row, 1978), pp. 280–290.
5. Boyce Rensberger, "The Nature-Nurture Debate I: On Becoming Human," *Science* 83 (April 1983): 41.
6. Rowe, *Biology and Crime*, p. 8, referring to Wilson, *Sociobiology: The New Synethsis*.
7. Stephen Schafer, *Theories in Criminology* (New York: Random House, 1969), p. 24. The quote from Marvin E. Wolfgang is from, "Cesare Lombroso," in *Pioneers in Criminology*, 2d ed., ed. Hermann Mannheim (Montclair, NJ: Patterson Smith, 1973), p. 232.
8. Cesare Lombroso, *Crime, Its Causes and Remedies*, trans. H. P. Horton (Boston: Little, Brown, 1911), p. 365.
9. Ibid., pp. 381–383.
10. Ronald L. Akers and Christine S. Sellers, *Criminological Theories: Introduction, Evaluation, and Application*, 5th ed. (New York: Oxford University Press, 2009), p. 49.
11. Thorsten Sellin, "The Lombrosian Myth in Criminology" (Letter to the Editor), *American Journal of Sociology* 42 (May 1937): 898–899. For a scathing criticism of Lombroso, see Alfred Lindesmith and Yale Levin, "The Lombrosian Myth in Criminology," in this same issue, pp. 653–671.
12. See Edwin H. Sutherland and Donald R. Cressey, *Principles of Criminology*, 5th ed. (Philadelphia: Lippincott, 1955), p. 55; 9th ed. (1974), p. 54; and the discussion in Chapter 3 of this text.

13. Wolfgang, "Cesare Lombroso," p. 288.

14. Nicole Rafter, "Cesare Lombroso and the Origins of Criminology: Rethinking Criminological Tradition," in *The Essential Criminology Reader*, ed. Stuart Henry and Mark M. Lanier (Boulder, CO: Westview Press, 2006), pp. 33–42; quotations are on pp. 39–40. See also Rafter, "Earnest A. Hooton and the Biological Tradition in American Criminology," *Criminology* 42, no. 3 (August 2004): 735–771.

15. Ernst Kretschmer, *Physique and Character*, trans. W. J. H. Sprott (New York: Harcourt Brace, 1926).

16. William H. Sheldon, *The Varieties of Human Physique: An Introduction to Constitutional Psychology* (New York: Harper & Row, 1940); Sheldon, *The Varieties of Temperament* (New York: Harper & Row, 1942); Sheldon, *Varieties of Delinquent Youth: An Introduction to Constitutional Psychiatry* (New York: Harper & Row, 1949); Sheldon, *Atlas of Men* (New York: Harper & Row, 1954). For a recent analysis of Sheldon's contributions, see Nicole Rafter, "Somatotyping, Antimodernism, and the Production of Criminological Knowledge," *Criminology* 45, no. 4 (November 2007): 805–834.

17. Juan B. Cortés with Florence M. Gatti, *Delinquency and Crime: A Biopsychosocial Approach* (New York: Seminar Press, 1972), p. 8.

18. Albert K. Cohen, Alfred Lindesmith, and Karl Schuessler, *The Sutherland Papers* (Bloomington: Indiana University Press, 1956), p. 289.

19. See Sheldon Glueck and Eleanor Glueck, *Physique and Delinquency* (New York: Harper & Row, 1956); Glueck and Glueck, *Five Hundred Criminal Careers* (New York: Knopf, 1930); Glueck and Glueck, *Later Criminal Careers* (New York: Commonwealth Fund, 1937); Glueck and Glueck, *Criminal Careers in Retrospect* (New York: Commonwealth Fund, 1943); Glueck and Glueck, *Unraveling Juvenile Delinquency* (New York: Commonwealth Fund, 1950).

20. Hermann Mannheim, *Comparative Criminology* (Boston: Houghton Mifflin, 1965), p. 241.

21. Cortés, *Delinquency and Crime*, p. 19.

22. Ibid., p. 19.

23. Ibid., p. 158.

24. Sheldon Glueck and Eleanor Glueck, *Of Delinquency and Crime* (Springfield, IL: Thomas, 1974).

25. Charles Goring, *The English Convict* (London: H. M. Stationery Office, 1919).

26. Marshall B. Jones and Donald R. Jones, "The Contagious Nature of Antisocial Behavior," *Criminology* 38 (February 2000): 25–46; quotation is on p. 26.

27. See, for example, Ronald L. Simons et al., "A Test of Various Perspectives on the Intergenerational Transmission of Domestic Violence," *Criminology* 33 (February 1995): 141–171.

28. For a detailed review of these early studies, see Karl O. Christiansen, "A Review of Studies of Criminality Among Twins" and "A Preliminary Study of Criminality Among Twins," in *Biosocial Bases of Criminal Behavior*, eds. Sarnoff A. Mednick and Karl O. Christiansen (New York: Gardner Press, 1977), pp. 89–108.

29. Sarnoff A. Mednick and Jan Volavka, "Biology and Crime," in *Crime and Justice: An Annual Review of Research*, Vol. 2, ed. Norval Morris and Michael Tonry (Chicago: University of Chicago Press, 1980), p. 97.

30. Glenn D. Walters and Thomas W. White, "Heredity and Crime: Bad Genes or Bad Research?" *Criminology* 27 (August 1989): 478.

31. Patricia A. Brennan and Sarnoff A. Mednick, "A Reply to Walters and White: 'Heredity and Crime,'" *Criminology* 28 (November 1990): 660–661. For a response, see Glenn D. Walters, "Heredity, Crime, and the Killing-the-Bearer-of-Bad-News Syndrome: A Reply to Brennan and Mednick," *Criminology* 28 (November 1990): 663–667.

32. Akers and Sellers, *Criminological Theories*, 5th ed., p. 61, referring to Michael Gottfredson and Travis Hirschi, *A General Theory of Crime* (Palo Alto, CA: Stanford University Press, 1990), pp. 47–63.

33. See Sarnoff A. Mednick et al., "Genetic Factors in Criminal Behavior: A Review," in *Development of Antisocial and Prosocial Behavior: Research, Theories, and Issues*, ed. Dan Olweus et al. (New York: Academic Press, 1986), pp. 33–50; Mednick et al., "Genetic Influences in Criminal Convictions: Evidence from an Adoption Cohort," *Science* 224 (1984): 891–894.

34. Gottfredson and Hirschi, *A General Theory of Crime*, p. 60.

35. Rowe, *Biology and Crime*, pp. 30–31.

36. Adrian Raine, "Biosocial Studies of Antisocial and Violent Behavior in Children and Adults," *Journal of Abnormal Child Psychology* 30, no. 4 (August 2002): 311–329.

37. Margaret A. Zahn, "Thoughts on the Future of Criminology—The American Society of Criminology 1998 Presidential Address," *Criminology* 37 (February 1999): 1–16, quotation is on p. 3.

38. Anthony Walsh, "Behavior Genetics and Anomie/Strain Theory," *Criminology* 38 (November 2000): 1075–1108; quotations are on pp. 1077, 1097, and 1098–1099.

39. Rafter, "Earnest A. Hooton and the Biological Tradition"; quotation is on p. 735. See also Rafter, *Creating Born Criminals* (Urbana: University of Illinois Press, 1997).

40. Rowe, *Biology and Crime*, p. 65.

41. Matt Robinson, *Why Crime? An Integrated Systems Theory of Antisocial Behavior* (Upper Saddle River, NJ: Pearson Prentice-Hall, 2004), quoted in John P. Wright et al., "Lombroso's Legacy: The Miseducation of Criminologists," *Journal of Criminal Justice Education* 19, no. 3 (November 2008): 325–338, p. 326.

42. Wright et al., "Lombroso's Legacy," p. 325.

43. Raine, "Biosocial Studies of Antisocial and Violent Behavior." All the information on obstetric factors comes from this source unless otherwise noted.

44. Adrian Raine et al., "Birth Complications Combined with Early Maternal Rejection at Age 1 Year Predispose to Violent Crime at Age 18 Years," *Archives of General Psychiatry* 51 (1994): 984–988.

45. Unless otherwise noted, the information in this and the following sections on neuroendocrinology, neurochemistry, and the autonomic nervous system is from Vicki Pollock et al., "Crime Causation: Biological Theories," in *Encyclopedia of Crime and Justice*, Vol. 1, ed. Sanford H. Kadish (New York: Macmillan, 1983), pp. 311–315.

46. Ibid., p. 311, referring to the study of Sarnoff A. Mednick et al., "EEG as a Predictor of Antisocial Behavior," *Criminology* 19 (August 1982): 219–229.

47. Pollock et al., "Crime Causation," p. 312.

48. "PET Imaging Brings New Advances in Patient Care and Research," *Mayo Magazine* (Fall/Winter 1999), p. 46.

49. "Discovery That Genes May Raise Panic Could Lead to New Therapies," *Pharma Marketletter* (2 February 2004), p. 1, a British newsletter referring to an article in the January 2004 *Journal of Neuroscience*, published in the United States.

50. "Neuroscientist/Psychiatrist Takes Helm at Flagship Primate Research Center," *Journal of the American Medical Association* 272 (28 September 1994): 907.

51. See Comment, "Premenstrual Syndrome: The Debate Surrounding Criminal Defense," *Maryland Law Review* 54, no. 2 (1995): 571–600; Thomas L. Riley, "Premenstrual Syndrome as a Legal Defense," *Hamline Law Review* 9 (February 1986): 193–202.

52. *Yates v. Texas*, 171 S.W.3d 215 (Tex.App.Houston, 1st Dist., 2005). For an excerpt and a case analysis, see Sue Titus Reid, *Criminal Law*, 8th ed. (New York: Oxford University Press, 2010), pp. 104–108.

53. "Bye Bye Blues: Falling Apart and Picking Up the Pieces with Postpartum Depression," *San Antonio Current* (25 April 2002), n.p.

54. "Mom's Life Sentence Is Cut: Postpartum Sufferer Who Killed Her Kids in '85 Will Go Free," *Chicago Tribune* (2 May 2009), p. 4C.

55. Colleen Kelly, Comment, "The Legacy of Too Little, Too Late: The Inconsistent Treatment of Postpartum Psychosis as a Defense to Infanticide," *Journal of Contemporary Health Law & Policy* 19 (Winter 2002): 247.

56. Ibid.

57. Rowe, *Biology and Crime*, p. 74, referring to the work of K. C. Jacobson and David C. Rowe, "Nature, Nurture, and the Development of Criminality," in *Criminology: A Contemporary Handbook*, 3d ed., ed. J. F. Sheley (New York: Wadsworth, 2000).

58. Raine, "Biosocial Studies of Antisocial and Violent Behavior."

59. Akers and Sellers, *Criminological Theories*, 5th ed., p. 57. See also Anthony Walsh, *Biosocial Criminology: Introduction and Integration* (Cincinnati, OH: Anderson, 2002).

60. "Roots of Crime: Hair May Hold the Secret," *American Bar Association Journal* 69 (December 1983): 1814.

61. Diana H. Fishbein and Susan Pease, *The Effects of Diet on Behavior: Implications for Criminology and Corrections* (Boulder, CO: National Institute of Corrections, June 1988), pp. 2–3, 32. See also the later work by Fishbein, *Biobehavioral Perspectives on Criminology* (Belmont, CA: Wadsworth, 2001).

62. See, for example, Mary Story and Diane Neumark-Sztainer, "Diet and Adolescent Behavior: Is There a Relationship?" *Adolescent Medicine* 9, no. 2 (January 1998): 283–298.

63. S. J. Schoenthaler and I. D. Bier, "The Effect of Vitamin-Mineral Supplementation on Juvenile Delinquency Among American Schoolchildren: A Randomized, Double-Blind Placebo-Controlled Trial," *Journal of Alternative Complement Medicine* 6, no. 1 (2000): 7–17.

64. National Council Against Health Fraud, "NCAHF Position Paper on Diet and Criminal Behavior," http://www.NCAHF.org/pp/diet.html, accessed 11 December 2010.

65. Adrian Raine et al., "High Autonomic Arousal and Electrodermal Orienting at Age 15 Years as Protective Factors Against Criminal Behavior," *American Journal of Psychiatry* 152 (November 1995): 1591–1600.

66. Pollock et al., "Crime Causation," p. 315.

67. Adrian Raine, "Autonomic Nervous System Factors Underlying Disinhibited, Antisocial, and Violent Behavior: Biosocial Perspectives and Treatment Implications," *Annals of the New York Academy of Science* 794 (September 1996): 46–59, as cited in the National Library of Medicine MEDLINE Database.

68. Adrian Raine et al., "Reduced Prefrontal Gray Matter Volume and Reduced Autonomic Activity in Antisocial Personality Disorder," *Archives of General Psychiatry* 57, no. 2 (February 2000): 119–129, as summarized in the National Library of Medicine MEDLINE Database.

69. Centers for Disease Control and Prevention, "Attention-Deficit/Hyperactivity Disorder (ADHD): Data and Statistics in the United States," http://www.cdc.gov/ncbddd/adhd/data.html, accessed 11 December 2010.

70. R. C. Kessler et al., "Prevalence, Severity, and Comorbidity of Twelve–Month *DSM-IV* Disorders in the National Comorbidity Survey Replication (NCS-R)," *Archives of General Psychiatry* 62, no. 6 (June 2005): 617–627.

71. "Attention Deficit Disorder, Part I," *Harvard Mental Health Letter* 11, no. 10 (April 1995): 1.

72. Ibid.

73. Ibid.

74. Ibid.

75. Ibid.

76. Drew H. Barzman, "Attention-Deficit Hyperactivity Disorder Diagnosis and Treatment," *Journal of Legal Medicine* 25 (March 2004): 23–38.

77. "Large Study on Mental Illness Finds a Global Problem," *New York Times* (2 May 2004), p. 16, reporting on a study published in the *Journal of the American Medical Association*.

78. "Health Information; Statistics," National Institute of Mental Health, http://www.nimh.nih.gov/health/topics/statistics/index.shtml, accessed 2 October 2010.

79. "Mental Health of Inmates Cited as Top Concern of Jail Managers," *Criminal Justice Newsletter* (1 August 2007), p. 5.

80. Lauren E. Glaze and Doris J. James, Bureau of Justice Statistics, "Mental Health Problems of Prison and Jail Inmates," (6 September 2006), http://bjs.ojp.usdoj.gov/index.cfm?ty=pbdetail&iid=789, accessed 2 October 2010. See also Doris J. James and Lauren E. Glaze, "Mental Health Problems of Prison and Jail Inmates," Bureau of Justice Statistics (September 2006, revised 14 December 2006), http://bjs.ojp.usdoj.gov/content/pub/pdf/mhppji.pdf, accessed 2 October 2010.

81. "Offenders with Health Problems Found to Fare Poorly After Prison," *Criminal Justice Newsletter* (17 March 2008), pp. 6–7.

82. Eric Silver, "Mental Disorder and Violent Victimization: The Mediating Role of Involvement in Conflicted Social Relationships," *Criminology* 40, no. 1 (February 2002): 191–212; quotations are on pp. 206–207.

83. See William Healy, *The Individual Delinquent* (Boston: Little, Brown, 1915); Franz Alexander and William Healy, *Roots of Crime* (New York: Knopf, 1935); William Healy and Augusta Bronner, *New Light on Delinquency and Its Treatment* (New Haven, CT: Yale University Press, 1931).

84. See Sigmund Freud, *New Introductory Lectures on Psychoanalysis*, ed. and trans. James Strachey (New York: Norton, 1933).

85. Hermann Mannheim, *Comparative Criminology* (Boston: Houghton Mifflin, 1965), p. 331.

86. Ibid., p. 332.

87. Herbert C. Quay, "Crime Causation: Psychological Theories," in *Encyclopedia of Crime and Justice*, Vol. 1, ed. Sanford H. Kadish (New York: Macmillan, 1983), p. 332.

88. Akers and Sellers, *Criminological Theories*, 5th ed., p. 74.

89. *Random House Compact Unabridged Dictionary*, special 2d ed. (New York: Random House, 1996), p. 1445.

90. For a brief discussion, see Akers and Sellers, *Criminological Theories*, 5th ed., p. 75.

91. American Psychiatric Association, *Diagnostic and Statistical Manual of Mental Disorders*, 4th ed. (Washington, D.C., 1994), pp. 645–650.

92. See, for example, Cyril Burt, *The Young Delinquent* (New York: Appleton, 1925); Sheldon Glueck and Eleanor Glueck, *One Thousand Juvenile Delinquents: Their Treatment by Court and Clinic* (Cambridge, MA: Harvard University Press, 1934); Healy and Bronner, *New Light on Delinquency and Its Treatment*.

93. See, for example, Karl F. Schuessler and Donald R. Cressey, "Personality Characteristics of Criminals," *American Journal of Sociology* 55 (March 1950): 476–486.

94. John Monahan and Henry J. Steadman, *Crime and Mental Disorder*, National Institute of Justice (Washington, D.C.: U.S. Department of Justice, September 1984).

95. Stanton E. Samenow, "Forty Years of the Yochelson/Samenow Work," in *The Essential Criminology Reader*, ed. Henry and Lanier, pp. 71–77. See also Samuel Yochelson and Stanton Samenow, *The Criminal Personality*, Vol. 1, *A Profile for Change* (New York: Aronson, 1976); Vol. 2, *The Change Process* (1977), Vol. 3, *The Drug User* (1987).

96. Samenow, "Forty Years," pp. 71, 72.

97. Ibid., p. 75.

98. Ibid., p. 76. For elaboration, see Stanton E. Samenow, *Before It's Too Late: Why Some Children Get into Trouble and What Parents Can Do About It* (New York: Three Rivers Press, 2001).

99. Akers and Sellers, *Criminological Theories*, 5th ed., p. 76.

100. See the discussion in Thomas J. Bernard et al., *Vold's Theoretical Criminology*, 6th ed. (New York: Oxford University Press, 2010), p. 67.

101. James Q. Wilson and Richard J. Herrnstein, *Crime and Human Nature* (New York: Simon & Schuster, 1985), pp. 148–172.

102. Richard J. Herrnstein and Charles Murray, *The Bell Curve: Intelligence and Class Structure in American Life* (New York: Free Press, 1994).

103. Paul M. Thompson et al., "Genetic Influences on Brain Structure," *Nature Neuroscience* 4, no. 12 (December 2001): 1253–1258.

104. Paul M. Thompson et al., "Structural Abnormalities in the Brains of Human Subjects Who Use Methamphetamine," *Journal of Neuroscience* 24, no. 26 (30 June 2004): 6028–6036.

105. Akers and Sellers, *Criminological Theories*, 5th ed., p. 55.

106. See Jean Piaget, *The Moral Judgment of the Child* (New York: Harcourt Brace Jovanovich, 1932).

107. Lawrence Kohlberg, *The Development of Modes of Moral Thinking and Choice in Years Ten to Sixteen*, PhD dissertation (Cambridge, MA: Harvard University, 1958).

108. Lawrence Kohlberg et al., *The Just Community Approach to Corrections: A Manual* (Niantic: Connecticut Department of Corrections, 1973).

109. Glenn D. Walters and Thomas W. White, "The Thinking Criminal: A Cognitive Model of Lifestyle Criminality," Sam Houston State University Criminal Justice Center, *Criminal Justice Research Bulletin* 4, no. 4 (1989): 8.

110. See B. F. Skinner, *Science and Human Behavior* (New York: Macmillan, 1953); Skinner, *Cumulative Record* (New York: Appleton-Century-Crofts, 1959).

111. Hans J. Eysenck, *Crime and Personality* (London: Routledge & Kegan Paul, 1977).

112. Gwynn Nettler, *Explaining Crime*, 3d ed. (New York: McGraw-Hill, 1984), p. 207.

113. Eysenck, *Crime and Personality*, p. 13.

114. Nettler, *Explaining Crime*, 3d ed., p. 297.

115. Ibid.

116. Wilson and Herrnstein, *Crime and Human Nature*; Jack P. Gibbs, "Review Essay," *Criminology* 23 (May 1985): 381.

117. Mednick and Volavka, "Biology and Crime," pp. 143–144; emphasis in the original.

118. Diana H. Fishbein, "Integrating Findings from Neurobiology into Criminological Thought: Issues, Solutions, and Implications," in *The Essential Criminology Reader,* ed. Henry and Lanier, pp. 43–68; quotation is on p. 66.

119. Diana H. Fishbein, "The Psychobiology of Female Aggression," *Criminal Justice and Behavior* 19 (June 1992): 99.

120. Thomas J. Bernard, "Angry Aggression Among the 'Truly Disadvantaged,'" *Criminology* 28 (February 1990): 73–96.

121. Raine, "Biosocial Studies of Antisocial and Violent Behavior."

122. See the Michigan provision, as explained in *People v. Ramsey*, 375 N.W.2d 297 (Mich. 1985). The statute is codified at MCL, Section 768.36 (2010).

123. See, for example, Alan Dershowitz, *The Abuse Excuse and Other Cop-Outs, Sob Stories, and Evasions of Responsibility* (Boston: Little, Brown, 1994). For a discussion of legal defenses, see Sue Titus Reid, *Criminal Law*, 8th ed. (New York: Oxford University Press, 2010), pp. 82–137.

124. *Porter v. McCollum*, 130 S.Ct. 447 (2009).

125. *Roper v. Simmons*, 543 U.S. 551 (2005). The other two cases are *Graham v. Florida*, 130 S.Ct. 2011 (2010) and *Sullivan v. Florida*, 130 S.Ct. 2059 (2010).

CHAPTER 5

Sociological Theories of Criminal Behavior I: The Social-Structural Approach

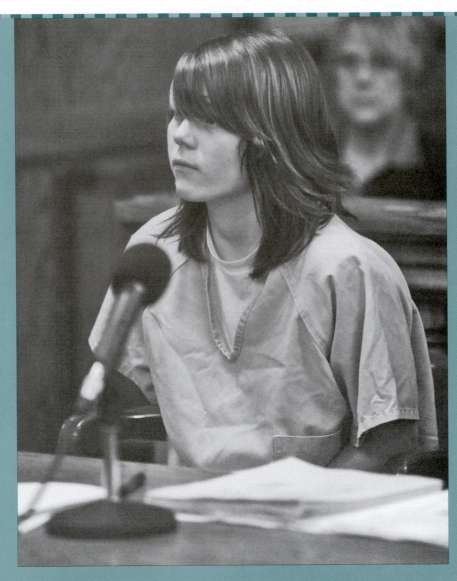

On 21 October 2009, 9-year-old Elizabeth Kay Olten left a neighbor's house to walk home but never made it. Her body was found in a shallow grave. Authorities alleged that 15-year-old Alyssa Bustamante (shown above in court) lured Olten to the Missouri woods (in which she had previously dug two graves), strangled the child, stabbed and slit the victim's throat, and buried her in a shallow grave. A gifted student, Bustamante had posted a YouTube video stating that her hobbies were "killing people" and "cutting."

CHAPTER OUTLINE

KEY TERMS

anomie
concentric circle
conflict
consensus
critical criminology
culture conflict theory
doing gender
ecological school
feminist theory
general strain theory (GST)
institutional anomie theory (IAT)
instrumental Marxism
left realist theorists
modernism

INTRODUCTION

This chapter analyzes sociological theories of criminal behavior, focusing on those that consider society's social structure or organization. The two basic approaches are consensus and conflict. The consensus approach views folkways, mores, and laws as reflections of society's values, which arise out of group sharing, especially through voting. The result is that some acts are defined as wrong, even criminal, although some crime is seen as inevitable and even functional. In the conflict approach, criminal behavior emerges as a conflict between groups within society. There is a struggle: Someone wins, someone loses. Making and enforcing laws are struggles, and those in power dominate the processes.

Previous chapters looked at beliefs that crime is the result of rational choice or that there is something about offenders, such as a biological or psychological characteristic, that leads them to commit crimes. This chapter turns to sociological explanations, discussing early ecological, anomie/strain, and subculture and related theories along with their modern counterparts. The relationship of family structure and power relationships to delinquency and crime are noted, followed by an analysis of the routine activity approach. Examination of the conflict approach and of critical criminology focuses on a brief history of these approaches and a discussion and critique of the major contemporary scholars and approaches. The chapter closes with an analysis of female criminality from a social-structural perspective.

The study of the causes of crime is important to sociology and criminology, but it can be a frustrating experience for students, many of whom find theory inherently difficult and complicated by the lack of agreement among scholars in the field. Some professors who serve as reviewers of this text suggest that several theories should be eliminated because the material is too confusing for students. However, it would be a disservice to students to tell them that one or even a few theories explain all criminal behavior. And many criminologists and other social scientists have made significant contributions to our understanding of criminal behavior. They and their research deserve attention and critique.

It is difficult to develop theories that explain human behavior, especially criminal behavior, because the behavior varies and the participants have different characteristics, experiences, and backgrounds. Consider, for example, the young criminals discussed in Exhibit 5.1 and try to develop your own sociological (or other) explanations for why they engaged in criminal acts.

Social science theory is complicated, and this gives rise to disagreement. Nevertheless, theory is important, and sociologists and criminologists have made great strides in their analyses of criminal behavior and other aspects of criminal justice systems. This chapter and Chapter 6 present the major approaches, along with evaluations, research, and current events that illustrate different crimes and criminals. This approach is intended to enable readers to see how a particular theory might be useful in explaining criminal behavior.[1]

Sociologists study the causes of crime from two perspectives: structure and process. The first views crime in relation to the social organization or structure of society and asks how crime is related to the social system. What are the characteristics of the situation or social *structure* in which crime takes place? Do crime rates vary as these situations or structures change? The second approach looks at the *process* by which criminals are produced, but it is not an individualistic approach. Sociologists look for *patterns* of variables and relationships that might explain how and why people engage in criminal acts.

Although sociological theories may be classified abstractly as structure or process, most do not fall exclusively into either category. Likewise, it is not possible to isolate sociological from nonsociological theories. For analysis, however, some categorizations may be made. This chapter focuses on social-structural approaches, and Chapter 6 discusses social-process approaches.

One further distinction is important. Some sociologists attempt to develop a *general* theory that will explain most, if not all, deviant or criminal behavior, whereas others focus on *specific* approaches, such as the study of persons who commit robbery in contrast to those who commit murder. Some try to identify factors that may be linked with criminal behavior. For example, cigarette smoking, problem drinking, illicit sexual behavior, illegal use of

5.1

Crimes of the Young: Do the Theories Explain Them?

In recent years, the media have focused on violent crimes committed by young people, many of whom are very young. Consider the facts of the following cases and determine whether any of the theories discussed in Chapters 4 and 5 might be useful in explaining the behavior. It might also be useful to review these examples after reading Chapter 6 and consider them again in subsequent discussions of how the criminal justice system should handle young people convicted of violent crimes.

On 21 October 2009, 9-year-old Elizabeth Kay Olten left a neighbor's house to walk home but never made it. Her body was found in a shallow grave. Authorities alleged that 15-year-old Alyssa Bustamante lured Olten to the Missouri woods (in which she had previously dug two graves), strangled the child, stabbed and slit the victim's throat, and buried her in a shallow grave. A gifted student, Bustamante had previously attempted suicide and spent 10 days in a mental health center in 2007. In 2009, she had posted a YouTube video stating that her hobbies were "killing people" and "cutting." She was alleged to have told police that she killed Olten because she "wanted to know what it felt like." Bustamante was charged as an adult with first-degree murder and was being held in custody as Missouri officials wrestled with the problem of how to house a 15-year-old girl accused of murder.[1]

Christian Romero, age 9, was charged with killing his father and his father's friend. A reason or motive for these killings may never be revealed, as the case did not go to trial. Romero was offered a plea bargain in which (1) he entered a guilty plea to negligent homicide in the death of the friend, Tim Romans, (2) the charge of killing his father, Vince Romero, was dropped, and (3) Romero was to undergo intensive probation and therapy at an in-patient facility but not be incarcerated.

In 2001, two Florida juveniles were found guilty of murder. Lionel Tate, age 14, was only 12 when he killed 6-year-old Tiffany Eunick, his young playmate. Tate claimed he was play wrestling with her in the home of his mother, Kathleen Grossett-Tate, a Florida Highway Patrol officer, who was in the home at the time. Prosecutors alleged that Tate beat Eunick severely, causing her death. He was tried in an adult criminal court, convicted of first-degree murder during aggravated child abuse, and given the mandatory sentence in Florida: life in prison without parole. Tate was perhaps the youngest person in the United States to receive that sentence. Ms. Grossett-Tate had rejected a plea bargain offer from the state: If her son had entered a guilty plea to second-degree murder, he would have served only three years in a juvenile detention center, followed by ten years' probation.

In December 2003, a Florida appellate court reversed Tate's conviction and sentence, ruling that because of his youth and his lack of prior exposure to the criminal justice system, he was constitutionally entitled to a hearing to determine whether he fully understood the charges against him and could rationally participate in the proceedings with his lawyer. Thus, Tate was entitled to a new trial. The prosecution offered Tate essentially the same plea bargain they had offered prior to his original trial. Tate accepted the plea deal and was released from prison to the custody of his mother in January 2004, four days before his seventeenth birthday. Tate was to undergo a psychiatric evaluation. He would be under house arrest for a year and then on probation for ten years.

In the fall of 2004, Tate violated the terms of his probation but was not jailed. In May 2005, he was charged with several crimes, to which he entered guilty pleas and then asked to withdraw them. He was permitted to withdraw his plea to robbery but not to weapons charges, since those were a violation of his probationary terms. He was sentenced to 30 years in prison for violating probation. That sentence was upheld in 2007.[2] In 2008, Tate accepted a plea bargain on the robbery charge, for which he will serve ten years in prison.

Nathaniel Brazill was also 14 when he was tried in a Florida adult criminal court, but he was convicted of second-degree murder and thus escaped the mandatory sentence of life without parole specified by Florida law for first-degree murder convictions. Brazill, who was 13 when he shot and killed his favorite teacher, faced a possible 25-years-to-life sentence. He received 28 years.

In May 2003, Brazill's conviction and sentence were upheld by a Florida court of appeals, and in 2004, the Florida Supreme Court refused to hear the case. Brazill's prosecutor, Marc Shiner, described the defendant as a killer whose "demeanor sends chills up my spine." But he also said that it was very difficult for him to prosecute a young man who was not much older than his own son. "There was something wrong with the picture. It just didn't fit. It didn't fit that you had a schoolteacher killed by a kid, either." Shiner subsequently became a defense attorney, and one of his first clients was a 16-year-old girl who was accused of killing her newborn son.[3]

Brazill filed his own appeal, which a trial judge ruled was not filed in a timely manner. In 2006, a Florida appeals court reversed that decision and sent the case back for another hearing. Brazill was not successful, however. In October 2009, a district court judge refused him the opportunity to argue his allegations of ineffective assistance of counsel. The judge ruled that even if there were errors in representation, the evidence against Brazill was so strong that those errors would not have made a difference in the result of Brazill's trial. In fact, the judge held, the evidence was strong enough to support a first-degree murder charge. Brazill completed a paralegal course in prison. His release date is 2028, at which time he will be 41 years old.[4]

(continued)

In June 1998, Luke Woodham, age 17, was convicted of charges stemming from his acts in the fall of 1997. After stabbing his mother to death, Woodham went to his high school in Pearl, Mississippi, and shot nine students, killing two, including his ex-girlfriend. Seven other students were wounded. Woodham is serving life in prison. According to prosecutors, Woodham slaughtered numerous cats in the weeks prior to the shootings for which he was convicted, and he is said to have laughed when he killed his own dog. Some authorities believe that animal abuse can lead to violence against humans.

_____

1. "Online Boast Is Dead Serious—I'm Alyssa and I Like 'Killing People,'" *New York Post* (21 November 2009), p. 19; "Girl, 15, Is Puzzler for Justice System Missouri Has no Place to Put a Girl Charged in a Violent Murder," *St. Louis Post-Dispatch* (22 November 2009), p. 1.

2. "Clemency Bid Clears Another Hurdle," *Sun-Sentinel* (Fort Lauderdale, FL) (24 June 2003), p. 1B; "Florida Youth Who Got Life Term for a Killing Is Freed at 16," *New York Times* (27 January 2004), p. 12. The case is *Tate v. State*, 864 So.2d 44 (Fla.Dist. Ct.App. 4th Dist. 2003), *reh'g. denied, State v. Tate*, 2004 Fla. App. LEXIS 2309 (Fla.Dist.Ct.App. 4th Dist. 2004); "Two Reprieves Lost: Tate Gets 30 Years," *Los Angeles Times* (20 May 2006), p. 8; "Hearing Held for Suspect in Tot's Beating Death," *Miami Herald* (18 January 2008), n.p. Tate's last appeal, in which his 30-year sentence for probation violation was upheld, was published without an opinion, *Tate v. State*, 961 So.2d 957 (Fla.Dist.Ct.App. 4th Dist. 2007).

3. "After Conviction of Boy, Prosecutor Switches Sides," *New York Times* (18 November 2002), p. 14; "Brazill's Attorney at New Trial Denied," *Sun Sentinel* (Fort Lauderdale, FL) (24 October 2009), p. 8B.

4. The case is *Brazill v. State*, 845 So.2d 282 (Fla.Dist.Ct.App. 4th Dist. 2003), *review denied*, 876 So.2d 561 (Fla. 2004), *and post-conviction proceeding, remanded, Brazill v. State*, 937 So. 2d 272 (Fla.Dist.Ct.App. 4th Dist. 2006).

drugs, aggressive behavior, and stealing have been found to occur together with enough frequency that some scholars refer to them as constituting problem behavior or a problem behavior syndrome. *Problem behavior* is defined as problematic or undesirable or as a source of concern for which societal response is required. Scholars have found that problem behavior is related to environmental and personality factors.[2] Some research suggests that problem behavior differs by gender.[3]

Studies of criminal behavior may focus on delinquents or adults. Specifically, with juveniles, a study conducted by 22 researchers working over a two-year period under the sponsorship of the Office of Juvenile Justice and Delinquency Prevention of the U.S. Department of Justice located a number of predictors that appeared related to delinquent behavior. The list is presented in Exhibit 5.2. Note that the first group of predictors consists of individual factors, and those would be included under the theories discussed in Chapter 4 of this text. The first two factors listed in Exhibit 5.2 are medical and physical factors; other individual factors include psychological ones, such as internalizing disorders (nervousness or withdrawal, worrying, and anxiety). Most of Exhibit 5.2 refers to factors that might be considered part of the social structure in which delinquency occurs; a few apply to the theories discussed in Chapter 6 of this text.

Ecological Theories

Early scholars studied crime through a variety of approaches, some of which influenced modern sociological theory. In particular, ecological theories are significant.

Ecology is the study of the distribution of phenomena and their relationship to their environment. The **ecological school** attempted to explain crime as a function of social change that occurs along with environmental change. At the root of this approach is the concept of *social disorganization*, which "is primarily concerned with the issue of social control: the ability of a neighborhood to regulate itself and to regulate the behavior of community residents and visitors to realize common goals, including a crime-free environment."[4]

The Chicago School and Its Impact

The early ecological school in the United States was centered during the 1920s and 1930s at the University of Chicago, where it was dominated by the works of Ernest W. Burgess, Robert Ezra Park, and others who attempted to explain the relationship between ecology and crime in Chicago. They saw the city as a living, growing, organic whole, and the various areas of the city as organs that served different functions.[5]

Studies of Chicago's areas of high crime rates and other forms of deviance suggested to researchers, such as David Matza, Harvey Zorbaugh, and Paul Cressey, that even the deviant's world was characterized by differentiated social roles, which were ordered and stratified with rules that were enforced. Subjects in the study had rewards and satisfactions, not all of which were deviant.[6] Some researchers, for example, Nels Anderson, Harvey Zorbaugh, and Paul Cressey, noted evidence of this approach in their studies of hobos and homeless men, who were found to have a stratified society, defined social roles, regulations, and traditions.[7]

The city's characteristics, social change, and distribution of people and their behavior have been studied by means of the **concentric circle**, an approach developed to

EXHIBIT 5.2

Predictors of Youth Violence

Individual Factors

- "Pregnancy and delivery complications
- Low resting heart rate [which might predispose one to aggressive and violent behavior]
- Internalizing disorders [nervousness or withdrawal, worrying, and anxiety]
- Hyperactivity, concentration problems, restlessness, and risk taking
- Aggressiveness
- Early initiation of violent behavior
- Involvement in other forms of antisocial behavior
- Beliefs and attitudes favorable to deviant or antisocial behavior

Family Factors

- Parental criminality
- Child maltreatment
- Poor family management practices
- Low levels of parental involvement
- Poor family bonding and family conflict
- Parental attitudes favorable to substance use and violence
- Parent-child separation

School Factors

- Academic failure
- Low bonding to school
- Truancy and dropping out of school
- Frequent school transitions

Peer-Related Factors

- Delinquent siblings
- Delinquent peers
- Gang membership

Community and Neighborhood Factors

- Poverty
- Community disorganization
- Availability of drugs and firearms
- Neighborhood adults involved in crime
- Exposure to violence and racial prejudices"

Source: J. David Hawkins et al., Office of Juvenile Justice and Delinquency Prevention, *Predictors of Youth Violence* (Washington, D.C.: U.S. Department of Justice, April 2000), http://www.ncjrs.gov/html/ojjdp/jjbul2000_04_5/pag3.html, accessed 3 October 2010.

study Chicago but thought to be applicable to other cities. The concentric circle theory divides the city into five zones. At the center of the city is Zone 1, the *central business district*. This zone is characterized by light manufacturing, retail trade, and commercialized recreation. Zone 2, surrounding the central business district, is the *zone of transition* "because it is in the immediate path of business and industrial expansion and has an ephemeral character." This zone is populated primarily by low-income people,

although typically it also has an area of high-cost luxury housing. Zone 3 is the *zone of working-class homes*, which is less deteriorated than the zone of transition and populated largely by "workers whose economic status enables them to have many of the comforts and even some of the luxuries the city has to offer." Zone 4, the *area of middle-class dwellers*, is populated largely by professional people, clerical forces, owners of small businesses, and the managerial class. On the outer edge of the city is Zone 5, the

Noted sociologists associated with the Chicago school of ecology argued that deteriorated areas of a city are conducive to juvenile and criminal behavior. Some modern theorists have contributed research findings that support the ecological approach. This photograph depicts one type of physical deterioration of a housing area: yards filled with trash.

commuters' zone. This zone includes satellite towns and suburbs. Many of the occupants vacate the area during the day and commute to the city for their employment.[8]

To explain crime, delinquency, and other vices, Burgess and Park stated that the key zone is Zone 2, the zone of transition. Because of the movement of businesses into this zone, it becomes an undesirable place to live, even though it previously claimed some of the most desirable housing in the city. Houses deteriorate. Zoning laws change. People who can afford to move out do so, and there is no prospect of improving the housing in the area without public subsidy. The population in the city is segregated by economic and occupational forces. Low-income persons, mostly unskilled workers, live in Zone 2, and frequently, this leads to racial and ethnic, as well as economic, segregation. The zone is characterized by warehouses, pawnshops, cheap theaters, restaurants, and a breakdown in the usual institutional methods of social control. The investigators hypothesized that crime, vice, and other forms of deviance would flourish in these socially disorganized environments.[9]

Clifford R. Shaw and Henry D. McKay, early ecological researchers, conducted several projects to determine the relationship between such factors as school truancy, young adult offenders, infant mortality, tuberculosis, and mental disorders and rates of delinquency and adult crime. They "noted that there is not a single instance in which they do not vary together. . . . On the basis of the facts presented, it is clear that delinquency is not an isolated phenomenon."[10]

Numerous criticisms have been directed at the early ecological studies, but these criticisms must be analyzed in light of the investigators' actual claims. Shaw and McKay did not conclude that the Zone 2 area *causes* crime, as some have suggested. In fact, they warned that cause-and-effect relationships should not be assumed just because high correlations between variables exist. Although Zone 2 may attract or collect criminals, another explanation of the higher crime and delinquency rates may be differential law enforcement. Police may be more likely to make arrests in Zone 2 than in other zones.

The Chicago studies found that areas with high rates and those with low rates of crime and delinquency were distinguished on the basis of physical status, economic status, and population composition as well as social values. Data from other cities supported these findings. Furthermore, despite changes in the population, rates of crime and delinquency remained highest in the zone of transition. Shaw and McKay concluded that crime-producing factors were inherent in the social and economic fabric of the community and constituted a normal reaction to living in a disorganized area.

Modern-day criminologists have praised the work of Shaw and McKay. In his presidential address before the American Society of Criminology in 2003, John H. Laub discussed the life course of criminology in the United States (more attention is given to the *life-course approach* in Chapter 6 of this text). In discussing what he called the *turning points* in the development of the discipline, Laub stated, "[O]ne can argue that the research of Clifford Shaw and Henry McKay has been most influential in the development of criminological theory." According to Laub, the primary reason is that Shaw and McKay moved away from the individualistic approaches to crime and focused on multiple levels of analysis. They studied the social-psychological aspects of crime and also crime and delinquency over time. They looked at issues such as industrialization, immigration, and urbanization and the effect those changes had on the family, church, peer groups, schools, and other traditional institutions. Changes in crime patterns could reflect differences in the level of social control exerted by those institutions.

In contrast to the cluttered yard full of trash in a development, pictured on p. 105, this mansion in a gated community in Miami Beach, Florida, would be presumed to have less crime.

"Thus, their interest was in the ecological, cultural and group processes of delinquency." Shaw and McKay also addressed the policy implications of their findings. Laub concluded as follows:

> Because of the scope and breadth of their research program, the seeds of virtually all the major schools of sociological criminology and delinquency theory can be found in Shaw and McKay's research. Their analysis focused on both the social organization and the individual aspects of crime and delinquency.[11]

Contemporary Research on Urban Crime and Delinquency

The mass migration of residents from the inner city to the suburbs of U.S. cities left the inner cities without support for many of their beautiful and large churches, some of which dated back two centuries. The migration left many cities without a sufficient tax base to maintain organizations and services. As a result, many inner-city areas are characterized by physical deterioration as well as high rates of crime, delinquency, and other social problems, such as the use and sale of illegal drugs, large numbers of residents on welfare, and high rates of illegitimacy and one-parent households. In recent years, some jurisdictions have made significant efforts to change these characteristics and improve the quality of life, buildings, and other characteristics of their inner cities.

The impact of environment on crime was investigated by Oscar Newman, who introduced the concept of *defensible space*. Newman believed that crime can be reduced by modifying the environment's physical features to the point that crime is more difficult to commit because the area gives the impression that the residents are in control.[12] For example, on the one hand, houses in certain neighborhoods may be considered too risky for crime in the summer because more people are outdoors and neighbors have a better view of the potential target. On the other hand, the fact that people go on vacation in the summer can make these houses more attractive targets during this time. Lighting is important, too; a well-lit area is less likely to become a target because of the increased possibility of detection.

Contemporary scholars, who have reanalyzed the social disorganization approach of the Chicago school, emphasize that, although ecology may not *cause* crime, problems within the ecological environment may undercut the influence of normal social control mechanisms. Perhaps the usual measures of social disorganization, such as social class or racial composition, are not really measures but *assumptions* of social disorganization. Underlying social class, race, poverty, mobility, or any other traditional measures of social disorganization are other factors that influence delinquent and criminal behavior. The key is to look at systems of social relationships that

may exert community-level social control. The argument is that the traditional forms of informal social controls that enable a community of people to keep order are undermined, altered, and rendered less effective by social disorganization. Thus, it is easier for delinquency and crime to develop and flourish. Modern researchers have attempted to measure the nature and extent of social controls within the communities characterized by disorganization. It has been suggested that three forms of social control may be increased in neighborhoods characterized by social organization:

- The *private order* of social control is based on the intimacy of primary groups. At this level, behavior is controlled through ostracism, ridicule, and criticism, and the stronger the primary relationships, the greater the level of social control.
- The *parochial system* of social control refers to the broader local interpersonal networks and the interlocking of the various local institutions. In communities characterized by social controls that extend beyond the families, children are socialized and controlled by the broader community.
- The *public order* refers to the external relationships that the community has with other communities and "focuses on the ability of the community to secure public goods and services that are allocated by agencies located outside the neighborhood."[13]

Investigators who attempted to measure social disorganization and social control by adding the factors of community supervision of teenage gangs, informal friendship networks, and participation in formal organizations, along with these traditional measures of social disorganization—social class, residential mobility, and family disruption—found that most of these external factors were related to social disorganization.[14]

Neighborhood characteristics that lead to concentrated social disadvantages, resulting in social disorganization, make it difficult for neighbors to look out for each other's property and exercise control over the community's children. They also make it less likely that residents will share trust and intervene in situations to aid the common good by maintaining social order and engaging in activities that are helpful in crime prevention, a process referred to as *collective efficacy*.[15]

Collective efficacy may be viewed as the opposite of social disorganization, which is frequently associated with such factors as poverty, race, and ethnicity. These and other factors have been examined as evidence of social disorganization when the key should perhaps be whether these (or other) factors are only indirectly associated with the social disorganization that accompanies crime. For example, there is evidence of higher rates of crime in African American neighborhoods, but there are studies that suggest this is the case because of the concentration of African Americans in extremely poor neighborhoods that are often isolated from the rest of the city's neighborhoods.[16] Possibly, the lack of resources and other factors in these neighborhoods, rather than race, leads to higher crime rates.

Rates of violence among and between racial and ethnic groups have also been examined. Researchers who studied violent crime within a Los Angeles, California, neighborhood that had transitioned to a predominantly Latino area from that of a predominately African American area concluded that social disorganization theory explained their finding of increased intergroup violence among both groups. The authors suggested that a breakdown in norms, not race, led to greater violence.[17]

Higher crime rates in neighborhoods may not always be explained by concrete factors. For example, it might seem logical that the return of parolees from prison to their former neighborhoods would be accompanied by increased crime. Researchers who studied the return of parolees to a Sacramento, California, neighborhood between 2003 and 2006 did find an increase in crime. Specifically, the authors found that the number of returning violent parolees was associated with an increase in some crimes, such as murder and burglary. However, the impact of violent parolees on burglary and aggravated assault appeared to diminish when the neighborhood had a large number of voluntary organizations, which helped reintegrate parolees back into the community. The positive effect was particularly strong when the voluntary organizations provided youth services. The researchers also found that the impact of parolees on robbery was moderated by the existence of greater residential stability.[18]

Residential mobility may also be associated with crime victimization. Scholars have emphasized the *push* factors (the negative features of the neighborhood, such as crime) and the *pull* factors (the favorable features, such as cleanliness, view, low crime rates, and so on) that affect mobility. In general, research has shown that crime victimization is associated with the movement of populations *out* of neighborhoods. There is also evidence that indirect *property* victimization (i.e., the victimization of others in the area) is linked to residential mobility out of the neighborhood. However, this is not the case with *violent* victimizations of others, perhaps because they may involve persons known to the victims and thus not threaten others.[19]

There is also evidence that poverty within a neighborhood is associated not only with property crimes but also with homicide and other forms of violence in the United States[20] as well as in other countries.[21] But some scholars take the position that it is not poverty, family disorganization, high residential mobility, or any other factors within neighborhoods that are linked to crime, but rather, the lack of control that neighbors have over each other is the key. All of these factors restrict the participation of neighbors in social organizations, which limits social control and facilitates criminal behavior. Law-abiding residents lose interest in community life and organizations and move away.[22]

Such positions are reminiscent of the *broken windows concept* of policing based on the belief that, when neighborhoods deteriorate socially and physically, they invite crime. Thus, it is important to remove minor offenders from the streets because they disrupt the quality of neighborhood life. If they are not removed, other residents will be frightened, predatory criminals will be attracted, and crime will escalate.[23]

Although strong social ties and social networks make it more likely that neighbors will intervene in inappropriate behavior for the common good, strong ties can also have a negative influence. For instance, respondents in an analysis of violent young people living in extremely disadvantaged urban neighborhoods reported that social ties may lead to the identity of persons who try to exert social control—for example, by reporting drug problems. Identity could result in violent retaliation. Thus, "local ties may undermine, rather than support, social control processes."[24]

Although much of the research on neighborhood disorganization and crime has been conducted in urban areas, studies of rural communities have also revealed an association between juvenile violence and crime and rates of residential instability, family disruption, and ethnic heterogeneity.[25]

Scholars have also looked at crime rates within disadvantaged neighborhoods in light of economic issues, such as unemployment, that occur in, but are not limited to, a city's zone of transition. In any area, changes in the business cycle might affect crime. The motivation to engage in criminal activities could be enhanced by the social strain that exists when individuals cannot meet their economic goals. Motivation to commit crimes might increase as the ability of society to control its members deteriorates. Economic conditions might also affect the opportunities persons have to commit crimes.[26]

Crime, such as homicide, has also been associated with the deprivation of resources, which is often characteristic of areas of social disorganization.[27]

These and many other contemporary findings suggest that social disorganization, which may exist for a variety of reasons but is often typical of the zone of transition, may influence crime and delinquency because it diminishes the impact of informal social controls within the community. However, to understand the complex interrelationships within a community, it is not sufficient to study only informal social controls. It is necessary to look at the *types* of informal social controls. One researcher contrasted *direct informal social controls* (the use of direct intervention) with *indirect informal social control* (using the services of formal authorities, e.g., the police). Overreliance on direct methods of intervention can lead to vigilantism; overreliance on the police or other formal agencies may weaken informal social controls by decreasing the willingness of residents to work with each other to solve local problems.[28]

The common theme of research on social disorganization and crime and delinquency is that crime, delinquency, and other forms of deviant behavior can flourish in disadvantaged neighborhoods because informal social controls are negatively impacted by social disorganization. But there is evidence that communities that manage to develop a spirit of solidarity and mutual trust, or collective efficacy, have lower rates of delinquency and crime. Specifically, in a recent study of violent urban youths, researchers concluded: "Collective efficacy exerts an independent influence on violent behavior and attenuates [weakens] the effect of unstructured socializing on this outcome."[29]

There is also evidence that authoritative parenting (described as parents who "combine support and nurturance with structure and control") is associated with such positive results, especially when authoritative parenting exists within a community characterized by high collective efficacy.[30]

In any event, the key factor in explaining crime, claim some criminologists, is found in the concept of **anomie**, or normlessness.

Émile Durkheim (1858–1917), a French sociologist, introduced and developed the concept of anomie in his writings about crime and suicide. His work has influenced modern sociologists, who have expanded and tested his concepts.

Anomie/Strain Theories

This section looks at the classic and earlier approaches in developing the concept of anomie and then at the contemporary contributions.

The Classic Anomie Approach

The introduction and development of classic anomie theory involve the work of two outstanding scholars, Émile Durkheim and Robert K. Merton.

Durkheim's Contributions

Émile Durkheim (1858–1917), a noted French sociologist, made significant contributions to the study of human behavior. According to Durkheim, crime has functional (or positive) consequences, such as fostering flexibility. It is impossible for all people to be alike and to hold the same moral consciousness. Some individuals differ from the collective type; inevitably, some of these divergences include criminal behavior—not because the act is intrinsically criminal but because the collectivity defines it as criminal. Durkheim saw crime as the product of norms. The concept of wrong is necessary to give meaning to right and is inherent in that concept. Even a community of saints will create sinners. For a society to be flexible enough to permit positive deviation, it must also permit negative deviation. If no deviation is permitted, societies become stagnant. Crime helps prepare society for such changes; it is one of the prices we pay for freedom.[31] Furthermore, crime is normal. No society can be exempt from crime: "There is . . . no phenomenon that presents more indisputably all the symptoms of normality, since it [crime] appears closely connected with the conditions of all collective life."[32]

In 1893, Durkheim introduced his version of the concept of *anomie*, which derives from a Greek word meaning "without norms." He was not the first to use the term, nor did he develop the concept as extensively as did American sociologist Robert K. Merton. But Durkheim was responsible for making the concept an integral part of sociology and criminology. He believed that one of society's most important elements was its social cohesion, or *social solidarity*, which represented a *collective conscience*. In explaining this phenomenon, Durkheim defined two types of solidarity: mechanical and organic.

According to Durkheim, primitive societies are characterized by *mechanical solidarity*, which is dominated by the collective conscience. The type of law manifests this dominance; the reason for law is to discourage individuals from acting in a way that threatens the collective conscience. As societies become larger and more complex, the emphasis in law shifts from the collective conscience to the individual wronged, and law becomes *restitutive*. This shift from mechanical to *organic solidarity* is characterized by an increased need for a division of labor, a division that may be forced and therefore abnormal, leading to the creation of unnatural differences in class and status. People are less homogeneous, and the traditional forms of social control, appropriate to a simple, homogeneous society, are not effective in controlling behavior. Greater loneliness, more social isolation, and a loss of identity result, with a consequent state of anomie, or normlessness, which replaces the former state of solidarity and provides an atmosphere in which crimes and other antisocial acts may develop and flourish.[33]

Durkheim had a strong impact on scholarly theorists, including most of those discussed in this chapter. His theory of the relationship between anomie and suicide and other social problems remains important today. Durkheim wrote a book on suicide,[34] seeing that extreme reaction as one result of normlessness, social isolation, and loss of identity. It is perhaps reasonable to revisit his contributions in light of some recent crimes, especially those involving young people, in which the perpetrators have killed themselves after committing multiple murders. The December 2007 shooting spree in an upscale department store in Nebraska's largest mall that took the lives of eight victims and wounded two others critically before the gunman, Robert A. Hawkins, 19, killed himself is one recent example. In an effort to understand and explain the senseless killings, reporters uncovered descriptions of Hawkins that sound like they might have come from Durkheim: "a young man facing depression, alienation, abandonment, rejection," a high school dropout, like a pound puppy that nobody wanted, and despondent over being fired from his job at McDonald's and losing his girlfriend, who recently ended their relationship. Some who knew him, however, described him as laid-back but not violent.[35]

The relevance of Durkheim is illustrated by recent research applying his contributions to modern developments. Global Focus 5.1 explains how Durkheim influenced a study of changing society in Russia.

Merton's Contributions

Durkheim's belief that crime is normal and his theory of anomie formed the basis of Robert K. Merton's (1910–2003) contributions to an understanding of criminal behavior. Merton's thesis was that social structures exert pressure for change. Some of that change is helpful to society; some of it is not. Merton sought to develop a way to analyze social and cultural changes in society by means of functional analysis. To him, the key concepts are those of "strain, tension, contradiction, or discrepancy between the component elements of social and cultural structure." *Social structure* refers to the approved social means, and *cultural structure* is the approved goals for achieving those means. The strain or tension between the goals and the means "may be dysfunctional for the social system in its then existing form; they may also be instrumental in leading to changes in that system. In any case, they exert pressure for change." Some persons may be pressured to behave in nonconforming rather than conforming ways. If evidence is found for this thesis, it will follow that nonconforming behavior is as normal as conforming behavior.[36]

GLOBAL FOCUS

5.1

Changes in Russian Society: An Analysis Based on Durkheim

Among the significant contributions of Émile Durkheim was his understanding of the effect of rapid social change on behavior.[1] Scholars studied the "sudden, widespread, and fundamental" changes that occurred after the dissolution of the former Soviet Union.[2] In their words, "The former social welfare system—with its broad guarantees of employment, healthcare, education, and other forms of social support—was dismantled in the shift toward democracy, rule of law, and a free-market economy." This situation provided an unusual and rare opportunity to assess the impact of social change upon behavior.

The researchers began their analysis with Durkheim's approach: To determine the cause of a social fact, one must look at the social facts that occurred before that fact. They then turned to Durkheim's distinction between mechanical and organic solidarity, which is discussed in this text. The researchers traced the changes in Russia and noted that high rates of crime were generated by rapid social change because the rapid changes reduced "the capacity of the society to regulate the escalating aspirations and expectations of its citizenry."[3] The result in Russia was "continued economic, social, and political instability" that affected all aspects of their lives.[4]

The researchers examined three major social problems: homicide, suicide, and alcohol-related deaths. They found:

that the Russian Federation experienced significant permanent increases in the level of homicides and alcohol-related deaths and a more dramatic, though short-lived, increase in the suicide rate in the years following the breakup of the Soviet Union. The reasons behind the differences in the functional forms of these relationships is [sic] beyond our capacity to determine with these data. Nonetheless . . . there can be no doubt that the breakup was associated with a rise in the level of deviant behavior within the Russian Federation.[5]

1. See Émile Durkheim, *Suicide*, trans. John A. Spaulding and George Simpson (New York: Free Press of Glencoe, 1951).
2. William Alex Pridemore et al., "An Interrupted Time-Series Analysis of Durkheim's Social Deregulation Thesis: The Case of the Russian Federation," *Justice Quarterly* 24, no. 2 (June 2007): 271–290.
3. Ibid., p. 274.
4. Ibid., p. 275.
5. Ibid., p. 284.

In further elaborating his concepts of goals and means, Merton first looked at goals, which are the aspirations of all individuals in the society. *Goals* are those things individuals believe are worth striving for. Second are the means by which those goals may be obtained. The *means* are socially approved methods and thus involve the norms, which are defined culturally. A society's norms define the goals and the methods by which those goals may be obtained. According to Merton, when there is a focus on the goals to the virtual exclusion of the norms, and when the socially approved means for obtaining the goals are not equally available to all, many people turn to unapproved and unacceptable means to achieve the goals. The result is a situation of normlessness, or anomie. Merton suggested that in contemporary American culture, the primary emphasis is on goals, not means, and the main goal is a monetary one.[37]

After examining American cultural patterns, Merton designed a typology to describe the methods, or modes, of adaptation that are available to those who react to society's goals and means. He identified five modes: conformity, innovation, ritualism, retreatism, and rebellion. These are *modes of adaptation*, not personality types. The first mode, *conformity*, refers to the acceptance of a society's goals and its approved means for achieving those goals. Conformity is the adaptation used most frequently. The second mode, *innovation*, represents acceptance of the goals but rejection of the means for obtaining them. For example, if a college degree is the goal, the student who adopts that goal but rejects the acceptable means for attaining it may cheat.

The third mode of adaptation is *ritualism*, which refers to a rejection of the goals but acceptance of the means. Often, people lose sight of the reasons for doing things, such as going to church, but continue the socially approved behavior, thus making a ritual out of it. The fourth mode, *retreatism*, the least common of the five adaptations, refers to the rejection of both the goals and the means. This adaptation occurs after a person has accepted both the goals and the means but has failed repeatedly to achieve the goals by legitimate means. At the same time, because of prior socialization, this individual is not able to adopt illegitimate means. The retreatist mode of adaptation rep-resents a nonproductive liability to conventional society, and it is characteristic of psychotics, autistic persons, outcasts, tramps, chronic drunkards, drug addicts, vagrants, and vagabonds.

Merton's final type of adaptation, *rebellion*, consists of rejecting the goals and means of the present society and attempting to establish a new social order. Merton said this adaptation is different from the others, as it represents an attempt to change the social structure rather than to make an individual adaptation within that structure. Merton's five types of adaptations are listed in Exhibit 5.3, along with an indication of whether each type accepts or rejects society's goals and the means of achieving those goals.

Merton's approach has been widely accepted and can be seen in the later development of subculture and related theories of crime, discussed later in this chapter.

Merton raised some criticisms of his own theory. It does not take into account social-psychological factors that might explain the adoption of one adaptation over the other. It does not examine rebellious behavior thoroughly, and it does not consider the social-structural elements that might predispose an individual toward one adaptation over another.[38]

Some have argued that Merton's theory of anomie does not explain the nonutilitarian element of much juvenile delinquency, which its perpetrators appear to engage in just for fun and not to meet society's specific goals. It has also been argued that the theory neither explains the destructive nature of some delinquent and criminal acts nor accounts for crime in societies where some goals are not seen as available to everyone. Finally, some critics argue that the theory has not been sufficiently tested empirically.[39]

Some scholars advocate abandoning Merton's approach;[40] others maintain that it remains a viable theory to explain delinquent and criminal behavior.[41] Alternatively, revisions of the theory have been suggested.[42]

Contemporary Approaches

Anomie/strain theories have been expanded and tested by numerous contemporaries with two approaches in particular standing out in the published research.

EXHIBIT 5.3

Summary of Merton's Anomie Theory

Robert K. Merton's approach to explaining the effect of anomie or strain on adaptations is to present five types of adaptations, which are based on acceptance of the society's goals and its institutionalized means for achieving those goals.

Type of Adaptation	Goals	Means
1. Conformity	Accept	Accept
2. Innovation	Accept	Reject
3. Ritualism	Reject	Accept
4. Retreatism	Reject	Reject
5. Rebellion	Rejects society's values and goals and substitutes new ones	

Messner and Rosenfeld: Institutional Anomie Theory (IAT)

Steven F. Messner and Richard Rosenfeld recommended extending Merton's ideas about the relationship between crime rates and such factors as culture, social structure, and anomie. They based their **institutional anomie theory (IAT)** (that term was not used at the original inception but emerged later) approach on an analysis of profit-motivated crimes, including both white-collar and common law crimes. Messner and Rosenfeld went beyond Merton's emphasis on the legitimate opportunity structure and maintained that eliminating social-structural obstacles to achieving goals would not reduce crime rates significantly. Their point was that the desire to succeed economically is so strong in America that all the country's social institutions have lost their ability to control behavior. The institutions promoted the goals of economic success but did not provide alternative definitions of success. For example, education "is regarded largely as a means to occupational attainment, which in turn is valued primarily insofar as it promises economic rewards."[43]

No matter how much wealth one has, there is pressure to accumulate more, and social institutions have little power to control the means of achieving goals. In addition, Messner and Rosenfeld went beyond Merton's emphasis on social class and looked at the family as well as economic, political, and educational institutions. They expanded their position to include other societies, including those in which the economy is not as dominant as it is in America. They argued that high crime rates are produced by institutional balance *per se* rather than just by the dominance of economic institutions. They also stated that the type of institutional dominance is related to the type of crime produced. For example, societies in which the political institutions dominate will tend toward moral cynicism that leads to political corruption; those dominated by economic institutions, as in America, will have more crimes associated with economic gain and success.[44]

In a subsequent publication, Rosenfeld and Messner summarized their position and the developments that had occurred since its inception. They concluded that research on their approach had been promising if not uniform in its findings. "In general, the theory's 'structural' propositions relating crime to the institutional balance of power have fared better . . . than its 'cultural' propositions linking crime to an anomic emphasis on the goal of material success." They concluded that a significant and permanent reduction in crime would require that we place less emphasis on extreme materialism and individualism. But those changes "must be accompanied by a corresponding shift in the institutional balance of power that strengthens the social control and social support functions of noneconomic institutions." As examples, Rosenfeld and Messner cited the civil rights and women's movements of the twentieth century, which resulted in massive changes for large populations of the society.[45]

Institutional anomie theory has generated considerable theoretical analysis and empirical research, although scholars have found some difficulties in the empirical testing of its propositions. Specifically, it is difficult to operationalize and measure the variables of culture, social structure, and institutional controls and compare them with crime rates.[46]

Other scholars have reported support for anomie and IAT. A recent test of the approach of Merton as well as that of Messner and Rosenfeld led the researchers to conclude:

- "Instrumental crime rates are significantly higher in areas where both a strong commitment to monetary success goals and a weak commitment to legitimate means exist.
- The tendency for this 'goals/means' value complex to translate into higher rates of instrumental crime is reduced in the context of higher levels of welfare assistance and more frequent socializing among families . . .
- [L]ow levels of educational and economic attainment and high levels of inequality enhance the degree to which commitment to monetary success translates into instrumental crime."[47]

Agnew: General Strain Theory (GST)

Other contemporary developments in anomie theory may be analyzed by looking at **general strain theory (GST)** as developed by Robert Agnew. *Strain theory* refers to the theories of social disorganization, anomie, and subculture that focus on negative social structures and relationships "in which others prevent the individual from achieving positively valued goals." Agnew maintained that strain theory should be expanded beyond the traditional emphasis on an individual's failure to achieve goals and include "all types of negative relations between the individual and others." He argued for a more comprehensive approach to the analysis of how strain is related to delinquent and criminal behavior but recognized that his theory was not developed fully.[48]

In 2006, Agnew published a book that developed his strain theory more fully.[49] He discussed three types of strain concepts that may produce deviance. First is the individual's failure to achieve his or her immediate and future goals. Agnew went beyond Merton's anomie theory to include the inability to achieve goals because of one's own inadequacies. In addition, he noted that the gap between one's expectations and achievements may result not only in disappointment but also in resentment or even anger. Agnew also included the person's impression that there is a difference between the *actual* outcome and what the outcome *should* be—that is, a fair and just outcome. This might be illustrated by students who expect an A on a test because they studied so hard; in their minds, an A would be a just result. Any grade below an A would be unjust and could lead to disappointment, even anger.

According to Agnew, a second type of strain occurs when an individual loses a source of stability, such as a loved one, through death or the dissolution of the personal relationship, such as the end of a romantic involvement. The person suffers strain through the loss of a stimulus that had a positive valuation.

The third of Agnew's strain types occurs when an individual is confronted with negative stimuli, such as difficulties in school, crime victimization, or abuse by family members. The young person cannot get away from school or family without acting in a deviant way, and that appears to be the solution to the troubled youth.

These three strains may lead to the development of negative emotions (e.g., anger, malicious envy, jealousy, frustration, depression, and fear). The resulting negative emotions "create pressure for corrective action, reduce the ability to cope in a legal manner, reduce the perceived costs of crime, and increase the disposition for crime." Further, the strains may "temporarily reduce social control and foster the social learning of crime."[50] Agnew's approach is presented in diagram form in Figure 5.1.

Agnew was not suggesting that crime is a reasonable, or even an effective, response to strain. He emphasized that crime is not a long-term solution to strain, but for some individuals, it may provide an effective short-term solution.[51]

Agnew's suggestions for reducing the strains that may lead to crime are as follows:

- "Attempt to eliminate those strains conducive to crime." This can be done through parent-training programs and antibullying programs.
- "Alter strains so as to make them less conducive to crime." This can be accomplished by establishing programs in schools and altering the ways criminal justice systems react to individuals.
- "Remove individuals from strains conducive to crime." Two examples are the establishment of group homes and programs that provide greater

opportunities (e.g., as rent subsidies) for the families of children who live in poor communities.
- "Equip individuals with the traits and skills to avoid strains" conducive to crime through social skills training, preschool enrichment programs, and vocational training.
- "Alter the perceptions/goals of individuals to reduce subjective strains" by teaching young people how to evaluate situations that might lead to aggressive behavior. Another method is to develop programs that assist young people in altering the goals that they may not be able to achieve through legal means.[52]

In addition to identifying negative emotion as a variable that provides a link between strain and criminal behavior, Agnew also included the variables of *social support* and *criminal peer association*. He argued that with proper social support, individuals are more likely to react to strain through appropriate behaviors rather than coping by adopting inappropriate responses. In contrast, associations with criminal peers may increase the chances that a person subjected to strain will react by engaging in delinquent or criminal behaviors. Association with criminal behavior may provide not only reinforcement for that behavior but the message that it is reasonable to blame others for the strain one faces.[53]

Although Agnew's development of strain theory has increased our understanding of the impact that strain has on future behavior, it does not explain all reactions to strain. In his more recent contributions, Agnew has specified the variables that he thinks are most likely to lead to delinquent or criminal behavior. Examples are strains that are high in magnitude, those that one views as unjust, and those that occur in social situations that undermine social control. The strains may be anticipated as well as real, and their impact on behavior may be linked to personality characteristics (discussed previously) as well as social learning (discussed in Chapter 6).[54]

Agnew recognized that most forms of strain "have only small to moderate overall effects on delinquency,"

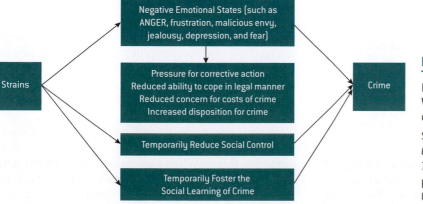

Figure 5.1

Robert Agnew: The Mechanisms by Which Strains Increase the Likelihood of Particular Crimes

Source: Robert Agnew, *Pressured into Crime: An Overview of General Strain Theory* (Los Angeles: Roxbury, 2006), p. 38, reprinted with permission from Oxford University Press.

and if strain theory is to be effective, "it must identify the factors that influence the reaction to strain." His recognition of the potential impact of personality characteristics implies that reactions to strain may be caused, at least in part, by biological and environmental factors.[55]

One test of strain theory verified Agnew's position in general but failed to support some of his findings, with the authors concluding: "In expanding the scope of strain theory, Agnew has only begun an important line of both theoretical and empirical work that we wish to see undertaken."[56]

A study of subjects in Russia, Greece, and the Ukraine found only limited support for GST (and that only in the Ukraine), leading the authors to conclude that further research is needed on this approach.[57]

Agnew's place among criminological theorists is one of high regard. As one scholar concluded, Agnew's development of GST "has developed into one of the leading social psychological theories of crime with a fairly developed body of research."[58]

Other researchers, while accepting that there is a link between strain and criminal offending, have questioned the direct impact of negative emotions on strain to create a criminal response. It may be that strain alone is sufficient to lead one to react in a criminal manner and that neither social support nor criminal peer associations explain this response.[59]

Cullen's Social Support Explanation

Agnew's position on the role of social support in explaining a person's reaction to strain was further developed by Francis T. Cullen. Some of Cullen's propositions are as follows:

- "America has higher rates of serious crime than other industrialized nations because it is a less supportive society. . . .
- The less social support there is in a community, the higher the crime rate will be. . . .
- The more support a family provides, the less likely it is that a person will engage in crime. . . .
- The more social support in a person's social network, the less crime will occur. . . .
- Social support lessens the effects of exposure to criminogenic strains. . . .
- Across the life cycle, social support increases the likelihood that offenders will turn away from a criminal pathway. . . .
- Anticipation of a lack of social support increases criminal involvement. . . .
- Giving social support lessens involvement in crime. . .
- Crime is less likely when social support for conformity exceeds social support for crime. . . .
- Social support often is a precondition for effective social control. . . ."[60]

The approaches of ecology, strain, and social support confront the fact that some people in our society are not sufficiently talented or qualified to achieve the symbols of success but may desire them. This raises interesting public policy questions, such as the following, articulated by criminological theorists:

> Do untalented people have the same rights as talented people to want material goods, the respect of their peers, and power and control over their own lives? Would society be well advised to provide untalented as well as talented people with legitimate opportunities to obtain these things? Or is the economy so dominant in American society that we cannot even consider such questions?[61]

A summary of ecological and anomie/strain theories is provided in Exhibit 5.4. The influence of these theories and approaches may be seen in some of the cultural transmission and related theories discussed in the next section.

Cultural Transmission Theories and Their Forerunners

The theory of anomie as developed by Durkheim and Merton established a framework for the emergence of theories and research on the structural characteristics of groups or cultures. Some approaches focused on a particular social class (e.g., the lower class), whereas others concentrated on the existence of a **subculture** (an identifiable segment or group characterized by specific patterns of behavior, folkways, and mores that set it apart from the rest of society) to explain delinquent and criminal behavior. The scholars did not agree on why certain norms existed within classes, groups, or subcultures, but they were influenced by the early study of gangs, a subject that is the focus of significant research today.

The Study of Gangs

The study of gangs has a long history, which includes significant contributions by sociologists.

The Earlier Works

Modern theories and studies of gangs were preceded by Frederic M. Thrasher's classic study (published in 1927). Thrasher viewed juvenile gangs developing in Chicago as a result of social disorganization in the zone of transition. He studied 1,313 Chicago gangs and noted that they emerged as a result of innocent play groups that came into conflict over space in the crowded and physically deteriorated areas of the inner city. Thrasher did not deny that gangs existed outside the slums, but he thought most were located in that area of the city.[62]

In his classic study, *Street Corner Society* (published in 1943), William F. Whyte disputed Thrasher's social disorganization theory. Whyte showed that slums are characterized by social organization but that their inhabitants may face a conflict between the status system of their cultures within the slums and that of the society's mainstream sys-

5.4   Ecological and Anomie/Strain Theories: A Summary

Ecological Theories

These theories attempt to explain crime as a function of social change that occurs along with environmental change; research centered around the University of Chicago in the 1920s and 1930s, dominated by the works of **Ernest W. Burgess** and **Robert Ezra Park** and their concentric circle theory.

The impact of environment on crime was developed further by **Oscar Newman's** concept of *defensible space*, stating that crime can be reduced by modifying the environment's physical features so that it appears residents are in control. Contemporary scholars, such as **Robert J. Bursik Jr., W. Byron Groves, Robert J. Sampson,** and **Harold G. Grasmick**, have reanalyzed the Chicago school approach.

Anomie/Strain Theories

■ The Classic Anomie Approach

This approach is characterized by **Émile Durkheim's** belief that crime is functional and exists in all societies; it is based on the concept of *anomie*, which means "without norms." The concept was further developed by **Robert K. Merton,** who believed that social structures exert pressure on some persons to behave in nonconforming rather than conforming ways. Merton analyzed this proposition by looking at the goals, along with the means of achieving them, in terms of five modes of adaptations, which are listed in Exhibit 5.3.

■ Contemporary Anomie/Strain Approaches

These approaches focus "on relationships in which others prevent the individual from achieving positively valued goals," according to **Robert Agnew**, whose *institutional anomie theory (IAT)* expands the concept of anomie beyond the failure of one to achieve desired goals. Agnew's categories of strain are enumerated in Figure 5.1. His work includes the collaboration of others, such as **Lisa M. Broidy**. Contemporary researchers also include significant work by **Steven F. Messner** and **Richard Rosenfeld**, who based their institutional anomie theory on an analysis of profit-motivated crimes. The contribution of **Francis T. Cullen** to the development of *social support theory* is also important.

---

tem. Thus, to move up within their milieu meant to excel in the rackets or in the politics of the slum. But this success was frowned on by the rest of society.[63]

In recent years, gang-related crimes have captured national and international attention, leading to increased research on the nature and causes of gangs and policies for preventing them. Even college texts on gangs are now appearing on the market, as illustrated by the 2008 publication of Kimberly Tobin's *Gangs: An Individual and Group Perspective*.[64] First we look at data on gangs.

Data on Gangs

Research on the extent of gang membership is illustrated by the publications of the Office of Juvenile Justice and Delinquency Prevention (OJJDP) of the U.S. Department of Justice (DOJ), which conducts an annual survey of youth gangs. The OJJDP reported a significant increase in gang activity in recent years.[65]

Data on gangs are also reported by the FBI. In July 2009, the FBI released estimates that as of 2008, approximately one million persons belonged to over 20,000 gangs in the United States. In many communities, these gang members commit as much as 80 percent of all crime. Gangs exist in all states, and although they are concentrated in urban areas, they can also be found in suburban and rural areas.[66]

Current Research and Policies

Recent research findings suggest that gang activity has changed significantly since the studies of Thrasher and others. Many of today's gangs, unlike those of the past, are associated with violence and illegal drugs. Although violence might have been characteristic of some early gangs, it appears to be the *focal* point of today's gangs. Whereas the gangs that were the focus of early sociological research may have fought over turf, today's gangs go to war over drug trafficking, even killing their own members if they become informers.

Scholars disagree on all of the variables associated with drug trafficking and gangs. Conclusions range from "gang members who sell drugs are significantly more violent than gang members that don't sell drugs and drug sellers that don't belong to gangs"[67] to "serious crime and violence occur regardless of the prevalence of drug dealing within the gang"[68] and "gang member involvement in drug sales does not necessarily result in more frequent violent offenses."[69]

Other recent findings concerning youth gangs are revealed through research conducted by the National Alliance of Gang Investigators Association (NAGIA), which, along with the FBI, concluded the following:

- Gang members use inexpensive and easily accessible technology (such as cell phones) to communicate with one another, and their knowledge of such technology makes it difficult for law enforcement to apprehend them.
- Gangs are migrating throughout the United States, bringing fear to many more communities, and as they do so, the traditional boundaries and alliances are blurred.
- It is difficult for jurisdictions to share ways of dealing successfully with gangs because definitions of

gangs, gang activities, and gang members are so varied.

- Gang activity is difficult to address because many communities are in denial concerning the existence of gangs in their areas.[70]

Because of the escalating numbers of gangs and gang members and their increasing engagement in violence, the OJJDP established the National Youth Gang Center (NYGC), with the following goals:

- "Collect and analyze gang-related data and generate annual surveys and reports. . . .
- Compile and analyze gang-related legislation. . . .
- Collect the most current gang literature. . . .
- Identify promising gang intervention and prevention strategies across the country. . . .
- Participate in and serve as the coordinator for the OJJDP-sponsored Youth Gang Consortium, which coordinates gang program development and information exchange among Federal, State, and local agencies."[71]

A 2009 criminology journal that focuses on the policy implications of research in criminology devoted a major portion of one journal to an analysis of data on gangs and included discussions of public policies concerning gang activities and how to control them.[72] Issues such as race and ethnicity and gender are key in these analyses.

Race and Ethnicity

Most of the earlier studies of gangs focused on youths who were white immigrants to the city, but more recent research has focused on minority youths in urban areas. Factors such as poverty, urbanization, and discrimination have been analyzed in an attempt to explain the higher gang memberships and arrests of minorities, especially Af-

rican Americans and Hispanic youths compared to whites. It was theorized that the decreasing job opportunities and increasing economic inequality in urban areas, which were heavily populated by minorities, contributed to the rise in gang membership. Young people living on the edge and with few opportunities to develop a positive self-concept turned to gang membership. It was also suggested that the lack of traditional controls from family, schools, and law enforcement, which characterized the depressed areas in which the minority youths lived, created threats that led to the violence characteristic of gang membership. Missing from many of these studies, however, was an investigation of whether there were common factors that distinguished minority and ethnic gangs from those with primarily white membership. Some current research indicates that ecological and economic stress factors are more characteristic of white gang members, while African American and Hispanic youth gang membership is more frequently associated with elements of social control (such as provided by family, school, and police) and street socialization (which occurs when youths spend time with friends who may be involved with alcohol and other drugs).[73]

It seems reasonable that researchers should go beyond the data on the characteristics of gang membership, which could easily lead to the conclusion that Hispanics and African American youths are more prone to such memberships, and investigate all of the variables associated with gangs.

Gender is also a variable that constitutes an issue in gang membership. Although evidence indicates that most gang members are male, female gang members have become more common in recent years.

Female Gangs

Earlier sociological researchers reported that female juveniles participated in gangs and that they did so for some of

Although historically gang members were usually male, young women are forming their own gangs, and there is evidence that they are becoming increasingly violent.

the same reasons as their male counterparts—for example, to find a sense of belonging that they had not found otherwise. Anne Campbell found that female gang members did not view themselves as criminals even when they engaged in behavior that violated the law. They rationalized their behavior by saying it was necessary in their social circles or by denying responsibility for what they did. Generally, female gang members were aggressive against other women but not against men.[74]

A report by the Chicago Crime Commission, based on a two-year study of female teen gangs, concluded the following:

[Girls in gangs] are stepping to the forefront, selling their own drugs, making their own decisions, and avenging their own wrongs. Females are willing to participate in the full range of violent criminal activity at the same rate and the same level—and sometimes more—as their male counterparts.[75]

Some scholars question whether women are becoming more violent as gang members, noting that female violence in this context may be a reflection of a generally more violent society.[76] It is suggested that researchers should spend more time studying the phenomenon of female gang membership, noting that the publications portray a "sobering perspective on gang life that normally is not portrayed in the popular media."[77]

Finally, in the study of the involvement of girls and women within gangs, it is important to analyze the social structure of the gangs of boys and young men to ascertain their attitudes toward female members. It has been reported that in gangs to which both boys and girls belong, the boys view girls with much greater acceptance than is the case in gangs to which only boys belong. In the latter, the boys tend to view girls and young women as unacceptable for gang membership.[78]

The Prevention of Gangs

Because of the apparent increase in and the violent nature of gangs, legislation and policies have been developed to cope with them. School administrators have taken measures to decrease gang activities. Extra security officers and metal detectors are utilized in an effort to eliminate the problem of lethal weapons. In some schools, students are forbidden to wear certain colors and insignia or to engage in activities, such as handshakes, commonly associated with local gangs.

As part of the Violent Crime Control and Law Enforcement Act of 1994, Congress included increased penalties for certain gang-related crimes and provided for the attorney general to "develop a national strategy to coordinate gang-related investigations by Federal law enforcement agencies."[79]

In an earlier effort to curb gangs, Chicago enacted an antiloitering ordinance that permitted police to disburse people gathered in a public place "with no apparent lawful purpose." In 2000, the U.S. Supreme Court decided the case of *City of Chicago v. Morales*, in which the Court held that the ordinance was unconstitutional because it was vague and gave police too much discretion to arrest people who might not be engaging in any illegal acts.[80]

In February 2000, Chicago tried again, with an ordinance designed to inconvenience gangs by disbursing them so frequently that they could not keep a hold on a community or an area within one. Three Hispanic men, who were among the first arrested under the new ordinance, challenged its constitutionality. On 19 March 2002, a judge in Chicago ruled that the ordinance was constitutional. According to Cook County (Illinois) Circuit Judge Mark Ballard, the U.S. Supreme Court's opinion in *Morales* drew a road map for an acceptable plan, and "the Chicago framers of the revised ordinance knew how to read the map."[81]

The Justice Policy Institute (JPI), a research and policy organization in Washington, D.C., reviewed the literature on gangs and concluded that more tough legislation, more police (approximately one-half of police departments had established special gang units by 1999), and more prison sentencing had not reduced gangs significantly. The institute also found that gangs do not commit most of the crime in the United States, that gang members are predominantly white (40 percent), that incarceration does not necessarily stop members' participation in gangs, that most members quit before they reach adult age, and that punitive measures against gang members may only increase their solidarity without reducing crime. The report cited the success of several programs over a 17-year period and concluded the following:

Rather than promoting antigang rhetoric and programs, policy makers should expand evidence-based approaches to help former gang members and all youth acquire the skills and opportunities they need to contribute to healthy and vibrant communities.[82]

The study of gangs is important to an understanding of the specific theories of cultural transmission developed by sociologists and criminologists. These theories may also be viewed in terms of both classic anomie and modern anomie/strain theories. We begin with a classic analysis of the impact of social class and subculture on delinquency.

The Lower-Class Boy and Middle-Class Measuring Rod

The 1955 publication of Albert K. Cohen's *Delinquent Boys*[83] set the stage for a new look at subculture theories as an explanation for delinquency. Cohen focused on young males who lived in economically disadvantaged neighborhoods but who were judged by the standards of the more affluent population. This discussion utilizes Cohen's language, as he referred to the "lower-class boy and the middle-class measuring rod." According to Cohen, the lower-class boy accepted the goals of the middle class but was unable to meet those goals by socially approved means. He was required to function within institutions that were run by middle-class people who judged him according to their standards and who expected everyone to strive for accomplishments and to succeed.

Cohen argued that the lower-class boy did not have the prior socialization that the middle-class boy had and thus was unprepared for aspiring to and achieving middle-class goals. He had been socialized to live for the present and to place more value on physical aggression than did the middle-class boy. He was less likely to have played with educational toys as a child, and he had lower aspirations. He found himself deprived of status compared with middle-class norms, and his life was further complicated because he accepted middle-class standards. He learned this acceptance from his parents, who wanted him to achieve at a higher level than they had, from the mass media, from the realization that some people did move up in the social hierarchy, and from the cultural emphasis on competition. The lower-class boy learned that the way to status and success was to adopt middle-class values, but he was not able to do so. The results were low self-esteem and major adjustment problems. To answer these problems, lower-class boys developed a subculture that inverted middle-class values.

Cohen said that the subculture was *nonutilitarian* (boys stole items "for the hell of it," not necessarily out of need), *malicious* (boys delighted in the discomfort they caused others), *negativistic* (the boys' norms were opposite those of society), and *versatile* (boys stole a variety of items). Two other characteristics were *short-run hedonism* (an emphasis on momentary pleasures) and *group automony* (resistance to outside pressures to conform).

Most of the reviews of Cohen's book have been positive; moreover, his theory has been given considerable recognition in sociological literature. Nevertheless, some criticisms have been raised. Cohen's statement that the lower-class boy measures himself by middle-class norms has been questioned. Cohen himself noted that some lower-class boys might not be concerned about middle-class values. But he argued that most children sought the approval of adults with whom they had significant contacts. Critics responded that Cohen was not convincing, and if there are class differences in socialization, it is reasonable to expect that they will affect the lower-class boy's perspective of how he is perceived by middle-class people. In addition, Cohen's description of the delinquent subculture as nonutilitarian, malicious, and negativistic has been criticized. Some of the activities Cohen described are not characteristic of lower-class gangs today but are characteristic of some middle-class delinquent groups, which were excluded from Cohen's theories. In contrast, many of today's lower-class gang activities are much more serious than those Cohen identified.[84]

Cohen's theory followed that of Merton's strain theory in that it looked at the social structure as producing the strain that leads youths to delinquent behavior. Cohen's position differed from that of Merton in that he did not place the emphasis on efforts to gain material or economic goals but, rather, on status and acceptance among one's peers.

Neutralization and Drift

In one sense, the *techniques of neutralization* approach developed by Gresham Sykes and David Matza and Matza's theory of *delinquency and drift* are social-process theories. They are considered here (rather than in Chapter 6) because of their relationship to the subculture theories, which involve an analysis of the social structure.

In stating their theory, Sykes and Matza attacked Cohen's assertion that delinquents develop values that differ from those of middle-class adult society as a reaction to their initial failure to accept those values and meet middle-class goals. First, Sykes and Matza argued that if delinquents had established a subculture with norms that differed from those of the larger society, they would not have exhibited shame or guilt when violating the social order. Second, many juvenile delinquents admire law-abiding citizens. They resent the attribution of criminal or immoral behavior to those who are important to them, for example, their mothers. They appear to recognize the "moral validity of the dominant normative system in many instances." Third, juvenile delinquents distinguish between appropriate victims and persons or groups considered inappropriate targets for their activities. Finally, delinquents do internalize and accept some of society's norms.

Sykes and Matza contended that delinquents may become committed to the dominant norms but may rationalize their deviance from those norms. They described the delinquents' attitudes not as a rejection of society's values, as Cohen suggested, but as an "apologetic failure. . . . We call these justifications of deviant behavior techniques of neutralization." Sykes and Matza argued that delinquents are "at least partially committed to the dominant social order," but they may rationalize their deviance from these norms. They are not rejecting society's values, as Cohen stated, but apologizing for their failure to attain society's goals.[85]

Some scholars believe that neutralization theory cannot be tested empirically; others have emphasized its importance and maintained that it can be tested and that the theory is important in "bridging the gulf that exists between social-structural analysis and social-psychological analysis."[86] One researcher, who analyzed the self-report responses of almost 10,000 persons in the workplace, found support for neutralization theory and concluded that those who dismissed the theory were premature in their judgment.[87]

A recent analysis of the impact of neutralization theory praised the work of Robert Agnew, whose work was cited as the strongest in support of the theory. The analysis cited practical aspects of the theory in the areas of crime prevention and offender treatment, especially the latter because it involves overcoming denial and challenging rationalizations.[88]

Another recent article reported on efforts to expand neutralization theory beyond its focus on conventional value systems to encompass a larger group of offenders, maintaining that the theory "can be applied to all types of offenders regardless of the degree to which conventional or unconventional values are important to them." This conclusion was based on interviews with a sample of African American offenders described as "hardcore, active, noninstitutionalized (uncaught) drug dealers, street robbers and carjackers." These self-admitted offenders made an effort to maintain their self-images in terms of the code of the street rather than conventional norms.[89]

Delinquency and Drift

Similar to neutralization theory is David Matza's theory of *delinquency and drift*. Matza's studies of delinquency adopted an approach that he called *soft determinism*. It is a middle-of-the-road position between the extremes of the classicists, who believed that crime was the product of free will, and the positivists, who argued that crime was the result of forces beyond the criminal's control. Matza's position was that although modern-day criminologists' theories incorporate different elements of determinism compared with those of the positivists of Cesare Lombroso's day, they have gone to an extreme. Although Matza did not adopt the doctrine of free will, he did argue that some movement should be made back in that direction, hence his soft determinism. He suggested that the delinquent *drifts* between conventional and criminal behavior, "responding in turn to the demands of each, flirting now with one, now with the other, but postponing commitment, evading decision."[90]

Differential Opportunity

When Richard Cloward and Lloyd Ohlin introduced their theory of **differential opportunity**, they said that their work was influenced by two schools of thought: Durkheim's and Merton's concepts of anomie, which focused on the pressures associated with deviance, and Edwin H. Sutherland's differential association theory (discussed in Chapter 6 of this text).[91]

Cloward and Ohlin maintained that sociological and psychological factors limit a person's access to both illegitimate *and* legitimate roles but that this is not recognized by other approaches. For example, the anomie approach views individuals from the perspective of the legitimate opportunity structure. The focus is on differential access to *legitimate* means of achieving goals, but the approach assumes either that illegitimate routes to success are freely available to all or that there is little significance in any differential to their availability. Thus, anomie theory recognizes that not all persons have equal access to the approved ways of becoming (e.g., a doctor), but it does not recognize that many persons do not have easy access to unapproved methods of achieving success, such as cheating, stealing, and so on. In contrast, Sutherland's differential association theory recognizes differential access to *illegitimate* opportunities but does not recognize differential access to legitimate opportunities.

Cloward and Ohlin's theory of differential opportunity structures unites the theories of anomie and differential association and considers the individual in terms of legitimate and illegitimate systems. Differential opportunity theory contains three types of subcultures: criminal, conflict, and retreatist. *Criminal subcultures* exist primarily in lower-class neighborhoods, in which successful criminals are more available and willing to assist young people in committing crimes. Conventional role models are less available. *Conflict subcultures* feature violence as a way of gaining status. Social controls are weak, and the area is populated with failures from conventional and criminal groups. Transiency and instability create disorganization in this area, and young people turn to violence as a result of the lack of an organized way to address their frustrations. Those who fail in the conflict and criminal subcultures tend to resort to the *retreatist subculture*, which is characterized by drug use.

Differential opportunity theory fostered extensive research and provided the basis for numerous programs aimed at crime prevention.[92] Criminologist Francis T. Cullen argued that the theory is more than a variation of Merton's strain theory. Differential opportunity theory is rooted in the Chicago school of ecology, and because of that, some have relegated it to historical status only. Cullen suggested that the theory be reexamined for its potential contributions to an analysis of crime causation.[93]

One of the problems with differential opportunity theory is the lack of precise, measurable definitions of the relevant concepts. In addition, Cloward and Ohlin did not specify the degree of organization that is required for a gang to fall within their theoretical framework. The empirical validity of the theory needs further analysis and testing.[94]

Despite these criticisms, differential opportunity theory identified an important element in the development of deviant behavior: the differences in the deviant's perceptions of the availability of illegitimate compared with legitimate opportunities and the belief in a greater chance of success through illegitimate sources.

Education and Delinquency

Violence in U.S. schools at all levels is a concern, as noted in Exhibit 5.5, which features recent data on school crime

EXHIBIT 5.5

School Crime and Safety: 2009

Violence in our nation's schools has been an issue in recent years, with national and international media attention focused on school shootings involving high schools as well as colleges and universities and even middle and elementary schools. In 2009 the Bureau of Justice Statistics (BJS) presented data from numerous sources to depict the nature and extent of school crime. Most of the data were based on 2007 (or 2007–2008) figures and include the following results:

- Students aged 12–18 encountered more nonfatal crimes during school hours than during nonschool hours. Both the rates for violent crime and for theft were higher at school than away from school.

- The crimes rates between 1992 and 2007 declined, but the rates between 2004 and 2007 did not decline.

- 4 percent of students said they were victimized at school during the previous six months, but most did not report serious victimizations.

- Black and Hispanic compared to white male students reported more threats and injuries from a weapon during school hours.

- Teachers in city schools reported threats of injuries or injuries more frequently than teachers in rural schools. Secondary school teachers reported more threats than elementary school teachers, but the latter reported more physical attacks.

- 85 percent of public school teachers reported that crimes occurred in their schools; 75 percent reported that violent crimes occurred, with 17 percent reporting serious violent incidents.

- 25 percent of teachers reported that student bullying occurred on a daily or weekly basis.

- 20 percent of public schools reported that gang acts occurred.

- 23 percent of students reported that their school had gangs.

- 22 percent of all students in grades 9–12 reported that they were offered, given, or sold illegal drugs.

- 10 percent of students aged 12–18 reported that they were victims of hate words, and 35 percent said they had seen hate words displayed (e.g., in graffiti).

- 32 percent of teachers reported that student absences affected their teaching, and 34 percent strongly agreed that their teaching was disrupted by bad student behavior.

- Students also reported that some of their classmates carried weapons, leading other student to fear for their safety; that they were afraid of being attacked by other students at school; that they had consumed alcohol on school property (45 percent in grades 9–12 had consumed alcohol in school or elsewhere); and that they had refused to attend a school function because of fear of violence.[1]

---

1. Rachel Dinkes et al., Bureau of Justice Statistics, *Indicators of School Crime and Safety: 2009* (10 December 2009), pp. v–vii, http://bjs.ojp.usdoj.gov/content/pub/pdf/iscs09.pdf, accessed 3 October 2010.

---

and safety. Attempts to explain school violence often focus on the fact that delinquents, compared to nondeliquents, are more likely to have poor educational achievements. What is not clear is why this is the case. Although there is some recent evidence that delinquents may have a lack of understanding of how their behavior affects educational goals,[95] researchers have also looked at the structure of educational institutions in an attempt to explain these and other criminal and delinquent acts. One of the approaches involved an extension of differential opportunity theory.

One measure of poor educational achievements is the extent of school dropouts. In a study of delinquency and school dropouts, Delbert S. Elliott and Harwin L. Voss attempted to modify and expand the differential opportunity theory of Cloward and Ohlin. Unlike Cloward and Ohlin, Elliott and Voss studied both genders and all social classes. The guiding principle for this extension of differential opportunity theory was that "both delinquent behavior and dropping out are alternative responses to failure, alienation, and selective exposure to these forms of behavior." Of the three contexts in which Elliott and Voss studied delinquency

and dropouts—the home, the school, and the community— the school would be the most important. For male and female dropouts, the strongest predictors were academic failure, school normlessness and social isolation, exposure to a dropout in the home, and commitment to peers. School "dropout is related to class while delinquency is not," and "a strong commitment to one's peers was conducive to delinquency, regardless of the extent of delinquency in that group." Elliott and Voss concluded that "peer culture itself is conducive to delinquency."[96]

The results of the Elliott and Voss study, shown in the following list, are relevant because they challenge the conclusions of some other cultural transmission studies of delinquency:

1. There appeared to be no relationship between delinquent behavior and social class or ethnic origins.

2. The degree to which students participated in extracurricular activities was not predictive of delinquency.

3. Delinquency among females compared with that of males was more frequently a response to alienation and rejection.

4. For males and females, the school context was more important socially than home or community.

5. Associations with delinquent friends, along with alienation and normlessness, were both causes and results of delinquency in both males and females.[97]

Refer back to Exhibit 5.2, which listed factors predictive of future violence. In elaborating on the school factors, the publication noted that academic failure, truancy, poor-quality schools, and dropping out of school have long been recognized as predictive of youth violence. The predictive value of poor academic achievement and subsequent violence has long been recognized and is higher for girls than for boys.

Other studies have associated school factors with truancy or delinquency. After reviewing the research, one scholar concluded as follows: "A variety of school-related variables have been consistently linked to delinquent behavior, including commitment to school, involvement in school, attendance at school, school social bonds, and school climate." The scholar continued: "Although these studies have provided valuable insights into the relationship between schools and delinquency, they have failed to address the influence of multiple levels (e.g., individuals and schools) associated with school delinquency." The scholar attempted to remedy this shortcoming of previous research by looking at individual and school-related factors and their relationship to school misbehavior. He found that "higher levels of school attachment, school commitment, and belief in school rules are associated with lower levels of misbehavior in school" and that "larger schools in urban areas explain variations in school misbehavior." He recommended more extensive research on the relationship between individual and school-related factors on student misbehavior.[98]

The importance of education in understanding delinquency and future adult criminality requires a reminder not to assume that the frequency with which poor academic performance occurs with delinquency[99] means that it *causes* that delinquency. In fact, in an extensive study published recently, the investigators concluded that although delinquency and academic failure often occur together, the delinquency is not *caused* by educational failure. Rather, the differences in academic performance appear related to differences in self-control. "In sum, our evidence suggests delinquency is not a response to academic failure."[100]

With regard to education, the variable of race is also important. An examination of adult incarceration rates of African Americans who attended predominantly black high schools compared to those who attended predominantly integrated schools disclosed that the incarceration rates were significantly higher among those from predominantly black high schools. These differentials increased over time.[101]

Finally, a structural analysis of the impact of education as a link to delinquency should also consider the impact of the family, which is discussed later in this chapter.

The Lower-Class Boy and Lower-Class Culture

Walter B. Miller focused his cultural transmission theory of delinquency on what he termed lower-class delinquents responding to lower-class cultures. First, Miller viewed the lower class as characterized by a *female-based household*; the family is organized around a woman. Men may be present but not in the stable form of marriage that was characteristic of the middle and upper classes. When present, the man in the lower class did not participate as fully in the rearing of children and in the economic support of the family as did men of other social classes. Second, Miller stated that the *one-sex peer* unit was the most significant unit for men and was the focus of other social classes.[102]

Miller viewed the lower class as characterized by six *focal concerns*, which he defined as "areas or issues which command widespread and persistent attention and a high degree of emotional involvement." He labeled these concerns as *trouble, toughness, smartness, excitement, fate,* and *autonomy,* resulting in a *cultural system* that distinguished the lower class from the middle and upper classes. Miller argued that this cultural system was growing more distinctive and that the size of the group that shared the tradition was also growing larger.

In contrast to Cohen's theory that the lower-class boy was engaging in reaction formation against middle-class values that he could not attain, Miller suggested that lower-class values came from the inherent characteristics of the lower class itself. When lower-class males acted according to the focal concerns that dominated the socialization within their social class, they conflicted with middle-class values.

An ecological study in Portland, Oregon, led the investigator to conclude that Miller's theory, although relevant as a tool for understanding the African American lower class, was not applicable to all lower-class areas.[103] A study in Seattle, Washington, reported that social class was not a significant factor in predicting delinquency.[104]

Evaluation of Cultural Transmission Theories

Cultural transmission theorists seek to explain the high rates of delinquency in the lower class as well as in subcultures. These researchers deserve a significant place in criminology, but their social class emphasis has limitations. They are criticized for placing too much emphasis on poverty and class delinquency, especially gangs. However, perhaps they responded to public concerns, fears, and demands for action, much like the current pressure on social scientists to study terrorism and homeland security.

Nevertheless, critics of the emphasis have a point, as noted in the research of James F. Short and F. Ivan Nye, who reminded us years ago that most people commit acts for which they could be adjudicated delinquent or criminal (although the extent and severity of the delinquent and criminal activity vary) and that social class is not significantly related to criminal behavior among the general population.[105]

John Hagan's research found that class was an important variable in explaining delinquent and criminal behavior but that the middle or upper class might be as significant as the lower class. Hagan concluded that access to *power* might be as important as lack of access to power.[106] In short, multiple factors might be involved in the analysis of social class and crime or delinquency, and the results may differ according to whether one uses official data or self-report studies as measures of crime and delinquency.[107]

Another issue involved in cultural transmission theories is how social class is measured. The usual measure is income (or in the case of juveniles, parental income). Francis T. Cullen and his collaborators, who reviewed the literature on delinquency and class, reported that the results varied according to how delinquency was measured. Furthermore, in their study of adolescents in a small midwestern town, these investigators "did not find class differences in reported delinquency" on either of two scales used for the research, but they did find that "having money enhances rather than diminishes delinquency." Delinquency may be a pleasurable pursuit, not a desperate move to acquire status. The more money adolescents have, the more likely they are to engage in **status offenses**, alcohol and other drug violations, and property crimes, although the amount of money to which they have access does not seem to affect their involvement in violent crimes.[108]

The relationship between social class and delinquent or criminal behavior is complex and confusing. As one critic noted, "Depending mainly on the measure of social class used, the relationship between class and violence is nonexistent, moderate, or relatively strong."[109]

Exhibit 5.6 contains a summary of cultural transmission theories and their forerunners.

Crime and the Family

A traditional approach to the link between the family and delinquency is that delinquency and broken homes are related variables. In Chapter 4, brief attention was given to the early studies associating crime and family structure. Several theories already discussed in this chapter relate delinquency to the family. Recent research suggests that the relationship between crime and delinquency and the family is complex. We look first at family social structures and then at family power relationships.

Family Social Structures

A recent reconsideration of the research on broken homes and delinquency reported the following:

- The research does not find consistent relationships between broken homes and severe offending.
- Research shows that many children from broken homes do not become delinquent.
- Separation and divorce of the parents "are more strongly associated with delinquency than are single-parent households per se."[110]

There is also evidence that the disruption of a family may influence children to engage in delinquent behavior at various times in their development. Thus, it may be necessary to analyze the relationship between a broken home and delinquent behavior over time.[111]

The type of family structure may also be important. For example, there is some evidence that behavior differs in terms of whether a child is living with two biological parents who are married compared to a child living with two unmarried biological parents and whether there are children by other relationships within the family structure. There is also evidence of "an unusually high rate of antisocial behavior" among children who live with one biological parent who cohabits with a nonbiological parent, especially if the custodial parent is the biological father.[112]

One key to understanding these research reports is to examine how schools react to their students' family structures. Officials are more likely to intervene in the families of adolescents when the adolescent in question is a girl with a mother but no father in the home. Another family structure that is considered predictive of delinquency is that of an adolescent boy with a stepfather in the home. Although there is evidence that some family structures are not closely related to delinquency,[113] other research has found some relationship between adult criminality and (1) family structure,[114] (2) family size (with delinquent and criminal behavior more frequent among those from large families),[115] and (3) the absence of one parent, although that relationship is not strong and exists mainly in cases of status offenses.[116]

The abuse of children within the family is also important in a consideration of the link between families and crime. Studies have revealed subsequent delinquency by both male and female child abuse victims, with more extensive delinquency reported among the victims of more severe abuse.[117] Furthermore, substance abuse by parents prior to conception as well as by the mother during pregnancy may cause injury to a fetus. Some of these children later exhibit disruptive behavior.[118]

EXHIBIT 5.6

Cultural Transmission Theories and Their Forerunners: A Summary

Gangs

Early developments were by **Frederic M. Thrasher**, who studied juvenile gangs in Chicago and viewed them as the result of social disorganization, which emerged as innocent play groups that encountered conflict over space in the crowded and physically deteriorated areas of the inner city. Thrasher's approach was disputed by **William F. Whyte**, who believed that slums were characterized by social organization, not disorganization, but that young people living there may face a conflict between the status system of their culture within the slums and the system of mainstream society. Recent research suggests that today's gangs differ significantly from these earlier ones, that they are often associated with violence and drugs, that race may be a factor, and that girls and young women are also affiliated with gangs.

The Lower-Class Boy and Middle-Class Measuring Rod

Albert K. Cohen's theory focuses on young males who live in economically disadvantaged neighborhoods but who are judged by middle-class standards, which they accept but are unable to meet because they lack proper socialization. The result is the development of a subculture that is nonutilitarian, malicious, negativistic, versatile, and characterized by short-run hedonism and group autonomy.

Neutralization and Drift

Gresham Sykes and **David Matza** disagreed with Cohen's position and argued instead that delinquents have developed values that differ from those of the middle class; in effect, they neutralize middle-class values.

Differential Opportunity

Richard Cloward and **Lloyd Ohlin** argued that sociological and psychological factors limit a person's access to both illegitimate and legitimate roles and, in their analysis of delinquency, focused on the differential access to *legitimate* means of achieving goals. They developed three types of subcultures: criminal, conflict, and retreatist. An attempt to modify and verify this approach was made by **Delbert S. Elliott** and **Harwin L. Voss**, who viewed delinquency and school dropouts in terms of academic failure, school normlessness and social isolation, exposure to a dropout in the home, and commitment to peers.

The Lower-Class Boy and Lower-Class Culture

Walter B. Miller's position was that lower-class boys who become delinquent are responding to a lower-class culture, which is characterized by a female-based household and the one-sex peer unit. Miller viewed the social structure of this class in terms of six focal concerns: trouble, toughness, smartness, excitement, fate, and autonomy, which combine to distinguish lower-class from middle-class culture.

There is also evidence that physical, emotional, psychological, sexual, and other forms of abuse of young children are associated with subsequent behavior problems, especially delinquent behavior. "The basic hypothesis is that exposure to any type of abusive condition disrupts the normal course of development and leads to maladaptive behaviors, including delinquency and drug use at later ages." This approach can be explained through developmental psychology, which emphasizes the impact of early childhood experiences on later behavior. But contemporary researchers emphasize that subsequent life events may impact behavior, even to the point of neutralizing early experiences. Thus, by dividing childhood maltreatment into four categories—never, childhood-only, adolescence-only, and persistent—and comparing the categories with subsequent delinquency and drug use, researchers found:

■ "no relationship between childhood-only maltreatment and adolescent delinquency or drug use; [but]. . .

■ a consistent impact of adolescence-only and persistent maltreatment on [adolescent delinquency or drug use]."[119]

Basing their study on a reconstruction of the research data of Sheldon Glueck and Eleanor Glueck (discussed in Chapter 4), Robert J. Sampson and John H. Laub found that although childhood family experiences are important, adult family experiences are also influential. Specifically, Sampson and Laub found that "job stability and marital attachment in adulthood are significantly related to changes in adult crime—the stronger the adult ties to work and family, the less crime and deviance."[120]

Sampson and Laub published a book about their expansion of the Gluecks' research. One scholar called this book a "tour de force in criminology. It brings to fruition Sheldon and Eleanor Glueck's pioneering research on juvenile delinquency, which, until now, has never completely received its rightful acclaim." The reviewer called Sampson and Laub "consummate theorists and statisticians" and noted that their work enhanced our understanding of social control theory (discussed in Chapter 6):

In a nutshell, when people have a reason and an opportunity to become interested in their school work, families, and jobs, they are more likely to view crime as a costly and untenable option—a basic message that should be heeded by policymakers interested in alleviating America's intractable crime problem.[121]

Refer again to Exhibit 5.2, which enumerates the factors found to be associated with youth violence. One group of those is family factors. Research on family factors has shown the following:

1. Juveniles with criminal fathers are much more likely to commit juvenile offenses or criminal acts.

2. Persons who are sexually abused (or physically abused in other ways) as children are more likely than others to engage in delinquent and criminal acts.

3. Lack of good family management is associated with subsequent delinquency and substance abuse. Poor family management includes lack of clear parental expectations, poor supervision and monitoring by parents, and severe and inconsistent discipline.

4. Low levels of parental involvement in children's activities may precipitate aggressive and violent behavior.

5. Exposure to high levels of parental discord may increase the probability of delinquent behavior.

6. Positive parental attitudes toward substance abuse may increase the chances the children will become violent.

7. Separation of children from their parents before those children are 10 may predict future violence.[122]

Another family structure issue that has been related to delinquency is that of the mother's age at the birth of her first child. Specifically, it has been shown that children born to younger mothers are more likely to engage in subsequent delinquency and violence and be arrested than are children whose mothers were older when they began childbearing. The relationship is much greater among white and Hispanic than among African American children. Research suggests that "early childbearing may initiate a cycle of adversity that affects multiple, subsequent generations."[123]

It is important to consider that the *type* of parenting, not the structure of the family, is the key variable linking the family to a child's delinquent behavior. Chapter 6 examines the theory of self-control as an explanation of delinquency and crime, and the major proponents of that theory maintain that effective parenting is directly related to the development of self-control. To develop proper self-control in their children, parents must monitor their behavior, recognize any deviance that occurs, and punish inappropriate behavior. It is maintained that parents must perform all three of these functions effectively to instill appropriate self-control in children and that self-control will insulate the children from delinquency.[124]

In a recent study of this approach, researchers reported "that low self-control is positively associated with involvement in delinquency." However, they also found that parenting "influences an individual's risk for delinquency in more ways than simply through its impact on self-control." They cited research on some of the possibilities (such as poor parenting creating anger in a child) and recommended more research on these issues.[125]

Poor parenting can be the result of a number of factors, one of which is power relationships, which has led researchers to develop an approach called **power-control theory**.

Family Power Relationships: Power-Control Theory

Social control theories of delinquent and criminal behavior are discussed in Chapter 6. Feminist theories are discussed later in this chapter. An approach that blends these theories while building on the Marxist tradition (also discussed later in this chapter) and that is relevant to this chapter's discussion of social-structural theories is *power-control theory*. The primary thesis of power-control theory is that authority within the workplace affects power within the family structure. These power relationships between parents affect the way they socialize and control their sons and daughters. Those practices "influence gender differences in both perceived risks of sanctions and risk preferences," which are "translated into gender differences in delinquency."[126]

In the words of power-control theory's major proponent, John Hagan, and his colleagues, "The core assumption of our theory is that the presence of power and the absence of control create conditions of freedom that permit common forms of delinquency."[127] The authors tested their theory on a Toronto, Canada, population. After responding to their critics, they proclaimed that the theory had merit.[128]

Hagan's power-control theory is an example of Marxist theory that introduces us to another factor ignored by many researchers—gender. According to Hagan, power-control theory "asserts that the class structure of the family plays a significant role in explaining the social distribution of delinquent behavior through the social reproduction of gender relations."[129] Parental power affects delinquency in terms of the way children are socialized into accepted gender roles. Parental power is linked to factors within the family as well as to the workforce outside the family.

In the development of power-control theory, Hagan and others noted that gender is important in explaining delinquency because most *reported* delinquent acts are committed by boys. Class is not as important as many theorists have claimed, but class and gender are seldom analyzed in the same study, a serious omission. Hagan and his associates also considered the power relationships of husbands *and* wives, emphasizing that the family's power structure is determined by the wife's outside employment as well as by that of the husband. In families characterized as *patriarchal* (meaning that the husband/father assumes the traditional breadwinner role and the wife/mother the traditional domestic role), fathers have more power and resources at work and at home, while mothers have less power, less ownership, and fewer resources at work and at home. This has been the dominant family type in contemporary Western industrial societies. Women are expected to keep greater control over their daughters, socializing them in traditional female gender roles. The daughter will have less freedom to take risks and engage in nontraditional gender behavior. When daughters are groomed for domestic life, their delinquency is not likely.

The opposite of the patriarchal is the *matriarchal* family, in which the female has the dominant work job and more power and resources at work and at home. In more balanced, or *egalitarian,* family structures, husbands and wives have jobs with similar power and authority, which is reflected in more equal authority and power within the family. The roles mothers and fathers play within the family are different. In the egalitarian family, daughters "gain a kind of freedom that is reflected in a reduced control by fathers and mothers and an increased openness to risk taking that, among adolescents, includes some common forms of delinquent behavior."[130]

Power-control theory states that as families become more balanced, there are changes in the ways parents socialize their children. And it might be expected that females would be more likely to take risks and become involved in traditionally male-oriented activities, including delinquency.

Although Hagan began his power-control theory development in an attempt to explain why males are generally more involved than females in delinquent behavior, in a later study he and his colleagues extended the theory to include the variable of how parental influence and support for dominant attitudes affect male as well as female delinquency. They found that differences in family structure, especially within patriarchal families, result in variations in the way families interact. This is particularly true with regard to the interaction between mothers and their sons. Hagan and others found support for their belief that in less patriarchal families, "the most pronounced effects of changes in family life may be in altering the control of sons by mothers." Specifically, mothers may reduce the impact of traditional patriarchal roles of power, "thereby discouraging a preference [among their sons] for risks and delinquency."[131]

Some researchers have questioned the validity of the approaches of Hagan and others. One critic, quoting from Hagan, suggested that Hagan's approach "deals not so much with a testable theory of crime as it does with the means by which 'meaningful questions about crime and delinquency can be asked, and begin to be answered.'"[132]

Another challenger to power-control theory suggested that the assumption that the type of household or family structure influences gender perceptions of risks and of being caught is not complete. The power-control position that females, compared with males, perceive a greater risk in being caught and punished if they engage in delinquent or criminal behavior and that the perception is greater for females reared in patriarchal family structures is supported but limited. It fails to account for the influence of informal social controls on females—specifically, the fear of shame or embarrassment. It is argued that research supports the belief that these factors "are at least equally [as], if not more, important for females" and that "among those individuals reared in more patriarchal households, the perceived threat of shame accounts for a significant proportion of the gender-crime relationship."[133]

There is also evidence that, although power-control variables explained gender differences among adolescents in the use of alcohol and tobacco, they did not explain victimization or support the position that mothers have more influence than fathers in controlling their children. There are indications, however, that mothers are more influential in controlling daughters, and fathers have more control over their sons.[134]

Despite the various attempts to test Hagan's theory of power control, it is difficult to draw conclusions regarding the theory's ability to explain crime because the studies do not involve a consistent definition of the variable of *power.*

The Routine Activity Approach

Another social-structural approach to explaining crime is the **routine activity approach**. In examining this approach, keep in mind that it was developed to explain crime victimization, and its popularity coincides with the development of studies of this area of criminal justice systems. Students might relate to some of this discussion in terms of their own lifestyles—both parents working long hours, eating from fast food takeouts on the way to soccer practice or even breakfast on the way to school, arriving home in the dark and so on—with such lifestyles providing the backdrop for the development of the routine activity approach.

Lawrence Cohen and Marcus Felson, who developed the routine activity approach, stated that crime may be explained as the convergence of three elements: (1) likely offenders (people who are motivated to commit crimes), (2) suitable targets (the presence of things that are valued and that can be transported fairly easily), and (3) absence of capable guardians (people to prevent the criminal activity). Human ecology is used to explain how legal activities increase the probability of illegal activities. For example, the movement of women into the workforce reduces the number of women at home during the day and increases the absence of capable guardians. Two-income families have greater spending power, and this may increase the number of desirable goods or suitable targets for crime. If these two elements converge in time and space with likely offenders, the crime rate increases. The absence of one of these elements may inhibit or prevent crime. Furthermore, "the convergence in time and space of suitable targets and the absence of capable guardians can lead to large increases in crime rates without any increase or change in the structural conditions that motivate individuals to engage in crime."[135]

In a private letter to this author, Felson explained his approach more fully as follows:

> The idea of the routine activity approach is to *bypass* traditional sociological theories, including those dealing with motivation and those of Cloward and Ohlin. Indeed, I selected the term "routine activity" to *distinguish* this approach from differential opportunity, which means something entirely different from what I mean. I also deliberately avoided the word "theory," calling it instead an "approach," hoping that this might exempt it from the usual muddle.[136]

Felson emphasized that his concept of *guardians* goes beyond formal guardians (such as the police and other actors in criminal justice systems) and extends to even more important guardians, such as the individuals who live in the community or even strangers who are willing to help prevent crime therein. Thus, it is the informal social control system that works to reduce and prevent crime within communities.[137]

Researchers have found the routine activity approach useful in explaining urban homicides,[138] the relevance of places (such as taverns and barrooms) in explaining crime rates,[139] youth victimization,[140] the victimization of single-parent families,[141] the differences between violence among men and women,[142] and the subculture of violence.[143] The routine activity approach has been linked with property crimes in general[144] and consumer fraud in particular,[145] along with street robberies.[146] It has been the foundation of an analysis of reactions to natural disasters, such as Florida's Hurricane Andrew.[147]

The routine activity approach has also been extended to feminist studies, which are discussed in greater detail later in this chapter. It has been applied to an analysis of sexual assaults of females by male college and university students,[148] resulting in such findings as men who drink heavily are more likely to be abusers and women who drink heavily, especially with their abusive dates, are more likely to be victimized or, in the words of routine activity, to become "suitable targets." These results concerning alcohol use do not apply strongly to drug use. However, there was evidence that male college and university students who were encouraged or supported by their peers to engage in sexually abusive behavior were more likely to do so than those who did not receive such encouragement or support. The most significant finding was that undergraduate men "who drank two or more times a week and who had friends who gave them peer support for both emotional and physical partner abuse were more than nine times as likely to report committing sexual abuse as men reporting none of these three characteristics." The authors concluded that teaching college and university women self-defense tactics and conducting rape awareness campaigns are not sufficient. "The male peer support network that legitimizes rape must be attacked and dismantled before women will be truly safer on campus."[149]

The routine activity approach has also been used to study victimization and criminal activity in other countries, finding some support in urban China with regard

Neighborhoods with high rates of criminal offenders may also have high rates of victimization. Each year, the Mardi Gras parade and other festivities in New Orleans bring a lot of joy, but as this little 3-year-old holds out her hands for trinkets, the background signs stating "Enough" are reminders, placed by church members, to symbolize that the residents of that neighborhood have been victimized by violent crime far too often.

to property offenses but noting that some flexibility is to adapt the approach to the distinct sociocultural features of the Chinese social structure.[150]

The routine activity approach has been utilized in policy analyses. For example, research indicated that adolescents were more likely to become involved in delinquent or criminal acts when they were involved in groups with unstructured and unsupervised time.[151] As a result, many jurisdictions established after-school programs to keep youths occupied in constructive legal activities. Analyses of some of those programs found positive results in the form of reduced delinquency and victimizations, especially when more highly educated staff were employed; when the programs were small in numbers of participants; when male staff were involved; and when youths were taught general social skills, self-management, and drug resistance.[152] This suggests that the use of the routine activity approach "provides a platform from which to expand and enrich our understanding of factors that influence program effectiveness."[153]

It can be concluded that although the routine activity approach has not been sufficiently tested, "most of the research done so far reports findings consistent with the theory."[154]

The routine activity approach is summarized in Exhibit 5.7.

The Conflict Perspective

Earlier in this chapter, we noted Durkheim's position that crime is functional and normal. A society that permits any kind of deviation can expect negative deviation and thus crime. We have seen that some scholars believe laws emerge because societies understand the need to institute a more formal system of social control. The laws emerge out of **consensus**. In addition, social scientists have conducted numerous studies of criminals and compared them with noncriminals under the assumption that these are two distinct groups.

These and other aspects of the traditional approaches to the study of crime are rejected by those who believe that laws emerge out of **conflict**, not consensus. Laws are enacted by those in power as a means of controlling those who are not in power. Furthermore, criminals do not necessarily differ from noncriminals, except possibly in the way society *reacts* to their behavior. Thus, a person who embezzles millions of dollars from his or her company may be handled quietly by the company's management, whereas a hungry homeless person who takes food from the farmers' market may be processed through the criminal justice system. Members of minority groups may be treated more harshly than those who come from the majority; women and men may be treated differently. Power and conflict may explain these differences.

The consensus approach views the emerging norms and laws of society as representative of the common feeling about what is right and proper; that is, they represent a consensus of views—a mechanism for maintaining social order. The conflict perspective holds that norms, values, and laws create dissension. Conflict thinkers do not agree on the nature of this process; in fact, they do not agree on what to call it. Nor have the thinkers in this field agreed with one another over time; for some, the process has been evolving, and their most recent positions differ from their earlier ones.

Background of the Modern Conflict Approach

Many of today's scholars trace modern criminology conflict theory back to the social and economic upheavals of the 1960s, including racial conflicts and the civil rights movement, protests against the Vietnam War, the recognition of inmates' constitutional rights, and the beginning of the modern feminist movement. The conflict approach can be traced much further back in history, however, and some scholars have done so. The study is a fascinating and informative one. In criminology, particular attention is given to the works of Karl Marx and Friedrich Engels and the impact their writings have had on theoretical and political perspectives.[155]

Marx has had a significant impact on the thinking and policies of the modern world. His works, along with those of Engels, were not focused directly on crime, but they have implications for its study.

EXHIBIT 5.7

Routine Activity Approach: A Summary

As stated by **Lawrence Cohen** and **Marcus Felson**, routine activity views crime as resulting from the convergence of three elements:

- Likely offenders (people who are motivated to commit crimes)
- Suitable targets (the presence of things that are valued and that can be transported fairly easily)
- The absence of capable guardians (people to prevent the criminal activity)

The emphasis is on a crime of places rather than a crime of persons. The approach has been tested in various settings and extended to feminist studies.

In the conflict perspective of Marx and Engels, crime may be viewed in terms of the social structure characterized by social class conflict, which they saw as an inevitable by-product of capitalism. Marx and Engels argued that private ownership of property resulted in the poverty of some members of society, as those who owned the means of production exploited those who did not. The latter turn to crime as a result of poverty. Marx and Engels believed that the capitalist system was the sole determinant of crime as well as the causative element in all social, political, religious, ethical, psychological, and material life—and that the only way to eliminate social problems was to change the system through social revolution. They believed that eliminating social class would eliminate conflict. Crime could be abolished. Obviously, this position differed from that of Durkheim's functional approach, which maintained that crime was a normal and inevitable part of society.

The deterministic approach of Marx and Engels may be contrasted to the *facilitating* approach of Frank Tannenbaum. Tannenbaum argued that criminals were as much a part of the community as scholars, inventors, scientists, and businesspersons and that the community must provide a facilitating environment for their behavior to exist. According to Tannenbaum, the community facilitated the development of criminal methods as well as its ideals and goals.[156]

A similar view was taken by Willem A. Bonger, a Dutch criminologist who examined the lives of primitive peoples and noted that they were characterized by altruism. This altruistic way of life, based on mutual help, could be explained only by the social environment, which was determined by the mode of production. Among these people, production was for personal consumption and not for trade. Furthermore, neither private property nor wealth existed. When food was abundant, all were fed; when it was scarce, all were hungry. Primitive people were subordinate to nature, and they were not egotistic. Society was characterized by social solidarity, which was the result of the economic system.[157]

In contrast, in a capitalist system, Bonger argued, people concentrated only on themselves, and that led to selfishness. Capitalism bred social irresponsibility and contributed to crime. It did not determine criminal behavior but made people more capable of becoming criminals. The economic system provided a *climate of motivation* for criminal behavior. Although influenced by Marx and his economic determinism, Bonger recognized the influence of facilitating factors in the environment.[158]

Bonger's theory was tested by scholars who examined international data from 100 countries. They found support for Bonger's position that capitalism is an important predictor of homicide rates, thus linking capitalism with crime. However, they found that demoralization (which they determined by measuring corruption) did not appear to be the link between capitalism and homicide, as Bonger had maintained. They concluded that their research, "showing the link between capitalism and homicide in countries with predominant Eastern religions," could be integrated with other criminological theories and that it reinforced Bonger's contributions to an understanding of criminal behavior.[159]

Culture and Group Conflict

Conflict may exist between cultures, between subcultures within cultures, and between interest groups. **Culture conflict theory** is concerned with the first of these possibilities and is illustrated by the work of sociologist Thorsten Sellin. Sellin maintained that criminal acts must be analyzed as conflicts among norms. For every person, there is a right (normal) and wrong (abnormal) way of acting in specific situations, and these conduct norms are defined by the groups to which the individual belongs. In the process of social differentiation, these norms clash with other norms; culture conflict is the inevitable result of conflict between conduct norms.

Sellin distinguished between *primary conflict*, which occurs when the norms of two cultures clash, and *secondary conflict*, which occurs within the evolution of a single culture. The first was exemplified by a father from Sicily who, while living in New Jersey, killed the man who seduced his 16-year-old daughter. The father was surprised to be arrested for committing a crime. In his country, such an act by a father was viewed as a defense of the family's honor. In contrast to primary conflicts, secondary conflicts "grow out of the process of social differentiation which characterizes the evolution of our own culture." Secondary conflicts develop when, during the normal growth of cultures from homogeneous to heterogeneous, social differentiation occurs. This in turn produces different social groupings, each with its own values and a lack of understanding of the other groups' values. The result is an increase in social conflict.[160]

Some criminologists disagree with Sellin's thesis that criminals and delinquents are responding to different norms. They argued that they are responding to the same norms, but there is a scarcity of rewards associated with those norms. Perhaps the way to resolve these differences is to recognize that cultural conflicts may account for some types of crime, especially among subculture groups, such as gangs, and among the foreign born, but that they do not explain all types of crime.

Conflict may also exist between interest groups within the same society, an approach developed by sociologist George B. Vold. Vold did not suggest that the conflicts between groups were *caused* by any abnormality. Rather, they were made by "natural human beings struggling in understandably normal and natural situations for the maintenance of the way of life to which they stand committed."[161] Examples are racial conflicts that involve violence between interest groups and the violent behavior accompanying conflict between the interest groups of management and labor. The focus is on conflicts between interest groups, not between subcultures or cultures. The conflict is thus "one of the principal and essential social processes in the functioning of society."[162]

Power and Conflict

Conflicts between groups involve another dimension emphasized by conflict theorists—power and authority. The concept of power, meaning the ability to secure compliance from an unwilling person, has been explored by historians, sociologists, economists, and philosophers.

A prominent contributor to the power concept of conflict is Austin T. Turk, who in his early works viewed society as organized into weak and powerful groups. The powerful dictated the proper norms for all and established the sanctions imposed if those norms were violated. Turk's position has some similarities with labeling theory (discussed in Chapter 6), thereby taking a social-process approach, for he suggested that the persons most likely to be designated criminal because of their law violations are members of the society's least powerful groups.[163] Turk's position is a social-structural one in that he saw the *structure* of social institutions as relevant to the labeling process.

Turk emphasized that criminologists must study the differences between the status and roles of legal *authorities* and *subjects*. He maintained that these two roles are differentiated in all societies and that authority–subject relationships are accepted because it is felt that they are necessary for the preservation of a social order that permits individuals to coexist. The problems arise when these two groups come into conflict, which is inevitable. The more sophisticated the subjects, the more likely they are to achieve their goals without coming into conflict with authorities. The less sophisticated the subjects, the more likely they are to use alternative tactics, such as force, to achieve their goals. If the subjects engage in activities that the authorities find very reprehensible, the authorities are more likely to arrest, convict, and assess long sentences, and the more powerful the authorities are, the more successful they will be in this effort.[164] Turk defined *criminality* as "a label imposed on subjects who resist the claims and impositions of authorities."[165]

Turk's conflict theory has been criticized for dismissing research suggesting that there is considerable consensus regarding crime, a criticism leveled at most conflict theorists. Turk's approach, however—viewing crime as a status that is conferred on those who do not follow the laws of society—points out the conflict between those in power and those not in power.[166] An attempt to test Turk's position empirically led two scholars to conclude that there is some support for the theory but that it should be tested further.[167]

Criminological research literature contains numerous examples of power conflicts between groups within society in such areas as race, gender, and class. But the relationships are complex; it is unreasonable to assume that disparities are always the result of discrimination.

Exhibit 5.8 contains a summary of this discussion on conflict criminology.

EXHIBIT 5.8

The Conflict Perspective: A Summary

Conflict Theory—Deterministic

Karl Marx and **Friedrich Engels** viewed crime in terms of the social structure characterized by social class conflict, which to them was an inevitable by-product of capitalism. Capitalism produces a system in which some people live in poverty; as a result, they turn to crime.

Conflict Theory—Facilitating

Frank Tannebaum believed that the community must provide a facilitating environment before individuals may turn to criminal behavior. **Willem A. Bonger** studied primitive societies, which he viewed as characterized by altruism, meaning that individuals help one another in various ways and are not egotistic. The society is characterized by social solidarity, which results from the economic system. In contrast, the *climate of motivation* is conducive to criminal behavior, which is created by capitalism and in which people concentrate only on their own individual needs.

Culture and Group Conflict

This view was characterized by the culture conflict theory of **Thorsten Sellin**, who analyzed criminal acts as conflicts among norms. He articulated two types of conflict: primary, which occurs when two cultures clash, and secondary, which occurs within a single culture. **George B. Vold** viewed conflict as existing between interest groups within the same society. An example would be racial conflicts.

Power and Conflict

This approach emphasized that power is an important concept within the conflict perspective. **Austin T. Turk** looked at the differences between the status and roles of legal authorities and their subjects. Turk viewed political organization as the result of, and characterized by, conflicts, with those in power having some control over the goods and services that might be available to others.

Critical Criminology

The influence of the early conflict theorists and of the noted historian, journalist, economist, socialist, and philosopher Karl Marx and his contemporaries is seen in a broader scope of criminological thought that emerged in the 1970s. The approach is called **critical criminology** or **radical criminology**. The literal meaning of *radical* is "origin" or "to get to the root of." *Critical* is used in the context of "skillful judgment" or "judging with severity." Two proponents stated that *radical criminology* encompasses the process of exploring and verifying "connections between social phenomena and economic reality." The concept refers to a policy of "changing things for the better," although "there is no firm consensus or precise definition of radical criminology, either with respect to its key concepts or its primary theoretical emphasis."[168]

Karl Marx (1818–1883) wrote after the massive changes that occurred during and after the Industrial Revolution (roughly from the mid-1700s to the mid-1800s). The revolution resulted in the replacement of hand tools with machinery, the development of industries, and massive social changes. Marx attempted to explain these social changes.

The impact of the environment on human behavior had been at the center of historical attempts to explain criminal behavior for centuries before Marx wrote. One of the earliest explanations of behavior involving the environment was based on an analysis of the economic conditions of the society in which the behavior occurred. It traced the explanation of criminal behavior back to Xenophon, Plato, Aristotle, and the Romans Virgil and Horace, as well as to the utopians, including Thomas More.[169]

The philosophies and writings of Karl Marx (1818–1883) form the basis for modern conflict perspectives. Marx, along with Friedrich Engels, presented a deterministic view that had implications for understanding criminal behavior from a social-structural vantage.

These early economic explanations of human behavior can be categorized by the degree of influence the economic environment was believed to exert. The view of *economic determinism* was set forth by Marx, who advocated that private ownership of property results in poverty, which distinguishes those who own the means of production from those whom they exploit for economic benefit. The exploited may turn to crime as a result of this poverty. Marx believed that the economic system was the sole cause of crime. Although he did not specifically develop a theory of criminal causation, Marx saw the mode of production as the causative element in all social, political, religious, ethical, psychical, and material life. He saw social revolution as the only way to bring about the necessary changes in the economic system.[170]

The influence of Marx is seen in the emergence of critical criminology, which came on the heels of the social turbulence that rocked the United States in the 1960s. Social conflict between different groups affected most Americans. It caused many to admit that discrimination and economic inequality were so widespread that new approaches were required to address the nation's problems. In 1973, Ian Taylor and his colleagues published *The New Criminology*, the first noted work to challenge traditional criminology and invite a new critical look at American criminal justice systems. This volume was followed two years later by *Critical Criminology* by the same authors.[171] These classic works were followed by numerous other Marxist critiques of all aspects of criminal justice systems.

Despite the recency of critical criminology as an approach to the study of crime and the lack of unity among critical criminologists, there are at least two basic elements common to all critical theorists: (1) a reliance on economic explanations of behavior and (2) a belief that the problem of crime cannot be solved within the existing confines of capitalism. Critical theorists are also united in their conviction that the eight *serious* property and violent crimes (those included in the FBI's *Uniform Crime Reports*) are not the most serious criminal threats to an organized society. Corporate, political, and environmental crimes pose a greater danger.

Critical criminologists direct attention to how structural conditions and social class inequality affect criminal behavior and official responses to crime. The emphasis is on social and economic conditions rather than on the characteristics of individual criminals. Critical theorists draw upon a Marxist orientation to analyze social relations and processes.[172]

The critical theorists' redefinition of crime emphasizes such issues as the violations of human rights on grounds of racism and sexism, unsafe and exploitive working conditions, substandard housing, corporate fraud, political and military crimes, inadequate medical care, and environmental pollution. It also emphasizes the lack of opportunity for every person to excel to his or her greatest potential because of policies dictated by the powerful.

According to critical theory, capitalism is an economic system that creates a class structure that benefits some members of society at the expense of others. Class membership determines how individuals relate to one another both economically and politically because economic ownership is related to political power. According to critical criminologists, the class bias in laws is reflected in social control. For example, individuals from the lower class are more likely to be arrested, convicted, and given harsh sentences than persons from the upper class. Yet, as we have already learned, self-report studies (unofficial data) show that crime is more evenly distributed among all classes than official figures reveal.

Critical criminologists contend that the social control of criminals is biased because criminal law focuses on behaviors in which the powerless are most likely to engage, such as public drunkenness. The class bias in law is also evident in the fact that many cases of harmful social behaviors of the upper classes are processed through civil and administrative law and not through criminal justice systems.

Critical criminologists focus on existing social and economic conditions in society and examine how these conditions affect individuals and classes as well as criminal activity. This is in direct contrast to conventional criminology, which concentrates on the actions of individuals. Critical criminologists also focus on criminal justice systems, analyzing the emergence and development of laws as well as law enforcement.

For purposes of analysis, the work of many critical criminologists may be categorized as *instrumental Marxism* or *structural Marxism*.

Instrumental Marxism

One school of thought in Marxist criminology maintains that in a capitalist society, the state is the instrument used by those in power to control everyone else, a position called **instrumental Marxism**. One of the prolific writers in this area, Richard Quinney, stated in 1974 that the "role of the state in capitalist society is to defend the interests of the ruling class."[173] In his early writings, Quinney viewed both the theory and practice of criminology as "a form of cultural production," or cultural politics, whose purposes should be to move us from the acceptance of a capitalist to a socialist society. He attempted to develop a social theory that supported socialist rather than capitalist development and to provide "the knowledge and politics for the working class, rather than knowledge for the survival of the capitalist class." According to Quinney, the necessary basis for the development of this position is Marxist theory and practice.[174]

In the earlier developments of his perspective, Quinney examined and rejected traditional criminological approaches and developed his own approach, which he called *critical philosophy*. According to Quinney, this approach permitted questioning everything and developing a new form of social life. Specifically, Quinney argued that traditional criminology had not questioned the legal order critically. He claimed that the state is a political organization that serves to maintain the interests of the ruling class over and against those of the ruled.[175]

Quinney proposed a socialist society in which the "goal is a world that is free from the oppressions produced by capitalism." In a socialist society, all will be equal, and all will share equally in the society's material benefits. A new human nature will arise, one that is liberated from acquisitive individualism and "no longer suffers the alienation otherwise inherent in the relations of capitalism." There will be no need for the state once classes, bureaucracy, and centralized authority are abolished. Law as it is known now will exist only in history.[176]

Quinney advocated that the traditional notion of causality in criminology should be abandoned, and the attempt to discover "what is" should be replaced by an approach that would try to understand "what is in terms of what *could* be." His purpose in developing what he called a theory of the *social reality of crime* was to "provide the ideas for correct thought and action. Only with a critical theory are we able to adequately understand crime in American society."[177]

Like many other critical criminologists, Quinney changed his position over time. His most radical work was written during the late 1960s and early 1970s, but during the middle 1970s, he became more closely identified with the Marxist position, arguing that the real conflict was between the ruling class and those who are victimized by that class. He maintained his belief, however, that the solution was the establishment of a socialist system.[178]

In more recent years, Quinney compared the spiritualism of Christianity with the moral position of Marxist philosophy.[179] He and his coauthor reaffirmed Quinney's Marxist position but added a new dimension—a "*criminology of peacemaking*—a nonviolent criminology of compassion and service. . . . There can be no solution to the problem of crime without peace and social justice. They are the beginning of a world free of crime."[180] Quinney and others expanded the field of inquiry beyond crime to include other areas in which they saw the state as an instrument of oppression: sexism, racism, imperialism, unsafe working conditions, inadequate medical care, substandard education, lack of employment opportunities, and other issues that are paramount today.

Two other early conflict writers of note were Herman Schwendinger and Julia Schwendinger. In 1970, the Schwendingers published an article in which they maintained that criminologists should extend their analyses beyond those acts traditionally defined as crime and include violations of human rights.[181] In subsequent writings, the Schwendingers reported the results of their analyses. Their study of rape was one example. They reported that women who were raped felt guilty about the crime because of the oppression and discrimination they suffered in a capitalist society.[182] The Schwendingers also conducted research in other areas of criminology—for example, on social class and delinquency, in which they questioned the conclusion that membership in the lower class explained most delinquency.[183]

Structural Marxism

Advocates of **structural Marxism**, such as William J. Chambliss and Robert Seidman, criticized the instrumental Marxist approach as static, too deterministic, too focused on economics, and inaccurate in its assumption that all law is used to the advantage of the ruling class and the disadvantage of those ruled. For example, laws regulating trade and commerce (e.g., antitrust laws designed to protect businesses from unlawful restraints that would reduce competition), employment discrimination, working conditions, wages, and consumer laws, to mention a few, aid the capitalist system but do not necessarily work in the interests of the ruling class.[184]

Although there is some divergence, the adherents of structural Marxism usually look for the underlying forces that shape law. They advocate that these forces may create a conflict between capitalism in general and any particular capitalist. Capitalism has its own agenda. Thus, to keep the system in effect, laws that operate against the interests of some capitalists may be enacted to keep capitalism running. For example, the state could enact legislation aimed at long-term goals that may hinder the short-term goals of some capitalists. Laws against employment discrimination are examples.[185]

Integrated Structural-Marxist Theory

Mark Colvin and John Pauly developed the concept of *integrated structural-Marxist theory*, which analyzes several control structures: work, family, school, peer groups, and social class. These scholars analyzed socialization within the family in terms of marketplace control as follows: Parents' class position is determined by the marketplace (those who own and control production exert control over workers). Negative work experiences resulting from the control structure of work (e.g., disagreements with those in power) alienate parents, who then develop more coercive controls within the family. These controls alienate juveniles, who have a greater probability of being placed in coercive control situations at school. These youths are more likely to be in inferior schools and to perform poorly. They have a greater tendency to associate with other alienated juveniles and to develop peer group control structures, which, in interaction with class-related, community, and neighborhood distributions of opportunities, lead to delinquency. In short, Colvin and Pauly claimed that major changes in delinquency cannot be made without changes in the root causes of that behavior.[186]

Critics reacted to Colvin and Pauly's approach by observing that (1) there has been little empirical research on the approach and (2) the limited research "reports positive but fairly weak empirical validity to the theory." Even significant support for the theory would not significantly distinguish it from non-Marxist theory. "Simply referring to the class position of parents and youth, especially when this is measured by occupational classifications similar to those used by non-Marxists, does not substantiate it as Marxist theory." To explain crime, Colvin and Pauly, along with others who espoused a position described as an integrated structural-Marxist approach that goes beyond capitalism (using such factors as racial and economic inequality, urban density, peers, family, and industrialization), are in effect relying "on concepts taken directly from the same 'traditional' criminological theories of which they have been so critical and which they have declared to be inadequate."[187]

Peacemaking

The earlier discussion of Richard Quinney's works mentioned that Quinney added a new dimension to criminology, which he called a *criminology of **peacemaking***. Quinney developed this approach with Hal Pepinsky, who defined *peacemaking* as "the art and science of transforming violent relations [power plays that some inflict on others] into safe, trustworthy, mutually respectful, balanced relations." Murder is an example of a power play inflicted on another person. Discrimination is an example of a power play inflicted on a group of people. War is an example of a power play against a society, and at the organizational level, an example of a power play is unsafe labor conditions. The conclusion was that criminologists should look at all of these examples of violence, not just those, such as murder, that have been traditionally covered by the discipline. The thesis is that any type of violence breeds more violence. Thus, capital punishment, though a legitimate exercise under law in some circumstances, is a violent act that breeds violence. According to Pepinsky, peacemaking is a process of seeking to identify ways of behavior that are appropriate and satisfying to all people; specifically, it attempts to find ways to "transform violent relations into good, constructive, and beautiful human relations."[188]

Peacemaking criminology has been criticized for its lack of ability to test its propositions empirically. In fact, it is argued that "there is little more than direct anecdotal evidence from which to evaluate peacemaking criminology."[189]

Left Realist Theories

Another radical approach to criminology is that of **left realist theorists**. These theorists advocate that left-wing scholars have placed too much emphasis on the crimes of the power elite to the exclusion of street crimes and their victims, who are mainly the poor in urban areas and, in particular, African Americans. The position is also a reaction against the conservative, or extreme right, law and order approach, which has resulted in such measures as longer sentences for adults and harsher treatment of juveniles. Left realism theory was introduced in 1987 in England by Jock Young[190] and other British scholars. They argued that *realism* is the recognition that most of the perpetrators of street crimes are men in the lower socioeconomic class, who in turn are responsible for most of the criminal treatment of women and minorities. The left realists maintain that most of the people who recognize these facts are conservatives.[191]

Left realists recognize that extreme poverty in high crime areas cannot explain criminal behavior, as not all poor people commit crime. They look at *relative* deprivation. Left realists acknowledge that relative deprivation can occur at any socioeconomic level, but the social structure places youths in the bottom tier of society without jobs and without hope for improving their situations. These youths form subcultures with other disenfranchised young people in their areas, and those subcultures may support delinquent and criminal behavior. Society should react to these issues by providing jobs, decent and affordable housing, and day care.[192]

Postmodernism

Another variation of critical criminology is an approach that looks at the meanings conveyed by language. The term **modernism** is associated with multiple approaches but includes the position that facts can be determined through use of the scientific method, which is objective. This approach, characteristic of the twentieth century, is utilized by most criminologists. **Postmodernism** is an approach that goes beyond modernism and looks closely at the full meaning of words, which may be used by those in power to impose their own values on others. There are various approaches within postmodernism, but essentially, this position in criminology analyzes the hidden power of words. Words intended to help may actually convey messages that hinder.[193]

We might choose as an example the Americans with Disabilities Act (ADA). It was enacted to provide opportunities for people who, because they are mentally or physically challenged, may not be able to compete in the job market or utilize services and products made available for other consumers. But the word *disability* in the statute carries a negative meaning. It suggests that the person described lacks control and needs help—for example, that the person is subordinate to those who do not face such challenges. In recent times, however, we have been using the terms *physically challenged* or *mentally challenged*, which suggest that the described person may be in control and able to make his or her own decisions and perhaps is not subordinate. In fact, the alleged purpose of the ADA

is to equalize the playing field, to create situations that empower physically and mentally challenged persons. Likewise, we talk about *cancer survivors* rather than *cancer victims*. The first reference conveys a different and more positive meaning than the second.

Postmodernism looks at language to determine how the powerful may use it to control and demean those with less power. In law, for example, the words used in statutes may imply racist or sexist meanings even if that was not the intention. In this regard, it is important to note that in recent years, many jurisdictions have rewritten their statutes to reflect the use of gender neutral terms rather than the traditional reference to "he" or "his" or "man."

Postmodernism may be contrasted to Marxist criminology primarily in that it "shifts attention from economic production to linguistic production."[194]

Exhibit 5.9 contains a summary of this discussion on critical criminology.

Evaluation of Critical Criminology

In 1974, criminologist Gresham Sykes wrote that the most serious criticism of critical criminology was that it was a "viewpoint, a perspective, or an orientation."[195] The concepts crucial to the theory, such as social class, are not defined clearly in terms that facilitate empirical testing. Consequently, little testing has been, or can be, done. Others disagree and maintain that a Marxist approach to the explanation of crime can be assessed quantitatively.[196] Some argue that empirical testing is not critical to a significant understanding of criminal behavior and criminal law. Empirical research is important only in the context of the scientific method. Postmodernists (referring to a variety of recent critical thinkers in the field of criminology) emphasize meaning, not universal measurable factors.

Critical criminology has produced a large body of literature, not all of which is Marxist. But it is the Marxist, or radical, approach that has drawn considerable criticism. In a review and critique of a series of original papers written by conflict criminologists, some of whom were Marxists, Ronald L. Akers, a sociologist and criminologist, commented on Marxist criminology. Akers, who acknowledged that he was acquainted personally and professionally with all of the authors whose papers he reviewed, stated that he found little empirical support for Marxist theory in criminology and that he disagreed with Marxism, thus rejecting Quinney's argument on the need for a socialist society. Akers accused Quinney of drawing static conclusions rather than deriving them from empirically tested propositions. Despite his criticism of critical criminology, Akers concluded: "[H]owever much I disagree with Marxist criminology, I believe we should continue to hear about it and respond to it."[197]

Others, such as Sykes, have pointed out that critical criminology "holds out the promise of having a profound impact on our thinking about crime and society." Conflict

EXHIBIT

5.9

Critical Criminology: A Summary

Critical criminology directs attention to how structural conditions and social inequality in class affect criminal behavior and official responses to crime. The emphasis is on social and economic conditions rather than on the characteristics of individual criminals. Those who advocate critical criminology draw upon a Marxist orientation of society to analyze social relations and processes. The approach may be divided into two areas: instrumental Marxism and structural Marxism. The other approaches that come under critical criminology are integrated structural-Marxist theory and power-control theory.

Instrumental Marxism

In a capitalist society, the state is the instrument used by persons in power to control everyone else. The major proponent, **Richard Quinney**, in his early work developed the concept of *critical philosophy*, an approach that permits us to question everything critically and to develop a new form of social life. Quinney spoke in favor of a socialist society free from the oppressions produced by capitalism. The emphasis should be on a social reality of crime, looking for what *ought* to be, not what *is*. Quinney argued that the real conflict is between the ruling class and its victims. In his later writings, he added the dimension of peacemaking, seeking a nonviolent criminology of compassion and service. **Herman Schwendinger** and **Julia Schwendinger** argued that criminologists should go beyond analyzing only crime and include the violation of human rights as well.

Structural Marxism

William J. Chambliss and **Robert Seidman** viewed the instrumental Marxist position as too static, too deterministic, too focused on economics, and inaccurate in its assumption that all law is used to the advantage of the ruling class and the disadvantage of those ruled.

Integrated Structural-Marxist Theory

Works by **Mark Colvin** and **John Pauly** focused on several social control structures, such as work, family, school, peer groups, and social class. Some of these can alienate parents, who then develop more controls within the family. This can alienate juveniles, who then have a greater probability of joining forces with other alienated youths, leading to delinquency.

Peacemaking

This approach was developed by **Richard Quinney** and **Hal Pepinsky** and defined by the latter as "the art and science of transforming violent relations [power plays that some inflict on others] into safe, trustworthy, mutually respectful, balanced relations." Peacemaking is a process of seeking to identify ways of behavior that are appropriate and satisfying to all people.

Left Realist Theories

These theories advocate that left-wing scholars have placed too much emphasis on the crimes of the power elite to the exclusion of street crimes and their victims, who are mainly the poor in urban areas and, in particular, African Americans. Critical criminologists have failed to recognize the *reality* of street crime among the poor and minorities and should apply their solutions to this reality. Unlike conservatives or right wingers, left realists do not explain street crime in terms of poverty, but they examine poverty in terms of the concept of *relative deprivation*.

Postmodernism

This approach looks closely at the full meaning of words, which postmodernists believe may be used by those in power to impose their own values on others.

---

or critical criminology forces a reexamination of notions of equality before the law and a consideration of whether equality really exists or whether "there is ample evidence that our ideals of equality before the law are being compromised by the facts of income and race in an industrial, highly bureaucratized social order. If a 'critical criminology' can help us solve that issue, while still confronting the need to control crime, it will contribute a great deal."[198]

Since Sykes published those comments in 1974, radical criminologists have conducted many studies, although they have not produced the extensive scholarship of other approaches and theories. Radical criminology must confront at least the following four criticisms:

1. "Radical criminology lacks empirical support.
2. Concepts in radical criminology are too abstract and cannot be measured.
3. Radical criminology is a faulty theory of crime because socialism has failed.
4. Cross-national studies of crime and justice disprove the conditions of radical criminology."[199]

Radical criminologists claim that all of these criticisms are either misleading or inaccurate. In addition, orthodox criminology, unlike radical criminology, has never refocused to consider the extremely harmful crimes committed by the middle and upper classes. Some examples are unnecessary surgery (seen by some as a form of violence), illegal air pollution, and workplace violations of health and safety rules, each of which kills more people annually than homicides. Yet orthodox criminologists pay little attention to these and other areas of concern that victimize people, and they continue to focus on street crimes.[200]

Social-Structural Theories and Female Criminality

Social-structural theories are also utilized to explain female criminality, but scholars do not agree on the nature or extent of female criminality. Until recently, little attention was given to female offenders. Various reasons have been suggested for this neglect. Female offenders constitute a much smaller percentage of offenders than their proportion in the population. Most of their crimes do not present a serious threat to society, except perhaps to its moral fiber, as in the case of prostitution and other sex crimes. Female inmates have not been seen as a serious social problem and have not engaged in prison violence to the same extent as male inmates. Because female inmates have been easier to manage than male inmates, most correctional facilities for women are less secure. Some widely held beliefs in this area have been challenged, however, as scholars have begun to take a closer look at women in criminal justice systems.

Crimes among women, as measured by official crime data, have been increasing, and for some crimes, as noted in Chapter 2, the increases for women have exceeded those for men. Furthermore, although violent crimes among women remain rare, there have been several cases in recent years in which women engaged in violence against their children (as in the case of Susan Smith of South Carolina, who strapped her little boys into the backseat of a car and drove into a lake, jumping out to save herself, or in the case of Andrea Yates of Houston, Texas, who in 2001 drowned her five children) or against strangers (as illustrated by the pickax murders for which Texas executed Karla Faye Tucker).

Execution of women is not common in the United States, and considerable attention was generated by Tucker's 1998 execution. Tucker was convicted of the brutal murders of two people; she claimed to have been rehabilitated in prison, and numerous people throughout the world called for Texas to spare her life. That call was refused. In 2002, Florida executed Aileen Wuornos, noted lesbian female serial killer/prostitute, who killed more than seven men in one year. In 2010, Virginia executed Teresa Lewis, its first woman in almost a century. Over 7,300 people made appeals to the state's governor to stay that execution.

The cases of Smith, Yates, Tucker, Wuornos, and Lewis received far more media attention than the "normal" crimes committed by women. Although these high-profile cases are unusual, the fact is that women are being convicted of more violent crimes today than in the past. Their participation in property crimes is increasing, too, even though men still surpass women in the official data for most crimes.

Attempts to explain female criminality today focus on women's liberation theories, strain theory, critical theory, and feminist theory.

Women's Liberation Theory

One explanation of the official increase in crimes by women is that, as women have become more liberated and have participated more extensively (and more equally) in the workforce, they have had more opportunities to commit crimes and have done so. The liberation of women approach may be subdivided into three areas: opportunity, economic marginality, and power control.

Opportunity Theory

In *Sisters in Crime*, published in 1975, criminologist Freda Adler set the stage for the debate on the extent and nature of female criminality from the perspective of women's liberation and the increased opportunity for women to commit crimes. According to Adler, the data revealed that crime among women was increasing and that more women were engaging in acts traditionally considered

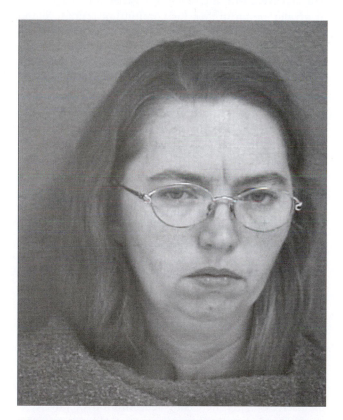

Criminologists differ in their explanations of crimes by women, with some claiming that women are more likely to commit crimes that are traditionally female (e.g., prostitution) or that are related to domestic issues. The arrest and conviction of Lisa Montgomery, 36, above, of Melvern, Kansas, illustrates the latter. Montgomery was accused of kidnapping and strangling Bobbie Jo Stinnett, 23, in December 2004, when Stinnett was eight months pregnant, cutting the fetus from Stinnett's body, and taking it home alive to pass off as her own. In October 2007, Montgomery was convicted by a federal jury and sentenced to death.

male rather than female crimes, leading some scholars to refer to the *masculinity hypothesis.* Women were becoming murderers, muggers, bank robbers, and members of organized crime (although they had not attained much success in the latter venture).[201]

Some criminologists supported Adler's position that female crime was increasing and becoming more violent, although not all agreed on why this was occurring.[202] Others criticized Adler's approach and suggested that any differences might be the result of methodological problems in collecting or analyzing the data.[203]

The second approach to the opportunity theory involving women's liberation was that of Rita James Simon. In one of her early works, Simon argued that female crime rates increased only in certain property crimes, such as larceny-theft, fraud, and embezzlement. She believed that the increase in those crimes could be explained by opportunity theory. More women were in the labor force, and they were working in a larger variety of jobs, leading to greater opportunities for committing crimes. Simon suggested that the propensities of men and women to commit crimes did not differ significantly; the difference is in opportunities. Thus, some refer to her approach as constituting the *opportunity hypothesis.* Simon's position was that women are more involved in economic crimes because they have more opportunities to commit these crimes. They are less involved in violent crimes because the frustrations that lead to the latter decrease as women become liberated.[204]

Economic Marginalization Hypothesis

Another interpretation of the relationship between women's liberation and crime is that girls and women who become delinquents or criminals are, for the most part, poor and unemployed or underemployed. As a result, they do not have access to legitimate ways to make money and earn a living for themselves and their families. They live on the edge of society. Although they may be more liberated, they do not experience greater access to legitimate ways of earning money. Their liberation has released men from their former positions of supporting women but has not provided women with the same opportunities that men (and boys) have to earn money and adequately support themselves. "This increasing feminization of poverty is an unintended consequence of women's liberation and is thought to be at the root of female crime."[205]

Power-Control Theory

Another approach to examining female crime in terms of women's liberation is that of John Hagan's *power-control theory,* discussed earlier in this chapter. It is argued that gender differences in delinquency and crime can be accounted for by the type of family structure and the extent to which parents exert control over their girls compared to their boys. This approach examines the relative power

of women in the family in terms of their occupational affiliations compared to the occupational positions of men within the family. In *patriarchial* families, the male commands greater authority; in *matriarchial* families, the woman commands greater authority. In families described as *egalitarian*, both male and female adult authorities command relatively equal authority. Mothers are more likely to exert more authority over the family in the matriarchial and egalitarian models (although less in the latter than in the former). In patriarchial families, the fathers are more likely to exercise greater authority than mothers, although even there, mothers will exercise more authority over female compared to male children.

Family structures and gender differences are also thought to be related to the risks children will take. It is argued that within the structure of patriarchial families, boys will take more risks and commit more delinquent acts than will girls because they are subjected to fewer controls. Boys also view risk taking as providing pleasure, and they do not perceive significant negative consequences for their actions. Within egalitarian families, the differences between the behavior of girls and boys are not as great, but there is still more delinquency on the part of boys compared to girls.

Hagan found some support for his power-control theory, but it has been questioned by others, including those who have found that Hagan's contention that mothers exert more control than fathers over children in general is not the case. Rather, mothers exert more control over daughters and fathers over sons. Some of the differences, however, may be due to sampling and measurement techniques.[206]

Critique of Women's Liberation Theory

The women's liberation approach has not received significant empirical support.[207] Darrell J. Steffensmeier and others have argued that the increase in female criminality actually began before the women's liberation movement. In earlier works, Steffensmeier agreed that there had been an increase in some kinds of crime among women, but he took the position that women were involved *primarily* in traditional female crimes such as shoplifting.[208] Steffensmeier also noted the lack of success of women in organized crime.[209] He, along with Renee Hoffman Steffensmeier, concluded that among male delinquents and criminals, women were regarded primarily as sex objects, wives, and mothers. Female delinquency continued to reflect traditional female gender roles; the women's movement has had little effect on this phenomenon.[210]

The findings of more recent research by Steffensmeier and Cathy Streifel "do not support the traditional liberation thesis" of female criminality. "Instead they show that trends in the female share of offending are largely a function of trends in formal policing, and less so of trends in the economic marginalization of females."[211]

Other scholars have supported Steffensmeier's argument that women are engaging in traditional female gender roles even when they commit crimes generally considered masculine.[212] It has also been argued that the same is the case with juveniles.[213]

Recent research on DUI arrests of women sheds light on why these arrests for women are gaining on those for men. Scholars who compared official arrest data with self-report data (see again the discussion on self-report data in Chapter 2) found that the gender gap for DUI violations was basically unchanged. The investigators concluded that the explanation of enhanced DUI arrest rates of women were explained by changes in the social structure of criminal justice systems. Simply stated, the "shifts in law and enforcement have enhanced the probability that women will be caught and dealt with formally for DUI." Changes in laws, such as lowering the level of alcohol intoxication that constitutes DUI, making the laws more gender neutral, and the concentrated effort of law enforcement officials to apprehend DUI drives, may have influenced the arrest data. The investigators concluded that if police had previously been more lenient toward women, that position has changed over time. "Ironically, women's liberation may have had greater effects on law-enforcement practices than on women's drunk-driving behaviors."[214]

This finding supports other conclusions that changes in law enforcement, targeting lower-level offenders, may impact the arrest rates of women. Thus, the appearance that woman are committing more crimes may simply be a reflection of a greater willingness of law enforcement officials to arrest women. There is evidence that such net-widening appears in the arrests of women and girls for the crimes of simple assault and juvenile robbery. In general, it makes female offenders more visible to law enforcement authorities in a society that is showing increasing interest in the punishment of lower-level offenders.[215]

Strain Theory

Earlier in this chapter, we looked at the contributions of Robert Agnew to the development of strain theory as an explanation of delinquency in particular and crime in general. Agnew also used his approach to examine gender and crime. He looked at the issue of why crime rates are generally higher among boys and men than among girls and women. He concluded that the explanation does not lie in greater strains among men and boys than among women and girls but, rather, in that the genders encounter *different types* of strains. They are socialized differently, and that creates different types of strains. The differences in sex-role socialization, said Agnew, also explain the differences in *types* of crimes (as well as the differences in the emotional reactions of the genders to crime). For example, the greater socialization of men and boys toward material success explains their higher arrests for most property crimes. The socialization of women and girls places an emphasis on social control and restricts criminal opportunities. According to Agnew,

> It is difficult to engage in serious violent and property crime when one spends little time in public, feels responsible for children and others, is burdened with the demands of others, and is under much pressure to avoid behaving in an aggressive manner.[216]

Agnew and Lisa M. Broidy utilized strain theory to explain not only why crime rates were higher among men than among women but also why women commit crimes at all. Broidy and Agnew suggested that men and women encounter different types of strains, that they react differently in terms of their emotions and their behavior, and that conditioning experiences help to explain these differences.[217] An empirical test of this approach showed some support for its ability to explain male versus female criminality.[218] However, a more recent analysis found stronger support for differential association/social learning theory (discussed in Chapter 6) than for social strain theory in explaining gender differences in substance abuse by incarcerated juvenile offenders.[219]

Broidy reported that most earlier tests of strain theory concentrated on the relationship between strain and crime. She extended her research on a sample of college students to include the role of negative emotions, such as anger, and legitimate coping strategies (cognitive, behavioral, emotional). She found some support for strain theory. "Central general strain theory variables—strain, negative emotions, and legitimate coping—all appear to be important in explaining the likelihood of criminal/illegitimate outcomes." However, Broidy concluded that the "nature of the relationship among these variables appears to be more complex than the theory suggests."[220]

Recent research has produced some support for Broidy and Agnew's analysis of the differences in strain when gender is concerned. One study reported support for the first two propositions (men and women experience different types of strains and they react differently) of their approach but only limited support for the third proposition (conditioning factors explain these differences). Specifically, the following findings were noted among African American adults:

- Women were more likely than men to report strains as a result of physical health, interpersonal relations, and gender roles within the family. Men were more likely to report work-related strains, which included racial as well as job-related strains. The one exception was that women as well as men reported financial strains.
- Women were more likely to react to strain by turning inward (depression and anxiety) rather than turning outward (anger).

■ The typical reaction of women (self-directed) was less likely to result in deviant, illegitimate coping behaviors than was the case with other-directed emotions, such as anger. This reaction was less strong, which may have been accounted for by the difficulty in measuring the effect of conditioning factors.[221]

Even more recently, research has revealed gender differences in the effect that serious strain (such as suicidal behavior by family and friends and violent victimization) has on men and women. Specifically, "depressive symptoms are positively predictive of all forms of deviance for females (suicidal thoughts, weekly drinking, running away, violence), but only some forms of deviance for males (suicidal thoughts, running away)."[222]

Critical Theory

Critical or radical criminology theory has also been utilized to explain the nature and extent of female criminality. Under this approach, the analysis of gender and crime emphasizes the subordinate position of women in society. Historically, women were treated as property, first of their fathers and then of their husbands. They were expected to take care of their families, bear and rear children, and engage in sexual relations with their husbands. Under the law in many jurisdictions, women did not have the authority to decline these roles. When they began working outside the home, women held inferior economic positions. There have been changes in the laws and social expectations, but some argue that those changes have not been sufficient.

Critical criminologists look at female offenders in terms of the economic structure and other conflicts within the social structure. Some suggest that female criminality is a function of the capitalist system that denies women equal access to the economic advantages men enjoy. If women spend most of their time at home, they do not have many opportunities to commit crimes. When they do engage in crime, they do so primarily in conjunction with their traditional roles as wives, homemakers, and mothers. They are prostitutes, they shoplift, or they engage in fraud. When they engage in violence, it is usually directed toward their children, husbands, or lovers. Critical criminologists' analyses of gender and crime go beyond attempts to explain the cause of crime and delinquency to explanations of all elements of criminal justice systems in terms of gender roles and power.

The discussion of John Hagan's power-control theory earlier in this chapter looked at his explanation of female delinquency and criminality. Hagan viewed society's capitalist-caused class issues as also appearing within families, and in that context, he examined gender issues. Hagan looked at the power-control issues of parents and children as well as of husbands and wives, noting the differences among patriarchal, matriarchal, and egalitarian families. These family structures were also considered by James W. Messerschmidt in his critical study of gender and crime.

Messerschmidt emphasized the need to consider hierarchical structures as well as economics. Most societies are patriarchal, with specific divisions of labor for men and women within the family. Primarily, women's roles have been related to their biological reproductive function. That women are subordinate to men economically and biologically, Messerschmidt asserted, explains why women engage in less criminal activity than men and why any criminal activity they do engage in is less serious. "Gender and class shape one's possibilities. . . . Criminality is related, then, to the interaction of patriarchy and capitalism and the structural possibilities this interaction creates."[223]

According to Messerschmidt, the lack of power explains female criminality as well as the violent crimes of lower-class men. Corporate crimes and sexual crimes committed by men against women (and children) may be explained by male power. These power relationships may explain particular types of crime, too, such as prostitution by women and rape and domestic violence by men.

Messerschmidt referred to his approach as **structured action theory**, which he said is necessary because power-control and strain theories do not explain the similarities between the criminal acts of girls and women, boys and men, as well as the differences *among* men and boys and *among* women and girls. In structured action theory, Messerschmidt distinguished between characteristics that designate *sex* (hair, clothing, etc.) and those that designate *gender* (the ways of acting that verify sex). He said we *do masculinity* or we *do femininity*, which means we act in ways to verify our sex. Masculinity and femininity are not static structures; we *do* them in specific situations, which are influenced by social structure and the constraints within that structure. "Not only are there many ways of **doing gender**—we must speak of masculinities and femininities— gender must be viewed as *structured action*, or what people do under specific social structural constraints."[224]

According to Messerschmidt, crime is a social practice that men engage in when other resources are not available to accomplish masculinity. This also explains social class and minority differentials in crime, for doing masculinity in the lower class might produce a different type of crime from that produced by middle- or upper-class boys in their efforts to "do masculinity."[225]

Messerschmidt's approach recognizes that race and class may play a role in criminal actions, but like other class and race theories, it cannot explain why crime is the resource used by some men (or boys) to do masculinity while law-abiding ways are utilized by others. Nor does it explain why crime is considered masculine, a position that feminist criminologists attack.

In the study of gender, critical criminology is also used to explain the victimization of women—for example, domestic violence leading to the battering of women by men. In many cases, domestic violence is accompanied by heavy drinking, and it is argued that violence and alcoholism "both represent the politics of domination" that exists between men and women in a domestic relationship.[226]

A study of violence among adolescents lends support to the theory of structural gender inequality as a factor in criminal behavior. Noting that other studies had reported considerable violence of females against males during adolescent dating, investigators reported that their evidence showed a striking difference between the violence of female and of male adolescents and that these differences could be explained by inequalities. Earlier research on courtship behavior had led scholars to conclude that violence against women occurred because of the power men had over them. In addition, when women were violent within romantic relationships, it was primarily the result of self-defense. Or perhaps courtship violence occurred in situations in which women and men exhibited gender parity. These studies, however, were described as uncovering "less serious forms of violence," and they tended "to treat gender as a sex category rather than as a social structure and meaning system that shapes behavior and its consequences." This study of urban African American youths living in dangerous communities and at high risk for, or already involved in, delinquent acts focused on the following: "youths' accounts of the broader gender dynamics within their peer culture, the nature of relationship conflicts, and the meanings youths brought to bear in their interrelationships of dating violence." The investigators examined "gender as an integral facet of everyday life that structures social action and shapes its interpretation." They concluded that although further research is needed, including comparisons with samples of adolescents who are not considered at high risk for delinquent or criminal behavior, their research "substantiates the importance of gender inequality in shaping the nature and consequences of partner violence, even when it is violence committed by young women."[227]

Finally, one study of female criminals suggested that, with respect to residential burglary, the varied behavior of men and women who interact in this street-life situation could be explained by traditional gender roles.[228]

What has been the impact of critical theory on the study of female criminality? It has been suggested that the addition of the analysis of gender inequality to critical criminology has advanced and enriched the field. "New questions are being asked, new perspectives are being introduced, and new solutions are being advanced."[229] Clearly, along with race and social class, gender is important in explaining the differences between male and female criminality.[230]

Feminist Theory

Meda Chesney-Lind and others have taken the position that the contributions of Freda Adler and Rita Simon do not constitute a sufficient explanation of female criminality, which requires the rethinking of criminological theory that they described as "a product of white, economically privileged men's experiences."[231] Chesney-Lind and Daly did consider the contributions of Adler and Simon to constitute **feminist theory**. Chesney-Lind referred to the works of Adler and Simon as "flawed theory building" that has been, for the most part, discredited by other researchers.[232]

Feminist scholars are not clear on what constitutes *feminist theory* in criminology, but a definition is necessary. This definition has been offered: *Feminism* and *feminist theory* are those theories that are based on "diverse perspectives that focus on women's interests, are overtly political, and strive to present a new vision of equality and social justice."[233]

Feminist scholars do agree that contributions to the development of feminist theory may be made by male as well as by female scholars and that the focus on female crime alone is not sufficient to qualify. The trend today is toward looking at the dominance of men over women (the patriarchal society) and the impact that has on crimes by and against women. This focus on the power of one gender over the other is similar to the focus on the power of one group over another, as illustrated by the earlier discussion of Messerschmidt's work. The use of the term *feminist* rather than *conflict* or *critical*, however, may connote a more special place for a focus on the subject of women and crime. Given the years of neglect of any attempt to explain female crime from a theoretical perspective, this labeling may be significant.

Feminist scholars go beyond an attempt to explain female criminality; like critical scholars, they also look at female victimization and at the treatment of women by criminal justice systems. For example, feminists have been particularly important in sensitizing us to the manner in which female victims of rape and other sexual assaults have been treated by police, prosecutors, and judges.[234]

Feminist scholars have also contributed to our understanding of the possible explanations of gender differences in violent delinquency. To illustrate, in an examination of gender and violence among juveniles, utilizing differential association theory (discussed in Chapter 6) and feminist theory and gender studies, researchers found evidence of subtler, indirect mechanisms influencing female violence, with more direct, overt ways affecting the violence of young males:

In short, the conclusion of our research is that violent delinquency is "gendered" in significant ways [through the socialization process]. . . . Specifically, boys are more violent than girls largely because they are taught more definitions favoring such behavior; girls are less violent than boys because they are controlled through subtle mechanisms, which included learning that violence is incompatible with the meaning of gender for them and being restrained by emotional bonds to family.[235]

Others have argued that the structural gendered differences of society must be considered in an examination of violent behavior. These differences are related to social associations, perceptions of risk, and the self-control (or its lack) that females and males encounter and develop. In addition, the violent behavior of males and females may often be distinguished by the social structure in which it occurs. For example, wives may kill their husbands after a long history of abuse; this is rarely the case with husbands killing their wives.[236]

Much remains to be done, however, in the explanations of delinquency and crime in terms of gender, as Media Focus 5.1 suggests.

Feminist explanations may have sensitized us to many issues regarding gender and crime, but there have been insufficient empirical studies to support their position. Ronald L. Akers and Christine S. Sellers maintain, "No direct tests of the gendered context of crime exist, and indirect tests demonstrate little support for the hypothesis of major differences in the etiology of male and female crime."[237] These theorists concluded as follows:

> Feminist theory is still in formation, and the paucity of direct tests of its hypotheses has not yet provided a clear evaluation of its empirical validity or policy usefulness.[238]

Exhibit 5.10 contains a summary of this discussion on theories of female criminality.

MEDIA FOCUS

5.1 The Media and School Shootings: A Look at Feminist Theory

The 1999 shootings at Columbine High School in Colorado as well as those at other schools have gained international media attention. Although some of the attention has focused on the social class of the schools targeted (most draw students from middle- or upper-class neighborhoods), little attention has been given to an analysis of the gender issues involved.

Two female scholars studied media reactions to Columbine and other schools that were the scenes of multiple shootings by students. In these studies, all of the offenders were male; 59 percent of the victims were female. Mona J. E. Danner and Dianne Cyr Carmody utilized the feminist approach in their analysis of the media treatment of these crimes. They defined their approach as one that placed women at the center of the inquiry or, in Danner's words, "a women-centered description and explanation of human experience and the social world."[1] The authors emphasized the importance of asking what the gender issues are in situations such as student shootings in schools.

In their analysis, the authors noted that when those persons closest to the shootings—the classmates and teachers—were asked why they thought the violence occurred, they frequently responded with statements such as "he was retaliating against a girlfriend" or "he was respond-

ing to being bullied." The grandfather of a suspect in one shooting was quoted as saying that the suspects selected their victims because of their gender: "It was not a random shooting." Yet some of the early media reports, featuring interviews with social scientists, referred to the culture of violence in our society, the easy availability of guns, the breakdown of the family, violence in movies, and so on. According to Danner and Carmody, "None of these experts commented on the gendered nature of the . . . shootings, suggested that violence is a means of asserting one's masculinity, or implicated violence against women and girls in any way."[2]

Danner and Carmody concluded: "The relative absence of expert and media attention to the social construction of gender encourages incomplete explanations of school violence, and therefore fosters ineffective policy recommendations."[3]

---

1. Mona J. E. Danner and Dianne Cyr Carmody, "Missing Gender in Cases of Infamous School Violence: Investigating Research and Media Explanations," *Justice Quarterly* 18 (March 2001): 87–114; quotation is on p. 89.
2. Ibid., pp. 107, 108.
3. Ibid., p. 110.

5.10 EXHIBIT

Theories That Address Female Criminality: A Summary

Opportunity Theory and Women's Liberation

These theories view the increase in female criminality as the result of greater opportunities for women in the workforce. **Freda Adler's** book *Sisters in Crime* states that the nature of female crime (toward that previously characterized primarily as male crime) changed when women began participating more extensively in the workforce. **Rita James Simon** took the position that female crime rates increased only in certain property crimes and that the increase is explained by opportunity theory—women had more chances to engage in crimes such as larceny-theft, fraud, and embezzlement. **Darrell J. Steffensmeier** argued that the increase in female criminality began before the women's liberation movement. In addition, women have been engaged primarily in traditional female crimes or, when engaging in traditional male crimes (e.g., murder), have assumed traditional female gender roles.

Strain Theory

Robert Agnew extended strain theory to an analysis of crime by girls and women, contending that the genders experience different kinds of strains because of the differences in the way they are socialized, and that explains the differences in delinquency and criminality.

Critical Theory

This theory emphasizes the subordinate position of women within society's economic structure in explaining the nature and extent of female crime and the criminal justice systems' reactions to those crimes. **James Messerschmidt** looked at hierarchical structures of society as well as economic systems. Women are viewed in most societies as subordinate to men in both areas, and thus, they engage in less crime, and the crimes they do engage in are less serious. Their possibilities in the criminal world are shaped by gender and class as well as by economics. Messerschmidt added what he called *structured action theory* to power-control and strain theories in explaining female crime. He distinguished between sex and gender and introduced the concept of *doing gender* to the study of crime. **Jody Miller** and **Norman A. White** studied violence among adolescents and found support for the feminist theory of gender inequality in explaining criminal behavior. Critical criminology is also used to explain gender differences in victimization and sentencing.

Feminist Theory

This theory looks at the dominance of men over women and the impact it has on crimes by and against women. Since criminology has been dominated by male researchers who have concentrated on male crime, the issue of gender roles in explaining crime and the reaction to crime have been ignored. Feminists aim to eliminate this bias in criminological research. **Meda Chesney-Lind** and **Kathleen Daly** are two of the major proponents of feminist theory; they emphasized that the traditional structure of patriarchy, with men dominating women, is as important as social class in understanding crime. Male dominance is seen in criminal justice systems as well as in criminological research, as men discriminate against women to reinforce traditional female gender roles.

Summary

Chapters 3 and 4 explored explanations of criminal behavior that focus on the individual criminal and his or her characteristics. This chapter examined explanations that focus on crime as a function of the social structure. Writings on these theories and approaches are extensive and involve numerous contributors. Several exhibits were provided to ease the difficulty students may have in outlining the presentation.

During the past several decades, the social-structural approach has been the most popular one of liberal theorists, many of whom concentrated on such characteristics as unemployment and other forms of economic deprivation. They viewed the entire society as being to blame for crime. Even violent crime was seen as the result of the social structure—the oppressed kill and steal to get even with a society that has wronged them.

Some writers see crime as a reflection of the family and other social institutions, and some offer psychological and psychiatric causes. However, the consensus of the liberal writings is that no matter what or who is blamed, severe punishment based on a concept of personal evil and wickedness is not appropriate. The principal problem in dealing with crime is to curb poverty, sexism, and racism.

The chapter began with a brief overview of the social-structural approach before focusing on the ecological school of thought. The Chicago-based studies of Park and Burgess and of Shaw and McKay were examined and critiqued. The impact of this school was viewed through the works of contemporary scholars, who conducted research on social disorganization as it relates to urban crime and delinquency.

The discussion of anomie and crime began with an analysis of the contributions of Émile Durkheim, who claimed that crime is normal and functional. His concept of anomie was discussed in the context of social solidarity and its relationship to deviant and criminal behavior. Anomie is an important concept in criminological theory. It was further developed by Robert K. Merton, who focused on American culture, which he analyzed by typologies, or modes of adaptation to societal goals and the acceptable means of attaining those goals. The contemporary institutional anomie theory (IAT) of Steven F. Messner and Richard Rosenfeld was also discussed, followed by an analysis of the general strain theory (GST) of Robert Agnew, which incorporates three types of strain. A look at Francis T. Cullen's development of social support completed the analysis of contemporary approaches to anomie/strain theories.

The influence of anomie on the emergence of cultural transmission theories to explain crime and, especially, delinquency was introduced with a look at the ecological theories of early gangs. Particular attention was given to the work of Frederic M. Thrasher in the Chicago area, but current data and research on gangs were also highlighted, including a discussion of female gangs and the race and ethnicity of gangs. The chapter also considered efforts to prevent gangs.

The discussion of gangs was followed by a look at the major cultural transmission theories that illustrate various ways of analyzing crime in terms of society's social and economic class structure. These approaches range from viewing the lower socioeconomic class as a subculture with norms differing from those of the rest of society to the assumption that crime and delinquency may be explained primarily in terms of differential access to legitimate or illegitimate ways of achieving goals. One aspect of opportunity theory is education, and the chapter noted the research on differentials between male and female school dropouts and delinquency. The problem of measuring class was noted in the context of evaluating cultural submission theories.

Gender is a relevant variable in any attempt to explain criminal or delinquent behavior. This chapter built on previous discussions of gender in analyses of the relationship between family structure and delinquency. It also included some of the latest research on the influences of family structure on the behavior of children and examined the nature of John Hagan's power-control theory and its explanation of family structure and delinquency and crime.

Scholars continue to refine social-structural analyses of criminal behavior, and the chapter summarized some of the more recent approaches, such as routine activity. This approach considers the availability of likely offenders, suitable targets, and the absence of "guardians"—people to prevent criminal activity from occurring. It is useful in explaining crime as well as victimization.

In recent years, considerable attention has been given to the study of crime by conflict theorists. The emergence of the conflict approach was viewed in the context of other societal changes, such as the civil rights movement. This section began with a look at the theories of Karl Marx and Friedrich Engels, along with those of Frank Tannenbaum and Willem A. Bonger. The contributions of Thorsten Sellin to an understanding of the impact of culture on group conflict were followed by an analysis of the impact of power on conflict. This section also looked at the contributions of Austin T. Turk and others.

The chapter gave extensive attention to critical (or radical) criminology, looking at the impact of Karl Marx on this area of criminology. Two types of Marxist criminology were distinguished—instrumental Marxism and structural Marxism—along with efforts to develop an integrated structural-Marxist theory. Peacemaking, left realist, and postmodern criminological approaches were explained before the chapter turned to an evaluation of critical criminology.

The final section of the chapter included an expanded and significantly updated discussion of social-structural theories and female criminality. Women and crime were examined first in terms of women's liberation theory, which included opportunity, economic marginalization, and power-control approaches, along with a critique of liberation theories. Next followed strain theory, conflict theory, and feminist theory. The study of female crime was neglected for years; feminists are now focusing attention on the phenomenon and applying traditional theories, along with new ones, to this important area of understanding crime.

The social-structural emphasis on explaining criminal behavior has lost some popularity in the United States. The swing is toward the criminal, who is presumed to think rationally and who, it is assumed, can be deterred from criminal activity if the correct disincentives are imposed. The contributions of social-structural theories must not be overlooked, however. In identifying social and political institutions as possible causes of crime, we have made significant changes, some that may be questioned and some that appear functional for individuals and for society. We have learned that it is important to consider crime from many perspectives.

Although this chapter's primary emphasis was on social structure, the approaches provide a basis from which process theories may be considered. For example, an environmental explanation of criminal behavior might include not only the ecology of the area in which the criminal behavior occurs but also the impact that the environment has on a person's decision to engage in criminal behavior. The process of becoming a criminal might be intertwined with the structure in which the behavior takes place. Thus, these social-structural explanations are important not only for their own merit in explaining criminal behavior but also for the framework they establish for process theories.

In developing an understanding of how to reduce crime, we need to assess sociological theories that are concerned with the *process* of becoming a criminal. The contributions of sociologists in this area are significant. The next chapter is devoted to those developments.

Study Questions

1. What is the difference between structure and process in the explanation of delinquent and criminal behavior?

2. List and define the zones of transition in the Chicago school, and explain their importance to modern criminology.

3. Contrast Durkheim's concept of anomie with its development by Merton.

4. Describe briefly the reaction to Merton's theory of anomie.

5. What is institutional anomie theory (IAT)? General strain theory (GST)? Discuss the importance of research in these areas.

6. Explain Cullen's social support approach to strain theory.

7. Evaluate the contributions of Thrasher and Whyte to the study of gangs. How do these early studies compare with today's research on gangs?

8. What do we know about female gangs?

9. What do we know about how to prevent gangs?

10. Briefly contrast the theories of the lower-class boy and the middle-class measuring rod with that of differential opportunity theory.

11. What is meant by neutralization and drift in relationship to delinquency?

12. What is the relationship between education and delinquency? Social class and delinquency?

13. Evaluate the studies of family structure and crime. What does Hagan's power-control theory contribute?

14. What is meant by the routine activity approach? Is it a reasonable explanation for crime? For victimization?

15. Evaluate Sellin's contributions to our understanding of conflict theory.

16. What is Austin Turk's position regarding conflict and criminality?

17. State briefly the history and importance of critical criminology.

18. Distinguish and evaluate instrumental, structural, and integrated-structural Marxism.

19. What is *peacemaking* criminology?

20. Define *left realist* criminology.

21. Explain *postmodernism* criminology.

22. Evaluate the contributions of critical criminology.

23. What is meant by women's liberation theory and crime? Briefly describe three types of liberation theory.

24. Apply strain and critical theory to an explanation of the crimes of women and girls.

25. Explain and critique feminist theory as an explanation of the crimes of women and girls.

Brief Essay Assignments

1. Explain the basis of the ecological school of crime, and discuss some of the early research supporting its position.

2. Discuss contemporary ecological research.

3. Compare the contributions of traditional anomie theorists with those of contemporary strain theorists.

4. Discuss the nature of modern gangs, and elaborate on gender and gangs.

5. Compare and contrast the major cultural transmission theories of delinquency and crime.

6. Compare the conflict perspective with that of critical criminology.

7. Explain how any of the theories in this chapter may be used to explain the criminality of girls and women.

Internet Activities

1. Go to the National Criminal Justice Reference Service website at http://www.ncjrs.gov and search gangs. What can you find out about current data on gangs? Is there any information on female gangs?

The Florida Department of Corrections has created a website to educate parents and the community about gangs to reduce their adverse impacts. Check out this site at http://www.dc.state.fl.us/pub/gangs/awareness.html. Review the site and critique the suggestions (sources accessed 2 October 2010).

2. Go to the website of the National Criminal Justice Reference Service at http://www.ncjrs.gov/ and click on Juvenile Justice. What is the rate of recidivism for juveniles? How many juveniles are sexually assaulted? What can you find out about early intervention strategies for juveniles at risk? Relate that information to the theories in this chapter (source accessed 2 October 2010).

Notes

1. For a concise but excellent overview and analysis of criminology theories, see Ronald L. Akers and Christine S. Sellers, *Criminological Theories: Introduction, Evaluation, and Application*, 5th ed. (Los Angeles: Roxbury, 2009). See also Charis E. Kubrin et al., *Researching Theories of Crime and Deviance* (New York: Oxford University Press, 2009).

2. Richard Jessor and Shirley Jessor, *Problem Behavior and Psychosocial Development—A Longitudinal Study of Youth* (New York: Academic Press, 1977).

3. Helene Raskin White, "Early Problem Behavior and Later Drug Problems," *Journal of Research in Crime and Delinquency* 29 (November 1992): 412–429.

4. Amie L. Nielsen and Ramiro Martinez Jr., "Reassessing the Alcohol-Violence Linkage: Results from a Multiethnic City," *Justice Quarterly* 20, no. 3 (September 2003): 445–469; quotation is on p. 451.

5. See Robert E. Park, "Human Ecology," *American Journal of Sociology* 42 (1936): 1–15; Park and Ernest W. Burgess et al., *The City* (Chicago: University of Chicago Press, 1925); Park and Burgess, *Introduction to the Science of Sociology* (Chicago: University of Chicago Press, 1921).

6. David Matza, *Becoming Deviant* (Englewood Cliffs, NJ: Prentice-Hall, 1969), p. 31.

7. Nels Anderson, *The Hobo* (Chicago: University of Chicago Press, 1923). See also Harvey Zorbaugh, *The Gold Coast and the Slum* (Chicago: University of Chicago Press, 1929); Paul Cressey, *The Taxi-Dance Hall* (Chicago: University of Chicago Press, 1932).

8. Noel P. Gist and Sylvia Fleis Fava, *Urban Society*, 5th ed. (New York: Thomas Y. Crowell, 1964), pp. 108–109.

9. See Ernest W. Burgess, "The City," in Park et al., *The City*, p. 51.

10. Clifford R. Shaw and Henry D. McKay, *Juvenile Delinquency and Urban Areas*, rev. ed. (Chicago: University of Chicago Press, 1972), p. 106; first published in 1942.

11. John H. Laub, "The Life Course of Criminology in the United States: The American Society of Criminology 2003 Presidential Address," *Criminology* 42, no. 1 (February 2004): 1–26; quotations are on pp. 9–10.

12. Oscar Newman, *Defensible Space* (London: Architectural Press, 1972).

13. Robert J. Bursik Jr. and Harold G. Grasmick, *Neighborhoods and Crime: The Dimensions of Effective Community* (New York: Lexington Books, 1993), pp. 4, 16, 17.

14. Robert J. Sampson and W. Byron Groves, "Community Structure and Crime: Testing Social Disorganization Theory," *American Journal of Sociology* 94 (1989): 774–802.

15. Robert J. Sampson et al., "Neighborhoods and Violent Crime: A Multilevel Study of Collective Efficacy," *Science* 277 (1997): 918–924.

16. For a review, see Thomas J. Bernard et al., *Vold's Theoretical Criminology*, 6th ed. (New York: Oxford University Press, 2010), pp. 143–144.

17. John R. Hipp et al., "Intergroup and Intragroup Violence: Is Violent Crime an Expression of Group Conflict or Social Disorganization?" *Criminology* 47, no. 2 (May 2009): 521–564.

18. John R. Hipp and Daniel K. Yates, "Do Returning Parolees Affect Neighborhood Crime? A Case Study of Sacramento," *Criminology* 47, no. 3 (August 2009): 619–656.

19. Min Xie and David McDowall, "Escaping Crime: The Effects of Direct and Indirect Victimization on Moving," *Criminology* 46, no. 4 (November 2008): 809–840.

20. For a review of the literature, see Gary LaFree, "A Summary and Review of Cross-National Comparative Studies of Homicide," in *Homicide: A Sourcebook of Social Research*, ed. M. Dwayne Smith and Margaret A. Zahr (Thousand Oaks, CA: Sage), cited in William Alex Pridemore, "A Methodological Addition to the Cross-National Empirical Literature on Social Structure and Homicide: A First Test of the Poverty-Homicide Thesis," *Criminology* 46, no. 1 (February 2008): 133–154.

21. Pridemore, "A Methodological Addition to the Cross-National Empirical Literature."

22. Bernard et al., *Vold's Theoretical Criminology*, 6th ed., p. 145.

23. See James Q. Wilson and George L. Kelling, "Police and Neighborhood Safety: Broken Windows," *Atlantic Monthly* 249 (March 1982): 28–38.

24. Deanna L. Wilkinson, "Local Social Ties and Willingness to Intervene: Textured Views Among Violent Urban Youth of Neighborhood Social Control Dynamics and Situations," *Justice Quarterly* 24, no. 2 (June 2007): 185–220; quotation is on p. 185.

25. D. Wayne Osgood and Jeff M. Chambers, "Social Disorganization Outside the Metropolis: An Analysis of Rural Youth Violence," *Criminology* 38, no. 1 (February 2000): 81–116.

26. David Cantor and Kenneth Land, "Unemployment and Crime Rates in the Post World War II United States: A Theoretical and Empirical Analysis," *American Sociological Review* 50 (1985): 317–332. See also Cantor and Land, "Unemployment and Crime Rate Fluctuation: A Comment on Greenberg," *Journal of Quantitative Criminology* 17, no. 4 (2001): 329–342.

27. See Kenneth Land et al., "Structural Covariates of Homicide Rates: Are There Invariances Across Time and Social Space?" *American Journal of Sociology* 95, no. 4 (1990): 922–963; Daniel P. Mears and Avinash S. Bhati, "No Community Is an Island: The Effects of Resource Deprivation on Urban Violence in Spatially and Socially Proximate Communities," *Criminology* 44, no. 3 (August 2006): 509–545; Thomas M. Arvanites and Robert H. DeFina, "Business Cycles and Street Crime," *Criminology* 44, no. 1 (February 2006): 139–164.

28. Barbara D. Warner, "Directly Intervene or Call the Authorities? A Study of Forms of Neighborhood Social Control Within a Social Disorganization Framework," *Criminology* 45, no. 1 (February 2007): 99–130.

29. David Maimon and Christopher R. Browning, "Unstructured Socializing, Collective Efficacy, and Violent Behavior Among Urban Youth," *Criminology* 48, no. 2 (May 2010): 443–474; quotation is on p. 443.

30. Ronald L. Simons et al., "Collective Efficacy, Authoritative Parenting and Delinquency: A Longitudinal Test of a Model Integrating Community– and Family-Level Processes," *Criminology* 43, no. 4 (December 2005): 989–1030; quotation is on p. 991 and is a reference to Ronald L. Simons et al., *Families, Delinquency and Crime: Linking Society's Most Basic Institution to Antisocial Behavior* (Los Angeles: Roxbury, 2004).

31. Émile Durkheim, *The Rules of Sociological Method* (New York: Free Press, 1964), p. 71; first published in 1938.

32. Ibid., p. 66.
33. Émile Durkheim, *The Division of Labour in Society* (New York: Free Press, 1964), pp. 374–388.
34. Émile Durkheim, *Suicide*, trans. John A. Spaulding and George Simpson (New York: Free Press of Glencoe, 1951).
35. "Searching for Clues to a Young Killer's Motivation," *New York Times* (7 December 2007), p. 22.
36. Robert K. Merton, *Social Theory and Social Structure*, enl. ed. (New York: Free Press, 1968), p. 176.
37. Ibid., pp. 189, 190, 192–193.
38. Ibid., p. 241. For a more recent statement by Merton, see Robert K. Merton, "On the Evolving Synthesis of Differential Association and Anomie Theory: Perspective from the Sociology of Science," *Criminology* 35 (August 1997): 517–525.
39. Edward Sagarin, *Deviants and Deviance: An Introduction to the Study of Disvalued People and Behavior* (New York: Holt, Rinehart & Winston, 1975), pp. 108–109.
40. See Ruth Kornhauser, *Social Sources of Delinquency* (Chicago: University of Chicago Press, 1978).
41. See Margaret Farnworth and Michael J. Leiber, "Strain Theory Revisited: Economic Goals, Educational Means, and Delinquency," *American Sociological Review* 54 (April 1989): 263–274.
42. See, for example, Scott Menard, "A Developmental Test of Mertonian Anomie Theory," *Journal of Research in Crime and Delinquency* 32 (May 1995): 136–174.
43. Steven F. Messner and Richard Rosenfeld, *Crime and the American Dream* (Belmont, CA: Wadsworth, 1994), p. 78. The fourth edition of this text was published in 2007.
44. Steven F. Messner and Richard Rosenfeld, "An Institutional-Anomie Theory of Crime," in *Explaining Criminals and Crime*, ed. Raymond Paternoster and Ronet Bachman (Los Angeles: Roxbury, 2001), pp. 151–160.
45. Richard Rosenfeld and Steven F. Messner, "The Origins, Nature, and Prospects of Institutional-Anomie Theory," in *The Essential Criminology Reader*, ed. Stuart Henry and Mark M. Lanier (Boulder, CO: Westview Press, 2006), pp. 164–173; quotations are on pp. 167 and 171.
46. See, for example, the work of Mitchell B. Chamlin and John K. Cochran, "Assessing Messner and Rosenfeld's Institutional Anomie Theory: A Partial Test," *Criminology* 33 (August 1995): 411–429.
47. Eric P. Baumer and Regan Gustafson, "Social Organization and Instrumental Crime: Assessing the Empirical Validity of Classic and Contemporary Anomie Theories," *Criminology* 45, no. 3 (August 2007): 617–664; quotation is on p. 617.
48. Robert Agnew, "Foundation for a General Strain Theory of Crime and Delinquency," *Criminology* 30 (February 1992): 47–87; quotations are on pp. 74 and 75.
49. Robert Agnew, *Pressured into Crime: An Overview of General Strain Theory* (Los Angeles: Roxbury, 2006).
50. Ibid., pp. 37–38.
51. Ibid., p. 48.
52. Ibid., pp. 175–186.
53. Agnew, "Foundation for a General Strain Theory," pp. 71–74.
54. See, for example, Agnew, *Pressured into Crime*; Agnew, *Juvenile Delinquency: Causes and Control* (Los Angeles: Roxbury, 2001); Agnew, "Building on the Foundation of General Strain Theory: Specifying the Types of Strain Most Likely to Lead to Crime and Delinquency," *Journal of Research in Crime and Delinquency* 38 (2001): 319–361.
55. Robert Agnew et al., "Strain, Personality Traits, and Delinquency: Extending General Strain Theory," *Criminology* 40, no. 1 (February 2002): 43–72; quotations are on pp. 43 and 44.
56. Raymond Paternoster and Paul Mazerolle, "General Strain Theory and Delinquency: A Replication and Extension," *Journal of Research in Crime and Delinquency* 31 (August 1994): 235–274; quotation is on p. 254. See also Robert Agnew, "Testing the Leading Crime Theories: An Alternative Strategy Focusing on Motivational Processes," *Journal of Research in Crime and Delinquency* 32 (November 1995): 363–398.
57. Ekaterina V. Botchkovar et al., "General Strain Theory: Additional Evidence Using Cross-Cultural Data," *Criminology* 47, no. 1 (February 2009): 131–173.
58. Joanne M. Kaufman, "Gendered Responses to Serious Strain: The Argument for a General Strain Theory of Deviance," *Justice Quarterly* 26, no. 3 (September 2009): 410–444; quotation is on p. 411.
59. Charles R. Tittle et al., "Strain, Crime, and Contingencies," *Justice Quarterly* 25, no. 2 (June 2008): 283–312.
60. Francis T. Cullen, "Social Support as an Organization Concept," *Justice Quarterly* 11, no. 4 (1994), reprinted in part in *Criminological Theory: Past to Present: Essential Readings*, ed. Francis T. Cullen and Robert Agnew (Los Angeles: Roxbury, 1999), pp. 236–245. See also Cullen et al., "Social Support and Social Reform: A Progressive Crime Control Agenda," *Crime and Delinquency* 45 (1999): 188–207.
61. Bernard et al., *Vold's Theoretical Criminology*, 6th ed., p. 170.
62. Frederic M. Thrasher, *The Gang*, abbrev. ed. (Chicago: University of Chicago Press, 1927, 1963).
63. William F. Whyte, *Street Corner Society* (Chicago: University of Chicago Press, 1943).
64. Kimberly Tobin, *Gangs: An Individual and Group Perspective* (Upper Saddle River, NJ: Prentice-Hall, 2008).
65. Arlen Egley Jr. et al., "Highlights of the 2008 National Youth Gang Survey," http://www.ncjrs.gov/pdffiles1/ojjdp/229249.pdf, accessed 2 October 2010.
66. Federal Bureau of Investigation, *National Gang Threat Assessment 2009*, http://www.fbi.gov/publications/ngta2009.pdf, accessed 2 October 2010.
67. Paul E. Bellair and Thomas L. McNulty, "Gang Membership, Drug Selling, and Violence in Neighborhood Context," *Justice Quarterly* 26, no. 4 (December 2009): 644–694; quotation is on p. 644.
68. J. Fagan, "The Social Organization of Drug Use and Drug Dealing Among Urban Gangs," *Criminology* 27 (1989): 633–699; quotation is on p. 660, cited in Bellair and McNulty, "Gang Membership," p. 645.
69. J.C. Howell and S. H. Decker, *The Youth Gangs, Drugs, and Violence Connection* (Washington, D.C.: U.S. Department of Justice, Office

of Justice Programs, Office of Juvenile Justice and Delinquency Prevention, 1999), p. 8, as cited in Bellair and McNulty, "Gang Membership," p. 645.

70. U.S. Department of Justice, Office of Community Oriented Policing Services, "Gangs," http://www.cops.usdoj.gov/default.asp?Item=1593, accessed 2 October 2010; "National Gang Threat Assessment Issued," Federal Bureau of Investigation (2 February 2009), http://www.fbi.gov/pressrel/pressrel09/ngta020209.htm, accessed 2 October 2010.

71. National Youth Gang Center, Office of Juvenile Justice and Delinquency, U.S. Department of Justice, "Federal Programs," http://ojjdp.ncjrs.org/pubs/gun_violence/sect08-f.html, accessed 2 October 2010.

72. See *Criminology and Public Policy* 8, no. 4 (November 2009): 667–732.

73. Adrienne Freng and Finn-Aage Esbensen, "Race and Gang Affiliation: An Examination of Multiple Marginality," *Justice Quarterly* 24, no. 4 (December 2007): 600–628. See this article for a summary of previous research.

74. Anne Campbell, "Self Definitions by Rejection: The Case of Gang Girls," *Social Problems* 34 (December 1987): 451–466.

75. Terry Carter, "'Equality with a Vengeance': Violent Crimes and Gang Activity by Girls Skyrocket," *American Bar Association Journal* 85 (November 1999): 22.

76. See Karen Heimer and Stacy DeCoster, "The Gendering of Violent Delinquency," *Criminology* 37 (May 1999): 277–318.

77. James C. Howell, Book Review, *Justice Quarterly* 17 (September 2000): 635, reviewing these books: Jody Miller, *One of the Guys* (New York: Oxford University Press, 2001); Mark Fleisher, *Dead End Kids: Gang Girls and the Boys They Know* (Madison: University of Wisconsin Press, 1998).

78. Jody Miller and Rod K. Brunson, "Gender Dynamics in Youth Gangs: A Comparison of Males' and Females' Accounts," *Justice Quarterly* 17, no. 3 (September 2000): 419–448.

79. Violent Crime Control and Law Enforcement Act of 1994, Public Law 103-322 (13 September 1994), Title XV, Section 150006(a) (2010).

80. *City of Chicago v. Morales*, 527 U.S. 41 (2000).

81. "Anti-Loiter Ordinance: Does It Have a Leg to Stand On?" *South Bend Tribune* (Indiana) (1 April 2002), p. 1C.

82. Judith Greene and Kevin Pranis, *Gang Wars: The Failure of Enforcement Tactics and the Need for Effective Public Safety Strategies*, Justice Policy Institute (July 2007), pp. 4–9; quotation is on p. 9, http://www.justicepolicy.org/images/upload/07-07_EXS_GangWars_GC-PS-AC-JJ.pdf, accessed 3 July 2010.

83. Albert K. Cohen, *Delinquent Boys: The Culture of the Gang* (New York: Free Press, 1955).

84. John I. Kitsuse and David C. Dietrick, "Delinquent Boys: A Critique," in *Society, Delinquency, and Delinquent Behavior*, ed. Harwin L. Voss (Boston: Little, Brown, 1979), pp. 238–245. For a recent analysis of Cohen's contributions, see J. Mitchell Miller et al., *Criminological Theory: A Brief Introduction* (New York: Pearson, 2008), pp. 118–120; Akers and Sellers, *Criminological Theories*, 5th ed., pp. 185–186.

85. Gresham Sykes and David Matza, "Techniques of Neutralization: A Theory of Delinquency," in *The Sociology of Crime and Delinquency*, 2d ed., ed. Marvin E. Wolfgang et al. (New York: Wiley, 1970), pp. 292–299.

86. John E. Hamlin, "The Misplaced Role of Rational Choice in Neutralization Theory," *Criminology* 26 (August 1988): 425–438.

87. Richard C. Hollinger, "Neutralizing in the Workplace: An Empirical Analysis of Property Theft and Production Deviance," *Deviant Behavior* 12, no. 2 (1991): 169–202.

88. W. William Minor, "Techniques of Neutralization," in *The Essential Criminology Reader*, ed. Henry and Lanier, pp. 100–108. The reference is to Robert Agnew, "The Techniques of Neutralization and Violence," *Criminology* 32 (1994): 555–580.

89. Volkan Topalli, "When Being Good Is Bad: An Expansion of Neutralization Theory," *Criminology* 43, no. 3 (August 2005): 797–835; quotations are on pp. 823 and 797, respectively.

90. David Matza, *Delinquency and Drift* (New York: Wiley, 1964), p. 28.

91. Richard A. Cloward and Lloyd E. Ohlin, *Delinquency and Opportunity: A Theory of Delinquent Gangs* (New York: Free Press, 1960). The following comments are from pp. 144–160.

92. See James F. Short Jr. et al., "Perceived Opportunities, Gang Membership, and Delinquency," *American Sociological Review* 30 (February 1956): 56–67.

93. Francis T. Cullen, "Were Cloward and Ohlin Strain Theorists? Delinquency and Opportunity Revisited," *Journal of Research in Crime and Delinquency* 25 (August 1988): 236.

94. For example, see Christopher J. Schreck et al., "On the Origins of the Violent Neighborhood: A Study of the Nature and Predictors of Crime-Type Differentiation Across Chicago Neighborhoods," *Justice Quarterly* 25, no. 4 (December 2009): 771–793.

95. See, for example, the research reviewed in Sonja E. Siennick and Jeremy Staff, "Explaining the Educational Deficits of Delinquent Youths," *Criminology* 46, no. 3 (August 2008): 609–636.

96. Delbert S. Elliott and Harwin L. Voss, *Delinquency and Dropout* (Lexington, MA: D. C. Heath, 1974), pp. 5, 204–205.

97. Ibid., pp. 206–207.

98. Eric A. Stewart, "School Social Bonds, School Climate, and School Misbehavior: A Multilevel Analysis," *Justice Quarterly* 20, no. 3 (September 2003): 575–604; quotation is on p. 575.

99. For a review of these earlier studies, see Eugene Maguin and Rolf Loeber, "Academic Performance and Delinquency," in *Crime and Justice: A Review of Research*, Vol. 20, ed. Michael Tonry (Chicago: University of Chicago Press, 1996), pp. 145–264.

100. Richard B. Felson and Jeremy Staff, "Explaining the Academic Performance-Delinquency Relationship," *Criminology* 44, no. 2 (May 2006): 299–320; quotation is on p. 315.

101. Gary LaFree and Richard Arum, "The Impact of Racially Inclusive Schooling on Adult Incarceration Rates Among U.S. Cohorts of African Americans and Whites Since 1930," *Criminology* 44, no. 1 (February 2006): 73–104.

102. Walter B. Miller, "Lower Class Culture as a Generating Milieu of Gang Delinquency," *Journal of Social Issues* 14 (1958): 5–19.

103. Kenneth Polk, "Urban Social Areas and Delinquency," *Social Problems* 14 (Winter 1967): 320–325; reprinted in *Ecology, Crime, and Delinquency,* ed. Harwin L. Voss and David M. Petersen (New York: Appleton-Century-Crofts, 1971), pp. 273–281.

104. Richard E. Johnson, "Social Class and Delinquent Behavior: A New Test," *Criminology* 18 (May 1980): 91.

105. See, for example, James F. Short Jr., "Differential Association and Delinquency," *Social Problems* 4 (January 1957): 233–239; F. Ivan Nye, *Family Relationships and Delinquent Behavior* (New York: Wiley, 1958). See also the earlier works of James S. Wallerstein and C. J. Wyle, "Our Law Abiding Lawbreakers," *Probation* 25 (April 1947): 107–112; Austin Porterfield, "Delinquency and Its Outcome in Courts and College," *American Journal of Sociology* 49 (November 1943): 199–208.

106. For a discussion of class and power as they relate to delinquency, see John Hagan et al., "The Class Structure of Gender and Delinquency: Toward a Power-Control Theory of Common Delinquent Behavior," *American Journal of Sociology* 90 (1985): 1151–1178.

107. See John Hagan, "The Poverty of a Classless Criminology—The American Society of Criminology 1991 Presidential Address," *Criminology* 30 (February 1992): 1–19.

108. Francis T. Cullen et al., "Having Money and Delinquent Involvement: The Neglect of Power in Delinquency Theory," *Criminal Justice and Behavior* 12 (June 1985): 171–192.

109. David Brownfield, "Social Class and Violent Behavior," *Criminology* 24 (August 1986): 435.

110. Cesar J. Rebellon, "Reconsidering the Broken Homes/Delinquency Relationship and Exploring Its Mediating Mechanism(s)," *Criminology* 40, no. 1 (February 2002): 103–135; citations omitted, quotation is on p. 103.

111. Ibid., p. 128.

112. Robert Apel and Catherine Kaukinin, "On the Relationship Between Family Structure and Antisocial Behavior: Parental Cohabitation and Blended Households," *Criminology* 46, no. 1 (February 2008): 35–70; quotation is on p. 35.

113. Richard E. Johnson, "Family Structure and Delinquency: General Patterns and Gender Differences," *Criminology* 24 (February 1986): 65–84.

114. See, for example, Joan McCord, "Some Child-Rearing Antecedents of Criminal Behavior in Adult Men," *Journal of Personality and Social Psychology* 37 (1979): 1477–1486.

115. See Nye, *Family Relationships and Delinquent Behavior.*

116. See Lawrence Rosen, "Family and Delinquency: Structure or Function?" *Criminology* 23 (1985): 553–573; Patricia Van Voorhis et al., "The Impact of Family Structure and Quality on Delinquency: A Comparative Assessment of Structural and Functional Factors," *Criminology* 26 (May 1988): 235–261.

117. Carolyn Smith and Terence P. Thornberry, "The Relationships Between Childhood Maltreatment and Adolescent Involvement in Delinquency," *Criminology* 33 (November 1995): 451–477.

118. See Timothy Brezina, "Adolescent Maltreatment and Delinquency: The Question of Intervening Processes," *Journal of Research in Crime and Delinquency* 35 (February 1998): 71–99.

119. Timothy O. Ireland et al., "Developmental Issues in the Impact of Child Maltreatment on Later Delinquency and Drug Use," *Criminology* 40, no. 2 (May 2002): 359–399; quotation is on p. 359.

120. Robert J. Sampson and John H. Laub, "Crime and Deviance over the Life Course: The Salience of Adult Social Bonds," *American Sociological Review* 55 (October 1990): 625.

121. Arthur J. Lurigio, "Going Backward to Move Forward in Criminological Theory and Research," *Criminal Justice and Behavior* 22 (June 1995): 200, reviewing Robert J. Sampson and John H. Laub, *Crime in the Making: Pathways and Turning Points Through Life* (Cambridge, MA: Harvard University Press, 1993).

122. J. David Hawkins et al., Office of Juvenile Justice and Delinquency Prevention, *Predictors of Youth Violence* (Washington, D.C.: U.S. Department of Justice, April 2000), pp. 3–5, http://www.ncjrs.gov/pdffiles1/ojjdp/179065.pdf, accessed 2 October 2010.

123. Greg Pogarsky et al., "The Delinquency of Children Born to Young Mothers: Results from the Rochester Youth Development Study," *Criminology* 41, no. 4 (November 2003): 1249–1286; quotation is on p. 1278.

124. Michael R. Gottfredson and Travis Hirschi, *A General Theory of Crime* (Palo Alto, CA: Stanford University Press, 1990).

125. Callie Harbin Burt et al., "A Longitudinal Test of the Effects of Parenting and the Stability of Self-Control: Negative Evidence for the General Theory of Crime," *Criminology* 44, no. 2 (May 2006): 353–396; quotation is on p. 381.

126. Brenda Sims Blackwell, "Perceived Sanction Threats, Gender, and Crime: A Test and Elaboration of Power-Control Theory," *Criminology* 38 (May 2000): 439–488; quotation is on p. 440.

127. John Hagan et al., "The Class Structure of Gender and Delinquency"; quotation is on p. 1174.

128. John Hagan, "Clarifying and Extending Power-Control Theory," *American Journal of Sociology* 95 (1990): 1024–1037.

129. John Hagan, *Structural Criminology* (New Brunswick, NJ: Rutgers University Press, 1989), p. 145.

130. John Hagan et al., "Class in the Household: A Power-Control Theory of Gender and Delinquency," *American Journal of Sociology* 92 (January 1987): 788–816; quotation is on p. 813.

131. Bill McCarthy et al., "In the Company of Women: Structure and Agency in a Revised Power-Control Theory of Gender and Delinquency," *Criminology* 37 (November 1999): 761–814; quotation is on p. 784.

132. Kyle L. Snow, "Contemporary Theories of Crime: Control and Socialization," Review Essay, *Criminal Justice and Behavior* 18 (December 1991): 493, quoting Hagan, *Structural Criminology*, p. 14.

133. Blackwell, "Perceived Sanction Threats, Gender, and Crime," pp. 439–488; quotations are on p. 477.

134. Brenda Sims Blackwell et al., "A Power-Control Theory of Vulnerability to Crime and Adolescent Role Exits Revisited," *Canadian Review of Sociology and Anthropology* 39 (2002): 199–218.

135. Lawrence E. Cohen and Marcus Felson, "Social Change and Crime Rate Trends: A Routine Activity Approach," *American Sociological Review* 44 (August 1979): 588–608; quotation is on p. 604.

136. Private letter from Marcus Felson to the author, 25 January 1988.

137. See Marcus Felson, *Crime and Everyday Life*, 3d ed. (Thousand Oaks, CA: Sage, 2002).

138. Steven F. Messner and Kenneth Tardiff, "The Social Ecology of Urban Homicide: An Application of the 'Routine Activities' Approach," *Criminology* 23 (May 1985): 241–267.

139. Dennis W. Roncek and Pamela A. Maier, "Bars, Blocks and Crimes Revisited: Linking the Theory of Routine Activities to the Empiricism of 'Hot Spots,'" *Criminology* 29 (November 1991): 725–753.

140. James Lasley, "Drinking Routines, Lifestyles, and Predatory Victimizations: A Causal Analysis," *Justice Quarterly* 6 (December 1989): 529–542.

141. Michael Maxfield, "Household Composition, Routine Activities, and Victimization: A Comparative Analysis," *Journal of Quantitative Criminology* (1987): 301–320.

142. See Robert M. O'Brien, "Exploring the Intersexual Nature of Violent Crimes," *Criminology* 26 (February 1988): 151–170.

143. See Leslie W. Kennedy and Stephen W. Baron, "Routine Activities and a Subculture of Violence: A Study of Violence on the Street," *Journal of Research in Crime and Delinquency* 30 (February 1993): 88–111.

144. See James L. Massey et al., "Property Crime and the Routine Activities of Individuals," *Journal of Research in Crime and Delinquency* 26 (November 1989): 378–400; Elizabeth Ehrhardt Mustaine and Richard Tewksbury, "Predicting Risks of Larceny Theft Victimization: A Routine Activity Analysis Using Refined Lifestyle Measures," *Criminology* 36 (November 1998): 829–857.

145. Kristy Holtfreter et al., "Low Self-Control, Routine Activities, and Fraud Victimization," *Criminology* 46, no. 1 (February 2008): 189–220.

146. William R. Smith et al., "Furthering the Integration of Routine Activity and Social Disorganization Theories: Small Units of Analysis and the Study of Street Robbery as a Diffusion Process," *Criminology* 38 (May 2000): 489–524.

147. Paul F. Cromwell et al., "Routine Activities and Social Control in the Aftermath of a Natural Catastrophe," *European Journal on Criminal Policy and Research* 3 (1995): 56–69.

148. Martin D. Schwartz and Walter S. DeKeseredy, *Sexual Assault on the College Campus: The Role of Male Peer Support* (Thousand Oaks, CA: Sage, 1997).

149. Martin D. Schwartz et al., "Male Peer Support and a Feminist Routine Activities Theory: Understanding Sexual Assault on the College Campus," *Justice Quarterly* 18, no. 3 (September 2001): 623–649, quotation is on p. 647.

150. Steven F. Messner et al., "Risks of Criminal Victimization in Contemporary Urban China: An Application of Lifestyle/Routine Activities Theory," *Justice Quarterly* 24, no. 3 (September 2007): 496–522.

151. See, for example, D. Wayne Osgood and Amy L. Anderson, "Unstructured Socializing and Rates of Delinquency," *Criminology* 42, no. 2 (May 2004): 519–550.

152. Denise C. Gottfredson et al., "Distinguishing Characteristics of Effective and Ineffective After-School Programs to Prevent Delinquency and Victimization," *Criminology and Public Policy* 6, no. 2 (May 2007): 289–318.

153. Carol A. Zimmerman, "Routine Activity Theory and the Handling of Children and Policy Makers," *Criminology and Public Policy* 6, no. 2 (May 2007): 327–336; quotation is on p. 334.

154. Akers and Sellers, *Criminological Theories*, 5th ed., p. 44.

155. See, for example, Karl Marx and Friedrich Engels, *The German Ideology* (New York: International Library, 1947); Marx and Engels, *The Communist Manifesto* (New York: International Library, 1930).

156. Frank Tannenbaum, *Crime and the Community* (Boston: Ginn, 1938).

157. Willem A. Bonger, *Criminality and Economic Conditions,* trans. Henry P. Horton (Boston: Little, Brown, 1916). This work was reissued with an introduction by criminologist Austin T. Turk (Bloomington: Indiana University Press, 1969).

158. C. Ronald Huff, "Conflict Theory in Criminology," in *Radical Criminology: The Coming Crises*, ed. James A. Inciardi (Beverly Hills, CA: Sage, 1980), p. 69.

159. Olena Antonaccio and Charles R. Tittle, "A Cross-National Test of Bonger's Theory of Criminality and Economic Conditions," *Criminology* 45, no. 4 (November 2007): 925–958; quotation is on p. 950.

160. Thorsten Sellin, *Culture, Conflict, and Crime*, Bulletin no. 41 (New York: Social Science Research Council, 1938), p. 105.

161. George B. Vold, *Theoretical Criminology* (New York: Oxford University Press, 1958), p. 208.

162. George B. Vold et al., *Theoretical Criminology*, 5th ed. (New York: Oxford University Press, 2002), p. 229. See also the latest edition of this text, updated and authored by Thomas J. Bernard et al., *Vold's Theoretical Criminology*, 6th ed. (New York: Oxford University Press, 2010).

163. Austin T. Turk, "Law as a Weapon in Social Conflict," *Social Problems* 23 (February 1976): 288.

164. See Austin T. Turk, *Political Criminality: The Defiance and Defense of Authority* (Beverly Hills, CA: Sage, 1982); Turk, *Criminality and Legal Order* (Chicago: Rand McNally, 1969).

165. Austin T. Turk, "Criminology and Conflict Theory," in *The Essential Criminology Reader*, ed. Henry and Lanier, pp. 185–190; quotation is on p. 186.

166. William V. Pelfrey, *The Evolution of Criminology* (Cincinnati, OH: Anderson, 1980), pp. 64, 68.

167. See Richard G. Greenleaf and Lonn Lanza-Kaduce, "Sophistication, Organization, and Authority-Subject Conflict: Rediscovering and Unraveling Turk's Theory of Norm Resistance," *Criminology* 33 (November 1995): 565–585.

168. Michael J. Lynch and W. Byron Groves, *A Primer in Radical Criminology*, 2d ed. (New York: Harrow & Heston, 1989), pp. viii, ix, 4.

169. Stephen Schafer, *Theories in Criminology* (New York: Random House, 1969), p. 256.

170. For an overview of Marx's contributions, see Bernard et al., *Vold's Theoretical Criminology*, 6th ed., pp. 268–271.

171. Ian Taylor et al., *The New Criminology: For a Social Theory of Deviance* (New York: Harper & Row, 1973); Taylor et al., eds., *Critical Criminology* (London: Routledge & Kegan Paul, 1975).

172. See Karl Marx, *Critique of Political Economy* (New York: International Library, 1904; originally published 1859).

173. Richard Quinney, *Criminal Justice in America* (Boston: Little, Brown, 1974), p. 95.

174. Richard Quinney, "The Production of Criminology," *Criminology* 16 (February 1979): 445, 455.

175. Richard Quinney, *Critique of Legal Order: Crime Control in a Capitalist Society* (Boston: Little, Brown, 1974).

176. Ibid., p. 165.

177. Richard Quinney, *Criminology: Analysis and Critique of Crime in the United States* (Boston: Little, Brown, 1974), pp. 37–41.

178. Richard Quinney, *Class, State and Crime: On the Theory and Practice of Criminal Justice* (New York: McKay, 1977), pp. 61–62, 165.

179. See Richard Quinney, *Social Existence: Metaphysics, Marxism, and the Social Sciences* (Beverly Hills, CA: Sage, 1982); Quinney, *Providence: The Development of Social and Moral Order* (New York: Longman, 1980).

180. Richard Quinney and John Wildeman, *The Problem of Crime: A Peace and Social Justice Perspective*, 3d ed. (Mountain View, CA: Mayfield, 1991), p. viii.

181. Herman Schwendinger and Julia Schwendinger, "Defenders of Order or Guardians of Human Rights?" *Issues in Criminology* 5 (1970): 113–146.

182. Herman Schwendinger and Julia Schwendinger, "Rape Victims and the False Sense of Guilt," *Crime and Social Justice* 6 (1976): 4–17.

183. See Herman Schwendinger and Julia Schwendinger, "The Paradigmatic Crisis in Delinquency Theory," *Crime and Social Justice* 18 (Winter 1982): 70–78; Schwendinger and Schwendinger, *Adolescent Subcultures and Delinquency* (New York: Praeger, 1985).

184. See, for example, William J. Chambliss and Robert Seidman, *Law, Order, and Power* (Reading, MA: Addison-Wesley, 1971).

185. Lynch and Groves, *A Primer in Radical Criminology*, 2d ed., p. 26.

186. Mark Colvin and John Pauly, "A Critique of Criminology: Toward an Integrated Structural-Marxist Theory of Delinquency Production," *American Journal of Sociology* 89 (November 1983): 513–551.

187. Akers and Sellers, *Criminological Theories*, 5th ed., pp. 248–249.

188. Hal Pepinsky, "Peacemaking," in *The Essential Criminology Reader*, ed. Henry and Lanier, pp. 278–285; quotations are on

pp. 278 and 279. See also Harold E. Pepinsky and Richard Quinney, eds., *Criminology as Peacemaking* (Bloomington: Indiana University Press, 1991).

189. John Randolph Fuller and John F. Wozniak, "Peacemaking Criminology: Past, Present, and Future," pp. 251–273, in *Taking Stock: The Status of Criminological Theory: Advances in Criminological Theory*, Vol. 15, ed. Francis T. Cullen et al. (New Brunswick, NJ: Transaction, 2006); quotation is on p. 264.

190. Jock Young, "The Tasks Facing a Realist Criminology," *Contemporary Crises* 11 (1987): 337–356.

191. See, for example, Walter S. DeKeseredy and Martin D. Schwartz, "Left Realist Theory," in *The Essential Criminology Reader*, ed. Henry and Lanier, pp. 307–315.

192. Ibid., pp. 309, 310.

193. See Bruce A. Arrigo, "Postmodern Theory and Criminology," in *The Essential Criminology Reader*, ed. Henry and Lanier, pp. 224–233.

194. Bernard et al., *Vold's Theoretical Criminology*, 6th ed., p. 279.

195. Gresham M. Sykes, "The Rise of Critical Criminology," *Journal of Criminal Law and Criminology* 65 (June 1974): 212–213.

196. Michael J. Lynch, "The Extraction of Surplus Value, Crime and Punishment: A Preliminary Examination," *Contemporary Crisis* 12 (1988): 329–344.

197. Ronald L. Akers, "Theory and Ideology in Marxist Criminology: Comments on Turk, Quinney, Toby, and Klockars," *Criminology* 16 (February 1979): 528, 543.

198. Sykes, "The Rise of Critical Criminology," p. 213.

199. Michael J. Lynch and Paul B. Stretesky, "The New Radical Criminology and the Same Old Criticisms," in *The Essential Criminology Reader*, ed. Henry and Lanier, p. 194.

200. Ibid., p. 194.

201. Freda Adler, *Sisters in Crime* (Prospect Heights, IL: Waveland Press, 1975; reprinted 1985), pp. 19–20. For a discussion of the *masculinity hypothesis*, see Rita J. Simon and Heather Ahn-Redding, *The Crimes Women Commit*, 3d ed. (Lanham, MD: Lexington, 2005).

202. See Richard Deming, *Women: The New Criminals* (Nashville, TN: Thomas Nelson, 1977).

203. See Darrell Steffensmeier, "Flawed Arrest 'Rates' and Overlooked Reliability Problems in UCR Arrest Statistics: A Comment on Wilson's 'The Masculinity of Violent Crime—Some Second Thoughts,'" *Journal of Criminal Justice* 11 (1983): 167–171.

204. Rita James Simon, *Women and Crime* (Lexington, MA: D. C. Heath, 1975).

205. Akers and Sellers, *Criminological Theories*, 5th ed, p. 277.

206. Ibid., p. 278.

207. See Coramae Richey Mann, *Female Crime and Delinquency* (Tuscaloosa: University of Alabama Press, 1984); Meda Chesney-Lind and Lisa Pasko, *The Female Offender: Girls, Women, and Crime*, 2d ed. (Thousand Oaks, CA.: Sage, 2004).

208. Darrell J. Steffensmeier, "Crime and the Contemporary Woman: An Analysis of Changing Levels of Female Property Crime, 1960–75," *Social Forces* 57 (December 1978): 566–584.

209. Darrell J. Steffensmeier, "Organization Properties and Sex-Segregation in the Underworld: Building a Sociological Theory of Sex Differences in Crime," *Social Forces* 61 (June 1983): 1010–1032.

210. Darrell J. Steffensmeier and Renee Hoffman Steffensmeier, "Trends in Female Delinquency: An Examination of Arrest, Juvenile Court, Self-Report, and Field Data," *Criminology* 18 (May 1980): 62–85.

211. Darrell J. Steffensmeier and Cathy Streifel, "Time-Series Analysis of the Female Percentage of Arrests for Property Crimes, 1960–1985: A Test of Alternative Explanations," *Justice Quarterly* 9 (March 1992): 77–103; quotation is on p. 77.

212. See Lee H. Bowker, *Women, Crime, and the Criminal Justice System* (Lexington, MA: D. C. Heath, 1978).

213. Meda Chesney-Lind and Randall G. Shelden, *Girls, Delinquency, and Juvenile Justice* (Pacific Grove, CA: Brooks/Cole, 1992). See also Chesney-Lind, *The Female Offender: Girls, Women, and Crime* (Thousand Oaks, CA: Sage, 1997).

214. Jennifer Schwartz and Bryan D. Rookey, "The Narrowing Gender Gap in Arrests: Assessing Competing Explanations Using Self-Report, Traffic Fatality, and Official Data on Drunk Driving," *Criminology* 46, no. 3 (August 2008): 637–672; quotation is on p. 662.

215. Ibid., p. 663, referring to the following works: Meda Chesney-Lind and Vickie Paramore, "Are Girls Getting More Violent?" *Journal of Contemporary Criminal Justice* 17 (2001): 142–166; David Garland, *The Culture of Control: Crime and Social Order in Contemporary Society* (Chicago: University of Chicago Press, 2002); Jennifer Schwartz and Darrell Steffensmeier, "The Nature of Female Offending: Patterns and Explanation," in *Female Offenders: Critical Perspective and Effective Interventions*, ed. Ruth Zaplin (Boston: Jones and Bartlett); Darrell Steffensmeier et al., "An Assessment of Recent Trends in Girls' Violence Using Diverse Longitudinal Sources: Is The Gender Gap Closing?" *Criminology* 43, no. 2 (May 2005): 355–406.

216. Robert Agnew, "An Overview of General Strain Theory," in *Explaining Criminals and Crime: Essays in Contemporary Criminological Theory,* ed. Raymond Paternoster and Ronet Bachman (Los Angeles: Roxbury, 2001), pp. 161–174; quotation is on p. 169.

217. See Lisa M. Broidy and Robert Agnew, "Gender and Crime: A General Strain Theory Perspective," *Journal of Research in Crime and Delinquency* 34 (August 1997): 275–306.

218. Paul Mazerolle, "Gender, General Strain, and Delinquency: An Empirical Examination," *Justice Quarterly* 15 (March 1998): 65–92.

219. Joan N. Neff and Dennis E. Waite, "Male Versus Female Substance Abuse Patterns Among Incarcerated Juvenile Offenders: Comparing Strain and Social Learning Variables," *Justice Quarterly* 24, no. 1 (March 2007): 106–132.

220. Lisa M. Broidy, "A Test of General Strain Theory," *Criminology* 39 (February 2001): 9–37; quotation is on p. 30. For a supporting study, see Nicole Leeper Piquero and Miriam D. Sealock, "Gender and General Strain Theory: A Preliminary Test of Broidy and Agnew's Gender/GST Hypotheses," *Justice Quarterly* 21, no. 1 (March 2004): 125–157.

221. Sung Joon Jang, "Gender Differences in Strain, Negative Emotions, and Coping Behaviors: A General Strain Theory Approach," *Justice Quarterly* 24, no. 3 (September 2007): 523–549; conclusions are on p. 543.

222. Kaufman, "Gendered Responses to Serious Strain," p. 439.

223. James W. Messerschmidt, *Capitalism, Patriarchy and Crime: Toward Socialist Feminist Criminology* (Totowa, NJ: Rowman & Littlefield, 1986), p. 41.

224. James W. Messerschmidt, "Masculinities and Theoretical Criminology," in *The Essential Criminology Reader*, ed. Henry and Lanier, pp. 214–220; quotation is on p. 218.

225. See James W. Messerschmidt, *Masculinities and Crime: Critique and Reconceptualization of Theory* (Lanham, MD.: Rowman & Littlefield, 1993), p. 85.

226. Marsali Hansen and Michele Harway, eds., *Battering and Family Therapy: A Feminist Perspective* (Newbury Park, CA: Sage, 1993), p. 217.

227. Jody Miller and Norman A. White, "Gender and Adolescent Relationship Violence: A Contextual Examination," *Criminology* 41, no. 4 (November 2003): 1207–1248; quotations are on pp. 1241, 1243, and 1244.

228. Christopher W. Mullins and Richard Wright, "Gender, Social Networks, and Residential Burglary," *Criminology* 41, no. 3 (August 2003): 813–839.

229. Quinney and Wildeman, *The Problem of Crime,* 3d ed., p. 85.

230. See, for example, Sally S. Simpson and Lori Ellis, "Doing Gender: Sorting Out the Caste and Crime Conundrum," *Criminology* 33 (February 1995): 47–81.

231. Kathleen Daly and Meda Chesney-Lind, "Feminism and Criminology," *Justice Quarterly* 5 (1988): 497–538; quotation is on p. 506.

232. Meda Chesney-Lind, "Girls' Crime and Woman's Place: Toward a Feminist Model of Female Delinquency," *Crime and Delinquency* 35 (1989): 5–29; quotation is on p. 19.

233. Jeanne Flavin and Amy Desautels, "Feminism and Crime," in *Rethinking Gender, Crime, and Justice: Feminist Readings*, ed. Claire M. Renzetti et al. (Los Angeles: Roxbury, 2006), pp. 11–28; quotation is on p. 12.

234. See, for example, Daly and Chesney-Lind, "Feminism and Criminology."

235. Karen Heimer and Stacy De Coster, "The Gendering of Violent Delinquency," *Criminology* (May 1999): 277–319; quotation is on pp. 305, 306.

236. See, for example, Darrell Steffensmeier and Emilie Allan, "Gender and Crime: Toward a Gendered Theory of Female Offending," *Annual Review of Sociology* 22 (1996): 262–283; Karen Heimer et al., "Opening the Black Box: The Social Psychology of Gender and Delinquency," *Sociology of Crime, Law, and Deviance* 4 (2006): 109–135, both cited in Akers and Sellers, *Criminological* Theories, 5th ed., p. 285.

237. Akers and Sellers, *Criminological Theories*, 5th ed., p. 287.

238. Ibid., p. 290.

CHAPTER 6

Sociological Theories of Criminal Behavior II: The Social-Process Approach

Social institutions are important in socializing children. In this first picture, parents are reading to their child at home. In the second, family members are attending religious services together. In the third, children are arriving by bus at their school. The environment of social institutions may have a significant impact on whether a child becomes a delinquent or law-abiding person.

INTRODUCTION

This chapter is concerned with the *process* by which people become criminals. Do they learn this behavior? If so, how and under what circumstances? The chapter begins with a discussion of learning theory, which includes a look at the development of imitation theory in the 1800s, followed by a brief look at the influence that today's media may have on imitative behavior. The chapter then turns to an analysis of the social learning theory called *differential association*. The influence of that theory is assessed in the light of recent reformulations of learning theory by sociologists and criminologists.

The next section of the chapter examines *control theories*, which are based on the assumption that criminal behavior occurs when society's normal methods of controlling people break down. The fourth section discusses *labeling theory*, which focuses on the process by which people who engage in certain acts come to be called (or labeled) criminal, whereas others who engage in those same kinds of behavior are not labeled. A section on *integrated theories* discusses numerous approaches to integrating theories of criminal behavior. The chapter closes with a conclusion to criminal behavior theories and an analysis of the policy implications of the theories of criminality that are explored in this chapter and in Chapter 5.

C hapter 5 discussed sociological theories that emphasize the relationship of criminal behavior to the social structure or organization of society. Whether the environment is seen as a determining or a facilitating factor in the causation of crime, the emphasis is on the environment's structure rather than on individual characteristics, as in the constitutional theories discussed in Chapters 3 and 4. One problem with the social-structural theories, however, is that they do not explain the *process* by which individuals turn to crime. This chapter analyzes social-process theories, which attempt to explain *how* individuals become criminals.

It is not possible to separate all sociological theories into the categories of social structure and social process. Some theories may be placed in both categories. For example, the neutralization theory of Gresham Sykes and David Matza, discussed in Chapter 5, explains the *process* by which a person neutralizes any inhibitions that he or she might have against violating laws. Yet the theory is also related to cultural transmission and subcultures, which are aspects of the social structure. Likewise, labeling theory is discussed in this chapter because it explains the *process* by which a person becomes a criminal; namely, the person is labeled by those in a position to make that determination. Others characterize labeling theory as a social-structural theory that has some similarities to conflict theory because it is through the social institutions that labeling occurs.

Social-process theories developed as sociologists and criminologists began to analyze the fact that not all people exposed to the same social-structural conditions respond in the same way. Some become law-abiding citizens, and others become criminals. Not all criminals respond in criminal ways in all circumstances; likewise, not all non-criminals observe the law at all times. To explain these differences, social scientists suggest that human behavior is learned and that criminal behavior may be acquired in the same way as any other behavior. This approach has also been taken by other disciplines.

Learning Theory

Various scholars have based their research on *learning theory*. The topic was introduced in Chapter 4's discussion of psychological theories. There, it was emphasized that learning may be accomplished by using other people as models and that motivations can come from biological and psychological factors. We noted the work of Hans J. Eysenck, who stressed the interrelationship between psychology and biology in explaining how humans learn to behave. This chapter adds the social factor, but first, it looks at other contributions that may have influenced the development of social concepts of learning theory.

Although learning theory has been developed by sociologists and psychologists to explain a variety of behaviors, this chapter's discussion of the theory focuses on criminal behavior.

Tarde's Imitation Theory

Gabriel Tarde (1843–1904), a forerunner of modern imitation theory, was born in southern France. After studying law, he was a magistrate for many years. He showed considerable interest in social problems and, as a judge, proved himself to be a deep thinker and profound philosopher. Reacting against Cesare Lombroso and the positivist school, Tarde argued that people are not born criminal; rather, they become criminal. He saw criminal behavior as the result primarily of social factors, a belief that constitutes one of his greatest contributions to criminology.[1]

Tarde rejected the biological and other physical theories of criminal behavior, but he did not become a social determinist. He thought people had some choice in their behavior, although he believed that when the ability to choose is impaired, people should not be held responsible for their criminal acts.[2]

Tarde's social-process theory of criminal behavior is reflected in his belief that all the "important acts of social life are carried out under the domination of example."[3] Upon this belief, he formulated his *theory of imitation*, through which he explained the process of acquiring criminal as well as noncriminal behavior. In developing his theory, Tarde distinguished between fashion and custom, both of which are forms of imitation. *Fashion* is characteristic of the imitation that takes place in crowds or cities where contact is close and frequent. *Custom* refers to the phenomenon that occurs in small towns and rural areas where contact is less frequent and change occurs less frequently. Since both fashion and custom are forms of imitation, each occurs to some degree within a society; fashion may uproot and create a new custom. Since fashion and custom are related to the degree of social contact, Tarde formulated his first law of imitation: "Men imitate one another in proportion as they are in close contact."[4]

Tarde's second law of imitation was that the *inferior imitates the superior*. Peasants imitate royalty; small-town and rural residents imitate the acts of city residents. Tarde wrote: "Infectious epidemics spread with the air or the wind; epidemics of crime follow the line of the telegraph."[5]

Tarde's third law of imitation was the *law of insertion*: "When two mutually exclusive fashions come together, one can be substituted for the other. When this happens, there is a decline in the older method and an increase in the newer method."[6] Tarde illustrated this position by noting the increase in the use of a gun rather than a knife for murder.

Tarde's neglect of the physical, psychological, and economic influences on behavior and his oversimplification of causation led most sociologists to reject his imitation theory. But according to sociologist Stephen Schafer, Tarde's "emphasis on the social origins of crime had a lasting impact on criminological thought in both Europe and America."[7]

The recent emphasis on the influence of the mass media on behavior has refocused attention on the possible impact of imitation on behavior, especially criminal behavior.

The Modern Media and Imitation

It is possible that delinquent and criminal behaviors are learned from the media rather than through association with other human beings. Whether the process is one of identification or imitation, the result is the same: What the media portray may influence how the audience behaves. Some of that impact may be seen in the concern over whether television has an effect on behavior. This concern raises the possibility of psychological and sociological explanations of the process by which a person becomes either deviant or law-abiding.

Television and the Internet are the primary sources of news for most Americans, many of whom may believe that the news they acquire is reasonably accurate. The issue here, however, is whether exposure to television (or other media, such as movies or the Internet) *causes* crime. There are arguments pro and con, and actual causation is difficult to prove. A Yale University psychology professor, who in 1960 began a study of the causes of aggression, visited his sample 10 years later and again in another 10 years; he reported a high correlation between violence and the amount of television watched. The professor stated that he "found that the violent programming [his subjects] had watched was related to the seriousness of the crimes they committed, how aggressive they were to their spouses, and even to how aggressive their own kids were."[8]

Writing in the 1970s, one of the most prominent psychological learning theorists, Albert Bandura, referred to the "reciprocal interaction between cognitive, behavioral and environmental determinants."[9] According to Bandura, research had shown that television, the most influential of the media for adolescents, had four types of effects on their social behavior:

1. The teaching of aggressive styles of conduct
2. The lessening of restraints on aggression
3. Desensitization and habituation to violence
4. The shaping of images of reality on which people base their actions

Bandura claimed that television could distort people's perceptions of the real world: "Heavy viewers see the society at large as more dangerous regardless of their educational level, sex, age, and amount of newspaper reading."[10]

Some of the attention given to the effects that violence on television and the Internet might have on the behavior of adults and children is anecdotal (i.e., based on individual stories rather than on empirical research). Crimes such as those discussed in Media Focus 6.1 may, however, help form people's attitudes about the influence of the media. Consider those crimes carefully. How do you react to each case in terms of a causal relationship between the criminal act and television viewing?

Researchers remind us that media exposure does not occur in a vacuum. Although most of the surveys of reactions to a particular television show, for example, occur

6.1 Crime as Imitation: Are the Media Responsible?

The following crimes were reported in the media during recent years. Each case stated that the media were the cause or a major cause of the crime. What questions would you raise in reaction to these cases?

1. In October 2009 in the village of Mont Vernon, New Hampshire, while her husband was out of town on business, a 42-year-old nurse was hacked to death with a machete in her bed. Her 11-year-old daughter, Jaimie, was maimed, knifed multiple times, and left for dead, but she subsequently recovered. Police say the perpetrators, allegedly four teenagers, did not know she survived until they checked the Internet the following day. The suspects charged with these crimes said they chose that particular home because it was in a rural area. One of the teens had just updated his Facebook page to state that "*Dexter* is such a funny show." *Dexter*, a television show, is about a serial killer.

2. T. J. Soloman, age 15, was accused of shooting six classmates (one died) at his high school in Conyers, Georgia. Police found a letter written by Soloman in which he stated his allegiance to the "brothers and sisters related to the trench coat mafia." That was a group in which Littleton, Colorado's, Columbine High School shooters, Eric Harris and Dylan Klebold, were fringe members. Just one month previously, Harris and Klebold had gone on a rampage at their high school, killing 14 students and one teacher before killing themselves. Soloman was reported to have boasted to other students that he could do a better job than the Columbine killers and that his school should have had a shooting long before. It was suggested that Soloman's knowledge of the Columbine shootings came from his exposure to television.[1]

3. A 15-year-old boy, who was accused of sexually abusing his 8-year-old half-sister for the previous three years, said he got the idea for the crime from watching television. The youth (along with his 13-year-old brother) testified that he had oral, anal, and vaginal sex with the child after their mother left for work in the mornings and before she returned in the afternoons. When asked by police how he learned these behaviors, the boy said, "I watched *The Jerry Springer Show*." When asked what that meant, he said he watched a show on incest. The program was characterized by lewd language and physical violence, but only one or two episodes dealt with incest. Still, one of those shows was entitled "I'm Pregnant by My Brother."[2]

4. After arresting a 17-year-old accused of murdering his stepmother and half-sister, police claimed the suspect was obsessed with the movie *Natural Born Killers*. Friends said the youth had been unhappy, had threatened to kill his family, and after seeing the movie, shaved his head and wore tinted glasses similar to those worn by the offender in the movie.[3]

5. A 17-year-old boy was convicted of murdering a woman, whom he stabbed and strangled. His defense was that he had watched the movie *A Clockwork Orange* several times and as a result "did bad things." The movie portrays a "marauding young Briton with a vacant stare who acts on his violent impulses." The movie character and his gang associates engaged in random rapes and murders on London's streets. The movie was nominated for several Academy Awards but was criticized for its portrayal of violence. After he received several death threats, the director withdrew the movie from circulation in Britain.

At his trial, the defendant testified that he did "bad things" only when he wore a black *Clockwork Orange* T-shirt, which he was wearing when he killed the victim.[4]

6. A 4-year-old boy accidentally shot and killed his 2-year-old sister. Authorities say the boy learned how to load a gun by watching television and learned to shoot by playing with his friend's air gun.[5]

7. The mother of a 5-year-old boy, who started a fire that killed his younger sister, claimed that the boy got the idea from the MTV cartoon "Beavis and Butt-Head," which promoted burning as fun. Shortly after the boy watched the cartoon, his mother caught him playing with matches. According to the fire chief who investigated the fire, "The children admitted they saw it on TV and thought they could do it, too."[6]

8. A 16-year-old, Mario Padilla, assisted by his 14-year-old cousin, stabbed Padilla's mother, Gina Castillo, 45 times while she sat at her computer. The teen stated that he had watched violent television programs since he was 7 years old, that he was influenced by them (in particular the "slice-and-dice" *Scream* movies), and that he encouraged parents not to let their children watch such programs. Padilla was sentenced to life in prison without the possibility of parole. Padilla reportedly told authorities that he and his cousin (who was sentenced to 25 years to life) robbed Castillo to buy costumes like those worn by the killers in *Scream* and that they planned to wear those while killing their classmates.[7]

---

1. "Colorado Killers Inspired Youth in Georgia Shooting, Note Says," *New York Times* (10 August 1999), p. 8.
2. "Youth Says He Got Idea for Sexual Abuse from Springer Show," *New York Times* (8 January 1999), p. 10.
3. "Police Seize Suspect Obsessed by a Movie," *New York Times* (11 November 1994), p. 9.
4. "Teen Found Guilty of Murder, Blames *A Clockwork Orange*," *Miami Herald* (23 June 1990), p. 3B.
5. "Boy, Four, Learned How to Load Gun from TV—He Kills Sister," *Miami Herald* (28 August 1991), p. 3B.
6. "Mother Blames a Deadly Fire on an MTV Cartoon," *New York Times* (10 October 1993), p. 14.
7. "Teenager: 'Scream' Films Inspired Me to Kill Mom," *St. Petersburg Times* (15 January 1998), p. 14; "Unkind Cut," *The Australian* (29 July 1999), p. M15.

right after the show is televised, we cannot assume a direct cause-and-effect relationship. The behavior must be examined in the total context in which it occurs, and the facts can be misleading. For example, women watch more television than men, yet crime rates are higher among men (although they are increasing at a faster rate among women than among men). Teens view less television than adults do, yet most property crimes are committed by teens and young adults (under 25). Clearly, something other than television is involved.

Scholars writing for an earlier National Institute of Justice review of research on the issue concluded that there is "no clear evidence of causal links" between television viewing and criminal behavior.[11] Research by other social scientists concluded that most of the research does *not* show a causal link between television and crime.[12] However, recent research reveals that watching television programs such as the popular ones that involve evidence (e.g., *CSI Miami*) is linked with an expectation among jurors that scientific evidence will be presented at trial, especially in rape (76 percent), breaking and entering (71 percent), murder or attempted murder (46 percent), and theft (59 percent) cases. Watching television may also influence conviction rates.[13]

The critical question is to determine the *processes* that are involved in reactions to the media and especially to violence. Psychological and sociological theories of behavior must be considered.[14] Many people who view the programs or movies in question do not engage in antisocial behavior. Why do they react in appropriate ways, whereas others who view the same material react in antisocial, even violent, ways? One scholar suggested the following explanation:

> The empirical and theoretical evidence suggests that . . . the effects of television's content depend in part on the extent to which contradictory messages are available, understood, and consistent. In the case of sex-role attitudes, messages from television are consistent and either absent or reinforced in real life, whereas in the case of aggressive behavior, most viewers receive contradictory messages from both sources. All viewers may learn aggression from television, but whether they act aggressively will depend on a variety of factors.[15]

The influence of television on crime has been measured in the context of publicity about capital punishment. One of the earlier scholars in this area found no relationship between television viewing of news about capital punishment and the incidence of homicide. The evidence did not support the assumption that publicizing executions deters homicides, nor did it support the assumption that publicity encourages and increases homicides. Such publicity may have communicated the impression that a person convicted of homicide was not likely to be executed, thus reducing any possible deterrent effect of capital punishment. But it seemed clear that "the current level of executions and media practices regarding executions in this country neither discourage nor promote murder."[16]

One social scientist's analysis of the impact of the media on crime covered many aspects of the relationship between the media, especially television, and criminal behavior. The research suggested that people are more aggressive socially because of the mass media, but social aggression was not always criminal, and most crime was not violent. The research implied that the relationship between the media and crime could be indirect and that the relationship was greater in property crimes than in violent crimes, with the possible exception of the impact of pornography. Further, there was some evidence of short-term imitation of media violence by children but mixed results of "an incorporation of violent behavior into the viewer's overall behavior pattern or a subsequent willingness among children to use violence as a problem-solving method."[17]

In 1998, after visiting and working with faculty and students who had witnessed the shootings at the Westside Middle School in Jonesboro, Arkansas, a psychology professor related his beliefs concerning the violence by young people in that incident and others. According to the professor, the behavior of the accused killers at Jonesboro, like many others, could be explained in part by the phenomenon of media-induced violence. The boys, who killed four students and a teacher and wounded 10 other people, were characterized by a lack of self-esteem and a sense of inferiority that, combined with media violence, can provoke violent behavior in young people who are "wannabes": "They want to be tough, they want to impress people, they want to make a bold statement and they don't know how. And then the media tells them how." The professor suggested that the media message was "killing is the route to greatness. Killing is the route to fame." The professor also suggested that specific types of role models on television may precipitate similar types of violence. He alleged that school shootings by white adolescent boys in 1997 and 1998 may have been influenced by the 1995 movie *The Basketball Diaries*. In that movie, the character played by *Titanic* star Leonardo DiCaprio entered a schoolroom and shot numerous teachers and children. "In doing so he became a role model that other white males desire to emulate." Movie producers and others rejected that analysis.[18]

The consideration of a possible impact of the media on crime, especially among young people, is not limited to the United States, as Global Focus 6.1 notes.

In reviewing three books on the relationship between the media and crime, one scholar explored the books' coverage of the impact of the media on crime victimization and the fear of crime as well as the commission of crime. Some of her conclusions were as follows:

- "[D]ata presented in the news, even when provided by seemingly unbiased sources, may be faulty and should be approached with caution. . . .
- [T]he news tends to focus on white, female victims, suggesting to their white, female viewers that their crime victimization potential is greater than is actually the case. . . .

6.1   Shooting Rampage in Finland: A Copycat Crime?

The possibility of imitation leading to copycat crimes was raised in 2007 after a teenager killed six students, a nurse, and the principal at his high school in Finland before committing suicide. After the shooting rampage, police stated that Pekka-Eric Auvinen, 18, may have been in contact through the Internet with 14-year-old Dillon Cossey, in Philadelphia, Pennsylvania, who had recently been arrested for planning an attack at his school. Both were alleged to have communicated through a myspace.com site that focused on the Columbine High School (Littleton, Colorado) killers, Eric Harris and Dylan Klebold, who killed 12 students and one teacher and wounded over 20 others before killing themselves in 1999.[1]

According to one media account,

More than eight years after the bloodiest high school massacre in U.S. history, Columbine has become a towering symbol of retribution and martyrdom among would-be imitators far beyond Littleton, Colo. . . . Eric Harris and Dylan Klebold have ascended to the status of folk heroes.[2]

Shortly after the shootings in Finland, two teenagers, aged 16 and 17, arrested in Stockholm, Sweden, and accused of conspiring to murder their principal and a janitor, were thought to have been inspired by the Finnish shootings.[3]

In Australia, Jason James Cousins, 30, was accused of posting a threat against students at Cambridge Park High School, which he once attended, stating that he would give the Finnish killer, whom he allegedly admired, four days of media attention before he began his own rampage.[4]

1. "School Shooters Use MySpace to Network," *UPI Release* (12 November 2007), n.p.
2. "Columbine Both Symbol, Obsession," *Philadelphia Inquirer* (15 November 2007), p 1.
3. "School Murder Plot," *Sunday Times* (Perth, Australia) (11 November 2007), p. 37.
4. "Net Threat to Shoot Students," *Daily Telegraph* (Australia) (14 November 2007), p. 13.

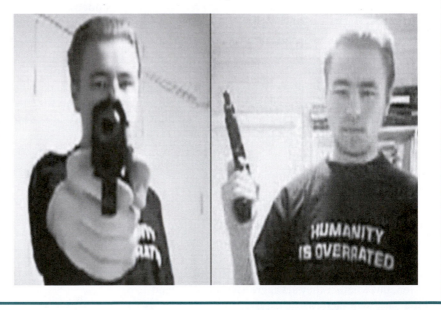

Crime as a function of imitation was raised after Pekka-Eric Auvinen, an 18-year-old Finnish student, began a shooting rampage at his high school, killing six students, a nurse, the principal, and himself. Auvinen reportedly had been in contact with an American student concerning other high school killings, including those at Columbine in Littleton, Colorado.

■ The media's coverage of drug problems in our society serves as a prop for the ideology of control and it has done so throughout its history. . . .
■ Not only do these accounts project representations that suggest that street crimes are the greater problem in Western societies, but they also portray offenders as crazed strangers who interact with the victims exclusively for the purpose of attacking or harming them."[19]

Whatever the media's impact might be in terms of imitation or copycat behavior, criminologists look at *social learning theory* as crucial to explaining the process by which people learn criminal behavior.

Social Learning Theory

Social learning theory in criminology is generally traced to the contributions of noted criminologist Edwin H. Sutherland ("widely recognized as the most important criminologist of the 20th century"[20]) and his **differential association** approach.

Sutherland's Differential Association Theory

When Sutherland was asked to write a criminology text in 1921, his primary interest was in the controversy that was raging between environmental and hereditary theories of behavior. Sutherland wanted to analyze criminal behavior by utilizing some of the prevailing sociological concepts. He was also interested in finding concrete causes of crime. As he examined the facts and issues, he decided that no concrete variables could explain crime. For example, the condition associated most frequently with crime is gender; that is, most people apprehended for crimes are men. But Sutherland said that it was obvious that gender was not the *cause* of crime. He turned to abstract explanations and decided that a learning process involving communication and interaction must be the principle that would explain all types of crime.[21]

In the 1939 edition of his text, Sutherland introduced the concept of differential association. As an explanation of criminal behavior, *differential association* is based on the premise that criminal behavior is learned in the same way that any other behavior is learned. Sutherland developed his concept of differential association into a theory to explain the *process* by which an individual engages in criminal behavior. Sutherland's theory has nine propositions.[22] They are discussed here, but for easy reference to the propositions alone, see Exhibit 6.1.

First, "criminal behavior is learned." In this proposition, Sutherland emphasized his belief that criminal behavior is not inherited. Nor did he believe that a person who has not been trained in criminal behavior invents that behavior. It must be learned.

Second, "criminal behavior is learned in interaction with other persons in a process of communication." That process involves gestures as well as verbal interactions. Third, "the principal part of the learning of criminal behavior occurs within intimate personal groups" (e.g., families). Sutherland did not believe that the media play an important role in the process. His approach should be understood in the context of pretelevision times.

Fourth, "the learning includes (a) techniques of committing the crime, which are sometimes very complicated, sometimes very simple; (b) the specific direction of motives, drives, rationalizations, and attitudes." Fifth, "the specific direction of motives and drives is learned from definitions of the legal codes as favorable or unfavorable." Sutherland pointed out that in American society, the definitions of legal codes are mixed: Some favor violating those codes, but others support compliance. The mixture creates cultural conflict with respect to legal codes.

Sixth, "a person becomes delinquent because of an excess of definitions favorable to violation of law over definitions unfavorable to violation of law." This statement is Sutherland's principle of differential association. Those who engage in criminal behavior do so because they have contacts with that type of behavior and are isolated from anticriminal behavior.

Seventh, "differential associations may vary in frequency, duration, priority, and intensity." This statement is a crucial one in Sutherland's theory, and it means that associations with criminal and noncriminal behavior vary in terms of those four elements. Sutherland stated that the first two, frequency and duration, did not need to be defined; their meaning is obvious. He suggested that *priority* is important in that behavior learned early in life might persist for a long time, but that is not always the case. In his view, "priority seems to be important principally through its selective influence." Finally, *intensity* "has to do with such things as the prestige of the source of a criminal or

EXHIBIT 6.1 — The Nine Propositions of Sutherland's Differential Association Theory

1. "Criminal behavior is learned.
2. Criminal behavior is learned in interaction with other persons in a process of communication.
3. The principal part of the learning of criminal behavior occurs within intimate personal groups.
4. When criminal behavior is learned, the learning includes (a) techniques of committing the crime, which are sometimes very complicated, sometimes very simple; (b) the specific direction of motives, drives, rationalizations, and attitudes.
5. The specific direction of motives and drives is learned from definitions of the legal codes as favorable or unfavorable.
6. A person becomes delinquent because of an excess of definitions favorable to violation of law over definitions unfavorable to violation of law.
7. Differential associations may vary in frequency, duration, priority, and intensity.
8. The process of learning criminal behavior by association with criminal and anticriminal patterns involves all of the mechanisms that are involved in any other learning.
9. While criminal behavior is an expression of general needs and values, it is not explained by those general needs and values since noncriminal behavior is an expression of the same needs and values."

Source: Edwin H. Sutherland, *Principles of Criminology*, 4th ed. (Philadelphia: Lippincott, 1947), pp. 6–7, emphasis omitted.

anticriminal pattern and with emotional reactions related to the associations." Sutherland acknowledged that it would be difficult to develop a precise formula to measure all of these four modalities.[23]

Eighth, "the process of learning criminal behavior by association with criminal and anticriminal patterns involves all of the mechanisms that are involved in any other learning." To Sutherland, the same learning theory that explained noncriminal behavior explained criminal behavior.

Ninth, "while criminal behavior is an expression of general needs and values, it is not explained by those general needs and values, since noncriminal behavior is an expression of the same needs and values." To Sutherland, the attempt to explain criminal behavior in terms of a person's needs or desires was as futile as trying to explain the behavior in terms of respiration: Breathing (like a need or desire) does not distinguish criminal from noncriminal behavior, although it is necessary for both.

Sutherland has had a "massive impact on criminology," according to some critics, primarily because he moved criminological thought away from biological and psychological theories to environmental influences. However, the theory was based on dated social learning theory, and the theory's propositions have proved difficult to test.[24]

In an attempt to test a portion of Sutherland's theory, one criminologist called the theory "the most truly sociological of all theories which have been advanced to explain criminal and delinquent behavior." However, this scholar also noted the difficulty of testing differential association.[25]

One early attempt to test differential association by measuring actual delinquency as reported by best friends led investigators to "question the postulate that differential association is a necessary and sufficient condition explaining delinquency."[26] In 1944, Sutherland considered this and other criticisms in a paper that was not published until after his death. Sutherland acknowledged that some of the criticisms were valid, and he concluded that criminal associations alone do not explain criminal behavior: "Rather, it is those associations plus tendencies toward alternate ways of satisfying whatever needs happen to be involved in a particular situation."[27]

Donald R. Cressey, who revised the text after Sutherland's death in 1950, acknowledged problems with differential association. The theory, he wrote,

is neither precise nor clear. . . . Most significantly, the published statement gives the incorrect impression that there is little concern for accounting for variations in crime and delinquency rates. This is a serious error in communication on Sutherland's part.[28]

Cressey believed that the theory needed to be reformulated, but he made no attempt to do so in subsequent editions of the text. He stated that due to the popularity of the theory, "It would be inappropriate to modify the statement in such a way that research work now in progress would be undermined."[29]

Cressey analyzed the criticisms and defended the theory against some of the attacks. He stated that one result of the theory's ambiguity and the critics' failure to read the theory carefully was the assumption that people become criminals because of their association with criminals or criminal patterns of behavior and attitudes. But, observed Cressey, the theory is that people become criminals because of an *overabundance* of associations with criminal compared with anticriminal behavior patterns.[30]

Some critics argued that a person can become a criminal without associating with criminals; therefore, differential association does not apply. That was not the point, said Cressey. One may be exposed to criminal attitudes and behavior without being exposed to criminals. For example, parents who teach their children not to steal may suggest that it is permissible to steal a loaf of bread if they are starving.

Differential association has produced extensive research findings; one of the most consistent among these in delinquency literature is the relationship between peer associations and delinquency. The influence of Sutherland is seen in empirical research concerning this relationship.[31]

Research has shown that the relationship between peer associations and delinquency involves several aspects of peer relations, all of which are consistent with Sutherland's position as well as with explaining (at least in part) the relationship between age and criminal behavior:

1. Differential *exposure* to delinquent peers, meaning the number of delinquent peers reported by respondents at different ages.
2. *Time* spent in the company of peers.
3. The *importance of friends* to respondents.
4. Respondents' *commitment or loyalty* to their own particular set of friends.[32]

It has also been argued that although peer attitudes affect delinquency, peer behavior is even more important, suggesting that delinquency does not result primarily from the influence of attitudes acquired from peers: "Rather, it more likely stems from other social learning mechanisms, such as imitation or vicarious reinforcement, or from group pressures to conform." It is suggested that for purposes of analysis, attitudes and behavior should be separated because "what peers do appears to be at least as important as what they think."[33]

Earlier reactions focused on the development and refinement of differential association. More recently, scholars have focused on testing it or rejecting it and replacing the theory with control or integrated theories, discussed later in this chapter. Some argue that differential association theory is sound but that further developments are needed. For example, it is difficult to measure the content of definitions favorable to law violations. In general, the theory "appears supported, but requires additional research to specify the concrete content of its abstract principles."[34]

Of the suggestions for revising Sutherland's theory, the most often cited and tested is Ronald L. Akers's learning theory, which Akers developed more thoroughly after his work with Robert L. Burgess.

Akers's Social Learning Theory

In an effort to provide a "more adequate specification of the learning process" required in the theory of differential association, Burgess and Akers developed a concept of **differential association-reinforcement**. Their purpose was to integrate Sutherland's theory with the principles of modern behavior theory. They assumed that in doing so, they could render differential association propositions more testable and at the same time make the learning processes easier to understand.[35]

Akers later refined social learning theory, although over the years his position has undergone revision. Today, he views his social learning theory as based on four basic concepts, which he and Christine Sellers defined as follows:

1. "*Differential reinforcement* refers to the balance of actual or anticipated rewards and costs, both social and nonsocial, that follow a behavior.
2. *Imitation* refers to engagement in behavior after observing similar behavior in others who have meaning to the individual.
3. *Definitions* refer to one's own attitudes that define the commission of an act as right or wrong, justified or unjustified.
4. *Differential association* refers to direct and indirect exposure, via associations with others, to patterns of behavior as well as to patterns of norms and values."[36]

Social learning occurs first in a process of differential association. The person interacts and identifies with groups (peer groups, family, schools, churches, and so on) that provide models for social reinforcements and behavior. The individual develops attitudes toward the behaviors and attaches definitions to those behaviors, defining them as good or bad, acceptable or unacceptable. These definitions help reinforce behavior and serve as cues for behavior. The more positive the definitions people have of a given behavior, the more likely they are to engage in it. According to Akers and Sellers, some definitions that are favorable to violating the law are so strong (e.g., radical definitions held by terrorists) that they essentially require one to follow them. But in most cases, definitions that are favorable to violating the law do not act as direct motivations to commit crimes. "Rather, they are conventional beliefs so weakly held that they provide no restraint or are

positive or neutralizing attitudes that facilitate law violation in the right set of circumstances."[37]

A person may associate with numerous groups, and the norms, values, and behaviors of the groups may differ; some may be deviant and others conforming. The direction chosen by an individual is determined by the "*relative balance* of reinforcements, definitions, and behavioral models."[38]

Akers and his students and colleagues conducted many tests of this social learning theory, including such areas as smoking among adolescents, deviant drinking among the elderly, and rape and sexual coercion. According to Akers and Sellers, the findings "demonstrated that the social learning variables of differential association, differential reinforcement, imitation, and definitions, singly and in combination, are strongly related to the various forms of deviant, delinquent, and criminal behavior studied."[39]

Akers and Sellers recognize that social learning theory has its critics and its limitations, but they contend that it is the "most strongly and consistently supported" of the social psychological theories advanced to explain delinquency and crime.[40]

In recent years, Akers has expanded his social learning theory into the social structure and social learning (SSSL) model, which combines social structure and social process. He advances four dimensions of social structure. First is *differential social organization*, which refers to the demographic variables in a given area, such as age and population density, that affect crime rates. Second is *differential location in the social structure*, which encompasses the characteristics of individuals, such as race and ethnicity, class, gender, marital status, and age, that determine their locations within groups. The third dimension of the social structure consists of *theoretically defined structural variables*, which includes anomie, group conflict, social disorganization, and other concepts that have been used by other theorists to identify social-structural conditions that may be related to high delinquency and crime rates. The fourth, and final, dimension is *differential social location*, which refers to memberships in primary, secondary, and reference groups such as the family or peer groups. Akers and Sellers concluded:

> The differential social organization of society and community, as well as the differential location of persons in the social class, race, gender, religion, and other structures in society, provides the general learning contexts for individuals that increase or decrease the likelihood of their committing crime.[41]

Akers and Sellers reported their findings after reviewing the research on social learning theory; they concluded that "the great preponderance of research conducted on social learning theory has found strong relationships in the theoretically expected direction between social learning variables and criminal, delinquent, and deviant behavior." They cited numerous studies that demonstrated the importance of peers in a youngster's development of delinquent and criminal behavior, including the following:

- "There is abundant evidence to show the significant impact on criminal and deviant behavior of differential association in primary groups such as family and peers. . . .

- [I]n general, parental deviance and criminality are predictive of the children's future delinquency and crime.

- Moreover, youngsters with delinquent siblings (especially same-sex older siblings) in the family are more likely to be delinquent, even when parental and other family characteristics are taken into account. . . .

- Other than one's own prior deviant behavior, the best single predictor of the onset, continuance, or **desistance** [ceasing, stopping] of crime and delinquency is differential association with conforming or law-violating peers. . . .

- Virtually every study that includes a peer association variable finds it to be significantly and usually most strongly related to delinquency, alcohol and drug use and abuse, adult crime, and other forms of deviant behavior."[42]

Akers and Sellers noted the importance of association with gangs to delinquent and criminal behavior. They concluded that the importance of social learning through differential association on delinquent behavior "is among the most fully substantiated and replicated findings in criminology," with only the factors of age and gender so consistently associated with crime and delinquency.[43]

Akers's social learning theory continues to generate research and reassessment. Despite its popularity, however, there are problems, as he and his collaborators have noted. Among the questions the theory raises is: Which comes first? Do young people become delinquent because they are reinforced in that type of behavior by delinquents, or are they delinquent and seek the company of others who behave similarly? According to Akers and Sellers, research accounts for the reciprocal relationship between the conduct of a person and his or her association with others. And social learning theory purports that through associations, one learns approved as well as disapproved behavior. Social learning theory would come into serious question only if it were found that "the onset of delinquency always or most often predates interaction with peers who have engaged in delinquent acts and/or have adhered to delinquency-favorable definitions." The theory would also not be supported "if the research evidence showed that whatever level of delinquent behavioral involvement preceded association with delinquent peers stayed the same or decreased rather than increased after the association." This has not been the case, however, according to Akers and Sellers.[44]

Other researchers agree. According to Mark Warr, "Although many investigations offer evidence of reciprocal effects, no study yet has failed to show a significant effect of peers on current and/or subsequent delinquency."[45] But Warr also offers this criticism: "[T]he generality of the theory has yet to be fully demonstrated. To be sure, the evidence of social learning is extensive and impressive . . . but it is concentrated disproportionately on tobacco, alcohol, and other drug use, and on relatively minor forms of deviance."[46] Akers and Sellers reacted to that statement by arguing that, with the possible exception of **self-control theory** (discussed later in this chapter), social learning theory has a broader scope than other criminological theories.[47]

This discussion of learning theories is summarized in Exhibit 6.2.

Control Theory

This section explores approaches that take a quite different approach from those discussed previously. **Control theory** refers to a group of theories or approaches that focus on explaining why people obey the law. The scholars developing this area of concern believe that it is natural for people to want to commit crimes; we have to be motivated *not* to do so. People obey the law because they are responding to appropriate social controls. They are socialized to obey rather than to disobey the law, and this socialization process requires a lot of work. Those who violate the law do so because the social controls are not working; their bonds to law-abiding persons have been broken or were never developed. Thus, criminals are not different kinds of people; they are not people who learned the wrong kind of behaviors. Rather, they are people who live in the wrong neighborhoods; they are people for whom social controls have, for whatever reason, been ineffective. Crime results when social controls are weakened or broken down; when controls are strong, crime does not occur. The problem is to try to explain what can be done in a positive way to elicit appropriate behavior. The issue is not "why do they do it?" but rather, "why don't we do it?" According to Travis Hirschi, whose social control approach is discussed later in this section, "There is much evidence that we would if we dared."[48]

The question, then, is not how to prevent criminal behavior but how to train people to engage in law-abiding behavior. Social control theorists take a variety of approaches.

Reiss and Nye's Control Theory

One of the first to apply control theory to delinquent or criminal behavior was Albert J. Reiss Jr., who maintained that such behavior results from the failures of two kinds of social controls. *Personal controls* are internalized, while *social controls* result from formal controls (e.g., laws) and

6.2

Learning Theory: A Summary

Tarde's Imitation Theory

Gabriel Tarde was a forerunner in developing theories about what are today called *copycat crimes*. He rejected the biological and psychological theories and did not believe in social determinism; rather, he said, behavior is the process of imitation. Tarde articulated three laws of imitation: (1) People imitate each other in proportion to their close contact; (2) the inferior imitates the superior; and (3) when two mutually exclusive behaviors occur together, one can be substituted for the other, resulting in the decline of the use of the older and an increase in the use of the newer.

Sutherland's Differential Association

Based on nine propositions (see Exhibit 6.1), **Edwin H. Sutherland's** theory of differential association advocates that all criminal behavior is learned, not inherited. Criminal behavior is learned through social interaction with others in the same way that noncriminal behavior is learned. The learning occurs primarily in small groups and includes techniques as well as motives and drives. Criminal behavior basically occurs when an individual has more definitions favorable to a deviant life than to a law-abiding life.

Akers's Social Learning Theory

Ronald L. Akers (joined in some of his early work by **Robert L. Burgess**) expanded differential association theory to include the principles of modern behavior theory. Behavior is strengthened by positive reinforcement and weakened by negative reinforcement—thus, his differential association-reinforcement theory. Individuals learn these reinforcements from peers, families, schools, and other institutions.

Akers's social learning theory developed four concepts: differential reinforcement, imitation, definitions, and differential association. More recently, Akers expanded his position to include four social-structural dimensions: differential social organization (e.g., age), differential location in the social structure (e.g., social class), theoretically defined structural variables (e.g., anomie or group conflict), and differential social location (e.g., memberships in primary, secondary, and reference groups, such as the family or peer groups).

---

informal controls (e.g., social sanctions from parents, schools, etc.).[49]

Shortly after Reiss's work was published, sociologist F. Ivan Nye analyzed delinquency using three control categories:

1. *Direct control*, by which punishment is imposed or threatened for misconduct and compliance is rewarded by parents.

2. *Indirect control*, by which a youth refrains from delinquency because his or her delinquent act might cause pain and disappointment for parents or others with whom the youth has a close relationship.

3. *Internal control*, by which a youth's conscience or sense of guilt prevents him or her from engaging in delinquent acts.[50]

Although Nye recognized that formal institutions, such as law, could influence social control, he believed that informal institutions, such as the family, were the most influential. Thus, the more an adolescent's needs are met within the family, the less likely the adolescent will be to look for satisfaction in unacceptable ways outside the family. Nye reported that he found associations between delinquent behavior and such family situations as lack of discipline, broken or disintegrated homes, insufficient parental affection toward the children, and even rejection. These associations were weak, however, and Nye was criticized for not clearly articulating exactly "how a particular aspect of

family relationships included in his study was connected to the concepts in his control theory." Furthermore, for some of the family attributes, such as social class, Nye did not show any connection to delinquency.[51]

Reckless's Containment Theory

Perhaps the best known of the early control theories was Walter C. Reckless's **containment theory**, which stressed that we live in a society that provides a variety of opportunities for conformity or nonconformity. Not everyone chooses the illegal opportunities; thus, social-structural theories that stress the availability of illegal and legal opportunities, the existence of a subculture, the location of goods and services within the city, population density, and other variables cannot explain all criminal behavior. What we need to know is *why* those phenomena affect some people and not others. That is, why are some of us immune to such influences in that our exposure to them is not followed by criminal behavior? Reckless suggested that the answer could be found in *containment theory*, which he defined as follows:

The assumption is that there is a containing external social structure which holds individuals in line and that there is also an internal buffer which protects people against deviation of the social and legal norms. The two containments act as a defense against deviation from the legal and social norms, as an insulation against pressures and pulls, as a protection against demoralization and seduction. If there are "causes" which lead to deviant behavior, they are negated, neutralized, rendered impotent, or are paired by the two containing buffers.[52]

There are two types of containment: outer containment and inner containment. *Outer containment* (or external control) might be called *social pressure*, and in simple societies, this kind of social control worked well. The community's social norms were taught to new members, who internalized them and were restrained by the community's reaction to any violation of these norms. Social ostracism could have been the most effective social control in simple societies or communities, but as societies became more complex, outer containment lost its effectiveness. People had to develop inner containment mechanisms to control their own behavior.

Inner containment (or internal control) referred to the ability to direct oneself, which is related to one's **self-concept**. According to Reckless, "One of the components of capability of self is a favorable self-image, self-concept, self-perception. The person who conceives of himself as a responsible person is apt to act responsibly."[53] A high goal level, especially regarding societal goals, and a high aspiration level geared to society's expectations are essential components of the self. Frustration tolerance and identification with society's values and laws are important. The opposite of this is alienation-the release of inner containment.

Reckless emphasized that the components of external and internal containment were *buffers*, not causes. They operated to help the individual refrain from succumbing to pressures to violate laws. If the buffers were strong, the individual was law-abiding; if the buffers were weak, the individual committed a crime. The buffers helped to neutralize the norms.

Despite the claims of Reckless and his associates that containment theory explained most delinquency and crime, that the theory might bring psychologists and sociologists together in the study of crime because it involved both disciplines, and that the theory, unlike many others, could be used in an individual case history,[54] the theory has been criticized severely. It cannot explain why people who do the same things are labeled differentially, and it is limited in its predictive ability. In addition, it includes a questionable measure of self-concept, along with a lack of control groups in some of the early works. The difficulty of measuring the strength or weakness of external and internal containment is a problem. Further, the theory does not explain why some children with bad self-concepts are not delinquent.

Containment theory may be most useful when combined with other approaches. In a comparison of containment theory with differential association theory, one criminologist concluded that the two theories are similar, except that differential association emphasizes the *process* of differential association, whereas containment theory emphasizes the *product* of socialization—the self-concept. Together, these theories can account for delinquency more fully than either one can separately.[55]

Travis Hirschi refined the elements of control theory, as noted later. But first, it is important to recall one other theory of delinquent behavior that is considered by some as a control theory: neutralization and drift. This theory was discussed in Chapter 5 as a social-structural theory and should be reviewed here.

Hirschi's Bonding Theory

In their review and critique of control theories of criminal behavior, Akers and Sellers stated: "All of the earlier control theories were superseded by the version proposed by Travis Hirschi, who remains today the major control theorist."[56]

Hirschi's control theory focused on social bonding. According to Hirschi, it is conforming behavior, not deviance,

Happy family gatherings are important in the positive socialization of children. In this picture, four generations celebrate the little girl's birthday.

that we must explain. The real question is *why*, with so many opportunities and pressures to commit crimes, most of us are law-abiding citizens most of the time. The basic concept of control theory, asserted Hirschi, is the individual's bond to society; delinquency is more likely when that bond is weakened. The bond has four components:

- *Attachment* to conventional persons
- *Commitment* to conventional behavior
- *Involvement* with conventional people
- *Belief* in conventional norms[57]

Attachment refers to the feelings we have toward others. If we have close ties to others, we are more likely to care what they think of our behavior; likewise, if we do not have close ties, we care less. The controlling of delinquency is tied to the attachments young people have to their parents. But Hirschi emphasized that attachment to peers may also control delinquency, even when those peers are not always law-abiding. It is the *attachment* that is most important; it is the lack of attachment that is conducive to delinquency.

Commitment refers to the investment one has in activities, such as getting an education. A person must measure the extent to which that investment would be lost by deviant behavior before he or she engages in deviance. Thus, commitment to conventional behavior, such as going to school, might be sufficient to cause someone to avoid jeopardizing that education by engaging in delinquent behavior. According to Hirschi, most people acquire goods and services that they do not want to lose; the risk of losing those is "society's insurance that [people] will abide by the rules."[58]

Most people are engaged in conventional activities, and this *involvement* does not permit them sufficient time to engage in delinquent or nonconventional activities. Hirschi noted: "Many people undoubtedly owe a life of virtue to a lack of opportunity to do otherwise."[59] Finally,

by *belief*, Hirschi means that a person accepts society's conventional norms and rules, believing that those general rules and laws (although not necessarily each specific one) are correct and should be obeyed. But individuals vary in the extent to which they have these beliefs, and "the less a person believes he should obey the rules, the more likely he is to violate them."[60]

Hirschi tested his theory on a sample of California youths using the self-report method of collecting data (discussed and analyzed in Chapter 2 of this text). The 4,000 junior and senior high school students in Hirschi's sample were given questionnaires designed to measure their attitudes toward friends, neighborhood, parents, school, teachers, and human relations. The students were asked to respond to six offenses, indicating for each whether they had (1) never committed the offense, (2) committed the offense more than one year ago, (3) committed the offense during the past year, or (4) committed the offense during the past year as well as more than a year ago. The offenses were referred to in the following question form:

1. Have you ever taken little things (worth less than $2) that did not belong to you?
2. Have you ever taken things of some value (between $2 and $50) that did not belong to you?
3. Have you ever taken things of large value (worth over $50) that did not belong to you?
4. Have you ever taken a car for a ride without the owner's permission?
5. Have you ever banged up something that did not belong to you on purpose?
6. Not counting fights you may have had with a brother or sister, have you ever beaten up on anyone or hurt anyone on purpose?[61]

The responses to these questions were used as an index of self-reported delinquency. In addition, questions

The impact of schools goes beyond the academic education of students. These high school students are discussing family and health issues in an informal school setting.

were asked about work, money, expectations, aspirations, participation in school activities, and use of leisure time. School records, including grades, and police records were also used as sources of data for the study.

The high association between low socioeconomic class and crime, found in the earlier studies using official crime data, had been questioned by self-report studies. Hirschi found strong evidence that this traditional association does not exist. Indeed, he noted very little association between social class, as measured by the father's occupation, and admitted or official delinquency, with the exception of a low incidence, by both measures, of delinquency among the professionals' sons. Hirschi did find, however, that boys "whose fathers have been unemployed and/or whose families are on welfare are more likely than children from fully employed, self-sufficient families to commit delinquent acts." Hirschi's research also disclosed that positive attitudes toward teachers and school were related to nondelinquent behavior. He suggested that the closer the ties to parents, the less likely it was that the youths would engage in delinquent acts. It was not the parent's status that was important but, rather, the child's *attachment* to the parent.[62]

Hirschi concluded that young people who are not very attached to their parents and to school are more likely to be delinquent than are those who have these kinds of attachments. He also found that youths who have positive attitudes toward their own accomplishments are more likely to believe in the validity and appropriateness of conventional laws and the moral rules of society than are youths who are negative about their own accomplishments.

Although Hirschi's California study was based on a sample of urban respondents, a study of a rural sample in New York State found support for Hirschi's control theory.[63] However, this study "failed to replicate a positive relationship between attachment to parents and attachment to friends. . . . [It] failed to show that attachment to friends increases the likelihood of delinquent behavior." The researcher concluded that researchers should go beyond measuring attachment to peers and try to discover the *type* of peer to whom the individual is attached before the analysis has validity for the prediction of delinquent behavior.[64]

Other scholars advocate that their findings showed that the type of peer did not matter[65] and that the likelihood of delinquent behavior seemed to decrease with attachment to conventional peers but to increase with attachment to delinquent peers.[66] The gender of friends mattered in deterring property crimes, with the friendships showing more influence over females than males. Females were more likely to have the type of friendships that investigators believed provided the bonding that deterred delinquent behavior: Their friendships were more intimate than those of males, they were more likely to occur in settings with more social control, they engaged in fewer risky behaviors than males, and they were more likely to discourage offending.[67]

Hirschi recognized that his control theory could not escape unscathed. In the first place, his theory "underestimated the importance of delinquent friends; it overestimated the significance of involvement in conventional activities." Hirschi decided that one should probably look at the relationship between delinquent activities and the person's self-concept or self-esteem. That relationship might be important in explaining "the potency of the adult-status items, such as smoking, drinking, dating, and driving a car." Although control theory can help us understand these relations, Hirschi noted, it leaves a lot unexplained. However, he concluded this early work on an optimistic note with regard to his theory: "I am confident that when the processes through which these variables affect delinquency are spelled out, they will supplement rather than seriously modify the control theory, but that remains to be seen."[68]

Perhaps a more serious challenge to Hirschi's theory has been raised by those who emphasized that most tests of the theory used cross-sectional data at a particular time rather than measures of the relationship of variables over time. Robert Agnew sampled young men at the beginning of their sophomore year in high school and again near the end of their junior year and suggested that Hirschi's control theory was more limited than Hirschi claimed. Agnew's study showed that Hirchi's theory did not predict delinquency among middle to older adolescents, although it might be important in predicting delinquency among younger adolescents.[69] Similar findings were reported in other research showing that adolescence should not be viewed as a unitary period but, rather, should be refined further by the factor of age.[70]

Despite these and other criticisms, the influence of Hirschi's bonding theory can be seen in an analysis that found communal school organization and student bonding were predictive of the lack of student disorder, delinquency, and victimization. *Communal school organization* was defined as the "organization of a school as a community, as indicated by supportive relationships between and among teachers, administrators, and students, a common set of goals and norms, and a sense of collaboration and involvement." Schools with high communal organization had better morale among both students and faculty, and students bonded with the faculty to a greater extent. Such schools had fewer behavior problems among students, less delinquency, and fewer victimizations of teachers and students by other students. The researchers made the analogy of the communal school organization to that of Sampson's concept of neighborhood collective efficacy, which was discussed in Chapter 5.[71]

Another tribute to Hirschi was noted in the 2003 presidential address to the American Society of Criminology, in which John H. Laub examined what he called the five turning points in the development of criminology. One of those was the contributions of Travis Hirschi in his 1969 publication, *Causes of Delinquency*. According to Laub, "Over the last 25 years, more than [the works of] any other scholar, Travis Hirschi's work has dominated intellectual discussion and substantially formed the research agenda for the field of criminology." This work, noted Laub, has been referred to by others as a "turning point in deviancy research," "a highly significant piece of research," and "a work of major consequence."[72]

Not all scholars agree completely with this analysis. In a 2009 publication, five criminology scholars acknowledged the importance of Hirschi's work but published their own analysis of the data on which Hirschi based *Causes of Delinquency,* in which, they argued, Hirschi was challenging the strain theory claim that the delinquency of African Americans might be caused by racial discrimination. The investigators concluded that delinquency prediction can be achieved by looking at *perceived racial discrimination.* "This finding suggests that Hirschi missed a historic opportunity to focus the attention of a generation of criminologists on how the unique experiences of African Americans may shape their criminality." If Hirschi had uncovered the impact of perceived racial discrimination's predictive ability regarding juvenile delinquency among African Americans "as opposed to arguing that the causes of crime are general and not race specific," other investigators might have paid more attention to the importance of the perception of racial discrimination. The scholars also noted the importance of considering perceived racial discrimination in treatment policies.[73]

Gottfredson and Hirschi's Self-Control Theory

In recent years, Hirschi has moved from his original social bonding theory and collaborated with Michael Gottfredson in developing a general theory of crime that focuses on self-control and purports to explain all acts of deviance and criminal behavior by all persons. In a 1990 book developing their general theory, Gottfredson and Hirschi referred to *self-control* as the "differential tendency of people to avoid criminal acts whatever the circumstances in which they find themselves."[74] In a later publication, they were more specific and referred to the "tendency to avoid acts whose long-term costs exceed their momentary advantages."[75] The implication apparently is that the new definition emphasizes *all* consequences rather than just *long-term* consequences.[76]

Gottfredson and Hirschi rejected the traditional theories of crime, arguing that in an attempt to answer the question of what causes crime, each discipline looks to its own central concepts. "Thus sociology looks to social class, culture, and organization; psychology looks to personality; biology looks to inheritance; and economics looks to employment or work."[77]

According to Gottfredson and Hirschi, all these explanations are incompatible with the nature of *crime,* which they defined as "an act of force or fraud undertaken in pursuit of self-interest."[78] They distinguished *crime* from *criminality,*

which, to them, refers to a person's *predisposition* to commit a crime. Criminality is a part of the personality trait that is central to the thesis of Gottfredson and Hirschi's approach, which is the concept of low self-control.

Gottfredson and Hirschi viewed behavior in terms of the classical view discussed in Chapter 3. People seek pleasure and avoid pain. Crime is a fast and easy way to attain quick pleasure; the issue is not what *causes* crime but what *constrains* it, and according to Gottfredson and Hirschi, the answer is low self-control.

Persons with low self-control have several common characteristics. First, they seek immediate gratification, with a "here-and-now" attitude, in contrast to persons with high self-control, who are able to defer gratification. Second, persons with low self-control look for simple ways to gratify their desires. Crime provides "money without work, sex without courtship, revenge without court delays." Third, they find in crime their need for acts that are exciting, risky, or thrilling. Criminal acts involve "stealth, danger, speed, agility, deception, or power." In contrast, persons with high self-control "tend to be cautious, cognitive, and verbal." Fourth, persons with low self-control have little stability in their lives; crimes do not provide stability in the form of a job or a career, friendships, or family ties. Little skill or planning is required to pursue crime; thus, persons with low self-control do not need or value cognitive or academic skills. Fifth, people with low self-control are "self-centered, indifferent, or insensitive to the suffering and needs of others." Thus, they can handle the fact that crime causes pain or discomfort for its victims. This does not mean those with low self-esteem are "routinely unkind or antisocial. On the contrary, they may discover the immediate and easy rewards of charm and generosity." Finally, persons with low self-control have little tolerance for frustration and tend to respond to situations physically rather than verbally.[79]

Gottfredson and Hirschi maintain that low self-control is primarily a product of poor parenting. Alternatively, when parents are supportive, show affection, and invest in their children, they may produce "a child more capable of delaying gratification, more sensitive to the interests of others, more independent, more willing to accept restraints on his activity, and more unlikely to use force or violence to attain his ends."[80]

Although self-control may improve over time as the result of better parenting or the influence of other social institutions, in most individuals, low self-control persists throughout life. Persons with low self-control are much more likely than persons with high self-control to engage in criminal activities throughout their lives.[81] Low self-control does not *cause* crime, but it interacts with crime opportunities. When an opportunity to commit a crime exists, a person with high self-control is not likely to commit the act; a person with low self-control may succumb.

Gottfredson and Hirschi claim that their theory is a general one that "explains all crime, at all times, and, for that matter, many forms of behavior that are not sanctioned by the state." That is a big claim, but the authors note that "modesty per se is not a virtue of a theory."[82]

Self-control theory has generated extensive research and theory development, with most studies supporting the theory. For example, Christine S. Sellers found some evidence that self-control may explain variables, such as drug and alcohol abuse, academic probation, excessive partying, and friendship loss, that are associated with courtship violence. These variables may be indicators of low self-esteem and low self-control. In addition, the theory may explain the fact that many persons who are involved in courtship violence are from homes in which domestic violence was experienced.[83]

In a test of self-control theory, Carter Hay examined parenting and its role in the development of a child's self-concept. Hay emphasized that Gottfredson and Hirschi "argue that the principal cause of individuals' low self-control is ineffective child rearing." In particular, the children of parents who do not watch them closely and who do not recognize and punish the child's deviant behavior will have low self-control. Those children are more likely to become deviant or delinquent than are their counterparts with higher self-control. But few studies have been conducted on the role of parenting in the development of self-control. In seeking to remedy this situation, Hay based his study on the theory of an early psychological approach to self-control, that of *authoritative parenting*, referring to parents who are both demanding and responsive. He tested two hypotheses regarding parenting and concluded that there is support for self-control theory but that the support was not overwhelming.[84]

Other scholars looked at parenting and self-control theory in a sample of 2,472 students, examining the relationship of parental management, attention-deficit hyperactivity disorder (ADHD) (for a discussion, see Chapter 4), and delinquent behavior. The following results were reported:

- "First, low self-concept was a strong predictor of both self-reported delinquency and self-reported arrests.
- Second, parental monitoring not only increased self-control, but had direct effects on both measures of delinquency.
- Third, the effects of ADHD on delinquency were largely through low self-control."[85]

Scholars have also tested the *stability thesis* of social control theory—that is, that low self-control not only is developed early in life but also persists over time. The role of parent socialization (according to Gottfredson and Hirschi, the main explanation for differences in self-control) in the self-control of adolescents was examined. With regard to the first issue, researchers found moderate stability of self-control in the short run but less in the long run for most but not all of a sample. Thus, one's self-control at age 7 is more similar to the self-control that one has at age 9 than to one's degree of self-control at age 15. The researchers also found that "parenting still matters for self-control

beyond childhood." They concluded that, overall, there is moderate support for self-control theory.[86]

Gottfredson and Hirschi's self-control theory of crime has also been used to explain criminal victimization. One study focused on a sample of African American female offenders who had committed a wide range of offenses, were considered high-rate offenders, were drug users (used illegal drugs at least three times in the previous 30 days), and were not in drug treatment, jail, prison, or any other institution. After interviewing the women and analyzing the data, the researchers concluded as follows:

> The results of this study corroborate that women who display low levels of self-control have a higher risk of violent victimization. Even after commonly applied demographic and lifestyle correlates of victimization were controlled, low self-control remained significant.[87]

Self-control theory, although well recognized and the focus of extensive research, remains controversial among researchers. Some scholars have taken the position that for self-control theory to be complete, other dimensions, such as psychopathy (rejected by Gottfredson and Hirschi), must be considered. It is argued that both psychopathy and low self-control reflect "a self-centered, antisocial personality" and that each construct "maps out a path to an antisocial life, in which immediate and selfish desires are gratified at the expense of both the rights and feelings of other people and one's own long-term interests."[88] It might be useful in examining these constructs to add that of *self-direction*, which is "comprised of elements of self-control and psychopathy, that appears to be significantly related to offending." This "fresh look" at crime would permit us to look at the causes of self-directed behavior along with that of antisocial behavior.[89]

In 2004, Hirschi articulated some revisions of social control theory, including a new definition of *self-control*, calling it "the tendency to consider the full range of potential costs of a particular act [which] moves the focus from the long-term implications of the act to its broader and often contemporaneous implications." In this new definition, self-control "is the set of inhibitions one carries with one wherever one happens to go."[90]

In what they called the first attempt to test this redefinition, two criminologists concluded that future studies of self-control should consider the *situational aspects* of the concept. According to these investigators, the new definition of self-control means that, at the point of making decisions regarding behavior, some people will consider potential cost factors and their prominence, but other people will consider a fewer number of factors and their prominence. Thus, the *situational aspect* of self-control is important, with some situations resulting in reactions of high self-control and others in low self-control. This approach might explain such phenomenon as why, for example, a police officer might engage in domestic battering or a bank official might embezzle. These individuals exhibit significant self-control in one situation but not in others.[91]

Some scholars have called for alterations of Gottfredson and Hirschi's theory. Some have found that parenting influences a child's risk for delinquency in more ways than social control does. Parental behavior may create anger in children, leading to delinquency.[92] In addition, there is some evidence that "low self-control is a condition that can be improved through appropriate intervention and social experiences."[93]

The research linking self-control and crime is extensive, but another aspect of Gottfredson and Hirschi's general theory is that self-control occurs through parental socialization, thus rejecting any influence of other fields, such as genetics. Recall Chapter 4's emphasis on integrating the findings of disciplines other than sociology into explanations of criminal behavior. Several investigators have tested the role of parenting in the development of self-control among twins. There appears to be a weak and inconsistent effect of parenting on self-control. It was suggested that self-control theory should be revised to include the large body of research that links behavior to biological factors, such as the effect of smoking and the use of drugs on the fetuses of pregnant women. Investigators also found that the type of methodology used to measure social variables (e.g., self-concept) influences findings.[94]

Terrie E. Moffitt has also emphasized the importance of going beyond self-control to explain delinquency and crime. She and others who base their research on neuropsychological and developmental psychological theories have found

support for biological and psychological influences on delinquency that cannot be explained by self-control.[95] This research was supported by other researchers, who compared public high school students in California with adolescents who were incarcerated in that state. They found support for Gottfredson and Hirschi's position that self-control, as exemplified by future orientation, was a significant predictor of offending, but they also found the biological factor of heart rate and the neuropsychological factor of spatial span to distinguish the two groups. They concluded the "take-home message is that proponents of Gottfredson and Hirschi's theory may wish to revisit the role of neurobiology in the determinants of self-control."[96]

Some scholars take the position that social control theory should incorporate opportunity theory (discussed in this text in Chapter 5). Two scholars who considered this proposal investigated the amount of time juveniles spend away from parental supervision and with their friends. They concluded that the effect that low self-control has on delinquency is at least related in part to the opportunities the juveniles have to commit delinquency acts.[97]

One final comment is that social control theory may be useful in predicting the consequences of low social control in other aspects of criminal justice systems. Investigators found, for example, that among offenders who come into contact with criminal justice systems, "those with lower levels of self-control are at greater risk of being arrested and convicted."[98]

A summary of the control theories just discussed appears in Exhibit 6.3. Other control theories exist and are

EXHIBIT 6.3 Control Theory: A Summary

Reiss and Nye's Control Theory
Albert J. Reiss Jr. maintained that criminal behavior results from the failures of two types of controls: personal (internalized) and social (formal controls, such as laws, and informal controls, such as social sanctions). F. Ivan Nye articulated three social control categories, which he believed could occur in formal institutions but took place primarily within the family: (1) direct control (parents threaten punishment for bad behavior and give rewards for good behavior), (2) indirect control (youth refuses to engage in delinquent behavior because it might hurt family or friends), and (3) internal control (youth's conscience or guilt prevents participation in delinquent acts).

Reckless's Containment Theory
According to Walter C. Reckless, there are two forms of containment that control behavior. First is outer containment, or external control, such as social pressure. Second is inner containment, or internal control, which refers to the ability to direct oneself. This ability is related to one's self-concept or self-image. These two control components are not causes of behavior; rather, they are buffers that operate to help the

person refrain from engaging in illegal acts. If the buffers are strong, the person is law-abiding; if they are weak, he or she commits a crime. These buffers neutralize society's norms.

Hirschi's Bonding Theory
Travis Hirschi looked at the question of why most people do not commit crimes. He believed the answer lies in social bonding, which includes four components: (1) attachment to conventional persons, (2) commitment to conventional behavior, (3) involvement with conventional people, and (4) belief in conventional norms.

Gottfredson and Hirschi's Self-Control Theory
Low self-control is the key element of the theory Travis Hirschi and Michael Gottfredson developed to explain crime. Persons with low self-control have several characteristics in common. They (1) seek immediate gratification, (2) look for easy or simple ways to gratify their desires, (3) find in crime their need for exciting, risky, or thrilling acts, (4) have little stability in their lives, (5) are self-centered and indifferent or insensitive to the needs of others, and (6) have little tolerance for frustration. Self-control arises through parental socialization.

discussed elsewhere. Developmental and life-course theories combine social control and social learning theories and are discussed in a later section of this chapter, along with other attempts to integrate criminology theories. Power-control theories were discussed in Chapter 5.

Labeling Theory

A final single theoretical approach to explaining crime is different from the others discussed. Most theories and explanations of criminal behavior look for the *cause* of the behavior or at least the process by which the behavior came about. Why did the individual commit the crime, and what can be done to prevent future criminal acts? The answer may be found in the individual physique, body build, chemical imbalance, hormones, or chromosomes. It may be found in the environment, or perhaps it is the result of some type of social process. The emphasis is on finding out *why* the person engaged in the behavior.

In contrast, **labeling theory** asks why the person was *designated* deviant. The critical issue is not the behavior itself but why the behavior was labeled deviant. Not all who engage in certain kinds of behavior are labeled deviant, but some are. What is the reason for this distinction? In 1962, sociologist Kai T. Erikson described this approach as follows:

> Some men who drink heavily are called alcoholics and others are not, some men who behave oddly are committed to hospitals and others are not . . . and the difference between those who earn a deviant title in society and those who go their own way in peace is largely determined by the way in which the community filters out and codes the many details of behavior which come to its attention.[99]

If criminal behavior is to be explained according to the responses of others rather than the characteristics of offenders, the appropriate subject matter is the *audience*, not the individual actors, for it is the existence of the behavior, not why it occurred, that is significant. Only the audience's response determines whether that behavior is defined as deviant, and those determinations may result in serious negative reactions.

Most of the popular reform movements discussed in this text, such as diversion, deinstitutionalization, decriminalization, due process for all, and many of the treatment modalities, are based on the belief that if people are not treated fairly and positively but, rather, are labeled negatively after being subject to questionable procedures, the results will be negative. Consequently, some states, such as Florida, have statutory provisions for withholding adjudication of a felony for persons who have been found guilty and are sentenced to probation. During the probationary period, the person does not suffer any of the negative effects of being labeled a *felon*, such as losing voting rights, being prohibited from running for public office, losing a job, and so on. Individuals who do not violate their probation for a specified period do not have felony records. One study of 95,519 Florida offenders examined their subsequent convictions. The investigators found that the felon label was "significantly and substantially" linked to an increased likelihood of repeat offenses and that the effect was stronger for whites and women compared to blacks, Hispanics, and males.[100]

The next sections consider the history and development of the labeling perspective and the effects of labeling, along with recent developments and an evaluation of labeling. In some respects, labeling is a social-structural approach, like conflict theory, but it is primarily a social-process theory because it attempts to explain labeling as a *process* by which some people who commit deviant acts come to be known as deviants whereas others do not.

The Emergence and Development of Labeling Theory

A 1938 statement by Frank Tannenbaum described labeling theory as follows:

> The process of making the criminal is a process of tagging, defining, identifying, segregating, describing, emphasizing, making conscious and self-conscious; it becomes a way of stimulating, suggesting, emphasizing, and evoking the very traits that are complained of.
>
> The person becomes the thing he is described as being.[101]

The labeling perspective was further developed by Edwin Lemert, who distinguished *primary* and *secondary* deviance (or deviation) as follows:

> Primary deviation is assumed to arise in a wide variety of social, cultural, and psychological contexts, and at best has only marginal implication for the psychic structure of the individual; it does not lead to symbolic reorganization at the level of self-regarding attitudes and social roles.
>
> Secondary deviation is deviant behavior or social roles based upon it, which becomes a means of defense, attack or adaptation to the overt and covert problems created by the societal reaction to primary deviation.[102]

To labeling theorists, primary deviance is relatively unimportant; it is secondary deviance that is more important because it is the *interaction* between the person labeled deviant and the labeler that counts. This approach is called *interaction theory*.

Another contributor to the early development of labeling theory was sociologist Howard S. Becker, who pointed out that because only some of the many people who break rules are considered deviant, we must distinguish between rule breaking and deviance. *Rule breaking* describes a person's behavior, but *deviance* describes the reaction of others to that behavior; thus, rule breaking is defined as deviant when engaged in by some, but not all, people. It is important to find out who is and who is not labeled deviant.[103]

Another early contributor to the development of labeling theory was Walter R. Gove, who stated that whether or not labeling occurs depends on (1) the time the act is committed, (2) who commits the act and who is the victim, and (3) society's perception of the consequences of the act.[104]

The Effects of Labeling

Labeling theory is based on the assumption that people respond to others in an informal and unorganized way until those others are placed in categories that lead to stereotyping, which causes corresponding responses. The response may become what sociologists call a *self-fulfilling prophecy*. The labeled person develops a self-concept consistent with the deviant label and acquires the knowledge and skills of the labeled status. Once labeled, the labelee has an almost impossible task of shedding that status. The effects of labeling may also snowball in that, once a person is stigmatized by a label, new restrictions are placed on legitimate opportunities. Hence, the labelee's probabilities of further deviance increase. Such a vicious circle is reinforced by the tendency of the public to believe that one who commits a crime will always be a criminal.

One act may not be enough to result in a negative label, but whether or not a person is labeled brings into play power differentials. Certain types of groups may be more likely than others to be labeled deviant: groups that do not have political power, groups that are seen to threaten persons in power, and groups that have low social status. The last is particularly important. Even when middle- and upper-class persons are suspected of committing conventional crimes, they are less likely than lower-class persons to be labeled criminal.[105]

Members of the upper socioeconomic class have greater access to attorneys and are more likely to know their legal rights. They are less likely to negotiate a plea or admit guilt. They have the symbols of the middle and upper classes, and those symbols are not associated with criminal status. For example, they are more likely to have strong family ties, to have a job, to have sufficient income, to speak fluently and knowledgeably, to be poised, to be able to rationalize their behavior, to have a record of continuous employment, and to have the respect of the community and of local law enforcement officials. They are more likely to have friends who may intervene at any stage in the legal process. They live in areas that are unlikely to be targets of drug raids. They are more likely to get probation if a condition of probation is that they obtain psychiatric or other professional services.[106]

Crime visibility is also a factor in determining whether a person is labeled criminal. People who live in ghettos are more likely to be visible when committing crimes. Because of their greater contact with public services, they are also more likely to be visible after crimes are committed. For example, many statutory rape cases are brought to the attention of the police through referrals from public welfare agencies. Thus, with the exception of high-profile cases, statutory rape may be punished primarily among the poor, whose victims become visible by applying for maternity aid from welfare authorities.

Empirical Research

Attempts have been made to test labeling theory empirically. In a classic study, Richard D. Schwartz and Jerome H. Skolnick measured the reaction of 100 employers to a potential employee with a "criminal" record. The employers were divided into four groups, and each group was shown a different folder on the prospective employee. Stated simply, the conclusion was that employers would not offer a job to a person with a criminal record. The second phase of this study included 58 doctors who had been sued for medical malpractice (a civil wrong rather than a criminal act) in Connecticut. There was no evidence that these doctors had lost patients because of the malpractice suits. Most of the doctors reported no change, and five specialists reported an increase in their number of patients.[107]

Schwartz and Skolnick warned of the problems comparing these two phases of their study. The doctors had a *protective institutional environment* that did not exist for the prospective employee. The doctors were permitted to continue using hospital facilities and had no difficulty getting malpractice insurance, although often at a higher rate. This protective institutional environment may eliminate the negative labeling process that normally occurs after one loses a court battle. Another possible reason for the different reactions in the study's two phases was that physicians were in short supply and unskilled laborers were not. But most probably, the difference in reaction was due to the doctors' occupational status and the protection they got from their profession. An interesting question left unanswered by this study was how a doctor would be labeled if he or she had been acquitted of a charge of assault and battery or some other *criminal* offense.

One example of the effect of labeling gained national attention in the 1970s. Eight sane researchers of varied backgrounds sought admission to the psychiatric wards of 12 hospitals throughout the United States. The hospitals were of different types; some had excellent treatment facilities, and others had poor ones. The researchers called the hospitals for appointments, and upon their arrival for the initial interviews, they feigned mental illness, stating that they heard voices. When asked about the significant events in their backgrounds, all related the events accurately; none had a history of pathological experiences. After admission to the hospital, all the pseudopatients acted like sane persons. All except one had been labeled schizophrenic, and none of the doctors or staff suspected the researchers' pseudopatient status. Once labeled insane, they were presumed insane by the staff, who interacted with them daily. Their behavior did not identify them as insane; the identity came from a label given to them upon admission. Thus, they differed from sane persons only in the label.[108]

Another study involved the simulation of prison life with student volunteers assigned to the roles of correctional officers and inmates. The experiment had to be terminated because of serious problems. Those in the experiment assigned to the role of correctional officers began behaving as if they derived pleasure "from insulting, threatening, humiliating and dehumanizing" those who were inmates. The ones who were assigned to be inmates became depressed, despondent, and helpless and acted in self-deprecating ways.[109]

Much of the more recent research on labeling theory has focused on juvenile delinquency. This research calls for refining the labeling theory approach. For example, gender roles should be considered. Male and female juveniles do not necessarily respond to labels in the same way.[110] Social class and race should be taken into account, along with whether the person is a first-time or a persistent offender.[111] The differences in reactions to negative and positive labeling should be measured.[112]

Recent Refinements of Labeling Theory

In recent years, scholars have developed refinements of traditional labeling theory. This section looks at three of those.

Braithwaite's Restorative Justice

John Braithwaite emphasized that labeling per se is not the issue. Labeling must be examined in the context of the total social structure. Labeling might cause some people to abandon criminal activity; it might cause others to continue in crime. What are the characteristics of the broader social context in which the behavior occurs that might explain whether the person becomes law-abiding or law-breaking? Braithwaite answered the question with his concept of **shaming**, defined as social disapproval that has the "intention or effect of invoking remorse in the person being shamed and/or condemnation by others who become aware of the shaming."[113]

In Braithwaite's view, shaming is important for social control, but the shaming should be of the criminal *act*, not the criminal. Shaming that goes far enough to stigmatize the person labeled is a process Braithwaite referred to as *stigmatization* or **disintegrative shaming**. This process can propel the individual into delinquent or criminal behavior. Disintegrative shaming does not involve any attempt to reintegrate the shamed person into society; it

stands in contrast to **reintegrative shaming**, in which attempts are made at reintegrating the offender into the community "through words or gestures of forgiveness or ceremonies to decertify the offender as deviant."[114] These reactions are more likely to reduce the negative effects of shaming, thus reducing the chances that the shamed person will continue in crime. According to Braithwaite, societies that demonstrate forgiveness and show respect but still take crime seriously have lower crime rates than those that humiliate and degrade criminals. Likewise, families that show love and respect for their children who misbehave are more likely to have law-abiding children than are families that degrade and demean their children.[115]

According to Braithwaite, a theory of crime should explain that most offenders are young, minority, male, and unemployed. They live in large cities and have low educational achievements and goals. They are the persons most likely to be targeted for disintegrative shaming, and because they do not have strong social bonds to society, they are also stigmatized, which pushes them toward criminal subcultures. In that environment, they have an opportunity to gain self-respect by rejecting those who reject them; thus, they are more likely to engage in deviant behavior. "In contrast, the consequence of reintegrative shaming is that criminal subcultures appear less attractive to the offender."[116]

In short, according to Braithwaite, reintegrative shaming will reduce and disintegrative shaming will increase the chances of future offending. Other scholars maintain, however, that the limited empirical studies do not provide support for this position.[117] Braithwaite acknowledged that not as much empirical testing as might have been expected has occurred. But although he recognizes the research results are mixed, and he and his colleagues are working on a revision of his approach, he notes the support he and one of his colleagues found in the first test of his theory. In his words,

> Australian nursing home inspectors with a reintegrative shaming philosophy were successful in substantially improving compliance with regulatory laws in the two years after inspections, but compliance substantially worsened when inspectors adopted a stigmatizing philosophy.[118]

One might, however, question whether that fact pattern involving administrative law applies to juveniles or adults violating criminal law.

Braithwaite's theory of reintegrative shaming has provided the basis for an important policy approach to crime prevention called **restorative justice**. This concept began in New Zealand but has spread throughout the United States and the world. Braithwaite defined *restorative justice* as encompassing the belief that "because crime hurts, justice should heal, and especially heal relationships." Braithwaite emphasized that restorative justice means that everyone involved in the pains of crime should have an opportunity to discuss how to repair that pain and how to prevent crime. He noted that aspects of restorative justice have become part of even those societies, such as the United States, Russia, and South Africa, where some of the highest imprisonment rates exist.[119]

The restorative justice approach provides both adults and juveniles with a wide range of programs that are designed to restore crime victims and the community. Examples are community work service, apologies to crime victims, restitution, and other programs to aid crime victims.[120] Exhibit 6.4 reproduces the Vermont statute on restorative justice. Note the leeway given to local jurisdictions to develop programs that fit within the spirit of that statute.

The obvious goal of restorative justice is to reduce delinquency and crime. Francis T. Cullen and his collaborators have advocated that restorative justice be linked with rehabilitation (discussed in Chapter 3 of this text) in an effort at crime reduction.[121] Others concluded that there has been insufficient research to make informed conclusions concerning the impact of restorative justice and other so-called faith-based programs on recidivism rates.[122]

Restorative justice has become important enough in the United States to generate special college courses and texts. Clifford K. Dorne's 2008 publication of *Restorative Justice in the United States* is an example. This text contains an overview of the approach along with research in the area.[123]

Finally, restorative justice also impacts crime victims. Research indicates it helps reduce victims' fear and anger, benefits their mental health, and increases forgiveness while reducing their posttraumatic stress syndrome effects suffered as a result of the victimization process.[124]

Matsueda's Reflective Appraisal

Another contributor to labeling theory was Ross L. Matsueda.[125] Matsueda based his approach on the much earlier theory of George Herbert Mead, whose classic *Mind, Self, and Society* was published in 1934.[126] Mead explored the concept of *self*, which he said was composed of many dimensions and developed through symbolic interactions with other individuals, some of whom are more significant than others. In the process of interacting, individuals often take the role of the other person and try to discern

---

EXHIBIT 6.4

Restorative Justice: The Vermont Approach

Vermont Statutes Annotated, Title 28, Section 2a (2010).

■ **Restorative justice**

"(a) State policy.—It is the policy of this state that principles of restorative justice be included in shaping how the criminal justice system responds to persons charged with or convicted of criminal offenses. The policy goal is a community response to a person's wrongdoing at its earliest onset, and a type and intensity of sanction tailored to each instance of wrongdoing. Policy objectives are to:

[1] Resolve conflicts and disputes by means of a non-adversarial community process.

[2] Repair damage caused by criminal acts to communities in which they occur, and to address wrongs inflicted on individual victims.

[3] Reduce the risk of an offender committing a more serious crime in the future, that would require a more intensive and more costly sanction, such as incarceration.

(b) Implementation.—It is the intent of the general assembly that law enforcement officials develop and employ restorative justice approaches whenever feasible and responsive to specific criminal acts, pursuant to sections [citations omitted], concerning court diversion, chapter [citations omitted], concerning sentencing, and the provisions of this title, concerning persons in the custody of the commissioner of corrections. It

is the further intent of the general assembly that such restorative justice programs be designed to encourage participation by local community members, including victims, when they so choose, as well as public officials, in holding offenders accountable for damage caused to communities and victims, and in restoring offenders to the law-abiding community, through activities:

[1] Which require offenders to:

[A] acknowledge wrongdoing and apologize to victims;

[B] make restitution for damage to the victims, consistent with provisions of [another statute; citation omitted];

[C] make reparation for damage to the community by fulfilling a community service; and

[D] when relevant, successfully complete treatment addressing the offense or other underlying problematic behavior, or undertake academic or vocational training or other self-improving activity.

[2] Which aid in the recovery of victims, recognizing that victims, particularly of violent crime, often suffer lifelong effects and, accordingly, must feel safe and involved in any program offered to assist them.

[3] Which help in identifying the causes of crime and ways community members and municipal and state government can reduce or prevent crime in the future."

how that person evaluates his or her behavior. Later in their development, they learn to generalize the roles of others, such as a group, a community, or a society. The behavior children exhibit, for example, may initially be labeled by family members as play or mischief (and Matsueda's theory is read by some to suggest that such informal labeling has a greater impact than formal labeling), but a larger group or the society may label that same behavior as bad, evil, deviant, or even delinquent. According to Matsueda,

> Eventually, this spiraling labeling process can leave the youth in the hands of juvenile justice officials—cut off from conventional society, stigmatized by parents and teachers, and left with a delinquent self-image. Thus, a self-fulfilling prophecy is set up: through this process of deviance amplification ... an otherwise conforming child may eventually respond to the initial labeling of harmless acts by confirming the delinquent label.[127]

Matsueda, along with a collaborator, studied data on juvenile delinquency and found support for their concept of **reflected appraisal**, which refers to a person's perception of how others view him or her. Those who believe that others view them as behaving in a delinquent manner in certain situations are more likely to engage in such behavior than are those who view others as expecting them to be law-abiding citizens.[128]

Sampson and Laub's Cumulative Disadvantages

Later in this chapter, we discuss **developmental and life-course theory**, but at this point, it is important to note that the **life-course** approach embraces labeling theory. According to Robert J. Sampson and John H. Laub, labeling theory is "truly developmental in nature, because of its explicit emphasis on processes over time."[129] Labeling theory leads to structural disadvantages, or what Sampson and Laub call **cumulative disadvantages**, in future life opportunities. Consequently, those who are labeled delinquent or criminal find that the event is a transitional one in their lives and that fewer legitimate opportunities will be available to them in the future because of the structural disadvantages. In the words of Sampson and Laub,

> Cumulative disadvantage is generated most explicitly by the negative structural consequences of criminal offending and official sanctions for life changes. The theory specifically suggests a "snowball" effect—that adolescent delinquency and its negative consequences (e.g., arrest, official labeling, incarceration) increasingly "mortgage" one's future, especially later life chances molded by schooling and employment. . . . The theoretical perspective in turn points to a possible indirect effect of delinquency and official sanctioning in generating future crime.[130]

In an effort to assess the importance of labeling in the development of cumulative disadvantages, researchers analyzed data ranging from adolescence to early adulthood. They looked at the relationship that official labeling might have on future criminal activity by producing negative consequences that reduced conventional opportunities, specifically education and job options. They found that educational attainment was affected by early labeling because the labeling decreased the chances the youths would finish high school. Lack of a high school education in turn affected future job opportunities. The researchers concluded as follows:

> Our results are consistent with the hypothesis that official intervention during adolescence influences criminal involvement as late as early adulthood when individuals become fully affected by blocked life chances shaped by education and employment. But, in addition to the indirect effects that both intervention by the police and the juvenile justice system have on adult crime, official intervention also directly influences subsequent criminality.[131]

It is possible, however, that intervening factors could affect the outcome found in this research.

Evaluation of Labeling Theory

In 1988, two scholars described labeling theory as "one of the most influential in the field of deviance over the past two decades."[132]

In 2009, Akers and Sellers looked at the reaction to labeling theory over the years. In the 1960s, the theory "captured the imagination of social science researchers, theorists, and practitioners," but by the 1970s, the theory was on the decline in popularity, with some of those who had originally supported the theory moving to other perspectives. Today, the theory continues to hold some advocates, especially those who combine it with other theories. Akers and Sellers concluded that the primary importance of labeling theory is that it "calls attention to the unintended consequences of social control." But the main weakness is that "it essentially ignores primary deviance and seriously underestimates the influence that other variables have on behavior in the first place and continue to have on its future occurrence."[133]

One of the most serious criticisms of labeling theory is that it is not a theory—it is a perspective. No systematic labeling theory has been developed. The empirical assessment of a theory requires that it produce testable propositions. Not only is that difficult with labeling theory, but according to one critic, "empirical tests of labeling theory are both impossible and ridiculous."[134]

A systematic theory cannot be created unless it has precisely defined terms that can be measured. Labeling theory's methodological problems are serious, and the data are poor. Thus, the research cannot be used to support the theory, but neither can it be used to reject it. For adequate testing, it is imperative that specific hypotheses be derived and tested after precise operational definitions have been articulated.[135]

One of the common criticisms of labeling theory is that it avoids the issue of causation and ignores the actual behavior in question. Labeling theory assumes that what one does is not the key to explaining behavior; the keys are who that person is and why he or she was labeled deviant. Not all would agree with that position, as the discussion of conflict and critical theory (see again Chapter 5) and evidence of discrimination against racial and ethnic groups or decisions based solely on gender might suggest.

Another criticism of labeling theory is that it views the actor, or labelee, as too passive, and it does not acknowledge the reciprocal relationship between the actor and the reactor. Most labeling theorists overemphasize the action of society and de-emphasize the action of the subject being labeled. Social interaction should receive greater attention.

Labeling theory may also be criticized for its lack of attention to the personality characteristics of those who engage in deviant behavior. To the labeling theorists, characteristics of the individual, such as personality traits, are not important in explaining behavior. It is the *reaction* to the person that is critical. Yet labeling theory does not explain differential law enforcement. Why do police arrest some and not others for the same offenses?

A final category of criticisms focuses on the assumption that labeling produces only negative results. It is possible that, in some cases, labeling a person *deviant* might deter that person rather than plunge him or her into further deviance. Whether or not the labeling process produces negative or positive results may depend on a number of factors that have been overlooked by labeling theorists.

First, it appears that labeling has different effects on the deviant at various stages of his or her career. Labeling might thrust a male juvenile delinquent into a criminal career but deter an adult female shoplifter. Perhaps the key element is peer support, not labeling. Labeling may create a subculture, thereby establishing peer support, especially among juveniles. In short, it matters who is labeled, who does the labeling, and how the label is applied.

A second factor concerns the confidentiality of the labeling. If the label is confidential and given to a nonprofessional deviant, that person may be more likely to abandon his or her deviant behavior than if the individual is already a professional and the label is public. Third, the result is more often positive than negative when the subject has some commitment to and is sensitive toward the person doing the labeling. For example, former alcoholics and drug addicts may be more successful than nonpeers, counselors, or psychiatrists in the rehabilitation of fellow deviants. Fourth, a person is more likely to abandon deviant behavior if the label of deviant, once given, can be removed easily.

Fifth, the reaction of friends and society is important in whether the label results in positive or negative behavior. If friends and others are supportive in assisting the individual to improve, the results are more likely to be positive. Sixth, most labeling theorists have overlooked the possibility that positive labeling can increase positive behavior.

Because of these and other criticisms, some scholars have argued that labeling theory is not very important. Others take the position that even if labeling does not cause delinquent and criminal behavior, it does cause problems that should be analyzed. For example, there is evidence that people who have been labeled mentally ill have negative feelings about both that label and the way others respond to them even after they are released from treatment. The more negative these feelings, the more difficult it may be for such persons to interact positively with others. They may try to hide the fact that they have been treated, they may avoid interaction with others, or they may project negative attitudes that do not exist in others. Thus, labeling theory should be modified and further developed rather than abolished.[136]

The major contributions to labeling theory are summarized in Exhibit 6.5.

Integrated Theories

This chapter, along with Chapters 3, 4, and 5, covers theories that attempt to explain delinquent and criminal behavior from various points of view. But none of these theories explains all crime, as we would like for a general theory to do, and some of the theories compete with each other. How do we evaluate or make sense out of them?

The authors of a concise but informative theory book discussed the issue and made several suggestions, some of which are also utilized by other scholars. The simplest approach is **singular theory assessment**, which involves evaluating one individual theory and the tests of that theory's propositions. This approach is used often, and most theories will generate some support despite the fact that theories are often difficult to test empirically. Two or more theories may be compared on the basis of the scope of their coverage of crime and the empirical support for them, a process referred to as **theory competition**. But they remain as individual theories.[137]

In an effort to develop a theory that can provide a broader explanation of crime and, ideally, reach a general theory of criminal behavior, social scientists in recent years have focused on **theoretical integration**, the combination of two or more theories to form a new one. The assumption is that the resulting theory will be superior to any of the individual theories standing alone. This is not an easy task. For example, some of the theories have contradictory underlying premises such as behavior is predetermined, behavior is learned. How do you combine those propositions?

6.5

Labeling Theories: A Summary

Frank Tannenbaum

According to **Frank Tannenbaum**, persons are tagged, labeled, or named—and whether the purpose of this process is punishment or reformation, disapproval is indicated.

Edwin Lemert

Edwin Lemert distinguished between (1) *primary deviation*, which arises in a wide variety of contexts and has only marginal implications for the individual's psychic structure, and (2) *secondary deviation*, which consists of deviant behavior that is a defense to society's reaction to one's primary deviation.

Howard S. Becker

Howard S. Becker distinguished between rule breaking and deviance, as some people who break rules are not considered deviant. *Deviance* is a label created by society and attached to some but not all people who engage in the described acts.

Braithwaite's Restorative Justice

John Braithwaite examined labeling theory in the context of the total social structure, which might cause some people to embrace criminal behavior and others to avoid it. His key word is *shaming*, which is a process of heaping social disapproval on a person until it induces remorse. Shaming is an important element of social control, and there are two types. *Disintegrative shaming* stigmatizes the subject, whereas *reintegrative shaming* consists of attempts to bring that person back into law-abiding society, which is done through a process of *restorative justice*.

Matsueda's Reflective Appraisal

Based on the symbolic interaction theory of George Herbert Mead, **Ross L. Matsueda's** approach focused on the development of an individual's self-concept. This process occurs through social interaction during which the person plays the role of the other in an effort to determine his or her reactions. Some of those reactions are negative, which may lead the role player to a self-fulfilling prophecy: "They say I am bad, so I will be bad." Thus, the initially harmless acts of a child, as defined by his or her parents, may be labeled bad by others. The spiraling labeling process may cause an otherwise conforming child to live up to the labels.

Sampson and Laub's Cumulative Disadvantage

According to **Ralph J. Sampson** and **John H. Laub**, the accumulation of structural disadvantages, over time, leads to cumulative disadvantages in future life opportunities, which may lead to delinquency and crime.

Theoretical integration can be accomplished in two ways. In the first, scientists examine the distinct but complementary aspects of various theories in an effort to reach a broader explanation, a process referred to as **sequential integration**. The second approach, **conceptual fusion**, involves linking together propositions of various theories that are somewhat different but similar enough to be combined, or fused.[138]

Despite the difficulties of theoretical integration, numerous scholars have attempted it (although most of these efforts are limited to integrating only a few theories). The following section focuses on some of these integrated theories.

Akers: Conceptual Absorption

In his earlier publications, Ronald L. Akers wrote about the overlap of several theories, including social learning, social bonding, labeling, conflict, anomie, and deterrence.[139] In subsequent work, he proposed theoretical integration by means of **conceptual absorption** (similar to conceptual fusion, just discussed), which he defined as "subsuming concepts from one theory as special cases of the phenomena defined by the concepts of another."[140] To illustrate, Akers suggested that the *belief* concept of social bonding theory could be absorbed into social learning theory's concept of definitions favorable or unfavorable to law violations. Thus, beliefs that propel one to violate the law or constrain one from doing so are similar to definitions favorable or unfavorable to violating the law. Likewise, the social bonding concept of *attachment*, which refers to one's closeness with others, such as peers and parents, can be absorbed by social learning theory's concept of the *intensity* of one's relationships.[141] It can be argued, however, that Akers's conceptual absorption may simply consume the concepts of other theories without really integrating those theories.

Developmental and Life-Course Theories

One of the most frequently analyzed theories in criminology today is the *developmental and life-course (DLC) theory* approach. In his 2002 address to the American Society of Criminology, David P. Farrington examined the key theoretical and empirical aspects of the theory, which, he stated, attempts to explain three main issues: "the development of offending and antisocial behavior, risk factors at different ages, and the effects of life events on the course of development." Farrington explored the 10 conclusions about delinquency and criminal behavior that are widely accepted and that must be explained by DLC (or any other) theory:

- "First, the prevalence of offending peaks in the late teenage years—between ages 15 and 19.
- Second, the peak age of onset of offending is between 8 and 14, and the peak age of desistance [stopping, ceasing the behavior] from offending is between 20 and 29.
- Third, an early age of onset predicts a relatively long criminal career duration and the commission of relatively many offenses.
- Fourth, there is marked continuity in offending and antisocial behavior from childhood to the teenage years and to adulthood. . . .
- Fifth, a small fraction of the population . . . commit a large fraction of all crimes. . . .
- Sixth, offending is versatile rather than specialized. . . .
- Seventh, the types of acts defined as offenses are elements of a larger syndrome of antisocial behavior. . . .
- Eighth, most offenses up to the late teenage years are committed with others, whereas most offenses from age 20 onwards are committed alone. . . .
- Ninth, the reasons given for offending up to the late teenage years are quite variable, including utilitarian ones . . . for excitement or enjoyment . . . , or because people get angry. In contrast, from age 20 onwards, utilitarian motives become increasingly dominant.
- Tenth, different types of offenses tend to be first committed at distinctively different ages."[142]

In general, DLC theories may be distinguished from the position taken by Hirschi and Gottfredson (in their general theory, discussed earlier in this chapter) on the relationship between age and crime. The DLC theorists disagree with the position of Hirschi and Gottfredson that once the child has developed low self-control or a tendency to misbehave, those characteristics remain essentially throughout life. Since it is the lack of self-control that, in their view, causes delinquency and crime, the causes of such deviance are the same at all ages. In contrast, DLC theorists take the position that *age-related variables*, not age per se, explain the changes in delinquent and criminal behavior. These theorists de-emphasize the importance of biology and early childhood experiences.[143]

The life course approach is based on the premises that development is an ongoing process that unfolds over the entire life span, and development involves interactions between the individual and the environment. . . . Predicting the life course of an individual based only on factors present at an early age ignores all of the causal factors that come into play later.[144]

Numerous researchers have worked on DLC theories. The works of several are summarized here.

Sampson and Laub: Age-Graded Theory

The DLC theory of Robert J. Sampson and John H. Laub is called **age-graded theory**, referring to age-graded, informal social controls such as the bonding that occurs within the family and schools, with peers, and in later life, with marriage and jobs. Sampson and Laub attempt to explain why people do *not* engage in delinquent and criminal offenses (assuming that offending is natural). They believe that people are inhibited from offending by their social bonds to the age-graded institutions mentioned here. Offenders make a decision to offend on a cost–benefit basis, which is related to their fund of **social capital**, defined as life-sustaining, positive relations with other people and institutions, which increase their bonding with society.

In his 2003 presidential address before the annual meeting of the American Society of Criminology, Laub focused on the life course of the discipline of criminology but made the analogy to the 17 years he and Sampson had spent developing their theory of the life course of criminal behavior. By *life course*, Sampson and Laub mean the paths through which a person travels during a life span. It examines change and continuity, internal and external forces, age, and other important variables.[145]

Some terms critical to life-course theory need to be defined. **Trajectories** are long-term patterns of behavior or lines of development (e.g., marriage, career, or parenthood) that consist of **transitions**, which are short-term events (e.g., a first job or even a first marriage). A third important concept is that of **turning points**, which refers to a "change in the life course" generated by the "interlocking nature of trajectories and transitions." Thus, the life-course theory examines the long-term view of a person's life, implying a strong connection between childhood and adulthood. But by also looking at behavior in terms of the shorter view, the theory acknowledges that life trajectories can be modified or redirected by transitions or turning points. According to Sampson and Laub, "Social institutions and triggering life events that may modify trajectories include school, work, the military, marriage, and parenthood."[146] These events give a person an opportunity to change the course of his or her life, in effect, to start over or to make new friends and associates and, at least to some extent, to discard the past life.

By gaining access to the data cards from the research of Sheldon Glueck and Eleanor Glueck (see discussion in Chapter 4), who sampled 500 delinquents and 500 nondelinquents and followed them for almost two decades, Sampson and Laub analyzed criminal and noncriminal behavior over much of the critical life span of the Gluecks' sample of boys/men.[147]

Sampson and Laub emphasize a fact we have known for a long time: Crime by teenagers is disproportionate to that of other age groups. Most researchers have concentrated on this age group in their formulations of theories about crime. Sampson and Laub believe that it is a mistake to ignore the implications that childhood behavior has for the *total life span* of criminal activity. Further, they criticize most researchers for largely ignoring "the link between social structural context and the mediating processes of informal social control."[148] It is not only the social structures within which one is raised that are important but also the social processes that occur within those structures that must be considered.

Like Gottfredson and Hirschi in their general theory, discussed earlier in this chapter, Sampson and Laub acknowledge that early childhood experiences are important in the development of self-control. Similar to the social bonding theory of Travis Hirschi, also discussed earlier in this chapter, Sampson and Laub's DLC theory maintains that when a person's social bonds to society become weak or nonexistent, delinquency and crime result. But unlike Gottfredson and Hirschi and others, Sampson and Laub reject the implication that adulthood experiences are of little relevance. "[W]e contend that social interaction with both juvenile *and* adult institutions of informal social control has important effects on crime and deviance."[149]

Sampson and Laub developed three propositions for their approach.

1. "structural context mediated by informal family and school social controls explains delinquency in childhood and adolescence;
2. in turn, there is continuity in antisocial behaviors from childhood through adulthood in a variety of life domains; and
3. informal social bonds in adulthood to family and employment explain changes in criminality over the life span despite early childhood propensities."[150]

Sampson and Laub were invoking both social control and learning theory, as they emphasized the learning processes that occur in the family. They contended that both abrupt turning points and gradual changes that occur as one matures, such as getting married or entering a career, would increase that individual's bonding to society. Thus, it is understandable that even those who are delinquent during youth will decrease their illegal activity as they grow older. But those who have negative experiences, or do not go through such changes as marriage and a career, may persist in illegal activities. Those who are strongly bonded with their spouses or attached to their jobs will be less likely to risk losing these and disrupting their lives by engaging in illegal behavior. Mark Warr referred to this approach as a "straightforward summary of control theory—strong ties to conventional institutions or persons create stakes in conformity and thereby inhibit deviance."[151]

But Warr noted limitations of Sampson and Laub's approach. He argued that it may not be marriage per se that inhibits crime but the fact that marriage leads spouses to change their social contacts significantly, and those changes are associated with desistance from crime. Thus, it is the peer influences that are at work. In his own research, Warr found strong support for this position.[152]

The issue of peer influences within marriage has been investigated by other scholars, some of whom thought that Warr's additions to Sampson and Laub's theory were advised but suggested that Warr needed to embellish his own approach. "He [Warr] emphasizes the fact that adult friends can either encourage or discourage criminal behavior, but fails to recognize that the same is true for romantic partners." Further, the assumption that romantic partners encourage people to desist from crime should be refined. According to DLC theory, this will be true only if the partner is conventional, not also antisocial. And research shows that people do tend to fall in love and marry people who are similar to themselves. So, if an antisocial criminal man marries the same type of woman, the marriage might not result in influencing him to change his social network and desist from crime. In short, it is important to look at the nature *and* quality of the relationship with romantic partners to assess the impact they will have on future criminal behavior. Thus, there is evidence that "a conventional romantic partner, strong job attachment, and conventional adult friends all served to moderate the chances that a woman with a delinquent history would graduate to adult crime." For men, however, the only factor that was influential was that of conventional adult friends.[153]

In a 2003 publication, Sampson and Laub reported the results of what they believed was the "longest longitudinal study of crime to date." This project examined "trajectories of offending over the life course of delinquent boys followed from ages 7 to 70." The researchers looked at the childhood characteristics, family background, and individual differences of the sample and reported that these factors alone were not predictive of the future offending of persistent criminals.[154]

In another publication, Sampson and Laub, along with Christopher Wimer, reported research findings supporting their position that marriage is one of life's transitions that is associated with desisting from criminal behavior, reducing it by approximately 35 percent.[155] Other researchers have reported that the effect of marriage on desisting from criminal behavior exists but is more pronounced for men than for women.[156]

Another of life's activities that Sampson and Laub found associated with reductions in criminal activity was stable employment, which, they argued, builds social capital and thus improves bonding with society. John Paul Wright and Francis T. Cullen studied the relationship of associating with prosocial coworkers to the changing of peer networks, criminal behavior, and drug use. They found some support for the reduction of misbehavior by stable employment. They emphasized that it is not only the *quality of the employment* that is important (as recognized by Sampson and Laub) but the *quality of the peer associations* as well.[157]

Sampson and Laub did not consider the impact of spirituality in desistance from crime. But others have found that spirituality, as measured by church attendance and reported perceived closeness to God, has positive effects on some persons.[158]

Although Sampson and Laub concentrated on the effects of positive life events as turning points in eliminating law-breaking activities, some researchers have found that *negative* events might also be positive turning points. For example, when those who have been engaging in law-breaking activities become crime *victims*, they may desist from criminal activity, especially if they perceive that they were in some way responsible for criminal acts that led to their victimization.[159]

Despite the extensive research of Sampson and Laub and of others responding to their work, there are some variables with regard to the life span and repeat offending that have not been tested rigorously. Some criminologists have argued, for example, that more research is needed on age-graded theory and the distinction between the *prevalence* of offending or *participation* in crime and the *frequency* (or incidence) of committing crimes. The former refers to whether or not one ever committed a crime and the latter to how often one commits crimes, a distinction made by Alfred Blumstein and his colleagues in a 1986 publication on criminal careers[160] (this topic is discussed in more detail in Chapter 8). For example, how does the life event of marriage relate to age and gender in the life span of desistance from crime?[161]

The influence of the work of Sampson and Laub on other criminologists has been enormous. Their classic work, *Crime in the Making*, has been described as

> perhaps the most influential life-course study of criminal behavior. . . . [It is] an ambitious effort . . . to put forth a theory of crime that attempts to explain misbehavior across the life course. . . . [The book is] now required reading for serious criminologists.[162]

Moffitt: Developmental Theory

In her psychological development theory, Terrie Moffitt considered the fact that not all teen offenders continue to commit criminal acts as adults but that most chronic adult offenders committed illegal acts as teens. Moffitt examined two categories of antisocial adolescents. The **adolescent limiteds** are those whose antisocial behavior peaks during adolescence and then declines. They constitute the majority of antisocial adolescents. They are strongly influenced by their peers. In contrast are those few antisocial adolescents who had social problems as children, began delinquent behavior early, and continued it. These juveniles are the **life-course persisters**, those young people who begin crime early in life, persist, and commit even more serious crimes as they mature. They are thought to have a neuropsychological deficit; they differ qualitatively from others. They have low self-control, exhibit difficult temperaments during childhood, may be impulsive, and may demonstrate hyperactivity. They may be expected to continue offending into adulthood, and they are not strongly influenced by their peers.[163]

Moffitt considered the relationship between race and her developmental theory. She argued that African American youths are more likely than whites to fit into both categories of adolescent limiteds and life-course persisters primarily due to their lack of opportunity to participate in the economic well-being of society. She referred to this as the *economic maturity gap*.[164] Scholars have found support for Moffitt's position, with recent research providing empirical evidence "that economic prospects generally, and the economic maturity gap in particular, account in large part for the observed race differences in criminal (and violent) offending in early adulthood."[165]

Other scholars have concluded that empirical tests are generally supportive of Moffitt's developmental theory, referred to as "one of the most influential psychological theories in contemporary criminological theory."[166]

Cullen and Colvin: Social Support or Coercion

Francis T. Cullen suggested that all criminological theory can be integrated around the concept of **social support**, which refers to social integration within group relationships in which individuals provide social, emotional, and material support for each other. The higher the level of social support, the less likely crimes will result. Cullen advanced 13 propositions concerning social support, concluding with the proposition that, in many cases, a precondition for social control is the existence of social support.[167] Cullen and Robert Agnew maintain that this approach explains much crime and that it adds a dimension of humanitarianism to efforts to control crime.[168]

In reacting to Cullen's approach, Mark Colvin argued that it is *coercion* (defined as "a force that compels or intimidates an individual to act because of the fear or anxiety it creates" and that "can also involve the actual or threatened removal of social supports"[169]) that unifies theories that explain crime.[170] Coercion may come from interpersonal sources, such as families, other individuals and small groups, or from impersonal sources, such as governments, the economy, or criminal justice agencies. Together, Cullen and Colvin proposed that crime is *caused* by coercion and *prevented* by social support. After a discussion of the policy implications of their proposal, Cullen and Colvin concluded as follows:

> To live up to our value of freedom while reducing crime, it is imperative that we offer social support to individuals and families that free them from coercive forces. Social support offers an avenue to freedom that fosters responsibility, mutual help, and trust. It is in this context of social support that freedom can coexist with low levels of crime.[171]

In a recent analysis of Colvin's differential coercion theory, which he acknowledged combines several theories (e.g., social control, general strain, general theory, control balance, structural Marxist, social support, and social learning), one scholar maintained that, although the research on the theory is limited, there is general support for it, showing, for example, that coercion "has a direct relationship with violent offending."[172]

Thornberry: Interactional Theory

Terence P. Thornberry combined social learning, social bonding, and social-structural theories into **interactional theory**. According to Thornberry, the interaction of adolescents with other people and institutions results in behavioral outcomes. Adolescents are not propelled toward certain forms of behavior, but behavior is learned through the process of *interaction* within the family, within schools, within other social institutions, and with peers. The chances of delinquency are reduced by a strong attachment to parents, commitment to school, and acceptance of society's conventional values; chances of delinquency are increased when these conditions do not exist. But it is the *interaction* over time, not just the child's perception and level of attachment and commitment, that is the key to explaining behavior.[173]

Thornberry emphasized that these interactions change over time; they are not static. He looked at three stages: early adolescence (ages 11 to 13), middle adolescence (ages 15 to 16), and late adolescence (ages 18 to 20). Thornberry advocated that, although weak social controls may be the fundamental cause of delinquency, they do not lead directly to delinquency (as classic control theory suggests). Rather, the weakening of controls permits a wider array of behavior, including conventional as well as delinquent and criminal behavior. Also, the interactions are reciprocal; so just as delinquent peer groups may increase the chances of an adolescent becoming delinquent, delinquent behavior may increase the chances of the person's movement toward a delinquent peer group. Thornberry also looked at the structural variables of class, race, gender, and community of residence, all of which, he claimed, set the stage for the social interactions discussed here.

In later works, Thornberry, along with Marvin D. Krohn, developed the *interactional theory perspective*, suggesting that social bonding and offending affect each other and that both change over time. Life events, such as joining a gang, are influential in this reciprocal interaction. Those juveniles who begin their delinquent activities later in their development differ from the early starters in degree but not in kind; in both categories, the key is interaction.[174]

The importance of the life event of gang membership on the development and duration of delinquency was investigated by numerous researchers, who built on the works of Thornberry and his collaborators, as well as other researchers who found higher delinquency among gang members than among nongang members. The important question is whether delinquency increases as the result of gang membership. Researchers have reported that "boys who join gangs are more delinquent before entering the gang than those who do not join." However, "drug selling, drug use, violent behaviors and vandalism of property increase significantly when a youth joins a gang. The delinquency of peers appears to be one mechanism of socialization." But the research also shows that when boys leave the gangs, they engage in delinquent behavior less frequently; thus, the influence of the gang is temporary.[175]

In their review of interactional theory, Cullen and Agnew acknowledged that the research is limited and the conclusions tentative, but they concluded that the research supported the importance of both developmental issues and reciprocal effects in explaining behavior. Cullen and Agnew also noted that Thornberry and Krohn had recently proposed a revision of their theory to include individual traits and biological variables as well as the consideration of other life stages.[176]

Krohn: Network Analysis

The social learning theory of differential association along with social bonding theories form the basis of a theory of *network analysis* proposed by Marvin D. Krohn. Networks are categorized as social or personal. *Personal network* refers to a person's ties to others, including individuals within the family, friends, church, and school. *Social network* includes sets of individuals or groups who are linked by friendship or other relationships. Individual behavior is constrained by social networks; that constraint could be toward conforming or toward delinquent behavior, with the direction depending on the number and the nature of those networks. For example, a youngster who lives in a small village where everyone knows everyone else will be more constrained than one who lives in a more anonymous setting.[177]

After looking at the nature of friendship networks among adolescents, one scholar concluded as follows:

> [C]ontrary to the common-sense idea that adolescents become involved in crime/delinquency because of a lack of social and/or human capital (e.g., social control and social disorganization theory) or due to an impulsive personality trait (e.g., self-control theory) adolescents become delinquent if they are located in friendship networks that support and facilitate delinquency.[178]

Kaplan: Self-Derogation

The **self-derogation theory** of Howard B. Kaplan suggests that young people become involved in drug use, delinquent or criminal behavior, or other deviant behaviors because they have low self-esteem or self-derogation. Kaplan proposed that the following factors, explained by the theories in parentheses, can be integrated into self-derogation theory:

- Stress caused by the inability or failure to live up to society's expectations (strain theory).
- School and family (control theory).
- The influence of deviant friends (social learning theory).
- Self-concept (labeling and symbolic interaction theories).

According to Kaplan, individuals take actions that maximize their positive self-image and minimize their negative self-image, a process he refers to as a *self-esteem motive*. Many people can achieve positive self-images through this process, but young people who are not able to do so may turn to deviant acts and deviant peers to enhance their own self-esteem and self-images. Kaplan and others tested the self-derogation theory primarily on adolescent drug abusers and found some support for it.[179]

Tittle: Control Balance

One of the most complex of the integrated theories is **control balance theory**, which attempts to combine deterrence, rational choice, conflict theory, social learning, anomie, and social bonding theories. It proposes to explain the *type* of criminal behavior in which people will engage as well as *why* they engage in criminal behavior. The major proponent of this approach, Charles Tittle, began his description of the theory with the following hypothetical situation.

You are a student in a class in which the teacher humiliates you, for example, by calling you stupid. What can you do? You could work very hard to prove to the teacher that you are not stupid, but that could take a long time and might not be worth the effort. Furthermore, the other students who heard the humiliating put-down might be gone by then. You could hit the teacher, but although that might bring personal satisfaction, it might also result in arrest, being charged with a crime, and being processed through the criminal justice system. Another option is to criticize the teacher to others and to engage in questionable behavior in class. But that might result in a low grade and limit your future opportunities. Wealthy students might get someone to act on their behalf or, although rare, buy the school, dismiss all the teachers, and start a new school. A final possibility Tittle suggested is that you give up, leave school, abandon your dreams, and become decadent. So, how do you react?

According to Tittle, under control theory, you would weigh the options for reducing or eliminating your humiliation with the cost of such action. In his words,

The central premise of the theory is that the amount of control to which people are subject relative to the amount of control they can exercise affects their general probability that they will commit specific types of deviance. Deviant behavior is interpreted as a de-

vice, or maneuver, that helps people escape deficits and extend surpluses of control. . . . [A person is predisposed to engage in delinquent, criminal, or other deviant acts as the result of] an unbalanced control ratio, in combination with a desire for autonomy and fundamental bodily and psychic needs.[180]

This view assumes that control theory is central in explaining why people conform, but it goes further and assumes that control is also crucial in explaining deviance. According to Tittle, those who are controlled by others may engage in deviant behavior to avoid or escape that control, while those who control others may engage in deviant behavior to continue that control. It is not control per se but, rather, *control balance*, meaning that people have about as much control over others as others have over them, that explains behavior. Those with the most control and those with the least control tend to be the most deviant. The more balanced the control ratio, the less likely it is that a person will engage in deviant behavior regardless of whether the direction of that imbalance is negative or positive.

Originally, Tittle divided control balance into several categories, but subsequently, he revised his theory, abandoned those categories, and classified deviant acts by **control balance desirability**. In 2004, he explained this concept as involving (1) the extent to which the actor will gain long-term control and (2) the extent to which the act can be done indirectly by the actor. An example would be the attempt of one company to drive another company out of business by massive price lowering. If it works, in the long run, the company will gain more control. Furthermore, the act is impersonal. Thus, the act has significant control balance desirability. In the revision of his theory, Tittle placed greater emphasis on self-control, stating that persons who engage in deviance are generally rational, and they select actions that will maximize their control balance desirability. Those who have low social control are likely to act more irrationally in their selections of behavior. For example, actors low in social control are more likely to hit the teacher in the situation described earlier; those higher in social control would be more likely to make efforts to get the teacher fired.[181]

Although Tittle related his theory to traditional variables, such as social class, race, gender, age, marriage, parenting, and so on, he recognized that the theory has not been tested directly. His theory is young, but some theorists have concluded, "Tittle's theory does a nice job of explaining deviance committed by several segments of society, including both skid-row bums and political and corporate criminals."[182]

Elliott, Ageton, and Cantor: Integrated Strain/Control

Perhaps the most recognized of the theories that integrate traditional strain, social control, and social learning theories is that of Delbert S. Elliott, Suzanne S. Ageton, and

Rachelle J. Cantor. These researchers proposed to develop a theory that would explain how delinquency is generated and maintained. They developed two paths, or a combination of conditions, through which adolescents move into delinquent behavior. Probably, the most frequent path involves "weak bonds to conventional society and exposure and commitment to groups involved in delinquent activity." The second path incorporates "(1) strong bonds to conventional society, (2) conditions and experiences which attenuate those bonds, and, in most instances, (3) exposure and commitment to groups involved in delinquency."[183]

Bonds or controls may be internal, which Elliott, Ageton, and Cantor referred to as *integration*, or they may be external, which they called *commitment*. Integration includes occupying conventional social roles and participating in activities, organizations, and institutions that are conventional. Integration also involves effective networks for sanctioning behavior. Commitment, or external bonds, includes "perceived legitimacy of conventional norms, normlessness, social isolation, societal estrangement, powerlessness, attachment to parents and peers, belief in conventional goals and values, and tolerance for deviance."[184]

Bonds may be reinforced or weakened by experiences or conditions, such as social disorganization within the family, school, or community; failures and successes; and labeling (both positive and negative). Even young people with strong bonds to society may become involved in deviant behavior when faced with one or more of these stressors. For example, although the most important socialization occurs within the family, if that process is not adequate, young people may become more bonded to their peers. If those bonds are stronger with delinquent than with conventional peers, the youths are more likely to become involved in deviant, delinquent, and even criminal behavior.

According to Cullen and Agnew, Elliott, Ageton, and Cantor found support for their integrated theory, concluding that the factor most predictive of delinquency (other than prior delinquent acts) is association with peers who engage in delinquent behavior. The impact of those associations was greater on individuals who had low social control, which was influenced by strain.[185] Recent support for the model was reported by investigators who studied offenders and their mentors.[186]

Robinson: Integrated Systems Theory of Antisocial Behavior

In his book *Why Crime? An Integrated Systems Theory of Antisocial Behavior*,[187] criminologist Matthew Robinson explained his position concerning theory integration, which is based on integrating academic *disciplines*, not just concepts or propositions. Robinson called his approach the **integrated systems theory** (IST). It begins with a list of

facts that we know about crime, such as most people who commit crimes begin as juveniles. Robinson claimed that IST is consistent with all of the facts about crime, and it is aimed at explaining the likelihood of engaging in antisocial behavior in general. Robinson listed six philosophical assumptions of his approach:

- "People choose whether or not to commit crime.
- People's choices are influenced by factors beyond their control.
- The facts that influence people's choices (and hence their behaviors) are risk factors and protective factors.
- These risk and protective factors exist among six levels of analysis, including cells, organisms, groups, communities/organizations, and society.
- Exposure to risk factors generally increases the risk of antisocial and criminal behavior, especially when exposure is frequent, regular, intense, and occurs early in life.
- Exposure to protective factors generally decreases the risk of antisocial and criminal behavior, especially when exposure is frequent, regular, intense, and occurs early in life."[188]

Risk factors have been identified in numerous academic disciplines, from biology to sociology. Robinson developed a time line involving risk factors that showed which factors are most likely to be influential at which time in a person's life. For example, genetics is most influential in early childhood, and employment is in early adulthood. Robinson concluded that "the more risk factors a person is exposed to during any stage of life, the more likely antisocial behavior will occur." These risk factors can be counteracted by protective factors.[189]

Robinson's developments are recent and have not yet been subjected to rigorous testing. However, criminologists have reacted favorably to the theory, with some describing Robinson's work as "perhaps the most ambitious, comprehensive interdisciplinary attempt so far to move integration of criminological theory to new heights."[190]

One reviewer wrote that Robinson's integrative theory makes "major contributions to criminology" and that his book "is a tour de force for the criminologist who wants to learn something about the biosocial perspective."[191] Finally, the Danish National Television made a documentary about Robinson's book on integrated theory.[192]

Agnew: General Theory

Robert Agnew, whose strain theory was discussed in Chapter 5, has also developed an integrated theory, which he referred to as a general theory that incorporates a broader range of variables than other integrated theories. For example, Agnew's general theory includes personality traits (e.g., irritability), measures of social support, and peer abuse. Agnew stated that his general theory incorporates all of the variables associated with other theories as well as the mechanisms associated with those theories. Finally, he said, it describes the relationships among the variables.[193]

Agnew classified the variables that cause crime into these five clusters associated with life domains:

- Self (irritability/low self-control)
- Family (poor parenting practices, no/bad marriages)
- School (negative school experiences, limited education)
- Peers (peer delinquency)
- Work (unemployment/bad jobs)[194]

According to Agnew, others organize the variables by theories, but there are too many variables for individual examination, and separating them may be misleading. For example, measuring the impact of family conflict is too narrow. When family is a risk factor, there are probably other influential variables that are associated with the family. It makes sense to combine all the family variables to measure the effect of the family on behavior. The same goes for other variables.[195]

Agnew continued with these propositions:

- "The life domains have reciprocal effects on one another which vary over the life course. . . .
- Crime affects the life domains and prior crime affects subsequent crime. . . .
- Life domains interact in affecting crime and one another. . . .
- Life domains have nonlinear [i.e., 'As the level of a life domain increases it has an increasingly larger effect on crime and the other domains'] and largely contemporaneous effects on crime and one another. . . .
- Biological factors and the larger social environment affect the life domains."[196]

Agnew concluded that his theory reflects the basic concepts and propositions of the major theories of crime and that it is more than a patchwork result. He believes that his theory provides an answer to the question of "why they do it?"—"although you, the reader, are the final judge."[197]

Farrington: Integrated Cognitive Antisocial Potential

We began our discussion of DLC theories with a reference to an address by David P. Farrington, in which he reviewed the life course of the discipline of criminology. In that presentation, Farrington discussed the "ten widely accepted conclusions about the development of offending that any DLC theory must be able to explain." He then offered his own contribution to integrated theory, which he referred to as the **integrated cognitive antisocial potential (ICAP) theory**. This theory, according to Farrington,

integrates concepts from strain, control, learning, labeling, and rational choice theories. The key concept of ICAP theory is *antisocial potential* (AP), which refers to a person's potential to engage in antisocial acts. It "assumes that the translation from antisocial potential to antisocial behavior depends on cognitive (thinking and decision-making) processes that take account of opportunities and victims." Farrington distinguished long-term from short-term AP. The former "depends on impulsiveness, strain, modeling, socialization processes, and life events." Short-term AP depends on "motivating and situational factors."[198]

Individuals can be placed on a continuum from low to high with regard to their AP (and this ordering persists over time). Few people have relatively high levels, but those are the persons most likely to commit deviant acts. AP levels vary with age and reach a peak during the teen years "because of changes within individuals in the factors that influence long-term AP (i.e., from childhood to adolescence, the increasing importance of peers, and decreasing importance of parents)." The primary factors influencing high AP are "desires for material goods, status among intimates, excitement, and sexual satisfaction. However, these motivations only lead to high AP if antisocial methods of satisfying them are habitually chosen." Those who have difficulty satisfying their needs through legitimate means—such as persons with low incomes, those who are unemployed, and those who are not successful in school—are most likely to engage in antisocial methods. They will also be influenced by physical capabilities and behavioral skills. As Farrington noted, a small child would have difficulty stealing a car.[199]

Long-term AP is influenced by the processes of attachment (children who are not attached to prosocial parents will have high AP) and socialization (children who are consistently punished for bad behavior and rewarded for good behavior will have low AP). Exposure to antisocial role models increases long-term AP as does impulsiveness, as those who are impulsive tend to act quickly without giving significant thought to their behavior. Life events affect AP; for example, AP decreases with marriage or moving from a high crime area, and it increases after separation or divorce. Interaction among these factors is also important. Thus, persons who are exposed to antisocial role models may have higher AP if they also experience poor socialization or strain. Biological factors (e.g., low intelligence) may also be important.[200]

With regard to his theory, Farrington concluded the following:

According to the ICAP theory, the commission of offenses and other types of antisocial acts depends on the interaction between the individual (with his immediate level of AP) and the social environment (especially criminal opportunities and victims). Short-term AP varies within individuals according to short-term energizing factors such as being bored, angry, drunk, frustrated, or being encouraged by male peers. Criminal opportunities and the availability of victims depend on routine activities. Encountering a tempting opportunity or victim may cause a short-term increase in AP, just as a short-term increase in AP may motivate a person to seek criminal opportunities and victims.[201]

The factors that determine whether a person with a particular level of AP actually commits a crime include the cognitive consideration of the costs and benefits of such behavior—for example, the material goods that might be secured; the chances of being apprehended by law enforcement officials; and the likely reaction of peers, parents, and partners—as well as the person's past experiences. According to Farrington, most people act in ways they think are rational, "but those with low levels of AP will not commit offenses even when (on the basis of subjective expected utilities) it appears rational to do so." And persons with high short-term AP levels—for example, levels caused by heavy drinking or anger—may commit offenses that are not rational. Further, as a result of the social learning process, the consequences of offending may create changes in long-term AP as well as in the cognitive level of future decisions.[202]

In concluding his address to the American Society of Criminology, upon receiving the prestigious Edwin H. Sutherland award, David P. Farrington acknowledged the need for significant future research on his and other integrated theories, but he said

> I am happy to end on an optimistic note. Given the current state of DLC theories and DLC knowledge, there seems great scope for cumulative advancement of knowledge and for widespread agreement about key facts that need to be explained and key assumptions that need to be included in DLC theories.[203]

Bernard and Snipes: Theory Integration Approach

Thomas L. Bernard and Jeffrey B. Snipes took yet another approach to integrating criminological theories. These scholars did not develop a new integration theory but, rather, suggested five points that must be included in a criminology theory that represents the existing theories and lends itself to empirical testing. Those points are as follows:

- Rather than focusing on the theories that have been proposed to explain crime, criminologists should focus on the variables related to criminal behavior and the relationship between and among those variables.
- Rather than focus on the validity of any given theory, criminologists should focus on the usefulness of theories to the scientific process.

- The process of trying to show that a theory is wrong (e.g., falsifying that theory) should give way to concentrating on risk factors and determining which theories explain most crime in terms of those risks. It is impossible to falsify a theory totally as crime is so complex that any theory probably has some explanatory ability. Risk-factor analysis, however, allows integration of theories because it permits grading theories from those that explain a lot of crime down to those that explain less crime.
- Theories that contradict each other cannot be integrated.
- The theory should state policy implications clearly.[204]

Conclusion to Integrated Theories

The theories discussed in this section give only a partial picture of the extensive efforts by social scientists to integrate theories about crime. Some of the theories have been tested; others have not. All have met with mixed success. One of the strongest reactions has been from Travis Hirschi, discussed earlier in this chapter in terms of his social bonding theory and general theory (with Gottfredson). Hirschi maintained that theories about crime should remain separate because they are not compatible; they have different perspectives and should be examined on their own merits. Those who propose integration theories are not integrating but, rather, developing new theories.[205]

In their discussion of integrated theories, Akers and Sellers concluded that reactions to the various attempts at integration were mixed, with some accepted and some even ignored. There appeared to be a willingness to accept these theories, "but there continues to be a considerable indifference and a healthy skepticism toward integration as a theory-building strategy."[206]

Others are more optimistic. They acknowledge that integrated theories have not received as much support as one might have predicted, but criminologists remain excited about this approach, and integration attempts and refinements can be expected to continue for years.[207]

Integrated theories are summarized in Exhibit 6.6.

Conclusion to Criminal Behavior Theories

We have looked at the various theories of criminal behavior: the economic, biological, physiological, psychological, psychiatric, and sociological approaches. All have methodological problems: Crime is difficult to define in operational terms, samples are limited, and follow-up studies are expensive and time-consuming. All the research today is plagued with an increasing lack of public interest in what caused the behavior; rather, the hue and cry is

6.6 EXHIBIT

Integrated Theories: A Summary

Conceptual Absorption
Ronald L. Akers and **Christine S. Sellers** advocate subsuming or combining into one theory the concepts of another. They believe their approach integrates social learning, social bonding, labeling, conflict, anomie, and deterrence theories.

Developmental and Life-Course (DLC) Theories
The DLC theories attempt to explain how offending and antisocial behavior develop, the risk factors persons face at different ages, and the effect that various life events have on development.

Age-Graded Theory
Robert J. Sampson and **John H. Laub** referred to age-graded informal social controls such as the bonding that occurs within the family and schools, with peers, and in later life, with marriage and jobs. A person's bonding with these age-graded controls inhibits delinquent and criminal behavior.

Developmental Theory
Terrie Moffitt, a psychologist, looked beyond a single dimension and distinguished two categories of antisocial adolescents: the *adolescent limiteds* (whose antisocial behavior peaks during adolescence and then declines) and the *life-course persisters* (who have social problems as children and continue their antisocial behavior even into adulthood).

Social Support or Coercion and Crime
Francis T. Cullen and **Mark Colvin** advocated that all criminological theory can be integrated around the concept of social support, which refers to social integration within group relationships in which individuals provide social, emotional, and material support for each other. The higher the level of social support, the less likely it is that crimes will occur.

An Interactional Theory of Delinquency
Terence P. Thornberry combined social learning, social bonding, and social-structural theories, claiming that delinquency is the result of the fact that children interact with their parents and others over time. All change is a result of these interactions, and all must be considered in explaining delinquent and criminal behavior.

Network Analysis
Marvin D. Krohn used social and personal networks to integrate social learning and social bonding theories.

Self-Derogation Theory
Howard B. Kaplan's concept of delinquent behavior is explained by low self-esteem or self-derogation. Persons have a self-esteem motive, meaning they take actions that maximize their positive self-image and minimize their negative self-image.

Control Balance Theory
Charles Tittle's theory concerns the ratio between how much a person needs to control and how much that person is able to control. The more balanced the control ratio, the less likely it is that the individual will engage in deviant behavior.

An Integrated Strain/Control Perspective on Delinquency
This theory developed by **Delbert S. Elliott, Suzanne S. Ageton**, and **Rachelle J. Cantor** integrates traditional strain, social control, and social learning theories.

Integrated Systems Theory of Antisocial Behavior
Matthew Robinson's approach integrates academic disciplines as well as concepts and propositions. He began with a list of facts we know about crime, looked at risk factors at six levels of analysis, and advocated that his approach was aimed at explaining antisocial behavior in general.

General Theory
Robert Agnew contended that his general theory incorporates a broader range of variables (e.g., personality traits) than other integrated theories, and he described the relationships among those variables.

The Integrated Cognitive Antisocial Potential (ICAP) Theory
David P. Farrington's effort to integrate strain, control, learning, labeling, and rational choice theories is based on the concept of long-term or short-term antisocial potential (AP), which refers to a person's potential to engage in antisocial acts.

The Theory Integration Approach of Thomas L. Bernard and Jeffrey B. Snipes
These scholars did not develop a new integration theory but, rather, suggested five points that must be included in a criminology theory that represents the existing theories and lends itself to empirical testing.

"Let the punishment fit the crime," although there is some evidence of a return to treatment rather than punishment. But gaining an understanding of the reasons for the behavior does not generally command a high priority in research funding.

What have we come to know about crime by analyzing official data? We know that most crimes are committed by men but that, according to *official* arrest data, some crimes have been increasing among women. We know that most crimes are committed by persons who are mobile and who live in large cities. We know that among juveniles, those who are closely bonded to their families and schools are less likely to commit delinquent acts or crimes than those who are not so closely bonded. We know that those who are unemployed and hovering at the bottom of society's class structure are more likely than those who are in the middle or at the top of the social structure to be apprehended for serious property crimes. But the official data must be considered along with data about white-collar crimes (discussed in Chapter 9), which involve greater financial losses to society than the serious property crimes of arson, larceny-theft, burglary, and motor vehicle theft.

We know that according to *official* data, a disproportionate amount of crime is committed by African Americans, and we know that most crimes are committed by persons who are not married. So, how do we make sense of these and other crime data? That is what the theories, and the tests of those theories, are about. If you become discouraged because we do not know *the* cause of crime, perhaps you can compare this venture to health problems for which we have not found *the* cause, problems such as cancer and the common cold. We know about the virus that causes AIDS, but we have not found a cure. Physical scientists continue forming and testing their theories in an effort to find answers to these and other health problems. Likewise, social scientists continue to work toward understanding the causes of crime.

Some social scientists look for a general theory to explain all crime (or perhaps all behavior); we have seen some of those approaches that look at the social-structural or social-process theories. In 1990, after reviewing 20 years of testing theories of criminal behavior, Thomas J. Bernard concluded that we had made tremendous progress in empirical research on crime but little progress on theoretical developments.[208] In 1991, Roland Chilton expressed his view that a general theory to explain all crime cannot be discovered: "Crime is too variable, too influenced by moral and political entrepreneurs to be seen as a unitary phenomenon."[209]

More recent research has, perhaps, been more promising, but criminologists still have a long way to go. As Thomas J. Bernard, Jeffrey B. Snipes, and Alexander L. Gerould stated in their analysis of the state of criminological theory, "criminology researchers simply have not fully sorted out the issues."[210] But they concluded that, taken together, the research does provide us with the following characteristics associated with criminal behavior:

1. "A history of early childhood problem behaviors and of being subjected to poor parental child rearing techniques, such as harsh and inconsistent discipline; school failure and the failure to learn higher cognitive skills such as moral reasoning, empathy, and problem solving.

2. Certain neurotransmitter imbalances such as low seratonin [*sic*], certain hormone imbalances such as high testosterone, central nervous system deficiencies such as frontal or temporal lobe dysfunction, and autonomic nervous system variations such as unusual reactions to anxiety.

3. Ingesting alcohol, a variety of illegal drugs, and some toxins such as lead; head injuries; and complications during subject's pregnancy or birth.

4. Personality characteristics such as impulsivity; insensitivity; a physical and nonverbal orientation; and a tendency to take risks.

5. Thinking patterns that focus on trouble, toughness, smartness, excitement, fate, and autonomy, and a tendency to think in terms of short-term rather than long-term consequences.

6. Association with others who engage in and approve of criminal behavior.

7. Weak attachments to other people, less involvement in conventional activities, less to lose from committing crime, and weak beliefs in the moral validity of the law.

8. A perception that there is less risk of punishment for engaging in criminal behavior.

9. Masculinity as a gender role."[211]

In addition, the researchers list these factors as increasing the probability of victimiztion: "Frequently being away from home, especially at night; engaging in public activities while away from home; and associating with people who are likely to commit crime."[212]

The authors concluded their theory text with their belief that, "Today, both liberals and conservatives increasingly rely on criminology theory and research to support their recommendations about crime policy."[213]

The fact that we have differences and problems with criminological research does not mean that we should abandon our efforts to develop and test theories that explain the causes of crime. It does mean that we must be careful in our interpretations of the existing theories, research, and data on crime.

It is important not to conclude that research on criminal behavior is hopeless. As sociologist George A. Lundberg stated in 1961, "Many of the fruits of science . . . can be used to advantage while still in the process of development. Science is at best a growth, not a sudden revelation. . . . We do not abandon cancer research because the patients of today may not be saved by it." Research in the social and physical sciences can be used "imperfectly and in part while it is developing."[214]

In reemphasizing the importance of theory, the editor of the leading professional journal in the field noted why the annual meetings of the American Society of Criminology require that research papers be grounded in theory. Robert J. Bursik Jr. quoted a passage from a 1963 book by noted sociologist Peter Berger entitled *Invitation to Sociology*: "Statistical data by themselves do not make sociology.

They become sociology only when they are sociologically interpreted, put within a theoretical frame of reference." Bursik emphasized that although anyone can take a set of data and explain what is there—for example, more men than women commit crime—"a truly criminological contribution to the field not only documents the 'what,' but also offers insightful arguments about the 'why.'" Bursik continued by noting that this is possible only "if the selection of variables upon which to focus and the interpretation of the patterns that are identified are grounded in theoretical considerations."[215]

But there is concern that criminologists are not being heard by policy makers (public policy is discussed next). As one criminologist lamented,

> Despite the annual publication of hundreds of peer-reviewed articles and textbooks proudly displayed at our annual conventions, policy makers are paying little if any attention to us. When Congress or state legislatures debate new crime bill legislation or the effectiveness of past actions, their first question is not, "What do the criminologists think?" I would venture that one would be hard pressed to cite another discipline that has been so ignored for such a long time. [Another scholar's] lament that criminology has been unable to evaluate the relative effects of various law enforcement strategies on illegal drug consumption use is another example of how impotent criminology is in shaping and improving criminal justice policy. . . . [With regard to policy changes] over the years I learned, . . . such efforts amounted to nothing more than spitting in the wind.[216]

In addition to theoretical formulations, it is critical that criminologists, sociologists, and other social scientists communicate their theoretical explanations and empirical findings in language that can be understood (and, we hope, accepted!) by those who are in a position to make policy decisions. The chapter closes with some examples of such decisions that are based on social science research.

Policy Implications of Criminal Behavior Theories

Public policy decisions regarding how to deal with crime are made at all levels of government as well as within other institutions, such as families, churches, and schools. These decisions may be made after a careful analysis of the research data; they may be made on the basis of intuition; they may be the result of political decisions; or they may involve all of these approaches. In most cases, we really do not know the reasons policy decisions are made. We may

be given reasons, but they are not always accurate. Part of the problem lies with social scientists, who do not always communicate their findings and theoretical developments in a manner that is readily accessible and fully understood by those in policy-making positions. At times, however, the latter simply refuse to listen. Still, it is important to consider the policy implications of what we know (or do not know) about crime.

Throughout this text, you will read about administrative rules and regulations, local ordinances, state and federal laws, court decisions, and even some constitutional challenges that will have an impact on the way we react to deviant, juvenile, and criminal behavior. We have already noted that even the definitions of the word *crime* are not always uniform. And even when we agree on what is a crime, we do not always count the acts or react to them in the same ways in various jurisdictions. It is suggested that as you progress through the text, you consider the theories you have learned in Chapters 3, 4, 5, and 6 and question their relevance to the policy decisions that have been made.

Let us consider a few examples. In his presidential address before the American Society of Criminology in November 2000, Roland Chilton spoke about public policy. He referred to a meeting in which a group of scientists were discussing murders that appeared to be drug related. Chilton suggested that it might be time to reexamine the government's policies regarding drug enforcement. The implication was that we might consider legalizing drugs. The response was that such a suggestion would not be "viable policy." In other words, it would not be politically acceptable. Chilton saw this response as a serious problem.[217]

In Chapter 10, we will look at some aspects of the criminalization of drugs in greater detail, but the purpose is not to advocate that drugs should be legalized. Rather, it is to examine the implications of the direction we have taken in the so-called war on drugs. Chilton referred to this war as "the folly of our time." By *folly*, he meant "a costly undertaking that has an absurd or ruinous outcome" or "conduct that lacks good sense, understanding, or foresight." According to Chilton, the U.S. drug policies are "one of the best examples of criminal justice folly in our lifetime. Our drug laws are indeed tragically foolish and excessively costly." And he noted, they consume enormous resources within criminal justice systems.

If research shows that the long sentences that we have been assessing for minor drug offenses have had little or no impact on drug sales (i.e., no impact on the big drug dealers), have had no impact on the rehabilitation of drug offenders, and have crowded many prisons almost beyond our capacity to process more serious offenders, should we refuse to look for new ways to deal with the issue? Or should we look more closely at the position taken in the fall of 2000 by California voters (and discussed later in

The U.S. Congress and state legislatures enact numerous statutes aimed at regulating behavior, especially criminal behavior. It is imperative that these politicians consider valid scientific evidence that supports or rejects the policies they consider. It is the responsibility of social and physical scientists to provide such evidence to the extent it is possible.

this text) and provide treatment rather than punishment for minor drug offenses? Since Chilton made this speech, some of the harsh drug laws have been revised, as we will note later.

Chilton ended his speech by stating: "Political viability is of little value if it produces foolish and unfair policies and practices."[218]

In connection with Chilton's thoughts, we might consider whether marijuana should be permitted for medicinal reasons and whether nonviolent drug offenders should be processed through special courts (discussed in Chapter 13). There is evidence that, "Drug use and criminal activity are substantially reduced for drug court participants while they are in the program" and that drug courts have "generated savings in jail costs, probation supervision, police overtime, and other criminal justice costs, and they have fostered savings outside of the criminal justice system as well." Specifically, it was reported that in a Baltimore treatment court, "Drug subjects who participated in ten or more consecutive days of certified drug treatment were much less likely to recidivate than were both untreated drug court subjects and control subjects."[219]

One criminologist concluded that the impact of the drug court movement "is hard to ignore. . . . [The] contribution of the drug court innovation leaves a mark on justice practices far beyond what consistently positive findings from the most rigorous evaluation of reoffending rates could probably ever produce."[220]

Not all public policies have shown positive results. Consider those requiring the mandatory arrests of alleged domestic batterers. Empirical analysis of problems that

resulted when such policies were implemented in Milwaukee, Wisconsin, suggested that increased prosecutions of those alleged to have engaged in domestic violence may result in court delays, increased recidivism prior to trial, and fewer convictions. Thus,

> Arresting more batterers does not necessarily result in more prosecutions. . . . [W]ell-intended policies regarding domestic violence can backfire. . . . Good intentions of policy makers need to be balanced with a realistic view of how the criminal justice system functions and what the actual effects of new policies are likely to be.[221]

Other research produced similar results, with the investigator concluding that although police should continue to be aggressive in domestic violence cases, "local officials should recognize that mandatory arrest laws could reduce the number of cases that enter the system." Furthermore, when the state awards domestic violence victims the custody of their children, it should provide those children with adequate protection and needed services.[222]

Another policy issue is what to do about repeat offenders. Later in this text, we consider special laws enacted in all states and the federal government to provide long sentences—such as 25 years to life without parole—for repeat offenders even when their offenses are not serious (although most do require a serious third offense to invoke the statutes). This situation has increased prison populations and contributed little to public safety.

Does it make sense that putting people in prison for longer periods of time will deter them from committing crimes as well as provide a warning to others? Yes, it might seem logical, but what did we learn from the classical theorists about letting the punishment fit the crime? Did it work then? Will it work now?

The importance of considering the policy implications of research and theory in criminology is dramatically illustrated by the most recent edition of the criminology theory book by Ronald L. Akers and Christine S. Sellers: *Criminological Theories: Introduction, Evaluation, and Application*. These scholars proclaimed the following:

> Every criminological theory implies a therapy or a policy. . . . All major criminological theories have implications for, and have indeed been utilized in, criminal justice policy and practice. Every therapy, treatment program, prison regimen, police policy, or criminal justice practice is based, either explicitly or implicitly, on some explanation of human nature in general or criminal behavior in particular.[223]

Akers and Sellers discussed the policy implications of criminological theories, giving detailed information on specific programs that have been instituted as a result of an acceptance of each theory. Their examples ranged from policies of involuntary sterilization to fundamental changes within institutions based on the theory that criminal justice policies have been sexist.

Finally, the American Society of Criminology published the papers on criminal justice policy presented by its members during the association's annual meeting in 2009. Charles Wellford suggested that rather than whining about the lack of attention to their research and recommendations, criminologists should acknowledge the scientific contributions they have made, become even more scientific in their research, and understand that more funding will be available as they accomplish these goals. In responding to Wellford, Thomas G. Blomberg stated his belief that criminologists today are more oriented toward going beyond publishing their research and trying to have an impact on public policy. In his words, "A large and growing number of us are already and will continue to actively pursue and evaluate various strategies for linking our research to policy and practice."[224]

Summary

This chapter examined theories that emphasize the *process* by which a person becomes a criminal. Many theories were discussed, and several exhibits were presented to summarize them for you.

The chapter began with a brief overview of learning theory before looking more closely at the contributions of Gabriel Tarde, who used his imitation theory to explain how people learn acceptable as well as deviant, delinquent, or criminal behavior. That set the backdrop for consideration of the modern media's influence on behavior, especially criminal behavior.

The chapter then turned to a more extensive analysis of Edwin H. Sutherland's theory of differential association. Sutherland viewed his theory as one that explains all behavior, not just deviance, delinquency, or crime. Individuals learn those behaviors in the same ways they learn acceptable behaviors. Sutherland's work influenced other social scientists, many of whom attempted to test the propositions of differential association.

A second type of learning theory is that of differential association-reinforcement theory, in which Burgess and Akers attempted to integrate Sutherland's theory with that of modern behavior theory and, eventually for Akers, the development of his own version of social learning theory.

The influence of sociology may be seen in the application of social control theories as a supplement to (or replacement for) psychological control theories (discussed in Chapter 4) in explanations of criminal and delinquent behavior. Control theories explain deviance in terms of a breakdown in social controls. Reiss and Nye's control theory approach looked at the impact of personal inner controls and external social structures on behavior. Reckless's containment approach viewed social controls as providing insulators or buffers against improper behavior. Hirschi developed control theory in terms of his position that it is conforming behavior that must be explained. He did so in terms of four components of social bonds: *attachment* to conventional persons, *commitment* to conventional behavior, *involvement* with conventional people, and *belief* in conventional norms. In testing his approach by means of self-report studies, Hirschi found a lack of support for the traditionally reported high association between low socioeconomic class and crime. Rather, he found that weak attachments to parents and to school are more predictive of delinquent and criminal behavior than class is and that positive attitudes toward one's own accomplishments are more characteristic of law-abiding than of law-violating youths.

Gottfredson and Hirschi developed a general self-control theory. They argued that low self-control, which results primarily from poor parenting, is the best predictor of criminal behavior. They attempted to measure the characteristics of persons with low self-control and relate them to criminal behavior.

The chapter next focused on labeling theory, which considers why, of all the people who engage in deviant, delinquent, or criminal behavior, some are processed through criminal justice systems while others are ignored. The emphasis is on the external labeling process rather than on the reason for the behavior in question. Labeling theory has been applied to criminal behavior since the 1930s but has received more attention in recent years. The chapter discussed the earlier works of Tannenbaum, Becker, and others before focusing on more recent research, much of which tests the approach utilizing juvenile subjects. The contributions of Braithwaite's restorative justice, Matsuda's reflective appraisal, and Sampson and Laub's cumulative disadvantages were examined.

A major section of this chapter's discussion of social-process theories was devoted to integrated theories. The elements of integration were explained, including the contributions of Akers's conceptual absorption approach. Extensive coverage was given to developmental and life-course theories, with emphasis on the age-graded approach of Sampson and Laub. This approach considers the age-graded, informal social controls such as the bonding that occurs within the family and schools, with peers, and in later life, with marriage and jobs. A person's bonding with these age-graded controls inhibits delinquent and criminal behavior. The section closed with an examination of Moffitt's developmental theory.

Cullen and Colvin attempted to integrate criminological theories around the concept of social support or coercion and proposed that crime is caused by coercion and prevented by social support. For Thornberry, social learning, social bonding, and social-structural theories can be combined into interactional theory, whereas Krohn used social and personal network analysis to integrate social learning and social bonding theories. Under Kaplan's self-derogation theory, delinquent behavior is explained by low self-esteem or self-derogation.

Tittle's control balance theory refers to the ratio between how much a person needs to control and how much that individual is able to control. The more balanced the control ratio, the less likely it is that a person will engage in deviant behavior. Elliott, Ageton, and Cantor utilized an integrated strain/control perspective to combine traditional strain, social control, and social learning theories. This approach is probably the most popular and accepted of the integrated theories.

Robinson's integrated systems theory of antisocial behavior is directed as integrating academic disciplines as well as theoretical concepts and propositions. Although recently developed, the theory has been well received in the profession and by the media.

Agnew contributed a general theory, which he believes integrates more than other theories, including such variables as personality traits generally excluded by other integrated theories. He classified the variables he considered into five categories: self, family, school, peers, and work.

A discussion of the integrated cognitive antisocial potential theory of Farrington, who claimed that his theory integrates strain, control, learning, labeling, and rational choice theories, was followed by a final approach at theory integration, that of Bernard and Snipes.

After a conclusion on integrated theories, the chapter continued with a brief analysis of criminal behavior theories. Social-process theories in particular have been instrumental in achieving a better understanding of criminal behavior. As a group, social-process theories may be more acceptable than other current approaches of sociologists and criminologists. The theories attempt to explain differential reaction to the social structure; they are based on the sociological proposition that criminal behavior is acquired through social interaction just as noncriminal behavior is acquired. The chapter closed with a discussion of some of the policy implications of sociological and criminological theories.

This chapter concludes the text's formal analysis of theories, although references are made to those theories throughout the remainder of the text. Chapter 7 begins the study of particular crimes.

Study Questions

1. Define *learning theory*.

2. What was Tarde's contribution to criminology, and what is its relevance today? What is the impact of the media on crime?

3. Discuss the contributions of Edwin H. Sutherland to criminology, and summarize the reactions to his major theoretical developments.

4. State the elements of differential association.

5. Discuss and evaluate Akers's social learning theory.

6. Explain the control theory of Reiss and Nye.

7. Explain and critique Hirschi's bonding theory.

8. Why is the self-control theory of Gottfredson and Hirschi considered a general theory?

9. Explain the primary difference between labeling theory and other explanations of deviant behavior.

10. Are the effects of labeling always negative? Discuss.

11. Explore Braithwaite's concept of restorative justice, and relate it to modern criminal justice systems.

12. Define *reflective appraisal*, and discuss Matsueda's development of this approach.

13. Define *cumulative disadvantages*, and discuss Sampson and Laub's development of this concept.

14. Discuss briefly the use of labeling theory to explain juvenile delinquency. What are the racial implications of the theory?

15. What is meant by integrated theories? Define and discuss *conceptual absorption*.

16. Name and briefly explain the integrated theories discussed in the chapter. Which do you think have the greatest promise for explaining delinquency and crime?

Brief Essay Assignments

1. Define and contrast *social learning theory* and *social control theory*, and compare the contributions of the major proponents of each.

2. Define, explain, evaluate, and discuss the impact of self-control theory as developed by Gottfredson and Hirschi.

3. Explain how labeling theory differs from social control theories.

4. Select the four most important integrative theories and explain your choices.

5. Discuss the policy implications of criminological theories.

Internet Activities

1. Learn about efforts to control violence in the media and the legal implications of those efforts by logging on to the Media Coalition site, http://www.mediacoalition.org/litigations.php, accessed 9 October 2010. What types of cases concerning efforts to censor the media have been filed? How should they be resolved?

2. Search newspapers, magazines, or journals, and the Internet for information on a recent well-publicized crime. Find out as much information as you can about the defendant(s), victim(s), and offense(s). In your opinion, do any of the theories discussed in this and the previous chapters explain or contribute to explaining the actions that occurred? If so, which one(s)?

Notes

1. See Gabriel Tarde, "Penal Philosophy," in *The Heritage of Modern Criminology*, ed. Sawyer F. Sylvester Jr. (Cambridge, MA: Schenkman, 1972), p. 84.

2. For further details on Tarde's theories, see Margaret S. Wilson Vine, "Gabriel Tarde," in *Pioneers in Criminology*, 2d ed., ed. Herman Mannheim (Montclair, NJ: Patterson Smith, 1973), p. 292. Tarde's book is *Penal Philosophy*, trans. R. Howell (Boston: Little, Brown, 1912).

3. Tarde, "Penal Philosophy," p. 90.

4. Vine, "Gabriel Tarde," p. 295.

5. Tarde, "Penal Philosophy," p. 94.

6. Vine, "Gabriel Tarde," p. 295.

7. Stephen Schafer, *Theories in Criminology* (New York: Random House, 1969), p. 239.

8. "Television Gets Closer Look as a Factor in Real Violence," *New York Times* (14 December 1994), p. 1.

9. Albert Bandura, *Social Learning Theory* (Englewood Cliffs, NJ: Prentice-Hall, 1977), p. vii.

10. Albert Bandura, "The Social Learning Perspective: Mechanisms of Aggression," in *Psychology of Crime and Criminal Justice*, ed. Hans Toch (New York: Holt, Rinehart & Winston, 1979), pp. 204–205.

11. J. Ronald Milavsky, *TV and Violence*, National Institute of Justice (Washington, D.C.: U.S. Department of Justice, 1988), p. 3.

12. James Q. Wilson and Richard J. Herrnstein, *Crime and Human Nature* (New York: Simon & Schuster, 1985).

13. Honorable Donald E. Shelton, "The 'CSI Effect': Does It Really Exist?" http://www.ojp.usdoj.gov/nij/journals/259/csi-effect.htm, accessed 3 October 2010.

14. See David Pearl et al., *Television and Behavior: Ten Years of Scientific Progress and Implications for the Eighties* (Washington, D.C.: U.S. Government Printing Office, 1982). For the full report, see J. Ronald Milavsky et al., *Television and Aggression: A Panel Study* (New York: Academic Press, 1983).

15. Tannis MacBeth Williams, "Summary, Conclusions, and Implications," in *The Impact of Television: A Natural Experiment in Three Communities*, ed. Tannis MacBeth Williams (New York: Academic Press, 1986), p. 411.

16. Walter C. Bailey, "Murder, Capital Punishment, and Television: Execution Publicity and Homicide Rates," *American Sociological Review* 55 (October 1990): 628–633; quotation is on p. 633.

17. Ray Surette, *Media, Crime, and Criminal Justice: Images and Realities* (Pacific Grove, CA: Brooks/Cole, 1992), pp. 108, 118.

18. "Media Violence Plays Part in Shootings: Ex-Army Ranger Argues TV, Films Affect Children," *Washington Times* (10 November 1998), p. 2.

19. Jana Bufkin, "Book Review Essay: Exploring the Media and Crime," *Criminal Justice Review*, 26, no. 1 (Spring 2001): 62–68; quotations are on pp. 63–64.

20. Ronald L. Akers and Christine S. Sellers, *Criminological Theories: Introduction, Evaluation, and Application*, 5th ed. (New York: Oxford University Press, 2009), p. 85.

21. Albert K. Cohen et al., *The Sutherland Papers* (Bloomington: Indiana University Press, 1956), p. 19.

22. Edwin H. Sutherland and Donald R. Cressey, *Criminology*, 10th ed. (Philadelphia: Lippincott, 1978), pp. 80–82, emphasis omitted; Edwin H. Sutherland, Donald R. Cressey, and David F. Luckenbill, *Criminology*, 11th ed. (Dix Hills, NY: General Hall, 1992).

23. Edwin H. Sutherland and Donald R. Cressey, *Criminology*, 5th ed. (Philadelphia: Lippincott, 1960), pp. 78–79.

24. Thomas J. Bernard et al., *Vold's Theoretical Criminology*, 6th ed. (New York: Oxford University Press, 2010), p. 193.

25. James F. Short Jr., "Differential Association and Delinquency," *Social Problems* 4 (January 1957): 233. See also Short, "Differential Association as a Hypothesis: Problems of Empirical Testing," *Social Problems* 8 (Summer 1960): 14–25.

26. Albert J. Reiss Jr. and Albert L. Rhodes, "An Empirical Test of Differential Association Theory," *Journal of Research in Crime and Delinquency* 1 (February 1964): 5–18; quotation is on p. 12.

27. Quoted in Cohen et al., *The Sutherland Papers*, p. 37.

28. Donald R. Cressey, "The Theory of Differential Association: An Introduction," *Social Problems* 8 (Summer 1960): 3.

29. Edwin H. Sutherland and Donald R. Cressey, *Criminology*, 9th ed. (Philadelphia: Lippincott, 1974), p. 78. This position was retained in the 10th edition, published in 1978.

30. Sutherland and Cressey, *Criminology*, 10th ed., p. 84.

31. See, for example, Ross L. Matsueda and Karen Heimer, "Race, Family Structure, and Delinquency: A Test of Differential Association and Social Control Theories," *American Sociological Review* 52 (1987): 826–840.

32. Mark Warr, "Age, Peers, and Delinquency," *Criminology* 31 (February 1993): 17–40, emphasis in the original; quotation is on p. 19.

33. Mark Warr and Mark Stafford, "The Influence of Delinquent Peers: What They Think or What They Do," *Criminology* 29 (November 1991): 851–866; quotations are on pp. 851 and 864.

34. Ross L. Matsueda, "The Current State of Differential Association Theory," *Crime and Delinquency* 34 (July 1988): 277–306; quotations are on p. 277.

35. See, for example, Robert L. Burgess and Ronald L. Akers, "A Differential Association-Reinforcement Theory of Criminal Behavior," *Social Problems* 14 (Fall 1966): 128–147.

36. Christine S. Sellers and Ronald L. Akers, "Social Learning Theory: Correcting Misconceptions," in *The Essential Criminology Reader*, ed. Stuart Henry and Mark M. Lanier (Boulder, CO: Westview Press, 2006), pp. 89–99; quotations are on p. 90. See also Ronald L. Akers et al., "Social Learning and Deviant Behavior: A Specific Test of a General Theory," *American Sociological Review* 44 (August 1979): 637–638.

37. Akers and Sellers, *Criminological Theories*, 5th ed., p. 91.

38. Sellers and Akers, "Social Learning Theory," p. 91.

39. Akers and Sellers, *Criminological Theories*, 5th ed., p. 104.

40. Sellers and Akers, "Social Learning Theory," p. 96.

41. Akers and Sellers, *Criminological Theories*, 5th ed., p. 96.

42. Ibid., pp. 99–101, citations omitted.

43. Ibid., pp. 102–103; quotation is on p. 102.

44. Ibid., p. 102.

45. Mark Warr, *Companions in Crime: The Social Aspects of Criminal Conduct* (Cambridge, UK: Cambridge University Press, 2002), p. 42.

46. Ibid., pp. 78–79, as quoted in Akers and Sellers, *Criminological Theories*, 5th ed., pp. 109–110. For a recent challenge to Akers's social learning theory, see Jonathan R. Brauer, "Testing Social Learning Theory Using Reinforcement's Residue: A Multilevel Analysis of Self-Reported Theft and Marijuana Use in the National Youth Survey," *Criminology* 4, no. 3 (August 2009): 929–970.

47. Akers and Sellers, *Criminological Theories*, 5th ed., p. 110.

48. Travis Hirschi, *Causes of Delinquency* (Berkeley: University of California Press, 1969), p. 34.

49. See Albert J. Reiss Jr., "Delinquency as the Failure of Personal and Social Controls," *American Sociological Review* 16 (1951): 196–207.

50. F. Ivan Nye, *Family Relationships and Delinquent Behavior* (New York: Wiley, 1958), as quoted in Akers and Sellers, *Criminological Theories*, 5th ed., p. 126.

51. Akers and Sellers, *Criminological Theories*, 5th ed., p. 126.

52. Walter C. Reckless, "Containment Theory," in *The Sociology of Crime and Delinquency*, 2d ed., ed. Marvin E. Wolfgang et al. (New York: Wiley, 1970), p. 402.

53. Ibid.

54. Walter C. Reckless, *The Crime Problem*, 5th ed. (Englewood Cliffs, NJ: Prentice-Hall, 1973), pp. 55–57; reprint of article from *Federal Probation* 25 (December 1961): 42–46.

55. Harwin L. Voss, "Differential Association and Containment Theory: A Theoretical Convergence," in *Society, Delinquency and Delinquent Behavior*, ed. Harwin L. Voss (Boston: Little, Brown, 1970), pp. 198, 206.

56. Akers and Sellers, *Criminological Theories*, 5th ed., p. 128.

57. Hirschi, *Causes of Delinquency*, pp. 16–34. This classic work was republished in 2002 (New Brunswick, NJ: Transaction, 2002).

58. Ibid., p. 21.

59. Ibid.

60. Ibid., p. 26.

61. Ibid., pp. 54, 56.

62. Ibid., pp. 72, 108, 132, 134.

63. See Michael J. Hindelang, "Causes of Delinquency: A Partial Replication and Extension," *Social Problems* 20 (Spring 1973): 471–487.

64. Rand D. Conger, "Social Control and Social Learning Models of Delinquent Behavior: A Synthesis," *Criminology* 14 (May 1976): 19, 35.

65. See Delbert S. Elliott and Harwin L. Voss, *Delinquency and Dropout* (Lexington, MA: Lexington Books, 1974).

66. Eric Linden and James C. Hackler, "Affective Ties and Delinquency," *Pacific Sociological Review* 16 (January 1973): 27–46.

67. Bill McCarthy et al., "Girl Friends Are Better: Gender, Friends, and Crime Among School and Street Youth," *Criminology* 42, no. 4 (November 2004): 805–835.

68. Hirschi, *Causes of Delinquency*, pp. 230–231.

69. Robert Agnew, "Social Control Theory and Delinquency: A Longitudinal Test," *Criminology* 23 (February 1985): 58, 59.

70. Randy L. LaGrange and Helene Raskin White, "Age Differences in Delinquency: A Test of Theory," *Criminology* 23 (February 1985): 36.

71. Allison Ann Payne et al., "Schools as Communities: The Relationships Among Communal School Organization, Student Bonding, and School Disorder," *Criminology* 41, no. 3 (August 2003): 749–777; quotation is on p. 751.

72. John H. Laub, "The Life Course of Criminology in the United States: The American Society of Criminology 2003 Presidential Address," *Criminology* 42, no. 1 (2004): 1–26; quotations are on pp. 11 and 12.

73. James D. Unnever et al., "Racial Discrimination and Hirschi's Criminological Classic: A Chapter in the Sociology of Knowledge," *Justice Quarterly* 26, no. 3 (September 2009): 377–409; quotations are on pp. 378, 379.

74. Michael R. Gottfredson and Travis Hirschi, *A General Theory of Crime* (Palo Alto, CA: Stanford University Press, 1990), p. 87.

75. Travis Hirschi and Michael R. Gottfredson, eds., *The Generality of Deviance* (New Brunswick, NJ: Transaction, 1994), p. 3.

76. See Alex R. Piquero and Jeff A. Bouffard, "Something Old, Something New: A Preliminary Investigation of Hirschi's Redefined Self-Control," *Justice Quarterly* 24, no. 1 (March 2007): 1–26; specific reference is on p. 16.

77. Gottfredson and Hirschi, *A General Theory of Crime.*, p. xiv.

78. Ibid., p. 15.

79. Ibid., pp. 89–90.

80. Ibid., p. 97.

81. Ibid., pp. 89, 95–97.

82. Ibid., p. 117.

83. Christine S. Sellers, "Self-Control and Intimate Violence: An Examination of the Scope and Specification of the General Theory of Crime," *Criminology* 37 (May 1999): 375–404.

84. Carter Hay, "Parenting, Self-Control, and Delinquency: A Test of Self-Control Theory," *Criminology* 39, no. 3 (August 2001): 707–736.

85. James D. Unnever et al., "Parental Management, ADHD, and Delinquent Involvement: Reassessing Gottfredson and Hirschi's General Theory," *Justice Quarterly* 20, no. 3 (September 2003): 471–500; quotation is on p. 471.

86. Carter Hay and Walter Forrest, "The Development of Self-Control: Examining Self-Control Theory's Stability Thesis," *Criminology* 44, no. 4 (November 2006): 739–774; quotation is on p. 757.

87. Eric A. Stewart et al., "Integrating the General Theory of Crime into an Explanation of Violent Victimization Among Female Offenders," *Justice Quarterly* 21, no. 1 (March 2004): 159–181; quotation is on p. 175.

88. Richard P. Wiebe, "Reconciling Psychopathy and Low Social-Control," *Justice Quarterly* 20, no. 2 (June 2003): 297–336; quotations are on pp. 299, 303.

89. Ibid., pp. 322, 323.

90. Travis Hirschi, "Self-Control and Crime," in *Handbook of Self-Regulation: Research, Theory, and Applications*, ed. Roy F. Baumeister and Kathleen D. Vohs (New York: Guilford Press, 2004), pp. 537–552; quotation is on pp. 543–544.

91. Piquero and Bouffard, "Something Old, Something New." The quotation from Hirschi is on p. 3 of this article and was taken from Hirschi, "Self-Control and Crime," p. 543.

92. See, for example, Mark Colvin, *Crime and Coercion: An Integrated Theory of Chronic Criminality* (New York: St. Martin's Press, 2000); Robert Agnew, "Foundation for a General Strain Theory of Crime," *Criminology* 30, no. 1 (February 1992): 47–88.

93. Callie Harbin Burt et al., "A Longitudinal Test of the Effects of Parenting and the Stability of Self-Control: Negative Evidence for the General Theory of Crime," *Criminology* 44, no. 2 (May 2006): 353–396; quotation is on p. 381.

94. John Paul Wright and Kevin M. Beaver, "Do Parents Matter in Creating Self-Control in Their Children? A Genetically Informed Test of Gottfredson and Hirschi's Theory of Low Self-Control," *Criminology* 43, no. 4 (November 2005): 1169–1202. For a more recent analysis, see John Wright et al., "Evidence of Negligible Parenting Influences on Self-Control, Delinquent Peers, and Delinquency in a Sample of Twins," *Justice Quarterly* 25, no. 3 (September 2008): 544–569.

95. See, for example, Terrie E. Moffitt, "Adolescence Limited and Life Course Persistent Antisocial Behavioral: A Developmental Taxonomy," *Psychological Review* 100 (1993): 674–701.

96. Elizabeth Cauffman et al., "Psychological, Neuropsychological and Physiological Correlates of Serious Antisocial Behavior in Adolescence: The Role of Self-Control," *Criminology* 43, no. 1 (February 2005): 133–176; quotation is on p. 159.

97. Carter Hay and Walter Forrest, "Self-Control Theory and the Concept of Opportunity: The Case for a More Systematic Union," *Criminology* 46, no. 4 (November 2008): 1039–1072.

98. Kevin M. Beaver et al., "Low Self-Control and Contact with the Criminal Justice System in a Nationally Representative Sample of Males," *Justice Quarterly* 26, no. 4 (December 2009): 695–715; quotation is on p. 710.

99. Kai T. Erikson, "Notes on the Sociology of Deviance," *Social Problems* 9 (Spring 1962): 308.

100. Ted Chiricos et al., "The Labeling of Convicted Felons and Its Consequences for Recidivism," *Criminology* 45, no. 3 (August 2007): 547–581. The Florida statute that permits deferred adjudication is Fla. Stat., Section 948.08 (2010).

101. Frank Tannenbaum, *Crime and the Community* (New York: Columbia University Press, 1938), pp. 19–20.

102. Edwin M. Lemert, *Human Deviance, Social Problems, and Social Control* (Englewood Cliffs, NJ: Prentice-Hall, 1967), p. 17.

103. Howard S. Becker, *Outsiders: Studies in the Sociology of Deviance* (New York: Free Press, 1963).

104. For more details on the development of labeling theory, see Walter R. Gove, ed., *The Labeling of Deviance: Evaluating a Perspective*, 2d ed. (Beverly Hills, CA: Sage, 1980).

105. See Edwin M. Schur, *Radical Nonintervention: Rethinking the Delinquency Problem* (Englewood Cliffs, NJ: Prentice-Hall, 1973).

106. Stuart L. Hills, Crime, *Power and Morality* (Scranton, PA: Chandler, 1971), pp. 19–21.

107. Richard D. Schwartz and Jerome H. Skolnick, "Two Studies of Legal Stigma," *Social Problems* 10 (Fall 1962): 136–141.

108. D. L. Rosenhan, "On Being Sane in Insane Places," *Science* 179 (January 1973): 250.

109. Craig Haney et al., "Interpersonal Dynamics in a Simulated Prison," *International Journal of Criminology and Penology* 1 (1973): 69–97; reprinted in *Examining Deviance Experimentally*, ed. Darrell J. Steffensmeier and Robert M. Terry (Port Washington, NY: Alfred, 1975), p. 223.

110. Melvin C. Ray and William R. Down, "An Empirical Test of Labeling Theory Using Longitudinal Data," *Journal of Research in Crime and Delinquency* 23 (May 1986): 169–194.

111. Malcolm W. Klein, "Labeling Theory and Delinquency Policy," *Criminal Justice and Behavior* 13 (March 1986): 47–79.

112. Gordon Bazemore, "Delinquent Reform and the Labeling Perspective," *Criminal Justice and Behavior* 12 (June 1985): 131–169.

113. John Braithwaite, *Crime, Shame, and Reintegration* (Cambridge, UK: Cambridge University Press, 1989), p. 100.

114. Ibid., pp. 100–101.

115. John Braithwaite, "Reintegrative Shaming," in *Explaining Criminals and Crime: Essays in Contemporary Criminological Theory*, ed. Raymond Paternoster and Ronet Bachman (Los Angeles: Roxbury, 2001), pp. 242–251; reference is to p. 244.

116. Braithwaite, *Crime, Shame, and Reintegration*; reprinted in *Criminological Theory, Past to Present*, 4th ed., eds. Francis T. Cullen and Robert Agnew (New York: Oxford University Press, 2011); quotation is on p. 254.

117. See Akers and Sellers, *Criminological Theories*, 5th ed., p. 162, referring to the following: Toni Makkai and John Braithwaite, "Reintegrative Shaming and Compliance with Regulatory Standards," *Criminology* 32 (1994): 361–386; Carter Hay, "An Exploratory Test of Braithwaite's Reintegrative Shaming Theory," *Journal of Research in Crime and Delinquency* 38 (2001): 132–153.

118. Makkai and Braithwaite, "Reintegrative Shaming and Regulatory Compliance," cited in John Braithwaite et al., "Reintegrative Shaming," in *The Essential Criminology Reader*, ed. Henry and Lanier, pp. 286–295; quotation is on p. 292.

119. John Braithwaite, "Encourage Restorative Justice," *Criminology and Public Policy* 6, no. 4 (November 2007): 689–696; reference is to p. 689.

120. See, for example, John Braithwaite, *Restorative Justice and Responsive Regulation* (New York: Oxford University Press, 2002); Daniel Van Ness and Karen Heetderks Strong, *Restoring Justice* (Cincinnati, OH: Anderson, 1997); Gordon Bazemore and Mark Schiff, eds., *Restorative Community Justice: Repairing Harm and Transforming Communities* (Cincinnati, OH: Anderson, 2001).

121. Francis T. Cullen et al., "The Virtuous Prison: Toward a Restorative Rehabilitation," in *Contemporary Issues in Crime and Criminal Justice: Essays in Honor of Gilbert Geis*, ed. Henry N. Pontell and David Shichor (Upper Saddle River, NJ: Prentice-Hall, 2001), pp. 265–286.

122. Akers and Sellers, *Criminological Theories*, 5th ed., pp. 171–172.

123. Clifford K. Dorne, *Restorative Justice in the United States* (Upper Saddle River, NJ: Prentice-Hall, 2008).

124. Braithwaite, "Encourage Restorative Justice," pp. 690–691.

125. Ross L. Matsueda, "Reflected Appraisals, Parental Labeling, and Delinquency: Specifying a Symbolic Interactionist Theory," *American Journal of Sociology* 97 (1992): 1577–1611, reprinted in *Criminological Theory: Past to Present*, ed. Cullen and Agnew, pp. 279–285.

126. George Herbert Mead, *Mind, Self, and Society* (Chicago: University of Chicago Press, 1934).

127. Matsueda, "Reflected Appraisals," p. 284.

128. Dawn J. Bartusch and Ross L. Matsueda, "Gender, Reflected Appraisals, and Labeling: A Cross-Group Test of an Interactionist Theory of Delinquency," *Social Forces* 75 (1996): 145–177.

129. Robert J. Sampson and John H. Laub, "A Life Course Theory of Cumulative Disadvantage and the Stability of Delinquency," in *Advances in Criminological Theory: Developmental Theories of Crime and Delinquency*, Vol. 7, ed. Terence P. Thornberry (New Brunswick, NJ: Transaction, 1997), pp. 133–161; quotation is on p. 138.

130. Ibid., pp. 147–148.

131. Jon Gunnar Bernburg and Marvin D. Krohn, "Labeling, Life Chances, and Adult Crime: The Direct and Indirect Effects of Official Intervention in Adolescence on Crime in Early Adulthood," *Criminology* 41, no. 4 (November 2003): 1287–1318; quotation is on p. 1313.

132. Daniel L. Dotter and Julian B. Roebuck, "The Labeling Approach Re-Examined: Interactionism and the Components of Deviance," *Deviant Behavior* 9, no. 1 (1988): 19.

133. Akers and Sellers, *Criminological Theories*, 5th ed., pp. 172, 174.

134. Charles R. Tittle, "Labelling and Crime: An Empirical Evaluation," in *The Labelling of Deviance*, ed. Walter R. Gove (New York: Halsted Press, 1975), chap. 6, pp. 157–179; quotation is on p. 158, citations omitted.

135. Ibid., p. 176.

136. See Bruce G. Link et al., "A Modified Labeling Theory Approach to Mental Disorders: An Empirical Assessment," *American Sociological Review* 54 (June 1989): 400–423; Link et al., "The Social Rejection of Former Mental Patients: Understanding Why Labels Matter," *American Journal of Sociology* 6 (May 1987): 1461–1500.

137. J. Mitchell Miller et al., *Criminological Theory: A Brief Introduction*, 2d ed. (New York: Pearson Education, 2008), pp. 194–202.

138. Ibid., pp. 202–204.

139. See Ronald L. Akers, *Deviant Behavior: A Social Learning Approach* (Belmont, CA: Wadsworth, 1973; 2d ed., 1977).

140. Akers and Sellers, *Criminological Theories*, 5th ed., p. 303.

141. Ibid.

142. David P. Farrington, "Developmental and Life-Course Criminology: Key Theoretical and Empirical Issues—the 2002 Sutherland Award Address," *Criminology* 41, no. 2 (May 2003): 221–255; quotations are on pp. 223–224.

143. See Akers and Sellers, *Criminological Theories*, 5th ed., pp. 318–319.

144. Michael L. Benson, *Crime and the Life Course: An Introduction* (Los Angeles: Roxbury, 2002); quotation is on p. 14.

145. Laub, "The Life Course of Criminology in the United States," pp. 3–4.

146. Robert J. Sampson and John H. Laub, "An Age-Graded Theory of Informal Social Control," in *Criminological Theory*, 3d ed., (2006)

ed. Cullen and Agnew, pp. 241–253; quotation is on p. 244. See also Sampson and Laub, *Crime in the Making: Pathways and Turning Points Through Life* (Cambridge, MA: Harvard University Press, 1993).

147. See the discussion by Cullen and Agnew, eds., in *Criminological Theory*, 3d ed., pp. 241–242.
148. Sampson and Laub, "An Age-Graded Theory of Informal Social Control," p. 243.
149. Ibid.
150. Ibid.
151. Mark Warr, "Life Course Transitions and Desistance from Crime," *Criminology* 36, no. 1 (February 1998): 183–216; quotation is on p. 184.
152. Ibid.
153. Ronald L. Simons et al., "A Test of Life-Course Explanations for Stability and Change in Antisocial Behavior from Adolescence to Young Adulthood," *Criminology* 40, no. 2 (May 2002): 401–434; quotation is on p. 429.
154. Robert J. Sampson and John H. Laub, "Life-Course Desisters? Trajectories of Crime Among Delinquent Boys Followed to Age 70," *Criminology* 41, no. 3 (August 2003): 555–592; quotations are on p. 555.
155. Robert J. Sampson, John H. Laub, and Christopher Wimer, "Does Marriage Reduce Crime? A Counterfactual Approach to Within-Individual Causal Effects," *Criminology* 44, no. 3 (August 2006): 465–508.
156. Ryan D. King et al., "The Context of Marriage and Crime: Gender, the Propensity to Marry, and Offending in Early Adulthood," *Criminology* 45, no. 1 (February 2007): 33–66.
157. John Paul Wright and Francis T. Cullen, "Employment, Peers, and Life-Course Transitions," *Justice Quarterly* 21, no. 1 (March 2004): 183–201.
158. See, for example, Peggy C. Giordano et al., "A Life-Course Perspective on Spirituality and Desistance from Crime," *Criminology* 46, no. 1 (February 2008): 99–132.
159. See, for example, Scott Jacques and Richard Wright, "The Victimization-Termination Link," *Criminology* 46, no. 4 (November 2008): 1009–1038.
160. See Alfred Blumstein et al., *Criminal Careers and "Career Criminals,"* (Washington, D.C.: National Academy Press, 1986). See also Blumstein et al., "Criminal Career Research: Its Value for Criminology," *Criminology* 26 (1988): 1–35; Blumstein et al., "Longitudinal and Criminal Career Research: Further Clarifications," *Criminology* 26 (1988): 57–74.
161. See, for example, Hanno Petras et al., "Participation and Frequency During Criminal Careers Across the Life Span," *Criminology* 48, no. 2 (May 2010): 607–638.
162. Wright and Cullen, "Employment, Peers, and Life-Course Transitions," pp. 184, 197.
163. Terrie E. Moffitt, "Adolescence Limited and Life Course Persistent Antisocial Behavior: A Developmental Taxonomy," *Psychological Review* 100 (1993): 674–701. See also Moffitt et al., *Sex Differences in Antisocial Behaviour: Conduct Disorder, Delinquency, and Violence in the Dunedin Longitudinal Study* (Cambridge: Cambridge University Press, 2001). For a test of Moffitt's theory, see Alex R. Piquero and Timothy Brezina, "Testing Moffitt's Account of Adolescence-Limited Delinquency," *Criminology* 39, no. 2 (May 2001): 353–370.
164. See Terrie E. Moffitt, "A Review of Research on the Taxonomy of Life-Course-Persistent and Adolescence-Limited Offending," in *Taking Stock: The Status of Criminological Theory*, ed. Francis T. Cullen et al. (New Brunswick, NJ: Transaction, 2006), pp. 502–521.
165. Dana L. Haynie et al., "Race, the Economic Maturity Gap, and Criminal Offending in Young Adulthood," *Justice Quarterly* 25, no. 4 (December 2008): 595–622.
166. Miller et al., *Criminological Theory: A Brief Introduction*, p. 79.
167. Francis T. Cullen, "Social Support as an Organizing Concept for Criminology: Presidential Address to the Academy of Criminal Justice Sciences," *Justice Quarterly* 11 (1994): 528–559.
168. Cullen and Agnew, ed. *Criminological Theory*, 4th ed., p. 590.
169. Mark Colvin, Francis T. Cullen, and Thomas Vander Ven, "Coercion, Social Support, and Crime: An Emerging Theoretical Consensus," *Criminology* 40, no. 1 (February 2002): 19–42; quotations are on pp. 19 and 20.
170. Mark Colvin, *Crime and Coercion: An Integrated Theory of Chronic Criminality* (New York: St. Martin's Press, 2000).
171. Colvin et al., "Coercion, Social Support, and Crime," p. 37.
172. Stephen W. Baron, "Differential Coercion, Street Youth, and Violent Crime," *Criminology* 47, no. 1 (February 2009): 239–268.
173. Terence P. Thornberry, "Toward an Interactional Theory of Delinquency," *Criminology* 25 (1987): 863–891.
174. Terence P. Thornberry and Marvin D. Krohn, "The Development of Delinquency: An Interactional Perspective," in *Handbook of Youth and Justice*, ed. Susan O. White (New York: Plenum, 2001). See also Thornberry and Krohn, *Taking Stock of Delinquency: An Overview of Findings from Contemporary Longitudinal Studies* (New York: Kluwer/Plenum, 2003).
175. Rachel A. Gordon et al., "Antisocial Behavior and Youth Gang Membership: Selection and Socialization," *Criminology* 42, no. 1 (February 2004): 55–87; quotations are on p. 56.
176. Cullen and Agnew, *Criminological Theory*, 4th ed., p. 559. See also Terence P. Thornberry and Marvin D. Krohn, "Applying Interactional Theory to the Explanation of Continuity and Change in Antisocial Behavior," in *Integrated Developmental and Life-Course Theories of Offending*, ed. David P. Farrington (New Brunswick, NJ: Transaction, 2005), pp. 183–210.
177. Marvin D. Krohn, "The Web of Conformity: A Network Approach to the Explanation of Delinquent Behavior," *Social Problems* 33 (1986): S81–S93, as cited in Akers and Sellers, *Criminological Theories*, 5th ed., p. 309.

178. Dana L. Haynie, "Friendship Networks and Delinquency: The Relative Nature of Peer Delinquency," *Journal of Quantitative Criminology* 18 (2002): 99–134; quotation is on p. 104.

179. Howard B. Kaplan, *Self Attitudes and Deviant Behavior* (Pacific Palisades, CA: Goodyear, 1975); Kaplan, "Drugs, Crime, and Other Deviant Adaptations," in *Drugs, Crime and Other Deviant Adaptations*, ed. Kaplan (New York: Plenum, 1995), pp. 3–46; Kaplan, "Empirical Validation of the Applicability of an Integrative Theory of Deviant Behavior to the Study of Drug Use," *Journal of Drug Issues* 26 (1996): 345–377.

180. Charles R. Tittle, "Control Balance Theory," in *Criminological Theory*, 4th ed., ed. Cullen and Agnew, pp. 571–589. The quotation is from Tittle, *Control Balance: Toward a General Theory of Deviance* (Boulder, CO: Westview Press, 1995), p. 142.

181. Charles R. Tittle, "Redefining Control Balance Theory," *Theoretical Criminology* 8 (2004): 395–428, with references to pp. 405, 406. For a discussion, see Cullen and Agnew, ed., *Criminological Theory*, 4th ed., pp. 571, 572.

182. Bernard et al., *Vold's Theoretical Criminology*, 6th ed., p. 335.

183. Delbert S. Elliott et al., "An Integrated Theoretical Perspective on Delinquent Behavior," *Journal of Research in Crime and Delinquency* (1979): 3–27, as reprinted in Cullen and Agnew, ed., *Criminological Theory*, 3d ed., pp. 537–550. See p. 548.

184. Ibid.

185. Ibid., p. 537.

186. Carlo Morselli et al., "Mentors and Criminal Achievement," *Criminology* 44, no. 1 (February 2006): 17–43.

187. Matthew Robinson, *Why Crime? An Integrated Systems Theory of Antisocial Behavior* (Upper Saddle River, NJ: Prentice-Hall, 2004).

188. Matthew Robinson, "The Integrated Systems Theory of Antisocial Behavior," in *The Essential Criminology Reader*, ed. Henry and Lanier, pp. 319–335; quotation is on p. 326.

189. Ibid., p. 333.

190. Stuart Henry and Mark M. Lanier, *Essential Criminology* (Boulder, CO: Westview Press, 2004), p. 351.

191. Anthony Walsh, Book Review, *Human Nature Review* 5 (31 December 2005): 87–94; quotation is on p. 93, http://www.human-nature.com/nibbs/05/awalsh.html, accessed 10 October 2010.

192. The film can be viewed online at http://www.dr.dk/DR2/Viden Om/Videnskab%20der%20udfordrer/Programmerne/20070615142459.html, accessed 5 January 2008.

193. Robert Agnew, *Why Do Criminals Offend? A General Theory of Crime and Delinquency* (Los Angeles: Roxbury, 2005), p. 208.

194. Ibid., p. 209.

195. Ibid., p. 210.

196. Ibid., pp. 210–213.

197. Ibid., p.214.

198. Farrington, "Developmental and Life-Course Criminology," pp. 223, 231.

199. Ibid., pp. 231, 232.

200. Ibid., p. 233.

201. Ibid.

202. Ibid.

203. Ibid., pp. 247–248. For a more recent statement on his ICAP theory in particular and life-course theories in general, see David P. Farrington, "Developmental and Life-Course Criminology: Theories and Policy Implications," in *Criminological Theory: A Life-Course Approach*, ed. Matt DeLisi and Kevin M. Beaver (Boston, MA: Jones and Bartlett, 2011), pp. 167–186.

204. Bernard et al., *Vold's Theoretical Criminology*, 6th ed., pp. 337–339.

205. Travis Hirschi, "Separate but Unequal Is Better," *Journal of Research in Crime and Delinquency* 16 (1979): 34–38; Hirschi, "Exploring Alternatives to Integrated Theory," in *Theoretical Integration in the Study of Deviance and Crime*, ed. Steven F. Messner, Marvin D. Krohn, and Allen E. Liska (Albany: State University of New York Press, 1989), pp. 37–49, both cited in Bernard et al., *Vold's Theoretical Criminology*, 6th ed., pp. 339–330.

206. Akers and Sellers, *Criminological Theories*, 5th ed., p. 320.

207. Miller et al., *Criminological Theory*, p. 205.

208. See Thomas J. Bernard, "Twenty Years of Testing Theories: What Have We Learned and Why?" *Journal of Research in Crime and Delinquency* 27 (November 1990): 330–347.

209. Roland Chilton, "Urban Crime Trends and Criminological Theory," *Criminal Justice Research Bulletin* 6, no. 3 (Huntsville, TX: Sam Houston State University Criminal Justice Center, 1991), p. 2.

210. Bermard et al., *Vold's Theoretical Criminology*, 6th ed., p. 347.

211. Ibid., p. 353.

212. Ibid.

213. Ibid., p. 364.

214. George A. Lundberg, *Can Science Save Us?* (New York: Longman, 1961), pp. 143–144.

215. Robert J. Bursik Jr., Editorial Statement, *Criminology* 39 (February 2001): n.p.

216. James Austin, "Why Criminology Is Irrelevant," *Criminology and Public Policy* 2, no. 3 (July 2003): 557–564; quotation is on p. 557.

217. Roland Chilton, "Viable Policy: The Impact of Federal Funding and the Need for Independent Research Agendas—The American Society of Criminology 2000 Presidential Address," *Criminology* 39, no. 1 (February 2001): 1–8.

218. Ibid., p. 7.

219. Denise C. Gottfredson et al., "Effectiveness of Drug Treatment Courts: Evidence from a Randomized Trial," *Criminology and Public Policy* 2, no. 2 (March 2003): 171–196; quotations are on pp. 173 and 190.

220. John S. Goldkamp, Reaction Essay: "The Impact of Drug Courts," *Criminology and Public Policy* 2, no. 2 (March 2003): 197–206; quotation is on p. 203.

221. Robert C. Davis et al., "Increasing the Proportion of Domestic Violence Arrests That Are Prosecuted: A Natural Experiment in

Milwaukee," *Criminology and Public Policy* 2, no. 2 (March 2003): 263–282; quotation is on p. 280.

222. Laura Dugan, "Domestic Violence Legislation: Exploring Its Impact on the Likelihood of Domestic Violence, Police Involvement, and Arrest," *Criminology and Public Policy* 2, no. 2 (March 2003): 283–312; quotation is on p. 283.

223. Akers and Sellers, *Criminological Theories*, 5th ed., p. 11.

224. Thomas G. Blomberg, "Advancing Criminology in Policy and Practice," in *Contemporary Issues in Criminal Justice Policy: Policy Proposals from the American Society of Criminology Conference* (Belmont, CA: Wadsworth Cengage Learning, 2009), pp. 25–30; quotation is on p. 29. Blomberg was responding to an article in the same journal: Charles F. Wellford, "Criminologists Should Stop Whining About Their Impact on Policy and Practice," pp. 17–24.

Part III

Types of Crime

The study of crime and criminal behavior necessitates a close look at types of crime, which is the focus of Part III. **Chapter 7** opens the discussion with an overview of the crimes people fear most: violent crimes against the person. The chapter explores the four serious violent crimes as categorized by the *UCR* (murder and nonnegligent manslaughter, forcible rape, robbery, and aggravated assault). It then focuses on other violent offenses, including domestic violence, hate crimes, stalking, and terrorism. Next, the chapter discusses the fear of crime, followed by an analysis of gun control and violence. It closes with a consideration of the media, pornography, and violent crime.

Chapter 8 covers the four serious property crimes as categorized by the *UCR* (burglary, larceny-theft, motor vehicle theft, and arson) as well as less serious crimes against property. Attention is given to professional career criminals and their activities, followed by a look at the sentencing of repeat offenders.

Chapter 9 considers crimes of the business world, noting the similarities and differences between these crimes and those discussed in **Chapters 7 and 8**. It covers government-related crimes, such as obstruction of justice; political crimes; and official abuse of power, such as civil rights violations. The chapter closes with an overview of methods for controlling these crimes.

Chapter 10 focuses on three major areas of criminal activity in the world today: drug use, drug trafficking, and organized crime.

CHAPTER 7

Violent Crimes

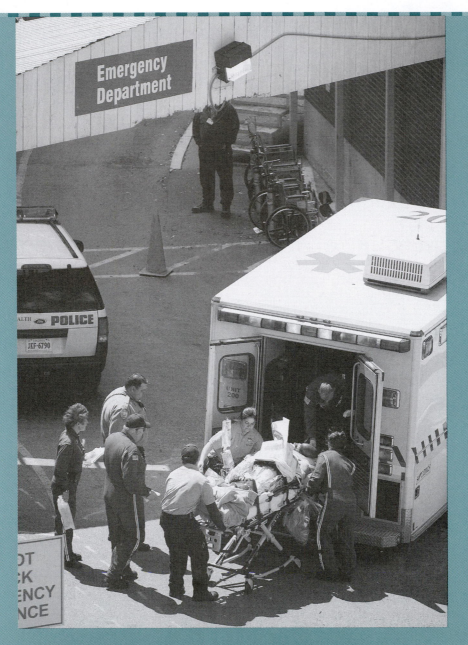

Violent crimes are down, but mass murders and random violence remain a concern. Here, emergency personnel remove victims from the Virginia Tech campus in Blacksburg, Virginia, in April 2007, after a gunman, Cho Seung-Hui, 23, a student, killed 32 students and faculty before turning the gun on himself.

CHAPTER OUTLINE

KEY TERMS

aggravated assault
asportation
assault
battered person syndrome
battery
child abuse
date rape
Department of Homeland Security (DHS)
domestic violence
elder abuse
false imprisonment
felony murder
forcible rape
hate crimes
home-invasion robbery
homicide
incest
intimate partner violence (IPV)
involuntary manslaughter
kidnapping
manslaughter
marital rape
murder
nonnegligent manslaughter
parental kidnapping
rape
rape shield
robbery

INTRODUCTION

This is the first of four chapters on types of crime. After discussing the study of types of crime and looking at an overview of violent crimes, the chapter considers violent crimes in greater detail. First, it focuses on the *UCR*'s four serious violent crimes: murder and nonnegligent manslaughter, forcible rape, robbery, and aggravated assault. A few other violent crimes included in *UCR* data are also selected for discussion. Considerable attention is given to the various types of domestic violence, including intimate partner violence (IPV), child abuse, and elder abuse, along with theories of domestic violence. Kidnapping, hate crimes, and stalking are overviewed, followed by an analysis of terrorism. Crimes of violence often create fear, which is examined, followed by a discussion of gun control. Finally, the chapter considers the impact of the media and pornography on violence, especially violence against children.

Violent crimes capture widespread attention, especially when the violence involves multiple murders, as illustrated by the November 2009 killings of 12 people at the U.S. Army base in Fort Hood, Texas. Major Nidal Malik Hasan, 39, a psychiatrist, was charged with the murders and the wounding of 31 in a rampage in which he was shot and wounded. Many of the victims were fellow soldiers with Hasan at the Texas base.

Nor are schools safe from violence. In February 2010, a man began shooting on a Littleton, Colorado, middle school yard, injuring two students before he was tackled by a math teacher. That community was the scene of the 1999 incident, when two teens killed 12 students and a teacher before killing themselves. Colleges and universities are not immune to violence either. In February 2010, a faculty meeting at the University of Alabama in Huntsville was the scene of a shooting that resulted in the deaths of three faculty members and the wounding of three others. The suspect, Amy Bishop, a biology professor, was said to be despondent over being denied tenure.

Mass murders are not common, but a closer look at murder rates over the years is important and provides interesting data. The 1980 murder rate in the United States was the highest annual rate in that century. *Newsweek* labeled 1981 as the "year that mainstream America rediscovered violent crime" and concluded: "Defying any cure, it overwhelms the police, the courts and the prisons—and warps U.S. life."[1] By 1989, violence had escalated to the point that one national news magazine headlined an article as follows: "Dead Zones: Whole Sections of Urban America Are Being Written Off as Anarchic Badlands, Places Where Cops Fear to Go and Acknowledge: 'This Is Beirut, U.S.A.'"[2]

Rates of murder and other violent crimes fell in the 1990s, but that was little comfort to a nation that experienced the bombing of the federal building in Oklahoma City, the killings by the Unabomber, and numerous violent acts committed on school grounds by juveniles with guns, some involving multiple murders. Many other crimes made it clear that our schools, our homes, and our workplaces were no longer safe from violent acts. There were highly publicized acts of domestic violence, such as those by O. J. Simpson (who was acquitted of criminal charges but found liable in a civil suit involving the deaths of his ex-wife and her friend) and Susan Smith (who strapped her little boys into the backseat of a car and drove it into a lake, jumping out in time to save herself). Many other nationally publicized crimes illustrated that dangers of violence lurked even among people who appeared to live ordinary lives. None of these crimes, however, compared with the terrorist attacks of 11 September 2001.

This chapter focuses on the four most serious violent crimes as defined by the Federal Bureau of Investigation (FBI), but it also includes discussions of other violent crimes, such as domestic violence (which often involves one or more of the four most serious violent crimes), kidnapping, hate crimes, stalking, and terrorism. Other features are the fear of crime, guns and violent crime, and finally, the mass media, pornography, and violent crime.

The Study of Types of Crime

Thus far, the text has analyzed criminal behavior using biological and other physical-characteristic theories of criminal behavior, as well as psychological, psychiatric, social-structural, and social-process approaches and theories. Some social scientists have also attempted to explain criminal behavior by looking at *types* of crime and criminals. Many early studies took this approach, focusing on the robber, the burglar, the thief, or the rapist.

In analyzing the study of criminal behavior in terms of typologies, sociologist Don C. Gibbons stated in 1975 that "the research . . . indicates that no fully comprehensive offender typology which subsumes most criminality within it yet exists." Gibbons concluded that typing criminals may be inappropriate in many cases.[3]

The emphasis in this chapter is on types of crime, not types of criminals. Some sociological analyses of types of criminals are discussed, but it is important to recognize that a rapist may also commit armed robbery. Furthermore, it does not necessarily follow that a person has committed the particular crime charged. For many reasons, defendants might not be charged with the crimes they are thought to have committed, or they may be charged with those crimes but be allowed to plead guilty to less serious offenses. For example, a defendant charged with forcible rape may be permitted to plead guilty to assault and battery. In official data, this offender is classified as one who committed assault and battery, not forcible rape.

These chapters on types of crime use the legal approach to define crime. This is not to suggest that other approaches are not important, but it is the legal elements of the definition that must be proved for a conviction in U.S. criminal justice systems. Thus, within the legal system, it is inappropriate to label a person a robber if the charges of robbery, a violent crime, have been dismissed and the defendant has been permitted to plead guilty to theft, a property crime. Likewise, it is inappropriate to call a person a rapist after he or she has been acquitted of rape.

In such cases, sociologists studying why people engage in robbery might include these persons in their samples. Some sociological studies are discussed, but it is important to understand that they are not always based on legal or mutually exclusive categories.

Serious Violent Crimes: An Overview

As noted in Chapter 2, for official crime data, the FBI's *Uniform Crime Reports* (*UCR*) include as serious crimes four violent crimes—murder and nonnegligent manslaughter, forcible rape, robbery, and aggravated assault. Exhibit 7.1 provides the *UCR* definition of each.

The *UCR* data for 2009 reveal that the number of violent offenses decreased 5.3 percent over 2008. Aggravated assault accounted for 61.2 percent of those crimes, with robbery accounting for 31.0 percent, forcible rape 6.7 percent, and murder and nonnegligent manslaughter 1.2 percent.[4] The individual *UCR* data for the four serious crimes are given as each crime is discussed later in this chapter.

The Bureau of Justice Statistics (BJS) reported that in 2009, both violent and property crime victimizations were lower than in 2008. Between 2000 and 2009, violent crime rates declined by 39 percent and property crime rates declined by 29 percent. There was a decline in every type of violent and property crimes (discussed in Chapter 8) during that period.[5]

Serious Violent Crimes: The Specific Offenses

Each of the four serious violent offenses as categorized by the *UCR* is discussed in this section.

Murder and Nonnegligent Manslaughter

The *UCR* combines **murder** and **nonnegligent manslaughter** and defines them as "the willful (nonnegligent) killing of one human being by another." This definition may appear simple, but not all willful killings are categorized as murder. Generally, the term **homicide** is used to refer to all killings, some of which may be lawful, as implied by this statute from the Washington State criminal code:

> Homicide is the killing of a human being by the act, procurement, or omission of another, death occurring at any time, and is either (1) murder, (2) homicide by abuse, (3) manslaughter, (4) excusable homicide, or (5) justifiable homicide.[6]

Some of those terms need further explanation. The killing of another person might be *justifiable homicide*, as when a police officer kills in the line of duty. A homicide may be *excusable*, such as taking the life of another person who is trying to inflict serious bodily harm on or kill you or others. Not all states have the provision of *homicide by abuse*, which involves a death that occurs as the result of abusing a child or an adult.

Note that the Washington State statute refers to killing a human being. In most jurisdictions, that would not include as murder the killing of a fetus because, historically, a fetus has not been considered a human being. California and some other states have altered that position. The California statute formerly stated that murder was "the unlawful killing of a human being, with malice aforethought." It was amended to provide as follows: "Murder is the unlawful killing of a human being, or a fetus, with malice aforethought." There are exclusions for acts such as legal abortions.[7]

The Protection of Unborn Children Act was enacted in 2004. This law created a separate federal crime for a person who harms or kills a fetus while committing an unlawful attack upon a pregnant woman.[8] It is also referred to as Laci and Connor's law—named after the mother and her unborn son who were killed by Laci's husband, Scott

EXHIBIT 7.1

UCR Definitions of Serious Violent Crimes

- **Murder and Nonnegligent Manslaughter:** "[Th]e willful (nonnegligent) killing of one human being by another." . . .
- **Forcible Rape:** "[T]he carnal knowledge of a female forcibly and against her will. Assault or attempts to commit rape by force or threat of force are also included; however, statutory rape (without force) and other sex offenses are excluded." . . .
- **Robbery:** "[T]he taking of or attempting to take anything of value from the care, custody, or control of a person or persons by force or threat of force or violence and/or by putting the victim in fear." . . .
- **Aggravated Assault:** "[A]n unlawful attack by one person upon another for the purpose of inflicting severe or aggravated bodily injury. This type of assault is usually accompanied by the use of a weapon or by means likely to produce death or great bodily harm. Attempts are included since it is not necessary that an injury result when a gun, knife, or other weapon is used which could and probably would result in serious personal injury if the crime were successfully completed. When aggravated assault and larceny-theft occur together, the offense falls under the category of robbery."

Source: Federal Bureau of Investigation, *Crime in the United States: Uniform Crime Reports 2009,* http://www2.fbi.gov/ucr/cius2009/about/offense_definitions.html, accessed 20 October 2010.

Peterson, who received the death penalty and resides on California's death row.

Other qualifications are required for a killing to be classified as a murder. Some statutes provide that death may occur at any time. In some jurisdictions, however, death must occur within the traditional period used under common law—one year and one day. This limitation was made because of the difficulties in determining the cause of death. In recent years, some states, either by court decision or legislative enactment, have changed that rule. For example, California has retained the theory of the **year-and-a-day rule** but expanded the time period to three years and one day. Under the California Penal Code, the prosecution is required to sustain the burden of proving that the killing was criminal if death occurred three or more years after that killing.[9]

There are other definitions of elements of the crime of murder that might distinguish one state from another and as a result might affect murder data. For example, murder requires an intent, or *mens rea,* but states differ in the words they use for intent and in their interpretations of those words. Some refer to an intent to kill, and others stipulate that an intent to inflict great bodily harm is sufficient. Still others find intent if a victim dies while a felony, such as a robbery or rape, is being committed. This type of murder is referred to as **felony murder.** Its definition might include a list of felonies to which it applies; for example, Maine lists committing or attempting to commit, "or immediate flight after committing or attempting to commit" murder, robbery, burglary, kidnapping, arson, gross sexual assault, or escape. Maine also requires that the resulting death be reasonably foreseeable.[10]

In addition to varying definitions of murder, statutes may distinguish degrees of murder, such as first, second, or third, with first-degree murder being the most serious.

Laci and Scott Peterson appeared to be a happily married couple awaiting the birth of their first child. But when Laci, eight months pregnant, disappeared the day before Christmas in 2003, law enforcement officers became suspicious of Scott. In March 2005, Peterson was convicted for the murders of his wife and unborn son. He is incarcerated in San Quentin, on California's death row.

Statutes may also distinguish murder from **manslaughter**, which may be divided into types. Generally, **voluntary manslaughter** refers to an intentional killing that takes place while the defendant is in the heat of passion and provoked by the victim—a situation that mitigates but does not excuse the killing. All circumstances must be examined to determine whether the crime is murder or manslaughter, and provocation must be such that it would cause a reasonable person to kill. As an example, California defines *voluntary manslaughter* as the unlawful killing of a human being without malice committed "upon a sudden quarrel or heat of passion."[11]

Involuntary manslaughter refers to a killing that was not intended. California defines the term as "the unlawful killing of a human being without malice. . . . in the commission of an unlawful act, not amounting to felony; or in the commission of a lawful act which might produce death, in an unlawful manner, or without due caution and circumspection." The provision excludes "acts committed in the driving of a vehicle,"[12] although those acts are included within some statutes and may be referred to as *vehicular homicide*, *vehicular manslaughter*, or even *DUI* (driving under the influence) *manslaughter*. Involuntary manslaughter may also be categorized as *negligent manslaughter* (deaths resulting from negligent but not criminal acts) or *failure-to-act manslaughter*, in which a person who has a legal duty to act fails to do so and thus causes the death of another person. Involuntary manslaughter is a serious offense that may result in a prison sentence.

Data

In 2009, the FBI reported 15,241 murder and nonnegligent manslaughter offenses, which represented a 7.3 percent decrease over the 2008 volume, a 9.0 percent decrease over the 2005 estimate, and a 2.2 percent decrease over the 2000 estimate.[13]

In 2009, men accounted for 89.7 percent of the homicide offenders and 77 percent of the victims. In terms of race, 51.6 percent of offenders were black and 46.3 percent were white. For victims, 48.7 percent were white and 48.6 percent were black. Almost 50 percent (48.6 percent) of the 2009 homicides were single victim/single offender situations.[14] Details of the 2009 data concerning the relationship between victims and their assailants appear in Figure 7.1.

Research on Murder

The theories covered in earlier chapters may be helpful in explaining murder. In an application of institutional anomie theory and social disorganization theory (both discussed in Chapter 5) to a comparison of homicide rates of African Americans and whites, investigators concluded that whites' greater access to resources (in contrast to the higher levels of disadvantage characteristic of African Americans in their sample) worked to lower homicide rates among them. Whites' available resources permitted them to gain the political power that was important to insulate them and their living and working areas from factors conducive to violent crimes. Greater resources also

Percent Distribution,[1] Volume by Relationship,[2] 2009

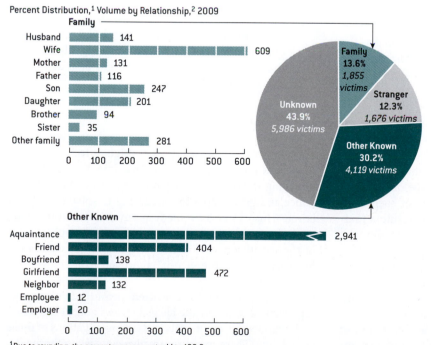

Figure 7.1

Murder by Relationship, 2009

Source: Federal Bureau of Investigation, "Expanded Homicide Data," *Crime in the United States: Uniform Crime Reports 2009*, http://www2.fbi.gov/ucr/cius2009/offenses/expanded_information/homicide.html, accessed 18 October 2010.

[1]Due to rounding, the percentages may not add to 100.0.
[2]Relationship is that of victim to offender.
NOTE: Figures are based on 13,636 murder victims for whom supplemental homicide data were received, and includes the 5,986 victims for whom the relationship was unknown.

permitted whites to exercise the informal social controls (e.g., intervening in a dispute or fight) that reduce or prevent violent crime. Resources also give whites access to the social, economic, and political institutions that foster social organization and thus prevent the social disorganization associated with higher violent crime rates.[15]

Researchers of violence, especially murder, have also examined gender. They focus on such explanations as biological differences, psychological problems that have developed after severe victimizations, and hormonal influences. Some investigators maintain that traditional explanations ignore the possibility that women make rational decisions to engage in violence. One study examined 106 violent incidents and the alleged circumstances under which they occurred as reported by the 67 women who committed them. Although these researchers described their study as only a first step, they reported challenges to the traditional explanations of female violence. Some women described their violent acts in ways supporting the common approaches to female crime (e.g., occurring within domestic situations, often as the result of victimization), but others gave as their rationale "the desire for money, respect, and reparation." Clearly, more research is needed, but the traditional notions that men and women engage in violence for different reasons are being challenged. The authors also found racial differences, with violence between partners more likely to occur between interracial than intraracial couples, and violence was especially more likely when the black partner was the male.[16]

The second of the serious violent crimes in the *UCR* is forcible rape.

Forcible Rape

Under the common law, **forcible rape** was defined as the unlawful carnal knowledge involving the penetration of a female vagina by a male penis and without the woman's consent.

The FBI's official data on **rape** include only the crime of *forcible rape*, defined by the *UCR* as unlawful sexual intercourse involving force by a man with a female victim (see Exhibit 7.1).

Technically, the FBI definition of forcible rape could include **marital rape**, which is forcible rape of a woman by her husband, but in fact, prosecutions of such cases rarely occur, and those that do occur rarely result in findings of guilt.

Historically, a husband had unlimited sexual access to his wife; she was expected, and in most cases, she herself expected, to comply with his sexual desires. Common law rape did not include the rape of a female spouse unless the husband forced his wife to have sex with another man. This common law provision became a part of most original U.S. rape statutes. Although some jurisdictions retain the common law approach, in recent years, many have changed their rules by statute or by judicial deci-

sions to permit forced sexual acts between spouses to be prosecuted as rape.

Research reveals that marital rape is much more prevalent than previously thought and probably exceeds all other kinds of forcible rape. Possibly, as many as one of every ten wives is victimized. According to the earlier works of David Finkelhor and Kersti Yllo, "The offender's goal, in many instances, appears to be to humiliate and retaliate against his wife and the abuse may often include anal intercourse."[17]

Another type of rape, **date rape**, could also be included in the FBI definition of *forcible rape*. *Date rape* refers to forced sexual intercourse during a situation in which the alleged victim has agreed to some forms of social contact but not sexual intercourse. This topic is discussed in more detail later in the chapter.

State statutes define *rape* in different ways. Some include only rape of girls and women; others include rape of both genders. Some statutes require actual penetration of the vagina by the penis; others include *rape by instrumentation*, involving the penetration of the genital or anal openings of another by a foreign object under specified circumstances.

One example of a rape statute is that of Georgia, under which only females can be rape victims and wives are not excluded as victims. Note that carnal knowledge of a female under the age of 10 (this does not require force) is considered *rape* rather than **statutory rape**.

> (a) A person commits the offense of rape when he has carnal knowledge of:
>
> (1) A female forcibly and against her will; or
>
> (2) A female who is less than ten years of age.
> Carnal knowledge in rape occurs when there is any penetration of the female sex organ by the male sex organ. The fact that the person allegedly raped is the wife of the defendant shall not be a defense to a charge of rape.[18]

Data

Before we look at forcible rape data, it is important to understand some of the factors that might affect those data. First is the reporting of this violent crime. Victims may be unwilling to report an alleged rape or to cooperate with police and prosecutors in attempting to solve the alleged crime. This can be a problem in any crime, but it is particularly significant in allegations of forcible rape because of the sensitive nature of the victimization as well as the historical "blame the victim" approach to investigations and prosecutions.

Most jurisdictions have enacted measures to encourage rape victims to report the alleged crimes and to cooperate with criminal justice officials in their investigations of those complaints. These measures involve counseling those who allege that they have been raped and imposing restrictions on the evidence that can be admitted during a rape trial.

Historically, only men were considered perpetrators of statutory rape, and only women were considered victims. This policy has changed, and increasingly, women are arrested and charged with statutory rape, especially in the school arena. Stephanie Ragusa, Tampa, Florida, middle school teacher, seen here with her attorney at her sentencing hearing, pleaded guilty to having had sex with two middle school students. Ragusa faced multiple charges, and conviction on all could have sent her to prison up to from 22 to 45 years. She was sentenced to 10 years (including the two she had already served), one of the stiffest sentences for this crime. She will be on probation after her release from prison, and for life she must register as a sex offender in the community in which she resides.

Evidence is protected by a **rape shield** statute, meaning that evidence of the alleged victim's past sexual experience generally cannot be admitted. Such evidence is embarrassing to the victim, who as a result may not wish to report the rape. The evidence is also not relevant. However, the widely publicized rape case against Los Angeles Lakers basketball star Kobe Bryant illustrated how the rape shield statute may not protect an alleged victim. The trial judge in the Bryant case approved a partial waiver of the rape shield statute because the evidence at issue was crucial to the issue of force. Media Focus 7.1 points out how the waiver of the rape shield statute and the resulting media publicity of sensitive evidence might discourage rape victims from reporting the offenses.

Three scholars who reviewed the literature and looked at rape reporting over a seven-year period investigated why alleged sex crime victims may not report their situations to law enforcement officers, especially if they are claiming they were raped by persons they knew. Investigators have identified the following four reasons that have accounted for *significant* underreporting of rape.

1. Sex crime victims may not fully understand what constitutes an illegal sexual act.
2. They may fear that the offender will harm them if they report the act.
3. They may be embarrassed or feel stigmatized.
4. They may think the law enforcement community will not do anything about the reporting.[19]

The researchers emphasized that since the early 1970s, law enforcement agencies have made policy changes designed to encourage sex crime victims to report their victimizations to authorities. Furthermore, statutory re-

visions now consider a wider range of acts within sex crimes, and males, spouses, and other domestic partners are included as potential victims. An alleged victim's prior sexual behavior may not be introduced as evidence unless it is related to acts of the accused perpetrator. In addition, victim counselors are available, rape crisis centers have been established, and so on.[20]

The first reason given for not reporting a rape—that rape victims may not fully understand the legal nature of forced sex—has some support in other recent research. Bonnie S. Fisher and her collaborators looked at the issue of whether women who are rape victims acknowledge the experience as rape. After reviewing earlier research on the issue and conducting their own study, these researchers concluded that their research supported the belief that acknowledging rape is a real problem. "We found that only about half the rapes were acknowledged by the victims. . . . [I]t appears that many college women who are raped are not fully aware that their victimization was not simply a sexual assault or a 'mistake' but a potentially serious criminal offense." The researchers concluded that the policy implications of these findings are extensive. Rape victims may blame themselves for the acts, and they may not get the benefit of available social, medical, and mental health services that they need. They may be victimized again, and rapists may not be processed through criminal justice systems.[21]

The FBI reported an estimated 88,097 forcible rapes in 2009, down 2.6 percent from 2008, 6.6 percent from 2005, and 2.3 percent from 2000. The 2009 *rate* of forcible rapes was 56.6 per 100,000 female inhabitants, representing a 3.4 percent decrease over the 2008 rate. Rapes by force accounted for 93 percent of the forcible rapes in 2009, and assaults or attempts to commit rape constituted 7 percent of the acts reported as rape.[22]

Media Impact on Rape Prosecutions

Two rape cases captured significant attention and led to speculation that they would hinder future investigations and prosecutions of alleged rape cases.

Kobe Bryant, a superstar basketball player with the Los Angeles Lakers, was accused of raping a young woman in a resort hotel in a small Colorado town in 2003. Bryant admitted that he had sexual relations with his accuser but insisted that the acts were consensual.

Media attention to the Bryant case was extensive, and the accuser's sexual history, although normally not admissible in court because of the Colorado rape shield statute (see the text for a discussion of rape shield statutes), was discussed in the media. The trial judge ruled that the evidence of any sexual conduct the complainant might have had shortly before and after the encounter with Bryant was relevant to the issue of injuries she claimed were caused by forced sex with the defendant. Thus, that evidence could be admitted. The judge also ruled that the complainant could not be referred to as the *victim* during court proceedings. The accuser's name and picture were published on the Internet and in the tabloid press despite the custom of not publishing the name of alleged rape victims. Finally, some of the documents in the case were (allegedly) inadvertently released. These and perhaps other factors (e.g., death threats) led the accuser to withdraw her willingness to go forward with the case, leading the prosecutor to ask for and the judge to grant a dismissal. The complainant continued with her civil case against Bryant. Legal commentators

Los Angeles Lakers' basketball player Kobe Bryant and his attorney, Pamela Mackle, walk into the Eagle County (Colorado) Justice Center for a preliminary hearing. The rape charges against Bryant were subsequently dropped after the alleged victim stated that she did not want to testify. Her civil suit against Bryant was settled out of court.

pointed out that the filing of that case before the conclusion of the criminal case hurt the prosecution because it suggested a financial motive. The civil case was settled out of court, and the terms were confidential.

Rape counselors and others were concerned that the media coverage in the Bryant case, along with the subsequent dismissal of the case, would discourage future victims from reporting to the police that they have allegedly been raped by well-known men. They may be correct, as the following information suggests.

Reporters for a New Jersey newspaper consulted four members of a local rape victim support group and also talked with the district attorney who prosecuted a high-profile rape and sodomy case (discussed next) involving a mentally impaired 17-year-old Glen Ridge, New Jersey, rape victim and several high school men. The prosecutor noted that information that was supposed to be the subject of private hearings in the Bryant case was being leaked to the media and that "This has a chilling effect on rape victims coming forth. . . . They are playing fast and loose with the rape shield law." The legal director of the Pennsylvania Coalition Against Rape proclaimed: "Because defense attorneys are trying to pierce the rape shield law, we are seeing the trial before the trial. The problem, even if information is not revealed in court, is that it's already been leaked and most people have heard of it. You can't unring the bell."[1]

The New Jersey report on rape victims quoted one alleged victim, a 20-year-old woman, as saying that the media coverage of the Kobe Bryant case kept her from filing a complaint after she was raped. "I can't watch the news.. . . [I]t aggravates the hell out of me . . . . People try to find something wrong with rape victims. . . . I don't want people looking at me differently or opening the wound that still hasn't healed about my being molested as a child."[2]

The Glen Ridge rape trial of 1989 occurred after a young woman was invited to the home of one of the defendants, where she engaged in some of the sex acts "voluntarily" with three persons while about one dozen others watched. Defense attorneys argued that the accuser was an aggressive temptress. Prosecutors alleged that the young woman, who had an IQ of 64 and the mental capacity of an 8-year-old, could not give legal consent to sex because of her mental condition. Three youths were convicted of first-degree aggravated sexual assault and sentenced to up to 15 years in a youth facility, but all were free pending their appeals, and all had completed college and were employed by 1997.

In 1997, the three convicted defendants were incarcerated, but Kyle Scherzer served only about 30 months of his seven-year sentence before being released. His twin brother, Kevin, and the third defendant, Christopher Archer, were sentenced to 15 years in prison.[3] Archer was released

7.1

MEDIA FOCUS continued

in August 2001. The Glen Ridge case became the subject of a television movie.

There are two sides to rape allegations. There is the possibility of a false claim against specific individuals, whose lives may be ruined in the process. In the spring of 2006, Durham, North Carolina, prosecutor Mike Nifong brought charges against three Duke University lacross players accused of raping a woman at a team party on 13 March 2006. The three denied the charges, and one produced evidence that he was not at the party at the time of the alleged sexual assaults. The media became highly involved in this event and may have been partially responsible for the eventual outcome: The state's Attorney General Roy A. Cooper, after investigation of the allegations, determined that there was no credible evidence that the defendants committed the alleged acts. He made the unusual decision of announcing that Nifong was overzealous

and that the players were innocent. Cooper considered filing criminal charges against the accuser but decided not to do that, stating that she may really believe that the alleged acts occurred.

Nifong was disbarred after the state bar found that he repeatedly lied and misrepresented facts in the case. He was convicted of lying in court and ordered to serve one day in jail. He was forced to resign his office. The three accused men filed charges against Nifong and the city for malicious prosecution. The case was settled out of court.

1. "Kobe Bryant Rape Case Seen Having a Chilling Effect: Some Fear Fewer Women Will Report Assaults," *The Record* (Bergen County, NJ) (15 June 2004), p. 1.
2. Ibid.
3. "Three Imprisoned 4 Years After Rape Trial," *Los Angeles Times* (1 July 1997), p. 9.

Victimization data published by the Bureau of Justice Statistics (BJS) in 2010 revealed a decline of 38.7 percent in rape/sexual assaults between 2008 and 2009 and a 56.9 percent decline between 2000 and 2009.[23] Recall that the FBI publishes data on crimes reported to the police, whereas National Crime Victimization Survey (NCVS) data are secured from a sample of the population that reports on questionnaires whether they have been victimized.

Research on Rape

Most studies of rapists do not separate out the violent rapist (who causes injuries other than those associated with the rape), who is thought to account for only a small percentage of rapes. Thus, it is not surprising that these studies suggest that most people convicted of rape are not deviant psychologically. In fact, a study conducted by Paul H. Gebhard and his collaborators reported that most men who raped adult women were not distinguishable from other men except for their sexual conduct. However, those convicted of statutory rape were rather impulsive individuals.[24]

Further insight into rapists comes from the work of Menachem Amir, who studied a sample of 646 forcible rape cases in Philadelphia. Amir found that most rapes were intraracial, with the rate much higher among African Americans than among whites; the offenders and victims were young, usually under 25, and were unmarried. Most of the offenders were unemployed and from the lower socioeconomic class. About one-half of the victims had a previous relationship, often a primary one, with the offenders. The majority of the victims were found to be submissive (although that could be because of fear), and

the majority of the incidents did not involve repeated intercourse or brutality.[25]

Myths about rapists were discussed by A. Nicholas Groth and H. Jean Birnbaum, who conducted clinical studies of 500 rapists. They reported that rape is more often an expression of nonsexual than of sexual needs. One-third of the sample were married men who had active sex lives with their wives, and the majority of the unmarried offenders had active sex lives with consenting women. According to Groth and Birnbaum, rape is not the result of sexual arousal but rather of an emotional problem. Most rapists are persons who lack secure and close emotional relationships with others. Groth and Birnbaum argued that sex is a motivating factor in some rapes, usually those occurring between persons who had a previous acquaintance, but sex is not the primary motivation for rape. In many cases, sex is not even a relevant variable.[26]

A further position is that sociological explanations are more relevant than other approaches in explaining the rapist. According to Larry Baron and Murray A. Straus, "Rape is a socially patterned phenomenon, not just a manifestation of individual psychopathology or other defects of personality, character or physiology." Rape is explained in terms of four theoretical approaches: gender inequality, pornography, social disorganization, and legitimate violence.[27]

Rape has been related to pornography as a negative influence on men as well as on potential female victims, but scholars do not agree on the relationship between pornography and criminal behavior (discussed later in this chapter). Labeling theory, learning theory, and conflict theory (all discussed in previous chapters) are also employed to explain rape. Other researchers suggest that rape is the result of sexual desire as well as a desire for power and control.

Robbery

The third serious violent crime according to the *UCR* is **robbery**. Two elements distinguish robbery, a form of theft, from larceny-theft, which is discussed in Chapter 8. In robbery, possessions are taken from a person by the use or threat of force (see Exhibit 7.1). Thus, robbery is not just a property crime but also a crime against the person, a crime that might result in personal violence. The use or threat of force must be such that it would make a reasonable person fearful.

The line between larceny-theft and robbery is difficult to draw in some cases. For example, if an offender grabs a purse, billfold, or other piece of property from the victim so quickly that he or she cannot offer any resistance, the act may be classified as larceny-theft or as robbery. If there is a struggle between the victim and the offender, the act is more likely to be classified as a robbery. Some jurisdictions classify robbery according to the degree of force used or threatened; thus, armed robbery is a more serious crime than robbery without a weapon.

A *weapon* may be defined in various ways and does not necessarily mean a gun, a knife, or some other obviously dangerous instrument. Some courts have held that a toy pistol may meet the weapon requirement, and others have held that hands can be a weapon.

An important element of both robbery and larceny-theft is an intent to steal—that is, an intent to deprive the owner of his or her possessions. Both also involve **asportation**, which means "taking away" the property. And whereas larceny-theft statutes may specify the amount of property that must be taken to constitute a degree or type of the crime, in robbery that is not an issue. The key element in robbery is that the perpetrator threatens to use force or in some other way intimidates the victim.

Although statutes may include robbery of a person in his or her home, that situation is so threatening that most jurisdictions, including the federal, have enacted special legislation to cover what is commonly called **home-invasion robbery**. A typical *home-invasion robbery* statute is that of Florida, which provides as follows:

> (1) "Home-invasion robbery" means any robbery that occurs when the offender enters a dwelling with the intent to commit a robbery, and does commit a robbery of the occupants therein.[28]

The seriousness of home-invasion robberies was demonstrated on 23 July 2007, when two men broke into a Connecticut home and held the family hostage for seven hours. The home invaders forced the wife to drive to her bank and withdraw $15,000. Later, the wife and mother, Jennifer Hawke-Petit, 48, was strangled after she and one daughter were sexually assaulted. They, along with the other daughter, were doused with gasoline before the house was set on fire, and all three died. The husband/

father, Dr. William A. Petit, was beaten but escaped. Citizens were outraged when they found out that the men charged in these crimes had been released from prison on parole (discussed in Chapter 15) after serving time for burglary. The 2009 publication of a book on the murders, based in part on interviews with one of the accused, led defense attorneys to ask for a postponement in the trial in November of 2009.[29] The trial of Joshua Komisarjevsky was pending as of this publication, but in October 2010, Steven J. Hayes was convicted of all charges against him (including murder) except arson. He was sentenced to death.

Data

The *UCR* reported that the volume of approximately 408,217 robbery offenses in 2009 represented a decrease of 0.8 percent from 2008 but a 2.2 percent increase over the 2005 estimates. Most (42.8 percent) of the 2009 robberies were committed on streets or highways, as Figure 7.2 shows. The average loss per robbery in 2009 was $1,244; the average loss per bank robbery was $4,029. In 42.6 percent of 2009 robberies, the perpetrators used firearms.[30]

Research on Robbery

Social scientists have studied robbery in an effort to explain this criminal behavior. Stewart D'Alessio and Lisa Stolzenberg looked at the role of the social and physical environment, analyzing convenience store robberies in Florida. They found

Figure 7.2

Locations of Robberies, Percentage Distribution 2008

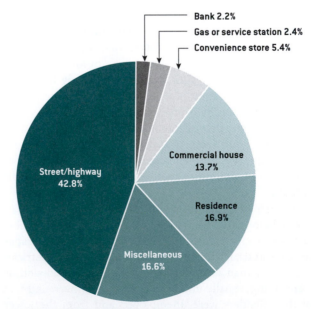

Note: Due to rounding, the percentages may not add to 100.0.

Source: "Robbery," Federal Bureau of Investigation, *Crime in the United States: Uniform Crime Reports 2009,* http://www2.fbi.gov/ucr/cius2009/offenses/violent_crime/robbery.html, accessed 18 October 2010.

that although "environmental factors are not important predictors of whether a convenience store is robbed," significant factors in determining the frequency of robbery are "parking lot size, degree of social disorganization surrounding the store, number of hours open, and whether gasoline service is provided." D'Alessio and Stolzenberg noted that it is difficult to predict where robberies will occur because robbers are not consistent in their target selections.[31]

In a similar vein, robberies from automated teller machines (ATMs) may be understood in terms of the geographical areas in which they occur. For example, the evidence that some drug addicts may commit robbery (or larceny-theft) to support their habits should lead to the avoidance of locating ATM machines in physical areas that are characterized by drug trafficking or that consist of a lot of abandoned property or liquor establishments that have high rates of crime. ATM machines should be located in areas with good lighting and lots of pedestrian and vehicle traffic. Recall the discussion in Chapter 5 about the routine activity approach, which suggests that capable guardians may serve as a deterrent to criminal activity. These and other suggestions were made in a report released by the Office of Community Oriented Policing Services (COPS).[32]

Some characteristics of career robbers were reported by Joan Petersilia and her colleagues. Their in-depth study of 49 inmates serving time for armed robbery in a medium-security facility in California disclosed that they all had served more than one prison term. The inmates had committed a total of 10,500 crimes; individuals had committed multiple crimes, ranging from six rapes to 3,620 drug sales. The inmates averaged 20 crimes per person per year. The level of criminal activity diminished with age. Most of the inmates had started their criminal careers with auto theft in their juvenile years, then moved to burglary and, as they got older, to robbery. They shifted to robbery because they could do it alone and therefore did not run the risk of being implicated by a partner. Robbery has the additional advantage of requiring few tools, having unlimited targets, and not usually requiring that the offender hurt anyone. Most of the career robbers did not earn much money from their crimes. Drugs and alcohol were involved in many cases.[33]

Criminologists have also looked at gender differences in robbery offenses. Jody Miller pointed out that, with the exception of rape, "robbery is perhaps the most gender differentiated serious crime in the United States." Miller focused her attention on female as compared with male street robbers. She reported that although the motivations of male and female robbers reveal gender similarities, the methods for committing the crimes show striking differences. "These differences," she concluded, "highlight the clear gender hierarchy that exists on the streets."[34]

In particular, Miller found that women are more likely to rob other women, which is considered by both male and female robbers an easier task than robbing men. Men are more likely to rob other men, which Miller suggested is one way of showing their masculinity. When women do rob men, they accomplish the task by reverting to behaviors that make men more vulnerable, such as flirting:

> Because they recognize men's perceptions of women, they also recognize that men are more likely to resist being robbed by a female, and thus they commit these robberies in ways that minimize their risk of losing control and maximize their ability to show that they're "for real."

Miller concluded that women, compared with men, do not engage in different techniques to meet specific needs while committing robberies. Rather, they are making practical choices in the gender-stratified environment of street crime. This is an environment in which "men are perceived as strong and women are perceived as weak."[35]

Aggravated Assault

An unlawful attack by one person on another for the purpose of inflicting severe or aggravated bodily injury is called **aggravated assault** (see Exhibit 7.1), which constitutes the fourth serious violent crime. Usually, this type of assault involves a weapon. *Attempts* are included in the official data for this crime.

An assault should be distinguished from a **battery**. Technically, a *battery* is unauthorized harmful or offensive touching, whereas **assault** is the threat to inflict immediate bodily harm. In common use, however, the term *assault* refers to the actual physical attack for the purpose of inflicting harm. The FBI category of *aggravated assault* includes only serious attacks; *simple assaults* are included under lesser offenses. Recall, however, that BJS victimization data on serious crimes include simple as well as aggravated assaults.

As they do with most other crimes, states differ in the way they define *assault* and *battery*. For example, the District of Columbia Penal Code defines *aggravated assault* as follows:

> (a) A person commits the offense of aggravated assault if:
>   (1) By any means, that person knowingly or purposely causes serious bodily injury to another person; or
>   (2) Under circumstances manifesting extreme indifference to human life, that person intentionally or knowingly engages in conduct which creates a grave risk of serious bodily injury to another person, and thereby causes serious bodily injury.[36]

Florida defines *aggravated battery* as follows:

> (1) (a) A person commits aggravated battery who, in committing battery:
>   1. Intentionally or knowingly causes great bodily harm, permanent disability, or permanent disfigurement; or
>   2. Uses a deadly weapon.

(b) A person commits aggravated battery if the person who was the victim of the battery was pregnant at the time of the offense and the offender knew or should have known that the victim was pregnant.[37]

Aggravated assault is the most common serious violent crime according to official FBI data, yet there is little research on this offense. An estimated 806,843 aggravated assaults were reported to police in 2009, representing a decline of 4.2 percent over 2008 and a decrease of 11.5 percent over the 2000 estimate. The rate of aggravated assaults was 262.8 offenses per 100,000 persons, representing an 18.9 percent decline in the rate for 2000.[38]

Some aggravated assaults may not be counted as such because they are defined as specific crimes occurring within the family. Domestic violence is a significant type of violence in today's world. It is discussed later in this chapter. Also, as with many other crimes, aggravated assault charges may be reduced to other crimes, such as, in these cases, simple assault.

Explanations of Violent Crime

Earlier theory chapters covered explanations of criminal behavior. Some of those approaches have been applied particularly to violent crimes. One example used data from Japan and is discussed in Global Focus 7.1.

Previous chapters also cited various theories for explaining the higher rates of both violent offenses and victimizations by African American youths. Some researchers attributed these results to community characteristics such as social disorganization, high crime rates, poverty, and violent neighborhoods. Others looked to social structures, such as family violence, corporal punishment of children, antisocial or criminal parents, and delinquent peer groups.

The violent neighborhood variable or, as Elijah Anderson phrased it, the "code of the street" thesis, suggests that the higher proportion of violence among African American compared with white children can be explained by the structural characteristics of the neighborhood as well as those of the families. Children living in "street" families—those with high levels of social disorganization, discrimination, and disadvantages caused by the social structure—grow up with a cultural code that is conducive to violence. These children have fewer opportunities for employment and social status, less social cohesion, more racial isolation, and more economic stress. They come from what Anderson called *street families*, which have fewer social controls and adopt the street culture, in contrast to *decent families*, which are committed to traditional values of hard work, education, and so on.[39]

Two researchers argued that Anderson's street code thesis needed further study. They analyzed data from 720 African American families in 259 neighborhoods and found overall support for the thesis. The researchers concluded that "neighborhood context, family characteristics, and racial discrimination directly influence adopting the street code, and partially influence violence indirectly through the street code."[40] In a more recent analysis, the same investigators concluded that their research generally supports Anderson's approach, although they recognized some limitations of their research. Still, they hoped their work would "encourage future investigations into the various ways that the structure and culture of neighborhoods affect adolescent violence in African American communities."[41]

These two investigators, along with another colleague, focused a study on childhood violence among African American children, utilizing both social-psychological and social-structural dimensions. Unlike other research that selected subjects from urban areas, they concentrated on youths from small towns and rural areas.[42] These investigators reported that violent neighborhoods do not necessarily produce violent children; clearly, social-psychological factors are important in explaining the violence. The evidence showed that parental use of violence and their children's association with violent peers were related to childhood violence. However, there was no significant relationship between childhood violence and corporal punishment. Youngsters who invested time in a street code that was conducive to violence were likely to engage in violence. The researchers found that neighborhood affluence had a positive influence on deterring childhood violence, suggesting that the resources such neighborhoods provide are important in turning children away from violence. Likewise, quality parenting was positively related to low childhood violence. Finally, children who observed violent acts were not necessarily likely to engage in violence; they might even become desensitized to such violence. The researchers concluded:

> Overall, our results suggest that simply living in a violent neighborhood does not produce violent children, but that family, peer, and individual characteristics play a large role in predicting violent offending among children. This suggests that childhood offending may have less to do with neighborhood crime levels than originally thought.[43]

Another researcher included ethnicity in her study of causes of violence, looking at the impact of social-psychological variables on the neighborhood structure as it related to violence. She concluded with regard to the relationship between race and ethnicity and violence, "Having witnessed and been victimized by violence is by far the most important social psychological process in explaining this relationship."[44]

One final example of research on violent crimes illustrates the use of theory to explain the phenomenon. Investigators examined data on sexual assaults against 674 college and university women in 12 institutions in eight

7.1   Explanations of Violence in Japan

GLOBAL FOCUS

Historically, Japan has had low rates of criminal violence. Researchers have attributed this to low levels of social disorganization resulting from a culture that places a high value on social bonding to other individuals, to the family, and to society in general. Japan has also had low levels of economic stress. In addition, certainty of punishment, long thought to be associated with low crime rates, has been a characteristic of Japanese culture. But during recent decades, these situations have changed, at least to some extent. Divorce and other aspects of social disorganization have increased, more wives and mothers have entered the workforce, the economic climate has deteriorated, and there is evidence that social and family ties have weakened. But crime rates continued to decrease.

Aki Roberts and Gary LaFree analyzed postwar violent crime trends in Japan and found support for the position that economic stress, the certainty of punishment, and the age structure (proportion of young males) but not social disorganization theory were reasonable explanations of the violent crime trends in homicide and robbery. Specifically, they found a significant relationship between unemployment and income inequality and the crime of robbery, al-though they did not find support for a significant relationship between unemployment and homicide. They found strong support for the relationship between the proportion of the population that were young males and the crimes of robbery and homicide. Although the researchers did not find strong support between crime and social disorganization (measured by divorce, urbanization, and female participation in the labor market), they suggested that other measures of social disorganization might produce different results. Roberts and LaFree declared that the importance of economic stress in explaining Japan's violent crime rates, which began to increase in the 1990s, should not be overlooked. Even though Japan's violent crime rates remain low compared with those of most other industrialized countries, "[I]f the Japanese economy continues to deteriorate, and levels of economic stress increase, the result may be an unwelcome change in Japan's historically low rates of violent crime."[1]

1. Aki Roberts and Gary LaFree, "Explaining Japan's Postwar Violent Crime Trends," *Criminology* 42, no. 1 (February 2004): 179–209; quotation is on p. 202.

---

southern states. They reviewed the literature on rape and noted several points of agreement among scholars:

1. Sexual assault is the only crime for which most victims are female children or adults.
2. The rate of sexual assault against women is 13 times as high as that against men.
3. Most female sexual assault victims know their assailants.
4. Most perpetrators of sexual assault are men.
5. Sexual assaults are thought to be the most underreported of all crimes, certainly of all violent crimes.[45]

These investigators noted that feminist theorists (discussed in Chapter 5) often explain sexual assaults as the result of a patriarchal social structure in which men are the more powerful of the two genders. The male culture perpetuates attitudes and values that are conducive to dominating and controlling women through sexual violence. Although women were clearly at a higher risk than men for sexual assaults, not all women experienced equal risk. The investigators proposed to use the routine activity approach (also discussed in Chapter 5) to enhance feminist theory as an explanation for sexual violence against women. Recall that the routine activity approach proposes that crime is not random but, rather, follows patterns that can be explained by situation and place, "and it examines how these interact with individual characteristics and behaviors."[46]

The investigators interpreted feminist theory (noting that not all theorists agree on the exact meaning of this approach) as viewing men as assaulting women in an effort to control or have power over specific women or women in general (by instilling fear in women that they will become sexual assault victims). Some studies of male sexual assault offenders support this position, even to the point of using the same language (e.g., "I hated her for what she did to me; I had to get even with her and hurt her"). Also, parts of the male culture support male aggression, even toward women, and neutralize any guilt male offenders might have about such behavior.[47]

Some support was found for the use of a routine activity approach as a complement to feminist theory in explaining sexual assault victimization of college and university women. Specifically, they found higher victimization risks among female athletes as well as women who more often engaged in drug use in public, belonged to more clubs, or went out more often at night for leisure activities. "These measures are indicators of exposure and proximity to potential offender male peer groups. . . . [These activities] all increase a woman's visibility to men who may be of the mind to sexually assault women." In contrast, women who more frequently went to movies were at a lower risk for sexual assault, for that is not an activity in which they are likely to encounter "male peer groups that may encourage members to sexually abuse women."[48]

There was no evidence that alcohol use, membership in a sorority, or demographic characteristics—all factors associated with sexual assaults in previous studies—were influential. There could be various explanations for these differences. Drug use may be more influential than alcohol use, the nonrandom sample may account for the differences, or measures of exposure to potential male offenders may be more important than membership in a sorority. Thus, for example, the higher risk rate among female athletes than among nonathletes may be explained by the fact that the athletes were more closely associated with a group of males viewed as potential offenders. In addition, female athletes may be viewed by male athletes as engaging in traditionally male activities and thus needing to be controlled. Finally, the research showed that women who came from more stable family backgrounds were less likely to become sexual assault victims than were women from less stable backgrounds. "Thus, this research indicates that women's risks of sexual assault in a hot spot for such victimization are primarily influenced by exposure to male peer groups or other potential offenders and by family stability while growing up."[49]

Other Violent Crimes

Despite the emphasis on the *UCR*'s Part I, four most serious violent crimes, many other crimes of violence are committed. Some of those are discussed in this section.

Domestic Violence

A discussion of violent crime is not complete without an analysis of **domestic violence**, which is an example of behavior that historically was not considered a violent crime. Crimes associated with domestic violence have been publicized widely in recent years, including the 2009 murders that occurred on Thanksgiving Day, when four relatives were murdered after eating dinner in Jupiter, Florida. Paul Michael Merhige, 35, of Miami, was accused of killing his pregnant sister, Lisa Knight; her twin sister; a 6-year-old cousin; and his 79-year-old aunt. Knight's husband, who was wounded, emerged from a coma in March 2010 and was told of the death of his pregnant wife. Merhige was charged with the crimes, and prosecutors were seeking the death penalty.

Domestic violence occurs within a setting where people can and should expect warmth, reinforcement, support, trust, and love. It has been considered a personal, domestic problem, not an act of violence. In early Roman and English law, parents had almost exclusive rights to discipline their children. These rights permitted physical punishment and even death. The Bible provided that a stubborn and rebellious child could be taken by the parents into the city and be stoned to death by the elders. The death sentence was permitted for children who cursed or killed

their parents. Historically, women were the property of their fathers and then of their husbands, who were allowed to punish them virtually without penalty and, as noted in the discussion of rape, engage them in sexual relations, even by force.

After the abuse of family members was no longer sanctioned as proper, little attention was paid to such abuse. It was considered a domestic matter and of little or no concern to the rest of society. Thus, although we have known about family violence for a long time, only recently have facts been pulled together into a general analysis of such violence.

In its 1982 report, the Task Force on Victims emphasized the seriousness of domestic violence. The report stated that domestic violence is more complex than violence against strangers. The task force recommended that the government appoint a new task force to study family violence. In September 1983, the U.S. attorney general announced the formation of the Task Force on Family Violence, but it was not until 1994 that Congress enacted the Violence Against Women Act, which is part of the Violent Crime Control and Law Enforcement Act. The act makes gender-based violence a violation of civil rights, giving victims a civil cause of action that, if successful, entitles them to attorney fees as well as damages.[50] Many of the provisions of the 1994 statute were reauthorized or strengthened, along with the addition of new programs, in the Violence Against Women Act of 2000.[51]

The difficulty of defining domestic violence and the fact that definitions vary from jurisdiction to jurisdiction create problems in collecting accurate data. Other problems in data gathering are that alleged victims are reluctant to report the crimes. Cases that are reported may be processed as some other crime (simple assault, aggravated assault, battery, sexual battery, and so on) and thus not be recorded as domestic violence. Many cases are dismissed without formal processing and do not become part of the official data. This may be particularly true with domestic violence cases reported from middle- and upper-income families in contrast to those from low-income families, especially those on welfare.

Domestic violence involves several types of violence; the next sections cover intimate partner violence, child abuse, and elder abuse.

Intimate Partner Violence (IPV)

Traditionally, social scientists have examined violence between spouses and former spouses, but **intimate partner violence** (IPV) also includes violence between romantic friends, sometimes referred to as *courtship violence*.

Data

It is difficult to collect data on IPV. Figure 7.1, presented earlier in this chapter, contains expanded homicide data by the relationship of the perpetrators and the victims. Some data focus only on IPV. For example, in 2006, the

Bureau of Justice Statistics (BJS) released data indicating that IPV declined between 1993 and 2004. During those years, 22 percent of the violent victimizations against women were nonfatal intimate partner victimizations. A later report in December 2007 showed a continued decline in 2005.[52]

In a 2007 publication on intimate partner violence, the BJS reported trend data from 1993 to 2005, which showed a decline in the reporting of intimate partner violence, with the reporting of such violence leveling off in 2001 and continuing through 2005. In 2005, IPV affected approximately 1 percent of households, or 1 in 320, with no changes in data between 2004 and 2005.[53] For the victims of nonfatal IPV, 98 percent of the women, compared to 84 percent of the men, were victimized by men. Most victims reported that their perpetrators were similar in age to their own. Most white victims (89 percent) were victimized by white offenders, and 95 percent of black victims were victimized by black offenders. The most common form of victimization was simple assault, most of which occurred at home between 6 PM and 6 AM (two-thirds of female victims, one-half of male victims). The use of alcohol or other drugs was present in approximately 43 percent of the cases of nonfatal IPV, with 7 percent occurring when the perpetrator was under the influence of both alcohol and illegal drugs. Male victims were more likely than female victims to be attacked by a perpetrator with a weapon, but males were more likely to face perpetrators with firearms.[54]

In 2009, the BJS published 2008 data along with trend data between 2003 and 2008, focusing on female violence victims but also including male IPV victims. The publication reported 552,000 nonfatal violent IPV acts against females aged 12 or over in 2008 compared to 101,000 against males. The nature of the offenses, by type of crime and gender of the victims, is noted in Table 7.1. The rates of IPV acts against females were higher for those over 18 than for those under that age and higher for black than for white females. Approximately 99 percent of the acts against females were committed by males. Nonfatal IPV acts against both females and males declined at about the same rate between 1993 and 2008, as graphed in Figure 7.3.[55]

Fatal IPV acts are also recorded. These acts include homicide or murder and nonnegligent manslaughter. Figure 7.4 graphs the number of such acts by gender of victims between 2003 and 2008, showing a decline for both males and females. Fourteen percent of the 2007 homicides were cases of IPV, with females constituting 70 percent of the victims who were killed by an intimate partner. Women were killed at twice the rate as men. Black women were twice as likely as white women to be killed by a spouse and four times more likely to be killed by a boyfriend or girlfriend. Only 2 percent of male IPV victims were killed by their spouses, and only 3 percent were killed by their girlfriends or boyfriends.[56]

Data also focus on court processing. A 2009 BJS report presented data on IPV cases processed in court in 2002. It reported that most victims were women and most offenders were men. The victim and the defendant were of the same gender in only 4 percent of the cases. Over 50 percent of persons charged with IPV were convicted, and 80 percent of them were sentenced to jail or prison.[57]

With regard to courtship violence, including date rape, some studies focus on college and university campuses, where IPV is more common than among noncollege young people. It is estimated that each year over 97,000 college and university students between the ages of 18 and 24 are victims of sexual assault or date rape, mostly in alcohol-related situations.[58]

Table 7.1

Violence by Intimate Partners, by Type of Crime and Gender of the Victims, 2008

	Total		Female		Male	
	Number	Rate	Number	Rate	Number	Rate
Overall violent crime	652,660	2.6	551,590	4.3	101,050	0.8
Rape/sexual assault	44,000	0.2	35,690	0.3[a]	8,310	0.1[a]
Robbery	38,820	0.2[a]	38,820	0.3[a]	—[b]	—[b]
Aggravated assault	111,530	0.4	70,550	0.5	40,970	0.3[a]
Simple assault	458,310	1.8	406,530	3.1	51,770	0.4

Note: Victimization rates are per 1,000 persons age 12 or older. The difference in male and female intimate partner victimization rates is significant at the 95% confidence level for overall violent crime, robbery, and simple assault. There is no significant difference in the rate of male and female intimate partner victimization for aggravated assault.

[a]Based on 10 or fewer sample cases.

[b]No cases were present for this category.

Source: Shannan Catalano et al., Bureau of Justice Statistics, *Female Victims of Violence* (September 2009, revised 23 October 2009), p. 1, http://bjs.ojp.usdoj.gov/content/pub/pdf/fvv.pdf, accessed 10 October 2010.

Figure 7.3

Nonfatal Violent Victimization Rate by Victim/Offender Relationship and Victim Gender, 1993–2008

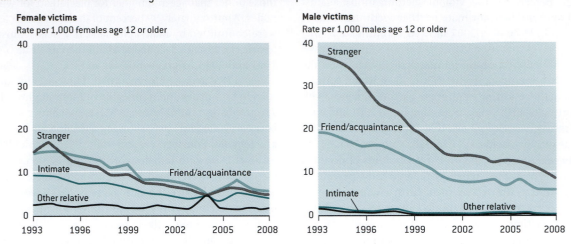

Source: Shannon Catalano et al., Bureau of Justice Statistics, *Female Victims of Violence* (September 2009, revised 23 October 2009), p. 2, http://bjs.ojp.usdoj.gov/content/pub/pdf/fvv.pdf, accessed 10 October 2010.

Figure 7.4

Homicides of Intimate Partners by Gender of Victim, 1993–2007

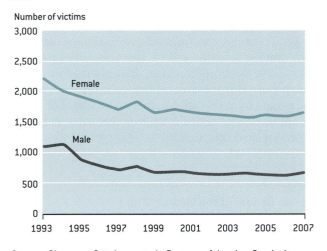

Source: Shannon Catalano et al., Bureau of Justice Statistics, *Female Victims of Violence* (September 2009, revised 23 October 2009), p. 3, http://bjs.ojp.usdoj.gov/content/pub/pdf/fvv.pdf, accessed 10 October 2010.

Explanations

Social scientists have attempted to explain IPV. First, why do some women commit IPV acts? Many women who strike or kill men allege that they do so in self-defense. One researcher found that women were seven times more likely than men to engage in domestic violence for self-defense either to avoid physical attacks or physical violence in the form of rape.[59]

One question often asked about women, the most frequent IPV victims, is why they remain in abusive re-

lationships. There are many myths based on public misunderstanding. Battered women are thought to be weak, sick, guilty (she nagged him until he beat her), lower class, and willing to take physical abuse for a meal ticket.[60]

Research on woman abused in IPV situations is limited in scope and depth, but the available studies suggest that the abused woman has characteristics similar to those of the man who abuses her. One study described female IPV victims in these terms:

[S]he is all ages, all ethnicities, from all socioeconomic groups, has a low level of self-esteem, and for the most part has very traditional notions of male and female behavior. She may feel that her husband is supposed to be in charge of the family, even if that means beating her; she must be supportive of him, even if that means allowing herself to be abused repeatedly. Her role as a woman includes marriage, even a bad marriage, and to leave the home would be to admit that she is a failure as a woman.[61]

The pioneering work on the issue of why an IPV abused woman remains in the relationship was conducted by Richard J. Gelles, who found three reasons these women do not leave their husbands. First, women are less likely to leave if the violence is not frequent or severe. Second, wives who were abused by their own parents are more likely to remain with abusive husbands than are those who were not abused as children. Third, the more resources and options a wife has, the more likely she is to leave an abusive spouse.[62]

Psychologist Lenore E. Walker characterized the IPV abuse woman as one who is

repeatedly subjected to any forceful or psychological behavior by a man in order to coerce her to do something he wants her to do without concern for her rights . . . [T]he couple must go through the battering cycle at least twice. . . . [And if] she remains in the situation, she is defined as a battered woman.[63]

In 1977, Walker coined the term **battered person syndrome** and supported it as a legal defense in a case involving a battered woman who was accused of murdering her husband. The defendant was acquitted, and Walker was on her way to a career as a recognized expert on the battered person syndrome. The defense has been accepted in many courts but rejected in others. Some jurisdictions have enacted statutes supporting the admissibility of expert testimony concerning the syndrome. The battered person syndrome is used in cases in which women allege that they have been raped and beaten by their partners over a long period of time.

The *fear* of further victimization involving serious injury or even death supports permitting women to use the battered person defense when they are charged with killing their husbands. Some experts argue that the fear of future violence is a factor that distinguishes female IPV victims from male victims, who are more likely than female victims to be able to leave the abusive relationship. Female victims are more likely to be tied economically to the men who abuse them. Furthermore, data suggest that once a woman is victimized by her spouse or lover, she is likely to be victimized again.[64]

Another issue in understanding IPV is explaining why someone becomes a perpetrator of this crime. Researchers have found that persons of all races and social classes are batterers. Statistically, battering may occur more often in the lower than in the upper classes, but that may be due to variations in reporting. There appear to be three major factors characteristic of men who batter their partners: frustration or stress, gender roles or learned behavior, and alcohol.[65] Stress may occur for many reasons. Frustration and stress may result from the man's sense of inadequacy as a male, as a provider, and as a father, a husband, or a lover. Insecurities may result from his extreme dependence on his partner coupled with his fear of losing her.

Gender roles, learned through the process of socialization, may be related to partner battering. Men learn to be aggressive and dominant and to expect women to be passive and subservient. Any show of superiority by the partner—for example, if she is employed and he is unemployed or if both are employed and she earns more money—may trigger a violent response. Many men and women adjust to changing gender roles without violence, but those who continue to hold traditional gender-role differentiations may be more likely to explode when the situation, by their definition, gets out of hand. This desire to maintain traditional gender-role stereotypes may explain the willingness of some women to tolerate the physical abuse.

The socialization process may trigger a violent reaction in the man. If he comes from a home in which his mother was battered (a characteristic of many batterers), he may have accepted violence as an appropriate way to handle the problems between men and women. If he was battered as a child, he may have decided that it is acceptable for the one who loves you to beat you as a method of control. Alcohol may also be a factor in abusive behavior. In some IPV situations, both spouses are under the influence of alcohol.

There is evidence that men who abused their wives or other partners were not violent in other relationships; that is, violent men tended to specialize. Either they abused partners and other family members or they abused nonfamily members, but they did not abuse both groups. Only 10 percent of the sample reported engaging in violence against both family and nonfamily. Further, those who engaged in violence outside the family were more likely to be blue-collar workers than those who engaged in violence against their families.[66]

One final area of discussion important to an understanding of IPV is feminist criminology (see again Chapter 5). Two of the noted researchers in this area, Kathleen Daly and Meda Chesney-Lind, applied feminist theory to an explanation of why men brutalize women in domestic relationships. Daly and Chesney-Lind advocated that rape and other forms of IPV are the "result and the linchpin of patriarchal systems, in which women's bodies and minds are subject to men's domination." They called for more regulations on pornography and changing laws concerning prostitution and intimate violence and rape. Daly and Chesney-Lind argued in favor of gender equality in criminal justice systems.[67]

Finally, it has been assumed that males who inflict IPV on their partners specialize in this type of violence, but some studies have reported that females who inflict IPV are the greater specialists, although they are generally reacting defensively. These findings suggest that current policies utilized by special domestic violence courts (discussed in Chapter 13), which react to male batterers as specialists, may be misdirected and that these special courts may not be treating female IPV perpetrators reasonably either. "Criminalizing the behavior of these women has serious consequences," which includes barring them from some jobs, public housing, and welfare benefits, while creating immigration status problems for them.[68]

Legal Reactions

We noted earlier the federal Violence Against Women Act. This act provides civil damages as well as numerous services for IPV victims. Most states have also enacted specific statutes aimed at IPV. An example is that of California, which provides as follows:

> (a) Any person who wilfully inflicts upon a person who is his or her spouse, former spouse, cohabitant, former cohabitant, or the mother or father of his or her child, corporal injury resulting in a traumatic condition, is guilty of a felony.[69]

Some jurisdictions have granted early release or even pardons to women who have been convicted and incarcerated for killing their spouses after being allegedly victimized by them.

Further, many jurisdictions have initiated policies involving mandatory arrests in IPV cases. This subject is discussed in greater detail in Chapter 12, but here it is important to raise the issue of whether mandatory arrests or special programs for battering spouses and others reduces the number of IPV acts. One recent study compared IPV batterers who were sentenced to special programs to those who were not. "The study found that neither the batterer program nor either of the two monitoring schedules produced a reduction of official re-arrest rates for any offense, for domestic violence, or for domestic violence with the same victim."[70]

Another issue with regard to arresting IPV perpetrators is whether this approach works. As noted earlier, the BJS reported in 2009, based on 2002 data, that over one-half of IPV defendants were convicted, with approximately 80 percent of those being incarcerated. One might argue that the conviction of only approximately one-half of defendants is not very high.[71]

A violent crime that is frequently connected with IPV is child abuse.

Child Abuse

In recent years, considerable media attention has focused on **child abuse**, a broad term used to include neglect, psychological, and physical abuse (including sexual abuse). Exhibit 7.2 provides the federal definitions of the acts included within child abuse. Note, however, that the federal statute permits states to provide their own definitions of child abuse and neglect; thus, data from various states may not be comparable.

Child abuse may include child stealing, or **parental kidnapping**, in which the parent who does not have legal custody takes the child without permission and refuses to return the youngster to his or her legal guardian or parent. Child abuse may include the involvement of children in pornography. Sexual abuse includes sexual activities that are voluntary in the sense that no force is used, but the child is coerced to act by the parent or other perpetrator. Children do not have the legal right to consent to sex.

Child abuse goes beyond abuse in the domestic scene; thus, some of the data are not limited to the home and family. For example, the Children's Bureau of the U.S. Department of Health and Human Services includes data for all children who are referred to state Child Protective Services (CPS). The latest bureau report on child maltreatment was based on 2008 data; during that year, an estimated 772,000 children were abuse or neglect victims, and nearly 3.7 million children received an investigation. In terms of types of abuse, 71.1 percent were neglect cases, 16.1 percent were victims of physical abuse, 7.3 percent were victimized by emotional or psychological abuse, 7.1 percent were victims of sexual abuse, and 2.2 percent were victims of medical maltreatment. Approximately 48.3 percent of the child victims were boys, and 51.3 percent were girls. The highest rates of victimization were inflicted on the youngest victims, with children younger than 4 constituting 32.6 percent of the maltreatment cases and children between 4 and 7 constituting 23.6 percent of the victims. In terms of race and ethnicity, the highest rates were among minorities. Most children were abused by one or both parents, but of those abused by only one parent, the mother was the most frequent perpetrator (39 percent of the cases).[72]

Children may be abused in many ways, including emotional and psychological as well as physical, but shaking a baby, as this teenage father is doing, is a common and physically dangerous method, which may lead to death, especially in a small child.

Child Abuse: Definitions and Types

7.2 EXHIBIT

"How Is Child Abuse and Neglect Defined in Federal Law?

Federal legislation lays the groundwork for States by identifying a minimum set of acts or behaviors that define child abuse and neglect. The Federal Child Abuse Prevention and Treatment Act (CAPTA), (42 U.S.C.A. 5106g), as amended by the Keeping Children and Families Safe Act of 2003, defines child abuse and neglect as, at minimum:

- Any recent act or failure to act on the part of a parent or caretaker which results in death, serious physical or emotional harm, sexual abuse or exploitation; or
- An act or failure to act which presents an imminent risk of serious harm. . . .

What Are the Major Types of Child Abuse and Neglect?

Within the minimum standards set by CAPTA, each State is responsible for providing its own definitions of child abuse and neglect. Most States recognize four major types of maltreatment: physical abuse, neglect, sexual abuse, and emotional abuse. Although any of the forms of child maltreatment may be found separately, they often occur in combination. In many States, abandonment and parental substance abuse are also defined as forms of child abuse or neglect.

The examples provided below are for general informational purposes only. Not all States' definitions will include all of the examples listed below, and individual States' definitions may cover additional situations not mentioned here.

Physical abuse is nonaccidental physical injury (ranging from minor bruises to severe fractures or death) as a result of punching, beating, kicking, biting, shaking, throwing, stabbing, choking, hitting (with a hand, stick, strap, or other object), burning, or otherwise harming a child, that is inflicted by a parent, caregiver, or other person who has responsibility for the child. Such injury is considered abuse regardless of whether the caregiver intended to hurt the child. Physical discipline, such as spanking or paddling, is not considered abuse as long as it is reasonable and causes no bodily injury to the child.

Neglect is the failure of a parent, guardian, or other caregiver to provide for a child's basic needs. Neglect may be:

- Physical (e.g., failure to provide necessary food or shelter, or lack of appropriate supervision)
- Medical (e.g., failure to provide necessary medical or mental health treatment)
- Educational (e.g., failure to educate a child or attend to special education needs)
- Emotional (e.g., inattention to a child's emotional needs, failure to provide psychological care, or permitting the child to use alcohol or other drugs)

These situations do not always mean a child is neglected. Sometimes cultural values, the standards of care in the community, and poverty may be contributing factors, indicating the family is in need of information or assistance. When a family fails to use information and resources, and the child's health or safety is at risk, then child welfare intervention may be required. In addition, many States provide an exception to the definition of neglect for parents who choose not to seek medical care for their children due to religious beliefs that may prohibit medical intervention. Sexual abuse includes activities by a parent or caregiver such as fondling a child's genitals, penetration, incest, rape, sodomy, indecent exposure, and exploitation through prostitution or the production of pornographic materials.

Sexual abuse is defined by CAPTA as "the employment, use, persuasion, inducement, enticement, or coercion of any child to engage in, or assist any other person to engage in, any sexually explicit conduct or simulation of such conduct for the purpose of producing a visual depiction of such conduct; or the rape, and in cases of caretaker or inter-familial relationships, statutory rape, molestation, prostitution, or other form of sexual exploitation of children, or incest with children."

Emotional abuse (or psychological abuse) is a pattern of behavior that impairs a child's emotional development or sense of self-worth. This may include constant criticism, threats, or rejection, as well as withholding love, support, or guidance. Emotional abuse is often difficult to prove and, therefore, child protective services may not be able to intervene without evidence of harm or mental injury to the child. Emotional abuse is almost always present when other forms are identified.

Abandonment is now defined in many States as a form of neglect. In general, a child is considered to be abandoned when the parent's identity or whereabouts are unknown, the child has been left alone in circumstances where the child suffers serious harm, or the parent has failed to maintain contact with the child or provide reasonable support for a specified period of time.

Substance abuse is an element of the definition of child abuse or neglect in many States. Circumstances that are considered abuse or neglect in some States include:

- Prenatal exposure of a child to harm due to the mother's use of an illegal drug or other substance.
- Manufacture of methamphetamine in the presence of a child.
- Selling, distributing, or giving illegal drugs or alcohol to a child.
- Use of a controlled substance by a caregiver that impairs the caregiver's ability to adequately care for the child."

Source: Child Welfare Information Gateway, "What Is Child Abuse and Neglect?" notes and citations omitted, http://www.childwelfare.gov/pubs/factsheets/whatiscan.cfm, accessed 18 October 2010.

Data on the sexual abuse of children were analyzed at the Crimes Against Children Research Center of the University of New Hampshire. The researchers concluded that the significant decline in reported child sexual abuse cases from 150,000 to 89,500 cases between 1992 and 2000 was not necessarily the result of fewer cases of sexual abuse. The reported decline, claimed these researchers, may have been the result of "a drop in the number of cases being identified and reported or by changes in practices of child protective agencies." Part of the apparent decline might have been due to a policy of tighter standards in questionable cases, such as those reported during divorce or custody battles. Part may have been due to a public backlash about false claims of child sexual abuse. The investigators considered these and other possible explanations but concluded that there was no clear evidence that any were correct.[73]

Two types of child sexual abuse deserve closer attention.

Statutory Rape

A sexual relationship with an underage person constitutes the crime of *statutory rape*, so called because it was not a common law crime to have sex with underage children; rather, the acts became criminal by statute. All states have statutory rape statutes, but they vary significantly in terms of the elements for the crime. Recent trends have been to alter the age at which a child may consent to sex as well as to vary the age of offenders. Thus, rather than criminalizing any sexual act by an adult of any age with a person under, for example, the traditional age of 16, the statutes might specify the difference in the ages of the parties, along with establishing a minimum age for the younger one. The Washington statutes (see Exhibit 7.3) provide examples, using the term *rape of a child* rather than *statutory rape*. These statutes make it clear that the seriousness of sex with a child takes into consideration a range of ages of the child and of the perpetrator rather than simply stating the maximum age of the child victim, a significant change from previous laws. Note that the statutes do not address the issue of consent. Consent cannot be legally given by children under the specified ages. Recall, however, from Chapter 1's coverage of the Genarlow Wilson case that Georgia changed its statutory rape statute, easing the penalties considerably for a factual pattern such as existed in that case.

Originally, only females could be considered statutory rape victims and only males could be perpetrators, but most jurisdictions have changed those statutes. In recent years, several cases involving female perpetrators (especially school teachers) and male victims (usually much younger) have been successfully prosecuted, with considerable media attention given to them. For example, Mary Kay Letourneau, 34, a married teacher with four children, served prison time for violating the Washington State sex laws by having sex with one of her male students, Vili Fualaau, who was 13 at the time (1996). Letourneau had a child by Fualaau and, after her first release from prison, violated the conditions of that release, saw the boy, had sex again, became pregnant, and had a second child by him. In the summer of 2004, Letourneau was released after spending seven and one-half years in prison. One of the conditions was that she could not see Faulaau. He, however, asked the court to release her from that condition, and the court agreed. The couple were wed on 20 May 2005, in a closely guarded ceremony at a winery outside Seattle, Washington.

There is evidence that sex between teachers and students is increasing, at least in terms of reporting. The New York State Board of Education reported a doubling of reported cases between 2001 and 2006. The data were published in the *New York Times* in June 2007 in an ar-

---

EXHIBIT 7.3

Rape of a Child: Statutory Rape

Revised Code of Washington (2010)

- **Section 9A.44.073. Rape of a child in the first degree.**

  (1) A person is guilty of rape of a child in the first degree when the person has sexual intercourse with another who is less than twelve years old and not married to the perpetrator and the perpetrator is at least twenty-four months older than the victim.

  (2) Rape of a child in the first degree is a class A felony.

- **Section 9A.44.076. Rape of a child in the second degree.**

  (1) A person is guilty of rape of a child in the second degree when the person has sexual intercourse with another who is at least twelve years old but less than fourteen years old and not married to the perpetrator and the perpetrator is at least thirty-six months older than the victim.

  (2) Rape of a child in the second degree is a class A felony.

- **Section 9A.44.079. Rape of a child in the third degree.**

  (1) A person is guilty of rape of a child in the third degree when the person has sexual intercourse with another who is at least fourteen years old but less than sixteen years old and not married to the perpetrator and the perpetrator is at least forty-eight months older than the victim.

  (2) Rape of a child in the third degree is a class C felony.

ticle that focused on the charges of aggravated sexual assault against a popular male teacher, who was accused by a 21-year-old woman. The accuser alleged that she and the teacher had sex while she was a student between the ages of 13 and 15.[74]

A report by the U.S. Department of Education stated that teachers sexually approach close to 10 percent of their young students and that 43 percent of those teachers are women.[75]

Incest

Sexual abuse of children, especially within the family, is a major type of child abuse today. The increased attention given nationally to this abuse has created a greater awareness of the crime of **incest**, which refers to sexual relations between family members who are considered by law too closely related to marry. Usually, children cooperate with the abusing parents, siblings, or other relatives because they are eager to please and do not understand what is going on. Most children also cooperate in the warning not to tell anyone about the sexual behavior. Because many cases of incest are not reported, the data on this crime are not accurate.[76]

Most cases of incest are between father and daughter. Father-son incest may occur, but less is known about this type of sexual abuse than about the other types. Most of the studies of incest are about father-daughter relationships, reporting that in most cases sexual abuse does not begin with sexual intercourse; other forms of activity may take place for years before sexual penetration. Abused daughters may have poor relationships with their mothers and not feel that they can turn to them when their fathers initiate sexual activity. Many men who have sexual relations with their daughters are having problems, often sexual, with their wives, and they see their wives as threatening and rejecting.[77]

There is evidence that most fathers deny the incestuous relationship or, if it is admitted, attribute it to overindulgence in alcohol or drugs. Many incestuous relationships begin when the daughter is very young. When confronted, some fathers rationalize the behavior in terms of teaching their daughters the facts of life or claiming that their daughters seduced them. Often, the mother is passive and possesses other traits characteristic of battered wives: extreme dependence on her husband, poor self-image, hostility, and jealousy of her spouse. In some cases, the mother becomes an accomplice or at least a witness. Very little has been written about brother-sister incest, thought to be the least damaging of all types of incest and usually transitory. Mother-son sexual relationships are reported infrequently, but they do exist. In fact, research shows that "the most traumatic form of incest is mother-son contact."[78]

The National Center for Victims of Crime posts a review of the literature on incest on its website, noting that some jurisdictions expand the crime of incest to include nonfamily members who are in positions of authority over a child. Some points are as follows:

- Forty-three percent of children who are abused are victimized by family members, and incest is the most common form of child abuse.
- Data are underreported, partially because of the victim's reluctance to report, but there is also evidence of a biochemically induced state of amnesia concerning the abuse.
- Inmates who abused children reported that three of every four victims were girls, but boy victims may be even more reluctant than girls to report the crime.
- Only approximately 24 percent of incest victims are abused by strangers.[79]

Explanations and Effects of Child Abuse

Social-structural factors were the focus of a national study of family violence, including child abuse, which was published in 1989. The investigator emphasized that the causes of child abuse are complex. Clearly, they are not attributed solely to mental illness or psychiatric disorder. A number of variables are involved, including "stress, unemployment and underemployment, number of children, and social isolation." After examining the social characteristics of the abusing parents, the social characteristics of the abused children, and the situational or contextual properties of the child abuse itself, the researcher concluded that if we are to treat and prevent the abuse of children, we must stop thinking of the abuser as a sick person who can be cured and begin working on social-structural factors, such as unemployment and child-rearing techniques.[80]

Some studies have reported that sexually abused children are more likely than nonabused children to engage in subsequent delinquent (or criminal) behavior. According to the National Council on Crime and Delinquency (NCCD), preventing child abuse is one way to prevent delinquency. The council noted that many juveniles who were serving time for delinquent acts were abused in their homes when they were younger.[81]

Medical researchers have reported the results of their findings that abused children may show exaggerated psychological reactions to subsequent stressful events. In particular, women showed hormonal changes when introduced to stressful events. The researchers stated that people are "born with a certain genetic constitution to handle many things, including stress. . . . But if the developing animal or human is faced with an extraordinary amount of stress, these systems are going to be changed in how they develop." One of the researchers, a professor of psychiatry, stated that persons who suffer from posttraumatic stress may relive those experiences during future stressful events. These events are defined as those that threaten life or serious bodily injury, which, of course, includes many experiences of child abuse.[82]

According to the Bureau of Justice Statistics, one in twenty men and one in four women in state prisons reported that they had been the victims of sexual abuse before they were 18; one in ten men and one in four women said they had been victimized by other forms of physical abuse.[83]

Some child abuse victims engage in violence against other children and their own parents while they are children; later, they may abuse their own children. Studies of juvenile offenders reveal that many child abuse victims were victims of child abuse or were witnesses to the abuse of other children or to domestic violence in their homes.[84]

The same is true of adult offenders. A study by the National Institute of Justice reported that two-thirds of convicted male felons in New York State said they had suffered child abuse. Some were abused sexually, and others were abused physically. Some reported being neglected but not physically or sexually abused. Physical abuse, cited most frequently, was reported by 35 percent of the inmates. Although only 14 percent reported sexual abuse, of those who were serving time for sexual offenses, 26 percent reported that they were sexually abused as children.[85]

Researchers refer to the continuation of violence in families over generations as the *cycle of violence* or the *intergenerational transmission of violence*. It is important to understand, however, that sexual (or nonsexual) abuse of children does not necessarily *cause* them to engage in the same kind of behavior against others. Different factors may also be influential.

Elder Abuse

Accurate data on **elder abuse** are not available because many of the crimes are not reported. There are other reasons, too, for inaccurate data. The crime is difficult to prove. The fact that elderly people fall often and bruise easily accounts for the majority of all home accidents. Because some doctors are not trained to detect abuse, many incidents do not come to the attention of those who collect the data.

One type of elder abuse that has gained attention in recent years is the abuse of elderly persons by members of their own families. This form of violence is referred to as the *King Lear syndrome* (after the aging character in Shakespeare's play who was mistreated by two of his daughters), *granny bashing*, and *parental abuse*. Elder abuse includes violent physical attacks as well as withholding food, stealing savings and Social Security checks, verbally abusing an elderly person, and threatening to send an elderly person to a nursing home.

It has been relatively recently that social scientists have begun to study family abuse of the elderly; thus, our knowledge of the problem is limited. The roots of the abuse may lie in child abuse. It may be the result of an attempt to do the right thing but an inability to cope with the problems of an aging parent or grandparent, coupled with the inability, because of guilt or expense, to place that parent in a nursing home.

Elder abuse also occurs outside the family. Elderly people die from neglect in nursing homes and other residences. With its large elderly population, Florida faces difficult problems in this area, and investigations reveal that most of the victims are elderly women. Most of the cases are reported by social services, followed closely by neighbors or friends. Some are referred by medical personnel. Elder abuse has led to both civil and criminal charges.[86]

One final problem for the elderly with regard to violent crime is their fear of becoming victims. This fear is realistic to the elderly but unrealistic in terms of actual data. Most violent crime victims are between the ages of 18 and 21.[87] As noted in earlier discussions, however, it is the possibility, not the probability, of becoming a crime victim that concerns the elderly.

Some jurisdictions have enacted statutes covering elder abuse. California is an example. Among that state's provisions is the following statement of need and purpose:

> (a) The Legislature finds and declares that crimes against elders and dependent adults are deserving of special consideration and protection, not unlike the special protections provided for minor children, because elders and dependent adults may be confused, on various medications, mentally or physically impaired, or incompetent, and therefore less able to protect themselves, to understand or report criminal conduct, or to testify in court proceedings on their own behalf.[88]

At the federal level, the U.S. Congress passed the Elder Justice Act as part of the Patient Protection and Affordable Care Act, which became law on 23 March 2010. The health care reform bill is extensive, and no attempt can be made here even to summarize it. However, it is important to note that in addition to health care for seniors, the new law contains provisions to provide tools to reduce crimes against the elderly, such as targeting them for various fraudulent acts.[89] The constitutionality of the law is in question.

There are situations in which persons may not be physically harmed by family members or others, but they may still be placed in fear. Kidnapping, hate crimes, and stalking are examples.

Kidnapping

Kidnapping (restricting the freedom of a victim against his or her will and removing the victim from one place to another) was mentioned earlier as a form of child abuse in which the noncustodial parent removes the child and flees with him or her. But the common form of kidnapping is committed by strangers, and many victims are abused and murdered. The victim need not be a child, although that is usually the case. Both parental and stranger kidnappings are considered here. Both crimes are similar to the crime of **false imprisonment** (the unlawful and knowing restraint of a person against his or her wishes so as to deny freedom) because they involve restricting the freedom of another. The crimes differ in the elements required to establish them, the seriousness of the offenses, and the punishments. Under the common law, *kidnapping* required the asportation (the removal from one place to another) of a victim from his or her own country to another. *False imprisonment* did not require this element. Sometimes called *false arrest*, false imprisonment referred only to the unlawful confinement of another person. Thus, kidnapping was the same as false imprisonment with the added element of asportation. Some jurisdictions do not define a separate crime of false imprisonment; likewise, some states do not define kidnapping as a separate crime if it is committed incidental to another crime. Asportation remains a required element of kidnapping in most jurisdictions. The California statute, reprinted here in part, is an example.

> Every person who forcibly, or by any other means of instilling fear, steals or takes, or holds, detains, or arrests any person in this state, and carries the person into another country, state, or county, or into another part of the same county, is guilty of kidnapping.[90]

Under the California statute, asportation might not be required if it can be shown that the offender had an intent to take the victim out of the state.[91]

The requirement of asportation avoids converting the less serious crime of false imprisonment into the more serious crime of kidnapping by finding the asportation element when it has nothing to do with the crime of kidnapping or by creating two crimes (false imprisonment and kidnapping) when only one occurred.

Some kidnapping statutes require that the victim be isolated in a *secret* place; others require only proof that there was an intent to isolate the victim. Some statutes define more than one degree of kidnapping, requiring aggravating circumstances for the more serious offense of first-degree kidnapping. Kidnapping a child for purposes of prostitution or pornography is an example of an aggravating circumstance; kidnapping for ransom is another. Frequently, the classic kidnapping is accompanied by other crimes, such as extortion, sexual assault, ransom demands, terrorism and torture, and murder.

Some jurisdictions define a separate crime of *child stealing*, or *parental kidnapping*. Congress passed the Parental Kidnapping Prevention Act of 1980, which permits federal authorities to issue warrants for parents who flee a state's jurisdiction to avoid prosecution for parental kidnapping. The statute also obligates states, under specified circumstances, to recognize the child custody determinations of other states.[92] The U.S. Supreme Court has held, however, that this statute does not give federal courts the power to resolve conflicting custody battle disputes between states.

That problem is for Congress to decide through appropriate legislation if states refuse to cooperate with the provisions of the federal act. Thus, if two states disagree in a child custody case, federal courts cannot solve that dispute in a civil action. Critics argue that this ruling makes U.S. courts powerless to deter parental kidnapping, for it does nothing to prevent a parent from kidnapping a child and going to another jurisdiction to avoid the custody decision of the home state.[93]

A major problem with child kidnapping cases is that parents who take children illegally from a custodial parent may be difficult, if not impossible, to locate. Some parents begin a new life with successful disguises for themselves and for their children; others move to foreign countries. Recent data suggest that such kidnappings are increasing and that they are very difficult to solve.[94]

One approach to handling alleged parental kidnapping cases is illustrated by an Ohio statute entitled *interference with custody*, which includes children "under the age of eighteen, or a mentally or physically handicapped child under the age of twenty-one" as well as adults institutionalized for mental retardation or mental illness and children under the state's juvenile custody. It is a crime for anyone "knowing the person is without privilege to do so or being reckless in that regard" to "entice, take, keep, or harbor" persons in the enumerated categories.[95]

In recent years, a few kidnapping cases have resulted in the safe return of victims. Elizabeth Smart, who was abducted from the bedroom she shared with her younger sister, was located nine months later. Two people were charged with kidnapping and other crimes, and in November 2009, one of the defendants, Wanda Eileen Barzee, pleaded guilty and asked for forgiveness. She has not been sentenced. Her husband, Brian David Mitchell, had not been tried, although in 2010 he was finally declared competent to stand trial. Shawn Hornbeck, kidnapped at the age of 11 in 2002, was located in 2007, along with another kidnapped victim, William "Ben" Ownby. Michael Devlin entered guilty pleas and is serving life sentences for various crimes, including rape and sexual assault in these cases. A final example is that of Jaycee Lee Dugard, kidnapped when she was 11 and held for 18 years before she was located in 2009. Dugard, who had two children during her captivity allegedly by the man accused of abducting her, convicted sex offender Phillip Garrido, was held in a shed in the backyard of the defendant and his wife, Nancy Garrido, also a defendant in this case. Both defendants were awaiting trial as of this writing. Dugard was awarded $20 million for damages.

Hate Crimes

The U.S. Congress enacted the Hate Crime Statistics Act in 1990, requiring that data on **hate crimes** be collected. The act, as amended, requires the FBI to collect data on hate or bias crimes, which include crimes that evidence prejudice against persons based on race, religion, ethnicity, disability, sexual perceived gender, sexual orientation, or gender identity. The 2009 provision is known as the Matthew Shepard and James Byrd Jr. Hate Crimes Prevention Act and is named for two hate crime victims.

In 1988, university student Matthew Shepard became a symbol of hate crimes after Russell A. Henderson and Aaron J. McKinney tortured and killed him, allegedly because he was gay. Both defendants were convicted and sentenced to life in prison. James Byrd Jr., an African American, was dragged to his death behind a truck in Texas in June 1998. Three white defendants were convicted in this case. Russell Brewer, 32, and Bill King, 25, were convicted of capital murder; Shawn Berry, 24, was sentenced to life in prison. The families of Shepard and Byrd fought for a decade for the 2009 revision of the federal hate crime statute, which was signed by President Barack Obama in the fall of 2009.[96]

States may also include some or all of these targets in their statutes. Some states do not have hate crime statutes but do provide enhanced penalties if the state can prove that a crime, such as aggravated assault or murder, was committed with a bias. The difficulty is with the proof, as illustrated by the case of Tyler Clementi, an 18-year-old Rutgers University student who jumped off the George Washington Bridge and to his death in the Hudson River in an apparent suicide on 22 September 2010. Two 18-year-old classmates, Dharun Ravi (Clementi's roommate) and Molly Wei, were accused of making a video of Clementi in a sexual encounter with another male and posting it on the Internet. Some people argued that Ravi and Wei should be charged with a hate crime, but others noted it would be difficult to prove the elements of that crime in this case.

Since the collection of hate crime data is so recent, trend data are limited, but the FBI publishes annual data on bias offenses, divided into five categories: racial bias, religious bias, sexual-orientation bias, ethnicity/national origin bias, and disability bias. Law enforcement must indicate one of these categories for each reported bias offense. The FBI defines a *single-bias incident* as "an incident in which one or more offense types are motivated by the same bias." It defines a *multiple-bias incident* as "an incident in which more than one offense type occurs and at least two offense types are motivated by different biases."

On 22 November 2010, the FBI released the 2009 hate crime data and made the following comments.

- "Of the 6,598 single-bias incidents, 48.5 percent were motivated by a racial bias, 19.7 percent were motivated by a religious bias, 18.5 percent were motivated by a sexual-orientation bias, and 11.8 percent were motivated by an ethnicity/national origin bais. Bias against a disability accounted for 1.5 percent of single-bias incidents.
- There were 4,793 hate crime offenses classified as crimes against persons. . . .

Figure 7.5

Hate Crimes: Behind the Bias

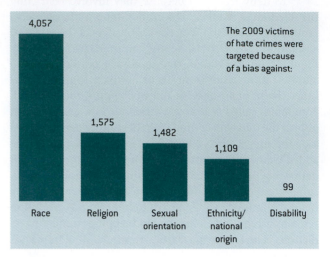

Source: Federal Bureau of Investigation, "FBI Releases 2009 Hate Crime Statistics" (22 November 2010), http://www.fbi .gov/news/pressrel/pressreleases/2009hatecrimestats_112210, accessed 16 December 2010.

- There were 2,970 hate crime offenses classified as crimes against property; most of these (83.0 percent) were acts of destruction/damage/ vandalism. . . .
- Of the 6,225 known offenders, 62.4 percent were white, 18.5 percent were black. . . ."[97]

The FBI reported that in 2009, law enforcement agencies reported 8,336 victims of hate crimes. A victim "may be an individual, a business, an institution, or society as a whole." Figure 7.5 graphs the 2009 victims by category of the type of bias for which they were targeted.

As with most other crimes, criminologists have applied theories to the explanation of hate crimes. An analysis of 2,031 hate crimes reported in Pennsylvania revealed that the frequency and the severity of hate crimes, along with the police response to them, were related to both community and individual influences. With regard to hate crime victims, investigators found the following:

- Hate crimes, both in rural and in urban areas, were relatively minor acts.
- There was a relationship between the type of victim and the severity of the hate crime, with antiracial incidents between African Americans and whites precipitating the more violent acts, while anti-Semitic targets more often involved low-level property crimes. Offenses against multiple groups were more likely to involve acts such as the distribution of hate literature.
- Types of hate crimes differed by counties with, for example, more crimes against gay victims occurring in rural than in urban areas, which were more

likely to be the scene of hate crimes against multiple target groups or Asians.[98]

These findings were analyzed in terms of social disorganization theory, which would imply that, like other crimes, hate crimes are more likely to occur in urban than in rural areas because of the weaker formal and informal social controls resulting from greater social disorganization. These researchers, however, found the opposite: Both personal and property hate crimes were significantly higher in rural than in urban areas. To explain this unexpected finding, the researchers suggested that rural people, compared with urbanites, may be more prejudiced and less accepting of outsiders. Or the actual frequency of hate crimes might be the same in urban areas, but those victims might be less likely to report them. Urbanites may consider hate crimes to be so frequent that they think law enforcement officials will not respond; so they do not report them. It is also possible that rural areas have fewer hate crimes, but they are more likely reported; because of their infrequency, they are taken more seriously.[99]

A significant legal decision with regard to hate crimes was made by the U.S. Supreme Court in 2003, when the Court upheld the Virginia Supreme Court, in the case of *Virginia* v. *Black,* in ruling unconstitutional a statute that provided:

> It shall be unlawful for any person or persons, with the intent of intimidating any person or group of persons, to burn, or cause to be burned, a cross on the property of another, a highway, or other public place.[100]

The *Black* case involved three defendants. The Virginia Supreme Court held that the statute in this case violated the defendants' First Amendment right to free speech, which has been interpreted to include symbolic speech. Eight U.S. Supreme Court justices viewed cross burning as a form of speech protected by the First Amendment. According to these justices, for a conviction to survive under the Virginia statute, prosecutors must prove beyond a reasonable doubt that the cross burning was for the purpose of intimidation rather than as an expression of symbolic speech. The constitutional defect with the Virginia statute was that it permitted an *inference* that if a cross were burned on the property of another, that act constituted *prima facie* [evidence sufficient to establish a fact—such as, in this case, intent to intimidate—without further evidence] evidence of an intent to intimidate.[101] Justice Clarence Thomas, the lone dissenter, described cross burning as a unique symbol of racial hatred and intimidation. In his view, the act itself is evidence of intimidation.[102]

Stalking

Some acts do not rise to the level of actual physical contact but are still frightening to potential victims. **Stalking** is an example. Although definitions differ, the Stalking Resource Center (SRC) of the National Center for Victims

of Crime defines the term as "a course of conduct directed at a specified person that would cause a reasonable person to feel fear." Included within this definition are the following behaviors:

- "making unwanted phone calls
- sending unsolicited or unwanted letters or e-mails
- following or spying on the victim
- showing up at places without a legitimate reason
- waiting at places for the victim
- leaving unwanted items, presents, or flowers
- posting information or spreading rumors about the victim on the internet, in a public place, or by word of mouth."[103]

The National Crime Victimization Survey (NCVS) published a January 2009 pamphlet reporting on 2006 stalking data, summarized as follows:

- "During a 12-month period an estimated 14 in every 1,000 persons age 18 or older were victims of stalking.
- About half (46%) of stalking victims experienced at least one unwanted contact per week, and 11% of victims said they had been stalked for 5 years or more.
- The risk of stalking victimization was highest for individuals who were divorced or separated—34 per 1,000 individuals.
- Women were at greater risk than men for stalking victimization; however, women and men were equally likely to experience harassment.
- Male (37%) and female (41%) stalking victimizations were equally likely to be reported to the police.
- Approximately 1 in 4 stalking victims reported some form of cyberstalking such as e-mail (83%) or instant messaging (35%).
- 46% of stalking victims felt fear of not knowing what would happen next.
- Nearly 3 in 4 stalking victims knew their offender in some capacity."[104]

Antistalking statutes are relatively new, with the first state statute enacted in California in 1990. The federal statute, the Interstate Stalking Punishment and Prevention Act, was enacted in the fall of 1996. This statute is aimed at stalking on federal property or across state lines.[105]

Some of the antistalking statutes have been invalidated by courts, taking the position that the laws are vague or too broad. For example, the Kansas antistalking statute was invalidated in 1996. That statute defined stalking as

> an intentional and malicious following or course of conduct directed at a specific person when such following or course of conduct seriously alarms, annoys, or harasses the person, and which serves no legitimate purpose.[106]

The Kansas Supreme Court held that this statute was void for vagueness because *alarms* and *annoys* are subjective terms and thus open to many interpretations. The court noted that there were no guidelines to enlighten persons on the meaning of when following a person becomes "alarming, annoying, or harassing." As defined, the crime of stalking "depends upon the sensitivity of the complainant." The court did hold, however, that the word *following* is not vague.

The Kansas statute was changed to read as follows:

Stalking is an intentional, malicious and repeated following or harassment of another person and making a credible threat with the intent to place such person in reasonable fear for such person's safety.[107]

A final type of stalking statute, *electronic stalking*, is new and has not yet been enacted in many jurisdictions. On 1 January 1999, California's computer stalking statute became effective. It constitutes an amendment to the state's stalking statute by adding that the term *credible threat* in the original statute means

a verbal or written threat, including that performed through the use of an electronic communication device, or a threat implied by a pattern of conduct or a combination of verbal, written, or electronically communicated statements and conduct, made with the intent to place the person that is the target of the threat in reasonable fear for his or her safety or the safety of his or her family, and made with the apparent ability to carry out the threat so as to cause the person who is the target of the threat to reasonably fear for his or her safety or the safety of his or her family. It is not necessary to prove that the defendant had the intent to actually carry out the threat.[108]

Researchers have conducted studies of stalkers and their victims. In an analysis of the problem for college and university women, investigators studied subjects for a seven-month period. During that time, slightly over 13 percent of the students reported being victimized by stalking. The researchers emphasized the seriousness of stalking but noted that few colleges and universities had policies concerned with the education and prevention of this crime. They emphasized the importance of the routine activity approach in explaining stalking and suggested that college and university women should be aware of the activities that underlie stalking: living alone, dating, going to bars. But as the researchers underscored, these are routine activities and difficult to avoid in that setting. More important, women should not be required to alter their routine activities to accommodate stalkers. Policies should be in place to reduce the chances of stalking victimizations in college and university (as well as other) settings. The researchers concluded that victimization by stalking "is a price of going to college that students should not have to bear or, if experienced, should not have to bear alone and without the support of institutional officials."[109]

Terrorism

A crime that frequently involves violence is **terrorism**. Most terrorism victims are innocent and unsuspecting persons who become the targets of violent attacks that frequently result in death. This was tragically demonstrated on 19 April 1995, when Timothy McVeigh bombed the federal building in Oklahoma City, killing 168 people, including 19 children in a day care center within the building, and injuring hundreds. This was the worst act of terrorism on American soil until the events of 11 September 2001, referred to as 9/11, when approximately 3,000 people died after carefully coordinated hijacked airplanes were flown into the Twin Towers of the World Trade Center in New York City, two of the tallest buildings in the world, representing the financial strength of the United States, and the Pentagon in Washington, D.C., one of the sources of U.S. government and military strength. A fourth hijacked plane, apparently headed for another Washington, D.C., building (perhaps the U.S. Capitol or the White House), was crashed by the terrorists in Pennsylvania after passengers apparently fought with them. The death toll for this greatest terrorist attack on American soil would have been much higher, but thousands were able to evacuate the World Trade Center towers before they collapsed. Other terrorist acts have occurred on foreign soils as well as in the United States. Terrorism is a worldwide concern today.

Terrorist attacks are not new to this country or other countries, but it was not until 1981 that the U.S. government perceived the threat of terrorism "to be serious enough to warrant classification as a major component of American foreign policy."[110] Accurate data on terrorism are not available, but it is obvious, as noted earlier, that some terrorist attacks have been costly both in terms of human lives and property.

Definitional Issues

Although there is little agreement on a definition of *terrorism*, most people have an idea of what it means. A broad legal definition is found in the American Law Institute's Model Penal Code, which defines *terrorist threats* as follows:

A person is guilty of a felony if he threatens to commit any crime of violence with purpose to terrorize another or to cause evacuation of a building, place of assembly, or facility of public transportation, or otherwise to cause serious public inconvenience, or in reckless disregard of the risk of causing such terror or inconvenience.[111]

Applied to the political arena, terrorism has been defined simply as "motivated violence for political ends."[112] The Task Force on Disorders and Terrorism of the National Advisory Commission on Criminal Justice Standards defined terrorism as "a tactic or technique by means of which a violent act or the threat thereof is used for the prime pur-

An honor guard salutes during the dedication of the memorial to the victims of the terrorist bombing of the federal building in Oklahoma City on 19 April 1995. A chair represents each of the victims.

pose of creating overwhelming fear for coercive purposes." Terrorism is a political crime but may also be a violent personal crime. Most terrorist acts are carefully planned, and to be effective, terrorists must manipulate the community to which the message is addressed. The inculcation of fear is paramount and deliberate; it is the real purpose of the activity, and an audience is important. In this respect, the terror involved in an individual robbery, for example, differs from terrorism. In the latter, the immediate victim is not the important focus; the emphasis is on the larger audience.[113] In this respect, terrorism differs significantly from violent personal crimes.

One final definition is relevant. Professor and security expert H. H. A. Cooper, a noted international authority and consultant on terrorism, stated that his own definition of terrorism had evolved during his lengthy teaching career. According to Cooper, "Terrorism is the intentional generation of massive fear by human beings for the purpose of securing or maintaining control over other human beings." He continued: "Terrorism is not a struggle for the hearts and minds of the victims nor for their immortal souls. Rather, it is, as Humpty Dumpty would have said, about who is to be master, that is all." It is a "naked struggle for power, who shall wield it, and to what ends." Cooper admitted that the definition of terrorism is "as needful and as illusory as ever." But he said, as with pornography, "we know it well enough when we see it."[114]

The Categories of Terrorism

The Task Force on Disorders and Terrorism (hereafter referred to as The Task Force), which was directed by Cooper, divided terrorism into six categories:

1. *Civil disorders*: "a form of collective violence interfering with the peace, security, and normal functioning of the community."

2. *Political terrorism*: "violent criminal behavior designed primarily to generate fear in the community, or a substantial segment of it, for political purposes."

3. *Nonpolitical terrorism*: terrorism that is not aimed at political purposes but that exhibits "conscious design to create and maintain a high degree of fear for coercive purposes, but the end is individual or collective gain rather than the achievement of a political objective."

4. *Quasi terrorism*: "those activities incidental to the commission of crimes of violence that are similar in form and method to true terrorism but which nevertheless lack its essential ingredient." It is not the main purpose of the quasi terrorists "to induce terror in the instant victim," as in the case of true terrorism. Typically, the fleeing felon who takes a hostage is a quasi terrorist, whose methods are similar to those of the true terrorist but whose purposes are quite different.

5. *Limited political terrorism*: "acts of terrorism which are committed for ideological or political motives but which are not part of a concerted campaign to capture control of the State." Limited political terrorism differs from real terrorism in the former's lack of a revolutionary approach.

6. *Official or state terrorism*: activities carried out by "nations whose rule is based upon fear and oppression that reach terrorist proportions."[115]

Terrorism may consist of acts or threats or both. The Task Force discussed several characteristics that distinguish modern terrorism from classical terrorism in its original form. First, as the result of our technological vulnerability, the potential for harm is greater today than in the past. This development, which includes improved intercontinental travel and mass communication, has increased the bargaining power of the modern terrorist. Television has carried the activities of terrorists to the entire world, giving modern terrorists more power than classical terrorists had. Finally, modern terrorists believe that through violence, they can maintain or increase hope for their causes.

Terrorism Victims

In one sense, all of society is victimized by terrorist acts. The action taken against the immediate victim is coercive and designed to impress others. Terrorism is not a victimless crime. The immediate victims may be involved incidentally, as when they are killed by a randomly placed bomb, or they may be selected with considerable discrimination, as, for example, when a prominent politician is assassinated or a businessperson is kidnapped. Terrorism is characterized by gross indifference toward the victims, which includes their dehumanization and their treatment as mere elements in a deadly power play.

The randomness of victimization by terrorism is illustrated by most of the more recent terrorist acts, such as the bombing of the federal building in Oklahoma City and the 9/11 terrorist attacks. The ultimate objective of the terrorist, particularly the political terrorist, is the establishment of a bargaining position, so the identity of the victims is unimportant in most cases. Kidnapping and taking hostages are terrorist techniques par excellence for this purpose. The victims are treated largely as objects to be traded for what the terrorist wants: money, release of prisoners, publication of manifestos, escape, and so on. These bargains are extralegal and rest on a recognition of the power of life and death that the terrorist holds over victims. This aspect raises the most serious social, political, and humanitarian issues for those who must make these awesome decisions affecting the lives and safety of the victims.

Terrorist victimization produces special individual and collective traumas. Many hostages and kidnap victims experience incongruous feelings toward their captors, and the events may constitute a serious challenge to their own value systems. The most striking manifestation of this is the **Stockholm syndrome**, named after an incident that occurred in the Swedish capital in 1973. The *Stockholm syndrome* is an incongruous feeling of empathy toward the hostage takers and a displacement of frustration and aggression on the part of the victims toward authorities. In some terrorist acts, such as those of 9/11, death and destruction occur so rapidly that the Stockholm syndrome concept is not applicable.

Another way many individuals are victimized by terrorist attacks is in the creation of fear that leads to changes in lifestyles. This result occurred among many Americans who were not direct victims of 9/11 but who feared additional terrorist acts. Perhaps the fear of flying that led many to cancel flights (or refuse to book them) after these events was the greatest manifestation of fear in reaction to the acts.

Faisal Shahzad, a naturalized U.S. citizen born in Pakistan, pleaded guilty in a Manhattan federal court to 10 counts for driving a car bomb into Times Square in New York City on 1 May 2010. He was apprehended by federal law enforcement authorities at JFK Airport as he was attempting to fly to Dubai. The terrorist attempt failed as the bomb did not explode. Shahzad admitted that he had been in Pakistan training with Taliban militants. He was sentenced to life in prison.

The Control of Terrorism: Federal Initiatives

What is the most effective way to respond to terrorism? If the government meets the demands of the terrorists, does that concession raise the specter of creating inconvenient or unreasonable precedents for the handling of future incidents? Ted Gurr, author of *Why Men Rebel*, said: "The most fundamental human response to the use of force is counterforce. Force threatens and angers men. Threatened, they try to defend themselves; angered, they want to retaliate."[116]

After terrorist attacks on U.S. planes, skyjacked in large numbers in the 1970s, the federal government took action. Security measures were required in all U.S. airports, and skyjacking decreased. But terrorists are adaptable, as demonstrated by their planting of bombs *outside* the secure areas of airports. It was obvious on 9/11 that although efforts to secure airports and aircraft had increased, they were not sufficient to prevent such attacks. The skyjackers boarded airplanes carrying box cutters, which were apparently used to subdue and murder flight attendants and pilots. And even with the increased security that followed those attacks, passengers have boarded planes with knives and guns. In December 2001, Richard Reid boarded a U.S.-bound flight in Paris, France, with explosives in his shoes. Umar Farouk Abdulmutallab, 23, a Nigerian national, was charged with attempts to destroy an aircraft bound for the United States from the Netherlands on 24 December 2010, in violation of a federal statute.[117] Even more stringent security measures were put into effect in the aftermath of these and other security breaches.

In the summer of 1995, President Bill Clinton urged Congress to pass his antiterrorism bill. After considerable negotiation, the House and Senate passed a bill, and President Clinton signed it shortly before the first anniversary of the Oklahoma City bombing. The Antiterrorism and Effective Death Penalty Act of 1996 restricts the legal opportunities for death-row and other inmates to appeal their sentences. It makes it more difficult for foreign terrorist groups to raise money in the United States and provides for easier deportation of alien terrorists. It authorizes money for fighting terrorism in the United States. The statute contains provisions for terrorism victims, such as mandatory restitution. There is also a provision for them to have access to closed-circuit television to view a trial that has been moved more than 350 miles from the venue in which they were victimized by a terrorist act.[118]

After 9/11, President George W. Bush proposed and Congress enacted several pieces of legislation to create new federal agencies and to empower those agencies and others in the fight against terrorism. The most significant changes occurred as a result of the quick passage of the **USA Patriot Act** (United and Strengthening America by Providing Appropriate Tools Required to Intercept and Obstruct Terrorism Act of 2001) in the fall of 2001. The act expanded the powers of the federal government to deal with terrorism.[119]

The National Homeland Security and Combating Terrorism Act of 2002 coordinates the federal agencies involved in domestic preparedness and those that coordinate plans for natural and human-made crises and emergency planning. The legislation provided for the creation of a White House Office of Combating Terrorism, empowered to oversee government-wide antiterrorism policies and coordinate threats, to be in charge of a national strategy to combat terrorism, and to exercise control over the budget for counterterrorism. A subsection of the act, the Homeland Security Information Sharing Act, contains provisions for requiring the federal government to share classified information, along with unclassified but sensitive information, with state and local law enforcement agencies.[120]

The Enhanced Border Security and Visa Entry Reform Act of 2002 is an extensive act designed to provide greater security with regard to granting foreigners permission to enter the United States.[121]

The Public Health Security and Bioterrorism Response Act of 2002 authorized $4.6 billion to fund measures to protect the United States against bioterrorist attacks. Among other provisions of this act are those aimed at increasing the ability of law enforcement officers to respond quickly and efficiently to bioterrorist attacks and funding for public health preparedness. It provides funding measures to increase the protection of the nation's supplies of food, drugs, and drinking water. It also contains provisions to allocate funds to state and local governments to assist law enforcement to improve their preparation for potential bioterrorist attacks.[122]

Two other federal agencies were designed to combat terrorism in the United States. The **Department of Homeland Security (DHS)** constituted the most extensive federal government reorganization in 50 years. The **Transportation Security Administration (TSA)** was created by the Aviation and Transportation Security Act (ATSA) enacted in November 2001. The TSA was developed to take on the screening functions for all commercial flights. This job had been performed by the Federal Aviation Administration (FAA), which was restructured by the statute. The TSA is a part of the DHS and is devoted to transportation security.

In an effort to determine more about terrorism and, in particular, the 9/11 terrorist acts, the U.S. Congress and the president created the National Commission on Terrorist Attacks upon the United States. The 9/11 Commission presented its report to Congress, to the president, and to the American people in the summer of 2004.[123]

Doing justice to the 567 pages of the authorized edition of the *9/11 Commission Report* is beyond the scope of a college text, but the report cannot go unnoted. Five Republicans and five Democrats reviewed over 2.5 million pages of documents, interviewed more than 1,200 people in 10 countries, held 19 days of hearings, and took testimony from 160 witnesses. The commissioners stated that their purpose was not to place blame but to understand, to learn, and to make recommendations. Among the comments on what the commissioners learned are the following:

> We learned about an enemy who is sophisticated, patient, disciplined, and lethal. The enemy rallies broad support in the Arab and Muslim world by demanding redress of political grievances, but its hostility toward us and our values is limitless. Its purpose is to rid the world of religious and political pluralism, the plebiscite, and equal rights for women. It makes no distinction between military and civilian targets. *Collateral damage* is not in its lexicon.[124]

The commission made the following major recommendations for reorganizing the government (some of these recommendations, including the national intelligence director, are provided by the Intelligence Reform and Terrorism Prevention Act of 2004):

- "unifying strategic intelligence and operational planning against Islamist terrorists across the foreign–domestic divide with a National Counterterrorism Center;
- unifying the intelligence community with a new National Intelligence Director;
- unifying the many participants in the counterterrorism effort and their knowledge in a network-based information-sharing system that transcends traditional governmental boundaries;
- unifying and strengthening congressional oversight to improve quality and accountability; and
- strengthening the FBI and homeland defenders."[125]

Chapter 12 discusses some of the recent federal legislation relating to the 9/11 Commission report. A recently published research article, summarized in Media Focus 7.2, emphasizes the impact of the media on our knowledge of terrorist acts.

The Fear of Crime

A typical reaction to violent crimes, especially terrorist acts, is fear. Numerous studies have been conducted on the fear of crime, what causes the fear, and how it may be alleviated. Research suggests that fear of crime varies according to where people live. Also, the nature of social interaction correlates with the degree of fear. And research confirms what most people think would be obvious: Fear is greater at night than during the day.[126]

The fear of crime has changed our lives in many ways. We must have exact change for buses and small bills for taxi drivers, who will not change large bills. We must lock our doors, bar our windows, and install burglar alarms, thus paying a high price for home security. Many people refuse to go out alone at night. Elderly people have suffered or even died from heat strokes in their apartments because they would not leave their homes during hot weather for fear of being burglarized or attacked. We worry that on Halloween our children might be given candy or other treats that have been laced with poison or have razor blades hidden inside. The fear of terrorist acts has made our lives more regulated, as illustrated by increased security not only at airports throughout the

---

MEDIA FOCUS

7.2   **Media Focus on Domestic Terrorism: An Analysis**

The media, along with research scholars, pay more attention to terrorist acts today than they did prior to 9/11, but according to a recent analysis, that attention s focused on only a few incidents. Criminologists who analyzed media reports on terrorist acts between 1980 and 11 September 2001 reported the amount and type of coverage given by the *New York Times* to the terrorist incidents. These researchers note that little research exists on this topic, with most of the analyses of the extensive media attention to crime focusing on homicides. They found that the media gave little attention to most terrorist acts but that they sensationalized some acts.

The media and terrorists have a symbiotic relationship in that terrorists need the media to publicize and sensationalize their acts, and the media capitalize on the acts to increase their ratings.

In their study, the investigators included 412 terrorist incidents, of which approximately 63 percent were completed, 24.8 percent were prevented, and 11.9 percent were suspected. Of the 412 incidents, the *New York Times* mentioned only 55.3 percent, or 228. The paper published almost 3.8 million words in more than 4,000 articles about those 228 incidents, with the average incident receiving 10 articles and 9,000 words. The researchers classified 48 percent of the articles as *incident stories*—that is, based

on facts, the circumstances in which those facts occurred, and the responses to them. The second group (52 percent) were classified as *general policy stories*. Some incidents resulted in extensive debate and even legislative and policy changes.

The Oklahoma City bombing had the highest number of words and articles, followed by the 9/11 acts. The researchers found that in discussing these and other terrorist acts, several characteristics appeared related to which acts were covered and to what extent.

> Incidents with casualties, linked to domestic terrorist groups, targeting airlines, or when hijacking is used as a tactic are significantly more likely to be covered and have more articles and words written about them.[1]

> These characteristics are consistent with those that explain media coverage of homicides and of the research concerning media coverage of international terrorist acts as well as media coverage of other issues.[2]

---

1. Steven M. Chermak and Jeffrey Gruenewald, "The Media's Coverage of Domestic Terrorism," *Justice Quarterly* 23, no. 4 (December 2006): 428–461; quotation is on p. 428.
2. Ibid., p. 457.

world but also at Times Square on New Year's Eve and at many other large public events.

Some of these fears are realistic; others are not. Americans are more likely to die from natural causes than from violent crime, but people do not always respond in terms of probabilities. Research suggests that women and the elderly have the greatest fears of violent crime, but as we have already noted, they are less likely than young people, or than men in general, to become victims. Still, both women and the elderly may perceive themselves as more vulnerable to crime and less able to protect themselves from violent predators than do men and the young. Compared with men, women take far more precautions to protect themselves. They are more likely to avoid being alone on the streets at night.

The nature of crimes against women is important in understanding their fear of violent crime, especially rape. This violent crime usually takes longer to commit than other crimes, thus increasing the victim's contact with the offender and the probability of additional personal injury. Studies of the effects of rape show that it is one of the most traumatic of all personal crimes. In addition, the victim may be blamed for the rape. Rape may be feared, too, because of the inaccurate belief that in most cases it involves violence that goes beyond that of the rape itself.

Researchers have also found that women's fear of rape influences their fear of other personal crimes, a phenomenon referred to as the *shadow of sexual assault*. Thus, for example, when a woman is facing a robbery, she may fear that in addition to being a robbery victim, she will become a rape victim.[127] Two researchers who examined national data on college and university women found support for the shadow thesis, with the data showing that "college women's fear of rape is an inseparable companion to fear of other offenses while on campus during the day and night." The researchers concluded that college and university officials should develop policies that focus on the potential offenders—college men—as well as educate college women concerning the risks and how best to empower themselves to avoid becoming rape victims.[128]

The fear of crime should be analyzed more carefully in terms of the environment and the cues that might create unrealistic fear. One attempt to do so was made by scholars who analyzed *fear spots*, defined as "those specific places or areas where individuals feel fear of being victimized but where crime may not be frequent or where the police may not have recorded any criminal incidents either during the day or at night." The results suggested that fear may be greater when people have little chance of escaping, when there are places for potential offenders to hide and wait for their prospective victims, and when there is lack of prospect (the ability to obtain an open view by looking into or walking through the area). For example, lack of sufficient lighting affects a person's ability to look through an area and perhaps even walk through the area.

If these factors are found to be widely applicable to the fear of crime, the relationship raises obvious policy issues: Local and state governments may call for more effective lighting, fewer obstructions, more open escape routes, and so on. It is reasonable to assume that "understanding the causes of fear will help to better understand the fear-generating process and to develop effective fear reduction strategies."[129]

Another factor that deserves further study is the relationship between race and the fear of crime. A report by the Bureau of Justice Statistics disclosed that African Americans are three times as likely as whites to express fear of crime in their neighborhoods.[130] In addition, there is evidence that African Americans are seen as *symbolic assailants*;[131] their presence in large numbers evokes fear of crime even when the crime level is not high. Further, criminal justice personnel may be influenced by stereotypes of African Americans as dangerous, which may account for the larger incarceration rates of African Americans. In fact, in a study of state prison incarceration rates, investigators concluded: "That the presence of Latinos is not associated with imprisonment rate growth indicates that it is not minorities in general, but blacks in particular, who are perceived as threatening."[132]

The media also impact the extent and nature of fear. Two scholars who reviewed the literature in this area concluded that the media "play a substantial role in shaping beliefs and fear of crime." Local television has more impact than national television, but that impact differs by type of community. Those who live in communities with low violent crime rates are not as influenced by mass media reports on local crimes as are those who live in communities with high violent crime rates. The researchers also found reaction differences by race. However, they did not find support for the belief that people with low risks of victimization (women, the elderly, and the affluent) are particularly influenced by media depictions of crime.[133]

The fear of crime may have contributed to the widespread ownership of guns. In fact, the earlier research on gun behavior explored what researchers referred to as the *fear and loathing* hypothesis, which meant that individuals carry guns because they fear or perceive that they might become crime victims. There is some support for this approach in the literature.[134] The next section examines some aspects of the use of weapons and crime.

Guns and Violent Crime

According to a 2010 Bureau of Justice report, 22 percent of all violent crimes in 2009 were committed by an offender who carried a weapon. In 8 percent of those crimes, a firearm was used, but 28 percent of all robberies involved a firearm.[135] Many suggestions have been made for reducing this violence.

One suggestion for reducing gun-related violence is referred to as *pulling levers*, which means to focus police efforts on the small number of persons who are responsible for most of the violent gun-related crime in the area. This generally involves gang-related persons, especially in urban areas. With a problem-oriented approach, police focus on a particular crime problem (e.g., gun-related homicides) and attempt to identify key offenders, groups, and behavior patterns identified with that problem. The police cooperate with other agencies, such as those involving social services and community resources, and design strategies for targeting the offenders and deterring their behavior. For example, law enforcement officials identify gang members who might be at risk of using guns for violent acts and tell them that if they do, all sanctions, or levers, will be used against them. The deterrence message in Boston was thought to be related to a 60 percent reduction in youth homicides. Comparable results followed a similar approach in Minneapolis.[136] A study of a deterrence intervention in Indianapolis also brought similar declines in homicides, leading the investigator to conclude that the results in these three cities are consistent and have promise for reducing homicides.[137] Finally, there is evidence that this problem-oriented approach was significant in reducing gun homicides and other violent gun-related acts in Lowell, Massachusetts.[138]

Part of the problem is to understand why people possess and carry guns. A recent study comparing adults and juveniles with regard to gun possession, carrying, and use found a greater willingness among juveniles, compared to adults, to carry guns. In their sample of adult and juvenile arrestees who reported experience with guns, the researchers found that "[J]uveniles were four times as likely to report carrying a gun on a daily basis and twice as likely to indicate that they had fired a gun in the last year when compared to adults." Once they have acquired a gun, juveniles are not likely to be deterred from carrying or using it by legislation or other gun control efforts. In contrast, in the face of gun control efforts, adults were more likely to be deterred from gun use, although not from gun acquisition.[139]

One suggestion for reducing gun-related violence is to enact legislation.

Gun Control Legislation

General gun control legislation at the federal level followed John Hinckley Jr.'s attempted assassination of President Ronald Reagan in 1981. The Brady Handgun Violence Prevention Act, called the *Brady bill* after Press Secretary James Brady, who was wounded during Hinckley's attack on the president, requires a five-day waiting period for purchasing handguns. When the permanent provisions of the Brady bill became effective, the statute covered all gun purchases, not just handguns.[140]

Lanette McDonald, whose son Derrion Albert was killed in Chicago on 24 September 2009 by a group of teens as he walked home from school, holds a sign outside the high school he attended. A vigil was held there in memory of her 16-year-old son, an honors student. Cell phone pictures recorded the group beating and kicking Albert to death. In December 2010, one teen, aged 14 at the time of the crime, was convicted of first-degree murder. Other teens were awaiting trial.

States and municipalities also have gun control statutes. A critical issue regarding gun control legislation, however, is the constitutionality of the statutes. In 2007, a three-judge panel of a federal court in Washington, D.C., held that, under the Second Amendment's provision of a "right to bear arms" (see Appendix A), individuals have a right to possess handguns in their homes. The panel of justices held that the strict gun control statute was too broad. The full court refused to review the case, and it was appealed to the U.S. Supreme Court, which agreed to hear the case. *District of Columbia v. Heller* involved Dick Heller, a D.C. special police officer, who had the authority to carry a firearm while on duty but was denied permission under a D.C. statute to keep a weapon at home. In a 5-to-4 decision, the U.S. Supreme Court held that the Second Amendment (see Appendix A) protects the right of an individual to possess a firearm in his home, even though it is not for purposes of the militia, and to use that firearm for traditional legal purposes, such as self-defense within the home.[141]

On 28 June 2010, as its term ended, the U.S. Supreme Court announced its decision in the case of *McDonald v. Chicago*. This case involved a Chicago *ordinance,* whereas the *Heller* case involved a *federal statute.* Thus, the case raised the issue of whether the Second Amendment also applies to a local ordinance. The Seventh Circuit had ruled that the amendment does not apply to states and their subordinates, municipalities. The Supreme Court disagreed.

The Chicago ordinance, which effectively banned essentially all citizens from possessing handguns, was challenged by citizens who alleged that the ordinance prevented their protecting themselves in their homes. One of the petitioners, Otis McDonald, a man in his 70s, was a community activist involved in policing strategies. He had received violent threats from persons dealing in illegal drugs. He and the other petitioners argued that the Chicago ordinance violated the Second Amendment as applied to the states through the Fourteenth Amendment. The city argued that the Second Amendment does not apply to the states. Justice Samuel Alito, who wrote the opinion for the majority, noted that over the years, the U.S. Supreme Court had held that most of the Bill of Rights (the first 10 amendments) are incorporated into the Fourteenth Amendment (and thus applied to the states). The Second Amendment is no exception. The amendment's provision for the right to bear arms applies to the states, for it involves a right that is "fundamental to our scheme of ordered liberty" and "deeply rooted in this Nation's history and tradition." He discussed at length the Court's history concerning these issues and the methods by which it has held that certain amendments in the Bill of Rights apply to the states through the Fourteenth Amendment. He rejected Chicago's argument that the right to bear arms is distinct from other Bill of Rights' provisions in that it involves "the right to possess a deadly implement" and this involves security issues. Justice Alito wrote that all of the constitutional provisions that restrict prosecution and law enforcement are in the same category.[142]

In his last day on the bench, after almost 35 years of service, the third longest in history, Justice John Paul Stevens, joined by Justice Stephen Breyer, wrote a scathing dissent. He looked at the meaning of *fundamental rights,* insisting that the concept includes those rights that define oneself, the ability to do that which affects one's destiny and that of his or family, "and the right to be respected as a human being. Self-determination, bodily integrity, freedom of conscience, intimate relationships, political equality, dignity and respect—these are the central values we have found implicit in the concept of ordered liberty in the Fourteenth Amendment." In other words, these rights are *fundamental.* Fundamental rights, such as the right to free speech protected by the First Amendment (see Appendix A), can

be regulated by the government but only if the regulations follow strict guidelines that have been established by the Court over the years. Justice Stevens did not view the right to possess a handgun in one's home to constitute one of those fundamental rights. He argued that the right to self-defense does not include the right to use certain weapons for that defense. "It is a very long way from the proposition that the Fourteenth Amendment protects the right of self-defense to the conclusion that a city may not ban handguns." The Second Amendment was adopted to "protect the states from federal encroachment." Stevens concluded his long dissent with these words:

> Although impressively argued, the majority's decision to overturn more than a century of Supreme Court precedent and to unsettle a much longer tradition of state practice is not, in my judgment, built "upon respect for the teaching of history, solid recognition of the basic values that underlie our society, and wise application of the great roles that the doctrines of federalism and separation of powers have played in establishing and preserving American freedoms." Accordingly, I respectfully dissent.[143]

This case does not mean that states and municipalities may not in any way restrict the possession of guns. Indeed, in terms of the facts of both of these cases decided by the U.S. Supreme Court, the right to bear arms is restricted to one's home. The Court did not give clear indications of the nature of gun control legislation that might be constitutional. It is now left to states and municipalities to redesign their statutes and ordinances, and numerous lawsuits can be expected over the various issues.

The Effects of Gun Control on Violence

Considerable research has been conducted on the effects of gun possession on violence and the escalation of violence as well as on the imposition of gun control policies to curb crimes. The results are often contradictory; a few studies are summarized here.

Criminologist Lawrence W. Sherman found that "directed police patrols in gun crime 'hot spots' can reduce gun crimes by increasing the seizures of illegally carried guns." When gun seizures by police increased by 65 percent, gun crimes decreased by 49 percent.[144]

Criminologists who looked at the effects of guns in the context of various threatening situations found that the effects of weapons did differ by situation. Attacks were less likely to follow threats when guns or knives were involved. With regard to the effects of guns, "the violence-increasing and violence-suppressing effects of gun possession and use almost exactly cancel each other out, making the net effect on the likelihood of the victim's death very close to zero." Thus, gun control may not only be ineffective in reducing crime, but permitting guns for self-defense may actually inhibit crime.[145]

Other scholars have reported different results with regard to whether the presence of weapons was likely to result in attacks. Two investigators "found that when a respondent possessed a gun or other weapon he was more likely to attack an opponent than when he did not have a weapon in his possession." But the attack was less likely by those with guns than by those in possession of weapons other than guns. It was suggested that the differences in findings between studies was due to the way the researchers defined the stages of conflict.[146]

These findings were questioned in a study of defensive gun use (DGU), in which researchers concluded that DGU may provide deterrence in some cases, but it does not in others. Specifically, DGU "does not significantly reduce the odds of injury for women or victims residing in low-income homes. The findings also indicate that the deterrent benefit of DGU is limited to urban settings." Thus, DGU is not "uniformly effective at reducing the likelihood of injury during assaults and robberies."[147]

A study of DGU among convicted felons found no support for the assumption that DGU provokes injuries. But the study raised questions about the deterrent effect of DGU, highlighting that, "[W]e are not yet in a position to conclude that a relatively large number of DGUs implies a large social benefit derived from the availability and use of guns." In conclusion, "The DGU concept must be more clearly elaborated and empirical evidence must continue to be gathered before these types of gun uses can be equated with clear social benefits."[148]

After an examination of the effects of drug dependence, gang membership, and gun possession on repeat offenses following the release of 332 young men aged 17 to 24 from prison, investigators concluded that although drug dependence and gang membership, along with race and institutional behavior, were predictive of repeat offenses after release, gun ownership was directly connected. Gun possession was so pervasive pre- and post-prison that it was impossible to measure any unique effect that it might have had on post-prison criminal acts. The researchers looked at the age-graded social control theory of Sampson and Laub and the control theory of Hirschi (see again Chapter 6) and noted the importance of working with institutionalized young men on reducing the impact that gang membership and drug involvement have upon their release from prison. Additionally, given the strong relationship between their institutional behavior and repeat offenses after release, attention should be given to prison programs that might improve that variable.[149]

An analysis by researchers for the Centers for Disease Control and Prevention (CDC) of dozens of studies of gun control laws led to the conclusion that there is "insufficient evidence to determine the effectiveness of any of the firearms laws." The researchers noted this does not mean that gun control laws are not effective, but the research does not prove it.[150]

Charles Wellford and others addressed the issue of what we know about gun violence control in a special issue of *Crime and Public Policy* in November 2005. In his editorial introduction, Wellford noted the lack of research and the lack of meaningful theories on violence and emphasized the need for greater research and theoretical attention to the relationship between gun control and violence. He stated, "With better data, research-driven theory, and research at the appropriate level of analysis, we can make progress. Until then research in this area will continue to be difficult to conduct and use."[151]

The Media, Pornography, and Violent Crime

This final section looks at the impact of the media and pornography on violent crime. Concern with the potential effect of the media on criminal behavior has been raised in particular by those who are fighting to control or eliminate pornography, especially when it involves minors. The 1986 publication of the final report of the Commission on Pornography (The Meese Report) focused nationwide attention on the link between pornography and aggressive behavior. The commission concluded that there is a causal link between some forms of aggressive behavior and pornography.

Two members of the commission issued a strong dissent from the finding that hard-core pornography may cause violent behavior. According to one of the dissenters, "the idea that eleven individuals studying in their spare time could complete a comprehensive report on so complex a matter in so constricted a time frame is simply unrealistic. . . . No self-respecting investigator would accept conclusions based on such a study." Many social scientists agree with this criticism. Others point out that the commission's conclusions contradict those of a 1970 presidential panel "which found no link between violence and sexually explicit material."[152]

In defense of its conclusions, some members of the commission argued that since 1970, the nature of sexually explicit material had changed and become more violent and more explicit.

Psychologists who have studied the effects of pornography on behavior have reported that there is little proof that laboratory studies of sexual aggression give evidence of sexual aggression in real life. It is more likely that antisocial attitudes and behavior toward women in particular occur after exposure to violent material regardless of whether that material is considered pornographic. According to one group of researchers, "no scientifically reputable data exist that indicate a pornography-violence connection in serial murders."[153]

Other researchers take the position that there may be a relationship between pornography and violence. Criminologist Ray Surette, whose analysis of the impact of the media on crime covers many aspects of the relationship between the media, especially television, and criminal behavior, suggested that we are more aggressive socially because of our mass media. But that social aggression is not always criminal, and most crime is not violent. Research implies that the relationship between the media and crime may be indirect and that it is greater in property than in violent crimes, with the possible exception of the impact of pornography. According to Surette,

> There is increasing evidence that even nonexplicit, non-X-rated depictions of sexual violence against women may evoke negative social effects such as trivializing rape and supporting aggression against women, and the potential influence of sexually violent material on predisposed males poses a clear danger.[154]

One study contradicted this statement and found no relationship between exposure to sexually oriented magazines and rape rates.[155] Another noted that, although sexually explicit material may be offensive to some, it has not been shown "sufficiently harmful to justify state intrusion."[156]

An unpublished report that surfaced in the summer of 2007, based on a study of 155 male inmates incarcerated at the Federal Correctional Complex in Butner, North Carolina (the only federal treatment center for sex offenders), could shed light on the impact of pornography on violence. The study was conducted by psychologists treating the inmates who volunteered to participate in the research. The therapists stated that the 155 men reported 1,777 victims, although only 75 had been identified prior to the sentencing of these offenders. The researchers concluded that there may be many more child abusers who are accessing child pornography on the Internet. Their research report was accepted for publication in the *Journal of Family Violence*, but prior to publication, it was withdrawn by the federal Bureau of Prisons, stating that the report did not meet agency standards. The therapists/researchers found that 85 percent of their sample of inmates convicted for online trafficking in child pornography reported having molested at least one child. This contrasted to estimates of between 35 and 40 percent in other studies. According to a board member of the National Center for Missing and Exploited Children, the prison study was based on a limited sample, but "even if these numbers turn out to be a bit fuzzy, the implications are astounding."[157]

Data on the dissemination of pornography are unreliable, but the U.S. Department of Justice (DOJ) has estimated that over 100,000 illegal websites post pornography, with more than 20,000 images posted on the Internet each week. Efforts to combat such postings of children resulted in the establishment of Project Safe Childhood, which "marshals federal, state, and local resources to better lo-cate, apprehend, and prosecute individuals who exploit children via the internet, as well as to identify and rescue victims." As an example of the efforts of this program, in November 2009, DOJ announced that William Travis Brown, 39, was sentenced to 20 years in prison followed by lifetime supervision for his conviction for transporting and possessing child pornography.[158]

There are, however, legal issues regarding the statutes that have been enacted to combat illegal pornography.

Legal Issues and Pornography

The U.S. Supreme Court has recognized the First Amendment right of free speech (see Appendix A) as embracing the right of adults to view certain forms of pornography. This does not include a right to view pornography involving minors, nor does it include a right to view obscenity. The problem comes in defining the term *obscene*. The Supreme Court has held that to be obscene a work must meet all the following criteria:

1. [T]he average person, applying contemporary community standards, would find that the work, taken as a whole, appeals to the prurient interest.
2. [T]he work depicts or describes, in a patently offensive way, sexual conduct specifically defined by the applicable state [or federal] law, and
3. [T]he work, taken as a whole, lacks serious literary, artistic, political, or scientific value.[159]

Prurient interest is defined legally as "a shameful or morbid interest in nudity, sex, or excretion."[160] The U.S. Supreme Court has ruled that state statutes must be judged by local, not national, standards.[161]

In addition to problems of defining what is meant by *obscene,* attempts to criminalize what people possess and view have run into other legal issues. In particular, issues have been raised recently with regard to the Internet and the viewing of child pornography.

Congress has made numerous efforts to protect children from pornography and other material that might be harmful to them. One of those laws was part of the Communications Decency Act of 1996 (CDA). In 1997, in the case of *Reno v. American Civil Liberties Union*, the U.S. Supreme Court held that two portions of the act aimed at preventing minors from accessing pornography on the Internet were unconstitutional. The CDA criminalizes the knowing transmission of obscene or indecent messages to any recipient under 18 and prohibits knowingly sending or displaying to a person under 18 any message "that, in context, depicts or describes, in terms patently offensive as measured by community standards, sexual or excretory activities or organs." Affirmative defenses are provided for those acting in good faith to exclude minors from viewing the material. After a discussion of the nature of the Internet, the U.S. Supreme Court stated that the World Wide Web is "both a vast library including millions of readily available and indexed publications and a sprawling mall offering goods and services."[162]

The U.S. Supreme Court described Internet pornography as extending "from the modestly titillating to the hardest core." The Court noted, however, that generally the sexually explicit materials are preceded by warnings about their context and that, unlike listening to materials on the radio or watching television, accessing materials on the Internet requires affirmative acts beyond that of turning a dial.

The U.S. Supreme Court's analysis was lengthy and involved complicated legal issues, but in essence, the Court held that the statute was unconstitutional because it was too broad. Statutes that infringe upon First Amendment free speech rights must be narrowly tailored, and this one was not. The act encompassed material that adults have a right to see, and in the view of the Supreme Court, there are no realistic and economically reasonable methods for preventing minors from viewing the material without infringing on the rights of adults. In the words of the U.S. Supreme Court,

> It is true that we have repeatedly recognized the governmental interest in protecting children from harmful materials. But that interest does not justify an unnecessarily broad suppression of speech addressed to adults. As we have explained, the Government may not "reduce the adult population . . . to . . . only what is fit for children." Regardless of the strength of the government's interest in protecting children, '[t]he level of discourse reaching a mailbox simply cannot be limited to that which would be suitable for a sandbox.'[163]

In 2003, however, the U.S. Supreme Court upheld a provision of the Children's Online Protection Act (COPA), which requires libraries to place filters on their computers so that children cannot access pornography when they ask to use library computers. Adults who wish to view pornography may have the filters removed. Failure to comply with the statute results in the loss of federal funds available to libraries to enhance their Internet access.[164]

Virtual Child Pornography

In 2002, the U.S. Supreme Court decided the case of *Ashcroft v. The Free Speech Coalition*.[165] This case was appealed from a lower federal court decision that held in 1999 that some provisions of the Child Pornography Prevention Act of 1996 (CPPA) violated the First Amendment of the U.S. Constitution. The act prohibits not only pornographic depictions of actual children but also "any visual depiction including any photograph, film, video, picture, or computer or computer-generated image or picture" that "is, or appears to be, of a minor engaging in sexually explicit conduct." The phrase "or appears to be" includes what is referred to as *virtual child pornography*, in which the computer is used to generate pictures of children or to change adult images to look like children, and the Supreme Court found that language too broad. A second portion of the statute on which the Supreme Court based its opinion criminalized any prohibited image "advertised, promoted, presented, described, or distributed in such a manner that conveys the impression" that it depicts "a minor engaged in sexually explicit conduct." The Supreme Court held that the phrase "conveys the impression" is too broad. The Court cited several examples of virtual child pornography that could result in prosecutions under the language of the statute but that are part of accepted literature, such as Shakespeare's *Romeo and Juliet*. Those characters are only 14, but the impression is that they consummated their relationship; that sex act could, under the language of the CPPA, be considered what "appears to be a minor engaged in sexually explicit conduct," even though adults played the parts.

The government's attorneys argued that virtual child pornography might encourage persons to become pedophiles and to molest children. The U.S. Supreme Court agreed that might happen but stated that the tendency of speech to encourage criminal behavior is not per se a reason to ban that speech. There is no clear evidence to support a causal relationship between viewing pornography and engaging in violent criminal behavior, but it is possible that if scientists could show such a relationship, the U.S. Supreme Court would hold differently in such cases. For now, though, the Court emphasized that the First Amendment right to free speech is the beginning of freedom and thought. And although children should not be permitted to view pornography, stated the Court, "speech within the rights of adults to hear may not be silenced completely in an attempt to shield children from it."[166]

Congress reacted to the case by passing the Prosecutorial Remedies and Other Tools to End the Exploitation of Children Today Act of 2003 (the PROTECT Act), a lengthy statute that contains provisions aimed at protecting children from kidnapping, sexual assaults, and other crimes as well as from pornography.[167] The statute was challenged in the case of *United States v. Williams* in which a federal court in Alabama reversed the pandering conviction of Michael Williams and upheld his conviction for possession of child pornography.[168]

Williams had posted on the Internet that he had good pictures of a child and would trade those for other pictures of toddlers. After several exchanges with an undercover law enforcement officer, Williams sent seven images of children, aged approximately 5 to 15, displaying their genitals or engaging in sexually explicit activity. A search of Williams's computer uncovered other depictions of child pornography as well as pictures of sadomasochistic conduct. Williams was arrested and charged with the aforementioned offenses.

The pandering charge at issue in this case was based on the act of advertising, promoting, presenting, distributing, or soliciting real or purported material "in a manner that reflects the belief or that is intended to cause another to believe" that the materials involve child pornography. The 11th Circuit held that those words are unconstitutionally broad because they could cover anyone who brags about having child pornography but does not actually possess any. The U.S. Supreme Court reversed the 11th Circuit in *Williams* and upheld the constitutionality of the PROTECT Act. According to Justice Antonin Scalia, who wrote the opinion for the Court, the First Amendment concerns in the previous statute were eliminated by the fact that the PROTECT Act limits the crime to the pandering of child pornography and the requirement that the panderer believes and states that the depictions are of real children or that he or she communicates in a way designed to make others so believe.[169]

In June 2004, the U.S. Supreme Court decided *Ashcroft v. The American Civil Liberties Union*. This case involved the amended child protection law enacted in 1998, the 1998 Child Online Protection Act (COPA), which had never taken effect due to an injunction. The COPA criminalizes knowingly placing on a commercial website within the unrestricted reach of minors material that is "harmful to minors." The lower courts had granted a preliminary injunction against the enforcement of the statute, and the U.S. Supreme Court upheld that position on the grounds that the statute violates the First Amendment right to free speech. According to the Court, the government did not show that less restrictive alternatives proposed by the Internet providers were not sufficient to meet the purpose of COPA. In fact, the U.S. Supreme Court stated that those alternatives "may be more effective than the provisions of COPA."[170]

In 2007, a lower federal appellate court issued a permanent injunction holding that COPA was a violation of the First Amendment free speech right, impermissibly broad, and ineffective. The judge's opinion stated that despite his regret at having to overturn another effort by Congress to protect children, "perhaps we do the minors of the country harm if First Amendment protections, which they will with age inherit fully, are chipped away in the name of their protection." The case was affirmed by the Circuit Court of Appeals, and the U.S. Supreme Court refused to review the case, thus permitting the decision to stand.[171]

Summary

This chapter covers a wide range of criminal activity. Its contents illustrate the difficulty of studying crime by types. Many categories of people commit the crimes covered in these discussions.

The chapter began with a brief discussion of criminal types and an overview of serious violent crimes. It then turned to an analysis of serious violent crimes. The four serious violent crimes, as categorized by the FBI's *Uniform Crime Reports*, were featured: murder and nonnegligent manslaughter, forcible rape, robbery, and aggravated assault. For each of these crimes (as well as those to follow in subsequent sections), data were given (when available), and social science research was considered. In particular, there was an emphasis on criminological theories as they have been applied to the crimes. Each crime was also defined and, in most cases, accompanied by an illustrative criminal statute. The recent data on serious violent crimes were noted along with attempts to explain them.

The chapter then looked at violent crimes that are not part of the FBI's four most serious crimes, although many are serious, with some resulting in death and thus involving one of the four serious violent crimes. The first focus on these violent crimes was domestic violence. The chapter gave a definition and a brief overview of the problems of collecting and analyzing data before detailing the major types of domestic violence: intimate personal violence (IPV), child abuse (including statutory rape and incest, along with a discussion of the long-term effects of child abuse), and elder abuse.

The next three individual violent crimes were those of kidnapping, hate crimes, and stalking. The discussions included examples of statutes as well as attempts to explain the commission of these crimes, such as social disorganization and the routine activity approach. In the hate crime discussion, reference was made to the recent U.S. Supreme Court decision on cross burning, *Virginia v. Black*, along with the most recent FBI data on hate crimes.

Considerable attention was given to terrorism, ranging from definitions and examples to recent legislative changes since the 9/11 terrorist attacks. In particular, the USA Patriot Act was analyzed, along with the development of the Department of Homeland Security (DHS) and the Transportation Security Administration (TSA). Finally, brief attention was given to the 9/11 Commission Report.

The fear of crime is an expected reaction to violence, but some fears are not realistic. Yet they are important, and the chapter looked at some of the ways women and the elderly, in particular, change their lifestyles because of their fears.

Violence is frequently associated with the use of weapons, especially guns. The discussion of gun control underscored legislative efforts to control such gun violence.

Finally, the potential effects of the media on behavior were analyzed in the context of pornography, a subject that is attracting more extensive research today. In particular, social scientists are exploring whether exposure to pornography is related to sexual offenses against women and children. A belief that there is a relation has led to more extensive legislation in this area, some of which has been challenged successfully as a violation of the constitutional right to free speech.

Study Questions

1. What are the problems with attempting to study crime by types, such as murder?

2. Define and analyze the following: the *year-and-a-day rule*, *mens rea*, *felony murder*, and *manslaughter*.

3. How have violent crime data changed in recent years?

4. Explain the relationship of gender and race to violent crime data.

5. What does research tell us about race, gender, and murder?

6. Should marital rape and date rape be included in the FBI category of forcible rape? Explain your answer.

7. Should statutory rape be included in the FBI category of forcible rape? Explain your answer. What should be the age limits regarding statutory rape?

8. Discuss the difficulties of getting accurate data on rape.

9. What do we know about males as rape victims?

10. Why do people rape?

11. Why is robbery considered a violent crime? What is meant by the element of asportation? By home-invasion robbery? What is the relationship between gender and robbery?

12. What is meant by "code of the street"?

13. What is the relationship between social-psychological variables and violent behavior?

14. How might the routine activity approach explain the violent victimization of college students?

15. What is meant by the "shadow of sexual assault"?

16. Distinguish between assault and battery.

17. Define *domestic violence,* and explain the limitations of the definition and the problems with gathering data on the crime. Define *intimate partner violence (IPV)*.

18. Explain the types of violence against children.

19. Distinguish statutory rape from incest, and discuss the implications of each crime.

20. Define *elder abuse*, and explore the types and implications of this form of domestic violence.

21. Contrast male and female batterers and the reasons for their violence.

22. Define *kidnapping*, and note recent examples.

23. Explore the various types of hate crimes, and discuss their implications. What are the legal implications of cross burning?

24. What is stalking, and why is the crime getting so much attention today?

25. What is meant by the word *terrorism*? Discuss two examples of recent terrorist acts. How should society react to those acts?

26. How does terrorism differ from other violent crimes?

27. How do terrorist victims differ from victims of other violent crimes?

28. What are the highlights of the Antiterrorism and Effective Death Penalty Act of 1996?

29. Discuss the implications of the fear of crime.

30. What is the relationship, if any, between pornography and crime?

31. Discuss recent U.S. Supreme Court decisions regarding gun control.

Brief Essay Assignments

1. Define each of the *UCR* serious violent crimes, and discuss the latest trends in data.

2. Discuss the theories, presented earlier in this text, that you think best explain each of the four *UCR* serious violent crimes.

3. Analyze the legislative reactions to the 9/11 terrorist attacks, and summarize the recommendations of the 9/11 Commission.

4. Analyze the recent developments in gun control.

5. Elaborate on the recent congressional attempts to prevent minors from viewing pornography on the Internet. How have courts reacted to these efforts?

Internet Activities

1. Stalking continues to be a frequent and serious crime in the United States. Learn more about the prevalence and impact of this crime by logging on to the National Center for Victims of Crime's Stalking Resource center, at http://www.ncvc.org/src/main.aspx?dbID=dash_Home, accessed 20 October 2010. What are the federal laws regarding this offense? Find your state statutes on this website. How are they similar to or different from federal laws?

2. To gain more information on hate crimes, log on to the FBI's "Hate Crime Statistics" website at http://www2.fbi.gov/ucr/cius2009/hate_crime/index.html, accessed 18 December

2010. Find out the characteristics of hate crime offenders and victims. At what types of locations do most hate crimes take place?

Notes

1. "The Plague of Violent Crime," *Newsweek* (23 March 1981), p. 46.
2. *U.S. News and World Report* (10 April 1989), pp. 20–21.
3. Don C. Gibbons, "Offender Typologies—Two Decades Later," *British Journal of Criminology* 15 (April 1975): 148, 152, 153.
4. Federal Bureau of Investigation, *Crime in the United States, Uniform Crime Reports 2009*, http://www2.fbi.gov/ucr/cius2009/offenses/violent_crime/index.html, accessed 19 October 2010.
5. Jennifer L. Truman and Michael R. Rand, National Crime Victimization Survey, *Criminal Victimization, 2009* (October 2010), p. 1, http://bjs.ojp.usdoj.gov/content/pub/pdf/cv09.pdf, accessed 18 October 2010.
6. Rev. Code Wash., Section 9A.32.010 (2010).
7. Cal Pen Code, Section 187(a) (2010).
8. Protection of Unborn Children Act, USCS, Article 18, Section 1841 (2010).
9. Cal Pen Code, Section 194 (2010).
10. M.R.S., Title 17-A, Section 202 (2010).
11. Cal Pen Code, Section 192(a) (2010).
12. Cal Pen Code, Section 192(b) (2010).
13. Federal Bureau of Investigation, *Crime in the United States: Uniform Crime Reports 2009*, http://www2.fbi.gov/ucr/cius2009/offenses/violent_crime/murder-homicide.html, accessed 18 October 2010.
14. Federal Bureau of Investigation, "Expanded Homicide Data," *Crime in the United States: Uniform Crime Reports 2009*, http://www2.fbi.gov/ucr/cius2009/offenses/expanded_information/homicide.html, accessed 18 October 2010.
15. María Veléz, Lauren J. Kirvo, and Ruth D. Peterson, "Structural Inequality and Homicide: An Assessment of the Black-White Gap in Killings," *Criminology* 41, no. 3 (August 2003): 645–672.
16. Candace Kruttschnitt and Kristin Carbone-Lopez, "Moving Beyond the Stereotypes: Women's Subjective Accounts of Their Violent Crime," *Criminology* 44, no. 2 (May 2006): 321–352.
17. David Finkelhor and Kersti Yllo, "Forced Sex in Marriage: A Preliminary Research Report," *Crime and Delinquency* 28 (July 1982): 459.
18. O.C.G.A, Section 16-6-1 (2010).
19. Eric P. Baumer et al., "Changes in Police Notification for Rape, 1973–2000," *Criminology* 41, no. 3 (August 2003): 841–872; paraphrased material is on p. 842, citations omitted.
20. Ibid., p. 864.
21. Bonnie S. Fisher et al., "Acknowledging Sexual Victimization As Rape: Results from a National-Level Study," *Justice Quarterly* 20, no. 3 (September 2003): 536–574, quotations are on pp. 566–567.
22. "Forcible Rape," Federal Bureau of Investigation, *Crime in the United States: Uniform Crime Reports 2009*, http://www2.fbi

.gov/ucr/cius2009/offenses/violent_crime/forcible_rape.html, accessed 18 October 2010.
23. Truman and Rand, *Criminal Victimization, 2009*, pp. 1, 2.
24. Paul H. Gebhard et al., *Sex Offenders* (New York: Harper & Row, 1965), pp. 197–205.
25. See Menachem Amir, "Forcible Rape," *Federal Probation* 31 (March 1967): 51–58; Amir, *Patterns in Forcible Rape* (Chicago: University of Chicago Press, 1971).
26. A. Nicholas Groth and H. Jean Birnbaum, *Men Who Rape: The Psychology of the Offender* (New York: Plenum, 1979), pp. 5–6.
27. Larry Baron and Murray A. Straus, *Four Theories of Rape in American Society: A State Level Analysis* (New Haven, CT: Yale University Press, 1989); quotation is on p. 57.
28. Fla. Stat., Section 812.135 (2010).
29. "Neighbors of Home Invasion Victims Demand Stricter Repeat-Offender Laws," *New York Times*, late ed. (16 August 2007), p. 4; "Petit Asks for Investigation," *Hartford Courant* (Connecticut) (7 November 2009), p. 1.
30. Federal Bureau of Investigation, "Robbery," *Crime in the United States: Uniform Crime Reports 2009*, http://www2.fbi.gov/ucr/cius2009/offenses/violent_crime/robbery.html, accessed 20 October 2010.
31. Stewart D'Allesio and Lisa Stolzenberg, "A Crime of Convenience: The Environment and Convenience Store Robbery," *Environment and Behavior* 22 (March 1990): 255–271; quotation is on p. 255.
32. *Robbery at Automated Teller Machines*, U.S. Department of Justice Resource Information Center (9 August 2006), http://www.cops.usdoj.gov/ric/ResourceSearch.aspx, accessed 18 October 2010.
33. Joan Petersilia et al., *Criminal Careers of Habitual Felons* (Washington, D.C.: U.S. Government Printing Office, 1978), pp. vii, xiii.
34. Jody Miller, "Up It Up: Gender and the Accomplishment of Street Robbery," *Criminology* 36 (February 1998): 37–66; quotation is on p. 60.
35. Ibid., p. 61. See also Jody Miller, "Feminist Theories of Women's Crime: Robbery as a Case Study," in *Of Crime and Criminality*, ed. Sally S. Simpson (Thousand Oaks, CA: Pine Forge Press, 2000), pp. 25–46.
36. D.C. Code, Title 22, Section 22–404.01 (2010).
37. Fla. Stat., Section 784–045 (2010).
38. "Aggravated Assault," Federal Bureau of Investigation, *Crime in the United States: Uniform Crime Reports 2009*, http://www2.fbi.gov/ucr/cius2009/offenses/violent_crime/aggravated_assault.html, accessed 18 October 2010.
39. See Elijah Anderson, *Code of the Street: Decency, Violence, and the Moral Life of the Inner City* (New York: W.W. Norton, 1999).
40. Eric A. Stewart and Ronald L. Simons, "Structure and Culture in African American Adolescent Violence: A Partial Test of the 'Code of the Street' Thesis," *Justice Quarterly* 23, no. 1 (March 2006): 2–33; quotation is on p. 2.
41. Eric A. Stewart and Ronald L. Simons, "Race, Code of the Street, and Violent Delinquency: A Multilevel Investigation of Neighborhood Street Culture and Individual Norms of Violence," *Criminology* 48, no. 2 (May 2010): 569–606; quotation is on p. 594.

42. Eric A. Stewart et al., "Assessing Neighborhood and Social Psychological Influences on Childhood Violence in an African-American Sample," *Criminology* 40, no. 4 (November 2002): 801–829.

43. Ibid., p. 821.

44. Joanne M. Kaufman, "Explaining the Race/Ethnicity-Violence Relationship: Neighborhood Context and Social Psychological Processes," *Justice Quarterly* 22, no. 2 (June 2005): 224–251; quotation is on p. 224.

45. Elizabeth Ehrhardt Mustaine and Richard Tewksbury, "Sexual Assault of College Women: A Feminist Interpretation of a Routine Activities Analysis," *Criminal Justice Review* 27, no. 1 (Spring 2002): 89–123; summarized material is on p. 89.

46. Ibid., p. 90.

47. Ibid., p. 91.

48. Ibid., p. 118.

49. Ibid., p. 119.

50. Violent Crime Control and Law Enforcement Act of 1994, Public Law 103–322 (13 September 1994), Title IV, "Violence Against Women."

51. Violence Against Women Act of 2000, P.L. 106–386 (2000).

52. Bureau of Justice Statistics, Department of Justice, "Intimate Partner Violence Declined Between 1993 and 2004," Press Release (28 December 2007), http://bjs.ojp.usdoj.gov/content/pub/press/ipvpr.cfm, accessed 18 October 2010; Shannan Catalano, Bureau of Justice Statistics, "Intimate Partner Violence in the United States," (December 2007), http://bjs.ojp.usdoj.gov/content/pub/pdf/ipvus.pdf, accessed 18 October 2010.

53 Patsy Klaus, *Crime and the Nation's Households, 2005* (Washington, Bureau of Justice Statistics (April 2007), pp. 1–2, http://bjs.ojp.usdoj.gov/content/pub/pdf/cnh05.pdf, accessed 21 October 2010.

54. Shannan Catalano, Bureau of Justice Statistics, "Intimate Partner Violence in the U.S.: Circumstances," (December 2007), pp. 1–5, http://bjs.ojp.usdoj.gov/content/intimate/circumstances.cfm, accessed 18 October 2010.

55. Shannan Catalano et al., Bureau of Justice Statistics, *Female Victims of Violence* (September 2009), p. 2, http://bjs.ojp.usdoj.gov/content/pub/pdf/fvv.pdf, accessed 18 October 2010.

56. Ibid., p. 3.

57. Erica L. Smith and Donald J. Farole Jr., Bureau of Justice Statistics, *Profile of Intimate Partner Violence Cases In Large Urban Counties* (October 2009), p. 1, http://bjs.ojp.usdoj/content/pub/pdf/pipvcluc.pdf, accessed 18 October 2010.

58. National Institute on Alcohol Abuse and Alcoholism (NIAAA), "A Snapshot of Annual High-Risk College Drinking Consequences," http://www.niaaa.nih.gov/Publications/Pages/default.aspx, accessed 18 October 2010.

59. Richard J. Gelles, "The Truth About Husband Abuse," in Gelles, *Family Violence* (Beverly Hills, CA: Sage, 1987), chap. 8, p. 137.

60. Mildred Daley Pagelow, *Women-Battering: Victims and Their Experiences* (Beverly Hills, CA: Sage, 1981), p. 54.

61. Donna M. Moore, ed., *Battered Women* (Beverly Hills, CA: Sage, 1979), p. 20.

62. Richard J. Gelles, *The Violent Home* (Beverly Hills, CA: Sage, 1974), pp. 95–110.

63. Quoted in *State v. Kelly*, 478 A.2d 364, 371 (N.J. 1984). See also Lenore Walker, *The Battered Woman* (New York: Harper & Row, 1979).

64. Bureau of Justice Statistics, *Preventing Domestic Violence Against Women* (Washington, D.C.: U.S. Department of Justice, August 1986), pp. 1–2.

65. Moore, *Battered Women*, pp. 16–19.

66. Elizabeth Kandel-Englander, "Wife Battering and Violence Outside the Family," *Journal of Interpersonal Violence* 7 (December 1992): 462–470.

67. Kathleen Daly and Meda Chesney-Lind, "Feminism and Criminology," in *Criminological Theory: Past to Present*, ed. Francis T. Cullen and Robert Agnew (Los Angeles: Roxbury, 1999), pp. 355–374; quotation is on pp. 360–361.

68. Leana A. Bouffard et al., "Gender Differences in Specialization in Intimate Partner Violence: Comparing the Gender Symmetry and Violent Resistance Perspectives," *Justice Quarterly* 25, no. 3 (September 2008): 570–594; quotation is on p. 590.

69. Cal Pen Code, Section 273.5 (2010).

70. Melissa Labriola et al., "Do Batterer Programs Reduce Recidivism? Results from a Randomized Trial in the Bronx," *Justice Quarterly* 25, no. 2 (June 2008): 252–282; quotation is on p. 252.

71. Smith and Farole, *Profile of Intimate Partner Violence Cases in Large Urban Counties*, p. 1.

72. U.S. Department of Health and Human Services, Children's Bureau, *Child Maltreatment 2008*, chap. 3, http://www.acf.hhs.gov/programs/cb/pubs/cm08/chapter3.htm#child, accessed 18 October 2010.

73. David Finkelhor and Lisa M. Jones, *Explanations for the Decline in Child Sex Abuse Cases* (Washington, D.C.: U.S. Department of Health and Human Services, 2004), as quoted in "Researchers Assess Soundness of Drop in Child Sex Abuse Reports," *Criminal Justice Newsletter* (12 March 2004), p. 1.

74. "Between Teacher and Student: Sex Cases and the Suspicions Are Increasing," *New York Times* (20 June 2007), p. 20.

75. Reported in "Counselor Is Charged: Youth Worker Helped Lover, 17, Flee Detention Center Outing, Police Say," *Baltimore Sun* (2 October 2009), p. 3.

76. See Anne L. Horton et al., *The Incest Perpetrator: A Family Member No One Wants to Treat* (Newbury Park, CA: Sage, 1989).

77. See Robert L. Geiser, *Hidden Victims: The Sexual Abuse of Children* (Boston: Beacon Press, 1979).

78. Ibid., p. 68.

79. "Incest," National Center for Victims of Crime, http://www.ncvc.org/ncvc/main.aspx?dbName=DocumentViewer&DocumentID=32360, accessed 18 October 2010.

80. Gelles, *Family Violence*, pp. 32–37, 42–53.

81. *Preventing Delinquency Through Improved Child Protection Services* (Washington, D.C.: Juvenile Justice Clearinghouse, 2001).

82. "Childhood Abuse and Adult Stress," *New York Times* (2 August 2000), p. 14; Rachel Yehuda, "Risk and Resilience in Posttraumatic Stress Disorder," *Journal of Clinical Psychiatry* 65 (2004): 29–36.

83. Caroline Wolf Harlow, *Prior Abuse Reported by Inmates and Probationers* (April 1999), p. 1, http://bjs.ojp.usdoj.gov/content/pub/pdf/parip.pdf, accessed 20 October 2010.

84. For a recent analysis of the effects on children of exposure to violence, see Christ L. Gibson et al., "Secondary Exposure to Violence During Childhood and Adolescence: Does Neighborhood Context Matter?" *Justice Quarterly* 26, no. 1 (March 2009): 30–57.

85. National Institute of Justice, *Early Childhood Victimization Among Incarcerated Adult Male Felons* (Washington, D.C.: U.S. Department of Justice, 1998), cited in "Two-Thirds of Prisoners Were Abused as Children, Study Finds," *Criminal Justice Newsletter* 29 (15 April 1998): 7–8.

86. See, for example, "'Every Death Was Avoidable,' Witness Says," *Times-Picayune* (New Orleans) (6 September 2007), p. 1.

87. See Patsy Klaus, Bureau of Justice Statistics Special Report, *Crimes Against Persons Age 65 or Older, 1993–2002* (Washington, D.C.: U.S. Department of Justice, January 2005).

88. Cal Pen Code, Section 368 (2010).

89. Patient Protection and Affordable Care Act, P.L. 111–148 (2010).

90. Cal Pen Code, Part I, Title 8, Chapter 3, Section 207(a) (2010).

91. See Cal Pen Code, Section 207(d) (2010).

92. USCS, Title 28, Section 1738A (2010).

93. *Thompson v. Thompson*, 484 U.S. 174 (1988).

94. See, for example, Carole S. Gailor and Cathy C. Hunt, "When a Parent Steals a Child Away," *Trial* 42, no. 13 (December 2006): 42–47.

95. Ohio Rev. Code Ann., Title 29, Chapter 2929, Section 2919.23 (2010).

96. The Matthew Shepard and James Byrd Jr. Hate Crimes Prevention Act is codified at USCS, Title 28, Section 534 (2010).

97. Federal Bureau of Investigation, "FBI Releases 2009 Hate Crime Statistics" (22 November 2010), http://www.fbi.gov/news/pressrel/pressreleases/2009hatecrimestats_112210, accessed 16 December 2010.

98. Mindy S. Wilson and R. Barry Ruback, "Hate Crimes in Pennsylvania, 1984–99: Case Characteristics and Police Responses," *Justice Quarterly* 20, no. 2 (June 2003): 373–398; excerpt is from pp. 391–395.

99. Ibid.

100. *Virginia v. Black*, 538 U.S. 343 (2003).

101. Va. Code Ann., Section 18.2-423 (2010).

102. *Virginia v. Black*, 538 U.S. 343 (2003).

103. Bureau of Justice Statistics Special Report, *Stalking/Intimidation*, http://bjs.ojp.usdoj.gov/index.cfm?ty=tp&tid=314, accessed 19 October 2010.

104. Ibid.

105. Public Law 104-201 (1997); USCS, Title 18, Section 2261 (2010).

106. Kan. Stat. Ann, Section 21-3438 (2009).

107. *State v. Bryan*, 910 P.2d 212 (Kan. 1999).

108. Cal Pen Code, Section 646.9(g) (2010).

109. Bonnie S. Fisher et al., "Being Pursued: Stalking Victimization in a National Study of College Women," *Criminology and Public Policy* 1, no. 2 (March 2002): 257–308; quotation is on p. 299.

110. Robert H. Kupperman, "Terrorism and Public Policy," in *American Violence and Public Policy: An Update on the National Commission on the Causes and Prevention of Violence*, ed. Lynn A. Curtis (New Haven, CT: Yale University Press, 1985), pp. 184, 188.

111. American Law Institute, *Model Penal Code*, Section 211.3.

112. Brian Crozier, *Terroristic Activity, International Terrorism Part 4: Hearings Before the Subcommittee to Investigate the Administration of the Internal Security Laws of the Senate Committee on the Judiciary*, 94th Cong., 1st Sess. 180 (1975), quoted in H. H. A. Cooper, "Terrorism: New Dimensions of Violent Criminality," *Cumberland Law Review* 9 (1978): 370.

113. National Advisory Committee on Criminal Justice Standards and Goals, *Disorders and Terrorism* (Washington, D.C.: U.S. Government Printing Office, 1976), p. 3.

114. H. H. A. Cooper, "Terrorism: The Problem of Definition Revisited," *American Behavioral Scientist* 44 (February 2001): 881–893; quotations are on pp. 883, 890, 891, and 892.

115. National Advisory Committee, *Disorders and Terrorism*, pp. 3–7.

116. Ted Robert Gurr, *Why Men Rebel* (Princeton, NJ: Princeton University Press, 1970), p. 232, quoted in Robert G. Bell, "The U.S. Response to Terrorism Against International Civil Aviation," in *Contemporary Terrorism: Selected Readings*, ed. John D. Elliott and Leslie K. Gibson (Gaithersburg, MD: International Association of Chiefs of Police, 1978), p. 191.

117. The defendant was charged with violating USCS, Title 18, Section 32 (2010).

118. Antiterrorism and Effective Death Penalty Act of 1996, 104th Cong., 2d Session, No. 104–518 (1996), codified at USCS, Title 18, Section 2254 (2010).

119. The USA Patriot Act of 2001, Public Law No. 207–296, revised and codified, USCS, Title 31, Section 5332 et seq. (2010).

120. Homeland Security and Combating Terrorism Act, Public Law 107–296 (2010).

121. Enhanced Border Security and Visa Entry Reform Act of 2002, USCS, Title 8, Section 7101 et seq. (2010).

122. Public Health Security and Bioterrorism Response Act of 2002, Public Law 107-188 (2010).

123. The commission was established by Public Law 107-306 (27 November 2002). The report is entitled *The 9/11 Commission Report: Final Report of the National Commission on Terrorist Attacks upon the United States*, authorized ed. (New York: Norton, 2004).

124. Ibid., p. xvi.

125. Ibid., pp. 399–400. The Intelligence Reform and Terrorism Prevention Act of 2004 is codified as Public Law 108-458 (2008).

126. For a review of the literature concerning these areas, see Bonnie S. Fisher and Jack L. Nasar, "Fear Spots in Relation to Microlevel Physical Cues: Exploring the Overlooked," *Journal of Research in Crime and Delinquency* 32 (May 1995): 214–239.

127. See, for example, K. F. Ferraro, *Fear of Crime: Interpreting Victimization Risk* (Albany: State University of New York Press, 1995); Ferraro, "Women's Fear of Victimization: Shadow of Sexual Assault?" *Social Forces* 75 (1996): 667–690.

128. Bonnie S. Fisher and John J. Sloan III, "Unraveling the Fear of Victimization Among College Women: Is the 'Shadow of Sexual Assault Hypothesis' Supported?" *Justice Quarterly* 20, no. 3 (September 2003): 633–659.

129. Fisher and Nasar, "Fear Spots in Relation to Microlevel Physical Cues," pp. 215, 236.

130. Bureau of Justice Statistics, *Crime and Neighborhoods* (Washington, D.C.: U.S. Department of Justice, 1994).

131. See Jerome H. Skolnick, *Justice Without Trial: Law Enforcement in a Democratic Society* (New York: Wiley, 1996).

132. David F. Greenberg and Valerie West, "State Prison Populations and Their Growth, 1971–1991," *Criminology* 39, no. 3 (August 2001): 615–653; quotation is on p. 640.

133. Ronald Weitzer and Charis E. Kubrin, "Breaking News: How Local TV News and Real-World Conditions Affect Fear of Crime," *Justice Quarterly* 21, no. 3 (September 2004): 497–521; quotation is on p. 515. See also Ted Chiricos et al., "Fear, TV News, and the Reality of Crime," *Criminology* 38 (August 2000): 755–786.

134. See J. D. Wright et al., *Under the Gun: Weapons, Crime, and Violence in* America (new York: Aldine de Gruyter, 1983); J. D. Wright et al., Armed *and Considered Dangerous: A Survey of Felons and Their Firearms* (New York: Aldine de Gruyter, 1994). For a review of these and other earlier studies in the area, see Adam M. Watkins et al., "Patterns of Gun Acquisition, Carrying, and Use Among Juvenile and Adult Arrestees: Evidence from a High-Crime City," *Justice Quarterly* 25, no. 4 (December 2008): 674–700; in particular, see pp. 675–677. But see also Chris Melde et al., "'May Peace Be with You': A Typological Examination of the Fear and Victimization Hypothesis of Adolescent Weapon Carrying," *Justice Quarterly* 26, no. 2 (June 2009): 348–375.

135. Truman and Rand, *Criminal Victimization, 2009*, p. 8.

136. See D. Kennedy, "Pulling Levers: Getting Deterrence Right," *National Institute of Justice Journal* (July 1998): 2–8; Kennedy and Anthony A. Braga, "Homicide in Minneapolis: Research for Problem Solving," *Homicide Studies* 2 (1998): 263–290, discussed in Edmund F. McGarrell et al., "Reducing Homicide Through a 'Lever-Pulling' Strategy," *Justice Quarterly* 223, no. 2 (June 2006): 214–231.

137. See McGarrell et al., ibid.

138. Anthony A. Braga et al., "The Strategic Prevention of Gun Violence Among Gang-Involved Offenders," *Justice Quarterly* 25, no. 1 (March 2008): 132–162.

139. Watkins et al., "Patterns of Gun Acquisition," pp. 690–691.

140. The Brady bill is codified at USCS, Title 18, Section 922 *et seq.* (2010).

141. *Parker v. District of Columbia*, 478 F.3d 370 (D.C. Cir. 2007), *reh'g. en banc, denied,* 2007 U.S. App. LEXIS 11029 (D.C. Cir. 8 May 2007), *and stay granted*, 2007 U.S. App. LEXIS 12467 (D.C. Cir. 24 May 2007), *and aff'd., District of Columbia v. Heller*, 554 U.S. 570 (2008).

142. *McDonald v. Chicago*, 130 S.Ct. 3020 (2010), cases and citations omitted.

143. *McDonald v. Chicago*, 130 S.Ct. 3020 (2010), Justice Stevens, dissenting, cases and citations omitted.

144. Lawrence W. Sherman et al., *The Kansas City Gun Experiment* (Washington, D.C.: National Institute of Justice, January 1995), p. 1.

145. Gary Kleck and Karen McElrath, "The Effects of Weaponry on Human Violence," *Social Forces* 69 (1991): 669–692, quotation is on p. 668. See also Kleck, *Point Blank: Guns and Violence in America* (New York: Aldine de Gruyter, 1991); Kleck, *Targeting Guns: Firearms and Their Control* (New York: Aldine de Gruyter, 1997).

146. William Wells and Julie Horney, "Weapon Effects and Individual Intent to Do Harm: Influences on the Escalation of Violence," *Criminology* 40, no. 2 (May 2002): 265–295; quotations are on pp. 288 and 289.

147. Stephen M. Schnebly, "An Examination of the Impact of Victim, Offender, and Situational Attributes on the Deterrent Effect of Defensive Gun Use: A Research Note," *Justice Quarterly* 19, no. 2 (June 2002): 377–398; quotations are on pp. 377 and 397.

148. William Wells, "The Nature and Circumstances of Defensive Gun Use: A Content Analysis of Interpersonal Conflict Situations Involving Criminal Offenders," *Justice Quarterly* 19, no. 1 (March 2002): 127–157; quotation is on p. 152.

149. Beth M. Huebner et al., "Gangs, Guns, and Drugs: Recidivism Among Serious, Young Offenders," *Criminology and Public Policy* 6, no. 2 (May 2007): 187–222.

150. Robert A. Hahn et al., Centers for Disease Control, *First Reports Evaluating the Effectiveness of Strategies for Preventing Violence: Firearms Laws*, http:www.cdc.gov/mmwr/preview/mmwrhtml/rr5214a2.htm, accessed 20 October 2010.

151. Charles Wellford, "Editorial Introduction: Special Issue on Gun Policy," *Criminology and Public Policy* 4, no. 4 (November 2005): 673–676; quotation is on p. 675. Volume 2, no. 3 (July 2003) of this journal carries a special section on "Handguns and Violent Crime," pp. 359–418.

152. "Two on U.S. Panel Dissent on Pornography's Impact," *New York Times* (19 May 1986), p. 13.

153. Daniel Linz and Edward Donnerstein, "Research Can Help Us Explain Violence and Pornography," *Chronicle of Higher Education* 39 (30 September 1992): 1.

154. Ray Surette, *Media, Crime, and Criminal Justice: Images and Realities* (Pacific Grove, CA: Brooks/Cole, 1992), p. 108.

155. Cynthia S. Gentry, "Pornography and Rape: An Empirical Analysis," *Deviant Behavior* 12 (July-September 1991): 277–288.

156. Alexis M. Durham III, "Pornography, Social Harm, and Legal Control: Observations on Bart," *Justice Quarterly* 3 (March 1986): 94–102; quotation is on p. 102. Durham was responding to an article by Pauline B. Bart, "Pornography: Hating Women and Institutionalizing Dominance and Submission for Fun and Profit: Response to Alexis M. Durham III," in the same journal, pp. 102–105.

157. "Debate on Child Pornography's Link to Molesting," *New York Times* (19 July 2007), p. 1; "Tech File: Teens Need to Know Online Actions Have Consequences," *San Jose Mercury News* (23 July 2007), n.p.

158. Federal Bureau of Investigation, Department of Justice Press Release, "Indiana Man Sentenced to 20 Years in Prison for Transporting and Possessing Child Pornography," http://indianapolis.fbi.gov/dojpressrel/pressrel09/ip112009.htm, accessed 20 October 2010.

159. *Miller v. California*, 413 U.S. 15 (1973), citations omitted.

160. *Black's Law Dictionary*, special deluxe 5th ed. (St. Paul, MN: West, 1979), p. 1104.

161. See, for example, *FW/PBS, Inc. v. City of Dallas*, 493 U.S. 215 (1990).

162. *Reno v. American Civil Liberties Union*, 521 U.S. 844 (1997).

163. *Reno v. American Civil Liberties Union,* 521 U.S. 844 (1997).

164. *United States v. American Library Association*, 539 U.S. 194 (2003).

165. *Ashcroft v. The Free Speech Coalition*, 535 U.S. 234 (2002).

166. *Ashcroft v. The Free Speech Coalition*, 535 U.S. 234 (2002). The Child Pornography Protection Act of 1966 (CPPA) is part of the Communications Decency Act of 1996. At issue in the case were USCS, Title 18, Sections 2256 (8)(B) and 2256(8)(D) (2010).

167. The Prosecutorial Remedies and Other Tools to End the Exploitation of Children Today Act of 2003 (the PROTECT Act), Public Law 108-21 (20100.

168. The promotion or pandering provision is codified at USCS, Chapter 18, Section 2252A(a)(3)(B) (2010), and the possession provision is codified at USCS, Chapter 18, Section 2252A(a)(5)(B) (2010).

169. *United States v. Williams*, 553 U.S. 285 (2008)

170. *Ashcroft v. American Civil Liberties Union*, 542 U.S. 656 (2004). The case has a long subsequent history, resulting in the injunction in 2007, *ACLU v. Gonzales*, 478 F.Supp. 2d 775 (E.D.Pa. 2007), *aff'd., ACLU v. Mukasey*, 534 F.3d 181 (3d Cir. 2008), *cert. denied*, 129 S.Ct. 2032 (2009). The Child Online Protection Act (COPA) is codified at USCS, Chapter 47, Section 231 (2010).

171. *ACLU v. Gonzales*, 478 F.Supp. 2d 775 (E.D.Pa. 2007), *aff'd. sub nom.*, 534 F.3d 181, *cert. denied*, 129 S.Ct. 1032 (2009).

CHAPTER **8**

Property Crimes

A devastated mother, Tina Meier, holds two pictures of her daughter, Megan, 13, who committed suicide after she received cyberbully messages on MySpace from the mother of one of her friends, who posed as a boy initially flirting with Megan and then making negative statements about her. Meier is now an activist for statutes criminalizing bullying.

KEY TERMS

arson
attempt crimes
burglary
CAN-SPAM Act
career criminals
carjacking
cohort
computer crime
constructive possession
counterfeiting
cybercrime
cyberphobia
cyberstalking
embezzlement
fence
forfeiture
forgery
fraud
grand larceny
identity theft
larceny-theft
petit larceny
phishing
recidivism
selective incapacitation
shoplifting

INTRODUCTION

This chapter discusses property crimes and begins with the four serious property crimes as defined by the FBI's *Uniform Crime Reports* (*UCR*): burglary, larceny-theft, motor vehicle theft, and arson. Because laws defining larceny-theft and burglary can be understood only in the light of their historical development, brief attention is given to the history of property crimes. The second section focuses on a sample of the lesser property crimes as categorized by the *UCR*: forgery, counterfeiting, and fraud; buying, receiving, and possessing stolen property; and embezzlement. Identity theft, one of the fastest-growing crimes in the United States, is discussed in detail. Computer crimes, also increasing at a fast pace, are analyzed in terms of types, control, and legal issues. The final section explores professional and career criminals, many of whom are engaged in property crimes. That section closes with a look at the latest U.S. Supreme Court case on sentencing repeat offenders.

"Law is never a mere abstraction. It is a very practical . . . matter. It represents the sum total of the rules by which the game of life is played . . . but this is quite a different game in different lands and in different times."[1] With those words, a noted law professor began his commentary on the development of property law. The emphasis on different times is significant; this chapter discusses some crimes that historically were not considered criminal. For example, taking something of value from another by fraud, deceit, or embezzlement was considered clever, not criminal. In business deals between people who knew each other well, it was usually the responsibility of all parties to ensure that they were treated fairly. Times changed, however, and as business and social conditions became more complex, it was necessary to change the laws governing business life.

In the following sections, property crimes are discussed by categories, beginning with the four that are included in the Federal Bureau of Investigation's list of serious offenses. The next section enumerates and discusses three crimes included in the FBI's categorization of less serious crimes. Attention is then given to such modern crimes as identity theft and computer crimes, followed by a discussion of professional versus amateur thieves, which sets the stage for a look at career criminals in the last section of the chapter.

Serious Property Crimes

The serious offenses of the *Uniform Crime Reports* (*UCR*), the official crime data of the FBI, include four property crimes: burglary, larceny-theft, motor vehicle theft, and arson. All are defined according to the FBI categorization in Exhibit 8.1. Property crimes affect significantly more people than violent crimes, and in 2009, they accounted for an estimated $15.2 billion in losses. The estimated 9,320,971 serious property crimes were 4.6 percent lower than the 2008 volume and 8.4 percent lower than the 2005 estimate. According to victimization data from the Bureau of Justice Statistics (BJS), between 2000 and 2009, there was a 29 percent drop in the property crime rate.[2]

In 2009, only 18.6 percent of all reported serious property crimes were cleared by arrest or exceptional means (compared to 47.1 percent of serious violent crimes). Larceny-theft had the highest clearance rate, 21.5 percent, of the serious property crimes.[3] Figure 8.1 shows the clearance figures for the three property crimes (excluding arson), in comparison to the four serious violent crimes.

Figure 2.2 in Chapter 2 graphed the percentage of U.S. households that reported experiencing property crimes, showing a decline of 29 percent between 2000 and 2009

EXHIBIT 8.1

Serious Property Crimes: *UCR* Definitions

- **Burglary**—"the unlawful entry of a structure to commit a felony or theft."
- **Larceny-theft**—"the unlawful taking, carrying, leading, or riding away of property from the possession or constructive possession of another."
- **Motor vehicle theft**—"the theft or attempted theft of a motor vehicle."
- **Arson**—"any willful or malicious burning or attempting to burn, with or without intent to defraud, a dwelling house, public building, motor vehicle or aircraft, personal property of another, etc."

Source: Federal Bureau of Investigation, *Crime in the United States: Uniform Crime Reports 2009*, "Offense Definitions," http://www2.fbi.gov/ucr/cius2009/about/offense_definitions.html, accessed 20 October 2010.

Figure 8.1

Percentage of Crimes Cleared by Arrests or Exceptional Means, 2009

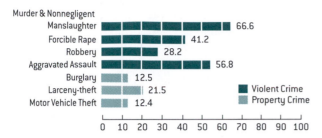

Source: Federal Bureau of Investigation, "Offenses Cleared," *Crime in the United States: Uniform Crime Reports 2009*, http://www2.fbi.gov/ucr/cius2009/offenses/clearances/index.html, accessed 20 October 2010.

(excluding 2006 and 2007). Figure 2.5 graphed the decreasing trends in property crime offenses between 2005 and 2009, as reported by the *UCR*.[4]

As noted previously, the elderly are not often crime victims. However, when they are victimized, they are most frequently subjected to property crimes. The 2009 BJS victimization data show that, as in previous years, the overall violent crime victimization rates decreased with a victim's age.[5]

The four property crimes are discussed in rank order, beginning with the most serious.

Burglary

The crime of **burglary** is frightening because it often involves the invasion of our most private places, our homes. To decrease the chances of being burglarized, many people move to another area, have expensive burglar alarm systems installed, alter their lifestyles, or take other precautionary measures. Avoiding burglary is thus costly for private lives, peace of mind, and daily living. It is also expensive for policing. In addition to the undetermined cost of investigating burglaries and processing those accused of this crime, police spend considerable time and money responding to burglar alarms. The problems can be expected to increase as more citizens arm their homes, their cars and in some cases, even their persons.

The *UCR* defines *burglary* as "the unlawful entry of a structure to commit a felony or theft" (see Exhibit 8.1). The evolution of burglary statutes illustrates the problems the common law courts had in interpreting the elements of the crime; some of these elements have been retained in recent legislation.

Common Law History

Under English common law, burglary was defined as breaking and entering the dwelling of another in the night with the intent to commit a felony. Burglary was punishable as

a separate offense from the felony committed, probably in an effort to plug legal loopholes regarding **attempt crimes**, which are difficult to prove and may carry penalties less severe than those for completed crimes. Making burglary a separate offense increased the chances of a conviction even when the state could not prove all the elements of the theft or other crime that took place after the breaking and entering occurred.

Numerous problems arose with the common law definition. What was meant by *breaking and entering*? The cases are fascinating and, in some instances, absurd. Early cases held that if the owner left the home unsecured, he (women were not permitted to own property) was not entitled to protection. A person who entered the home through an open door or window without permission could not be convicted of burglary. If the door or window was partly open, opening it further to enter was not breaking and entering. It was not necessary for the homeowner to lock the doors or windows, only to close them.

The requirement of *entering* also presented problems. If a person used an instrument to open the building and if only the instrument entered the building, that action did not constitute entering unless the instrument was used in the commission of the felony for which the premises were entered. However, the entry by any part of the offender could constitute an entry. In addition, the offender could be held to have met the entering element of the crime by sending in a child or another person who could not be held legally responsible. In that situation, the adult offender was held to have entered constructively.

The phrase *dwelling of another* raised interesting legal problems. Because a person's home was his castle, breaking and entering that dwelling was a heinous crime punishable by death. The occupant did not need to be present; indeed, he could have been absent for a long time, but it had to be that person's dwelling place. An unfinished house would not count even if the workers slept there. In some circumstances, the word *dwelling* included barns, stables, and other buildings on the premises.

Under common law, to constitute burglary, the offense had to be committed during the night. The difference between night and day was defined as "whether the countenance of a man could be discerned by natural light even though the sun may have set. Artificial light or moonlight, regardless of their intensity, would not suffice." Finally, to be convicted of burglary, the offender had to intend to commit a felony while inside the dwelling. Passing through the home to commit a felony elsewhere would not suffice.[6]

Over the years, the meaning of burglary has been changed to the extent that modern statutes bear little resemblance to the common law definition. They are much broader; most do not require breaking, and they may cover entry at any time into any kind of structure.

An example of a modern statute that differs from the common law is the New York statute, which permits a burglary charge when a person "knowingly enters or remains unlawfully in a building with intent to commit a crime therein." This provision refers to all degrees of burglary and is the sole definition of third-degree burglary. To constitute first- or second-degree burglary, the act must meet other elements that range from being "armed with explosives or a deadly weapon" to displaying "what appears to be a pistol, revolver, rifle, shotgun, machine gun or other firearm." Notice also that the statute refers to an intent to commit a *crime*, not an intent to commit a felony. Thus, a burglary charge could be brought against one who entered with the intent to commit a misdemeanor.[7]

Under many modern burglary statutes, a person may be convicted of burglary as well as the crime for which the burglary was committed. For example, Maine's burglary statute covers one who "enters or surreptitiously remains in a structure, knowing that that person is not licensed or priviliged to do so, with the intent to commit a crime therein." The statute also contains the following provision:

> A person may be convicted both of burglary and of the crime which the person committed or attempted to commit after entering or remaining in the structure.[8]

Problems of interpreting the elements of burglary remain, but it appears clear that the crime involves invading the right of a person to possess and thus have exclusive control over property belonging to another.

Data

An estimated 2,199,125 burglaries occurred in 2009 representing a 1.3 percent decrease over 2008, an increase of 2.0 percent compared to 2005, and an increase of 7.2 percent over the estimates of burglaries in 2000. The 2009 burglaries cost an estimated $4.6 billion in losses to victims, with an average loss per burglary of $2,096. Burglaries accounted for 23.6 percent of all serious property crimes in 2009. Most of the burglaries (72.6 percent) were of residential structures, with most of those for which the time was known occurring during the day.[9]

Victimization data also present interesting information concerning burglary. According to victimization data released by the Bureau of Justice Statistics (BJS), in 2009, household burglaries declined by 2.6 percent over 2008, with 3,188,620 households experiencing at least one burglary.[10]

Analysis of Burglary

Burglary and burglars have been studied from several approaches. Some sociologists have studied the people convicted of burglary (often combined with those who commit larceny-theft) and tried to discover whether these types of criminals have any distinguishable characteristics. Others have looked at the circumstances surrounding the crime—for example, the type of establishment burglarized, the value of the loss, the type of entry, and the hour of the day or night when the crime occurred. Still others have looked at the characteristics of the area in which the crime occurred. Some researchers have concentrated on the characteristics of the actual burglaries.

The most extensive research on burglary has been in the area of professional or career criminal studies, which may include all serious property crimes. These studies require greater analysis and are discussed later in this chapter. It is not always possible to separate the burglary offenders from the studies of career criminals, but a significant number of persons convicted of burglary are habitual or professional criminals.

Most persons apprehended for burglary are young unskilled males. In urban areas, they are disproportionately nonwhite. Older and more talented burglars are more likely to steal alone, whereas young and female burglars

Some criminals are quite bold in committing their crimes. This potential burglar is preparing to force open the front door and enter illegally despite adequate lighting and the presence of vehicles on the street.

are more likely to steal in groups. Most do not travel far from their homes to commit their crimes, choosing accessible victims and those of their own race.

Neal Shover has written extensively on burglary, beginning with his PhD dissertation in 1971, in which he suggested that we should attempt to "correct" burglars as well as make it more difficult for them to succeed in their crimes. Shover studied 88 incarcerated burglars while gathering data for his dissertation, which, along with his more recent works, is referred to later in this chapter in the section on career criminals.[11]

Richard Wright and other researchers studied active burglars in the field who were not incarcerated. Such fieldwork is difficult and at times dangerous, but researchers who studied 105 active residential burglars concluded that this approach is important and meaningful. Seventy-five percent of the burglars would not have been included in a sample of incarcerated burglars. Of these, 44 percent reported that they had never been arrested for burglary, and 35 percent responded that they had been arrested for burglary one or more times but had not been convicted. An analysis of the data on the 105 burglars supported other studies, discussed later, that suggest a few offenders commit most of the crimes. Of the 105 burglars, 34 percent said they committed fewer than 5 burglaries a year, and 7 percent stated they committed 50 or more burglaries per year.[12]

Paul F. Cromwell's study of burglars, which involved a sample of 30 active residential burglars over a two-year period, led him to conclude that burglars are less rational and more opportunistic than previous research suggested. Most burglars "are easily deterred or displaced from one target site to another. Situational factors such as the presence of a dog, an alarm system, security hardware, and alert neighbors may be the most effective deterrents."[13]

One scholar looked at burglary from the perspective of multiple variables. Matthew B. Robinson summarized his conclusions concerning crime prevention policy based on his analyses of residential burglary patterns and the environment. The studies were conducted at private apartment complexes near a large state university in a southeastern U.S. city. Robinson concluded that burglary prevention can be aided by changes at the individual, group, community, organization, and societal levels.[14]

Specifically, individuals should alter their lifestyles in such a way as to increase irregular pedestrian and automotive traffic. Those living alone should vary their schedules and activities; those living with others should attempt to maximize the times someone is visible at the residence. At the group level, those looking for roommates should seek persons with different schedules. At the community level, neighbors should become acquainted with each other and look out for each others' homes. At the organizational level, various crime prevention policies can be adopted by police and other departments. An obvious one is crime prevention alert signs in the area. At the societal

level, Robinson suggested employer policies that provide more flexible work schedules, thus enabling employees to be home at varying times and, of course, educational campaigns concerning burglary prevention. Robinson concluded: "Citizens who seek to alter their physical and social environments should focus on increasing surveillability, reducing accessibility, changing their lifestyles, and getting involved in community crime prevention activities."[15] This study thus offered some support for the routine activity approach discussed in Chapter 5.

Studies of burglary also show that the crime is social. Burglary involves networking, through which criminals share information and knowledge and dispose of stolen goods. In his earlier works, Neal Shover emphasized that a good burglar is one who can get along with other burglars.[16]

Other scholars have explored the networking variable with regard to women and burglary; this subject has received little research attention despite the fact that women are involved in more burglaries than any other serious crime with the exception of larceny-theft. The limited research suggests that women and men take into consideration the prevailing beliefs about the proper roles of each gender even when they are involved in daily, routine, and mundane tasks. This process can result in limiting the opportunities of both genders but especially of women and particularly with regard to street-life crimes.[17]

An analysis of gender and burglary lends further support to a link between burglary and social networking. Among other findings were the following:

- Most of the burglars began this crime in intimate, small groups of older friends, family, or street associates.
- Men and women differed in the nature of those small groups, with women more often introduced to burglary by their boyfriends and men by same-gender peers.
- Men and women did not differ significantly on their motivations; most burglarized to support a party lifestyle (e.g., illicit drug use) or to attain the symbols (e.g., jewelry) of success. However, some men used the money for sexual conquests, whereas some women used it to buy necessities for their children. These differences mirror the gender characteristics of the low-income urban neighborhoods from which the sample was derived. Women, who often head their households, are the primary caregivers and providers for their children. Men gain their status by being able to spend money and appearing economically self-sufficient.
- Both men and women had two objectives in selecting a target: It had something of value and it was unoccupied. But men had greater access to information on these objectives, as they often had legitimate jobs as home remodelers; none of the women

had these jobs. Some women, however, were able to use sex to gain access to this information from men who lived in those houses.

- Some of the men but none of the women expressed a preference for burglarizing alone, with some of the women expressing a need for help in breaking into a building.[18]

The research showed that female burglars capitalized on their gender in several ways. For example, when men and women worked together, women were rarely first to enter the target building. In some cases, however, petite women might be first because their small size enabled them to get into tight places. In general, the roles available to women were limited, some by their choices and others by the men in the group. Men who engaged in "women's work" during burglaries did so only when women were not available to do that work, during the early stages of their careers, or when such work was viewed as part of an apprenticeship in career building. In contrast to men, women tended to view their gender as an advantage. If they were apprehended during a burglary, they could blame the crime on the men, and the criminal justice systems would be lenient with them. Even if this is not true, they acted as if it were. Finally, with regard to leaving a life of crime, the men suggested that might happen when they settled down with the right woman; the women said it would occur only if they left the wrong man. So "it is clear that they are working at cross purposes—the men talk about the need to *make* a tie, the women about the need to *break one*."[19]

Another issue in the study of burglary is that of preventing the crime. Two English scholars examined 21 burglary reduction schemes. Recall that in our discussion of the routine activity approach, Cohen and Felson (see again Chapter 5) stated that for crimes to occur, there must be a motivated offender, the opportunity to commit the crime, and the absence of a capable guardian. Thus, it is important not only to remove opportunities for crimes but also to ensure that people *perceive* that those opportunities have been removed (or at least reduced). This is most effectively done through publicity. Cohen and Felson found evidence that publicity is an "effective crime prevention tool and that many different types of publicity have been associated with burglary reduction schemes." The English scholars suggested even more innovative approaches, such as calling people to tell them about burglary prevention programs in their neighborhoods. Although these calls might have the effect of assuring people that something is being done to reduce burglary (or other crimes) in their neighborhoods, it is also possible they might have the undesired effect of increasing people's fear of crime (review Chapter 7's discussion of the fear of crime).[20]

Crime prevention is not simple. Research suggests that it is not sufficient to inform people that an act is wrong and will not be tolerated. We do not know enough about "how much publicity, and what sort of publicity, is necessary to achieve" the goals of crime reduction. The answers to these issues require a better understanding of why offenders make the decisions they make. Offenders know from experience that they may get caught, they may be arrested, and they may be prosecuted, but they also know that they probably will not serve time, certainly not a lot of time. "Thus, any attempts to use publicity to prevent or deter crime must be credible or they will contribute to the very real perception that the system is not really serious about prevention and intervention efforts."[21]

It has been suggested that although publicity might be effective in preventing home burglaries and driving under the influence, it is not as likely to be effective in preventing crimes such as murder or illicit drug use. Further, publicity of crime prevention may "increase fear of crime and distort the public's understanding of crime."[22]

One final study of burglary relating to prevention considered this crime in terms of daylight versus nighttime targeting. It was concluded that burglaries may be explained by both the routine activity approach and rational choice theory in that targets were apparently selected in terms of when they would be less covered by capable guardians, and thus, the offender would be less likely to be seen during the crime.[23]

Larceny-Theft

Daily news media accounts remind us that **larceny-theft** is a common crime in the United States as well as in the rest of the world. Larceny-theft involves several types of acts and may be defined differently in various jurisdictions. The FBI defines *larceny-theft* as "the unlawful taking, carrying, leading, or riding away of property from the possession or **constructive possession** [the condition of having the power to control an item along with the intent to do so] of another." The crime does not include embezzlement, forgery, passing worthless checks, or confidence games, although some of these theft crimes are discussed later in this chapter. It does include "crimes such as shoplifting, pocket-picking, purse-snatching, thefts from motor vehicles, thefts of motor vehicle parts and accessories, bicycle thefts, etc., in which no use of force, violence, or fraud occurs."[24] Larceny-theft is a broad category that can be understood only in light of its historical development.

Common Law History

Larceny-theft, the first theft crime in English history, was a common law crime, meaning that it was created by judges in deciding cases, not by Parliament in passing statutes. Larceny-theft was defined as a crime committed when a person misappropriated the property of another by taking that property from the possession and without the consent of the owner. The crime did not include the misappropriation of property that one already had. For example, if your boss gave you a sheep and asked you to take it to a customer and you decided to keep the sheep, that act was not larceny because you already had the sheep in your possession.

One of the reasons for requiring that the property be taken from the possession of another was that the seriousness of the offense lay not in the act of taking possession but in doing so under circumstances that might cause the owner to retaliate, perhaps in a violent way. In addition, taking possession by deceit, fraud, or embezzlement was not considered larceny-theft because such methods demonstrated that the thief was smarter than the property owner, and that was not a crime. It was the responsibility of the property owner to watch business dealings more carefully.

Another feature of early English common law is very important to an understanding of how larceny-theft laws evolved. Larceny-theft was a felony, and at one period in English history, all felonies were punishable by death. Early statutes provided that if the value of what was stolen did not exceed a specified amount, the punishment might be imprisonment rather than death, but the amount was relatively small, equivalent to approximately the price of a sheep.

Many English judges were reluctant to impose the death penalty in cases of **grand larceny** (in contrast to the lesser crime of **petit larceny**), so they began looking for technical ways to avoid finding the defendant guilty. One method was to find something peculiar about the way the property had been taken. The result was the development of many loopholes in the law of larceny-theft. Subsequently, statutes were passed to fill these gaps in the law, resulting in a patchwork of laws on theft that "are interesting as a matter of history but embarrassing as a matter of law enforcement."[25]

Data

Larceny-theft is the least likely of the eight serious *UCR* crimes to be reported, but it is the most frequently committed of the four serious property crimes, constituting an estimated 67.9 percent of all serious property crimes in 2009. According to the official *UCR* data, the number of larceny-theft offenses in 2009 (an estimated 6,327,230 offenses) decreased by 4.0 percent over 2008 (and showed a 9.2 percent decline over 2000). The larceny-theft rate decreased by 4.8 percent over 2008 and 16.8 percent over 2000. In 2009, larceny-theft victims lost an average of $864 per offense, for an estimated total of $5.5 billion.[26]

According to victimization data, in 2009, approximately 133,210 personal thefts (includes pocket picking, completed purse snatching, and attempted purse snatching) were reported, down 3.3 percent from the previous year.[27] Figure 8.2 graphs the distribution of larceny-thefts by category.

Caution must be used in interpreting these data. In our discussion of robbery, we noted that one of the differences

Figure 8.2

Larceny-Theft: Percentage Distribution, 2009

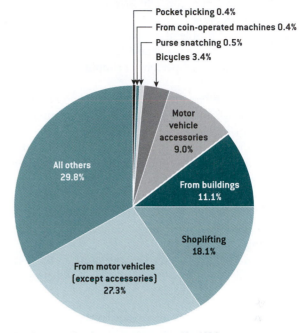

Note: Due to rounding, the percentages may not add to 100.0.

Source: Federal Bureau of Investigation, "Larceny-Theft," *Crime in the United States: Uniform Crime Reports 2009,* http://www2 .fbi.gov/ucr/cius2009/offenses/property_crime/larceny-theft. html, accessed 20 October 2010.

between larceny-theft and robbery is the use or threat of violence in the latter. We used the example of purse snatching, categorized by the FBI as larceny-theft. But if sufficient force or threat of force is used, purse snatching should be classified as robbery. This kind of distinction makes it necessary to realize that when we compare robbers with thieves, we may not be talking about significantly different types of criminals.

As noted in Figure 8.2, the FBI includes numerous specific theft crimes within the category of larceny-theft: pocket picking, purse snatching, shoplifting, theft from motor vehicles, theft of motor vehicle accessories, theft from buildings, theft of bicycles, and theft from coin-operated machines. Shoplifting is one of the most frequent. Special attention is given to this type of larceny-theft.

Focus on Shoplifting

The illegal removal of merchandise from stores by customers or by persons posing as customers constitutes the crime of **shoplifting**. Most shoplifters do not take large amounts of merchandise, with an average loss of $181.[28] That is an official figure, however; as noted later, not all suspected shoplifting is reported to police. The National Association for Shoplifting Prevention (NASP) reports that more than $35 million is stolen daily from retailers, representing a yearly total of over $13 billion. Other facts reported by the NASP are as follows:

- "There are approximately 27 million shoplifters (or 1 in 11 people). . . .
- There is no profile of a typical shoplifter. Men and women shoplift equally as often.
- Approximately 25 percent of shoplifters are kids. . . .
- Many shoplifters buy and steal merchandise in the same visit. Shoplifters commonly steal from $2 to $200 per incident. . . .
- Shoplifters say they are caught an average of only once in every 48 times they steal. They are turned over to the police 50 percent of the time. . . .
- The excitement generated from 'getting away with it' produces a chemical reaction resulting in what shoplifters describe as an incredible 'rush' or 'high' feeling. . . .
- Drug addicts, who have become addicted to shoplifting, describe shoplifting equally as addicting as drugs."[29]

Shoplifters come from all income levels and from both minority and majority populations; the types of items they steal vary widely. Apprehended shoplifters report that even after they are caught, it is difficult to stop stealing. Their crimes are usually not premeditated, and most shoplifters are nonprofessionals who do not commit other types of crimes. According to the NASP, shoplifters "never steal an ashtray from your house and will return to you a $20 bill you may have dropped."[30]

It is reasonable to expect that in a depressed economy, shoplifting might increase. According to a June 2010 report, retail shrinkage (includes employee theft as well as shoplifting and other forms of loss) actually decreased between 2008 and 2009, representing a $33.5 billion loss in 2009 compared to a loss of $36.5 billion the previous year. The largest loss, $14.4 billion (43 percent), was due to employee theft, followed by an $11.7 billion (35 percent) loss from shoplifting. A loss of $4.9 billion (14.5 percent) was due to administrative error. The remainder, $4.9 billion (3.8 percent), was from vender fraud.[31]

Many comments about shoplifting are not based on systematic studies, but one recognized study merits attention. In 1964, Mary Owen Cameron's classic study of shoplifting distinguished between the *snitch* (the pilferer) and the *booster* (the commercial or professional shoplifter). Cameron concluded that "most shoplifting, including pilfering, appears to be chronic, habitual or systematic behavior." She found that in addition to the booster and the snitch, there might be a group of shoplifters who committed the offense because of an "unexpected urge to steal" or who were overcome "by an unpremeditated desire for a particular object."[32]

Cameron's data showed that the majority of shoplifters were not associated with a criminal subculture. Most were women, and over 90 percent probably were never convicted of another offense. Usually, they had not thought about the possibility of being arrested, although they had given consideration to the possibility of being caught.

When apprehended, many shoplifters in Cameron's study used the excuses and rationalizations characteristic of juveniles caught in a delinquent act. They did not manifest psychotic symptoms, and few were repeat offenders. Many had childhood experiences with groups in which older children taught them the techniques of successful pilfering. The items taken were generally for the shoplifter's personal use rather than for resale and profit. Most of the female shoplifters were from families with modest budgets. They stole luxury items that could not come out of the family budget without sacrificing other needs of the family rather than items they bought frequently. They rationalized that it was better to steal from the department store than from the family budget.

Pilferers, in contrast to other shoplifters, did not think of themselves as thieves, and when arrested, they resisted the definition of their behavior as theft. The arrest, however, forced them to realize that the behavior was not only bad but also illegal. At this stage, many pilferers became upset, even hysterical. In contrast, professional shoplifters, upon finding it impossible to talk their way out of an arrest, accepted the inevitable. The pilferers feared their family's reactions and did not expect in-group support for the illegal behavior. The act of apprehension was sufficient to deter most of them from further illegal activity of this kind.

A more recent analysis of shoplifting is available from the U.S. Department of Justice, which published a report that characterized shoplifting as "one of the most common but least detected and reported crimes." It referred to one study estimating that only about 1 in 150 shoplifters is apprehended by the police. The report focused on what police departments need to do with regard to shoplifting. It criticized the police and alleged that they pay little attention to shoplifting, leaving the responsibility for apprehending offenders to store owners and managers. The report emphasized that shoplifting can significantly affect the profits of stores, especially in deprived neighborhoods; it can even result in the closure of some stores. Unlike other research on shoplifting, this report concluded that most shoplifters are young people and men. Thus, stores that cater to young men and boys are particularly vulnerable to shoplifting, as are stores located in neighborhoods that are populated by large numbers of drug users. Since many shoplifters are teens, the most vulnerable times for store owners and managers are those when schools are not in session. Schools that open onto streets rather than into malls and stores in busy areas with more casual shoppers (in contrast to those with a regular clientele) are more vulnerable to shoplifting. There is little evidence that signs stating that shoplifters will be prosecuted are effective in deterring the crime or that identifying the most frequently shoplifted items with a sign and large red star is effective. It was suggested that merchants should be permitted to assess restitution at the scene.[33]

One food market in the New York City area uses the immediate restitution/shaming approach to shoplifting. The store's security officers seize the identification of shoppers who are caught shoplifting. They photograph the shoplifters holding the items they stole and threaten to embarrass them by displaying those pictures on large monitors in the store, along with calling the police. The store's clientele is heavily populated by immigrants, and deportation is a fear if convicted of a crime; thus, many of the apprehended will pay the demanded restitution. The legality of this approach is questionable and may constitute extortion, but thus far, no complaints have been filed with the local police department or the district attorney's office.[34]

According to the NASP, most shoplifters are nonprofessionals who steal for many reasons "mostly related to common life situations and their personal ability (or inability) to cope. They include people who are depressed, frustrated, anxious, influenced by peers, thrill seekers or kleptomaniacs."[35]

Finally, in a study of shoplifting by use of a hidden camera, investigators found that approximately 8.5 percent of customers engaged in shoplifting. Overall, whites shoplifted as frequently as nonwhites. The race-gender grouping most likely to shoplift were Hispanic females, and the least likely were white females. The best predictors of shoplifting were behavioral characteristics: scanning the store for security devices, looking around, and sampling products. The most likely to have shoplifted were those persons who left the store without making purchases.[36]

Motor Vehicle Theft

The *UCR* tabulates motor vehicle theft separately from other serious thefts. The FBI defines this crime as "the theft or attempted theft of a motor vehicle. . . . The definition excludes the taking of a motor vehicle for temporary use by those persons having lawful access." An estimated 794,616 motor vehicle thefts were reported in 2009, down 17.1 percent from the previous year, a decrease of 35.7 percent over 2005, and a 31.5 percent decrease over 2000. The estimated total loss from motor vehicle thefts in 2009 was $5.2 billion, with an average of $6,505 per incident. Most of the thefts (72.1 percent) involved automobiles.[37]

In 2009, the *UCR* reported 181,797 arrests for motor vehicle theft.[38] As noted earlier (see again Figure 8.1), motor vehicle theft was close with burglary for the lowest clearance rate of all serious property or violent crimes. This low level of clearance means that motor vehicle theft is a fairly safe crime to commit.

The crime of carjacking, as pictured here, involves takng the car from the driver by force. Personal injury and death have occurred in some cases.

The BJS National Crime Victimization Survey (NCVS) data revealed that 735,770 households reported motor vehicle theft in 2009, which was 8.4 percent fewer than in 2008.[39]

Carjacking: Property or Violent Crime?

The difficulty in differentiating between property crimes and violent crimes is illustrated by **carjacking**, which refers to auto theft by force or threat of force. The usual procedure is for the carjackers to force people out of their cars and then steal the cars. Personal injury and death have occurred in some cases, and a few are described in Exhibit 8.2.

Because of the violent nature of carjacking and the increase in the reported number of these crimes, the FBI announced in September 1992 that carjacking was a new priority in the bureau's Operation Safe Streets program. This program was established earlier in approximately 40 cities for the purpose of combating violence associated with drugs and gang activities.[40]

In July 2004, the BJS published an analysis of carjacking data between 1993 and 2002 that included the following:

- Approximately 34,000 carjackings occurred each year. About 45 percent of attempted carjackings were completed.
- Carjacking rates were lower during the last five years of the period than during the first five years.
- Men, blacks, and Hispanics were more often carjacking victims than women, whites, and non-Hispanics.
- Most carjackings (93 percent) occurred in cities or suburbs.
- Most carjackings did not result in injury to the victims; most injuries that did occur were minor. However, in 74 percent of the carjackings, a weapon was used.
- In 56 percent of the cases, more than one offender was involved.
- Males committed 93 percent of the crimes, with 3 percent committed by men and women together.

8.2 — EXHIBIT

Carjacking: A New Fear

In December 2009, the month in which the FBI published preliminary motor vehicle theft data for the first six months of the year, noting that offenses were down 18.7 percent over the previous year, several carjackings were reported. In mid-December, a motorist was flagged down on a Pennsylvania road. He stopped and was told that a friend was having a heart attack in the stopped vehicle. Would he please help? The Good Samaritan was forced to drive his car to an ATM and withdraw money. The victim was later released, but the carjacker had his identity from the ATM machine transaction.[1]

Also in December 2009, the daughter of Tennessee Senator Bob Corker called her father to report that she was a carjack victim just two blocks from the Washington, D.C., police station. The carjackers stopped Julia Corker, 22, to ask directions, at which point she was pulled out of her car, choked, and thrown to the ground. Corker was temporarily unconsciousness but awoke in time to see her SUV being driven away. Corker, who was holding her cell phone when attacked, called her father, who was in the area. He rushed to assist her, as did a couple she had encountered on the sidewalk earlier. The car was equipped with OnStar, and the police were able to track its location and arrest the suspected carjackers, Steven Alston, 25, and Dewalden Conner, 22, who was dressed as a woman. Both men pleaded guilty. Conner was sentenced to two years in prison. Alston was sentenced to nine years.[2]

Some carjacking victims are not so fortunate as to escape without serious physical injuries or death. A 2004 news article focused on the carjacking and rape of a 21-year-old woman who had only recently returned from military service in Iraq. She was a college student with a bright future who was in the wrong place at the wrong time. While Kimberly Horton waited for the light to turn green in a Los Angeles, California, suburb so she could continue on her way to visit her parents in the Los Angeles area, she was forced out of her car, shot in the head, and left dying on the sidewalk. Two hours later, her Honda Accord was pulled over by officers. An 18-year-old suspect was arrested but released for lack of evidence that he stole the car or knew anything about the carjacking.[3]

In 1992, Pamela Basu, 34, of Maryland, was forced from her BMW by two men who stole the car and drove it two miles. Basu, whose left arm was restrained by the shoulder strap of the car, was dragged to her death. The driver swerved into a barbed-wire fence, apparently trying to dislodge Basu's body. "Before finally ridding themselves of the fatally injured woman, they stopped to toss her 22-month-old daughter from the car." The daughter, found in her car seat, survived. One man, age 27, and one juvenile, age 16, were arrested 90 minutes later.[4]

Kissimmee, Florida, the home of Disney World and other amusement parks, was the scene of a 1992 carjacking that involved four victims, only two of whom survived. According to three of the four suspects, all of whom were African Americans, one of the survivors, an African American female, was spared because of her race. During the carjacking, the three male victims were ordered to remove their clothes and lie down in a field, where each was shot in the back of his

- Most carjackings (63 percent) occurred within five miles of the victim's home.
- Of the completed carjackings, 98 percent were reported to the police; 58 percent of attempted carjackings were reported.
- In 25 percent of the carjackings, the victims' total property was recovered; in 78 percent of the cases, partial or complete recovery occurred.[41]

Carjacking data are not as readily available as data for some other crimes. Some jurisdictions record carjackings as motor vehicle theft. And the separate crime of carjacking is not included among the FBI's serious property or violent crimes.

The Anti Car Theft Act of 1992, a federal statute, defines *carjacking* as an act in which a person approaches a car "with the intent to cause death or serious bodily harm" and "by force and violence or by intimidation" removes (or attempts to remove) the driver forcibly for purposes of stealing the car. The crime carries a sentence of not more than 15 years unless there is bodily injury, in which case

the maximum penalty is 25 years. If the victim dies as a result, the offender may be sentenced to a fine and "any number of years up to life, or both, or the death sentence." In addition, the statute increases penalties for other crimes related to car theft. The first trial under this statute is referred to in Exhibit 8.2. The statute's constitutionality was upheld by a federal court in 1995, and the U.S. Supreme Court refused to hear the case on appeal, thus permitting the lower appellate court's decision to stand.[42]

Analysis of Motor Vehicle Theft

Despite the attention given to the violent aspects of carjacking, most motor vehicle thefts do not involve violence. Some studies report that many motor vehicle theft arrestees are young people who steal cars for *joy rides*. A second reason for car theft is *short-term transportation*, and a third is *long-term transportation*. The latter purpose is given by persons from a lower socioeconomic background who are older than the joy riders. They paint or alter the cars in other ways to disguise them. Other offenders steal

EXHIBIT 8.2 continued

head. The male survivor, who was wounded by a gunshot to the hand he held over his head, feigned death. The female victim was forced to watch the executions.[5]

The suspects were apprehended, and one defendant entered a guilty plea, provided that he would testify against the other defendants and that state prosecutors would not seek the death penalty in a pending state case. The trial of the other three accused constituted the first trial under the federal carjacking statute, which became effective in October 1992. In April 1993, the three remaining defendants were convicted of abducting the three men and murdering two of them.[6]

With their husbands at their sides, the mothers of the victims asked the judge to impose the harshest penalties on all the defendants. One said: "They had no sympathy for my son. I have no sympathy for them. . . . My son was brutally murdered and I feel no remorse for [the defendants]. And there has to be a place in hell for the three of them." Calling the crimes "cold-blooded and pitiless," the judge imposed identical terms: life without parole plus 25 years for the defendants' convictions in federal court on charges of conspiracy, armed carjacking resulting in death, and using a firearm during a felony.[7]

In the subsequent state trial, two of the defendants were convicted of murder and kidnapping. The defendant who admitted that he pulled the trigger was sentenced to die in Florida's electric chair (Florida now offers inmates under a death sentence a choice between the chair and lethal injection). Attorneys for one of the others argued that since their

client did not pull the trigger he should not be convicted. The prosecutor disagreed and stated:

> The fact that the pack has a leader doesn't change the wolves in the pack into sheep. . . . When you run with the pack, you share in the kill. This was a pack, a pack of hungry wolves looking for prey.[8]

This defendant was sentenced to life in prison. The fourth defendant, who testified against his friends in the federal trial, was not tried on state charges.

1. "Police Investigate Carjacking, Kidnapping," Homepage, *Pennsylvania News* (15 December 2009), http://www.wgal.com/news2197890/detail.html, accessed 26 December 2009.
2. "Attack on Senator's Child Gets Carjacker Two Years," *Washington Post* (2 July 2010), p. 5B.
3. "Crime Rate Puts Residents on Edge: Statistics Show Rise in Number of City Incidents Since 2000," *Daily News of Los Angeles* (20 June 2004), p. 1SC.
4. "A New Terror on the Road: Carjacking Puts Fear in the Driver's Seat," *Newsweek* (23 November 1992), p. 31.
5. "Three Men Get Life Plus Twenty-Five Years in Carjacking," *Orlando Sentinel* (27 April 1993), p. 1B.
6. "Two Found Guilty in Carjack Deaths," *St. Petersburg Times* (11 February 1994), p. 5B.
7. Ibid.
8. "Carjack Killer Sentenced to Electric Chair," *St. Petersburg Times* (26 July 1994), p. 4B.

for *profit*, intending to sell the cars (or strip them and sell their parts) rather than use the cars for transportation. Many of these offenders operate in groups that resemble highly organized businesses. A final reason for stealing motor vehicles is to use them in the *commission of another crime*, such as robbery. This category constitutes a small portion of motor vehicle thefts.[43]

Arson

The fourth serious property crime is **arson**, defined by the *UCR* as "any willful or malicious burning or attempting to burn, with or without intent to defraud, a dwelling house, public building, motor vehicle or aircraft, personal property of another, etc." The *UCR* definition includes only fires that are found to be set maliciously or willfully. Fires of unknown or suspicious origin are excluded.[44]

Arson was not originally categorized by the FBI's *UCR* as a serious property offense. By congressional mandate in October 1978, which became effective in 1979, arson was moved from a Part II to a Part I offense. Procedures were developed for reporting the crime, but the *UCR* emphasized that care must be used in interpreting arson data, particularly trend data, which might be affected significantly by better reporting procedures rather than by increased volume and higher rates.

Data

Estimated arson offenses reported in 2009 totaled 58,871, representing a 10.8 percent decrease over 2008. The most frequent targets were structures (residential, storage, public, etc.), accounting for 44.5 percent, with 28.4 percent of arsons targeting mobile property. The average value loss per arson was $17,411.[45]

Despite its seriousness, arson did not receive much attention historically. The crime, however, has been in the news frequently during the last decade. Numerous church fires, which occurred primarily in southern states and involved very old buildings with predominantly African American congregations, led Congress to enact the legislation described in Exhibit 8.3.

Arson of other structures has also resulted in extensive property damage as well as personal injuries and deaths. For example, in March 1990, a blaze in the Happy Land Social Club in New York City killed 87 people. It was the worst fire in that city since 1911 and the worst in the nation since 1986, when 97 people died in a hotel fire in Puerto Rico. The Happy Land Social Club victims died within minutes after the fire began. Julio Gonzalez, convicted of starting the fire, was sentenced to 25 years to life in prison on each count of murder and felony murder. By law, the sentences must be served concurrently. He will be eligible for parole after serving 25 years. He went to the club to talk to his former girlfriend, Lydia Feliciano, who was an employee. The club's bouncer evicted Gonzalez after he quarreled with Feliciano, who had jilted him. Gonzalez returned later and started the fire. Feliciano was one of the six survivors of the fire.[46]

Although the dry conditions in the state of California result in frequent fires, the devastation that occurred in October 2007 was tragic, with 10 deaths, the loss of 2,000 homes, and the destruction of 780 square miles of land. One fire was apparently started by a 10-year-old boy who was playing with matches. No charges were filed, but his case was turned over to the state's Department of Children and Family Services. The fire forced 15,000 people to evacuate their homes and resulted in the destruction of 21 homes and 38,000 acres of land.[47]

Analysis of Arson

Analysis of arson has focused on the crime, not the criminal, and some sociological theories discussed in earlier chapters have been utilized. For example, arson has been attributed to "patterns of systematic speculation in transitional neighborhoods," racial problems, and capitalism. The scale and complexity of this crime call into question our deviance theories.[48]

One study of convicted arsonists analyzed them by types. *Revenge arsonists* are the most prevalent type. Most are family members or friends who have been involved in an argument with the people against whom they seek revenge. Many are intoxicated at the time of the crime.

EXHIBIT 8.3

Church Burnings: Congress Reacts

The frequent burnings of churches in which the congregations were predominantly or entirely African American led President Bill Clinton to appoint the National Arson Task Force to investigate whether the arsons were racially motivated. In 1997, the task force concluded that the rash of arsons against African American churches was not the result of a national conspiracy. Nevertheless, the church burnings prompted Congress to enact the Church Arson Prevention Act. This statute provides grants to assist congregations in rebuilding their churches, most of which were located in southern states. It doubles to 20 years the maximum sentence for arson of a house of worship. It permits the federal government to become involved in arson cases in which racial hatred appears to be a factor.[1]

The statute may not be as effective as hoped, however, because arson cases are difficult to investigate, and connecting them with racial hatred presents challenging evidentiary issues.

1. The statute amends USCS, Title 18, Section 247, Damage to Religious Property (2010).

Revenge arsonists are potentially more dangerous than other types, and they make little attempt to conceal their acts.[49]

Many *vandalism arsonists* are teenagers who think it is fun to destroy property by fire. These arsonists often work in pairs or groups, in contrast to other types, who work alone most of the time. *Crime-concealment arsonists* are offenders who set fires to conceal other crimes that they have committed—for example, burglary or murder. *Insurance-claim arsonists* set fires so they can make false claims against their insurance companies. These arsonists frequently commit their crimes during the day, in contrast to crime-concealment arsonists, who usually work at night.

Excitement arsonists are often intoxicated and set fire to inhabited buildings at night for the fun they find in the activity. Perhaps the next type, *pyromaniacs*, best fits the common stereotype of arsonists. These are the pathological fire starters who do not seem to commit the crime for any practical or financial reason but, rather, because of an irresistible impulse.

Another type is the perpetrator who commits *arson for hire* or for profit. Most of these arsonists are never caught, and therefore, little is known about their characteristics. Finally, the *serial arsonist* is difficult to explain. Jay Scott Ballenger of Yorktown, Indiana, is serving over 42 years in prison for arson in 26 churches in eight states in the 1990s. Ballenger refers to himself as "a messenger of Lucifer, the archangel who became Satan."[50]

Some recent arsonists defy attempts to explain their behavior. It is particularly difficult to explain arson by professional firefighters, yet two major fires in 2002 were set by firefighters. In June of that year, 138,000 acres, 133 homes, 466 outbuildings, and 1 commercial building in four counties southwest of Denver were destroyed by a fire started by Terry Lynn Barton, 38, an employee of the U.S. Forest Service. This $39.1 billion fire, the largest in the state's history, required the efforts of thousands of firefighters working for three weeks. In December 2002, Barton pleaded guilty to starting the fire and subsequently lying to federal authorities about that act. Barton was sentenced to six years in federal prison followed by 15 years of probation. She must also pay millions in restitution. She was sentenced to the maximum, 12 years, for aggravated arson, on the state charges, but those were successfully challenged on procedural grounds in the state courts. Barton was released in June 2008 and required to perform 1,500 hours of community service in at least one of the counties damaged by her crime.[51]

In October 2003, a part-time firefighter entered a guilty plea to starting a 2002 fire in Arizona. It merged with another fire started by a person who was not prosecuted; it was a signal fire started by a woman lost in the forest and attempting to signal for help. This most destructive fire in that state's history consumed more than 450,000 acres and destroyed approximately 500 homes. Leonard Gregg, 29, who said he started the fire to create work for himself, originally claimed that he was not competent to stand trial. After

spending time in a federal prison hospital, he was declared competent to stand trial and subsequently entered a guilty plea. In March 2004, the judge sentenced Gregg to 10 years in prison and ordered him to pay over $27 million in restitution to the fire's victims. One news analyst pointed out that at the rate of $100 per month, which Gregg was ordered to pay, it would take him 23,235 years to pay the full restitution. The sentencing judge stated that he hoped Gregg would seek professional help for his psychiatric problems and that he would realize the full impact of his acts.[52]

In 2007, Van Bateman, 57, was sentenced to two years in federal prison, three years' probation, and a $5,000 fine and was ordered to pay $10,390 in restitution to the U.S. Forest Service for arson in the Coconino National Forest in Arizona. Bateman was a 34-year veteran firefighter, who, along with other firefighter experts, said they often started fires without permits to avoid the hassle of getting the permits.[53]

Also in 2007, three college students were sentenced to serve two years each in state prison for their respective roles in starting fires at rural Alabama churches. Matthew Cloyd, 21, Benjamin Moseley, 20, and Russell DeBusk Jr., also 20, entered guilty pleas to arson and burglary in the burning of five churches. Moseley also entered a guilty plea to animal cruelty after shooting a cow. The students said they were drunk and driving through the countryside when they committed these acts. Two received eight years and one was given seven years in federal prison for burning seven churches. They will serve their state terms after they complete their federal sentences; then all will be required to perform 300 hours of community service work for the church congregations and pay a total of $3.1 million in restitution.[54]

There have been some medical studies of arsonists, and three are mentioned here. One study examined the mental health records of 283 arsonists. It reported that 90 percent of those offenders had a history of mental health problems, and 36 percent had been diagnosed as schizophrenic or bipolar. Only three of the sample were diagnosed as having pyromania; 64 percent were abusing alcohol or other drugs at the time they committed arson. Many of the patients were both delusional and angry.[55]

An English study included only female arsonists and violent offenders who were in custody. These women were compared with a control group. The investigators found that female arsonists were more likely to have a background of sexual abuse as children and a history of self-inflicted violence. The investigators suggested that the female arsonists were unable to vent their hostilities toward other persons, so they did so toward property. This effort at displaced aggression might have enhanced their self-esteem, which they had not succeeded in achieving by other means.[56]

Finally, a report on the research that measured **recidivism** among fire setters concluded that the literature does not support the assumption that those who set fires are inherently dangerous persons.[57]

Lesser Property Crimes: A Sample

The *UCR* enumerates and collects data on less serious, or Part II, offenses. Despite the FBI categorization of these crimes as less serious property crimes, at some levels, they are *more* serious than burglary, larceny-theft, motor vehicle theft, and arson. The total economic loss may be greater, and the erosion of society's moral fiber may be more significant. More attention is given to these issues in Chapter 9, which discusses business- and government-related crimes.

Several of the *UCR*'s Part II property offenses are considered here. The FBI definitions of these crimes are listed in Exhibit 8.4.

Forgery, Counterfeiting, and Fraud

The FBI lists and defines **forgery** and **counterfeiting** together, as noted in Exhibit 8.4. **Fraud** is also included here because crimes involving checks as negotiable instruments may involve forgery and fraud. The most common type of forgery is *check forgery*, which was studied in depth by an early sociologist, Edwin M. Lemert, whose work became a classic.

Many people who engage in check forgery are not professionals, but amateurs, called *naive check forgers* by Lemert, who applied his closure theory of analysis in studying them. According to Lemert, persons who are isolated socially and facing situations that tend to create further isolation (e.g., divorce, unemployment, or alcoholism) may encounter problems that they perceive can be solved only with money. Check forging is seen as a way to eliminate or at least reduce those problems—a way to get closure. Lemert found that check forgers did not associate with other criminals or engage in other types of crime. Many were nonviolent and likable persons, older and more intelligent than most other criminals.[58]

Another frequently committed theft crime is stealing credit cards or credit card numbers. Such thefts may be covered under identity theft, discussed later in this chapter. Credit card thefts may also be connected with organized crime, discussed in Chapter 10. Muggers, prostitutes, burglars, and other offenders connected with organized crime steal credit cards and sell them to credit card rings. The estimated loss per year from credit card theft and fraud is impossible to measure because much goes undetected. However, for both individuals and for businesses and financial institutions, the losses are significant.

Credit card theft may be connected to other crimes. For example, in December 2009, the U.S. Department of Justice (DOJ) announced a plea agreement leading to a guilty plea by Albert Gonzalez, 28, of Miami, Florida, for "conspiring to hack into computer networks supporting major American retail and financial organizations, and to steal data relating to tens of millions of credit and debit cards." Under the terms of the plea, Gonzalez would not ask for less than 17 years in prison, and the prosecutor would not ask for more than 25 years. Gonzalez pleaded guilty to 19 counts of conspiracy, computer fraud, aggravated identity theft, and other charges. The DOJ did not state an estimated dollar amount attributed to Gonzalez's crimes but did describe them as involving "one of the most complex and large scale identity theft cases in history."[59]

There are numerous ways offenders acquire checks and credit cards illegally. They steal them through pickpocketing or mugging or by stealing cars, purses, briefcases, or other items that contain the cards. They may burglarize a house and steal checks and cards. They may make counterfeit checks or cards or alter existing ones. They intercept checks in the mail and cash them or intercept

---

EXHIBIT 8.4

Selected Lesser Property Crimes: *UCR* Definitions

Forgery and Counterfeiting

"The altering, copying, or imitating of something without authority or right, with the intent to deceive or defraud by passing the copy or thing altered or imitated as that which is original or genuine; or the selling, buying, or possession of an altered, copied, or imitated thing with the intent to deceive or defraud. Attempts are included."

Fraud

"The intentional perversion of the truth for the purpose of inducing another person or other entity in reliance upon it to part with something of value or to surrender a legal right. Fraudulent conversions and obtaining of money or property by false pretense. Confidence games and bad checks, except forgeries and counterfeiting, are included."

Embezzlement

"The unlawful misappropriation or misapplication by an offender to his/her own use or purpose of money, property, or some other thing of value entrusted to his/her care, custody, or control."

Stolen Property; Buying, Receiving, Possessing

"Buying, receiving, possessing, selling, concealing, or transporting any property with the knowledge that it has been unlawfully taken, as by burglary, embezzlement, fraud, larceny, robbery. Attempts are included."

Source: Federal Bureau of Investigation, *Crime in the United States: Uniform Crime Reports 2009,* "Offense Definitions," http://www2.fbi.gov/ucr/cius2009/about/offense_definitions.html, accessed 20 October 2010.

blank checks and complete them. They may gain access to an individual's personal identification information or manufacture and market illegal cards. Some offenders set up false websites that request credit card information, perhaps informing a person electronically that his or her bank account will be closed unless certain information is forwarded to the website. They may also engage in computer crimes, breaking into information contained by others, such as retailers, and accessing those accounts.

There are many kinds of fraud in addition to credit card fraud. Some of these are discussed in Chapter 9.

Stolen Property: Buying, Receiving, Possessing

The *UCR* includes the buying, receiving, or possessing of stolen property as a Part II offense. To make money on their acquisitions, thieves must make arrangements to exchange the goods for money or other merchandise. In many instances, a **fence** is involved. A *fence* is a person who disposes of stolen goods. Often, fences are professionals connected with organized crime.

Researchers have given considerable attention to the role of the fence in property crimes. Sociologist Darrell J. Steffensmeier's *The Fence: In the Shadow of Two Worlds* covered many aspects of fencing, including a discussion of the process of becoming and being a fence.[60] Another sociological analysis of fences was conducted by Neal Shover, whose primary focus was the professional burglar. Shover found that fences could be distinguished by three characteristics: "(1) the *scale* of their operation, (2) the *frequency* of purchase, and (3) their *degree of product specialization*."[61]

The routine activity approach (discussed in Chapter 5) has been used in the anlaysis of offenders who engage in receiving stolen property. According to this approach, demographic variables such as gender, age, ethnicity, and income appear to be related to whether a person is offered stolen property for purchase and whether the individual to whom it is offered is motivated to buy. But these variables do not influence whether or not the person buys the stolen property. It appears that the opportunity to buy stolen property and, to a lesser degree, the motivation to buy are more important than demographic variables in determining whether the purchase is made.

> Routine activities theory predicts that potential buyers and potential sellers of illegal goods must converge in time and space before an illegal transaction can occur. This convergence is facilitated when the life styles of buyers and sellers bring them together. . . . Younger persons and males were much more likely than older persons or females to be offered stolen goods for sale. These groups are also more likely than other groups to engage in "high risk" activities which might bring them into physical proximity with sellers of stolen goods.[62]

Embezzlement

As mentioned earlier, under the common law, if the property of another had been entrusted to you and if you had kept the property, even against the wishes of the owner, you would not have committed larceny-theft. Gradually, it was decided that misappropriation of the property entrusted by the owner to another person should be a crime. But since larceny-theft was a felony and all felonies carried the death penalty, there was a reluctance to place such acts in that category. The solution was to create a new crime category that carried lighter penalties.

Embezzlement refers to the misappropriation or misapplication of property or money entrusted to the care, custody, or control of the offender. The crime may involve greater economic loss than larceny-theft but result in a less severe sentence. Today, many jurisdictions have a general theft statute that covers most, if not all, types of theft, including larceny-theft and embezzlement. The California theft statute is an example.

> Every person who shall feloniously steal, take, carry, lead, or drive away the personal property of another, or who shall fraudulently appropriate property which has been entrusted to him, or who shall knowingly and designedly, by any false or fraudulent representation or pretense, defraud any other person of money, labor or real or personal property . . . is guilty of theft.[63]

A statute as broadly worded as this includes the new kinds of theft that have come to our attention in recent years. Despite the possibility of including all types of theft in one statute, some jurisdictions have enacted special statutes to cover certain thefts, such as one that has been described as the fastest-growing property crime in the world: identity theft.

Embezzlement is frequently combined with other crimes. In June 2010, an attorney, Michael Scott Margulies, 56, of Minneapolis, pleaded guilty to embezzling approximately $2 million from his clients and his law firm. He also entered a guilty plea to wire fraud (discussed in Chapter 9 of this text). He committed embezzlement by forging checks, submitting fraudulent expense reports and invoices, and false documentation. He faced up to 20 years in federal prison.[64]

Identity Theft

The *UCR* lists and tabulates data on all of the crimes discussed thus far, but some of those crimes overlap with the growing crime called **identity theft**. *Identity theft* involves stealing Social Security numbers, bank code numbers, and other personal identifiers that may reveal financial information. This information is then used to steal the victim's personal financial resources. A recent BJS special report on identity theft was published in June 2010 and based on 2007 data. The BJS defines *identity theft* as the "unauthorized use or attempted use of a credit card, existing accounts such as checking accounts, misuse of personal information, or multiple types at the same times."[65] Exhibit 8.5 contains additional information from this and a later report.

Identity theft victims may spend months or even years trying to erase the false charges from their credit reports and clear their names, and law enforcement officials face significant roadblocks trying to apprehend identity theft thieves.

Media Focus 8.1 contains additional information about identify theft in the United States.

In 1998, the U.S. Congress enacted the Identity Theft and Assumption Deterrence Act, which, under most circumstances, carries a penalty of a maximum prison term of 15 years, a fine, and the **forfeiture** of any personal property used (or intended to be used) in committing the crime. Among other actions, the statute provides that a crime is committed by one who

knowingly transfers, possesses, or uses, without lawful authority, a means of identification of another

person with the intent to commit, or to aid or abet, or in connection with, any unlawful activity that constitutes a violation of Federal law, or that constitutes a felony under any applicable State or local law.[66]

Federal law also includes other statutes, such as those governing credit card fraud, computer fraud, and mail fraud, that may be used to prosecute schemes to commit identity theft. All these crimes are felonies and carry penalties up to 30 years in prison, a fine, and criminal forfeiture. On 4 December 2003, in an effort to thwart identity theft, President George W. Bush signed into law the Fair and Accurate Credit Transactions Act of 2003, which improved the accuracy of consumer records and imposes additional requirements on lenders and others.[67] Financial fraud and identity theft are also problems in other countries, as noted in Global Focus 8.1.

Anyone might become an identity theft victim, but the most targeted industry for **phishing**, which is one type of identity theft, is financial services. *Phishing* is defined

---

EXHIBIT 8.5   Identity Theft: The Extent

"Type of identity theft

- In 2007, half of all victimized households, accounting for nearly 4 million households, experienced the unauthorized use or attempted use of a credit card account.
- The second-most common type of identity theft in 2007, experienced by 1.9 million households, involved the unauthorized use or attempted use of existing accounts, such as a bank, checking or debit, or cellular phone account.

Head of household characteristic

- Households headed by individuals age 65 or older were less likely than any other age groups to be victims of attempted or successful identity theft.
- A lower percentage of Hispanic households (5.2%) experienced identity theft or attempted identity theft than non-Hispanic households (6.8%).

Household income

- Households with incomes of $75,000 or more experienced a higher rate of identity theft than households in lower income brackets.
- Households with one person were less likely or somewhat less likely to experience identity theft than households with two or more persons age 12 or older.

Financial loss

- In 2007, 32% of households victimized by identity theft reported a financial loss of $500 or more.
- Households experiencing the theft of personal information were more than twice as likely as households with thefts of credit cards, other existing accounts, or multiple types to report that no money was lost due to the identity theft.
- Among households experiencing the misuse of personal information, those with a financial loss reported an average household loss of $5,650.
- Across all victimized households reporting a financial loss, the average amount lost per household was $1,830."[1]

In a later report, published in December 2010, the BJS reported that, "Although the total financial cost of identity theft was nearly $17.3 billion . . . less than a quarter (23%) of identity theft victims suffered an out-of-pocket financial loss from the victimization."[2]

---

1. Lynn Langton and Katrina Baum, Bureau of Justice Statistics, *Identity Theft Reported by Households, 2007—Statistical Tables* (June 2010), p. 2, http://bjs.ojp.usdoj.gov/content/pub/pdf/itrh07st. pdf, accessed 20 October 2010.
2. Lynn Langton and Michael Planty, Bureau of Justice Statistics, *Victims of Identity Theft, 2008* (December 2010), p. 1, http://bjs.ojp .usdoj.gov/content/pub/pdf/vit08.pdf, accessed 16 December 2010.

8.1 Identity Theft: Statements by the Media

MEDIA FOCUS

During the past few years, the media have frequently focused on the growing crime of identity theft, which is reaching epidemic proportions. These accounts are informative and, ideally, will alert us to a crime that can cause severe economic damage as well as time lost in trying to eliminate the problems caused when someone steals our identities. Media reports range from papers in our largest cities to those in our smallest villages and include local and national radio and television stations. Following are a few examples.

In June 2009, the *New York Times* published a lengthy article entitled "A New Ailment: Medical ID Theft." The article began with the facts surrounding the medical identity theft from Brandon Sharp, of Houston, Texas, a healthy 37-year-old who had never been to an emergency room yet was charged with a large bill for services at one. In addition, he received a $19,000 bill for a Life Flight air ambulance service from a remote location with which he was unfamiliar. He also received bills for emergency room services from places he had never been. Such medical identity theft may occur in many ways, including theft by medical personnel.[1]

In July 2006, the *New York Times* published an article entitled "Identity Thief Finds Easy Money Hard to Resist." The article featured Shiva Brent Sharma, then 22, who, by the time he was 20, had been arrested three times for identity theft. Sharma said he did not keep track of the money he stole, but he knew he obtained $20,000 in a day and a half on at least one occasion. Sharma used the Internet to commit most of his crimes, learning how to deceive individuals into sending him personal financial information and using it to wire money to his own accounts. He was sentenced to two to four years in a New York correctional facility.[2]

Three years earlier, the *New York Times* had published an article entitled "Identity Theft Victimizes Millions, Costs Billions." This article was based on a report issued that day by the Federal Trade Commission, noting that 3.3 million Americans were identity theft victims the previous year and that the losses cost $3.8 billion to consumers and $32.9 billion to businesses.[3]

By 2008, the estimate of identity theft victims was over 9.9 million; in 2009, Federal Reserve Chairman Ben Bernanke and his wife, Ann, were identity theft victims. And a private security firm took out a full-page ad in a national paper soliciting customers for its theft protection services.[4]

A January 2003 bank journal called identity thieves a new breed of criminals. This article referred to the November 2002 arrest of Phillip Cummings, 33, accused of masterminding a $2.7 million ring of identity theft. The case was thought to be the largest loss from identity theft in the United States to that point. Cummings was accused of stealing more than 30,000 passwords used by financial institutions while he was employed by a software company that connected those financial institutions with credit bureaus on the World Wide Web. Cummings sold the passwords for $30 each to a partner, who downloaded them and sold the resulting credit reports to an identity theft ring of 20 persons. In January 2005, Cummings was sentenced to 14 years in a federal prison and ordered to forfeit $1 million in proceeds after he entered a guilty plea to conspiracy, wire fraud, and identity theft. Prosecutors estimated that Cummings and his partner helped the other 20 persons to steal between $50 million and $100 million.[5]

1. "A New Ailment: Medical ID Theft," *New York Times* (13 June 2009), p. 1B.
2. "Identity Thief Finds Easy Money Hard to Resist," *New York Times* (4 July 2006), p. 1.
3. "Identity Theft Victimizes Millions, Costs Billions," *New York Times* (4 September 2003), p. 16.
4. "5 Things Everyone Should Know About Identity Theft," Lifelock ad in *USA Today* (4 November 2009), p. 6C.
5. "Identity Theft: A New Breed of Criminals," *Bank Technology News* 16, no. 1 (January 2003): 1; "Identity Thief Gets 14 Years," *Electronic Payments Week* 2, no. 3 (18 January 2005), p. 0.

by the Federal Trade Commission as a "high-tech scam that uses spam or pop-up messages to deceive you into disclosing your credit card numbers, bank account information, Social Security number, passwords, or other sensitive information." Phishing is a way Internet scammers lure people into their nets. They go fishing for information, but it is now called *phishing*. Here is how it works. The potential victim receives an email or a pop-up message that appears to be from a company with which he or she does business. Usually, the message states that you need to update or verify personal information. You are directed to a website that appears, but is not, legitimate. The purpose of that website is to trick the unsuspecting consumer into releasing personal identification information that is then used by the scammer to commit an illegal act. The FTC warns that legitimate companies do not ask for such personal information by email; thus, to avoid being scammed, never give out such information by email.[68]

Phishing illustrates the relationship between identity theft and computer crimes.

8.1 **Fraud and Identity Theft: International Issues**

Financial fraud, especially that resulting from identity theft, often of credit cards, has spread rapidly to other countries in the world. In August 2008, federal prosecutors charged 11 people with stealing and selling over 40 million credit and debit card numbers. The accused were from Estonia, Ukraine, China, and Belarus as well as from the United States. The alleged mastermind, Albert "Segvec" Gonzalez, of Miami, Florida, faces life in prison if convicted on charges of wire fraud, access device fraud, aggravated identity fraud, computer fraud, and conspiracy. It was alleged that the defendants hacked into WiFi networks and installed "sniffer" programs that gave them access to card numbers and passwords. They allegedly dumped the information into Ukranian and Latvian servers and stored it on servers in other countries as well, including the United States. According to the indictment, the personal information was then used to withdraw money from ATMs. Federal agents investigated this case for three years before issuing the indictments. The director of the Secret Service claimed this to be the "largest, most sophisticated identity-theft ring ever prosecuted by the DOJ [Department of Justice]."[1]

In December 2009, computer hackers known as the Russian Business Network were under investigation by the FBI. It was alleged that the group, a Russian Internet gang previously accused of cybercrimes involving child pornography, fraud, and identity theft, hacked into U.S. banks and stole millions of dollars. These accusations surfaced as President Obama named Howard Schmidt as head of cybersecurity. Obama had stated that defending against cyberattacks had become a "national security priority." Some of the banks that were allegedly targeted disclaimed any FBI investigation into their banks. The Russian gang, previously headquartered in St. Petersburg, Florida, had moved its headquarters to China.[2]

The commission of fraud, identity theft, and other crimes was suspected in the June 2007 solving of a mystery that had existed since 1998, when an antique jewel was stolen from a castle in Vienna. The nineteenth-century jewel, which was made for Queen Elizabeth of Austria, was found in 2007 in a home in Winnipeg, Canada. Canadian police suspected that the theft was part of an elaborate and highly organized criminal group that engaged in such crimes in Europe, Africa, and Canada. The eight persons arrested, including the suspected leader, Gerald Daniel Blanchard, faced 41 charges, including trafficking in credit card data, fraud, and organized crime offenses. Blanchard pleaded guilty to 16 charges and was sentenced to eight years in prison.[3]

1. "11 Charted in Global Theft, Sale of 40 Million Card Numbers," *Washington Post* (6 August 2008), p. 01D.
2. "Russian Hackers 'Stole Millions from Citibank,'" *The Guardian* (London) (23 December 2009), p. 14.
3. "Winnipeg Police Recover Antique Jewel Stolen in Vienna," *Hamilton Spectator* (Ontario, Canada) (2 June 2007), p. 3; "Leader of Global Theft Ring Gets Eight Year Prison Sentence," *Daily Herald-Tribune* (Grande Prairie, Alberta, Canada) (8 November 2007), News Section, p. 9.

Computer Crimes

Computers have revolutionized the way we do business and, in many respects, the way we think and act. Computers fascinate and challenge many people; others may develop an intense fear of computers or of the Internet called **cyberphobia**; and a few people may even become violent, attacking the computer. Computers are also used to commit crimes.

The cost of **computer crime** is unknown, but estimates run into billions of dollars. Within the category of computer crime is **cybercrime**, which is a computer crime that involves the Internet. The most damaging cybercrime is identity theft, but computer viruses are also costly, with estimates as high as $400 billion a year or more.[69] A medium-sized company with a computer virus can spend over a million dollars a year cleaning computers of the virus, and to that must be added the cost of lost employee productivity. Cleaning an infected computer can take hours; the average cost is between $100 and $300 per machine. In April 2009, the Pentagon announced that in the previous six months it had spent $100 million on cyberattacks. In 2008, the Pentagon had to take 1,500 computers offline because of a cyberattack, and later that year, it banned the use of external flash drives because of a detected virus threat.[70]

Data on cybercrime are probably understated because some businesses and individuals may not want to report it. But the latest BJS National Computer Security Survey (NCSS) showed that of the almost 8,000 businesses responding, 67 percent suffered at least one cybercrime incident in the previous year. The most common type of crime was a computer virus, reported by 52 percent of the respondents. Viruses accounted for 60 percent of the system downtime suffered by the businesses. In almost 75 percent of the reported crimes, employees (or contractors) of the businesses were the perpetrators. Telecommunications businesses accounted for 82 percent of the reported crimes. Exhibit 8.6 contains more information from the national survey, including the definitions of the groups of crime.[71]

More recent data come from the Internet Crime Complaint Center (IC3), which was established in 2000 as the

Computer hacker Kevin Mitnick arrives at a news conference after his release from serving five years in a federal prison in California. After his release, Mitnick, one of the nation's most notorious computer hackers and at one time the FBI's most wanted hacker, began working as an internationally recognized computer security expert.

Internet Fraud Complaint Center. In its 2009 annual report, the IC3 indicated that the number of reported complaints between 2008 and 2009 increased by 22.3 percent. The estimated loss to victims was $559.7 million. Figure 8.3 graphs the yearly comparison of complaints received by the IC3 between 2000 and 2009, and Figure 8.4 graphs the yearly dollar loss of those complaints between 2001 and 2009.

In addition to the expense and inconvenience that a computer virus causes for individuals and businesses, there is the possibility that a virus can infect a computer with information leading to criminal charges. Julian Green, 45, of western England, claimed that the 172 images of child pornography on the hard drive of his computer were put there by a computer virus. Green, who suffers chronic pain as the result of a degenerative disk disease, spent nine days in prison and three months in a halfway house. During that time, he had only limited visits with his 7-year-old daughter, who discovered the images and told her father. Green sought to have the computer cleaned; that was successful, although he still had problems with the computer, which would connect to the Internet even when no one was in the house. Someone alerted the police, Green's home was searched, and the computer was seized. The police found no evidence of child pornography in the house, just on the hard drive of the computer. Green claimed he did not put it there and had no idea how it got there.[72] The criminal charges against Green were eventually dropped.

One final type of computer crime that is becoming a growing menace is **cyberstalking**. Stalking was discussed in Chapter 7 and should be reviewed here. In cyberstalking, the Internet, email, or some other form of electronic

Figure 8.3

Cybercrime: Yearly Comparison of Complaints Received by the Internet Crime Complaint Center (IC3)

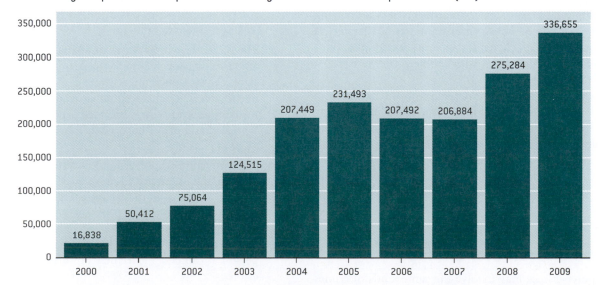

Source: Internet Crime Complaint Center (IC3), Bureau of Justice Assistance, U.S. Department of Justice, *2009 Internet Crime Report* (2010), p. 4, http://www.ic3.gov/media/annualreport/2009_IC3Report,pdf, accessed 18 December 2010.

Figure 8.4

Cybercrime: Yearly Dollar Loss (in Millions) of Complaints Referred to the Internet Crime Complaint Center (IC3)

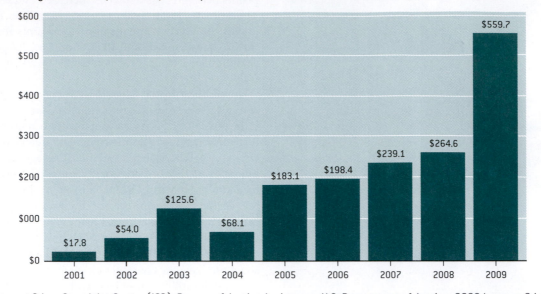

Source: Internet Crime Complaint Center (IC3), Bureau of Justice Assistance, U.S. Department of Justice, *2009 Internet Crime Report* (2010), p. 4, http://www.ic3.gov/media/annualreport/2009_IC3Report,pdf, accessed 18 December 2010.

communication is used for stalking, harassing, or annoying an individual. In some cases, individuals have been physically threatened by their stalkers. Recent examples of *cyberbullying* have caught the attention of the media. Consider, for example, the case of Megan Meier, 13, who committed suicide after she received cyberbullying from an alleged boy named Josh, who flirted and then made cruel statements, such as the world would be a better place without Megan. Problems with prosecuting such cases are noted later, but the issue of cyberbullying and its association with suicide are of great concern. On 28 June 2010, for example, the *New York Times* carried a front page "above the fold" article about cyberbullying, continuing with two full additional pages of text.[73] Some forms of cyberbullying may be considered hate crimes, as noted in Chapter 7's discussion of Tyler Clementi's apparent suicide after photos of his sexual encounter with another male were placed on the Internet.

Two criminologists who looked into the relationship between cyberbullying and suicide and have a forthcoming article on the subject have established the Cyberbullying Research Center on the Internet. They defined *cyberbullying* as "willful and repeated harm inflicted through the use of computers, cell phones, and other electronic devices." They concluded that, according to their research, "all forms of bullying were significantly associated with increases in suicidal ideation."[74]

Types of Computer Crimes

Computer crimes may involve the same kinds of crimes discussed elsewhere in this chapter as well as those discussed in previous chapters except that a computer is used in the perpetration of the crime. According to white-collar crime expert August Bequai, "Computer crime may also take the form of threats of force directed against the computer itself. . . . Computer crime cases have one commonality: the computer is either the tool or the target of the felon."[75]

A special jargon is used to describe computer crimes:

1. *Data diddling*, the most common, the easiest, and the safest technique, involves changing the data that will be put into the computer or that are in the computer.

2. The *Trojan horse* method involves instructing the computer to perform unauthorized functions as well as its intended functions.

3. The *salami technique* refers to taking small amounts of assets from a larger source without significantly reducing the whole. For example, one might, in a bank account situation, instruct the computer to reduce specified accounts by 1 percent and place those assets into another account.

4. *Superzapping* Because computers at times malfunction, there is a need for what is sometimes called a "break glass in case of emergency" computer program. This program will "bypass all controls to modify or disclose any of the contents of the computer." In the hands of the wrong person, it can be an extremely powerful tool for crime.

5. *Data leakage* involves removing information from the computer system or computer facility.[76]

EXHIBIT 8.6

Cybercrime Against Businesses

The president's National Strategy to Secure Cyberspace, issued in February 2003, focused on improving data collection on cybercrime as well as ways to prevent it. The U.S. Department of Justice (DOJ) subsequently announced that the Bureau of Justice Statistics (BJS) and the Department of Homeland Security's (DHS) National Cyber Security Division would conduct a national survey of businesses, the National Computer Security Survey (NCSS), in an effort to meet the goals of the president's orders. In an earlier study, the BJS found that almost three-fourths of businesses were cybercrime victims in 2001.[1]

In its latest survey data analysis, based on the 2005 survey and published in 2008, the BJS noted these critical definitions along with some of its findings:

"The NCSS documents the nature, prevalence, and impact of cyber intrusions against businesses in the United States. . . . [The] three general types of cybercrime" are as follows:

- *Cyber attacks* are crimes in which the computer system is the target. Cyber attacks consist of computer viruses (including worms and Trojan horses [discussed in the chapter]), denial of service attacks, and electronic vandalism or sabotage.
- *Cyber theft* comprises crimes in which a computer is used to steal money or other things of value. Cyber theft includes embezzlement, fraud, theft of intellectual property, and theft of personal or financial data.
- *Other computer security incidents* encompass spyware, adware, hacking, phishing, spoofing, pinging, port scanning, and theft of other information, regardless of whether the breach was successful or damage or losses were sustained as a result."

[Here are some of the findings.]

"Computer virus infections were the most prevalent cybercrime among businesses . . . . detected by 52% of responding businesses. . . . Cyber fraud was the most common type of cyber theft. . . .

"86% of victimized businesses detected multiple incidents. . . .

"91% of businesses detecting cybercrime incurred losses. . . .

"Cybercrime resulted in monetary loss of $867 million among businesses responding to the survey.

"Two-thirds of computer security incidents were targeted against critical infrastructure businesses. . . .

"Insiders were involved in cyber theft for 74% of businesses. . . .

"Most businesses did not report cyber attacks to law enforcement authorities."[2]

---

1. U.S. Department of Justice, Office of Justice Programs, News Release, "National Computer Security Survey Announced" (9 February 2006), http://bjs.ojp.usdoj.gov/index.cfm?ty=pbdetail&iid=413, accessed 20 October 2010. The 2001 study by the Bureau of Justice Statistics is available in a Technical Report, *Cybercrime Against Business* (Washington, D.C.: U.S. Department of Justice, March 2004).

2. Ramona R. Rantala, Bureau of Justice Statistics Special Report, *Cybercrime Against Businesses, 2005* (17 September 2008, revised 21 March 2010), pp. 1–7, http://bjs.ojp.usdoj.gov/index.cfm?ty=pbdetail&iid=371, accessed 20 October 2010.

Controlling Computer Crimes

Legislation regulating computer crimes is relatively recent and reflects the varying definitions of this type of crime. Passage of a federal statute did not occur until the enactment of the Comprehensive Crime Control Act of 1984. Before that act, computer crimes were prosecuted under other statutes, such as those covering mail fraud and wire fraud, which excluded some types of computer crimes. In addition, the penalties were considered inadequate for computer crimes. The 1984 act has been amended several times.[77]

In 2003, Congress passed legislation, which was signed by the president and entitled the **CAN-SPAM Act** (Controlling the Assault of Non-Solicited Pornography and Marketing); it became effective in January 2004. Among other requirements, this act directed the Federal Trade Commission to adopt a rule requiring a mark or notice on spam that contains sexually explicit material. Violation of this requirement can result in criminal as well as civil penalties.[78]

In 2003, the Bush administration issued its *National Strategy to Secure Cyberspace*, a lengthy document detailing the need for eliminating cyberspace crime. According to that report, "cyberspace is the nervous system" of all U.S. public and private infrastructures, such as "agriculture, food, water, public health, emergency services, government, defense industrial base, information and telecommunications, energy, transportation, banking and finance, chemicals and hazardous materials, and postal and shipping." The report concluded that the "healthy functioning of cyberspace is essential to our economy and our national security." The report enumerated eight major initiatives and actions that must be instituted to secure U.S. cyberspace. As noted earlier, data collection and analysis are part of that initiative.[79]

A particular cybercrime statute aimed at identity theft was passed in 2008. The Identity Theft Enforcement and Restitution Act (ITERA) targets spam, phishing, and identity theft. The statute eliminated the previously required $5,000 in damages before the statute could be invoked. The statute also made it easier to file claims in federal court even when the information did not cross state lines, and it expanded the definition of *cyberextortion*.[80]

President Barack Obama appointed Howard A. Schmidt as the nation's chief of cybersecurity. Schmidt also served in the Bush administration. In May 2010, the Worldwide Cyber Security Summit was held in Dallas, Texas, attended by computer techs from around the world. In January 2010, the *Christian Science Monitor* emphasized that cybercrime has "reached a new era" but that many do not realize its potential impact. The article noted that in 2008, an estimated $1 trillion in intellectual property was stolen online and that the "human spy on the scene is being replaced by cybersleuths at a computer terminal." These spies are becoming more organized and are now operating much like international drug cartels (discussed in Chapter 10 of this text).[81]

Prosecution of computer crimes may, however, be difficult, as illustrated by the recent prosecution of Lori Drew, who was accused of posting information on the Internet to harass Megan Meier, mentioned earlier. Drew, 49, was indicted under the federal Computer Fraud and Abuse Act (CFAA) for setting up a false account on MySpace, pretending to be the boy, Josh, who made cruel statements to Meier after flirting online with her. Drew was convicted of accessing a computer without proper authorization, essentially for violating the terms of service of MySpace. She was acquitted of intentionally inflicting emotional distress. On appeal, a federal court held that the website rules were unconstitutionally vague.[82]

States have also made plans to combat cyberspace crimes, but it is possible that the enactment of statutes designed to prevent computer crimes will not be as effective as some would like to think. First, many establishments might not want the public to know that their employees committed crimes with the company's computers. Second, in addition to a lack of reporting or willingness to prosecute and the difficulties of apprehension and prosecution, law enforcement officials may not have the technical expertise to solve computer crimes, and most cases that go to trial are highly technical, costly, and extremely time-consuming. Finally, as noted in the *Drew* case, constitutional issues may preclude successful prosecutions.

A Legal Focus on Computer Crimes

This section focuses on one legal issue regarding computers, and that one is chosen because of its significance and the fact that it has not been resolved by federal courts. One of the terms of probation for persons convicted of computer crimes has been that they are prohibited from using the Internet or, in some cases, a computer for any reason.

Lori Drew, 49, leaves federal court after her sentencing hearing in Los Angeles. Drew was charged under the federal Computer Fraud and Abuse Act (CFAA) for setting up a false account on MySpace and pretending to be a boy, Josh, who made cruel statements to Megan Meier, 13, after flirting online with her. Meier committed suicide. Drew was convicted of three misdemeanor accounts of accessing a computer without proper authorization, essentially for violating the terms of service of MySpace. The jury deadlocked on a conspiracy charge. The judge delayed sentencing pending decision on a defense motion to dismiss the charges against Drew. The judge, who ruled in Drew's favor, said the MySpace rules were unconstitutionally vague.

We look at three lower federal court cases with different holdings on the issue.

In *United States v. Paul*, the Fifth Circuit Court of Appeals upheld a lower court's probation condition that the defendant, Ronald Scott Paul, "shall not have, possess or have access to computers, the Internet, photographic equipment, audio/video equipment, or any item capable of producing a visual image" during his three years of supervised release following his five-year prison term. Paul had entered a guilty plea to knowingly possessing child pornography after investigators found child pornography on his computer along with emails discussing child pornography. The Fifth Circuit held that the probationary terms were appropriate in view of Paul's offenses, which included seeking boy lovers. According to the court, the computer and Internet bans were "reasonably related to Paul's offense and to the need to prevent recidivism and protect the public." The U.S. Supreme Court refused to review the case, thus leaving the lower appellate court's decision standing.[83]

In contrast, in 2004, the Second Circuit Court of Appeals ruled that prohibitions such as the above are unconstitutional. In *United States v. Lifshitz*, the defendant, Michael Lifshitz, pleaded guilty to receiving child pornography on his computer. As part of his probationary terms, Lifshitz was required to have a monitoring device on his computer. That device would permit probation officers to monitor his computer use at any time; in addition, Lifshitz was required to submit to an examination of his computer and all his computer equipment at any time. He argued on appeal that these restrictions constituted unreasonable searches and seizures and thus were unconstitutional. The Second Circuit agreed that the restrictions might be too broad and sent the case back to the lower court for reanalysis. In an earlier case, the Second Circuit had also ruled that a ban on a defendant's use of the Internet, which would preclude his use of email, reading a newspaper online, or checking the weather, was too broad.[84]

In 2003, the Eighth Circuit Court of Appeals upheld an Iowa lower court's imposition of probation terms prohibiting the use of a computer by a defendant who was convicted of having child pornography on his computer.[85]

It is not uncommon in a field of emerging law that lower courts differ in their decisions on similar issues. At some point, the U.S. Supreme Court must resolve these differences.

Professional and Career Criminals

Some criminals work alone. Occasional thieves may steal for something they need; employees may embezzle money from their employers. Such people steal consistently over a number of years but never develop the skills, techniques, and attitudes of professional thieves. Other criminals are considered, and consider themselves, trained professionals; they may possess the skills, techniques, and attitudes that are common to many noncriminal professional people. Usually, they steal for profit. They may have long criminal careers, during which they may serve prison terms, one of the hazards of their occupation.

For years, professional thieves have captured the interest of scholars as well as the public. They have been featured in the media, and they have provided sociologists with interesting research opportunities. This discussion begins with an earlier analysis of the professional thief before proceeding to the more recent approach, which focuses on the career of the persistent offender.

Professional Criminal Behavior: The Early Approach

Numerous writers on professional crime have pointed out that over time there has been little change in conceptual categories of professional crime. The professional criminal, such as the professional thief, manifests highly developed career behavior patterns characterized by nonviolence, a high degree of skill, loyalty toward the loosely organized group rather than toward individuals, association with other professional as opposed to amateur criminals, long careers with few arrests, and an outlook that views noncriminals as people who deserve to be victimized. Professional criminals have a status hierarchy that is related to a combination of skill and an expectation of high profits. They are not from the extremes of poverty. They start crime later in life than other criminals, and the peer group becomes important in terms of reinforcing their deviant self-concepts and attitudes.[86]

The classic study of professional criminals was conducted by Edwin H. Sutherland, who talked extensively with a thief who had been in the profession for more than 20 years. Sutherland asked the thief to write on several topics. He submitted the manuscript to other professional thieves and talked with still others, finding that none disagreed with the account. Sutherland described the theft profession as a group way of life that had all the characteristics of other groups—techniques, codes, status, traditions, consensus, and organization. He pointed out that these characteristics are not pathological. In addition, apprenticeship and tutelage by professional thieves are prerequisites, and an individual must be recognized by professional thieves to become one.[87]

Contemporary Conceptualizations of Professional Thieves

Traditional conceptions of professional criminals are criticized for relying mainly on anecdotes and case studies and for not utilizing systematic sociological approaches.[88] Few attempts were made to test hypotheses; professional crime was confused with full-time crime, the latter being engaged in by individuals who did not have the skills and other characteristics of professional criminals. More recent studies have attempted to eliminate these and other criticisms.

Under the auspices of the 1967 President's Crime Commission, several investigators determined that the professional thief was characterized by decreased specialization. According to this study, the professional thief was "in business to cash in on opportunities and thus must not specialize too narrowly, for that increases the possibility of missing opportunities. Such characterizations of professional criminals indicate a radical change from the more traditional conceptualizations." Professional thieves must be versatile because of an emphasis on hustling, which means using all available means for victimizing others to make illegal gains for oneself. Further characteristics of contemporary professional criminals, in contrast to prior ones, were found to be an increased reliance on fences and longer careers because of increased agreements with prosecutors, which may reduce the probability of incarceration and the time spent behind bars if incarcerated. In many cases, the professional thief's selection of work depended on available opportunities rather than on his or her preferred criminal activity.[89]

Neal Shover's studies suggest that burglars are not highly specialized, although there is some evidence of short-term specialization. Shover found that, in contrast to the rest of the population, who might be viewed as honest, burglars did not see themselves as thieves: "The *good burglar* sees himself, then, as different from most people only in the methods he uses to steal."[90] Shover also found that most burglars were young African American men. Most performed their work in concert with others. The social organization and other characteristics may differ according to the type of burglar. For example, the *high-level burglar's* social organization might resemble that of the military. High-level burglars earned more than *low- or middle-level burglars*; for them, burglary was a way of life.

> Misfits in a world that values precise schedules, punctuality, and disciplined subordination to authority, high-level thieves value the autonomy to structure life and work as they wish. . . . Only the infirmities of age and diminishing connections significantly dampen their criminal activities.[91]

The study of professional crime shows the intricate pattern of social interaction that develops, which in many cases is a subculture. It shows the close relationship to acceptable patterns of business relationships, emphasizing shrewdness and even condoning fraud and swindles. According to criminologist Don C. Gibbons, "The law violator is no less a product of society than the moral, upright citizen, and both of them have much more in common than they are likely to acknowledge."[92]

Career Criminals: The Modern Approach

The skills, knowledge, attitudes, and values of professional criminals that were emphasized by early researchers may not be as much of a concern to the public as **career criminals** are. Today, the emphasis is on the repeat offender, especially when that offender is violent. Most people are not concerned with whether the offender is professional; in fact, an amateur violent criminal may be more feared than a professional nonviolent criminal. Nor is there a great concern for the attitudes and group affiliations of the person who burglarizes a home. There is concern, however, about why some offenders continue to repeat crime.

Repeat property offenders, for example, are distinguished from professional criminals in the former's lack of skill and absence of a complex interactional pattern. These criminals see themselves as society's victims. They do not feel guilty about their behavior. In comparison to professional criminals, they are more hostile toward law enforcement officials and toward society, their parents, and occupational roles. Most remain in crime through middle age, at which point some change to noncriminal activities. Some studies suggest that an increasing number of amateurs are involved in bank robberies and car thefts; others suggest that these offenders have rather stable criminal careers. It has also been reported that repeat or semi-professional burglars are predominantly young nonwhite men and that most burglary victims are from the lower socioeconomic class. A study of African American armed robbers disclosed that most were older than other felons, with predominantly lower-class urban origins, a history of criminal activity as teenagers, and an unstable family background.[93]

Wolfgang's Studies of Delinquency Cohorts

Many modern studies of chronic career offenders are based on the approach developed most extensively in the now classic studies of Marvin E. Wolfgang and his colleagues. These researchers utilized a **cohort** (a universe of persons defined by some characteristic) of 10,000 boys born in Philadelphia in 1945 who were available for study when they became 18 in 1963. According to official police reports, 65 percent of the boys had not been arrested before their eighteenth birthday. About one-third had prior contact with police. Of those, 46 percent of the delinquents stopped after the first offense, and of those who committed more than one offense, 35 percent had no more than three offenses. Fewer than 7 percent had five or more arrests; these repeat or chronic offenders committed 57 percent of all crimes attributed to the cohort of 10,000.[94]

Wolfgang repeated this approach in a study of 14,000 boys born in 1958, and he found some similarities with the earlier study. A small percentage, around 7 percent, committed most of the crimes. In this second study, the repeat offenders committed an even higher percentage of the crimes of their cohort, including 75 percent of the reported rapes and robberies. They constituted a chronically violent, although small, group of young men who began their criminal careers early and continued engaging in criminal activities into adult life.[95]

Other studies of delinquent cohorts have disclosed similar patterns of involvement with law enforcement, with a small percentage of the sample showing relatively high rates of repeat offenses.[96] Studies provide some evidence that high-rate juvenile offenders continued their criminal activities into adulthood.[97] Such findings raise interesting research as well as ethical questions, such as, "How can we identify the potential career criminals prior to the beginning of their careers and, if that can be done, with what result?" If effective prediction scales can be constructed, the results could be used for crime prevention and other social programs.[98] If most crimes are committed by only a few people, it can be argued that taking those people out of circulation, a process called **selective incapacitation**, would cut the crime rate significantly. As a result, it would "take the criminal justice system out of the business of dealing with social problems and put it to work doing what it alone can do: Identifying and removing from circulation people whose continued freedom would jeopardize the safety of the community."[99]

Earlier policy expectations of reduced crime through selective incapacitation seemed obvious to many law enforcement officials; special units to identify and track career criminals were established. However, few of these programs were evaluated, and "those which were evaluated failed to show strong positive results in either conviction rates or sentence severity." Evaluations of police department repeat offender programs suggested that the programs had some success, but even success in identification and prosecution raises important issues. First, which suspects should be targeted? Second, will the improved efforts of defense lawyers erase the efforts of police and prosecution?[100] Finally, the programs raise the ethical and legal question of invading the privacy of targeted persons.

In addition to the ethical problems involved in predicting which juveniles (or adults) might become recidivists are several practical problems. In short, how do we accurately predict recidivism? Research on California and Massachusetts career criminals who engaged in dangerous behavior found some characteristics that assist in the identification of offenders who frequently commit violent crimes. This information may be useful to prosecutors in deciding priority in prosecutions.[101]

Rand Studies of Career Criminals

Rand Corporation researchers have published numerous documents based on their extensive studies of habitual or career offenders. Their research, which collected data through the self-reports of offenders, focused on the small percentage of offenders who committed many offenses. In analyzing these studies, recall the discussion in Chapter 2 of the pros and cons of collecting data by the self-report data (SRD) method.

The first Rand sample involved 49 California prison inmates. The next study utilized a sample of 624 inmates from five California prisons selected to represent all male inmates in that state in terms of custody level, age, offense, and race. The study focused on the criminal activities of the inmates during the three years prior to their current incarcerations.[102] A third sample was larger: 2,190 jail and prison inmates in California, Michigan, and Texas.

The first Rand study found that most offenders were not specialized in their crimes. At any given time, the offenders engaged in a variety of criminal activities. Few

criminals committed crimes at a high rate; most did so at a fairly low rate, and the rate of violent crime among these inmates was very low. These findings were confirmed in the second study. During the three years prior to their current incarcerations, most of the inmates committed several other kinds of crime. Of those who reported having committed a crime other than the type for which they had been incarcerated, 49 percent listed more than four other crimes. As in the earlier study, a few inmates committed most of the reported crimes.

The Rand investigators found that neither age nor a prior prison term was strongly associated with offense rates, but self-concept was significant: "High-rate offenders tended to share a set of beliefs that were consistent with their criminal lifestyle—e.g., that they could beat the odds, that they were better than the average criminal, that crime was exciting, and that regular work was boring."[103]

The largest sample, in the third Rand study, was selected to check on possible problems in the first two samples and to include lesser offenses normally represented by jail populations. Analysis of data from this study confirmed that most offenders reported committing few crimes, and only a few reported committing many crimes. Offenders were placed into categories, the most serious being those who reported robberies, assaults, and drug deals. These offenders were termed *violent predators*. Most reported having committed these three crimes at high rates while also engaging in numerous other crimes. The factors that distinguished the violent predators from other inmates were the following:

- Youth
- Onset of crime (especially violent crime) before age 16
- Frequent commission of both violent and property crime before age 18
- Multiple commitments to state juvenile facilities
- Unmarried and with few family obligations
- Employed irregularly and for short times
- Frequent use of hard drugs as a juvenile
- Use of heroin at costs exceeding $50 per day
- Use of multiple combinations of drugs[104]

Researchers offered the following conclusions: Offenders identified as career criminals viewed themselves as criminals; they expected to return to crime after release from prison; they began their criminal careers early in their juvenile years; they were hedonistic, viewing crime as "a safe and enjoyable way to obtain the good life"; and they viewed themselves as proficient criminals. They represented only 25 percent of the sample, but they committed 58 percent of all reported armed robberies, 65 percent of burglaries, 60 percent of auto thefts, and 46 percent of assaults. The investigators pointed out that criminal justice systems might benefit by directing their incarceration efforts at these types of offenders rather than at other offenders (the majority) who do not exhibit these characteristics. The study noted that career property offenders can be identified and that some of them commit violent crimes, but the study did not provide any evidence "of an identifiable group of career criminals who commit only violence."[105]

Many studies are limited by the fact that the data represent official reports only, but the Rand research, based on self-report data, is said to be more reliable.[106]

The BJS Report

In June 1983, the BJS issued a Special Report on Career Criminals, which utilized data on offenders from across the country.[107] A random sample of 11,397 male and female inmates was interviewed; respondents were questioned extensively about their criminal careers. Since the major purpose of the study was to examine careers, only inmates who were at least 40 years old at the date of last admission to prison were selected for intensive study.[108]

Data in the BJS study were analyzed according to four types of offenders. The typologies were concerned with three of the major stages of life: adolescence (7–17 years), young adulthood (18–39 years), and middle age (40 years and older). The sample was divided as follows:

Type 1: Offenders who engaged in criminal activity in all three stages
Type 2: Offenders who engaged in criminal activity in all but young adulthood
Type 3: Offenders who engaged in criminal activity in all but adolescence
Type 4: Offenders who engaged in criminal activity in middle age only

Type 1 and Type 2 offenders engaged in some criminal activity during adolescence. Type 2 offenders did not engage in criminal activity during young adulthood. They were law-abiding during that time but returned to criminal activity in middle age. They represented a small percentage of the inmate population, but it is significant that 92 percent of those offenders who reported criminal activity during adolescence continued with criminal activity during young adulthood and into middle age. These are the Type 1 offenders.

Perhaps the most surprising finding of this study was that the Type 4 offenders, those middle-aged offenders who did not engage in criminal activity as adolescents or as young adults, represented almost half of all the inmates who entered prison in middle age. The BJS report explained this finding in terms of the reasons for incarceration. Many persons arrested for property offenses are incarcerated for those offenses only if they have prior criminal records. But those who commit violent personal crimes are likely to be incarcerated even without a prior criminal record. Therefore, in an analysis of the crimes for which offenders are currently incarcerated, it is important to consider their prior records. Thus, the fact that 40 percent of the inmates in the BJS study were

serving time for property offenses, not violent crimes, does not necessarily mean that society is incarcerating too many people for nonviolent crimes. Violence has been a part of the past record of many of these property offenders. The BJS report suggested that, although the study did not investigate the issue, it is likely that the high rates of incarceration for violent crimes of the offenders older than 40 represent domestic violence.

The NIJ Overview of Repeat Offenders

In 1989, the National Institute of Justice (NIJ), under the authorship of Lawrence Sherman, published an overview on repeat offenders, defining them as "people who commit serious criminal offenses at a high rate and over a long period." According to Sherman, these criminals do not specialize; they commit a variety of crimes, and they differ in the extent to which they commit crimes. They commit the majority of serious, detected crimes, although they do not constitute a majority of criminals.

Sherman noted that ethical, practical, and technological problems exist when authorities track these repeat offenders. One view shared by many is that offenders are responsible for crimes they have committed but not for crimes they *may* commit at some future date. Yet, identifying repeat offenders and arresting them for crimes may reduce crime significantly. Some cities attempted to do this; they established repeat offender programs among the police as well as prosecutors. Sherman concluded:

> Repeat offender programs seem likely to expand and proliferate. With the scarce resources of modern criminal justice confronted by growing demands, policy makers must increasingly establish priorities. The idea of focusing scarce resources on repeat offender programs—even with all the errors of prediction and ethical questions of such programs—provides an attractive basis for choosing which criminal justice course to take.[109]

The Young Criminal Years of the Violent Few

Another study of criminal careers that has gained wide attention is that by Donna Martin Hamparian, published in 1985. In an introduction to one of Hamparian's works, the administrator of the Office of Juvenile Justice and Delinquency Prevention, which funded the research, explained that the study extended those of Wolfgang and his associates and of the Rand Corporation. He described that research "as important as anything else we have learned in recent years." He continued, referring to the Hamparian study: "Probably the most significant contribution of this study is the increased knowledge of the characteristics of those offenders who are likely to continue their criminality into adulthood."[110] Hamparian's work was based on a cohort of 1,222 people born between 1956 and 1960. She described the juvenile arrests of these young people from 1962 to 1978 and "follow[ed] the cohort members through their early adult careers, if any, up to mid-1983." The major conclusions of Hamparian's study were as follows:

1. Most violent juvenile offenders make the transition to adult offenders.
2. There is continuity between juvenile and adult criminal careers.
3. A relatively few chronic offenders are responsible for a disproportionate number of crimes.
4. The frequency of arrests as adults declines with age.
5. Incarceration has not slowed the rate of arrest—in fact, the subsequent rate of arrest increases after each incarceration.[111]

Recent Research

Criminal careers have been the focus of considerable research in recent years. The researchers do not always agree on the issues. One approach, led by Michael Gottfredson and Travis Hirschi, takes the position that it is not important to study criminals over a time period and analyze the progression of their activities to understand crime. Gottfredson and Hirschi maintain that their self-control, or general, theory of crime (see again Chapter 6) explains all crime, and it is not relevant how many crimes were committed by a particular offender: "[T]he causes of criminal acts are the same regardless of the number of such acts."[112] Furthermore, it is not important to look at stages in the careers of criminals in an effort to distinguish criminal types and when they cease committing crimes or increase their activities. Gottfredson and Hirschi contended that, over time, all criminals lose their propensity to engage in crime. There is no need to study the impact of unemployment or other factors on crime because these factors are unimportant in explaining the behavior.

The second position, illustrated by the work of Alfred Blumstein and his collaborators, views career criminal behavior in terms of its stages. These researchers argued that factors that influence the beginning of crime may not influence a criminal career or its decline. For example, people might begin stealing or selling illegal drugs because they have no other source of income. But as their income needs are fulfilled, they may not abandon theft; some other reason might be necessary to explain the continuation of the criminal activity at this subsequent stage.

Yet other factors might explain why an individual ceases engaging in criminal activity, a process Blumstein and his colleagues refer to as *desisting* (defined and discussed in Chapter 6).[113] Further, career criminals differ in characteristics and may be analyzed by groups. Career criminals must be studied over a time period (longitudinal studies) in an effort to understand the factors that might influence various stages of their criminal careers. Such a study should distinguish between criminals and noncriminals, analyze a criminal career by the frequency of offending, and analyze the termination of a criminal career. These

three categories are referred to as innocents, desisters, and persisters. *Innocents* have never been involved with law enforcement. *Desisters* are offenders with a relatively low probability of repeating criminal behavior, and *persisters* have a relatively high probability of repeating criminal acts.[114]

Blumstein and his colleagues concluded that their approach, in contrast to the single-factor approach of Gottfredson and Hirschi, "allows for the possibility that different factors could influence these different facets of a criminal career." In contrast, "the single-factor approach presumes that all aspects of a criminal career are influenced by the same factors in the same way."[115]

Both approaches have been analyzed by David F. Greenberg, who developed a mathematical formula model of criminal careers. He concluded that much of the empirical research utilized in the dispute concerning the study of criminal careers "is entirely irrelevant to it. . . . Findings that seem to point to one conclusion can take on a different significance when viewed from a different perspective."[116]

In response, Blumstein and his colleagues concluded that Greenberg's position did not detract at all from their work and that Greenberg had made an important contribution to the debate on research on criminal careers "by presenting a much more explicit representation of the Gottfredson-Hirschi position than had previously been available." Blumstein and his collaborators conceded that the study of criminal careers needed more work, and in the future, it might become obvious that a simpler approach to the study is warranted. They pointed out that their main concern with Gottfredson and Hirschi was not their single-factor approach per se but "their unwillingness to consider more complex possibilities."[117]

In response, Greenberg argued that the debate over criminal careers has been mainly empirical, not theoretical, and the lack of a link to theory means that much work remains. Greenberg stated that when research on criminal careers "is conducted with greater attention to procedures that do not bias the research in favor of one model over the other, I predict that both positions will require modification."[118]

When asked to write a comment on the debate concerning the two models for approaching the study of criminal careers, Kenneth Land said, "I responded that this would be somewhat like trying to referee a fight between King Kong and Godzilla—with a substantial likelihood of being crushed in the middle, regardless of what I say."[119]

Considerable research on career criminals has been published by University of Cambridge (England) professor David P. Farrington. Farrington, along with his British and American colleagues, reviewed the most recent research on delinquency careers and analyzed data from the Seattle (Washington) Social Development Project. These data constitute a longitudinal study of 808 youths. The researchers compared data from court records with those of self-reports. They emphasized that most criminal career studies are based on official records of arrests and convictions. The problem with this approach is that official records do not capture the full range or the total number of crimes committed by the studied offenders. Self-reports by offenders capture more offenses but may also be inaccurate if the respondents lie or forget. Previous studies showed that delinquency peaked between about ages 15 and 17 and declined in the 20s (although these ages differed by types of crimes, with shoplifting peaking earlier than, for example, drug use). Farrington and his collaborators studied delinquents aged 11–17. Information was collected from court records, students, parents, school records, and teachers. Self-report data and juvenile court records were available for burglary, vehicle theft, larceny, robbery, assault, vandalism, marijuana use, and drug selling.[120] Here are some of the findings:

1. "The prevalence of offending increased with age in both the court and self-report data. . . .

2. [T]he prevalence of offending was higher in self-reports for all eight types of offenses. The two prevalence estimates [of the two measures] were most similar for vehicle theft . . . and most dissimilar for marijuana use. . . .

3. [I]ndividual offending frequency . . . was much higher in self-reports (49.2 per offender on average) than in court records (4.6 per offender on average). . . .

4. The self-report data . . . show a steady increase in individual offending frequency from age 11 to age 17. . .

5. Continuity in the prevalence of offending . . . . was generally highest for drug offenses and lowest for property [burglary, vehicle theft, and larceny] offenses.   . . .

6. [A]s expected, an early age of onset predicted a large number of offenses in both self-reports and court referrals. . . .

7. The probability of a self-reported offender being referred to court increased with the number of offenses committed. . . . However, the probability of a court referral after an offense decreased with the number of offenses committed, which suggests that the more frequent offenders might be more skilled at avoiding court referrals."[121]

Farrington and his collaborators concluded that, in general, offending was greater as measured by self-reports than by court records, and offending increased with age, with a sharp increase in court referrals for those respondents between ages 12 and 13. Both measures revealed continuity in offending with age, with the continuity greater in court referrals. The measure of the variance of offending frequency by age showed that while it remained constant according to official court records, it increased according to self-reports. Both measures showed a small percentage

of offenders committing most of the offenses, but this finding was greater when measured by self-reports than by court records. There was, however, a significant overlap between the two measures, meaning that both targeted some of the same chronic offenders. Most self-reported offenses were not referred to court, and this was particularly the case with drug offenses. Only approximately 1 in 1,000 offenses of marijuana use were court referred, and 1 in 10 vehicle theft offenses were reported. On the average, a delinquent was not referred to court until 2.4 years after the first self-reported offense. The majority of the chronic offenders were referred to court at some time, and the probability of such referral increased sharply in the categories of ages 11 and 12 and ages 13 and 15.[122]

The researchers concluded as follows:

[I]n self-reports, prevalence and individual offending frequency were higher, the age of onset was earlier, and the continuity and concentration of offending were greater. Self-reports and court referrals agreed in showing that the prevalence of offending increased during the juvenile years and that an early onset predicted a large number of offenses in total. The main difference in delinquency career results concerned the sharp increases in the prevalence of court referrals, and in the probability of an offender being referred to court, between ages 12 and 13; the fact that early onset (age 11–12) predicted a high frequency of offending in court referrals but not in self-reports; and the fact that the individual offending frequency increased with age in self-reports but not in court referrals.[123]

A 2008 research analysis of specialization among criminals raised the issue of the relationship between specialization and age. This study was based on data from and about a sample of more than 2,000 serious offenders who were incarcerated under the California Youth Authority in the 1980s. The investigator found some support for the influence of age on specialization, especially with regard to property and violent offenses, but less support for the influence of age on drug and miscellaneous offenses. The investigator distinguished between explaining crime specialization by an individual *propensity* to commit those crimes in contrast to an explanation that those crimes were committed primarily because of the *opportunity* to do so. This study was not, however, theoretically based and did not support either position for explaining why some criminals specialize in committing certain crimes. However, the results led the investigator to suggest that it is reasonable to conclude that opportunity theory is a better explanation.[124]

These and other findings could lead one to conclude that theory and public policy regarding criminal careers will differ according to the method by which data on the problem are secured. Consequently, research reports should be analyzed carefully before making important policy changes. In terms of policy, however, it is assumed today that repeat offenders are different from other offenders and that they should be punished more severely. The issues surrounding the enhancement of penalties for repeat offenders are discussed further in Chapter 13, but at this point, it is reasonable to take a quick look at the sentencing of repeat offenders.

Sentencing Repeat Offenders: The U.S. Supreme Court Rules

Criminologists may offer varying explanations for why some people are repeat offenders; defense attorneys in individual cases may argue that their clients should not receive long sentences for certain crimes. But the U.S. Supreme Court has held that, under proper circumstances, long sentences for repeat offenders do not violate the U.S. Constitution.

In 2003, the U.S. Supreme Court decided two cases involving three-strikes legislation, which is discussed in Chapter 13. One of those cases is noted briefly here. In *Ewing v. California*, the Court held that California's repeat offender statute did not violate the cruel and unusual clause of the Eighth Amendment (see Appendix A). Gary Ewing walked out of a pro golf shop with three golf clubs priced at $399 each. He did not pay for the clubs, which he concealed in his pants leg. Ewing was convicted and sentenced to 25 years to life in prison. Ewing's prior record consisted of numerous felony convictions, and he was on parole when he stole the golf clubs. The U.S. Supreme Court upheld Ewing's sentence and noted that, although the current three-strikes legislation was relatively new, for years states had utilized repeat offender sentencing laws. Among other comments, the Court stated the following:

> These laws responded to widespread public concerns about crime by targeting the class of offenders who pose the greatest threat to public safety: career criminals. . . . When the California Legislature enacted the three strikes laws, it made a judgment that protecting the public safety requires incapacitating criminals who have already been convicted of at least one serious or violent crime. Nothing in the Eighth Amendment prohibits California from making that choice.[125]

Summary

This chapter explored the most prevalent property crimes historically and currently. It began with a look at the four serious property crimes as defined by the FBI's *Uniform Crime Reports*: burglary, larceny-theft, motor vehicle theft, and arson.

Burglary is a common law crime with a fascinating history, a knowledge of which is necessary for a complete understanding of the treatment of this serious property crime today. Burglary has been studied by sociologists, but since many burglars are repeat offenders, the analysis of this crime is frequently included within studies of career criminals.

Originally, larceny-theft was a felony and carried the death penalty. The intricacies of the traditional laws concerning this serious crime were explored historically to see how the law has developed. Larceny-theft remains a serious crime, but it no longer carries the death penalty in the United States, and some of the elements required for the crime have changed. Larceny-theft, however, continues to embody a variety of crimes. One of those, shoplifting, was reviewed in terms of social science research.

The third serious property crime, motor vehicle theft, is committed frequently in the United States, but the clearance rate is so low that it has not permitted significant sociological research on those who commit the crime. Attention was also given to carjacking, a serious but less frequently committed crime than other motor vehicle thefts. Carjacking may be considered a property crime, but it is also a crime that may, and often does, result in injuries or even deaths and thus may be considered a violent crime.

The fourth serious property crime, arson, was moved by the FBI from its list of less serious crimes to that of serious offense status in 1979. That means data are not available for long-term trends. Estimates suggest that arson is increasing, with some evidence saying that it is one of the fastest-growing of the four serious property crimes.

The second section of the chapter covered some Part II, or less serious, property offenses as defined by the *UCR*: forgery, counterfeiting, and fraud; buying, receiving, and possessing stolen property; and embezzlement. These crimes may be categorized officially as less serious, but the economic and other losses from these crimes cause some people to consider them more serious than the four property crimes categorized by the *UCR* as serious.

Special attention was given to identity theft. This discussion presented practical as well as theoretical information. Significant attention was also given to the growing number of computer crimes, including cyberstalking, Internet fraud, and cyberbullying.

Since many property crimes involve career criminals and professional thieves, the final section of the chapter was devoted to the major studies of career criminals. That discussion showed the extent of disagreements among scholars in the field.

Property crimes do not always receive as much popular press as violent crimes because they are less dramatic, but the effect on the American public is significant, and the volume of property crimes far exceeds the volume of violent crimes. Many of the property crimes are subtle in their execution, and unlike common street crimes, many property crimes are committed by people with white-collar positions. The importance of these and other crimes related to business organizations makes it necessary to devote an entire chapter to them—Chapter 9.

Study Questions

1. Comment on the nature of the 2009 *UCR* data on serious property crimes.

2. Discuss the historical and current general requirements for establishing that a burglary has occurred.

3. Briefly discuss sociological findings about burglary.

4. Define *larceny-theft*, and discuss the historical development of the crime.

5. How does larceny-theft compare to other property crimes? What do recent data show about this crime?

6. What do we know about shoplifting?

7. Why is motor vehicle theft considered a serious crime? What is unique about the clearance rate of this crime?

8. Why was it necessary to have a federal carjacking statute?

9. Do you think carjacking should be categorized as a property or a violent crime? Explain your answer.

10. Comment on the nature and extent of arson.

11. List and explain six types of arsonists.

12. Explain briefly the following crimes: forgery; counterfeiting; fraud; buying, receiving, and possessing stolen property; and embezzlement.

13. Explain why identity theft is potentially such a serious crime.

14. Define *phishing*.

15. What is cybercrime? How serious is it? What can be done to control it?

16. Define *cyberstalking* and *cyberbullying*.

17. Discuss two major studies of career criminals.

18. What did the U.S. Supreme Court hold regarding long sentences for repeat offenders? Discuss the Court's reasoning.

Brief Essay Assignments

1. Explain the differences between burglary and larceny-theft.

2. Explore some of the sociological theories that might be applicable to the property crimes covered in this chapter.

3. What are the issues regarding attempts to curb cybercrime and, in particular, cyberstalking?

4. Discuss the potential methods for deterring repeat offenders, and relate your discussion to a U.S. Supreme Court decision regarding long sentences for these offenders.

Internet Activities

1. Log on to the Bureau of Justice Statistics website at http://bjs.ojp.usdoj.gov, accessed 20 October 2010, and read the article on carjacking by Patsy A. Klaus, "Carjacking, 1993–2002." How does carjacking differ from motor vehicle theft? According to the findings, how often were weapons used in the crime? What types of weapons were used? What percentage of carjackings were committed by a lone offender? What is the gender issue regarding carjacking offenders? What are the race and gender characteristics of victims?

2. Check the U.S. Department of Justice's Computer Crime and Intellectual Property Section (CCIPS) website at http://www.cybercrime.gov, accessed 20 October 2010. This site provides a comprehensive collection of publications, reports, and news updates involving various types of crimes related to intellectual property, computers, and the Internet.

Notes

1. Rollin M. Perkins, *Criminal Law*, 3d ed. (Mineola, NY: Foundation Press, 1982), p. 289.

2. Jennifer L. Truman and Michael R. Rand, Bureau of Justice Statistics, National Crime Victimization Survey, *Criminal Victimization, 2009* (October 2010), p. 1, http://bjs.ojp.usdoj.gov/content/pub/pdf/cv09.pdf, accessed 18 October 2010.

3. Federal Bureau of Investigation, "Offenses Cleared," *Crime in the United States, Uniform Crime Reports 2009*, http://www2.fbi.gov/ucr/cius2009/offenses/clearances/index.html, accessed 20 October 2010.

4. Federal Bureau of Investigation, *Crime in the United States, Uniform Crime Reports 2009*, http://www2.fbi.gov/ucr/cius2009/offenses/property_crime/index.html, accessed 20 October 2010.

5. Truman and Rand, *Criminal Victimization, 2009*, p. 4.

6. For a discussion of the historical development of the law of burglary, see Wayne R. LaFave and Austin W. Scott Jr., *Criminal Law*, 2d ed. (St. Paul, MN: West, 1986), pp. 702–706, from which this summary was taken.

7. New York Penal Code, Sections 140.20-140.30 (2009).

8. M.R.S.A., Title 17-A, Section 401 (2009).

9. "Burglary," Federal Bureau of Investigation, *Crime in the United States: Uniform Crime Reports 2009*, http://www2.fbi.gov/ucr/cius2009/offenses/property_crime/burglary.html, accessed 20 October 2010.

10. Truman and Rand, *Criminal Victimization, 2009*, p. 1.

11. Neal Shover, *Burglary as an Occupation*, PhD dissertation (Urbana-Champaign: University of Illinois Department of Sociology, 1971).

12. Richard Wright et al., "A Snowball's Chance in Hell: Doing Fieldwork with Active Residential Burglars," *Journal of Research in Crime and Delinquency* 29 (May 1992): 148–161.

13. Paul F. Cromwell et al., *Breaking and Entering: An Ethnographic Analysis of Burglary* (Newbury Park, CA: Sage, 1991), p. 40.

14. Matthew B. Robinson, "From Research to Policy: Preventing Residential Burglary Through a Systems Approach," *American Journal of Criminal Justice* 24, no. 2 (Spring 2000): 169–179.

15. Ibid.

16. See Neal Shover, "Structures and Careers in Burglary," *Journal of Criminal Law, Criminology, and Police Science* 68 (1972): 540–549; Shover, "The Social Organization of Burglary," *Social Problems* 20 (1973): 499–514.

17. Christopher W. Mullins and Richard Wright, "Gender, Social Networks, and Residential Burglary," *Criminology* 41, no. 3 (August 2003): 813–839.

18. Ibid.

19. Ibid., quotation is on p. 835.

20. Shane D. Johnson and Kate J. Bowers, "Opportunity Is in the Eye of the Beholder: The Role of Publicity in Crime Prevention," *Criminology and Public Policy* 2, no. 3 (July 2003): 497–524.

21. Scott H. Decker, Reaction Essay: "Advertising Against Crime: The Potential Impact of Publicity in Crime Prevention," *Criminology and Public Policy* 2, no. 3 (July 2003): 525–530; quotations are on pp. 526 and 529.

22. Lorraine Mazerolle, "The Pros and Cons of Publicity Campaigns as a Crime Control Tactic," *Criminology and Public Policy* 2, no. 3 (July 2003): 531–540; quotation is on p. 535.

23. Timothy Coupe and Laurence Blake, "Daylight and Darkness Targeting Strategies and the Risks of Being Seen at Residential Burglaries," *Criminology* 44, no. 2 (February 2006): 431–464.

24. Federal Bureau of Investigation, "Larceny-Theft," *Crime in the United States: Uniform Crime Reports* 2009, http://www2.fbi.gov/ucr/cius2009/offenses/property_crime/larceny-theft.html, accessed 16 October 2010.

25. Perkins, *Criminal Law*, 3d ed., p. 291. For a history of the development of the law of theft, see Jerome Hall, *Theft, Law and Society*, rev. ed. (Indianapolis, IN: Bobbs-Merrill, 1952), chap. 1–4.

26. Federal Bureau of Investigation, "Larceny-Theft."

27. Truman and Rand, "Criminal Victimization, 2009, p. 1.

28. "Offense Analysis," Federal Bureau of Investigation, *Crime in the United States: Uniform Crime Reports 2009*, http://www2.fbi.gov/ucr/cius2009/data/table_23.html, accessed 20 October 2010.

29. "Shoplifting Statistics," National Association for Shoplifting Prevention, National Learning and Resource Center, http://www.shopliftingprevention.org/WhatNASPOffers/NRC/PublicEducStats.htm, accessed 20 October 2010.

30. Ibid.

31. "Retail Fraud, Shoplifting Rates Decrease," National Retail Federation, http://www.nrf.com/modules.php?name=News&op=viewlive&sp_id=945, accessed 20 October 2010.

32. Mary Owen Cameron, "An Interpretation of Shoplifting," in *Criminal Behavior Systems: A Typology*, ed. Marshall B. Clinard and Richard

Quinney (Cincinnati, OH: Anderson, 1986), p. 109, reprinted from Mary Owen Cameron, *The Booster and the Snitch: Department Store Shoplifting* (New York: Free Press, 1964).

33. Department of Justice Response Center, *Shoplifting*, summarized in "Police Need Smart Approach to Shoplifting, Report Says," *Criminal Justice Newsletter* 32, no. 21 (21 November 2002): 6, 7.

34. "Shoplifting Suspects Choice: Pay or Be Shamed," *New York Times* (22 June 2010), p. 1.

35. Peter Berlin, National Association for Shoplifting Prevention, National Learning and Resource Center, "Why Do Shoplifters Steal?" http://www.shopliftingprevention.org/WhatNASPOffers/NRC.htm, accessed 20 October 2010.

36. Dean A. Dabney et al., "Who Actually Steals? A Study of Covertly Observed Shoplifters," *Justice Quarterly* 21, no. 4 (December 2004): 693–728.

37. Federal Bureau of Investigation, "Motor Vehicle Theft," *Crime in the United States 2009*, http://www2.fbi.gov/ucr/cius2009/offenses/property_crime/motor_vehicle_theft.html, accessed 20 October 2010.

38. Federal Bureau of Investigation, "Persons Arrested," *Uniform Crime Reports 2009*, http://www2.fbi.gov/ucr/cius2009/data/table_29.html, accessed 20 October 2010.

39. Truman and Rand, *Criminal Victimization, 2009*, p. 1.

40. "FBI Announces Plans for Anti-Carjacking Task Forces," *Criminal Justice Newsletter* 23 (1 September 1992): 5.

41. Patsy A. Klaus, Bureau of Justice Statistics, Crime Data Brief, *Carjacking, 1993–2002* (Washington, D.C.: U.S. Department of Justice, Office of Justice Programs, July 2004), pp. 1–2, http://bjs.ojp.usdoj.gov/content/pub/pdf/co2.pdf, accessed 20 October 2010.

42. *United States v. Bishop*, 66 F.3d 569 (3d Cir. 1995), *cert. denied*, 516 U.S. 1066 (1996). The Anti Car Theft Act of 1992 is codified at USCS, Title 18, Section 2119 (2010).

43. Charles McCaghy et al., "Auto Theft," *Criminology* 15 (November 1977): 367–381.

44. Federal Bureau of Investigation, "Arson," *Uniform Crime Reports 2009*, http://www2.fbi.gov/ucr/cius2009/offenses/property_crime/arson.html, accessed 20 October 2010.

45. Ibid.

46. "Happy Land Arsonist Sentenced to 25 Years to Life for 87 Deaths," *New York Times* (20 September 1991), p. 12B.

47. "No Arson Charge for California Boy," *UPI Release* (14 November 2007), n.p.

48. James P. Brady, "Arson, Fiscal Crisis, and Community Action: Dialectics of an Urban Crime and Popular Response," *Crime and Delinquency* 28 (April 1982): 247–270.

49. Nolan D. C. Lewis and Helen Yarnell, *Pathological Firesetting (Pyromania)* (New York: Nervous and Mental Disease Monographs, 1951). See also James A. Inciardi, "The Adult Firesetter: A Typology," *Criminology* 8 (August 1970): 145–155.

50. "Church Continues Its Recovery from Arson," *Indianapolis Star* (14 June 2001), p. 01W.

51. "Guilty Plea in Huge Fire in Colorado," *New York Times* (7 December 2002), p. 16; "Barton Enters Prison for Hayman Fire," *Denver Post*

(23 March 2003), p. 1B; "Embers of Anger, Mercy Hayman Fire Starter's Return Stirs Old Emotions," *Denver Post* (9 June 2008), p. A–01. *People v. Barton*, 121 P.3d 224 (Colo.Ct.App. 2004), *modified and reh'g. denied*, 2005 Colo. App. LEXIS 164 (Colo.Ct.App. 2005), *cert denied*, 2005 Colo. LEXIS 894 (Colo. 2005), *and subsequent appeal, remanded*, 174 P.3d 786 (Colo. 2008).

52. "Fireman Admits Setting Blaze; Faces 10 Years," *Arizona Republic* (21 October 2003), p. 1B; "'Rodeo' Arsonist to Pay $28 Mil, Serve 10 Years," *Arizona Republic* (9 March 2004), p. 1B.

53. "Ex-Firefighter Gets Two Years for Coconino Blazes," *Arizona Republic* (5 June 2007), p. 1.

54. "Three Receive State Prison Terms," *Mobile Register* (Alabama) (13 April 2007), p. 2B.

55. E. C. Ritchie and T. G. Huff, "Psychiatric Aspects of Arsonists," *Journal of Forensic Science* 44 (July 1999): 733–740, as reported on MEDLINE.

56. S. Noblett and B. Nelson, "A Psychosocial Approach to Arson-A Case Controlled Study of Female Offenders," *Medicine, Science, and the Law* 41 (October 2001): 325–330, as reported on MEDLINE.

57. Brett Adam, "'Kindling Theory' in Arson: How Dangerous Are Firesetters?" *Australian Journal of Psychiatry* 38, no. 6 (2004): 419–425, as reported on MEDLINE.

58. Edwin M. Lemert, "An Isolation and Closure Theory of Naive Check Forgery," *Journal of Criminal Law, Criminology and Police Science* 44 (September/October 1953): 301–304. See also Norman S. Hayner, "Characteristics of Five Offender Types," *American Sociological Review* 16 (February 1961): 96–102.

59. U.S. Department of Justice, "Major International Hacker Pleads Guilty For Massive Attack on U.S. Retail and Banking Networks," Press Release (29 December 2009), http://www.justice.gov/criminal/cybercime/gonzalezPlea.pdf, accessed 20 October 2010.

60. Darrell J. Steffensmeier, *The Fence: In the Shadow of Two Worlds* (Totowa, NJ: Rowman & Littlefield, 1986). See also Marilyn E. Walsh, *The Fence—A New Look at the World of Property Theft* (Westport, CT: Greenwood Press, 1977).

61. Shover, *Burglary as an Occupation*, p. 152.

62. Paul F. Cromwell and Karen McElrath, "Buying Stolen Property: An Opportunity Perspective," *Journal of Research in Crime and Delinquency* 31 (August 1994): 295–310; quotation is on p. 306.

63. Cal Pen Code, Section 484 (2010).

64. United States Department of Justice, District of Minnesota, "Former Lindquist & Vennum Attorney Pleads Guilty to Embezzling $2 Million from His Clients and the Firm," Press Release (8 June 2010), http://www.justice.gov/usao/mn/econ/econ0440.pdf, accessed 20 October 2010.

65. Lynn Langton and Katrina Baum, Bureau of Justice Statistics, *Identity Theft Reported by Households, 2007* (June 2010), p. 1, http://bjs.ojp.usdoj.gov/content/pub/pdf/itrh07st.pdf, accessed 20 October 2010.

66. USCS Title 18, Section 1028(a)(7) (2010).

67. Fair and Accurate Credit Transactions (FACT) Act of 2003, Public L. 108–159 (2010).

68. Federal Trade Commission, "Identity Thief Goes 'Phishing' for Consumers' Credit Information" (21 July 2003), http://www.ftc.gov/opa/2003/07/phishing.shtm, accessed 20 October 2010.

69. "Security," *Washington Internet Daily* 6, no. 129 (6 July 2005): 1.

70. "A Costly Effort to Fight Cyber Attacks," *Boston Globe* (8 April 2009), p. 10.

71. Ramona R. Rantala, Bureau of Justice Statistics Special Report, *Cybercrime Against Businesses, 2005* (17 September 2008), p. 1, http://bjs.ojp.usdoj.gov/index.cfm?ty=pbdetail&iid=371, accessed 20 October 2010.

72. "Acquitted Man Says Virus Put Pornography on Computer," *New York Times* (8 November 2003), p. 1C.

73. "Online Bullies Pull School into the Fray," *New York Times* (28 June 2010), p. 1.

74. Sameer Hinduja and Justin W. Patchin, "Cyberbullying Research Summary: Cyberbullying and Suicide," Cyberbullying Research Center, http://www.cyberbullying.us/cyberbullying_and_suicide_research_fact_sheet.pdf, accessed 20 October 2010.

75. August Bequai, *Computer Crime* (Lexington, MA: D. C. Heath, 1978), p. 4.

76. Discussed in National Criminal Justice Information and Statistics Service, *Computer Crime: Criminal Resource Manual* (Washington, D.C.: U.S. Government Printing Office, 1979), pp. 9–29.

77. USCS, Title 18, Section 1030 (2010).

78. CAN-SPAM Act of 2003, USCS, Chapter 15, Section 7701 (2010).

79. Department of Homeland Security, *The National Strategy to Secure Cyberspace,* pp. x, 1, http://www.dhs.gov/xlibrary/assets/National_Cyberspace_Strategy.pdf, accessed 20 October 2010.

80. Identity Theft Enforcement and Restitution Act of 2008, Title II, P.L. 110–326 (2008). For a discussion, see Richard Acello, "Feds Ready to Tackle Cybercrime," *ABA Journal* 95 (February 2009): 37.

81. "Google and China: The New Era of Cybercrime: Corporations Need to More Fully Acknowledge the Cybercrime Threat and Step Up Their Defenses," *Christian Science Monitor* (26 January 2010), editorial page.

82. *United States v. Drew*, 259 F.R.D. 449 (C.D.Cal. 2009). The Computer Fraud and Abuse Act (CFAA) is codified at USCS, Title 18, Section 1030 (2010).

83. *United States v. Paul*, 274 F.3d 155 (5th Cir., 2001), *cert. denied*, 535 U.S. 1002 (2002).

84. *United States v. Lifshitz*, 369 F.3d 173 (2d Cir. 2004).

85. *United States v. Fields*, 324 F.3d 1025 (8th Cir. 2003).

86. For a more complete discussion of these issues, along with numerous citations of sociological works on professional criminals, see Gregory R. Staats, "Changing Conceptualizations of Professional Criminals: Implications for Criminology Theory," *Criminology* 15 (May 1977): 49–65.

87. Edwin H. Sutherland, *The Professional Thief* (Chicago: University of Chicago Press, 1937).

88. For an example of some of the earlier works, see David Maurer, *The Big Con* (New York: Signet, 1962); Maurer, *Wiz Mob: A Correlation*

of the Technical Argot of Pickpockets with Their Behavior Pattern (Gainesville, FL: American Dialect Society, 1955).

89. Leroy Gould et al., *Crime as a Profession* (Washington, D.C.: U.S. Government Printing Office), cited in Staats, "Changing Conceptualizations of Professional Criminals," p. 60.

90. Shover, *Burglary as an Occupation*, p. 194, emphasis in the original.

91. Neal Shover, "Burglary," in *Crime and Justice: A Review of Research*, Vol. 14, ed. Michael Tonry (Chicago: University of Chicago Press, 1991), p. 92.

92. Don C. Gibbons, *Society, Crime, and Criminal Careers: An Introduction to Criminology*, 4th ed. (Englewood Cliffs, NJ: Prentice-Hall, 1983), p. 279.

93. For a general discussion, see ibid., pp. 284–288.

94. Marvin E. Wolfgang et al., *Delinquency in a Birth Cohort* (Chicago: University of Chicago Press, 1972). See also Wolfgang et al., *From Boy to Man, from Delinquency to Crime* (Chicago: University of Chicago Press, 1987).

95. See Marvin E. Wolfgang, "Delinquency in a Birth Cohort II: Some Preliminary Results." Paper prepared for the Attorney General's Task Force on Violent Crime, Chicago, 17 June 1982, cited in Patrick A. Langan and Lawrence A. Greenfeld, Bureau of Justice Statistics, *Career Patterns in Crime* (Washington, D.C.: U.S. Department of Justice, June 1983), p. 2.

96. See, for example, Lyle W. Shannon, *Assessing the Relationship of Adult Criminal Careers to Juvenile Careers* (Iowa City: Iowa Urban Community Research Center, University of Iowa, 1981).

97. See Jan Chaiken et al., *Varieties of Criminal Behavior: Summary and Policy Implications* (Santa Monica, CA: Rand Corporation, 1982).

98. See Alfred Blumstein et al., "Delinquency Careers: Innocents, Desisters, and Persisters," in *Crime and Justice: An Annual Review of Research*, Vol. 6, ed. Michael Tonry and Norval Morris (Chicago: University of Chicago Press, 1985), pp. 187–219.

99. Michael Gottfredson and Travis Hirschi, "Career Criminals and Selective Incapacitation," in *Controversial Issues in Crime and Justice*, ed. Joseph E. Scott and Travis Hirschi (Newbury Park, CA: Sage, 1988), p. 291.

100. Allan F. Abrahamse et al., "An Experimental Evaluation of the Phoenix Repeat Offender Program," *Justice Quarterly* 8 (June 1991): 141–168; quotation is on p. 143.

101. Marcia Chaiken and Jan Chaiken, *Redefining the Career Criminal: Priority Prosecution of High-Rate, Dangerous Offenders* (Washington, D.C.: U.S. Department of Justice, National Institute of Justice, 1990).

102. See Mark A. Peterson et al., *Who Commits Crimes? A Survey of Prison Inmates* (Cambridge, MA: Oelgeschlager, Gunn & Hain, 1981).

103. Peter W. Greenwood with Allan Abrahamse, *Selective Incapacitation*, prepared for the National Institute of Justice (Santa Monica, CA: Rand, 1982), p. 19.

104. Jan Chaiken et al., *Varieties of Criminal Behavior*, pp. v, vi, vii.

105. Mark A. Peterson et al., *Doing Crime: A Survey of California Prison Inmates* (Santa Monica, CA: Rand, 1980), pp. vii–xii.

106. See, for example, Julie Horney and Ineke Haen Marshall, "An Experimental Comparison of Two Self-Report Methods for Measuring Lambda," *Journal of Research in Crime and Delinquency* 29 (February 1992): 102–121.

107. Patrick A. Langan and Lawrence A. Greenfeld, Bureau of Justice Statistics, Special Report, *Career Patterns in Crime* (Washington, D.C.: U.S. Department of Justice, June 1983).

108. Ibid.

109. Lawrence Sherman, *Repeat Offenders*, National Institute of Justice (Washington, D.C.: U.S. Department of Justice, 1989), p. 3.

110. Alfred S. Regnery, quoted in the Introduction to Donna Martin Hamparian et al., *Young Criminal Years of the Violent Few* (Washington, D.C.: U.S. Department of Justice, June 1985).

111. Hamparian et al., *Young Criminal Years of the Violent Few*, p. 22.

112. Michael Gottfredson and Travis Hirschi, *A General Theory of Crime* (Stanford, CA: Stanford University Press, 1990), p. 241.

113. See again Chapter 6 for a discussion of *desistance*.

114. Alfred Blumstein et al., "Delinquency Careers: Innocents, Desisters, and Persisters," in *Crime and Justice,* Vol. 6, ed. Tonry and Morris, pp. 187–219.

115. Quoted in Arnold Barnett et al., "Not All Criminal Career Models Are Equally Valid," *Criminology* 30, No. 1 (February 1992): 133–140; quotation is on p. 133.

116. David F. Greenberg, "Modeling Criminal Careers," *Criminology* 29, No. 1 (February 1991): 17–46; quotation is on pp. 17–18.

117. Quoted in Barnett et al., "Not All Criminal Career Models Are Equally Valid," p. 138.

118. David F. Greenberg, "Comparing Criminal Career Models," *Criminology* 30, No. 1 (February 1992): 141–147; quotation is on p. 144.

119. Kenneth Land, "Models of Criminal Careers: Some Suggestions for Moving Beyond the Current Debate," *Criminology* 30, no. 1 (February 1992): 149.

120. David P. Farrington et al., "Comparing Delinquency Careers in Court Records and Self-Reports," *Criminology* 41, no. 3 (August 2003): 933–958.

121. Ibid., pp. 952–954.

122. Ibid.

123. Ibid., pp. 954–955.

124. Todd A. Armstrong, "Are Trends in Specialization Across Arrests Explained by Changes in Specialization Occurring with Age?" *Justice Quarterly* 25, no. 1 (March 2008): 201–222.

125. *Ewing v. California*, 538 U.S. 11 (2003). See also *Lockyer v. Andrade*, 538 U.S. 63 (2003). The statute in question is Cal Pen Code, Section 667(b) (2010).

CHAPTER 9

Business- and Government-Related Crimes

This diverse work group of employees appears quite happy, and although most workers probably function within the legal limits of the criminal law, some, either individually or with coworkers, engage in conspiracy, fraud, and other types of white-collar crimes, many of which have far-reaching consequences. For example, the bankruptcy filing by the energy giant Enron Corporation (once the seventh-largest company on the Fortune 500 list), headquartered in Houston, Texas, resulted in the unemployment of over 4,500 workers, along with the loss of retirement accounts, the erosion of public confidence in corporations, and the trials and convictions of several corporate executives.

KEY TERMS

antitrust laws
blackmail
bribery
conspiracy
contempt
conversion
corporate crime
enterprise liability
extortion
false pretense
graft
habeas corpus
insider information
insider trading
Irangate
obstruction of justice
official misconduct in office
perjury
securities
strict liability
under color of law
vicarious liability
Watergate
white-collar crime

INTRODUCTION

This chapter covers crimes committed within businesses and in governments, although many of them may also be committed in other contexts. Most of the chapter focuses on crimes of the business world. The history of larceny-theft, discussed in Chapter 8, provides a background for this chapter. Many of the business activities defined as crimes are not viewed by everyone as crimes but, rather, as shrewd business transactions, just as they were perceived historically. There is little agreement on the definitions of business crimes or on how to control these illegal activities.

The chapter begins with a discussion of the problem of defining business-related crimes and proceeds to an analysis of the extent, prosecution, and impact on society of these crimes. The basis for legal liability is also discussed, followed by an analysis of types of business-related crimes.

In a similar vein, the discussion of government-related crimes covers some acts that previously were considered acceptable or at least were overlooked in our society. Today, those acts are crimes, and government officials are coming under closer scrutiny in their personal as well as public lives.

The analysis of types of crime, which began in Chapter 7 with violent crimes and continued in Chapter 8 with property crimes, proceeds in this chapter to look at business- and government-related crimes. These crimes involve property and may involve violence, but most can be distinguished from the violent and property crimes discussed in the previous two chapters.

The crimes discussed in this chapter have less obvious victims than most of those covered in Chapters 7 and 8. The victims may be individual consumers or the general public. Even when the victim is a particular person, the relationship between the offender and the victim is not always obvious. Business-related crimes differ from ordinary serious property crimes and personal violent crimes in the violation of public trust that is involved in many cases. Likewise, the government-related crimes described in the latter part of this chapter may not have obvious victims, and certainly, the violation of public trust is a factor in these crimes.

There are, however, some similarities between the crimes covered in this chapter and those discussed previously. In many cases, the same kinds of actions are involved. In the past, as we saw in Chapter 8, some of these practices were accepted, even admired; others were considered unethical but not illegal. Today, enhanced technology, combined with the complexity and heterogeneity of business transactions and the inability of individual consumers to protect themselves, has brought about increased regulation of business transactions. Likewise, many actions (private as well as public) of government officials that were acceptable in the past are illegal today. Or if they were illegal in the past, they were virtually ignored. Some of today's regulations of business- and government-related crimes are part of the criminal law; others are covered by civil law or administrative law.

Business-Related Crimes: An Overview

Before we look at specific business-related crimes, it is important to notice the difficulties of defining these crimes. That discussion is followed by a brief look at the extent and prosecution of business-related crimes, a sociologi-

cal analysis of these crimes, and the basis of legal liability for them.

Definitional Problems

A difficult problem in analyzing *business-related crimes* is to define the concept. Social scientists disagree about the best way to categorize crimes associated with occupations and businesses. The most familiar term, **white-collar crime**, is not defined uniformly. The term was coined by Edwin H. Sutherland in his 1939 presidential address to the American Sociological Society and developed in a later published work.[1]

By *white-collar crime*, Sutherland meant "a crime committed by a person of respectability and high social status in the course of his occupation." Examples are embezzlement by a banker and price fixing by physicians. Sutherland recognized that his definition excluded crimes such as murder, adultery, and intoxication "since these are not customarily a part of [a person's] occupational procedures." He also realized that his approach excluded some crimes committed by persons who were "wealthy members of the underworld, since they are not persons of respectability and high social status."[2]

Sutherland became interested in white-collar crime because studies of crime were usually based on samples of institutionalized criminals, most of whom were poor. Sutherland observed that most of the crimes committed by upper-class people (especially crimes associated with their occupations) were not handled by criminal courts. Rather, they were processed through administrative agencies. Even if those agencies found the individuals responsible for the alleged acts, the offenders were not considered criminals and were not included in studies and theories of criminal behavior. In developing his concept of white-collar crime, Sutherland was not trying to redefine these types of crimes. Nor was he saying that we should consider white-collar offenders criminals and process them in the criminal courts rather than through administrative agencies. He was saying that if we want to know why crimes are committed, it is just as important to study white-collar offenders, who are processed through administrative agencies, as it is to study the crimes of those who are processed through the criminal courts and incarcerated in penal institutions.

Sutherland's limitation of white-collar crimes to occupational crimes of the upper class has been rejected by most authorities. In defense of Sutherland's approach, however, August Bequai emphasized that Sutherland was reacting to the social and economic situation of the 1930s, in which "only the wealthier classes had access to the requisite machinery necessary for the enactment of many of the crimes included in his concept of white-collar crime."[3]

With developments in technology and mass communications, more people acquired the opportunity to engage in white-collar crime. Bequai argued that instead of defining white-collar criminals by social class, we should define them by the methods they use to commit the crimes. He pointed out that even though white-collar criminals may use force occasionally, they are primarily distinguished from the common felon by "guile, deceit, and concealment."[4]

The crimes that might be included in a definition of white-collar crime are extensive; therefore, categorization is difficult. In 1970, Herbert Edelhertz concluded that the best categorization was to classify the various crimes "by the general environment and motivation of the perpetrator," and for that purpose, he suggested the following:

1. "Crimes by persons operating on an individual, ad hoc basis, for personal gain in a nonbusiness context. . . .
2. Crimes in the course of their occupations by those operating inside businesses, Government, or other establishments, or in a professional capacity, in violation of their duty of loyalty and fidelity to employer or client . . .
3. Crimes incidental to and in furtherance of business operations, but not the central purpose of such business operations . . .
4. White-collar crimes as a business, or as the central activity of the business. . . ."[5]

In a discussion of the problems of measuring white-collar crime, three basic categories might be utilized: (1) the type of offender (e.g., Sutherland's higher socioeconomic class), (2) the type of offense (e.g., economic crimes), and (3) the organizational culture. But it is impossible to use the "type of offender" approach when analyzing crime by *UCR* data because the FBI compilation does not include measures of socioeconomic status.[6] The same would be true of an approach that looked to the motivation of the offender, as is the case of the aforementioned categorization by Edelhertz.

The Federal Bureau of Investigation (FBI) defines *white-collar crime* as

those illegal acts which are characterized by deceit, concealment, or violation of trust and which are not dependent upon the application or threat of physical force or violence. Individuals and organizations

commit these acts to obtain money, property, or services; to avoid the payment or loss of money or services; or to secure personal or business advantage.[7]

If that definition of white-collar crime is utilized for research purposes, the only FBI data from the *UCR* are arrest data for the crimes of fraud, forgery and counterfeiting, embezzlement, and what the FBI lists as *all other offenses*, although those are not broken down by crimes that fit this definition. Recall from Chapter 2's discussion that, for the eight serious violent and property crimes (Part I offenses), the *UCR* includes tabulations of numbers of crimes known to the police, crime rates, and arrest data. But for all other crimes (Part II offenses), only arrest data are available.

Our ability to measure the crimes that fall within the white-collar crime category should be improved with the government's new system: the National Incident-Based Reporting System (NIBRS), also discussed in Chapter 2. Many of those crimes can be considered white-collar offenses and are discussed in this chapter (in addition to those already discussed in Chapter 8). Some crimes that are in the NIBRS classifications but are not discussed in this book are as follows: contract fraud, corrupt conduct by jurors, defense contract fraud, employment agency and education-related scams, false advertising and misrepresentation of products, home improvement frauds, impersonation, insurance fraud, jury tampering, crimes that come under the Racketeer Influenced and Corrupt Organizations (RICO) Act (discussed in Chapter 10), religious fraud, sports bribery, telephone fraud, travel scams, and welfare fraud.[8]

In some circumstances, it is difficult to draw the line between business-related crimes and legitimate business activities. Most people would agree that the crimes discussed in the first part of this chapter should be designated business-related crimes, but in some cases, the acts might be considered sharp business practices rather than crimes.

It is important to an understanding of business-related crime that **corporate crime** be distinguished from white-collar and other business crimes. *Corporate crime* is a form of white-collar crime, but unlike the latter, it may involve individuals or small groups of individuals acting within their professional or occupational capacity. Sociologist Marshall B. Clinard defined *corporate crime* as organizational crime that occurred "in the context of extremely complex inter-relationships. . . . Here it is the organization, not the occupation, that is of prime importance."[9] A more precise distinction between the two is as follows:

If a policy making corporate executive is acting in the name of the corporation and the individual's decision to violate the law is for the benefit of the corporation, as in price-fixing violations, the violation would constitute corporate crime.

If, on the other hand, the corporate official acts against the corporation, as in the case of embezzlement, and is financing benefits in a personal way from his official connections with the corporation, his acts would constitute white-collar or occupational crime.[10]

Early studies of white-collar crime focused on *individuals* who committed their crimes in secret. The lack of attention to corporate crime may have been due, first, to the complexity of the crimes and the corporate structure. A thorough understanding of corporate crime requires expertise in areas that have not been part of the traditional training of social scientists. Second, the regulation of corporate crime is frequently carried out in administrative agencies rather than in courts. Many sociologists and criminologists are not as familiar with the functions of these agencies as they are with judicial court processes. Investigation and prosecution of white-collar crime cases have also been problems. Third, research funds have been more readily available for the study of conventional crime than for corporate crime. Fourth, the public has not been as concerned with white-collar crime as it has been with conventional crime.

Why change the emphasis today from individual white-collar or business crimes to corporate crime? First, the number and size of corporations increased significantly during the twentieth century. Today, most business activities, along with many social and political activities, are influenced or controlled by corporations. The number of federal and state regulations has also increased dramatically.

Second, although the media gave little publicity to the prosecution of corporate crimes during the time of Sutherland's studies, that is not the case today. The media give considerable attention to modern business-related crimes, particularly when public officials are involved. Third, the earlier efforts of consumer advocates and others had a significant impact on public concern with corporate crime and on the increasing legislative efforts to curb such crime. Fourth, increasing concern with the environment, coupled with the realization that many corporations contribute to its pollution, led to the creation of the federal Environmental Protection Agency (EPA) and to legislation in this area.

A fifth reason for today's focus on corporate crime is the realization that, in concentrating crime control on the poor, the crime problem was not being solved. Furthermore, crimes committed by middle- and upper-class persons and by corporations were ignored. Similarly, the civil rights and prison reform movements of the 1960s and 1970s, along with the short sentences imposed on business and government offenders, focused attention on differential treatment in criminal justice systems. Finally, both Marxist and neo-Marxist writings in criminology have focused on this differential treatment (see again Chapter 5).[11]

Extent

Although we do not have exact figures for the extent of white-collar or business crimes, we do know that the amount and cost are extensive (estimated to be more than $300 billion annually[12]), and some experts believe there has been an increase in the actual number of business crimes. The editor of a white-collar crime trade journal aimed at lawyers and investigators said: "White-collar crime is spinning through the roof. It's spinning new varieties daily and the incidence and amounts of money being stolen are incredible."[13]

Experts also note that changes in the way chief executive officers were paid led to greater incentives for managers to manipulate the books so that earnings appeared higher than they actually were. Some examples are noted later in this chapter. Significant increases in the number of reported accounting and disclosure cases have occurred, along with increases in all kinds of fraud but particularly health care fraud and theft of trade secrets. Also on the rise have been reports of bankruptcy, procurement, and government fraud. Civil suits associated with these and other business-related crimes have increased. New crimes—such as identity theft (discussed in Chapter 8)—primarily connected with the Internet have fueled the increase in business-related crimes. In addition, private groups have reported large increases in the number of frauds related to borrowing money from investors and banks.[14]

Prosecution

Although most of the violent and property crimes discussed in Chapters 7 and 8 are prosecuted in state courts because they involve violations of state statutes, many of the prosecutions of crimes discussed in this and the following chapter occur in federal courts. They are prosecuted by U.S. attorneys, who are appointed by the president and confirmed by the U.S. Senate. These attorneys report to the U.S. attorney general through the deputy attorney general.

The U.S. attorneys and their assistant attorneys and staffs handle civil as well as criminal cases. The criminal caseload is more diverse than ever before. In the 1990s, U.S. attorneys focused on the following priority areas for criminal prosecutions: violent crime, narcotics, immigration, organized crime, white-collar crime, government regulatory offenses, child support recovery crimes, and civil rights violations.[15] Since the 9/11 terrorist attacks, however, federal prosecutors have focused more on terrorism and less on white-collar and government-related crimes, as noted in the strategic plan for fiscal years 2007–2012 published by the U.S. Department of Justice (DOJ). The priorities are listed as follows, in rank order, with terrorism declared "the Nation's greatest threat."

- "To detect and prevent terrorism
- To combat violent crime
- To combat computer crime, especially child pornography, obscenity, and intellectual property theft
- To combat illegal drugs

- To attack corporate and public corruption
- To promote civil rights and civil liberties"[16]

Impact on Society

Another important aspect of white-collar or business-related as well as government-related crimes is the impact these crimes have on society in terms of the loss of trust and security as well as personal and business fortunes. Perhaps the actions and words of the outgoing chair of the Securities and Exchange Commission (SEC) in 1987, explaining why he donated $20 million to the Harvard Business School for an ethics program, best emphasize the impact on the country's moral fiber that can result when persons of status and power engage in illegal acts:

> I've been very disturbed most recently with the large numbers of graduates of leading business and law schools who have become convicted felons. Some of those we're bringing cases against are . . . the cream of the crop, and that's what is so shocking and causes concern.[17]

The extent and nature of business-related crimes and the possible explanations can be connected to several theories discussed in Chapters 5 and 6. Some of those theories are noted in the next section.

A Sociological Analysis

Despite the difficulties of defining and categorizing business-related crimes, sociologists have identified some characteristics that distinguish offenders in these cases from other offenders. Most often, sociologists use the phrase *white-collar offenders*, noting that these offenders differ from nonbusiness offenders primarily in their higher socioeconomic status and their occupational respectability and prestige. Most white-collar offenders do not perceive themselves as criminals but, rather, as honest people taking advantage of a good business situation. Often, even when they recognize the law-breaking aspect of their behavior, they rationalize it by claiming that either the laws are wrong or the laws do not apply to them. Criminologist Donald R. Cressey illustrated this position in his study of trust violators, who were able to redefine their positions and convince themselves that their behavior was noncriminal. They were not stealing; they were borrowing. They acted as they did because of unusual circumstances, a financial problem that they could not share with others, and a belief that the only way to solve that problem was through embezzling.[18]

Another question of interest to sociologists and criminologists is whether business-related crimes are learned and, if so, how? Edwin H. Sutherland argued that his theory of differential association (see again Chapter 6) was an appropriate theory for explaining the behavior. He used biographical or autobiographical descriptions as data and noted examples of the "diffusion of criminal practices from one situation to another" as evidence that the theory of differential association is useful in explaining white-collar crime.[19]

Other sociologists have pointed out the relevance of differential association, although Marshall B. Clinard argued that the theory cannot explain *all* white-collar crime and that personality factors are also important. Clinard enumerated such individual personality traits as the following:

> egocentricity, emotional insecurity or feelings of personal inadequacy, negative attitudes toward other persons in general, the relative importance of status symbols of money as compared with nationalism, and the relative lack of importance of one's personal, family or business reputation.[20]

Other scholars have examined why some organizational executives comply or do not comply with business regulations and found that four theories offer partial explanations, although not one of them alone is sufficient. Of those four theories—opportunity, control, subculture, and differential association (all discussed in previous chapters of this text)—the one that offered the most explanatory power was opportunity theory (see again Chapter 5).[21]

More recent researchers have challenged the early sociological theorists, who tended to analyze white-collar crime and white-collar criminals as separate or distinct from other types of crime and other criminals. Travis Hirschi and Michael R. Gottfredson maintained that it is possible to "outline a general theory of crime capable of organizing the facts about white-collar crime at the same time it is capable of organizing the facts about all forms of crime."[22] (Recall the discussion of Gottfredson and Hirschi's general theory of crime in Chapter 6.)

Rather than beginning with offenders, as many theorists do, Hirschi and Gottfredson began with an analysis of criminal events. They looked for the characteristics of criminal events that make all crime attractive to potential offenders. According to Hirschi and Gottfredson, the common characteristics are the avoidance of pain and the seeking of pleasure rather than money, success, or peer approval. To provide maximum pleasure, the events must occur immediately, be easy to accomplish, and have a certainty of outcome. White-collar crimes, like other crimes, satisfy these characteristics for those in a position to commit them.[23]

Hirschi and Gottfredson concluded that theories that analyze crime by offender typologies—that is, those that compare rapists with burglars with white-collar criminals—should be replaced by their general theory that analyzes the properties of crime. According to them, "the distinction between crime in the street and crime in the suite is an *offense* rather than an *offender* distinction, that offenders in both cases are likely to share similar characteristics."[24] Their theory is based on a combination of control and opportunity theory. Criminals have low self-control, and when presented with an opportunity to engage in criminal activity, they are more likely to do so than are persons with a high level of self-control. Thus, self-control and opportunity are the key variables in explaining crime, including white-collar crime.[25]

Some scholars have rejected this approach. Darrell Steffensmeier questioned the two researchers' database (Hirschi and Gottfredson used official *UCR* data on fraud and forgery) as being unrepresentative of *actual* white-collar crime. Steffensmeier argued that on the basis of gender, age, and race, the offender characteristics of white-collar criminals differ from those of other criminals.[26]

Other scholars have rejected the Gottfredson-Hirschi theory's implication that, in general, white-collar criminals are as versatile and as prone to deviance as common offenders are. They insist that motivation is a factor in white-collar crime and that its omission in Gottfredson and Hirschi's approach is a mistake. Rather, there are "three paths or routes to white-collar crime along which motives, opportunities, and self-control operate differently." The first is that of persons who are impulsive and who pursue their own selfish interests through fraud whenever the opportunity arises. These white-collar criminals fit Gottfredson and Hirschi's theory; they are like criminals who commit non-white-collar crimes. Persons following this path have high offending rates.[27]

The second route is followed by persons with high self-control, who calculate their behavior and act aggressively while engaging in crime in pursuit of ego gratification. In between these two routes are persons whose level of self-control is adequate for most situations but who take advantage of criminal opportunities when they have personal problems, such as financial hardships. Gottfredson and Hirschi's theory, it is argued, cannot explain these offenders because it does not account for the influence that different circumstances might have on an individual's behavior.[28]

Another control theory that is used to explain white-collar crime is that of control balance theory (CBT) developed by Charles R. Tittle. Recall from Chapter 6's discussion of Tittle's CBT theory that it analyzes the control a person exercises in relationship to the control he or she experiences, which is the *control balance*. A *control surplus* exists when there is an excess of control exercised compared to control experienced; that is, you exercise more control over others than is exercised over you. The opposite, an excess of control experienced compared to control exercised, constitutes a *control deficit*; that is, others exercise more control over you than you exercise over them. It is expected that a control deficit contributes to repressive forms of deviance, whereas a control surplus is related to autonomous forms of deviance, meaning that the actors escape control over themselves by others and exercise more control over others.[29]

Nicole Leeper Piquero and Alex R. Piquero attempted to test CBT in the context of corporate crime. Specifically, they looked at autonomous deviant acts of exploitation that might be explained by CBT. For example, Tittle advocated that if a corporate agent wished to dump toxic waste into a river, he or she would calculate that the people most harmed, such as those engaged in fishing and farming along the river, would not be in a position to complain; thus, by dumping, the corporate agent would extend his or her control over these people and suffer few, if any, consequences.[30]

Piquero and Piquero believed their study was the first to test the application of CBT to corporate and white-collar crime. They gathered data from a sample of adults enrolled in college and university business courses and asked them to respond to hypothetical scenarios concerning sales fraud. They found support for the hypothesis that exploitative corporate behavior is related to control surpluses rather than control deficits.[31]

Other theories have also been used to explain white-collar and corporate crime. In a recent test of rational choice theory (recall the discussion in Chapter 5, noting this theory is based on the belief that individuals will commit a crime if they perceive that its benefits outweigh its costs), researchers added the dimension of the *desire-for-control* (DC) concept from psychology, thus combining personality theory with rational choice theory. DC refers to the desire one has to be in control of everyday life events. These scholars studied a sample of managers in training and business (MBA) students in the context of decision-making scenarios presented by the researchers. In general, they found that DC is important and that persons in corporate positions are influenced by individual, situational, and personality characteristics. Specifically, the respondents with high DC were more likely than respondents with low DC to respond that they would engage in corporate violations. Apparently, their need for control would propel them to do whatever was necessary to gain that control. However, the researchers recognized and discussed the limitations of their study. One was the small number of female respondents and the need to consider that gender might be a significant factor in explaining decisions in the corporate world. They also suggested that personality variables might have a different effect by level of position within the same organization.[32]

The issue of gender and white-collar crime has been explored by some investigators. It was addressed by the National White Collar Crime Center, which published a brief article on women and white-collar crime, pointing to crime data based on consumer complaints to the Internet Fraud Complaint Center (IFCC). These data suggested that 17.7 percent of the white-collar crime victims identified women as the perpetrators of the fraud by which they were victimized. The report emphasized that women have assumed greater roles in the economy as more of them have become the primary source of income for their families. After reviewing the various theories that have been utilized to explain the increase of women in white-collar crime, the investigator concluded that "motivating factors, occupations, opportunities, and access to information and people have contributed to the increase in white collar crimes committed by women." One problem with the analysis, however, must be considered in any conclusions regarding white-collar crimes, and that is how the data are collected. For example, one cited study referred to women who were convicted for larceny-theft, fraud, and forgery. Although those crimes may fall within the definition of white-collar crime per se, they do not necessarily represent what we traditionally think of as white-collar crimes. Thus, stealing groceries from a store, although the act might constitute a theft crime, is not comparable to using a position of power to embezzle money. Researchers must be careful to ensure that they are measuring more than simple theft when they designate a perpetrator a white-collar or business criminal.[33]

Finally, there is evidence that historically women have been prone to victimization by fraud and other white-collar crimes.[34]

Basis of Legal Liability

The general principles underlying the basis of legal liability for criminal behavior have been discussed. Those principles also apply to the crimes presented in this and the following chapter. In these two chapters, however, we are also concerned with acts that may result in criminal liability for the behavior of others. Several legal theories underscore how this is possible.

First, persons may be convicted of a crime under a theory of **strict liability**. For example, a person who serves or sells liquor to an underage customer may be held criminally liable even though he or she did not know that the customer was under age. Second, under a theory of **vicarious liability**, a person may be held criminally liable for the acts of another person. A bar owner may be held liable for the crime of selling to an underage person even if that crime was committed by an employee and without the knowledge of the owner. Third, under the theory of **enterprise liability** (also called *corporate liability*), corporate officers and officials may, in some circumstances, be held criminally liable for the acts of their employees.

Types of Business-Related Crimes

Many criminal acts may be classified as business-related crimes. Some are committed primarily by individuals acting alone; others require more than one person; still others are committed primarily by corporations. This section briefly discusses several crimes. Other crimes are given more attention in following sections or in Chapter 10. Some were also discussed in Chapter 8, as they often involve the theft of property. It is important to understand, however, that property crimes discussed elsewhere may also be white-collar or business-related crimes, and they may occur on a large scale, even involving numerous employees within a company or corporation.

Statutes criminalizing the acts discussed in this chapter may differ from jurisdiction to jurisdiction, but there are common elements. As noted earlier, many of these crimes are prosecuted in federal courts; thus, primarily federal statutes are used to illustrate the crimes. **Conspiracy** is discussed first because it is often combined with other property and violent crimes.

Conspiracy

It is assumed that when people act together in criminal acts, they may be more dangerous than when they act alone; thus, statutes have been enacted to punish group actions. *Conspiracy* may involve a crime of violence against a person, such as murder, or a property crime, such as distributing counterfeit money. Persons charged with other crimes may also be charged with conspiracy if there is evidence of the additional elements that constitute conspiracy. They may be convicted of the base crime (e.g., murder) as well as conspiracy (conspiracy to commit murder) or of only one of the crimes. Conspiracy is frequently combined with crimes committed within the business setting.

Under the common law, *conspiracy* was defined as an agreement between two or more persons to commit an *unlawful* act or to achieve by unlawful means an act that was not in itself unlawful. The unlawful acts need not be carried out for conspiracy to occur. Although the word *unlawful* might be interpreted to mean "criminal," early English and American courts interpreted it to include acts that are "corrupt, dishonest, fraudulent, immoral, and in that sense illegal, and it is in the combination to make use of such practices that the dangers of this offense consist."[35] Thus, conspiracy is a useful tool for prosecutors because it is defined broadly, and a person can be charged with the conspiracy as well as the predicate crime, such as burglary.

Today, some jurisdictions specify that the act that is the focus of the alleged conspiracy must be a *crime*, whereas others use the term *unlawful act*; still others specify which crimes (or class of crimes) may form the basis of a conspiracy. For example, New York limits *conspiracy in the first degree to* only the most serious felonies.[36]

Congress has enacted a general conspiracy statute,[37] but federal criminal law also includes a number of specialized conspiracy statutes.

Conspiracy differs from other crimes in that the *act* requirement may be the agreement, which is the essence of conspiracy.[38] The agreement may be verbal and inferred from the facts and circumstances of the case. Conspiracy is a complicated crime and often difficult to prove.

Avoidance or Evasion of Taxes

Tax fraud is a crime that may be committed individually or with others. Perhaps the most commonly recognized tax fraud charge is that of evasion of federal (or state) income tax. The federal statute is as follows:

> Any person who willfully attempts in any manner to evade or defeat any tax imposed by this title or the payment thereof shall, in addition to other penalties provided by law, be guilty of a felony and, upon conviction thereof, shall be fined not more than $100,000 ($500,000 in the case of a corporation), or imprisoned not more than 5 years, or both, together with the costs of prosecution.[39]

Some elements and interpretations of this statute should be noted. First, the *attempt* completes the crime; eventual success in avoiding or evading taxes adds nothing to the crime. Second, Congress intended that if willfulness, a tax deficiency, *and* an intent to defeat the tax are proved beyond a reasonable doubt, a felony has been committed.[40] Third, the avoidance or evasion of income tax must be *willful*, not just accidental, and "willfulness may not be inferred solely from proof of understated taxes. A specific intent to evade or defeat the tax must be proved by independent evidence of willful affirmative acts."[41]

A recent prosecution for federal tax evasion ended in November 2009, when Bernard Kerik, former New York City police commissioner, hailed as a hero for his efforts in leading that department during the terrorism events of 11 September 2001, entered guilty pleas to eight criminal charges. The charges included tax evasion and lying to the White House when he was under consideration for the position of head of the Department of Homeland Security. Kerik was ordered to pay $188,000 in restitution and faced prison sentences of up to 61 years. He was under house arrest, where he wore an electric monitor, until he was ordered to report for his four-year sentence in federal prison.

In July 2010, high-profile celebrity defense attorney Mickey Sherman pleaded guilty to two misdemeanor charges of willful failure to pay federal income taxes in 2001 and 2002. He paid the tax bills eventually but still owed about $1 million in penalties and interest at the time of his plea. Sherman, a frequent TV commentator on criminal law issues, had not been sentenced but, according to his attorney, was hoping to avoid a prison sentence and losing his license to practice law. His law partner, Joseph Richichi, who faced five years in prison, was sentenced to 16 months in 2007 for failure to pay more than $600,000 in taxes.[42]

One way to evade federal income tax is to launder income through foreign banks. By November 2009, more than 14,700 Americans had disclosed their foreign bank accounts in response to an amnesty program. Those who did not come forward faced civil and criminal fines and

Bernard Kerik, former New York City police commissioner, hailed as a hero for his efforts in leading that department during the terrorism events of 11 September 2001, stands outside the federal court in Washington after pleading not guilty to eight criminal charges, including tax evasion and lying to the White House when he was under consideration for the position of head of Homeland Security. Kerik subsequently entered guilty pleas and was sentenced to four years in prison. He said he had been wronged but pleaded guilty because he was "financially helpless." In May 2010, he reported to prison to begin serving his sentence, which is longer than the federal guidelines for his offenses. At the sentencing, the judge stated that Kerik had used 9/11 for "personal gain and aggrandizement." Kerik is appealing.

possibly prison terms if their names appeared on the list that UBS, a Swiss banking giant, agreed to give to the Internal Revenue Service (IRS) as the result of its admission that the bank sold offshore services that facilitated U.S. income tax evasion. Approximately 4,450 American names (holding $18 billion at one point) were on the list the bank was to give over.[43]

Like most of the crimes in this chapter, income tax fraud charges may be combined with other charges, as illustrated by indictments filed on 23 June 2010 against former Detroit mayor, Kwame Kilpatrick: ten counts of mail fraud, three counts of wire fraud, five counts of filing a false tax return, and one count of tax evasion. With regard to the charges of tax crimes, the U.S. prosecutors alleged that Kilpatrick had unreported taxable income of at least $640,000 between 2003 and 2008, "including cash, private jet flights, and personal expenses paid for by the Civic Fund," which was a fund to be used for improving the lives of citizens of Detroit and surrounding communities. Kilpatrick allegedly used these funds to pay for summer camp for his own children, moving expenses, car rentals, yoga and golf lessons, golf clubs, a personal residence, and other unauthorized and illegal expenditures. Kilpatrick was in a state prison for a probation violation after he was sentenced to one and a half to five years in prison in a felony text-message scandal about which he lied to authorities. The federal investigation that led to the June indictments had gone on for approximately five years, with 10 suspects already having entered guilty pleas to various charges.[44]

As many cities and states faced financial budget crises, especially in 2009 and 2010, efforts were increased to collect back state income and other taxes. New York, for example, was facing a $3 billion budget gap in November 2009 and was issuing tax warrants against individuals and businesses, even going after some persons who were already in prison. At the time, the state had 1.2 million active tax cases. The state had some success, with The Walt Disney Corporation paying $3.3 million in corporate taxes in July.[45]

Bribery and Extortion

Historically, **bribery** was defined as corruption in the administration of justice. The modern concept of bribery includes the voluntary gift or receipt of anything of value in corrupt payment for an official act already done or to be done or with the corrupt intent to influence the action of a public official or any person involved with the administration of public affairs. The federal statute covers bribery and **graft**, which is defined as the offering, giving, soliciting, or receiving of anything of value in connection with the procurement of materials under a federal defense program.[46] Exhibit 9.1 discusses a recent bribery case involving an individual. Bribery can also be applied to corporations, as illustrated by the 2009 forfeiture of $700 million by J. P. Morgan Securities. The company was charged with bribing friends of Alabama county commissioners "as part of a scheme to win lucrative business from the county to sell bonds and trade in derivatives."[47]

Bribery statutes are not broad in scope, and courts generally limit bribery to actions within the *official* capacity of the public servant. State bribery statutes vary but may include the receiving or soliciting, as well as the giving or offering, of a bribe. Iowa's statute provides an example of a state bribery statute. Notice that the first part covers *any* person, and the second part refers to the *officers or employees* of the state.

Any person who gives, pays, or offers, directly or indirectly, to any officer or employee of this state authorized to perform any of the duties prescribed by this chapter or by the regulations of the secretary, any money or other thing of value, with intent to influence said officer or employee in the discharge of any such duty, shall be deemed guilty of a felony . . . [penalty stated] and any officer or employee of this state authorized to perform any of the duties prescribed by this chapter who accepts any money, gift, or other thing of value from any person, given with intent to influence the officer's or employee's official action, or who receives or accepts from any person engaged in intrastate commerce any gift, money, or other things of value given with any purpose or intent whatsoever, shall be deemed guilty of a felony and shall, upon conviction thereof, be summarily discharged from office and shall be punished . . . [remaining penalty follows].[48]

Although the two crimes are similar, bribery should be distinguished from **extortion**, or **blackmail**, which refers to obtaining property from others by wrongful use of actual or threatened force, fear, or violence or the corrupt taking of a fee by a public officer, **under color of law** (discussed later in this chapter), when that fee is not due.[49] Exhibit 9.2 features a press release about an extortion case involving a large amount of money. That press release illustrates the interlocking of some of the crimes discussed in this and the previous chapter because the computer was an integral part of the attempt to extort $17 million.

Readers will perhaps be most familiar with two recent cases. The first concerns allegations against Dutchman Joran van der Sloot, thought to be responsible for the disappearance and probable death of Natalee Holloway, a high school student on vacation in Aruba in 2005. Van der Sloot is alleged to have extorted money from Holloway's mother in exchange for being told the location of her daughter's remains. In July 2010, a federal grand jury indicted him on charges of wire fraud and extortion.

The second case involved attempts by Robert Halderman to extort $2 million from night talk show host David Letterman. Halderman, a former producer for the CBS show *48 Hours*, tried to blackmail Letterman by threatening to publish information concerning Letterman's extramarital affairs. In a plea agreement that prohibits Halderman from publicizing any of the information he had about Letterman and saved the defendant from a potential 15-year sentence, Halderman entered a guilty plea and was sentenced to six months in prison.

Embezzlement

The crime of *embezzlement*, discussed as a property crime in Chapter 8, involves having rightful possession of the property of another and intending to deprive the owner of

Bribery: A Former U.S. Congressman Convicted

William J. Jefferson, 62, who was defeated for reelection to the U.S. Congress (from Louisiana) in 2008, was convicted of bribery and other charges stemming from his unlawful dealings that violated the Foreign Corrupt Practices Act (FCPA). Jefferson brokered business deals in Africa using his office to enrich himself and his family. The FCPA prohibits corporate bribery overseas, and Jefferson was the first single individual to be charged under this statute.

Federal authorities alleged that Jefferson solicited over $500,000 in bribes, $90,000 of which prosecutors found wrapped in foil in a freezer in his home. Jefferson's congressional office was raided in 2006, constituting the first time federal officials searched the office of a member of Congress. The raid was challenged, and both political parties condemned it. But a judge upheld the search and seizure as constitutional, although an appeals court ruled that part of the raid was illegal and ordered some of the seized documents returned to Jefferson. Jefferson challenged the indictment on the grounds that it violated the Speech and Debate clause of the U.S. Constitution, which provides immu-

nity for legislative acts by members of Congress. Jefferson, a member of a House Ways and Means subcommittee, was indicted for using that position to solicit and receive bribes "from persons and business entities. In exchange, he promoted their products and services to government officials in Africa." The lower federal court held that the indictment focused on acts that went beyond Jefferson's official duties and did not violate the Speech and Debate clause. The circuit court agreed, and the U.S. Supreme Court refused to review the issue.[1]

Jefferson was convicted of 11 of 16 counts and sentenced to 13 years in prison. He was free on bail pending his appeal.

---

1. *United States v. Jefferson*, 546 F.3d 300 (4th Cir. 2008), *cert. denied*, 129 S.Ct. 2383 (2009). The Speech or Debate clause is from the U.S. Constitution, Art. 1, Sec. 6, Cl. 1. Among other crimes, Jefferson was convicted of two counts for soliciting bribes, six counts of wire fraud, three counts of money laundering, obstruction of justice, and racketeering.

---

that property wrongfully. The crime evolved because, under the common law, a person under rightful possession of property could not be charged with larceny-theft.

Embezzlement requires that the property to which one has been entrusted is converted to his or her own use or possession; thus, **conversion** (the process of using the property or goods of another for one's own use and without permission) is required. Conversion is a serious interference with property, not just a movement of that property.

Some statutes define the property that can be the target of embezzlement; others define the crime more broadly and even include real property. Some jurisdictions have a separate statute to cover embezzlement by public officials, making the penalty more severe for them than for others. Finally, some jurisdictions do not distinguish between embezzlement and larceny-theft.[50]

The seriousness of embezzlement by public officials is indicated by the 2009 conviction of Sheila Dixon, mayor of Baltimore, Maryland. Dixon was convicted of using a $500 gift card intended for needy families and purchasing items, including electronics, for herself and others. Under a plea arrangement, Dixon pleaded guilty and was sentenced to probation after resigning her office.[51]

Embezzlement can also be charged as other crimes. In November 2009, federal prosecutors charged Donna White, 46, of Avondale, Louisiana, and Daniel Kinney, 44, of Whitesville, Kentucky (White's sister's boyfriend), each with one count of wire fraud. They pleaded guilty to embezzling $13 million between August 1995 and 29

October 2007 by stealing checks and funds belonging to White's employer and depositing those funds to their personal accounts. They each faced 20 years in federal prison. White was sentenced to 40 months and Kinney to 78 months, each followed by three years' probation. They were required to pay $12.7 million in restitution.[52]

Securities and Investment Crimes

Recent investigations into the accounting and other business practices of high-level executives in national corporations such as Enron, Tyco, WorldCom, ImClone, and Adelphia, along with the resulting financial losses of their employees and investors, have focused renewed attention on crimes committed in the corporate world. Some of the questionable or illegal acts occurred within the highly regulated securities business in the United States.

Securities include stocks, bonds, notes, and other documents that represent a share in a company or a debt of a company. *Securities fraud* includes acts of illegal manipulation or deception that affect the exchange of securities. Normally, these illegal acts involve the omission or misrepresentation of material facts.

The U.S. securities industry is administered by the Securities and Exchange Commission (SEC). The organization came under intense scrutiny and criticism in 2008 and 2009 as the case of Bernard L. Madoff unfolded. Madoff pleaded guilty to a $65 billion scheme to defraud, ruining the financial fortunes of scores of people. He was sentenced to 150 years in prison, and by the end of 2009,

Wi-Fi Hacker Pleads Guilty to Attempted $17,000,000 Extortion

"Paul J. McNulty, United States Attorney for the Eastern District of Virginia, announced that Myron Tereshchuk, 42, of Hyattsville, Maryland, pled guilty . . . to one count of attempting to extort $17 million over the Internet. The maximum potential sentence is 20 years imprisonment and a $250,000 fine.

"For more than a year, the defendant harassed MicroPatent, an intellectual property firm that produces and distributes patent and trademark information. The defendant sent MicroPatent's clients hundreds of emails, many of which were 'spoofed' to resemble authentic MicroPatent correspondence. The emails contained statements derogatory to MicroPatent, attached sexually explicit patent applications, and disclosed MicroPatent documents that were believed to have been confidential. The defendant obtained the confidential information by gaining unauthorized access to MicroPatent's computer network and by searching through the trash set out to be collected by a shredding company at MicroPatent's location in Alexandria, Virginia. The defendant sent emails anonymously by using equipment from his automobile to gain unauthorized access to unsecured wireless computer networks in residences and businesses in Maryland and Virginia. Once the defendant had access to the networks, he often sent the emails using accounts of AOL customers without their knowledge or authorization.

"On February 3, 2004, the defendant began sending a series of extortionate emails to the president of MicroPatent using the alias 'Bryan Ryan' and a free Yahoo email account. To further hide his identity, the defendant accessed the Yahoo account through unsecured wireless access points and the unauthorized use of the University of Maryland computer network and students' accounts. In the emails, the defendant demanded $17 million or he would disclose additional MicroPatent proprietary information and launch distributed denial-of-service attacks against intellectual property attorneys' computer systems worldwide.

"Based on one of the messages, the FBI believed the defendant might be the person attempting the extortion. Thereafter, the FBI, with the assistance of Yahoo, AOL, and the University of Maryland, was able to catch the defendant in the act of sending emails to the president of MicroPatent. At the time of the defendant's arrest at his automobile on March 10, 2003, he was in possession of his laptop, an antenna, and other computer equipment.

"The FBI searched the defendant's residence on March 10, 2004, and found not only computers and other items related to the attempted extortion, but also the components for hand grenades, the formula and items necessary for making Ricin, and literature about poisons. . . .

"United States Attorney Paul J. McNulty stated, 'While the Internet has brought our society many benefits, it is also being used by a wide variety of criminals. Some of these criminals have the technical savvy to use new means to try to conceal their identities. This case is proof, however, that law enforcement is keeping up with technological advances and will catch these offenders.'"[1]

The defendant was sentenced to 41 months in federal prison.

1. News Release, United States Attorney's Office, Eastern District of Virginia (8 June 2004).

---

he was in the infirmary of the North Carolina prison in which he was incarcerated. Although the exact reason for his hospitalization was not known, it was reported that his injuries were consist with an assault, which was denied by Madoff and by prison officials.[53]

Investigations of Madoff's associates continued despite his claim that he acted alone in his scheme. Former computer programmers Jerome O'Hara and George Perez were charged with falsely running programs that made it appear that Madoff secured the increases in stock investments that he claimed. Daniel Bonventre, Madoff's former operations chief, was indicted on federal charges, including conspiracy, tax fraud, and securities fraud. All of these men have entered guilty pleas. Former aide Frank DiPascali Jr. pleaded guilty in August 2009 to federal charges in this case in a bid for leniency in sentencing. DiPascali was jailed, but in June 2010, he was granted bail under very stringent conditions, including posting a $10 million bond with $2 million in cash

or property. He was required to forfeit all but about $300,000 of his family's property and had already given the government his yacht, jewelry, and other items. Federal prosecutors were seeking forfeitures from other Madoff employees, including Annette Bongiorno (40 years with Madoff) and Joann Crupi (25 years with Madoff) claiming that the moneys sought could be traced to Madoff's fraud. Both women were indicted for fraud and conspiracy.[54]

Civil claims were also made against others, including the estate of Jeffrey M. Picower, who drowned at his oceanfront home in Florida while rumors were swirling concerning his possible role in the Madoff scheme. Lawyers for investors who lost money contended that Picower and other investors who withdrew large sums of money before the Madoff fraud scheme unraveled should be required to pay their gains into a fund for Madoff's victims. Picower's widow agreed to a $7.2 billion settlement for the victims' fund.[55]

Not all prosecutions are successful, however, as federal prosecutors learned in November 2009, when a quick jury verdict acquitted two former Wall Street hedge fund managers, Ralph Cioffi and Matthew Tannin, of Bear Stearns. The fund's failure in 2007 contributed to the demise of Bear Stearns, now a part of JPMorgan Chase & Company. Both defendants were found not guilty of securities fraud, and Cioffi was acquitted of insider trading. It was alleged that they defrauded investors of $1.6 billion. The Securities and Exchange Commission brought a civil suit against the two, and that was still pending.[56]

Numerous statutes apply to securities crimes, but two are dominant. The Securities Act of 1933 requires the registration of all securities that are to be sold to the public. It requires complete information is given regarding the stock offering and its issuer. The buying and selling of stock, along with the over-the-counter trading of stock, are regulated by a second statute, the Securities Exchange Act of 1934.[57]

Under penalty of law, these (and other) criminal statutes prohibit the use of any device, scheme, or artifice to defraud. They forbid making any untrue statements of material fact that might affect the buying and selling of stock. The statutes also forbid all acts that are intended to defraud or deceive potential stock purchasers. Intent is a crucial element of the crimes associated with securities. Another element is that interstate commerce must be used in the commission of the crimes charged under these securities statutes. Mail and wire fraud charges (discussed later in this chapter), conspiracy, and other crimes may fall within securities statutes. There are a variety of ways to defraud investors and otherwise violate securities laws.

The FBI investigates securities and commmodities crimes within its Financial Crimes Section (FCS). The FBI estimates that losses from these crimes run into the billions annually. Figure 9.1 provides a graph of pending cases between 2005 and 2009. As of the end of fiscal year 2009, the FBI was investigating 1,510 cases. The agency had secured 412 indictment/informations, 306 convictions, $8.1 billion in restitution orders, $63.4 million in recoveries, $126 million in seizures, and $12.8 million in fines. Between 2005 and 2009, FBI investigations into open securities and commodities fraud increased by 33 percent.[58]

Several high-profile securities and related fraud cases are noted in Exhibit 9.3.

Insider Trading

One type of securities crime that has gained considerable attention is **insider trading**. *Insider trading* exists when officers, directors, and stockholders who hold more than 10 percent of the stock of a corporation listed on a national exchange buy and sell corporate shares. **Insider information** is known to these officers before it is available to the public. Federal law requires that such transactions be reported monthly to the SEC. This requirement is meant

Figure 9.1

Securities and Commodities Fraud Pending Cases

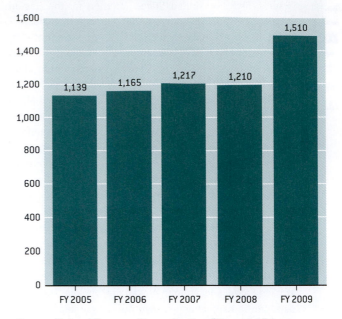

Source: Federal Bureau of Investigation, "Financial Crimes Report to the Public: Fiscal Year 2009," p. 8, http://www.fbi.gov/stats-services/publications/financial-crimes-report-2009, accessed 22 October 2010.

to ensure that insiders are not taking undue advantage of the investing public by trading information that enables them to make large profits on their investments at the expense of other investors.

Like most other areas of criminal law, the laws covering insider trading have changed rapidly and are complicated. Some information may be traded without criminal liability, but there are gray areas. Since 1986, when several cases of insider trading were prosecuted successfully, the U.S. Department of Justice (DOJ) has won numerous large cases. The DOJ argued successfully in the 1986 cases that the defendants had gone too far. Most of the cases involved selling information about corporate takeovers. Ira B. Sokolow, a 32-year-old investment banker, was convicted and sentenced to one year and a day in prison and three years' probation after he admitted that he sold information about pending takeovers to Dennis B. Levine, the central figure in the largest illegal insider trading scheme uncovered at that time.

One of the key defendants in the 1986 prosecutions was Ivan F. Boesky, a leading Wall Street stock market speculator who cooperated with federal officials by permitting a secret recording of his conversations with other investors. Boesky agreed to pay a $100 million fine and to plead guilty to one criminal charge (if others were dropped). He was sentenced to three years in prison and served about two. Boesky was barred from the investment business for the rest of his life. He was released from prison in April

EXHIBIT

9.3

High-Profile Securities and Accounting Fraud Cases

The December 2001 bankruptcy filing by the energy giant Enron Corporation (listed as the seventh-largest company on the Fortune 500 list), headquartered in Houston, Texas, resulted in the unemployment of over 4,500 workers, along with the loss of approximately $2 billion in pension plans, $60 billion in market value, and the erosion of public confidence in corporations. Within six months, federal prosecutors, after a six-week trial, had won a conviction for obstruction of justice against Enron's accounting firm, Arthur Andersen, one of the largest accounting firms in the world, which was placed on five years' probation and fined $500,000. In June 2004, a federal court upheld that conviction, but in June 2005, the U.S. Supreme Court reversed and remanded the case.[1]

Enron's chief financial officer (CFO), Andrew Fastow, was accused of creating partnerships with others to enrich himself and to misrepresent Enron's profits. He faced 78 counts of federal violations. His wife, Lea, was charged with several crimes of aiding her husband by hiding money from the off-the-books partnerships and other questionable business ventures. She negotiated a plea with prosecutors and, in July 2004, began serving a one-year prison term for her guilty plea to evading taxes.

Andrew Fastow initially pleaded not guilty but subsequently agreed to cooperate with the government. He pleaded guilty to two charges of conspiracy and agreed to forfeit $23.8 million of the money he acquired as a result of his illegal business transactions while CFO of Enron and to spend 10 years in prison. The trial judge sentenced him to 6 years, stating that 10 was too long.[2] Fastow is due for release from prison in December 2011.

Other former Enron executives entered guilty pleas or were convicted, but by far, the most watched cases were those of Enron's founder Kenneth L. Lay and the company's former chief executive officer (CEO) Jeffrey Skilling. Lay was convicted but died before sentencing. According to the rules of criminal procedure, since Lay could not appeal, his conviction was vacated. Skilling was convicted and sentenced to 24.3 years in prison. With good behavior and participation in a substance abuse program, Skilling could reduce the time he must serve by 54 days a year. At Skilling's sentencing, the judge stated that his crimes "imposed on hundreds if not thousands a life sentence of poverty [as a result of losing their jobs and pensions]."[3]

On 24 June 2010, the U.S. Supreme Court decided the case of *Skilling v. United States*. Skilling was convicted of charges

Lea Fastow, left, spouse of former Enron chief financial officer Andrew Fastow, arrived with one of her attorneys at the federal building in Houston, Texas. Fastow pleaded guilty to one misdemeanor count of filing a false tax return and was sentenced to one year in prison. After her release, her husband began serving his six-year term for two counts of conspiracy.

(continued)

9.3

that included conspiracy to commit "honest services" wire fraud.[4] A unanimous U.S. Supreme Court vacated Skilling's conviction under the statute, which prohibits schemes "to deprive another of the intangible right of honest services." According to the Court, that covers only bribery and kickback schemes, and to extend it further would raise a vagueness issue. Skilling did not prevail on his argument that he did not receive a fair trial because of pretrial publicity, with the Court holding 6-3 that the trial was fair. But since Skilling's convictions rest on the "honest services" statute and did not involve bribery or kickback schemes, the case was returned to the lower court to determine whether the errors were harmless. It is possible that some of the charges against Skilling will not be retried or that his sentence will be reduced. Skilling maintained that he did not intend to deprive anyone of honest services but was only acting to improve the value of Enron's stock. He was accused of conspiring to commit fraud against stockholders by misrepresenting the company's financial situation.[5]

Following Enron into bankruptcy was telecommunications giant WorldCom, the second-largest long-distance carrier in the United States. In June 2002, WorldCom officials announced that they had overstated the company's cash flow by more than $3.8 billion. That figure rose to over $11 billion with subsequent investigations. In July 2002, the company filed for bankruptcy. In August 2003, two former WorldCom executives, chief financial officer Scott D. Sullivan and controller David F. Myers, were arrested, handcuffed, and taken to the federal district courthouse, where bail was set: $2 million for Myers and $10 million for Sullivan. In March 2004, criminal charges of securities fraud, false filings, and conspiracy to commit securities fraud were filed against former WorldCom CEO Bernard Ebbers just hours after Sullivan pleaded guilty to securities fraud and filing false documents with the SEC. At his plea, Sullivan said he did not engage in those acts for personal gain but to lead WorldCom out of what he thought to be temporary financial problems.[6] Myers also pleaded guilty. Ebbers, 63, was convicted and sentenced to 25 years in prison, with no chance of release until he serves 85 percent of that term. The sentencing judge said she realized this is a life sentence for Ebbers but that a shorter sentence would not reflect the seriousness of his crimes. In the summer of 2006, the conviction was upheld by a federal court, and in 2007, the U.S. Supreme Court declined to review the case.[7]

Finally, several members of the founding family of Adelphia Communications Corporation were indicted for conspiracy and securities, wire, and bank fraud. John J. Rigas, 79, his sons Timothy and Michael, and former assistant treasurer Michael C. Mulcahey were alleged to have run the company "not for the benefit of the public shareholders but for the benefit of the Rigas family." Among other expenses, the defendants were accused of using company money to buy timber rights to protect the view at their home (cost of $25 million), to pay their condo fees, and to purchase stocks ($822 million). John Rigas was accused of drawing $1 million a month in cash advances. He and his son, Timothy, were convicted of securities fraud, bank fraud, and conspiracy. Mulcahey was acquitted. The jury deadlocked on the charges against Michael Rigas. Rather than face another trial, he entered a guilty plea to charges of making a false entry to an accounting record. He was sentenced to 10 months of home confinement, followed by 14 months of court supervised probation, and fined $2,000. John Rigas, 80, was sentenced to 15 years in prison and Timothy Rigas to 20 years. Although initially free pending their appeals, both were ordered to report to federal prison in August 2007. On appeal, the convictions were upheld with the exception of one count of bank fraud, which was reversed and remanded for acquittal. The lower court was ordered to resentence the appellants based on its findings. The appellants appealed to the U.S. Supreme Court, which refused to hear their cases.[8] At resentencing, the sentence for each defendant was reduced by three years; their motions for new trials were denied. In October 2010, the U.S. Supreme Court refused to hear their appeal.[9]

1. *United States v. Andersen*, 374 F.3d 281 (5th Cir. 2004), *rev'd., remanded*, 544 U.S. 696 (2005). The data are from "Former Executive for Enron Gets Sentence of 16 Months," *New York Times* (29 September 2009), p. 7B

2. "Fastow Sentenced to 6 Years," *New York Times* (27 September 2006), p. 1C.

3. "Skilling Sentenced to 24 Years," *New York Times* (24 October 2006), p. 1B.

4. See USCS, Title 18, Sections 371, 1343, and 1346 (2010).

5. *United States v. Skilling*, 554 F.3d 529, *aff'd. in part and vacated in part, remanded, Skilling v. United States*, 130 S.Ct. 2896 (2010).

6. "Ex-CEO Ebbers Is Charged in $11 Billion WorldCom Scandal over Accounting," *New York Law Journal* 231 (3 March 2004): 1.

7. "WorldCom Ex-CEO Gets 25 Years," *Washington Post* (17 July 2005), p. 3; *United States v. Ebbers*, 458 F.3d 110 (2d Cir. 2006), *cert. denied*, 549 U.S. 1274 (2007).

8. "Rigases, Their Ilk Sing Same Song," *Denver Post* (10 August 2007), p. 1C; "Adelphia Prosecutor Begins His Closing: Rigases Looted Company, He Says," *Washington Post* (17 June 2004), p. 4E; "Business Briefs," *New York Times* (4 March 2006), p. 2C; *Rigas v. United States*, 490 F.3d 208 (2d Cir. 2007), *cert. denied*, 552 U.S. 1242 (2008).

9. *United States v. Rigas*, 583 F.3d 108 (2d Cir. 2009), *cert. denied*, 2020 U.S. LEXIS 7717 (U.S. 4 October 2010).

1990 and became a key government witness in other cases involving Wall Street scandals.

Michael Milken, the executive who presided over the junk bond operation of securities firm Drexel Burnham Lambert, pleaded guilty to six felony counts (none having to do with insider trading; he was indicted on 98 counts) and agreed to pay a $600 million fine. His 10-year prison term was the longest sentence assessed against any defendant in the Wall Street insider trading scandals. Milken entered a federal prison in 1991, but in August 1992, a federal judge reduced his sentence to two years. After serving 22 months in prison, Milken was released to a halfway house in January 1993. Subsequently, he was released on probation, diagnosed with prostate cancer, founded and partially financed the Association for the Cure of Cancer of the Prostate, and appeared to be on the road to rehabilitation as far as criminal activity was concerned. In 1996, his probation was extended while the SEC investigated some of his financial dealings; in 1997, the government announced that it was focusing on obstruction of justice charges against Milken.[59]

In March 1998, Milken agreed to pay the SEC $47 million; in exchange, federal prosecutors dropped their investigation into his possible parole violation and terminated his probation.

Many problems arose in the prosecution of insider trading cases despite the government's success in the 1980s. One problem was that there were no federal statutes aimed specifically at insider trading. Congress attempted to alleviate this in 1988 by enacting a statute encompassing insider trading and increasing the penalties that could be assessed for securities violations of this type.[60]

Sarbanes-Oxley (SOX) Act

As a result of the corporate frauds in recent years, Congress enacted the Sarbanes-Oxley (SOX) Act of 2002. When President George W. Bush signed the bill on 30 July 2002, he declared: "Today I sign into law the most far-reaching reform of American business practices since the time of Franklin Delano Roosevelt." The SOX was also viewed by others as the most important legislation in securities regulation since the passage of the Securities Exchange Act of 1934, discussed at the beginning of this section. The SOX applies only to publicly held companies, but some are suggesting that privately held corporations should follow its requirements. The law is complex and beyond the scope of this book, but it is important to look at a few requirements that do relate to issues of interest to criminologists.

The SOX is the first and only statute that provides for whistle-blower claims that target financial wrongdoing. Thus, an employee who is fired for reporting financial fraud may seek protection under the SOX. It is assumed that providing legal protection to employees who suspect fraud will encourage them to report the infractions and

will serve as a deterrent to business persons who might think about engaging in fraud.

The SOX requires the chief executive officer and chief financial officers of public companies to certify that the financial statements they compile fairly represent the company's actual financial health. The company's management is required to publish its assessment of the effectiveness of the company's internal controls over financial reporting. The company's auditors are under similar requirements. The act makes it unlawful, under most circumstances, for a company to extend credit to any director or executive officer. The company's general counsel is required to report up the line if he or she suspects any accounting or securities violations. Conviction for failure to comply with these requirements can result in a heavy fine and a prison sentence. The act directed the U.S. Sentencing Commission (discussed in Chapter 13) to recommend increased penalties for securities violations and to reconsider the penalties for violations of all white-collar crimes. The commission did so, and the penalties were increased in 2003.[61]

Although subsequently the U.S. Supreme Court has held that the federal sentencing guidelines are not mandatory, some federal courts have made it clear that light sentences, even those resulting from plea bargains, may not be upheld by appellate courts.[62]

The SOX was before the U.S. Supreme Court in its 2009–2010 term, with a decision handed down on the last day of the term. In *Corporate Accountability Free Enterprise Fund v. Public Company Accounting Oversight Board*, the Court upheld the constitutionality of the SOX by a 9-0 vote but split 5-4 on the issue of how the members of the oversight board, which are appointed by the SEC, can be removed.[63]

Antitrust Violations

Laws designed to ensure fair competition and free enterprise in the private economic marketplace are known as **antitrust laws**. Historically, the common law attempted to limit restraints on trade and to control monopolies and excessive profits of intermediaries, or middlemen. During the second half of the nineteenth century, Congress expressed concern over abusive practices of large corporations by enacting the Interstate Commerce Act of 1887 and the Sherman Antitrust Act of 1890. The latter has two main provisions:

Sec. 1: Every contract, combination in the form of trust or otherwise, or conspiracy, in restraint of trade or commerce . . . is declared to be illegal [and is a felony punishable by fine and/or imprisonment]. . . .

Sec. 2: Every person who shall monopolize, or attempt to monopolize or combine or conspire with any other person or persons, to monopolize any part of the trade or commerce among the several States, or with foreign nations, shall be deemed guilty of a felony [and is similarly punishable].[64]

The purpose of Section 1 is to prohibit two or more competing parties from acting together to fix prices, which is a violation of federal law under the Sherman Antitrust Act. One problem with the court decisions based on this statute, however, is that there is not a clear definition of *price fixing*. Another difficulty is distinguishing between the legal exchange of information between businesspeople, such as trade associations that disseminate trade news and data, and illegal conduct in the exchange of information that tends to restrain trade unreasonably.

Section 2 of the Sherman Antitrust Act focuses on the control of monopolistic power. Troublesome issues under this section include definitions of the product market, the geographic market, and the market share. The prosecution must prove an illegal purpose and intent along with market structure and power.

The Sherman Act contains criminal and civil penalties. The Department of Justice has jurisdiction to prosecute criminal actions, whereas the Federal Trade Commission is limited to administrative and civil jurisdictions. Under the Sherman act, privately injured parties may sue for treble damages and attorney's fees.

Environmental Crime

Protection of the environment for future generations and for those of us enjoying life today has become a matter of significant local, state, and national concern in the United States as well as globally. Most of the attempts to regulate acts that damage the environment involve administrative or civil law. Chapter 1 distinguished these types of law from criminal law, noting that unless the criminal law is invoked, technically, people (and corporations) who violate regulations are not criminals. Perhaps, as sociologist Edwin H. Sutherland argued, sociologists should study these violators to develop theories of why people violate administrative regulations and civil laws, but it is important to distinguish cases brought in the criminal courts from those processed through administrative agencies or civil courts. Unfortunately, this distinction is not always made, which leads people to think that corporations violating administrative regulations or civil laws have violated criminal laws.

There is a question, however, of which type of law—civil, administrative, or criminal—is the most effective regulatory measure. If people suffer property damage and personal injury when regulations and laws are violated, would they be compensated more adequately by filing civil suits and getting court orders for the agencies to discontinue the violations and pay damages to the victims? Or would society (and individual victims) be compensated more adequately if violators were prosecuted in criminal courts? Or should both civil and criminal laws be utilized?

Despite the large number of environmental violations that are processed through administrative agencies, today the criminal law is used more frequently in an effort to prevent environmental pollution and other crimes and punish those who engage in the acts covered by state and federal statutes. The reason is that civil penalties may not carry sufficient stigma to be a deterrent. Civil cases can last for years, and businesses may consider the resulting fines just another cost of doing business.

The primary agency charged with protecting the environment is the Environmental Protection Agency (EPA). Although some congressional attempts at regulating the environment occurred earlier, as noted in Exhibit 9.4, the EPA was not established until 1970

> in response to the growing public demand for cleaner water, air and land. Prior to the establishment of the EPA, the federal government was not structured to make a coordinated attack on the pollutants that harm human health and degrade the environment. The EPA was assigned the daunting task of repairing the damage already done to the natural environment and to establish new criteria to guide Americans in making a cleaner environment a reality.[65]

The federal government has enacted numerous civil and criminal laws aimed at preventing environment pollution and related crimes. Those statutes include the Comprehensive Environmental Response, Compensation, and Liability Act of 1980 (CERCLA), the Resource Conservation and Recovery Act (RCRA), which was enacted in 1976 and amended subsequently, and the Clean Water Act. The RCRA was passed for the purpose of providing the EPA with a tool for regulating the generation, transportation, disposal, storage, and cleanup of hazardous waste.[66]

The Environment and Natural Resources Division (ENRD) of the U.S. Department of Justice is charged with enforcing environmental and natural resources litigation. The ENRD, which is headed by Ignacia S. Moreno, assistant attorney general, had 6,000 cases pending in December 2009. It "has represented virtually every federal agency in courts all over the United States and its territories and possessions."[67]

One type of environmental crime is the improper disposal of hazardous wastes. While physical scientists look for better methods of disposal, government agencies wrestle with enforcing the statutes and administrative rules developed to control the disposal. Consumer advocates and political activists campaign to alert the public to the hazards of industrial waste and to apply pressure to regulatory agencies charged with the responsibility of enforcing environmental protection laws. Protection of the environment is not without controversy because regulations to protect the environment may, and often do, conflict with business interests.

The improper disposal of toxic waste may create hazards for all living creatures and plants. Although medi-

EXHIBIT 9.4

The Environmental Protection Agency (EPA)

In 1970, President Richard Nixon ordered the development of the Environmental Protection Agency (EPA). Today, that agency, headed by Lisa P. Jackson, employs 17,000 individuals in specialties such as engineering, science, policy analysis, law, information management, and computer science. The EPA's mission is to protect human health and the environment. Its purpose "is to ensure that

- all Americans are protected from significant risks to human health and the environment where they live, learn and work;
- national efforts to reduce environmental risk are based on the best available scientific information;
- federal laws protecting human health and the environment are enforced fairly and effectively;
- environmental protection is an integral consideration in U.S. policies concerning natural resources, human health, economic growth, energy, transportation,

agriculture, industry, and international trade, and these factors are similarly considered in establishing environmental policy;

- all parts of society—communities, individuals, businesses, and state, local and tribal governments—have access to accurate information sufficient to effectively participate in managing human health and environmental risks;
- environmental protection contributes to making our communities and ecosystems diverse, sustainable and economically productive; and
- the United States plays a leadership role in working with other nations to protect the global environment."

Source: Environmental Protection Agency, http://www.epa.gov/aboutepa/whatwedo.html, accessed 22 October 2010.

cal scientists do not know the extent and nature of the relationship between these hazards and human life and welfare, several health problems—such as cancer; genetic mutation, birth defects, and miscarriages; and damage to the lungs, liver, kidneys, or nervous system—have been linked to toxic waste. Contamination of water supplies is one of the greatest hazards of toxic waste.

Other legislative attempts to prevent environmental crime include provisions aimed at damage to the environment caused by terrorist acts; these are part of the Uniting and Strengthening America by Providing Appropriate Tools Required to Intercept and Obstruct Terrorism Act of 2001 (the USA Patriot Act). In May 2007, Chelsea D. Garlach, age 30, was sentenced to nine years in prison for her role in a group of radical environmentalists, called "terrorists" by the sentencing judge. The group engaged in arson and other destructive acts at numerous sites, burning what they considered threats to the environment. The judge ignored the defense argument that the acts were not terrorist because they were aimed at the destruction of property, not people. According to the judge, it was the defendant's intention "to scare, frighten and intimidate people and government through the very dangerous act of arson." Among other targets of the defendant's arson were 30 sport utility vehicles at a dealership. Labeling the actions in this case *terrorist* enabled the judge to give longer sentences than would be possible under traditional arson statutes.[68]

In October 2007, British Petroleum (BP) agreed to pay more than $370 million for environmental crimes and fraud cases resulting from a 2005 Texas refinery explosion, leaks in the Alaska pipeline, and attempts to manipulate the market. British Petroleum agreed to plead guilty to

violating the Clean Air Act and other statutes in exchange for the dropping of some charges.[69]

In 2010, BP agreed to place $20 billion in a compensation fund for those suffering damages due to the oil spill in the Gulf off New Orleans after a BP-leased rig exploded in April, killing 11 people and causing an oil spill. It was the greatest environmental disaster in U.S. history. No criminal charges had been filed, but it was suggested that BP's actions might be considered grossly negligent or even willful misconduct. British Petroleum will be liable for civil damages; whether criminal prosecutions result will be determined later.[70]

But criminal prosecutions are rarely successful in such cases, and even when they are, defendants rarely serve prison time for violating environmental laws. Even in the case of the *Exxon Valdez* (the worst oil spill in U.S. history prior to the BP disaster), which occurred when an Exxon tanker ran aground in Alaska in 1989 and dumped millions of gallons of oil into Prince William Sound, the captain, Joseph J. Hazelwood, was acquitted of the most serious charges against him, including reckless endangerment, criminal mischief, and operating a vessel while intoxicated. Hazelwood, who had gone below to his cabin and left a third mate in charge of the tanker's voyage through the sound, was thought to have been drinking, but the jury did not believe the state proved he was intoxicated. Hazelwood's conviction on a single charge of misdemeanor negligence was overturned on an immunity issue,[71] after which Congress toughened the maritime laws.

In 2009, the first ship's pilot to be sentenced to prison for an oil spill, Captain John Cota, was given the maximum sentence of 10 months in prison for his role in a 2007 oil spill in San Francisco Bay. Cota pleaded guilty to two misdemeanor charges of water pollution when he ran the ship into the Bay Bridge, dumping more than 53,000 gallons of fuel oil, which spread along 26 miles of coast and killed more than 2,400 birds. The estimated cost of cleanup was $70 million. The ship's operating company, Fleet Management, Ltd., was scheduled to go on trial in September 2009 but, in August of that year, entered a plea agreement with prosecutors. The company agreed to plead guilty to criminal charges of obstruction, making false statements, and negligent discharge of oil and to pay a $10 million fine as well as to put in effect a compliance plan for training. Two million of the fine will be used to fund marine environmental projects in San Francisco Bay.[72]

States also prosecute for environmental crimes, as illustrated by the case against Eastman Kodak, which was fined $2.15 million in criminal and civil penalties for violating New York's environmental statutes. The company pleaded guilty to two misdemeanor violations for illegally disposing of hazardous waste and failing to report a toxic spill until five days after the spill was discovered.

Nobody served prison time in the New York case, but in another case in that state, defendants were not so fortunate. Evelyn Berman Frank, head of a New York company charged with illegal sewage-sludge dumping, was sentenced to five years' probation and 500 hours of community service for her role in the offense. After Frank violated the terms of her probation, she was sentenced to a jail term. One of her daughters, Susan B. Frank, was sentenced to four months in jail, followed by four months of home confinement for polluting New York Harbor with hazardous sewage sludge. Another daughter, Jane Frank Kresch, was sentenced to one year and a day in prison. For years, the Frank family ran a maritime business in New York, and Evelyn Frank was known as the Tugboat Empress and the Dragon Lady.[73]

Environmental crimes are also a problem in other countries, as Global Focus 9.1 indicates.

Products Liability and Crime

Consumers who are injured by defectively designed, manufactured, or constructed products may sue for civil damages, but the issue for this discussion is whether products liability cases should also be prosecuted in criminal courts.

On 13 September 1978, Ford Motor Company was indicted by a grand jury in Elkhart, Indiana, for three counts of reckless homicide stemming from the fiery crash of a Ford Pinto that left three teenagers dead. The victims died from burns suffered when the Pinto burst into flames after a low-speed rear-end collision. Although Ford was acquitted on 13 March 1980, this was a pivotal case concerning the criminal liability of corporations for the grossly negligent acts of their employees.

The Ford case and others illustrate the interrelationship, and often confusion, between civil and criminal law.

The families of victims in these cases sued and won large judgments for wrongful deaths, and surviving victims of other such crashes were compensated for their injuries. Some settled out of court; others took their cases to trial.

The Pinto represented Ford's attempt in the early 1970s to produce a compact car that would sell for $2,000. The design and production were on a rush schedule. The reasons for considering the design of this car defective are complicated, but at issue was the location of the fuel tank. For design reasons, it was placed behind rather than over the rear axle, as was the custom in other compacts at that time. Because this made the car less crush-resistant, death by fire was more probable in a Pinto than in other compact cars. Evidence revealed that the design defects were known to Ford's corporate executives, who were warned of the dangers. The cost of adding additional crush space was $15.30 per car, but high-level officials decided to go ahead with the project for cost-saving and time reasons. The appellate court in one case concluded as follows:[74]

Grimshaw v. Ford Motor Company

Through the results of the crash tests Ford knew that the Pinto's fuel tank and rear structure would expose consumers to serious injury or death in a 20 to 30 mile-per-hour collision. There was evidence that Ford could have corrected the hazardous design defects at minimal cost but decided to defer correction of the shortcomings by engaging in a cost–benefit analysis balancing human lives and limbs against corporate profits. Ford's institutional mentality was shown to be one of callous indifference to public safety. There was substantial evidence that Ford's conduct constituted "conscious disregard" of the probability of injury to members of the consuming public.

The Grimshaw case illustrates how gross negligence can be used in a civil suit to award punitive damages to a plaintiff. The fact that Ford was acquitted in the criminal trial does not mean that another corporation will not be convicted in a similar case. Corporations engaging in conduct that is grossly negligent or reckless may find themselves convicted of crimes.

In fact, in December 1999, SabreTech, a corporation involved with aircraft maintenance, was convicted of charges stemming from the 11 May 1996 fatal crash of a ValuJet Airlines plane. All 110 persons on board the flight from Miami to Atlanta were killed when the plane went down in fire in the Florida Everglades. Initially, SabreTech, which shipped oxygen generators on the fatal ValuJet flight, was charged with 110 counts of murder and 110 counts of manslaughter, but those were dropped. Other state charges were dropped in exchange for a no contest plea to one count of unlawful transporting of hazardous waste. The company was convicted of multiple federal charges of recklessly causing hazardous materials

9.1 Environmental Crimes in Other Countries

GLOBAL FOCUS

China has now surpassed the United States as the largest emitter of the life-threatening polluter carbon dioxide. The country with 1.3 billion people goes through 1.9 billion tons of coal yearly. Sixteen of the twenty most polluted cities in the world were in China in 2002, a year when more than one-half of all Chinese cities were polluted. The Chinese insisted that the pollution comes from American, Japanese, and European companies operating within the country to benefit from cheap labor and resources.

In 2007, the Chinese government stated that companies that pollute would be closed down and that the future of China depends on "environmentally friendly industries." The country was under pressure to eradicate or at least reduce pollution before the Olympics were held in Beijing.[1]

A June 2007 report by the international Environmental Investigation Agency (EIA) emphasized that organized crime and corrupt governments were converting environmental exploitation and crime into a big business that rivaled the drug trade. Gangs were involved in poaching elephants, resulting in a profit of hundreds of millions of dollars to the offenders. Customs officials were bribed by officials of fake companies, who shipped illegal ivory from Zambia to Malawi for packing and then shipment to other countries. The killing of elephants, along with other wildlife crimes, was threatening the highly lucrative tourist industry.[2]

From 2008 through 2009, an investigation was ongoing into allegations that Canadian firm Goldcorp, the largest gold mining corporation in the world, had polluted land and rivers in Honduras, killing livestock and causing illnesses to humans. Goldcorp was closing down its mine, but villagers argued that the damage had been done and the company should pay. At a time when gold prices were soaring throughout the world, it was feared that more corporations would violate the environmental protection laws and open new mines.[3]

In early 2009, authorities in Britain announced the arrest of 12 suspects for allegedly shipping electronics (e.g., televisions) to developing countries in violation of environmental laws. Under European and British law, functioning electronics may be shipped out of the country to underdeveloped countries, where there is a big market for the resale of these still usable products. However, if the electronics are not functioning, they are considered hazardous waste and cannot be legally exported. It was reported that gangs were involved in this illegal exporting, with so-called waste tourists going to England to secure the products and then exporting them to developing countries for profit. The result:

Tonnes [*sic*] of defunct electronic equipment sent from Britain to countries including Ghana and Nigeria ends up each year on waste dumps where "scavenger children" pick through the detritus looking for bits of wire, circuit board and cathode-ray tube. The precious or heavy metals in the components can be extracted by setting light to their plastic and glass coatings but that produces a dense cloud of potentially toxic chemicals.[4]

The process is thus dangerous to children and to the environment.

1. "Pollution: Foreign Firms Get the Blame—CHINA," *The Australian* (28 June 2007), p. 33.
2. "Governments 'Ignoring Environmental Crime,'" *Global News Wire—Europe Intelligence Wire* (8 June 2007), n.p.
3. "Honduras Begins Inquiry After Villagers Claim Gold Mining Company Polluted Fields and Rivers," *The Guardian* (London) (1 January 2010), p. 20.
4. "Man Held After Tonnes [*sic*] of Illegal E-waste Are Exported to Africa; 'Scavenger Children' at Risk from Toxic Fumes Produced by Broken Equipment," *The Independent* (London) (7 November 2009), p. 22.

to be transported and one count of improperly training employees in the handling of such materials. On appeal, only the latter charge was upheld. ValuJet was not charged criminally.[75]

As of this writing, no criminal charges had been filed in the Toyota recalls in 2009 and 2010, which resulted from sudden acceleration due to sticking gas pedals. In April 2010, the company agreed to pay a record $23 million fine for its slow response in reporting to the government possible rollover dangers in nearly 10,000 Lexus SUVs. Federal law requires that disclosures of possible safety defects be made within five business days. According to government officials, Toyota knew of the defect in late September 2009 but did not issue its recall of the vehicles until late January 2010. Regarding the recall of

cars with sticking accelerators, investigations and hearings were continuing in a case of Koua Fong Lee, who was convicted of criminal vehicular homicide when his 1996 Toyota Camry rear ended an Olds Ciera, which was stopped at a red light in 2006, killing two and wounding another, who died subsequently. Lee was in prison for these crimes despite his claims that he applied his brakes. Based on new evidence about the car's defects and other issues, Lee was subsequently freed from prison and is suing Toyota in a civil case.[76]

Products liability issues also extend to other areas, such as food and drugs. In a decision involving a company charged with violations of the Federal Food, Drug and Cosmetic Act, the U.S. Supreme Court emphasized the importance of protecting the consumer from adulterated food.

In a case before the Supreme Court, rats in the company's warehouse contaminated the food. According to the Court, the only defense permitted in these cases is the defendant's evidence that he or she was powerless to correct or prevent the violation.[77]

Workplace Violations

Employers must provide their employees with a safe working environment. At the federal level, the Occupational Safety and Health Act (OSHA) was enacted in 1970, but the government was not as active in enforcing that statute as has been the case with other federal statutes. In fact, only 68 cases were prosecuted during the first 36 years after OSHA was enacted, and of those that were successful, defendants spent a total of 42 months in jail. During that same time period, approximately 341,000 employees died at work.[78]

Consequently, state-level prosecutions are important and are illustrated by California. After a discussion of prosecutions under that state's statute, two scholars concluded that although the "number of prosecutions may be small, . . . like a barking dog, their very presence may deter thousands of violations." In distinguishing the criminal from the civil nature of workplace violations, the authors stated as follows:

> None of these cases . . . involved intentional deaths. They were all the result of either a reckless or negligent act, or a failure to act. Nonetheless, in each case the defendant violated his duty of care to another human being. Under California law, the acts or omissions were criminal. The deaths or injuries were not accidents.[79]

Like many other illegal acts, workplace violations are often treated under administrative law rather than criminal law, and the debate will continue over which is the best approach. In some cases, both administrative or civil law and criminal law will be employed, as illustrated in the following case.

When a fire spread quickly through the chicken-processing plant of Imperial Food Products, Inc., in Hamlet, North Carolina, in 1991, 25 persons died and 56 were injured. Numerous violations of federal and state requirements were cited, including blocked exits. The owner, Emmett Roe, who was concerned about theft of chicken parts, reportedly ordered the blockage. There were not enough exits for emergencies, and the facility did not have a sprinkler system. Because of these and other violations, Roe was charged with both civil and criminal liability. The insurance company paid $16.1 million in settlements. Roe was charged with numerous counts of manslaughter, along with his son, Brad, and another plant supervisor. The elder Roe agreed to plead guilty if charges against the other two defendants were dropped. Prosecutors accepted the deal, and Roe was sentenced to 19 years in prison, far

fewer than the maximum of 250 years for 25 counts of manslaughter. He served a little more than four years in prison. Upon his release, he moved to Georgia and obscurity. Roe's company was fined $808,150 for the violations, which were viewed as willful. Civil lawsuits were filed by survivors against 41 companies whose products within the plant were alleged to have aided the spread of the fire or added toxic products to the smoke.[80]

A scholarly analysis of media reactions to the Imperial Food case is featured in Media Focus 9.1.

A more recent example of criminal charges demonstrates how serious those charges can be when, within a workplace environment (and in this case, a business to which the public was invited), gross negligence leads to multiple injuries and deaths. The case involved a deadly fire in a Rhode Island nightclub in 2003. Jeffrey A. Derderian and his brother Michael A. Derderian, owners of the nightclub, were indicted for involuntary manslaughter, along with Daniel M. Biechele, who was the tour manager for the band Great White.

The fire started when Biechele set off three pyrotechnical devices, creating sparks, which ignited the polyurethane that had been installed to reduce sound. Approximately 400 people were inside the building, which quickly burst into flames, killing 100 people and injuring 200. According to the state's attorney general, the brothers were charged with criminal negligence based on the way they operated the club and misdemeanor manslaughter because they allegedly did not maintain the soundproofing in a fireproof manner. The criminal negligence charges against Biechele stemmed from allegations that he discharged the devices negligently. The manslaughter charges were based on the failure of the band to get a permit to use fireworks inside the building.[81]

Biechele, who agreed to testify against the Derderian brothers, pleaded guilty to 100 counts of involuntary manslaughter, after which the criminal negligence charges were dropped. Biechele was sentenced to four years in prison. He was released on parole in March 2008 after serving 22 months. His request for parole was supported by numerous relatives of the fire's victims. The Derderian brothers entered no contest pleas to involuntary manslaughter charges. Jeffrey Derderian was sentenced to 500 hours of community service and three years on probation. Michael Derderian was sentenced to four years in prison. He was scheduled for release in October 2009 but was released early because of earned time due to good behavior. He vowed to work, along with his brother and partner in the business, toward establishing a fund for the education of children whose parents died in the fire. He also stated that he would be willing to speak about his prison experiences if that might deter others from violating the law. Some victims' families, however, fought his early release, stating that he had not shown proper remorse for his acts.[82]

Holding employers and owners criminally liable for the injuries and deaths of their employees (and customers)

9.1

The Media and Corporate Crime

MEDIA FOCUS

This chapter discussed Edwin H. Sutherland's contributions to the study of white-collar crime. Sutherland emphasized that most of these crimes are handled by administrative agencies and are not processed through the criminal courts.

More recently, scholars have researched the issue of how the media react to certain crimes of the business world. For example, a scholarly analysis of newspaper coverage of the Imperial Food case discussed in this text illustrated that corporate crime is not always considered *real* crime. Although

the papers did not attempt to blame the workers or avoid the issue of negligence or the horrors of the injuries and deaths, the articles did not show any perspective of viewing corporate violence as criminal. No reports of criminal acts were mentioned in the papers until the government took legal action by returning indictments for manslaughter.[1]

1. John P. Wright et al., "The Social Construction of Corporate Violence: Media Coverage of the Imperial Food Products Fire," *Crime and Delinquency* 42 (January 1995): 37–53.

raises many issues with regard to the lack of security, especially with the increase in violent crimes in the workplace. Workplace violations may also be prosecuted under environmental crime statutes, as illustrated by Exhibit 9.5.

One of the lead prosecutors in the DOJ's investigation of the case discussed in Exhibit 9.5 wrote an article about the case. He pointed out the limitations of prosecuting workplace violations under OSHA, mentioned earlier, which is the main federal statute for such prosecutions. Under OSHA, an employer may be charged with a crime only if the employee dies as a result of the workplace

violations. However, the DOJ successfully prosecuted the employer noted in Exhibit 9.5 for violating environmental crime statutes and secured what was thought to be the longest sentence ever imposed on a defendant for knowingly exposing someone to hazardous waste.[83]

One additional area of concern in the workplace that should be mentioned is criminal responsibility for negligent hiring—failure to do a thorough background check before hiring an employee who subsequently commits criminal acts on the job. This issue may be raised in the hiring of Amy Bishop, University of Alabama biology professor who

9.5

Workplace Violations and Criminal Law

EXHIBIT

Employers are required by law to provide a safe working environment for their employees, but until recently, no criminal action was taken in most cases if they did not do so. In 2000, however, Allan Elias was sentenced to 17 years in prison, the longest term ever assessed to a defendant charged with an environmental crime. Elias was the owner of a chemical-reprocessing facility, Evergreen Resources, in a small Idaho town. On 26 August 1996, he ordered 20-year-old Scott Dominguez and other employees, without the benefit of any safety equipment despite their pleas for such, to clean sludge from the bottom of a 25,000-gallon tank that contained sodium cyanide. Dominguez suffered permanent brain damage as a result of the exposure. In addition to his prison sentence, Elias was ordered to pay Dominguez $5 million in restitution.[1]

The U.S. Court of Appeals for the Ninth Circuit held that the criminal prosecution of Elias was appropriate under the federal Resource Conservation and Recovery Act. In 2002, the U.S. Supreme Court refused to review the case, thus leaving the conviction and sentence standing.[2]

A special agent with the Environmental Protection Agency (EPA) in Seattle, who worked on this case, was one of the authors of *The Cyanide Canary*. A review of that book stated as follows:

The Cyanide Canary is a marvelously suspenseful tale full of male camaraderie, long drives to small towns in the middle of nowhere, suspicious laborers terrified of losing their jobs, the saintly family of Scott Dominguez and, on the other side, that leering scummy, remorselessly lying Elias, who in trying to avoid justice makes as many moves as an octopus in a handbag.

Of course, Elias was a stooge of a larger corporation; even after his Evergreen Resources closed, he remained on the payroll of Kerr-McGee, to the tune of more than $41,000 a month. . . . [The book] is a bona fide thriller pitting joyous, decent good guys against a villain without a scintilla of redeeming social value.[3]

1. "Adding Up Pollution Prosecutions," *National Journal* (21 October 2000), p. 330.
2. *Elias v. United States*, 2001 U.S. App. LEXIS 27064 (9th Cir. 2001), *cert. denied*, 537 U.S. 812 (2002). The statute is codified at USCS, Title 42, Section 6928(3) (2010).
3. Carolyn See, "Slime and Punishment," *Washington Post* (24 September 2004), p. 3C.

allegedly shot and killed three colleagues at a faculty meeting on 12 February 2010 in Huntsville, Alabama, possibly as a result of being denied tenure. At issue regarding her hiring is whether her employers should have discovered that she shot and killed her brother in 1986. She was not charged in that shooting at the time; it was ruled an accident. Bishop also threatened police with a shotgun at an automobile dealership, where she attempted to get a car for her escape. The case was reopened with an inquest into that shooting in April 2010; in June, a judge refused to release those results to the public. Bishop was indicted on first-degree murder charges in her brother's death.[84]

Mail and Wire Fraud

Although most fraud charges are brought in state courts, we have seen examples of securities and other types of fraud that are prosecuted in federal courts. In particular, the use of mail and wire services has led to the commission of crimes across state lines, which gives the federal government jurisdiction. Congress enacted the federal fraud statutes to criminalize the use of the postal services or wires to carry out an interstate scheme to defraud people of money or other property rights. The mail fraud statute was originally passed in 1872 and is the oldest of the federal statutes covering crimes traditionally prosecuted in state courts.[85] The wire fraud statute, which was enacted in 1952, provides the same penalties as the mail fraud statute for defendants convicted of using "wire, radio, or television communications in interstate or foreign commerce" for the purpose of fraud.[86]

Mail and wire fraud statutes constitute an important tool in the government's efforts to combat white-collar crime because the statutes are broad and flexible. In 1984, Congress added a section on *bank fraud* to the federal statute. It provides for sanctions against writing checks with insufficient funds as well as crimes associated with the failure of banks and other financial institutions.[87]

A successful mail or wire fraud case requires the government to prove three elements:

1. A scheme or artifice formed with the intent to defraud
2. Using or causing the mails or wire to be used
3. In furtherance of the scheme

The government is not required to show that the scheme was successful or even that victims suffered losses; it has to show only that the defendant had the specific intent to defraud.[88]

To satisfy the *use* requirement, the defendant is not required to be directly involved in using the mail or wire, and the victim does not have to receive the information through either means. But there must be evidence that either the mail or the wire actually was used and that its use was a reasonably foreseeable result of the defendant's actions.

The final element does not require that the mail or wire be essential to the scheme but only that either or both are useful to the defendant or closely related to the scheme. This requirement is illustrated by the case of *Schmuck v. United States*, in which the U.S. Supreme Court held that, for a conviction under this statute, the mails do not have to be an essential element of the crime as long as they are incident to an essential part of the scheme. In *Schmuck*, the defendant, a Wisconsin used-car distributor, "purchased used cars, rolled back their odometers, and then sold the automobiles to Wisconsin retail dealers for prices artificially inflated because of the low-mileage readings." The dealers then sold the cars at higher prices to their customers. The resale of each used automobile was completed when the retail dealer submitted a title application form to the Wisconsin Department of Transportation on behalf of the buyer of the car. The title to the car could not be transferred without submission of a Wisconsin title, which was secured through the mails.

Schmuck argued that the mail fraud statute does not apply unless the mail "affirmatively assists the perpetrator in carrying out his fraudulent scheme." The U.S. Supreme Court did not agree and held that a rational jury could find that under the facts of this case, the "title-registration mailings were part of the execution of the fraudulent scheme, a scheme which did not reach fruition until the retail dealers resold the cars and effected transfers of title."[89]

Because the mail and wire fraud statutes are broad, they are useful for prosecution in numerous situations, such as the use of the mail or wire to commit bribery, extortion, political corruption, or fraud within business and government settings. Defendants may also be charged with conspiracy to commit mail or wire fraud or many other charges.

An example of multiple charges involved a California man who was charged with defrauding a Baptist minister of his almost $1 million retirement fund. Nicholas Roblee, also known as Nicholas Richmond, pleaded guilty to four counts of wire fraud and money laundering. Roblee, 35, who was the president and chief executive of Premier Marketing and Investments, Inc., told the Reverend Calvin A. Harper in Cincinnati that he would receive at least a 70 percent return per month if he liquidated his retirement fund of $925,000 and reinvested the money in gold, gold concentrate, and other precious metals. In his plea agreement, Roblee admitted that he and others received more than $4.8 million from 40 investors. According to prosecutors, only $2 million was returned to investors, while $1 million was used to pay for Premier's overhead. In addition, Roblee spent $800,000 on himself (for such items as a down payment on a $1.5 million home, limousines, guards, and an attempt to buy a male strip club) and $200,000 on an adult-content website. Roblee was sentenced to five years in prison.[90]

Although Roblee was successful in obtaining money from his victims, success is not required for a conviction on mail or wire fraud charges. In that sense, federal mail and wire fraud are distinguishable from **false pretense**, which requires a successful effort.

Wire fraud cases, combined with other crimes, may result in severe penalties. In September 2009, Richard Monroe Harkless, 65, of Riverside, California, was sentenced to 100 years in prison for his role in a fraudulent scheme that collected more than $60 million from approximately 600 investors. Harkless was convicted of three counts each of mail and wire fraud and one count of money laundering. Once Harkless realized the federal prosecutors were investigating him, he diverted millions of dollars into accounts in Belize and Mexico.[91]

Financial Institution Fraud

A federal bank fraud statute was enacted in 1984. It was patterned after the mail fraud statute and provides as follows:

> Whoever knowingly executes, or attempts to execute, a scheme or artifice—
> (1) to defraud a financial institution; or
> (2) to obtain any of the moneys, funds, credits, assets, securities, or other property owned by, or under the custody or control of, a financial institution, by means of false or fraudulent pretenses, representations, or promises; shall be fined not more than $1,000,000 or imprisoned not more than thirty years, or both.[92]

This statute includes *check kiting* (writing checks without sufficient funds), one of the most common forms of bank fraud, as well as crimes associated with the failure of banks and other financial institutions. Federal prosecutors place a high priority on prosecuting persons responsible for the failure of savings and loans and other financial institutions. The backlog of cases was so extensive by 1989 that Congress extended the *statute of limitations* (the time period during which a lawsuit may be filed) for bank fraud and other financial institution offenses from 5 to 10 years.[93]

The Savings and Loan (S&L) crisis of the 1980s and early 1990s that resulted in the collapse of financial loan institutions was, in the words of the deputy director of the FBI, dwarfed by the failure of banks and other financial institutions in 2008 and 2009. The difference was $160 million in the earlier period compared to $1.2 trillion in the latter years. The financial crisis involved numerous problems and institutions, but as the FBI emphasized, mortgage fraud (discussed below) was one of the most significant.[94]

Early in the administration of Barack Obama as president the DOJ began preparing to increase prosecutions for financial fraud. A spokesperson for the U.S. Department of Justice stated, "It will be a top priority of the Justice Department to hold accountable executives who have engaged in fraudulent activities." Mortgage fraud was one of the targets.[95]

Mortgage Fraud

With the downturn in the U.S. economy beginning in 2008, unemployment climbed to more than 10 percent, and the housing market and other areas suffered severe setbacks; this made selling houses difficult and, in many cases, impossible. Homes and businesses were foreclosed, and predators engaged in fraudulent practices. Mortgage fraud became a reality for many people.

In December 2009, the FBI announced that federal prosecutors had secured indictments against five persons alleged to have engaged in at least 35 fraudulent mortgage schemes totaling $14.6 million. The FBI alleged that the defendants targeted desperate homeowners who were close to losing their homes through foreclosure, made false promises to help them avoid these drastic measures, "engaged in real estate transactions with straw purchasers,

Sholom Rubashkin, 50, was convicted of 86 counts of financial fraud charges in the Agriprocessors slaughterhouse case in Postville, Iowa. Although a first-time offender, Rubashkin was sentenced to 27 years in prison, two years longer than prosecutors recommended. This was an unusually long sentence for financial fraud crimes. Rubashkin is appealing. The kosher meat-packing plant gained national and international attention when a May 2008 raid resulted in the detention of several hundred illegal immigrants, including children, and the subsequent deportation of many of them.

and obtained dozens of fraudulent mortgages." In addition, the indictment alleged the following:

> The defendants took whatever equity the homeowner had left, funneled it through various shell corporations they controlled, used some of it to pay the new mortgages, and put the rest of the equity into their own bank accounts. . . .
>
> This sort of fraudulent activity not only preys on desperate homeowners, it weakens our financial institutions, destroys neighborhoods by leaving properties abandoned, and devalues the homes of innocent neighbors.[96]

In June 2010, the FBI announced that it had made 485 arrests in Operation Stolen Dreams, an effort that targeted mortgage fraudsters and constituted the largest effort ever made to apprehend offenders committing mortgage fraud. The effort had resulted in the recovery of over $147 million; 191 civil enforcement actions had been completed. Homeowners lost an estimated $2.3 billion in the mortgages involved in this fraud. U.S. Attorney General Eric Holder said, "Mortgage fraud ruins lives, destroys families and devastates whole communities. . . . We will use every tool available to investigate, prosecute and prevent mortgage fraud, and we will not rest until anyone preying on vulnerable American homeowners is brought to justice."[97]

Health Care Fraud

Health care fraud, a growing problem in the United States, is a relatively new area of focus for the FBI. According to the FBI, within the agency's White-Collar Crime Program, health care fraud investigations are among the highest priority, with higher priority given only to public corruption and corporate fraud investigations. It was estimated that the total health care expenditures in the United States would be approximately $2.26 trillion in 2010, and by 2016, that cost would exceed $4.14 trillion, about 19.6 percent of the gross national product.[98]

There are numerous ways to commit health care fraud, but the FBI listed these as the most common:

- "Hospitals, doctors, pharmacists, and other care providers submitting fake bills for services never rendered—or overcharged;
- Service providers charging insurance for unnecessary and costly procedures;
- Doctors selling prescriptions to patients for cash;
- Companies billing insurance for expensive equipment but providing poor substitutes;
- Crooked docs enticing patients to visit their offices for 'free services' or gifts, then stealing their personal information and using it to file fake claims."[99]

Most of health care fraud occurs in Medicare (federal government-provided comprehensive medical health care for persons 65 and older and for the disabled at any age) and Medicaid (federal government health care provisions for low-income persons). In November 2009, a government financial report indicated that in the previous fiscal year (including the first three months of 2009) the $440 billion Medicare program paid out $47 billion in fraud claims, approximately three times that of the previous year. That increase may have been caused by the change in the methodology the Department of Health and Human Services requires for documentation rather than actual increases in fraud, but the figures are still significant. Claims have included those from dead doctors and for shoes for amputees, along with claims that have little or nothing to do with an individual patient's particular medical problem. "Patients, many of them new citizens who barely speak English, are sometimes recruited by brokers who go door to door offering hundreds of dollars for use of their Medicare numbers."[100]

Health care fraud is easier to commit in federal programs because of the size of the programs and the inability of management to respond quickly. It can take months of paperwork to make price adjustments in government programs, leading to overpayment. Claims processed in government programs can fail to catch these overpayments.

According to the FBI, one of the most alarming trends in health care fraud is the willingness of medical persons and others to perform unnecessary surgeries or prescribe unneeded treatments and medications to secure fraudulent money. Developing technology has resulted in the evolution of health care fraud schemes facilitated by computers and other technological equipment. One FBI initiative to combat such developments is the Internet Pharmacy Fraud Initiative, which focuses on Internet sources through which fraudulent prescriptions are sold. It also targets physicians who write fraudulent prescriptions as well as pharmacies and other sources of counterfeit and diverted pharmaceuticals.

Other agencies and programs have also evolved to combat medical fraud. For example, the Auto Accident Insurance Fraud Initiative, started in 2005, focuses on fraudulent claims arising out of staged accidents. Existing agencies are also utilized in the fight against medical fraud. The FBI works with the U.S. Postal Services, Drug Enforcement Administration, Federal Trade Commission, and other federal agencies to secure information on fraud within the Medicare Prescription Drug Program (Part D). FBI agents investigate fraud in such areas as public health care programs, the prescription and sale of medical equipment, actions of hospitals, physicians, home health care agencies, drug diversion programs, physical therapy, and pain management. They also look into chiropractic care, prescription drugs, and identity theft of physician identifiers for the purpose of fraudulently billing the government or private health insurance programs.

Prosecutions of health care fraud have been aided by several congressional statutes. The Health Insurance Portability and Accountability Act of 1996 (HIPAA) and the Balanced Budget Act of 1997 (BBA) increased the penalties and provide financial incentives for fighting health care and other kinds of fraud.[101] Federal (and some state) statutes also provide incentives for whistle-blowers: Part of the recovered money goes to the person who reports the alleged medical care fraud offenses. For example, a whistle-blower who was the vice president for sales of a pharmaceutical company in Illinois was awarded $77 million for reporting a fraud issue in his company. The company, TAP Pharmaceutical Products, Inc., was assessed a $875 million fine after a six-year investigation.[102]

An important prosecutorial tool is the False Claims Act (FCA), which prohibits a person from knowingly submitting false claims to secure money from the federal government.[103] The act permits individuals (often employees) to submit civil claims regarding health care fraud and receive payment for successful claims. In December 2009, the DOJ settled a case in which it had alleged that a Michigan health care provider (Genesys Health System) had submitted false claims to Medicare between 2001 and 2007. Genesys agreed to pay $669,413. The whistle-blower who reported the abuse to the government received $133,882 from the settlement.[104] Although this case involved a civil judgment, it could have had criminal implications and thus illustrates the power that federal prosecutors have in such cases.

In 2009, the Department of Justice and the Department of Health and Human Services joined forces to combat health care fraud by establishing the Healthcare Fraud Prevention and Enforcement Action Team (HEAT). Among other plans, HEAT increased the number of Medicare Fraud Strike Force operations from those in South Florida and Los Angeles to include ones in Detroit and Houston. These strike forces involve federal, state, and local agents in fighting health care fraud. They identify fraud hot spots and begin investigations with the goal of bringing civil and criminal charges and conducting successful prosecutions.[105]

The FBI emphasizes that to be successful in detecting and prosecuting health care fraud, the agency needs not only the support of other federal agencies, such as Health and Human Services, the Food and Drug Administration, and the Internal Revenue Service. It also needs the assistance of private organizations with which the agency works, such as the National Health Care Anti-Fraud Association and the National Insurance Crime Bureau to the Blue Cross Blue Shield Association.[106]

Government-Related Crimes

A variety of crimes may be committed *against* the government; this section focuses on one: **obstruction of justice**. Governments may also commit crimes against their citizens. In either case, these crimes may be the same as those discussed in the text thus far, but attention is given here to political crimes, official corruption, and civil rights violations.

Obstruction of Justice

Some of the crimes discussed previously, such as bribery, may take on additional criminal impact when they are engaged in for the purpose of obstructing justice. Tampering with a jury; intimidating witnesses; bribing or attempting to bribe witnesses, attorneys, judges, or other court personnel; refusing to produce evidence ordered by the court; and refusing to appear when ordered by the court are some of the acts that may constitute obstruction of justice. The phrase refers to acts that interfere with the orderly processes of civil and criminal courts. The crime may be committed by judicial and other officials, in which case it might constitute the crime of **official misconduct in office**. This refers to any willful, unlawful behavior by public officials in the course of their official duties. The misconduct may consist of an improperly performed official act or a failure to act by one who has a legal duty to act.

An example of obstruction of justice comes from a case involving two attorneys who tried to convince a convicted drug dealer that on payment of $50,000 they would have his four-year prison sentence reduced to 15 months. The attorneys were convicted and sentenced to five years for each charge; the sentences were to be served concurrently. The convictions were upheld on appeal.[107]

Obstruction of justice charges may be brought against individuals, businesses, or corporations. For example, Lewis "Scooter" Libby, top aide to Vice President Dick Cheney during the George W. Bush administration, was convicted of obstruction of justice and **perjury** (making false statements under oath in a judicial proceeding) in the investigation into the leak of the identity of Valerie Plame, a Central Intelligence Agency (CIA) operation officer. Libby was sentenced to 30 months in prison, which President Bush subsequently commuted, meaning that Libby did not serve prison time, although his probation (two years) and $250,000 fine remained.

A charge of obstruction of justice is often brought in cases in which prosecutors believe they cannot prove more serious crimes. To illustrate, the prosecution of Martha Stewart, who founded Martha Stewart Living Omnimedia, a billion-dollar business empire, was successful on the obstruction of justice charges. Charges of securities fraud were dropped, with the judge stating there was insufficient evidence for those charges. Stewart was accused of lying to federal authorities with regard to the arrangements she made with her stockbroker concerning selling her ImClone stock, a sale that saved her approximately $45,000. Her shares were sold the day before an announcement that the federal government had rejected the company's request for approval to market an experimental cancer drug. That announcement resulted in a significant decline in the value of ImClone stock, but Stewart's stock had already been sold, leading to the allegation that she had inside information about the situation. She was never charged with insider trading, but in the ensuing investigation, she was charged with tampering with evidence, engaging in conspiracy with her broker, and lying to the federal authorities who questioned her. Stewart served five months in a federal prison followed by probation and house arrest.[108]

Closely associated with obstruction of justice is the crime of **contempt**, which may be civil or criminal. In the federal system (also in state systems), Congress's contempt power is its power to respond to actions that obstruct the legislative process. Congress can punish a violator by issuing a *criminal contempt* citation, but Congress also has the power to use its *civil contempt* power to remove the obstruction. Congress may coerce compliance through its *inherent contempt* powers.[109] Courts may use their contempt powers in actions that are believed to disrupt the judicial process, and courts have both civil and criminal contempt powers.

Political Crimes and Official Misuse of Power

Until recently, little attention was paid to crimes committed by U.S. government officials against private citizens. This changed after the criminal violations during **Watergate** (the name of the building where the 1972 break-in at the offices of the Democratic headquarters occurred). The scandal erupted during the administration of President Richard M. Nixon and led to his resignation as the first U.S. president to resign in disgrace. Nixon was pardoned by his successor, President Gerald Ford, but some officials in the Nixon administration were indicted, tried, and convicted. Several served prison sentences.

The Watergate scandal became a symbol of the abuse of power by the government, with part of its name used in subsequent scandals. For example, the Iran-Contra scandal, which began to unfold in 1986, was referred to as **Irangate**. That affair involved numerous allegations concerning the illegal sale of arms to Iran in exchange for the release of U.S. hostages there and the use of some of the profits from those sales to buy arms for the anticommunist Contra rebels in Nicaragua.

Several government officials were convicted of various crimes related to the Iran-Contra scandal. The highest-ranking government official to be indicted in the Iran-Contra affair was Caspar W. Weinberger, defense secretary under President Ronald Reagan, who was indicted for lying to Congress. Although one charge against him was dropped, Weinberger was scheduled to go on trial in January 1993. On 24 December 1992, President George H. W. Bush issued pardons for Weinberger and other officials associated with Irangate.

Independent counsel Lawrence E. Walsh was furious with President Bush about the pardons. He suggested that the trial of Weinberger would have given prosecutors and the American people the last chance to explore the role that former President Ronald Reagan and then Vice President George Bush may have played in the Iran-Contra scandal. According to Walsh,

> President Bush's pardon of Caspar Weinberger and other Iran-Contra defendants undermines the principle that no man is above the law. It demonstrates that powerful people with powerful allies can commit serious crimes in high office—deliberately abusing the public trust without consequence.[110]

The Watergate investigations were possible under the Ethics in Government Act (or independent counsel act), enacted in 1978 and subsequently amended, to ensure accountability in government. The act provides for the appointment of independent counsel to investigate alleged abuses of power within the executive department of the government. In 1988, the U.S. Supreme Court upheld the constitutionality of the act.[111]

In the intervening years, other incidents of government misconduct have occurred, including allegations against the FBI. In 2001, FBI officials admitted that the agency had failed to disclose over 4,000 documents to defense attorneys in the Oklahoma City bombing case. The execution of Timothy McVeigh, scheduled for 11 May 2001, was postponed until 11 June 2001 to give his attorneys time to consider the documents. McVeigh's attorneys argued that the federal government had perpetrated a fraud on the court by not disclosing the documents. Although the matter was being investigated, and the trial judge was critical of the FBI's withholding of evidence, neither that judge nor the appellate court was willing to postpone the execution again. McVeigh decided not to appeal this decision to the U.S. Supreme Court, and he was executed on 11 June. Chapter 12 contains additional discussions of the FBI.

Civil Rights Violations

In recent years, attention has focused on one of the most offensive types of abuse of power by government, the violation of civil rights.

Domestic Civil Rights Historically

On 2 July 1964, President Lyndon B. Johnson signed into law the Civil Rights Act of 1964. In observing the fortieth anniversary of this historic legislation, on 2 July 2004, President George W. Bush proclaimed that the United States is a better place because of the legislation but that much needs to be done to remedy bigotry and ensure equality for all people. President Bush quoted the words of slain civil rights leader Martin Luther King Jr., who told us that we should not rest until "justice rolls down like waters and righteousness like a mighty stream."[112]

The applicable civil rights statute is as follows:

Whoever, under color of any law, statute, ordinance, regulation, or custom, willfully subjects any inhabitant of any State, Territory, or District to the deprivation of any rights, privileges, or immunities secured or protected by the constitution or laws of the United States, or to different punishments, pains, or penalties, on account of such inhabitant being an alien, or by reason of his color, or race, that are prescribed for the punishment of citizens, shall be fined not more than $1,000 or imprisoned not more than one year, or both; and if death results shall be subject to imprisonment for any term of years or for life.[113]

After a two-year battle between President George H. W. Bush and Congress, a new civil rights act was enacted in November 1991. Among other provisions of relevance here are the violations of civil rights that carry criminal as well as civil penalties.[114]

In a case involving police brutality, a federal appellate court held that the civil rights statutes were not limited to cases involving "race, color or alienage." According to the court in *Miller v. United States*, "all people regardless of taint or degradation so long as they are inhabitants of a state, territory or district are within the statute's protective embrace. Even suspected criminality or accomplished incarceration furnish[es] no license for the destruction of guaranteed constitutional rights."

In *Miller*, the defendant police officer had activated his K-9 police dog to attack the suspect for seven or eight minutes.[115]

The highly publicized Rodney King case illustrated the importance of federal civil rights legislation. The four white Los Angeles police officers accused of beating King during his 1991 arrest were tried for the violation of King's federal civil rights (they had previously been acquitted of charges in a state trial). Three of the officers were charged with beating King for 81 seconds, and the fourth, Sergeant Stacey Koon, with failure to restrain the three officers. Two of the officers (Timothy Wind and Ted Briseno) were acquitted of civil rights charges. Laurence Powell and Stacey Koon were found guilty and each sentenced to 30 months in prison. A federal appeals court upheld the convictions but ordered the trial court to reconsider the sentences, which were shorter than the federal sentencing guidelines for their offenses. Koon and Powell appealed to the U.S. Supreme Court, which upheld the principle of judicial discretion under the federal guidelines. The U.S. Supreme Court agreed with the lower court's decision to reduce the sentence because of the victim's misconduct in the incident, the susceptibility of the defendants to abuse by other inmates, and the burdens they had sustained with successive prosecutions (state and federal). The Supreme Court reversed and remanded the case for reconsideration because it abused its discretion "in relying on the other two factors . . . career loss and low recidivism risk."

Justin A. Volpe (left), former New York City police officer, with his attorney before entering a guilty plea for the charge of beating and sodomizing Haitian immigrant Abner Louima. Volpe entered the plea after the trial began and damaging testimony was introduced. Volpe was sentenced to 30 years in prison without parole.

The lower court did not impose longer sentences when it reconsidered the case.[116]

Numerous other examples of police mistreatment of citizens have come to light in recent years. Of particular note are three in New York City. In 1999, Justin A. Volpe pleaded guilty to sodomizing Abner Louima, a Haitian immigrant, and threatening to kill Louima if he reported the incident. Volpe was sentenced to 30 years in prison. In 2001, Louima accepted an $8.7 million civil settlement of his claims against the city for this brutality.[117]

In 2000, a jury acquitted four white New York City police officers who fired 41 times, killing an unarmed West African immigrant, Amadou Diallo. An anonymous juror reported that the prosecution did not prove its case beyond a reasonable doubt.[118] In 2008, three New York City police officers were acquitted in the death of Sean Bell on his wedding day after 50 bullets were fired into the unarmed black man as he reached for his cell phone. In February 2010, U.S. attorneys announced that they did not have sufficient evidence to prosecute the officers for violation of Bell's federal civil rights and were closing the case.

Other civil rights violations that have gained significant attention since 2001 are those associated with terrorist acts.

Terrorism and Civil Rights

Since the 9/11 terrorist attacks on the United States, numerous challenges have been made to government actions taken because of alleged terrorist threats. Some of these challenges deal with criminal procedure, but some involve civil rights. The focus of most challenges is the USA Patriot Act, a major piece of legislation that was enacted shortly after the 9/11 terrorist attacks and amended subsequently. The statute was designed to provide law enforcement officers and prosecutors with additional tools for combating terrorism. One of the controversial provisions involves delaying informing suspects that their property has been searched and items seized pursuant to a warrant. Another is permitting the government to obtain certain records and other items to protect against international terrorism or espionage (which has been interpreted by some to permit the government to monitor the reading

A mourner wears a T-shirt with the picture of Sean Bell, 23, while waiting in line to pay his last respects to Bell, who was killed just hours before he was scheduled to marry Nicole Paultre, the mother of his two children. Bell and two other unarmed men were attending Bell's bachelor party at a strip club and were shot outside the club when Bell reached for his cell phone. The New York City police officers fired 50 bullets. They were all acquitted of state charges, and in February 2010, U.S. attorneys announced that they did not have sufficient evidence to prosecute the officers for violation of Bell's federal civil rights and were closing the case. In May 2010, a judge ruled that the civil suit filed by Bell's estate against the police involved in the shooting and the city of New York could go forward. In June 2010, one of the officers, Michael Carey, asked the court to release him from the civil suit and then sued Bell's estate, alleging that Bell injured him prior to the shooting and that he was acting in self-defense.

habits of everyone by obtaining copies of library records, bookstore purchases, and the like). And another is detaining aliens indefinitely and without judicial authorization for minor visa violations. This section discusses some of the lawsuits that involve allegations of civil rights violations by the government.[119]

Some of the cases tested the tension between national security and civil rights and between the executive and the judicial branches of government.[120] The U.S. Supreme Court ruled that all persons in U.S. custody, even foreign nationals, have a right to know why they are being detained, the right to consult with an attorney, and the right to have a hearing before a neutral judge.[121]

In an effort to limit the impact of the Supreme Court's decision, the Republican-led Congress, during its final weeks of control, passed the Military Commissions Act of 2006, signed by President George Bush in October of that year. The act strips all U.S. courts of jurisdiction to hear the **habeas corpus** actions (literally, "you have the body"; it refers to actions filed by persons in custody questioning the right to be detained) filed by alien detainees if the president has determined that they are *enemy combatants* (persons suspected of terrorist acts against the United States). Until the U.S. Supreme Court ruled, these persons could be held indefinitely and without being charged with a crime. The act grants that power to special military tribunals. The bill alarmed many immigration attorneys because the broad definition of *enemy combatant* appears to include many aliens who, before their deportations, have been traditionally afforded an administrative law hearing and a series of appeals through the Board of Immigration Appeals and the federal courts. The law was viewed as continuing the trend of limiting or eliminating relief to all aliens accused of terrorism-related acts.[122]

In 2008, the U.S. Supreme Court considered the constitutionality of the Military Commissions Act in two cases involving 37 detainees and combined for hearing and decision. The Court held the act unconstitutional because it stripped U.S. courts of their jurisdiction in habeas corpus petitions filed by enemy combatants. As a result of *Boumediene v. Bush*, all persons held by U.S. officials once again have the right to challenge their detention before a neutral judge in U.S. courts. According to Justice Anthony Kennedy, who wrote the opinion for the Court's majority of five justices, the provision of military tribunals to hear habeas corpus petitions from those detained at the U.S. Naval Station at Guantánamo Bay is not an adequate substitute for the procedural protections provided by the U.S. Constitution.

> We hold that petitioners may invoke the fundamental procedural protections of habeas corpus. The laws and Constitution are designed to survive, and remain in force, in extraordinary times. Liberty and security can be reconciled; and in our system

they are reconciled within the framework of the law. The Framers decided that habeas corpus, a right of first importance, must be a part of that framework, a part of that law.[123]

Constitutional issues with regard to terrorism and the potential erosion of civil rights are also discussed in Chapter 11.

Controlling Business- and Government-Related Crimes

The sampling of business- and government-related crimes in this chapter pertains to those that may be committed by individuals in a business or government setting or by executives acting on behalf of a corporation. One issue in analyzing government- or business-related crimes is whether the civil or criminal law should be invoked. Another is whether corporate managers should be held criminally liable for the actions of their employees or whether the civil law is sufficient for these cases.

We have distinguished between criminal and civil law and noted that in some cases corporations (or noncorporate employers) may be held criminally liable for the acts of their employees. Earlier in this chapter, we discussed Sutherland's argument that social scientists who study crime should include violators of white-collar crimes in their research even if those violations are handled by administrative agencies or by civil rather than criminal courts.

It is important to keep in mind that the issue is not whether we should attempt to prevent or regulate business- and government-related crimes but which is the best control method. Deciding that the civil law is the best response does not mean that the misconduct is considered less serious; it simply means that the civil law is perceived as the best method of control. Criminal charges are hard to prove; negligence is easier. Civil and criminal law are not mutually exclusive, but we must consider the costs in time, attorney fees, and court personnel that are involved in an unsuccessful criminal prosecution. It is also important to understand that administrative regulation may be more effective than either the civil or the criminal law in controlling corporate conduct.

In the final analysis, business-related crimes are a lot like other crimes.

> Although they differ systematically from common-crime offenses, the white-collar crimes committed by those we studied have a mundane, common, every-day character. Their basic ingredients are lying, cheating and fraud, and for every truly complicated and rarefied offense there are many others that are simple and could be carried out by almost

anyone who can read, write, and give an outward appearance of stability.[124]

Regardless of what we think about sentencing those who break the statutes discussed in this chapter compared with those who commit traditional property and violent crimes, new sentencing provisions for white-collar criminals went into effect in November 1991 upon recommendation of the U.S. Sentencing Commission, an independent administrative agency within the federal judiciary. (The commission and its purpose are discussed in Chapter 13.) According to the commission, the purpose of the new guidelines was to provide just and adequate deterrence, the same purpose that is behind the sentencing guidelines for other crimes. The commission added one new purpose that is not part of its guidelines for other crimes. The new guidelines contain incentives for corporations and other organizations to develop internal mechanisms for "preventing and detecting criminal conduct." The sanctions are severe, but they may be mitigated by corporations that utilize effective compliance programs aimed at prevention and detection. The guidelines emphasize restitution to victims and sanctions that amount to death for corporations that are primarily criminal in nature (this is accomplished by divesting them of their assets). There are fines (the typical sanction for most offenses) that represent the seriousness of the offense and the ability of the corporation to pay. The supervision of the U.S. Probation Office assures compliance with imposed sanctions.[125]

Penalties for white-collar crimes were increased again in 2001, 2002, and 2003, although some of those sentences have been challenged (see Chapter 13). In another effort to curb financial and other business crimes, in July 2010, Congress passed and President Obama signed the Restoring American Financial Stability Act of 2010. The law's stated purpose is "to promote the financial stability of the United States by improving accountability and transparency in the financial system, to end 'too big to fail,' to protect the American taxpayer by ending bailouts, to protect consumers from abusive financial practices, and for other purposes." Among other provisions, the law established a panel charged with the responsibility of detecting risks to the U.S. financial systems.[126]

Summary

This chapter focused on crimes of the business world as well as those committed by and against the government. Although many of these crimes are economic, personal injury or death may result from crimes such as faulty design or construction of products or environmental pollution. The erosion of trust and the violations of civil rights that occur when government officials commit crimes destroy the confidence citizens have in the ability of the government to protect them and treat them fairly.

The discussion began with the problem of defining white-collar crime and looking at the contributions of Sutherland and subsequent sociologists who followed his development of the term. Particular attention was given to the term *corporate crime* and an explanation of how it differs from business-related or white-collar crimes. The various bases for legal liability were also discussed.

The main thrust of the chapter was an examination of numerous examples of business- and government-related crimes. Some, such as embezzlement, are committed primarily by individuals in secret; others, like conspiracy, by definition involve more than one person. Specific business-related crimes, ranging from income tax evasion to health care fraud, were discussed. All were updated with the latest information concerning statutes, data, and cases.

Federal and state government officials also commit crimes, and this chapter delved into some of those, such as political crimes and the official misuse of power. Attention was given to civil rights violations by government officials.

The control of business and government crimes is a problem faced directly by the U.S. Sentencing Commission, which has recommended increasing the penalties for many offenses discussed in this chapter. There are some differences, however, between the commission's approach to these crimes and their approach to common crime offenses, such as larceny-theft or burglary. Whether these differences are reasonable is a subject of debate. Whether criminal penalties are more effective than civil penalties is also a subject of debate.

The types of crimes and offenders discussed in this chapter cannot always be distinguished from those involved in organized crime. Chapter 10 completes the discussion of types of crime and criminals by looking at drug abuse, drug trafficking, and organized crime.

Study Questions

1. Distinguish between white-collar crime and corporate crime.

2. Comment on data regarding the extent of business-related or white-collar crimes in the United States.

3. Discuss the contributions of Edwin H. Sutherland to our understanding of white-collar crime.

4. Enumerate the social and political factors that might account for the current emphasis on corporate crime. Can these crimes be explained by any sociological theories discussed earlier in the text?

5. Distinguish strict liability, vicarious liability, and enterprise liability, and relate each to white-collar crime.

6. Why is tax evasion a serious offense?

7. Define *bribery*, *extortion*, *blackmail*, and *graft*.

8. Is conspiracy a civil or a criminal offense? Discuss.

9. Define *embezzlement* and *conversion*.

10. What is insider trading?

11. Explain the purpose and the provisions of the Sarbanes-Oxley Act (SOX) of 2002. What did the U.S. Supreme Court decide in 2010 regarding this statute?

12. What is the purpose of antitrust laws?

13. How effective have we been in prosecuting environmental crimes? Should BP be criminally prosecuted for the oil spill in the gulf?

14. What is the relationship between products liability and crime?

15. Should employers be held criminally liable for workplace violations that lead to injury or death? Explain your answer.

16. Define *fraud*. Discuss two types.

17. Distinguish between obstruction of justice and official misconduct in office.

18. Explain what is meant by Watergate and Irangate.

19. What is meant by *civil rights*?

20. Define *enemy combatant*.

Brief Essay Assignments

1. Explain and evaluate the use of administrative rather than criminal law to control business-related crimes. Use the Enron case to illustrate your discussion, paying attention to the recent U.S. Supreme Court decision in the case of *Skilling v. United States*.

2. Discuss the contributions of sociologists to our understanding of white-collar crime.

3. Analyze recent convictions for securities and related crimes, and discuss the impact these crimes have had on the economy and the morale of the U.S. people.

4. Explain what is meant by civil rights violations, and relate your answer to the concept of enemy combatants.

Internet Activities

1. Go to the Web and search for recent news and events concerning business- or government-related crimes. What was the offense? Who was involved? What are the short- and long-term impacts of the acts? Who are the victims? Which sociological theories might explain the behavior? If the offender has been convicted and sentenced, do you think the sentence is fair? Do you think the sentences imposed for business- or government-related crimes should be more or less severe than those imposed for other serious property crimes? Why?

2. Check out information about white-collar crime at Cornell's Legal Information Institute website at http://topics.law.cornell.edu/wex/white-collar-crime and the FBI's website at http://www.fbi.gov/about-us/investigate/white_collar/whitecollarcrime, accessed 18 December 2010, and answer the following questions.

a. Which document gives the federal government the power to regulate white-collar crimes?

b. Name and define four white-collar crimes that were not discussed in this chapter.

c. Approximately how much money does the Untied States lose yearly due to income tax fraud?

d. What is bankruptcy fraud?

Notes

1. Edwin H. Sutherland, *White Collar Crime* (New York: Holt, Rinehart & Winston, 1959, 1961, originally published in 1949 by Dryden Press). In 1983, an uncut version of Sutherland's work was published. This version restores the names and case histories and contains an introduction by Gilbert Geis and Colin Goff. It was published by Yale University Press, New Haven, Connecticut.
2. Sutherland, *White Collar Crime*, 1983 ed., p. 9.
3. August Bequai, *White-Collar Crime: A 20th-Century Crisis* (Lexington, MA: D. C. Heath, 1978), p. 2.
4. August Bequai, "Wanted: The White Collar Ring," *Student Lawyer* 5 (May 1977): 45.
5. Herbert Edelhertz, *The Nature, Impact and Prosecution of White-Collar Crime*, U.S. Department of Justice, Law Enforcement Assistance Administration (Washington, D.C.: U.S. Government Printing Office, 1970), pp. 19–20.
6. Cynthia Barnett, *The Measurement of White-Collar Crime Using the Uniform Crime Reporting (UCR) Data* (Washington, D.C.: U.S. Government Printing Office, 6 March 2002), p. 1.
7. U.S. Department of Justice, Federal Bureau of Investigation, *White Collar Crime: A Report to the Public* (Washington, D.C.: U.S. Government Printing Office, 1989), p. 3.
8. Barnett, *The Measurement of White-Collar Crime*, p. 7.
9. Marshall B. Clinard, *Illegal Corporate Behavior* (Washington, D.C.: U.S. Government Printing Office, October 1979), Abstract.
10. Ibid., p. 18. For a brief but excellent overview of corporate crime, see Nancy K. Frank and Michael J. Lynch, *Corporate Crime, Corporate Violence: A Primer* (New York: Harrow & Heston, 1992).
11. See James W. Messerschmidt, *Capitalism, Patriarchy, and Crime: Toward a Socialist Feminist Criminology* (Totowa, NJ: Rowman & Littlefield, 1986), pp. 99–129.

12. "White-Collar Crime," Cornell University's Legal Information Institute, http://topics.law.cornell.edu/wex/white-collar_crime, accessed 22 October 2010.

13. "Downturn and Shift in Population Feed Boom in White-Collar Crime," *New York Times* (2 June 2002), p. 1.

14. Ibid.

15. *Statistical Report: United States Attorney General's Office, Fiscal Year 1996* (Washington, D.C.: U.S. Department of Justice, 1997), pp. 1–4.

16. Department of Justice, "Matters of Justice: An Overview of Major Issues and Trends," *Fiscal Years 2007–2012 Strategic Plan*, p. 1, http://www.justice.gov/jmd/mps/strategic2007-2012/matters_of_justice.pdf, accessed 22 October 2010.

17. John S. R. Shad, quoted in *American Bar Association Journal* 73 (1 June 1987).

18. Donald R. Cressey, *Other People's Money: A Study in the Social Psychology of Embezzlement* (New York: Free Press, 1953), p. 30.

19. Sutherland, *White Collar Crime*, 1983 ed., p. 234. See also Edwin H. Sutherland, "Is 'White Collar Crime' Crime?" *American Sociological Review* 10 (April 1945): 132–139.

20. See Marshall B. Clinard and Richard Quinney, eds., *Criminal Behavior Systems: A Typology* (New York: Holt, Rinehart & Winston, 1967), p. 134.

21. Toni Makkai and John Braithwaite, "Criminological Theories and Regulatory Compliance," *Criminology* 29 (May 1991): 191–217.

22. Travis Hirschi and Michael R. Gottfredson, "Causes of White-Collar Crime," *Criminology* 25, no. 4 (November 1987): 949.

23. Ibid., p. 959.

24. Ibid., pp. 970–971.

25. See Michael R. Gottfredson and Travis Hirschi, *A General Theory of Crime* (Stanford, CA: Stanford University Press, 1990), pp. 23, 180–201.

26. Darrell J. Steffensmeier, "On the Causes of 'White-Collar' Crime: An Assessment of Hirschi and Gottfredson's Claims," *Criminology* 27, no. 2 (May 1989): 345–358. For a response by Hirschi and Gottfredson, see "The Significance of White-Collar Crime for a General Theory of Crime," *Criminology* 27 (May 1989): 359–371.

27. Michael L. Benson and Elizabeth Moore, "Are White-Collar and Common Offenders the Same? An Empirical and Theoretical Critique of a Recently Proposed General Theory of Crime," *Journal of Research in Crime and Delinquency* 29 (August 1992): 152–172.

28. Ibid.

29. See Charles R. Tittle, *Control Balance: Toward a General Theory of Deviance* (Boulder, CO: Westview Press, 1995) and the discussion in Chapter 6 of this text.

30. See Tittle, *Control Balance*, p. 164, referred to in Nicole Leeper Piquero and Alex R. Piquero, "Control Balance and Exploitative Corporate Crime," *Criminology* 44, no. 2 (May 2006): 397–429; citation is on p. 404.

31. Piquero and Piquero, "Control Balance and Exploitative Corporate Crime," p. 424.

32. Nicole Leeper Piquero et al., "Integrating the Desire-for-Control and Rational Choice in a Corporate Crime Context," *Justice Quarterly* 22, no. 2 (June 2005): 252–280.

33. Sandy Haantz, "Women and White Collar Crime," National White Collar Crime Center (October 2002), http://www.nw3c.org, accessed 29 June 2010. For more information on white-collar crime, see Gilbert Geis, *White-Collar and Corporate Crime* (Upper Saddle River, NJ: Prentice-Hall, 2007); Stephen Rosoff et al., *Profit Without Honor* (Upper Saddle River, NJ: Prentice-Hall, 2007).

34. See, for example, George Robb, "Women and White-Collar Crime: Debates on Gender, Fraud and the Corporate Economy in England and America, 1850–1930," *British Journal of Criminology* 26, no. 6 (2006): 1058–1072.

35. *State v. Burnham*, 15 N.H. 396 (1844).

36. NY CLS Penal, Section 105.17 (2010).

37. USCS, Title 18, Section 371 (2010).

38. For a brief discussion of this and other elements of the crime of conspiracy, see Sue Titus Reid, *Criminal Law*, 8th ed. (New York: Oxford University Press, 2010), pp. 60–68.

39. USCS, Title 26, Section 7201 (2010).

40. See *United States v. Coppola*, 300 F.Supp. 932 (D.C.Conn. 1969), *aff'd.*, 425 F.2d 660 (2d Cir. 1969).

41. *United States v. Berger*, 325 F.Supp. 1297, 1303 (S.D.N.Y. 1971), *aff'd.*, 456 F.2d 1349 (2d Cir. 1972), *cert. denied*, 409 U.S. 892 (1972).

42. "TV Lawyer's Partner a Tax Cheat," *New York Post* (6 April 2007), p. 10.

43. "14,700 Americans Tell I.R.S. of Foreign Accounts," *New York Times* (18 November 2009), p. 1B.

44. Department of Justice, "Former Detroit Mayor Kwame Kilpatrick Indicted on Fraud and Tax Charges," Press Release (23 June 2010); "City Hall Probe Snares Dozens," *Detroit News* (24 June 2010).

45. "New York Stps Up Its Pursuit of Tax Delinquents to Raise Cash," *New York Times* (10 November 2009), p. 28.

46. USCS, Title 18, Section 201 et seq. (2010).

47. "Morgan to Pay $700 Million in Bribe Case," *New York Times* (5 November 2009), p. 1B.

48. Iowa Code, Section 189A.19 (2010).

49. See USCS, Title 18, Section 1951(b)(2) (2010).

50. See, for example, Va. Code Ann., Title 18.2, Ch. 5, Art. 4, Section 18.2-111 (2010).

51. "Theft and Embezzlement Trial Begins for Mayor of Baltimore," *New York Times* (10 November 2009), p. 14.

52. "Bookkeeper Sentenced for $13 Million Theft," *Times-Picayune* (New Orleans) (12 March 2010), p. 3B.

53. "The Year in Review," *Los Angeles Times* (30 December 2009), p. 1B.

54. "Two Women Indicated as Participants in Madoff Scheme," *New York Times* (19 November 2010), p. 4B.

55. "Madoff Investors to Be Paid," *Wall Street Journal Abstracts* (4 May 2010), p. 4C; "Deal Recovers $7.2 Billion for Madoff Fraud Victims," *New York Times* (18 December 2010), p. 1.

56. "Pair Are Cleared of Fraud Charges," *Los Angeles Times* (11 November 2009), p. 1B; "Obama Pushes Financial Fight," *Chicago Tribune* (20 April 2010), p. 19C.

57. USCS, Title 15, Section 77a et seq. (2010).

58. Federal Bureau of Investigation, "Financial Crimes Report to the Public: Fiscal Year 2009," pp. 5, 7, 9, http://www.fbi.gov/stats-services/publications/financial-crimes-report-2009/, accessed 22 October 2010.

59. "Milken Leaves Prison for Halfway House Stint," *Orlando Sentinel* (5 January 1993), p. 1D; "Michael Milken," *Dallas Morning News* (29 January 1995), p. 1J; "Now, Obstruction of Justice Is Focus of Milken Inquiry," *New York Times* (14 November 1997), p. 4C.

60. Insider Trading and Securities Fraud Enforcement Act of 1988, USCS, Title 15, Section 78(a) (2010).

61. The Sarbanes-Oxley Act of 2002, Public Law 107-204, is codified, as amended, in various sections of the federal securities statutes in Titles 15 and 28 of the USCS (2010).

62. See *United States v. Martin*, 455 F.3d 1227 (11th Cir. 2006); *United States v. Crisp*, 454 F.3d 1285 (11th Cir. 2006). Several later cases have been decided as well. For a discussion, see Reid, *Criminal Law*, 8th ed., pp. 354–361. In particular, see *Kimbrough v. United States*, 552 U.S. 85 (2007).

63. *Free Enterprise Fund v. Public Company Accounting Oversight Board*, 2010 U.S. LEXIS 5524 (2010).

64. USCS, Title 15, Section 1 et seq. (2010).

65. Environmental Protection Agency (EPA), http://www.epa.gov, accessed 10 January 2010. For a concise overview of the EPA's organization and function, see Ronald G. Burns, Michael J. Lynch, and Paul Stretesky, *Environmental Law, Crime, and Justice* (New York: LFB Scholarly Publishing, 2008), pp. 73–96.

66. RCRA is codified at USCS, Title 42, Sections 9601 et seq. (2010). CERCLA is codified at USCS, Title 42, Section 9607 et seq. (2010). The Clear Water Act is codified at USCS, Title 33, Section 1252 et seq. (2010).

67. Environment and Natural Resources Division, "AboutENRD," http://www.justice.gov/enrd/About_ENRD.html, accessed 22 October 2010.

68. "Radical Environmentalist Gets 9-Year Term for Actions Called 'Terrorist,'" *New York Times* (26 May 2007), p. 8. The USA Patriot Act, revised and codified, can be found at USCS, Title 31, Section 5332 (2010).

69. "BP Deal Doesn't Close Book," *Houston Chronicle* (26 October 2007), p. 1.

70. "Obama Determinted to Make BP Pay," *The Australian* (15 June 2010), p. 34.

71. See *Hazelwood v. State*, 836 P.2d 943 (Alaska Ct.App. 1992), *aff'd. in part and rev'd in part, remanded*, 866 P.2d 827 (Alaska 1993), *rev'd., remanded*, 946 P.2d 875 (Alaska, 1997), *on remand*, 962 P.2d 196 (Alaska Ct.App. 1998).

72. "Pilot Gets Max Term: 10 Months," *San Francisco Chronicle* (18 July 2009), p. 1C; "Nation Digest," *Washington Post* (14 August 2009), p.2; "Ship Owner Pleads Guilty in S. F. Bay Spill," *Los Angeles Times* (14 August 2009), p. 11; "Shipping Firm Sentenced to Pay $10 Million for Causing Cosco Busan Oil Spill," *San Jose Mercury News* (19 February 2010), n.p.

73. "Barge Owner Gets Probation for Harbor Dumping," *New York Times* (7 November 1990), p. 1; "Two Sentenced for Dumping Toxic Sludge," *New York Times* (14 November 1996), p. 6B; "Sotheby's and Christie's Face Mounting Suits in Antitrust Case," *New York Times* (21 February 2000), p. 1.

74. *Grimshaw v. Ford Motor Company*, 174 Cal. Rptr. 348, 384 (4th Dist. 1981).

75. "Service Company Must Pay $11 Million in ValuJet Crash," *New York Times* (15 August 2000), p. 20; "Ten Years After ValuJet Flight 592: Changes Made After the Tragic 1996 Everglades Crash Have Contributed to an Unprecedented Safety Record for the U.S. Aviation Industry," *Miami Herald* (11 May 2006), State and Regional News, n.p.; "Airlines Still Put Revenue Above Safety, Some Say," *Palm Beach Post* (11 May 2006), p. 1A. The case is *United States v. SabreTech, Inc.*, 271 F.3d 1018 (11th Cir. 2001), *appeal after remand*, 2003 U.S. App. LEXIS 12231 (11th Cir. 2003).

76. "State Action Is Next in Lee Case," *Star Tribune* (Minneapolis, MN) (22 November 2010), p. 12.

77. *United States v. Park*, 421 U.S. 658 (1975).

78. See the media article by one of the lead prosecutors in the case of *United States v. Elias* (discussed in this chapter in Exhibit 9.5): David M. Uhlmann, "The Working Wounded," *New York Times* (27 May 2008), p. 23. The cited data are from the National Safety Council and the Bureau of Labor Statistics.

79. Ira Reiner and Jan Chatten-Brown, "When It Is Not an Accident, but a Crime: Prosecutors Get Tough with OSHA Violations," *Northern Kentucky Law Review* 17, no. 1 (1989): 85–103; quotation is on p. 103.

80. "Watch on the Media," *Liability Week* 8 (2 August 1993): n.p.; Bureau of National Affairs, "Job Safety: OSHA to Ease Federal Enforcement Role After Upgrades to North Carolina Program," *Daily Report for Executives* (8 March 1995), p. 45; "Still Burning: After a Deadly Fire, a Town's Losses Were Just Beginning," *Washington Post* (10 November 2002), p. 1F.

81. "3 Men Are Indicted in Fire at Rhode Island Nightclub," *New York Times* (10 December 2003), p. 14.

82. "Tentative Settlement Is Reached with TV Station in Fatal Nightclub Fire," *New York Times* (3 February 2008), p. 20; "R.I. Nightclub Owner Freed from Prison: Vows to Aid Kin of '03 Fire Victims," *Boston Globe* (26 June 2009), p. 3.

83. Uhlmann, "The Working Wounded."

84. "The Amy Bishop Case," *Boston Herald* (14 April 2010), p. 7.

85. See USCS, Title 18, Section 1341 (2010).

86. USCS, Title 18, Section 1343 (2010).

87. USCS, Title 18, Part I, Chapter 63, Section 1344 (2010).

88. See USCS, Title 18, Section 1341 et seq. (2010).

89. *Schmuck v. United States*, 489 U.S. 705 (1989).

90. "Porn Investor," *City News Service* (3 May 2004), n.p.; "Encino Man Is Charged with Bilking Minister," *Los Angeles Times* (8 March 2003), Part 2, p. 4. For an extensive recent analysis of mail and wire fraud, see Marissa Pezo, "Mail and Wire Fraud: Twenty-Second Annual Survey of White Collar Crime," *American Criminal Law Review* 44, no. 2 (22 March 2007): 745(24).

91. Federal Bureau of Investigation Los Angeles, Department of Justice, "Operator of MX Factors Sentenced to 100 Years in Prison for Ponzi Scheme That Cost Victims $39 Million," Press Release (28 September 2009), http://losangeles.fbi.gov/, accessed 22 October 2010.

92. USCS, Title 18, Section 1344 (2010).

93. See USCS, Title 18, Section 3293 (2010).

94. John S. Pistole, Deputy Director, Federal Bureau of Investigation, Statement Before the House Committee on the Judiciary "FBI Efforts to Combat Mortgage Fraud and Other Frauds, (1 April 2009), http://www.fbi.gov/news/testimony/2009-testimonies, accessed 22 October 2010.

95. "Financial Fraud Rises as Target for Prosecutors," *New York Times* (12 March 2009), p. 1.

96. Federal Bureau of Investigation, Department of Justice, Press Release, "Five Indicted in Foreclosure Rescue and Mortgage Fraud Scheme: Scam Involved Lawyers, Mortgage Brokers, and More Than $14.6 Million in Loans," http://philadelphia.fbi.gov/doj-pressrel/pressrel09/ph120809a.htm, accessed 18 December 2010.

97. Federal Bureau of Investigation, "Financial Fraud Enforcement Task Force Announces Results of Broadest Mortgage Fraud Sweep in History," Press Release (17 June 2010).

98. Federal Bureau of Investigation, "Financial Crimes Report to the Public: Fiscal Year 2009," Press Release, pp. 9, 10, http://www.fbi.gov/publications/financial/fcs_report2009/financial_crime_2009.htm, accessed 27 June 2010.

99. Federal Bureau of Investigation, "Health Care Fraud," http://fbi.gov/publications/financial/fcs_report2007/financial_crime_2007.htr, accessed 4 January 2010.

100. "Report Details Billions Lost in Medicare Fraud," *Washington Post* (16 November 2009), p. 6.

101. Health Insurance Portability and Accountability Act of 1996 (HIPAA), Public Law No. 104-191, 110 Stat. 1936 (1996); Balanced Budget Act of 1997 (BBA), Public Law No. 105-33, 111 Stat. 251 (1997).

102. "A Whistle-Blower Rocks an Industry," *Business Week*, no. 3788 (24 June 2002), p. 126.

103. False Claims Act, USCS, Chapter 31, Section 3729 et seq. (2010).

104. U.S. Department of Justice, "Michigan Health Care Provider to Pay United States $669,413 to Settle False Claims Allegations," http://www.justice.gov/opa/pr/2009/December/09-civ-1384.html, accessed 22 October 2010.

105. U.S. Department of Justice, "Remarks as Prepared for Delivery by Attorney General Eric Holder at the HEAT Press Conference on Detroit Takedown," http://www.justice.gov/ag/speeches/2009/ag-speech-0906241.html, accessed 22 October 2010.

106. Robert S. Mueller III, Director, Federal Bureau of Investigation, "Motor City Strike Force/Health Care Fraud Press Availability" (24 June 2009), http://www.fbi.gov/pressrel/speeches/mueller064209.htm, accessed 3 January 2010.

107. *United States v. Machi*, 811 F.2d 991 (7th Cir. 1987).

108. Richard A Booth, "It's Not a Good Thing, but It's Not a Crime," *Legal Intelligencer* 230, no. 35 (23 February 2004): 13.

109. For a discussion, see Morton Rosenberg and Todd B. Tatelman, "Congress's Contempt Power: A Sketch," *Congressional Research Service (CRS) Reports and Issue Briefs* (1 August 2007), n.p.; James Hamilton et al., "Congressional Investigations: Politics and Process," *American Criminal Law Review* 44, no. 3 (22 June 2007): 1115.

110. "Independent Counsel's Statement on the Pardons," *New York Times* (25 December 1992), p. 10.

111. Ethics in Government Act, Public Law 95-521, codified at USCS, Chapter 28, Sections 591-599 (2010). For a discussion, see Joseph S. Hall et al., "Independent Counsel Investigations: Fourteenth Survey of White Collar Crime," *American Criminal Law Review* 36, no. 3 (22 June 1999): 890 et seq. The U.S. Supreme Court upheld the act in *Morrison v. Olson*, 487 U.S. 654 (1988).

112. "Bush Marks Anniversary of the Civil Rights Act," *New York Times* (2 July 2004), p. 16.

113. USCS, Title 18, Section 242 (2010). Civil liabilities are covered in USCS, Title 42, Sections 1983 and 1985 (2010).

114. Civil Rights Act of 1991, P.L. 102-166, 105 Stat. 1071 et seq. (21 November 1991).

115. *Miller v. United States*, 404 F.2d 611 (5th Cir. 1968), *cert. denied*, 394 U.S. 963 (1969).

116. *United States v. Koon*, 34 F.3d 1416 (9th Cir. 1994), *aff'd. in part, rev'd. in part, remanded, Koon v. United States*, 515 U.S. 1190 (1995).

117. "New York Settles in Brutality Case," *New York Times* (13 July 2001), p. 1.

118. "Mother Responds Angrily to Decision in Diallo Case," *New York Times* (29 April 2001), p. 29.

119. The original USA Patriot Act was Public Law No. 107-56, 115 Stat. 272 (26 October 2001). The 2005 revision is referred to as the USA Patriot Improvement and Reauthorization Act of 2005, Public Law No. 109-177, 120 Stat. 192 (9 March 2006). The USA Patriot Act, revised, is codified at USCS, Title 42, Section 5332 et seq. (2010).

120. See, for example, *Padilla v. Hanft*, 432 F.3d 582 (4th Cir. 2005).

121. *Rasul v. Bush*, 542 U.S. 466 (2004).

122. Military Commissions Act of 2006, Public Law 109-366, 120 Stat. 2600 (2006).

123. *Boumediene v. Bush*, 553 U.S. 723 (2008).

124. David Weisburd et al., *Crimes of the Middle Classes: White-Collar Offenders in the Federal Courts* (New Haven, CT: Yale University Press, 1991), p. 171.

125. See U.S. Sentencing Commission, *Supplementary Report on Sentencing Guidelines for Organizations* (30 August 1991).

126. "Tougher Federal Sentences Loom for White-Collar Crime," *Broward Daily Business Review* (10 May 2001), p. 12; "Obama Signs a Contentious Overhaul of the U.S. Financial System," *New York Times* (22 July 2010), p. 1. The Restoring American Financial Stability Act of 2010 is S. 3217 (111th Congress, 2nd Session) (2010).

CHAPTER 10

Drug Abuse, Drug Trafficking, and Organized Crime

Andrew Luster, Max Factor cosmetics heir, walks out of the Puerto Vallarta police station in Puerto Vallarta City, Mexico, on 18 June 2003. Luster, who fled the United States during his California trial on charges of raping three young women after slipping date rape drugs into their drinks, was convicted in absentia and sentenced to 124 years in prison. After his capture in Mexico, he was extradited to the United States to begin serving his sentence.

CHAPTER OUTLINE

KEY TERMS

bootlegging
drug
drug abuse
drug paraphernalia
drug trafficking
extradition
fetal abuse
immunity (criminal)
loan sharking
Mafia
money laundering
organized crime
Racketeer Influenced and Corrupt Organizations (RICO)
racketeering
syndicate

INTRODUCTION

This chapter focuses on drug abuse, drug trafficking, and organized crime. The activities involved in these areas may include some or all of the property and violent crimes that have been discussed previously. All of the areas on which the chapter focuses are costly to the involved individuals as well as to society. Less obvious but nevertheless extensive damage is thrust upon individuals daily by the activities of those associated with organized crime, which has infiltrated legitimate as well as illegitimate businesses throughout the world.

The first two chapters of Part III covered violent and property crimes. Usually, violent and property crimes can be differentiated, but all crimes do not fit neatly into one of these categories. As already noted, an act of stealing, such as a purse snatching, may be either larceny-theft (a property crime) or robbery (a violent crime) depending on the circumstances of the act.

The three crime categories covered in this chapter involve both property and violent crimes. Drug abuse involves the illegal purchase and possession of drugs and **drug paraphernalia**. In some, perhaps many, cases, other crimes are committed to secure money for the drugs. Illegal drug trafficking, which may or may not be linked with organized crime, involves violent as well as property-related crimes. Organized crime results in extensive property losses to businesses and individuals; the hierarchy within organized crime is known for its use of violence to accomplish established goals.

Those who commit the ordinary property and violent crimes discussed in previous chapters are similar in some ways to those who commit the crimes discussed in this chapter. They may do so for personal or business gain or for political reasons. Early sociological analyses noted the interrelationships between business-related crimes and organized crime. Some argued that the relationship is one of mutual benefit, whereas others believed that the structure of legitimate society is necessary for the successful existence of organized crime. But clearly, one of the important components of both drug trafficking and organized crime is that many people abuse drugs.

Drug Abuse

Chapter 1 discussed the use of the criminal law to control behavior that some people might consider none of the law's business. **Drug abuse** is one area in which many people believe the criminal law either should not be employed or should be more restricted.

One of the major problems in analyzing drug abuse is to understand the terms, beginning with the word **drug**, which may be defined as follows:

> An article intended for use in the diagnosis, cure, mitigation, treatment, or prevention of disease in man or other animals and any article other than food intended to affect the structure or any function of the body of man or other animals.[1]

As so defined, the word *drug* is positive. Drugs are to be used for medical reasons. Some drugs, however, have been defined as illegal, and in this chapter, we consider those drugs as well as the abuse of legal drugs. Drugs include alcohol, marijuana, cocaine, heroin, and other substances. In many cases, it is impossible to separate the excessive use of alcohol from the abuse of other drugs in terms of effect

because many people who abuse one substance also abuse others. So, what is meant by *drug abuse*? Some define the words in terms of addiction, but clearly, in the criminal law, one may abuse drugs without being addicted; so in this text, we use the American Social Health Association's definition of *drug abuse*: "the use of mood modifying chemicals outside of medical supervision, and in a manner which is harmful to the person and the community."[2] That definition is rather broad, but it does capture the essence of this chapter's focus: harmful behaviors involving drugs. However, as we will see, not everyone agrees that using such drugs as marijuana is harmful. Others will disagree, and we will look at evidence to support both positions.

Finally, with regard to definitions, it is important to remember that crimes involving drugs must be defined by the *criminal* law. Definitions of some drugs that are discussed in this chapter appear in Exhibit 10.1.

Data

The Substance Abuse and Mental Health Services Administration Agency (SAMHSA) is the major source of data on the abuse and illegal use of alcohol, other drugs, and tobacco among noninstitutionalized populations aged 12 and older. The SAMHSA sponsors an annual survey on drug use and health. A summary of the latest available survey is presented in Exhibit 10.2.

High school age students are often the subjects of drug abuse studies. A survey that tracks drug use among teens is the Monitoring the Future (MTF) study, which is funded by the National Institute on Drug Abuse. When this study was initiated in 1975, 30.7 percent of high school seniors reported using an illicit drug in the month prior to the study. This use declined in the years prior to 1992 and then began rising again before another drop between 1997 and 1998. Of particular concern has been the increase in the use of marijuana in this age group. Between 1991 and 1998, the use of marijuana in the month prior to the survey increased from 13.8 percent to 22.8 percent among high school seniors.[3]

The December 2003 MTF survey was the twenty-ninth annual survey of high school seniors; eighth- and tenth-grade students were added in 1991. The surveys indicated that illicit drug use among teens peaked in 1996 or 1997 (depending on the grade) and then began declining among eighth-graders and remaining steady among students in the upper grades. The 2003 data showed a statistically significant drop in illicit drug use among eighth- and tenth-grade students and a slighter drop among high school seniors. In the 2003 survey, fewer students in each of the surveyed grades said they had ever used illicit drugs, but 13 percent of the surveyed eighth-graders, 28 percent of the tenth-graders, and 35 percent of the high school seniors responded that, in the 12 months prior to the survey, they smoked marijuana. In all three grades, there was a

EXHIBIT

10.1

Drugs: A Sample of Definitions and Facts

Cocaine

"A white crystaline narcotic alkaloid extracted from coca leaves. Used as a local anesthetic. A 'controlled substance' as included in narcotic laws."[1]

Heroin

"Narcotic drug which is a derivative of opium and whose technical name is diacetyl-morphine. It is classified as a Class A substance for criminal purposes and the penalty for its possession is severe."[2]

Marijuana

"An annual herb, *cannabis sativa*, having angular rough stem and deeply lobed leaves. . . .

Marijuana is also commonly referred to as 'pot,' 'grass,' 'tea,' 'weed,' or 'Mary Jane'; and in cigarette form as a 'joint' or 'reefer.'"[3]

Hallucinogenic drugs

"Hallucinogenic substances are characterized by their ability to cause changes in a person's perception of reality. Persons using hallucinogenic drugs often report seeing images, hearing sounds, and feeling sensations that seem real, but do not exist. In the past, plants and fungi that contained hallucinogenic substances were abused. Currently, these hallucinogenic substances are produced synthetically to provide a higher potency."[4]

Club Drugs

The so-called club drugs, which have become popular in recent years and are often abused by teens and others at dances and "raves" because they enable party-goers to dance all night, consist of the following: MDMA/Ecstasy, Rohypnol, GHB, and ketamine.[5] The Office of National Drug Policy defines these drugs as follows:

"MDMA is a synthetic, psychoactive drug chemically similar to the stimulant methamphetamine and the hallucinogen mescaline.

"The tasteless and odorless depressants Rohypnol and GHB are often used in the commission of sexual assaults due to their ability to sedate and intoxicate unsuspecting victims. Rohypnol, a sedative/tranquilizer, is legally available for prescription in over 50 countries outside the U.S. and is widely available in Mexico, Colombia, and Europe. . . .

"GHB, available in an odorless, colorless liquid form or as a white powder material, is taken orally, and is frequently combined with alcohol. In addition to being used to incapacitate individuals for the commission of sexual assault/rape, GHB is also sometimes used by body builders for its alleged anabolic effects.

"The abuse of ketamine, a tranquilizer most often used on animals, became popular in the 1980s, when it was realized that large doses cause reactions similar to those associated with the use of PCP, such as dream-like states and hallucinations. The liquid form of ketamine can be injected, consumed in drinks, or added to smokable materials. The powder form can also be added to drinks, smoked, or dissolved and then injected. In some cases, ketamine is being injected intramuscularly."[6]

---

1. *Black's Law Dictionary, Special Deluxe Fifth Edition* (St. Paul, MN: West Publishing, 1979), p. 233.
2. Ibid., p. 654.
3. Ibid., p. 871.
4. Office of National Drug Control Policy, *Drug Facts: Hallucinogens*, http://www.whitehousedrugpolicy.gov/drugfact/hallucinogens/index.html, accessed 28 October 2010, footnotes omitted.
5. Office of National Drug Control Policy, *Drug Facts: Club Drugs: Overview*, http://www.whitehousedrugpolicy.gov/drugfact/club/index.html, accessed 28 October 2010, footnotes omitted.
6. Office of National Drug Control Policy, *Drug Facts: Club Drug Facts and Figures*, http://www.whitehousedrugpolicy.gov/drugfact/club/club_drug_ff.html, accessed 28 October 2010, footnotes omitted.

---

significant increase in the awareness of the harmful effects of marijuana, possibly due to the National Youth Anti-Drug Media Campaign by the Office of National Drug Control Policy (ONDCP) and the Partnership for a Drug-Free America, which began their efforts in October 2002. Perhaps even more encouraging in the 2003 survey was the fact that the proportion of tenth-graders and high school seniors who reported that they had used the club drug Ecstasy in the previous 12 months fell by more than one-half since 2001. The use of Ecstasy by eighth-graders was down considerably, although not as much as for the other two categories of students. By 2006, the survey revealed a 23 percent decline in the use of any illicit drug over the previous five years. The study reported declines in cigarette smoking, the use of marijuana, steroids, Ecstasy, and methamphetamines, but high levels of abuse of Vicodin, a painkiller, and a doubling since 2002 of the use of OxyContin (also a painkiller) among eighth-graders (although the use declined among twelfth-grade students). The 2007 report showed some encouraging news, especially among eighth-graders, who reported a decline of almost 1 percent in lifetime use of any drug, a decline from 14.8 percent to 13.2 percent of past year's use, and the continued decline in the use of alcohol. Cigarette use among eighth-graders declined to its lowest level since the surveys first included that group. Both eighth- and

EXHIBIT 10.2

2009 National Survey on Drug Use and Health: A Summary

- "In 2009, an estimated 21.8 million Americans aged 12 or older were current (past month) illicit drug users, meaning they had used an illicit drug during the month prior to the survey interview. This estimate represents 8.7 percent of the population aged 12 or older. Illicit drugs include marijuana/hashish, cocaine (including crack), heroin, hallucinogens, inhalants, or prescription-type psychotherapeutics used nonmedically.

- The rate of current illicit drug use among persons aged 12 or older in 2009 (8.7 percent) was higher than the rate in 2008 (8.0 percent).

- Marijuana was the most commonly used illicit drug. In 2009, there were 16.7 million past month users. Among persons aged 12 or older, the rate of past month marijuana use and the number of users in 2009 (6.6 percent or 16.7 million) were higher than in 2008 (6.1 percent or 15.2 million) and in 2007 (5.8 percent or 14.4 million).

- In 2009, there were 1.6 million current cocaine users aged 12 or older, comprising 0.7 percent of the population. These estimates were similar to the number and rate in 2008 (1.9 million or 0.7 percent), but were lower than the estimates in 2006 (2.4 million or 1.0 percent).

- Hallucinogens were used in the past month by 1.3 million persons (0.5 percent) aged 12 or older in 2009, including 760,000 (0.3 percent) who had used Ecstasy. The number and percentage of Ecstasy users increased between 2008 . . . and 2009.

- There were 7.0 million (2.8 percent) persons aged 12 or older who used prescription-type psychotherapeutic drugs nonmedically in the past month. These estimates were higher than in 2008 (6.2 million or 2.5 percent), but similar to estimates in 2007 (6.9 million or 2.8 percent).

- The number of past month methamphetamine users decreased between 2006 and 2008, but then increased in 2009. The numbers were 731,000 (0.3 percent) in 2006, 529,000 (0.2 percent) in 2007, 314,000 (0.1 percent) in 2008, and 502,000 (0.2 percent in 2009).

- Among youths aged 12 to 17, the current illicit drug use rate increased from 2008 (9.3 percent) to 2009 (10.0 percent). Between 2002 and 2008, the rate declined from 11.6 to 9.3 percent.

- The rate of current marijuana use among youths aged 12 to 17 decreased from 8.2 percent in 2002 to 6.7 percent in 2006 and remained unchanged at 6.7 percent in 2007 and 2008, then increased to 7.3 percent in 2009.

- Among youths aged 12 to 17, the rate of nonmedical use of prescription-type drugs declined from 4.0 Percent to 2.9 percent in 2008, then held steady at 3.1 percent in 2009.

- The rate of current Ecstasy use among youths aged 12 to 17 declined from 0.5 percent in 2002 to 0.3 percent in 2004, remained at that level through 2007, then increased to 0.5 percent in 2009. . . .

- From 2002 to 2009, there was an increase among young adults aged 18 to 25 in the rate of current nonmedical use of prescription-type drugs . . . driven primarily by an increse in pain reliever misuse. . . . There were decreases in the use of cocaine . . . and methamphetamine. . . .

- Among persons aged 12 or older in 2008–2009 who used pain relievers nonmedically in the past 12 months, 55.3 percent got the drug they most recently used from a friend or relative for free. Another 17.6 percent reported they got the drug from one doctor. Only 4.8 percent got pain relievers from a drug dealer or other stranger, and 0.4 percent bought them on the Internet. Among those who reported getting the pain reliever from a friend or relative for free, 80.0 percent reported in a follow-up question that the friend or relative had obtained the drugs from just one doctor.

- Among unemployed adults aged 18 or older in 2009, 17.0 percent were current illicit drug users, which was higher than the 8.0 percent of those employed full time and 11.5 percent of those employed part time. However, most illicit drug users were employed. . . .

- In 2009, 10.5 million persons aged 12 or older reported driving under the influence of illicit drugs during the past year. This corresponds to 4.2 percent of the population aged 12 or older, which is similar to the rate in 2008 (4.0 percent) and the rate in 2002 (4.7 percent). In 2009, the rate was highest among young adults aged 18 to 25 (12.8 percent)."

Source: U.S. Department of health and Human Services, Substance Abuse and Mental Health Services Administration Office of Applied Studies, *Results from the 2009 National Survey on Drug Use and Health: Volume I. Summary of National Findings,* (September 2010), pp. 1–2, http://www.oas.samhsa.gov/NSDUH/2k9NSDUH/2k9ResultsP.pdf, accessed 30 October 2010.

twelfth-graders showed declines in methamphetamine abuse from 2006 to 2007. But the abuse of prescription drugs continued to be an issue.[4]

In 2008, the abuse of prescription drugs, especially Vicodin ("abused at unacceptably high levels") continued to be a concern, with 15.4 percent of twelfth-graders reporting the illegal use of prescription drugs within the previous year. The 2008 data indicated that although marijuana use among teens continued to decline, that decline appeared to have leveled off. However, the latest report, issued in December 2010, indicated that the daily use of marijuana increased significantly among all three grades and that "most measures of marijuana use increased among eighth-graders." The 2010 data also showed significant increases in the use of Ecstasy and "continued high levels of prescription drug abuse."[5]

Particular attention is given to teen use of the drug Ecstasy (also referred to as MDMA). This drug was created in 1912 as an appetite depressant. It was also prescribed by medical doctors to facilitate psychotherapy. In 1988, the U.S. Congress designated Ecstasy a Schedule I drug, the most serious of the five categories used by Congress to classify drugs. Schedule I drugs are considered to have a high potential for abuse and have, according to the federal law, "no currently accepted medical use in treatment in the United States."[6] Exhibit 10.1 contains more information about Ecstasy, along with a few other drugs (see again Exhibit 10.1). The harmful effects of such drug use are discussed later in this chapter.

Another area in which drug abuse is an issue is the workplace. The U.S. Department of Labor (DOL) reports data from several sources. In 2010, the DOL reported the following data concerning drug abuse.

- In 2007, 75.3 percent of the illicit drug users over age 18 were employed. Of the binge drinkers, 79.4 percent were employed.
- About 2.9 percent of workers reported that they had worked while under the influence of drugs, while 3.1 percent used drugs while on duty or just prior to reporting for work.
- Approximately 1.8 percent of employed adults used alcohol before going to work; 7.1 percent consumed alcohol during the workday.
- Workers who abuse drugs and alcohol were more likely to have missed more than two days of work during the year, to have worked for more than one employer, and to have missed more than two days due to injury or illness.
- Substance abuse by a worker affected other workers, resulting in loss of productivity and negative attitudes. Some workers reported "having been put in danger, having been injured, or having had to work harder, to re-do work, or to cover for a coworker as a result of a fellow employee's drinking."[7]

Data indicate that drug abuse is more common in some occupations and professions than others. Specifically, alcohol abuse and illicit use of other drugs are highest among those in food service and construction, but other jobs showing significant problems with alcohol abuse are auto mechanics, laborers, and light-truck drivers.[8]

Race may also be a factor in substance abuse. There is evidence that deaths associated with motor vehicle crashes are more prevalent for Native Americans than for other groups. Death from cirrhosis of the liver is higher among ethnic and minority groups than among whites. Mortality rates from alcohol are highest among African American men "even though alcohol use tends to be more moderate for African Americans than for whites or Hispanics."[9]

Finally, age may be a relevant variable, with 14 percent of elderly patients in emergency rooms, 20 percent in psychiatric wards, and 6 to 11 percent who are admitted to hospitals exhibiting alcohol problems. Further, among women who are 60 or older, "substance abuse and addiction to cigarettes, alcohol, and psychoactive prescription drugs are at epidemic levels." One study indicated that women are more likely than other groups to become addicted after taking small amounts of these substances.[10]

Not all who abuse drugs are arrested, but as Table 10.1 demonstrates, most drug abuse arrests, 82.3 percent, are for the *possession* of illegal drugs, not for their sale or manufacture. Among possession arrests, by far the greatest percentage, 44.3 percent, is for marijuana.

Table 10.1

Percentage of Arrests for Drug Abuse Violations, 2009

Sale/Manufacture	Total: 18.4 Percent
Heroin or cocaine and their derivatives	7.1
Marijuana	6.0
Synthetic or manufactured drugs	1.7
Other dangerous nonnarcotic drugs	3.5
Possession	**Total: 81.6 Percent**
Heroin or cocaine and their derivatives	17.7
Marijuana	45.6
Synthetic or manufactured drugs	3.7
Other dangerous nonnarcotic drugs	14.6

Source: Federal Bureau of Investigation, *Crime in the United States, Uniform Crime Reports 2009* (September 2010), http://www2.fbi.gov/ucr/cius2009/arrests/index.html, accessed 30 October 2010.

The abuse of prescription drugs has been mentioned already, but it deserves more attention. According to the ONDCP, "Prescription drugs account for the second most commonly abused category of drugs, behind marijuana and ahead of cocaine, heroin, methamphetamine, and other drugs." The ONDCP emphasizes that abuse of prescription drugs "poses a unique challenge because of the need to balance prevention, education, and enforcement, with the need for legitimate access to controlled substance prescription drugs."[11]

Persons engaging in the abuse of prescription drugs are often referred to treatment centers, not to criminal justice agencies, thus limiting data on the problem. The most commonly abused drugs are painkillers (e.g., OxyContin and Percocet), drugs prescribed for some sleep disorders and anxiety (e.g., Valium and Xanax), and stimulants prescribed to treat obesity, attention-deficit hyperactivity disorder (ADHD), and other conditions. Recall that the latest survey of drug use among students expressed concern about the high rates of continued use of Vicodin. Some of these drugs may be obtained through the Internet without a prescription.[12]

Drug abuse is also a concern in the U.S. armed forces. Almost 40 percent of U.S. Army personnel who committed suicide in recent years were taking psychotropic drugs. Although failed relationships are linked to many of the suicides, experts believe drugs are also a factor, with abuse of prescription drugs a serious area of concern.[13]

In December 2009, the Pentagon released a study of 28,000 troops, revealing that in 2008, 20 percent had abused prescription drugs and that 13 percent were suffering from posttraumatic stress disorder (PTSD), up from 9 percent in 2005. Thirty percent of those with multiple deployments were characterized by psychological problems.[14]

Finally, drug abuse impacts populations differently. Illegal weekly drug use is more likely reported by African Americans, and heavy alcohol use is more likely reported by Hispanics, with whites and African Americans following. Native Americans are more likely than other groups to be involved in alcohol-related vehicle fatalities, and African American men are more likely than other groups to die from alcohol-related problems.[15]

The Impact of Drug Abuse

Although some people consider the use of controlled substances a personal, private issue and not harmful, there is evidence to the contrary. First, we look at the effects of drug abuse on the abuser.

Effects on the Abuser

The full range of the effects of drugs on the abuser is beyond the scope of this text, but it is important to note some of the reactions one might experience with drug abuse. These effects are not limited to the use of illegal drugs; they also apply to the legal abuse of alcohol by adults (along with the illegal possession and consumption by underage persons) and to the misuse of prescribed drugs.

The first negative reaction to a person who abuses drugs may be the harmful side effects to that individual's health. Some effects of club drugs, for example, are confusion, depression, paranoia, sleeplessness, anxiety, a craving for drugs, muscle tension, blurred vision, sweating, tremors, rapid eye movement, chills, involuntary teeth clenching, nausea, and fainting. Individuals with circulatory problems or heart disease may enhance their risks with those diseases by taking Ecstasy. They may also experience kidney failure, hyperthermia, or dehydration. The effects of Ecstasy may last for a long time, even up to two years in the case of side effects such as memory or sleep loss.[16]

The National Institute of Drug Abuse (NIDA) reports research findings indicating that chronic use of Ecstasy might cause long-term brain damage. Some of the health problems caused by Ecstasy and other drugs may lead to death.[17]

Men who use Ecstasy to enhance their sexual abilities while taking Viagra may increase their risks of stroke or heart attack as well as their chances of contracting the HIV virus that causes AIDS.[18]

There are also harmful effects from the use of other club drugs. The drug Rohypnol can cause muscle relaxation if lower doses are used, but with higher doses, this drug may result in loss of muscle control, partial amnesia, and even loss of consciousness. The effects of Rohypnol appear within 15 to 20 minutes and may last from four to six hours or even longer; thus, it is one of the drugs used for date rape. Loss of consciousness may also occur from taking GHB. This drug may cause drowsiness, severe respiratory depression, nausea, seizure, and even a coma. The use of Ketamine can cause a person to lose control for an hour or so, but the drug can result in impairment to the senses, judgment, and coordination for up to 24 hours.[19]

Marijuana use may also have harmful side effects, such as increased heart rate, panic attacks, impaired memory and learning, and respiratory infections. The regular use of marijuana can produce some of the same respiratory problems characteristic of tobacco smokers. According to the NIDA, since marijuana has significantly more carcinogenic hydrocarbons than tobacco smoke, it has the potential to cause lung cancer. There is also evidence that frequent use of marijuana may impair critical thinking.[20]

In addition to the negative effects that drugs may have on users are the effects they may have on others. Persons under the influence of controlled substances may (and do) drive and cause injury and death to themselves as well as to others. They may engage in abusive, harassing, or obnoxious, even violent, behavior, offending, injuring, or killing others. Their drug abuse may have a negative impact on their friends and families.

One area of focus with regard to the effects of drug abuse on others is the harm that substance abuse may cause to the unborn children of female abusers.

Fetal Abuse

A recent area of concern is **fetal abuse**, leading some states, as noted in Chapter 7, to change their homicide statutes to include killing a fetus. The issue here, however, is whether the substance abuse of a pregnant woman, when that abuse causes birth defects or the death of the fetus, should form the basis for a criminal charge against the mother, especially in view of the following evidence. Babies born to mothers who drink alcohol or take other drugs during pregnancy are more likely to be born with fetal alcohol syndrome, drug addiction, and to develop leukemia during infancy. Mothers who smoke are more likely to give birth to underweight babies and those with mental disabilities than are mothers who do not smoke. Yet, there is evidence that many women smoke (or drink) during pregnancy despite all the warnings, and some even binge drink, which puts their pregnancies in the high-risk category.[21]

Studies (on rats) showed that Ecstasy exposure early in a pregnancy can affect the chemistry of the brain of the fetus. There is also evidence that fetuses exposed to Ecstasy during pregnancy, compared with a control group that had not been exposed, had more difficulty adjusting to a new environment.[22] In another study of pregnant rats, it was found that the offspring of mothers who were given a marijuana-related chemical were more likely than the unexposed offspring in a control group to have memory lapses and to be hyperactive. It was emphasized that studies of the effects on fetuses of drug use by pregnant humans are difficult because of the problem of controlling for other issues, such as smoking cigarettes, drinking alcohol, or abusing other drugs. Although the study of rats does not necessarily apply to the study of humans, the researchers concluded: "Our findings suggest that both pregnant and lactating women should avoid using marijuana."[23]

One study concluded that the height and weight deficits found among babies born to women who drink alcohol during their pregnancies may extend into the child's teen years. "Researchers found that even mothers who drank less than an average of one drink per day during pregnancy put their children at risk of decreased weight, height, head circumference and skinfold thickness at age 14. The size of the deficits was directly related to the amount of alcohol consumed." The researchers noted, however, that most of the subjects were poor, and thus, the results might not be applicable to affluent pregnant women, suggesting that factors other than alcohol (e.g., poor nutrition) might be involved.[24]

Some jurisdictions have prosecuted pregnant women who abuse alcohol and other drugs, but most prosecutions have not resulted in convictions. In September 2007, a Missouri court held that it was improper to charge a pregnant woman with the crime of child endangerment after the mother and child both tested positive for marijuana and methamphetamines. The court noted that 15 other states had considered the issue, but only South Carolina has a statute that encompasses, in effect, homicide by child abuse by a pregnant woman whose act or omission causes the death of a fetus. The court suggested that social services would be an appropriate agency to handle such issues. In June 2010, the Kentucky Supreme Court held that it was unconstitutional under that state's law to prosecute a pregnant woman for wanton endangerment in the first degree because she ingested drugs during her pregnancy. At birth, the child tested positive for cocaine.[25]

South Carolina did invoke its statute in the case of a pregnant homeless drug addict, Regina McKnight, age 24.

Evidence that a pregnant woman's consumption of alcoholic beverages may cause injury to her fetus has led some jurisdictions to go beyond warnings and enact criminal statutes, arresting and prosecuting women when such fetal injuries (or deaths) occur.

McKnight smoked crack cocaine during her pregnancy; her stillborn baby was delivered when McKnight was eight and one-half months pregnant. McKnight's first trial ended in a mistrial; she was convicted at her second trial. The South Carolina Supreme Court upheld McKnight's conviction, and the U.S. Supreme Court refused to review the case. McKnight was sentenced to 12 years in prison.[26]

The U.S. Supreme Court has ruled, however, that pregnant women suspected of drug abuse may not be tested for drugs without their permission if the purpose of the test is to alert police to their substance abuse. According to the Supreme Court, even with the possibility that the substance abuse could endanger the fetus, if the woman does not consent or if law enforcement officials do not have a warrant, a drug test is an unconstitutional search and seizure.[27]

Another result of drug abuse and drug trafficking is that they are changing the nature of cities, towns, and even rural villages.

Drugs and the Community

The infestation of the inner-city ghetto with drugs, especially those associated with gangs, has been a focus of social science research and law enforcement attention for decades. Considerable attention was given to the study of gangs in Chapter 5, with notations that illegal drugs were often involved in gang activity. That was emphasized in 2004, as the Los Angeles Police Department (LAPD) increased its efforts to combat gangs in that city.[28] In 2004, Los Angeles was referred to as the gang capital of the nation, with Chicago close behind. The Los Angeles police chief at that time, William Bratton, referred to gangs as the greatest terrorist threat in America, the "emerging monster of crime in America," killing more people than terrorists do. Phillip J. Cline, Chicago's police superintendent, stated in 2004 that gangs had killed more people in his city than had organized crime.[29]

By 2007, Chief Bratton had been given another term in Los Angeles; gang homicides in that city were down, with 42 fewer in the first six months compared to the same period in 2006. Overall, homicides in Los Angeles were down 22 percent through June 2007 compared to June 2006, an important drop because gang homicides account for approximately 56 percent of all homicides in that city. Despite this decline, Chief Bratton stated that gangs remained a serious concern, with overall gang crime up 15 percent in the first six months of 2007.[30] Bratton left as chief in 2009; gangs were still a problem.

The deadly combination of drugs and gangs is also found in the nation's schools. Investigators found a high correlation between the presence of drugs (and guns) in schools and gangs. Students who reported that illegal drugs were readily available in their schools were much more likely to report the presence of gang members than were students who did not report readily available drugs.[31] Perhaps even more shocking was a headline in 2007, "Slaughter in Our Cities: Chicago School Kids Are Getting Killed at a Faster Pace Than Illinois Soldiers." Then presidential candidate Barack Obama, a Chicago resident, noted that 32 children were killed in the city's schools during the previous school year. He quoted the FBI as saying that the United States had more gang members than police officers on its streets.[32]

Large cities are not the only focus of gangs and drugs. Although the two are not always combined, the presence of drugs in even small-town America has become a serious problem in some areas. One news article focused on Lovell, Wyoming, a town of only 2,264 that had twice the national average of methamphetamine use. One-half of the time of Lowell's seven police officers was consumed with crimes related to this drug. In the previous two years, 70 people were arrested for crimes associated with the drug. Parents lost custody of children they forgot to feed while they were under the influence of the drug, and burglaries increased at an alarming rate. Some people quit their jobs, sold their houses, and concentrated on selling drugs. The little town lost income and people; as a result, three of its four grocery stores, a movie theater, a Sears store, and a few other businesses closed. According to the article, this situation was typical of other small towns in Wyoming, the nation's least-populated state, but one overrun with demand for the synthetic drug.[33]

Two years prior to the aforementioned article, the *New York Times* focused an article on drugs in rural areas. The article highlighted Prentiss, Mississippi, with its magnificent and expensive homes owned by drug dealers who earned their money selling crack, methamphetamine, marijuana, and OxyContin. "They are the most visible manifestation of an explosion of rural drugs and crime that is overwhelming local law enforcement agencies and bringing the sort of violence normally associated with poor neighborhoods of big cities."[34]

Drug abusers and drug traffickers have also infiltrated other living areas where they might not be expected, such as Harborview Terrace, a New York City public housing project for persons who are at least 62 years old and the disabled. Young people moved in illegally, dealing in drugs, some openly, and threatening to injure or kill anyone who defied them or reported them. Legal residents lived in fear, suffered in silence, and armed themselves with weapons in case of invasion.[35]

These events are particularly important in view of the 2002 U.S. Supreme Court decision *HUD* v. *Rucker*, upholding a federal law that permits evicting public housing tenants if anyone in their residences, including guests, used illegal drugs—even if those drugs are outside the premises and the tenant had no knowledge of these acts. Two of the four elderly residents who were served eviction notices by the Oakland (California) Housing Authority had grandsons living with them; unknown to the tenants, these relatives were smoking marijuana in the parking lot. Another evictee had a caregiver who was frequently apprehended with cocaine. The fourth had a mentally disabled daughter who was three blocks from the apartment when she was found with cocaine. The U.S. Supreme Court, in upholding the eviction statute, emphasized that drugs lead to the physical deterioration of housing developments as well as to violence in the form of muggings, robbery, and even murder. Thus, it was reasonable for Congress, because of the significant expenditure of federal funds in these housing developments, to enact legislation to permit no-fault evictions to "provide public and other federally assisted low-income housing that is decent, safe, and free from illegal drugs."[36]

Campus and Intimate Partner Violence

The use of illegal drugs and alcohol is frequently associated with intimate partner violence (IPV) (see Chapter 7 for a discussion of this crime). One area in which illegal drug use may be related to IPV is on U.S. college and university campuses. Frequent studies report that alcohol and other drugs are problems in these venues. In fact, alcohol abuse is one of the most prevalent mental health problems among college students, who generally drink more than their noncollege counterparts. Many are binge drinkers (defined as five or more drinks in a row for men and four or more for women on one or more occasions during a two-week period). According to the Centers for Disease Control and Prevention, one-half of college binge drinkers engage in such behavior frequently, meaning three or more times within a two-week period. It is estimated that one-third of college students abuse alcohol and that 1 in 17 is alcohol dependent. Most of these students deny that they have a drinking problem, and few seek treatment. In addition to the problems these college drinkers cause for themselves are the so-called secondhand effects. These are the effects they have on others by engaging in loud, boisterous behavior; vomiting; or engaging in aggressive behavior, including sexual and nonsexual assaults, property damage, driving under the influence, and so on.[37]

Specifically, a study conducted by the Harvard School of Public Health found that college and university students who did not abuse alcohol encountered secondhand effects of others' drinking, such as the following:

- "60.5 percent had study or sleep interrupted
- 53.6 percent had to take care of a drunken student
- 29.3 percent had been insulted or humiliated
- 20.1 percent experienced an unwanted sexual advance (women)
- 18.6 percent had a serious argument or quarrel
- 13.6 percent had property damaged
- 9.5 percent had been pushed, hit, or assaulted
- 1.3 percent had been a victim of sexual assault or date rape (women)"[38]

In April 2010, the president of Reed, a prestigious private college in Portland, Oregon, was told to "rein in drug use on his campus." He was informed that federal authorities planned to send undercover law enforcement officials to his campus during a forthcoming festival to attempt to arrest drug offenders. Reed College "has long been known almost as much for its unusually permissive atmosphere as for its impressively rigorous academics." It was stated that two words come to mind when one hears the name Reed: brains and drugs. In 2008, a Reed student died from a heroin overdose.[39]

The Bureau of Justice Statistics (BJS) analyzed data on violent victimizations of college students (compared to nonstudents). Those data are presented in Exhibit 10.3, which also covers variables such as race and gender, along with the time of day or night when the crimes occurred. The report included information on alcohol and drug abuse, pointing out that 4 in 10 victims of violence perceived that their offenders were under the influence of alcohol or other drugs; 37 percent were unsure.[40]

Other research shows a strong relationship between alcohol and physical violence, especially sexual violence. Persons who have been drinking or using illegal drugs compared with nonabusers are much more likely to be violent crime victims. In one medical study, heterosexual women aged 18–30 were asked about IPV and drugs. The study reported that the women who used marijuana or other drugs compared with women who did not were more likely to be victimized by IPV.[41]

Criminologists who study victimization have suggested several explanations. Perhaps people who drink put themselves in a position where they are likely to be victimized. They associate with likely perpetrators, they are more likely to frequent bars and other places where violence might occur, and their close friends and partners are more likely to drink. Thus, opportunity theory explains their victimization. Social scientists state it this way:

> [O]pportunity explanations suggest that drinkers are more likely to come in contact with motivated offenders, while situational explanations suggest that potential offenders become motivated (or disinhibited) in response to victim's drinking.[42]

Data from the National Violence Against Women survey of men and women aged 18 and older indicated that, although individual drinking habits do not predict victimization while persons are not drinking, they are highly predictive of victimization while those individuals are drinking. Drinking is a much stronger predictor of victimization for sexual than for other physical assaults. Also, drinking is a much greater predictor of male than of female victimization, with men who are physically assaulted by their female intimates much more likely than woman to be drinking at the time of the assault by an intimate. The researchers did not find evidence that women are more likely than men to elicit violence when they are

EXHIBIT 10.3

Violent Victimization of College Students

- "Male college students were twice as likely to be victims of overall violence than female students (80 versus 43 per 1,000).
- White college students had somewhat higher rates of violent victimization than blacks and higher rates than students of other races (65 versus 52 and 37 per 1,000 respectively).
- For females, nonstudents were over 1.5 times more likely than college students to be a victim of a violent crime (71 versus 43 per 1,000). For males, students and nonstudents were equally likely to be the victim of a violent crime (about 80 per 1,000).
- For both whites and blacks, nonstudents had higher rates of violent victimization than college students (81 and 83 versus 65 and 52 per 1,000).

- Hispanic college students and nonstudents experience violence at similar rates.

Characterisitcs of Violent Victimizations of College Students

- 58 percent were committed by strangers.
- 41 percent of offenders were perceived to be using alcohol or drugs.
- 93 percent of crimes occurred off campus, of which 72 percent occurred at night."

Source: Katrina Baum and Patsy Klaus, Bureau of Justice Statistics, *Violent Victimization of College Students* (January 2005), p. 1, http://bjs.ojp.usdoj.gov/content/pub/pdf/vvcs02.pdf, accessed 31 October 2010.

---

drinking. "We see no evidence that intoxicated women are assaulted because they are stigmatized or because they elicit a social control reaction." It appears more likely that intoxicated men are more likely than intoxicated women to provoke violence, especially from their partners. But it also appears likely that "drinking plays an important role in increasing vulnerability to sexual attack. We cannot tell if drinking impairs the victim's judgment, leads to risky behavior, or incapacitates the victim." The evidence shows that men and women are similar when the relationship between alcohol and victimization is analyzed. This suggests "that sexual assaults are not a social control response to women's drinking."[43]

One of the types of sexual assault associated with alcohol and illegal drug use, especially on college campuses, is date rape (discussed in Chapter 7). Although date rape may be accomplished without the use of drugs, it is frequently associated with them. Rape victims may have been drinking excessively by choice, or they may drink only one or more drinks that are laced (without their knowledge) with one of the club drugs, most often GHB, which is odorless and tasteless. Thus, the victim cannot detect that the drug has been placed into the drink. The victim can lose consciousness within 20 minutes and, after the rape, not recall that it occurred.

The use of club drugs for date rape gained international attention in January 2003 when Andrew Luster, grandson of the founder of Max Factor (a cosmetics company), was charged with secretly lacing the drinks of his dates with Ecstasy and then raping them. Most of the alleged victims could not recall these events, but Luster had videotaped them. During the trial, Luster, who was charged with 87 criminal counts, was free on $1 million bail and required to wear an electronic ankle bracelet. He was able to break the system and disappeared, not showing up one day for his trial, which was conducted in his absence. Luster was convicted and sentenced to 124 years in prison. He was apprehended in Mexico in June 2003 and returned to the United States to begin his sentence.

The possible impact of alcohol and other drugs on campus life was raised in May 2010, when Yeardley Love, 22, a Lacrosse player and student at the University of Virginia in Charlottesville, was found dead in her off-campus apartment after her roommate reported that she was not responsive and may have consumed large amounts of alcohol. Another of the university's Lacrosse players, George Huguely V, was arrested and charged with murdering his former girlfriend. He was being held in jail without bond. In 2008, Huguely was arrested for public drunkenness and resisting arrest, but university officials were not aware of that fact. The University of Virginia now has a policy requiring all students to report arrests and convictions before they access university computers.[44]

Another issue regarding drug abuse is its economic cost to individuals and to society.

Economic Cost

The Office of National Drug Control Policy (ONDCP) conducted a 10-year study of the overall economic cost of drug abuse to society, estimating the yearly cost to be over $180 billion. "This value represents both the use of resources to address health and crime consequences as well as the loss of potential productivity from disability, death and withdrawal from the legitimate workforce."[45] That report was published in 2004. In 2010, the Innovators Awards program, established by the Robert Wood Johnson Foundation, headquartered at The Johns Hopkins University School of Medicine in Baltimore, Maryland, and focusing on combating substance abuse, estimated the annual cost of drug abuse at $414 billion annually. The

Chilean police officers escort Joran van der Sloot (left) to an airplane to be returned to Chile, where he was charged with the murder of Stephany Flores (right), seen visiting the Inca ruins in Cuzco. Flores was brutally murdered on 30 May 2010 in a Peruvian hotel room registered to van der Sloot, who was seen on videotape entering that room with her earlier, leaving alone, and then returning with coffee. Van der Sloot was a suspect in the 2005 disappearance of Natalie Holloway, who was vacationing in Aruba with her senior class and last seen with van der Sloot. A recognized party guy, van der Sloot was known to have problems with alcohol and drugs.

organization posted a figure of $166 billion for alcohol abuse, pointing out that employee costs of health care are twice as expensive for those who have alcohol problems as for those who do not. Additionally, 527,000 emergency room visits occur annually as the result of drug abuse. An estimated 100,000 deaths annually are the result of alcohol abuse, and one of every four deaths annually can be attributed to the excessive use of alcohol, tobacco, or illicit drugs.[46]

Another cost of drugs is that of incarcerating drug offenders. Although the exact data for this cost are not available, some figures can be considered. As later discussions show, the number of inmates in local, state, and federal correctional institutions has increased significantly in recent years. Many of the drug offenders are in federal prisons, where they accounted for over one-half of the total of all federal inmates in 2006.[47] In its December 2009 report, the BJS did not update these data but did note that the number of blacks incarcerated for drug offenses in state prisons decreased between 2000 and 2006. However, the number of whites and Hispanics incarcerated in state prisons for drug offenses increased. "Consequently, the overall number of sentenced drug offenders in state prison increased by 14,700 prisoners."[48] Data for 2009 were not available at the time of publication.

Yet another area in which drug abuse creates an impact on individuals, families, and society is in its connection with criminal activity.

Criminal Activity

One of the stated reasons for criminalizing the use of drugs is that substance abuse has been associated with criminal acts. Exhibit 10.4 presents information from the Office of National Drug Control Policy (ONDCP) on the relationship between crime and the use of drugs. This table is a summary of the types of criminal acts associated with drug abuse. Specifically, those who are arrested frequently test positive for recent illegal drug use. Those who are incarcerated state that they were frequently under the influence of drugs when they committed their offenses. Offenders often commit crimes to support their drug abuse habits. And in many cases, drugs are associated with violent crimes. Despite these associations, the ONDCP emphasized that studies of the relationship between drugs and crime should be interpreted cautiously for the following reasons:

- "Most crimes result from a variety of factors (personal, situational, cultural, economic); even when drugs are a cause, they are likely to be only one factor among many.

- What is meant by 'drug-related' varies from study to study; some studies interpret the mere presence of drugs as having causal relevance whereas other studies interpret the relationship more narrowly.
- Reports by offenders about their drug use may exaggerate or minimize the relevance of drugs; drug-use measures, such as urinalysis, [which] identifies only very recent drug use, are limited."[49]

Social scientists have conducted research on the relationship between drugs and crime. In his work published more than 20 years ago, after conducting interviews with 356 heroin users who had a long history of drug use, criminologist James A. Inciardi concluded: "The data . . . clearly demonstrate not only that most of the heroin users were committing crimes, but also that they were doing so extensively and for the purpose of drug use support." Inciardi's account of the world of drugs was based on his own street research in Miami and New York and on interviews with persons who used, dealt, or trafficked in heroin and cocaine.[50]

Inciardi studied the relationship between crack cocaine use and crime. He and a colleague emphasized that the evidence does not show that drug use *causes* crime—or enslaves drug abusers in a life of crime—because many of the abusers had already engaged in criminal activity before they turned to drugs. But

It is clear to us that drugs are driving crime. That is, although drug use does not necessarily initiate criminal careers among users it freezes users into patterns of criminality that are more intense and unremitting than they would have been without drugs.[51]

Researchers who have analyzed the works of Inciardi and others concerning the relationship between substance abuse and crime found support for most of the earlier findings and concluded, "The most plausible conclusion is that drugs and crime are related by mutual causation: crime affects drug use and drug use affects crime."[52]

Prison and Jail Overcrowding

Every aspect of criminal justice systems is affected by drug abuse and efforts to control it. Courts are crowded, creating a backlog of cases in the civil division as the courts try to process those in the criminal division. More defense lawyers, prosecutors, judges, and court staff positions are needed along with more courtrooms and other facilities. And although jail and prison population growth has slowed in recent years in some jurisdictions, many correctional facilities remain overcrowded in large part because of the number of drug offenders sentenced to serve time for, or awaiting trial for, drug abuse offenses.

According to the FBI, the area of crime with the highest arrests in 2009 was drug offenses (representing 1,603,582 of 13,687,241 arrests).[53] As noted earlier in this chapter, most drug arrests (81.6 percent in 2009) were for possession (see again Table 10.1 for details) rather than sales.

EXHIBIT 10.4

Summary of the Relationship Between Drugs and Crime

Drugs/Crime Relationship	Definition	Examples
Drug-defined offenses	Violations of laws prohibiting or regulating the possession, use, distribution, or manufacture of illegal drugs.	Drug possession or use. Marijuana cultivation. Methamphetamine production. Cocaine, heroin, or marijuana sales.
Drug-related offenses	Offenses to which a drug's pharmacologic effects contribute; offenses motivated by the user's need for money to support continued use; and offenses connected to drug distribution itself.	Violent behavior resulting from drug effects. Stealing to get money to buy drugs. Violence against rival drug dealers.
Drug-using lifestyle	A lifestyle in which the likelihood and frequency of involvement in illegal activity are increased because drug users may not participate in the legitimate economy and are exposed to situations that encourage crime.	A life orientation with an emphasis on short-term goals supported by illegal activities. Opportunities to offend resulting from contacts with offenders and illegal markets. Criminal skills learned from other offenders.

Source: Office of National Drug Control Policy, *Drug-Related Crime*, http://www.whitehousedrugpolicy.gov/publications/factsht/crime/index.html, accessed 31 October 2010.

Defendants convicted of drug offenses have been primarily responsible for the recent overcrowding of prisons, especially in the federal system, forcing some jurisdictions to consider alternatives to long, mandatory sentences for nonviolent drug offenders. This facility is in California, a state with serious overcrowding problems, which has led inmates to file lawsuits concerning their treatment.

Arrests for drug abuse violations declined by 6 percent between 2000 and 2009.[54]

The problems of prison and jail overcrowding are, in large part, due to convictions, previous arrests, and long sentences for drug abuse violations. For example, between 1997 and 2004, the number of federal and state prison inmates incarcerated for drug violations increased by 57,000, and in 2004, an estimated 333,000 inmates were in prison for drug violations. They constituted 21 percent of all state inmates and 55 percent of all federal inmates.[55] And although there has been a move recently to reduce sentence lengths for drug offenses (discussed later), the long-term effects of earlier sentencing practices on jail and prison populations must be acknowledged. In 2010, in a posting on "The Human Cost of Substance Abuse," an organization that combats substance abuse indicated that more than one-third of the increase in state prison inmate populations and 80 percent of the increase in federal populations since 1985 were the result of drug offense sentences.[56]

Michael Tonry, in his widely acclaimed book *Malign Neglect*, stated the problem as follows: "Drug-offense sanctions are the single most important cause of the trebling of the prison population in the United States since 1980."[57]

Influence on Criminal Justice System Personnel

The nation's declared war on drugs (discussed later in this chapter) presents all criminal justice system personnel with some of their most challenging problems. More than 20 years ago, it was alleged that the escalation of drug trafficking and drug abuse had resulted in corruption, violence, enormous expense, and a crushing blow to all elements of criminal justice systems. Drug offenders had created a "new underworld" within prisons, resulting in the use of drugs to corrupt correctional officers.[58]

Police also face the serious problem of fighting illegal drugs with inadequate resources while drug offenders tempt them. In 2010, San Francisco prosecutors dropped approximately 1,000 drug cases because of a scandal in the police crime lab. Evidence in other cases was sent to outside labs for testing, and prosecutors planned to file charges, where appropriate, when the lab results were returned. The San Francisco police lab was closed on 9 March 2010 after allegations that Deborah Madden, a longtime employee, had stolen cocaine evidence for personal use. Madden, a civilian, admitted using cocaine. She retired in March 2010 after 29 years in the police lab.[59]

As of 20 December 2010, Madden had not been charged with a crime. However, prosecutors had notified defense attorneys in hundreds of cases that the expert testimonies of Madden and of Ann Marie Gordon, toxicology lab supervisor, might not be accurate and could have undermined the defense of their cases. Gordon misrepresented her role with regard to tests she said she performed in a previous job. These issues should have been communicated to defense attorneys *before* their clients' trials. It was alleged that the crime lab was understaffed and unable to perform second tests when needed. For example, Tylenol PM could show up as cocaine and require a second test to disprove the first test. "One of the most notorious examples of misidentification was the 2007 arrest of Don Bolles, a punk rock musician, after a substance found inside his car tested positive for a date rape drug. The substance was later confirmed to be Dr. Bronner's Magic Soap, as Mr. Bolles had claimed, and the charges were dropped."[60]

Madden also had a previous conviction for domestic violence. This conviction was not, as required by current procedures, disclosed to defense attorneys. Some of the officials involved in the investigation, who failed to disclose this information, were demoted.[61]

As a result of these and other problems, some people are calling for changes in laws regulating drugs, especially sentencing provisions.

The Debate over Drug Laws

Statutes governing the use and sale of controlled substances, with cases interpreting those statutes, have proliferated over the years. A brief look at these laws and cases is important to an understanding of the current situation because the use of the criminal law to control substance abuse illustrates the successes and problems associated with attempting to control this behavior. We look first at efforts to control alcohol production and consumption and then at the legislation pertaining to other drugs.

The Federal Approach

Alcohol is blamed for thousands of deaths each year along with personal, property, and economic problems. Thus, alcohol creates more than individual personal problems. There have been numerous attempts to legislate alcohol use and abuse.

In 1919, the government enacted the Eighteenth Amendment (see Appendix A) to the U.S. Constitution, prohibiting the manufacture, sale, and transportation of intoxicating liquors. The Eighteenth Amendment did not prohibit drinking liquor, although it attempted to make liquor more difficult to obtain. But violations of the law were rampant, and **bootlegging** (the illegal production, use, or sale of alcoholic beverages) became widely accepted. The experiment failed and national Prohibition was repealed in 1933 (see Appendix A, Amendment 21). The result is that we can legally make, sell, and drink liquor. But the criminal law is still used to regulate driving under the influence of alcohol and the age at which consumers may legally buy and possess liquor along with other regulations.

These uses of the criminal law may be considered appropriate, but they must be distinguished from defining as criminal all manufacture and sales of alcohol (as during Prohibition) or public drunkenness. Many persons arrested for public drunkenness are poor, unemployed, and suffering from acute personal problems. Most are arrested more than once, and many spend so much time in jail that they have been described as serving a life sentence on the installment plan. Such persons are not aided by being placed in jail, and as a result of enforcing criminal laws in this area, the police are diverted from other, more important functions.[62]

The criminal law is used even more extensively to regulate the sale of other drugs. Although in the latter half of the 1800s and in the early part of the 1900s drugs could be purchased in the United States by anyone without penalty, laws were gradually passed to regulate the sale and the possession of drugs.

Although some states had enacted legislation to regulate drugs, the federal government first took action in 1914 when the U.S. Congress restricted the sale and possession of heroin, opium, and cocaine. The Harrison Act of 1914 was originally intended as a tax measure, but it was quickly perceived as restricting the sale, prescription, and use of drugs. Congress added more restrictions to the act over the years, along with enacting other statutes for controlling the use of drugs.

The War on Drugs

The modern federal war on drugs began with President Richard M. Nixon and developed more extensively during the administration of President Ronald Reagan. Legislation under the Reagan administration focused primarily on drug trafficking, especially by those associated with organized crime. In 1982, the FBI was assigned jurisdiction over drug offenses, leading Attorney General William French Smith to declare: "For the first time since its establishment over fifty years ago, the full resources of the FBI will be added to our fight against the most serious crime problem facing our nation—drug trafficking." The FBI's efforts were coordinated with those of the Drug Enforcement Administration (DEA), U.S. attorneys, other agencies in the U.S. Department of Justice (DOJ), and other federal agencies.[63]

In June 1982, President Reagan appointed a special group of government agency heads and instructed them to report back to him with suggestions on how to fight drug abuse. Four years later, he signed into law the Anti-Drug Abuse Act of 1986, which increased penalties for federal drug-related offenses and provided funding for drug prevention, education, and treatment.[64] Also that year, President Reagan issued an executive order authorizing federal agencies to establish programs for drug testing of federal employees.

As part of the war on drugs, Congress enacted the Anti-Drug Abuse Act of 1988, which directed the president to examine the extent and nature of the drug problem and to propose policies for dealing with it. The Office of National Drug Control Policy (ONDCP) was established and located in the Executive Office of the President, with the director appointed by the president and confirmed by the Senate. Exhibit 10.5 gives the purposes of the ONDCP and states the proposed budget for the Obama administration's drug control policy for 2011.

Federal law requires the president's office to publish an annual statement concerning its drug policy. On 11 May 2010, Gil Kerlikowske, director of the National Drug Control Policy, spoke about the new five-year policy of the Obama administration, outlining this five-year goal strategy:

- "Reduce the rate of youth drug use by 15 percent;
- Decrease drug use among young adults by 10 percent;
- Reduce the number of chronic drug users by 15 percent;
- Reduce the incidence of drug-induced deaths by 15 percent; and
- Reduce the prevalence of drugged driving by 10 percent."[65]

EXHIBIT 10.5

National Drug Control Policy: 2011 Budget and Strategy

"The Office of National Drug Control Policy (ONDCP or Office) is the President's primary source of support for drug policy development and program oversight. The Office advises the President on national and international drug control policies and strategies, and works to ensure the effective coordination of anti-drug control programs within the National Drug Control Program agencies.

For the period October 1, 2010 through September 30, 2011, ONDCP is requesting $401,446,000 and 99 full-time equivalents (FTE)....

ONDCP's major responsibilities include:

- Developing a *National Drug Control Strategy* (*Strategy*);
- Developing a consolidated National Drug Control Budget (*Budget*) to implement the *Strategy* and certifying whether the drug control budgets proposed by National Drug Control Program agencies are adequate to carry out the *Strategy*;
- Coordinating, overseeing and evaluating the effectiveness of Federal anti-drug policies and programs of National Drug Control Program agencies responsible for implementing the *Strategy*;
- Conducting policy analysis and research to determine the effectiveness of drug programs and policies in accomplishing the *Strategy's* goals;

- Encouraging private sector, state, local and tribal initiatives for drug prevention, treatment and law enforcement;
- Designating High Intensity Drug Trafficking Areas (HIDTA) and providing overall policy guidance and oversight for the award and management of Federal resources to HIDTAs in support of Federal, state, local and tribal law enforcement partnerships within these areas;
- Overseeing the Drug-Free Communities Program, which provides grants to community anti-drug coalitions to reduce substance abuse among our youth;
- Managing a National Youth Anti-Drug Media Campaign designed to prevent youth drug use with messages for youth and their parents and mentors; and,
- Developing and issuing the National Interdiction Command and Control Plan (NICCP) to ensure the coordination of the interdiction activities of all the National Drug Control Program agencies, and ensure consistency with the *Strategy*."

Source: Executive Office of the President; Office of National Drug Control Policy; Fiscal Year 2011, "Congressional Budget Submission," pp. 1–2, http://www.ondcp.gov/policy/Congress_budget_submission.pdf, accessed 31 October 2010.

The details of the new approach were not fully developed and published as of the publication of this text, and of course, their effectiveness could not yet be evaluated. Thus, the following discussion is based on the drug policies of previous administrations.

Analysis of the War

In recent years, the U.S. war on drugs has been severely criticized. Critics argue that the war denies to some sick people the drugs needed for treatment; they note that drugs such as marijuana and heroin help in the treatment of cancer pain, nausea due to radiation and chemotherapy, and glaucoma (an eye disease that results in the loss of vision and can cause blindness). The legalization of marijuana for medicinal purposes was discussed briefly in Chapter 1 and is discussed in more detail later in this chapter.

With regard to the war on drugs, an internationally acclaimed drug policy expert, Arnold S. Trebach, stated in 1988 that, although they victimized millions, drug policies brought little benefit to anyone. According to Trebach, "We do not now have, and never had, the capability to manage a successful war on any drug."[66]

Other social scientists have also been critical of the war on drugs. Sociologists traced what they described as the failure of the war on drugs back to the efforts of Harry Anslinger, director of the Federal Bureau of Narcotics

(FBN) from 1930 until his retirement (which, they allege, was forced) in 1962. During that period, according to sociologists, Anslinger used measures to discredit, humiliate, and harass Alfred Lindesmith, a sociologist and researcher who argued for approximately four decades that drug addicts should be treated, not punished. One of Anslinger's methods was to discredit a Canadian film, *Drug Addict*, that was developed for training police and drug counselors. The film embraced the following themes, also supported by Lindesmith:

1. that addicts and traffickers are recruited from all races and classes;
2. that high-level drug traffickers are white;
3. that law enforcement only targets low-level dealers;
4. that addiction is a sickness;
5. that addiction[s] to legal and illegal drugs are essentially the same;
6. that cocaine is not necessarily addictive; and
7. that law enforcement control of drugs is, in the final analysis, impossible.[67]

The sociologists concluded that "in hindsight [the film] appeared to be the last and best chance to create a rational and humane policy on narcotics." Anslinger and his colleagues at the FBN, however, persuaded Congress "to stiffen drug penalties and thus set the nation on a course that has led to its current failed policy."[68]

Over the years, various presidents have claimed success for their efforts to control or eradicate illegal drugs; others have ignored the issue or said very little. The George W. Bush administration claimed success in its efforts. In fact, the subtitle of one of its articles on the 2008 drug strategy proposal was "A Record of Accomplishment." This article pointed out that when President Bush took office, drug use had been increasing but was met mainly with ambivalence or resignation that nothing would work. The Bush administration set as its goal reducing drug use among youths by 10 percent in two years and 25 percent within five years. President Bush claimed success because, according to the article, drug use had decreased by 23.2 percent "just 1.8 percentage points short of the 25 percent goal."[69]

Although not all scholars or politicians would agree with the sociological analysis of the Bush administration claims, many people do oppose legalizing drugs. It is doubtful that anyone would seriously conclude that we have won the war on drugs or even that we are moving in that direction, especially with our punitive approach of mandatory and long sentences. A more careful analysis of drug sentencing laws is called for.

Sentencing Practices

Many social scientists have been critical of the legislative attempts that have involved longer and mandatory minimum sentences. "Scholarly research generally concludes that increasing the severity of penalties will have little, if any, effect on crime," a conclusion that is "applicable to offenders of drug offenses." It is alleged that:

> Observers of the criminal justice system who in general agree on little else have joined in arguing that increased penalties for drug use and distribution at best have had a modest impact on the operation of illicit drug markets, on the price and availability of illicit drugs, and on consumption of illicit drugs.[70]

Chapter 3's discussion of deterrence theory is relevant here. The approach maintains that increasing penalties for crimes is based on the assumption that long prison sentences will deter people from committing crimes. The war on drugs has been based primarily on this theory. Yet, a comparison of the recidivism of convicted felons placed on probation with those sentenced to prison found "no support for the deterrent effect of imprisonment. . . . [but rather] found compelling evidence that offenders who were sentenced to prison had higher rates of recidivism and recidivated more quickly than offenders placed on probation." Investigators concluded as follows:

> Coupled with the findings of previous research questioning the deterrent effect of punishment, our results provide persuasive evidence that it is time to

rethink the War on Crime and the War on Drugs. It seems clear that extending the crime control policies of the past decades will result in an increasingly large prison population but will not produce the predicted reduction in crime.[71]

A more recent study, published in 2010 and also conducted by criminologists, concluded that "at least among those facing drug-related charges, incarceration and supervision seem not to deter subsequent criminal behavior."[72]

Another issue that should be considered in sentencing drug offenders is whether the government's approach has a differential impact on persons of color and the poor. An analysis of National Institute of Justice publications concerning drug control led scholars to conclude that the war on drugs perpetuates the image of the poor and minorities as a "criminal class." Furthermore, "minorities and the poor are affected disproportionately by drug control campaigns, which lead to their overrepresentation in arrests, prosecutions, convictions, and incarcerations." It can be concluded that research "not only ignore[s] the scholarly literature on race, class, and drugs but also fail[s] to include research by other government agencies . . . that document such biases in drug control."[73]

Other areas of racial discrimination with regard to the drug war have been suggested. Michael Tonry, a law professor, alleged that racial disparities in drug sentencing had "steadily gotten worse since 1980." Tonry cited as one example the differential sentences Congress provided for possession of powder cocaine and crack cocaine.[74] Crack, which is less expensive, is used more by African Americans; powder is used more by whites. The sentencing differential was 100 to 1. And although the U.S. Sentencing Commission recommended changing this ratio for a decade, it was not accomplished until recently and even then to a lesser degree than some think it should. Federal sentencing policies are discussed in more detail in Chapter 13.

African Americans have argued that they are more often selected for drug prosecutions, but in 1996, in *United States v. Armstrong*, the U.S. Supreme Court ruled that a defendant who alleges racial bias regarding prosecutorial discretion must show that similarly situated persons of other races are not prosecuted. This case involved crack cocaine, and the Supreme Court held that the appellants did not show racial bias in the prosecutions of the crime.[75] In 2007, the U.S. Supreme Court revisited the issue, and that case is also discussed in Chapter 13.[76]

Changes have also been made in legislation to *increase* the penalties for some drug violations at the federal level, especially in the area of club drugs. In 2000, President Bill Clinton signed into law a bill that increased the penalties for the possession, manufacturing, and sale of GHB, making these crimes federal and providing for penalties of up to 20 years in prison. The drug was reclassified as a Schedule I drug, the most serious in the government's drug categories. Recall that Schedule I drugs cannot legally be prescribed for any reason other than research approved by the federal government.[77]

State Approaches

In addition to the federal government's efforts, states have waged their own wars on drugs. Some state antidrug laws have been upheld; others have been declared unconstitutional. In 1991, the U.S. Supreme Court held that a Michigan statute providing for a life sentence without possibility of parole for possession of more than 650 grams (about 23 ounces) of cocaine did not violate the cruel and unusual punishment clause of the Eighth Amendment to the U.S. Constitution (see Appendix A).[78]

Other state laws have also been tested in the courts. The most severe, those of New York, known as the *Rockefeller laws*, were enacted in 1973 during the administration of New York Governor Nelson Rockefeller. In 2001, attempts were made to ease the Rockefeller laws. New York Governor George E. Pataki supported those attempts and even proposed a comprehensive reform in 2002, but no changes were made. Even former U.S. drug czar General Barry R. McCaffrey called for a revision of the New York drug laws, contending that the harsh laws had done nothing to combat drug abuse but had led to the significant increase in prison populations.[79]

In 2004, an organization known as Drop the Rock (DTR) called for the revision of New York's harsh drug laws, noting that there were over 18,300 state inmates incarcerated for drug offenses, most of them minor offenders with no history of violence. Ninety-three percent of them were minorities, although there was evidence that most drug dealers and most drug users were white. Drop the Rock estimated that the state would save $245 million a year ($270 million estimated in 2010) by revising the Rockefeller laws and concluded, "After 30 years, it is long past time to remove the stain of these wasteful, unjust and racist laws from New York's penal code."[80]

In December 2004, the New York legislature passed and Governor Pataki signed a bill to revise the harsh Rockefeller drug laws. Among other provisions, the new statute reduced the minimum sentences for 446 drug offenders currently in the state's prisons, and life sentences for certain drug offenses were eliminated. Sentence ranges were reduced for certain nonviolent offenders (e.g., from 15 to 25 years to life to 8 to 20 years), and prison-based drug treatment programs were expanded. When he signed the bill, the governor stated that the released offenders would "be given another chance to lead a productive life free of drugs and crime."[81]

Other changes were made in New York's drug laws in 2005, but some argued that the changes still were not sufficient. In 2007, the state Commission on Sentencing Reform held hearings on how to revise the laws further. Some of the organizations appearing before that commission pointed out that over 14,000 people were still in New York prisons under long drug sentencing statutes. These inmates constituted 38 percent of the total prison population, and more than 90 percent were blacks and Hispanics. According to one testimony, the laws were "unfair, unjust and cruel . . . [T]hey destroy lives rather than rehabilitating them. They are enforced with blatant racial and ethnic bias."[82]

The fight continues in New York to "drop the rock," as indicated by Exhibit 10.6, which contains data published to support the efforts of the Drop the Rock organization to reduce New York's drug sentences even further. In 2009, additional changes were made in New York's Rockefeller drug laws. Among other provision, judges were given greater discretion to shorten the prison terms of some nonviolent offenders, but mandatory minimum sentences remained.[83]

Other states have reduced penalties for drug offenses; some have done so in favor of treating rather than punishing minor nonviolent drug offenders. In 2002, Michigan made significant changes in its drug law, as the following quotation from a newswire indicates:

> Public Acts 676, 666, and 670 of 2002 eliminate most of the state's Draconian mandatory minimum sentences for drug offenses. Judges can now use sentencing guidelines to impose sentences based on a range of factors in each case, rather than solely drug weight, and lifetime probation for the lowest-level offenders has been replaced with a five-year probationary period. Earlier parole is now possible for some prisoners, at the discretion of the parole board.[84]

These changes involve reducing sentences; some people are calling for legalization of some statutes regulating the sale and possession of drugs. We look first at the debate in general, then at permitting small amounts of marijuana possession, and finally, at the legalization of the sale of marijuana for medicinal purposes only.

The Legalization Debate

Many agree that some aspects of substance abuse should be included in the criminal law. The production and sale of dangerous narcotics are examples. There is not much agreement, however, on the criminalization of the possession of small amounts of drugs such as marijuana, the use of which is considered by many people to be a private matter. Others say the drug is dangerous. They may cite the evidence from New York City regarding increased violence associated with the drug, which has become rather expensive in that city. According to police, shootings related to marijuana use and sales have gone up. One area police chief stated, "Some people may think the drug is benign, but the distribution network certainly is not."[85] This view of marijuana as a dangerous drug was portrayed

EXHIBIT 10.6

What Are the Rockefeller Drug Laws?

"Enacted in 1973, the Rockefeller Drug Laws require lengthy prison terms for the possession or sale of a relatively small amount of drugs.

There are nearly 12,000 people in New York's prisons incarcerated under the drug laws, most of them minor offenders with no history of violent behavior.

It costs New York $520 million a year to imprison drug offenders.

Almost 90% of the people locked up in New York for drug offenses are African American or Latino, despite research showing that the majority of people who use and sell drugs are white.

Research shows that drug treatment is less expensive than imprisonment and more successful in reducing drug-related crime.

Repealing the Rockefeller Drug Laws would save the fiscally strapped state approximately $270 million per year.

After over 35 years, it is long past time to remove the stain of these wasteful, unjust and racially biased laws from New York's penal code.

It is time to Drop the Rock!"

Source: Drop the Rock, http://www.droptherock.org, accessed 29 June 2010.

---

by the media in a *New York Times* article featured in Media Focus 10.1.

Others argue that the prosecution of marijuana possession is not an effective use of the criminal law and should be legalized, as least for some reasons. The first is the possession of small amounts of marijuana.

Decriminalization of Marijuana Possession for Personal Use

Another use of the criminal law to control substance abuse is that of laws prohibiting growing, distributing, and prescribing marijuana for any purpose. The sale and possession of marijuana are serious offenses with long penalties in many states. According to the National Organization for the Reform of Marijuana Laws (NORML), since 1973, fifteen states and the District of Columbia have made some changes in their statutes regarding marijuana possession, with some jurisdictions decriminalizing the possession of small amounts of this drug. For example, the possession of less then one ounce of marijuana in your residence or home is not an offense in Alaska.[86]

Decriminalization of Marijuana for Medicinal Purposes

As noted in Chapter 1, in the federal system, marijuana is a Schedule I drug, meaning it cannot be prescribed by doctors for any reason. Nor can research be conducted without the federal government's permission. Yet, in California and several other states, it is legal under *state* law to use marijuana for medicinal reasons with an appropriate prescription. The drug relieves pain and other symptoms of some diseases and is tolerated by some patients who do not respond well to approved medications.

In the past, federal authorities took the position that because the prescription of marijuana for medicinal reasons violated federal law, they had jurisdiction to prosecute persons who violated state laws permitting the use. When challenged, especially during the Bush administration, the feds had some success. The U.S. Supreme Court

reversed a lower federal court in California and ruled that the necessity defense is not available to a defendant who grows marijuana for medicinal reasons. That means the defendant charged with violating the federal Controlled Substance Act by growing marijuana cannot defend that this was done because the drug was necessary for medical treatment. The U.S. Supreme Court reasoned that when Congress included marijuana as a Schedule I drug and provided no exceptions, that is exactly what Congress meant. However, federal prosecutors wanted to avoid the harsh criminal penalties of the federal statute and thus petitioned the California Supreme Court to issue an injunction prohibiting anyone from providing marijuana for medicinal reasons. The California Supreme Court did so, and that permits federal prosecutors to process through the civil rather than the criminal court anyone who allegedly grows, sells, or uses marijuana for medicinal purposes in that state.[87]

Beyond criminal charges, however, are other issues with regard to permitting the medicinal use of marijuana in some states. For example, a panel of the Ninth Circuit Court of Appeals ruled in a California case that the government could not revoke the medical licenses of physicians who prescribed marijuana for medicinal reasons. A hearing by the full court was denied, and the U.S. Supreme Court refused to review the case, thus leaving the lower court's decision standing.[88]

In 2005, the U.S. Supreme Court, in *Gonzales v. Raich*, a case involving two persons who were using marijuana (under a physician's care) to ease the pain of their illnesses, held that state laws permitting the medicinal use of marijuana do not override the federal statute prohibiting such use. According to the Court, Congress has the constitutional authority under the Commerce clause to regulate the sale of drugs even though the drugs in question were not shown to have entered interstate commerce. The case was sent back to the lower federal court, and in March 2007, a panel of that court held that although

10.1   A Media View of Marijuana and Violence

Today, many people advocate the legalization of marijuana, basing their positions on the belief that the drug is not a dangerous one. Unlike crack cocaine, the advocates proclaim, marijuana is not associated with violence. New York City police take a different view, as related in a *New York Times* article entitled "Violent Crimes Undercut Marijuana's Mellow Image." A person who reads only the title, as many probably did, could reasonably conclude that violence is associated with marijuana.

A closer reading of the article, however, leads to the conclusion that police are associating violence with the *sale* of marijuana but not its use. For example, one police official stated: "The marijuana trade in New York City is controlled and run through the use of violence." Another stated that the number of marijuana-related drive-by shootings and other killings had increased in recent years. The cited examples were of persons who made large profits from the sale of the drug. But officials acknowledged that they do not keep data on marijuana-related killings, so these pronouncements may be misleading and even inaccurate. Still, the media headline is impressive; it will convince many of its position. A closer reading, however, reveals that it is the *profit* in selling marijuana that is associated with the violence. Advocates of legalizing the sale of marijuana argue that if the drug were legal, prices would decline, decreasing the high profits from the sale of the drug—and thus reducing the violence. This position, too, is an assumption that may not be accurate.

1. "Violent Crimes Undercut Marijuana's Mellow Image," *New York Times* (19 May 2001), p. 1.

---

it sympathized with Angel McClary Raich, she had not presented uncontroverted evidence that she needed marijuana to survive; thus, she did not have legal grounds to be exempted from the federal law. Raich, 41, who had an inoperable brain tumor along with other medical problems, argued that marijuana kept her alive. Specifically, she testified that it was the only drug that relieved her pain and stimulated her appetite. The panel stated that it "recognizes the use of marijuana for medical purposes is gaining traction." However, it "has not yet reached the point where a conclusion can be drawn that the right to use medical marijuana is 'fundamental.'"[89]

Despite the legalization of marijuana for medicinal purposes in some states, courts have held that, in some circumstances, employers may terminate the employment of employees who use marijuana for medicinal reasons. In 2006, an Oregon court held that an employer may terminate the employment of an employee who refused a drug test for marijuana despite permission under state law to use the drug.[90] In 2008, the California Supreme Court upheld the right of an employer to terminate an employee for the use of marijuana for medicinal reasons.[91] And in April 2010, the Oregon Supreme Court upheld the right of an employer to terminate the employment of an

Angel Raich, who suffers from several physical problems, including a brain tumor, is held by her husband and attorney, Robert Raich. The couple fought for the right to use medical marijuana to help with pain control. Although California permits such usage, the federal government does not. In 2005, the couple lost their legal battle before the U.S. Supreme Court.

employee who used marijuana for medicinal reasons during the course of employment.[92]

The Treatment Approach

Another approach to drug abuse is to reduce or discontinue punishment and focus on treatment.

Statutory Changes in Drug Treatment

In 2000, California enacted an amendment (to become effective in 2001) to its statute covering possession of controlled substances. It provided for treatment rather than punishment for first- or second-time minor drug offenders. California's Proposition 36, also known as the Substance Abuse and Crime Prevention Act, does not apply to persons who sell or manufacture drugs, but it does apply to minor drug offenders who violate their parole. Funds provided for treatment may not be used for drug testing, and once an offender has completed his or her treatment program, the conviction is dismissed.[93]

Exhibit 10.7 contains a portion of the California statute; notice the references to drug treatment. An analysis of the results of this legislation concluded that for every $1 the state spent on treatment programs under this statute, it saved $2.50, a savings of $173 million over a 30-month period. For offenders who actually completed the treatment programs, the savings was much higher: $4 for every $1 spent.[94]

Drug Courts and Education

One area of drug treatment that is increasing across the country is drug courts, which are discussed in more detail in Chapter 13. Arrests, trials, and convictions for drug offenses, especially with the stiff penalties many jurisdictions impose on drug offenders, have increased the strain on federal and state courts as well as on jails and prisons, as already noted. The use of drug courts as a means of diversion from adult criminal courts is an effort to relieve that pressure. Drug courts are supervised by judges and involve intensive community-based treatment and supervision programs aimed at rehabilitating nonviolent drug offenders.

A 2007 study of 6,500 offenders processed through a Portland, Oregon, drug court between 1991 and 2001 compared the participants with other drug offenders not processed through drug courts. The result was lower arrests for reoffending five or more years after release and lower costs (approximately $6,744 per person). The recidivism rates did, however, vary depending on the judge's drug court experience and the program's stability.[95]

Also in 2007, a blue-ribbon commission that studied the sentencing of drug offenders in New Jersey reported that it made more sense to rehabilitate than to incarcerate offenders. The panel recommended extending the state's drug court program, which permits drug offenders to attend an inpatient rehabilitation program for six months. If the offenders are drug free for the next five years, they are not required to serve time in jail or prison. The commission emphasized that the treatment program is less than one-third the cost of prison. The commission's chair stated, "Somewhere along the way there's got to be a realization that the drug issue, for the most part, is a health issue." The commission also recommended that some of-

EXHIBIT 10.7

The California Statute for First- and Second-Time Drug Offenders

Possession of Controlled Substances; Probation; Exceptions

"[a] Notwithstanding any other provision of law, and except as provided in subdivision [b], any person convicted of a nonviolent drug possession offense shall receive probation. As a condition of probation the court shall require participation in and completion of an appropriate drug treatment program. The court shall impose appropriate drug testing as a condition of probation. The court may also impose, as a condition of probation, participation in vocational training, family counseling, literacy training and/or community service. A court may not impose incarceration as an additional condition of probation. Aside from the limitations imposed in this subdivision, the trial court is not otherwise limited in the type of probation conditions it may impose. Probation shall be imposed by suspending the imposition of sentence. No person shall be denied the opportunity to benefit from the provisions of the Substance Abuse and Crime Prevention

Act of 2000 based solely upon evidence of a co-occurring psychiatric or developmental disorder. To the greatest extent possible, any person who is convicted of, and placed on probation pursuant to this section for a nonviolent drug possession offense shall be monitored by the court through the use of a dedicated court calendar and the incorporation of a collaborative court model of oversight that includes close collaboration with treatment providers and probation, drug testing commensurate with treatment needs, and supervision of progress through review hearings.

In addition to any fine assessed under other provisions of law, the trial judge may require any person convicted of a nonviolent drug possession offense who is reasonably able to do so to contribute to the cost of his or her own placement in a drug treatment program." [The statute then specifies the types of offenders who are excluded from this statute.]

Source: Cal Pen Code, Title 8, Section 1210.1 (2010).

fenders be permitted to attend the rehabilitation program on an outpatient basis.[96]

What can society do beyond or in addition to drug courts to reduce substance abuse and drug offenses? Certainly, education is a key factor. Education programs, aimed especially at teens and preteens, encouraging them to avoid beginning the use of illegal drugs and abuse of prescription drugs are a start. Education has been part of recent federal drug policy and is utilized by some states. For example, Arizona enacted a statute under which the state provides technical and other forms of assistance to school districts that request such help. The purpose is to provide instruction on the harmful effects of alcohol and other drugs (specifically mentioning marijuana and other dangerous drugs such as date rape drugs and tobacco) on the individual user as well as on the fetus of a pregnant woman. The educational programs may be part of existing courses.[97]

Drug Testing

Drug testing is another a part of the efforts to combat drug abuse. The U.S. Supreme Court has held that under some circumstances random drug testing among public school students is not a violation of their constitutional rights.[98] But is drug testing effective in deterring the illegal use of drugs? One study compared drug use among Oregon high school athletes who were subjected to drug tests with the drug use of other high school athletes who were not subject to drug tests. The study found less drug use among the students subjected to random drug testing. But the largest study of drug use among high school students, involving 76,000 participants (see the earlier discussion of the MTF study), reported no significant difference in drug use in schools where students were subject to random drug testing and those where they were not. The researcher concluded that drug testing is "the kind of intervention that doesn't win the hearts and minds of children. I don't think it brings about any constructive changes in their attitudes about drugs or their belief in the dangers associated with using them." The National Institute on Drug Abuse responded that several more studies were needed.[99]

The U.S. Supreme Court has not ruled on whether random drug testing is constitutional for all students, not just those in athletics or extracurricular activities. But according to a medical sociologist, "Random student drug testing is expensive and inefficient. School districts across the country are in financial crisis. The millions of dollars proposed for testing could be used more wisely, having a real rather than symbolic impact on high school drug use." After an Ohio school spent $35,000 per year drug testing 1,473 students and only 11 tested positive for drugs, school officials canceled the program and used the money to hire a full-time counselor and provide prevention programs that reached all students.[100]

Closely related to the problem of substance abuse is drug trafficking.

Drug Trafficking

Billions of dollars in profits are generated annually through illegal drug sales, and the crime of **drug trafficking** results in "incalculable costs on individuals, families, communities, and governments worldwide." According to the most recent national commission, drug trafficking is the most serious problem in organized crime throughout the world. The commission emphasized that although the influence of organized crime is significant, the individual user of illegal drugs must also be a target of control; without the demand from users, there would be no illegal drug market.[101]

First, we look at drug trafficking and then at organized crime.

Drug Trafficking Dynamics

Although some illegal drugs are produced in the United States, significant quantities are smuggled into the country, which is difficult to detect for a number of reasons. The drugs may be hidden in innovative ways and brought in through many points of entry into the United States by air, sea, and land. This makes it difficult for law enforcement officers to apprehend smugglers at U.S. borders.

Some drugs are smuggled into the United States (or any other country) in small amounts, which are valuable because of the high prices they command. Drugs are also smuggled in large shipments, divided, and then sold to dealers. The purity of the drugs may be diluted. There may be several stages in the processes of receiving, distributing, and selling drugs, and the processes may cover a large geographic area, be highly organized, and involve many people.

Violence is common in drug trafficking. It is used to reduce or eliminate competition, expand markets, and intimidate anyone who interferes. That includes witnesses as well as law enforcement and other personnel. Drug informers and anyone who cheats, steals from, or lies to a drug dealer may be killed.

Another characteristic of drug traffickers is that they may attempt to corrupt public officials. Police are said to be at highest risk because of their arrest power, but corruption occurs at other levels as well. Some examples are as follows:

- Selling information about upcoming police raids, agents, and police information.
- Accepting bribes to tamper with evidence or committing perjury to protect an illegal drug dealer.
- Stealing drugs from police property rooms or laboratories for personal use or sale.
- Stealing drugs or money for personal use from sellers and users without arresting them.
- Extorting money or property from drug dealers in exchange for failure to arrest them or to seize their drugs.[102]

Although a few people make millions from illegal drug trafficking, most drug dealers are not wealthy. Many of the lower-level drug dealers are drug addicts whose habits consume their profits; these offenders may spend a lot of their time in jail or prison.

Finally, **money laundering** plays an important role in drug trafficking. *Money laundering* is a process of concealing the existence, source, and disposition of money secured from illegal sources. The term is derived from the reference criminals make to "dirty" money that is "laundered clean" so that it can be used openly and without suspicion regarding its origin. Large sums of money obtained by selling illegal drugs are channeled through legitimate sources to make it appear that the money was obtained legally. The transaction might be as simple as sending the cash to another country or as complex as taking over a bank. Large amounts of cash are difficult to handle and easily stolen. Drug trafficking money may be secured in foreign banks or invested in legitimate stocks, bonds, businesses, or other sources. More complicated money laundering schemes may involve multiple transactions and financial institutions in several countries.[103]

In some countries, drug trafficking involves *cartels* in which producers of the drugs join together to control production, distribution, and pricing to gain a monopoly. Such arrangements are generally illegal in the United States due to its antitrust laws, but they are prominent in some other countries.

Selected Drug Cartels

Three drug cartels are discussed. Two are noted for their historical position in drug trafficking, and the third for its current impact.

Two drug cartels in Colombia, South America, are thought at one time to have controlled approximately 80 percent of the cocaine traffic in the world. The cartels are named after cities.

The Medellin Cartel

The Medellin cartel started in the late 1970s and involved numerous drug lords who found it more feasible to work as a group than to work individually. They pooled their cocaine and smuggled it into other countries. The cartel became widely known in 1986 when U.S. attorneys drew up an indictment for many of the cartel members and publicized their efforts. According to a news article, "the indictment labeled the cartel the world's biggest drug-smuggling organization and charged it with producing 58 tons of cocaine between 1978 and 1985."[104]

The 1991 surrender in Bogotá, Colombia, of Pablo Escobar, one of the most wanted criminals in the world and a billionaire drug baron, meant that all the most influential leaders in the Medellin cartel were either in prison or dead. It was alleged that Escobar ordered the killing of hundreds of Colombians, whose officials hoped that his surrender would make Colombia a safer place to live. Prior to turn-

ing himself in, Escobar declared that he would surrender if his president promised that he would not face **extradition** (the process by which an accused is removed from one jurisdiction—usually a state or a country—to another for purposes of proceeding with legal actions, such as a trial) to the United States, which was holding 10 indictments against him for murder and drug trafficking. Escobar surrendered and was housed in a private, luxurious, high-security prison located in the hills with an excellent view.[105] In 1992, he and nine of his associates escaped from prison. In 1993, Escobar was killed, essentially ending the power and influence of the Medellin cartel.

Despite the waning influence of the Medellin cartel, described by the U.S. State Department as "one of the most ruthless and violent criminal organizations the world has ever known" (the cartel was alleged to have killed hundreds of police officers and about 40 judges in Colombia), one of its founders, Fabio Ochoa-Vasquez, was said to have continued to run his drug trafficking from his Colombian prison cell. Ochoa was in prison from 1991 to 1997 after surrendering to Colombian authorities in 1990. In 2001, he was extradited to the United States, where, in 2003, he was convicted of conspiracy to possess with intent to distribute cocaine and conspiracy to import cocaine into the United States. He was sentenced to 30 years and five months in prison. In 2005, the 11th Circuit upheld his conviction and sentence, and in 2006, the U.S. Supreme Court refused to hear his appeal.[106]

The Cali Cartel

The Cali cartel (or Cali Mafia) existed alongside the Medellin, and it was suggested that the two cartels divided the lucrative U.S. drug markets between themselves. After the decline of the Medellin, the Cali cartel expanded and gained more power. It was thought to have grossed $7 billion in 1994 in the United States alone and, by 1995, to be in control of 80 percent of the world's cocaine. In 1995, a federal drug enforcement agent said of the cartel, "This is probably the biggest organized-crime syndicate there has ever been. . . . For their impact, profit and control, they're bigger than the Mafia in the U.S. ever was."[107]

The Cali cartel has been distinguished from the Medellin cartel by the differences in the ways violence was used against public officials. Escobar and his colleagues engaged in the assassinations of high-level public officials. It was claimed that the Cali cartel members engaged in violence against public officials only if the officials interfered directly with the cartel's business. Another difference was in the attempt to gain publicity. One drug expert stated that unlike Medellin members, when Cali cartel members ordered a hit, they did not "leave their calling cards."[108]

In June 1995, U.S. officials unsealed a 161-page indictment charging 59 persons allegedly connected to the Cali cartel with conspiring to smuggle more than 200 tons of cocaine into the United States. The indictment alleged that from about 1983, the cartel met the **Racketeer Influenced and Corrupt Organizations (RICO)** Act's criterion to be defined as an *enterprise*. (This statute is discussed later in this chapter.) Specifically, the indictment alleged that the cartel was

> a group of individuals and entities, foreign and domestic, associated in fact for the purposes of importing and distributing cocaine, laundering the proceeds and profits of cocaine trafficking through the use of foreign and domestic corporations and financial institutions, concealing the source and true owners of the finances for the acquisition of these assets and protecting the leaders of the Enterprise from arrest and prosecution.[109]

Subsequent sections of the indictment contained specific charges of **racketeering** (an organized conspiracy to attempt or to commit extortion or coercion by use of force or threats; discussed later in this chapter), conspiracy, money laundering, obstruction of justice, murder, extortion, and other crimes. It was alleged that drugs were smuggled into the United States in frozen broccoli boxes, cement posts, and other such items and shipped to storage and distribution points throughout the country. Global Focus 10.1 illustrates one of the more recent smuggling methods.

Included among the 59 defendants were six U.S. lawyers. Their indictments raised the ire of the criminal defense bar, who claimed that the lawyers were unfairly targeted by U.S. law enforcement officials. Prosecutors argued that the indicted lawyers stepped over the line between acceptable representation of their clients and criminal activity. Four of the six attorneys entered guilty pleas; two went to trial. Their first trial ended with acquittals for the most serious charges (racketeering) and a deadlocked jury on four conspiracy charges. Subsequently, they were convicted of racketeering and money laundering conspiracy but not of drug trafficking conspiracy. Both faced life

in prison; one was sentenced to five years and the other to more than seven years.[110]

Although some DEA agents claimed to this author in 1995 that the administration had broken the back of the Cali cartel, there was evidence that the impact of this cartel continued. In July 2001, Segundo Quinones was sentenced to 30 years in prison. Quinones was the captain of a fishing trawler, the *Layneyd*, which the government seized in connection with a Tampa, Florida-based investigation called Operation Panama Express. At the time of Quinones's sentencing in July 2001, the investigation had resulted in the seizure of 80 tons of cocaine worth $1.6 billion. The *Layneyd* was carrying 4 tons of cocaine when it was seized.[111]

Said to be one of the largest drug probes in U.S. history, this operation also targeted Joaquin Mario Valencia-Trujillo, the new leader of the Cali cartel. In February 2004, the Colombian Supreme Court agreed to extradite Valencia-Trujillo to the United States for trial on drug trafficking, money laundering, operating a continuing criminal enterprise, conspiring to import and distribute cocaine, and other drug-related charges. Valencia-Trujillo, considered the most important catch of Operation Panama Express, was a multimillionaire and an influential leader in the Cali cartel. In February 2007, he was sentenced to 40 years in prison after being convicted of drug smuggling and conspiracy. Prosecutors claimed that Valencia-Trujillo, 49, smuggled more than 100 tons of cocaine into the United States each year at one point in his career. Valencia-Trujillo was also required to forfeit $110 million. Two years later, one of his lieutenants, Ivan Gongzlez-Bejarano, was sentenced to life in prison.[112]

In December 2003, two brothers who were imprisoned in 1995 for their involvement in the Cali cartel were indicted for continuing to run the cartel from their foreign

---

GLOBAL FOCUS

10.1 Methods Used for Smuggling Cocaine and Heroin into the United States

Among the many methods for smuggling drugs is by the use of *mules*, persons who swallow the drugs and smuggle them into a country within their bodies. Humans, even children, are used as mules, but the process is dangerous because the drugs can leak out of the packages and cause serious injury or death.

In 2005, law enforcement authorities in Medellin, Colombia, found 10 purebred puppies that were allegedly to be used as drug couriers. Packets of liquid heroin had been inserted into the stomachs of six puppies by means of surgery (others were allegedly awaiting surgery). Only three of the six puppies survived the surgeries. One of the puppies, a Rottweiler, was adopted by the Colombian National Police. Heroina, as she was nicknamed, assists the police in their canine unit. This playful puppy's nickname is a combination

of the Spanish words for *heroin* and *heroine*. Colombian officers adopted the two male mules as pets. The implanted heroin was worth about $2 million on the street.[1]

Also in 2006, police apprehended a drug ring in Medellin that was using elderly people as drug couriers, paying each old-age pensioner $5,000 a trip to go to Miami with drugs.[2]

---

1. "Pup Will Bite Back: Littlest Drug Mule to Work for the Narcs," *Daily News* (New York) (3 February 2006), p. 3; "Heroin Implants Turned Dogs into Drug Mules, U.S. Says," *New York Times* (2 February 2006), p. 22.
2. "World News IN BRIEF: Elderly Used as Drug Mules," *The Independent* (London) (17 March 2006), p. 28.

prison cells. Miguel Rodríguez-Orejuela and Gilberto Rodríguez-Orejuela were two of the founders of the Cali cartel. They, along with nine others, were alleged to have run the cartel through the elder son of Miguel, William Rodríguez-Abadia, who was in charge of the day-to-day operations of the cartel's illegal transactions. The two brothers were accused of "trafficking more than 55 tons of cocaine, laundering $2 billion in proceeds and silencing witnesses with money and murder."[113]

The man believed to be the third-ranking leader of the Cali cartel, Daniel Serrano Gomez, reportedly the accountant, turned himself in to authorities in Colombia in December 2003. He, too, was wanted in the United States for drug trafficking offenses.[114] Miguel Rodríguez-Orejuela and Gilberto Rodríguez-Orejuela were extradited to the United States. In November 2006, both entered guilty pleas and were sentenced to 30 years in prison and ordered to forfeit $2.1 billion of the money they made from drug trafficking.[115]

The DEA has reported more indictments and arrests. In June 2004, two indictments, representing 29 months of work in the project called the Caribbean Initiative, were unsealed, naming more than 50 drug traffickers from seven countries. The primary target of this investigation was Elias Cobos-Munoz.[116] He was extradited to the United States in April 2005 and subsequently entered a guilty plea to conspiracy to import cocaine into the United States. He was sentenced to 235 months in prison, followed by five years of supervised release.[117]

Mexican Drug Cartels

In January 2009, U.S. law enforcement officials returned 15 indictments in the Chicago, Illinois, area, alleging that the targets were affiliated with the La Familia Michoacana, a major Mexican drug cartel known for violence, including beheading its enemies. All of those named in the indictments were charged with conspiracy to distribute cocaine; some faced other drug-related charges.[118]

In October 2009, officials arrested over 300 persons in 38 cities in what they called their largest strike at Mexican cartels operating within the United States, again focusing on the La Familia cartel. Almost one-third of the arrests were in Dallas, Texas, described by authorities as "an area that drug traffickers are trying to dominate." In announcing the arrests, U.S. Attorney General Eric Holder stated, "The sheer level and depravity of violence that this cartel has exhibited far exceeds what we have, unfortunately, become accustomed to from other cartels."[119]

By 2010, the United States was spending $1.3 billion on its Merida Initiative, enacted to provide assistance to the Mexican government in its efforts to eradicate drug cartels within that country. President Obama asked Congress for another $310 million for this effort in 2011.[120] In April 2010, the leaders in several Caribbean nations asked to be included within the initiative. They stated that as Mexico cracked down on its cartels, some drug traffickers were threatening security and increasing the crime problems in the waters around their countries.[121] Mexican authorities were not highly successful in their crime control efforts. As they struggled to contain drug cartels, those arrested, convicted, and incarcerated within the country's overcrowded prisons were known to continue trafficking drugs from their prison cells. The *New York Times* printed a major article on the problem, stating, "Easy Escapes Point to Cartels' Use of Jails as a Base of Operations for Business."[122]

These recent indictments, extraditions, and convictions illustrate that some cooperation between the United States and other nations has occurred, but they also illustrate the difficulties of eliminating illegal drug trafficking.

In October 2008, Mexican authorities arrested drug cartel leader Eduardo Arellano Felix. In this photo, Felix was presented to the media after his arrest following a shootout in the violent border city of Tijuana, the birthplace of the Arellano Felix cartel. Eduardo Felix was one of the international drug traffickers most sought by the United States. With his arrest, all the Felix brothers and many of their lieutenants are either dead or in custody. It was hoped that would lead to the demise of the cartel. Mexico has been increasing the extradition to the United States of wanted suspects, but it refuses to extradite anyone who might face the death penalty.

The Control of Drug Abuse and Drug Trafficking

Throughout the previous discussions in this chapter, we have looked at the problems of drug abuse and drug trafficking. We have discussed some control efforts, one of which is legislation, examples of which are noted here. For instance, the U.S. Congress reacted to the spread of Ecstasy by proposing the Ecstasy Anti-Proliferation Act of 2000, which instructed the U.S. Sentencing Commission to draft harsher penalties for trafficking in this drug. Those new sentences became effective 1 November 2001 and increased by 300 percent (from 15 months to five years) the penalty for trafficking 800 MDMA pills. The penalty for trafficking 8,000 pills was increased by nearly 200 percent, from 41 months to 10 years.[123]

In March 2010, a Texas defendant was sentenced to 14 years in federal prison (with no chance of parole) and ordered to forfeit $2 million to the government for his role in a drug-trafficking conspiracy involving Ecstasy. He was the last of 28 defendants to be sentenced in this conspiracy.[124]

Bills introduced in the U.S. Congress in 2002 and 2003 were designed to crack down on Ecstasy and other club drugs. The Reducing Americans' Vulnerability to Ecstasy (RAVE) Act amended existing federal laws to increase the civil and criminal penalties for persons responsible for putting teenagers at risk of using Ecstasy and other club drugs by preventing the leasing, renting, or profiting from any place in which the drugs are used. That bill was signed into law by President George W. Bush in April 2003 and constitutes an amendment to the controlled substance provision of the Comprehensive Drug Abuse and Prevention Act of 1970.[125]

A second approach to controlling both individual abuse and drug trafficking has been to increase the length of prison sentences. However, long sentences for drug offenses must be considered in terms of their full impact on criminal justice systems. We have already noted that long sentences overcrowd prisons. We have looked at evidence suggesting that long sentences are not particularly effective deterrents in the war against drugs. Here we will look at some of the other side effects.

It is very costly to investigate and prosecute drug trafficking cases because of the sophisticated techniques required for intelligence gathering. Trials are long and complicated. Drug traffickers are known to intimidate or even kill witnesses. Danger to witnesses requires the government to protect some through the Witness Security Program (commonly called the Witness Protection Program). This program is sponsored by U.S. marshals and provides a new identity and a new location for persons who aid the government in dangerous, high-profile prosecutions. This is a very expensive process, and not everyone wishes to have a new identity.

But even if suspects are convicted and receive long sentences, it is not clear they will serve time in prisons rather than in plush detention facilities, as noted earlier in the case of Escobar. Nevertheless, prison sentencing remains the primary approach in the drug control strategy. In fact, several sections of the Violent Crime Control and Law Enforcement Act of 1994 involve enhanced penalties for drug offenses, including drug trafficking in prisons.[126]

As we conclude these sections on drug abuse and drug trafficking, it is pertinent to note that in March 2001 the government released a report based on a study by 15 economists, criminologists, and psychiatrists assembled by the National Research Council (an arm of the National Academy of Sciences) during the Clinton administration. The report took no position on the controversial issue of whether we should focus on punishment or treatment of drug offenders. However, it did conclude that the data and research available on what works in reducing the demand and supply of drugs are so poor that no reasonable assessments can be made. The report concluded that "even what might seem the simplest measures of success in the battle against illegal drugs are unreliable."[127]

Organized Crime

For a long time, the crimes of the underworld have been a source of mystery and excitement. They have captured our attention through fictional works such as *The Godfather*, a novel published in 1969 and subsequently made into a movie, both of which have enjoyed immense success.

The ability of underworld criminals to elude law enforcement is well known; in many cases, underworld activities have provided services and commodities that, although labeled illegal by statute, are considered sources of pleasure in our daily lives. In these cases, unsuccessful law enforcement may not be viewed as a problem; indeed, attempts to enforce the law may be regarded as a nuisance. **Organized crime** has infiltrated legitimate businesses in many cases to the extent that the relationship between organized crime and legitimate society is one of cooperation.

The cost of organized crime to society is impossible to determine. It goes beyond the loss of property and life and includes the high cost of attempts to control and eradicate it.

The Concept of Organized Crime

The first problem in an analysis of organized crime is to define the concept. There is little agreement on the definition. In some countries, the term *organized crime* is synonymous with *professional crime*. It is true that all professional crime is to some extent organized. Early sociologists used the term *organized crime* to describe professional criminals in contrast to amateur criminals.

According to sociologist Alfred Lindesmith, organized crime is "usually professional crime . . . involving a system of specifically defined relationships with mutual obligations and privileges." Edwin H. Sutherland and Donald R. Cressey defined *organized crime* as the "association of a small group of criminals for the execution of a certain type of crime."[128] These definitions include any small group of criminals who organize to engage in their professional work.

In recent years, the term *organized crime* has been used more narrowly. Many people think of organized crime as a national or international **syndicate** that infiltrates businesses at the local, national, and international levels. This view is not accepted by most social scientists; thus, it is important to distinguish between the two major approaches to defining organized crime: (1) the law enforcement perspective and (2) the social and economic perspective.

The most common view of organized crime is the *law enforcement perspective*. In its 1967 report, the President's Commission on Law Enforcement and Administration of Justice defined *organized crime* as "a society that seeks to operate outside the control of the American people and their working government." According to that report, organized crime involves thousands of criminals. They operate in a complex organizational structure, and they have rules that are more rigid and more strictly enforced than those of legitimate government. Money and power are their goals. They infiltrate legitimate as well as illegitimate businesses.[129]

A second approach views organized crime as "an integral part of the nation's social, political, and economic life—as one of the major social ills, such as poverty or racism, that grew with urban living in America." Organized crime does involve minority groups, but that involvement is seen by this second perspective as the *process* by which those groups begin to establish themselves and gain power in society. As more acceptable avenues for this process become available, the criminals may move into legitimate enterprises while other groups move into organized crime to begin the process of integration into the society.[130]

Another version of this functional perspective comes from economists, who view organized crime as just another economic enterprise. Organized crime supplies goods and services to customers seeking them. Even when the supply is considered illegal by the government at a given time—for example, liquor during Prohibition—the economic process is the same as it would be if the enterprise were not defined as criminal. In organized crime, however, the *proceeds* from these illegal sales are used to engage in other illegal activities, such as corrupting public officials to gain protection from prosecution or bribing jurors to avoid conviction.[131]

These two approaches to the concept of organized crime have some common elements. In both perspectives, the activity is organized and goes on beyond the life of any one particular member. Both perspectives see the need for and the existence of some degree of protection, which is obtained by corrupting public officials. Both perspectives view organized crime as a way of providing illegal goods and services demanded by the public. These similarities have led to the following definition of *organized crime*:

> a persisting form of criminal activity that brings together a client-public which demands a range of goods and services defined as illegal. It is a structure or network of individuals who produce or supply those goods and services, use the capital to expand into other legitimate or illegitimate activities, and corrupt public officials with the aim of gaining their protection.[132]

The National White Collar Crime Center has a shorter definition, similar to the preceding one, but it adds these dimensions: "Its [organized crime's] continuing existence is maintained through the use of force, threats, monopoly control, and/or the corruption of public officials."[133]

Despite these attempts to articulate a definition of organized crime that is broad enough to include the two perspectives, the view persists of organized crime as roughly synonymous with the national (or international) crime syndicate characterized by Italian membership. This perspective has obvious implications in terms of attempts to eradicate or control organized crime. It leads to a focus on catching the notorious underworld criminals rather than on making changes in the social system. The lack of a generally accepted definition of organized crime also results in a variety of definitions throughout the states.[134]

The History and Organization of Organized Crime

Many scholars believe that organized crime was not pervasive before the twentieth century and that its development as a large-scale operation was a result of Prohibition, discussed earlier in this chapter. They trace the history of organized crime to the Volstead Act, the Eighteenth Amendment, passed in 1919, which made it illegal to sell and distribute alcohol. The "Great Experiment," as some called Prohibition, "provided a catalyst of opportunity that caused organized crime, especially violent forms, to blossom into an important force in American society."[135] Our puritanical approach to the suppression of vice, of which Prohibition was an example, provides a fertile bed for the growth of organized crime. It can provide the services consumers want but are forbidden by law to obtain.

A study of the history of organized crime must include brief mention of the reports of four major official studies. The Committee to Investigate Crime in Interstate Commerce (named the Kefauver Committee, after Estes Kefauver, its chair) found widespread involvement of organized crime in gambling and other forms of racketeering.[136] The Select Committee on Improper Activities in the Labor or

Management Field (the McClellan Committee) reported numerous incidents of organized criminal activity among labor unions.[137] The 1967 President's Commission on Law Enforcement and Administration of Justice (or simply, the President's Commission) found that in American cities, organized crime was widespread, dominating activities such as gambling, narcotics traffic, and **loan sharking**. In addition, organized criminals had invested some of their money in legitimate businesses in which they had some indirect control.[138] The National Advisory Committee on Criminal Justice Standards and Goals, which issued its report on organized crime in 1976, concluded that organized crime had infiltrated legitimate as well as illegitimate businesses and was spreading rapidly.[139]

In July 1983, President Ronald Reagan expressed his concern for the need to combat organized crime in the United States by naming a 20-person organized crime commission. That commission was headed by Judge Irving R. Kaufman of the U.S. Court of Appeals for the Second Circuit. It issued an interim report in 1984 and a final report on labor and management racketeering in 1986. The work of the commission was not without controversy from outside, but even the members disagreed among themselves on the final report. Nine of them questioned the methods used for reaching conclusions and accused the commission of mismanaging time, staff, and money.[140]

The 1967 President's Commission described organized crime as a highly organized structure with the lords of the underworld at the top. These persons made all the important decisions, and since few were detected, not much was known about their career patterns. At the bottom were those who dealt directly with the public and resembled conventional offenders in their career patterns.[141]

Organized crime is directed by a syndicate, a group of persons who organize to carry out their mutual financial interests. There is disagreement about whether there is one syndicate or several syndicates in charge of all organized crime in the United States. Some, such as the Kefauver Committee, contended that there was one syndicate, the **Mafia**, operating out of New York and Chicago and run by Italians from Sicily.[142] Others denied the existence of the Mafia.[143] The word *Mafia* refers to a secret, highly organized, hierarchical group involved in racketeering, smuggling, drug trafficking, and other illegal criminal activities. The term is used to encompass other organized crime syndicates, as will be seen below.

According to the 1967 President's Commission, organized crime was controlled by 24 groups known as *families*. The size of a family ranged from 20 to 700 members. The families operated as criminal cartels in large American cities; most cities had only one family, although New York City had several. Each family was headed by a *boss*, who had complete authority over the family and could be overruled only by the national advisory commission. Reporting to the boss was the *underboss*, who, like the vice

president of a company, acted in the absence of the boss and served as a mediator between the boss and lower-level management. The *consigliere*, or counselor, held a position analogous to that of a legal adviser in a corporation. The lieutenants, or *caporigima*, were the intermediaries, or middlemen, in the management structure. They served as buffers between the boss or underboss and internal or external conflicts. The lower-level management comprised soldiers who "operate[d] the illegal enterprises on a commission basis or own[ed] illicit or licit businesses under the protection of the family."[144]

Many social scientists disagree with this bureaucratic analogy, which they say is too rigid to explain the social, economic, and political dynamics of the organized crime family. They describe the family in *kinship terms*, maintaining that organized crime families are called *families* because many are tied by marriage or blood and because they exhibit some of the complex ties characteristic of families.[145] Others analyze organized crime in terms of an economic system and as an organization of power relationships.[146]

The 1967 President's Commission concluded that the organized crime families were in frequent communication and that their membership was exclusively Italian. The name of the organization had been changed from the Mafia to *La Cosa Nostra* (LCN), which means "our thing." The 24 groups controlled other groups that often had members from diverse ethnic backgrounds. The ultimate authority in the organization was the *commission*, which served primarily as a judicial body. It was made up of 9 to 12 men, not all of equal rank and power. The respect they commanded and the power they wielded appeared to be related to their own wealth, their tenure on the commission, and their positions as heads of large families or groups.[147]

In its 1986 report, a subsequent presidential commission did not precisely define the terms *Mafia* and *La Cosa Nostra* and insisted that, although the report centered on LCN, organized crime was broader than that. However, LCN was the "group most entrenched in labor and business," infiltrating legitimate business more frequently than any other organized crime group.[148]

Despite the focus on the Mafia and LCN, it is important to emphasize that organized crime is much broader today than ever before, extending to other countries as well.

Organized Crime and Legitimate Business

Organized crime infiltrates many illegitimate businesses, such as prostitution, pornography, gambling, and illegal drug trafficking. It is important to understand, however, that all these (and other) crimes are also committed without any involvement with organized crime. But organized crime also controls legitimate businesses. In 1972, a federal court in Michigan underscored the involvement of organized crime in legitimate businesses. An excerpt from that case follows.[149]

United States v. Aquino

The Congress finds that (1) organized crime in the United States is a highly sophisticated, diversified, and widespread activity that annually drains billions of dollars from America's economy by unlawful conduct and the illegal use of force, fraud, and corruption; (2) organized crime derives a major portion of its power through money obtained from such illegal endeavors as syndicated gambling, loan-sharking, the theft and fencing of property, the importation and distribution of narcotics and other dangerous drugs, and other forms of social exploitation; (3) this money and power are increasingly used to infiltrate and corrupt legitimate business and labor unions and to subvert and corrupt our democratic processes; (4) organized crime activities in the United States weaken the stability of the Nation's economic system, harm innocent investors, interfere with free competition, seriously burden interstate and foreign commerce, threaten the domestic security, and undermine the general welfare of the Nation and its citizens.

The following sections give an overview of the infiltration of organized crime into the health care, food, construction, and cartage industries.

The Health Care Industry

Chapter 9 contained information about fraud in the health care industry, noting that this type of fraud costs billions of dollars annually. In his testimony before a Senate committee in March 1995, FBI Director Louis J. Freeh stated that organized crime had "penetrated virtually every legitimate segment of the health care industry." Freeh alleged that doctors, chiropractors, and attorneys had been corrupted by organized crime and that the list of schemes was extensive.[150]

In 1999, the U.S. General Accounting Office (GAO) issued a report on the infiltration of organized crime into the health care industry. It concluded that organized crime was "carving out a role in Medicare, Medicaid, and private insurance health care fraud throughout the country." The GAO identified several fraud schemes, such as using patient brokering, in which "runners" are paid to recruit "patients" to go to health clinics for medical care they do not need. In some cases, these "patients" are paid a portion of the "runner's" fee. The results of this and other types of schemes are increasing medical costs as well as the risk that medical benefits will be exhausted for some individuals whose names are used in the schemes.[151]

The Food Industry

The federal government's most recent commission reported that New York is a unique market for organized crime not only because of the "myriad of goods and services it offers" but also because one-half of the members of LCN are in that state. Organized crime has gained control over a significant portion of the meat industry, a large industry in New York and in the country. Ten percent of consumer spending on beef in this country each year comes from the five New York City boroughs; it is assumed that figures are comparable for the poultry industry. Whereas meat and poultry production and distribution had been conducted at local levels, today the industry is vast, complex, and particularly susceptible to infiltration by organized crime. Its members have several advantages over lawfully operated businesses: lower wages, cash from other operations to subsidize their businesses, and a willingness "to use threats or violence to advance their business interests."[152]

Organized crime continues to maintain a strong hold over the food industry in New York City and to use its captive labor unions and reputation for violence to "extort, bribe, cartelize, and otherwise pervert the free market." However, some progress has been made. In 1995, local officials recommended that the city take over the Fulton Fish Market, the largest wholesale seafood distribution center in the country and a company with a history of problems associated with organized crime. Mayor Rudolph Giuliani, who as a prosecutor vowed that the "mob will be crushed," achieved some success in his efforts. By 1996, it was thought that organized crime's control over the Fulton Fish Market had been cut. Giuliani announced regulations that permitted the city, which owned at least part of the wholesale meat and produce markets, to conduct background checks on all persons who worked in those industries, take fingerprints, check criminal records, and maintain files on all workers.[153]

By 1997, it was alleged that the mayor's policies had resulted in lowered costs of fish and garbage removal (discussed later) and had "sent a signal that businesses and consumers no longer have to accept the mob as a fact of life."[154] In 2005, when the Fulton Fish Market was moved to the Bronx, it was thought that organized crime had lost its stronghold over the market, but the city kept a watch on it.[155]

Another example of the infiltration of organized crime into the food industry involved related areas (cosmetics and other items from retailers). Local, state, and federal law enforcement authorities joined in a two-year investigation and found evidence that millions of dollars worth of merchandise had been stolen for resale in Dayton, Ohio. In January 2004, authorities arrested most of those named in a 20-person indictment involving organized crime. The stolen articles were sent to warehouses to be remarked, and some were given extended expiration dates. WalMart, Target, and Kroger unknowingly bought back some of their own merchandise. In addition to the property losses this organized crime ring caused were the health dangers. For example, baby food was kept at very high temperatures during the exchanges, thus likely causing it to spoil. The suspects were charged with conspiracy to transport stolen goods across state lines, conspiracy to sell and receive stolen property that had crossed state lines, and possession and unauthorized use of food stamp benefit cards. In March 2004, a grand jury indicted the alleged mastermind of this theft/conspiracy ring, Amjad Salem, 39, and others and added to the charges those of money laundering and money laundering conspiracy. In 2006, Salem was convicted and sentenced to 132 months in prison and ordered to pay $2,669,848.80 in restitution.[156]

Indictments of crimes committed in the food industry are not always associated with organized crime, although the charges may sound as if they were. In 2010, a federal grand jury indicted Frederick Scott Salyer (the former owner of SK Foods) on charges of quashing competition and selling tomato products at inflated prices. Salyer was indicted on racketeering charges along with conspiracy, obstruction of justice, and wire fraud.[157]

The Construction Industry

At the time of its study, the latest presidential commission on organized crime estimated that the construction industry accounted for approximately 8 percent of the annual gross national product and that organized crime added about 20 percent to construction costs. The commission found a substantial infiltration of organized crime in the construction industry in New York City but stated that government responses to the situation had "generally been sporadic and inconsistent. Recent developments had shown more promise," but organized crime has the capability of avoiding and eliminating competition readily.[158]

In 2004, a member of New Jersey's Casino Control Commission wrote an 80-page opinion. He alleged that organized crime was so widespread in the construction industry of that state that incidental contacts between legitimate business persons "with disreputable characters within the confines of their industry may have been unavoidable and, to some extent, even inevitable." Because of the possibility of innocent involvements with organized crime, the judge recommended that Interstate Industrial Corporation be permitted to continue working in Atlantic City, New Jersey, even though it was alleged to have had contacts with organized crime and, as a result, was barred from work in New York City.[159]

In January 2007, Laborers' Local 394 in Elizabeth, New Jersey, was placed under trusteeship after a hearing judge declared that it retained ties to organized crime. The construction company owners had once boasted that not a nail was driven in New Jersey unless they got a piece of it.[160]

Organized corruption in the construction industry has been targeted in neighboring countries as well. In November 2009, Toronto, Canada, police arrested 10 people allegedly tied to a money-laundering scheme headed by the Hells Angels biker gang. The investigation began in

Organized crime has infiltrated many otherwise legitimate businesses, such as construction, escalating prices for all concerned. It is estimated that the construction business accounts for approximately 8 percent of the total U.S. gross national product.

2007, and with the arrests in 2009, police seized houses, cars, and money.[161]

The Garbage Carting Industry

Under the leadership of Mayor Rudolph Giuliani, New York City prosecutors charged 23 companies, four trade associations, and 17 individuals with using violence and intimidation to control the city's garbage collection. Garbage carting in that city was controlled almost entirely by these companies, which were in the hands of the Gambino and Genovese crime families. Prosecutors alleged that garbage carting had been controlled by organized crime in New York City for more than 50 years. The inflated prices as a result of the infiltration of organized crime were illustrated by the cost for carting at one building: $10,000 under the terms of a contract won by a new group compared with $100,000 charged by the organized crime-controlled industry.[162] New Yorkers were paying the highest garbage collection rates in the country, twice those of Chicago and three times those of Los Angeles.[163]

In October 1997, the courts convicted two men alleged to be the most influential Mafia members behind the hold of organized crime over the carting industry. Joseph Francolino Sr. and Alphonse Malangone were found guilty of the most serious charges, those dealing with the state's organized crime control statute. Fourteen of their associates had already pleaded guilty in the five-year investigation. The indictment "estimated that the group had inflated costs for 200,000 customers in the city by as much as $400 million a year." The sentences for these defendants included prison terms up to 30 years and fines totaling $32 million.[164]

Mayor Giuliani convinced New York's city council to permit the application of background checks (similar to those applied in the food industry) in the garbage carting industry. The mayor believed that prosecution of organized crime members would not be sufficient to break the hold they had on the city's legitimate industries. "Too often, when top crime figures were indicted or convicted, they were simply replaced by others who kept the corruption going." The city's refusal to grant permits to those with any connections to organized criminals was thought to result in greater access to competitive bids (in contrast to the monopoly held by organized crime for years). This lowered costs to the industry and eventually to consumers.[165]

A book by Rick Cowan and Douglas Century, reviewed by attorney Robert Knightly, claimed that the garbage collection industry cartel in New York City was broken in 1996 by a detective who, while wired, infiltrated the industry for three years. It was said that organized crime controlled the garbage carting industry from the mid-1950s until 1996. A 1995 indictment contained 114 charges against 17 persons and their four trade associations. The trial began in May 1997 and lasted eight months. The investigating detective, Rick Cowan, was on the stand all summer. By the end of the trial, all defendants except two had entered guilty pleas; after 12 days of deliberation, the jury convicted those two, who were sentenced to prison.[166]

The Control of Organized Crime

These examples, especially those in the garbage carting industry, illustrate that organized crime is difficult to eliminate or control despite the limited success in New York City. Persons involved in organized crime receive significant support from the criminal groups with which they associate. Often, the efforts of these specialized groups focus on gaining a monopoly over a particular kind of criminal activity, such as prostitution. They operate through threats, intimidation, bribery, and violence, and they are often successful.

Organized crime figures clearly enjoy the support of their colleagues. Few top officers are ever apprehended,

but when they are, the higher-ups "fix" the situation and get them released. Organized crime figures also find protection from outsiders, in some cases including the police, attorneys, and judges. For example, in 1998, Jose Grana Sr. entered a guilty plea in federal court to the charge of conspiring to participate in the affairs of the police department through a pattern of racketeering. He admitted that he bribed West New York, New Jersey, police officers to protect his multimillion-dollar gambling business. Several others, including Grana's son, were also charged in a case alleged to involve the police department's acceptance of over $600,000 to protect businesses in prostitution, gambling, and illicit liquor sales. Grana was fined $30,000 and sentenced to 62 months in prison. His son was fined $25,000 and sentenced to 60 months in prison. Alexander V. Oriente, the former police chief of West New York, was sentenced to four years in prison and fined $50,000. The court found that Oriente "had personally presided over a corrupt operation that resulted in $2.5 million to $5 million in bribes and kickbacks from gamblers and pimps."[167]

In many cases, organized crime members may gain **immunity (criminal)** from prosecution through their political control in a locality. Furthermore, to some extent, the public is tolerant of the activities of organized crime because of public demand for the goods and services provided. Organized criminals evade the law by infiltrating legitimate businesses, which cannot complain to law enforcement authorities because of their own involvement. Finally, the statutes available for prosecuting organized crime have not always been effective.

Statutory Measures

Legal efforts to control organized crime include several statutes. Robbery; extortion by force, threat, or fear; and extortion under color of law are criminalized by the Hobbs Act, which traces its history to the Anti-Racketeering Act of 1934.[168] The Hobbs Act and other federal statutes were used to prosecute individual crimes, but additional and more powerful tools were needed.

Congress enacted the Organized Crime Control Act of 1970, which has been amended in subsequent years. The stated purpose of this act is

> to seek the eradication of organized crime in the United States by strengthening the legal tools in the evidence-gathering process, by establishing new penal prohibitions, and by providing enhanced sanctions and new remedies to deal with unlawful activities of those engaged in organized crime.[169]

Part of the 1970 legislation was the Racketeer Influenced and Corrupt Organizations (RICO) statute, which has been called the *new darling* of the prosecutor's tools, replacing conspiracy. This designation refers to the fact that RICO is a very broad statute. Although it was designed to prosecute organized crime, it is broad enough to encompass many white-collar crimes. The RICO statute does not create specific *individual* statutes for crimes, such as robbery or extortion, but refers to *patterns* of offenses. Specifically, RICO prohibits the following:

1. The use of income derived from a *pattern of racketeering* to acquire an interest in an enterprise
2. Acquiring or maintaining an interest in an enterprise through a pattern of racketeering activity
3. Conducting or participating in an enterprise's affairs through a pattern of racketeering activity
4. Conspiring to commit any of these offenses[170]

Racketeering refers to the process of engaging in a racket such as extortion or conspiracy for the purpose of obtaining an illegal goal by means of threats. The discussion of the garbage carting industry in New York City earlier in this chapter illustrates the concept: placing persons in fear through threats if they compete in the industry. Those who engage in racketeering may demand money (or something else of value) under threat of violence in return for protection from law enforcement officials, or any other of a number of activities, and so ruin the victim's business by, for example, driving up prices.

The RICO statute contains numerous other provisions. To illustrate, since its major purpose is to eradicate organized crime in the United States, one section of RICO strengthens the legal tools for gathering evidence and adds new remedies, including higher damage awards. To aid the prosecution in gathering information, RICO gives the witness immunity in return for testifying in court or before Congress.

The RICO statute illustrates the difficulty of separating organized crime from white-collar crime, even for purposes of analysis. It is a very broad and flexible statute used for prosecutions against businesspeople; medical, legal, and other professionals; labor union leaders; government officials; and others charged with a variety of white-collar crimes. The statute expands federal law enforcement powers significantly.

The federal RICO statute lists the crimes that may form the basis of a RICO offense. These 24 federal and 8 state crimes are called *predicate* crimes because they establish a basis for a RICO violation. Although each predicate crime may constitute racketeering, RICO requires a *pattern* of racketeering activity, which includes at least two predicate crimes within a 10-year period.[171]

The RICO statute specifies that an enterprise involves "any individual, partnership, corporation, association or other legal entity, and any union or group of individuals associated in fact although not a legal entity." It includes legal enterprises, but the enterprise, according to the U.S. Supreme Court, must have an ongoing formal or informal organization whose associates function as a continuing unit.[172]

Congress intended RICO as a statute to embrace serious cases—those involving major violators who engage in a pattern of racketeering activity. Many states also have RICO-type statutes.

The RICO statute is an effective prosecutorial tool because of its breadth of coverage and the fact that it provides both criminal and civil causes of action. In addition, the statute provides stiff penalties, including jail and prison terms as well as treble damages and attorney fees for civil violations. But perhaps its most damaging and controversial element is the provision for forfeiture of "any interest . . . acquired or maintained" in violation of the statute. The statute gives the government broad powers "to preserve the availability of the property subject to forfeiture."[173]

The forfeiture provision in particular has raised legal issues. Generally, forfeiture involves civil proceedings, which have a lower burden of proof than criminal proceedings. Under current provisions, the government may seize the property of a drug trafficking suspect even if that person has been acquitted of criminal charges. Prosecutors have done both: brought criminal charges and seized property. Some lower courts have held that the dual actions violate the constitutional rights of the accused not to be tried twice for the same offense (see Appendix A, Fifth Amendment, concerning double jeopardy) and that prosecutors must choose civil forfeiture or criminal proceedings, not both. The U.S. Supreme Court has held that civil forfeiture proceedings do not constitute punishment and thus do not violate the double jeopardy provision if coupled with criminal proceedings. In *Bennis v. Michigan*, the Supreme Court held that the Fourteenth Amendment's due process clause (see Appendix A) does not prohibit forfeiture proceedings against an innocent owner who was not aware that the property would be used in a crime. *Bennis* involved a petitioner who was co-owner of a car in which her husband forfeited her interest as well as his when he used their car for engaging in sex with a prostitute. Finally, courts have imposed sanctions on attorneys who use RICO improperly—for example, by filing frivolous lawsuits.[174]

In 1998, the U.S. Supreme Court put the brakes on the amount that may be forfeited when persons are arrested. In *United States v. Bajakajian*, a sharply divided Court (voting 5–4) held that a forfeiture intended as punishment is unconstitutional if the amount is "grossly disproportional" to the offense. Specifically, the Supreme Court held that it was disproportional to seize $357,144 in undeclared cash that a Los Angeles man and his family attempted to take in their suitcases on a flight to Cyprus. According to the Court, the only crime the suspect committed was failure to report carrying over $10,000 of currency when leaving the United States for another country.[175]

Statutory measures are also available to control money laundering. Until 1986, money laundering per se was not a crime. Prior to that time, any illegal activities connected with money laundering were prosecuted under the Bank

Secrecy Act of 1970, which requires banks to report any domestic transaction of more than $10,000.[176]

The Money Laundering Control Act of 1986 makes money laundering per se illegal and encompasses new offenses related to money laundering and violations of currency transactions.[177] Some provisions of the Anti-Drug Abuse Act of 1986 are also useful in prosecutions of money laundering activities.[178]

The Money Laundering Prosecution Improvement Act of 1988 includes provisions that enable financial institutions to require additional information from those who purchase checks, traveler's checks, or money orders in amounts of $3,000 or more. In addition, this legislation authorizes the treasury secretary to target some types of institutions or geographic areas for further reporting requirements.[179] The Suspicious Activity Reporting (SAR) Act of 1996 requires banks to report persons who deposit more than $5,000 if the bankers suspect those funds came from an illegal source. But the provisions are sufficiently vague that bankers might overlook illegal transactions and risk being fined or report legal ones and risk losing customers.[180]

Since the 9/11 terrorist attacks in the United States, money laundering statutes have been strengthened. Recall our earlier discussions of the USA Patriot Act. Among other provisions, this act tightens the Bank Secrecy Act and money laundering statutes and requires banks to develop new programs and guidelines for knowing their customers well. It imposes significant new anti-money laundering requirements, especially on money that may have been used to finance terrorist acts against the United States. The U.S. Treasury Department has the authority to interpret the USA Patriot Act, and those interpretations are broad. The act applies to "all financial institutions," and that may include many programs and fund managers not previously covered by anti-money laundering statutes. The act requires bankers and other professionals to monitor money that may be laundered and used for terrorist acts. Private bankers in south Florida complained that, in effect, the government was using private resources to do its own policing. "In South Florida, where many financial institutions do business with foreign governments and foreign nationals, community banks are spending top dollar to train employees, buy new software and develop new policies to comply with the new law." The president and chief executive officer of one south Florida bank complained that the legislation was requiring bankers to rework their policies and described the act as "an emotional piece of legislation in response to 9/11." Some bankers complained that the requirements would do little more than reduce the profits of banks.[181]

Many states also have money laundering statutes. The Texas statute is an example:

> (a) A person commits an offense [of money laundering] if the person knowingly;
>> (1) acquires or maintains an interest in, receives, conceals, possesses, transfers, or transports the proceeds of criminal activity;

>> (2) conducts, supervises, or facilitates a transaction involving the proceeds of criminal activity; or
>> (3) invests, expends, or receives, or offers to invest, expend, or receive, the proceeds of criminal activity or funds that the person believes are the proceeds of criminal activity.
>> (4) finances or invests or intends to finance or invest funds that the person believes to further the commission of criminal activity.

Under that statute, it is not required that the accused have knowledge "of the specific nature of the criminal activity giving rise to the proceeds."[182]

Prosecutions and Trials

Several examples illustrate the government's failures and successes in prosecuting organized crime figures. We begin with some of the most recent cases, several of which are not yet completed.

In March 2010, federal prosecutors announced the return of indictments against eight defendants: Theodore Persico Jr., Michael Persico, Thomas Petrizzo, Edward Garofalo Jr., James Bombino, Louis Romeo, Alicia Dimichelle, and Mike Lnu. Some of those named are affiliated with organized crime families. The charges include racketeering conspiracy, wire fraud conspiracy, extortion, and embezzlement—for example, from welfare benefit and pension plans. The primary targeted organized crime family is the Colombo family.[183]

The Colombo organized crime family was the focus of an indictment in Boston in December 2009, when three Massachusetts men and one from Arkansas were charged with racketeering conspiracy. Ralph F. Deleo, Franklin M. Goldman, Edmond Kulesza, and George Wylie Thompson were charged with conspiracy to violate RICO. According to officials, the crimes with which these persons are charged "pose a threat to American society."[184]

In October 2009, indictments were returned against 29 persons, including six building inspectors of the New York City Buildings Department (which has a history of corruption scandals). The suspects were accused of granting permits in exchange for bribes, along with other crimes, such as extortion. Members of the Luchese crime family were targeted in these indictments.[185]

Also in October 2009, members and associates of the Bonanno organized crime family of La Cosa Nostra were indicted on 33 counts of the following crimes:

- racketeering
- racketeering conspiracy
- assault in-aid-of racketeering
- conspiracy to commit assault in-aid-of racketeering
- threatening to commit a crime of violence in-aid-of racketeering
- use and possession of a firearm in relation to a crime of violence
- bank fraud

- illegal gambling
- extortion conspiracy
- obstruction of justice
- perjury[186]

Federal officials have had some success in trials. In May 2004, the trial of Joseph Massino, 61, began with the prosecutors stating that this trial "is about the vicious, violent, cunning and murderous rise to power of Joseph Massino." Massino, the reputed head of the Bonanno crime family, was alleged to have killed other mob members. In his opening statement, Massino's lawyer argued that mob members were pressured into making those allegations. In addition, the same torture methods reportedly used in Iraq were also used at the Metropolitan Detention Center in New York City, which housed the informants who were to testify against his client.[187]

One of the witnesses who testified against Massino was his brother-in-law, Salvatore Vitale, who said that he personally participated in many murders ordered by Massino. In 2004, Massino was convicted of murder, racketeering, arson, money laundering, loan sharking, gambling, and extortion. He faced a mandatory life sentence for these convictions, but sentencing was withheld pending Massino's testimony against other alleged mob members. He began testifying in February 2005, apparently leading several key mob figures to plead guilty to murder and other crimes. Thus, they avoided trials that, if they led to convictions, would have resulted in the defendants' families losing their financial assets. Massino could have received the death penalty for a murder committed in 1999. But after he admitted his role in eight murders, he told the feds where the bodies were located. His wife turned over $7.6 million in cash and $267,000 in gold that he received in his illegal activities. Therefore, the government offered Massino a plea deal: two life terms, thus sparing him the death sentence.[188]

In April 2004, the Gambino family boss, Peter Gotti, 64, a retired garbage man and brother of the late John J. Gotti (discussed later in this chapter), was sentenced to nine years and four months in prison for racketeering and money laundering. Upon completion of that sentence, he is to begin serving 25 years in prison for participating in an unsuccessful plot to murder Sammy Gravano, who testified against mob members. In 2007, a federal court affirmed that decision.[189]

In 1988, Anthony "Fat Tony" Salerno, the alleged boss of the Genovese crime family, along with eight other defendants, was convicted of racketeering. Salerno died in prison in 1992. In 1989, Gene Gotti and John Carneglia were found guilty of drug trafficking, sentenced to 50 years in prison, and fined $75,000 each. Reputedly, both were officers in the Gambino crime family.[190]

In 1987, John J. Gotti, who the government alleged was the leader of the most powerful Mafia family, was acquitted of federal racketeering and conspiracy charges. In 1990, Gotti was acquitted of assault and conspiracy charges. But in 1992, he was on trial again. The federal prosecutor argued that Gotti had used violence to work his way to the top of organized crime, including arranging the murder of his predecessor, former Gambino boss Paul Castellano. Gotti was indicted on 13 counts, including gangland murders, conspiring to murder, gambling, loan sharking, obstruction of justice, and tax evasion. Gotti's trial drew attention from the media and from well-known persons. After his conviction and during his sentencing, Gotti supporters held a vigil outside the courthouse. Some alleged that he did not get a fair trial; others said that they did not know why the government would spend millions of dollars to try Gotti. "All I know is he was very nice to me and my family," said one supporter who asked not to be identified. Gotti and his codefendant were convicted of all 13 counts and sentenced to life in prison without the possibility of parole. Although Gotti did not speak at his sentencing, his codefendant did. He declared his innocence of the charges for which he was convicted but admitted that he was "guilty of being a good friend of John Gotti. And if there were more men like John Gotti on this earth, we would have a better country."[191]

Gotti was incarcerated in one of the most secure federal prisons, located in Marion, Illinois, from which it was alleged that he continued to dominate the Gambino crime family through contacts with his son and his brother. Gotti and his attorney were optimistic that Gotti's sentence would be reversed, but in October 1993, a federal court upheld the verdict, and the U.S. Supreme Court refused to review the case.[192]

Because of his ill health (cancer of the head, neck, and throat), Gotti was moved to the U.S. Medical Center for Federal Prisoners in Springfield, Missouri. In June 2001, his family told the media that although Gotti had not complained, he was not getting adequate medical care. Gotti died in prison in June 2002.

Gotti's son, John A. Gotti, followed in his father's path and became the reputed leader of the crime family his father had led. But he, too, was apprehended by authorities. In 1998, it was reported that federal officials had offered a plea bargain to the younger Gotti and 10 other mob members who were scheduled for trial in January 1999. Bruce Cutler, Gotti's attorney, said his client was not accepting a plea bargain (reported to involve a 10-year sentence if he would plead guilty to lesser crimes than the major racketeering charges). Gotti was charged with extorting the former owners of a New York City nightclub and profiting from the Gambino family's rackets in "gambling, loan sharking, prepaid telephone card frauds and shakedowns of construction companies in the New York metropolitan area." Gotti was denied bail and jailed from January 1998 until a federal judge ordered his release on bail in August of that year. Cutler had proposed a $10 million bail package, which was financed by 35 "ordinary, common folk of means and good reputation" (in Cutler's words) who put up their homes as collateral. Cutler also proposed that Gotti would pay for the cost of surveillance by a firm hired by the government. His bail package included home confinement. By December 1998, however, Cutler was suggesting that Gotti might go back to jail voluntarily because he could not pay all of his bills. Most of his assets were frozen by prosecutors, and he was paying $21,000 a month for the security coverage. Cutler had asked the judge for a rehearing on the bail package. Prosecutors opposed his motion.[193]

In December 1998, allegedly upon the strong advice of his father, Gotti refused the government's plea bargain offer of a six-and-a-half-year prison term and a $1 million fine in exchange for a plea to lesser charges. Gotti faced up to 20 years in prison and the forfeiture of approximately $20 million in assets if convicted on all the acts for which he was charged. The government faced a long, expensive, complicated trial with the possibility of acquittals for Gotti and his colleagues because of problems with some of the witnesses. Government prosecutors stated that this was their last plea bargain offer, but shortly before his 1999 trial began, John A. Gotti pleaded guilty in exchange for a maximum sentence of seven years and three months.[194]

In October 2006, after hung juries in three trials of John A. Gotti, the prosecutor announced that he did not believe it was "in the interest of justice" to try Gotti again; Gotti was free. His attorney said it was not unusual to try a person three times, but it would be unusual to try a defendant a fourth time; that would just be a case of "playing the law of averages."[195] Gotti was tried a fourth time, however, and in December 2009, the jury deadlocked; in January 2010, the prosecutor announced that Gotti would not be retried.

In August 1998, Nicholas "Little Nick" Corozzo was given an eight-year prison sentence, a light sentence considering his "virtual lifetime of racketeering activity" and a plea agreement that he accepted, which would have put him in prison for 10 years. That agreement was dropped when Corozzo failed to pay the $500,000 in restitution to which he and two others had agreed. Although the prosecutor recommended a long sentence, the judge imposed a light one. Corozzo, 64, was released from a federal prison in Kentucky in June 2004. It was feared that with Peter Gotti and John A. Gotti both in prison, Corozzo might become the new boss of the Gambino crime family.[196]

Thomas Gambino, a reputed captain in the Gambino family, which was named after his late father, was sentenced to five years in prison but was free on $500,000 bail pending appeal. He lost that appeal in July 1995, but he was permitted to remain free pending an appeal to the U.S. Supreme Court, which in 1996 refused to hear the case. Gambino was incarcerated on 3 January 1996. He was not eligible for parole, but he was released in 2000 because of good behavior.[197]

In January 1993, officials arrested Anthony Salvatore "Gaspipe" Casso, a fugitive from justice who was thought to be one of the most dangerous of current U.S. Mafia leaders. He had disappeared two days before his 1990 trial on federal racketeering charges was to begin. Casso was reputed to be the acting boss of the Luchese crime family. He was apprehended as he stepped out of his shower and was taken into custody wearing only a towel.[198]

In 1995, Casso began cooperating with federal prosecutors. He informed them that three mobsters plotted to kill 75-year-old Eugene Nickerson, the judge who was scheduled to preside over their racketeering trial. Casso provided information on other former "colleagues," leading six of them to plead guilty in exchange for seven-year prison terms rather than face trials and the probability of much longer prison terms, such as life without parole. In March 1995, Casso pleaded guilty to racketeering charges, which included multiple murders. Under a plea agreement with federal prosecutors, he was to be given a lighter sentence than would be normal for one who participated in 15 murders (he claimed 37) as well as other violent crimes. Casso's agreement to testify against other mobsters earned him the desired plea agreement. In 1998, however, the agreement was rescinded on the grounds that while in prison, Casso bribed correctional officers to smuggle liquor and food for him. He also lied about some of the persons against whom he testified. In July 1998, Casso was sentenced to 15 life sentences.[199]

In June 2001, Salvatore Gravano, known as "Sammy the Bull," pleaded guilty to selling Ecstasy pills in Arizona. Gravano testified against John J. Gotti, his former Gambino crime family boss. Gravano had been in the federal Witness Protection Program but left it to sell Ecstasy with his son and a former business partner. The latter, when confronted with the possibility of prison, gave the government information on Gravano. Gravano was convicted and sentenced to 20 years in prison on the drug charge.[200]

These and other successful prosecutions have been due in part to the willingness of mob members to testify against their colleagues, a situation that would not have occurred in the distant past. The government rewards them for their cooperation, usually by giving them lesser sentences than they would otherwise receive. In extreme cases, when the informants are threatened by other mob members, they may be placed in the federal Witness Protection Program discussed earlier in this chapter. A spokesperson for the program has stated that the system has never lost a witness who followed the rules.[201]

Even with the power of RICO as a prosecutorial tool, not all organized crime prosecutions are successful. After a four-month trial, in July 2001, seven reputed Mafia members were acquitted of multiple murders and other charges. The reputed mob boss Joseph Merlino and six codefendants faced 36 charges, including racketeering, extortion, drug trafficking, gambling, attempted murder, and murder.[202]

One final recent trial of organized crime figures is referred to as the *Family Secrets* trial. It was one of the largest organized crime trials in Chicago and originally involved 14 men, known in their organized crime family world as the *Chicago Outfit*. Two died before trial; one was too ill to be tried; six entered guilty pleas. Four of the remaining defendants were convicted of racketeering conspiracy: James Marcello, 65; Joey "The Clown" Lombardo, 78; Frank Calabrese Sr. 70; and Paul "the Indian" Schiro, 70. The fifth defendant, Anthony Doyle, 62 and a retired Chicago police officer, was not charged with any

of the 18 gangland-type murders alleged to be at the heart of the case. The jury convicted Marcello, Calabrese, and Lombardo of 10 of those murders but deadlocked on the other 8 murders, including the only murder with which Schiro was charged. The elder mobsters faced 20 years in prison on the racketeering convictions; conviction of even one murder could result in a life sentence.[203]

Summary

This chapter completes the analysis of types of crimes and types of criminals by looking at drug abuse, drug trafficking, and organized crime, three areas of criminal behavior that are receiving increasing attention nationally and internationally. The chapter began with a brief overview of these crimes, their similarities, and their differences.

The discussion of drug abuse began with definitional issues and proceeded to look at the recent data on the extent and impact of drug abuse. The impact of drugs on the abuser was discussed in detail, noting the physical effects of several drugs. A section on fetal abuse explored the effect that drug abuse may have on the fetuses of pregnant women and considered whether such abuse should be processed within the criminal law.

The impact of drug abuse on communities was noted, with attention given not only to large cities, such as Los Angeles, but also to rural areas, where drug abuse may be increasing. The impact of gangs and drugs was noted, followed by a look at the impact of drugs on college and university campuses and especially on intimate partner violence in those settings.

The economic cost of substance abuse is enormous to both individual abusers and their families, to governments, and to society. The chapter explored the annual cost of drug abuse, which runs into the billions. Next was a discussion of the relationship between drug abuse and criminal activity, which is not fully understood, although we do know that many who abuse drugs are also involved in crime. And it is a fact that much of the overcrowding of jails and prisons results from drug abuse sentences. Drug abuse also presents criminal justice personnel, such as police and correctional officers, with temptations that may lead to corruption.

A section on the debate over drug laws explored federal and state laws, looking in particular at the federal war on drugs and its critics. Particular attention was given to social science research on the impact (or the lack thereof) of stiff drug laws on drug abuse, including the issue of whether these laws have a deterrent effect. Attention was given to the relationship between drug sentencing practices and race.

The punitive reaction to drug abuse by states was illustrated by a discussion of the New York Rockefeller laws. Recent reactions to those laws were noted, followed by an analysis of the debate over whether drug use should be legalized. In particular, attention was given to the legalization of the possession of small amounts of marijuana for personal use as well as for medicinal purposes. The reaction of the government and the courts to such laws was noted.

A big issue today is whether drug abuse should remain within the criminal law, given its punitive reactions, or should instead be the focus of treatment. We know the drug abuser needs treatment, but we are not sure whether that approach will be successful in reducing drug abuse. California's enactment of a statute with a treatment rather than a punishment orientation to first- and second-time drug offenders will provide us with some information about this approach.

With regard to treatment, brief attention was given to drug courts (discussed in detail in Chapter 13) and to educational programs drafted to encourage young people to avoid drug use and abuse. Drug testing was considered, especially in terms of whether it is a deterrent to illegal drug use.

The discussion of drug trafficking included a look at the dynamics of this serious area of criminal activity before focusing in particular on two Colombian drug cartels (the Medellin cartel and the Cali cartel) and Mexican drug cartels. The history and nature of these cartels were discussed, along with prosecutions and sentences of cartel members as well as other attempts to control drug trafficking.

Finally, with regard to drug abuse, the chapter explored the control of drug abuse and drug trafficking. This section examined recent legislation designed to curb drug abuse and drug trafficking.

The last major section of the chapter contained an analysis of organized crime. It examined the law enforcement perspective and the social and economic perspectives before proceeding with an analysis of the concept of organized crime. The history and structure of organized crime were examined briefly.

Organized crime infiltrates legitimate as well as illegitimate businesses; it provides goods and services that the public wants despite their illegality. Attention was given to the infiltration of organized crime into four types of otherwise legitimate businesses: health care, food, construction, and garbage carting. Such infiltrations provide group support for the activities of organized crime, and thus, its control is made more difficult. The discussion of controlling organized crime focused on statutory efforts and prosecutions, with some of the government's successful trials discussed.

A study of criminal types makes it clear that crime is difficult to analyze by types; categories, even legal ones, are not discrete. There is considerable overlap among the activities involved in crimes of property and of violence and in the characteristics of people who engage in these activities. These four chapters may illustrate that there are more similarities than differences in criminal types. Often, the difference lies not in the behavior itself but in the reaction to it. Thus, it is appropriate that attention be given to the official reaction to criminal behavior through an analysis of U.S. criminal justice systems, the focus of Part IV.

Study Questions

1. What is meant by drug abuse? What do we know about the numbers of people who abuse drugs and the type of drug abuse?

2. Summarize the findings of recent studies of data on drug abuse and its effect on abusers.

3. What is fetal abuse, and how should the law relate to this issue?

4. Drug abuse occurs primarily in large cities. Comment on this statement.

5. Elaborate on the impact and nature of drug abuse on college and university campuses.

6. Discuss the economic impact of drug abuse.

7. What, if any, is the relationship between drug abuse and criminal behavior?

8. To what extent, if any, does drug abuse contribute to prison and jail overcrowding? To corruption of law enforcement personnel?

9. Explain what is meant by the war on drugs, and evaluate the impact this approach has had on controlling drug abuse.

10. What are the Rockefeller laws? Have they been effective in controlling drug use?

11. Should marijuana possession be legalized? Why or why not?

12. What recent efforts have been made to treat rather than punish drug offenders?

13. Comment on the legal issues regarding the use of marijuana for medicinal purposes.

14. What effect, if any, might drug courts and educational programs have on drug abuse?

15. What might be the impact of random drug testing on drug abuse?

16. Outline the dynamics of illegal drug trafficking.

17. Distinguish between the Medellin and the Cali cartels. Comment on Mexican drug cartels.

18. What efforts are being made to control drug abuse and drug trafficking?

19. Define *money laundering*, and discuss its importance.

20. Define *racketeering*, and discuss the impact of RICO.

21. Analyze the concept of organized crime.

22. Distinguish between the two major approaches to the study of organized crime.

23. Explain the hierarchy of an organized crime family.

24. State briefly the relationship of organized crime to the following businesses: health care, food, construction, and garbage carting.

25. How successful has the government been in controlling organized crime? Be specific in your answer.

Brief Essay Assignments

1. Discuss the impact of drug abuse on the abuser, the fetus of a pregnant woman, and the community in which the abuser lives.

2. What is the relationship, if any, between drug abuse and crime?

3. Do you think criminalizing drugs leads to corruption of the police? Of correctional officers?

4. Trace the development of federal reactions to drug abuse.

5. Discuss recent treatment orientations for drug abuse and evaluate their effectiveness.

6. Evaluate the assertion that there is little difference between organized crime and white-collar crime.

Internet Activities

1. Using your Web browser, search for more information about fetal abuse. What are the arguments for and against criminalizing fetal abuse? Which arguments do you support? What other social and political issues are intertwined in this complex debate? To get started, go to the following website for information about fetal abuse and the law: http://www.motherjones.com/ politics/2000/06/fetal-abuse, accessed 31 October 2010.

2. The United States is not the only country in which organized crime and other issues discussed in this chapter are serious problems. Go to the United Nations Office on Drugs and Crime website, http://www.unodc.org/unodc/en/organized-crime/index .html, accessed 31 October 2010, and look at the following topics: human trafficking, organized crime, money laundering, terrorism prevention, and illicit drugs.

Notes

1. *Black's Law Dictionary*, special deluxe 5th ed. (St. Paul, MN: West, 1979), p. 446.

2. Quoted in Howard Abadinsky, *Drug Abuse: An Introduction* (Chicago: Nelson-Hall, 1989), p. 2.

3. Executive Office of the President, Office of National Drug Control Policy, *Drug Use Trends* (Washington, D.C.: Drug Policy Information Clearinghouse, June 1999), p. 2.

4. Office of National Drug Control Policy, News Release (19 December 2003), http://www.monitoringthefuture.org, accessed 5 July 2004. The 2006 data are from "Monitoring the Future Survey, Oveview of Findings 2006," National Institute on Drug Abuse (NIDA), http://www.nida.nih.gov/newsroom/06MTF06Overview.html, accessed 23 January 2008, p. 1. The 2007 data are from NIDA, Press Release, "Monitoring the Future Survey, Overview of Findings 2007," http://www.drugabuse.gov/newsroom/07/MTF07Overview.html, accessed 31 October 2010.

5. Monitoring the Future Survey, "Overview of Findings 2008" (December 2009), http://www.drugabuse.gov/newsroom/08/MTF08Overview.html accessed 31 October 2010; National Institutes of Health, National Institute on Drug Abuse, "Teen Marijuana Use Increases," http://www.drugabuse.gov/pdf/news/NR121410.pdf, accessed 18 December 2010.

6. Schedules of Controlled Substances, USCS, Title 21, Section 812(1) (2010).

7. Department of Labor, "General Workplace Impact," http://www.dol.gov/asp/programs/drugs/workingpartners/stats/wi.asp, accessed 31 October 2010.

8. Innovators Combating Substance Abuse, "Facts About Substance Abuse," http://www.innovatorsawards.org/facts, accessed 30 October 2010.

9. Ibid.

10. Ibid.

11. Office of National Drug Policy Control, "Drug Facts: Prescription Drugs," http://www.whitehousedrugpolicy.gov/drugfact/prescrptn_drgs/index.html, accessed 31 October 2010.

12. "Drugs Just a Click Away: Online Pharmacies Can Make Dangerous Drugs Easy to Get, but Also Can Promote Better Health Care," *State Legislature* 33, no. 6 (1 June 2007): 45.

13. Mark Thompson, "America's Medicated Army" (June 2008), http://www.time.com/time/nation/article/0,8599,1811858,00.html, accessed 31 October 2010.

14. "Pentagon Plays Catchup as Toll of Repeat Combat Duty Rises," *Christian Science Monitor* (17 December 2009), p. 1.

15. Innovators Combating Substance Abuse, "Facts About Substance Abuse."

16. "Chronic Ecstasy Use May Promote Long-Term Neuropsychiatric Damage," *Alcoholism and Drug Abuse Weekly* 14, no. 30 (5 August 2002): 6.

17. National Institute of Drug Abuse, "MDMA/Ecstasy," http://www.nida.nih.gov/DrugPages/MDMA.html, accessed 31 October 2010.

18. "Men Combining Viagra, Illicit Drugs, to Heighten Sexual Experience," *Alcoholism and Drug Abuse Weekly* 13, no. 33 (3 September 2001): 8.

19. The information on the effects of club drugs comes from the Office of National Drug Control Policy, *Club Drugs*, http://www.whitehousedrugpolicy.gov/drugfact/club/index.html, accessed 31 October 2010.

20. National Institute on Drug Abuse, cited in Office of National Drug Control Policy, *Drug Facts: Marijuana*, www.whitehousedrugpolicy.gov/drugfact/marijuana/index.html, accessed 31 October 2010.

21. "Many Women Drink Alcohol During Pregnancy," *Alcoholism and Drug Abuse Weekly* 15, no. 5 (3 February 2003): 8.

22. "Ecstasy May Affect Fetus in Early Pregnancy," *Alcoholism and Drug Abuse Weekly* 15, no. 34 (8 September 2003): 7.

23. "Prenatal Marijuana Exposure May Pose Health Risks," *Science Weekly* 163, no. 14 (5 April 2003): n.p.

24. "Drinking in Pregnancy Yields Long-Term Deficits," *Alcoholism and Drug Abuse Weekly* 14, no. 40 (21 October 2002): 7.

25. "Missouri Court of Appeals Western District Case Summaries," *Missouri Lawyers Weekly* (17 September 2007). The Missouri case is *State v. Wade*, 232 S.W.3d 663 (Mo.Ct.App. 2007). The Kentucky case is *Cochran v. Commonwealth*, 315 S.W.3d 325 (Ky. 2010). The Kentucky statute is KRS, Section 508.060 (2010).

26. *State v. McKnight*, 576 S.E.2d 168 (S.C. 2003), *cert. denied*, 540 U.S. 819 (2003), *post conviction relief granted*, McKnight v. State, 661 S.E.2d 354 (S.C. 2008). This relief was concerned with other issues, such as ineffective assistance of counsel. The South Carolina statute, which is entitled Homicide by child abuse, is codified at S.C. Code Ann., Title 16, Section 16-3-85 (2009).

27. *Ferguson v. Charleston*, 532 U.S. 67 (2001).

28. "Los Angeles Police Department and FBI Officials Continue Their Crackdown on Gangs in South Central," *National Public Radio Transcript* (28 January 2004), n.p.

29. "Rise in Killings Spurs New Steps to Fight Gangs," *New York Times* (17 January 2004), p. 1; "Bratton Shuffles LAPD Brass: Department to Focus on 'Top 10 Percent,'" *Daily News of Los Angeles* (18 November 2003), p. 3N.

30. "Homicide Rates Decline in the Southland," *Los Angeles Times* (18 July 2007), p. 1B; "Panel Presses for Details on Gang Programs," *Daily News of Los Angeles*, Valley Edition (20 July 2007), p. 3N.

31. James C. Howell and James P. Lynch, *Youth Gangs in Schools* (Washington, D.C.: U.S. Department of Justice, Office of Justice Programs, Office of Juvenile Justice and Delinquency Prevention, August 2000), p. 1.

32. "Slaughter in Our Cities; Chicago School Kids Are Getting Killed at a Faster Pace Than Illinois Soldiers," *Pittsburgh Post-Gazette* (18 July 2007), p. 7B.

33. "Across Rural America, Drug Casts a Grim Shadow: Methamphetamine Spurs Crime and Sorrow," *New York Times* (4 January 2004), p. 10.

34. "As Drug Use Drops in Big Cities, Small Towns Confront Upsurge," *New York Times* (11 February 2002), p. 1.

35. "With Drugs in Open, the Elderly Live Behind Locks," *New York Times* (2 May 2004), p. 31.

36. *HUD v. Rucker*, 535 U.S. 125 (2002).

37. Elissa R. Weitzman, "Social Developmental Overview of Heavy Episodic or Binge Drinking Among U.S. College Students," *Psychiatric Times* (1 February 2004), p. 57.

38. "College Binge Drinking in the 1990s: A Continuing Problem. Results of the Harvard School of Public Health 1999 College Alcohol Study," *Journal of American College Health* 48 (March 2000): 208, quoted in White House Initiative on Educational Excellence for Hispanic Americans, http://www.yic.gov/drugfree/alcabuse.html, accessed 31 October 2010.

39. "Reed College's President Is Told to Crack Down on Campus Drug Use," *New York Times* (27 April 2010), p. 13.

40. Katrina Baum and Patsy Klaus, Bureau of Justice Statistics, *Violent Victimization of College Students, 1995–2002* (January 2005), p. 1, http://bjs.ojp.usdoj.gov/content/pub/pdf/vvcs02.pdf, accessed 31 October 2010.

41. Maria Testa et al., "Women's Substance Use and Experiences of Intimate Partner Violence," *Addict Behavior* 28, no. 9 (December 2003): 1649–1664.

42. Richard B. Felson and Keri B. Burchfield, "Alcohol and the Risk of Physical and Sexual Assault Victimization," *Criminology* 42, no. 4 (December 2004): 837–859; quotation is on p. 838.

43. Ibid., pp. 853, 855.

44. "Death of Cockeysville Woman Spurs 'Day of Dialogue' at UVA," *Baltimore Sun* (25 September 2010), p. 1.

45. *The Economic Costs of Drug Abuse in the United States 1992–2002*, Office of National Drug Control Policy (December 2004), http://www.ncjrs.gov/ondcppubs/publications/pdf/economic_costs/economic_costs.pdf, accessed 31 October 2010.

46. Innovators Combating Substance Abuse, "Facts about Substance Abuse."

47. William J. Sabol et al., Bureau of Justice Statistics, *Prisoners in 2006* (December 2007), p. 10 http://bjs.ojp.usdoj.gov/content/pub/pdf/p06.pdf, accessed 31 October 2010.

48. William J. Sabol et al., Bureau of Justice Statistics, *Prisoners in 2008* (December 2009), p. 6 http://bjs.ojp.usdoj.gov/content/pub/pdf/p08.pdf, accessed 31 October 2010.

49. Office of National Drug Control Policy, *Drug-Related Crime*, http://www.whitehousedrugpolicy.gov/publications/factsht/crime/index.html, accessed 31 October 2010.

50. James A. Inciardi, "Heroin Use and Street Crime," *Crime and Delinquency* 25 (July 1979): 335–346; Inciardi, *The War on Drugs: Heroin, Cocaine, Crime, and Public Policy* (Palo Alto, CA: Mayfield, 1986).

51. James A. Inciardi and Anne E. Pottieger, "Drug Use and Street Crime in Miami: An (Almost) Twenty-Year Retrospective," in *The American Drug Scene*, 3d ed., ed. James A. Inciardi and Karen McElrath (Los Angeles: Roxbury, 2001), pp. 319–342; quotation is on pp. 337–338.

52. Scott Menard et al., "Drugs and Crime Revisited," *Justice Quarterly* 18 (June 2001): 269–299; quotation is on pp. 269–270.

53. Federal Bureau of Investigation, *Uniform Crime Reports: Crime in the United States 2009*, "Arrests," (September 2010), http://www2.fbi.gov/ucr/cius2009/arrests/, accessed 31 October 2010.

54. Federal Bureau of Investigation, *Crime in the United States 2009*, "Arrests," Table 32 (September 2010), http://www2.fbi.gov/ucr/cius2009/data/table_32.html, accessed 31 October 2010.

55. Christopher J. Mumola and Jennifer C. Karberg, Bureau of Justice Statistics, *Drug Use and Dependence, State and Federal Prisoners, 2004* (October 2006, revised 19 January 2007), pp. 1, 4, http://bjs.ojp.usdoj.gov/content/pub/pdf/dudsfp04.pdf, accessed 31 October 2010.

56. Innovators Combating Substance Abuse, "Facts About Substance Abuse."

57. Michael Tonry, *Malign Neglect: Race, Crime, and Punishment in America* (New York: Oxford University Press, 1995), p. 81.

58. "Explosive Drug Use in Prisons Is Creating a New Underworld," *New York Times* (30 December 1989), p. 1.

59. "1,000 San Francisco Drug Cases To Be Dismissed in Lab Scandal," *San Jose Mercury News* (California) (1 April 2010), n.p.; "D.A. Alerts Defense Attorneys with Regard to Experts' Problems," *San Francisco Chronicle* (15 June 2010), p. 1.

60. "In Scandal's Wake, Police Turn to Cheap, Quick Test for Drugs," *New York Times* (27 August 2010), p. 17.

61. "Police Alerted to Drug Case Face Demotion," *San Francisco Chronicle* (21 August 2010), p. 1.

62. See the classic study by David J. Pittman and C. Wayne Gordon, *Revolving Door* (New York: Free Press, 1958).

63. *Justice Assistance News* 3 (March 1982).

64. Anti-Drug Abuse Act of 1988, USCS, Title 8, Section 1108(a)(43)(F) (2010).

65. Gil Kerlikowske, "Launching America's New Approach to the Drug Problem," Of Substance Blog, http://ofsubstance.gov/blogs/pushing_back/archive/1020/05/10/51127.aspx, accessed 31 October 2010.

66. Macmillan Publishing Company, News Release concerning the book by Arnold S. Trebach, *The Great Drug War* (New York: Macmillan, 1988).

67. John F. Galliher et al., "Lindesmith v. Anslinger: An Early Government Victory in the Failed War on Drugs," *Journal of Criminal Law and Criminology* 88 (Winter 1988): 661–682; quotation is on pp. 670–671.

68. Ibid., p. 681.

69. "The President's National Drug Control Strategy: February 2007: Introduction, A Record of Accomplishment," The Office of National Drug Control Policy, http://biblio.colmex.mx/cei/Docs/DrugStrategy_07.pdf, accessed 31 October 2010.

70. Jacqueline Cohen et al., "A Hierarchical Bayesian Analysis of Arrest Rates," *Journal of the American Statistical Association* 93 (1998): 1260–1270; quotation is on p. 1260, as cited in Cassia Spohn and David Holleran, "The Effect of Imprisonment on Recidivism Rates of Felony Offenders: A Focus on Drug Offenders," *Criminology* 40, no. 2 (May 2002): 329–357; quotation is on p. 330.

71. Spohn and Holleran, "The Effect of Imprisonment," pp. 350, 351, 352–353.

72. Donald P. Green and Daniel Winik, "Using Random Judge Assignments to Estimate the Effects of Incarceration and Probation on Recidivism Among Drug Offenders," *Criminology* 48, no. 2 (May 2010): 357–388; quotation is on p. 358.

73. Michael Welch et al., "Decontextualizing the War on Drugs: A Content Analysis of NIJ Publications and Their Neglect of Race and Class," *Justice Quarterly* 15 (December 1998): 719–742; quotations are on p. 734.

74. Michael Tonry, "Racial Politics, Racial Disparities, and the War on Crime," *Crime and Delinquency* 40 (October 1994): 475, 483–488. See also Tonry, *Malign Neglect*.

75. *United States v. Armstrong*, 517 U.S. 456 (1996).

76. See *Kimbrough v. United States*, 552 U.S. 85 (2007).

77. The statute is codified at USCS, Title 21, Section 812(b) (2010).

78. *Harmelin v. Michigan*, 501 U.S. 957 (1991).

79. "End the Rockefeller Laws," *Wall Street Journal Abstracts* (25 May 2004), p. 16.

80. "Drop the Rock, Repeal the Rockefeller Drug Laws," http://www.droptherock.org/, accessed 31 October 2010.

81. "New York Governor Signs Legislation to Reform Drug Laws," *Alcoholism and Drug Abuse Weekly* 16, no. 48 (20 December 2004): n.p.

82. "Drug Laws Need Changing, Advocates Say," *Journal News* (Westchester County, NY) (29 August 2007), p. 14.

83. "New York Is Set to End Drug Laws Requiring Prison," *New York Times* (26 March 2009); "The High Cost of Empty Prisons," *New York Times* (12 October 2009), p. 23.

84. "Mandatory Minimum Drug Sentences Toppled in Michigan," *U.S. Newswire* (27 December 2002), n.p.

85. "Violent Crimes Undercut Marijuana's Mellow Image," *New York Times* (19 May 2001), p. 1.

86. To view the statutory provisions of each jurisdiction, access http://www.norml.org/index.cfm?Group_ID=4516, and click on the state of your choice, accessed 31 October 2010.

87. *United States v. Oakland Cannabis Buyers' Cooperative*, 532 U.S. 483 (2001), *injunction granted sub nom.*, 2002 U.S. Dist. LEXIS 10660 (N.D.Cal. 2002).

88. *Conant v. Walters*, 309 F.3d 629 (9th Cir. 2002), *cert. denied*, 540 U.S. 946 (2003).

89. *Gonzales v. Raich*, 545 U.S. 1 (2005), *on remand*, Raich v. Gonzales, 500 F.3d 850 (9th Cir. 2007).

90. *Washburn v. Columbia Forest Products, Inc.*, 134 P.3d 161 (Or. 2006).

91. *Ross v. Ragingwire Telecom*, 174 Pac.3d 200 (Ca. 2008).

92. *Emerald Steel Fabricators Inc. v. Bureau of Labor and Industries*, 230 P.3d 518 (Or. 2010).

93. Substance Abuse and Crime Prevention Act (Proposition 36), Cal Pen Code, Section 1210.1 (2010).

94. "Study of California Prop. 36 Shows Savings to Taxpayers," *Criminal Justice Newsletter* (2 April 2007), p. 4.

95. *The Impact of a Mature Drug Court over 10 Years of Operation*, NPC Research (Portland, OR, 2007), as summarized in "Drug Court Study," *Criminal Justice Newsletter* (1 August 2007), p. 8.

96. "Rehab, Not Jail: Plan Due for Drug Offenders," *New Jersey Lawyer* 16, no. 10 (5 March 2007): 2.

97. Arizona Revised Statutes, 15-712 (2010).

98. See *Veronia School District 47J v. Acton*, 515 U.S. 646 (1995), permitting drug testing of athletes; *Board of Education v. Earls*, 536 U.S. 822 (2002), permitting drug testing of all middle and high school public school students who participate in extracurricular activities.

99. "Study Finds No Sign That Testing Deters Students' Drug Use," *New York Times* (17 May 2003), p. 1, reporting on an article in the *Journal of School Health* (April 2003).

100. Marsha Rosenbaum, "Random Student Drug Testing Is No Panacea," *Alcoholism and Drug Abuse Weekly* 16, no. 15 (12 April 2004): 5.

101. President's Commission on Organized Crime, Report to the President and the Attorney General, *America's Habit: Drug Abuse, Drug Trafficking, and Organized Crime* (Washington, D.C.: U.S. Government Printing Office, 1986), pp. 5–13.

102. Bureau of Justice Statistics, *Drugs, Crime, and the Criminal Justice System* (Washington, D.C.: U.S. Department of Justice, December 1992), referring to a study by David L. Carter, "Drug-Related Corruption of Police Officers: A Contemporary Typology," *Journal of Criminal Justice* 18 (1990): 88.

103. Carter, "Drug-Related Corruption of Police Officers," p. 62.

104. "No. 1 Drug Lord Gives Up, Flies to Posh Prison," *St. Petersburg Times* (20 June 1991), p. 1.

105. Ibid.

106. "Colombian Drug Figure Is Guilty in U.S. Dealing," *New York Times* (29 May 2003), p. 16; U.S. State Department, "Fabio Ochoa Was Founding Member of Notorious Medellin Cartel," News Release (28 August 2003), n.p. The case is *United States v. Ochoa-Vasquez*, 428 F.3d 1015 (11th Cir. 2005), *cert. denied*, 549 U.S. 952 (2006).

107. "Outwitting Cali's Professor Moriarty," *Time* (17 July 1995), p. 30.

108. "Colombia's Weak Courts Hamper Police Efforts to Control Drugs," *Miami Herald* (23 October 1992), p. 1.

109. Grand Jury Indictment, U.S. District Court, Southern District of Florida, case of *United States v. Miguel Rodríguez-Orejuela et al.*, p. 4. The statute is USCS, Title 18, Section 1961 (2010).

110. "Lawyers Weigh Effects of Conviction of Missing Colleague," *New York Times* (9 August 1998), p. 24.

111. "Drug Boat Captain's Sentence: Thirty Years," *Tampa Tribune* (14 July 2001), p. 3.

112. "Colombian Drug Leader Gets 40-Year Term," *St. Petersburg Times* (Florida) (2 February 2007), p. 3B; "A Quiet Sentence," *Tampa Tribune* (17 January 2009), p. 2.

113. "Brothers Ran Drug Cartel from Behind Bars, Grand Jury Says," *Miami Herald* (23 December 2003), n.p.

114. "Suspected Drug Cartel Accountant Surrenders," *Los Angeles Times* (28 December 2003), p. 16.

115. "Cali Cartel Front Man Pleads Guilty and Is Sentenced on Money Laundering Charges," *PR Newswire US* (11 May 2007), n.p.

116. "Authorities Break Up Major Caribbean Cocaine Operation," *South Florida Sun-Sentinel* (24 June 2004), n.p.

117. "Narcotics Conspirators Sentenced to Prison," *States News Service* (19 October 2005), n.p.

118. "15 Indictments in Chicago Are Tied to Mexican Cartel," *New York Times* (21 January 2009), p. 12.

119. "Epicenter of Bust Arrests Highlight La Familia Cartel's Battle for North Texas," *Dallas Morning News* (23 October 2009), p. 1.

120. "A Wave of Arrests, Then Quiet Releases, in Mexico," *Washington Post* (26 April 2010), p. 1.

121. "Drug War Squeezing Caribbean, Leaders Say," *Baltimore Sun* (17 April 2010), p. 9.

122. "Mexico's Drug Traffickers Continue Trade in Prison," *New York Times* (11 August 2009), p. 1.

123. The Ecstasy Anti-Proliferation Act of 2000 is codified as Section 3664 of Pub. Law 106-310 (2010).

124. U.S. Department of Justice, "Texas Man Sentenced to 14 Years in Prison in Massive Ecstasy Conspiracy," Press Release (11 March 2010), http://kansascity.fbi.gov/dojpressrel/pressrel10/kc031110.htm, accessed 31 October 2010.

125. Comprehensive Drug Abuse and Prevention Act of 1970, USCS, Title 21, Sections 801-966 (2010).

126. Violent Crime Control and Law Enforcement Act of 1994, Public Law 103-222 (13 September 1994). See Title IX, Drug Control.

127. "Drug Research Inadequate, White House Panel Finds," *New York Times* (30 March 2001), p. 15.

128. Quoted in Francis A. J. Ianni and Elizabeth Reuss-Ianni, "Organized Crime," in *Encyclopedia of Crime and Justice*, Vol. 3, ed. Sanford H. Kadish (New York: Macmillan, 1983), p. 1095.

129. President's Commission on Law Enforcement and Administration of Justice, *The Challenge of Crime in a Free Society* (Washington, D.C.: U.S. Government Printing Office, 1967), p. 187.

130. Ianni and Reuss-Ianni, "Organized Crime," p. 1095.

131. Ibid., p. 1097.

132. Ibid., p. 1096.

133. National White Collar Crime Center, *Organized Crime* (September 2002), p. 1. The NW3C is located in Fairmont, West Virginia. It can be located on the Internet at http://www.nw3c.org/, accessed 31 October 2010.

134. Ianni and Reuss-Ianni, "Organized Crime," p. 1096.

135. Howard Abadinsky, *Organized Crime*, 3d ed. (Chicago: Nelson-Hall, 1993), p. 95.

136. Estes Kefauver, *Crime in America* (New York: Doubleday, 1951).

137. Robert F. Kennedy, *The Enemy Within* (New York: Harper & Row, 1960).

138. President's Commission, *The Challenge of Crime*, pp. 187–210.

139. National Advisory Committee on Criminal Justice Standards and Goals, *Organized Crime* (Washington, D.C.: U.S. Government Printing Office, 1973).

140. The commission was established by Executive Order, No. 12435, July 28, 1983; see USCS, Title 96, Section 1961 (2010). The interim report is *The Cash Connection: Organized Crime, Financial Institutions, and Money Laundering* (Washington, D.C.: U.S. Government Printing Office, 1984). The final report is the President's Commission on Organized Crime, Report to the President and the Attorney General, *The Edge: Organized Crime, Business, and Labor Unions* (Washington, D.C.: U.S. Government Printing Office, March 1986).

141. The President's Commission on Law Enforcement and Administration of Justice, Task Force Report, *Organized Crime* (Washington, D.C.: U.S. Government Printing Office, 1967), p. 7.

142. See U.S. Senate Special Committee to Investigate Organized Crime in Interstate Commerce, *Third Interim Report*, Senate Report No. 307, 83d Cong., 1st Sess. (Washington, D.C.: U.S. Government Printing Office, 1951). The report is abridged in Kefauver, *Crime in America*.

143. Giovanni Schiavo, *The Truth About the Mafia* (New York: Vigo Press, 1962).

144. Ianni and Reuss-Ianni, "Organized Crime," p. 1101.

145. See Francis A. J. Ianni and Elizabeth Reuss-Ianni, eds., A *Family Business: Kinship and Social Control in Organized Crime* (New York: Russell Sage, 1972).

146. See Joseph L. Albini, *The American Mafia: Genesis of a Legend*, Reprint (New York: Irvington, 1979).

147. President's Commission, *The Challenge of Crime*, pp. 192–193.

148. Ibid., p. xviii.

149. *United States v. Aquino*, 336 F.Supp. 737, 739 (D.C. Mich. 1972).

150. "Congress Told That Organized Crime Has Penetrated Health Care Industry," *Criminal Law Reporter* 56 (29 March 1995): 1595.

151. "Health Fraud Is Fertile Ground for Career Criminals," *Insurance Fraud* 6 (November 1999), n.p.

152. President's Commission, *The Edge*, pp. 213–214.

153. "About Crime: How to Reform a Fishy Business," *Newsday* (New York) (3 March 1995), p. 34; "New York Mayor Expands War on Mob," *Dallas Morning News* (7 July 1996), p. 4.

154. "The Mob and the Markets," *New York Times* (12 April 1997), p. 18.

155. "Fulton Fish Starts Fresh," *Small Business Report* (12 March 2007), p. 19.

156. "Beavercreek Man Headed Stolen-Goods Ring, Police Say," *Dayton Daily News* (23 January 2004), p. 1; "Creek Man Indicted in Stolen-Food Case," *Dayton Daily News* (25 March 2004), p. 3B; "Dayton Man Sentenced for His Role in Stolen-Goods Trafficking Ring," *States News Service* (12 March 2006), n.p.

157. "U.S. Lays Out Case Against Tomato Kingpin," *Los Angeles Times* (19 February 2010), p. 1.

158. President's Commission, *The Edge*, pp. 217–228.

159. "Mob Ties May Be Innocent, Casino Panel Member Says," *New York Times* (20 April 2004), p. 4B.

160. "Married to Mob, Union Is Whacked," *Star Ledger* (Newark, NJ) (30 January 2007), p. 22.

161. "Quebec Corruption Crackdown Yields 10 Arrests," *Globe and Mail* (Canada) (4 November 2009), p. 7.

162. "Today's News Update," *New York Law Journal* (23 June 1995), p. 1; "Monitors Appointed for Trash Haulers," *New York Times* (23 December 1995), p. 31.

163. "The Garbage Wars: Cracking the Cartel," *New York Times* (30 July 1995), Section 3, p. 1.

164. "Two Convicted as Masterminds of Mob's Hold on Private Garbage Collection," *New York Times* (22 October 1997), p. 19; "Business and Technology: Criminal Justice Defendants in New York City

Carting Trial Hit with Prison Terms, Fines," *IAC (SM) Newsletter Database (TM)* (Business Publishers, Inc., Solid Waste Report) (18 December 1997): 28, Section no. 50, ISSN: 0038-1128.

165. "Texas Company Agrees to Buy Mafia-Linked Waste Hauler," *New York Times* (23 January 1996), p. 1B; "Progress Against Organized Crime," *New York Times* (1 July 1996), p. 12.

166. "The Lawyer's Bookshelf," *New York Law Journal* 230 (11 August 2003): 2. The book is Rick Cowan and Douglas Century, *Takedown: The Fall of the Last Mafia Empire* (New York: Putnam's Sons, 2003).

167. "Defendant Admits Bribery in Police Corruption Case," *New York Times* (9 September 1998), p. 25; "Ex-New Jersey Police Chief Who Ran a Corrupt Force Is Sentenced and Fined," *New York Times* (6 January 2000), p. 4B.

168. USCS, Title 18, Sections 1951 et seq. (2010).

169. Section 1 of Public Law 91-452, 84 Stat. 922 (2010).

170. USCS, Title 18, Section 1962 (2010). For an analysis of RICO, see "Racketeer Influenced and Corrupt Organizations: Twenty-Second Annual Survey of White Collar Crime," American Criminal Law Review 44, no. 2 (22 March 2007): 901 et seq.

171. USCS, Title 18, Section 1961 (5) (2010).

172. *United States v. Turkette*, 452 U.S. 576 (1981).

173. USCS, Title 18, Sections 1963(a)(b-h) and 1964(c) (2010).

174. *Bennis v. Michigan*, 516 U.S. 442 (1996); *Fred A. Smith Lumber Co. v. Edidin*, 845 F.2d 750 (7th Cir. 1988).

175. *United States v. Bajakajian*, 524 U.S. 321 (2001).

176. Bank Secrecy Act of 1970, USCS, Title 31, Sections 5311-5326 (2010).

177. USCS, Title 18, Sections 1956 and 1957 (2010).

178. USCS, Title 21, Section 5324 (2010). See also the RICO statute, USCS, Title 18, Sections 1961 et seq. (2010).

179. USCS, Title 31, Sections 5325-5326 (2010).

180. "Suspicious Activity; Reporting Rules Rely on Bank's Good Judgment," *New York Law Journal* (4 April 1996), p. 5.

181. "Patriotic Duty: New Laws Burden Community Banks, Hinder Profitability," *Miami Daily Business Review* 77, no. 33 (25 July 2002): 1.

182. Tex. Penal Code, Chapter 34, Section 34.02 (2010).

183. Federal Bureau of Investigation, Department of Justice, "Indictment Unsealed Charging Colombo Family Administration Member Theodore Persico and Seven Others," News Release (9 March 2010), http://newyork.fbi.gov/dojpressrel/pressrel10/nyfo030910.htm, accessed 31 October 2010.

184. Federal Bureau of Investigation, Department of Justice, "Colombo Family "Street Boss' Indicted as Head of Massachusetts RICO Crew," News Release, http://boston.fbi.gov/dojpressrel/pressrel09/bs121709.htm, accessed 31 October 2010.

185. "Mob Infiltration Seen in City Agency," *New York Times* (2 October 2009), p. 24.

186. Federal Bureau of Investigation, "Bonnano Organized Crime Family Ruling Panel Member, Captains, Soldiers, and Associates Indicted for Racketeering, Assault, and Other Offenses," http://newyork.fbi.gov/dojpressrel/pressrel09/nyfo100709.htm, accessed 31 October 2010.

187. "Grisly Crimes Described by Prosecutors as Mob Trial Opens," *New York Times* (25 May 2004), p. 23.

188. "More Mob Figures Plead Guilty," *Newsday* (New York), City Edition (12 February 2005), p. 13; "Don's Last Deal: Mob Boss Talks, Wife 'Buys' Him Life in Jail," *Daily News* (New York) (24 June 2005), p. 3.

189. "Gambino Crime Boss or Not, Peter Gotti Gets 9-Year Prison Term," *New York Times* (16 April 2004), p. 19. The case is *United States v. Gotti*, 2004 U.S. Dist. LEXIS 45 (S.D.N.Y. 2004), *aff'd. sub nom.*, 489 F.3d 115 (2d Cir. 2007), *cert. denied sub nom.*, 552 U.S. 969 (2008).

190. "Gotti Brother Sentenced to Fifty Years," *Miami Herald* (8 July 1989), p. 6.

191. "Gotti Sentenced to Life in Prison Without the Possibility of Parole," *New York Times* (24 June 1992), p. 1.

192. "After Court Setback, Gotti Faces a Decision," *New York Times* (4 May 1994), p. 16. The case is *United States v. Lacascio and Gotti*, 6 F.3d 924 (2d Cir. 1993), *cert. denied, United States v. Gotti*, 511 U.S. 1070 (1994).

193. "Gotti's Son and Co-Defendants Are Said to Reject Plea Deals," *New York Times* (11 September 1998), p. 3B; "'Common Folk' Put Up Homes for Mob Suspect," *New York Times* (18 October 1998), p. 30; "Younger Gotti Says Bail Costs and Seizures Impoverish Him," *New York Times* (2 December 1998), p. 27.

194. "Gotti Rejects Deal, Heeding Father's Words, Friends Say," *New York Times* (29 December 1998), p. 15; "Gotti Offered Lighter Term as Setbacks Hamper U.S.," *New York Times* (1 February 1999), p. 3B.

195. "After Three Attempts to Convict Gotti, Prosecutors Decide Against Making It Four," *New York Times* (21 October 2006), p. 11B.

196. "Gotti Pal Gets Eight Years in Prison," *Daily News* (New York) (20 August 1998), p. 8.

197. *United States v. Gambino*, 818 F.Supp. 536 (E.D.N.Y. 1995), *aff'd.*, 59 F.3d 353 (2d Cir. 1995), *cert denied*, 517 U.S. 1187 (1996). See also "A Gambino Goes to Jail in 1993 Case," *New York Times* (4 January 1996), p. 6B; "Wiseguy Fires at Trusty Clintons," *New York Post* (1 July 2001), p. 7.

198. "New York Mobster Convicted of Murder," *Miami Herald* (16 June 1992), p. 17; "FBI Arrests Mafia Chieftain in a Hideaway in New Jersey," *New York Times* (20 January 1993), p. 16.

199. "Mafia Chiefs Prefer Jail to Trial Gamble," *The Times* (London) (2 April 1994), Overseas News Section, n.p.; "Plea Deal Rescinded, Informer May Face Life," *New York Times* (1 July 1998), p. 4B; "Rubout King 'Gaspipe' Gets Life Fifteen Times," *New York Post* (9 July 1998), p. 10.

200. "Gravano Pleads Guilty to Selling Drugs," *New York Times* (30 June 2001), p. 12; "An Ill Gravano a No-Show at Court Hearing," *The Record* (Bergen County, NJ) (11 January 2006), Local, p. 2L.

201. "Gotti Guns for Mafia Superbrass," *Sunday Times* (4 June 1993), Overseas News Section, n.p.; "Gotti Tries to Rope Bull," *Daily News* (New York) (4 January 1996), p. 7.

202. "Seven Reputed Mafia Figures Are Acquitted of Murder," *New York Times* (21 July 2001), p. 7.

203. "'One Less Clown in the Circus:' Jury Pins 10 Murders on Outfit Figures Joey Lombardo, Frank Calabrese Sr. and James Marcello," *Chicago Sun Times*, Final Edition (28 September 2007), p. 10

PART FOUR

Criminal Justice Systems

Part IV consists of three chapters to introduce criminal justice systems. **Chapter 11** focuses on an overview, beginning with a discussion of the basic concepts of U.S. criminal justice systems, followed by a look at the systems effect of changes and an analysis of the exercise of discretion. After a walk through the various stages of the systems from investigation to release, the chapter turns to an analysis of selected constitutional rights of defendants. The chapter considers victims' rights.and compares those with defendants' rights. It closes with an analysis of U.S. criminal justice systems, looking at race and ethnicity, socioeconomic status, and gender.

CHAPTER **11** U.S. Criminal Justice Systems

CHAPTER **12** Police

CHAPTER **13** Court Systems

Chapter 12 covers policing in its historical perspective as well as its modern developments. Public and private policing are compared and contrasted. Personnel issues are highlighted, and a section on the nature of policing covers basic police functions as well as police subcultures and the impact of AIDS on policing. Police decision making, discretion in policing, and police misconduct are also covered. The chapter analyzes various ways to control policing and closes with a brief analysis of terrorism and policing.

Chapter 13's overview of court systems distinguishes among the types of courts; describes the roles of lawyers and judges; and gives accounts of pretrial processes, trials, sentencing, and appeals. The chapter closes with a look at the problems of court congestion and court violence.

CHAPTER 11

U.S. Criminal
Justice Systems

Jeff Pierce, center, holds hands with his aunt Louise Burris, left, and his sister-in-law Esty Pierce during a news conference at the Joseph Harp prison in Lexington, Oklahoma. Pierce was released from prison after serving 15 years of a 65-year sentence for a rape that he did not commit. He was freed after DNA evidence exonerated him. The police chemist, Joyce Gilchrist, who testified against him, was fired from her job. Other cases in which Gilchrist testified were also examined.

KEY TERMS

adversary system
anticipatory search warrant
arraignment
arrest
bail
bail bond
booking
burden of proof
charge
crime control model
criminal justice systems
defendant
discretion
due process
due process model
equal protection
grand jury
indictment
information
initial appearance
inquisitory system
jurisdiction
jury
magistrate
Miranda warning
peremptory challenge

INTRODUCTION

In this chapter, we begin our look into U.S. criminal justice systems by analyzing the philosophy on which they rest. The chapter opens with a discussion of the two major concepts of the adversary system: due process and equal protection. It then examines the effects of changes within criminal justice systems along with the importance of discretion. Although criminal justice systems, even within the United States, may differ from one jurisdiction to another, all have the same essential stages. Those are examined individually.

The next section of the chapter analyzes four of the basic constitutional rights of defendants: the right to be free from unreasonable searches and seizures, the right not to testify against oneself, the right to counsel, and the right to trial by a jury. These and other constitutional rights are recognized to ensure that the government follows proper procedures in apprehending, charging, and trying people for alleged criminal acts. Victims' rights are important, too, and the chapter looks at those rights and considers how they may conflict with defendants' rights. A brief assessment of U.S. criminal justice systems with reference to race and ethnicity, socioeconomic status, and gender is followed by a new topic that looks at a June 2010 U.S. Supreme Court decision that considers the impact of potential terrorist acts on First Amendment rights.

This chapter provides an overview of U.S. **criminal justice systems** by examining the basic philosophy and concepts on which those systems rest. Criminal justice systems are based on the philosophy that the defendant's dignity must be recognized and that he or she is innocent until proven guilty beyond a reasonable doubt by the government, which must follow proper procedures in presenting its case. Violation of these rules impairs defendants' rights and threatens the foundation of U.S. criminal justice systems.

Concepts of U.S. Criminal Justice

The U.S. criminal justice systems guarantee numerous constitutional and statutory rights to persons who are charged with crimes. Those rights are based on the philosophies on which the systems rest.

The Philosophy of the Adversary System

The major characteristic of U.S. criminal justice systems is that they rest on the **adversary system**. This approach presumes that the best way to get the facts in a dispute is to have a contest between the two sides—the government, the prosecuting attorney (who together represent society), and the victim (in a criminal trial) versus the defense attorney and the defendant. In contrast is the **inquisitory system**, under which the accused is presumed guilty and must prove his or her innocence.

The primary difference between the adversary and the inquisitory systems is the presumption of innocence versus the presumption of guilt, which affects the **burden of proof**. Under the adversary system, the prosecution has the burden of proving guilt; under the inquisitory system, the defense has the burden of proving innocence. This is a major difference because, in U.S. justice systems, the burden of proof is critical. In criminal cases, the burden is *beyond a reasonable doubt*; in civil cases, it is a *preponderance of the evidence*. Proving in a criminal case that a defendant is guilty beyond a reasonable doubt is a heavy burden. However, we impose that stringent standard on the government because of its greater resources and because we believe that it is better to release a guilty person than to convict an innocent one.

The adversary system has aroused considerable criticism, some of which is justified, but it is important to understand its philosophy. It is based on the concepts of **due process** and **equal protection** for all criminal defendants, as provided by the Fourteenth Amendment to the U.S. Constitution (see Appendix A), which states, in part: "[N]or shall any State deprive any person of life, liberty, or property, without due process of law; nor deny to any person within its jurisdiction the equal protection of the law." Both due process and equal protection are difficult to define and have been the subjects of numerous court decisions.

Due Process

A former U.S. Supreme Court justice attempted to explain *due process* in the following frequently quoted statement:

> "Due Process," unlike some legal rules, is not a technical conception with a fixed content unrelated to time, place and circumstances. . . . [It] cannot be imprisoned within the treacherous limits of any formula. Representing a profound attitude of fairness between man and man, and more particularly between the individual and government, "due process" is compounded of history, reason, the past course of decisions, and stout confidence in the strength of the democratic faith which we possess. Due process is not a mechanical instrument. It is not a yardstick. It is a process.[1]

The importance of due process may be underscored by referring to the earlier and often cited work of Herbert L. Packer, who wrote about the conflict between the **crime control model** of criminal justice and the **due process model**. The goal of the crime control model is quick and efficient processing of people who are accused of violating the law. This model, said Packer, is similar to an assembly line. The due process model is more of an obstacle course because of its emphasis on procedures that protect defendants' right. Within criminal justice systems, support for the due process model comes mainly from the courts and defense attorneys. The main support for the crime control model comes from the prosecution and the police.[2]

Packer made these observations in the 1960s, but his comments are still relevant. By the provisions of our state and our federal constitutions, particularly the Bill of Rights and the U.S. Supreme Court decisions interpreting them, we have criminal justice systems that are based on the due process model. There is no question, however, that observation of defendants' due process rights creates obstacles for law enforcement. If authorities could accuse anyone of a crime regardless of available evidence, could search and seize at will, could interrogate suspects for unlimited periods of time when those suspects did not have an attorney, could physically and psychologically coerce confessions, and could violate other recognized due process rights, convictions would be easier. That approach could also increase law violations, however, if people became angry about the process. And as the discussion that follows indicates, it definitely would increase wrongful convictions. Although some people argue that our system has gone too far in recognizing the rights of the accused, others argue that it has not gone far enough.

Equal Protection

Like due process, equal protection is a critical concept of U.S. criminal justice systems. Stated simply, *equal protection* prohibits treating people differently because of their gender, race, nationality, ethnicity, religion, disability, and so on. Thus, minorities may not be excluded from juries because they are minorities, and persons may not be excluded because of their gender. But at times, it is difficult to prove that what appears to be discrimination is just that—rather than a legitimate use of discretionary power.

An example of this problem occurs when officials target African Americans because of their race, a concept referred to as **racial profiling**, which is presented later in this chapter and, in more detail, in Chapter 12. Chapter 10 discussed the fact that minorities have argued that they are targeted because of their race. When that issue was before the U.S. Supreme Court in the *Armstrong* case (see again Chapter 10), the Supreme Court held that, although the alleged discrimination would be a violation of equal protection, the defendants had not proved that such discrimination actually occurred in their cases.[3]

The Reality of the Adversary System

The U.S. adversary system does not always work as intended, and innocent people are convicted. Although many people argue that wrongful convictions are the result of inevitable mistakes, some authorities dispute that position. According to criminologist C. Ronald Huff, "a substantially significant number of cases . . . are . . . attributable either to professional dishonesty and deception or to professional incompetence."[4] A study by Huff reported that up to 1985 in the United States, 345 people were wrongly convicted of capital crimes and 25 of them were executed.[5] Exhibit 11.1 presents recent examples of wrongful convictions.

In his 2002 presidential address before the American Society of Criminology, Huff reviewed his work on wrongful convictions. He incorporated the views of Packer (discussed earlier) with those of other scholars to explain what he called the *ratification error* (rubber-stamping decisions made at lower levels). According to Huff, mistakes made at lower levels are ratified by others as the cases move through criminal justice systems. This process serves both the crime control and the due process models, "neither of which adequately addresses the needs of the innocent defendant."[6]

More recent information on wrongful convictions comes from The Innocence Project, a nonprofit law clinic at the Benjamin N. Cardozo School of Law in New York City. This organization works on cases in which DNA (deoxyribonucleic acid, contained in all body cells, which provides a rather precise way to identify persons if the sample of body fluids containing DNA is large enough for thorough testing) can show conclusively that the accused could not have committed the crime for which he or she has been convicted. The project, begun in 1992 by Barry C. Scheck and Peter J. Neufeld, reported in 2010 that, since the first DNA exoneration in 1989, 261 persons had been exonerated (as noted in Exhibit 11.1), with the following leading causes for the wrongful convictions:

- Mistaken eyewitness identification testimony occurred in 75 percent of the cases. Of that group, for those cases in which race was known, at least 40 percent involved cross-racial eyewitness identification.
- Invalid or improper forensic science was involved. Either the evidence was not subjected to rigorous testing, the testing was improperly done, or improper conduct occurred in the testing or the expert testimony in court.
- False confessions and incriminating statements were at issue in approximately 25 percent of the cases.[7]

According to The Innocence Project, of the 261 exonerees, 17 were on death row at some time, 155 were African American, and the real perpetrator was identified in 116 of the cases. Approximately one-half of those exonerated received some financial compensation, with 27 states, the District of Columbia, and the federal government providing compensation for wrongfully convicted persons.[8]

In November 2007, the *New York Times* published an article relating the findings of its reporters, who located and interviewed 137 of the inmates freed to date. Approximately one-third of the 137 were able to "find a stable footing in the world," but approximately one-sixth returned to prison or became addicted to alcohol or other drugs. Approximately one-half "had experiences

EXHIBIT 11.1

Wrongful Convictions: Innocent Defendants Are Released

Here are just a few of the 261 wrongful convictions documented as of October 2010. But first, there are some general facts about wrongful convictions as reported by The Innocence Project, which tracks the cases and works to win release for those who are wrongfully convicted.

- "Seventeen people had been sentenced to death before DNA proved their innocence and led to their release.
- The average sentence served by DNA exonerees has been 13 years.
- About 70 percent of those exonerated by DNA testing are members of minority groups.
- In almost 40 percent of the cases profiled here, the actual perpetrator has been identified by DNA testing.
- Exonerations have been won in 34 states and Washington, D.C."[1]

Joseph Lamont Abbitt, 2 September 2009

Joseph Abbitt served 14 years for two rapes he did not commit. On 2 May 1991, an intruder entered a home in Winston-Salem, North Carolina, where he remained for over an hour, bound the feet of two sisters, ages 13 and 16, and raped them. Abbitt was convicted primarily on the basis of the eyewitness testimony of the two victims. He had been in the sisters' home previously and had lived in the same neighborhood. Abbitt was convicted of burglary, kidnapping, and rape and sentenced to two life terms plus 110 years. His convictions were upheld. Although police were not required to keep evidence in such cases at that time, the rape kits were preserved. In 2005, Abbitt asked the North Carolina Center on Actual Innocence to assist him with his efforts at release. The first test of the evidence was inconclusive; subsequent tests excluded him as the perpetrator of the rapes.[2]

Thomas Lee Goldstein, May 2004

Two months after a state court judge overturned his conviction, Thomas Lee Goldstein was released after 24 years in prison for a murder he did not commit. Prosecutors held

Goldstein for two months after the judge's decision and then admitted that they did not have the evidence to retry him. He was convicted primarily on the basis of the testimony of a jailhouse informer who later recanted. Goldstein left prison with a $200 check, but he could not cash it until his attorney drove him to a Veterans Affairs center to get proper identification. Even there, he had bad luck; the computers were down, and the agency had no record of his three years of service as a U.S. Marine. His first night out of prison, his lawyer took him to dinner, where he had a beer and a Mexican dinner. The next day, he called an old girlfriend "hoping for a wild day of sex. Of course she was not home, so I went to the law library instead." Goldstein, 55, became a paralegal in a small law firm, working for his attorney on civil claims against the system that took the best years of his life.[3]

In 2007, a federal court held that Goldstein had the legal right to sue the prosecutor and his deputy for their respective roles in his wrongful conviction. But in 2009, by a 9-0 vote, the U.S. Supreme Court reversed, holding that the officials had absolute immunity for actions engaged in during the course of their respective roles. The case was sent back to determine whether any actions were outside the scope of their job assignments.[4]

Peter Limone, February 2001

Peter Limone served 33 years, 2 months, and 5 days before he was released from prison in February 2001. Limone, who was on death row for four years, was released at age 66. His wife, who was convinced of his innocence, visited him regularly and supported their four children during his incarceration. Limone and three other defendants were convicted of murder based primarily on the testimony of a witness whom the FBI had reason to know would perjure himself on the stand. Furthermore, the FBI permitted these men to languish in prison through appeals. Finally, after much research and many motions, Limone and another inmate (two of them had already died) were released. In June 2004, a federal appeals between those extremes, drifting from job to job and leaning on their families, lawyers or friends for housing and other support." The exonerated defendants complained that they received little if any help from criminal justice systems, pointing out that we have programs for released drug dealers but nothing for released innocent persons. The article emphasized that although many of these 137 individuals were at a disadvantage before they entered prison (e.g., more than one-half had not finished high school and many had not held regular jobs for a significant time period), others "had been leading lives of stability and accomplishment." Many were from states that provide no financial compensation for exonerated inmates.[9]

Before we close this discussion on wrongful convictions, it is reasonable to consider a study published by law professor Samuel R. Gross and his colleagues at the University of Michigan in 2004. These scholars noted that since 1989, at least 328 wrongful convictions had been uncovered. In 254 of those, the charges were dismissed after new evidence (e.g., DNA) was assessed. In addition, 42 persons were pardoned by a governor who thought they were innocent on the basis of new evidence; 28 were retried and acquitted. In four cases, the states acknowledged the innocence of convicted persons who had since died. These 328 persons served a total of 3,400 years in prison; 61 percent of those exonerated had been convicted of murder, 37 percent of rape. Only three of the cases were for robbery, which is

---

EXHIBIT 11.1 continued

court upheld a judge's ruling that Limone and Joseph Salvati could sue the retired FBI agent and a former police detective. The judge ruled that the agents were not entitled to immunity from civil suit. Excerpts from that opinion demonstrate the magnitude of the case.

Limone v. United States

The conclusions that the plaintiffs have asked me to draw—that government agents suborned perjury, framed four innocent men, conspired to keep them in jail for three decades—are so shocking that I felt obliged to analyze this complex record with special care in order that the public, and especially the parties, could be fully confident of my conclusions.

I have concluded that the plaintiffs' accusations that the United States government violated the law are proved. . . .

Now is the time to say and say without equivocation: This "cost" to the liberty of four men, to our system of justice is not remotely acceptable. No man's liberty is dispensable. No human being may be traded for another. Our system cherishes each individual. We have fought wars over this principle. We are still fighting those wars.

Sadly, when law enforcement perverts its mission, the criminal justice system does not easily self-correct. We understand that our system makes mistakes; we have appeals to address them. But this case goes beyond mistakes, beyond the unavoidable errors of a fallible system. This case is about intentional misconduct, subornation of perjury, conspiracy, the framing of innocent men. While judges are scrutinized—our decisions made in public and appealed—law enforcement decisions like these rarely see the light of day. The public necessarily relies on the integrity and professionalism of its officials.

It took nearly thirty years to uncover this injustice. It took the extraordinary efforts of a judge, a lawyer, even a reporter, to finally bring out the facts. Proof of innocence in this democracy should not depend upon efforts as gargantuan as these.

[The court discussed the civil actions involved in the case] . . .

The government's position is, in a word, absurd. The law they cite does not apply to the extraordinary facts of this case. The issue here is not discretion but abuse, not independent charging decisions but the framing of four innocent men, not the failure to produce exculpatory evidence but procuring convictions by misrepresentation, not letting perjured testimony proceed uncorrected but facilitating it. . . .

In the end I conclude that the defendant is liable to these men and their families. As to damages, plaintiffs' loss of liberty, and, in effect, a lifetime of experiences, is obviously not compensable. To the extent that damages can approach this task, my total award is One Hundred One Million, Seven Hundred Fifty Thousand, And 00/100 ($101,750,000.00) Dollars.[5]

---

1. The Innocence Project, "Innocent Project Case Profiles," http://www.innocenceproject.org/know/, accessed 29 October 2010.

2. The Innocence Project, "Know the Cases: Browse Profiles: Joseph Abbitt," http://www.innocenceproject.org/Content/Joseph_Abbitt.php, accessed 29 October 2010.

3. "No New Trial in '79 Killing: Inmate Is Free," *New York Times* (3 May 2004), p. 9; "Starting Over, 24 Years After a Wrongful Conviction," *New York Times* (21 June 2004), p. 14.

4. *Goldstein v. City of Long Beach*, 481 F.3d 1170 (9th Cir. 2007), rev'd., remanded sub nom., 129 S.Ct. 855 (2009).

5. *Limone v. United States*, 497 F.Supp.2d 143 (D.Mass. 2007), aff'd., 579 F.3d 79 (1st Cir. 2009).

committed four times as often as rape. The researchers suggested that the 328 cases were only illustrative and that perhaps thousands of persons are serving time for crimes they did not commit. The fact that the exonerations were primarily for murder and rape demonstrated that "we are most likely to convict innocent defendants in those cases in which their very lives are at stake." These are the cases that get the most attention by lawyers and others looking for errors; if that same degree of attention was given to all crimes, we would probably see a much higher number of wrongful convictions.[10]

In recent years, most states have enacted legislation that changed procedures in criminal cases and, among other provisions, now give inmates greater access to DNA and other information that might help them in their appeals. Closer scrutiny is being taken of crime labs that process DNA and other evidence, and eyewitness testimonies are being questioned more carefully.[11]

MEDIA FOCUS

11.1 Juveniles in Adult Jails

For over a century, U.S. criminal justice systems have viewed juvenile offenders as needing the care and protection of a special system. They have been processed through juvenile, not criminal, courts. There have been exceptions, and the incarceration of juveniles in adult jails and prisons has been a concern that has increased in recent years. The numbers are significant: In 2010, the Bureau of Justice Statistics reported that on 30 June 2009, 7,220 inmates held in local jails were juveniles (persons under the age of 18). Of those juveniles, 5,847 were held as adults; 1,373 were held as juveniles.[1]

A *New York Times* article about the issues that have arisen with the incarceration of juveniles in adult jails and prisons noted that Colorado, Louisiana, Pennsylvania, Texas, Washington, and other states had made special arrangements for their juvenile offenders. In most cases, this involved seg-

regating juveniles from adult inmates. These changes were the result of the recommendations made by the American Correctional Association (ACA). The ACA suggested limiting the number of juveniles who are transferred to adult criminal courts and subsequently incarcerated in adult jails and prisons; it also suggested that for those juveniles who are tried and convicted as adults, special provisions should be made.[2]

Juveniles who are incarcerated in adult jails and prisons may be (and often are) physically or sexually assaulted by adult inmates. In fact, there is evidence that they are "five times as likely to be sexually assaulted, twice as likely to be beaten by staff, 50 percent more likely to be attacked with a weapon, and eight times as likely to commit suicide as children confined in juvenile facilities."[3] Juveniles in adult jails or prisons may also learn even more about crime from

Juveniles who are detained in adult jails rather than in special juvenile facilities may be abused by other inmates and are more likely than their counterparts in juvenile facilities to return to crime after they are released. The Campaign for Youth Justice and other organizations report that juveniles in adult jails are at extreme risk for sexual abuse, and the jail experience is detrimental to their mental health (http://www.campaignforyouthjustice.org/, accessed 30 October 2010).

MEDIA FOCUS continued

11.1

their older colleagues. They are more likely than their counterparts in juvenile institutions to return to crime after their release. They also have a public felony conviction record in contrast to the private adjudications of the juvenile court.

It is not just the influence of adult inmates that provides a negative factor when juveniles are housed with them. Juveniles in corrections have different needs. Anyone who has ever fed a growing teen knows that additional food is one of those needs. For example, some juvenile inmates, when asked what the most important motivator in prison was, responded, "pizza." One official said that this response "shows that [juvenile inmates] are adolescents. They live very much for the minute—which makes them very dangerous inmates. They're not like adult inmates, who will listen to orders of a correctional officer."[4]

Pennsylvania attempted to meet its problems with juvenile inmates sentenced to prison by building a $71 million facility exclusively for teenage inmates. Pine Grove, a 500-bed institution, opened in January 2001. Florida enacted a statute requiring that juvenile inmates sentenced to adult prisons must be incarcerated in separate units. And in Texas, juvenile inmates are housed in a separate wing of an adult prison. They spend about one-half of their time in school and the rest in counseling.[5]

---

1. Todd D. Minton, Bureau of Justice Statistics, *Jail Inmates at Mid-year 2009, Statistical Tables* (June 2010), p. 9, http://bjs.ojp.usdoj.gov/Content/pub/pdf/jim09st.pdf, accessed 30 October 2010.
2. "States Adjust Adult Prisons to Needs of Youth Inmates," *New York Times* (7 July 2001), p. 1.
3. "Children in Adult Jails: Factsheet," Building Blocks for Youth, http://www.buildingblocksforyouth.org/issues/adultjails/factsheet.html, accessed 30 October 2010.
4. "States Adjust Adult Prisons to Needs of Youth Inmates."
5. Ibid.

Other Special Characteristics of U.S. Criminal Justice Systems

Two additional characteristics are important to an understanding of all U.S. criminal justice systems. The first is the *systems effect* of all elements and procedures; the second is *discretion*.

The Systems Effect

The U.S. criminal justice systems are composed of processes as well as structures. A change in one process or structure has an impact on other elements within the system. Consider the remarks of the late William H. Rehnquist while he was Chief Justice of the U.S. Supreme Court. In 1992, Rehnquist warned that the trend toward federalizing crimes was clogging the federal court system. Rehnquist was referring to the congressional practice of enacting new statutes that make federal crimes of acts previously processed only in state courts. In 1999, Rehnquist issued the warning again, referring to the propensity of Congress to respond to every highly publicized crime and create new federal crimes or increase sentences. Consider, for example, the area of drug offenses. Chapter 10 noted the increase in prison populations resulting from increased convictions and longer sentences for these offenders in both the state and federal systems. These increases at the state and federal levels have also had a significant impact on other parts of criminal justice systems. Courts are congested, and this requires more facilities, more personnel, and more resources.

Another example of the systems effect results from the trend in recent years to try juveniles as adults. Many states provide that juvenile cases involving serious offenses (especially violent ones) may be transferred to criminal courts. When the young people in these cases are convicted and sentenced to prison, they are usually sent to adult facilities, most of which are not prepared to handle the special needs of juvenile offenders. It would appear that little thought was given to this issue when the statutes were enacted, but now, with the increase in juveniles sentenced to prison (rather than to juvenile facilities), authorities must face new problems. And although we are often critical of the media for sensationalizing crimes, a news article presented the issues in a manner that was informative and thought-provoking. The article is summarized in Media Focus 11.1.

This is not to suggest that the arrests, prosecutions, trials, and incarcerations of violent juveniles are not warranted. Rather, it shows how attempts to handle a situation within one area of criminal justice systems may create problems in other areas.

A second special characteristic of criminal justice systems that deserves more attention is the use of discretion.

Discretion

The U.S. criminal justice systems permit wide **discretion**. There are not enough law enforcement officers to enforce all laws. Total enforcement is impossible, as well as unwise, because there may be extenuating circumstances that justify not enforcing some laws. If all laws are not enforced, authorities must make decisions concerning which laws to enforce and which suspects to apprehend. Law enforcement officers must decide how to allocate their time, which investigations to conduct, and whether a search is reasonable in a given situation.

Discretion is also exercised by other criminal justice professionals. Prosecutors must decide when to file charges and which ones to file. They must decide whether to drop or reduce charges and whether to seek indictments. Judges set bail or other conditions of pretrial release. They may accept or deny pleas or plea bargains, requests by defense or prosecution to drop or reduce charges, or any other motions from the attorneys. Some judges have sentencing discretion; they may or may not revoke probation. Defense attorneys have discretion in many areas of defending their clients. Correctional officers may have discretion regarding inmate classification, discipline, and job assignments. Parole authorities may have discretion to determine (or in some systems, only recommend) parole or parole revocation.

Discretion is an inevitable feature of criminal justice systems. Although guidelines, laws, and constitutional amendments may be passed to regulate it, discretion cannot be eliminated. Properly used, it is functional for the system. Many cases should not be prosecuted or tried, and a refusal to arrest (or to make any other decision that may appear lenient) may be the best approach in some instances.

One result of discretion is that the number of cases proceeding through criminal justice systems is considerably smaller than the number coming to the attention of the police. Most felonies that come to the attention of the police will not result in arrests, and as Figure 11.1 points out, most arrests that result in arraignments will not be processed through the entire criminal justice systems. Some of the accused are juveniles who are transferred to juvenile courts. Some of the remaining adult defendants' cases are dismissed without any charges being filed; in other cases, felony charges are reduced to misdemeanors or misdemeanors to violations. Some arrestees negotiate pleas, and only a small percentage of persons charged with crimes actually proceed to trial. And not all defendants who are found guilty at trial or who plead guilty are sentenced to jail or prison.

There are many reasons for the decrease in cases through the various criminal justice stages. In addition to the effect that the exercise of discretion by police or court officials may have, cases may be dismissed because victims or witnesses refuse to testify, and prosecutors do not have enough evidence for convictions without those testimonies. Those involved may agree to testify but fail to appear in court at the appropriate time. Improper or inaccurate statements by attorneys or witnesses, or illegal police behavior during arrest or investigation, may lead the trial judge to exclude evidence vital to the case. Without that

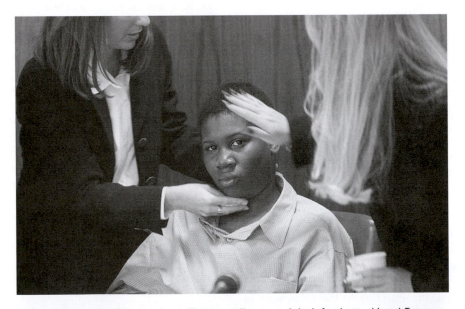

Plea bargains are offered to juveniles as well as to adult defendants. Lionel Tate was only 12 when he killed his playmate and only 14 when he was tried and convicted in 2001 as an adult and sentenced to life in prison without a chance of parole. In 2003, a Florida court ordered a new trial, ruling that Tate was entitled to a hearing on the issue of whether he understood the charges against him and could participate in his defense. The prosecutor offered the same plea bargain that Tate's mother had rejected on his behalf prior to trial. Tate was released to his mother's custody in January 2004. Later that year, Tate violated the terms of his release but was not jailed until he was arrested in 2005 for allegedly committing several crimes, including armed robbery. He entered guilty pleas and was sentenced to 30 years in prison. Subsequently (as noted in Exhibit 5.1), Tate asked to withdraw those pleas on the grounds that his attorney was incompetent, but in October 2007, Tate's 30-year prison term was upheld.

Figure 11.1

Typical Outcome of 100 Felony Defendants Arraigned in State Courts in the 75 Largest Counties, May 2006

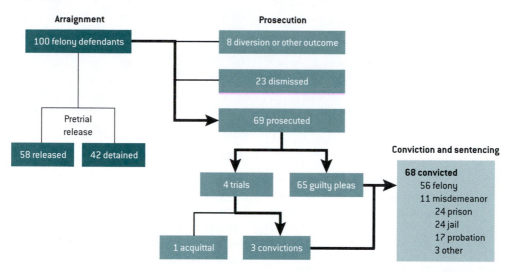

Source: Thomas H. Cohen and Tracey Kyckelhahn, Bureau of Justice Statistics, *Felony Defendants in Large Urban Counties, 2006* (May 2010), p. 1, http://bjs.ojp.usdoj.gov/content/pub/pdf/fdluc06.pdf, accessed 31 October 2010.

evidence, a conviction is unlikely, so the judge may dismiss the case.

One final point on discretion is important. Juries, police, prosecutors, and judges do not want to release (through acquittal, light sentencing, case dismissals, etc.) people who are dangerous, and they suffer intense criticism if they do so. This may lead police, court officials, juries, parole boards, and others to exercise discretion conservatively. That is, in an effort to maintain a safe society, criminal justice professionals may restrain a defendant who is not dangerous. Mistakes may be inevitable and impossible to control, but the system must keep a watchful eye on those who make discretionary decisions for improper reasons, such as to suppress racial minorities or other groups not in current favor with the decision makers.

The Stages in U.S. Criminal Justice Systems

Although criminal justice systems in the United States vary considerably, they do share many features. These systems consist of four basic components: police, prosecution, courts, and corrections. The *police* (and other law enforcement authorities) are responsible for entering most people into the system and are also involved in some pretrial procedures. The police are very important, and Chapter 12 focuses on them.

The second major component in a criminal justice system is the *prosecution.* The decision to prosecute is crucial.

It involves the discretion of a *prosecuting attorney*, who brings the charges against the accused, and a *defense attorney*, who represents the accused, or the **defendant**.

Prosecutors and defense attorneys function within criminal court systems. *Courts,* the third major component of criminal justice systems, are presided over by *judges.* The roles of judges, prosecutors, and defense attorneys are discussed in Chapter 13, along with the structure of courts and the concepts of punishment and sentencing.

The final component of criminal justice systems is *corrections,* which includes the detainment of some defendants in jail before trial (discussed later in this chapter); their confinement in jails, prisons, and other facilities after conviction (discussed in Chapter 14); and the supervision of offenders within the community (the focus of Chapter 15).

Criminal justice systems also feature similar stages, beginning with the investigation of a reported crime. For easy and quick reference, the stages are listed in Exhibit 11.2. This is merely an overview of the stages. Most of them are discussed in greater detail elsewhere, along with the racial and ethnic, gender, and age issues associated with them, where applicable.

Investigation Prior to Arrest

When police receive a complaint or are observers at a crime scene, they may make an investigation. Police may interview witnesses and obtain information that leads to an arrest. During the investigation, police may detain a suspect briefly and may search for weapons.

Arrest

Most police encounters do not result in an **arrest**, and police have wide discretion at this stage. When a person is arrested, he or she is taken into custody (usually to the police station).

The investigation of scenes in which crimes are alleged to have occurred is extremely important and must be conducted carefully, skillfully, and as quickly as possible. All evidence that might pertain to the crime or crimes must be preserved and analyzed. In this scene, two members of the Omaha Crime Lab Unit in Nebraska enter the Von Maur department store after a shooting spree. The alleged gunman killed nine people, including himself.

Booking

When the police arrive at the police station with an arrested suspect, the suspect undergoes **booking**—his or her name and the location, time, and purpose of the arrest are entered in the police arrest book, or log. The suspect may be fingerprinted, photographed, and released after booking if it is determined that a crime was not committed or that there is not sufficient evidence to hold that suspect pending further investigation.

Initial Appearance

Most states have a statutory requirement that, after arrest, the suspect must be taken quickly before a magistrate for an **initial appearance**. The **magistrate**, presumed to be a neutral party, must tell the suspect his or her rights and explain the **charge** (accusation of a crime) against him or her.

Preliminary Hearing

The defendant may waive the **preliminary hearing** in which the evidence against the accused is considered. If the hearing is not waived, the government's evidence is examined. At this time, the magistrate may either dismiss the charges or bind the suspect over to the **grand jury** for an indictment or to the prosecuting attorney for an information. The magistrate may grant **bail** and set the amount of the **bail bond** or refuse bail or other forms of release.

Information

If a grand jury is not used, the prosecutor may return an **information**, an accusation based on the evidence available from police officers or private citizens. An *information* is a formal legal document sufficient to send a suspect to trial.

Indictment

In some jurisdictions, the prosecutor must bring formal charges and have the approval of the grand jury, which, after examining the evidence, returns an **indictment**, or a true bill. The indictment serves the same purpose as the information; it requires the suspect to appear before a court that has **jurisdiction** to hear the charges. The grand jury, a specified number of private citizens chosen randomly, meets at periodic intervals to consider whether to indict suspects presented by the prosecution. The grand jury may also conduct investigations on its own.

The Fifth Amendment to the U.S. Constitution (see Appendix A) provides that in federal cases, felonies must go through the process of indictment by a grand jury. Some state laws require this process, too. The grand jury may refuse to return an indictment.

Arraignment

After an information or indictment is secured, the suspect must appear before a court for an **arraignment**. After hearing the formal charges and again being informed of his or her rights, the defendant may enter a plea for the first time. If the plea is *not guilty*, a trial date is set. If the defendant has a choice of a trial by a judge or by a jury, that decision is made at this stage. Certain pretrial motions may be made, such as a motion to change the **venue** of the trial or to admit or suppress evidence.

Reduction of the Charge

For a number of reasons, the charge or charges against a defendant may be reduced. The defendant may agree to plead guilty to lesser charges rather than stand trial on the original charge. At any of the stages in criminal justice systems, the prosecutor may drop charges (although this may require the permission of the judge), or the judge may dismiss charges or entire cases.

Trial

If the case is not dismissed or the defendant does not plead guilty, the case is set for **trial**. Most criminal cases do not go to trial but are resolved prior to that stage. Most trials of minor offenses are brief, lasting perhaps less than an hour or two. In complex cases, the trial may continue for weeks or months. Witnesses are questioned by attorneys, victims may testify, and physical evidence, such as weapons allegedly used in the crime, may be introduced. Rules of evidence are complex, and motions challenging them require rulings by trial judges and may be the subject of appeals.

Sentencing

After the defendant pleads guilty or is found guilty at a trial, the judge enters a judgment of conviction and sets a date for sentencing. Sentencing in minor cases may occur immediately. In cases involving defendants who have been convicted of several offenses or of one or more serious offenses, normally the judge sets sentencing for a future date

Trial judges preside over trials and issue rulings regarding evidence and other issues, but one of their most important roles is to impose sentences on guilty defendants.

to permit time for presentence investigations and recommendations. In some instances, the judge determines the sentence; in others, the jury may do so. In some cases, the jury recommends a sentence, but the judge is not required to follow that recommendation; in other cases, the judge must follow the jury's recommendation.

Appeals and Remedies

Defendants may have legal grounds on which to appeal their convictions to an appellate court. They may challenge their confinement through various postconviction remedies, such as the writ of habeas corpus, which is a constitutional challenge to the legality of detention. Through this frequently used procedure, inmates argue that they are being confined illegally because the conditions of confinement violate a federally guaranteed constitutional right.

Incarceration

Convicted persons may be incarcerated in detention centers, jails, prisons, work camps, or other facilities. Others may be permitted to return to the community with or without supervision; many are placed on probation, the most frequently imposed sentence.

Release

Upon completion of their sentences, inmates must be released unless they are confined under special statutes that permit the further detention of persons deemed dangerous to society (e.g., some sex offenders). Some inmates are released before the end of their sentences through the parole process (see Chapter 15). Inmates on parole may be returned to prison to serve the remainder of their terms if they violate parole conditions. Some correctional systems release inmates early to reduce prison overcrowding. Some systems are under federal court orders to keep their inmate populations at or below a specified level.

Selected Constitutional Rights of Defendants

The framers of the Constitution were concerned that the federal government might become too strong, so they added the Bill of Rights (see Appendix A) to provide further protections for individuals. In early decisions, the U.S. Supreme Court ruled that the Bill of Rights restricts only the *federal* government, but gradually, the Supreme Court has held that most of the constitutional provisions also apply to the states through the Fourteenth Amendment, which is reprinted in Appendix A.

The basic rights guaranteed by the U.S. Constitution have been interpreted over the years by the U.S. Supreme Court. The procedural safeguards we all have as the result of the Constitution and U.S. Supreme Court case law are very important. For example, the prosecution is required to prove its case beyond a reasonable doubt. Defendants cannot be forced to testify against themselves, and their persons and possessions cannot be searched unreasonably. They are entitled to be notified of the charges against them, to have impartial and public trials by juries of their peers, and to be represented by counsel. If they cannot afford counsel, it must be provided at the state's expense (the same is true of the federal system). Defendants may be tried only once for the same offense, and they are presumed innocent until proven guilty. Now we examine some of these constitutional rights. The law regarding these rights is complex, and no attempt is made to explain every right or every element of the rights in the following sections.

The Right to Be Free from Unreasonable Searches and Seizures

According to the Fourth Amendment of the U.S. Constitution (see Appendix A), the "right of the people to be secure in their persons, houses, papers, and effects, against unreasonable searches and seizures, shall not be violated." The key word is *unreasonable*. Unreasonable searches and seizures are prohibited because, according to the U.S. Supreme Court, the Constitution guarantees citizens a reasonable expectation of privacy. In some cases, the invasion of privacy is allowed to protect society, but in most instances, a search without a valid **search warrant** is a violation of the Fourth Amendment.

The search warrant is to be issued by a neutral magistrate (judge) only after a finding of **probable cause**, which

means that in light of the facts of the case, a reasonable person would think that the evidence sought exists and that it may be found in the place to be searched. The probable cause requirement also applies when an officer is searching without a search warrant, which is permitted only in limited circumstances.

The U.S. Supreme Court has upheld the constitutionality of an **anticipatory search warrant**, which is a warrant for a future search of a particular place at a particular time. The case of *United States v. Grubbs* involved a defendant, Jeffrey Grubbs, who purchased from a website a videotape containing child pornography. The website was operated by an undercover postal inspector. On the basis of these facts and an affidavit that the videotape would be delivered to Grubbs's home at a controlled time and that the warrant would not be executed until the package had been delivered and taken into the home, federal agents secured a search warrant. That warrant contained two attachments indicating the home address and the information sought. The affidavit was not included in the warrant. When the package was delivered to Grubbs's home, his wife signed for it and took it into the house. A few minutes later, when Grubbs left the home, he was detained by federal agents, who then entered the home and began the search. After reading the search warrant, Grubbs admitted that he had the tape. At trial, the judge denied the defendant's motion to exclude the videotape because the search warrant did not contain the affidavit stating the triggering events and was thus defective. Grubbs pleaded guilty but reserved his right to appeal.[12]

On appeal, Grubbs argued that anticipatory search warrants are not constitutional because they violate the requirement that warrants must be issued only upon probable cause. So if the police execute the warrant before the stated triggering event has occurred, they do not have reason to believe the items in question are at the searched place; thus, they do not have probable cause. The Court rejected this position and stated that "Because the probable cause requirement looks to whether evidence will be found when the search is conducted, all warrants are, in a sense, 'anticipatory.' In the typical case where the police seek permission to search a house for an item they believe is already located there, the magistrate's determination that there is probable cause for the search amounts to a prediction that the item will still be there when the warrant is executed." With regard to whether the anticipatory warrant was defective because it did not contain the affidavit with the triggering information, the Court held that it was not defective because the Fourth Amendment "does not require that the triggering condition for an anticipatory search warrant be set forth in the warrant itself."[13]

Despite its preference for warrants, the U.S. Supreme Court allows some exceptions, but they are few, specifically established, and well delineated. Some common types of searches are explored next.

Vehicle Searches

Under some circumstances, police may stop and search vehicles that they have reason to believe contain evidence of criminal activity or contraband, such as illegal drugs. For example, if police stop a driver whose vehicle matches the description of a car that was used for leaving the scene of a robbery, they may search the vehicle without a warrant. In other circumstances, a warrant is necessary, although in some cases the methods by which the police get information that leads to the granting of a warrant have been questioned.

In *Illinois v. Gates*, the U.S. Supreme Court considered the kinds of facts that police must produce to convince a magistrate that they have probable cause to obtain a warrant to search an automobile.[14] In *Gates*, the Bloomingdale, Illinois, police department received an anonymous letter stating that two specified people, a husband and his wife, were engaging in illegal drug sales and that on 3 May the wife would drive their car to Florida. The letter alleged that the husband would fly to Florida to drive the car back to Illinois with the trunk loaded with drugs and that the couple had about $100,000 worth of drugs in the basement of their Illinois home. After receiving this information, a police officer secured the address of the couple and confirmed that the husband had made a 5 May reservation to fly to Florida. Surveillance revealed that the suspect took the flight and spent the night in a motel room registered to his wife. The next morning, he left in a car with a woman. The license plate of the car was registered to him. The couple were driving north on an interstate highway used frequently for traveling from Florida to Illinois. On the basis of these facts, the police secured a search warrant for the couple's house and automobile.

The police, with warrants, were waiting for the couple when they returned to their home in Illinois. The officers searched the house and car and found drugs, which the state introduced as evidence at the trial. The U.S. Supreme Court upheld the issuance of the search warrant and subsequent admission of the seized evidence at trial. The Court established a "totality of circumstances" test for determining whether probable cause to issue a search warrant exists when informants provide information. In *Gates*, independent police verification of the allegations from the anonymous source provided sufficient information on which a magistrate could have probable cause to issue the warrants. Neither the anonymous letter alone nor the police's conclusions concerning the reliability of the informant were sufficient for probable cause. However, the extensive corroborating evidence obtained by the police, coupled with the letter and the police's conclusions, provided a reliable basis for issuing the search warrant.

The use of anonymous tips to provide evidence of a crime, giving police the right to stop a vehicle, was tested in 1990 in *Alabama v. White*. The U.S. Supreme Court held that an anonymous tip, furnished by a person who was not previously known to the police, could provide sufficient information and reasonable suspicion to justify an initial stop of a vehicle when the police had corroborated the informant's data by independent investigatory work. In this case, the informant alleged that the suspect, Vanessa White, would leave a specific apartment, get into a brown Plymouth station wagon with a broken right taillight, and drive to a named motel. She would be carrying illegal drugs. On the basis of this information, the police staked out the apartment building, located the described vehicle, and followed that vehicle when White (of whom they had no physical description) entered the car and drove away. The officers stopped the vehicle and told the driver that they suspected she was carrying illegal drugs. White consented to a search, and illegal drugs were found. She was arrested, tried, and convicted. On appeal, White argued that the police did not have reasonable suspicion for the initial stop. The U.S. Supreme Court disagreed and emphasized that the police corroborated the information supplied by the anonymous caller.[15]

Although in *White*, the suspect gave permission for the automobile to be searched, the U.S. Supreme Court has ruled that some warrantless searches of automobiles are allowable even without a suspect's permission. In *United States v. Ross*, the Supreme Court held that when police have probable cause to search a lawfully stopped automobile, even without a warrant, they may search any containers inside the car that might be used to conceal the object of the search.[16] Thus, if the car is stopped because police have probable cause to believe that it contains illegal drugs, they may search any container that is capable of concealing drugs. However, it has been held that a warrantless search of a bag in the trunk of a car, and thus out of the suspect's immediate reach and control, may not be conducted incident to a lawful arrest.[17]

Many issues surround the search of containers within an automobile. In 1991, the U.S. Supreme Court held that, even in the absence of probable cause, the search of a container within the automobile is proper when the suspect consents to a search of the car. In *Florida v. Jimeno*, police stopped a car that they believed contained illegal drugs and asked for permission to search the car. The suspect agreed, and the police opened a brown bag that they found on the floor of the car. That bag contained illegal drugs.[18]

In *United States v. Johns*, the U.S. Supreme Court ruled that the search of a container within the automobile need not be conducted immediately, and it upheld the warrantless search of containers taken from a truck that police had probable cause to believe contained marijuana. The search of the containers was not conducted for several days.[19]

In *Colorado v. Bertine*, the U.S. Supreme Court upheld the search of a suspect's vehicle after the suspect was arrested for driving while intoxicated. One officer drove the suspect to the police station while another took inventory of his vehicle, which had not yet been towed. This search, conducted without a search warrant, was upheld because "there was no showing that the police, who were following standardized procedures, acted in bad faith or for the sole purpose of investigation." In addition, police were responsible for the vehicle since they were having it towed.[20]

The U.S. Supreme Court has made some interesting decisions with regard to the investigatory stop as well as searches and seizures. For example, in 2000, all nine justices agreed that a person in suspicious circumstances, who flees upon seeing police officers, creates reasonable grounds for officers to stop and investigate, but they disagreed on how that principle should apply to the facts in the case. The scene in *Illinois v. Wardlow* was an area of Chicago characterized by heavy trafficking in illegal narcotics. When Wardlow saw police cars, he fled. He was chased down an alley by an officer, who determined that the suspect was carrying a gun. Five members of the U.S. Supreme Court believed these circumstances gave officers grounds for a stop and search. Chief Justice William H. Rehnquist, writing for that majority, said, "The determination of reasonable suspicion must be based on common-sense judgments and inferences about human behavior." He added, "Headlong flight—wherever it occurs—is the consummate act of evasion; it is not necessarily indicative of wrongdoing, but it is certainly suggestive of such." In a dissenting opinion, Justice John Paul Stevens argued: "Among some citizens, particularly minorities and those residing in high crime areas, there is also the possibility that the fleeing person is entirely innocent, but, with or without justification, believes that contact with the police can itself be dangerous, apart from any criminal activity associated with the officer's sudden presence."[21]

In 2000, the U.S. Supreme Court refused to uphold a case involving a search based on information from an informant. In *Florida v. J. L.*, an anonymous person called the Miami-Dade, Florida, police and told them that a young male who was African American, wearing a plaid shirt, and carrying a gun was standing at a named bus stop. When police arrived at that point they saw three African American males, one of whom was wearing a plaid shirt. He did not appear to have a gun and he did not act suspiciously. The only reason for the police to suspect any of these three young men was the anonymous tip, but they did frisk all three and found a gun on the one wearing the plaid shirt. The young man was only 15, so his full name is not used; thus, J. L. He was charged with carrying a concealed weapon and with firearm possession by a person under 18. At the trial, the defense motion to exclude the gun was granted; that was reversed by an intermediate appeals court but upheld by the state supreme court. Florida appealed that decision to the U.S. Supreme Court, which ruled in favor of the trial court. According to the U.S. Supreme Court, the anonymous tip alone was not a sufficient reason for the officers to search the three males, and thus, the gun found during that illegal search could not be used at trial.[22]

One issue of significance with regard to the investigatory stop is that police have been accused in many cities of engaging in racial profiling, which occurs when police stereotype persons as law violators based solely on their race. Generally, the complaints are brought by African Americans who allege that police have stereotyped them as law violators.

Like race, ethnicity is also an unacceptable reason for the police to stop a person. According to one federal appeals court, "Hispanic appearance is, in general, of such little probative value that it may not be considered as a relevant factor where particularized or individualized suspicion is required" for a stop. Three Mexicans were stopped about 115 miles east of San Diego, California, by U.S. Border Patrol agents, who gave five reasons for stopping them. One of those reasons was their Hispanic appearance.[23]

The U.S. Supreme Court has also held that when police act on some basis other than individualized suspicion, the reasons they take such actions should be considered in determining whether they violated a suspect's rights. In *Indianapolis v. Edmond*, several Indianapolis motorists brought an action to get a determination on whether police could use K-9 dogs to circle their cars and search for illegal drugs while other officers were checking driver's licenses and car registrations. The Court did not uphold this practice, in which police admitted that the primary purpose of their stops was to search for illegal drugs. The case did not, however, answer the question of how the Court would rule if searching for drugs was a secondary purpose.[24]

In December 2003, in *Maryland v. Pringle*, the U.S. Supreme Court considered the issue of whether police may search all occupants of an automobile after they find one occupant in possession of illegal drugs. In this case, the police stopped a driver because he was speeding. When the driver opened the glove compartment to get the car registration, the police officer saw cash; he then asked to search the car. The driver consented to the search, during which the police found illegal drugs in the armrest of the back seat. None of the occupants would admit responsibility for the drugs, so the police arrested all of them. Subsequently, Joseph Pringle, who was in the passenger side of the front seat, waived his *Miranda* rights and admitted that he owned the drugs and that the other two did not know he had them, at which point the others were released. Pringle was tried and convicted of drug possession with intent to sell; his sentence was 10 years with no parole. After Pringle lost his first appeal, he appealed to the highest appellate court in Maryland. The Maryland Court of Appeals reversed on the probable cause issue. It stated the fact that the police found drugs in the back seat of the car was not sufficient evidence to find probable cause to arrest a passenger in the front seat. The U.S. Supreme Court held that the arrest was proper. The car was stopped at 3:16 AM; a large amount of cash and illegal drugs were found during a legal search based on the driver's consent. These combined facts constituted probable cause to arrest all the occupants because it was reasonable to assume that they all knew about the cash and the drugs. According to Justice Rehnquist, who wrote for the majority, "The probable cause standard is incapable of precise definition or quantification into percentages because it deals with probabilities and depends on the totality of the circumstances."[25]

The U.S. Supreme Court has also considered whether police may stop motorists when officers have no reason to think they have committed a crime. In *Illinois v. Lidster*, police stopped all motorists at the intersection at which a fatal hit-and-run accident had occurred a week earlier. The police handed out fliers describing the accident and requesting information or witnesses to that accident. One driver, in attempting to stop, almost hit the officer. The driver was given a sobriety test, arrested, and convicted of driving while intoxicated. In a 4–3 vote, the Illinois Supreme Court overturned the conviction, holding that the roadblock was an unconstitutional stop, not a proper investigatory tool. The roadblock did not produce a witness, but one did respond to a television story about the accident. Thus, it could be argued that it is unreasonable to stop motorists in this manner when other methods of getting information are more useful. Despite that reasoning, the U.S. Supreme Court upheld the stop and arrest of Robert Lidster. In doing so, the Court referred to *Indianapolis v. Edmond*, in which the Court did not uphold roadblocks "whose primary purpose [was] to detect evidence of ordinary criminal wrongdoing." In that case, the police used sniffing dogs to detect drug violations, and the Court held that police may establish roadblocks only when there are "special needs, beyond the normal need for law enforcement," such as apprehending drunk drivers. In *Lidster*, the primary purpose of the police roadblock was not to detect whether a crime was being committed by the driver or other occupants of the stopped vehicle. Rather, it was to get information on another crime that had been committed previously at that venue.[26]

The U.S. Supreme Court has decided a case concerning whether police may use drug-sniffing dogs to search a car after they stop the driver for speeding or for other reasons but have no facts to support a belief that the car contains illegal drugs. The suspect in *Illinois v. Caballes* was stopped by a state trooper for driving six miles over the speed limit. While that officer was writing a speeding ticket, another one arrived and released his drug-sniffing dog, which called attention to the trunk. A search of the trunk revealed over $250,000 of marijuana. The suspect was convicted, sentenced to 12 months in prison, and assessed a $256,136 fine, which was the exact value of the illegal drugs. The case was affirmed by the Illinois Court of Appeals but reversed by the Illinois Supreme Court, which held that there were no facts to suggest illegal drug activity, and thus, the search turned a routine traffic stop into a drug investigation. The U.S. Supreme Court reversed, holding that there was no constitutional violation in the search and seizure. The U.S. Supreme Court ruled that the search did not violate any right of privacy. It took only 10 minutes, which did not create an unreasonable delay. Further, the use of the drug-sniffing dog did not reveal any information "other than the location of a substance that no individual has any right to possess." The two dissenting justices argued that, as a result of this decision, "every traffic stop could become an occasion to call in the dogs, to the distress of the law-abiding population."[27]

In 2007, a unanimous U.S. Supreme Court held that when officers stop a car, all passengers in that car have the same right as the driver to challenge that stop. In *Brendlin v. California*, the police, without any reason to believe the car was being operated unlawfully, stopped a driver to check the car's registration, recognized one of the passengers and verified that he was a parole violator, and then arrested and searched that passenger and found illegal drug paraphernalia. The Court held that the passenger had a right to challenge the stop and resulting arrest, search, and seizure. According to the unanimous Court, no reasonable passenger in that situation would feel free to leave without police permission; thus, it was a seizure.[28]

One final issue regarding a warrantless search and seizure after a driver is arrested was answered in 2009 in *Arizona v. Gant*. Justice John Paul Stevens, who wrote the opinion for the Court, acknowledged that since a 1981 decision, it has been assumed that once police arrest a driver or occupant of a car, they may search the vehicle even without a warrant. In *Gant*, the suspect, Rodney Gant, was arrested on the basis of an outstanding warrant for driving with a suspended license. He was handcuffed and restrained in the police squad car when his car was searched. The police found cocaine in a jacket pocket in the back seat of his vehicle and seized that evidence. Gant was convicted of possession of a drug for sale and possession of drug paraphernalia. He was sentenced to three years in prison. The U.S. Supreme Court held that the police search of Gant's car was a violation of the search-incident-to-an arrest exception. Gant was not in a position to reach and destroy any evidence in his car. Furthermore, the arrest of Gant for driving with a suspended license did not provide police with a reasonable belief that his car contained evidence of drug violations. Thus, they could have waited to secure a search warrant before conducting the search. Justice Stevens emphasized the Court's position by quoting a previous case stating that "searches conducted outside the judicial process, without prior approval of a judge or magistrate, are per se unreasonable under the Fourth Amendment," subject to a few exceptions and concern for the safety of police officers and others and the possible destruction of evidence.[29] This case leads to the logical discussion of seizing the person.

Person Searches

A seizure and search of the person is the most intrusive of all searches and constitutes the greatest invasion of privacy. The U.S. Supreme Court has articulated definitions of what constitutes a *search* and a *seizure* and the circumstances under which they are appropriate. First is the issue of what constitutes a seizure of the person.

In a 1980 case, the U.S. Supreme Court held that a seizure occurs when, under all the circumstances, a reasonable

Police are permitted to pat down a suspect and search for weapons to secure the safety of officers and others in the area, as shown in this photo of an arrested suspect. While one officer pats down the suspect, the other officer calls in the arrest to the police department.

person would not think he or she was free to leave.[30] The *free to leave test* arose in *Florida v. Bostick*, in which police boarded a bus bound for Atlanta, Georgia, from Miami, Florida, while it was stopped temporarily in Fort Lauderdale, Florida. Bostick consented to a search of his luggage; illegal drugs were found, and he was arrested.[31]

In *Bostick*, the appellant argued that he was not free to leave because the bus on which he was riding was ready to depart when officers boarded to search. He claimed that the officers did not have reasonable suspicion that any of the passengers were carrying illegal drugs or contraband. The U.S. Supreme Court held that its *free to leave* test has some limitations in cases such as a bus on which one is already a passenger. The test of a reasonable search and seizure under these circumstances is "whether a reasonable person would feel free to decline the officers' requests or otherwise terminate the encounter." The Supreme Court sent the case back for retrial using that test.

The issue of when a reasonable person feels free to leave while police are searching was at issue in *United States v.*

Drayton. The U.S. Supreme Court ruled that when police board a bus to search for drugs or for other purposes, they are not required to tell passengers that they do not have to cooperate by answering police questions. Reasonable people know they are free to leave rather than answer questions, so the fact that police board a bus does not mean they have seized it. Justice David H. Souter, a dissenter in the case, emphasized that the police took control of the bus and that no reasonable person would have been expected to believe that he or she was free to leave or to refuse to answer questions.[32]

Another case illustrates the U.S. Supreme Court's development of the law of seizure as it relates to persons. In *California v. Hodari D.*, the Court held that when police are chasing a fleeing suspect, that person is not seized until apprehended, and this is true no matter how much force police use. Thus, a "show of authority" by police does not amount to a seizure of the person.[33]

Next are the issues of what constitutes a search, how extensive the search of the person may be, and whether the search requires a warrant. Clearly, police may conduct a warrantless search of a suspect after making a valid arrest. This warrantless search is permitted because of the necessity for arresting officers to protect themselves and others as well as to preserve evidence of a crime. The legality of the search is determined by the legality of the arrest.[34]

Even without an arrest, police may conduct warrantless searches under some circumstances, although those searches are limited. In *Terry v. Ohio*, the U.S. Supreme Court acknowledged that officers must be able to protect themselves and others, so it is reasonable to permit them to pat down a suspect for weapons even though the officers do not have probable cause to arrest. In *Terry*, a police officer with 39 years of experience in law enforcement encountered three suspicious men. The officer believed the men were checking out a store for the possibility of a burglary or robbery. After he approached the men and asked their names, the officer conducted a pat-down search for weapons. Two of the men had weapons.[35]

Terry permits officers to conduct a pat-down search for weapons. The case did not rule concerning the discovery of contraband, such as illegal drugs. In 1993, in *Minnesota v. Dickerson*, the U.S. Supreme Court articulated the *plain feel* doctrine (similar to the *plain view* doctrine, discussed later). According to the Court, if, during a *Terry* search and before an officer has concluded that the suspect is not armed, the officer feels a contraband item "whose contour or mass makes its identity immediately apparent," that item may be seized without a warrant. In *Dickerson*, the officer's suspicion was aroused because of the suspect's evasive behavior when he saw officers as he exited a building commonly known as a crack house. In the course of a proper pat-down search for weapons (none were found), the officer detected a small lump, which felt like it was wrapped in cellophane, in the pocket of the suspect's nylon jacket. On the basis of his experience, the officer decided the object was crack cocaine. He seized the object and arrested the suspect. Subsequent tests confirmed that it was crack, and the suspect was charged with possessing a controlled substance.[36]

In a subsequent case, a lower federal court upheld a search and seizure involving a frisk in which an officer used his fingertips to press and probe a suspect's crotch. When the officer felt a hard object that felt to him like crack cocaine, he asked the suspect to drop his pants. During this process, the officer used his own body to shield the suspect from the view of others, thus preserving his privacy to a reasonable extent, according to the court.[37]

In 2009, the U.S. Supreme Court held that a pat-down search is permitted of a passenger when a car is stopped for a traffic violation even when that passenger is being questioned for a matter unrelated to the traffic stop. In *Arizona v. Johnson*, three Arizona police who were members of the state's gang task force ordered three men to exit a vehicle, which had been stopped after the officers ran a check and discovered an insurance-related violation. According to the Court, the pat down was permitted under *Terry* because police had a reasonable belief that the procedure was necessary for the officers' safety. In *Johnson*, police questioned a passenger about gang activity, which was totally unrelated to the reason for stopping the vehicle. The officer had asked a question about gangs after Lemone Johnson, upon questioning, said he did not have identification but that he was from Eloy, Arizona, which the officer knew to be home to a Crips gang. She also noticed that when Johnson exited the vehicle, he kept his eyes on the officers and that he was wearing clothing consistent with that worn by Crips members. He was carrying a police scanner in his pocket, which the officer thought unusual, as most people do not carry those unless they are trying to evade law enforcement officials. Based on these observations, the officer concluded that Johnson might be carrying a weapon; so she patted him down. When the officer felt the butt of a gun, Johnson began to resist, and the officer cuffed him and placed him under arrest. A unanimous U.S. Supreme Court reversed the Arizona Supreme Court in this decision, emphasizing that the initial stop must be lawful (as it was), but after that stop, if the police have reasonable suspicion that they (or others) are in danger, they may pat down for weapons even though they do not have probable cause to do so.[38]

Some jurisdictions are more restrictive than the U.S. Supreme Court in determining proper searches and seizures. For example, a New York court has held that it was not proper for an officer to remove an object from the waistband of a woman while he was frisking her after stopping the vehicle in which she was riding. The stop of the vehicle was lawful. The officer testified that he felt the hard object and asked the woman what it was; she refused to tell him, so he seized what turned out to be crack cocaine. The state argued that the officer feared for his safety when he could not tell the nature of the object and that he should not have to wait for the "glint of steel" before seizing such an object. Under *Terry*, he should be permitted to continue searching until he was sure no weapons were present. The New York court took the position, however, that a bulge discovered during a frisk cannot be seized unless it looks or feels like a weapon.[39]

Some body searches are even more intrusive and more offensive. In *Rochin v. California*, the U.S. Supreme Court stated its position on one method of searching a person for evidence of a crime.[40]

Rochin v. California

Having "some information that [petitioner here] was selling narcotics," three deputy sheriffs of the County of Los Angeles, on the morning of July 1, 1949, made for the two-story dwelling house in which Rochin lived with his mother, common-law wife, brothers and sisters. Finding the outside door open, they entered and then forced open the door to Rochin's room on the second floor. Inside they found petitioner sitting partly dressed on the side of the bed, upon which his wife was lying. On a "night stand" beside the bed the deputies spied two capsules. When asked "Whose stuff is this?" Rochin seized the capsules and put them in his mouth. A struggle ensued, in the course of which three officers "jumped upon him" and attempted to extract the capsules. The force they applied proved unavailing against Rochin's resistance. He was handcuffed and taken to a hospital. At the direction of one of the officers a doctor forced an emetic solution through a tube into Rochin's stomach against his will. This "stomach pumping" produced vomiting. In the vomited matter were found two capsules which proved to contain morphine.

Rochin was brought to trial . . . on the charge of possessing "a preparation of morphine." . . . Rochin was convicted and sentenced to sixty days' imprisonment. The chief evidence against him was the two capsules. . . .

[W]e are compelled to conclude that the proceedings by which this conviction was obtained do more than offend some fastidious squeamishness or private sentimentalism about combatting crime too energetically. This is conduct that shocks the conscience, illegally breaking into the privacy of the petitioner, the struggle to open his mouth and remove what was there, the forcible extraction of his stomach's contents—this course of proceedings by agents of government to obtain evidence is bound to offend even hardened sensibilities. They are methods too close to the rack and the screw to permit of constitutional differentiation.

The U.S. Supreme Court has upheld some intrusive body searches. It upheld the search of a woman suspected of smuggling drugs at the border. A search of her rectum produced a cocaine-filled balloon. A strip search was conducted only after the authorities, with probable cause to believe the suspect was smuggling drugs, conducted a pat-down search, which revealed that the suspect's abdomen was firm and that she was wearing plastic underpants lined with a paper towel. Using this evidence, authorities secured a warrant to conduct a strip search. Subsequently, the suspect excreted 88 balloons containing 80 percent pure cocaine hydrochloride. In upholding the detention and strip search, the U.S. Supreme Court emphasized that the right to privacy is diminished at the border and frequently must give way to the government's right to enforce laws. The test established by the Court for border strip searches is whether customs officials, "considering all the facts surrounding the traveler and her trip, reasonably suspect that the traveler is smuggling contraband in her alimentary canal."[41]

Strip searches of defendants detained in jail pending trial are permitted under some circumstances. In 1979, in *Bell v. Wolfish*, the U.S. Supreme Court used a reasonableness test in deciding that the strip searches of inmates after they returned from the visitors' room were necessary for security.[42]

Routine strip searches of persons arrested for violating traffic ordinances are not permissible, even when those persons are booked temporarily at the police station, unless the police have probable cause to believe that the suspects are hiding drugs or weapons. A federal appellate court held that the civil rights of a woman arrested for two minor traffic offenses were violated when she was strip searched after her arrest. The court emphasized that the fact that this arrestee would come into contact with other jailed inmates was not a sufficient reason to conduct a strip search under *Bell v. Wolfish*. Violence and drugs are not normally associated with the offenses for which she was arrested. Thus, more information is needed to justify a strip search of a person apprehended for traffic violations.[43]

One final case on strip searches is perhaps the best known of recent cases. In *Safford v. Redding*, decided in 2009, the U.S. Supreme Court held that a search of an Arizona middle school honors student was unconstitutional. Sarah Redding had no disciplinary record, but one of her friends, who was found with drugs in her possession, told school officials that Redding had given her the drugs. Redding was called to the office, where she was shown the drugs (four white prescription-strength ibuprofen 400-milligram pills) and asked whether she knew anything about them. She said she did not. She was told that someone reported that she did know. Officials asked to search her belongings, and she consented. No drugs were found.

Redding was then taken to the nurse's office, where two female employees told her to open her bra, revealing her breasts, so they could examine her clothing for drugs. Redding was told to remove her shoes, socks, and jacket. Her stretch pants and T-shirt had no pockets; she was asked to remove both, leaving her in her underpants and bra. She was instructed to pull the bra to the sides and shake it and then to pull the elastic waist of her underpants out, thus exposing her pelvic area. Redding, who consented to the search because she was too frightened to refuse, later said it was the "most humiliating experience of her life." Again, no drugs were found.

According to the U.S. Supreme Court, the search of a student, though permitted in some circumstances, must be reasonable from the beginning, and this one was not. It was based solely on the self-serving accusation of a student who was caught with drugs. Although the Court found that the search violated Redding's right to privacy, it also found that three of the defendants, under the facts of this case, had qualified immunity. The case was remanded to determine the liability of the school district.[44]

Home Searches

Searches of the home are permissible, as seen earlier in *Illinois v. Gates*, but the U.S. Supreme Court restricts the circumstances under which they may be conducted and limits the areas that may be searched. The landmark case on this issue is *Mapp v. Ohio*.[45]

Mapp v. Ohio

It appears that Miss Mapp was halfway down the stairs from the upper floor to the front door when the officers, in this highhanded manner, broke into the hall. She demanded to see the search warrant. A paper claimed to be a warrant was held up by one of the officers. She grabbed the "warrant" and placed it in her bosom. A struggle ensued in which the officers recovered the piece of paper and as a result of which they handcuffed appellant because she had been "belligerent" in resisting their official rescue of the "warrant" from her person. Running roughshod over appellant, a policeman "grabbed" her, "twisted [her] hand," and she "yelled [and] pleaded with him" because "it was hurting." Appellant, in handcuffs, was then forcibly taken upstairs to her bedroom where the officers searched a dresser, a chest of drawers, a closet and some suitcases. They also looked into a photo album and through personal papers belonging to the appellant. The search spread into the rest of the second floor including the child's bedroom, the living room, the kitchen and a dinette. The basement of the building and a trunk found therein were also searched. The obscene materials for possession of which she was ultimately convicted were discovered in the course of that widespread search.

At the trial no search warrant was produced by the prosecution, nor was the failure to produce one explained or accounted for. At best, "there is, in the record, considerable doubt as to whether there ever was any warrant for the search of the defendant's home."

The seized evidence was used against Mapp at her trial, and she was convicted. The U.S. Supreme Court reversed.

In 1980, the U.S. Supreme Court emphasized the importance of protecting the privacy of the home, noting that "the Fourth Amendment has drawn a firm line at the entrance to the house. Absent exigent circumstances, that threshold may not reasonably be crossed without a warrant."[46] In 1984, the Supreme Court held that the Fourth Amendment prohibited the warrantless entry of police into a suspect's home to arrest him for a civil, nonjailable traffic offense.[47] In 1995, the Supreme Court reversed the conviction in an Arkansas case in which police, with a search warrant, identified themselves but then entered the unlocked main door of the suspect's home without knocking and seized illegal drugs, a gun, and ammunition. A unanimous U.S. Supreme Court held that in this case it was necessary to "knock and announce." But the Supreme Court left open the possibility that under some circumstances (such as those involving officer safety, escaped inmates, or destruction of evidence), the knock rule might not be required.[48]

However, if police have a legal right to enter a home (or office or other structure), it is permissible, under the *plain view doctrine*, to seize some evidence without a warrant. This privilege was established by the U.S. Supreme Court in 1971 in *Coolidge v. New Hampshire*.[49] In 1987, in *Arizona v. Hicks*, the Supreme Court held that probable cause is required to invoke the plain view doctrine, and in 1990, the Court permitted a warrantless "protective sweep," defined as "a quick and limited search of premises, incident to an arrest and conducted to protect the safety of police officers or others. It is confined narrowly to a cursory visual inspection of those places in which a person might be hiding."[50]

In some cases, searches near the home may also be conducted. The U.S. Supreme Court has held that persons have no reasonable expectation of privacy for garbage left outside the *curtilage* (the enclosed space of buildings and grounds immediately surrounding the home), and thus, it may be searched without a warrant.[51] The Supreme Court did not answer the question of whether a search would be lawful if the garbage was left within the curtilage. A lower federal appellate court reached that issue in 1991 and ruled that the search would be permissible provided the garbage was left under circumstances making it "readily accessible" to the public. If the garbage appears abandoned and exposed to the public, its owner no longer has a reasonable expectation of privacy protecting it from search and seizure.[52]

The U.S. Supreme Court has upheld a warrantless aerial surveillance of a defendant's fenced backyard. The search revealed that marijuana plants were growing there.[53] The Supreme Court's holding was based on the assumption that, in general, a person does not have a reasonable expectation of privacy that would preclude a search of items left in public view or abandoned or obtained by consent.

A case closely related to home searches was decided in 2001 when the U.S. Supreme Court held that, if police believe a suspect will destroy evidence if left alone, they may hold that person outside the home while seeking a search warrant. In the case of *Illinois v. McArthur*, police approached Charles McArthur outside his trailer home in Sullivan, Illinois, and told him that his estranged wife informed the police that McArthur had marijuana hidden under his couch. McArthur refused to let the police in, and for about two hours, they held him outside, refusing to let him go inside alone. The Supreme Court held that this detention was appropriate.[54]

In an important case upholding the right of privacy, in 2001, the U.S. Supreme Court held, in a 5–4 ruling, that police must first secure a warrant before using a device that detects heat to determine whether an individual was growing marijuana in his home. In *Kyllo v. United States*, the police secured a search warrant and located over 100 marijuana plants growing in the suspect's home under lights. The warrant was secured after a device called Agema Thermovision 210 detected a hot spot in the home. Police had also examined electric bills and analyzed some tips before concluding that the suspect was growing the illegal drug under high-intensity lamps in his home. The heat-detection device located one place in the house that was particularly hot. The issue in the case was whether aiming that device at a private home from a public street constitutes a search. The Court held that it does, with the majority stating that, with regard to searches and seizures, U.S. Supreme Court precedents draw "a firm line at the entrance to the house," and "That line . . . must be not only firm but bright."[55]

In *Hudson v. Michigan*, decided by a 5–4 vote in 2006, the U.S. Supreme Court refused to exclude evidence obtained by police when they entered a home a short time (approximately three to five seconds) after knocking and announcing their presence. They had a warrant to search for illegal drugs and weapons, and they found both. The state conceded that the *knock and announce* rule was violated, so the only issue on appeal was whether the evidence should have been excluded. The Court held that was not required, noting that according to its own precedent, the exclusionary rule is applied only when its deterrent effect outweighs its substantial social costs.[56]

Also in 2006, the U.S. Supreme Court held that police may not enter a home to search without a warrant if one occupant objects. In *Georgia v. Randolph*, police went to the home of the complainant wife and her husband. In the presence of her husband, the wife told police that her husband used illegal drugs. When the police requested permission to search the house, the wife consented, but the husband refused. The police conducted the search and found evidence of illegal drug use. They secured a search warrant and found more evidence, all of which was used against the suspect at trial after his motion to suppress was denied. He was convicted and appealed. The U.S. Supreme Court, by a 5–3 vote (recently appointed Justice Samuel

Alito did not hear oral arguments and thus did not vote), held that the search as to the husband was unconstitutional, and thus, the evidence seized should have been excluded.[57]

The Right Not to Testify Against Oneself

The Fifth Amendment to the U.S. Constitution (see Appendix A) states that no person "shall be compelled in any criminal case to be a witness against himself." The reason behind this right has been expressed as follows:

> We do not make even the most hardened criminal sign his own death warrant, or dig his own grave, or pull the lever that springs the trap on which he stands. We have through the course of history developed a considerable feeling of the dignity and intrinsic importance of the individual man. Even the evil man is a human being.[58]

The right not to testify against oneself includes the right to be free of physical and mental methods for extracting confessions, as illustrated by excerpts from two cases. The first case, *Brown v. Mississippi*, gives an example of physical brutality used to elicit confessions from several African American defendants. The only evidence on which the defendants could have been convicted was their involuntary confessions secured after several whippings. The defendants were convicted and sentenced to death. The Mississippi Supreme Court upheld the convictions. The U.S. Supreme Court reversed. The Court's comments, after describing the beating of the first defendant, were as follows.[59]

Brown v. Mississippi

The other two defendants were also arrested and taken to the same jail. On Sunday night, April 1, 1934, the same deputy, accompanied by a number of white men, one of whom was also an officer, and by the jailer, came to the jail, and the two last named defendants were made to strip and they were laid over chairs and their backs were cut to pieces with a leather strap with buckles on it, and they were likewise made by the said deputy definitely to understand that the whipping would be continued unless and until they confessed, and not only confessed, but confessed in every matter of detail as demanded by those present; and in this manner the defendants confessed the crime, and as the whippings progressed and were repeated, they changed or adjusted their confession in all particulars of detail so as to conform to the demands of their torturers. When the confessions had been obtained in the exact form and contents as desired by the mob, they left with the parting admonition and warning that, if the defendants changed their story at any time in any respect from the last stated, the perpetrators of

the outrage would administer the same or equally effective treatment. . . .

Because a State may dispense with a jury trial, it does not follow that it may substitute trial by ordeal. The rack and torture chamber may not be substituted for the witness stand.

. . . It would be difficult to conceive of methods more revolting to the sense of justice than those taken to procure the confessions of these petitioners, and the use of the confessions thus obtained as the basis for conviction and sentence was a clear denial of due process.

After the prohibition against extracting confessions through physical brutality, some jurisdictions began to concentrate on psychological methods such as interrogation in a police-dominated atmosphere in which the accused is questioned for long periods without rest and without counsel. The interrogator pretended to have evidence of the suspect's guilt and suggested rationalizations for his or her behavior in an attempt to minimize the moral seriousness of the act. Under such pressure, many suspects confessed.

After some of these interrogation techniques were used on Ernesto Miranda, he signed a confession stating that his statement was voluntary. On the basis of that testimony and other evidence, Miranda was convicted of kidnapping and rape and sentenced to 20 to 30 years in prison for each offense, the sentences to run concurrently.

In its 1966 decision in *Miranda v. Arizona*, the U.S. Supreme Court emphasized the possibility that under the kinds of psychological pressures used by police on Miranda and other suspects, innocent persons might confess. The Supreme Court said that in our system of law, with the tremendous powers of the state in a criminal trial, it is necessary to give defendants procedural safeguards to avoid conviction of the innocent as well as coerced confessions from the guilty. The Supreme Court interpreted the Fifth Amendment right not to have to testify against oneself as requiring that the police must tell the accused of the specifics of that right. The procedures that the police must follow in the **Miranda warning** are explained by the Supreme Court in the following excerpt from the case.[60]

Miranda v. Arizona

As for the procedural safeguards to be employed, unless other fully effective means are devised to inform accused persons of their right of silence and to assure a continuous opportunity to exercise it, the following measures are required. Prior to any questioning, the person must be warned that he has a right to remain silent, that any statement he does make may be used as evidence against him, and that he has a right to the presence of an attorney, either retained or appointed. The defendant may waive effectuation of these rights, provided the waiver is made voluntarily, knowingly and intelligently. If, however, he indicates in any manner and at any stage of the process that he wishes to consult with an attorney before speaking, there can be no questioning. Likewise, if the individual is alone and indicates in any manner that he does not wish to be interrogated, the police may not question him. The mere fact that he may have answered some questions or volunteered some statements on his own does not deprive him of the right to refrain from answering any further inquiries until he has consulted with an attorney and thereafter consents to be questioned.

The purpose of this case was to ensure that police do not wear down suspects until they give in and make statements that might incriminate them. The decision created an immediate controversy. Reactions ranged from the cry that we were licensing people to kill, rape, rob, and steal to the argument that all the decision did was to extend to all defendants the rights that the U.S. Constitution has always guaranteed and that the rich have always enjoyed. In evaluating these criticisms, it is important to understand that the U.S. Supreme Court is not trying to free guilty people but, rather, to ensure that the rights of the accused are recognized. In many retrials, defendants are convicted again. For example, Miranda was retried without the confession. He was convicted and sentenced to prison. After his release from prison, he was involved in a fight in which he was killed.

The *Miranda* decision has led to extensive litigation. A few decisions illustrate the range of questions considered by the U.S. Supreme Court. In *Oregon v. Mathiason*, the Court considered whether the *Miranda* warning must be given to a person who went to the police station and confessed after an investigator had left a card at his home. The card invited the suspect, who was on parole, to go to the police station. The police alleged that the suspect went to the station to talk voluntarily, was told that he was under arrest, and then was questioned without an attorney. The *Miranda* warning was not given. The police told the defendant that his fingerprints were found at the scene of the crime. That was not true, but when the defendant heard the assertion, he confessed. The U.S. Supreme Court held that the confession was not obtained in violation of the suspect's *Miranda* rights: "*Miranda* warnings are required only where there has been such a restriction on a person's freedom as to render him 'in custody.'"[61] The words *in custody* are key, as some of the following cases illustrate.

In *Minnesota v. Murphy*, the U.S. Supreme Court considered whether the *Miranda* warning must be given by a probation officer when talking to a client about another crime. When questioned by his probation officer, a probationer admitted that he had raped and murdered a teenage girl. The confession was used against the probationer, who was convicted. On appeal, defense attorneys argued that their client's constitutional rights had been violated because his probation officer had not given him the *Miranda* warning. The Supreme Court ruled that the *Miranda* warning was not required.[62]

If a suspect invokes the right to remain silent until an attorney is present, the police may not interrogate until counsel has been provided, although there is an issue of how long invoking the right to counsel and remaining silent stay in effect. In *Edwards v. Arizona*, the U.S. Supreme Court addressed this issue. The defendant invoked his right to be silent and his right to an attorney; the police left but came back to the jail the following day and began questioning him again. Edwards confessed. The confession was used against him at his trial, and he was convicted. The lower courts held that his confession was admissible because Edwards answered questions during the second interrogation even though he was again given the *Miranda* warning. The Supreme Court disagreed and held that, although police may question a suspect who "initiates further communication, exchanges, or conversations with the police," the police may not initiate that interrogation the following day without providing the suspect with an attorney. Once a suspect invokes the *Miranda* rule, there is a presumption that any subsequent waiver is involuntary, and the burden of proof for the police to prove that was not the case is a heavy one. Thus, police should not question the suspect unless an attorney is present.[63]

But when does the presumption of involuntariness end? In 2010, the U.S. Supreme Court visited the *break-in-custody* issue that was apparently created by *Edwards*. *Shatzer v. Maryland* involved an appellant inmate who was approached by police while he was incarcerated for a crime. Shatzer was given his *Miranda* warning after which he stated that he did not want to talk to police, who wanted to question him about a different crime, allegedly having sexually abused his 3-year-old son. Shatzer was in prison for sexual abuse in an unrelated case. The officers left and closed the case. Another detective returned in two years and gave Shatzer the *Miranda* warning after which he signed a waiver of his rights. The detective then began questioning Shatzer, who made incriminating statements which were used against him at trial. He was convicted. The U.S. Supreme Court held that, although Shatzer was "in custody" of police when taken by a detective to a private area of the prison for interrogation, he was not in "continuous custody" while in prison because he was returned to the general population after the first questioning. Prior to the second questioning, Shatzer was in the custody of prison officials, not of the police. Thus, for *Miranda* purposes, he was not "in custody," and therefore, when he was questioned the second time, he was entitled to the *Miranda* warning. However, he was not entitled to a presumption that his waiver prior to that second questioning was involuntary; thus, police were not required to meet the heavy burden required when the presumption exists. There was no reason to assume that Shatzer's change in heart (e.g., his willingness to answer police questions) was coerced because he was not in custody when he signed the waiver. Thus, his waiver need not be scrutinized under the strict guidelines the Court has established for those waivers that are made after a suspect in custody had requested an attorney and indicated that he did not want to talk to police until he had one. The *Miranda* waiver was properly admitted at Shatzer's trial.[64]

The *Miranda* rule does not require that police refrain from questioning a suspect who has requested counsel during a court appearance for a separate crime. In *McNeil v. Wisconsin*, the U.S. Supreme Court ruled that when a suspect requested counsel during his initial appearance in court on an armed robbery charge, that request did not bar police from questioning the suspect on other charges (murder, attempted murder, and burglary) for which he waived his *Miranda* rights and made incriminating statements. He was convicted on the basis of those statements. He appealed, arguing that his invoking the *Miranda* requirements for the robbery charge applied to all questioning, even that for other charges. The U.S. Supreme Court

did not agree and held that the *Miranda* rule is *offense-specific.*[65]

Controversy over the *Miranda* rule had led to attempts to abolish it, but in 2000, in *Dickerson v. United States*, the U.S. Supreme Court ruled that a 1968 congressional attempt to overrule *Miranda* was unconstitutional. In an opinion written by Chief Justice Rehnquist, the Supreme Court held that the *Miranda* rule is a constitutional one and beyond the power of Congress to change. Congress had enacted the 1968 statute two years after the Supreme Court decided the *Miranda* case, but it had not been invoked by federal prosecutors, who apparently feared that it might not be held constitutional. According to Chief Justice Rehnquist, writing for the majority of seven justices, "*Miranda* announced a constitutional rule that Congress may not supersede legislatively."[66]

As Exhibit 11.3 indicates, in 2010, there was a movement to limit the *Miranda* rule in cases involving terrorist

---

EXHIBIT 11.3

The Miranda Rule in Transition?

In 1966, in *Miranda v. Arizona,* discussed in the text, the U.S. Supreme Court held that when suspects are arrested, they must be given what came to be known as the *Miranda* warning. Suspects must be told they have a right to remain silent; that anything they say can and will be held against them; they have a right to an attorney; and if they cannot afford an attorney, one will be provided for them. Also noted in the text was the 2000 case, *Dickerson v. United States*, in which the U.S. Supreme Court upheld the *Miranda* warning against efforts to abolish it.[1]

In 2010, after an attempted bombing in Times Square in New York City, the Obama administration began talking about supporting an emergency exception to the *Miranda* warning that would apply only to suspects of terrorist attacks. Attorney General Eric H. Holder Jr. and other members of the president's administration announced the support of such an exception despite their previous assurance that the provisions of U.S. criminal justice systems were sufficient to handle terrorist suspects successfully.

Some exceptions to the *Miranda* warning are permitted, but there is concern that more extensive exceptions are needed in the case of terrorist suspects. The push for congressional permission gained momentum after the questioning of the Times Square attempted bombing suspect, Faisal Shahzad, who gave authorities several leads during the three hours he was questioned prior to being given the *Miranda* warning. Likewise, after the attempted bombing of a plane preparing to land in Detroit after a flight from Amsterdam on 25 December 2009, police interrogated the suspect, Umar Farouk Abdulmutallab, who was on board the aircraft, for almost an hour before giving him his *Miranda* warning. Both of these interrogations were arguably justifiable under the "immediate public safety" exception to the *Miranda*

warning (see Chapter 12's discussion of the exclusionary rule).

Attorney General Holder justified the questioning of these two suspects because the U.S. Supreme Court had not placed time limits on the public safety exception to the *Miranda* rule. But Holder appeared to support a congressional statute rather than executive orders to change the rule. According to Holder, we need Congress to come up with an exception that does not violate the U.S. Constitution but is "also relevant to our time and the threat that we now face."[2]

On 29 July 2010, Adam Schiff introduced the Questioning of Terrorism Suspects Act of 2010 in the U.S. House of Representatives. It is described as a "bill to declare the sense of Congress that the public safety exception to the constitutional requirement for what are commonly called Miranda warnings allows for unwarned interrogation of terrorism suspects." The proposed legislation would amend the federal statute to assure "the admissibility of certain confessions made by terrorism suspects, and for other purposes." The federal statute in question provides that in "any criminal prosecution brought by the United States or by the District of Columbia, a confession, as defined [in another subsection] . . . shall be admissible in evidence if it is voluntarily given."[3]

---

1. See *Miranda v. Arizona*, 384 U.S. 436 (1966) and *Dickerson v. United States*, 530 U.S. 428 (2000).

2. "Administration Supports Limits on *Miranda* Rule," *New York Times* (10 May 2010), p. 1.

3. Questioning of Terrorism Suspects Act of 2010, 2010 Bill Tracking, H.R. 5934, introduced 29 July 2010 and referred to committee. The federal statute at issue is Section 3501(a) of Title 18 of the *U.S. Code* (2010).

suspects. As of press time, there was no official proposal in this regard, although a bill had been introduced into the U.S. House of Representatives, as indicated in Exhibit 11.3.

The timing of the *Miranda* warning was raised in *Missouri v. Seibert* in which the police questioned the suspect, then gave her the *Miranda* warning, and then questioned her again. The assumption in this "question-first" approach is that the suspect will confess again even after the *Miranda* warning is given. The facts of *Seibert* involved a mother who confessed to her role in setting her mobile home on fire, which resulted in the death of an 18-year-old mentally retarded young man who was living there. Seibert's young son, who had cerebral palsy, had died in his sleep in the home. Seibert, who feared that she would be charged with neglecting her son because his body had bed sores, agreed with her sons and their friends on a scheme of setting the home on fire with the 18-year-old inside, thereby making it appear that the ill son had not been left alone. Police questioned her a few days later and she confessed; they then gave her the *Miranda* warning and questioned her again, reminding her of her prewarning confession. She confessed again. The first confession was excluded, but the second one was admitted because it occurred after the defendant received the *Miranda* warning. Seibert was convicted of second-degree murder. The Missouri Supreme Court reversed; the U.S. Supreme Court upheld that decision, ruling that the second confession was virtually continuous with the first, which, having been given before the *Miranda* warning, was not admissible.[67]

What happens if the suspect does not want to listen to police give the *Miranda* warning? *United States v. Patane* involved suspect Samuel F. Patane, a convicted felon who was prohibited from possessing a gun. When police went to Patane's home in Colorado Springs, Colorado, to arrest him for allegedly violating a temporary restraining order (he was accused of telephoning his former girlfriend in violation of the restraining order), they began to give him the *Miranda* warning. But Patane interrupted them, saying he knew his rights. The police, who had been told by a probation officer that Patane had a gun, asked about the gun. Patant was hesitant but eventually directed police to the gun in his bedroom. The federal appeals court ruled that the gun should have been excluded as evidence at trial. The U.S. Supreme Court reversed, noting that no statements made by the defendant were used against him; the *Miranda* warning is for the purpose of protecting a defendant from harmful testimony; thus, the exclusionary rule (see discussion in Chapter 12) did not apply.[68]

In 2009, the U.S. Supreme Court removed some restrictions from requirements regarding when police may interrogate a suspect without his or her lawyer present. *Montejo v. Louisiana* involved a defendant who was convicted of first-degree murder and sentenced to death. When first questioned by police, Jessie Jay Montejo said he wanted to see an attorney. The police said they would "not really recommend that." The suspect answered questions but at

one point said he did not want to answer any more questions without an attorney. He was informed that he was under arrest, and he responded that he would talk. The police said they could not talk to him now that he requested an attorney, but he answered, "I don't want no attorney." These conversations were on tape, but the tape stopped there and resumed later. Police said they were confirming with their supervisors that the suspect had withdrawn his request for an attorney. Three days later, the suspect was taken to court for a required "72-hour hearing" at which the judge ordered the appointment of counsel for Montejo, who said nothing at the hearing. Later that day, Montejo accompanied the police, at their request and after being read his *Miranda* rights, on a hunt for the murder weapon. The suspect had earlier told police that he threw the weapon into a lake. Montejo told the police he had an attorney; they said they checked the records and that he did not have an attorney. The police asked Montejo to write a letter to the victim's wife apologizing for the robbery and murder of her husband. He complied. That statement was admitted at trial; Montejo was convicted and sentenced to death. The Louisiana Supreme Court affirmed. The U.S. Supreme Court reversed and remanded for further findings given the disputed facts. The Court held that if Montejo

> made a clear assertion of the right to counsel when the officers approached him about accompanying them on the excursion for the murder weapon, then no interrogation should have taken place unless Montejo initiated it. Even if Montejo subsequently agreed to waive his rights, that waiver would have been invalid had it followed an "unequivocal election of the right."[69]

A 2010 case decided by the U.S. Supreme Court interpreted the meaning of the *Miranda* warning's requirement that a suspect must be "clearly informed" prior to custodial questioning and informed that among other rights, he or she has the right to consult with a lawyer and to have that lawyer's assistance during questioning. In *Florida v. Powell*, the suspect was given the *Miranda* warning by the Tampa, Florida, police, using these words: "You have the right to talk to a lawyer before answering any of our questions" and "[y]ou have the right to use any of these rights at any time you want during this interview." Powell argued that it was not clear that he could have an attorney with him throughout the questioning. The U.S. Supreme Court held that although the warning could have been stated more clearly, it did meet the *Miranda* requirements.[70]

In June 2010, the U.S. Supreme Court held that if a suspect wishes to remain silent, he or she must clearly state that; otherwise, the police may interrogate. In *Berghuis v. Thompkins*, a divided Supreme Court (5-4 vote) held that a suspect cannot invoke the right to remain silent by remaining silent. The case involved Van Chester Thompkins, who was accused of murder. Thompkins was handed a form with five statements constituting the

Miranda warning as used in that jurisdiction. He was asked to read the last statement. The police testified that they wanted to ensure that he could read. He did so but refused to sign the statement when asked to do so. At no time did he ask for an attorney or state that he wanted to remain silent. He was seated in a chair with an armrest like those in many classrooms. The police interrogated him for three hours, during which time he said very little except to mention that his chair was hard and that he did not want a peppermint. He did answer "yes" to these questions: "Do you believe in God?" "Do you pray to God?" and "Do you pray to God to forgive you for shooting that boy down?" He refused to make a written confession. His "yes" answers were used against him at trial. He was convicted and sentenced to life without parole. The Court held that there were no violations of the suspect's rights. He gave a confession, and he was not coerced. He waived his rights by not stating that he did not want to be interrogated. The newest justice, Sonia Sotomayor, joined by the other three dissenting justices, wrote, in part, the following:

> Today's decision turns *Miranda* upside down. Criminal suspects must now unambiguously invoke their right to remain silent, which, counterintuitively, requires them to speak. At the same time, suspects will be legally presumed to have waived their rights even if they have given no clear expression of their intent to do so. Those results, in my view, find no basis in *Miranda* or our subsequent cases and are inconsistent with the fair-trial principles on which those precedents are grounded. . . . I respectfully dissent.[71]

It is reasonable to assume that defendants will continue to challenge issues concerning the *Miranda* warning, just as they raise questions concerning the right to counsel.

The Right to Counsel

The Sixth Amendment (see Appendix A), which provides that in all criminal prosecutions the accused shall have "the Assistance of Counsel for his defense," became part of the Bill of Rights in 1791. But it was not until 1963 and 1972, as a result of two important cases, that the right to counsel became a reality for most defendants. The discussion begins with the 1963 decision *Gideon v. Wainwright* and traces the evolution of this important right.[72]

Clarence Earl Gideon was not a violent man, but he had been in and out of prison for various law violations. At his trial for breaking and entering a poolroom with the intent to commit a misdemeanor, an act that constituted a felony under Florida law, Gideon represented himself but argued that he needed a lawyer. Because he could not afford to retain counsel, he requested the court to appoint an attorney at the state's expense. The judge replied that under Florida law, an indigent was not entitled to a court-

Clarence Earl Gideon's appeal to the U.S. Supreme Court led to the 1963 ruling that indigent defendants are entitled to appointed counsel in all felony cases, not just those involving a death sentence. Subsequent cases extended this right to appointed counsel to less serious offenses.

appointed attorney except when charged with a crime that could result in the death sentence.

After telling the judge that "the United States Supreme Court says I am entitled to be represented by Counsel," Gideon conducted his own defense "about as well as could be expected from a layman," according to the Supreme Court. Gideon was convicted and sentenced to five years in prison. On 8 January 1962, the U.S. Supreme Court received a large envelope from Florida prisoner number 003826. Gideon, who had printed his request in pencil, asked the Supreme Court to hear his case.

The U.S. Supreme Court agreed to hear Gideon's case and appointed Abe Fortas, an attorney with a prestigious Washington, D.C., law firm, to represent him. Fortas convinced the Supreme Court that it should overrule a previous case in which it had held that the right to counsel appointed at the government's expense if the defendant is indigent applied only to capital cases. The Supreme Court, reviewing that earlier decision and other cases, explained the reasons that counsel is important, as the following excerpt from the *Gideon* decision illustrates.

Gideon v. Wainwright

Not only these precedents but also reason and reflection require us to recognize that in our adversary system of criminal justice, any person haled into court, who is too poor to hire a lawyer, cannot be assured a fair trial unless counsel is provided for him. . . . The right of one charged with crime to counsel may not be deemed fundamental and essential to fair trials in some countries, but it is in ours. From the very beginning, our state and national constitutions and laws have laid great emphasis on procedure and substantive safeguards designed to assure fair trials before impartial tribunals in which every defendant stands equal before the law. This noble ideal cannot be realized if the poor man charged with crime has to face his accusers without a lawyer to assist him. A defendant's need for a lawyer is nowhere better stated than in the moving words of Mr. Justice Sutherland in *Powell v. Alabama*: "The right to be heard would be, in many cases, of little avail if it did not comprehend the right to be heard by counsel. Even the intelligent and educated layman has small and sometimes no skill in the science of law. If charged with crime, he is incapable, generally, of determining for himself whether the indictment is good or bad. He is unfamiliar with the rules of evidence. Left without aid of counsel he may be put on trial without a proper charge, and convicted upon incompetent evidence irrelevant to the issue or otherwise inadmissible. He lacks both the skill and knowledge adequately to prepare his defense, even though he may have a perfect one. He requires the guiding hand of counsel at every step in the proceedings against him. Without it, though he be not guilty, he faces the danger of conviction because he does not know how to establish his innocence."

Since Gideon was convicted of a felony, technically, the case applied the right to appointed counsel only to felony cases. In 1972, in *Argersinger v. Hamlin*, clarified in 1979 in *Scott v. Illinois*, the U.S. Supreme Court held that the right to appointed counsel applies to misdemeanors when conviction would result in the *actual* deprivation of a person's liberty.[73]

An important question not answered by *Gideon* is how soon after apprehension a suspect is entitled to appointed counsel. In *Escobedo v. Illinois*, the U.S. Supreme Court ruled that the right to counsel begins before the trial.[74] The Supreme Court has decided numerous cases involving the right to counsel during the pretrial and trial phases. In *Brewer v. Williams*, the Court emphasized that whatever else the right to counsel may mean, it "means at least that a person is entitled to the help of a lawyer at or after the time that judicial proceedings have been initiated against him."[75] In *Maine v. Moulton*, the U.S. Supreme Court underscored the importance of the right to counsel prior to trial by stating that "to deprive a person of counsel during the period prior to trial may be more damaging than denial of counsel during the trial itself."[76]

The right to counsel involves the right to retain counsel of one's choice for those who can afford to do so. In 2006, the U.S. Supreme Court reversed the conviction of an inmate who was refused the right to retain his preferred

attorney. In *United States v. Gonzalez-Lopez*, the defendant, Cuauhtemoc Gonzalez-Lopez, charged with marijuana possession in the eastern federal district court in St. Louis, initially retained a local attorney but subsequently retained Joseph H. Low IV, an experienced California defense attorney, who had recently secured a favorable plea bargain for his client in the same court. When lawyers, such as Low, are not already admitted to practice before the court in which their client is scheduled to be tried, they must request the judge to admit them provisionally to try the case. Usually, this request is granted, but there were issues of procedural impropriety on the part of Low, and the judge revoked the temporary provision. Low was also unsuccessful on appeal. Gonzalez-Lopez was represented by other counsel. Low was denied permission to assist and was, in fact, ordered not to sit at counsel table and to have no contact with the defendant during the proceedings. The defendant was convicted and sentenced to 24 years in prison. The U.S. Supreme Court justices agreed that the trial judge should have granted the motion for Low to represent Gonzalez-Lopez, but they disagreed on what remedy should be provided as a result of this error. The justices split 5-4, with the majority holding that, even though the trial was fair, the right to defense counsel includes the right of defendants to retain the attorney of their choice. The U.S. Supreme Court ruled that the right to counsel is so important that when defendants are, in effect, denied the opportunity to retain the attorney of their choice, their convictions must be reversed and they are entitled to new trials, represented by the counsel they choose to retain and "believe to be the best."[77]

The right to counsel is of little value unless the attorney who represents the defendant provides an effective defense. Thus, the right to counsel means the right to effective assistance of counsel, but there is little consensus on the meaning of *effective* assistance.

Lower federal courts have considered this issue, but their answers have varied. A 1984 decision illustrates ineffective counsel. When the defendant's attorney fell asleep during the trial, the court ruled that this was inherently prejudicial. According to the court, an unconscious or sleeping counsel is equivalent to no counsel at all.[78]

In a more recent case, a panel of three judges on the Fifth Circuit Court of Appeals remanded to the trial court a case involving an alleged sleeping attorney. The panel ruled that there was no evidence concerning when and how long the attorney slept and thus how much information he might not have heard. Therefore, it was not possible to determine whether the inmate (who had been on death row for 16 years when he filed his petition regarding alleged ineffective assistance of counsel) had been prejudiced. Neither the judge nor the prosecutor noticed the defense attorney sleeping, although some jurors and the court clerk testified that he did sleep. The judges sent the case back to the trial court to determine whether more evidence existed. In August 2001, the full appellate court upheld the lower court's initial decision, stating that, "In such circumstances, the Supreme Court's Sixth Amendment jurisprudence compels the presumption that counsel's unconsciousness prejudiced the defendant." The U.S. Supreme Court refused to hear the case; thus, the lower appellate court decision stands.[79]

The U.S. Supreme Court has, however, heard and decided other cases concerning the effective assistance of counsel. In 1984, the Court decided two cases on this subject. The first case involved a defendant whose attorney specialized in real estate. He had virtually no experience in criminal law and only 25 days to prepare a defense. The second involved a death row inmate who argued that he did not have effective counsel at the nonjury sentencing stage. In announcing its decision in both cases in *Strickland v. Washington*, the U.S. Supreme Court reinstated the convictions of the defendants, thus overruling the lower federal courts' rulings. According to the Supreme Court's opinion, "The benchmark for judging any claim of ineffectiveness must be whether counsel's conduct so undermined the proper functioning of the adversarial process that the trial cannot be relied on as having produced a just result." To win on the issue of ineffective assistance of counsel, a defendant must be able to prove that his or her attorney's errors "were so serious as to deprive the defendant of a fair trial, a trial whose result is reliable." In *Strickland*, the Supreme Court gave some guidelines for determining whether a defendant has had effective counsel; some of those guidelines are listed in Exhibit 11.4.[80]

In 1993, the U.S. Supreme Court held that defense counsel was not ineffective when the defense attorney failed to object to a decision that was subsequently overruled. Thus, the second requirement of *Strickland*, concerning whether

counsel's action prejudiced the defendant, requires more than a mere showing that the outcome would have been different had counsel not made the mistake. Perhaps one error would result in ineffective assistance of counsel, but the point is that the totality of counsel's actions must be considered.[81]

In 2000, the U.S. Supreme Court held that an appellant had ineffective assistance of counsel when the attorney failed to file an appeal within the 60 days permitted for such action. In *Roe v. Lucio Flores Ortega*, the defendant gave no instructions to his attorney about filing or not filing an appeal. In such cases, ruled the Supreme Court, the question must be asked: Did the attorney consult with the defendant regarding an appeal? "We employ the term 'consult' to convey a specific meaning—advising the defendant about the advantages and disadvantages of taking an appeal, and making a reasonable effort to discover the defendant's wishes." The U.S. Supreme Court held that there is a constitutional duty to consult "when there is reason to think either (1) that a rational defendant would want to appeal . . . or (2) that this particular defendant reasonably demonstrated to counsel that he was interested in appealing." But the appellant must prove that the ineffective assistance prejudiced him. The case was returned to the lower court to enable the appellant to offer proof that he would have been granted an appeal had his counsel petitioned for one.[82]

In 2003, the U.S. Supreme Court ruled in *Wiggins v. Smith* that a defendant had ineffective assistance of counsel when his attorney failed to conduct a "reasonable investigation" into his client's social background. That background included physical torment, sexual molestation, repeated rape while in foster care, and severe privation and abuse

---

EXHIBIT 11.4

The U.S. Supreme Court and Effective Assistance of Counsel

Until recently, the U.S. Supreme Court had not given much help to lower courts in interpreting what is meant by *effective assistance of counsel*. In its 1984 decision in *Strickland v. Washington*, the Court established a two-pronged test: (1) whether the counsel's performance was deficient and (2) whether it prejudiced the defendant. The Court was not very specific, however, on what those two tests mean. Here are some comments from that and other opinions, all cited by the Court in *Strickland*. Can you tell what is meant by effective assistance of counsel by reading these statements?

1. Counsel must be a reasonably competent attorney whose advice is "within the range of competence of attorneys in criminal cases."
2. To show ineffective assistance of counsel, defendants must show that "counsel's representation fell below an objective standard of reasonableness."
3. Counsel owes the client "a duty of loyalty, a duty to avoid conflicts of interest." Counsel must consult with his or

her client, advocate that client's cause, and keep the client informed of the important developments in his or her case.
4. Counsel has a duty "to bring to bear such skill and knowledge as will render the trial a reliable adversarial testing process."

Are these statements vague? According to the U.S. Supreme Court, it is not possible to articulate more specific general standards that could be applied to all cases. Each case must be analyzed individually in the light of the particular facts. "More specific guidelines are not appropriate. . . . The proper measure of attorney performance remains simply reasonableness under prevailing professional norms."

Source: Summarized from *Strickland v. Washington*, 466 U.S. 668 (1984); citations omitted.

while living with his alcoholic, absentee mother during the first six years of his life. Kevin Wiggins had diminished mental capabilities and was often homeless. All of these experiences meet the criteria the U.S. Supreme Court has used to determine mitigating circumstances that should be considered prior to sentencing.[83]

In 2002, in *Bell v. Cone*, the U.S. Supreme Court held that a Tennessee death row defendant who petitioned the Court did have adequate representation by counsel. Gary Cone alleged that his trial counsel was inadequate for these reasons:

1. He did not present mitigating evidence during the sentencing phase.
2. He did not put Cone on the stand to testify.
3. He did not present a final argument in the case.

The U.S. Supreme Court held that these reasons, along with the facts that the defense attorney was treated for mental illness and subsequently committed suicide, were too minor to constitute ineffective assistance of counsel.[84]

In 2005, the U.S. Supreme Court held that a defendant did not have adequate counsel because his trial attorney neglected to read the record of a prior rape conviction, which revealed that the defendant was of limited mental capacity, was an abused child, and probably suffered from fetal alcohol syndrome and schizophrenia.[85] This case was cited with approval by the Court in 2009, in *Porter v. McCollum*, in which the Court unanimously reversed the death penalty of the appellant because at his sentencing phase his attorney failed to present evidence of mitigating factors, such as the defendant's abusive childhood and his mental instability that occurred after his service in combat.[86] In 2010, however, in *Wood v. Allen*, the Court held that no error occurred when defense counsel made a strategic decision not to call an expert witness to testify concerning the defendant's borderline mental retardation. There was no evidence that the decision prejudiced the defense.[87]

Finally, in 2010, the U.S. Supreme Court considered the issue of how much mitigating evidence defense counsel may be required to present in a death penalty case. After citing the extent of the evidence presented in *Bobby v. van Hook*, the Court concluded that defense counsel is not required to search for all mitigating evidence, and at some point, such a search can become merely cumulative. In addition, in this case, there was no evidence that the appellant was prejudiced by counsel's decision not to research and present further evidence at the penalty phase.[88]

The Right to Trial by Jury

Among other rights, the Sixth Amendment (see Appendix A) to the U.S. Constitution provides: "In all criminal prosecutions, the accused shall enjoy the right to a speedy and public trial, by an impartial jury of the State and district wherein the crime shall have been committed."

The **jury** system is very important in the United States, which has approximately one-half of all criminal jury trials in the world. In some countries, such as Great Britain, the use of the jury system is declining. Other countries, such as Japan and India, have abolished the jury system, and some countries use professionals to serve as jurors.

The importance of the right to a jury trial was emphasized by the U.S. Supreme Court in 1968 in *Duncan v. Louisiana*: "Providing an accused with the right to be tried by a jury of his peers gave him an inestimable safeguard against the corrupt or overzealous prosecutor and against the compliant, biased, or eccentric judge." The Supreme Court said, however, that this right does not apply to all crimes. It excludes a category of petty crimes or offenses.[89]

The U.S. Supreme Court has held that the right to a jury trial does not extend to persons charged with driving under the influence (DUI). In deciding whether a crime is petty and therefore does not qualify for a jury trial, the Supreme Court looks primarily at the severity of the penalty that might be imposed if the defendant is convicted and incarcerated. In general, a possible sentence of six months or more in prison is considered sufficient to invoke the right to a jury trial.[90] Some states provide greater access to jury trials than is required by the U.S. Constitution.

The right to a jury trial is based on the belief that the defendant is entitled to have his or her case decided by those who represent community values. In that regard, the jury may ignore facts and acquit a defendant even when the facts clearly point to guilt, a process called *jury nullification*.

The U.S. Constitution provides that a defendant has the right to a trial in the state and county in which the crime is deemed to have occurred (see Appendix A, Sixth Amendment). But the defendant is permitted to ask the court to move the trial elsewhere if it appears that he or she cannot get a fair trial in that jurisdiction. In other words, the defendant may ask for a change of venue.

A defendant is entitled to a trial by a jury representative of the community, but that does not mean that he or she is entitled to a jury of any particular composition. Rather, it means that the lists from which jurors are selected must not exclude groups based on criteria such as gender, race, religion, or ethnic background. It addition, it means that actual jury selection may not proceed in a discriminatory manner. But neither must juries be selected in a totally random manner.

During the jury selection process, attorneys (or the judge) question those in the jury pool, a process called **voir dire**, which means "to speak the truth." The trial judge or the attorneys may excuse potential jurors for *cause*, meaning that they are presumed to be biased in the case. A person may be presumed biased because of prior associations with the defendant, the judge, or the attorneys or for any number of other reasons, such as the way he or she answers questions.

A second method of excusing potential jurors is through a **peremptory challenge**. When attorneys use this method, they do not need a cause or a reason. The number of peremptory challenges is limited, although the number varies by jurisdiction and by type of case.

In *Batson v. Kentucky*, the U.S. Supreme Court overturned part of an earlier decision and held that prosecutors may not use the peremptory challenge to exclude African Americans from juries because they believe they will favor their own race. *Batson* was concerned primarily with issues of evidence, but its effect was to make it easier for minority defendants to prove racial discrimination in the composition of the trial jury. Defendants must show that they are members of a defined minority group, that the prosecutor used the peremptory challenge to remove persons of that group from the jury, and that these and other facts "raise an inference that the prosecutor used the practice to exclude the [potential jurors] on account of their race." The prosecution would then have the burden of proving that the exclusion was not based on racial discrimination.[91]

Batson involved an African American defendant challenging the prosecutorial exclusion of African American jurors. In 1991, in *Powers v. Ohio*, the U.S. Supreme Court ruled that a white defendant could challenge a prosecutor's systematic exclusion of African American jurors. The right at stake here is the right of jurors excluded on the basis of their race. The right to a fair trial implies the right of ordinary citizens to participate in the criminal justice system, and their primary way of doing so is through jury duty.[92]

In *Hernandez v. New York*, the U.S. Supreme Court upheld a prosecutor's exclusion of two prospective Latino jurors in the trial of a Latino defendant. The Supreme Court accepted the prosecutor's argument "that the specific responses and demeanor of the two individuals during *voir dire* caused him to doubt their ability to defer to the official translation of Spanish-language testimony."[93]

In a case involving the trial of a Hispanic defendant, a New York court found unacceptable the prosecutor's reasons for using peremptory challenges to excuse the only three Hispanics in a jury pool. The prosecutor alleged that the computer background of one Hispanic would make him too analytical for the jury. Another, a school security officer, was excused for having had too much contact with young people, which might prejudice him toward the young defendant. A third was excused for various reasons, one of which was that the prosecutor thought he was not sufficiently intelligent. This dismissed potential juror had a high school education; white potential jurors with only high school educations were not dismissed. Two of the three were alleged to have had too many contacts with police, a situation normally thought to be favorable to the prosecution. The court concluded that the prosecution used race as a basis for excluding these potential jurors.[94]

In *Georgia v. McCollum*, the U.S. Supreme Court held that the defense may not use peremptory challenges to discriminate on the basis of race. According to the Supreme Court, the trial court erred when it refused to grant the prosecutor's request to prevent the white defendants from using peremptory challenges to eliminate African Americans from the jury. The defendants in this case were accused of committing crimes against African Americans.[95]

In 2003, the U.S. Supreme Court decided a case in which the defendant, Thomas Miller-El, an African American, who was within one week of execution, argued that his constitutional right to a jury of his peers was violated when the prosecution eliminated 10 of the 11 African Americans in the jury pool. Miller-El's motion to strike the jury prior to trial was not granted, and he was convicted. The lower federal court of appeals rejected his request for review; the U.S. Supreme Court held that the defendant should have been granted a hearing by that court. The case was reheard, and the federal court held that Miller-El did not state with clear and convincing evidence that the state had erred in its decision. In June 2005, the U.S. Supreme Court again reversed the case.[96] In 2008, Miller-El pleaded guilty in exchange for a life sentence.[97] In 2009, his case, which was originally tried in Dallas, Texas, was cited in another case in that city. A county judge ruled that the prosecutors had unfairly stacked the jury against a black defendant, James Broadnax, accused of two murders, when they struck all blacks from the jury. The judge ordered that one black be added to the jury to replace one of the selected white jurors. Broadnax was convicted and sentenced to death.[98]

The U.S. Supreme Court applied *Batson* to gender-based peremptories in a *civil* case. In *J.E.B. v. T.B.*, a paternity case, the state used its peremptory challenges to exclude 9 men from the jury. The case was heard by a jury of 12 women, who decided that the defendant fathered the child in question and should be ordered to make child support payments. The defendant's objection to the use of peremptory challenges to exclude male jurors was rejected by the trial judge and the Alabama Court of Civil Appeals. The Alabama Supreme Court refused to hear the case, but the U.S. Supreme Court held that the exclusion was improper because "gender, like race, is an unconstitutional proxy for juror competence and impartiality."[99]

The right to a jury of peers does not include the right of young adults to be tried by a jury composed of other young adults. The absence of young adults on the jury does not necessarily mean that the young defendant's right to be tried by a jury of peers was violated. The defendant must show that the underrepresented group has characteristics that can be defined easily and that the group has common attitudes, experiences, or ideas in addition to a community of interest.[100]

Another issue in selecting an impartial jury concerns the attitudes and beliefs of potential jurors. These attitudes may be so prejudicial that the defendant could not possibly get a fair trial. This issue arises most frequently in the context of capital cases. Should people who are opposed to the death penalty be excluded from juries in capital cases? Most states base their rules concerning jury selection in capital cases on a footnote of a 1968 Supreme Court opinion. In

Witherspoon v. Illinois, the Court said that potential jurors could be excused for cause if they made it

> unmistakably clear (1) that they would *automatically* vote against the imposition of capital punishment without regard to any evidence that might be developed at the trial of the case before them or (2) that their attitude toward the death penalty would prevent them from making an impartial decision as to the defendant's *guilt*.[101]

In *Wainwright v. Witt*, the U.S. Supreme Court said that it does not require a ritualistic adherence to the footnote in *Witherspoon*; the proper test for excluding a juror because of views on capital punishment does not require a conclusion that the juror would vote automatically against capital punishment or that the person's bias had to be clear. The test established was whether the person's views on capital punishment would prevent or substantially impair him or her from performing the duties of a juror.[102]

In 2007, the U.S. Supreme Court made it easier for prosecutors to challenge potential jurors for cause in death penalty cases. In *Uttecht v. Brown*, the Court ruled, by a 5–4 vote, that appellate courts should defer to trial courts in their decisions regarding whether potential jurors would be able to consider voting for the death penalty. This case involved inmate Cal Coburn Brown, who raped, robbed, tortured, and murdered a woman in Washington and two days later robbed, raped, tortured, and attempted to murder a woman in California. Brown was convicted for the California crimes and sentenced to life in prison. In the trial of his Washington State crimes, he was convicted and sentenced to death. During jury selection, the state asked for three potential jurors to be excused for cause on the grounds that they could not be impartial in considering assessing the death penalty. Brown objected and appealed. The court of appeals held that it was proper to exclude one juror but that the other two in question were appropriately seated for the trial. During the voir dire, the state sought and succeeded in having 47 of 98 potential jurors excluded on the basis of cause; that is, they could not be impartial in imposing the death penalty. The U.S. Supreme Court reversed the lower appellate court with regard to the two jurors. After reviewing precedent, the Court articulated four reasons for excusing jurors for cause in a death penalty case.[103]

Uttecht v. Brown

These precedents establish at least four principles of relevance here. First, a criminal defendant has the right to an impartial jury drawn from a venire that has not been tilted in favor of capital punishment by selective prosecutorial challenges for cause. Second, the State has a strong interest in having jurors who are able to apply capital punishment within the framework state law prescribes. Third, to balance these interests, a juror who is substantially impaired in his or her ability to impose the death penalty under the state-law framework can be excused for cause; but if the juror is not substantially impaired, removal for cause is impermissible. Fourth, in determining whether the removal of a potential juror would vindicate the State's interest without violating the defendant's right, the trial court makes a judgment based in part on the demeanor of the juror, a judgment owed deference by reviewing courts.

Deference to the trial court is appropriate because it is in a position to assess the demeanor of the venire, and of the individuals who compose it, a factor of critical importance in assessing the attitude and qualifications of potential jurors.

The right to a trial by an impartial jury also means that the jurors must not be prejudiced by the media. Defendants cannot have a fair trial if, because of pretrial publicity, the jurors have already made up their minds about the case. Therefore, the U.S. Supreme Court has issued rulings concerning when pretrial publicity is prejudicial to the defendant. Perhaps the most publicized of these rulings was *Sheppard v. Maxwell*, decided in 1966. Dr. Sam Sheppard was convicted of his wife's murder and served 10 years in prison before his conviction was overturned. At his second trial, he was acquitted.[104]

During Sheppard's trial, private telephones were installed to allow the press to transmit their stories as quickly as possible. One station was permitted to set up broadcasting equipment in the room next to the jury deliberation room. With the crowd of media persons and the public, it was impossible for Sheppard to talk privately with his counsel in the courtroom during the trial. Nor was it possible inside the courtroom for counsel to approach the judge out of the jury's hearing. The jurors were also exposed to the news media.

These and many other facts were considered by the U.S. Supreme Court before reversing Sheppard's conviction. The Court's opinion stressed the importance of the media's First Amendment rights to free speech but also the more important right of the defendant to be tried before an unbiased jury (see Appendix A). In conclusion, the Court declared:

> With his life at stake, it is not requiring too much that [a defendant] be tried in an atmosphere undisturbed by so huge a wave of public passion. . . . The theory of our system is that the conclusions to be reached in a case will be induced only by evidence and argument in open court, and not by any outside influence, whether of private talk or public print.[105]

The Court referred to the trial as having a "Roman holiday" atmosphere, complete with murder, mystery, society, and sex.

The influence of publicity on the jury faced the U.S. Supreme Court again in 1979 when it considered the issue of whether the press could be barred from a pretrial hearing. In *Gannett Co., Inc. v. Depasquale*, the Supreme

Court recognized the importance of openness but refused to recognize a constitutional right of the public to be present at pretrial hearings. The decision reopened the power struggle between the press and the Court and between the rights of the public and the rights of the defendant.[106]

In subsequent decisions, *Gannett* has been eroded. In *Richmond Newspapers, Inc. v. Virginia*, the U.S. Supreme Court ruled that the public and the press have a constitutional right of access to criminal trials (*Gannett* dealt with pretrial hearings), but that right is not unlimited. Before trials can be closed, however, the government must explore other alternatives.[107]

Richmond was criticized in the U.S. Supreme Court's later decision in *Globe Newspaper Co. v. Superior Court*, which involved a Massachusetts statute that was interpreted by the Massachusetts court to require that the press be excluded during the testimony of a sexual abuse victim who was under the age of 18. The Supreme Court did not agree that blanket exclusion in such cases is appropriate, stating that the facts of each case must be analyzed, and the state must show a compelling reason for excluding the press. Although preserving the psychological welfare of the victim may constitute a compelling state interest, the Supreme Court said that can be done on a case-by-case analysis by looking at the age and maturity of the victim, the victim's wishes, the nature and circumstances of the crime, and other relevant variables.[108]

The U.S. Supreme Court has held that "the qualified First Amendment right of access to criminal proceedings applies to preliminary hearings" in some circumstances. Those hearings may be closed only if (1) it can be shown that the defendant would not get a fair trial if it were open to the public and press, and (2) a fair trial cannot be provided by less drastic alternatives than closing the trial to the public.[109]

Trial judges have the responsibility of attempting to assess media impact on potential or actual jurors. Judges should take prophylactic measures before the jury is prejudiced and it becomes necessary to declare a mistrial.

In 2010, the U.S. Supreme Court held that the right to a public trial includes the right to have the voir dire of the jury open to the public.[110]

Finally, the right to a trial by jury includes the right to have a jury determine facts relevant to sentencing. These issues are noted in Chapter 13 in the context of the sentencing discussion.

Victims' Rights

The discussion thus far has focused on a sample of the constitutional rights of criminal defendants. Some believe the pendulum has swung too far; defendants have too many rights, society is not protected, and victims are ignored.

The decade of the 1980s was characterized by a strong movement toward the recognition of victims' rights evidenced by the implementation of changes directed toward the needs and concerns of crime victims in criminal justice systems. The movement continued and is characterized by two approaches. The first is to increase victims' participation in criminal justice systems; the second is to provide victim compensation.

Throughout most of our history, victims have been ignored by criminal justice systems. In the past decade, many jurisdictions have tried to remedy this situation, and they have done so in a variety of ways. For example, the California Penal Code provides that all crime victims and witnesses be treated with "dignity, respect, courtesy, and sensitivity."[111] The specific provisions of that code are reprinted in Exhibit 11.5.

Many witnesses and victims need financial and other kinds of assistance before they can participate in criminal court proceedings. They may need financial aid for transportation to court, parking, child care, or other reasonable expenses. They may need medical care and psychological counseling.

One of the ways victims have been recognized is to permit them to participate in criminal justice systems, such as negotiation proceedings with prosecutors and defense attorneys and even with offenders. Many jurisdictions have instituted special training programs to increase the understanding that law enforcement officers, prosecutors, judges, and others have of the needs of victims and witnesses. Arrest policies have been revised in many systems. Problems such as domestic violence and child abuse are treated as criminal acts, not as domestic problems that should be under the jurisdiction of someone other than criminal justice professionals. Victims may be permitted to express their concerns and opinions on issues such as sentencing or plea bargaining.

Victims' rights, however, may not infringe upon defendants' rights. In *Booth v. Maryland*, the U.S. Supreme Court held that the defendant's constitutional rights are violated when a victim impact statement (VIS) contains certain information, such as the severe emotional impact of the crime on the family, the personal characteristics of the victim, and the family members' opinions and characterizations of the crime and of the offender. When the issue arose in the sentencing phase of a capital case, the Court emphasized the concern that decisions in such serious cases should be based on reason, not emotion. Thus, the jury should not hear information that "can serve no other purpose than to inflame the jury and divert it from deciding the case on the relevant evidence concerning the crime and the defendant."[112]

Subsequently, the U.S. Supreme Court reversed itself on that ruling as well as another. In *Payne v. Tennessee*, the Court ruled that VISs may be used at capital sentencing hearings: "A state may legitimately conclude that evidence about the victim and about the impact of the murder on the victim's family is relevant to the jury's decision as to whether or not the death penalty should be imposed."[113]

EXHIBIT

11.5

California Penal Code: Rights of Victims and Witnesses of Crimes

Statutory Rights

"(a) The following are hereby established as the statutory rights of victims and witnesses of crimes:

(1) To be notified as soon as feasible that a court proceeding to which he or she has been subpoenaed as a witness will not proceed as scheduled, provided the prosecuting attorney determines that the witness' attendance is not required.

(2) Upon request of the victim or a witness, to be informed by the prosecuting attorney of the final disposition of the case.

(3) For the victim, the victim's parents or guardian if the victim is a minor, or the next of kin of the victim if the victim has died, to be notified of all sentencing proceedings, and of the right to appear, to reasonably express his or her views, have those views preserved by audio or video means, and to have the court consider his or her statements.

(4) For the victim, the victim's parents or guardian if the victim is a minor, or the next of kin of the victim if the victim has died, to be notified of all juvenile disposition hearings in which the alleged act would have been a felony if committed by an adult, and of the right to attend and to express his or her views.

(5) Upon request by the victim or the next of kin of the victim if the victim has died, to be notified of any parole eligibility hearing and of the right to appear, either personally or by other means, to reasonably express his or her views, and to have his or her statements considered.

(6) Upon request by the victim or the next of kin of the victim if the crime was a homicide, to be notified of an inmate's placement in a reentry or work furlough program, or notified of the inmate's escape.

(7) To be notified that he or she may be entitled to witness fees and mileage.

(8) For the victim, to be provided with information concerning the victim's right to civil recovery and the opportunity to be compensated from the Restitution Fund.

(9) To the expeditious return of his or her property which has allegedly been stolen or embezzled, when it is no longer needed as evidence.

(10) To an expeditious disposition of the criminal action.

(11) To be notified, if applicable, if the defendant is to be placed on parole.

(12) For the victim, upon request, to be notified of any pretrial disposition of the case.

(13) For the victim, to be notified by the district attorney's office of the right to request, upon a form provided by the district attorney's office, and receive a notice, if the defendant is convicted of any of the following offenses:"

[The code lists assault with intent to commit rape, sodomy, oral copulation].

"(14) When a victim has requested notification pursuant to paragraph (13), the sheriff shall inform the victim that the person who was convicted of the offense has been ordered to be placed on probation, and give the victim notice of the proposed date upon which the person will be released from the custody of the sheriff."

Source: Cal Pen Code, Title 17, Section 679 (2010), citations to other statutes omitted.

A second area of focus in victims' rights is the development of victims' compensation programs. In many cases, what victims need most is financial compensation for the property losses they have incurred, medical expenses, or both. All 50 states have enacted **victims' compensation legislation**, and more than 25 states have constitutional provisions for compensation. Enforcement has been a problem, however, and several states have created special agencies to ensure the enforcement of victim compensation provisions. Still, funding for these programs is a problem in many jurisdictions. The federal program is used to illustrate some of the provisions and problems of victim compensation programs.

Congress passed the Victim and Witness Protection Act of 1982 (VWPA), which, with subsequent amendments, applies to victims of offenders tried in federal courts. The findings and statement of purpose of the act emphasize that without the cooperation of crime victims and witnesses, the criminal justice processes could not function. However, historically, crime victims and witnesses have been ignored by the system or "simply used as tools to identify and punish offenders." The legislation recognizes that victims "suffer physical, psychological, or financial hardship first as a result of the criminal act and then as a result of contact with a criminal justice system unresponsive to the real needs of such victims." The act calls for elimination of harassment of victims and witnesses and establishes guidelines for the fair treatment of both. It specifies many other problems faced by witnesses, noting that its purpose is to correct these in the federal system and to provide a model for state victim compensation legislation.[114]

In 1998, after numerous drafts, the Senate Judiciary Committee passed a proposed constitutional amendment concerning victims' rights. One of the compromises in the proposal was that compensation would be limited to violent crime victims, thus excluding property crime victims. This decision caused a split among some victims' advocate groups.[115]

In 2000, the crime victims' rights constitutional amendment advanced to the Senate but was withdrawn after its sponsors requested that it not be voted on. They apparently knew they did not have the necessary two-thirds vote to pass the proposal. The Clinton administration had expressed its willingness to support an amendment but had reservations about some of the provisions of the particular proposal. Eventually, the administration advised the amendment's sponsors that it would not support the proposal because the concerns of the White House had not been addressed. For example, the White House had insisted on a statement providing that "nothing in [the amendment] shall be construed to deny or diminish the rights of the accused." Proponents of the amendment feared that statement would mean that any time a defendant asserted that his or her rights were being negatively impacted by a victim, the victim's rights would not be recognized.[116]

With regard to the concern about defendants' rights, at its annual meeting in 1997, the American Bar Association considered the implications of the growing victims' rights movement and approved these principles:

1. Defendants' rights should not be diminished.
2. Victims' rights should not diminish the ability of the trial court to "efficiently and fairly" manage courtroom proceedings.
3. Victims' rights should not diminish prosecutorial discretion in charging and plea negotiations.
4. Violations of a victim's rights should not give rise to a new cause of action against any public official or public office.
5. Government resources for implementing victims' rights should be fully funded.
6. The term *victim* should be defined.
7. Each jurisdiction should be able to develop its own victims' rights procedures.[117]

In 2000, Congress unanimously authorized another five years of life for the Violence Against Women Act of 1994. This occurred again in 2005 as the Violence Against Women and Department of Justice Reauthorization Act of 2005. President Bush signed the bill on 5 January 2006. The act contains provisions for victims, especially of domestic violence. Additional programs were approved, along with funding for legal counsel for civil cases brought by victims of domestic violence, stalking, and sexual harassment.[118]

New provisions include addressing the abuse of elderly and disabled victims; improving protective orders, especially across state lines; providing grants for coordinating the work of victims advocates, police, and prosecutors; broadening the definition of cyberstalking to include harassment through email or other electronic means; offering grants for shelters for battered women and children; and expanding some provisions to include crimes such as date rape.

Recent legislative action at the federal level is encouraging to victims. Although the proposed constitutional amendment was withdrawn by its sponsoring senators, a new federal bill was passed by the Senate and the House and signed by the president in 2004. In part, the Crime Victims' Rights statute provides the following rights for victims:

1. "The right to be reasonably protected from the accused
2. The right to reasonable, accurate, and timely notice of any public court proceeding, or any parole proceeding, involving the crime or of any release or escape of the accused
3. The right not to be excluded from any such public court proceeding, unless the court, after receiving clear and convincing evidence, determines that testimony by the victim would be materially altered if the victim heard other testimony at that proceeding
4. The right to be reasonably heard at any public proceeding in the district court involving release, plea, sentencing, or any parole proceeding
5. The reasonable right to confer with the attorney for the Government in the case
6. The right to full and timely restitution as provided in law
7. The right to proceedings free from unreasonable delay
8. The right to be treated with fairness and with respect for the victim's dignity and privacy"[119]

Finally, in an effort to curb human trafficking, which consists primarily of recruiting (or selling) women and girls into prostitution, Congress enacted the Trafficking Victims Protection Act in 2000, with subsequent amendments. The purposes of Congress in enacting that legislation, along with some of its findings on the issue, are presented in Global Focus 11.1.

Defendants' Rights Versus Victims' Rights

As the previous discussion suggests, efforts to compensate victims and to involve them in criminal justice systems may conflict with defendants' rights. One of the most frequently raised issues that creates conflicts between victims and defendants is whether or not a sexual abuse victim,

11.1 Sex Trade and Victimization: An International Problem

In January 2006, President George W. Bush signed into law the Violence Against Women and Department of Justice Reauthorization Act of 2005. This bill reauthorized the Violence Against Women Act (VAWA), which was first signed into law in 1994. It provided funding for rape crisis centers, sexual assault services, educational curriculums to improve teens' access to court services, and domestic abuse victims' services. In addition, it continued efforts to abolish the national and international trafficking of persons, mainly women and children, sold into sex and other forms of slavery. The VAWA also reauthorized the Community Oriented Policing Services (COPS) program, which is discussed in Chapter 12.[1]

In 2005, the United States enacted the Trafficking Victims Protection Reauthorization Act (TVPRA, reauthorizing a 2000 statute and its subsequent amendments). This act has many provisions, including training border guards to detect persons engaging in human trafficking and to provide services for trafficking victims. The TVPRA provides three approaches to preventing trafficking: economic alternatives, public awareness, and consultation. It provides funds for establishing programs to keep young girls in school, for training women to become involved in economic decision making, and for "grants to nongovernmental organizations to accelerate and advance the political, economic, social, and educational roles and capacities of women in their countries."[2]

Trafficking in humans, especially women and girls in the sex industry, is a worldwide problem. In some Asian countries, for example, women and girls are viewed as commodities. In the nineteenth century, Asians were the first to engage in trafficking women and girls on a large scale. Chinese and Japanese women were sold to brothels in other countries. Prostitution had become acceptable in many parts of the world. In Holland, for example, prostitution is legal. In Sweden, although it is illegal to buy sex, it is not illegal to sell sex.[3]

Prostitution is illegal in the United States, with the exception of a few rural Nevada counties. According to feminist criminologists, there are two positions with regard to the crime of prostitution. One view is that prostitution is the ultimate expression of sexual freedom: Any woman of age can do whatever she chooses with her body. The other position is that prostitution is the ultimate degradation, as the act portrays women as valuable only for the pleasure of men.[4]

When Congress enacted the Trafficking Victims Protection Act in 2000, it referred to trafficking as "contemporary manifestions of slavery" and included within the statute the following findings:

1. "As the 21st century begins, the degrading institution of slavery continues throughout the world. Trafficking in persons is a modern form of slavery, and it is the largest manifestation of slavery today. At least 700,000 persons annually, primarily women and children, are trafficked within or across international borders. Approximately 50,000 women and children are trafficked into the United States each year.

2. Many of these persons are trafficked into the international sex trade, often by force, fraud, or coercion. The sex industry has rapidly expanded over the past several decades. It involves sexual exploitation of persons, predominantly women and girls, involving activities related to prostitution, pornography, sex tourism, and other commercial sexual services. The low status of women in many parts of the world has contributed to a burgeoning of the trafficking industry.

3. Trafficking in persons is not limited to the sex industry. This growing transnational crime also includes forced labor and involves significant violations of labor, public health, and human rights standards worldwide.

4. Traffickers primarily target women and girls, who are disproportionately affected by poverty, the lack of access to education, chronic unemployment, discrimination, and the lack of economic opportunities in countries of origin. Traffickers lure women and girls into their networks through false promises of decent working conditions at relatively good pay as nannies, maids, dancers, factory workers, restaurant workers, sales clerks, or models. Traffickers also buy children from poor families and sell them into prostitution or into various types of forced or bonded labor.

5. Traffickers often transport victims from their home communities to unfamiliar destinations, including foreign countries away from family and friends, religious institutions, and other sources of protection and support, leaving the victims defenseless and vulnerable.

6. Victims are often forced through physical violence to engage in sex acts or perform slavery-like labor. Such force includes rape and other forms of sexual abuse, torture, starvation, imprisonment, threats, psychological abuse, and coercion.

7. Traffickers often make representations to their victims that physical harm may occur to them or others should the victim escape or attempt to escape. Such representations can have the same coercive effects on victims as direct threats to inflict such harm.

8. Trafficking in persons is increasingly perpetrated by organized, sophisticated criminal enterprises. Such trafficking is the fastest growing source of profits for organized criminal enterprises worldwide. Profits from the trafficking industry contribute to the expansion of organized crime in the United States and worldwide. Trafficking in persons is often aided

11.1

by official corruption in countries of origin, transit, and destination, thereby threatening the rule of law."

[The statement pointed out that many other crimes are involved in the commission of trafficking and that victims are subject to serious health risks, including deadly diseases. Some victims are even brutalized and beaten to death. It then continued to emphasize the global nature of trafficking in human slavery.] . . .

23. "The United States and the international community agree that trafficking in persons involves grave violations of human rights and is a matter of pressing international concern. . . .

24. Trafficking in persons is a transnational crime with national implications. To deter international trafficking and bring its perpetrators to justice, nations including the United States must recognize that trafficking is a serious offense. This is done by prescribing appropriate punishment, giving priority to the prosecution of trafficking offenses, and protecting rather than punishing the victims of such offenses. The United States must work bilaterally and multilaterally to abolish the trafficking industry by taking steps to promote cooperation among countries linked together by

international trafficking routes. The United States must also urge the international community to take strong action in multilateral fora to engage recalcitrant countries in serious and sustained efforts to eliminate trafficking and protect trafficking victims."[5]

1. Violence Against Women and Department of Justice Reauthorization Act of 2005, Public Law 109-162 (2006). The Violence Against Women Act of 1994 is Public Law 103-322. The Violence Against Women Act of 2000 is Public Law 106-386.
2. For a discussion and critique, see Takiyah Rayshawn McClain, "An Ounce of Prevention: Improving the Preventative Measures of the Trafficking Victims Protection Act," Vanderbilt Journal of Transnational Law 40, no. 2 (1 March 2007), p. 579 et seq.
3. Ibid.
4. Jody Raphael, "Compensating for Abuse: Women's Involvement in the Sex Trade in North America," in *Rethinking Gender, Crime, and Justice: Feminist Readings*," ed. Claire M. Renzetti, Lynne Goodstein, and Susan L. Miller (Los Angeles: Roxbury, 2006), p. 125.
5. Trafficking Victims Protection Act, USCS, Title 22, Section 7101, Purposes and Findings (2010).

particularly a young one, must testify in person in court or whether someone may testify as to what the victim said (hearsay evidence).

Normally, hearsay evidence is not allowed because it denies the defendant the opportunity to confront and cross-examine the witness. However, testifying in court can be a traumatic, even impossible task for some victims, especially young ones who have been sexually assaulted. This is true particularly when the alleged offender is a victim's relative. The U.S. Supreme Court considered this issue in 1988 in *Coy v. Iowa*, in which the defendant was accused of sexually assaulting his child. In this case, the Court did not say that defendants' rights would prevail in all cases but, rather, that the Court would carefully scrutinize any blanket requirements that infringe on defendants' rights.[120]

A question that was not answered by this case was answered in 1990 by the U.S. Supreme Court. In *Maryland v. Craig*, the Court held that a defendant's Sixth Amendment right to confront witnesses at trial (see Appendix A) does not require all confrontations to be face to face. In upholding a Maryland statute that permits a child who is the alleged victim of sexual abuse to testify outside the courtroom via television, the Supreme Court said that this is permissible provided the reliability of the child's testimony can be determined by other means.[121] Each case must be judged on its individual facts.

One final comment regarding the friction between a defendant's rights and those of the alleged victim arose in the case of basketball star Kobe Bryant (see again the discussion in Chapter 7), who was on trial for the alleged rape of a Colorado woman. The trial judge granted Bryant's motion that the woman could not be referred to as the *victim* during the court proceedings. It would prejudice the defendant for the term *victim* to be used, thus signifying that a crime had indeed been committed against her. The judge ruled that after the trial began, the woman's name would be used, and the only label used in court to refer to the parties would be the term *defendant* to refer to Bryant. Bryant's attorneys had objected to that term. Until the trial, since the victim's name had not been released, she was to be referred to as the *alleged victim*. Women's rights groups objected to these decisions regarding the victim. A spokeswoman for the Colorado Coalition Against Sexual Assault stated: "Rape is one of the most underreported crimes, and one of the major reasons is the fear of not being believed or of losing one's privacy. . . . We have seen those fears exponentially magnified in this case."[122]

As Media Focus 7.1 noted, the criminal case against Kobe Bryant was dropped after the alleged victim refused to testify. In March 2005, the alleged's victim's civil case against Bryant was settled out of court. The settlement details were not disclosed.

U.S. Criminal Justice Systems: An Assessment

This chapter began with a discussion of the important concepts of due process and equal protection, the backbones of the adversary philosophy of U.S. criminal justice systems. The chapter exposed some flaws in that system, such as wrongful convictions, illegal searches and seizures, and ineffective assistance of counsel. Throughout the text, there are other examples of flaws, but this section pays particular attention to the ways criminal justice systems negatively impact people because of extralegal variables, such as race or ethnicity, gender, or socioeconomic status. Many of the research articles examine more than one of these variables. For example, in an analysis of the sentencing of females for misdemeanors, one investigator found that sentencing was not directly related to race or ethnicity but was indirectly related along with other variables. Specifically, "Black and Hispanic females were more likely to receive jail sentences than their White counterparts due to differences in socioeconomic status, community ties, prior record, earlier case processing, and charge severity."[123]

Some constitutional law scholars and some social scientists argue that modern U.S. criminal justice systems have failed to live up to the promises of the nation's Constitution. For example, social scientist John Braithwaite began his Sutherland award presentation to the American Society of Criminology meeting in 2004 (recall that Edwin Sutherland was a recognized criminologist; some refer to him as the "dean of American criminology") with these statements:

> The criminal justice system could be seen as the most dysfunctional of the major institutional accomplishments of the Enlightenment. . . . There is progress in banning the stoning of evil women and in displacing decapitation with incapacitation. Yet the indecencies of carceral [a *carcer* is a place of detention and not punishment] systems are also profound and they fail the fundamental criminal justice purpose of making our persons and property safe. Modern societies throw more and more resources at their criminal justice systems, yet the accomplishments of that spending in safety are unremarkable.[124]

It is contended that some officials within criminal justice systems develop responses and take action based on race and ethnicity, socioeconomic status, physical or mental disability, age, gender, or some other extralegal characteristic, making decisions regarding criminal culpability and potential dangerousness on one or more of those variables. Researchers differ in their theories regarding when and under what circumstances stereotyping occurs. The

reasons are complicated; the research is extensive and cannot be reviewed here, but the conclusion is simple: Variables beyond those that are legally permitted (e.g., the nature of the crime and previous criminal history) influence decision making in sentencing and other criminal justice decisions.[125]

Race and Ethnicity

Perhaps the best examples of the suggestion that extralegal variables are involved in making decisions in criminal justice systems are race and ethnicity. To illustrate, research on drug offenders in Washington State revealed differences in treatment that apparently reflected stereotypes of both white and black offenders. Specifically, "[T]hose white offenders who most closely resemble the stereotype of a dangerous drug offender receive significantly harsher treatment than other white offender groups, while among black offenders, it is the defendants who least resemble a dangerous drug offender who receive substantially different—in this case, less punitive—treatment than other black offenders."[126]

For years, researchers have reported that, when white and black defendants are compared, whites get the most lenient sentences. However, many studies reveal that when legal issues, such as criminal background, are considered, the suspected discrimination disappears. Other researchers have reported that, when sentencing of whites, blacks, and Hispanics is considered, the most lenient sentences are assessed to white defendants and the harshest to Hispanics.[127]

Research also suggests racial and ethnic disparities in pretrial processes. Although legal characteristics are the most predictable of pretrial decisions, when race and ethnicity are relevant, there are three major results:

- "First, racial disparity is most notable during the decision to deny bail and for defendants charged with violent crimes.
- Second, ethnic disparity is most notable during the decision to grant a non-financial release and for defendants charged with drug crimes.
- Third, when there is disparity in the treatment of Black and Latino defendants with similar legal characteristics, Latinos always receive the less beneficial decisions."[128]

A recent study of pretrial release procedures reported that race played a significant role, with black defendants less likely to be released prior to trial. However, the study did not find race to be a significant factor in the amount of bail set or in the likelihood that the defendant would post bail. The investigators concluded that these results suggested courts view black defendants as more dangerous than white defendants and thus are less likely to release them prior to trial.[129]

Another study found that the variable of race is important in shaping how the public perceives the city's drug problem. Sociologists at the University of Washington found that "blacks are significantly overrepresented among Seattle's drug delivery arrestees." Officials explained this overrepresentation by the emphasis law enforcement places on arrests for possession of crack cocaine (recall Chapter 10's discussion of the disparity between punishments for crack compared to powder cocaine arrests and see Exhibit 13.7 regarding changes), the priority officials place on outdoor drug venues, and the concentration of law enforcement in geographic areas that are racially heterogeneous. But the investigators found that these three reasons were not based on legally permissible variables, such as citizen complaints of drug deliveries. They concluded that their research suggests "that blacks are substantially overrepresented among those arrested for drug delivery in Seattle and that the organizational practices that produce this outcome are difficult to explain in race-neutral terms."[130]

Blacks constitute only 13 percent of the population but almost one-half of prison populations and account for 16 percent more recidivists than white males within three years of release from prison. Such data led researcher Joan Petersilia, in discussing the reentry of inmates into society, to proclaim: "Race is the elephant sitting in the living room."[131]

Researchers in Florida found that racial inequality had a much greater effect on recidivism among black males than on white males in that state. They suggested that future research should consider the social context of the areas into which inmates are released. "Prisoners are not released into a social vacuum, but instead reenter communities with differing levels of economic inequities that potentially constrain their ability to pursue conventional lifestyles. The ability of released prisoners to desist from crime is affected not simply by their own attributes, but by the characteristics of the broader social context they reenter."[132]

Perhaps the higher rates of repeat crimes among blacks are attributed to the *racial threat perspective*. This approach suggests that as a minority population increases, leading to conflict, the majority will take measures to ensure its own control. One measure is economic—that is, by keeping the minority from getting the jobs the majority wishes to keep. Another is power, meaning the majority is threatened by the possible increase in power of the minority, so it increases social control measures to ensure that the minorities do not gain power.[133] This could, of course, explain higher arrests of minorities. It is also possible, however, that as long as the crimes are committed against other minorities, they will be mainly ignored, representing a *benign neglect approach*.[134]

Researchers examined black arrest rates in light of these perspectives, but rather than viewing racial threat only in terms of the size of the black population, they also looked at racial inequality and black immigration patterns. They examined how the "concentration of black disadvantage" (concentration of the population in poor areas with limited job opportunities) might affect rearrest rates of blacks. The researchers found a lack of support for the racial threat perspective; specifically, they found that the "size of the black population and black immigration has a negative impact on black arrest rates in urban cities." But they found that the arrest rates were impacted by high levels of black concentrated disadvantage. The explanation may be simple: Blacks in poor areas have less power to avoid arrest, are seen as a greater threat than are whites, and thus, whites exercise more social control in the form of more arrests.[135]

Investigators have also found support for the community context in explaining the higher rates of violence among black than among white youths, concluding that

> (1) community and family contexts are predictive of ability, achievement and violence, (2) black more than white children must contend with distressed environments that inhibit healthy child development, and (3) the relative exposure of blacks over whites to disadvantaged community structures explains the greater involvement in violence among black adolescents. These findings imply policies that focus on the social and structural obstacles that individuals and groups confront.[136]

The variables of both race and class may be at issue. A recent analysis of neighborhoods and crime tested six theories, with researchers finding support for some but not for others. In general, they concluded that "not only is the composition of race and class in neighborhoods important for explaining crime rates, but also that the distribution of race and class *within* neighborhoods has important effects." Those neighborhoods with racial/ethnic heterogeneity were higher in all types of crimes committed by strangers, while violent crimes were associated with overall and within racial/ethnic group income inequality. This suggests that relative deprivation may be a greater factor in crime when the perception is that others of your own race/ethnicity have more economic resources than you do.[137]

Other studies have given particular attention to socioeconomic factors and crime.

Socioeconomic Status

Decision making in criminal justice systems is also associated with socioeconomic status. "There is a substantial body of research that demonstrates a connection between poor economic conditions and punitive criminal justice policy, particularly the use of imprisonment."[138] Researchers claim it is not poverty or unemployment per se but the changing nature of employment, along with attitudes that develop as a result, that is at issue. Workers who lose their jobs cannot find comparable ones, and there is evidence that the resulting resentment toward those they believe are "getting something for nothing" affects their punitive attitudes. Thus, researchers have found that economically insecure persons may develop blame and punitive attitudes toward immigrants, welfare recipients, and beneficiaries of affirmative action programs. It appears that "punitiveness toward criminals is, in fact, part of a general constellation of resentment toward, and scapegoating of, . . . the 'undeserving poor.'"[139]

The importance of socioeconomic status and crime has been studied extensively not only with regard to crime rates but also with regard to recidivism. Studies indicate that when offenders are released from incarceration, the rate of recidivism is lower for those who return to rich or affluent neighborhoods than for those who return to disadvantaged areas.[140]

Gender

One final area of alleged discrimination is gender. It is important to analyze gender issues within criminal justice systems rather than to assume that empirical evidence regarding male offenders and male victims is applicable to females. For example, according to one gender expert, drug policies within the past few decades have had a "profound and disproportionate impact on the number of women who have been arrested and sentenced to prison."[141] This is particularly the case with regard to minority women, many of whom are poor and for whom crack (in contrast to powder) cocaine became the drug of choice.[142] Recall from previous discussions the differential sentencing of drug offenders in terms of this drug.

Despite some improvements in criminal justice system practices, women have been been negatively impacted by some changes. For example, it is argued that arresting women in intimate personal violence situations, even when they allegedly initiate victimization of their partners, may not be equitable. The reason is that even in those situations men may have initiated the interaction that led to confrontation and that they are stronger and cause more serious personal injuries than do women.[143]

As Chapter 14 explores, women also encounter differences, which may be viewed as discriminatory in some instances, when incarcerated.[144] Also, female professionals in criminal justice systems have been subjected to differential treatment.[145]

Not everyone agrees with feminist criminologists, however, and as we will see in subsequent discussions, some argue that women have received positive advantages within criminal justice systems. For example, they receive preferential treatment while incarcerated, are assessed shorter sentences compared to men, and so on.

In concluding this brief analysis of criminal justice systems, it is relevant to mention that researchers must apply theories to their analysis of the systems. Criminal justice theory should not be limited to an application to crime and crime rates but should embrace the entire system, including all of the stages mentioned in this chapter.

Theory lies at the heart of any social science discipline. It defines the parameters of how we think about our objects of study, and provides us the lenses through which we filter our subject matter in order to make sense of complex phenomena. It gives us our organizing concepts, frames our research questions, guides our scholarly interpretations, and is an unavoidable presence in crime control policy, practice, and decision-making.[146]

The U.S. Criminal Justice Systems and Terrorism

In recent years, especially since the attacks on U.S. soil on 11 September 2001, criminal justice agencies and professionals, policy makers, leaders in all areas of life, and U.S. citizens have been forced to make significant changes. Throughout this text, where relevant, terrorism and related issues have been (or will be in future chapters) noted. To end this chapter on U.S. criminal justice systems, however, we focus on one area of federal constitutional provisions and the U.S. Supreme Court interpretation that was handed down in June 2010.

The case of *Holder v. Humanitarian Law Project* raised issues regarding antiterrorism laws and their impact on the constitutional rights to free association and free speech. The case involved a challenge to a federal statute that bans material support for designated terrorist groups. That statute makes it a crime to "knowingly provid[e] material support or resources to a foreign terrorist organization."[147] The U.S. secretary of state has the power to determine the meaning of *foreign terrorist organization*. The phrase *material support or resources* is defined by the statute as follows:

> any property, tangible or intangible, or service, including currency or monetary instruments or financial securities, financial services, lodging, training, expert advice or assistance, safehouses, false documentation or identification, communications equipment, facilities, weapons, lethal substances, explosives, personnel . . . and transportation, except medicine or religious materials.[148]

In brief, plaintiffs, including the Humanitarian Law Project (HLP) (and HLP's president, a retired administrative law judge), wished to provide money and services for the *lawful* humanitarian and political activities of two organizations deemed included within the reach of the federal statutes. They feared prosecution if they did so and thus brought this action challenging the constitutionality of the federal statute. They alleged that it is vague and that it violated their rights to free association and free speech. The U.S. Supreme Court held that the statute did not violate any constitutional rights; the organizations are "so tainted by their criminal conduct that any contribution to such an organization facilitates that conduct." The three dissenting justices agreed with the majority that the statute is not unconstitutionally vague but disagreed that it did not violate First Amendment rights. Recognizing the constitutional power and responsibility of the executive branch of government to protect the security of the United States, the dissent emphasized the power of the Court to determine the constitutionality of statutes. They cited an earlier case in which the Court stated that "a state of war is not a blank check . . . when it comes to the rights of th[is] Nation's citizens."[149]

The dissent argued that the Court had not carefully examined the government's justification for the statute and concluded as follows:

> [The Court] has failed to insist upon specific evidence, rather than general assertion. It has failed to require tailoring of means to fit compelling ends. And ultimately it deprives the individuals before us of the protection that the First Amendment provides.[150]

Summary

This chapter introduced U.S. criminal justice systems and thus provided the background for the remaining chapters in this part of the book. After distinguishing the adversary system from the inquisitory system, the discussion proceeded to an explanation of the important concepts of due process and equal protection. Two special characteristics of U.S. criminal justice systems—the systems effect and the use of discretion—were explored, followed by an overview of the major stages in U.S. criminal justice systems.

The major portion of the chapter focused on a discussion of the constitutional rights of defendants. Attention was given to significant discussions of four specific constitutional rights: the right to be free of unreasonable searches and seizures (focusing on vehicles, persons, and homes), the right not to testify against oneself, the right to counsel, and the right to a trial by a jury of one's peers. The recognition of victims' rights was discussed, followed by a look at the potential conflicts that arise between the rights of defendants and those of victims.

This chapter showed some of the inevitable tensions and controversies in U.S. criminal justice systems. On the one hand, we believe in individual rights; we do not think the police or any other government officials should be able to interfere in our personal lives without just cause. On the other hand, we want to walk the streets safely, so we want adequate police protection from crime. When we are victimized, we want our property back and our medical bills paid, and we want the defendants brought to justice. It may be impossible to achieve all these goals. Finally, the chapter considered the impact that terrorism has had on our criminal justice systems, focusing on the decision by the U.S. Supreme Court in June 2010, *Holder v. Humanitarian Law Project*.

The tremendous power of the government, a power that can—in the hands of the ruthless—violate our constitutional rights even to the point of conviction for a crime we did not commit, requires us to provide and maintain some protection for those accused of crime. In protecting their rights, we protect the rights of us all. This need was demonstrated in *A Man for All Seasons*, a play about the life, trial, and execution of English humanist, author, and statesman Sir Thomas More. More, who lived from 1478 to 1535 (and in 1935 was canonized by the Roman Catholic Church), stated: "Yes, I'd give the Devil benefit of law, for my own safety's sake."[151]

Yet, because it is necessary to have the power of law enforcement and the power of prevention, it is essential that we have a professional police force, the focus of Chapter 12.

Study Questions

1. Define *adversary system* and *inquisitorial system*.

2. Define *due process* and *equal protection*.

3. What is meant by the systems effect of criminal justice systems?

4. Analyze the role of discretion in criminal justice systems.

5. List and define the major steps in U.S. criminal justice systems.

6. Define *probable cause*, and analyze its importance with regard to search warrants. Why does the U.S. Supreme Court prefer search warrants to warrantless searches?

7. State the implications of searches outside but in the vicinity of a home.

8. Should more intrusive body searches be permitted at U.S. borders? Why or why not?

9. Explain the reasons for the *Miranda* warning, and discuss the implications of recent U.S. Supreme Court decisions concerning this controversial precedent.

10. Explain the meaning of Clarence Earl Gideon's case, and analyze its implications for the right to counsel.

11. Define *jury nullification*, and discuss its implications.

12. Under what circumstances should a change of venue be permitted?

13. Define *voir dire* and *peremptory challenge*, and discuss these concepts in relationship to jury selection based on gender, race, and age. What, if any, role should disability play in jury selection?

14. Discuss the implications of a belief in capital punishment to jury selection in a capital case.

15. Explain the role of the media in a defendant's right to a fair trial.

16. To what extent should victims be permitted to participate in the trials and sentencing of their offenders? To what extent should victims be compensated for their suffering?

17. What is meant by human trafficking, and what measures have been taken to reduce or eliminate this problem?

18. Discuss potential conflicts between recognizing victims' rights and defendants' rights.

19. Should the threat of terrorism impact our constitutional rights? Relate your answer to a recent case.

Brief Essay Assignments

1. Distinguish the adversary from the inquisitory system, and discuss the roles of due process and equal protection in the adversary system.

2. Discuss the meaning of *wrongful convictions*, give examples, and analyze the impact of these convictions on criminal justice systems.

3. Summarize the development of the law of search and seizure with regard to the following: vehicles, homes, and persons.

4. What is meant by *effective assistance of counsel*? Critique the legal developments, and relate them to the importance of the right to counsel.

5. Discuss the legal implications of the *Miranda* rule.

6. Analyze U.S. criminal justice systems in terms of the variables of race and ethnicity, socioeconomic status, and gender.

Internet Activities

1. Check out the Northwestern University School of Law's Center on Wrongful Convictions, http://www.law.northwestern.edu/wrongfulconvictions, and the Innocence Project, http://www.innocenceproject.org/, accessed 30 October 2010. Both organizations are dedicated to assisting individuals who have been wrongfully convicted of crimes.

2. For more information on victims' rights, log on to the National Center for Victims of Crime, http://www.ncvc.org/ncvc/main.aspx, accessed 30 October 2010, and check the Victim Law link for ways to research victims' rights.

Notes

1. *Joint Anti-Fascist Refugee Committee v. McGrath*, 341 U.S. 123, 162–163 (1951), Justice Felix Frankfurter concurring.
2. Herbert L. Packer, "The Courts, the Police, and the Rest of Us," *Journal of Criminal Law, Criminology, and Police Science* 57 (September 1966): 238–243. See also Herbert L. Packer, *The Limits of the Criminal Sanction* (Palo Alto, CA: Stanford University Press, 1968).
3. *See United States v. Armstrong*, 517 U.S. 456 (1996).
4. C. Ronald Huff, "Wrongful Conviction: Societal Tolerance of Injustice," *Social Problems and Public Policy* 4 (1987): 113.
5. "Twenty-Five Wrongfully Executed in U.S., Study Finds," *New York Times* (14 November 1985), p. 13.
6. C. Ronald Huff, "Wrongful Conviction and Public Policy: The American Society of Criminology 2001 Presidential Address," *Criminology* 40, no. 1 (February 2002): 1–18. See also C. Ronald Huff et al., *Convicted but Innocent* (Thousand Oaks, CA: Sage, 1996); David Sudnow, "Normal Crimes: Sociological Features of the Penal Code in a Public Defender Office," *Social Problems* (Winter 1965): 255–276; William S. Lofquist, "Whodunit? An Examination of the Production of Wrongful Convictions," in *Wrongly Convicted: Perspectives on Failed Justice*, ed. Sandra D. Westervelt and John A. Humphrey (New Brunswick, NJ: Rutgers University Press, 2001).
7. The Innocence Project, "Facts on Post-Conviction DNA Exonerations," http://www.innocenceproject.org/Content/351PRINT.php, accessed 29 October 2010.
8. Ibid. See also Barry Scheck et al., *Actual Innocence* (New York: Doubleday, 2000).
9. "Vindicated by DNA, but a Lost Man on the Outside," *New York Times* (25 November 2007), p. 1.
10. "Michigan Study Raises Prospect of Thousands of False Convictions," *Criminal Justice Newsletter* (3 May 2004), p. 2.
11. "DNA Exoneration Brings Change in Legal System," *New York Times* (1 October 2007), p. 1.
12. *United States v. Grubbs*, 547 U.S. 90 (2006).
13. *United States v. Grubbs*, 547 U.S. 90 (2006).
14. *Illinois v. Gates*, 462 U.S. 213 (1983).
15. *Alabama v. White*, 496 U.S. 325 (1990).
16. *United States v. Ross*, 456 U.S. 798 (1982).
17. See *United States v. Perea*, 986 F.2d 633, 643 (2d Cir. 1993).
18. *Florida v. Jimeno*, 500 U.S. 248 (1991).
19. *United States v. Johns*, 469 U.S. 478 (1985).
20. *Colorado v. Bertine*, 479 U.S. 367 (1987).
21. *Illinois v. Wardlow*, 528 U.S. 119 (2000).
22. *Florida v. J.L.*, 529 U.S. 266 (2000).
23. *United States v. Montero-Camargo*, 208 F.3d 1122 (9th Cir. 2000), *cert. denied*, 531 U.S. 889 (2000).
24. *Indianapolis v. Edmond*, 531 U.S. 32 (2000).
25. *Maryland v. Pringle*, 540 U.S. 366 (2003).
26. *Illinois v. Lidster*, 540 U.S. 419 (2004).
27. *Illinois v. Caballes*, 543 U.S. 405 (2005).
28. *Brendlin v. California*, 551 U.S. 249 (2007).
29. *Arizona v. Gant*, 129 S.Ct. 1710 (2009). The 1981 case is *New York v. Belton*, 453 U.S. 454 (1981). The quotation is from *Katz v. United States*, 389 U.S. 347 (1967), footnotes omitted.
30. *United States v. Mendenhall*, 446 U.S. 544 (1980).
31. *Florida v. Bostick*, 501 U.S. 429 (1991).
32. *United States v. Drayton*, 536 U.S. 194 (2002).
33. *California v. Hodari D.*, 499 U.S. 621 (1991).
34. See *United States v. Robinson*, 414 U.S. 218 (1973).
35. See *Terry v. Ohio*, 392 U.S. 1 (1968).
36. *Minnesota v. Dickerson*, 508 U.S. 366 (1993).

37. *United States v. Ashley*, 37 F.3d 678 (D.C.Cir. 1994).
38. *Arizona v. Johnson*, 129 S.Ct. 781 (2009).
39. *People v. Clark*, 625 N.Y.S.2d 306 (App.Div.3d Dept. 1995), *aff'd.*, 86 N.Y.2d 824 (N.Y.App. 1995).
40. *Rochin v. California*, 342 U.S. 165, 166, 172 (1952).
41. *United States v. Montoya de Hernandez*, 473 U.S. 531 (1985).
42. *Bell v. Wolfish*, 441 U.S. 520 (1979).
43. *Masters v. Crouch*, 872 F.2d 1248 (6th Cir. 1989), *cert. denied, Frey v. Masters*, 493 U.S. 977 (1989).
44. *Safford Unified School District # 1 et al. v. Redding*, 129 S.Ct. 2633 (2009).
45. *Mapp v. Ohio*, 367 U.S. 643, 644 (1961).
46. *Payton v. New York*, 445 U.S. 573, 589–590 (1980).
47. *Welsh v. Wisconsin*, 466 U.S. 740 (1984).
48. *Wilson v. Arkansas*, 514 U.S. 927 (1995).
49. *Coolidge v. New Hampshire*, 403 U.S. 443 (1971).
50. *Arizona v. Hicks*, 480 U.S. 321 (1987).
51. *California v. Greenwood*, 486 U.S. 35 (1988).
52. *United States v. Hedrick*, 922 F.2d 396 (7th Cir. 1991), *cert. denied*, 502 U.S. 847 (1991).
53. *California v. Ciraola*, 476 U.S. 207 (1986). See also *Florida v. Riley*, 488 U.S. 445 (1989).
54. *Illinois v. McArthur*, 531 U.S. 326 (2001).
55. *Kyllo v. United States*, 533 U.S. 27 (2001).
56. *Hudson v. Michigan*, 547 U.S. 586 (2006).
57. *Georgia v. Randolph*, 547 U.S. 103 (2006).
58. Edward Bennett Williams, quoted in Alexander B. Smith and Harriet Pollack, *Crime and Justice in a Mass Society* (Waltham, MA: Xerox, 1972), p. 194.
59. *Brown v. Mississippi*, 297 U.S. 278 (1936).
60. *Miranda v. Arizona*, 384 U.S. 436 (1966).
61. *Oregon v. Mathiason*, 429 U.S. 492 (1977).
62. *Minnesota v. Murphy*, 465 U.S. 420 (1984).
63. *Edwards v. Arizona*, 451 U.S. 477, 484–485 (1981).
64. *Maryland v. Shatzer*, 130 S.Ct. 1213 (2010).
65. *McNeil v. Wisconsin*, 501 U.S. 171 (1991).
66. *Dickerson v. United States*, 530 U.S. 428 (2000).
67. *Missouri v. Seibert*, 540 U.S. 600 (2004).
68. *United States v. Patane*, 542 U.S. 630 (2004).
69. *Montejo v. Louisiana*, 129 S.Ct. 2079 (2009).
70. *Florida v. Powell*, 130 S.Ct. 1195 (2010).
71. *Berghuis v. Thompkins*, 2010 U.S. LEXIS 4379 (2010).
72. *Gideon v. Wainwright*, 372 U.S. 335 (1963), overruling *Betts v. Brady*, 316 U.S. 455 (1942), citations and footnotes omitted.
73. *Argersinger v. Hamlin*, 407 U.S. 25, 37 (1972); *Scott v. Illinois*, 440 U.S. 367 (1979).
74. *Escobedo v. Illinois*, 378 U.S. 478 (1964).
75. *Brewer v. Williams*, 430 U.S. 387, 398 (1977).
76. *Maine v. Moulton*, 474 U.S. 159 (1985).
77. *United States v. Gonzalez-Lopez*, 548 U.S. 140 (2006).
78. *Javor v. United States*, 724 F.2d 831 (9th Cir. 1984).
79. *Burdine v. Johnson*, 66 F.Supp. 2d 854 (S.D. Tex. 1999), *stay denied, motion granted, in part, motion denied, in part*, 87 F.Supp.

2d 711 (S.D.Tex. 2000), *vacated, remanded*, 231 F.3d 950 (5th Cir. 2000), *reh'g., en banc granted*, 234 F.3d 1339 (5th Cir. 2000), and *on reh'g. aff'd.*, 262 F.3d 336 (5th Cir. 2001), *cert. denied sub nom., motion granted*, 535 U.S. 1120 (2002).
80. *Strickland v. Washington*, 466 U.S. 668 (1984).
81. *Lockhart v. Fretwell*, 506 U.S. 364 (1993).
82. *Roe v. Lucio Flores-Ortega*, 528 U.S. 470 (2000).
83. *Wiggins v. Smith*, 539 U.S. 510 (2003).
84. *Bell v. Cone*, 535 U.S. 685 (2002).
85. *Rompilla v. Beard*, 545 U.S. 374 (2005).
86. *Porter v. McCollum*, 130 S.Ct. 447 (2009).
87. *Wood v. Allen*, 130 S.Ct. 841 (2010).
88. *Bobby v. van Hook*, 130 S.Ct. 13 (2010).
89. *Duncan v. Louisiana*, 391 U.S. 145, 149 (1968).
90. *Blanton v. North Las Vegas*, 489 U.S. 538 (1989).
91. *Batson v. Kentucky*, 476 U.S. 79 (1986). The earlier case is *Swain v. Alabama*, 380 U.S. 202 (1965).
92. *Powers v. Ohio*, 499 U.S. 400 (1991).
93. *Hernandez v. New York*, 500 U.S. 352 (1991).
94. *People v. Rodriguez*, 211 A.D. 2d 275 (N.Y.App.Div. 1st Dept. 1995).
95. *Georgia v. McCollum*, 505 U.S. 42 (1992).
96. *Miller-El v. Dretke*, 545 U.S. 231 (2005).
97. "Double Murder Trial to Begin," *Dallas Morning News* (8 August 2009), p. 1B.
98. "Black Juror Seated: Judge Orders Change After All-White Panel Picked in Murder Case," *Dallas Morning News* (31 July 2009), p. 1B.
99. *J.E.B. v. Alabama ex rel. T.B.*, 511 U.S. 127 (1994).
100. See *Barber v. Ponte*, 772 F.2d 982 (1st Cir. 1985) (*en banc*), *cert. denied*, 475 U.S. 1050 (1988).
101. *Witherspoon v. Illinois*, 391 U.S. 510, 522 (1968), emphasis in the original.
102. *Wainwright v. Witt*, 469 U.S. 412 (1985).
103. *Uttecht v. Brown*, 551 U.S. 1 (2007), cases and citations omitted.
104. *Sheppard v. Maxwell*, 384 U.S. 333 (1966).
105. *Sheppard v. Maxwell*, 384 U.S. 333, 349 (1966).
106. *Gannett Co., Inc. v. DePasquale*, 443 U.S. 368 (1979).
107. *Richmond Newspapers, Inc. v. Virginia*, 448 U.S. 555 (1980).
108. *Globe Newspaper Co. v. Superior Court*, 457 U.S. 596 (1982).
109. *Press-Enterprise Co. v. Superior Court*, 478 U.S. 1 (1986).
110. *Presley v. Georgia*, 130 S.Ct. 721 (2010).
111. Cal Pen Code, Title 17, Section 679 (2010).
112. *Booth v. Maryland*, 482 U.S. 496 (1987), *overruled in part; Payne v. Tennessee*, 501 U.S. 808 (1991).
113. *Payne v. Tennessee*, 501 U.S. 808. The other case that was overruled is *South Carolina v. Gathers*, 490 U.S. 805 (1989).
114. USCS, Title 18, Section 1512, note 5(a)(1)(2) (2010).
115. "Judiciary Committee Approves Constitutional Amendment," *Criminal Justice Newsletter* 29 (1 June 1998): 5.
116. "Constitutional Amendment Fails to Win Senate Approval," *Criminal Justice Newsletter* 30 (16 May 2000): 1, 2.

117. "ABA Takes Stands on Victims' Rights, Needle Exchange Programs," *Criminal Law Reporter* 61 (20 August 1997): 1458.

118. Violence Against Women and Department of Justice Reauthorization Act of 2005, Public Law 109-162 (2005).

119. Crime Victims' Rights Act, USCS, Title 18, Section 3771(a)(1)–(8) (2010).

120. *Coy v. Iowa*, 487 U.S. 1012 (1988).

121. *Maryland v. Craig*, 497 U.S. 836 (1990).

122. "Judge Rules Bryant Accuser May Not Be Called 'Victim,'" *New York Times* (2 May 2004), p. 14.

123. Pauline K. Brennan, "Sentencing Female Misdemeanants: An Examination of the Direct and Indirect Effects of Race/Ethnicity," *Justice Quarterly* 21, no. 1 (March 2006): 60–95; quotation is on p. 60.

124. John Braithwaite, "Between Proportionality & Impunity: Confrontation → Truth → Prevention," *Criminology* 43, 2 (May 2005): 283–306; quotation is on p. 283.

125. Sara Steen et al., "Images of Danger and Culpability: Racial Stereotyping, Case Processing, and Criminal Sentencing," *Criminology* 43, no. 2 (May 2006): 435–468.

126. Ibid., p. 435.

127. Darrell Steffensmeier and Stephen Demuth, "Ethnicity and Judges' Sentencing Decisions: Hispanic-Black-White Comparisons," *Criminology* 39, no. 1 (February 2001): 145–178. See this source for a review of race, ethnicity, and sentencing.

128. Traci Schlesinger, "Racial and Ethnic Disparity in Pretrial Criminal Processing," *Justice Quarterly* 22, no. 2 (June 2005): 170–192; quotation is on p. 170.

129. Tina L. Freiburger et al., "The Impact of Race on the Pretrial Decision," *American Journal of Criminal Justice* 35, no. 1/2 (Spring 2010): 76–86; quotation is on p. 76.

130. Katherine Beckett et al., "Race, Drugs, and Policing: Understanding Disparities in Drug Delivery Arrests," *Criminology* 44, no. 1 (February 2006): 105–138; quotations are on pp. 105, 130–131.

131. Joan Petersilia, *When Prisoners Come Home: Parole and Prisoner Reentry* (New York: Oxford University Press, 2003), p. 30.

132. Michael D. Reisig et al., "The Effect of Racial Inequality on Black Male Recidivism," *Justice Quarterly* 24, no. 3 (September 2007): 408–434; quotation is on p. 427.

133. For an explanation of the *racial threat perspective*, see Hubert M. Blalock, *Toward a Theory of Minority Group Relations* (New York: Wiley, 1967).

134. See Allen E. Liska and Mitchell B. Chamlin, "Social Structures and Crime Control Among Macrosocial Units," *American Journal of Sociology* 87 (1981): 413–426.

135. Karen F. Parker et al., "Racial Threat, Concentrated Disadvantage and Social Control: Considering the Macro-Level Sources of Variation in Arrests," *Criminology* 43, no. 4 (December 2005): 1111–1134.

136. "Beyond the Bell Curve: Community Disadvantage and the Explanation of Black-White Differences in Adolescent Violence," *Criminology* 43, no. 4 (December 2005): 1135–1168; quotation is on p. 1158.

137. John R. Hipp, "Income Inequality, Race, and Place: Does the Distribution of Race and Class Within Neighborhoods Affect Crime Rates?" *Criminology* 45, no. 3 (August 2007): 665–698.

138. Michael J. Hogan et al., "Economic Insecurity, Blame, and Punitive Ideology," *Justice Quarterly* 22, no. 3 (September 2005): 392–411; quotation is on p. 396 and cites several research articles in support of the statement.

139. Ibid., p. 405.

140. Charis E. Kubrin and Eric A. Stewart, "Predicting Who Reoffends: The Neglected Role of Neighborhood Context in Recidivism Studies," *Criminology* 44, no. 1 (February 2006): 165–198.

141. Lynne Goodstein, "Introduction," in *Rethinking Gender, Crime, and Justice*, ed. Claire M. Renzetti et al. (Los Angeles: Roxbury, 2006), pp. 1–10.

142. See, for example, Susan E. Martin, "Female Drug Offenders and the Drug/Crime Subculture: Gender, Stigma, and Social Control," in *Rethinking Gender, Crime, and Justice*, ed. Renzetti et al., pp. 107–124.

143. Goodstein, "Introduction," in *Rethinking Gender, Crime, and Justice*, ed. Renzetti et al., p. 7. See also Joanne Belknap and Hillary Potter, "Intimate Partner Abuse," in the same source, pp. 168–184.

144. See Tammy L. Anderson, "Issues Facing Women Prisoners in the Early Twenty-First Century," in *Rethinking Gender, Crime and Justice*, ed. Renzetti et al., pp. 200–212.

145. See the following articles in Renzetti et al., eds., *Rethinking Gender, Crime, and Justice*: Merry Morash et al., "Workplace Problems in Police Departments and Methods of Coping: Women at the Intersection," pp. 213–227; Cynthia Siemsen, "Women Criminal Lawyers," pp. 228–239; Michelle L. Meloy et al., "Women on the Bench: The Voices and Experiences of Female Judges," pp. 240–261; Mary K. Stohr, "'Yes, I've Paid the Price, but Look How Much I Gained': The Struggle and Status of Women Correctional Officers," pp. 262–277.

146. Peter B. Kraska, "Criminal Justice Theory: Toward Legitimacy and an Infrastructure," *Justice Quarterly* 23, no. 2 (June 2006): 167–185; quotation is on pp. 167–168.

147. *Holder v. Humanitarian Law Project*, 130 S.Ct. 2705 (2010). The statute is codified at USCS, Title 18, Section 2339B(a)(1) (2010).

148. USCS, Title 18, Secttion 2339A(b)(1) (2010).

149. *Hamdi v. Rumsfeld*, 542 U.S. 507 (2004).

150. *Holder v. Humanitarian Law Project*, 130 S. Ct. 2705 (2010), Justice Breyer, with whom Justices Ginsburg and Sotomayor, join, dissenting.

151. Robert Bolt, *A Man for All Seasons* (New York: Vintage Paperbacks, Random House, 1962), pp. 37–38.

CHAPTER 12

Police

Police officers engage in many community services as well as engage in traffic control, order maintenance, and law enforcement. This officer is taking the opportunity to relate to a child in a positive manner by getting down to her level and demonstrating the good biking safety of wearing a helmet.

KEY TERMS

constable
exclusionary rule
frankpledge
good faith exception
harmful error
hundred
inevitable discovery exception
INTERPOL
police
posse
proactive
reactive
sheriff
shires
tithing
watch system

INTRODUCTION

This chapter begins with a brief history of policing and discusses the levels of U.S. public police systems, including border patrol and campus security, before turning to a

INTRODUCTION continued

brief analysis of international policing and private security. Police personnel, the type of training and education that police officers have had historically, and recent efforts to recruit more women and minorities are noted. A section on the nature of policing focuses on its organization and three police functions: law enforcement, order maintenance, and provision of community services. We examine the way time is allocated among these three functions and the conflicts and stresses that develop as a result. Police decision making is analyzed, especially the decisions concerning whether to arrest and whether or not to use deadly force. Police misconduct is discussed, followed by a consideration of the control of policing. The chapter closes with a look at the impact of terrorism on policing.

This chapter covers one of the most important groups of people in American society: the **police**, who are entrusted with the right to protect the citizenry, even when protection requires force. More is demanded of police than of most other professionals. They are expected to be brave and not to show fear, shock, surprise, or hurt, even in the face of life's most serious tragedies. They are trained to make decisions quickly and with the calm, cool rationality that most people exhibit only in nontraumatic situations. They are expected to solve many problems for which society has not found solutions and, in some instances, to perform their jobs in a hostile, even violent, environment. They are instructed to treat citizens with respect, even when harassed, threatened, and verbally and physically abused.

Police occupy one of the most controversial positions in contemporary society. Although they are feared at times, they are indispensable in a modern, complex nation, especially when there is trouble. But many people are not comfortable with police and may react negatively when stopped by them. Police may retaliate with their attitudes, their comments, and in some cases, their weapons.

A word of warning is in order for this chapter. Of the many subjects covered in a criminology course, policing may be the most controversial. Policing has moral, religious, philosophical, ethical, and political overtones for many people. Attitudes about who should become police officers and how they should perform their jobs may be based on emotions and politics as well as knowledge, experience, reason, and practicality. In addition, in one chapter, it is impossible to skim even the surface of issues that surround policing; this chapter provides an overview of only some areas of concern.

The chapter begins with a look at policing historically and then proceeds to discuss the various policing levels in the United States before exploring security at U.S. borders and focusing on campuses and related areas of security. International policing is considered briefly and private security is examined before the chapter focuses on police personnel. That sections analyzes qualifications for policing, considers recruitment and training issues, and concentrates in some detail on the hiring of women and minorities in policing.

The nature of policing is examined in terms of the three primary police functions as well as policing models, time allocation, conflicting expectations, stress, the police subculture, and AIDS and law enforcement.

Police decision making is a crucial issue, and this chapter supplements Chapter 11's analysis of the right to stop and question and adds the dimension of the sociology of arrest. Racial profiling is examined more thoroughly, and the use of force is discussed in legal and practical terms, along with an analysis of the need for and restrictions on vehicle pursuits. Particular attention is given to the intervention of police in intimate personal violence cases.

The police misconduct section covers classic analyses as well as more recent examples and an analysis of corruption. Considerable attention is given to the various ways policing can be controlled, including control through police departments, the community, the U.S. Department of Justice, and the courts. A final section covers terrorism and policing.

The Emergence of Formal Policing

Chapter 1 discussed the informal social controls that characterized early, primitive societies and that exist to some extent in modern societies. As societies become more complex, formal methods of control become necessary; policing is an important part of that control. As laws emerge, police are needed to enforce them. A brief historical look at policing illustrates the background of modern police systems.

The history of policing began with *informal policing* in which all members of a community were responsible for maintaining order. In medieval England, policing was conducted through a system called **frankpledge**, or mutual pledge. Ten families constituted a **tithing**; within a tithing, each member was responsible for the acts of all other members.

Later, a **hundred** was developed, made up of 10 tithings. The hundred was under the charge of a **constable**, who can be considered the first police officer and was responsible for taking care of the weapons of the hundred. Subsequently, hundreds were combined to form **shires**, which were analogous to present-day counties. The shire was under the direction of an officer, appointed by the king, who was called a shire-reeve, a term that came to be pronounced **sheriff**.

With the growth of more complex societies, these informal methods of policing became ineffective. An increased division of labor, a more heterogeneous population, and a lack of social solidarity led to a *transitional type* of policing—for example, the **watch system**, which existed in England and in colonial America. In the watch system, bellmen walked throughout the city ringing bells and providing police services. Later, they were replaced by a permanent watch of citizens and still later by paid constables.

Dissatisfaction with the watch system led to the emergence of the modern type of policing, a movement that began in London. Londoners protested the ineffectiveness of the watch system for dealing with the problems of increased industrialization, rising levels of crime, and a perceived increase and greater severity of public riots. They agitated for a formal police force. Some believed that a police force constantly patrolling the streets would reduce and eventually eliminate crime in the streets. Others feared that the concentration of power that would be necessary for a formal police force would lead to abuses, especially if the force were a national one. Eventually, the conflict between these two positions was resolved by the establishment of local police systems.[1]

The first modern police force, the Metropolitan Police of London, was founded in 1829 by Sir Robert Peel. The men employed by the force were called *peelers* or *bobbies*. The officers worked full time; they wore special uniforms, and their primary function was to prevent crime. They were organized by territories and reported to a central government. Candidates had to meet high standards to qualify for a position. Bobbies were respected by Londoners, but recent incidents of corruption, incompetence, and alleged racism have tarnished the image of the once highly esteemed London bobbies.[2] A brief description of policing in England and Wales appears in Global Focus 12.1.

In time, the rest of England and other countries followed London's example. Some developed a centralized police system; others, including the United States, developed a decentralized one.

Public Policing in the United States

Many aspects of the English policing system were brought to the American colonies. Typically, a constable was in charge of towns, and the sheriff had jurisdiction over policing counties. Before the American Revolution, governors appointed by the English Crown filled these positions, but after the Revolution, most constables and sheriffs were selected by popular vote.

Many of the colonies adopted the English watch system. As early as 1631, Boston had a watch system; New Amsterdam (later New York) developed one in 1643. The New York City system was said to be typical of the watch system of policing in this country. Bellmen regularly walked throughout the city ringing bells and providing police services. They were replaced by a permanent watch of citizens, who were succeeded by paid constables. Professional, full-time police were not appointed in New York City until 1845.

One of the most familiar kinds of policing, which is still found in a few rural areas, was the **posse**. Under the posse system, the sheriff could call citizens over a certain age to assist in law enforcement.

Law enforcement officials were paid by local governments in some of the early American policing systems. In others, however, they were paid by private individuals. According to an analysis of police history,

> By the nineteenth century, American law enforcement was a hodgepodge of small jurisdictions staffed by various officials with different power, responsibilities, and legal standing. There was no system, although there were ample precedents for public policing.[3]

Informal policing came under attack early in the United States, as it had in England. It was realized that this system did not provide the expertise and efficiency that were needed to deal with urban riots and the increasing crime and violence that occurred as the country became more industrialized and complex.

Recognition of the need for a formal police system led to the development of a professional police force in Boston in 1837. By the late 1880s, most American cities had established municipal police forces. Today, those departments are complex as well as controversial. And unlike the system in England, the U.S. policing systems emerged as decentralized.

Rural, County, Municipal, and State Policing

United States policing systems operate at the local, state, and federal levels. Rural, county, and municipal police agencies may be found at the local level. Most studies of police focus on municipal policing, although the majority of police agencies are located in small towns, villages, or counties. Rural policing may be the responsibility of only one officer, and these systems must depend on county police agencies for assistance. Officers who work in rural

12.1 Policing in England and Wales

GLOBAL FOCUS

"There are 43 police forces in England and Wales, each responsible for a certain area of the country. Other police forces, such as the British Transport Police, the Ministry of Defence Police, and The Port of London Authority Police are responsible for the policing of particular installations. They are maintained and provided resources by central and local government agencies, with immediate oversight by local county committee councils and magistrates (police authorities). The Metropolitan Police Force polices London and is directly answerable to the UK Government Minister. The UK Government Minister is responsible both for crime control and other interior affairs."[1]

"The chief officer of each police force, the Chief Constable, is not answerable to anyone on operational matters, but is accountable to the committee on matters of efficiency. He or she must prepare an annual report on the work of the force concerned. Local police authorities select a force's most senior officers, subject to the approval of the Home Secretary. The Chief Constable can also appoint other officers. With the exception of the Metropolitan Police, all police forces are required to undergo statutory inspection by Her Majesty's Inspectorate of Constabulary."

"Some common services to police forces are provided centrally. The most important of these is the compilation of criminal records information. Liaison with the International Criminal Police Organization (Interpol) is provided by the Metropolitan Police. Other central bodies are the National Drugs Intelligence Unit and a National Criminal Intelligence Service (NCIS)."

Although the British police have traditionally been held in high esteem, in 2007, the London police force was questioned after a jury found the force (but not any individual officer) guilty of breaching safety laws in the 2005 death of an innocent person. In July 2005, police fired seven shots at Jean Charles de Menezes as he boarded a subway train. The deceased was wrongly identified as one of four suspects thought to have been involved in bombing the London underground the previous day, killing 52 people. The police were charged with "a serious lack of planning, chaotic communication and a failure to correctly identify a suspect." The Metropolitan Police Service was fined $364,000 and ordered to pay legal fees in the amount of $798,000. The victim's family was not satisfied. Police Commissioner Ian Blair said, "It is important to remember that no police officer set out that day to shoot an innocent man."[2]

In 2009, the de Menezes family settled with the Metropolitan Police Service for the cost of their attorney fees and a financial judgment in exchange for dropping all legal action. The litigants issued this statement:

> The commissioner of police of the metropolis and representatives of the de Menezes family are pleased to announce that all litigation between them arising out of the tragic death of Jean Charles de Menezes has been resolved.
>
> The members of the family are pleased that a compensation package has been agreed which enables them to put these events behind them and move forward with their lives.[3]

Since the police shooting of de Menezes, other deaths have occurred at the hands of London's Metropolitan Police: Stephen Lawrence, Blair Peach, and Ian Tomlinson. Tomlin-

A London police officer stands guard. The London bobbies have been widely recognized and respected, but in recent years, allegations of impropriety, including racism, have surfaced.

12.1 GLOBAL FOCUS continued

son, allegedly a passerby with his hands in his pockets, was walking away from police at a protest rally in front of the bank of England when he was shot on 1 April 2009. His family claimed there was a police cover-up; others alleged that the incident "changed" policing in London. For example, four months later at another protest scene, "the police entered into dialogue with protesters before the event, policed with a 'community-style' operation and used virtually no surveillance, stop and search or riot equipment."[4]

Other criticisms have focused on the Metropolitan Police Service, among them the agency's expenditures on air travel, which rose by more than one-third in 2009 and "the amount spent on business class tickets alone exceeding the cost of all flights in the previous two years." According to the department's spokesperson, the department books economy seats when possible, and the increase in the number of flights was due to "investigation and security work."[5]

1. This and the following two paragraphs are quoted from Coretta Phillips et al., Bureau of Justice Statistics, U.S. Department of Justice, *World Factbook of Criminal Justice Systems: England and Wales*, http://bjs.ojp.usdoj.gov/content/pub/ascii/WFBCJENG.TXT, accessed 18 May 2010.
2. "The World: London Jury Faults Police in Shooting," *Los Angeles Times* (2 November 2007), p. 3.
3. "De Menezes Family Settles," *The Guardian* (London) (24 November 2009), p. 5.
4. "National: Policing Protest: After Tomlinson: How One Man's Death Changed Policing," *The Guardian* (London) (26 November 2009), p. 8.
5. "Met Police Under Fire," *The Independent* (London) (30 December 2009), p. 8.

---

areas may not have sufficient training. Many work long hours without the prospect of assistance from county officers, and they are paid less than their urban counterparts. Rural policing can be rewarding for those who enjoy knowing everyone in the community and who like being involved in many activities and maintaining high visibility. Lower crime rates (particularly lower rates of violence), along with less complexity in police and community structures, may be seen as positive elements. Although crime rates have increased in many rural areas, rarely do they involve the violence characteristic of cities.

County policing may cover large geographic areas, creating problems for officers when they need assistance from other areas. Some county (and rural) police agencies may contract with other police agencies for services, a process that is complicated when the county system covers a large territory. Normally, the primary law enforcement officer in the county system is the sheriff, who may have numerous other duties, such as collecting county taxes, supervising some government activities, or even serving as the county coroner.

Reliance by rural villages on county law enforcement officials has been challenged in recent years because of the reduction in staff within counties. The usual backups may no longer be available. For example, in the small New Hampshire village in which this author lives, the county sheriff's office cut back its availability, and the village found it necessary to add a third full-time police officer. Fortunately, the local residents agreed to the increase in the police department budget to facilitate this addition, but that is not always the case. It is impossible for two full-time officers to police even a small village, especially with vacations and sick leave that are necessary. Further, all violations and misdemeanors are prosecuted by the police chief (or another officer or an attorney appointed by the chief). Most are not legally trained, and one could argue that a person who arrests and prosecutes has a conflict of interest. The state of New Hampshire does not see it that way.

Municipal police departments are larger and more complex than rural or county departments. They have higher costs and deal with higher crime rates and a more diverse population, but the officers are often better trained, better paid, and more highly educated. Most of the discussion in this chapter relates to municipal police departments.

Policing at the state level is divided into state police and state patrol. Although their duties may vary from state to state, patrol officers are primarily responsible for traffic control. They are uniformed officers, and they may have jurisdiction to enforce some state laws, but they do not have general powers of state law enforcement. That responsibility lies with the state police. State police officers, in contrast to the state patrol, have enforcement powers over certain regulations, such as those concerning fishing and gaming, gambling, horse racing, and the sale of alcoholic beverages.

Policing at the Federal Level

Most U.S. crimes involve violations of state statutes or local ordinances. Although the United States does not have a national police force, there are congressional statutes that cover federal crimes. These federal statutes are enforced by more than 50 federal agencies, of which the largest and best known is the Federal Bureau of Investigation (FBI) in the Department of Justice (DOJ), which is considered first.

The DOJ was created by a congressional act in 1870, but the office of the attorney general was established by the

Judiciary Act of 1789. The AG, who was to be one person working part time, was charged with the following:

> to prosecute and conduct all suits in the Supreme Court in which the United States shall be concerned, and to give his advice and opinion upon questions of law when required by the President of the United States, or when requested by the heads of any of the departments, touching any matters that may concern their departments.[4]

Today, the DOJ is headed by an attorney general, Eric Holder, to whom a deputy attorney general reports. Numerous other administrators report to the attorney general through his deputy attorney general.

One of the primary agencies within the DOJ is the Federal Bureau of Investigation. Among other responsibilities, the FBI is in charge of collecting and disseminating national crime data, published in the *Uniform Crime Reports (UCR)*, discussed in Chapter 2 of this text. The primary function of the FBI is investigative. FBI agents investigate crimes over which federal courts have jurisdiction, but when requested, they may investigate crimes under the jurisdiction of state and local law enforcement agencies.

The history of the FBI is one of controversy. The agency was headed by J. Edgar Hoover from 1924 until his death in 1972, and during much of that time, it enjoyed prestige and power. Some scholars allege, however, that under Hoover the FBI was characterized by corruption and other scandals.[5] In recent years, the FBI has been faced with lawsuits over hirings and promotions (alleging discrimination against minorities), harassment of agents, and allegations of fraud and other improper behavior on the part of those employed in the FBI lab. The latter allegations were the subject of an intensive investigation by the DOJ, which issued a report on the topic in 1997. The DOJ found no evidence of some of the allegations; others were supported. The FBI established a timetable for correcting the problems and agreed to pay Frederic Whitehurst, an FBI chemist who first made the allegations, the sum of $1.1 million. The whistle-blower was reinstated in his job, from which he had been suspended. He reported to work and resigned, as was required by the settlement agreement. The FBI agreed to drop all disciplinary charges against Whitehurst, and the DOJ agreed to pay his legal fees of $258,580.[6]

In July 1993, President Bill Clinton named federal Judge Louis J. Freeh to replace the embattled FBI Director William S. Sessions. By August 1996, Freeh was under fire, but he remained in office for nearly five more years, resigning in 2001. President George W. Bush nominated Robert S. Mueller III, a U.S. prosecutor, to the position. Mueller faced a tough job; the FBI came under severe criticism in 2001, when the execution of Timothy McVeigh, convicted of the Oklahoma City bombings, was postponed after it was disclosed that the FBI had withheld thousands of documents from the defense. Mueller was confirmed

FBI director, Robert S. Mueller III, speaking from the agency's headquarters in Washington, D.C.

and remains in office as of this writing. Exhibit 12.1 notes additional issues that erupted in subsequent years and cast the FBI in a negative light.

After the 9/11 terrorist attacks, the Bush administration recommended the creation of the Department of Homeland Security (DHS). Congress approved a cabinet-level position for this new agency, which combined 22 former federal agencies (not including the CIA and FBI).[7] The creation of the DHS constituted the most extensive federal government reorganization in 50 years. It was initially headed by Tom Ridge, who resigned in 2005 and was followed by Michael Chertoff. After President Barack Obama was elected, Janet Napolitano was nominated and confirmed to the position.

One new agency since 9/11, and part of the DHS, is the Transportation Security Administration (TSA) (see again Chapter 7). This agency's primary function is to secure modes of transportation and is probably best known for its presence at airport security, previously the function of the Federal Aviation Administration (FAA), which was restructured.

Many other federal agencies are also involved in law enforcement or licensing. For example, the Food and Drug

12.1 The Federal Bureau of Investigation Under Fire

The Federal Bureau of Investigation (FBI) has come under attacks in recent years, especially since the terrorist attacks of 11 September 2001. In April 2004, when the special commission investigating those attacks issued two interim reports, the FBI was the target of scathing criticism. Thomas H. Kean, chair of the commission, said of the FBI: "This is an agency that does not work. It makes you angry. And I don't know how to fix it."[1] The reports included details from which one could conclude that the FBI and CIA missed opportunities to prevent the 9/11 attacks. The bipartisan commission called for an overhaul of intelligence agencies and the creation of a cabinet-level intelligence czar to oversee all intelligence gathering, including that of the FBI as well as the CIA and other agencies. That was done and is discussed later in this chapter. The commission's final report was published in 2004; it was discussed in Chapter 7.

In July 2001, members of the U.S. Senate expressed outrage at the reports that 449 weapons and 184 laptop computers were missing from the inventory of the FBI. According to the *New York Times*, "Lawmakers said the latest lapse indicated that the bureau could no longer reliably manage its basic operations." Utah's Senator Orrin G. Hatch called the problem "simply inexcusable," and went on to say, "Lax administrative controls over sensitive materials like these cannot be tolerated." Vermont Senator Patrick J. Leahy said, "There are some very, very serious management problems at the F.B.I."[2]

These revelations came shortly after the guilty plea of Robert P. Hanssen, a former FBI agent who was accused of spying for Moscow since 1985. Hanssen pleaded guilty to 15 counts of espionage, attempted espionage, and conspiracy. As the result of his plea, 6 of the 21 counts against him were dismissed, and he did not receive the death sentence but, rather, life without parole.

Before his arrest, Hanssen was a respected member of the FBI, a family man, and an openly religious person. Most who knew and worked with him were shocked by his arrest and the revelation that he gave some of the United States' most sensitive security secrets to Russia.

More recently, FBI Director Robert S. Mueller III testified before the House Judiciary Committee (20 May 2009), stating that counterterrorism had become the bureau's top priority since 9/11, with counterintelligence and cybersecurity the next priorities. On 16 September 2009, Mueller testified before the Senate Judiciary Committee that the "men and women of the FBI have adopted to our country's ever-changing needs" by developing the intelligence necessary to combat terrorism. But after 5 November 2009, the agency was under attack again as the tragic events at Fort Hood, Texas, unfolded. On 8 December 2009, Director Mueller announced that he had appointed former FBI Director William H. Webster to head an investigation into those events. Major Nidal Malik Hasan, an army psychiatrist, was charged with 13 counts of premeditated murder and 32 counts of premeditated attempted murder. According to Mueller's press release in December, "It is essential to determine whether there are improvements to our current practices or other authorities that could make us all safer in the future."[3]

Military officials began a military hearing in October of 2010 to determine whether there was enough evidence for a court-martial; if so, Hasan could face the death penalty.

1. "Fixing FBI Failure," *Courier-Journal* (Louisville, KY) (18 April 2004), p. 2D.
2. "Senators Criticize F.B.I. for Its Security Failures," *New York Times* (19 July 2001), p. 16.
3. Federal Bureau of Investigation, "Director Asks Judge Webster to Conduct Independent Review," Press Release (8 December 2009), http://www.fbi.gov, accessed 10 November 2010.

Administration (FDA) oversees enforcement of laws regulating the sale and distribution of food and drugs. The Internal Revenue Service (IRS) is charged with enforcing laws regulating federal income tax.

Border security is a current focus of state and federal policing; thus, special attention is devoted to this area.

Security at U.S. Borders

The largest employer in the federal system is the U.S. Customs and Border Protection (CBP) agency, with more than 52,000 employees. The CBP began in 2003 and combines the "inspectional workforces and broad border authorities of the U.S. Customs Service, U.S. Immigration and Naturalization Service (INS), the U.S. Border Patrol, and the Animal and Plant Health Inspection Service." It "is tasked with stopping terrorists, terrorist weapons, illegal drugs, aliens, and materials harmful to agriculture from entering at, or between, ports of entry." The CBP is located within the DHS along with numerous other federal law enforcement agencies.[8] State and private agencies also provide law enforcement security in the United States.

Problems resulting from illegal immigration have resulted in increased concern and attention in recent years. According to the DHS, approximately 11 million illegal aliens were living in the United States in 2006, with approximately 6 million of those from Mexico. In May 2006, President Bush announced that he would order National Guard troops to the borders as a stopgap measure to prevent illegal aliens from entering the country. On 26 October 2006, President Bush signed the Secure Fence Act of 2006, which provides for 700 miles of new "virtual" fence along the United States/Mexico border.[9] Funding is an issue, however, and in March 2010, Secretary of Homeland Security Janet Napolitano stated that her office would divert about $50 million headed for that project to other areas of need at the border, such as laptops, radios, thermal-imaging devices, and so on.[10] But in May 2010, it was announced that an additional 1,200 National Guard would be dispatched to the Southwest borders of the United States, and the administration would be asking for more money to secure those borders. In August 2010, the House and Senate quickly passed, and President Obama signed, a bill authorizing $600 million for 1500 new border agents and other increased security measures at the borders.[11]

How serious is the problem of illegal immigration? In 1980, the country had an estimated 3 million illegal immigrants. In 2007, an estimated 12 million and in March 2009 an estimated 11.1 million illegal immigrants lived in the United States.[12]

Numerous provisions, some codified into statutes, were put into place in an attempt to track persons coming into and going out of the United States and to eliminate illegal immigration. Local jurisdictions passed ordinances, such as punishing landlords who rent to illegal aliens or businesses that employ them. Existing deportation measures were activated or new ones established. Federal courts faced significant increases in immigration appeals, and immigration officers faced huge backlogs of applications for citizenship. The importance of immigration issues was emphasized in 2010 when, for the first time in its history, the American Society of Criminology published major proceedings from its annual meeting (held in 2009). The title of the book, *Contemporary Issues in Criminal Justice Policy*, reflects the organization's current emphasis on policy. A section of this publication focuses on immigration issues and policies.[13]

In 2010, Arizona enacted a new immigration statute that resulted in a national and international negative reaction, including strong criticism from President Obama, who stated that the statute threatened

> to undermine basic notions of fairness that we cherish as Americans, as well as the trust between police and our communities that is so crucial to keeping us safe.[14]

Among other provisions, the Arizona statute permits law enforcement authorities to question and even detain anyone suspected of being in the country illegally. It requires individuals to carry immigration documents. Failure to do so is a state misdemeanor. The first lawsuit challenging the statute was filed on 17 May 2010 by the Mexican American Legal Defense and Education Fund and other groups as a class action. They argued that the statute would lead to racial profiling of peoples of color. Thus, it violates the Equal Protection clause of the U.S. Constitution and violates federal responsibility with regard to immigration.[15]

Other lawsuits were filed quickly, including one by the Obama administration on 6 July 2010. The government argued that the Arizona statute violated the Supremacy Clause of the U.S. Constitution because it usurped federal authority regarding immigration laws. On 28 July 2010, Judge Susan Bolton of the federal District Court of Arizona issued an injunction against the enforcement of the four most controversial portions of the statute. Judge Bolton permitted the remaining sections of the law to go into effect on 29 July 2010, as scheduled. Arizona appealed that decision, and a panel of three judges of the Ninth Circuit Court of Appeals heard oral arguments on 2 November 2010. The decision of that court was pending as of 23 December 2010.[16]

On the last day of its 2009–2010 term, the U.S. Supreme Court agreed to hear an earlier case concerning Arizona's 2007 immigration statute that "requires employers in the state to use a federal electronic system to verify their workers are eligible for employment. Those who knowingly hire illegal immigrants are penalized with suspension or revocation of their business licenses." One law school dean predicted that this case, *Chamber of Commerce of the United States v. Candelaria*, may be "potentially the biggest immigration ruling of the past 30 years."[17]

The U.S. Supreme Court has decided several immigration cases recently. In *Fernandez-Vargas v. Gonzales*, the Court reversed several lower federal courts and held that a 1996 statute may be applied even to immigrants who entered the United States prior to the date that statute became effective.[18]

In *Lopez v. Gonzales*, the U.S. Supreme Court held that any drug crime that is a felony under federal law but only a misdemeanor under state law is not necessarily an aggravated felony under immigration laws.[19] In *Carachuri-Rosendo v. Holder*, the Court cited this case as precedent in June 2010, when it decided an appeal by a permanent immigrant legally in the United States, where he had lived since age 5. His common-law wife and four children as well as his mother and sisters are U. S. citizens. The appellant was arrested in Texas for two drug offenses. The first offense, for which he received a 20-day jail sentence, was for possession of a small amount of marijuana. The second offense, for which he received a 10-day jail sentence, was for possession of one anti-anxiety pill, Xanax, for which he did not have a prescription. Although Texas law provides for a sentence enhancement for a second related offense, the state did not seek an enhancement, but after the second conviction, federal prosecutors began removal proceedings. The defendant agreed that he was subject to federal removal proceedings but argued that he was eligible for "discretionary cancellation of removal" because, as required by federal statute, he had not committed an aggravated felony. The Texas judge held that the second offense constituted an aggravated felony, the lower appeals courts upheld that decision, and the U.S. attorney general argued in their favor. The U.S. Supreme

Court reversed, holding that the possession of one Xanax tablet without a prescription and without the state having enhanced the penalty due to a prior conviction does not constitute conviction of a felony punishable under the Controlled Substances Act and thus subject the defendant to deportation.[20]

Crime by immigrants is an articulated issue of significant concern. For almost a century, this issue has been a focus of some U.S. criminologists, but in recent years, it has been given even more scrutiny as the above case indicates. In a recent article, criminologists reviewed the major research of the past century, noting studies showing that crime rates are actually low among immigrants, especially first-generation immigrants. In particular, they noted that "immigrants who live in neighborhoods with high concentrations of immigrants are especially law-abiding." The authors referred to a 2006 *New York Times* article in which criminologist Robert Sampson[21] suggested that the falling crime rates in the United States during the 1990s and early into this century might have been the result of increased immigration.[22]

Further, social scientists are focusing on the issue of whether illegal immigrants are more likely to be recidivists. Two investigators provided data on the recidivism of 517 deportable and 780 nondeportable aliens from the Los Angeles County Jail and found no significant difference, thus lending "no support to the ubiquitous assertion that deportable aliens are a unique threat to public safety."[23]

Other research will no doubt follow, but these recent findings should cause careful reexamination of U.S. immigration policies at the country's borders and beyond.

Campuses and Other Security Areas

Another area of security that may be public or private (discussed later) and that is growing in importance, expense, and complexity is security at schools, colleges, and universities. The killing of 32 students and himself by a Virginia Tech University student in April 2007, the killing of five students and himself by a former student at Northern Illinois University in February 2008, the murders of a student near Auburn University in Georgia and near the University of North Carolina in Chapel Hill in 2008, and the 2010 murder of a University of Virginia student and lacrosse player, Yeardley Love, allegedly by another lacrosse player and student at the same university, George Huguely, among others, tragically illustrate the need for increased security on campuses and in neighborhoods where students usually live and socialize. Exhibit 12.2 focuses on campus security.[24]

One of the problems school administrators face regarding campus security is the issue of privacy. Statutes protecting student privacy limit access to their records. The U.S. Department of Education has proposed changes to these federal statutes to enable campus administrators and law enforcement officers greater access to information that might assist them in preventing campus crime. For example, the Virginia Tech University student had a history of mental health issues which campus administrators missed because of their interpretation of the privacy statutes.[25]

A final area of security that needs attention is shopping malls, which could be a focus of terrorist threats and clearly have been the scenes of violence. Examples are the acts of a gunman who killed eight shoppers and himself at a Von Maur department store in Omaha, Nebraska, in December 2007 and the fatal shooting of five women in a Chicago area department store in February 2008.

Most shopping malls are located on private land, and in recent years, many of these malls have been the focus of criminal activity. With their sprawling facilities and large parking lots and garages, they are ripe for criminal activity. Although most are safer than city streets, businesspeople are understandably concerned about the safety and welfare of their clients and their employees. Private civil lawsuits brought successfully by those who are victimized in malls are also a factor in the use of private security to minimize crime in malls.

According to a study prepared for the National Institute of Justice, shopping mall security has not improved significantly since 9/11. A major problem, according to the study, is that most shopping malls are protected by private rather than public security and that the standards are lower. Another issue is that many businesses in shopping malls do not have close relationships with local police and do not wish to deal with security problems, preferring to ignore them rather than spend the money to deal with them.[26]

International Policing

Although this chapter focuses on U.S. policing, international policing is crucial. Global Focus 12.2 gives a brief sketch of the International Criminal Police Organization, or as it is most commonly known, **INTERPOL**.

Private Security

The problems that arise from decentralized policing, such as understaffed and underfunded public police agencies, accompanied by increased concern with crime, especially violent crime, have led many people to turn to private security firms for protection. Today, private (compared with public) security employs more people and is more expensive. Many people see private security as supplemental to public security. Its focus is in specialized areas such as proprietary (in-house) security, guard and patrol service, alarm services, private investigations, armored car services, manufacturers of security equipment, locksmiths, and security consultants and engineers. A miscellaneous

EXHIBIT **12.2**

Campus Security

Violence on college and university campuses was highlighted in April 2007 when shots were fired on the Virginia Tech campus in Blacksburg, Virginia. A lone shooter killed 32 students and faculty members before committing suicide. A state report issued in September of that year criticized university officials for their delay in communicating to the campus after the first two students were killed in a dormitory, some two hours before the gunman, a student, Seung Hui Cho, entered a classroom in another building and began firing again. College and university administrators across the country reacted with shock and concern, looking more carefully at their own security measures and emergency plans.

The state's review of this worst campus shooting spree in U.S. history was revised and published in late 2009. It stated that some administrators locked down their facilities and warned their own families about one and one-half hours before they alerted the rest of the campus. Both the first and the revised state reports concluded that with proper and timely warnings, lives could have been saved. The administration was also faulted for not contacting the first victim's family. Emily Hilscher lived for three hours and was taken to two hospitals before she died. A spokesman for the university declared that the report was not accurate.[1]

Shortly after fall classes began in 2007, several schools had occasion to test their emergency procedures. As soon as they got word that two students had been shot on 21 September, Delaware State University quickly notified students to remain in their rooms and lock the doors. At Saint John's University in Queens, New York, students, faculty, and staff were notified by text messaging that a gunman was on campus. An orderly process led them to seek safety as directed by security officers; the campus was locked down for three hours. And on the first day of classes at the University of Colorado at Boulder, students who had signed up for the text-message warning system received notice that a stabbing had occurred and the terrace was closed. The victim was treated at a local hospital and released, the perpetrator was apprehended, and no other persons were harmed. But thousands more students signed up immediately for text-message notification of emergencies.[2]

Many of the measures taken by campus security are necessary but costly. For example, the text-message alert system cost $25,000 at one university, where officials anticipate spending $150,000 for an alarm warning system. Another spent $750,000 on its emergency alert system, and one campus police department spent $13,800 for 15 long-range rifles. Additional deadbolts for residence halls cost $71,000, and one university received a bid for $2.7 million to install an emergency lockdown system on campus.[3]

In 2009, the Bureau of Justice Statistics announced that grants were available for persons interested in participating in the 2010 Survey of Campus Law Enforcement Agencies. The previous survey was conducted in 2004–2005. It reported that approximately 75 percent of four-year colleges and universities had a police force with sworn officers, and 67 percent had armed officers. The new survey will no doubt show increases in those numbers. According to the 2004–2005 survey, campus security officers performed such functions as the following:

- special events security (98 percent)
- dispatching calls for service (92 percent)
- traffic enforcement (89 percent)
- property crime investigation (86 percent)
- building lockup (85 percent)
- parking enforcement (84 percent)
- violent crime investigation (81 percent)[4]

---

1. "Virginia Tech Faulted Anew on Shootings," *New York Times* (5 December 2009), p. 1.
2. "Violence Tests the Security on Campuses," *New York Times* (30 September 2007), p. 21.
3. Ibid.
4. Brian A. Reaves, Bureau of Justice Statistics, *Campus Law Enforcement, 2004–05* (February 2008), p. 4, http://bjs.ojp.usdoj.gov/content/pub/pdf/cle0405.pdf, accessed 10 November 2010.

---

category includes guard dogs, drug testing, forensic analysis, and honesty testing.[27]

Private security services may be traced to Allan Pinkerton, who founded Pinkerton's Security Services in 1850. Headquartered in New York City, Pinkerton's was the largest of the private security firms and was responsible for the familiar term *private eye*. Like many other security firms, Pinkerton's contracted to supply private security officers, investigative services, electronic surveillance devices, and private consultants.[28]

Since 9/11, the demand for private security has increased. Several private firms have emerged to accommodate the demand, with one, Insite Security, in New York, stating that its lower-profile assignments grew approximately 33 percent in 2002 and again in 2003. The cost for private security services varies from $300 to $1,200 a day for a bodyguard. It can be even higher if special skills, such as speaking another language or training in martial arts, are required. Rates are also usually higher in large cities, such as New York and Los Angeles.[29]

12.2   INTERPOL

"INTERPOL is the world's largest international police organization, with 188 member countries. Created in 1923, it facilitates cross-border police co-operation, and supports and assists all organizations, authorities and services whose mission is to prevent or combat international crime.

"INTERPOL aims to facilitate international police co-operation even where diplomatic relations do not exist between particular countries. Action is taken within the limits of existing laws in different countries and in the spirit of the Universal Declaration of Human Rights. INTERPOL's constitution prohibits 'any intervention or activities of a political, military, religious or racial character.' . . .

"Each INTERPOL member country maintains a National Central Bureau (NCB) staffed by national law enforcement officers."

This is the mission statement posted by INTERPOL on the Internet. A recent case source gives some indication of how far-reaching this international source can be. In 2007, INTERPOL posted the picture of a suspected pedophile, who had been shown on the Internet sexually abusing children. The images were altered digitally, but experts working with INTERPOL unscrambled the maze and produced an iden-

tifiable image. Approximately 350 people supplied tips to INTERPOL, which identified the suspect. The organization withheld his name but stated that he was a 32- year-old teacher in South Korea, thought to be hiding in Thailand. Other news sources released his name as Christopher Paul Neil, suspected of having sex with at least 12 boys, some as young as 6.[1] In November 2007, Neil, a Canadian, was captured in Thailand, where he was teaching schoolchildren.[2]

In 2008, Neil pleaded guilty to sexually abusing a 13-year-old boy and was sentenced to three years and three months in prison. A few months later, he was convicted of holding that boy's 9-year-old brother against his will. Neil was sentenced to five more years in prison.[3]

---

1. INTERPOL, http://www.interpol.int/public/icpo/default.asp, accessed 10 November 2010.
2. "An Accused Child Molester in Jail and Waiting for a Court Date," *CNN Newsroom* (16 October 2007).
3. "Canadian Gets 5 Years on New Sex Conviction," *Toronto Star* (23 November 2008), p. AA03. Note: Some other sources said the new sentence was an additional nine years.

Some additional data on private security came from the executive director of the National Association of Security Companies (NASCO) in his testimony before the House Homeland Security committee on 1 May 2007:

- NASCO employs 450,000 trained security guards.
- Nationally, less than 700,000 persons are employed by public law enforcement agencies, while private security companies employ approximately 2 million people. Approximately 75 percent of the privately employed guards work for contract security companies.
- Most of the regulation of contract security is at the state level, with 40 states having licensing requirements. The trend is toward more stringent requirements, with states like California and New York leading the way.[30]

Another type of private security that is growing rapidly is private employment of public police. Questions of liability and conflict of interest have been raised, but proponents argue that trained police officers are better qualified to perform the tasks of private security than other persons are.[31]

Another issue is the cost of private security to society as well as to the individual. For example, private use of alarm systems for residences has resulted in the waste of law enforcement time to answer false alarms. A DOJ study

reported that of the 38 million burglar alarms to which the police responded in one year, 98 percent were false alarms. They cost police an estimated $1.5 billion and represented from 10 to 25 percent of all calls to police.[32]

One final issue with regard to private security is the growth of private security contractors who serve in Iraq and other countries to protect U.S. citizens. In September 2007, agents of one of the firms, Blackwater Worldwide, the largest of the U.S. government's security contractors, were accused of killing civilians in Baghdad. Blackwater USA guards said they were fired on while escorting a U.S. convoy; Iraq says Blackwater guards fired first. Seventeen Iraqis were killed; others were wounded. The Iraqi government completed its investigation first and demanded that the company be withdrawn from Iraq. The FBI concluded that at least 14 of the shootings were unjustified. Blackwater, the largest private security firm in Iraq, with 1,000 personnel, was paid billions for its contracts with the United States to provide security in Iraq. Most of those contracts were with the U.S. Department of State.[33]

In April 2010, five former officials of Blackwater were indicted by U.S. prosecutors for weapons violations and making false statements during criminal investigations. The company, which changed its name in 2009 to Xe Services and worked to reshape its image after the murder allegations, was still headed by its founder, Erik Prince (who was not named in these indictments) until December 2010, when the company's sale was final. In December 2009, indictments against five former Blackwater guards charged with manslaughter in the 2007 shootings were dismissed; one guard had pleaded guilty. The U.S. government, however, continued its criminal investigations into the company's operations, including a focus on alleged bribes of Iraqi officials to permit the company to continue to operate in Iraq after the 2007 shootings. In August 2010, Xe Services agreed with the U.S. State Department to pay $42 million to settle export violation cases. The company did this apparently to avoid criminal charges. The settlement permits Xe Services to continue to get contracts with the U.S. government.[34]

Police Personnel

According to the FBI, as of 31 October 2009, law enforcement agencies in the United States employed 1,021,456 people, of whom 706,886 were sworn officers and 314,570 were civilians. Men constituted 73.7 percent of the sworn officers and 39.0 percent of the civilians.[35]

One of the most important aspects of policing is the recruitment, selection, education, and training of officers. Until recently, most police officers were young, white males with a high school education or less. The training they received was at times inadequate for the wide range of duties they performed. Although that picture has changed, there is room for improvement.

Qualifications for Policing

A primary consideration in recruiting potential police officers is: What kind of characteristics of policing should be emphasized? First, an attempt should be made to portray policing to recruits in as realistic a manner as possible. Many of the issues discussed in this chapter are not known to all potential recruits, and those issues are important. They dispel the myth engendered by movies and television that policing consists of one exciting moment after another. In reality, many police are never involved in a crisis situation; most never fire a gun in the line of duty; and much of their time is consumed by routine, mundane work such as filling out forms and waiting for something to happen.

Second, police departments should focus on the qualities that are important to policing, such as intelligence, good judgment, compassion, tact, courage, objectivity, honesty, emotional stability, and integrity. Third, law enforcement departments should recruit persons who have developed the skills that enable them to use discretion wisely.

Fourth, psychological factors are important because policing is stressful (see the section on police stress later in this chapter). Handling racial tensions in a society in which these tensions appear to be increasing rather than decreasing is not an easy job. Today's law enforcement

officers are being accused of misconduct for acts they may believe they conducted appropriately. They may perform their jobs correctly but be suspended pending an investigation, which is the policy in most departments when, for example, a suspect is killed by an officer.

Fifth, temperament and personality are important considerations for policing. Early studies reported that police were emotionally maladjusted, cynical, authoritarian, and impulsive. They were described as being more rigid, punitive, physically aggressive, assertive, and lacking in self-confidence than most other people and as having a preference for being supervised.[36] It is necessary to analyze the results of these studies carefully. Although some studies show that many police officers are cynical, others suggest that they are not cynical toward all aspects of policing. Still others have argued that cynicism is not a trait of police but, rather, a label from society. Police are a heterogeneous, not a homogeneous, group of people who become less, not more, cynical as they grow older and as their length of service on the police force increases. Some reports contend that whatever traits police officers have, such as authoritarianism or punitiveness, were acquired on the force because recruits do not demonstrate these traits when they begin policing.[37]

In earlier studies of police, the emphasis was on personality, with the assumption that if we could attract different types of people, the quality of policing would improve. But the U.S. Commission on Civil Rights found that the standards used for selecting police recruits do not accurately measure the specific qualities needed for quality job performance. The commission stressed the importance of psychological testing. Analyses of some psychological test results suggest that police applicants are healthier psychologically and more homogeneous than some other applicant groups.[38]

Psychological tests are important, but unless we know how they relate to the specific functions that police must perform, the results will be of little help. We cannot analyze policing without looking at what police do and evaluating the conflicts and stresses they encounter. We need to know their priorities, which are not necessarily related to factors such as background or an authoritarian or nonauthoritarian personality.[39]

The question of the level of education that should be required of police recruits is also a sensitive and controversial issue. Although it might be assumed that experts agree that higher education is important for policing, that is not necessarily the case. Two criticisms of police education must be considered. First, the quality of the earlier educational programs developed specifically for police was questioned. Many of the curricula focused on technical courses and neglected the broad liberal arts courses that might help officers develop more understanding of the people they encounter. Second, some questioned whether the goal of a college education for police officers is reasonable. Supporters argue that education increases police officers' sensitivity to issues concerning race and gender and gives additional insights into some of the particular law enforcement and other problems they face on duty. However, others contend that there is no evidence that higher education has a positive effect on policing.

Another criticism of higher education prerequisites for police applicants is that the requirement might shrink the applicant pool, especially of minority candidates. Additionally, some police unions have expressed opposition to requiring college courses. There is also concern that police education and training have neglected the broader experiences that would enable individuals to tackle many of the professional problems encountered in policing.[40]

It is also possible that the routine work of policing is less bearable for a college-educated person than for one who has not obtained a college degree. The officer may become bored with the lack of challenge and intolerant of people who have not shared the same kinds of educational experiences. After a review of the literature, two investigators concluded that "intelligence and education do not guarantee success" in policing and that a college degree may "give rise to more dissatisfaction and higher wastage."[41]

In contrast, other investigators concluded:

> We find that higher education has two important roles to play. One is to carry education beyond the classroom in ways that encourage broad reform. The other is to help make improvements in police training and education in ways that at least will produce higher levels of civility, and might even encourage a more humanistic police professionalism.[42]

It is difficult, however, to increase the educational requirement for police recruits. For example, a few years back, the Plano (Texas) Police Department initiated a requirement that all recruits must have a college degree. The department officials wanted the police force to look more like the residents of that upscale Dallas suburb. Officials knew this would be difficult because that year the department lost six experienced officers, whose total years of experience were equal to those of 74 of the youngest officers.[43]

How does one recruit such experience *and* require college degrees? It apparently seemed impossible in Plano. The department now permits these alternatives to a four-year college degree: 60 semester hours of college credit from an accredited institution plus either two years as a full-time, paid, sworn law enforcement officer or three years of active military service.[44]

Police Recruitment and Training

The establishment of an effective and efficient police force requires careful recruitment, selection, and training. The extensive qualifications, along with the risk law enforcement officers face and the low salaries, make recruitment

difficult. Some of the issues in recruiting are mentioned in Media Focus 12.1.

The difficulties in recruiting police officers have led some agencies to advertise, offer incentives, and even lower standards. For example, some departments have relaxed the drug exclusions, having found that they were too strict. The FBI previously refused to hire a recruit who had used marijuana 15 or more times. In January 2007, the agency changed its policy to relax this rule. The current policy is stated in Exhibit 12.3.

Recruitment and selection must be followed by adequate training of law enforcement officers. Basic police training should range from firing weapons to understanding the ordinances and laws that the officer will be responsible for enforcing. It should include training in the social services that must be performed. Special attention should be given to training those officers who will patrol schools, some of which have experienced violence, as noted earlier.

The importance of adequate police training was underscored by a 1989 U.S. Supreme Court decision, *City of Canton, Ohio v. Harris*, in which the Court held that inadequately trained police could lead to civil liability on the part of the department. The Supreme Court did, however, limit that liability to situations in which the officer's training amounted to "deliberate indifference to the rights of persons with whom the police come into contact."[45]

Finally, with regard to law enforcement training, today's officers need special training in counterterrorism in addition to all of the innovative investigative techniques, such as infrared (thermal) imagers, computers, information systems, off-land vehicles (e.g., boats) in some jurisdictions, use of animals, and so on.

In addition to providing adequate training of officers, police departments need to diversify their personnel. Almost three decades ago, the U.S. Commission on Civil Rights emphasized the need for law enforcement departments to represent the composition of the populations they serve. The commission noted that a lack of minorities leads to increased tensions and violence in some predominantly minority neighborhoods with high crime rates. Residents of those areas may be reluctant to cooperate with crime prevention efforts if they think they will be discriminated against by police. Women, the most frequent victims of rape and other sexual assaults, may be less willing to report these crimes if there are no women on police forces. Minorities who have been mistreated by white police may not trust them in future interactions. Thus, efforts should be made to recruit female and minority police officers.

Female and Minority Officers

In recent years, the presence of women and racial and ethnic minorities in policing has increased although, as noted earlier in this chapter, most sworn law enforcement

12.1   Policing as Portrayed by the Media

Perhaps it is understandable that a national newspaper such as the *New York Times* would publish a front-page article entitled "City Police Work Losing Its Appeal and Its Veterans."[1] The 2001 article went beyond the personnel problems of the New York City Police Department and mentioned similar problems in other large cities. Police departments across the country were having difficulty recruiting young officers while facing an increased number of retirements, some of them early. Further, it was becoming more difficult to entice qualified officers to move up the ranks, especially to that of police chief.

The problems of recruiting police officers as well as police chiefs did not stop with the entry-level and top positions. Departments were having difficulty getting officers to take the sergeant's exam and sergeants to take the exam for promotion to lieutenant because lieutenants do not receive overtime pay. The police culture also has an impact on recruiting. As one head of a management and consulting firm stated: "There has been a big change in the culture of policing in the past few years, as lifestyle becomes more important than the sense of public service."

Some argue that the media are partly responsible for the current difficulties in recruiting police and, especially, chiefs. For example, when the new Seattle police chief was out for a run on his own time, saw a woman who had passed out, administered mouth-to-mouth resuscitation, and took her to the hospital, the local media that evening gave only cursory attention to these facts. But significant attention was given to a police chase that resulted in injury to a pedestrian, with the police blamed for those injuries.

Although the media continue to report negative aspects of policing, as perhaps is their duty, the media portrayal of police (and firefighters) after 9/11 took a different perspective, at least for a while. Considerable attention was given to the memorial services for the officers who died in the terrorist acts of that day, their accomplishments during their lives, and their remaining families. And apparently, the public took a more sympathetic view toward police as well as a greater interest in their jobs. Applications to attend the police academies of some jurisdictions increased. Most important, there appeared to be a greater understanding of the potential for

violence for those who work to protect us from the criminal acts of others.

The problems associated with publishing positive reports on policing were illustrated by a study of attempts by law enforcement to market community-oriented policing programs. Information about long-term crime fighting is just not as exciting as real crime. Even in areas where police officials and the media had excellent relations, articles on community policing received slight attention. As the researchers remarked, "Crime makes headlines; community policing does not."[2]

By 2007, although many departments were still having difficulty recruiting, and some had lowered age, weight, and other physical requirements, other departments were reporting success in recruiting. In May of that year, the *New York Times* ran an article entitled, "A Race for Jobs in Police Depts. on Long Island." According to this report, 28,000 people signed up to take the Suffolk County police test on 9 June 2007, and some of those came from across the country. That jurisdiction had a starting salary of $57,811, much higher than in neighboring departments, and with overtime pay, many officers made over $100,000—in a jurisdiction with a declining crime rate. Only a high school education was required.[3]

The Suffolk Police Department Web page in 2010 posted a salary for police officers with three years of service to be $97,958 (2007 labor contract) with excellent benefits, including 13 sick days the first year, 26 by the third year, such days to be cumulative.[4]

1. "City Police Work Losing Its Appeal and Its Veterans," *New York Times* (30 July 2001), p. 1. All of the information prior to note 2 is summarized from this article.
2. Steve Chermak and Alexander Weiss, *Identifying Strategies to Market Police in the News*, National Criminal Justice Reference Service (2001), http://www.ncjrs.gov/App/Publications/abstract.aspx?ID;eq194130, accessed 10 November 2010.
3. "A Race for Jobs in Police Depts. on Long Island," *New York Times* (22 May 2007), p. 1.
4. Suffolk County Police Department, http://www.cp.suffolk.ny.us/police/recruitment.htm, accessed 19 May 2010.

personnel are white males, and most of the nonsworn employees are white women.

Women and minority officers face problems in policing as well as in recruiting. Early studies of minority police officers emphasized their role conflicts. For example, an earlier scholarly analysis revealed some evidence that African American offenders expected African American officers to give them a break. If the officers were lenient, this along with many other actions resulted in criticism from white peers.[46]

Some minority officers complain that they are not accepted by white officers, although most say they believe white officers will come to their aid when they need help. In a 2010 text on policing, the author, a police officer and scholar, presented his ideas about policing and minorities. He noted the historical intertwining of black people and policing but the lack of attention paid to the research and thoughts of black scholars regarding how to police their communities. Christopher Cooper argued that we should listen to minorities rather than tell them to forget their

EXHIBIT 12.3   Federal Bureau of Investigation's Employment Drug Policy

"The FBI is firmly committed to a drug-free society and work place. Therefore, the unlawful use of drugs by FBI employees is not tolerated. Furthermore, applicants for employment with the FBI who currently use illegal drugs will be found unsuitable for employment. The FBI does not condone any prior unlawful drug use by applicants. We realize, however, some otherwise qualified applicants may have used drugs at some point in their pasts. The following policy sets forth the criteria for determining whether any prior drug use makes an applicant unsuitable for employment, balancing the needs of the FBI to maintain a drug-free workplace and the public integrity necessary to accomplish the FBI's intelligence and law enforcement missions. Applicants who do not meet the listed criteria should not apply for any FBI position."

Criteria

"Under the FBI's current Employment Drug Policy, an applicant will be found unsuitable for employment if they:

- Have used any illegal drug (including anabolic steroids after February 27, 1991), other than marijuana, within the past ten years, or engaged in more than minimal experimentation in their lifetime. In making the determination about an applicant's suitability for FBI employment, all relevant facts, including the frequency of use, will be evaluated.

- Have used marijuana/cannabis within the past three years, or have extensively used marijuana/cannabis or over a substantial period of time. In making the determination about an applicant's suitability for FBI employment, all relevant facts, including the recency and frequency of use, will be evaluated.

"You can easily determine whether you meet the FBI's illegal drug policy by answering the following questions:

1. Have you used marijuana at all within the last three years?
2. Have you used any other illegal drug (including anabolic steroids after February 27, 1991) at all in the past 10 years?
3. Have you ever sold any illegal drug for profit?
4. Have you ever used an illegal drug (no matter how many times or how long ago) while in a law enforcement or prosecutorial position, or in a position which carries with it a high level of responsibility or public trust?

"If you answered Yes to any of these questions, you are not eligible for employment with the FBI."

Source: Federal Bureau of Investigation, "Employment Drug Policy," http://www.FBIjobs.gov/52.asp, accessed 10 November 2010.

---

blackness. In his own words, "I choose to notice my societal position as a black man in America. To discard it is to avoid realizing and challenging the injustices that come with my social position. The same people who tell you to forget who you are, are the same people who will not let you forget who you are."[47]

Clearly, the hiring and promotion of minority officers should be a priority. Legal measures have pointed in that direction, although with some mixed results. For example, a 2009 jury trial in federal court resulted in a split decision for Greenwich (Connecticut) police officers. Nine jurors deliberated for four days after a ten-day trial and decided that five of the eight minority plaintiffs were denied opportunities for premium-pay assignments and promotions. They will share a $157,000 damage award, including damages for emotional distress. Two of those officers were awarded additional damages for being subjected to a hostile work environment.[48]

Hiring and promoting women should also be a focus of police departments. Women have made progress in policing since the first woman became a police officer on 1 April 1908, when Lola Baldwin was hired in Portland, Oregon.[49] But they still do not represent significant numbers in police departments, having made only slight gains in the past two decades according to a July 2010 BJS report,

which stated that approximately 100,000 women are state and federal sworn officers in law enforcement agencies. The FBI was 19 percent female; the federal Bureau of Prisons (BOP) was 14 percent, but the highest percentage in federal agencies was the Offices of Inspectors General (25 percent). Among the 13 largest police departments, Detroit led in 2007 with 27 percent women who were full-time sworn officers, followed by Philadelphia with 25 percent, down to a low of 9 percent in Las Vegas Metro. When all police departments were considered, women constituted an average of 18 percent of full-time sworn officers in local police departments that employed more than 2,000 sworn officers. In contrast, women represented only 6 percent of all sworn officers nationwide in local police departments that employed between 1 and 10 full-time sworn officers and 4 percent of those in small sheriff's offices.[50] Figure 12.1 graphs the percentage of full-time sworn law enforcement female officers in state and local law enforcement agencies between 1987 and 2007.

Female police officers report problems both on and off the job. With regard to the latter, some female police say they are not accepted as friends by male officers in after-hours social activities. Some female officers report that they have experienced rejection by male colleagues and even by the public whom they serve. Critics have argued

Minorities and women have made some gains in police department hirings. These two officers are launching a search with the aid of the canine patrol.

that women cannot handle the physical aspects of policing, but physical differences between men and women do not in themselves mean that women are less capable than men.[51]

One scholar referred to what she called the "culturally mandated patterns governing male/female interaction" and concluded: "In sum, a woman officer faces barriers and handicaps that are built into both the formal and informal work structures." Although the "most blatant barriers" that kept women from being recruited as police officers for years have fallen, and the numbers of women in policing are increasing, there are still barriers to advancement.[52]

Some feminist social scientists maintain that research supports the allegation that "police women do experience unique workplace stressors, including sex discrimination, language harassment, lack of role models and mentors, and the demands of emotional work to respond to these difficulties."[53] Other women might argue that these issues in no way distinguish female police officers from women in many other professions.

The National Center for Women and Policing (NCWP) states that recruiting women into policing is hindered by their differential treatment within police departments, including "discrimination, harassment, and intimidation." But the NCWP claims there are positives. Female police officers are less likely to use force than communication skills and thus, are more capable than men of diffusing a tense situation. They are less likely than male officers to be named in a civil suit or cited for violence. The NCWP surveys women in policing yearly, but their last posting on their Web page concerns 2001 data. Still, if those data are compared to the latest (2009) from the FBI, it is clear that women have made little progress in the ranks of sworn officers, now accounting for only approximately 12 percent of sworn officers. Exhibit 12.4 contains information on a national study of women and policing conducted and published by the NCWP.[54]

Figure 12.1

Percentage of Full-time Sworn Law Enforcement Officers Who Are Women Among State and Local Law Enforcement Agencies, 1987–2008

Source: Lynn Langton, Bureau of Justice Statistics, *Women in Law Enforcement, 1987–2008* (June 2010), p. 3, http://bjs.ojp.usdoj.gov/content/pub/pdf/wle8708.pdf, accessed 9 November 2010.

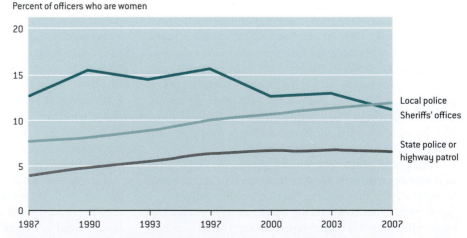

Note: Data on state police and highway patrol agencies were obtained from the Federal Bureau of Investigation's *Uniform Crime Reports*. Data on local police departments and sheriffs' offices were obtained from the BJS Law Enforcement Management and Administrative Statistics (LEMAS) series.

In a provocative analysis of that study and in reporting on her own study of women in policing, a retired division chief with the Miami-Dade (Florida) Police Department concluded as follows:

> Law enforcement remains a highly masculine profession. In order for law enforcement to truly represent the diversity of communities served . . . there must be a concerted effort to increase the percentage of women officers from the current 12 percent. In other occupations, 46.3 percent are women [citation omitted]. The integration of women into command levels will demonstrate to future promotional candidates that their departments have a commitment to diversity.[55]

There have been some efforts to promote women and minorities to upper-level policing. A few women and minorities have served as police chiefs in major cities. The first woman to hold that position in Detroit, Michigan, the nation's tenth-largest city, was an African American woman, Ella Bully-Cummings, who assumed the position in 2003 at age 46. Bully-Cummings led the department during turbulant times, with the department under federal monitoring to correct problems of excessive police use of force and mistreatment of inmates, which were uncovered during an investigation by the U.S. Department of Justice. Bully-Cummings retired in 2008. In 2009, the executive director of the Michigan Association of Chiefs of Police noted that 12 women "were leading the state's 600 or so law enforcement agencies." That is not a large number, but it was twice the figure of 10 years previously.[56]

The need to increase the number of women in international policing has also been emphasized. In October 2009, a female senior United Nations (UN) officer called for the hiring of more women as she praised an agreement between INTERPOL (see earlier discussion in this chapter) and the UN to "strengthen police units in peacekeeping missions around the world." The Police Division of the UN Department of Peacekeeping Operations (DPKO) set as its goal increasing the number of women from 8 percent in 2009 to 20 percent in 2014 and, eventually, achieve a 50-50 ratio of men and women in UN policing.[57]

The Nature of Policing

Historically, police had greater responsibility for enforcing the peace than for enforcing criminal laws or traffic ordinances. Their functions were to find homes and shelters for women who might be lured into prostitution; to handle riots and other civil disturbances; to regulate garbage disposal, street sanitation, and explosives; and to inspect bars, liquor stores, and other businesses that required licensing. Numerous social service functions were also part of their jobs.

In earlier times, police did not investigate criminal activities; that was the alleged victim's responsibility. Once the alleged victim identified the suspect, the police would assist with apprehension. Alleged victims paid police for helping them regain stolen property. Thus, officers who became experts in finding stolen property could expect greater gain. This action led to specialization in police

---

EXHIBIT 12.4

Women in Policing

The following information is from a national study of large police departments which was conducted by the National Center for Women in Policing (NCWP) (a division of the Feminist Majority Foundation) in 2001 and published in 2002. Here are the latest data from their annual surveys.

- "Over the last ten years, the representation of women in large police agencies has slowly increased from 9% in 1990 to 12.7% in 2001—a gain of less than 4%. This under-representation of women is striking, given that women account for 46.5% of the adult labor force.

- "There is now mounting evidence that the slow pace of increase in the representation of women in large police agencies has stalled or even possibly reversed. The percentage of women in large police agencies was 14.3% in 1999, 13.0% in 2000, and 12.7% in 2001.

"This discouraging trend is primarily concentrated among municipal and state agencies, and raises the question of whether women will ever reach equal representation or gender balance within the police profession. . . . One possible explanation for the stall or even decline in women's representation within sworn law enforcement is the decrease in the number of consent decrees mandating the hiring and/or promotion of women and/or minorities. Among surveyed agencies, eight consent decrees expired in the period of time from 1999 to 2002, yet only two consent decrees were implemented since 1995, and only six were implemented in the entire decade. Without the consent decrees imposed to remedy discriminatory hiring and employment practices by law enforcement agencies, even the marginal gains women have made in policing would not have been possible."

Source: National Center for Women in Policing (a division of the Feminist Majority Foundation), *Women in Policing: 2001* (April 2002), http://www.womenandpolicing.org/PDF/2002_Status_Report.pdf, accessed 10 November 2010.

forces. The practice of getting paid for their services made police give careful attention to those who had the means to pay.

The nature of policing has changed, but today, most policing differs from the image held by the public and preferred by police—that of the officer chasing and catching dangerous criminals. Considerable time is spent in routine, boring, and nondangerous activities. But the system has developed a structure that gives the greatest rewards for dangerous activities and the fewest for routine functions. This situation creates problems for police, for their departments, and for their communities. Thus, it is important to look at all police functions. The following discussion focuses on municipal or local policing.

Police Functions

Law enforcement is only one of several police functions, as Exhibit 12.5 demonstrates. Since information gathering may and usually does occur in all three police functions, most discussions categorize the three basic police duties as law enforcement, order maintenance, and service-related functions.

Law Enforcement

The law enforcement function of policing involves the power to stop, question, detain, and arrest people who violate the law. Law enforcement powers range from stopping traffic violators to apprehending persons suspected of committing serious felonies, which may involve the use of deadly force. Police gather information and file reports, both important, although at times monotonous, functions. Securing information may involve investigating crimes, a critical function. The successful prosecution of a case often depends on meticulous, professional, and precise investigative techniques by police. Police must also preserve the evidence they obtain and ensure that its integrity is maintained and that it is available for subsequent criminal trials. Police may be called to testify regarding any or all of these procedures as well as to identify the evidence and the suspect.

Chapter 11 discussed some of the restrictions that the U.S. Constitution places on police powers, but it is important to understand that police powers to affect the lives of citizens remain wide and significant. Perhaps the enormity of what the police can legitimately do is best illustrated by a 2001 case in which the U.S. Supreme Court held that police may make a full custodial arrest when they see someone breaking the law—even a minor infraction for which a small fine is the maximum penalty. The case involved a Texas mother, Gail Atwater, who, while driving (with her children in the car), was stopped by police for failure to wear her seat belt, as required by Texas law. Atwater was handcuffed and taken to the police station where she was held until she posted a $310 bond. The maximum penalty for the violation was $50. In a 5–4 decision, a bitterly divided U.S. Supreme Court ruled in *Atwater v. City of Lago Vista* that the police had not violated Atwater's constitutional rights when they made the arrest.[58]

It is also important to understand that law enforcement powers do not give police great crime prevention abilities. In a provocative and often cited work published in 1968, Herbert L. Packer described what the role of police should be in the area of law enforcement: "Ideally, police should be seen as the people who keep the law of the jungle from taking over."[59]

In their exercise of discretion, police may create problems if they engage in what is referred to as a *zero tolerance* policy. The approach is perhaps best illustrated by the tenure of William J. Bratton (who retired in 2009 as the Los Angeles police chief) when he was the police commissioner in New York City during most of the first term of Mayor Rudolph Giuliani. Bratton made changes in the police department at all levels and focused his zero tolerance policy on quality-of-life issues, such as removing beggars, prostitutes, petty drug dealers, graffiti scribblers, and other minor offenders from the streets. His approach followed the "broken windows" approach to policing, which was first introduced by James Q. Wilson and George Kelling in 1982. The broken windows concept was based on the belief that if minor offenders who disrupted the quality

EXHIBIT 12.5

Police Functions

"The roles of police officers are:

- **Law enforcement**—Applying legal sanctions (usually arrest) to behavior that violates a legal standard.
- **Order maintenance**—Taking steps to control events and circumstances that disturb or threaten to disturb the peace. For example, a police officer may be called on to mediate a family dispute, to disperse an unruly crowd, or to quiet an overly boisterous party.
- **Information gathering**—Asking routine questions at a crime scene, inspecting victimized premises, and

filling out forms needed to register criminal complaints.
- **Service-related duties**—A broad range of activities, such as assistance of injured persons, animal control, or fire calls."

Source: Bureau of Justice Statistics, *Report to the Nation on Crime and Justice: The Data*, 2d ed. (Washington, D.C.: U.S. Department of Justice, 1988), p. 62.

of life were not removed from the streets, people would be frightened, predatory criminals would be attracted, and crime would escalate.[60]

Bratton and Giuliani credited the zero tolerance approach and other changes in New York City with the significant decrease in crime in that city during the late 1990s. But not everyone agreed. After examining the city's crime rates and other factors and comparing them with those in the city of San Diego, which embraced a problem-oriented approach to policing (discussed later in this chapter), one scholar stated that she found "strong evidence that effective crime control can be achieved while producing fewer negative impacts on urban neighborhoods." Among the negative impacts found in New York City was a significant increase in the filing of citizen complaints before the Civilian Complaint Review Board along with lawsuits alleging police misconduct and abuse.[61]

Other scholars also questioned the impact of the zero tolerance approach to policing in New York City in the 1990s. One study scrutinized robbery and homicide rates in the city and concluded that the effect of zero tolerance on these rates was, at best, modest.[62] Other recent research focused on the homicide rates, policing, and drugs in New York City in the 1990s and found some support for the broken windows explanation of the decline in homicide rates as well as for what the investigators called the "crack-cocaine/drug activity" approach. Specifically, these results showed that the homicide rates decreased as misdemeanor arrest rates increased and the use of cocaine decreased. The scholars issued warnings, however, about the need to analyze the relationships further and to consider the possible negative effects of changes in policing on issues of social justice.[63]

The results of the zero tolerance policy of New York City's police department illustrate the systems effect discussed previously in this text. If a crackdown on minor offenders, who may be viewed as nuisances on the streets, results in substantial judgments against the city and the police department when citizens complain of violations of their civil rights, the "cure" may be worse than the "disease."

Zero tolerance policing is also referred to as quality-of-life policing, problem-solving policing, community policing, and order maintenance policing. These terms are noted in the following discussions, beginning with order maintenance policing

Order Maintenance

The second function of policing, *order maintenance*, was defined by James Q. Wilson as the "management of conflict situations to bring about consensual resolution." By *order*, Wilson meant the "absence of disorder, and by disorder is meant behavior that either disturbs or threatens to disturb the public peace or that involves face-to-face conflict among two or more persons." An example is domestic disputes. According to Wilson, it is crucial that police, rather than some other professionals, respond to calls involving domestic disputes because such incidents may (and often do) result in violence. Wilson argued that order maintenance is the most important function of police work. Furthermore, police have wide discretion in all areas and often must make decisions in situations characterized by intensive conflicts and hostile participants.[64]

Wilson's position was shared by George L. Kelling, who studied the historical development of policing in the United States. Kelling concluded that as police work becomes more professional, greater emphasis is placed on law enforcement, which is measured more easily than order maintenance. This reduces the emphasis on order maintenance and leads to negative effects without resulting in a decreased crime rate. Kelling, like Wilson, said the evidence pointed out that when police are involved in order maintenance, the relationship between the police and the community is improved. The result is reduced fear of crime and greater cooperation of citizens with the police in crime control.[65]

Carl B. Klockars disagreed with Kelling and Wilson, taking the position that, historically, Americans have considered law enforcement the primary function of policing. To shift that focus would not reduce the crime rate and would decrease the ability of police to respond to more serious problems and violations. Klockars did not take the position that order maintenance is an unimportant police function but only that a greater emphasis should be placed on law enforcement.[66]

In terms of specifics, order maintenance has been divided into two categories of focus: social incivilities and physical incivilities, defined as follows:

> Physical incivilities often include such things as broken windows and vacant lots, while social incivilities include loitering, loud parties, drug sales and prostitution. Within contemporary theories highlighting the importance of incivilities, social and physical incivilities are unique characteristics of neighborhoods causally linked to a number of important outcomes including crime.[67]

Suggestions for increasing the police role in order maintenance have been made. Examples are:

- Involving police in inmate reentry programs
- Changing police reactions to potential student riots
- Involving local police in preventing the trafficking of women in sex trades

With regard to the first suggestion, a report by the Urban Institute's Justice Policy Center, which concluded that the "primary mission of law enforcement is to maintain peace and order," emphasized that this role of police is threatened by inmates who leave prison and reenter society. Thus, it makes sense to have police involved in reentry programs.[68]

With regard to police reaction to potential student riots, a report by scholars at the University of Cincinnati pointed out that most students present in a situation that may turn into rioting do not participate in illegal activities. Police, however, may cause the situation to escalate, or they may initiate illegal activity by their reactions to student crowds in circumstances that often produce illegal behavior, such as crowds after a sporting event. These events often occur late at night, involve intoxicated students including those from other schools, and involve property damage. None of the policies police used in these situations had been evaluated; thus, researchers suggested that police, working with college and university personnel as well as community officials, develop and test policies that might decrease the possibilities of rioting. One example might be to require students to obtain permits to host large gatherings. In addition to notifying police that the gathering is anticipated, permits set conditions for the event, declare the expected number of attendees, and set controls on the availability of alcohol and the conditions that must be met for the proposed group activity. "These restrictions can lessen the likelihood of a disturbance, as well as hold the hosts responsible for any negative outcomes."[69]

The last suggestion for improving order maintenance in policing is to change the traditional notion that illegal human trafficking is primarily an immigration problem and thus should be in the jurisdiction of federal law enforcement. Human trafficking usually involves poor and uneducated women or young girls, who are promised good jobs if they leave their homes in other countries and come to the United States. Seventy percent of the women victimized in this way are brought into the country for purposes of sexual exploitation. These women should be viewed as victims, not as sex offenders. They should be provided protection by local police, who should be involved in reducing prostitution and other sexual offenses in which these women might be forced to participate, as provided by the victims of Trafficking and Violence Protection Act of 2000, discussed earlier.[70]

Some recent research, claim its authors, lends "considerable credibility to Wilson and Kelling's perspective that policing disorder can generate crime-prevention gains." Research in Lowell, Massachusetts, produced evidence that "the more focused and specific the strategies of the police are and the more tailored the strategies are to the problems the police seek to address, the more effective the police will be in controlling crime and disorder."[71]

There are, however, some negative aspects of order maintenance policing, and the approach has been questioned by criminologists. Some insist that the definitions of the key terms—*order* and *disorder*—are not clear and could lead to discrimination against lower-class cultures.[72]

It has also been argued that order maintenance policing may require stops that are perceived by the targeted individuals as police harassment, especially when only minor actions are questioned. A recently published study of the reaction of young men to such police stops led the investigators to conclude that "order maintenance policing

strategies have negative implications for police legitimacy and crime control efforts via their potential to damage citizens' views of procedural justice."[73]

Finally, the broken windows concept and order maintenance policing raise this critical question:

> Even if public order *is* a desirable goal, we should ask whether the police are the right institution to enforce it. Should the task of order maintenance remain with the police or, instead, largely include the efforts of community institutions and groups? As it stands, mandated police crackdowns on disorder constitute a top-down approach to fighting crime. A perhaps more palatable bottom-up approach would be to enlist the efforts of neighborhood residents by, for example, informally mobilizing neighborhood cleanups or creating neighborhood watches.[74]

Service-Related Duties

The final major function of policing is to engage in a variety of service-related duties. Some people who do not know how to solve a problem (e.g., killing a snake in the house or getting a cat out of a tree) call the police department for help. Although some service functions are important because of their relationship to crime control and police–community relations, we should not expect police to engage in activities unrelated to law enforcement, at least not in metropolitan areas. In rural areas, however, police may insist on performing such services. Those of us who live in such areas are pleased that our local police check on the elderly during winter storms (even shoveling snow for those who need it!), park their squad cars on the street near the grammar school every day when students are arriving and leaving, attend most community functions, engage in "welfare checks" throughout the community, and perform other service functions.

It is also the case that many so-called service issues may lead to law enforcement issues. For example, a report on juveniles explored the various ways local law enforcement and social services were dealing with the problems associated with juveniles who run away from home. The police role may be secondary, and most issues should perhaps be handled by social service agencies. But the presence of the police 24 hours a day on the streets means they may be the first to come into contact with runaway juveniles. It was also suggested that police analyze their data on calls for service to determine whether any particular families had repeated problems with juveniles. Police should work with social service agencies in developing policies as well as facilities for placement of such youths.[75]

Policing Models

The structure and manner in which policing occurs may be analyzed by models. The professional model is the traditional approach, and the community-oriented model involves a community emphasis as well as a problem-solving approach to policing.

Professional Model

The *professional model* of policing is a highly bureaucratic approach characterized by a hierarchical organizational structure in which the police chief is the central authority. All department heads report to the chief. Department heads have subordinates who report directly to them. The chain of command is clear, and the organization has many rules and regulations, with little input from subordinates in regard to making and enforcing them. The police department is organized around specialized functions such as personnel and training, data processing, traffic, patrol, homicide, and sex crimes.[76]

The professional model is efficient; decisions may be made quickly and easily, and the internal control of subordinates is facilitated. The structure may result in high productivity, but its rigidity may cause dissatisfaction among subordinates and result in a department that is too authoritarian and units that are too specialized.

The professional model of policing lasted throughout most of the twentieth century but was gradually replaced by other models with a variety of names but involving a community orientation.

Community-Oriented Policing

Dissatisfaction with the professional model led to an approach referred to as *community-oriented policing*, which involves a problem-solving approach by police along with community involvement. *Problem-oriented policing* (POP) is characterized by a less extensive division of labor within the police department, fewer rules and regulations, and fewer authority levels than was characteristic of traditional policing. The emphasis is on gaining the necessary knowledge required for solving problems, and power comes from accomplishing that goal rather than from a title. Problem-oriented policing permits greater participation by subordinates and is based on the assumption that police departments can be more effective if the expertise and creativity of all, including patrol officers, are utilized to solve underlying problems.

Problem-oriented policing looks at calls to police not as unique events or incidents to be processed individually but as part of a network of events. It looks for patterns of events and attempts to derive solutions. For example, instead of relying on legal categories such as burglary or robbery, officers are told to group calls into problem categories. What is traditionally called a robbery might be part of a network of prostitution-related thefts committed in specific hotels. By alerting potential customers, hotel owners and managers, and local businesses and by talking to the prostitutes, police may secure additional and significant information. The focus is on underlying *causes* or problems, not on the incident that precipitated an individual call. Problem-oriented policing relies on **proac-**tive rather than **reactive** policing. Although police remain somewhat reactive, the major thrust of POP is that police attention is shifted, as police utilize their experiences within the community to attempt to solve the problems that lie beneath those calls for service.[77] Problem-oriented policing was introduced by Herman Goldstein in 1979, developed and tested by others, and expanded by Goldstein in a 1990 publication.[78]

It is maintained that rather than focus on problems, police should focus on *signals*, which may be defined as a "sign that has an effect." Signals determine how specific incidents influence how people think and act about their own safety and security. Police should engage in *reassurance policing*, reacting to the signals that are important to their constituents and helping to reduce the causes of citizen perceptions of disorder and risk. Police thus see the signals as others see them and, in their attempts to reduce the causes, act beyond crime to provide enhanced security for the community.[79]

Considerable attention has been given to community-oriented policing in recent scholarly literature as well as by state legislatures, the U.S. Congress, and police departments. The Violent Crime Control and Law Enforcement Act of 1994 created an office to promote community-oriented policing at local levels: the Community Oriented Policing Services (COPS).[80]

George L. Kelling referred to the emphasis on community-oriented policing as follows: "A quiet revolution is reshaping American policing. Police in dozens of communities are returning to foot patrol." Kelling noted that many police were asking citizens what they perceive as their most pressing problems and what they thought might be done to solve them. Fear of crime is one of the concerns mentioned most frequently, and many police departments are addressing that issue.[81]

Although community policing differs among the various jurisdictions, Herman Goldstein identified its common characteristics:

- The involvement of the community in getting the police job done
- The permanent assignment of police officers to a neighborhood to cultivate better relationships
- The setting of police priorities based on the specific needs and desires of the community
- The meeting of these needs by the allocation of police resources and personnel otherwise assigned to responding to calls for public assistance[82]

Community-oriented policing may increase police accountability to the community, increase public cooperation with police, reduce fear of crime, and assist police and the community in solving society's problems with illegal drugs. According to the director of COPS, community policing is about "building relationships and solving problems."[83]

One of the important features of community policing is a return to foot patrol. This practice, reminiscent of earlier days, along with the use of horses or bicycles, makes officers less anonymous, more integrated into their communities, and more accountable to the public. Police are encouraged to view citizens as partners in crime prevention. In addition, more decision making at the patrol level means that those who are best informed of the problems in the community are the ones making important policing decisions.[84]

The return to foot patrol began in Flint, Michigan, and spread to other cities. Experiments of foot patrol in Flint and in Newark, New Jersey, produced the following results:

- When foot patrol is added in neighborhoods, levels of fear decrease significantly.
- When foot patrol is withdrawn from neighborhoods, levels of fear increase significantly.
- Citizen satisfaction with police increases when foot patrol is added in neighborhoods.
- Police who patrol on foot have a greater appreciation for the values of neighborhood residents than police who patrol the same areas in automobiles.
- Police who patrol on foot have greater job satisfaction, less fear, and higher morale than officers who patrol in automobiles.[85]

The Flint study revealed a significant (40 percent) reduction in telephone calls for service when police engaged in aggressive foot patrol. A small reduction in crime occurred. Likewise, officials in Seattle, Washington, reported that community policing was successful in improving the quality of life for residents and in reducing overall crime.[86]

Wesley G. Skogan, who studied many community-oriented policing programs, commented positively on the results of Chicago's program, calling it one of the most substantial programs he had evaluated. Residents stated that their perceptions of police were more positive and that they saw reductions in crime. These reductions were verified by official data.[87]

President Bill Clinton gave strong support to COPS during his two administrations. In 1994, the Clinton administration announced the down payment on its campaign promise to put 100,000 more police officers on the streets by offering federal grants for hiring police. Later that year, Congress passed a crime bill that contained a provision for the promised 100,000 officers. Under this legislation, the federal government provided 75 percent of the cost of employing new officers up to a total of $75,000 each during the first three years of a grant. After that, the communities were responsible for the full cost unless waivers were granted by the U.S. attorney general. Not all communities were eligible for the grants.[88]

The COPS program is controversial, and under the Bush administration, COPS budgets were slashed to the point of essentially making the program useless. The budget fights between the Bush administration and the Democrats came while social scientists were concluding that the COPS legislation resulted in a significant reduction in both property crime in cities with a population of over 100,000 but no significant effect in those under 100,000.[89] Others concluded that the funding had "little to no effect on crime."[90]

On 1 February 2010, President Barack Obama released his request for $730.3 million for the 2011 COPS budget. A major portion of that request, $60 million was for the COPS hiring program, which, "if enacted by the Congress would assist in reaching the Administration's goal of an additional 50,000 police officers."[91]

Another federal funding program, since dropped, that provided assistance to localities to fight crime was the Local Law Enforcement Block Grants (LLEBG), created by a 1997 amendment to the 1994 Violent Crime Control and Law Enforcement Act.[92] Unlike the COPS grants, the LLEBG were not limited to police departments but were available to other local agencies for crime fighting and public safety purposes. In some respects, this program had fewer restrictions than COPS grants. Much of the expenditures were used to purchase equipment and technology, but some was used to hire additional law enforcement officers. Although the LLEBG program was second only to COPS in the amount of total federal government spending, it received less attention by social science researchers. However, one study published in 2008 reported "fairly convincing evidence that LLEBG funding led to reductions in serious crime throughout the United States."[93] The relationship between such grants and crime reduction is complex, however, and these findings may not be as accurate as their author proclaims.[94]

Time Allocation

Regardless of the model followed, policing involves many problems and issues, one of which is time allocation. As noted earlier, there is disagreement over which of the three functions—law enforcement, order maintenance, and service-related activities—is the most important and how time should be allocated among these functions. In his study mentioned earlier, James Q. Wilson reported that 38 percent of police time was spent in service-related duties, followed by 30 percent in order maintenance, 22 percent in information gathering, and only 10 percent in law enforcement.[95]

Those figures differed from a study in Chicago conducted two years earlier by Albert J. Reiss Jr. He found that 58 percent of all calls to the police department involved requests about criminal matters and 30 percent were about noncriminal matters.[96]

Later studies, some based on observations of police on patrol rather than on analyses of calls to police departments, showed that although police spent more time on law enforcement than on any other activity, less than one-third of police activities involved crimes.[97] One study reported that only 17 percent of calls to police were for nonviolent crimes and 2 percent were for violent crimes. Among the other reasons for calls, the largest percentages were requests for information (21 percent), suspicious circumstances (12 percent), public nuisances (11 percent), traffic problems (9 percent), a citizen giving information (8 percent), and interpersonal conflict (7 percent).[98]

Some changes have been made in police agencies to facilitate calls. In 1996, President Bill Clinton asked for a national community policing number that could be used to reduce nonemergency calls to emergency 911 numbers. That requirement was approved in 1997, and some cities now use a 311 number for nonemergency calls to police. Researchers who studied the impact of a 311 system in Baltimore, Maryland, reported that the changes "can greatly facilitate police efforts to better handle citizen calls for police service," provided some changes are made within the agencies to provide for those nonemergency calls.[99]

The use of a 311 call system to police shifts the burden to citizens to determine which calls are really emergencies and thus require dialing 911 and which are calls for service that can wait. If service calls come in on the 911 system and result in a significantly delayed police response, callers may think the police are noncaring, when in reality, they are setting priorities, as they must do. Thus, having a 311 call system benefits both citizens and police. Police reaction to the 311 calls for service "can be more careful [because those calls are] unrelated to the immediacy of a crime to be investigated."[100]

The use of a 311 system, theoretically, gives police more time to devote to proactive policing. But how should they utilize that time? One method of focusing efforts is the use of CompStat, which is a shortened form of *computer comparative statistics*. CompStat is a system attributed to Commissioner William Bratton and developed while he was in New York City. As mentioned earlier, Bratton and his administration were credited, as least by some, with the significant reduction in crime in that city, and it is alleged that CompStat was the reason. CompStat was described by William F. Walsh as "a goal-oriented strategic management process that uses computer technology, operational strategy and managerial accountability to structure the manner in which a police department provides crime-control services." The process was acclaimed by the Ford Foundation and the John F. Kennedy School of Government at Harvard University.[101]

At the center of the CompStat approach is the computerization of information about crime. Crime data are processed, mapped, and analyzed, and the results are sent on a regular basis to operational managers, who have the power and the responsibility to discuss the information with their subunits. They are held accountable for appropriate problem-solving responses.[102]

One expert on policing and racism writes that the use of CompStat prevents crime because it enables police to dispatch officers to areas where crime happens. She maintains that blacks are supportive of the system, with 68 percent of those in a survey approving way the New York City police commissioner does his job. She insists that the higher incidences of stops of black compared to whites is not racist but, rather, an indication of where crime has occurred. She concluded, "No public policy change of the last quarter-century has done as much for the city's poor and minority neighborhoods as CompStat policing."[103]

Not everyone agrees, however, as discussions throughout this text suggest. Further, CompStat is not a quick fix to lower crime rates. It requires major changes in organizational structure and thinking, and we do not yet know whether its use will have long-term success in reducing crime.[104]

The broken windows concept, discussed earlier in this chapter, was key to New York's approach to the use of CompStat. The emphasis was on cleaning up the streets: arresting minor offenders whose presence may suggest that the police are not in control. Administrators took pride in and gave police credit for the fact that New York City became a cleaner city and a safer place to live as the police took back the streets. Not all criminologists agree, however. Some who studied the crime rates of the 1990s insist that more careful and scientific evaluations are necessary before the conclusions of the politicians and the police can be accepted.[105]

An example was the increased arrests for smoking marijuana in public view (MPV) which, by 2000, had reached a total of 51,267 compared to 1,851 arrests in 1994 (when the city began the broken windows concept for arrests), an increase of 2,770 percent. Researchers who studied these arrests concluded that African Americans and Hispanics were disproportionately represented, and there was "no good evidence that it contributed to combating serious crime in the city. If anything, it had the reverse effect." It was a very expensive experiment, and thus, concluded the researchers, "an extremely poor trade-off of scarce law enforcement resources."[106]

CompStat and similar programs, at least theoretically, help direct the unassigned time of officers so they can be more productive in their time allocations. But one study found that although a considerable amount of police time was spent uncommitted, proactive strategies were not well articulated by supervisors; they were vague, general, and not operationalized. These researchers, in studying policing in Baltimore, found that patrol officers had over three-fourths of their time unassigned but that they had few directives on how to spend that time profitably. They typically went on routine patrol or backed up other colleagues on calls to which they had not been assigned. Only 6 percent of their unassigned time was directed by supervisors.[107]

Conflicting Expectations

The variety of police functions and the lack of consensus on how police do or should allocate their time create conflicts over expectations police have for themselves and for other people, including their colleagues and supervisors. Any variations in the traditional functions of police may create conflicting expectations. In addition, police are expected to prevent crime, which they cannot do effectively even with citizens' support, which they do not always get. When police do prevent crimes, there is no way to measure what they have done. When police engage in order maintenance and service-related functions, they may face hostility in the former and unreasonable demands in the latter; that is, they are asked to solve problems for which they do not have solutions.

In addition to expecting the impossible, society is frequently unclear about what police should be expected to do in a given situation. Are they to enforce the law in all situations, or should they ignore some violations? Because particular communities may expect different types of behavior, police may follow those expectations even when they are not legal. Consider a neighborhood composed of persons whose lifestyles include knifings, narcotics, and domestic quarrels. Residents may expect law enforcement to ignore the laws regulating those behaviors, and officers may find resistance when they try to enforce those laws.

A study of the reaction of Chicago police to the ambiguity of their roles as patrol officers made the point clearly. Most officers said they preferred not to have patrol duty. Among the many reasons they listed for preferring other duty assignments—more interesting work, higher pay, greater prestige, and greater freedom—the most important was "the officer has a better sense of what is expected of him."[108]

Police officers also face conflicts over human misery versus evil. When they arrive at the scene of an accident or other tragedy, they must control their emotions. An officer cannot punish a parent who is accused of beating a child, nor can he or she get sick at the sight of a mangled body. Police must act with objectivity and perform their jobs as efficiently as possible regardless of the circumstances.

Police face conflict between efficiency and the constitutional rights of suspects and between honesty and the dishonest activities of some of their colleagues. Police officers may feel conflict between fear and courage—the desire to be courageous while realizing that they are risking their own health or lives. Order maintenance may take officers into hostile environments. Persons who called for help may consider the situation an emergency, but because the officers have been involved in many similar situations, they have learned by experience that the caller's version of the incidents may not be reliable. Consequently, the police may not be as sympathetic as the caller desires, and the caller may become upset at this apparent lack of understanding. Furthermore, because only a few calls to police result in arrests, complainants may think that police are not doing their jobs. The problem is that most crimes are property crimes with no clues or witnesses. Even if a suspect is found, officers must fulfill the requirements for making an arrest, and often, those cannot be met.

Finally, police experience conflicting expectations with regard to strategies of police administration. This area of strain arises as officers observe administrators wavering between traditional arrest-oriented versus problem-solving policing, reactive versus proactive policing, and traditional versus community-oriented policing.

Police Stress

Role conflicts and other problems create stress for police. Formerly considered a personal problem, stress is now viewed as a corporate problem because of the effect it has on employees. Some businesses retain a professional counselor to assist employees who have difficulty handling stress. Stress causes physical illnesses and results in higher medical costs, lower productivity, absenteeism, and premature death. All of this may be costly for businesses as well as for the affected individuals, their families, and friends.

Although all people may encounter some stress in their jobs, there is evidence that stress is high among air traffic controllers, lawyers, dentists, physicians, psychiatrists, and law enforcement officers as well as law enforcement administrators. Some argue that law enforcement is the most difficult among all jobs emotionally and psychologically because of the possibility of physical danger. Stress may account for the high divorce rate among police, a rate that according to some studies is higher than in most (or all) other professions.[109] Furthermore, stress in policing may be attributed to many factors, including the police organization itself.[110]

There is one major difference between policing and most other professions: Police are trained to injure or kill. If the situation requires it, they are expected to use force; indeed, they may be sanctioned for not doing so. Officers who kill, however, may be isolated by their colleagues. The routine procedure is to suspend officers pending the investigation of a shooting. Even when the investigation shows that the officer was justified in the killing, he or she may continue to experience stress.

Another stressor in policing is the fear of the police and their families that the officers may be injured or killed in the line of duty. Although most officers are never victimized by the violence of others, the *possibility* of such violence is greater for them than for people in most, if not all, other professions. In September 2010, the FBI issued data for police killings in 2009, stating that 48 officers (47 males and 1 female) were killed feloniously that year, 7 more than in 2008. Thirty-six of the 48 killed officers were wearing body armor at the time of their deaths.[111] According to the news media, 20 percent more officers were killed by gunfire in 2010 than in 2009.

The stress of policing reaches beyond the individual officer. The effects of stress on police and their families as well as their colleagues have led some departments to initiate stress-reduction programs. Some of these programs involve appointing psychologists or other professionals trained in stress reduction to be available to law enforcement officers in the work environment. Others are comprehensive programs that include inpatient treatment facilities and services for law enforcement officers who suffer from job-related stress. Eating and sleeping disorders, alcohol and drug addiction, posttraumatic stress, and obsessive-compulsive and anxiety disorders are examples of the problems that may be treated.

An extreme manifestation of stress among policing is that of suicide, highlighted in 2003 by the suicide of David Brame, police chief in Tacoma, Washington, who killed himself after fatally shooting his wife, Crystal. These acts were witnessed by the Brame's two young children, aged 8 and 5. In the summer of 2004, a woman who claimed that Brame raped her in 1988 sued the police department for $2 million. The 45-year-old woman claimed that even though investigators believed her story, no criminal investigation was initiated and that Brame, then a patrol officer, was subsequently promoted up the ladder until he became the police chief. A yearlong investigation, which ended in February 2005, concluded that former Tacoma assistant police chief, Catherine Woodard, violated city rules when she did nothing about her knowledge of death threats, domestic violence, and sexual harassment concerning Brame. Crystal's family filed a lawsuit for $75 million; it was settled for $12 million in 2005.[112]

In Oregon, in April 2003, a 32-year-old detective, Benjamin Crosby, went to the police station at midnight and left a note outside warning that his body was inside and that his death would be the result of suicide, not homicide. He also left letters, including one to his 7-year-old son. Although his colleagues did not know it, Officer Crosby had been despondent, as stated in his letters.[113]

The Centers for Disease Control and Prevention report that police officers are at an increased risk of heart disease and may face an increased risk of suicide.[114] After eight California Highway Patrol (CHP) troopers committed suicide during an eight-month period in 2006 (five times the rate of national law enforcement), the CHP developed training programs for suicide awareness and prevention. Other large law enforcement departments are doing likewise. For example, the Los Angeles Police Department employs numerous psychologists in its Behavioral Science Services.[115]

Police stress may also lead officers to engage in violence. In 2007, Tyler Peterson, 20, a sheriff's officer, fired 30 rounds and killed six young people gathered in a home to eat pizza and watch movies as part of their high school homecoming weekend. Included among the victims was a young woman with whom Peterson had been in a relationship for a few years, but the relationship had ended. Peterson was killed by police in an exchange of gunfire.

Stress among police may result in domestic violence. The National Center for Women and Policing (NCWP)

reports that domestic violence in police households is far more common than among nonpolice households. Studies report as many as 40 percent of police living in households characterized by this crime compared to 10 percent in the general population. Victims may be in far more danger, too, because police have guns, know the location of all shelters for abused persons, and know how "to manipulate the system to avoid penalty and/or shift blame to the victim." Further, the victims may fear calling the police, believing that the offender's colleagues will protect him or her.[116]

The Police Subculture

One of the ways that police officers attempt to cope with stress is to isolate themselves, forming a subculture and associating only with other officers and their families. Social solidarity among police may be the result of the danger that police face, which necessitates the need to help one another. It may be caused by suspiciousness, where police develop a perceptual shorthand to help identify people who might commit an unlawful act. It may be the result of the conflicting demands placed on police. It is difficult for some officers to make friends among nonpolice. Researchers note that the police subculture is characterized by "three guiding beliefs," which include bravery, autonomy, and secrecy. "The police subculture stresses these sentiments and teaches new officers the value of adopting these attitudes—and the consequences of not conforming."[117]

All of these beliefs serve to isolate police and are functional to some extent. They allow the police to relate to the public without the undue strain that might result if they were apprehending and arresting their friends. The opposing view is that police isolation is detrimental to police and a disservice to the public. It prevents police from seeing the public's point of view.

An exploration of the police subculture illustrated its importance by noting the role the subculture plays when a police officer is killed in the line of duty. The rituals of the services are important and have an impact nationwide. Police from other cities often gather (frequently on motorcycles) in a huge show of support for policing, respect for their slain colleague, and sympathy for the family. Police funerals "tend to re-awaken the significance of what is meant by being a cop."[118] Certainly, that appeared to be the case as thousands mourned the loss of police (and firefighters), along with many others, after the 9/11 terrorist acts.

AIDS and Law Enforcement

A final issue regarding the nature of policing is that the possibility of the transmission of the human immunodeficiency virus (HIV), which causes acquired immune deficiency syndrome (AIDS), by health care professionals to their patients, has created concern among law enforcement personnel. AIDS is a serious disease for which no cure is available. Policing brings officers into close contact with many people, some of whom are suffering injuries that include the loss of blood and other body fluids that carry and can transmit HIV. The converse is citizen attitudes and the concern of other officers about coming into contact with officers who carry HIV.

Although there is no evidence that HIV is transmitted by casual contact, many people are concerned about contacts with persons infected with the virus. Colleagues may react negatively to an officer who has AIDS. As a result, police who are HIV positive or have AIDS may be afraid to let others know of their condition, fearing that they will be "banished from the wider police fraternity in which most of them came of age, a sort of blue reservoir of strength that they are used to turning to for solace. They cannot imagine telling their colleagues they have a disease that many officers believe is an affliction only of gay men, drug addicts, prostitutes and the homeless." Some police departments employ specialists to work with officers who have AIDS or who are HIV positive.[119]

Police Decision Making

Police have considerable decision-making discretion in the performance of their jobs. The decision to interfere with the freedom of another person, even if momentarily, is an extremely serious one. People do not like to be stopped by police; it is a frightening and confusing experience, and some may perceive the police action as unlawful discrimination. Their perceptions may be correct. Police reject this conclusion, saying that they stop people only when they have legal reasons for doing so. The issue is more pronounced when the possibility of an arrest exists. The police officer is not only interfering momentarily with freedom but is also setting in motion a process that may result in stigmatization and incarceration.

The decision to stop and question someone or to take a suspect into custody is governed by case and statutory law. This body of law is technical and complicated. Chapter 11 focused on the importance of search warrants. This discussion focuses on the right to stop and question an individual. The law in this area is related primarily to the *legal seriousness* of the suspected crime, although some studies have found that legal seriousness plays a small part in the police decision to apprehend. Most of the problems that police are called on to resolve are not of a legally serious nature; they are minor problems in which arrests are not usually made. Thus, police may base their decisions to apprehend on criteria other than the legal seriousness of an alleged crime. According to some critical criminologists, policing "reinforces and maintains the class structure of society through its focus on behaviors most likely to be engaged in by the working class and marginal popula-

tions."[120] Not all agree, however, and it is important to analyze what police are legally permitted to do.

The Right to Stop and Question

Police must have probable cause to arrest, but probable cause is not required to stop and question in some circumstances. For instance, it is permissible for police officers to stop a person who acts suspiciously. They may stop the person and ask for identification, but they may not detain him or her unreasonably, nor may they stop *classes* or *categories* of people to harass them. A key California case illustrates what the police may not do.

On numerous occasions, white police officers stopped a tall, muscular, 36-year-old black man with long hair who jogged frequently in a predominantly white neighborhood. They asked for identification on about 15 occasions over a two-year period. Several times, when the jogger refused to identify himself or to answer other questions, he was arrested. He was convicted once and spent several weeks in jail.

According to police, the jogger committed a misdemeanor when he violated a California statute that labeled as *disorderly conduct* the behavior of a person "who loiters or wanders upon the streets or from place to place without apparent reason or business or who refuses to identify himself and to account for his presence when requested by any peace officer to do so, if the surrounding circumstances are such as to indicate to a reasonable man that the public safety demands such identification."[121]

In deciding that the statute was void because it was vague, the U.S. Supreme Court articulated the importance of individual freedoms. In *Kolender v. Lawson*, the Supreme Court acknowledged that the police must be able to exercise some discretion in stop-and-question situations but struck down the California statute because, in enacting it, the legislature had not provided sufficient guidelines for that discretion. According to the Supreme Court, the statute left individuals free to walk or jog the streets only at the "whim of any police officer."[122]

It is important to understand that the problem with this statute was not that it permitted an initial stop but that there were no standards by which to judge why the police were stopping the jogger. This gives police too much discretion and permits them to stop people for illegal reasons, such as race.

The issue of what type of probable cause is required for the police to stop a person and ask questions arose in *Whren v. United States*, decided by the U.S. Supreme Court in 1996. This case involved two African American men whose vehicle was observed by plainclothes officers in an unmarked vehicle in a high drug area in Washington, D.C. The officers noticed that the suspect's vehicle remained for an unusually long time at a stop sign (thus obstructing traffic), after which the driver turned without signaling and drove away at an unreasonable speed. The vehicle was stopped, allegedly to warn the driver about traffic violations. As the officers approached the vehicle, they noticed that the passenger was holding plastic bags, which appeared to contain crack cocaine. Both the driver and the passenger were arrested, charged with federal drug violations, tried, and convicted. On appeal, the defendants argued that the police did not have probable cause to believe they were violating drug laws but, rather, stopped them as an excuse to see whether they had illegal drugs. A unanimous U.S. Supreme Court upheld the stop, emphasizing that the police had a legal right to pull over the vehicle because of a traffic violation. Lack of probable cause to suspect that the driver and his passenger were in possession of illegal drugs was immaterial.

During the same term, the U.S. Supreme Court held in *Ornelas et al. v. United States* that when appellate courts consider cases involving investigatory stops and warrantless searches, they must undertake their own independent review of the lower court rulings. In other words, appellate courts may not treat those rulings deferentially, looking only for clear error or abuse of discretion. They must look at all the facts on which the lower courts based their rulings. According to the Supreme Court's opinion, this more detailed and careful review will result in unifying precedent and will encourage police to seek warrants when reasonable.[123]

In subsequent cases, the U.S. Supreme Court has held that during routine traffic stops, police may order *passengers* out of cars. Thus, in 1997, in *Maryland v. Wilson*, the Supreme Court extended the 1977 case of *Pennsylvania v. Mimms*, which upheld the right of police to order the *driver* out of a car after the officer made a legitimate traffic stop.[124]

The Right to Search a Home

In 1997, in *Richards v. Wisconsin*, the U.S. Supreme Court held that the knock-and-announce rule of *Wilson v. Arkansas* (decided in 1995 and mentioned in Chapter 11) could not be diluted by a blanket waiver for all drug cases. In *Richards*, the Supreme Court held that if police have a reasonable suspicion that "exigent circumstances" exist, they may enter a home by force without announcing their presence. Such circumstances might be the possible destruction of drugs or other evidence. But the U.S. Supreme Court ruled that the issue must be decided on a case-by-case basis, with careful attention given to the particular facts of each case. In *Richards*, several officers arrived at a motel where the suspect had allegedly been selling drugs out of his room. One officer was dressed as a maintenance man. Richards opened the door (with the chain on) when the officers knocked, but when he saw an officer in uniform, he slammed the door and locked it. The officers kicked in the door and found cash and cocaine during their search. Richards sought to have the evidence excluded. The Wisconsin Supreme Court recog-

nized a blanket rule for waiving the knock-and-announce rule in felony drug cases. The U.S. Supreme Court rejected that holding but did allow the use of the evidence against Richards on the grounds that exigent circumstances existed.[125]

Wilson and *Richards* did not answer the question of whether property damaged during the entry should factor into the determination of whether a no-knock entry was reasonable. During its 1997–1998 term, the U.S. Supreme Court held that a careful reading of those two cases leads to the conclusion that the lawfulness of entering without announcing does not depend on whether property is damaged in the process. In *United States v. Ramirez*, the police broke a window in a garage attached to a house. They took this action to prevent the suspect from getting to the weapons thought to be stored there. When the

Aiyana Jones, 7, was shot and killed when a Detroit police officer's weapon discharged on 16 May 2010 while police were executing a search warrant for a murder suspect. A reality TV show was filming the police actions. Criticism of the filming and its potential impact on the tragedy led to the resignation of the police chief, the city's third chief in two years. The police department has been under the supervision of a federal monitor since 2003.

suspect discovered that the breakage was caused by police officers, not burglars, he surrendered. The Supreme Court held that breaking the window without announcing their presence was a reasonable action by the police under the circumstances.[126]

Finally, by standing on its precedent holdings that decisions regarding the constitutionality of searches must depend on the totality of circumstances, in 2003, in *United States v. Banks,* the U.S. Supreme Court upheld a forced entry by police into an apartment after waiting only 15 to 20 seconds. After knocking and announcing "police search warrant" and getting no response, the police used force to enter the apartment of LaShawn Banks, whom they suspected of selling cocaine from his home. Banks was in the shower and did not hear the police knock and announce. The Ninth Circuit Court of Appeals had held that the force was unreasonable because the search warrant was a week old and there were no exigent circumstances that warranted such quick action and destruction of property. But the U.S. Supreme Court ruled unanimously in favor of the use of force, thus upholding the search, which resulted in finding weapons, crack cocaine, and other evidence of drug dealing.[127]

The dangers of using force to break into a home were illustrated in May 2010. Detroit police threw a device that makes a loud noise and a bright flash into a home and entered immediately, weapons drawn, looking for a murder suspect in the killing of a 17-year-old. Seven-year-old Aiyana Jones, who was sleeping on the couch in the living room, was killed when an officer's gun discharged during an interchange of action with the child's grandmother. The officer was suspended with pay pending an investigation.

The Sociology of Arrest

The U.S. Supreme Court has held that "it is not the function of police to arrest . . . at large and to use an interrogating process at police headquarters in order to determine whom they should charge before a committing magistrate on 'probable cause.'"[128]

The decision to stop and arrest is a powerful one. Police do not stop all people who they think are violating a law. What explains police decisions to stop and arrest? Sociologists and criminologists have studied police discretion in making the decision whether to arrest and have presented interesting findings. First, the decision whether or not to arrest may be related to the officer's safety concerns. An observational study of police decision making with regard to arrest revealed that police officers who expressed concerns about safety were less likely to arrest than were officers who did not express such concerns. Further, the officers who expressed safety concerns were less likely to arrest if they were accompanied by a female rather than a male research observer.[129]

Another variable in the decision whether or not to arrest is the officer's perception of community standards and attitudes and the homogeneity between the police and the community. A study of police activities in relation to community characteristics examined what police do after their initial apprehension of a suspect. The general finding was that police acted differently in various settings:

- "Police appear to be more active in racially mixed neighborhoods.
- In racially heterogeneous neighborhoods, police have a greater propensity to offer assistance to residents and to initiate more contacts with suspicious persons and suspected violators. . . .
- In high-crime areas police are less likely to stop suspicious persons, suggesting that the findings evidence a higher level of general police activity in racially mixed neighborhoods. . . .
- Suspects confronted by police have a higher average probability of being arrested in lower-status neighborhoods than in higher-status areas.
- Police are more apt to exert coercive authority in minority and racially mixed communities."[130]

The investigator emphasized that these findings do not mean that police are more prone to arrest African Americans than whites; rather, the *context* of the alleged criminal activity is an important factor in the decision to arrest.

Community expectations may influence police decisions not to investigate or not to apprehend suspects in some areas. For example, police may not consider places like narrow alleys and abandoned buildings and cars areas that the community wishes to be investigated even though they are known to be used for illegal purposes. After they become familiar with an area, the officers know what behaviors to expect, and they may tolerate behavior in one area that would not be considered permissible in another.

Arrests may reflect the preferences of complaining victims, as found in an earlier but extensive and classic study by Donald Black. He found that arrests were more likely when suspects were disrespectful and when they were stopped for serious crimes. Black suggested that these factors, not race per se, accounted for higher arrest rates among African Americans than among whites. Others disagree and insist that police discriminate against African Americans and other minorities in arrests. The solution to this problem is difficult, for as Black's study and many others have shown, police are lenient in their routine arrest practices. Most people who could be arrested are not arrested even when they are apprehended by police.[131]

Research in 24 police departments produced some support for the demeanor hypothesis. The researchers considered the display of disrespect but did so along with other variables. For example, in nontraffic contexts, they found that an officer's decision to arrest was not influenced by the suspect's apparent intoxication (from alcohol or other drugs) alone but by that fact combined with the suspect's show of disrespect for the officer. Additionally, they did

After allegations in the 30 June 2009 arrest by a white officer of Harvard University scholar Henry Louis Gates Jr, second from the left, for disorderly conduct for allegedly trying to break into his own home, President Barack Obama called the arrest "stupid." Amid allegations that the arrest was an example of racial profiling, an investigation ensued and concluded that there was no evidence of such and that both the officer, Sergeant James Crowley, and Gates were at fault (Gates accused the police of racism). President Obama invited Gates and Crowley to the White House, where Vice President Joe Biden joined them in the Rose Garden for the "beer summit."

not find that officers made arrest decisions based on race, gender, ethnicity, or age, but they expected respect from all suspects.[132]

Racial Profiling: Myth or Reality?

Others would disagree with the preceding conclusion, however, as illustrated by the increasing number of incidents of alleged racial profiling in which minorities claim that they are arrested because they are "driving while black."[133] Such complaints have led some police departments to collect data on traffic stops in an effort to determine whether their officers are engaging in racial profiling, as noted in Exhibit 12.6.

Ethnicity may also be an issue in racial profiling. In 2000, the Ninth Circuit Court of Appeals held that it is not permissible to use ethnicity as a factor in deciding whether to stop an individual suspected of a crime. The court noted the large number and rapid growth rate of Hispanics in California and concluded that despite a 25-year-old U.S. Supreme Court decision ruling that racial appearance is an appropriate factor for deciding whether a person should be stopped by police, this is not acceptable today. According to the U.S. Supreme Court, "Hispanic appearance is, in general, of such little probative value that it may not be considered as a relevant factor where particularized or individualized suspicion is required." The case of *United States v. Montero-Camargo* involved three Mexicans who were stopped by the U.S. Border Patrol in 1996, about 115 miles east of San Diego. The agents, responding to a tip, gave five factors they considered in their decision to stop the suspects, one of which was their Hispanic appearance. The U.S. Supreme Court refused to review the case, thus permitting the Ninth Circuit's decision to stand.[134]

There is little empirical research on racial profiling, although there is recent evidence showing that "both race and personal experience with profiling are strong predictors of attitudes toward profiling and that, among blacks, social class affects views of the prevalence and acceptability of the practice."[135] Ron Akers and Christine Sellers concluded that most research on racial profiling is descriptive and does not account for the intentions or motivations of the arresting police officers. Because those are an integral part of the racial profiling concept, they must be investigated before reasonable conclusions can be drawn.[136]

Clearly, the issue of whether police discriminate against minorities is sensitive and difficult; researchers describe it as "one of the most difficult issues facing contemporary American society." After analyzing data from the Miami-Dade (Florida) Police Department, researchers found mixed results concerning whether police discriminate in stops and subsequent actions. Although they did not find evidence of discrimination in the decision to make traffic stops, they did find that police engaged in disparate treatment of minorities in some subsequent activities, such as record checks, which were more likely to be run on black (or Latino) than on white motorists.[137]

It is, however, the *perceptions* of minorities regarding police that may influence their reactions to them and their feelings of discriminatory treatment. Considerable research shows that the cumulative negative experiences of young black men with police influence their perceptions of the police.[138] Data released in 2007 concerning police stops in New York City revealed that blacks constituted over one-half of the soaring number of people stopped by police in that city in 2006.[139]

In 2010, the media reported that although blacks and Latinos were nine times as likely as whites to be stopped by New York City police, they were not more likely to be arrested. In 2009, police made more than 575,000 stops, a record number of "stop and frisks," which led to 34,000 arrests and the confiscation of 762 guns. Blacks and Latinos

EXHIBIT 12.6

U.S. Police and Racial Profiling

The U.S. Department of Justice (DOJ) as well as state and local agencies have investigated many police departments and found evidence of racial profiling. As the result of complaints of brutal treatment in police stops of Hispanics in East Haven, Connecticut, the DOJ investigated that city's police department. On 15 April 2010, it sent a letter to the town's attorney warning that its initial investigation revealed that the department was "a shambles, with no modern rules of conduct for officers, no check on their use of force, inadequate training and no functioning citizen complaint system." The mayor told the police chief to turn in his badge and gun and placed him on administrative leave. Yale law students who prepared the complaint filed with the DOJ said that a statistical analysis of the data they secured from the police department under the Freedom of Information Act supported allegations by Hispanic residents claiming that they were racially profiled by the police.[1]

In 1999, the DOJ put the New Jersey state police under a monitoring system after finding evidence of racial profiling. The event that triggered the investigation was that police shot three unarmed men during a traffic stop in 1998. The white police officers had stopped a van carrying African American and Latino men. The officers claimed that they stopped the van because their supervisors had told them that minorities were more likely than whites to violate drug laws. Race is not permitted as a reason for police stops unless the individual in question fits the description of a crime suspect for whom the police are looking. The New Jersey investigation revealed that African Americans were stopped more often than whites solely because of their race and that, once stopped, they were more often discriminated against.[2]

In 2002, New Jersey state police officers involved in this shooting were permitted to plead guilty to misdemeanor charges of obstructing the investigation and lying about the facts. They were fined $280 each and not sentenced to prison, although they did lose their jobs and had to sign statements that they would never again seek employment as law enforcement officers. At the sentencing, the judge, who acknowledged that the officers were following what they were taught, told them: "You are victims not only of your own actions but of the system that employed you." In 2007, the DOJ lifted the federal monitoring from the New Jersey state troopers.[3]

Recent research suggests that police behavior when they stop minorities can help alleviate allegations of racial profiling. According to these researchers, "Several studies have shown that citizens, and blacks especially, are much more likely to cooperate with officers when they are given a reason for the stop, and that people put a premium on officers' being polite, listening to citizens, and explaining their actions."[4]

Numerous other allegations of racial profiling, along with lawsuits filed by alleged victims, have occurred, but one major problem is proof. Criminologists who examined studies and cases on racial profiling concluded: "The current state of research on racial profiling leaves courts and policy makers ill equipped to reach reliable conclusions about the possible unequal treatment of minorities by the police." But they noted, "[A] comprehensive study of racial profiling is complex, difficult, and expensive to conduct."[5]

One study of police discretionary decision making during traffic stops led investigators to conclude that, although police form opinions regarding minority suspects' behavior, they do not make official decisions based on those opinions. Rather, police appear to wait for what the researchers refer to as a *clearer prompt* before making an official stop. For example, they wait for a traffic violation or some other legal incident before they stop a vehicle or a suspicious person. Thus, it is necessary to "distinguish between officers who use race as a guide in decision making and those officers who use race as a discriminatory tool."[6]

Despite the difficulty of collecting accurate data on racial profiling, some jurisdictions are attempting to do so. In 2004, the largest of these studies was published in Texas, where a statute that took effect in 2001 requires law enforcement agencies to collect data on police stops. The data collection process began 1 January 2002. The 2004 report indicated that three of every four agencies reported stopping African Americans and Latinos more often than whites. Six of seven agencies reported that searches were conducted more frequently when the suspects were African American or Latino compared with white.[7] These data alone do not show racial profiling, and the data do not detail in how many cases illegal drugs or other contraband was found. It is possible that the more frequent stops and searches do not indicate racial discrimination and that other (and legal) factors account for what otherwise appears to be racial profiling. That conclusion, however, is probably not a logical one to many people.

It might appear obvious that the solution to racial profiling is to hire more minorities, but there is some evidence that although white officers are more likely to make arrests, black officers are more likely to arrest when the suspects are black.[8]

---

1. "Connecticut Town Grapples with Claims of Police Bias," *New York Times* (23 April 2010), p. 19.

12.6
EXHIBIT continued

2. "New Jersey Enters into Consent Decree on Racial Issues in Highway Stops," *Criminal Law Reporter* 66 (5 January 2000): 251.

3. "New Jersey Troopers Avoid Jail in Case That Highlighted Profiling," *New York Times* (15 January 2002), p. 1; "Two New Jersey Troopers Resign in New Race Profiling Scandal," *New York Times* (10 May 2003); "Uninformed Consent," *New York Times* (23 September 2007), p. 15.

4. Ronald Weitzer and Steven A. Tuch, "Perceptions of Racial Profiling: Race, Class, and Personal Experience," *Criminology* 40 (May 2002): 435–456; quotation is on p. 452. See also Lorie Fridell et al., *Racially Biased Policing: A Principled Response* (Washington, D.C.: Police Executive Research Forum, 2001).

5. Michael R. Smith and Geoffrey P. Alpert, "Searching for Direction: Courts, Social Science, and the Adjudication of Racial Profiling Claims," *Justice Quarterly* 19, no. 4 (December 2002): 673–703; quotation is on p. 699.

6. Geoffrey P. Alpert et al., "Police Suspicion and Discretionary Decision Making During Citizen Stops," *Criminology* 43, no. 2 (February 2005): 407–434; quotation is on p. 427.

7. "Large Study of Traffic Stops Finds Race Disparities in Texas," *Criminal Justice Newsletter* (27 February 2004), p. 3.

8. Robert A. Brown and James Frank, "Race and Officer Decision Making: Examining Differences in Arrest Outcomes Between Black and White Officers," *Justice Quarterly* 23, no. 1 (March 2006): 96–126.

were the focus of almost 490,000 of the stops. The Center for Constitutional Rights claimed that the data showed racial profiling; the police commissioner denied that charge and argued that the police were suppressing crime with their stops and frisks. A police spokesperson stated that the Rand Corporation analyzed police stops in that city in 2007 and found no evidence of racial profiling.[140]

The BJS has reported data on the race, ethnicity, and gender of drivers stopped and searched by police, but the data are not recent. Although published in 2007, the data, the latest available as of this writing, were from 2005. The publication reported that over one-half of police searches after stops were with consent and that illegal substances were found in 11.6 percent of all searches. Of the 64,000 in the sample, those most likely to have had face-to-face contact with police were males, whites, and younger persons. The most common reason was a traffic stop, and most who were stopped said the police acted properly after the stop, with 86 percent reporting that they thought they were stopped for legitimate reasons. Over one-half of the traffic stops were for speeding. More than one-half of the stopped drivers were ticketed, but 17.7 percent reported that a verbal warning was the most serious reaction of the police who stopped them. Males were more likely than females to be ticketed or arrested; younger drivers were more likely than older ones to experience serious action by the police. Males, blacks, and younger persons were more likely to experience the use of force by police. Of those, 83 percent thought the force was excessive, with approximately 80 percent of contacts involving force being initiated by police.[141]

With regard to gender and police stops, in their study of police traffic stops in Miami-Dade County (Florida), researchers found that police were "significantly more suspicious of men than of women . . . and suspicion was strongly associated with the decision to arrest."[142]

With regard to racial discrimination in police stops, investigators who studied stops in North Carolina found "only weak evidence of racial disparity in stops by officers of the state highway patrol but stronger evidence in those made by local police officers."[143]

Investigators emphasize the need to face racial issues directly or, as one researcher argues, make them "salient" within police departments and with the public. When this happens, police may "move toward training, supervision, and policies that will encourage officers to think about the effect racial biases may have in their work."[144]

The End Racial Profiling Act (ERPA) of 2010 (originally introduced in 2007) was pending before the U.S. House of Representatives, but no action had been taken on the bill since July 2010, when it was referred to the judiciary committee.[145]

Perhaps lawsuits are the only solution. In 2008, civil rights attorneys reached a settlement agreement for their clients who brought legal action against the Maryland State Police. Under the terms of the settlement, the state was required to pay attorney fees, monetary damages to the plaintiffs, and the expenses for an outside consultant to assess how the state police were developing and administering policies concerning racial profiling. One of the plaintiffs said, "More than 12 years after being wrongfully pulled over, harassed, and humiliated . . . I can finally tell my son that justice is possible when your rights have been violated in America." The state was also required to give the plaintiffs copies of all the policies, training materials, orders, and other specified materials from a 2003 consent decree on the issue of racial profiling.[146]

The final solution, however, probably rests with police departments, where recruitment, hiring, training, accountability, and appropriate departmental policies are crucial. In an analysis of all of these issues, investigators concluded as follows:

This is a new era of policing—one characterized by new tools and skills for dealing with complex and highly charged issues. Reflecting this changed profession, progressive chiefs and sheriffs across the nation are acknowledging the problems of racially biased policing and widespread perceptions of its practice and implementing initiatives to bring about critically needed, constructive change.[147]

The Use of Force

Laws regulating the use of force differ, but usually, officers may not use deadly force unless they or other persons are threatened with serious bodily harm or death. They may use as much nondeadly force as is reasonably necessary to make an arrest, control a crowd, or engage in any other legitimate police functions.

Generally, a police officer cannot use deadly force to apprehend a misdemeanant (someone who commits a misdemeanor, a less serious offense than a felony), but in some states, the act of fleeing is a felony. If a person flees *after* an arrest, the officer may be permitted to use deadly force, even if the original offense for making the arrest was a misdemeanor. Until recently, most jurisdictions permitted officers to fire at a fleeing felon, but those policies have changed. Today, federal and many local and state law enforcement agencies prohibit the use of deadly force unless human life is threatened.

Even when a statute permits police to fire at a fleeing felon, the courts may rule that under some circumstances this action violates the felon's constitutional rights. In 1983, in Tennessee, an officer fired at a 15-year-old who had allegedly broken into an unoccupied residence in a suburban area. The boy was killed by the police officer, who had been taught that it was legal to fire at a fleeing felon.

The boy's father filed a lawsuit against the Memphis police for violating his son's civil rights. In *Tennessee v. Garner*, the trial court held that the statute and the police officer's actions were constitutional. The court of appeals reversed the decision. The U.S. Supreme Court held that the Tennessee statute was "unconstitutional insofar as it authorizes the use of deadly force against . . . an apparently unarmed, nondangerous fleeing suspect." The Supreme Court stated, "It is not better that all felony suspects die than that they escape. Where the suspect poses no immediate threat to the officer and no threat to others, the harm resulting from failing to apprehend him does not justify the use of deadly force to do so." The Supreme Court emphasized, however, that the statute in question might be appropriate in cases when the officer's firing is based upon probable cause to believe that the suspect poses a threat of serious physical harm or death to the officer or to others.[148]

Even with the restrictions on deadly force placed on the police by *Tennessee v. Garner*, problems with police use of force remain. Allegations of police use of force and brutality are featured frequently in the media, ranging from physical abuse and harassment to the illegal use of weapons that results in serious injury or death. The issue of excessive force arises most often in civil suits brought against police and police departments. Examples are the 1991 beating of Rodney King in Los Angeles and the 1997 beating of Haitian immigrant Abner Louima in New York (see again Chapter 9, concerning the conviction of officer Justin Volpe in this latter case). Other officers were also convicted in the Louima case, but in March 2002, an appellate court overturned on technical grounds the conspiracy to obstruct justice convictions of Charles Schwarz (whose protestations of innocence had captured national attention, including a February 2001 segment of CBS's *60 Minutes*), Thomas Bruder, and Thomas Wiese. There was a possibility that these officers could have been charged under another federal statute under which the appellate court stated that there might be sufficient evidence to support convictions.[149] But federal prosecutors chose not to file additional charges, and the state did not file any charges. The officers had been acquitted of assault charges.

In March 2007, three New York City police detectives pleaded not guilty in the death of Sean Bell, a 23-year-old black male, who was leaving a bar on the day he was to be married. Two of Bell's friends were also wounded. Fifty shots were fired that night of 25 November 2006. Two of the detectives are black; one is white. The officers were acquitted of all charges in April 2008.

A 2006 BJS report regarding citizen complaints about police use of force indicate that during 2002, more than 26,000 citizen complaints were filed against police in departments with 100 or more sworn offices. Approximately 33 percent of these complaints were not sustained, 25 percent were unfounded, 23 percent resulted in exoneration of the targeted officers, 8 percent were sustained, and 9 percent were disposed of in another way (e.g., withdrawn).[150]

In 2009, one of the official publications of the American Society of Criminology, *Criminology and Public Policy*, carried a series of articles on police use of force. The articles were introduced by an expert in this area, Geoffrey P. Alpert. Alpert noted that "police use of force will always be controversial," but he emphasized that as we learn more about the use of force, we should be better able to reduce the negatives outcomes of such force. There is evidence that police distort their recollections of the facts that led to the use of force; 94 percent admitted that in one study.[151] According to Alpert, it is important to train officers to make decisions under stress and to train the public to understand "why facts may be recalled differently and at different times by officers."[152]

It is difficult to compare the studies of police use of force because they are not consistent on their definitions and measurements of *use of force*. Second, the use of force does not occur often, leading us to question whether any differences are important. Third, the most important issue, the use of *excessive* force, has not been studied frequently. Fourth, national estimates of the use of nonlethal force are not available.[153]

Finally, any use of force policies depend on adequate training of police officers. Police may at times be required to make split-second decisions. Their administrators "must provide tools to their officers so that they can make those difficult decisions."[154]

Vehicle Pursuits

The issue of how police use deadly force also arises in vehicle pursuits, highlighted in June 2010, when Sister Mary Celine Graham, 83, of St. Benedict's Day Nursery in Harlem, New York City, was stuck and killed by a robbery suspect leading police on a high-speed chase just a few blocks from the nursery where she worked.

Some jurisdictions have restricted the use of high-speed chases because of the danger involved, along with the fact that most of these chases involve relatively minor offenses, usually traffic violations. The Los Angeles Police Department, for example, which had more high-speed chases than any other city (60 percent of which were the result of traffic violations or other minor infractions), changed its policy and prohibits high-speed chases except in the case of serious crimes and with a helicopter tracking the police.[155] In 2007, the LAPD chief, William Bratton, announced that his office was working with OnStar and General Motors to perfect the process of using a global positioning system to stop the car of a fleeing suspect with, literally, the flick of a switch.[156]

In October 2009, a high-speed chase was avoided in Visalia, California, when operators at General Motors stopped an SUV, the target of a suspected carjacking, that police were preparing to chase. It was the first time the company had signaled a command to a car to disable the gas pedal in a potential police high-speed chase.[157]

Police Intervention in Intimate Personal Violence Cases

One final area of police decision making that we cover is deciding what to do when called for an alleged intimate personal violence (IPV) dispute. Recall that Chapter 7 covered several issues regarding IPV along with a brief history of this crime. The focus here is on whether IPV is prevented or exacerbated by police intervention and whether police should have the discretion to arrest or, rather, should be governed by a *mandatory* arrest policy. In short, does a mandatory arrest policy reduce recidivism among those who batter their spouses or other intimate partners?

The research in this area is extensive, with earlier publications, such as those of Lawrence W. Sherman, showing a significant decrease in domestic violence under a policy of mandatory arrest.[158] An analysis of those studies, based on a sample of 4,032 men who battered their partners, sug-

gests that arresting the batterer has some positive results, revealing "consistent but modest reductions in subsequent offenses targeting the original victim that [are] attributable to arresting the suspect." However, some batterers do continue to attack the original victim, and a factor that is more predictive (than arrest) of which ones will continue to batter is the suspect's prior arrest record. The research implied that although the results "lend limited support for policies favoring arrest over informal police responses to intimate partner violence. . . . new policies replacing or enhancing arrest that target potential repeat offenders might produce larger reductions in intimate partner violence."[159]

Others emphasize that there are some unintended consequences of mandatory arrests. First, there is some "disturbing evidence of racial bias" because, according to official arrest data, men of color are more likely to be recidivists in IPV. Research indicates, however, that white men are equally if not more likely to be recidivists. Thus, overpolicing in those areas that are occupied predominantly by minorities could lead to racial bias in arrest. In addition, a mandatory arrest policy has consequences for women and girls who may be perpetrators of IPV. Several studies reveal significant increases in the arrest of women and girls for IPV when a mandatory arrest policy is implemented. Women, especially girls, are more likely to be placed in detention. Some argue this is because women are becoming more violent, but it is also possible that the increased detention rates are the result of increased arrests, not all of which may be necessary. Some studies show that although arrests for both men and women increase when a mandatory policy for IPV is implemented, the increase is significantly higher for women and girls.[160] Perhaps reducing (or abolishing) arrests for status offenses (which were always significantly higher for girls than for boys) has been replaced by arrests for IPV, which may also be recorded as simple or aggravated assaults.

In some IPV cases, both parties are arrested. Arresting the alleged victim creates problems for that person in subsequent court trials, such as for child custody as well as the assault and battery trial. In addition, the wishes of the alleged victim may be important. Taking away control of his or her life at a time when control is important may have a negative impact. Further, the alleged victim may be in a better position than police to determine what is best. For example, a female who reports IPV may have greater understanding than police on whether she would be in less danger if the alleged partner is not arrested, especially since we know that batterers keep their victims in the relationship through threats of physical violence if they leave. The person who is arrested will be released, probably soon; he or she might be even more dangerous because of the arrest than would have been the case with other types of intervention.[161]

Intervention has also become a reaction to elder abuse cases, but here, too, the results are disturbing. There is, for example, some evidence that subsequent abuse is more likely to occur after social service or police intervention. Specifically, in one study, investigators found that subsequent abuse and new calls regarding alleged abuse were more likely in families that had intervention in the form of home visits and education than in those that had only education on elder abuse (pamphlets, posters, and elder abuse programs in public housing where elderly people lived).[162]

In recent years, significant changes have been made in police department policies concerning reactions to complaints of IPV. In fact, some researchers state the changes have been rapid and "almost unprecedented." The studies concerning their results are contradictory. "Considerable positive change *has* occurred. However the limitations and repercussions have yet to be satisfactorily addressed."[163]

Another issue in police intervention in IPV cases is that these situations may be dangerous for law enforcement officers. An example is the killing of two officers (and the serious injury of another) in Odessa, Texas, in September 2007. The three officers responded to a domestic call, which resulted in a standoff for hours before Larry White, 58, shot and killed the two officers and wounded the third. The complainant escaped the house unharmed. When officers could not enter the house through the front door, they went to the back door, and the accused came out shooting.[164]

Some jurisdictions handle domestic violence cases in special courts. Domestic violence courts are discussed in Chapter 13.

Police Misconduct

Considerable attention has been given to police misconduct, especially widespread corruption in large cities. According to sociologist Lawrence W. Sherman, "a public official is corrupt if he accepts money or money's worth for doing something that he is under a duty to do anyway, that he is under a duty not to do, or to exercise a legitimate discretion for improper reasons."[165] This section looks at the police departments of New York City, Los Angeles, and Atlanta.

New York Police Department (NYPD)

In response to an article charging widespread police corruption in the New York City Police Department, the city's major established the Knapp Commission in May 1970. This commission found that corruption was pervasive within the NYPD and that rookies were subjected to such strong pressures that many succumbed and became corrupt, whereas others became cynical. This cynical attitude was attributed to the departmental belief that corruption should not be exposed and to the code of silence among officers concerning the corrupt activities of their peers.[166]

In the 1980s, officials of the NYPD reported that only a small percentage of the city's police officers were characterized by corruption or other forms of misconduct. The officials claimed that undercover tests of integrity, whereby some officers were assigned to make secret reports on the behavior of other officers, had eliminated organized corruption. Officials noted, however, that the institutionalized, organized corruption found by the Knapp Commission had been replaced by a new type of activity: cheating scams, such as abuse of sick leave, overtime, and military leave. Some officers were charged with theft and drug violations.

In May 1992, five active NYPD officers and one retired officer were arrested and charged with drug violations in what police called the "most flagrant charge of drug corruption in the city's police force in six years."[167] The following month, the FBI began investigating the allegations. In July, four officers and two persons retired from the NYPD were arrested for stealing and fencing thousands of counterfeit Chanel handbags.[168] By September, even the highest-ranking officer in charge of stopping corruption admitted that the task was very difficult: "There has never been a time in this job when we've been presented with more corruption hazards than in the last five years, because of the drug situation."[169]

The Mollen Commission, which conducted a major investigation into alleged corruption in the NYPD, published its final report in 1994. The report compared current corruption patterns with those identified earlier in the Knapp Commission report. The earlier report found that most officers were *grass-eaters* (those who take bribes routinely) and few were *meat-eaters* (those who look for opportunities to go beyond bribes to more serious crimes). The 1994 report concluded that the current situation was the reverse: "Minor corruption is no longer systemic among the ranks . . . . But the 'meat-eaters' are the rule rather than the exception among corrupt cops today."[170]

With regard to corruption in the NYPD, researchers analyzed the data of all officers who were involuntarily separated from the department between 1975 and 1996. Following are some of their conclusions:

- "*Pre-employment history matters.* Officers whose life histories include records of arrest, traffic violations, and failure in other jobs are more likely than other officers to be involuntarily separated from the NYPD.
- *Education and training matter.* Officers who hold associate or higher degrees are less likely than those who do not to be involuntarily separated. . . .
- *Diversity matters.* As the NYPD has become more diverse, it has become better behaved.
- *Race still matters, but apparently only for black officers.* As the representation of Hispanic and Asian officers in the NYPD has increased, their involuntary separation rates have decreased and become

virtually indistinguishable from those of white officers. . . . Black officers' involuntary separation rates have also decreased, but remain higher than those for other racial groups."[171]

Charges of misconduct against NYPD officers have continued. The 2008 acquittal of NYPD officers accused in the killing of an innocent bystander, Sean Bell, was noted earlier in this chapter. In early 2010, three NYPD officers went on trial for the alleged abuse of Michael Mineo during an arrest for smoking marijuana. All three officers were acquitted.

Not all are acquitted, however. In the fall of 2009, Bernard B. Kerik, New York's former police commissioner, surrendered to authorities at the Federal Correctional Institution in Cumberland, Maryland, to begin serving a four-year prison term after he entered guilty pleas to eight felonies, including tax fraud and lying to White House officials. Kerik was nominated by President George W. Bush to head the Department of Homeland Security but withdrew his name after he was accused of accepting renovations to his New York apartment from a construction firm that allegedly had ties to organized crime. He was described by federal prosecutors "as a corrupt official who sought to trade his authority for lavish benefits." When he entered his plea, just before he was scheduled to go on trial, Kerik said he would offer no excuses for his behavior and would learn from his mistakes.[172]

Los Angeles Police Department (LAPD)

The Los Angeles Police Department, still feeling the effects of the 1991 Rodney King beating, which was captured on video by an amateur photographer and shown throughout the world, faced another corruption crisis. This one, the Rampart scandal (so called because it took place in the department's Rampart Division), was described as "the worst corruption scandal in [LAPD] history." The scandal began in 1999 when Officer Rafael Perez, who had been caught stealing cocaine from the evidence room, entered into a plea agreement with prosecutors. Perez alleged that in a unit that had little oversight, officers routinely planted evidence on suspects, covered up crimes such as unjustified shootings, lied on reports, and beat gang members. In the fall of 2000, three officers who were convicted of framing gang members and planting evidence were convicted. In December 2000, a judge overturned those convictions and ordered a new trial, ruling that prosecutors had not presented sufficient evidence for those convictions and that the jury had misunderstood its instructions.

Hundreds of cases were reexamined as a result of Perez's allegations. Numerous officers were fired, and an investigation into the department resulted in a 350-page report on its problems. Perez was sentenced to five years in prison. In November 2000, the city settled for $15 million

with Javier Francisco Ovando, a former gang member, paralyzed after being shot by Perez and Nino Durden in 1996. The officers claimed that Ovando shot at them, and they responded in self-defense. Ovando was convicted and sentenced to 23 years in prison, but an LAPD internal report concluded that he was framed by the police, who planted the gun on him. Ovando was released from prison after serving almost three years. The investigation concluded in early 2003 with no recommendations for further prosecutions. However, the new LAPD chief, William J. Bratton (who replaced Bernard Parks, who resigned under pressure in April 2002), called for further investigation into the Rampart scandal. Another commission was appointed in early 2004, headed by Connie Rice, described by the *Los Angeles Times* as "the firebrand civil rights attorney who has made a career out of suing the LAPD." The nine-member commission was empowered to conduct an investigation. In a July 2006 report, "Rampart Reconsidered," the Rice commission reported that the police department should be significantly expanded and other changes made or the city would be ripe for another Rampart scandal. Chief Bratton appointed a task force to enact the reforms.[173]

In June 2007, Chief Bratton was unanimously given a second five-year term, the first chief to get one since 1992. As noted earlier, he retired from that position in 2009.

Three LAPD officers alleged that they were falsely arrested and falsely prosecuted after the Rampart scandal erupted. A jury ruled that their constitutional rights were violated and awarded each officer $5 million plus interest and attorney fees. In 2008, the Ninth Circuit Court of Appeals upheld that decision and that judgment award, finding that the jury could reasonably have concluded that the cases against the officers were based on inadequate evidence, and that was "indicative of official policy." One of the attorneys for the officers said that the LAPD "frequently throws officers under the bus" when there is a political crisis and that it is time to realize that "officers are not expendable."[174]

Atlanta Police Department (APD)

Although the NYPD and the LAPD are often in the news, they are not the only police departments with police misconduct issues. In April of 2007, the U.S. Department of Justice announced that it would be investigating the Atlanta Police Department for what prosecutors called a "culture of misconduct." This occurred after Kathryn Johnston, 92, was killed in a November 2006 shootout with police, who knocked down her door after securing a "no-knock" warrant for a drug raid. Two officers, who admitted that they planted drug evidence in her home after Johnston was killed by police, pleaded guilty to manslaughter and violating Johnston's federal civil rights. Atlanta's mayor appointed a civilian review board to investigate the claims that police have obtained search warrants based on fabricated evidence of drug deals along with other alleged misconduct. In June 2010, the department's interim police chief announced that he had fired two more officers and disciplined six others involved in the shooting, stating, "Policing is a difficult job, no doubt, but we must be expected to comply with the very laws that we are sworn to uphold." Fourteen officers were involved in misconduct in this incident; five already entered guilty pleas to federal charges, and four of those officers are serving prison terms. The no-knock warrant was based on false information from an informant.[175]

Analysis of Corruption

Policing is rich in opportunities for corruption, but opportunity is not the only important variable. Variation in police corruption may depend on a police department's type of organization. James Q. Wilson analyzed police departments according to what he termed *styles* of law enforcement: the service style, the legalistic style, and the watchman style. These styles were found related to the degree of police corruption; the greatest degree is found in the watchman style.[176]

The *watchman style* emphasizes order maintenance over law enforcement; that is, the law is used to maintain order rather than to regulate conduct. In a department characterized by the watchman style, the police chief tries to limit the discretionary authority of patrol officers. A primary concern is that no one rocks the boat within the department. Police are recruited locally, paid low salaries, given minimum training, not rewarded for higher education, and expected to have other jobs—all factors that may make them more susceptible to corruption.

The *legalistic style* emphasizes specialization, promotional opportunities, and higher education along with attempts to recruit from the middle class. The law is seen as a means to an end; the police officer tries to be an impersonal agent of the law, uses formal rather than informal sanctions, issues traffic tickets at a high rate, and emphasizes law enforcement over order maintenance or community services.

The *service style* combines law enforcement and order maintenance. Emphasis is on community relations, with police on patrol working out of specialized units (e.g., narcotics or sexual assault crimes units) and a decentralized command. The pace of work is more leisurely, and more promotional opportunities are stressed. Corruption is not a serious problem, and police are expected to live exemplary private lives.

According to Lawrence W. Sherman, police corruption is a problem of both external opportunity and the individual's response. It can be explained only by a close analysis of both variables. Sherman applied theories of community structure and anomie (recall Chapter 5's discussion), which state that the degree of anomie depends on the gap between goals and the means to achieve them. Sherman emphasized that anomie can affect the corrupters

and the corruptees and that an occupational group might suffer anomie not characteristic of the entire community. Police might have an occupational anomie and therefore be more susceptible to bribes than are members of other occupational groups. In addition, recruits redefine themselves radically in a relatively short period of time, and the process of accepting bribes begins. The key factor is the extent of the corruption in the work group to which the officer is assigned. The process goes by stages, beginning with police perks—free coffee and meals—moving to a free drink after work, and then to money offered by a motorist. If the officer participates in these stages, he or she may be considered ready by colleagues to be cut in on gambling deals. That offer is hard to turn down, for it represents a chance to participate in the social solidarity of colleagues. Some officers move on to bribes from prostitutes, pimps, or brothel operators and finally into narcotics. Police officers may stop anywhere along the ladder because of their self-concepts, but they are influenced in where they stop by the group definition of how far they can go.[177]

The Control of Policing

The discussions of police stress and corruption are not meant to imply that all or even most officers or administrators are included or that the problems are unique to policing. They may, however, be more obvious and even more critical in this profession because of the power of the police and the fact that police officers have access to weapons. But because problems do exist, it is important to consider methods for controlling policing. Several approaches are used. We begin with internal controls.

Police Professionalism and Departmental Control

In the final analysis, only police can control policing. Police must be professionals. Discretion is vital in policing, and thus, the legislature, the courts, and the community cannot control all police activities. According to Jerome H. Skolnick,

> The needed philosophy of professionalism must rest on a set of values conveying the idea that police are as much an institution dedicated to the achievement of legality in society as they are an official social organization designed to control misconduct through the invocation of punitive sanctions. . . . [W]hat must occur is a significant alteration in the ideology of police.[178]

The importance of professionalism was dramatized by a study published by James Leo Walsh in 1970. Walsh reported that the attitudes and behavior of police are not explained by the social variables of class, ethnicity, age, rank, gender, race, and authoritarianism but, rather, by the impact of professionalism.[179]

It is important, however, that the public is not misled; police professionalism must be real, not illusory. Thus, in his 1974 work, Peter K. Manning, a scholar of police behavior, contended that police adopt an impossible mandate "that claims to include the efficient, apolitical, and professional enforcement of the law." Because they cannot meet that mandate, they resort to appearances of professionalism that include creating a bureaucracy in the police organization (which they see as the best and most efficient way to run the organization) and using technology to suggest a scientific perspective of crime. They also collect official data and use them to show how efficient the police are and devise styles of patrol that they see as part of bureaucratic efficiency. The police develop secrecy, one of their most effective sources of power, because it enables them to act without exposing what they are doing, such as cooperating with organized crime rather than fighting it. Appearances are important, too, because police need convictions for their arrests. For a high rate of convictions, police may cooperate with prosecutors in persuading people to plead guilty to lesser offenses. They operate on the assumption that all of the people they arrest are guilty and that, if the police apply enough pressure, suspects will confess.[180]

Police departments need to consider revising policies—such as those that prohibit lateral entry—that result in promotions only from within the department. Some experts have suggested that police departments develop specialized units (and some do), such as a domestic unit, a juvenile unit, and a substance abuse unit with an emphasis on peacekeeping, leaving most of the traditional law enforcement functions to other officers. Still other supporters of professionalism have suggested the creation of crisis intervention units because police receive so many disturbance calls involving family members and friends that might erupt into violence. The aim is to prevent violence. Various methods have been tried, and one that has received considerable attention in recent years is mandatory arrests of suspects in IPV cases even when the alleged victim does not want to press charges. This control method was discussed earlier in the chapter.

Community Control

A second method for controlling policing is through the community. In 1981, the U.S. Commission on Civil Rights stated that perhaps "the most valuable asset these officers can possess is credibility with the community they serve."[181] Good police–community relations are particularly important today because racial and other conflicts between police and the community may escalate into violence. These conflicts reflect larger societal problems, which police cannot solve, but police can work to improve public perceptions of their activities. Actual or perceived negative relationships may lead to violence. An earlier study reported that people who had positive images of the police were more likely to cooperate with the police in crime control. Least likely to cooperate were those who perceived that they were discriminated against—minorities and the poor—and who happened to be the most frequent crime victims.[182]

There is evidence that most people are pleased with the work of police. A 2008 Gallup Poll that quizzed people about various U.S. institutions found that 58 percent had "a great deal" of confidence in police, with only the military (71 percent) and small businesses (60 percent) obtaining a higher percentage for that response. The U.S. Supreme Court received only a 32 percent response for that confidence level.[183]

Research on police–community relations in Los Angeles suggested that police can improve their relationships with the public and their images by making informal contacts with the community through meetings and other local events. Researchers surveyed residents of four Los Angeles neighborhoods, ranging from one with high violent crime rates to one with low rates. They measured the respondents' views of social cohesion in their neighborhoods. Those who reported high social cohesion had more positive images of the police, but regardless of the level of social cohesion, informal contacts between police and residents improved the image the latter had of the former. The research at first appeared to confirm that of other studies reporting that whites have better images of police than do minorities, but when the factor of type of neighborhood was considered, the researchers concluded that disorder is a key variable. The researchers did not find that negative media images influenced attitudes toward the police. Almost two of every three residents said that their attitudes toward police were based on their own experiences or those of people they knew. Only one-third said the mass media were an influence. Finally, crime victimization was influential. While 85 percent of those who were not crime victims had positive attitudes toward police performance, only 70 percent of property crime victims and 57 percent of violent crime victims reported positive images of the police. The researchers concluded: "Speaking to officers on patrol or at community events was associated with a positive opinion of police performance, whether or not the resident lived in a disorderly neighborhood."[184]

These results also suggest that community-oriented policing is one way to improve relationships between the police and the community. Another is the involvement of citizens in establishing standards and policies and in enforcing disciplinary action. Civilian review boards were utilized in earlier years, but they were opposed by police; most boards did not last long and had little power. The U.S. Civil Rights Commission noted the problems with these boards but also suggested that some outside review of alleged police misconduct is appropriate.[185] Historically, according to some scholars, community involvement in police policy making and discipline has been a failure.[186] Today, however, some communities are again looking at the possibilities for cooperation in improving the relationship between law enforcement and policing. As noted earlier, Atlanta now has a civilian review board to look into complaints about policing.[187]

Control Through the U.S. Department of Justice (DOJ)

The U.S. Department of Justice has the authority to intervene in police departments that appear to be violating the civil rights of their constituents. The DOJ may conduct investigations and, upon relevant findings, place the department under the supervision and control of federal monitors. It can require a *consent order*, which is a legal document mandating specific reforms. A statute enacted in 1994 provides greater enforcement powers to the DOJ to prosecute police who violate the law. It permits investigation and prosecution of *patterns or practices* of department-wide misconduct in local police departments. It also authorizes the U.S. attorney general to "acquire data about the use of excessive force by law enforcement officers" and directs him or her to "publish an annual summary of the data."[188] The DOJ placed the Los Angeles Police Department (LAPD) under a consent decree in 2001, and it was removed in 2009. According to the assistant attorney general for DOJ's civil rights division, under that consent order, the LAPD regained public confidence and crime decreased.[189]

More recently, the DOJ became involved with the New Orleans Police Department (NOPD). This was the result of a request for federal oversight from the city's new mayor, Mitch Landrieu, but it was clear that the DOJ was headed in that direction. According to the local media, the NOPD needs federal assistance for reform in "recruiting, training, operating protocols, and disciplinary procedures." The media continued with specifics, referring primarily to the "abuses like the unjustified shooting of civilians at the Danziger Bridge after Katrina and its subsequent cover-up." The mayor's request to DOJ stated, "It's clear that nothing short of a complete transformation is necessary and essential to ensure safety for the citizens of New Orleans." Meanwhile, four NOPD officers had admitted they were involved in a cover-up with regard to the Danziger Bridge shootings; more charges were expected.[190]

In June 2010, five officers were indicted in the death of Henry Glover, 31, whose remains were found in an abandoned, burned car. It was alleged that the defendants beat and kicked Glover, killed him, placed his body in a car, burned the car, and then covered up the crimes. Three officers were convicted. The police chief announced

that any officer who lied about anything would be fired immediately.[191]

Control Through the Courts

Another method for controlling policing is through the courts. This may take several forms. Some departments, after investigations by the U.S. Department of Justice, discussed earlier, have been put under the control of monitors appointed and overseen by federal courts. The departments are given lists of specifics that must be corrected before those monitors are removed. Other departments are placed under federal monitors after a lawsuit.

The first police department placed under a federal monitor was Pittsburgh, Pennsylvania, in 1997. When the legal director of the American Civil Liberties Union (ACLU) moved to Pittsburgh in 1991, he asked a police officer for directions and got only a response of expletives. Five years later, the ACLU sued the police department on behalf of 65 residents for frequent violations of civil rights. The result was an agreement that the department would have a monitor and would consent to numerous changes. The federal oversight ended in 2002. In June 2003, it was proclaimed that "residents, civil libertarians, civil leaders and the police officers themselves say Pittsburgh has a more effective and humane police department."[192]

Federal monitoring, however, is expensive. In 2003, it was estimated that monitoring, along with the changes to which the Detroit Police Department had agreed, might cost that city more than $100 million over the five-year monitoring period. The cost of renovating jail holding cells alone could cost $50 million. Other requirements included improved medical care and screening of inmates for physical and mental health problems and potential suicides, training of officers and auditing regarding new policies such as use of force and requirements of inmate hygiene, a computer warning system to flag officers who are having problems, and more nutritional food for inmates. The cost of the federal monitor and her staff was an estimated $5 to $10 million. In addition, the police department was required to pay for a campaign to teach residents how to file complaints against the police and to equip police cars and holding cells with video cameras. By January 2006, halfway through the original monitoring period, the federal monitor reported that the city had not come close to fulfilling the federal mandate. By October 2007, only 54 of the 177 changes the city promised to make had been made. A federal judge, with reluctance, agreed to extend the compliance deadline until 2011.[193]

In April 2010, the new federal monitor, Robert Warshaw (who took over from Sheryl Robinson Wood, who was forced to resign), reported that the Detroit Police Department was in compliance with 44 percent of the required reforms. This was a 29 percent increase over his first report, filed three months earlier. In that report, the monitor expressed concern that over 1,100 complaints of excessive force by police had not yet been processed.[194]

After a review of the various methods of citizen complaint review boards, researchers concluded that the process is important, but no one method is a key answer. Further, any model must permit due process for police as well as accountability to the public.[195] Police may be falsely accused and maliciously prosecuted, and when that happens, they are entitled to compensation, as illustrated by the earlier discussion of three officers with the LAPD.

Another court method for controlling policing is through excluding evidence obtained by violating suspects' rights or by awarding civil damages.

The Exclusionary Rule

The **exclusionary rule** (which requires excluding from a court proceeding any evidence that was seized illegally) was developed by the U.S. Supreme Court in 1914 as a method for deterring police from conducting illegal searches and seizures in the federal system. The Supreme Court stated that, in federal trials, the prohibition against unreasonable searches and seizures would not be effective unless all illegally seized evidence was excluded from trial. In 1961, the Court held that the exclusionary rule also applies to cases tried in state courts.[196]

It is difficult, if not impossible, to determine whether the exclusionary rule does in fact deter police from improperly seizing evidence because illegal searches may not be reported. The research on the issue is inconclusive. There is evidence, however, that the existence of the rule has led some police departments to increase the quantity and quality of police training, thus educating officers more extensively in what they may and may not do in the area of search and seizure.[197]

The exclusionary rule also serves a symbolic purpose. If police violate suspects' rights to obtain evidence for use in trials, the government is setting a negative example. According to the U.S. Supreme Court, when this occurs, the government becomes a lawbreaker: "It breeds contempt for law; it invites . . . anarchy."[198]

In recent years, the exclusionary rule has come under attack, with some calling for its abolition or at least its modification. Generally, the arguments on this side of the issue are the reverse of the arguments in favor of the rule. First is the argument concerning symbolism, which is based on the view that when people see defendants they believe to be guilty going free because of a technicality, respect for the law and for the criminal justice system is undermined. It is the *perception* of letting guilty suspects go free that is crucial.

Second, abolitionists contend that the exclusionary rule should be eliminated because it results in the release of guilty people. Third, the possibility of having evidence excluded from a trial because it was not seized properly leads defendants to file numerous motions to suppress evidence, which takes up a lot of court time and contributes to court congestion. In criminal cases, objections to searches or seizures are two of the issues raised most frequently.

The U.S. Supreme Court has held that some exceptions are applicable to the exclusionary rule. Under the **good faith exception**, evidence that is obtained illegally should not be excluded from trial if it can be shown that the officers secured the evidence in good faith—that is, if they reasonably believed that they were acting in accordance with the law. The U.S. Supreme Court adopted the good faith exception in *Massachusetts v. Sheppard*.[199]

In 2004, the U.S. Supreme Court limited the good faith exception by holding that it did not apply in a case in which the application for a search warrant and the sworn affidavit for that warrant both contained the list of weapons to be sought in the search, but the search warrant did not contain that list. Neither the agent nor the magistrate who signed the warrant caught this clerical error. The occupant of the house was given a copy of the warrant but not of the affidavit. The police found no weapons, and the occupant sued for a Fourth Amendment (see Appendix A) violation. In another case, *Groh v. Ramirez*, the U.S. Supreme Court agreed that the good faith exception did not apply; the warrant, with no list of particulars, violated the Fourth Amendment's particularity requirement.[200]

The U.S. Supreme Court's good faith exception to the exclusionary rule does not require that all states adopt the exception. States may grant defendants greater protection than is required by the federal Constitution, and some have done so.[201]

Another exception to the exclusionary rule adopted by the U.S. Supreme Court is the **inevitable discovery exception**. In *Nix v. Williams*, the Supreme Court held that illegally seized evidence is admissible if police would have found it later by legal methods. In *New York v. Quarles*, the Supreme Court recognized a public safety exception, holding that there are some circumstances in which police are justified in conducting a search or asking questions without first giving the *Miranda* warning. In those instances, illegally obtained evidence is admissible at trial.[202]

In subsequent cases, the U.S. Supreme Court has held that when officers who had a warrant to search one apartment but, without realizing it, searched a different apartment and found illegal drugs, that evidence may be used in court because the officers acted in good faith. Excluding that evidence would not deter officers from making such searches because they had acted in the belief that they were searching the apartment identified in the warrant.[203]

The U.S. Supreme Court has ruled that defendants' rights are not violated when police, acting in good faith, lose or destroy evidence that could have been used to establish innocence. In *Arizona v. Youngblood*, police failed to perform chemical tests on the victim's semen-stained clothes or to refrigerate that evidence for subsequent tests. Test results might have shown that the defendant was not the assailant in that case.[204]

In *Arizona v. Fulminante*, a sharply divided U.S. Supreme Court held that the Constitution does not require the automatic exclusion from trial of a coerced confession. According to the Court, a coerced confession is to be evaluated like any other evidence, with the trial judge deciding whether the error was harmless. If so, the confession may be admitted. However, if the confession constituted **harmful error**, meaning that it affected a constitutional right of the defendant and thus is a serious error rather than a simple technical one, the evidence must be excluded.[205]

There is some concern that the U.S. Supreme Court may erode the exclusionary rule, as evidenced by its 2009 decision, *Herring v. United States*, decided by a 5–4 vote. Excerpts of that case are reproduced in Exhibit 12.7.

Criminal and Civil Liability

Another method for attempting to control misconduct by police officers and their supervisors is through criminal and civil liability. Civil litigation against law enforcement officers and their departments and municipalities is extensive, as illustrated by the $8.7 million settlement in New York City for the police brutality suffered by Abner Louima, discussed in Chapter 9. And as noted earlier in this chapter, the City of Los Angeles settled for $15 million with one victim, Javier Francisco Ovando, a former gang member who said he was shot in the head and chest and then framed by police. Ovando was paralyzed by the attack. The city council also approved millions in other settlements stemming from that scandal.[206]

Many legal reasons may be used in these civil suits. The U.S. Supreme Court has held that inadequate training is an acceptable reason, provided the plaintiff can prove that the negligence amounts to deliberate indifference by the police department. That case, *Canton v. Harris*, was discussed earlier.[207]

Civil lawsuits may also be brought by plaintiffs who allege that their federal civil rights have been violated. For example, in *Jackson v. Brister*, police were summoned to a bank where a person was attempting to cash a forged check. When the customer saw the police, she quickly exited the bank, got in her car, and sped away. The police followed, and the high-speed chase resulted in a crash of the suspect's car with another car, killing the driver. The estate of the deceased sued the police department and the city for civil damages for wrongful death. The case was appealed to the Mississippi Supreme Court, which ruled that the usual immunity provided to police for civil damages does not apply when officers act recklessly with disregard for human life. The department policies permit high-speed chases only when a serious crime has been committed and when a reasonable person would assume that the alleged suspect is more dangerous to the community than a high-speed chase is. In this particular case, noted the Mississippi court, the police could have gotten the license plate number, located the suspect, and arrested her, thus making a high-speed chase unnecessary.[208]

Cases involving civil liability are difficult to win against police. In a case decided in 2009, the U.S. Supreme Court held that police have qualified immunity from civil liability from violating the Fourth Amendment if they enter a home to search without a warrant after they get a signal from an informer who is inside the house. The appellant, in *Pearson v. Callahan*, alleged that police gave $100 to the informer to buy illegal drugs from Afton Callahan. Callahan admitted the informer to his home, and the informer signaled to the police. The police entered without a warrant, searched the home, found illegal drugs, and arrested Callahan. He was tried and convicted. The state courts ruled that the police action constituted an unconstitutional search and excluded the evidence. Callahan sued Pearson and other law enforcement agents. The U.S. Supreme Court did not rule on the constitutionality of the search but held that the officers had qualified immunity from civil liability because the unlawfulness of their conduct had not been clearly established.[209]

Terrorism and Policing

The terrorist acts on U.S. soil on 9/11 changed the way policing must be performed. No longer may police be primarily reactive to what goes on around them; they must be proactive, thinking and acting ahead of criminal acts because the impact of terrorist acts leaves no room for error. It is an age of intelligence-led policing (ILP) now, and police departments must retrain and rethink how they secure their communities and the nation, just as the TSA has had to redesign security at airports. Policing scholars state that the primary concern of ILP is to "prevent crime and terrorist attacks through effective communication and coordination." They describe ILP as the

> strategic integration of intelligence, with an emphasis on predictive analysis derived from the discovery of hard facts, information, patterns, and good crime analysis. . . . Ultimately, the goal of ILP is to provide a fundamental intelligence system that informs objective decision making on how to combat crime and terrorism.[210]

The National Commission on Terrorist Attacks upon the United States emphasized the lack of intelligence gathering and sharing prior to the 9/11 attacks. The commission's recommendations were controversial, but some have been implemented, as noted in Chapter 7 of this text.[211] But what is not controversial is that terrorist threats at home and abroad require that all law enforcement agencies be proactive.

12.7

The Exclusionary Rule: A New View

In January 2009, by a 5–4 vote, the U.S. Supreme Court decided *Herring v. United States*,[1] in which the Court refused to uphold the exclusionary rule after police made a mistake in executing a warrant. In *Pearson v. Callahan*,[2] the Court held that the police are immune from liability if they enter a home to search without a warrant after they get a signal from an informer who is inside the house. Some believe these cases are forerunners to the abolition of the exclusionary rule, which results in the exclusion of evidence from trial if there were improprieties in the methods of securing that evidence. Chief Justice John Roberts wrote the opinion in *Herring v. United States*, which is excerpted here.

Herring v. United States

The Fourth Amendment forbids "unreasonable searches and seizures," and this usually requires the police to have probable cause or a warrant before making an arrest. What if an officer reasonably believes there is an outstanding arrest warrant, but that belief turns out to be wrong because of a negligent bookkeeping error by another police employee? The parties here agree that the ensuing arrest is still a violation of the Fourth Amendment, but dispute whether contraband found during a search incident to that arrest must be excluded in a later prosecution.

Our cases establish that such suppression is not an automatic consequence of a Fourth Amendment violation. Instead, the question turns on the culpability of the police and the potential of exclusion to deter wrongful police conduct. Here the error was the result of isolated negligence attenuated from the arrest. We hold that in these circumstances the jury should not be barred from considering all the evidence.

On July 7, 2004, Investigator Mark Anderson learned that Bennie Dean Herring had driven to the Coffee County Sheriff's Department to retrieve something from his impounded truck. Herring was no stranger to law enforcement, and Anderson asked the county's warrant clerk, Sandy Pope, to check for any outstanding warrants for Herring's arrest. When she found none, Anderson asked Pope to check with Sharon Morgan, her counterpart in neighboring Dale County. After checking Dale County's computer database, Morgan replied that there was an active arrest warrant for Herring's failure to appear on a felony charge. Pope relayed the information to Anderson and asked Morgan to fax over a copy of the warrant as confirmation. Anderson and a deputy followed Herring as he left the impound lot, pulled him over, and arrested him. A search incident to the arrest revealed methamphetamine in Herring's pocket, and a

pistol (which as a felon he could not possess) in his vehicle. There had, however, been a mistake about the warrant. The Dale County sheriff's computer records are supposed to correspond to actual arrest warrants, which the office also maintains. But when Morgan went to the files to retrieve the actual warrant to fax to Pope, Morgan was unable to find it. She called a court clerk and learned that the warrant had been recalled five months earlier. Normally when a warrant is recalled the court clerk's office or a judge's chambers calls Morgan, who enters the information in the sheriff's computer database and disposes of the physical copy. For whatever reason, the information about the recall of the warrant for Herring did not appear in the database. Morgan immediately called Pope to alert her to the mixup, and Pope contacted Anderson over a secure radio. This all unfolded in 10 to 15 minutes, but Herring had already been arrested and found with the gun and drugs, just a few hundred yards from the sheriff's office. Herring was indicted in the District Court for the Middle District of Alabama for illegally possessing the gun and drugs. He moved to suppress the evidence on the ground that his initial arrest had been illegal because the warrant had been rescinded. The Magistrate Judge recommended denying the motion because the arresting officers had acted in a good faith belief that the warrant was still outstanding. Thus, even if there were a Fourth Amendment violation, there was "no reason to believe that application of the exclusionary rule here would deter the occurrence of any future." . . . [The Court reviewed the judicial history of the case.]

When a probable cause determination was based on reasonable but mistaken assumptions, the person subjected to a search or seizure has not necessarily been the victim of a constitutional violation. The very phrase "probable cause" confirms that the Fourth Amendment does not demand all possible precision. . . .

The Fourth Amendment protects "[t]he right of the people to be secure in their persons, houses, papers, and effects, against unreasonable searches and seizures," but "contains no provision expressly precluding the use of evidence obtained in violation of its commands." Nonetheless, our decisions establish an exclusionary rule that, when applicable, forbids the use of improperly obtained evidence at trial. We have stated that this judicially created rule is "designed to safeguard Fourth Amendment rights generally through its deterrent effect." . . .

EXHIBIT continued

12.7

The Coffee County officers did nothing improper. Indeed, the error was noticed so quickly because Coffee County requested a faxed confirmation of the warrant. The Eleventh Circuit concluded, however, that somebody in Dale County should have updated the computer database to reflect the recall of the arrest warrant. The court also concluded that this error was negligent, but did not find it to be reckless or deliberate. That fact is crucial to our holding that this error is not enough by itself to require "the extreme sanction of exclusion." . . .

The fact that a Fourth Amendment violation occurred—i.e., that a search or arrest was unreasonable—does not necessarily mean that the exclusionary rule applies. Indeed, exclusion "has always been our last resort, not our first impulse," and our precedents establish important principles that constrain application of the exclusionary rule.

First, the exclusionary rule is not an individual right and applies only where it "'result[s] in appreciable deterrence.'" We have repeatedly rejected the argument that exclusion is a necessary consequence of a Fourth Amendment violation. Instead we have focused on the efficacy of the rule in deterring Fourth Amendment violations in the future.

In addition, the benefits of deterrence must outweigh the costs. "We have never suggested that the exclusionary rule must apply in every circumstance in which it might provide marginal deterrence." . . . The principal cost of applying the rule is, of course, letting guilty and possibly dangerous defendants go free—something that "offends basic concepts of the criminal justice system." "[T]he rule's costly toll upon truth seeking and law enforcement objectives presents a high obstacle for those urging [its] ap-

plication." [The Court discussed the precedent cases concerning the exclusionary rule.] . . .

Indeed, the abuses that gave rise to the exclusionary rule featured intentional conduct that was patently unconstitutional. . . .

To trigger the exclusionary rule, police conduct must be sufficiently deliberate that exclusion can meaningfully deter it, and sufficiently culpable that such deterrence is worth the price paid by the justice system. As laid out in our cases, the exclusionary rule serves to deter deliberate, reckless, or grossly negligent conduct, or in some circumstances recurring or systemic negligence. The error in this case does not rise to that level.

We do not suggest that all recordkeeping errors by the police are immune from the exclusionary rule. In this case, however, the conduct at issue was not so objectively culpable as to require exclusion. . . . If the police have been shown to be reckless in maintaining a warrant system, or to have knowingly made false entries to lay the groundwork for future false arrests, exclusion would certainly be justified under our cases should such misconduct cause a Fourth Amendment violation. . . .

We conclude that when police mistakes are the result of negligence such as that described here, rather than systemic error or reckless disregard of constitutional requirements, any marginal deterrence does not "pay its way."

1. *Herring v. United States*, 555 U.S. 135 (2009), citations omitted.
2. *Pearson v. Callahan*, 555 U.S. 135 (2009) (2009).

Summary

The chapter began with a brief history of policing and an overview of U.S. public police systems, including a look at the recently established Department of Homeland Security and Transportation Security Administration, security at U.S. borders, and campuses and other security areas. The chapter then looked briefly at international policing and examined the role of private security. Private security has grown significantly, passing public policing in both numbers of employees and total costs. The growth of private security raises many questions, including the fairness issue—is adequate security available only for those who can afford it?—and quality control.

A key question in policing concerns the qualifications of police officers. The desired qualifications must be articulated before departments engage in the critical recruitment, training, and education of police. This chapter's overview of qualifications included a look at the psychology of policing. The chapter also examined the need to increase the numbers of women and minorities in policing. Much of the chapter was devoted to discussing police functions: law enforcement, order maintenance, and community services, along with the controversies that surround them. Policing models were discussed, with particular attention given to recent developments in community-oriented policing. The chapter examined public attitudes toward the police and the hostility police encounter from the public. These and other conflicts and problems have led some police officers to withdraw into themselves, to develop a code of secrecy, and to become isolated from society.

Policing is a stressful job, and some of the causes of stress were discussed, along with one reaction, the development of a subculture. The rapid spread of HIV and its impact on policing were examined. Police discretion in decision making was analyzed in the context of the initial stop, questioning, and arrest followed by home searches.

Special attention was given to racial profiling, including recent investigations into police departments concerning this area of policing.

The use of force, especially deadly force, is an issue of national concern today. The use of dangerous, high-speed vehicle pursuits was discussed, too, including the latest cases in this important area of policing. Police intervention in IPV cases was analyzed, with consideration given to whether mandatory arrests are effective in deterring further incidents of IPV.

The chapter then turned to a discussion of police misconduct, which detailed traditional approaches to police misconduct as well as relevant and recent examples of disciplinary issues in highly publicized cases. Particular attention was given to corruption problems in the police departments of New York City, Los Angeles, and Atlanta before turning to an analysis of police corruption.

Efforts to control police misconduct are made through the use of police professionalism and departmental control, the community, the U.S. Department of Justice, and the courts. The latter topic featured a recent case decided by the U.S. Supreme Court in which it refused to extend the exclusionary rule. Criminal and civil liability as methods of controlling policing were noted. Finally, brief attention was given to policing in a world of terrorism.

Experts have concluded that research on policing has not been adequate because we do not know enough about the police, who occupy one of the most important roles in our criminal justice systems. But we do know the tremendous impact their behavior can have on us as individuals and as a society. We need to understand that the behavior that touches our lives so deeply is significant for police officers as well. Most of them are hardworking and underpaid public servants who are not engaging in corruption or the misuse of police power. They deserve the support of the community in their efforts.

Study Questions

1. Explain briefly the meanings of these words in the historical context of policing: *frankpledge, hundred, shires, constable,* and *watch system.*

2. In what ways, if any, did the watch system influence policing in this country?

3. Briefly describe policing in Wales and in England.

4. Summarize recent issues with the FBI.

5. Analyze security at U.S. borders.

6. What, if any, special security concerns do colleges and universities have? Shopping malls?

7. Define and explain the purpose of *INTERPOL.*

8. Analyze private security in the United States and private security hired by the United States to protect its troops in foreign countries.

9. What should be the minimum qualifications for an entry-level police officer? Defend your answer.

10. What should be included in police training?

11. How have women and minorities been accepted in police departments? What problems do they face? What contributions do they make?

12. Briefly outline the law enforcement duties of policing.

13. Define and discuss the implications of zero tolerance policies in policing. Why is order maintenance important?

14. What is meant by *broken windows* as far as policing is concerned?

15. What influence do you think the media have on policing?

16. What type of service functions should police be expected to perform?

17. Describe and evaluate the professional model of policing, and contrast it with community-oriented policing.

18. What is the status of COPS?

19. How should police time be allocated among the three major policing functions?

20. Discuss the major role conflicts officers might encounter in policing.

21. What are the major factors contributing to police stress?

22. Define police *subculture*, and evaluate the concept.

23. What unique problems are presented to policing by the spread of AIDS?

24. Under what circumstances may police stop and question?

25. Explain and evaluate the no-knock rule and the knock-and-announce rule.

26. What have sociological studies shown us about arrest procedures and policies?

27. Discuss racial profiling.

28. Explain the importance of *Tennessee v. Garner* to police use of deadly force.

29. What position do you think we should take regarding high-speed police vehicle pursuits?

30. Should police be required to arrest in intimate personal violence cases?

31. What have the New York City, Los Angeles, and Atlanta police departments taught us about policing?

32. What are the prospects for controlling policing through community action?

33. What role does the DOJ play in policing? Illustrate with a recent example.

34. What is the role of federal courts in policing?

35. How can police be controlled through civil lawsuits or criminal charges?

Brief Essay Assignments

1. Distinguish among policing levels in U.S. systems, and discuss the most recent changes in policing at the national level.

2. Contrast and evaluate public and private policing.

3. Describe the three major police functions: law enforcement, order maintenance, service-related duties. Which function should have priority? Why?

4. Define *racial profiling*, and discuss its implications for policing and for the public image of policing.

5. Discuss police corruption historically, and indicate the major types of corruption today.

6. Define the exclusionary rule, state the reason it exists, and critique the policy. What are the recognized exceptions to the rule?

Internet Activities

1. Check out a local law enforcement agency on the Web. How many sworn officers does the agency have? How many civilian personnel? Does the department provide crime data for your area? Is there any information on community policing or problem-solving activities and/or programs? Does the department have any specialized investigative units, such as homicide, property, narcotics, juvenile? Sites such as http://www.officer.com and http://www.copseek.com offer search engines and links to find most law enforcement agencies on the Web. Both sites accessed 9 November 2010.

2. The National Center for Women and Policing website at http://www.womenandpolicing.org/ provides data, links, and publications on a variety of issues related to women and law enforcement. What are the issues this site covers? Is there any information on female police in your area? Site accessed 9 November 2010.

3. Check the website for the National Black Police Association, http://www.blackpolice.org, accessed 9 November 2010. What can you discover about the concerns of black police officers?

Notes

1. These methods of policing are discussed in Richard J. Lundman, *Police and Policing: An Introduction* (New York: Holt, Rinehart & Winston, 1980), pp. 15–17.

2. See, for example, "Lawrence Police Team Disbanded," *Evening Standard* (London) (24 April 2006), p. 19.

3. David H. Bayley, "Police: History," in *Encyclopedia of Crime and Justice*, Vol. 3, ed. Sanford H. Kadish (New York: Free Press, 1983), p. 1124.

4. U.S. Department of Justice, "Statutory Authority," http://www.usdoj.gov/02organizations/about.html, accessed 9 November 2010. The statute is The Judiciary Act of 1789, Chapter 20, Section 35, 1 Stat. 73, 92-93 (1789). The 1870 statute is codified at Chapter 150, 16 Stat. 162 (1870).

5. Tony Poveda, *Lawlessness and Reform: The FBI in Transition* (Pacific Grove, CA: Brooks/Cole, 1990), p. 1.

6. "F.B.I. to Pay Whistle-Blower $1.1 Million in a Settlement," *New York Times* (27 February 1998), p. 13.

7. The legislation concerning Homeland Security is Title 6 of the United States Code Service (2010).

8. Brian A. Reeves, Bureau of Justice Statistics, *Federal Law Enforcement Officers, 2004* (July 2006), p. 2, http://bjs.ojp.usdoj.gov/content/pub/pdf/fleo.04.pdf, accessed 9 November 2010. For more information on this agency, consult its webpage at http://www.cbp.gov, accessed 9 November 2010.

9. Secure Fence Act of 2006, Public Law 109–367 (2006).

10. "Budget Cut for Fence on Border," *New York Times* (17 March 2010), p. 12.

11. "National Guard Will Be Deployed To Aid At Border," *New York Times* (26 May 2010), p. 1; "Obama Signs Border Bill to Increase Surveillance," *New York Times* (14 August 2010), p. 8.

12. Pew Hispanic Center, "U.S. Unauthorized Immigration Flows Are Down Sharply Since Mid-Decade," http://pewhispanic.org/reports/report.php?ReportID=126, accessed 22 December 2010.

13. Natasha A. Frost et al., *Contemporary Issues in Criminal Justice Policy: Policy Proposals from the American Society of Criminology Conference* (Belmont, CA: Cengage Wadsworth, 2010), pp. 193–250.

14. "Arizona Enacts Stringent Law on Immigration," *New York Times* (24 April 2010), p. 1.

15. Ibid. The Arizona legislation is Senate Bill 1070, signed by the governor on 23 April 2010. To read the complaint, access the website of the Mexican American Legal Defense and Educational Fund (MALDEF), http://maldef.org/news/releases/maldef_and_other_civil_rights_05172010/, accessed 9 November 2010.

16. See *United States of America v. State of Arizona,* 703 F.Supp. 2d 980 (D.Ariz. 2010), reversed or upheld, 9th. Cir. 2010 (or 2011). The preliminary injunction covers Ariz. Rev. Stat, Sections 11-1051(B), 13-1509, 13-2928(c)), and 13-388(A)(5) (2010).

17. The quotation is from "Supreme Court to Hear Challenge to a 2007 Arizona Immigration Law," (30 June 2010), http://www.abajournal.com, accessed 9 November 2010. The case is *Arizona Contrs. Ass'n. v. Napolitano,* 526 F.Supp.2d 968 (D.Ariz. 2007), cert. granted, *Chamber of Commerce of the United States v. Candelaria,* 130 S.Ct. 3498 (2010).

18. *Fernandez-Vargas v. Gonzales,* 549 U.S. 30 (2006).

19. *Lopez v. Gonzales,* 549 U.S. 47 (2006).

20. *Carachuri-Rosendo v. Holder,* 130 S.Ct. 2577 (2010). The applicable federal statutes are USCS, Title 8, Section 1229b(a)(3) and USCS, Title 8, Section 1101(a)(43) (2010). The federal Controlled Substances Act is codified at USCS, Title 18, Section 924(c)(2) (2010).

21. Robert Sampson, "Open Doors Don't Invite Criminals: Is Increased Immigration Behind the Drop in Crime?" *New York Times* (11 March 2006), p. 27.

22. John Hagan et al., "The Symbolic Violence of the Crime-Immigration Nexus: Migrant Mythologies in the Americas," *Criminology and Public Policy* 7, no. 1 (February 2008): 95–112; quotation is on p. 107.

23. Laura J. Hickman and Marika J. Suttorp, "Are Deportable Aliens a Unique Threat to Public Safety? Comparing the Recidivism of Deportable and Nondeportable Aliens," *Crime and Public Policy* 7, no. 1 (February 2008): 59–92; quotation is on p. 59.

24. For information on the number of law enforcement officers at your campus, check http://www2.fbi.gov/ucr/cius2009/data/table_79.html, accessed 9 November 2010, and click on your state.

25. "Plan Would Ease Privacy Rules in Wake of Virginia Tech Shootings," *Criminal Justice Newsletter* (1 April 2008), p. 1. The statutes at issue are: the Health Insurance Portability and Accountability Act (HIPAA) of 1996, Pub. L. 104-191 and the Family Educational Rights and Privacy Act (FERPA) (also known as the Buckley Amendment), USCS, Title 20, Section 1232g (2010).

26. Robert C. Davis et al., *An Assessment of the Preparedness of Large Retail Malls to Prevent and Respond to Terrorist Attack,* National Institute of Justice, http://www.ncjrs.gov/pdffiles1/nij/grants/216641.pdf, accessed 9 November 2010.

27. William C. Cunningham et al., *Private Security: Patterns and Trends* (Washington, D.C.: U.S. Department of Justice, August 1991), pp. 1, 2.

28. See William C. Cunningham and Todd H. Taylor, "Ten Years of Growth in Law Enforcement and Private Security Relationships," *The Police Chief* 1 (June 1983): 30, 31.

29. "Not Just for Celebrities: Private Security Service," *New York Times* (7 March 2004), p. 8.

30. Joseph Ricci, Executive Director National Association of Security Companies, statement before the House Homeland Security Committee, 1 May 2007, *CQ Congressional Testimony*. See also the company's web page, http://www.nasco.org, accessed 9 November 2010.

31. Cunningham et al., *Private Security,* pp. 3, 4.

32. "Alarms Without the Burglars Put Strain on Police Budgets," *New York Times* (17 January 2003), p. 1, referring to a study by the U.S. Department of Justice.

33. "Hired Guns Help Wage War in Iraq," *The Advertiser* (Australia) (6 October 2007), p. 72. See also "Former Blackwater Employees Accuse Security Contractor of Defrauding Government," *Washington Post* (12 February 2010), n.p.

34. "Federal Prosecutors Indict 5 Ex-Officials of Blackwater," *New York Times* (17 April 2010), p. 8; "Blackwater Reaches $42 Million Settlement with U.S. over Export Violations," *New York Times* (21 August 2010), p. 8.

35. Federal Bureau of Investigation, *Uniform Crime Reports: Crime in the United States, 2009,* http://www2.fbi.gov/ucr/cius2009/data/table_74.html, accessed 9 November 2010.

36. See Arthur Niederhoffer, *Behind the Shield: The Police in Urban Society* (New York: Doubleday, 1969).

37. For an earlier analysis of cynicism among police chiefs, see John P. Crank et al., "Cynicism Among Police Chiefs," *Justice Quarterly* 3 (September 1986): 343–352.

38. Bruce N. Carpenter and Susan M. Raza, "Personality Characteristics of Police Applicants: Comparisons Across Subgroups and with Other Populations," *Journal of Police Science and Administration* 15 (March 1987): 16.

39. Michael K. Brown, *Working the Street: Police Discretion and the Dilemmas of Reform* (New York: Russell Sage, 1981), pp. xii, 7.

40. David L. Carter et al., *The State of Police Education: Policy Direction for the 21st Century* (Washington, D.C.: Police Executive Research Forum, 1989), p. 15.

41. Elizabeth Burbeck and Adrian Furnham, "Police Officer Selection: A Critical Review of the Literature," *Journal of Police Science and Administration* 13 (March 1985): 62.

42. Agnes L. Baro and David Burlingame, "Law Enforcement and Higher Education: Is There an Impasse?" *Journal of Criminal Justice Education* 10 (Spring 1999): 57–74; quotation is on p. 70.

43. "Out of the Blue: Six Senior Officers Leave Plano Force: City Gears Up Recruiting Effort to Fill Shoes of Law Enforcement Veterans," *Dallas Morning News* (3 February 2006), p. 1B.

44. Plano Police Department, http://www.plano.gov/Departments/ Police/Employment/, accessed 9 November 2010.

45. *City of Canton, Ohio v. Harris*, 489 U.S. 378 (1989).

46. Nicholas Alex, *Black in Blue: A Study of the Negro Policeman* (New York: Appleton-Century-Crofts, 1969).

47. Christopher Cooper, "An Afrocentric Perspective on Policing," in Roger G. Dunham and Geoffrey P. Alpert, *Critical Issues in Policing: Contemporary Readings*, 6th ed (Long Grove, Illinois: Waveland Press, 2010), 362–386; quotation is on p. 362.

48. "Split Decision for Officers Alleging Bias in Promotions," *New York Times* (31 July 2009), p. 18.

49. "Female Police Chiefs, a Novelty No More," *New York Times* (6 April 2008), http://www.nytimes.com/2008/04/06/nyregion/ nyregionspecial2/06Rpolice.html?scp=18sq=female, accessed 9 November 2010.

50. Lynn Langton, Bureau of Justice Statistics, *Women in Law Enforcement, 1987–2008* (June 2010), pp. 1, 2, http://bjs.ojp.usdoj.gov/ content/pub/pdf/wle8708.pdf, accessed 9 November 2010.

51. Nancy L. Herrington, "Female Cops—1992," in *Critical Issues in Policing: Contemporary Readings*, 3d ed., ed. Roger G. Dunham and Geoffrey P. Alpert (Prospect Heights, IL: Waveland Press, 1997), pp. 385–390; quotations are on p. 388.

52. Susan E. Martin, "Women Officers on the Move," in *Critical Issues in Policing: Contemporary Readings,* 5th ed., ed. Roger G. Dunham and Geoffrey P. Alpert (Long Grove, IL: Waveland Press, 2005), pp. 350–371; quotations are on pp. 362, 368.

53. Merry Morash et al., "Workplace Problems in Police Departments and Methods of Coping: Women at the Intersection," in *Rethinking Gender, Crime, and Justice*, ed. Claire M. Renzetti et al. (Los Angeles: Roxbury, 2006), pp. 213–227; quotation is on p. 216.

54. National Center for Women and Policing, *Equality Denied: The Status of Women in Policing: 2001*, pp. 4–5, http://www.womenand ppolicing.org/PDF/2002_Status_Report.pdf, accessed 9 November 2010.

55. Karin Montejo, "Women in Police Command Positions," in *Critical Issues in Policing*, ed. Dunham and Alpert, 6th ed, pp. 387–404; quotation is on p. 400.

56. "Sense of Urgency Needed in Reforming Detroit Police," *Detroit News* (17 July 2004), p. 7D; "Shattering the Blue Glass Ceiling: Women Make Gains in Police Work Statewide," *Detroit Free Press* (26 January 2009), p. 1.

57. "Calling for More Female Police, UN Officer Welcomes New Pact with INTERPOL," UN News Centre, http://www.un.org/apps/news/story. asp?NewsID=32634&CR=police&CR1=, accessed 9 November 2010.

58. *Atwater v. City of Lago Vista*, 532 U.S. 318 (2001).

59. Herbert L. Packer, *The Limits of the Criminal Sanction* (Stanford, CA: Stanford University Press, 1968), p. 283.

60. See James Q. Wilson and George L. Kelling, "Police and Neighborhood Safety: Broken Windows," *Atlantic Monthly* 249 (March 1982): 28–38. For a critical analysis of this work, see Samuel Walker, "'Broken Windows' and Fractured History: The Use and Misuse of History in Recent Police Patrol Analysis," reprinted in *Critical Issues in Policing*, 6th ed, ed. Dunham and Alpert, pp. 419–431; originally published in *Justice Quarterly* 1 (1984): 57–90.

61. Judith A. Greene, "Zero Tolerance: A Case Study of Police Policies and Practices in New York City," *Crime and Delinquency* 45 (April 1999): 171–187, quotation is on p. 171.

62. Richard Rosenfeld et al., "The Impact of Order-Maintenance Policing on New York City Homicide and Robbery Rates: 1988-2001," *Criminology* 45, no. 2 (May 2007): 355–384.

63. Steven F. Messner et al., "Policing, Drugs, and the Homicide Decline in New York City in the 1990s," *Criminology* 45, no. 2 (May 2007): 385–414.

64. James Q. Wilson, *Varieties of Police Behavior: The Management of Law and Order in Eight Communities* (Cambridge, MA: Harvard University Press, 1968), p. 21. For a discussion of Wilson's definition and its modern counterpart, see Wesley G. Skogan, "Broken Windows: Why-and How-We Should Take Them Seriously," *Criminology and Public Policy* 7, no. 2 (April 2008): 195–202.

65. See George L. Kelling, "Order Maintenance, the Quality of Urban Life, and Police: A Line of Argument," in *Police Leadership in America: Crisis and Opportunity*, ed. William A. Geller (Chicago: American Bar Foundation, 1985), p. 297.

66. Carl B. Klockars, "Order Maintenance, the Quality of Urban Life, and Police: A Different Line of Argument," in *Police Leadership in America*, ed. Geller, p. 316.

67. Todd Armstrong and Charles Katz, "Further Evidence on the Discriminant Validity of Perceptual Incivilities Measures," *Justice Quarterly* 27, no. 2 (April 2010): 280–304; quotation is on p. 281.

68. See Urban Institute Justice Policy Center, *Prisoner Reentry and Community Policing: Strategies for Enhancing Public Safety*, http://www.urban.org, accessed 22 June 2010.

69. Tamara D. Madensen and John E. Eck, U.S. Department of Justice, Office of Community Oriented Policing Services, *Student Party Riots* (February 2006), http://www.cops.usdoj.gov/files/RIC/ Publications/student_party.pdf, accessed 9 November 2010.

70. Graeme R. Newman, U.S. Department of Justice, Office of Community Oriented Policing Services, *The Exploitation of Trafficked Women* (February 2006), http://www.cops.usdoj.gov/files/RIC/ Publications/e02061007.pdf, accessed 9 November 2010.

71. Anthony A. Braga and Brenda J. Bond, "Policing Crime and Disorder Hot Spots: A Randomized Controlled Trial," *Criminology* 46, no. 3 (August 2008): 577–608; quotations are on pp. 597–598. With regard to focusing on "hot spots," see Stephen D. Matrofski et al., "Rethinking Policing: The Policy Implications of Hot Spots of Crime," in *Contemporary Issues in Criminal Justice Policy*, ed. Frost et al.,

pp. 251–264; in the same book these two responses: Edward A. McGuire, "Taking Implementation Seriously," pp. 265–270; Ralph B. Taylor, "Hot Spots Do Not Exist, and Four Other Fundamental Concerns About Hot Spot Policing," pp. 271–278.

72. See, for example, Charis E. Kubrin, "Making Order of Disorder: A Call for Conceptual Clarity," *Criminology and Public Policy* 7, no. 2 (May 2008): 203–214. This article also contains a concise review of the literature on recent research on order maintenance policing.

73. Jacinta M. Gau and Rod K. Brunson, "Procedural Justice and Order Maintenance Policing: A Study of Inner-City Young Men's Perceptions of Police Legitimacy," *Justice Quarterly* 27, no. 2 (April 2010): 255–279; quotation is on p. 255.

74. Kubrin, "Making Order of Disorder," p. 209, emphasis in the original. See this article for examples of this approach.

75. Kelly Dedel, U.S. Department of Justice, Office of Community Oriented Policing Services, *Juvenile Runaways* (February 2006), http://www.cops.usdoj.gov/files/RIC/Publications/e12051223.pdf, accessed 9 November 2010.

76. See the President's Commission on Law Enforcement and the Administration of Justice, *Task Force Report: The Police* (Washington, D.C.: U.S. Government Printing Office, 1967).

77. John D. Reitzel et al., "Problem-Oriented Policing," in *Critical Issues in Policing*, 6th ed., ed. Dunham and Alpert, pp. 450–462.

78. Herman Goldstein, "Improving Policing: A Problem-Oriented Approach," *Crime and Delinquency* 25 (1979): 236–258. See also Goldstein, *Problem-Oriented Policing* (Philadelphia: Temple University Press, 1990); Gary Cordner, "Fear of Crime and the Police: An Evaluation of a Fear-Reduction Strategy," *Journal of Police Science and Administration* 14 (1986): 223–233; John Eck and William Spelman, *Problem-Solving: Problem-Oriented Policing in Newport News* (Washington, D.C.: Police Executive Research Forum, 1987); James Q. Wilson and George L. Kelling, "Making Neighborhoods Safe," *Atlantic Monthly* (February 1989): 46–52.

79. Martin Innes, "What's Your Problem? Signal Crimes and Citizen-Focused Problem Solving," *Crime and Public Policy* 4, no. 2 (May 2005): 187–200. See this journal for additional research on POP.

80. The Violent Crime Control and Law Enforcement Act of 1994 is codified at USCS, Title 18, Section 1030 et seq. (2010).

81. George L. Kelling, *Police and Communities: The Quiet Revolution* (Washington, D.C.: U.S. Department of Justice, June 1988), p. 1.

82. Herman Goldstein, "Toward Community-Oriented Policing: Potential, Basic Requirements, and Threshold Questions," *Crime and Delinquency* 33 (January 1977): 7.

83. Office of Community Oriented Policing Services, "Message from the Director," http://www.cops.usdoj.gov/Default.asp?Item=2306, accessed 9 November 2010.

84. "Community Policing in the 1990s," *National Institute of Justice Journal* 225 (August 1992): 3.

85. George L. Kelling, National Institute of Justice, *Foot Patrol* (Washington, D.C.: U.S. Department of Justice, 1989), p. 3.

86. National Institute of Justice, *Community Policing in Seattle: A Model Partnership Between Citizens and Police* (Washington, D.C.: U.S. Department of Justice, August 1992).

87. "Community Policing in Chicago Gets High Marks from Evaluators," *Criminal Justice Newsletter* 26 (3 July 1995): 1.

88. Violent Crime Control and Law Enforcement Act of 1994, Public Law 103–322 (13 September 1994). The community policing statute, referred to as "Cops on the Beat," is codified at USCS, Title 42, Section 3796 et seq. (2010).

89. Jihong "Solomon" Zhao et al., "Funding Community Policing to Reduce Crime: Have COPS Grants Made a Difference?" *Criminology and Public Policy* 2, no. 1 (November 2002): 7–32.

90. John L. Worrall and Tomislav V. Kovandzic, "COPS Grants and Crime Revisited," *Criminology* 45, no. 1 (February 2007): 159–190; quotation is on p. 159.

91. Office of Community Oriented Policing Services, "President Obama Releases FY2011 Budget Request for the COPS Office," http://www.cops.usdoj.gov/Default.asp?Item=2359, accessed 9 November 2010.

92. P.L. 105–119 (H.R. 2267) (26 November 1979).

93. John L. Worrall, "The Effects of Local Law Enforcement Block Grants on Serious Crime," *Criminology and Public Policy* 7, no. 3 (August 2008): 32–-350; quotation is on p. 344.

94. See the following discussions: Kenneth C. Land, "Editorial Introduction: Federal Support of Local Law-Enforcement Agencies, Pooled Time-Series Designs, and the Challenges of Evaluation Research," *Criminology and Public Policy* 7, no. 3 (August 2008): 319–324; in the same journal, Alfred Blunstein, "Policy Essay: Federal Support of Local Criminal Justice Operations," 351–358; Thomas B. Marvell and Carlisle E. Moody, "Policy Essay: Can and Should Criminology Research Influence Policy?": 359–366.

95. See Wilson, *Varieties of Police Behavior*, p. 18.

96. Albert J. Reiss Jr., *The Police and the Public* (New Haven, CT: Yale University Press, 1971), pp. 63, 64, 71.

97. Richard J. Lundman, "Police Patrol Work: A Comparative Perspective," in *Police Behavior: A Sociological Perspective*, ed. Richard J. Lundman (New York: Oxford University Press, 1980), p. 55.

98. Eric J. Scott, *Calls for Service: Citizen Demand and Initial Police Response* (Washington, D.C.: U.S. Department of Justice, July 1981), p. 26.

99. Lorraine Mazerolle et al., "Managing Citizen Calls to the Police: The Impact of Baltimore's 3-1-1 Call System," *Criminology and Public Policy* 2, no. 1 (November 2002): 97–123; quotation is on p. 99.

100. Leslie W. Kennedy, "Issues in Managing Citizens' Calls to the Police," *Criminology & Public Policy* 2, no. 1 (November 2002): 125–132, quotation is on p. 126.

101. William F. Walsh, "COMPSTAT: An Analysis of an Emerging Police Managerial Paradigm," in *Critical Issues in Policing*, 6th ed., ed. Dunham and Alpert, pp. 197–211; quotation is on p. 197.

102. Walsh, "COMPSTAT," p. 202.

103. Heather MacDonald, fellow at the Manhattan Institute, "Fighting Crime Where the Criminals Are," *New York Times* (26 June 2010), p. 17.

104. Walsh, "COMPSTAT," p. 209.

105. See, for example, Richard Rosenfeld et al., "Did Ceasefire, Compstat, and Exile Reduce Homicide?" *Criminology and Public Policy* 4, no. 3 (August 2005): 419–450; James J. Willis et al., "Compstat and Bureaucracy: A Case Study of Challenges and Opportunities for Change," *Justice Quarterly* 21, no. 3 (September 2004): 463–496.

106. Bernard E. Harcourt and Jens Ludwig, "Reefer Madness: Broken Windows Policing and Misdemeanor Marijuana Arrests in New York City, 1989–2000," *Criminology and Public Policy* 6, no. 1 (February 2007) 165–182; quotation is on p. 176.

107. Christine N. Famega et al., "Managing Police Patrol Time: The Role of Supervisor Directives," *Justice Quarterly* 22, no. 4 (December 2005): 540–559.

108. Wilson, *Varieties of Police Behavior*, p. 53.

109. See Terry Eisenberg, "Job Stress and the Police Officer: Identifying Stress Reduction Techniques," in *Job Stress and the Police Officer: Identifying Stress Reduction Techniques*, ed. William H. Kroes and Joseph J. Hurrell, Proceedings of Symposium, Cincinnati, Ohio, May 8–9, 1975 (Washington, D.C.: U.S. Government Printing Office, 1975).

110. See, for example, the recently published analysis of interviews with over 500 officers conducted by Dennis J. Stevens, *Police Officer Stress: Sources and Solutions* (Upper Saddle River, NJ: Prentice-Hall, 2008).

111. Federal Bureau of Investigation, "About Law Enforcement Officers Killed and Assaulted, 2009" (September 2010), http://www2.fbi .gov/ucr/killed/2009/, accessed 9 November 2010.

112. "Woman Files Claim in Brame Case," *Seattle Post-Intelligencer* (17 July 2004), p. 3B; "Woodard's Silence Broke City Rules," *News Tribune* (Tacoma, WA) (1 March 2005), p. 1.

113. "Sherwood Officer Remembered for His Caring," *The Oregonian* (29 April 2003), p. 1B.

114. Centers for Disease Control, http://www.cdc.gov, accessed 20 May 2010.

115. "Suicide on the Force," *Newsweek* (19 March 2007), p. 14; "CHP Confronts New Danger: Suicide," *Inside Bay Area* (California) (10 January 2007), n.p.

116. National Center for Women and Policing, "Police Family Violence Fact Sheet," http://www.womenandpolicing.org/violenceFS.asp, accessed 9 November 2010.

117. Victor E. Kappeler et al., "Breeding Deviant Conformity: The Ideology and Culture of Police," in *Critical Issues in Policing*, 6th ed., ed. Dunham and Alpert, pp. 265–291; quotation is on p. 267.

118. Peter J. Mercier, "Review of John P. Crank, *Understanding Police Culture*," *American Journal of Criminal Justice* 24 (Fall 1999): 153.

119. "A Silent Fraternity: Officers with H.I.V.," *New York Times* (2 August 2000), p. 23.

120. Michael J. Lynch and W. Byron Groves, *A Primer in Radical Criminology*, 2d ed. (New York: Harrow & Heston, 1989), p. 87.

121. Cal Pen Code, Section 645(e) (1982).

122. *Kolender v. Lawson*, 461 U.S. 352, 358 (1983).

123. *Whren v. United States*, 517 U.S. 806 (1996); *Ornelas et al. v. United States*, 517 U.S. 690 (1996).

124. *Maryland v. Wilson*, 519 U.S. 408 (1997); *Pennsylvania v. Mimms*, 434 U.S. 106 (1977).

125. *Richards v. Wisconsin*, 520 U.S. 385 (1997); *Wilson v. Arkansas*, 514 U.S. 927 (1995).

126. *United States v. Ramirez*, 523 U.S. 65 (1998). The federal no-knock statute is codified at U.S. Code, Title 18, Section 3109 (2010).

127. *United States v. Banks*, 540 U.S. 31 (2003).

128. *Mallory v. United States*, 354 U.S. 449, 456 (1957).

129. Richard Spano, "Concerns About Safety, Observer Sex, and the Decision to Arrest: Evidence of Reactivity in a Large-Scale Observational Study of Police," *Criminology* 41, no. 3 (August 2003): 909–932.

130. Douglas A. Smith, "The Neighborhood Context of Police Behavior," in *Communities and Crime*, ed. Albert J. Reiss Jr. and Michael Tonry (Chicago: University of Chicago Press, 1986), pp. 313–341.

131. Donald Black, "The Social Organization of Arrest," *Stanford Law Review* 23 (June 1971): 1104–1109.

132. Robin Shepard Engel et al., "Further Exploration of the Demeanor Hypothesis: The Interaction Effects of Suspects' Characteristics and Demeanor on Police Behavior," *Justice Quarterly* 17 (June 2000): 235-259.

133. See Patricia Warren et al., "Driving While Black: Bias Processes and Racial Disparity in Police Stops," *Criminology* 44, no. 2 (August 2006): 709-737.

134. *United States v. Montero-Camargo*, 208 F.3d 1122 (9th Cir. 2000), *cert. denied sub nom.*, 531 U.S. 889 (2000).

135. Ronald Weitzer and Steven A. Tuch, "Perceptions of Racial Profiling: Race, Class, and Personal Experience," *Criminology* 40, no. 2 (May 2002): 435–456; quotation is on p. 435.

136. Ronald L. Akers and Christine S. Sellers, *Criminological Theories: Introduction, Evaluation, and Application*, 5th ed. (New York: Oxford University Press, 2009), p. 225.

137. Geoffrey P. Alpert et al., "Investigating Racial Profiling by the Miami-Dade Police Department: A Multi-Method Approach," *Criminology and Public Policy* 6, no. 1 (February 2007): 25–56.

138. For a review of the literature, see Rod K. Brunson, "'Police Don't Like Black People': African American Young Men's Accumulated Police Experiences," *Criminology and Public Policy* 6, no. 1 (February 2007): 71–102.

139. "Number of People Stopped by Police Soars in New York: Blacks Represent More Than Half of All Cases," *New York Times* (3 February 2007), p. 10.

140. "Minorities Frisked More, but Arrest Rate Is Same," *New York Times* (13 May 2010), p. 22.

141. Matthew R. Durose et al., Bureau of Justice Statistics, *Contacts Between Police and the Public, 2005* (April 2007), http://bjs.ojp .usdoj.gov/content/pub/pdf/cpp05.pdf, accessed 9 November 2010.

142. Michael R. Smith et al., "Differential Suspicion: Theory Specification and Gender Effects in the Traffic Stop Context," *Justice Quarterly* 23, no. 2 (June 2006): 271–295; quotation is on p. 271.

143. Warren et al., "Driving While Black," p. 710.

144. David A. Harris, "The Importance of Research on Race and Policing: Making Race Salient to Individuals and Institutions Within Criminal Justice," *Criminology and Public Policy* 6, no. 1 (February 2007): 5–24; quotation is on p. 16.

145. 2010 Bill Tracking HR 465748 (2010).

146. "Legal Settlement Reached in Racial Profiling Lawsuit," *Criminal Justice Newsletter* (15 April 2008), pp. 6–7.

147. Lorie Fridell and Michael Scott, "Law Enforcement Agency Responses to Racially Biased Policing and the Perceptions of Its Practice," in *Critical Issues in Policing,* 6th ed., ed. Dunham and Alpert, pp. 343–360; quotation is on p. 359. For a more thorough discussion, see Fridell, *By the Numbers: A Guide to Analyzing Race Data from Vehicle Stops* (Washington, D.C.: PERF, 2004).

148. *Tennessee v. Garner,* 471 U.S. 1 (1985).

149. "High Profile Lawyer Team in Louima Brutality Suit Is Raising Questions of Overkill," *New York Times* (9 November 1997), p. 17; "Five Cops Face Fed Trial in Louima Attack," *Daily News* (New York) (19 September 1998), p. 10; "Conviction Voided on Second Officer in Louima Attack," *New York Times* (1 March 2002), p. 1.

150. Matthew J. Hickman, Bureau of Justice Statistics, *Citizen Complaints About Police Use of Force* (June 2006), p. 1, http://bjs.ojp.usdoj.gov/content/pub/pdf/ccpuf.pdf, accessed 9 November 2010.

151. David A. Klinger and Rod K. Brunson, "Police Officers' Perceptual Distortions During Lethal Force Situations: Informing the Reasonableness Standard," *Criminology and Public Policy* 8, no. 1 (February 2009): 117–140.

152. Geoffrey P. Alpert, "Interpreting Police Use of Force and the Construction of Reality," *Criminology and Public Policy* 8, no. 1 (February 2009): 111–115; quotations are on pp. 111 and 113. See also the following articles in that journal: Robin S. Engel and Michael R. Smith, "Policy Essay: Perceptual Distortion and Reasonableness During Policy Shootings," pp. 141–152; Kenneth J. Novak, "Policy Essay: Reasonable Officers, Public Perceptions, and Policy Challenges," pp. 153–162; William Terrill, "Policy Essay: The Elusive Nature of Reasonableness," pp. 163–172.

153. For a discussion, see Robin S. Engel, "Editorial Introduction: Revisiting Critical Issues in Police Use-of-Force Research," *Criminology and Public Policy* 7, no. 4 (November 2008): 557–562. See also the following articles in that journal: Matthew J. Hickman et al., "Toward a National Estimate of Police Use of Nonlethal Force," pp. 563–604; David A. Klinger, "Policy Essay: On the Importance of Sound Measures of Forceful Police Actions," pp. 605–618; Michael R. Smith, "Policy Essay: Toward a National Use-of-Force Data Collection System: One Small (and Focused) Step Is Better Than a Giant Leap," pp. 619–628.

154. Lorie A. Fridell, "Use-of-Force Policy, Policy Enforcement, and Training," in *Critical Issues in Policing*, 6th ed., ed. Dunham

and Alpert, pp. 513–531; quotation is on p. 513. See also the following articles in that reader: James J. Fyfe, "The Split-Second Syndrome and Other Determinants of Police Violence," pp. 466–480; Jeffrey J. Noble and Geoffrey P. Alpert, "State-Created Danger: Should Police Officers Be Accountable for Reckless Tactical Decision Making?" pp. 481-495; Kenneth Adams, "What We Know About Police Use of Force," pp. 496–512.

155. "New Pursuit Rules Held a Week: Police Intend to Work Out Kinks Before Changing Policy," *Los Angeles Daily News* (3 May 2003), p. 3N.

156. "New Technology to End High-Speed Police Chases," *CBS News Transcripts: The Early Show* (9 October 2007). 7 AM.

157. "To Catch a Thief," *Grand Rapid Press* (Michigan) (20 October 2009), p. 16.

158. See, for example, Lawrence W. Sherman, *Policing Domestic Violence: Experiments and Dilemmas* (New York: Free Press, 1992); Lawrence W. Sherman and R. A. Berk, "The Specific Deterrent Effects of Arrest for Domestic Assault," *American Sociological Review* 57 (1992): 680–690; Sherman et al., *The Milwaukee Domestic Violence Experiment. Final Report* (Washington, D.C.: Crime Control Institute, 1990).

159. Christopher D. Maxwell et al., "The Preventive Effects of Arrest on Intimate Partner Violence: Research, Policy and Theory," *Criminology and Public Policy* 2, no. 1 (November 2002): 51–79; quotations are on pp. 51–52.

160. For a review of the studies, see Meda Chesney-Lind, "Criminalizing Victimization: The Unintended Consequences of Pro-Arrest Policies for Girls and Women," *Criminology & Public Policy* 2, no. 1 (November 2002): 81–90; quotation is on p. 82.

161. Drew Humphries, "No Easy Answers: Public Policy, Criminal Justice, and Domestic Violence," *Criminology and Public Policy* 2, no. 1 (November 2002): 91–95.

162. *Results from an Elder Abuse Prevention Experiment in New York City* (Rockville, MD: National Criminal Justice Reference Service), referred to in "Study Suggests Intervention Increases Chance of Elder Abuse," *Criminal Justice Newsletter* 31, no. 24 (11 January 2002): 6.

163. Eve S. Buzawa and Carl G. Buzawa, "Traditional and Innovative Police Responses to Domestic Violence," in *Critical Issues in Policing*, 6th ed., ed. Dunham and Alpert, pp. 137–167; quotation are on pp. 160, 161.

164. "Two Officers Are Killed in Texas, *New York Times,* Late Edition (10 September 2007), p. 21.

165. Lawrence W. Sherman, ed., *Police Corruption: A Sociological Perspective* (New York: Doubleday, 1974), p. 6.

166. *The Knapp Commission Report on Police Corruption* (New York: Braziller, 1972), p. 260.

167. "New York Officers Charged with Running Drug Ring," *New York Times* (8 May 1992), p. 14.

168. "New York Officers Held in Huge Theft of Handbags," *New York Times* (10 July 1992), p. 16.

169. "Official Says Police Corruption Is Hard to Stop," *New York Times* (20 September 1992), p. 6.

170. "Police Corruption in New York Found Rarer but More Virulent," *Criminal Justice Newsletter* 25 (15 July 1994): 1, reporting on the Mollen Commission report released 7 July 1994.

171. James F. Fyfe and Robert Kane, National Institute of Justice, *Bad Cops: A Study of Career-Ending Misconduct Among New York Police Officers* (September 2006), http://www.ncjrs.gov/pdffiles1/nij/grants/215795.pdf, accessed 9 November 2010.

172. "Kerik Gets 4 Years in Prison for Tax Fraud and Lies," *New York Times* (19 February 2010), p. 17.

173. "Los Angeles Settles Lawsuit Against Police," *New York Times* (22 November 2000), p. 18; "Bad Cops: Rafael Perez's Testimony on Police Misconduct Ignited the Biggest Scandal in the History of the L.A.P.D.: Is It the Real Story?" *The New Yorker* (21 May 2001), p. 60; "Bratton Oks Task Force for Reforms," *Los Angeles Times* (19 July 2006), p. 4B.

174. "Rampart Officers' Civil Award Upheld," *Los Angeles Times* (15 July 2008), p. 1B. The case is *Harper v. City of Los Angeles*, 533 F.3d 1010 (9th Cir. 2008).

175. "Officials Investigate Broad Corruption in Atlanta Police Dept.," *New York Times* (27 April 2007), p. 16; "Police Oversight Panelists Go West," *Atlanta Journal-Constitution* (30 September 2007), p. 14D.

176. Wilson, *Varieties of Police Behavior*, pp. 140–226.

177. Sherman, *Police Corruption,* pp. 1-39; 196–201.

178. Jerome H. Skolnick, *Justice Without* Trial, 2d ed. (New York: Wiley, 1975), pp. 238–239.

179. James Leo Walsh, "Professionalism and the Police: The Cop as Medical Student," *American Behavioral Scientist* 13 (May/August 1970): 705–725.

180. Peter K. Manning, "The Police: Mandate, Strategies, and Appearances," in *Crime and Justice in America: A Critical Understanding,* ed. Jack D. Douglas (Boston: Little, Brown, 1974), pp. 171, 186–191.

181. U.S. Commission on Civil Rights, *Who Is Guarding the Guardians?* p. 2.

182. See Paul S. Benson, "Political Alienation and Public Satisfaction with Police Services," *Pacific Sociological Review* 24 (January 1981): 45–64.

183. Cited in Roger G. Dunham and Geoffrey P. Alpert, "The Foundation of the Police Role in Society," in *Critical Issues in Policing*, 6th ed., ed. Dunham and Alpert, pp. 3–16; material referred to is on p. 7.

184. Cheryl Maxson et al., *Factors That Influence Public Opinion of the Police* (Rockville, MD: National Criminal Justice Reference Service, 2003).

185. U.S. Commission on Civil Rights, *Who Is Guarding the Guardians*? p. 163.

186. See Jack R. Greene, "Police and Community Relations: Where Have We Been and Where Are We Going?" in *Critical Issues in*

Policing, 2d ed., ed. Roger G. Dunham and Geoffrey P. Alpert (Prospect Heights, IL: Waveland Press, 1993), pp. 349–368.

187. For a recent analysis of the role of citizen complaints in controlling police conduct, see Jeff Rojek et al., "Addressing Police Misconduct: The Role of Citizen Complaints," in *Critical Issues in Policing*, 6th ed., ed. Dunham and Alpert, pp. 292–312.

188. See USCS, Title 42, Sections 14141–14142 (2010).

189. "Justice Department to Review New Orleans's Troubled Police Force," *New York Times* (18 May 2010), p. 14.

190. "Landrieu Asks Justice to Evaluate NOPD: Request Could Lead to Federal Oversight in Some Areas," *Times-Picayune* (New Orleans, LA) (6 May 2010), p. 1; "Editorial: A Needed Partnership," *Times-Picayune* (New Orleans, LA) (6 May 2010), p. 6B. See also "Justice Department to Review New Orleans's Troubled Police Force."

191. Editorial, "Cleaning up the Force," *Times-Picayune* (New Orleans) (22 December 2010), p. 3B.

192. "Feds Shape Up Pittsburgh Department: After Five Years of Oversight, Residents Say Cops More Humane," *Detroit News* (29 June 2003), p. 11.

193. "Detroit Cop Reform Tab May Top $100 Million," *Detroit News* (29 June 2003), p. 1; "Detroit Police Reform Failing," *Detroit News* (19 January 2006), p. 1B; "Detroit Cops Struggle to Meet Goals for Reform," *Detroit News* (21 October 2007), p. 1.

194. "Police Monitor Cites Improvements," *Detroit Free Press* (16 April 2010), p. 8; "Detroit Police Fixes Lagging, New Monitor Says, *Detroit News* (16 January 2010), p. 1.

195. Jeff Rojek et al., "Addressing Police Misconduct: The Role of Citizen Complaints," in *Critical Issues in Policing*, 6th ed., ed. Dunham and Alpert, pp. 29–2-312.

196. *Weeks v. United States*, 232 U.S. 383 (1914); *Mapp v. Ohio*, 367 U.S. 643 (1961).

197. Stephen H. Sachs, "The Exclusionary Rule: A Prosecutor's Defense," *Criminal Justice Ethics* 1 (Summer/Fall 1982): 31, 32. This journal contains a symposium on the pros and cons of the exclusionary rule and is an excellent source on the topic.

198. *Olmstead v. United States*, 277 U.S. 438, 485 (1928), Justice Brandeis, dissenting.

199. *Massachusetts v. Sheppard,* 468 U.S. 981 (1984). See also *United States v. Leon*, decided the same day, 468 U.S. 897 (1984).

200. *Groh v. Ramirez*, 540 U.S. 551 (2004).

201. See *State v. Novembrino*, 491 A.2d 37 (N.J.Sup. 1985).

202. *Nix v. Williams*, 467 U.S. 431 (1984); *New York v. Quarles*, 467 U.S. 649 (1984).

203. *Maryland v. Garrison*, 480 U.S. 79 (1987).

204. *Arizona v. Youngblood,* 488 U.S. 51 (1988).

205. *Arizona v. Fulminante*, 499 U.S. 279 (1991).

206. "Los Angeles Settles Lawsuit Against Police," *New York Times* (22 November 2000), p. 18.

207. *Canton v. Harris*, 489 U.S. 378 (1989).

208. *Jackson v. Brister*, 838 So.2d 274 (Miss. 2003).

209. *Pearson v. Callahan*, 129 S.Ct. 808 (2009).

210. Robert W. Taylor and Jennifer Elaine Davis, "Intelligence-Led Policing and Fusion Centers," in *Critical Issues in Policing*, 6th ed., ed. Dunham and Alpert, pp. 224–244; quotation is on p. 224.

211. National Commission on Terrorist Attacks upon the United States, *The 9/11 Commission Report* (Washington, D.C.: U.S. Government Printing Office, 2004).

CHAPTER 13

Court Systems

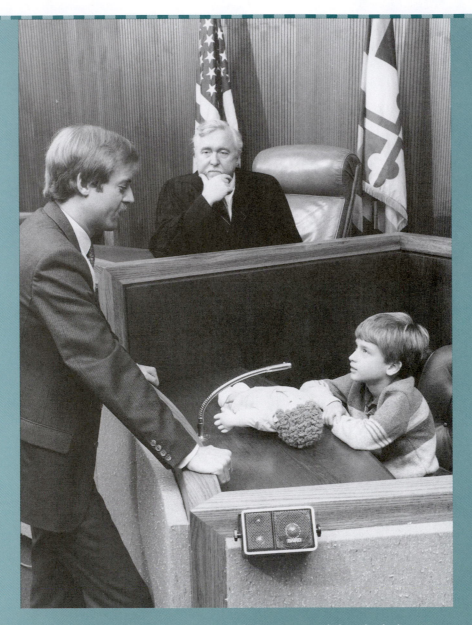

Young children may be afraid to testify in court, and they lack the experience and knowledge required for some kinds of statements, especially in sexual abuse cases. One way prosecutors have dealt with these problems is to use anatomically correct dolls, which enable children to demonstrate what allegedly happened.

KEY TERMS

appeal
appellant
appellee
capital punishment
certiorari
community service
corporal punishment
defense attorney
deferred prosecution
determinate sentence
dual court system
fine
good-time credit
indeterminate sentence
judge
judicial review
juvenile delinquent
mediation
pardon
parens patriae
plea bargaining
presumptive sentencing
preventive detention
prosecuting attorney
public defender
restitution
sentence
sentence disparity

INTRODUCTION

This chapter analyzes criminal court systems. A general overview is followed by a focus on four specialized courts: juvenile, domestic violence, drug, and mental health. The role of lawyers in criminal justice systems includes a more specific discussion of the roles of the prosecution and the defense in criminal cases. The next step, pretrial processes, leads to the topics of pretrial release, bail, and plea bargaining. In the section dealing with the trial of a criminal case, the right to a speedy trial and the role of the judge and jury are presented. The analysis of sentencing focuses on the current sentencing issues of alleged disparity, three strikes and you're out, the crack/ powder cocaine sentencing differentials, race and ethnicity discrimination, gender discrimination, and the control of sentence disparity. This latter topic explores federal sentencing guidelines and the recent U.S. Supreme Court cases dealing with them.

The increasing attention given to capital punishment, especially to the persons released from death row after DNA tests or other evidence revealed their innocence, warrants a focus on this topic. That section details the data on capital punishment, discusses the legal issues, and explores the question of whether capital punishment is a deterrent. It also examines the debate concerning whether persons should be given the death penalty for murders they committed as juveniles. Finally, it looks at the future of capital punishment.

In the last three sections of the chapter, attention is given to the appeals process in criminal courts, to court congestion and some solutions to the problem, and to courts and violence.

Courts may be considered the crux of criminal justice systems. Within them, pretrial, trial, and posttrial motions, petitions, appeals, and other processes, such as plea bargaining and sentencing, occur. Some of these processes involve not only the legal profession and law enforcement but also the public.

The importance of courts was emphasized by U.S. Supreme Court Chief Justice Earl Warren when he declared in the late 1950s: "The delay and the choking congestion in federal courts . . . have created a crucial problem for constitutional government in the United States. . . . [These delays are] compromising the quantity and quality of justice available to the individual citizen, and, in so doing, . . . leav[ing] vulnerable throughout the world the reputation of the United States."[1]

Since the 1950s, the situation has deteriorated in both state and federal courts at trial and appellate levels. Court congestion results in delayed trials. Many accused who are not released before trial endure long jail terms in overcrowded facilities. Because their court-appointed attorneys are so busy, defendants may not see them during that period. The accused are left with many questions, no answers, and a long wait under stressful conditions. Those who are incarcerated before trial may face more obstacles in preparation for trial and in the reactions of the juries at trial.

The injustices created by an overworked court, in which most cases must be decided quickly and with little individualized attention, are obvious, as is the lack of preparation time available to overworked prosecutors and defense attorneys. The inefficiency and injustice of crowded court dockets and delayed trials project to the public a tainted image of criminal justice systems.

The intricate details of court systems are not presented here; this discussion is a simple overview of the general structure of federal and state courts.

Court Systems: An Overview

The framers of the U.S. Constitution established three branches of government—legislative, executive, and judicial. Despite some overlap, these branches are separate and independent, at least in theory. Courts are part of the judicial branch and are empowered to hear and decide legal issues. Some courts have the power to determine whether acts of the other two branches of government, the executive and the legislative, fall within constitutional provisions. This power of **judicial review**, which was established by the U.S. Supreme Court in its historic 1803 decision, *Marbury v. Madison*,[2] represents the courts' greatest authority. The highest court of each state determines the constitutionality of that state's laws according to its own constitution. The U.S. Supreme Court decides whether statutes, lower court decisions, or executive acts violate the U.S. Constitution or federal statutes.

An understanding of some legal terms and concepts is necessary for an analysis of how courts function. One

In this typical courtroom scene of a jury trial, the jury is to the right, the defense and prosecution tables are in the center, and the judge is at the rear left. The witness is to the judge's left, and the court reporter is in front of the witness. The bailiff stands by the jury box. An attorney is questioning the witness.

of the most important terms is *jurisdiction*, which refers to the power of the court to hear and decide a case. Jurisdiction may be limited by subject matter. For example, some courts may hear only domestic dispute cases, such as divorce, child custody, or adoption. Jurisdiction may be limited by type of case, such as civil or criminal. In criminal courts, jurisdiction may be limited by whether the case involves a felony, a misdemeanor, or a lesser act, such as a violation. Jurisdiction may also be limited in terms of persons wishing to bring an action, or it may be limited by geographic area.

Jurisdiction may be original, concurrent, exclusive, or appellate. *Original jurisdiction* refers to the court that has the power to hear the case first—that is, the court that may try the facts of the case. If more than one court has jurisdiction, the courts have *concurrent jurisdiction*. When only one court can hear a particular case, that court has *exclusive jurisdiction*. Most decisions of lower courts may be appealed; the courts that have the power to hear and decide those appeals have *appellate jurisdiction*.

Because it is thought that the law needs stability, most courts follow a rule of *stare decisis*, which means they abide by, or adhere to, previously decided cases. The law is flexible, too, and courts may overrule (specifically or by implication) their previous decisions. It is important to distinguish between the *rule* of the court and the *dicta* of the judges or justices. At times, justices or judges expound on issues that are not part of the court's ruling. Even if these comments represent the opinion of a majority of the court, they must be recognized as *dicta* and not confused with the *holding* or *rule of law* of the case, which is based solely on the facts at issue in that particular case. For this reason, it is necessary to read cases carefully.

Courts decide legal issues utilizing a process called *legal reasoning*, which involves a case-by-case analysis. A decided case (precedent) is analyzed, and the facts of a

pending case are applied to it. It is argued that the facts at issue are similar enough that the holding of the precedent case should apply or dissimilar enough that it should not apply. Since the facts differ from case to case, *legal reasoning* becomes a crucial part of the legal process.

In announcing decisions, U.S. appellate courts usually give written opinions, which may be accompanied by *dissenting opinions* provided by the judges or justices who did not vote with the majority. Judges and justices who concur in the court's opinion may wish to make some additional comments. If so, they write *concurring opinions*. Some opinions are written by justices who concur with part of the court's decision and dissent from the remainder or by those who concur in the court's result but not in its reasoning.

In the United States, court decisions are recorded in official reporters. Decisions of the U.S. Supreme Court are recorded officially in the *U.S. Reports* and are cited as follows: *Gideon v. Wainwright*, 372 U.S. 335 (1963). Prior to being printed in the *U.S. Reports*, U.S. Supreme Court cases may be found in other sources, such as *U.S. Law Week* (*USLW*) and the Supreme Court Reporter (S.Ct.). The cases may be obtained through computer services shortly after the written opinion is released. As soon as a decision is announced, it becomes binding law unless otherwise noted by the court deciding the case. Decisions of the U.S. Supreme Court are binding on all federal courts and on state courts where applicable—that is, where federal statutory or constitutional rights are involved. For more information on how to read a court citation, see Appendix B.

Dual Court Systems

The United States has a **dual court system** consisting of state and federal courts, as diagrammed in Figure 13.1. State

Figure 13.1

The U.S. Dual Court System

Arrows indicate usual avenues of appeal; there may be some exceptions. State court systems are explained in more detail in Exhibit 13.1.

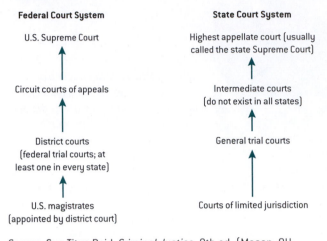

Source: Sue Titus Reid, *Criminal Justice*, 8th ed. (Mason, OH: Atomic Dog [Thomson Custom Solutions], 2008), p. 164.

crimes are prosecuted in state courts and federal crimes in federal courts. Criminal court systems differ from state to state, but all states have trial courts and appellate courts. In some states, trial courts may hear the serious cases (felonies) as well as the less serious ones (misdemeanors). In other jurisdictions, one level of courts hears felony cases, and the other hears misdemeanors. All states have appellate courts, and some states have an intermediate level of appellate courts. Others have only one court of appeals, usually called the *state Supreme Court.* Texas and Oklahoma have two highest courts of appeals, one for criminal and one for civil cases. In those two states, cases may not be appealed from the highest civil to the highest criminal courts, or vice versa.

Exhibit 13.1 contains more details on state court systems. This exhibit, a very general overview, briefly describes the structure and jurisdiction typical of each level. In addition, jurisdictions may have specialized courts, such as bankruptcy courts, probate courts, tax courts, juvenile courts, domestic violence courts, drug courts, and mental health courts. The last four of these types are discussed in this chapter because of their close relationship to criminal justice systems.

Some acts may involve a violation of both state and federal law, in which case the accused may be tried for the state crime in the state court and the federal crime in the federal court. For example, Terry L. Nichols was tried on federal charges in the federal district court in Denver, Colorado, for his role in the bombing of the U.S. federal building in Oklahoma City in 1995. He was convicted of conspiracy and involuntary manslaughter and sentenced to life without parole. Apparently in an effort to sentence Nichols to death, Oklahoma prosecutors tried him on 161 state murder charges (at a cost of over $4 million). Nichols was convicted on all of those charges, but the jury deadlocked on the death penalty. The trial judge sentenced Nichols to 161 life sentences without parole.

The federal courts established by Article III of the federal Constitution are the U.S. Supreme Court, the U.S. courts of appeals, the U.S. district courts, and bankruptcy courts. The Constitution permits Congress to establish additional courts (under Article I) that do not have full judicial power, such as the U.S. tax court, the U.S. court of military appeals, and the U.S. court of veterans' appeals.

The federal *district courts* are the trial courts in the federal system. Cases may be appealed from those courts to the *circuit courts of appeals,* which are called the U.S. courts of appeals (they also hear cases from federal administrative agencies). The highest federal court is the *U.S. Supreme Court,* basically an appellate court, although it also has limited original jurisdiction. The lower federal courts and the state courts are separate systems; a state court is not bound by the decision of a lower federal court in its district. Cases may be appealed to the U.S. Supreme Court from a state court only if a federal statutory or constitutional right is involved and the U.S. Supreme Court justices vote to hear the case. Map 13.1 indicates the geographic boundaries of the U.S. courts of appeals and U.S. district courts; thus, the Eleventh Circuit Court of Appeals has jurisdiction over Alabama, Georgia, and Florida cases. The Court of Appeals for the Federal Circuit "has nationwide jurisdiction to hear appeals in specialized cases, such as those involving patent laws and cases decided by the Court of International Trade and the Court of Federal Claims."[3]

Trial and Appellate Courts

Trial courts hear the factual evidence of a case and decide the issues of fact. These decisions may be made by a jury or by a judge if the case is tried without a jury. When a trial court has ruled against a defendant, he or she may have a right of **appeal** both in the state and in the federal court systems, although the defendant does not (except in a few specific types of cases) have the right to appeal to the highest court. Appellate courts hear and decide only a small percentage of appealed cases. These courts do not try the facts, such as those determining the defendant's guilt or innocence. In essence, they try the lower courts. The **appellant**—the defendant who was convicted at trial and is appealing that conviction—alleges errors in the trial court proceeding (e.g., hearsay evidence admitted, illegal confession admitted, minority groups excluded from the jury) and asks for a new trial or an acquittal. The **appellee**—the prosecution at trial—argues either that errors did not exist or, if they did, they were not reversible errors; that is, they did not prejudice the court against the ap-

EXHIBIT 13.1   Structure, Jurisdiction, and Function of State Court Systems

Court	Structure	Jurisdiction
Highest state appellate court (usually called the Supreme Court)	Consists of five, seven, or nine justices, who may be appointed or elected; cases decided by this court may not be appealed to the U.S. Supreme Court unless they involve a federal question, and then there is no right of appeal except in limited cases.	If there is no intermediate appellate court, defendants convicted in a general trial court will have a right to appeal to this court; if there is an intermediate appellate court, this court will have discretion to limit appeals with few exceptions such as in capital cases.
Intermediate appellate court (also called court of appeals; exists in approximately half of the states)	May have one court that hears appeals from all general trial courts or may have more than one court, each with appellate jurisdiction over a particular area of the state; usually has a panel of three judges.	Defendants convicted in general trial court have right of appeal to this level.
General trial courts (also called superior courts, circuit courts, court of common pleas)	Usually state is divided into judicial districts, with one general trial court in each district, often one per county; courts may be divided by function, such as civil, criminal, probate, domestic.	Jurisdiction to try cases usually begins where jurisdiction of lower court ends, so this court tries more serious cases; may have appellate jurisdiction over cases decided in lower courts.
Courts of limited jurisdiction (also called magistrate's courts, police courts, justice of peace courts, municipal courts)	Differs from state to state; some states divide state into districts, with each having the same type of lower court; in other states, courts may be located in political subdivisions, such as cities or townships, in which case the structure may differ from court to court; may not be a court of record, in which case the system will permit trial *de novo* in general trial court; particularly in rural areas, magistrates may not be lawyers and may work only part time.	May be limited to specific proceedings, such as initial appearance, preliminary hearing, issuing search and arrest warrants, setting bail, appointing counsel for indigent defendants; jurisdiction of cases is limited to certain types, usually the lesser criminal and civil cases, some jurisdictions may hear all misdemeanors—others are limited to misdemeanors with minor penalties.

Source: Sue Titus Reid, *Criminal Justice*, 8th ed. (Mason, OH: Atomic Dog [Thomson Custom Solutions], 2008), p. 165.

---

pellant, and therefore, the conviction should stand, and a new trial should not be granted.

The appellate court may affirm or reverse the lower court's decision. Usually, when a decision is reversed, the case is sent back for another trial (or resentencing); that is, the case is *reversed and remanded*. This does not necessarily mean that the defendant is free; in fact, in most criminal cases that are reversed and remanded, the defendant is retried and convicted. These retrials do not violate the Fifth Amendment prohibition against being tried twice for the same offense (see Appendix A). But if the defendant is found not guilty at trial, he or she may not be retried for that offense, although prosecutors might appeal the case on a point of law to get a ruling that may be of benefit in future trials.

Focus on Specialized Courts

This section focuses on four specialized courts typical of state court systems today: juvenile courts, domestic violence courts, drug courts, and mental health courts. The juvenile court has existed since 1899, when the first court was established in Illinois. Domestic violence, drug, and mental health courts are of more recent origin.

Juvenile Courts

Before looking in some detail at juvenile courts, a brief look at data is relevant. Although shooting sprees by juveniles capture the nation's attention, the facts show that juvenile crime is on the decline. The Office of Juvenile Justice and Delinquency Prevention, which is part of the U.S. Department of Justice, issued a lengthy report in 2006, reporting on trend data through 2002. We will use that report, hereafter referred to as the *OJJDP 2006 Report*, for trend data and supplement it with the 2009 *Uniform Crime Report* arrest data.[4]

The *OJJDP 2006 Report* disclosed the following, among other data:

- In 2002, the number of murders by juveniles dropped to its lowest level since 1984.
- In 2002, 1 in 12 murders involved a juvenile offender.
- The drop in minority males killing minority males with firearms drove the decline in murders by juveniles.

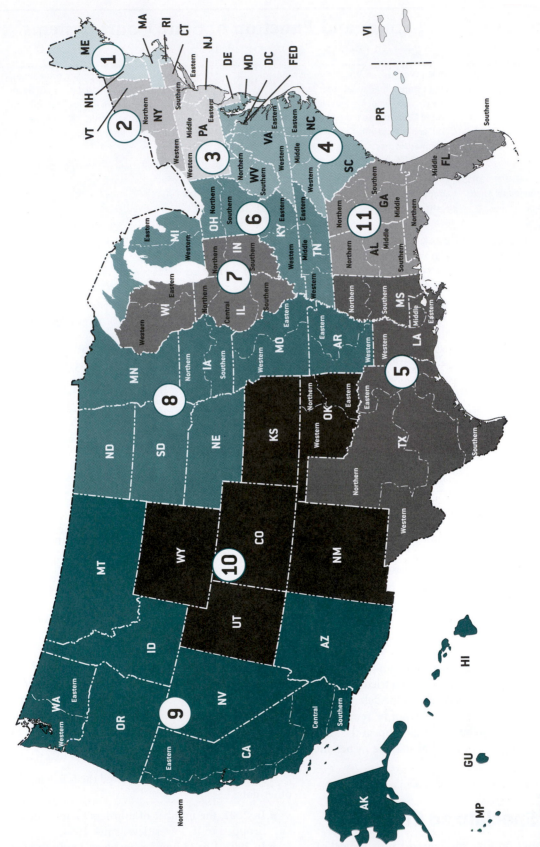

Map 13.1

Geographic Boundaries of U.S. Courts of Appeals and U.S. District Courts

Source: U.S. Courts, http://www.uscourts.gov/UScourts/images/CircuitMap.pdf, accessed 8 November 2010.

- The female proportion of youths entering the juvenile justice system for law violations has increased.
- In 2003, the juvenile violent crime arrest rate was lower than it was before its increase in the late 1980s.
- From 1998 through 2003, the juvenile arrest rate for property crimes declined sharply.
- After years of stability, the juvenile arrest rate for larceny-theft declined annually from 1995 to 2003.
- More than half of the arrests for arson in 2003 involved juveniles.
- The juvenile arrest rate for simple assault more than doubled between 1980 and 2003—up 138 percent.[5]

The *UCR* data for 2009 show that arrests of juveniles (persons under 18) dropped 20.2 percent (down 15.0 percent in serious violent crimes and down 20.3 percent in serious property crimes) from 2000, declining in seven of the eight serious crime categories, as follows: murder and nonnegligent manslaughter (down 0.6 percent), forcible rape (down 31.9 percent), aggravated assault (down 27.2 percent), burglary (down 20.9 percent), larceny-theft (down 15.1 percent), motor vehicle theft (down 59.6 percent), and arson (down 35.3 percent). However, during that same time period, arrests of juveniles for robbery increased by 18.0 percent. The arrests of juveniles in 2009 were down 8.9 percent from those of 2008, while arrests of adults during that year were down only 1.2 percent.[6]

In general, juveniles are processed by *state* juvenile courts, although as we will see later, some are processed in *state* criminal courts. There is no separate federal juvenile system, but federal statutes do permit, under limited circumstances, the processing of juveniles in federal district courts and even their sentencing to federal prisons.[7]

State statutes define who comes under the jurisdiction of the juvenile court, and the oldest age for *original jurisdiction* in delinquency matters ranges from 15 through 17, although most states have higher ages for juveniles apprehended for status offenses, such as running away from home. However, statutes also provide that juvenile courts may extend jurisdiction over juveniles (up to age 24 in some states) for some purposes that are considered to be in the best interests of the juveniles and the public. A minority of states have statutes that set the *minimum* age for juvenile court jurisdiction, ranging from age 6 to age 10.[8]

The juvenile court is based on the philosophy that a **juvenile delinquent** should be treated separately and differently from adults. Historically, it was assumed that in the juvenile court the judge would act as a parent treating a child, a concept called **parens patriae**, which literally means "parent of the country." The concept began in England and involved giving the sovereign the power to oversee children who were abused or neglected; it did not include delinquent children. The child's best interests

were to be the controlling factor. The system that began in the United States included children who were incorrigible, not obeying their parents or other significant adults. Later, delinquent children were added to the court's jurisdiction. Prior to the development of the juvenile court, children in the United States were processed in adult courts.

The parens patriae approach of the early juvenile courts embodied a philosophy of treatment and rehabilitation rather than punishment. In this milieu, it was assumed that lawyers were not necessary and that the due process and equal protection concepts so important in adult criminal court systems were not necessary. Unfortunately, the system did not work as visualized. Juveniles were often punished, not treated. They were detained in adult jails and prisons; decisions were not made in their best interests.

According to the first juvenile case to reach the U.S. Supreme Court, *Kent v. United States*, decided in 1966, the juvenile court structure constituted "an invitation to procedural arbitrariness." The U.S. Supreme Court stated that the "original laudable purpose of juvenile courts" had been eroded, and there was growing concern "that the child receives the worst of both worlds; that he gets neither the protection accorded to adults nor the solicitous care and regenerative treatment postulated for children."[9]

The following year, in 1967, the U.S. Supreme Court decided *In re Gault*. Gerald Gault was a 15-year-old boy who was accused of making obscene phone calls to a Mrs. Cook. Police took Gault into custody without notifying his parents. They were not shown the petition that was filed against Gault the following day. Mrs. Cook did not appear to testify against Gault, who was not represented by counsel. The judge decided to commit Gault to the state institution until he reached his majority. The maximum legal penalty for an adult who committed the acts of which Gault was accused was a fine of $5 to $50 or a two-month jail sentence. The case was appealed to the U.S. Supreme Court on the denial of these six basic rights:

1. Notice of the charges
2. Right to counsel
3. Right to confrontation and cross-examination
4. Privilege against self-incrimination
5. Right to a transcript of the proceedings, and
6. Right to appellate review

Despite the fact that some texts still have inaccurate information about the holding of this case, the U.S. Supreme Court actually ruled in favor of Gault on only the first four issues. The Court made no ruling on the right to a transcript of the proceedings and the right to appellate review.[10]

In subsequent years, the U.S. Supreme Court has extended to juveniles processed in juvenile courts some but not all of the due process and equal protection rights available to defendants processed in adult criminal courts. But there is evidence that even the due process requirements of *Gault* have not been fulfilled. A study of the Maryland system, conducted and published by the American Bar Association (ABA), reported the following:

1. Many juveniles waive their right to counsel because no one has sufficiently explained the importance of that right to them.
2. Most courts in the study did not even keep track of the number of juveniles who waive their right to counsel.
3. Many juvenile court officials continue to believe that the juvenile proceedings should be adversarial.
4. Those juveniles who are represented by counsel are often represented by less than ideal counsel, characterized by a lack of preparation and advocacy. "At least 90 percent of detained youth did not even know their public defender's name."
5. Most public defenders who represent juveniles spend very little time with their clients.

The ABA study concluded that most juveniles who are processed through the juvenile court are not adequately represented by counsel and are detained in secure facilities for punishment, not treatment. The ABA recommended that juveniles not be permitted to waive their right to counsel until they converse with an attorney and that defense counsel who represent juveniles should receive specialized training and additional resources. Furthermore, juvenile courts should be monitored to ensure that minorities, the mentally ill, and youths with disabilities are properly processed, and we should cease the practice of using secure detention facilities for juveniles.[11]

Among other constitutional rights that the U.S. Supreme Court has extended to juveniles are the following: the right to have court decisions based on the adult criminal court standard of beyond a reasonable doubt (*In re Winship*[12]) and the right not to be tried twice for the same offense (*Breed v. Jones*[13]). In 1992, the U.S. Supreme Court held that juveniles may not be punished more harshly in sentencing than would have been permissible had they been tried in an adult criminal court (see *United States v. R.L.C.*[14]). The U.S. Supreme Court has not held that the right to a trial by jury extends to the juvenile court (see *McKeiver v. Pennsylvania*[15]), although some states do extend that right. States are permitted to extend but not restrict constitutional rights that the U.S. Supreme Court has ruled applicable to juveniles.

In recent years, concern with serious crimes among juveniles has led to a push for more stringent treatment. Processing juveniles through the juvenile court has been replaced in some jurisdictions with the adult criminal court. All states now provide by statute that juveniles accused of some serious crimes (e.g., murder and rape) may be transferred to adult courts. When that occurs, the

courts must provide those juveniles with all the constitutional provisions for adults. The transfer process may be accomplished by a judicial waiver (also called *certification, remand, or bind over;* the process is usually limited to certain ages, offenses, and conditions—e.g., use of a firearm), statutorily provided concurrent jurisdiction (both the adult and the juvenile court have jurisdiction), or legislative exclusion (e.g., a juvenile accused of murder must be tried in the adult criminal court). Some states also provide for *reverse certification*, meaning that if the statute grants jurisdiction to the adult criminal court, the court may transfer the case to the juvenile court.[16]

The transfer of juveniles to adult criminal courts has been criticized by some juvenile court judges. According to the National Council of Juvenile and Family Court Judges, the "assumption is that . . . [adult] criminal courts will be tougher and can serve as a more effective deterrent for juvenile crime. . . . This assumption is not borne out by the facts."[17]

A study of legislative waivers in three jurisdictions came to the conclusion that it may be time to rethink waivers, as the overall data do not support deterrence.[18] The Campaign for Youth Justice, an organization dedicated to ending the practice of trying young people in adult criminal courts, published its conclusions on the issue of waivers in a document entitled *The Consequences Aren't Minor.* Here are some of the key findings:

- "The overwhelming majority of youth who enter the adult court are not there for serious, violent crimes. . . .
- The decision to send youth to adult court is most often not made by the one person best considered to judge the merits of the youth's case—the juvenile court judge.
- Access to effective legal counsel is a deciding factor on whether a youth is prosecuted as an adult.
- Youth of color are disproportionately affected by these policies.
- Female youth are affected too, but little is known about them.
- The consequences for prosecuting youth in adult court 'aren't minor.'
- The research shows that those laws do not promote public safety.
- These laws ignore the latest scientific evidence on the adolescent brain—the same evidence that informed the U.S. Supreme Court's decision to bar the juvenile death penalty. . . .
- The public should invest its dollars by strengthening the juvenile justice system."[19]

A panel of experts designated by the Centers for Disease Control and Prevention concluded, "Youths tried as adults and housed in adult prisons commit more crimes, often more violent ones, than minors who remain in the juvenile justice system."[20]

Successful constitutional challenges have been made to some automatic waivers from juvenile to criminal courts. For example, the Delaware provision that a juvenile who turns 18 before trial should be transferred to an adult criminal court automatically if one or more listed crimes (e.g., murder) were charged was held to violate the state and federal constitutions because it removed from the judiciary the authority to make the transfer decision. In essence, the decision was made by the prosecutor, who had the power to effect a transfer by bringing charges of a listed offense.[21]

There is also an issue of the impact that trial in an adult criminal court has on a juvenile. A limited but recent study of juveniles who were transferred to adult criminal courts, compared with similarly situated ones who were not transferred, found that the transferred juveniles were negatively impacted at sentencing. The study also found differences in terms of the counties in which the juveniles were processed.[22]

What is the future of the juvenile court? A criminologist who studied the public perception of this specialized court found "lingering appeal" for it, with the public retaining the belief that some juveniles are treatable.[23] Other criminologists propose a *blended sentence approach* that would utilize the juvenile court and the adult criminal court "to work in concert to impose developmentally appropriate punishments" in homicide cases, which are the most frequent in which juvenile cases are transferred to adult courts for trial. They argue that, in effect, "kids are different." They are physically and neurologically different, and as a result, they are less capable of understanding the full consequences of their actions.[24] These arguments were influential when the U.S. Supreme Court considered the death penalty for juveniles (discussed later in this chapter), and they are relevant to the issue of whether juveniles should be assessed life without parole (LWOP). It is argued that LWOP is inappropriate for juveniles and that it may negatively impact minorities compared with whites.

With regard to the issue of discrimination against minorities, in 2007, the Equal Justice Initiative (EJI), a private, nonprofit organization that provides legal representation for those who have been denied due process and equal protection, identified 73 inmates in 19 states who were serving life without parole for crimes they committed when they were 13 or 14 years old. Thirty-six of those 73 were black, 22 were white, 7 were Hispanic, 8 were of other races. The EJI filed lawsuits on behalf of some of those 73 persons.[25]

The use of LWOP for juveniles was considered by the United Nations, which voted 185 to 1 to support a resolution calling for its abolition. The United States was the only member opposing that resolution.[26]

In 2010, the U.S. Supreme Court considered the issue of LWOP and held that the sentence is cruel and unusual under the facts of *Graham v. Florida*. The Court's opinion is excerpted in Exhibit 13.2. That same day, the Court dismissed a second case from Florida. *Sullivan v. State* also involved a teen, Joe Harris Sullivan, who was arrested at the age of 13 for allegedly sexual assaulting an elderly woman after he and two older codefendants committed a burglary in her residence. Sullivan's attorney said that his client was one of only two teens nationwide who had been sentenced to LWOP without committing a crime other than homicide at the age of 13. The U.S. Supreme Court had agreed to review both Florida cases but dismissed Sullivan's case, stating that the decision to review it was "improvidently granted." The justices may have made that decision based on the fact that the *Graham* case applied more widely given his age, because there were some procedural issues with that case, or for any other reason. As a result of the Court's decision in *Graham*, Sullivan has a legal basis to petition for resentencing.[27]

Domestic Violence Courts

Earlier discussions in this text focused on intimate personal violence (IPV). The increasing concern with IPV and, especially, with protecting its victims has led to the development of specialized courts, which are generally referred to as *domestic violence courts*. Similar to the other specialized courts discussed in this chapter, domestic violence courts emphasize the need for one court to focus its personnel and resources on the processing of alleged perpetrators as well as the protection of alleged victims. Research on the effectiveness of these courts is sparse, but there is some evidence. One study found that 40 to 50 percent of domestic violence cases involved substance abuse and that the specialized courts were successful in getting the offenders into substance abuse treatment programs. Further, the offenders in these treatment programs were less likely to reoffend against the same victims.[28]

A study of four domestic violence courts in San Diego, California, where the first such court was introduced in 1997, found that the specialized courts focusing only on IPV were able to solve problems faster and with lower recidivism rates. This study emphasized that the judge hears all phases of a case from the initial filings through the monitoring of treatment. In this jurisdiction, prior to the existence of the specialized domestic violence court, some offenders appeared before as many as nine judges. This made it easier for the offenders to succeed in ignoring some court orders and to delay enrolling in the 52-week required domestic violence education program. The study emphasized that the sooner the offender gets into a treatment program, the more effective it will be and recommended that counseling be made available when the offender is still in custody.[29]

But is treatment always effective? In a Florida study on male IPV perpetrators, investigators separated the offenders into two groups: One received probation and court-mandated counseling; the other received only probation.

EXHIBIT 13.2

Life Without Parole Is Cruel and Unusual
Punishment for Juveniles

Graham v. Florida[1]

On 17 May 2010, the U.S. Supreme Court decided this case concerning the sentence of life without parole (LWOP) for a juvenile who did not commit homicide. The excerpt explains the facts and the Court's response. Justice Anthony Kennedy delivered the opinion of the court.

"The issue before the Court is whether the Constitution permits a juvenile offender to be sentenced to life in prison without parole for a nonhomicide crime. The sentence was imposed by the State of Florida. Petitioner challenges the sentence under the Eighth Amendment's Cruel and Unusual Punishments Clause, made applicable to the states by the Due Process Clause of the Fourteenth Amendment.

"Petitioner is Terrance Jamar Graham. He was born on January 6, 1987. Graham's parents were addicted to crack cocaine, and their drug use persisted in his early years. Graham was diagnosed with attention deficit hyperactivity disorder in elementary school. He began drinking alcohol and using tobacco at age 9 and smoked marijuana at age 13. . . .

[Graham and three other juveniles were charged with attempted robbery and armed burglary with assault or battery when Graham was 16. He entered guilty pleas under a plea agreement, which was accepted by the court. Adjudication was withheld and he was sentencened to concurrent three-year probation terms.] "Graham was required to spend the first 12 months of his probation in the county jail, but he received credit for the time he had served awaiting trial. . . ."

[Less than six months after Graham was released, he was arrested in a home invasion robbery case in which weapons were involved. His probation officer notified the court that his client had violated the terms of his probation by associating with people in criminal activities and being in possession of a firearm. Approximately a year later, hearings were held on these issues, with Graham appearing before a different judge. Graham was found guilty of the two original charges, armed burglary and attempted armed robbery, and sentenced to the maximum sentence that the law permitted for each charge: life for the first and 15 years for the second. Florida had abolished its parole system, which meant that Graham would be in prison for his entire life unless he received clemency from the executive branch. The Court reviewed its precedent cases concerning cruel and unusual punishment in sentencing. The Court considered state statutes, noting that LWOP sentences for juveniles who have not committed homicides are rare, with only 129 juveniles serving the sentence at that time. Of those, 77 were in Florida, and the other 52 were in only 10 other states.]

"Once in adult court, a juvenile offender may receive the same sentence as would be given to an adult offender, including a life without parole sentence. . . .

"For example, under Florida law a child of any age can be prosecuted as an adult for certain crimes and can be sentenced to life without parole. The State acknowledged . . . that even a 5-year-old, theoretically, could receive such a sentence . . . The sentencing practice now under consideration is exceedingly rare. And 'it is fair to say that a national consensus has developed against it.'"

[The Court stated that national consensus is not the final determinant of whether a sentence is cruel and unusual; that determination is for the Court. The Court referred to its decision in *Roper v. Sullivan*, when it held that capital punishment for juveniles is cruel and unusual. The Court saw no reason to revisit that decision.]

"The Court has recognized that defendants who do not kill, intend to kill, or foresee that life will be taken are categorically less deserving of the most serious forms of punishment than are murderers. . . .

"It follows that, when compared to an adult murderer, a juvenile offender who did not kill or intend to kill has a twice diminished moral culpability. The age of the offender and the nature of the crime each bear on the analysis.

"As for the punishment, life without parole is 'the second most severe penalty permitted by law.' . . . The State does not execute the offender sentenced to life without parole, but the sentence alters the offender's life by a forfeiture that is irrevocable. It deprives the convict of the most basic liberties without giving hope of restoration . . . [except for clemency. The Court quoted another court that overturned a LWOP sentence for a juvenile as saying] that LWOP 'means denial of hope; it means that good behavior and character improvement are immaterial; it means that whatever the future might hold in store for the mind and spirit of [the convict], he will remain in prison for the rest of his days.' [The Court then reviewed its precedent cases concerning LWOP for adults.] . . .

"Life without parole is an especially harsh punishment for a juvenile. Under this sentence a juvenile offender will on average serve more years and a greater percentage of his life in prison than an adult offender. . . .

"With respect to life without parole for juvenile nonhomicide offenders, none of the goals of penal sanctions that have been recognized as legitimate—retribution, deterrence, incapacitation, and rehabilitation—provides an adequate justification. [The Court discussed each of there goals]. . . .

"In sum, penological theory is not adequate to justify life without parole for juvenile nonhomicide offenders. This determination; the limited culpability of juvenile nonhomicide offenders; and the severity of life without parole sentences all lead to the conclusion that the sentencing practice under consideration is cruel and unusual. This Court now holds

13.2

EXHIBIT continued

that for a juvenile offender who did not commit homicide the Eighth Amendment forbids the sentence of life without parole. . . .

"Terrance Graham's sentence guarantees he will die in prison without any meaningful opportunity to obtain release, no matter what he might do to demonstrate that the bad acts he committed as a teenage are not representative of his true character, even if he spends the next half century attempting to atone for his crimes and learn from his mistakes. The State has denied him any chance to later demonstrate that he is fit to rejoin society based solely on a nonhomicide crime that he committed while he was a child in the eyes of the law. This the Eighth Amendment does not permit. [The Court notes that LWOP is rejected the world over but emphasizes that is not the controlling reason for its holding. The majority concludes its opinion]:

"The Constitution prohibits the imposition of a life without parole sentence on a juvenile offender who did not commit homicide. A State need not guarantee the offender eventual release, but if it imposes a sentence of life it must provide him or her with some realistic opportunity to obtain release before the end of that term. The judgment of the First District Court of Appeals of Florida affirming Graham's conviction is reversed, and the case is remanded for further proceedings not inconsistent with this opinion."

Citation: *Graham v. Florida*, 130 S.Ct. 2011 (2010). Justice Stevens wrote a brief concurring opinion, joined by Justices Ginsburg and Sotomayor; Justice Roberts wrote a concurring opinion; Justice Thomas wrote a lengthy opinion with which Justice Scalia joined and Justice Alito joined in part and also submitted his own brief opinion.

After one year, the results showed "no significant differences [between the two groups] . . . in their attitudes, beliefs, and behaviors regarding domestic violence; both groups were equally likely to engage in both minor and severe partner abuse." The investigators found no significant differences between the two groups in re-arrest rates.[30] Other researchers warn that mandatory arrest with no follow-up may not solve any problems. "Unless criminal justice responses deal with the violence that gave rise to the arrest, intervention is unlikely to be effective and repeat offenses should be expected."[31]

Criminologists who researched the effectiveness of a domestic violence court in South Carolina found that the court was effective in enhancing both law enforcement and victim safety. After the court was established, domestic violence arrests increased, but compared with a control sample, those offenders processed through the domestic violence court had significantly lower re-arrest rates for domestic violence. The researchers concluded that the findings underscored the "benefits of a coordinated response to domestic violence and the ability of local communities to act in a proactive manner toward the crime of domestic violence."[32]

Domestic violence courts have the ability to mobilize and coordinate services that can be used not only to protect the victim but also to punish and rehabilitate the offender. In a provocative article briefly tracing the history of official reaction to domestic violence, researchers suggested that institutions that have dealt with the issue are male dominated and favor "masculine approaches to implementing domestic violence policy." That began with legislation that permitted men to discipline their wives, even physically. The authors concluded that the move-

ment to mandatory arrest with no treatment provisions should give way to "more collaborative, interagency approaches. . . . These strategies need to focus on equalizing the power of social service agencies with that of the police to provide services to both the victims and offenders of DV [domestic violence.]"[33]

Drug Courts

Chapter 10 explored various aspects of substance abuse and associated crimes. The chapter presented a discussion of treatment rather than punishment for some substance abusers. In many jurisdictions, treatment is coordinated through specialized drug courts. Drug courts are also used to relieve the pressures of congestion in other courts. They began in Miami, Florida, in 1989. The Office of National Drug Control Policy describes a *drug court* as follows: "Supervised by a sitting judge, a drug court is an intensive, community-based treatment, rehabilitation, and supervision program for drug offenders."[34]

State drug courts spread throughout the Unites States aided by federal grants, which were part of the Violent Crime Control and Law Enforcement Act of 1994. That legislation provides federal funds and technical support for the development of drug courts for nonviolent drug offenders. All states have drug courts, which, according to the National Institute of Justice (NIJ), have coerced many drug offenders into treatment programs. These programs have been found to be more effective than incarceration alone. The majority of persons who enter drug treatment programs drop out before completing the programs. However, the structure of drug courts, according to the NIJ, provides a link between supervision by the courts and treatment. This results in a longer and more successful period of participation by drug offenders.[35]

Drug courts vary in size, type, and function. Some focus on offenders convicted of driving while under the influence of alcohol and are referred to as DWI/drug courts, with an emphasis on deterring drunk driving. Some focus on reintegrating children into their families after they have been removed because of their parents' drug abuse. Others focus on rehabilitative programs and services for substance abusers. Even though they vary, drug courts have the same general goals: to reduce drug abuse and crime and to rehabilitate drug abusers. A model of drug courts includes numerous components, which are listed in Exhibit 13.3.

Although some criticize drug courts as ineffective and too lenient, a study of New York's drug courts concluded that these courts are more effective than prisons in reducing recidivism and that they do so at significantly lower costs. Specifically, the report stated that drug offenders who completed supervised drug court treatment programs were 29 percent less likely to be recidivists than those who served prison time. The report stated that the treatment of 18,000 nonviolent drug offenders in the New York drug courts had saved the state approximately $254 million in expenses relating to incarceration.[36]

Authors of a study of the Ohio drug court program proclaimed: "By endorsing the view that treatment, when combined with strict judicial monitoring, can be an effective tool in reducing recidivism, drug courts hold more promise than traditional policies that rely on incarceration and stricter sentences." This study found that drug offenders who had participated in drug court treatment programs were, on the average, 15 percent less likely to be re-arrested than were their counterparts who did not participate.[37]

Similar results were reported by investigators who studied 235 drug offenders randomly assigned to a drug treatment court (DTC) or to "treatment as usual." The researchers found less recidivism among those assigned to the DTC, and they emphasized the importance of drug treatment programs and drug courts. They disagreed with the advocates of an approach referred to as *coerced abstinence*, which involves screening parolees and probationers for drug abuse, administering frequent drug tests, and applying sanctions when continued drug use is discovered. Coerced abstinence does not involve drug treatment or judicial monitoring, as is characteristic of drug treatment courts.[38]

In addition to evaluating whether drug courts work, researchers should consider two other factors: First, if the courts work, they should ask why. Second, what is the role drug courts play "as catalysts for broader change in the judicial system?"[39] Further, policy makers need to accept the fact that drug courts are not a magic bullet; there are failures. Policy makers must be prepared to counter the arguments that drug courts are soft on crime and that coercive treatment increases the chances that the offenders (overrepresented by minorities) will eventually be incarcerated. An examination of these concerns in a Baltimore drug court did not uncover evidence to support them.[40]

In 2010, in his request for the 2011 budget, President Obama's administration emphasized the importance of drug courts in the following statement:

The . . . National Drug Court Institute (NDCI) . . . was created as the training arm of the National Association of Drug Court Professionals (NADCP) by ONDCP [Office of National Drug Control Policy] in 1997. It continues to provide quality training and technical assistance to the drug court field through research-driven solutions that address the changing needs of treating substance-abusing offenders. Drug Courts are a comprehensive tool and proven

---

EXHIBIT 13.3

Drug Courts: Key Components

The National Criminal Justice Reference Service proposes the following components for all drug courts:

- "Incorporating drug testing into case processing.
- Creating a non-adversarial relationship between the defendant and the court.
- Identifying defendants in need of treatment and referring them to treatment as soon as possible after arrest.
- Providing access to a continuum of treatment and rehabilitation services.
- Monitoring abstinence through frequent, mandatory drug testing.
- Establishing a coordinated strategy to govern drug court responses to participants' compliance.

- Maintaining judicial interaction with each drug court participant.
- Monitoring and evaluating program goals and gauging their effectiveness.
- Continuing interdisciplinary education to promote effective drug court planning, implementation, and operations.
- Forging partnerships among drug courts, public agencies, and community-based organizations to generate local support and enhance drug court effectiveness."

Source: National Criminal Justice Reference Service, "Drug Courts: Summary," http://www.ncjrs.gov/spotlight/drug_courts/Summary.html, accessed 8 November 2010.

solution for reducing the public health and safety threats of drug abuse. With 2,300 Drug Courts operational today, many trained by NDCI, approximately 120,000 Americans annually receive the help they need to break the cycle of addiction.

NDCI's goal is to enhance court functioning and promote the utilization of evidence-based services within the drug courts to ensure long-term sustainability of programs through an education and training component.

NDCI develops, delivers, evaluates, markets, and expands the training and resources available to Drug Court professionals.[41]

The ONDCP marked the twentieth anniversary of drug courts in 2009 by noting that 1.2 million people were currently participating in drug court programs, and for them, the organization proclaimed, "Drug Court . . . is a passport to a new way of life." According to ONDCP, 70 percent of participants complete their treatment within a year, and 75 percent of those "never see another pair of handcuffs. This reduction in substance abuse and crime directly translates to $3.36 saved for every dollar invested in Drug Court."[42] Skeptics of these claims may wish to return to Chapter 11 and reread the critiques of the government's war on drugs.

Finally, at the annual meeting of the National Association of Drug Court Professionals in June 2010, U.S. Attorney General Eric Holder told the participants that drug courts, a top priority in the Department of Justice, must be available to more addicts, especially juveniles. "You have proven that redemption and rehabilitation are possible."[43]

Mental Health Courts

The final specialized courts that we consider are those that process mental health cases. One method for relieving congestion in criminal courts is to process mentally challenged persons through specialized courts rather than through criminal justice systems. According to the Bureau of Justice Statistics, more that one-half of all jail and prison inmates have a mental health problem. Almost one-fourth of those persons, compared to one-fifth of inmates who did not have mental health problems, had served three or more prior incarcerations.[44]

In recent years, policy makers have sought to find alternatives to cycling mentally challenged persons through prisons and jails. In 2000, Congress enacted a provision for mental health courts. The bill, passed unanimously by the Senate and by a voice vote in the House, provides federal grants for up to 100 programs to establish special mental health courts, which target offenders who are charged with nonviolent offenses or misdemeanors. The statute provides for training law enforcement and judicial personnel to identify persons who should qualify

for the special programs. There is a provision for "voluntary outpatient or inpatient mental health treatment, in the least restrictive manner appropriate, as determined by the court, that carries with it the possibility of dismissal of charges or reduced sentencing upon successful completion of treatment." The legislation also provides for the centralized management of all charges against a defendant. Finally, the statute provides for "continuing supervision of treatment plan compliance for a term not to exceed the maximum allowable sentence or probation for the charged or relevant offense and, to the extent practicable, continuity of psychiatric care at the end of the supervised period."[45]

Mental health courts have also been established in numerous states, and although they are relatively recent, there is some research evidence concerning their effectiveness. A summary of the research is presented in Exhibit 13.4.

Courts play a significant role in criminal justice systems, and this section would not be complete without mentioning a recent attempt at solving criminal justice issues through courts. New York is conducting a two-year experiment with *attendance courts*. These courts are designed to assist parents and school officials with chronically truant children. The courts do not have the power to punish the children but, rather, are designed to provide counseling and tutoring "as well as occasional tough talk by retired judges in hearings every two weeks."[46]

The roles of lawyers are crucial in courts. The next section looks at the roles of the prosecution and defense in adult criminal courts.

The Role of Lawyers in Criminal Court Systems

In criminal cases, lawyers act as defense or prosecuting attorneys, and each role is very important. Lawyers have an ethical obligation to abide by the rules of the courts in which they practice as well as by the rules and ethics of the legal profession, state and federal procedures and laws, and constitutional mandates.

Prosecution

One important role of attorneys in criminal cases is that of the prosecution. The **prosecuting attorney** presents the case for the state or federal government (federal prosecutors are called *U.S. attorneys*) and is responsible for securing and organizing the evidence against the defendant and for arguing cases that go to trial. Prosecutors have wide discretion. In most cases, they have the power to decide whether or not to prosecute; their decisions are virtually unchecked. Those who decide to proceed with a case over which they have jurisdiction must return an *information*, an official document that initiates prosecution. Some cases

EXHIBIT 13.4

Mental Health Courts: A Summary of Research

The Justice Center for The Council of State Governments has published a summary of research on mental health courts. Included in that publication are the following:

- "Mental health courts accept individuals charged with a wide variety of offenses and may focus on individuals charged with misdemeanor crimes, felonies, or both. . . .
- Most courts accept primarily individuals diagnosed as having (or who show signs of having) serious mental illnesses. . . .
- Many mental health court participants have co-occurring substance use disorders. . . .
- Mental health court 'team members' usually include a judge, representatives from the prosecutor's office and defense bar, probation or parole officers, and a case manager and/or representatives from the mental health treatment system. . . .
- Mental health court teams employ a variety of sanctions tailored to participants' specific circumstances to encourage them to comply with the terms of participation and their treatment plans. . . .
- In some instances, mental health courts use jail time as a sanction for noncompliance. . . .
- Research strongly suggests that mental health court participants have lower rates of new criminal charges while under court supervision than individuals with mental illnesses who go through the traditional criminal court system. There is some empirical evidence to support the belief that this trend may continue

after graduation, when individuals are no longer supervised by the court. . . .

- There is some research to suggest that mental health court participants have lower rates of recidivism after one year of participation than before enrolling in the court. No studies have found that participants are *more* likely to be arrested. . . .
- There is some research to suggest that the criminal justice outcomes of mental health court participants who graduate are better than those of individuals who start but do not complete the program or whose cases are processed by the traditional court system. . . .
- There is some research to suggest that mental health courts are a more effective means of connecting individuals with treatment services than the traditional court system or jails. . . .
- There is some empirical evidence to support the belief that, when compared with participants' mental health status before enrollment, mental health courts have a positive effect on participants' mental health. . . .
- There is some research to suggest that over time mental health courts have the potential to lead to cost savings through lower recidivism and the associated jail and court costs and through a reduction in use of the most expensive types of mental health treatment."

Source: Lauren Almquist and Elizabeth Dodd, Council of State Governments Justice Center, *Mental Health Courts: A Guide to Research-Informed Policy and Practice* (New York 2009), pp. 7–26.

Defense lawyers and prosecutors often disagree, sometimes in front of the jury as well as the judge, but the roles of both are extremely important in adversary systems, such as those in the United States.

must begin with a grand jury indictment, but even then, prosecutors have great power.

The Fifth Amendment requires, in part, that "no person shall be held to answer for a capital, or otherwise infamous crime, unless on a presentment or indictment of a Grand Jury, except in cases arising in the land or naval forces, or in the Militia, when in actual service in time of War or public danger." A grand jury, composed of private citizens, hears evidence presented by the prosecution. If the grand jury believes there is sufficient evidence that the accused committed the crime or crimes in question, it returns an indictment, which begins the official prosecution of the case. In most cases, the prosecutor has considerable control over the grand jury.

Prosecutors have wide discretion in determining which charges to bring or whether to present the case to the grand jury. For example, a person suspected of first-degree murder in a state that has the death penalty could be charged with second-degree murder, which does not carry the death penalty. In some states, that defendant could be charged with first-degree murder but not capital murder. He or she could be charged with first-degree murder, but after conviction and at the sentencing hearing, the prosecutor might not ask for the death penalty. It is also possible that the prosecutor could charge the suspect with manslaughter depending on the circumstances of the killing.

Prosecutors may drop charges after they have been filed. This decision may, but does not always, require the judge's permission. Once a defendant has been convicted, the prosecutor may also be influential in the sentencing process. Prosecutors may differ widely in their recommendations.

Prosecutorial discretion is necessary in criminal justice systems. No system can state in advance all cases that should be prosecuted. Decisions must be made in light of the offense, the offender, and the resources of the system. On the one hand, it would be a foolish waste of resources for a prosecutor to insist on taking to trial a case in which the evidence is so weak that there is no chance of a conviction. On the other hand, it would be an abuse of discretion to pursue or dismiss a case because the defendant is of a particular race, religion, or gender or because of other extralegal reasons.

There is evidence, however, that prosecutors are influenced by some extralegal characteristics. Investigators looking into prosecutions in federal courts did not find evidence of charge dropping associated with age, race, or ethnicity, but they did find that charges were more likely to be reduced in the cases of female compared to male defendants.[47]

Another study of prosecutorial discretion suggested that, in cases involving alleged IPV, prosecutors may view women more as victims than as offenders. The study looked at four variables: the decision to file charges, the decision to file as a felony rather than a misdemeanor, the decision to dismiss the case for lack of sufficient evidence, and the decision to reduce a felony to a misdemeanor or violation of probation.[48]

Prosecutors also have enormous power over other aspects of criminal justice systems. For example, we have already discussed the policy of mandatory arrests in domestic violence cases (see again Chapter 12). Those policies require the police to arrest, but they do not require the prosecution to prosecute. The mandatory arrest policy, though, could put pressure on prosecutors to continue with cases when they do not have strong evidence. Mandatory arrest policies may clog the system, pushing prosecution of more cases than the system can handle and thus increasing the time between arrest and trial. Defendants who must remain in jail during that period are negatively

The ethical standards of the legal profession and the philosophy of U.S. criminal justice systems place on prosecutors the responsibility of "doing justice," not just convicting. Prosecutors who violate the rules may be disciplined, and in some cases, even charged with criminal violations. Mike Nifong, who brought rape and other charges against three Duke University lacrosse players in the spring of 2006 and persisted in his prosecution despite weak evidence, eventually lost his job, was disbarred, and in 2008, filed for bankruptcy. The three players were declared innocent after an outside investigation.

impacted, and this is especially troubling if they are later acquitted or charges are dropped. Further, mandatory arrests may unnecessarily create jail overcrowding.

The American Bar Association's *Standards for Criminal Justice* specify that it is the duty of the prosecutor to "seek justice, not merely to convict."[49] Consequently, the prosecutor is not free to use any means available to convict a defendant. Serious problems are caused by overzealous or unscrupulous prosecutors, as was evident when Michael Nifong prosecuted three white Duke University lacrosse players in 2006. The defendants were accused of raping a black woman, who was hired to dance at a party they attended. Despite weak evidence, exposed by the attorneys of the accused as well as by the media, Nifong persisted in his efforts to prosecute the players. This persistence led the university to cancel the rest of the lacrosse season and cost the coach his job. The three young men were suspended from the university while they, their families, and their attorneys battled to clear their names. Nifong was accused of engaging in a political battle to win an election (which he won). Finally, in light of mounting evidence questioning the charges, Nifong dropped the rape charges but left intact the charges of lesser sexual assaults and kidnapping. In 2007, Nifong recused himself, and the state investigated the charges, announcing later that not only were the charges being dropped but that the evidence showed the players were innocent. Nifong was disbarred, resigned, and spent a night in jail for criminal contempt. He also faced other charges. The players brought civil charges against Nifong, the police, the lab personnel involved in the case, and the city for pursuing the prosecution of a weak case for political reasons. The suit referred to the prosecution of the three players as "one of the most chilling episodes of premeditated police, prosecutorial and scientific misconduct in modern American history."[50]

A more recent case, yet to be retried as of this writing, also illustrates the implications of a prosecutor's misuse of power. In March 2010, a judge in New Orleans granted a new trial to a defendant who was convicted of five counts of capital murder in 2006. Judge Lynda Van Davis ruled that the failure of the prosecutors to turn two key pieces of evidence over to the defense in a timely manner constituted reversible error. The prosecutors did not inform the defense of a plea agreement made with an informant who testified against the defendant, Michael Anderson. The second piece of evidence, a videotaped interview by the prosecution of a key witness, in which that witness contradicted parts of her trial testimony, was not given to the defense until five months after their client was convicted. The district attorney's appeal of the judge's ruling was denied; a new trial for Anderson, who was held without bond, was set for May 2011.[51]

Courts have decided some cases involved alleged prosecutorial misconduct. In 2004, in *Banks v. Dretke*, the U.S. Supreme Court overturned the death sentence of a Texas inmate, Delma Banks, because of prosecutorial miscon-

duct. Prosecution witnesses lied regarding the degree to which the prosecution rehearsed them, and when prosecutors heard testimony that they knew was false, they did not, as the Supreme Court stated, "raise a red flag." The U.S. Supreme Court ruled that Banks had a right to challenge his conviction as well as to be entitled to the vacating of his death penalty sentence. According to the Court, "When police or prosecutors conceal significant exculpatory or impeaching material in the state's possession, it is ordinarily incumbent on the state to set the record straight." The defense is not required to prove that prosecutors' statements are false; rather, the defense has a right to assume that they are truthful.[52]

One problem in controlling prosecutorial discretion, however, is that there are few checks. For example, later in this chapter, we discuss federal sentencing guidelines. Those guidelines, by statute, provide that U.S. attorneys can file what is called a *departure for substantial assistance.* In other words, when a defendant gives substantial assistance to prosecutors with regard to another case or defendant, the prosecutor may request that the judge grant a substantial departure from the sentencing guidelines. This provision of the federal sentencing law is often invoked in drug cases, many of which carry long, mandatory minimum sentences. According to U.S. Sentencing Commission data, approximately 20 percent of defendants receive departures for substantial assistance. An analysis of the use of these departures in crack cocaine versus powder cocaine cases disclosed that women were more likely than men and whites were more likely than blacks to receive the departures. In some of their categories, the investigators found that prosecutors were more likely to file motions for substantial departures in the more serious cases and in those in which defendants had more extensive criminal histories. These findings could mean that prosecutors were trying to adjust sentences that defendants would otherwise get; it could reflect their charging decisions—for example, charging women for serious offenses even though they played minor roles in the crimes. Or the results could reflect the belief that serious offenders were more help to the government than were minor offenders.[53]

One final issue that is important to an understanding of prosecution involves a process called **deferred prosecution**. Under deferred prosecution, the defendant must acknowledge the accused criminal act, and if the judge accepts the agreement between the defense and the prosecution, prosecution will be deferred for a specified number of years. If, during that period, the defendant is found guilty of another crime, the earlier admission can be used against him or her in a prosecution on the crime for which prosecution was deferred.

Defense

The Sixth Amendment provides, in part, "In all criminal prosecutions, the accused shall enjoy . . . the assistance of counsel for his defense." The attorney representing the defendant in a criminal trial is the **defense attorney**. The function of a defense attorney is to protect the legal rights of the accused.[54] The defendant in U.S. criminal justice systems is entitled to a fair trial in which the state must prove guilt beyond a reasonable doubt and in accordance with proper procedures. It is not the function of the defense attorney to prove the defendant's innocence. Attorneys are as bound by the ethics of their profession in the defense of persons they think committed the acts charged as in the defense of those they believe to be innocent. The function of defense attorneys is to give their clients the best legal advice and representation they can within the law and ethics of the legal profession. Once this function is recognized, the defense of a person who may have committed the criminal act in question is understandable.

This discussion is not meant to suggest that defense attorneys do not abuse the adversary system; some do, as noted in Chapter 11's discussion of the right to counsel, which includes the right to *effective* assistance of counsel. Unfortunately, abuses of the system may receive a lot of publicity even though they are isolated instances that do not reflect on the entire defense bar. But even when abuse occurs, it must be distinguished from the *philosophy* of the system. That philosophy is one of the strongest points of U.S. criminal justice systems—that all persons are presumed innocent until proven guilty and that they may be punished only after the government proves guilt beyond a reasonable doubt without violating the accused's constitutional rights. An indigent accused is entitled to counsel at the government's expense. The focus here is on the types of systems for providing that counsel.

Three types of systems are used to provide defense attorneys for indigent defendants. First, attorneys may be *assigned* to particular indigent defendants. Usually, assignments are made by judges from lists of attorneys who have agreed to serve in this capacity. Second, some jurisdictions use *a contract* system in which a bar association, private law firm, or individual attorney contracts with the government to provide legal assistance for indigent defendants. Third, many jurisdictions use **public defender** systems to provide legal representation for indigent defendants.

All methods of providing attorneys for indigents have been criticized, although there is some evidence that defense attorneys for indigent defendants perform their services very well. An earlier study, conducted by the National Center for State Courts, reported that "attorneys who represent indigent defendants perform as well as, and by some measures better than, privately retained defense lawyers."[55]

A court-appointed attorney with a large caseload (in New York, some public defenders had as many as 700 cases a year, leading to a statute to limit caseloads), low compensation, low status, and inadequate resources cannot be expected to provide the best legal defense. One issue is that the state does not fund (or fund sufficiently)

its public defender systems, leaving it to localities to do so. This results in underfunding as well as disparity among the various counties.

In May 2010, the highest court in New York, the New York Court of Appeals, held 4–3 in a bitterly fought suit that the plaintiff's challenge to the state's public defender system can proceed because it raises questions about fundamental fairness in the state's criminal justice system. The New York suit was filed on behalf of Kimberly Hurell-Harring and 19 others. Hurell-Harring alleged that her public defender did little for her other than to recommend that she enter a guilty plea to her felony charge. New York's system consists of appointments of Legal Aid societies consisting of private attorneys appointed by the courts, along with local public defenders. There is no state-supported system of public defenders.[56]

In February 2002, the American Bar Association adopted the following 10 principles of a public defense delivery system:

- "The public defense function, including the selection, funding, and payment of defense counsel, is independent.
- Where the caseload is sufficiently high, the public defense delivery system consists of both a defender office and the active participation of the private bar.
- Clients are screened for eligibility, and defense counsel is assigned and notified of appointment, as soon as feasible after clients' arrest, detention, or request for counsel.
- Defense counsel is provided sufficient time and a confidential space within which to meet with the client.
- Defense counsel's workload is controlled to permit the rendering of quality representation.
- Defense counsel's ability, training, and experience match the complexity of the case.
- The same attorney continuously represents the client until completion of the case.
- There is parity between defense counsel and the prosecution with respect to resources and defense counsel is included as an equal partner in the justice system.
- Defense counsel is provided with and required to attend continuing legal education.
- Defense counsel is supervised and systematically reviewed for quality and efficiency according to nationally and locally adopted standards."[57]

Other challenges to public defender systems occur with regard to the defense of defendants charged with capital offenses, as we will note later in this chapter.

The burden of improving public defender systems rests in two places. First, the legal profession should be challenged to discover ways to attract more qualified attorneys into criminal defense work; these may include greater prestige and rewards for such work and requiring better law school preparation for criminal cases. Second, society must provide the money and resources necessary to make criminal justice systems work as conceptualized. When that is not done, injustice may and often does result, as emphasized by Chapter 11's discussion of wrongful convictions and ineffective assistance of counsel.

More than 80 percent of defendants are indigent and must depend on public defender systems. According to the attorney who filed the suit, "Nearly 50 years after the Supreme Court held that criminal defendants have a right to meaningful counsel, the state's highest court has held that New York may well be violating that right every day." The state's governor, David Patterson, vowed to work with the judge on changing New York's public defender system, declaring, "We both agree that the current system is a disgrace."[58]

Pretrial Processes

Chapter 11 briefly covered the main stages that occur from the investigation of a crime through the pretrial, trial, and sentencing phases. The body of law and sociological literature on these processes is extensive. This section focuses on two of the most controversial processes: pretrial release and plea bargaining.

Pretrial Release

One of the most critical periods of criminal justice proceedings is the time between arraignment and trial. The purpose of pretrial release is to enable the defendant to prepare for trial while avoiding the harmful effects of detention. The stage is critical, and there is evidence that being detained rather than released pending trial has negative effects on defendants. To illustrate, a recent study of juveniles who were transferred to adult criminal court (as well as adults in those courts, compared to similarly situated ones who were not transferred) demonstrated "how individuals who cannot make bail may become disadvantaged at subsequent stages of the court process by virtue of their custody status."[59]

The enormous problems faced by incarcerated defendants extend beyond the most obvious one, deprivation of liberty. Pretrial detainees may lose their jobs and acquire the stigma attached to a jail term. They face days of loneliness and idleness, with limited opportunities to talk to and visit with family and friends. Often, they are confined along with those who have been convicted of crimes and are serving jail terms. These conditions exist even though pretrial detainees are *legally innocent of a crime*.

There are various types of release systems, as indicated in Exhibit 13.5. According to the Bureau of Justice Statistics' (BJS) latest data, published in June 2010 and covering 2006 data on the 75 largest counties, 58 percent of felony defendants were released from jail prior to the final disposition of their cases. Most were released under some kind of financial arrangement, with 42 percent released on surety bond, 8 percent on deposit bond, and 6 percent on full cash bond. Of the bonded defendants, approximately 6 percent had conditions attached such as electronic monitoring. Of those released without financial arrangements, 28 percent were released on their own recognizance. All scheduled court appearances were met by 82 percent of released defendants, but 33 percent committed some type of infraction during their release and 18 percent were arrested for a new offense. Almost two-thirds of released defendants were convicted, with 95 percent of those convictions obtained as the result of a guilty plea. The probability of conviction was highest for the offense of driving under the influence and lowest for assault. Seventy-three percent of the convicted felony defendants were sentenced to prison compared to only 57 percent of defendants convicted of misdemeanors.[60]

In an earlier report, the BJS reported that female defendants were more likely to be released than were males, 74 percent to 60 percent. Non-Hispanic whites (68 percent) were more often released than Hispanics (55 percent). Released defendants waited approximately three times longer than detained defendants for their cases to be adjudicated. Released defendants who were charged with pretrial misconduct were generally younger, male, black, and Hispanic. The least likely pretrial-released defendants to be charged with misconduct were those who were charged with murder or rape. Their rates of misconduct were about one-half the rates of defendants released on charges of motor vehicle theft, drug trafficking, or burglary.[61]

The Bail System

Courts use several methods for releasing defendants prior to trial, but the most controversial is the bail system. The bail system began in England to ensure the presence of defendants at trials, which were held infrequently because judges traveled from one jurisdiction to another. Facilities for detaining defendants before trial were terrible and expensive to maintain. Sheriffs preferred to have someone else take care of defendants who were awaiting trial and so relinquished them to other people, usually friends or relatives. These people served as *sureties*. If the defendants did not appear for trial after they had been placed on bail, the sureties were tried. The party furnishing bail was reminded that he or she had the powers of a jailer and was expected to produce the accused for trial. This policy of private sureties was followed in America but was replaced subsequently by a system of posting a bail bond. Several types of bail bond systems are used, as Exhibit 13.5 notes.

Early U.S. court cases made it clear that the purpose of bail is to ensure the defendant's presence at trial, not to punish defendants or to protect society. The U.S. Supreme Court has ruled that "bail set at a figure higher

EXHIBIT 13.5

Types of Pretrial Release Used in State Courts

Type of Release	Defendant	Financial Liability for Failure to Appear	Liable Party
Financial			
Surety bond	Pays fee (usually 10 percent of bail amount) plus collateral if required, to commercial bail agent.	Full bail amount	Bail agent
Deposit bond	Posts deposit (usually 10 percent of bail amount) with court, which is usually refunded at successful completion of case.	Full bail amount	Defendant
Full cash bond	Posts full bail amount with court.	Full bail amount	Defendant
Property bond	Posts property title as collateral with court.	Full bail amount	Defendant
Nonfinancial			
Release on recognizance (ROR)	Signs written agreement to appear in court (includes citation releases by law enforcement).	None	
Conditional (supervised) release	Agrees to comply with specific conditions such as regular reporting or drug use monitoring.	None	N/A
Unsecured bond	Has a bail amount set, but no payment is required to secure release.	Full bail amount	Defendant
Emergency release	Released as part of a court order to relieve jail crowding.	None	N/A

Source: Thomas H. Cohen and Brian A. Reaves, Bureau of Justice Statistics, *Pretrial Release of Felony Defendants in State Courts* (November 2007), p. 3, http://bjs.ojp.usdoj.gov/content/pub/pdf/prfdsc.pdf, accessed 10 November 2010.

than the amount reasonably calculated to [ensure that the defendant will stand trial] is 'excessive' under the Eighth Amendment [prohibition against cruel and unusual punishment]."[62]

According to federal rules and some state statutes, bail may be denied in capital cases and in noncapital cases in which the defendant has a history of fleeing to avoid prosecution. The reason in both cases is consistent with the original purpose of bail—to ensure the presence of the accused at trial. Until recently, this was the *only* legitimate purpose of bail. In 1970, with the passage of the District of Columbia Court Reform and Criminal Procedure Act, **preventive detention** was recognized as a legitimate purpose of bail in that jurisdiction. This statute permits judges to deny bail to defendants charged with dangerous crimes if the government has clear evidence, including consideration of the accused's past and present pattern of behavior, that release would endanger public safety.[63] Some states have similar provisions.

In 1984, Congress passed a comprehensive reform of the federal criminal code, including a provision for preventive detention. Detention is authorized if no conditions of release will reasonably assure "the appearance of the person as required and the safety of any other person and the community." The act provides that those arrested for drug offenses are presumed dangerous or likely to flee; thus, they may be detained pending trial unless they can prove that it would be reasonably safe for them to be released. The constitutionality of this provision was chal-

lenged, and the U.S. Supreme Court ruled in favor of the provision in *United States v. Salerno*, decided in 1987.[64]

Like many other aspects of criminal justice systems, the use of bail has been associated with extralegal variables. For example, numerous studies note that unemployed persons are more likely than employed persons to be incarcerated after conviction or detained before trial. It is argued that as unemployment increases and the unemployed are perceived as threats by the middle and upper classes, judges will be more punitive, imposing longer sentences or detaining more persons. That argument, however, has been questioned.[65]

Other extralegal factors associated with bail are race and ethnicity. Research on the racial and ethnic impact of bail or detention decisions has shown that Hispanics were more likely than whites or even African Americans to be detained prior to trial, and when bail was set, they were most likely to have higher bail. Four elements of the pretrial process resulted in the more frequent pretrial detention of minorities:

- "Black and Hispanic defendants are more likely than white defendants to be denied bail.
- Hispanic defendants are less likely to receive a nonfinancial release option (e.g., ROR [release on own recognizance]) than either white or black defendants.
- The amount of bail required for release is higher for Hispanic defendants than white defendants; there is no black–white difference in bail amount.

■ Hispanic and black defendants are more likely than white defendants to be held on bail because of an inability to post bail. Indeed, the inability to 'make bail' accounts for the majority of black and Hispanic defendants' overall greater likelihood of pretrial detention."[66]

These research findings were similar to others showing that Hispanics are disadvantaged in criminal justice systems.[67]

An additional problem with bail is that many defendants cannot pay the full amount of bail, thus making bail more available to the wealthy than to the poor. One system designed to remedy this problem is the professional bail bondsman/woman system. In return for a fee, the bail bondsman/woman posts bond for the accused defendant. Theoretically, if the defendant does not appear for trial, the bondsman/woman is required to forfeit the money. In practice, bond forfeitures are rarely enforced. Furthermore, some bondsmen/women do not have the necessary money to pay in cases of forfeiture. To avoid this situation, some jurisdictions require them to prove their ability to pay in case of forfeiture. The bond system has been criticized, and some states have placed legislative restrictions on the system or eliminated it entirely.

Plea Bargaining

Another controversial pretrial process is **plea bargaining**, a process of negotiation between the prosecution and the defense in which the defense agrees to plead guilty to the current charge(s) or to lesser charge(s) in exchange for the prosecutor's promise to recommend a light sentence, drop other charges, or make some other concession. The consequences of refusing a plea bargain may be severe and are illustrated by the two juvenile cases discussed in Exhibit 5.1 (see again Chapter 5).

Not all guilty pleas are the result of plea bargaining despite the fact that most convictions are the result of guilty pleas. Some guilty pleas are based on the defense's decision that pleading guilty is the best choice, even in the absence of a plea bargain offer from the prosecution. Likewise, prosecutorial decisions to reduce or drop charges may be the result of prosecutorial discretion unrelated to a bargain with the defense.

Plea bargaining received the recognition of the U.S. Supreme Court in 1971 when it was approved as a means of managing overloaded criminal dockets. The Supreme Court declared plea bargaining to be "an essential component" of the criminal process, which "properly administered . . . is to be encouraged."[68] Supporters of plea bargaining argue that the process is necessary because of the tremendous number of criminal cases. Further, plea bargaining saves the state money and time. Not all cases need to go to trial; defendants and society are better served by settling some cases out of court.

Opponents of plea bargaining argue that not all judges and prosecutors honor the deals made between the prosecution and the defense and that innocent defendants may be encouraged to plead guilty. Critics express concern that some deals are too good for defendants, that those charged with serious offenses are permitted to plead guilty to less serious offenses, and that some defendants charged with violent offenses get off too lightly. Another problem is that plea bargaining may reduce or even eliminate the exposure of errors made in the judicial process prior to pleading.

The U.S. Supreme Court has placed restrictions on plea bargaining, but the Court has upheld the prosecutor's right to threaten to secure a grand jury indictment against the defendant on a more serious charge if the defendant does not plead guilty to the existing charge, as the next case illustrates.

In *Bordenkircher v. Hayes*, the defendant was under indictment for passing a hot check for $88.30. The sentence that could have been imposed upon conviction of that offense was two to ten years. The prosecutor told the defendant that he would recommend a five-year sentence if the defendant would plead guilty. If the defendant refused to do so, the prosecutor said he would seek an indictment under the state's Habitual Criminal Act, which provided that upon conviction of a third felony, a defendant would receive a mandatory life sentence. The defendant refused to accept the offer, went to trial, and was convicted. In a separate proceeding, it was found that he had two prior felony convictions. He was sentenced to life in prison as required by the Habitual Criminal Act. In a 5–4 decision, the U.S. Supreme Court emphasized that although the state may not retaliate against a defendant who chooses to exercise a legal right, "in the 'give-and-take' of plea bargaining, there is no such element of punishment or retaliation so long as the accused is free to accept or reject the prosecution's offer."[69]

To constitute a valid plea bargain, the defendant's plea must be knowledgeable and voluntary. In determining whether a plea is voluntary, courts consider whether a defendant was represented by counsel; if so, the plea is less likely to be considered involuntary. Furthermore, prosecutors are not permitted to engage in harassment, misrepresentation, unfulfilled promises, or promises that have no relation to proper prosecutorial business, such as a bribe, to coerce a defendant to accept a plea bargain.[70]

An example of an improper plea bargain occurred in an Arizona case. The appellate court held that a guilty plea based on a prosecutor's promise not to oppose the defendant's efforts to obtain conjugal visits with his wife during his incarceration was invalid. Stating that conjugal access is an irrational basis for entering a guilty plea, the court ruled that including this understanding within the plea bargain suggests psychological pressure that invalidates the voluntariness of the defendant's plea.[71]

A 1995 U.S. Supreme Court decision, *United States v. Mezzanatto*, involved the federal procedural rule that permits plea bargaining. That rule specifies that statements made by the defendant in the course of a plea bargain may not be used against that defendant at trial if the plea negotiations fail. The rule does not state whether the defendant may waive that provision.[72] In *Mezzanatto*, the defendant agreed to the prosecutor's demand that any statement made during plea negotiations could be used against him if the case went to trial. During the negotiations, the defendant admitted some involvement in the alleged crime, but his evasiveness led the prosecution to break off negotiations. When the defendant was cross-examined during trial, some of his statements were inconsistent with those he made during plea bargaining. The evidence of those prior inconsistent statements was admitted at trial, and the defendant was convicted. The court of appeals reversed. The U.S. Supreme Court reversed that decision, holding that the exclusionary provision of the federal rule could be and was waived by the defendant in this case.[73]

States are free to abolish plea bargaining, and some have done so. But where plea bargaining is retained, its goals must be fairness, less delay, less disparity among sentences, and sentences closer to those that would result from trial. To achieve these goals, the parties to the negotiation must have a reasonable perception of the conviction and sentencing probabilities. The defendant should not be forced to accept a higher-bargained conviction or sentence because he or she is in jail, is unable to afford an attorney, has not seen the presentence report, or is represented by a public defender who does not have the time or resources to go to trial. Nor should prosecutors be forced to offer bargains with reduced charges or low sentences because of limited resources.

Finally, one researcher, trained in law and the social sciences, investigated one unit of a highly structured plea bargaining system in Seattle, Washington, and concluded that although efficiency was achieved in 70 percent of the cases, it was not clear that justice was achieved. Compared to traditional plea bargaining models, this jurisdiction's model gave more power to prosecutors than to defense attorneys. That change did not seem to alter attorneys' behavior in the processing of "normal crimes," but it did appear to create tension in the processing of more complex criminal cases.[74]

The Trial of a Criminal Case

The trial of a criminal case involves numerous complicated legal procedures. After a quick overview of the trial process, this section focuses on two major issues in criminal cases: the right to a speedy trial and the roles of the judge and jury.

Although most defendants enter a plea and do not proceed to trial, the trial is a crucial element of criminal justice systems. In recent years, the trial has become the focus of television, with some trials televised in their entirety, although some judges do not permit television cameras in the courtroom.

Even when an entire trial is televised, there are proceedings that take place elsewhere (e.g., in the judge's chambers) that are crucial to the trial proceedings. Judges meet frequently with the prosecution and defense attorneys to work out the details of how the trial will progress. These parties may discuss the need to streamline the presentation of evidence—for example, by reducing the number of witnesses. They may discuss the failure of one party to convey informational documents to the other side, as ordered by the judge in the discovery process. Attorneys may be penalized or the trial may be delayed if these procedures are not followed properly.

Throughout the trial, attorneys may file motions with the court, and those motions may affect the remainder of the trial. For instance, a successful motion to exclude specific evidence that the opposing side planned to introduce may make it necessary for that side to change its strategy. Also, throughout the trial, the plea bargaining process may continue, and at any time, the defendant, if he or she chooses, may be permitted to enter a plea and thus avoid or halt the trial.

At some point, however, unless the case has been decided by a plea, the trial begins with jury selection. In some complicated cases, this might take days, weeks, or even months. Once the jurors are selected and sworn, opening statements may be made, first by the prosecution and then by the defense. During the opening statements, the respective sides may give a glimpse of what they hope to accomplish during the presentation of evidence. When it is time for that stage, the prosecution presents its evidence first. After each witness finishes testifying, the defense may ask questions in a process called *cross-examination*, after which the prosecution may reexamine its witnesses, and the defense may re-cross. After all of the prosecution witnesses are presented and the prosecution rests its case, the defense may present its case.

The defense is not required to present witnesses or other evidence. In some cases, it will not do so; in effect, the defense rests after the prosecution has presented its case. Why would the defense do this? The defense attorney may believe that the state's evidence is not strong enough to prove the defendant guilty beyond a reasonable doubt. Furthermore, the defense might weaken its position by putting on witnesses, especially the defendant. Defendants are not required to testify, and many do not do so. Even an innocent defendant may hurt the defense by testifying.

After all the evidence is presented, each side may—but is not required to—offer a closing statement. Again, motions might be made. For example, the defense might make a motion for the judge to direct the jury to acquit the defendant based on the lack of credible evidence to convict. The judge may, but rarely does, grant this motion.

After the closing arguments and processing of any motions, the judge instructs the jury regarding the law in the case. Usually, both the defense and the prosecution submit information to the judge for that charge; the judge may or may not adopt their language. After the charge is given to the jury, the jurors retire to the jury room and deliberate regarding the evidence presented during the trial. They may be sequestered from then until they reach a verdict (in rare cases, they may be sequestered as soon as they are sworn in). Or they may be permitted to go home at night with instructions not to discuss the case with anyone and not to read newspapers or watch media concerning the case.

If the jury cannot reach a verdict after a reasonable time, the judge will declare a mistrial. If the jury reaches a verdict, it will be read in open court after all parties have been notified and given a reasonable time to assemble. After the verdict, the jurors may be dismissed. In some jurisdictions, they will be told to return at a specified time to hear evidence concerning the sentence if the defendant has been convicted. In other jurisdictions, a new jury may be selected for the sentencing hearing, or the hearing will be in front of a judge only.

After the defendant is sentenced, he or she may have legal grounds for an appeal. Those who appeal may or may not be released pending the outcome of that appeal. If they are held in custody, they may receive credit for that time served. Those who are sentenced to prison normally will be taken to a facility for classification prior to assignment to a state or federal prison.

The Right to a Speedy Trial

The Sixth Amendment provides, in part, "In all criminal prosecutions, the accused shall enjoy the right to a speedy and public trial." This right does not preclude the defense or the prosecution from asking for and being granted continuances when additional time is needed to prepare. It does mean that the prosecution and defense may not delay unreasonably. Most of the statutes specify some circumstances under which trials may be legitimately delayed, but those provisions are the subject of extensive litigation. An example is the federal provision that delays may occur when they are necessary to "serve the ends of justice."

What constitutes an unreasonable delay must be decided on a case-by-case basis. One decision held that even a 10-year delay between indictment and trial did not deny a defendant her right to a speedy trial. The defendant was charged with conspiracy to import cocaine. To avoid apprehension and prosecution, she fled the jurisdiction prior to the indictment. The government had made diligent efforts to locate her for trial but was unsuccessful for 10 years.[75]

In contrast, in 1992, the U.S. Supreme Court held that a defendant who was indicted in 1980 but not arrested until 1988 had been denied his right to a speedy trial. The defendant in *Doggett v. United States* left the country in 1980 and returned in 1982. The government thought he was still out of the country and made little effort to find him. Justice David Souter wrote the opinion for a divided U.S. Supreme Court stating that such delays compromise the reliability of a trial. A delay of this magnitude, which was the result of "inexcusable oversights" on the government's part, "far exceeds the threshold needed to state a speedy trial claim."[76]

The trial judge is responsible for monitoring all pretrial procedures and deciding when delays are reasonable and when they are not.

The Trial Decision: Judge or Jury

Although most cases do not go to trial, trials are a crucial part of criminal justice systems, and both judges and juries play a significant role in them. In a criminal trial, the **judge** is the referee. Theoretically, judges are neither for nor against a particular position or issue but are committed to the fair implementation of the rules of evidence and law. Judges must present the case to the jury with a charge in which they explain the law applicable to the case and give instructions that jurors must follow in arriving at a verdict. Judges may have significant influence over the jury through their attitudes, their rulings, and their charges. They have an impact on those who testify and on those who are parties to the trial. Trial judges should be considerate and uphold the highest standards of justice in their courtrooms. The position of the trial judge is a powerful one; although judges may be overruled, most cases are not appealed.

Some criminal cases are tried before a judge only, but most involve juries. Some authorities believe that the jury system is among the great achievements of English and American jurisprudence, whereas others criticize it. Sociologists have studied the jury system to gather data on some of the issues, and these studies have become widely recognized in the literature.

Although critics believe that the jury system is an ineffective method for determining facts (the results of empirical research are not clear), there is some support for the system's efficiency and accuracy.[77] The U.S. Supreme Court has held that juries understand the evidence presented at trials, but some critics question that conclusion.[78]

An analysis of the responses of more than 500 jurors in death penalty cases led to the conclusion that "jurors are not playing by the rules." The Capital Jury Project studied how jurors in death penalty cases understood and applied the law and whether they made arbitrary decisions. The findings disclosed that about half (50.7 percent) of jurors made their determinations about sentencing before they had heard the sentencing evidence. In capital cases in jurisdictions where juries were involved in sentencing as well as determining the guilt or innocence of the defendant, jurors are required to determine guilt or innocence first. The court holds a separate sentencing hearing, which can involve evidence that may not be admitted at trial; thus, the defendant does not have the benefit of this evidence if jurors have already made up their minds about sentencing. Considerations of possible punishment should not influence the issue of whether the defendant is guilty.[79]

The jury has the ultimate power to end a trial with an acquittal; it also has the power to convict an innocent person. The role of the media in jury decisions is also crucial, as illustrated by Media Focus 13.1, which shows the potential impact of the media in causing a mistrial.

An interesting point regarding the judge and jury relates to which is more likely to convict a defendant. A law professor who analyzed convictions in federal courts stated as follows:

> The figures contradicted one of the oldest pieces of conventional wisdom in the legal profession: That defendants get more sympathy from a jury than a judge. . . . [Although the conviction rates were similar prior to the introduction of federal sentencing guidelines in 1988, in the 14 years he examined] the conviction rate of federal juries increased to 84 percent, while that of federal judges decreased to 55 percent.[80]

Sentencing

One of the most important stages in criminal justice systems is **sentencing**. For offenders, sentencing determines the punishments that are imposed and thus how they will spend the coming months or years. For some, sentencing determines whether they will live or die. For society, the sentencing decision necessitates not only action in particular cases but also recognition of the philosophies that underlie the punishment concept. Punishment philosophies, upon which a **sentence** may be based, were discussed in Chapter 3.

Historically, many types of sentences have been imposed. They range from **corporal punishment**, much of it so painful and brutal that it resulted in death, to probation, the sentence used most frequently in the United States today (see Chapter 15). Offenders may be required to pay a **fine**, to make **restitution**, or to perform **community service**. Fines are being assessed more frequently, even in cases of violent crimes. Some offenders are incarcerated in prisons or jails, the focus of Chapter 14.

The Sentencing Process

The three basic sentencing models are legislative, judicial, and administrative, and most systems employ one or more of these types. In the *legislative model*, the legislature establishes by statute the length of the sentence for each crime. For example, a burglary conviction carries a sentence of 10 years. Under this model, the judge has no discretion at sentencing, and prison authorities or parole boards are not allowed discretion in determining when

---

13.1 | The Jury and the Tyco Trial: The Media Reports

MEDIA FOCUS

In 2002, L. Dennis Kozlowski, former chief executive, and Mark H. Swartz, former chief financial officer, of Tyco International Ltd. were indicted for defrauding the company of $600 million through unauthorized and excessive spending. Their first trial ended in a mistrial, and some charges were dropped. The second trial began in January 2005, with Kozlowski and Swartz facing 31 counts of stock fraud, conspiracy, grand larceny, and falsifying business records. Both men were convicted.

The Tyco mistrial was granted by the judge after the media ran extensive coverage of the allegations that one juror, initially known only as juror No. 4, flashed an OK sign to the defense team. Ruth B. Jordan, 79, a retired history teacher with a law degree, later said that she did not flash an OK sign to the defense, that such a gesture would have been inappropriate as well as "unbelievably stupid." Jordan did say, however, that she would have voted to acquit because she did not believe that the prosecution had proved the element of intent beyond a reasonable doubt.

After Jordan was identified by name in at least two newspapers, she received a letter, which she told the judge was disturbing but not threatening. The letter asked how she could disgrace her family by not seeing that the two men were obviously guilty. In declaring the mistrial, Judge Michael Obus blamed the media. He stated that the media put pressure on the jury as a result of the "notoriety that was brought to bear on one particular juror, whose name and background have been widely publicized in the media, lawfully, but in violation of the convention that is ordinarily observed and wisely observed." Jordan had been called such names as "holdout Granny," "Batty Blueblood," and a "braggart." A sketch of her was published in the media along with information obtained by reporters, who interviewed the staff in the building where she lived.

Some criticized the judge for calling a mistrial after the trial had gone on for six months. The jurors could have been sequestered or their mail censored to provide the protection they needed to reach a decision unbiased by the media or other outsiders. Judges are reluctant, however, to sequester a jury, especially one in a case predicted to last for months.

Source: Summarized from several media sources, including "Behind the Tyco Mistrial" and "Judge Faults Media's Moves," both appearing in the *Wall Street Journal* (5 April 2004), p. 1B.

the inmate is released. This type of sentence is called the **determinate sentence**.

In the *judicial* model, the judge decides the length of the sentence within a range established by the legislature. For example, the legislature determines that, for burglary, the sentence is from 5 to 10 years, and the judge imposes a sentence within that range. In the *administrative* model, the legislature establishes a wide range of imprisonment for a particular crime. For example, the legislature determines that for armed robbery, the sentence is one day to life, a sentence that is imposed by the judge after the defendant is convicted. The decision to release the inmate is made later by an administrative agency, usually a parole board. The type of sentence imposed in this model is called the **indeterminate sentence**.

There is considerable debate over which of the three sentencing models should be used. In recent years, the trend has been away from the administrative model and indeterminate sentencing and toward the legislative model and determinate sentencing. But even this trend illustrates that most sentencing is a combination of the three models. For example, some of the recent legislation permits determinate sentences established by the legislature to be altered judicially if a given case has certain mitigating or aggravating circumstances. This approach is called **presumptive sentencing**.

Presumptive sentencing differs from flat or determinate sentencing in that it does not remove all judicial discretion. It does, however, check the abuse of that discretion by establishing that a deviate sentence is presumed to be improper. Thus, when the sentence is appealed, the sentencing judge has the burden of proving that there were justifiable reasons for deviating from the recommended sentence.

Various combinations of sentence types are also used. A defendant may be fined and incarcerated, fined and placed on probation, or fined and ordered to pay restitution. There are combinations of probation and incarceration, too, including the following:

Split sentences—the court specifies a period of incarceration to be followed by a period of probation.

Modification of sentence—the original sentencing court may reconsider an offender's prison sentence within a limited time and change it to probation.

Shock probation—an offender sentenced to incarceration is released after a period of time in confinement (the shock) and resentenced to probation.

Intermittent incarceration—an offender on probation may spend only weekends or nights in jail.[81]

Any of the sentencing models or combinations may be affected by other factors. Power may be given to the governor to commute a life sentence to a specified term of years. The state governor (or the president in the federal system) may have the power to **pardon** an offender. Sentences may also be commuted by the governor or the president. For example, in July 2007, President George W. Bush commuted the sentence of Lewis "Scooter" Libby Jr., the former top aide to Vice President Dick Cheney. Libby was convicted of perjury and obstruction of justice, sentenced to two and one-half years in prison, and ordered to pay a $250,000 fine. The case involved the revelation of the name of Valerie Plame, a CIA undercover operative, after her husband published an article critical of the Bush administration. The effect of the Bush commutation was that Libby's convictions and fine remained intact, but he was not required to serve prison time.

It is also possible that sentence length may be reduced in accordance with **good-time credit** because of the inmate's good behavior or for time served without an evaluative measure, such as in jail awaiting trial.

Sentencing Issues

Earlier in the text, we discussed trends toward treatment rather than punishment, especially with regard to drug offenses. In addition to this trend, there are other sentencing issues that have gained significant attention. In this section, several of those are addressed.

Sentence Disparity

The earlier movement toward determinate and longer sentences was based on concern with rising crime rates and also with alleged **sentence disparity**, a concept used frequently and seldom defined. To some, sentence disparity occurs when two people convicted of the same crime are given different sentences by their respective judges. Others claim that disparity exists when legislatures of different states set different penalties for the same offense; thus, robbery with a firearm may result in a 25-year sentence in one state and a 15-year sentence in another. Still others say that sentence disparity exists only when similarly situated offenders receive quite different penalties for the same offense. It is a disparity if a three-time offender in one jurisdiction receives 5 years for armed robbery whereas a three-time offender in another receives 15 years for the same offense.

One sentencing practice that was adopted in an attempt to reduce recidivism is habitual offender statutes, manifested in what is referred to as *three-strikes legislation*. These statutes vary significantly from jurisdiction to jurisdiction, thus leading to charges of sentence disparity.

Three Strikes and You're Out

Legislation referred to as **three strikes and you're out**, available in the federal as well as state systems, is illustrated by the California statute. It provides for a mandatory sentence of from 25 years to life in prison for conviction of a third felony if prior felonies were for serious or violent crimes. It also provides for tougher sentences for first- and second-time felons and requires an offender to serve 80 percent of a sentence before release from prison. This mandatory minimum time before release is referred to as **truth in sentencing** and has been adopted in many jurisdictions.[82] Both approaches were criticized by judges, attorneys, and prison wardens, among others, and the California courts decided several cases on the issue. But in 2003, the U.S. Supreme Court upheld the California three-strikes legislation. The case of *Ewing v. California* is presented briefly in Exhibit 13.6.

Both the truth-in-sentencing and the three-strikes policies illustrate the systems effect mentioned often in this text. With inmates serving longer terms under both of these policies, courts, jails, and prisons have become overcrowded, an issue that was discussed in Chapter 10 with regard to drug sentences and is also discussed later in this chapter. The following chapters contain additional information on the corrections crisis in California, much of which can be attributed to the state's three-strikes legislation, the most stringent system in the nation. A scholarly analysis of the California three-strikes legislation emphasized that this legislation has added so many inmates to the state's prison populations that between 2009 and 2014, tens of thousands of them will become "a permanent residue in the California correctional system." A legislative attempt to change the three-strikes legislation in California failed in 2004, with 53 percent of those voting rejecting Proposition 66, which, among other provisions, would have resulted in the release of many nonviolent offenders and required that the third strike for sentences purposes must be a violent or serious felony to trigger a life sentence. Early polls showed that a majority of the state's voters favored the proposed changes, but last-minute efforts by the state's governor, along with a massive advertising campaign to defeat the proposition, were successful.[83] Subsequent chapters will outline the federal court orders that now control the California system as a result primarily of its overcrowding.

EXHIBIT 13.6

Three Strikes and You're Out

The California three-strikes sentencing legislation provides for the mandatory sentence for persons convicted of a third felony, which may be any felony although the first two must be serious or violent ones. Harsher penalties are also mandated for second felony convictions.[1]

The California statute has resulted in harsh sentences for offenders convicted of a third felony that is not serious or violent, such as the 25-year sentence for stealing a pizza imposed on Jerry Dewayne Williams, age 27. His prior convictions were for robbery, attempted robbery, drug possession, and unauthorized use of a vehicle. At his three-strikes trial, prosecutors described Williams as a career criminal who terrorized little kids. "[W]e think our children can sit down in peace in broad daylight, without a 6-foot 4-inch 220-pound ex-con threatening them and taking away food from them."[2]

Williams's sentence and others precipitated protests, but judges who followed the letter of the law had no choice but to impose the harsh penalties. In February 1997, a judge reduced some of Williams's prior felonies to misdemeanor convictions, thus making him eligible for release in 2 rather than 23 years. Judges in other cases have also challenged the three-strikes mandates. One prosecutor asked for a life sentence for a 43-year-old offender who was found guilty of stealing a $22 Mighty Ducks baseball cap from a shopping mall store. Thomas Kiel Brown was a candidate for the harsh penalty because he had two prior serious felony convictions (for robbery and grand theft). The judge commented: "No judge I know wants to let dangerous criminals loose in the community. But I'm sure the taxpayer doesn't want to spend more than $500,000 to put a petty thief in jail for stealing a cap."[3]

Various legal challenges were brought against the California three-strikes legislation, but the key decision came from the U.S. Supreme Court in 2003, when that Court upheld two three-strikes cases, one from California. In *Ewing v. California*, the Supreme Court held that a 25-years-to-life prison sentence for a repeat felon was not a violation of the cruel and unusual punishment clause of the Eighth Amendment (see Appendix A). Gary Ewing, who was on parole from a nine-year prison term, walked out of a golf pro shop with three golf clubs, priced at $399 each, concealed in his pants leg. An employee noticed Ewing limping and called the police, who apprehended him in the parking lot. Ewing, who had been convicted of numerous crimes previously, was convicted of felony grand theft of personal property in excess of $400. The court found that he had been convicted of four previous felonies; thus, the three-strikes sentencing law applied. According to the U.S. Supreme Court, "Ewing's sentence is justified by the State's public-safety interest in incapacitating and deterring recidivist felons, and amply supported by his own long, serious criminal record [which included nine separate incarcerations] . . . To be sure, Ewing's sentence is a long one. But it reflects a rational legislative judgment, entitled to deference, that offenders who have committed serious or violent felonies and who continue to commit felonies must be incapacitated."[4]

---

1. See Cal Pen Code, Title 16, Section 667 (2010).
2. "Theft of Pizza Slice Nets a Twenty-Five-Year Term," *New York Times* (5 March 1995), p. 11.
3. "Judges Hail Change in Their Role," *Los Angeles Times* (21 June 1996), p. 1.
4. *Ewing v. California*, 538 U.S. 11 (2003). The other case is *Lockyer v. Andrade*, 538 U.S. 63 (2003).

Another serious and perhaps unexpected result of the three-strikes legislation is that, apparently because of the seriousness of this approach (long or even life sentences), more defendants are challenging their convictions rather than pleading guilty. In the first few years of the three-strikes legislation in California, for example, the state experienced a 4 percent increase in trials in no-strike cases, a 9 percent increase in two-strikes cases, and a 41 percent increase in three-strikes cases. The increases were not uniform throughout the state, but many judges said that to accommodate the increases, they had to shift resources from civil to criminal courts.[84]

Three-strikes legislation strains criminal justice systems and causes disruption for judges, prosecutors, public defenders, and jail officials. It has also created an increased shortage of jurors. California already had a shortage, but with the increase in trials due to three-strikes legislation, the problem escalated. Finally, judges and jurors may look for ways to avoid the harsh penalties of the law. Juries can always refuse to convict if they think the mandatory penalty is too severe. Judges have several options, one of which is to reduce the current felony charge to a misdemeanor in some cases.

In conclusion, it could be argued that attempting to deter crime by incarcerating repeat offenders for longer periods of time increases costs and personnel problems in all areas of criminal court systems. But it offers no evidence that crime is significantly reduced.

This discussion is not meant to support the position that we should not incarcerate inmates for long periods of time. Rather, it illustrates the effect that changes in one part of the system may have on other elements of the system. Normally, there is little or no planning for the potentially negative side effects of what initially appears to be a great idea for combating crime.

Crack/Powder Cocaine Sentencing Reform

Earlier discussions in this text noted the 100-1 ratio in crack/powder cocaine sentences with the harsher penalties assessed for possession of crack, more often used by minorities than by whites. Racial discrimination in sentencing in general is discussed later; this analysis focuses on the sentencing laws regarding crack and powder cocaine, a disparity on which debate has raged for years. Some progress has been made in changing the sentencing ratio.

In May 2007, the U.S. Sentencing Commission recommended to Congress that the sentences for crack cocaine be lowered. Congress did not reject those recommendations, and as provided by law, they became effective 1 November 2007. Under the new guidelines, the average sentence was reduced from ten years and one month to eight years and ten months. In December 2007, the Sentencing Commission, by a unanimous vote, applied the new guidelines retroactively and estimated that approximately 19,500 crack cocaine offenders who were sentenced under the original and harsher guidelines could have their sentences lowered. The new guidelines went into effect on 3 March 2008, at which time The Sentencing Project, a research and advocacy reform organization, announced that the average sentence reduction would be a little over two years. "Releases are subject to judicial review and will be staggered over 30 years."[85]

On 3 August 2010, President Barack Obama signed the Fair Sentencing Act of 2010. This new law became effective on 1 November 2010. A brief summary of the provisions of the act is contained in Exhibit 13.7.[86]

Race and Ethnicity Discrimination

While scholars argue over whether criminal justice systems do or do not discriminate on the basis of extralegal factors (e.g., age, race and ethnicity, or gender), many people continue to believe that they do. Generally, this belief is based on the knowledge that convictions and sentences (as well as arrests) involve a disproportionate number of African Americans and other minorities. Despite arguments that these differentials are the result of such legal factors as prior criminal records, current offense, and other legally relevant variables, many remain unconvinced.

Law professor Michael Tonry, who studied race and sentencing, concluded that racial disparities have "steadily gotten worse since 1980." Tonry attributed this primarily to the increased penalties for drug violations. Specifically, he was referring to the 100–1 ratio of sentence length for conviction for possessing crack cocaine compared to sentences for conviction for possessiong powder cocaine. Crack cocaine use is more common among African Americans, whereas powder cocaine use is more characteristic of whites.[87]

Many lower courts that have heard cases on the issues involving statistical differences in sentencing have held that these differences do not prove racial discrimination.[88]

In Chapter 10, we noted that in *United States v. Armstrong*, the U.S. Supreme Court held that selective prosecutions in cases involving the 100-1 ratio of sentences for violations of crack cocaine to those for violations of powder cocaine do not alone support a claim of racial discrimination despite the fact that minorities more often use crack than powder cocaine (which is much more expensive).[89] As noted, the Fair Sentencing Act of 2010 changed the sentencing ratio to 18–1 but will not affect drug offenders already sentenced under the previous law.

Not everyone agrees with the U.S. Supreme Court analysis. The Sentencing Commission emphasized that in 2010, over 60 percent of the inmates in U.S. prisons were racial and ethnic minorities. On any given day, one of every eight U.S. black males in their 20s was in prison or jail, and three-fourths of all persons incarcerated for drug offenses were persons of color. The Sentencing Commission, citing two studies, attributed these disproportionate numbers to the U.S. war on drugs, especially the crack/

The Fair Sentencing Act of 2010

On 28 July 2010, the U.S. Congress passed the Fair Sentencing Act of 2010. The act was signed by President Barack Obama on 3 August 2010. It went into effect on 1 November 2010.

The main purpose of this new sentencing law was to change the 100-to-1 ratio disparity between sentences for convictions of crack cocaine compared to those for powder cocaine. The new law established a ratio of 18-to-1. The law is not retroactive; thus, it does not affect defendants who were sentenced prior to 1 November 2010. The statute also eliminated the five-year mandatory minimum prison sentence for simple possession of crack cocaine. It increases some penalties, such as those for drug offenses that involve certain vulnerable victims, violence, and other specified ag-

gravating factors. The statute contains provisions regarding drug courts (e.g., requiring collecting data on them) and many other provisions.

U.S. Attorney General Eric Holder issued a press release on 28 July 2010. He congratulated the Congress on passing the new bill. He stated that the bill "will go a long way toward ensuring that our sentencing laws are tough, consistent, and fair."[1]

1. U.S. Department of Justice, Statement of the Attorney General on Passage of the Fair Sentencing Act, Press Release (28 July 2010), http://www.justice.gov/opa/pr/2010/July/10-ag-867.html, accessed 7 November 2010. Fair Sentencing Act of 2010, P.L. 111-220 (2010).

cocaine sentence disparity.[90] With regard to overcrowded prisons (discussed in Chapter 14), The Sentencing Commission made this statement:

Changes in sentencing law and policy, not increases in crime rates, explain most of the six-fold increase in the national prison population. These changes have significantly impacted racial disparities in sentencing, as well as increased the use of "one size fits all" mandatory minimum sentences that allow little consideration for individual characteristics.[91]

The debate over whether criminal justice systems discriminate against minorities arises frequently in the context of capital punishment. Several extensive studies have been made in this area, but the U.S. Supreme Court remains unconvinced that the research substantiates unconstitutional discrimination, as demonstrated in the Court's 1987 decision in *McCleskey v. Kemp*. McCleskey used an empirical analysis by law professor David Baldus and his collaborators to demonstrate that capital punishment is assessed more frequently when the victim is white compared to African American and, to a lesser extent, when the offender is African American rather than white. The implication, claimed McCleskey's attorney, is that the lives of whites are more valued than are those of African Americans; thus, those who kill whites are more likely to get the death penalty than are those who kill African Americans. The Supreme Court would agree only that the study "indicates a discrepancy that appears to correlate with race. Apparent disparities in sentencing are an inevitable part of our criminal justice system." But the Supreme Court did not believe the study demonstrated "a constitutionally significant risk of racial bias."[92]

Some racial disparity may not be readily obvious. For example, cases are decided by different modes. Some are the result of negotiated or nonnegotiated plea bargains. Some are tried before juries, and others are tried only

before judges. Some result in convictions. Is it possible that the mode of conviction is related to racial and ethnic disparity? One study found that courtroom discretion and downward departures of sentence guidelines (i.e., imposition of sentences for *less* time than is recommended by sentencing guidelines) were more related to legal factors (e.g., the nature of the offense) than to extralegal factors (e.g., race).[93] But a later study looked more closely at courtroom discretion, considering the mode of conviction and downward departures. It reported that extralegal factors, including race, had more influence on the sentencing decisions. Compared with white defendants, African American and Hispanic defendants had a greater chance of receiving sentences that were beyond the guidelines and a smaller chance of receiving those that were below them. The relationship is complex, though, and investigators recommend further research.[94]

There were some changes in the number of blacks compared to whites in prisons due to drug convictions. In 2009, The Sentencing Project announced the results of its comparison of government data between 1999 and 2005, showing a decline of 21.6 percent of blacks and an increase of 42.6 percent of whites incarcerated for drug crimes. Possible explanations were changes in drug use, the methods of trafficking drugs, the use of drug courts for diversion, the rise in the use of methamphetamine (more commonly used by whites), and the decrease in some states in the number of prison sentences due to budget cuts.[95] Despite these changes, the proportion of blacks to whites in prisons remains disparate.

Gender Discrimination

Gender differences have also been noted in sentencing. In an often-cited work published in 1950, Otto Pollak stated that women were given preferential treatment in criminal justice systems primarily because of the chivalry of the men in power in those systems.[96] Subsequent researchers have agreed, noting that throughout much of the world, women are given preferential treatment in sentencing because of such extralegal factors as their family ties, their roles as the primary caregivers of their children, their mental health, a view of women as victims, and their economic dependence. A 1994 review of the literature in this area reported that women were less likely than men with comparable crimes to receive a harsh sentence in 8 to 26 percent of the cases, with sentences for men averaging 12 months longer than those for women. According to researchers of the differential sentencing of men and women in New Zealand, "Such research supports the hypothesis that women are treated more leniently than men in the criminal justice system, but we know relatively little about when and how this sex-based differential takes place." The New Zealand study found support for the earlier studies; the authors suggested that because of similarities between the criminal justice systems and the structure of gender roles in that country and in other Western countries, the results might be generalized. They also noted that the results "raise pivotal questions about policy and law, and the treatment of women and men in criminal justice."[97]

Feminist scholars suggest that even though women may at times be given lighter sentences than men, criminal justice systems also treat women and girls more harshly in circumstances designed to keep them in submissive roles. For example, girls who ran away from home or engaged in other status offenses were more likely to be processed through the juvenile courts than were boys who engaged in similar behavior.[98]

There is also research to support the consideration of several variables, such as marital status, employment, race, offense type, the presence of children in the home, and other factors that are associated with the judicial sentencing of women. After reviewing this body of research, scholars concluded that women in general do not receive leniency in sentencing but that leniency is used selectively. It is used more often when women behave in traditional roles (e.g., wife and mother) and when they commit offenses that have been traditionally associated with women (e.g., minor property crimes). A study in Minnesota found that although gender alone was not a factor in sentencing, there was evidence that both before and after sentencing guidelines, female offenders with children in the home were treated more leniently in sentencing. This might be just and positive in that it represents a concern for the welfare of children. Perhaps justice requires us to be more lenient when sentencing both women and men who have dependent children.[99] In that regard, it is relevant to note that in sentencing Lea W. and Andrew Fastow, both convicted in the Enron case (see again Exhibit 9.3 in Chapter 9), the judge granted their request that they not serve their prison time simultaneously to enable one parent to care for their two small children.

The Sentencing Project reported pertinent data on women and sentencing for drug offenses and alleged that drug sentencing policies have a negative impact on women as well as African Americans and Hispanics. Although, as we noted in Chapter 2, women represent a much smaller percentage of offenders than men, their numbers have been increasing at more rapid rates. The Sentencing Project (citing data from the Women's Prison Association) attributed that to drug policies, especially the mandatory minimum sentences. One-third of female inmates are in prison for drug offenses, and of those women, a disproportionate percentage are minorities.[100]

What explains the changes in female offender populations? After a review of many of the feminist explanations for sentencing, two scholars concluded that the research on gender discrimination and sentencing is similar to other allegations of disparity.

> The strongest effect on criminal justice decisions comes from legally relevant, non-discriminatory factors, such as the seriousness of the charged offenses and the criminal characteristics of the offenders. Gender disparities favoring women exist, but they have less effect than legally relevant variables.[101]

That quotation would suggest that all is fair and just in U.S. sentencing. Not all researchers agree with this position. They argue that sentence disparity still exists and suggest ways to control it.

Control of Sentence Disparity

Two approaches are being used to control sentence disparity. In the first, discretion is left with the judge, but efforts are made to control that discretion. In the second, discretion is removed from the judge and placed with the legislature. Traditionally, judges have had wide discretion at the sentencing stage, and various methods have been suggested for controlling it. The threat of removal or being pressured to resign is one approach. This has worked in some cases, particularly when citizens have organized court watches (actually sitting through trials and sentencings to keep an eye on judicial decision making) and publicized controversial sentencing decisions. Recently, however, considerable attention has been given to the establishment of model sentencing guidelines.

Sentencing Guidelines: An Overview

Sentencing guidelines are seen as a way to control discretion without abolishing it while correcting the disparity that can result from individualized sentencing. A judge who has an offender to sentence may consider the offender's background, the nature of the offense, or other variables without any guidelines. When sentencing guidelines are used, the difference is that the relevance of these variables may have been researched; thus, the judge has a benchmark for reasonable penalties under the circumstances involved in that case.

There are drawbacks to sentencing guidelines. First, some are just guidelines, and there is nothing (except pressure) to prevent judges from ignoring them. In other cases, judges must give written reasons for deviating from the guidelines, which may specify general conditions under which the judge may impose a sentence outside the guidelines. Second, it is argued that the presence of guidelines has not reduced sentence disparity significantly. Third, there has not been sufficient analysis of the processes used in establishing the guidelines. Finally, even if the sentencing guidelines are effective in reducing sentence disparity among judges, the system has no effect on the prosecutor's virtually unchecked discretion in deciding which charges to file, whether to plea bargain (and if so, how), and what to recommend for sentencing.

Federal Guidelines

Perhaps the most controversial sentencing guidelines have been the federal guidelines recommended by the U.S. Sentencing Commission and established as a result of the 1984 revision of the federal criminal code.[102] Those guidelines became law on 1 November 1987 and subsequently have been amended. They were, and they remain, highly controversial, and initially, some federal judges refused to enforce them. Others declared them unconstitutional; some judges held that they were constitutional but unwise.

In *Mistretta v. United States*, the U.S. Supreme Court reviewed the history of federal sentencing, including the emphasis on rehabilitation accompanied by indeterminate sentencing, which theoretically gives judges the opportunity to impose a sentence tailored to the rehabilitative needs of an individual offender. After discussing the constitutional issues, the Supreme Court held that the federal guidelines did not violate federal constitutional rights.[103]

Reactions to the federal sentencing guidelines continued to vary. The U.S. Sentencing Commission claimed that the guidelines had reduced disparities.[104] However, an early study reported by the ABA noted that since the guidelines had been enacted, sentences for young African American men were "significantly higher" than sentences for young white men.[105]

A law professor recommended that the federal sentencing guidelines "be relegated to a place near the Edsel in a museum of twentieth-century bad ideas." A federal district judge in Connecticut claimed: "We should face the possibility that the basic premise of the guidelines— that the human element should be wiped away from the sentencing process and replaced by the clean, sharp edges of a sentencing slide rule—is itself highly questionable." Numerous federal judges and attorneys expressed their opposition to the federal sentencing guidelines, and many called for their abolition.[106]

In 2003, the ABA appointed the Kennedy Commission, named after U.S. Supreme Court Associate Justice Anthony M. Kennedy, who spoke to the 2003 annual ABA meeting and challenged lawyers to pay more attention to

sentencing. Specifically, Justice Kennedy called for more judicial discretion in criminal sentencing. In June 2004, when Justice Kennedy accepted the Kennedy Commission's report, he stated: "'Tough on crime' should not be a substitute for thoughtful reflection or lead us into moral blindness."[107]

The Kennedy Commission issued numerous resolutions, which were adopted by the ABA's House of Delegates during its August 2004 annual meeting. A summary of those resolutions is presented in Exhibit 13.8. The U.S. Department of Justice strongly opposed the Kennedy Commission resolutions.[108]

One final issue of critical importance is whether the federal sentencing guidelines actually reduce sentencing disparity. A recent study of three federal U.S. district trial districts "found mixed support for the notion that the federal sentencing guidelines created consistency in the sentencing outcomes of judges." The authors found "little if any" evidence of the "judicial lawlessness" that led a federal judge in 1972 to call for a federal sentencing commission to establish sentencing guidelines.[109]

U.S. Supreme Court and Sentencing Guidelines

The U.S. Supreme Court has decided several cases involving the federal sentencing guidelines. In 2004, in *Blakely v. Washington*,[110] the Court held that the Washington (State) sentence structure was unconstitutional. Blakely had entered a guilty plea to kidnapping his estranged wife, Yolanda. Blakely bound Yolanda with duct tape, forced her into a wooden box by threatening her with a knife, placed the box in his truck, and drove to a friend's house in Montana. The couple's son was in a car following the truck. Blakely's purpose in committing this crime was to pressure Yolanda to abandon her plans to divorce him.

Blakely was charged with first-degree kidnapping, which had a statutory maximum sentence of 10 years in prison. Under a plea deal with the prosecutor, Blakely was permitted to plead to a lesser charge, for which the sentencing guidelines recommended a maximum sentence of 53 months. The sentencing judge, stating 32 findings of fact on which he based his decision that Blakely acted with deliberate cruelty, added 37 months to the recommended maximum of 53 months. The U.S. Supreme Court held that, in sentencing, defendants have a right to have a jury determine *all* facts that might lead to sentence enhancement.

In reversing Blakely's sentence, the majority of the U.S. Supreme Court justices said they were adhering to the controversial precedent case of *United States v. Apprendi*, decided in 2000. Apprendi was accused of firing shots into the home of African American neighbors, stating that he did not want them living there (Apprendi subsequently denied making that statement). Apprendi pleaded guilty to two counts of second-degree possession of a firearm for an unlawful purpose and one count of third-degree unlawful possession of a bomb. The judge found that

EXHIBIT 13.8

Summary of Recommendations of the ABA Justice Kennedy Sentencing Commission

In August 2004, the House of Delegates of the ABA considered the recommendations of the Kennedy Commission appointed by the ABA in 2003. The recommendations were accepted and became part of ABA policy. In summary, they include the following:

- "Repealing mandatory minimum sentences.
- Providing for guided discretion in sentencing, consistent with *Blakely v. Washington*, 542 U.S. 296 (2004), while allowing courts to consider the unique characteristics of offenses and offenders that may warrant an increase or decrease in a sentence.
- Requiring sentencing courts to state the reason for increasing or reducing a sentence, and allowing appellate review of such sentences.

- Considering diversion programs for less serious offenses, and studying the cost effectiveness of treatment programs for substance abuse and mental illness.
- Giving greater authority and resources to an agency responsible for monitoring the sentencing system.
- Developing graduated sanctions for violations of probation and parole."

Source: American Bar Association Justice Kennedy Commission Reports with Recommendations to the ABA House of Delegates, August 2004, http://www.abanet.org/crimjust/kennedy/JusticeKennedy-CommissionReportsFinal.pdf, accessed 10 November 2010.

---

the defendant acted with the intent required by the hate crime statute, which provides sentence enhancement for a crime if it can be shown that the defendant acted with bias; the judge then enhanced Apprendi's penalty in accordance with that statute. The U.S. Supreme Court held that any fact (other than a prior conviction) that can be used to enhance a sentence must be submitted to the jury and found to be true beyond a reasonable doubt.[111]

In 2005, the U.S. Supreme Court decided two cases involving issues left unanswered by *Blakely*: (1) whether, if a trial judge alone conducts fact-finding at the sentencing hearing, that violates the defendant's Sixth Amendment rights and (2) whether the federal sentencing guidelines are still viable.

The first case, *United States v. Booker*, involved Freddie J. Booker, who was convicted of possessing and distributing crack cocaine. When Booker was arrested, the police seized 92.5 grams of the illegal drug. Under the federal sentencing guidelines, that amount of illegal drugs, added to Booker's 23 prior convictions, would result in a prison sentence of a little less than 22 years. At the sentencing hearing, the judge added 20 more ounces of cocaine because Booker had told detectives that he sold that amount in the months prior to his arrest. The judge also concluded that Booker committed perjury at the trial and thus added an obstruction of justice conviction. These additional factors enabled the judge to sentence Booker to 30 years. The circuit court of appeals reversed.[112]

The second case, *United States v. Fanfan*, involved Ducan Fanfan, who was convicted in Maine in 2003 of conspiring to distribute at least 500 grams of *powder* cocaine. At the sentencing hearing, the prosecution offered evidence that Fanfan also dealt in *crack* cocaine, which, as noted earlier, carried a significantly longer penalty than

offenses associated with powder cocaine. The federal sentencing judge initially gave Fanfan a 16-year sentence. But on the basis of *Blakely*, which was decided four days prior to Fanfan's sentence hearing, the judge reduced that sentence to six and one-half years, basing that sentence on the amount of drugs considered by the jury in its fact-finding. The U.S. Supreme Court agreed to review the case directly from the trial decision, thus bypassing the First Circuit Court of Appeals in Boston.[113]

Booker and *Fanfan* were decided as companion cases in January 2005. The U.S. Supreme Court released 124 pages consisting of two separate 5–4 majority opinions. The opinion written by Justice John Paul Stevens states that the Sixth Amendment guarantee of a right to trial by jury is violated when a sentence is based on facts determined only by a judge. The second opinion, written by Justice Stephen G. Breyer, reduces the federal sentencing guidelines to an advisory role. According to Breyer, "The district courts, while not bound to apply the guidelines, must consult those guidelines and take them into account when sentencing." But Breyer noted that Congress could act when he said, "The ball now lies in Congress' court. The national legislature is equipped to devise and install, long-term, the sentencing system compatible with the Constitution, that Congress judges best for the federal system of justice. . . . Ours is not the last word."[114]

But Congress did not act, and during its 2006–2007 term, with federal courts disagreeing on how to resolve the issues left by these cases, the U.S. Supreme Court heard two cases that involved some of the unanswered questions. The first case, *Rita v. United States*, concerned whether a sentence in the federal guidelines is *presumed* to be reasonable, which would effectively limit or eliminate an appeal should that sentence be imposed. The issue arose in the case of Victor Rita, who was convicted of offenses related to providing false testimony before a grand jury. The defendant argued before the trial court that the guidelines were unreasonable in his case and that he should be given a lighter sentence due to his health, his fear of being abused in prison, and his distinguished military service. The U.S. Supreme Court upheld the lower court's ruling that the imposed sentence was reasonable because it was within the federal sentencing guidelines. Thus, a decision that falls within the federal sentencing guidelines is reasonable.[115]

The second case, *Claiborne v. United States*, concerned what a federal judge is required to do to justify imposing a sentence that is significantly shorter than that of the sentencing guidelines. Specifically, prosecutors challenged a 15-month prison sentence imposed on a defendant who was convicted of possession with intent to distribute crack cocaine. The federal sentencing guidelines provide for a three-year minimum sentence for this offense. Unfortunately, the 23-year-old defendant in this case was murdered shortly before the Court's decision was announced, and the Court vacated the case.[116]

The U.S. Supreme Court continued its analysis of federal sentencing guidelines by deciding two cases on 10 December 2007. The facts of each are included, and one is excerpted, in Exhibit 13.9.

The U.S. Supreme Court has also decided recent cases concerning state sentencing laws. In 2007, the Court invalidated a California criminal sentencing law in *Cunningham v. California*, a case involving a defendant who was convicted of the continuous sexual abuse of a child. Under California law, this offense is punishable by a lower term sentence of 6 years, a middle term of 12 years, or an upper term of 16 years. California law required the trial court to impose the middle term unless there was evidence of mitigating or aggravating circumstances. In *Cunningham*, the trial judge had imposed the upper term of 16 years after finding, by a preponderance of the evidence, six aggravating circumstances. The U.S. Supreme Court reversed, holding that the aggravating circumstances must be determined by a jury, which is required to find facts by the higher evidence standard of beyond a reasonable doubt. According to the majority opinion, "Factfinding to elevate a sentence from 12 to 16 years, our decisions make plain, falls within the province of the jury."[117]

In March 2005, the U.S. Supreme Court decided *Shepard v. United States*. This case reexamined the role of judges in sentencing. Recall that in the *Apprendi* case, the Court ruled that any fact, other than a prior conviction, that is used in sentence enhancement must be determined by a jury. *Shepard* involved a defendant who had previously entered guilty pleas to four burglaries, but the necessary details of those crimes did not appear in the plea agreement. The appeals court had ruled that the trial court should have inquired into police reports to determine whether any of those prior felonies met the requirements

of the federal statute under which Shepard was convicted. That statute, the Armed Career Criminal Act (ACCA), provides for enhanced penalties for offenders who have been convicted of specified prior violent felonies. Burglary counts as a violent felony only if it occurred in a building or enclosed space, such as a house; burglarizing a car or boat does not count. The federal district court ruled that the prosecutor did not present sufficient evidence that the prior burglaries qualified Shepard (who entered a guilty plea to being a felon in possession of a firearm) for the 15-year mandatory minimum sentence under the federal statute. The judge imposed a sentence of three years. The appellate court reversed and, in effect, ordered the lower court to impose the 15-year mandatory minimum sentence.[118]

The U.S. Supreme Court, by a 5–3 vote (Chief Justice William H. Rehnquist did not participate in the case), reversed the decision of the appellate court. Justice David H. Souter, who wrote the majority opinion, stated that *Apprendi* and other recent precedent cases limit trial judges to official court documents when they investigate the nature of prior felonies for purposes of sentence enhancement. Thus, in Shepard's case, the trial judge should not have gone beyond the official transcript of the plea bargaining process to determine whether Shepard's prior burglaries met the requirements for sentence enhancement under the ACCA.

These recent sentencing cases handed down by the U.S. Supreme Court were analyzed by social scientists in an August 2007 edition of *Criminology and Public Policy*. The various articles explained the cases and suggested avenues of research that might be attempted to determine whether the cases achieved the goal of limiting (or erasing) sentencing disparity. But according to one scholar, "[A]ssessment of the sentencing impact of most of these cases will be difficult. . . . In most states, these Supreme Court decisions may have more long-term effect on charging practices and sentencing laws and guidelines than on sentencing decisions."[119]

Another scholar focused on the impact of *Booker* on federal sentencing, looking at average sentence lengths and other issues before and after that decision. He concluded that although there were some changes in sentence lengths after the *Booker* decision, for most crimes, sentences remained relatively stable.[120]

Sentence disparity cannot be erased by dealing only with sentencing; discretion before and after sentencing must also be considered. Thus, "policy makers need to be more cautious with any conclusion about the relative benefits of presumptive versus voluntary guidelines."[121]

In reacting to these articles on the impact of the recent U.S. Supreme Court decisions, a member of the District of Columbia Sentencing Commission stressed the importance of a *scientific* basis for sentencing decisions, noting that at the time the U.S. Supreme Court is requiring a stronger *legal* basis for sentencing, we are tolerating a

Sentence Guidelines: The U.S. Supreme Court Speaks

Two key sentencing cases involving judicial discretion to depart significantly from federal sentencing guidelines were decided by the U.S. Supreme Court in 2007. Both appellants were drug offenders. In *Gall v. United States*, the Supreme Court upheld the trial court's decision to put the defendant, Brian Michael Gall, on probation for 36 months rather than sentence him to prison after he entered a guilty plea to conspiracy to distribute MDMA (also referred to as *Ecstasy*), which is a class C felony and carries a prison term within the guidelines, with the length of that term depending on the facts of the case. The defendant made a motion for a downward departure from the federal sentencing guidelines. Based on his limited prior criminal record, age, cooperation with the government, remorse, postoffense rehabilitation (he was a college student), and several other reasons, the judge decided on probation rather than prison.[1]

The facts of the second case and the sentencing issues are explained in the following excerpt from the case.[2]

Kimbrough v. United States

This Court's remedial opinion in *United States v. Booker* [discussed in this text's chapter] instructed district courts to read the United States Sentencing Guidelines as "effectively advisory." In accord with [the federal statute], the Guidelines, formerly mandatory, now serve as one factor among several courts must consider in determining an appropriate sentence. *Booker* further instructed that "reasonableness" is the standard controlling appellate review of the sentences district courts impose. . . .

The question here presented is whether, as the Court of Appeals held in this case, "a sentence . . . outside the guidelines range is per se unreasonable when it is based on a disagreement with the sentencing disparity for crack and powder cocaine offenses." We hold that, under *Booker*, the cocaine Guidelines, like all other Guidelines, are advisory only, and that the Court of Appeals erred in holding the crack/powder disparity effectively mandatory. A district judge must include the Guidelines range in the array of factors warranting consideration. The judge may determine, however, that, in the particular case, a within-Guidelines sentence is "greater than necessary" to serve the objectives of sentencing. In making that determination, the judge may consider the disparity between the Guidelines' treatment of crack and powder cocaine offenses.

In September 2004, petitioner Derrick Kimbrough was indicted in the United States District Court for the Eastern District of Virginia and charged with four offenses: conspiracy to distribute crack and powder cocaine; possession with intent to distribute more than 50 grams of crack cocaine; possession with intent to distribute powder cocaine; and possession of a firearm in furtherance of a drug-trafficking offense. Kimbrough pleaded guilty to all four charges.

Under the relevant statutes, Kimbrough's plea subjected him to an aggregate sentence of 15 years to life in prison. . . . [The Court discussed the details of the application of the guidelines to this case and the much longer sentence that would have been involved. The Court continued]:

A sentence in this range, in the District Court's judgment, would have been "greater than necessary" to accomplish the purposes of sentencing set forth in [the applicable statute]. As required by [the statute], the court took into account the "nature and circumstances" of the offense and Kimbrough's "history and characteristics." The court also commented that the case exemplified the "disproportionate and unjust effect that crack cocaine guidelines have in sentencing." In this regard, the court contrasted Kimbrough's Guidelines range of 228 to 270 months with the range that would have applied had he been accountable for an equivalent amount of powder cocaine: 97 to 106 months, inclusive of the 5-year mandatory minimum for the firearm charge. Concluding that the statutory minimum sentence was "clearly long enough" to accomplish the objectives listed in [the statute], the court sentenced Kimbrough to 15 years, or 180 months, in prison plus 5 years of supervised release. . . .

[The Court discussed the similarities between the two types of cocaine and noted the dissimilarity in sentencing for violating the statutes for powder and crack cocaine. The Court also discussed the history of the legislation and the development of the federal sentencing commission and its mission, its reasons for the differential sentencing, and its efforts to change that differential in recent years. The Court discussed the impact of *Booker* on sentencing guidelines and concluded] . . .

While rendering the Sentencing Guidelines advisory, we have nevertheless preserved a key role for the Sentencing Commission. As explained in [other cases], district courts must treat the Guidelines as the "starting point and the initial benchmark." Congress established the Commission to formulate and constantly refine national sentencing standards. Carrying out its charge, the Commission fills an important institutional role: It has the capacity courts lack to "base its determinations on empirical data and national experience, guided by a professional staff with appropriate expertise."

13.9 *continued*

EXHIBIT

We have accordingly recognized that, in the ordinary case, the Commission's recommendation of a sentencing range will "reflect a rough approximation of sentences that might achieve [the statute's] objectives." The sentencing judge, on the other hand, has "greater familiarity with . . . the individual case and the individual defendant before him than the Commission or the appeals court." He is therefore "in a superior position to find facts and judge their import in each particular case." In light of these discrete institutional strengths, a district court's decision to vary from the advisory Guidelines may attract greatest respect when the sentencing judge finds a particular case "outside the 'heartland' to which the Commission intends individual Guidelines to apply." On the other hand, while the Guidelines are no longer binding, closer review may be in order when the sentencing judge varies from the Guidelines based solely on the judge's view that the Guidelines range "fails properly to reflect [statutory] considerations."

1. *Gall v. United States*, 552 U.S. 38 (2007).
2. *Kimbrough v. United States*, 552 U.S. 85 (2007), cases and citations omitted.

relatively weak standard of empirical evidence in that we are not sufficiently evaluating sentencing and corrections policies.[122]

Finally, knowledge of sentencing practices and policies is limited, and in the words of a criminologist;

We must do better at documenting and understanding the impact and effects of existing policies so that we can describe the past reliably and can potentially predict the impact of future guidelines.[123]

This completes our analysis of some key issues in sentencing, but the recent attention devoted to one type of sentence warrants further exploration.

Capital Punishment

A major issue in recent years has been the increased use of **capital punishment**. Although capital punishment was used extensively in the past, in 1972, a U.S. Supreme Court decision, *Furman v. Georgia*, temporarily halted its use. *Furman* invalidated the Georgia capital punishment statute, ruling that capital punishment cannot be imposed arbitrarily and unfairly and that to do so violates the Eighth Amendment's ban on the infliction of cruel and unusual punishment (see Appendix A).[124] The Supreme Court left the door open for states to enact different capital punishment statutes, and many of them did.

Data and Cost

In 1977, Gary Mark Gilmore became the first person to be executed since the *Furman* decision. Gilmore gave up his right to appeal and was killed by a Utah firing squad. In June 2010, double murderer Ronnie Lee Gardner was executed by firing squad in Utah, probably the last to be executed by that method. In 2004, Utah changed its statute from permitting a choice of methods to requiring that execution be by lethal injection. Persons sentenced to death prior to 2004 may still choose.[125]

In 1979, John Spenkelink was executed in Florida's electric chair and became the first involuntary execution since *Furman*. Figure 13.2 graphs the distribution of executions between 1976, when executions were resumed, and 22 December 2010. It also contains pie charts of the data on victims and offenders in death penalty cases.

The Death Penalty Information Center (DPIC) provides extensive data on capital punishment. Since the cost of incarceration is frequently used as an argument in favor of capital punishment, the following facts, accumulated and published by the DPIC, are presented.

- "The California death penalty system costs taxpayers $114 million per year beyond the costs of keeping convicts locked up for life. Taxpayers have paid more than $250 million for each of the state's executions.
- In Kansas, the costs of capital cases are 70% more expensive than comparable non-capital cases, including the costs of incarceration.
- In Maryland, an average death penalty case resulting in a death sentence costs approximately $3 million. . . .
- The most comprehensive study in the country found that the death penalty costs North Carolina $2.16 million per execution *over* the costs of sentencing murderers to life imprisonment. The majority of those costs occur at the trial level.
- Enforcing the death penalty costs Florida $51 million a year above what it would cost to punish all first-degree murderers with life in prison without parole. Based on the 44 executions Florida had carried out since 1976, that amounts to a cost of $24 million for each execution.
- In Texas, a death penalty case costs an average of $2.3 million, about three times the cost of imprisoning someone in a single cell at the highest security level for 40 years."[126]

Figure 13.2

U.S. Death Penalty Facts: 1976–2010

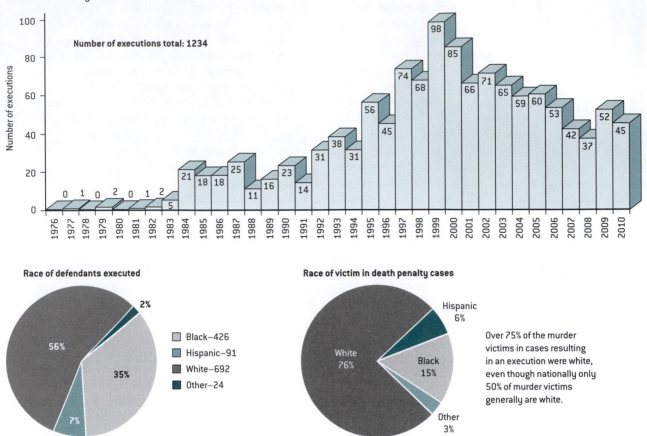

Source: Death Penalty Information Center, "Facts About the Death Penalty" (updated 5 November 2010), http://www
.deathpenaltyinfo.org/documents/FactSheet.pdf, accessed 22 December 2010.

Georgia spent more than $3 million in defense costs (no figure was available for the cost of prosecution) trying Brian Nichols for capital punishment in the 2005 shooting death of a judge and three other victims. Nichols offered to plead guilty in exchange for a life sentence, but the state insisted on a trial. In 2008, Nichols was convicted and sentenced to life in prison.[127]

The cost of death penalty cases is causing some jurisdictions to delay trials. The New Mexico Supreme Court halted two murder trials because the pay for defense attorneys was so low that the court did not believe the defendants could get effective assistance of counsel.[128] In 2009, the bill that ended capital punishment in that state replaced the penalty with life without parole. New Mexico Governor Bill Richardson said it was a difficult decision but "the potential for . . . execution of an innocent person stands as anathema to our very sensibilities as human beings."[129] New Jersey abolished the death penalty in 2007 primarily for cost reasons (those on death row remain under that sentence but no future defendants will receive it).[130]

Other jurisdictions are making efforts to settle death penalty cases rather than go to trial. In one Arizona county,

judges were refusing to delay capital trials and forcing attorneys to consider settlements, and there appeared to be some evidence that the pressure was working.[131]

Legal Death Penalty Issues

The U.S. Supreme Court, along with lower courts, has decided scores of cases on capital punishment; all of them cannot be reviewed here, but a few are noted.

Considerable concern has been expressed about the lack of expertise of attorneys who try death penalty cases, especially those who handle capital appeals. Recall Chapter 11's discussion of the right to counsel, which includes a right to the *effective* assistance of counsel. After five years of debate and discussion, in October 2004, Congress enacted the Justice for All Act of 2004, which contains a provision known as the Innocence Protection Act. This act provides grants to assist states in improving the quality of legal representation in capital cases. The act also contains provisions for victims as well as for extending the use of DNA tests in criminal cases.[132]

Another legal issue is whether mentally ill persons can be executed. In 2002, the U.S. Supreme Court held that it

Thomas Miller-El, Texas death row inmate, reacts after being told that the U.S. Supreme Court had granted him a stay of execution. Miller-El was scheduled to be executed on 21 February 2002 for the 1985 shooting of hotel clerk Douglas Walker when the Supreme Court agreed to hear his appeal. In that appeal the Court instructed the lower federal court to reconsider the evidence submitted by Miller-El in his claim that the prosecution had violated his constitutional rights by the manner in which it excluded African Americans from his jury. The lower court reconsidered but denied the claim on the merits. The U.S. Supreme Court reviewed the case again and on 13 June 2005 reversed and remanded. Miller-El accepted a plea bargain in 2008. In exchange for a life sentence, he pleaded guilty.

is unconstitutional to execute *mentally retarded* offenders. *Atkins v. Virginia* involved an appellant, Daryl R. Atkins, who has an IQ of 59. Atkins was on death row for a murder he committed when he was 18 (see again Exhibit 4.4, Chapter 4). In deciding this case, however, the Supreme Court did not give guidelines for determining mental retardation.[133]

In March 2003, James Colburn, who was severely mentally ill, having been diagnosed with paranoid schizophrenia, was executed in Texas. In May 2004, Kelsey Patterson, a diagnosed schizophrenic, was executed in Texas after the governor refused to follow the recommendation of the state pardons and parole board and the U.S. Supreme Court refused to hear the case.

In 2007, the U.S. Supreme Court, in *Panetti v. Quarterman*, ruled by a 5–4 vote that a mentally ill murderer who

did not have a rational understanding of why the state planned to execute him could not be executed. A brief excerpt explains the majority's position.[134]

Panetti v. Quarterman

We . . . find no support in [a precedent case] . . . for the proposition that a prisoner is automatically foreclosed from demonstrating incompetency once a court has found he can identify the stated reason for his execution. A prisoner's awareness of the State's rationale for an execution is not the same as a rational understanding of it. [Precedent] does not foreclose inquiry into the latter.

This is not to deny the fact that a concept like rational understanding is difficult to define. And we must not ignore the concern that some prisoners, whose cases are not implicated by this decision, will fail to understand why they are to be punished on account of reasons other than those stemming from a severe mental illness. The mental state requisite for competence to suffer capital punishment neither presumes nor requires a person who would be considered "normal," or even "rational," in a layperson's understanding of those terms. Someone who is condemned to death for an atrocious murder may be so callous as to be unrepentant; so self-centered and devoid of compassion as to lack all sense of guilt; so adept in transferring blame to others as to be considered, at least in the colloquial sense, to be out of touch with reality. Those states of mind, even if extreme compared to the criminal population at large, are not what petitioner contends lie at the threshold of a competence inquiry. The beginning of doubt about competence in a case like petitioner's is not a misanthropic personality or an amoral character. It is a psychotic disorder.

Petitioner's submission is that he suffers from a severe, documented mental illness that is the source of gross delusions preventing him from comprehending the meaning and purpose of the punishment to which he has been sentenced. This argument, we hold, should have been considered.

In June 2010, the U.S. Supreme Court agreed to review a California death penalty case involving an inmate whose attorney did not present evidence of his mental illness to the jury during the penalty phase of his case. Scott Pinholster's death sentence was reversed by the Ninth Circuit Court of Appeals, and the Court will consider whether that holding should remain in the case of *Cullen v. Pinholster*. Pinholster was convicted of two murders during a 1984 burglary.[135]

A major legal issue the U.S. Supreme Court considers in death penalty cases is the role of the jury in assessing the penalty. In 2002, the U.S. Supreme Court decided *Ring v. Arizona*, in which it held that the aggravating factor that required the judge, under Arizona law, to sentence an offender to death upon conviction of murder must be determined by the jury, not by the judge. The Arizona statute specified that the hearing on aggravating factors should be before the court alone. If the judge found one aggravating circumstance and "no mitigating circumstances sufficiently substantial to call for leniency," the defendant must be sentenced to death. The Supreme Court ruled that the aggravating factor was thus an element of the crime and therefore required a finding beyond a reasonable doubt, and as with all other factual issues, the defendant was entitled to have that decision made by a jury.[136] In 2004, the U.S. Supreme Court held that *Ring* does not apply retroactively to cases that were already final on direct review before the case was decided.[137]

In 2003, in *Wiggins v. Smith*, the U.S. Supreme Court reversed the conviction of Kevin Wiggins, who was convicted of the murder of a 77-year-old woman who lived in the apartment complex where Wiggins was employed. Wiggins's attorneys did not present to the jury any information on their client's background, and the defendant was quickly convicted and sentenced to death. The information that was not presented included the following: Wiggins's mother was an alcoholic and frequently left the children to fend for themselves, including rummaging through garbage to obtain food. She once forced Wiggins's hand onto a hot burner, which required that he be hospitalized. She had sex with men on the same bed in which the children slept. She locked the kitchen and beat the children when they broke in looking for food. Wiggins was placed in foster care when he was 6 years old. He was physically abused in two foster homes; in the second one, he was raped by his foster father. When he was 16, Wiggins ran away from foster care and lived on the streets. The U.S. Supreme Court held that the failure to present this evidence prejudiced Wiggins's case. Further, it was standard practice in that jurisdiction for the defense to present the court with a social history, and funds were available for the defense to hire a social worker for this purpose. Wiggins's lawyers had chosen not to do so.[138]

On 16 April 2008, the U.S. Supreme Court decided *Baze v. Rees*, brought by two inmates who raised the issue of whether there is a sufficient probability that proper procedures for administering lethal injection would not be followed in Kentucky, resulting in sufficient pain to constitute cruel and unusual punishment. According to Chief Justice John Roberts, who announced the Court's 7–2 decision, the petitioners had not sustained their burden of proving "that the risk of pain from maladministration of a concededly humane lethal injection protocol, and the failure to adopt untried and untested alternatives, constitute cruel and unusual punishment." There is some risk of pain in any method of execution, and "the Constitution does not demand the avoidance of all risk of pain in carrying out executions." In his concurring opinion, Justice Clarence Thomas stated that an execution method

"violates the Eighth Amendment only it if is deliberately designed to inflict pain."[139]

The dissent in *Baze* emphasized that the first of three drugs administered during Kentucky's lethal injection is for the purpose of sedating the inmate. If that drug is not administered properly, the next two drugs will cause excruciating pain. Thus, the case should be returned to Kentucky to consider whether the failure to include specific safeguards utilized by other states "poses an untoward, readily avoidable risk of inflicting severe and unnecessary pain."[140] Executions in all states had been on hold since 25 September 2007, but after the *Baze* decision, on 6 May 2008, Georgia executed William Earl Lynd by lethal injection.

The issue of pain during lethal injection along with other issues surrounding this execution method are under consideration in California, stemming from a 2006 case in which U.S. District Judge Jeremy Fogel noted five problems with procedures in the case of *Morales v. Tilton*. The state proposed revisions to its procedures in 2007; the matter was not yet resolved as of June 2010, when the state's Office of Administrative Law rejected the proposed lethal injection procedures, stating they were unclear, conflicted with state law, or did not properly state the reasons for the procedures. The procedures also must be subjected to public review before they can become law. The state received about 20,000 comments, most of which were critical of the proposal. Executions in California had been on hold since that 2006 decision. Changes were made in the execution procedures, and the state scheduled the execution of Albert Greenwood Brown Jr. for 30 September 2010. However, the execution was scheduled just three hours before the expiration of one of the drugs (sodium thiopental) used in executions. That drug is in short supply due to major production problems. This has caused execution delays in other states as well, and California could not get a new supply of the drug until 2011. A federal court judge ordered a stay of Brown's execution, stating that California was rushing to execute Brown before the expiration of the drug, and that did not leave the judge sufficient time to consider whether the state had met the constitutional requirements of precedent cases concerning the drugs used in lethal injections. A law professor reacted to this turn of events with the following statement:

> The back and forth of this case stems from the underlying question of whether certain procedures violate the eighth amendment banning cruel and unusual punishment and whether the cocktail of chemicals constitutes gratuitous pain—but that sidesteps the issue of whether people really have the stomach for the death penalty anymore. . . . This case raises questions about the purpose of the death penalty in today's society.[141]

A key capital punishment case was decided by the U.S. Supreme Court in 2008. *Kennedy v. Louisiana* involved the issue of whether capital punishment for the rape but not murder of a *child* is disproportionate to the crime and thus violates the Eighth Amendment. The U.S. Supreme Court had previously held that the death penalty is disproportionate for the crime of rape but not murder of an *adult* woman, and in *Kennedy*, the Court held that is also the case when the victim is a child.[142]

One final capital punishment case of note was before the U.S. Supreme Court during its 2010–2011 term. In March 2010, the Court granted a stay of execution about one hour before Hank Skinner was to be executed in Texas. In May 2010, the Court agreed to review his case in which he argued that Texas should be required to perform DNA testing on some additional evidence in his case. Original testing of only some of the evidence placed him at the scene of the murders of his girlfriend and her two sons, and he did not dispute that evidence. He did maintain, however, that he was innocent of the murders. The Texas Court of Criminal Appeals rejected his claims for further DNA testing. His plea to the U.S. Supreme Court was to be permitted to make his motion as a civil rights claim rather than as part of his death penalty appeal, which has more stringent requirements. The case was argued before the U.S. Supreme Court on 13 October 2010. A decision was expected prior to the end of the Court's 2010–11 term.[143]

Deterrence and Capital Punishment

Chapter 3 discussed deterrence along with other punishment philosophies. Deterrence theory is often explored in relation to capital punishment. Does the possibility of a death sentence deter potential murderers? Earlier research on this topic was dominated by the work of sociologist Thorsten Sellin, who reported that he found no support for any deterrent effect of the death penalty.[144] After analyzing Sellin's work and that of others in the same period, Richard O. Lempert observed that the researchers in general realized the necessity of controlling for factors that might be important in measuring the deterrent effect of capital punishment. But they did not use "the techniques of modern mathematical social science to hold these factors constant." Lempert then reviewed some of the work of more recent researchers who used these modern techniques but still failed to find support for deterrence theory.[145] Lempert concluded:

The strength of the research reviewed thus far rests not in individual studies but on the work taken as a whole. Deterrent effects of capital punishment have been given many different kinds of chances to appear. If capital punishment has any strong deterrent effects, it is likely that some deterrence would have been evident. While it is impossible to prove a negative, this failure to find a deterrent effect provides reason to believe that none exists.[146]

Some of the earlier studies actually found higher homicide rates in states with capital punishment compared with states without the death penalty. On the basis of their analysis of homicide rates between 1930 and 1970, Daniel Glaser and Max S. Zeigler found that the existence of capital punishment on the statute books was not a significant deterrent to homicide. Therefore, "[a] state should express its abhorrence of homicides not through the coldblooded means of capital punishment but through severity and certainty in its confinement penalties for those who kill."[147]

William C. Bailey, in his analysis of Glaser and Zeigler's study, decided that their methodology was questionable and that their conclusions were contradicted by other studies.[148] In responding to Bailey's publications, Glaser said, among other comments, that he had not argued eliminating the death penalty would decrease homicide rates. Rather, "advocating the death penalty is not as expressive of outrage at murder as is opposition to the death penalty," and one effective way the state could encourage alternatives to violence is by eliminating this form of violence.[149]

Another early scholar on the effect of the death penalty was Isaac Ehrlich, an economist whose work formed the basis for the U.S. solicitor general's arguments before the U.S. Supreme Court in the *Furman* case, discussed earlier in this chapter. According to Richard O. Lempert, Ehrlich's 1975 article was important because it was used to support the position that executions deter homicides. Lempert quickly added his own analysis that Ehrlich found no support for deterrence theory and that his work "stirred up the pond, but only to muddy the waters at a time when we need to see clearly."[150]

More recently, scholars have looked at the issue of capital punishment and deterrence in Texas, which has the highest number of executions. They found no support for deterrence theory and concluded that executions were not related to murder rates.[151] Other scholars agreed.[152]

Ronald L. Akers and Christine S. Sellers reviewed much of the literature on the deterrent effect of capital punishment and concluded as follows:

With some exceptions, neither the existence of capital punishment nor the certainty of the death penalty has been shown to have a significant effect on the rate of homicides. Findings show that there is some deterrent effect from the perceived certainty of criminal penalties, but the empirical validity of deterrence theory is limited.[153]

Juveniles and Capital Punishment

One final capital punishment issue that is addressed concerns the execution of juveniles. In 2005, in *Roper v. Simmons*, the U.S. Supreme Court considered the issue of whether the U.S. Constitution's prohibition against cruel and unusual punishment prohibits executing a person who was under 18 at the time he or she committed murder. The appellant in this case was Christopher Simmons, who was 17 on 8 September 1993, when he and a 15-year-old accomplice broke into the home of Shirley Crook. Crook was home and recognized Simmons because the two had previously been involved in the same automobile crash. Prosecutors stated that Crook, 46, was bound, gagged, driven around in her minivan, beaten when she tried to get free, and then pushed off a railroad trestle to drown in the river below.[154]

In *Simmons*, the U.S. Supreme Court ruled that executing a person for a crime committed before the age of 18 violates the Eighth Amendment's prohibition against cruel and unusual punishment. According to Justice Anthony M. Kennedy, who wrote for the majority of five justices, "The age of 18 is the point where society draws the line for many purposes between childhood and adulthood," and 18 is "the age at which the line for death eligibility ought to rest."[155]

The Future of Capital Punishment

Scholars continue to debate the morality of capital punishment and to conduct research on its possible deterrent effect. Many people support capital punishment and express fascination about its details, but there is evidence that when faced with the alternative of a life sentence without parole for murder, a growing number of people support that alternative. A Gallup Poll found that 65 percent of respondents (down from 80 percent in an earlier poll) favored the death penalty. But when the respondents were given a choice of the death penalty or life without parole, 48 percent chose life without parole compared to 47 percent who chose the death penalty. In a study of police chiefs asked to indicate which of several provisions they thought should be increased to combat crime, an increased

use of the death penalty was listed last. Finally, in a study of the current and former presidents of the top societies for criminologists, 88 percent responded that they did not believe the death penalty is a deterrent to murder.[156]

Most countries today do not have the death penalty, and as Global Focus 13.1 notes, in October 2007, many countries recognized a special day to call for its abolition. Some U.S. states have a moratorium on capital punishment, but executions spiked in 2009, as indicated by the graph presented earlier in Figure 13.2. In November 2007, the ABA released a three-year study of capital punishment systems in the United States. The ABA, which has 400,000 members and has not taken a position for or against capital punishment, concluded that the systems in Indiana, Georgia, Ohio, Alabama, and Tennessee were so faulty that they should be halted immediately, and serious problems were found in every state system. Among other findings were the following:

- Significant racial disparities in the imposition of the death penalty, particularly with regard to the race of the victim.
- Inadequate indigent defense programs.
- Lack of policies regarding knowledge required of defense attorneys with reference to mentally challenged clients.
- Lack of policies concerning control of prosecutorial discretion.
- Errors or fraud in crime laboratories.
- A lack of uniformity in implementing nationally recognized best practices in eyewitness identification procedures as well as the recording of interrogations of suspects.[157]

As noted, New Mexico and New Jersey recently abolished capital punishment, and some states (e.g., Illinois) have moratoriums on capital punishment pending resolu-

---

GLOBAL FOCUS

13.1   European Union and World Leaders Mark Day Against the Death Penalty

"Member nations of the European Union and the Council of Europe marked October 10th as 'European Day Against the Death Penalty,' an action to underscore the continent's firm commitment to ending executions throughout the world. Leaders from the EU and the Council of Europe launched the initiative during an October 9th conference in Lisbon, Portugal.

"On October 10 in New York at the United Nations, a press conference also marked the 'World Day Against the Death Penalty' with international human rights leaders urging support for a resolution calling for a global moratorium on executions. . . . In Lisbon, European Commission President Juan Manuel Barroso noted, 'The European Union is unreservedly opposed to the use of capital punishment under all

circumstances and has consistently called for the worldwide abolition of this punishment.'

"**One hundred and thirty-three countries** have abolished the death penalty in practice or in law. Regional press conferences calling attention to the day were also held in Morocco, Puerto Rico and the Democratic Republic of Congo."[1]

---

1. "European Union and World Leaders Mark Day Against the Death Penalty," Death Penalty Information Center, emphasis in the original, quoting European Union Press Release (9 October 2007); World Coalition Against the Death Penalty Press Release (10 October 2007), http://www.deathpenaltyinfo.org/node/1849, accessed 8 November 2010.

tion of issues raised by courts or legislators. In the final analysis, the higher costs of execution compared to life without parole may be the deciding factor in many jurisdictions.

Appeals and Other Legal Challenges

Several legal challenges to a criminal conviction, sentence, and subsequent incarceration are available. Defendants who have legal reasons to believe mistakes were made in their trials may have grounds for an appeal. Immediately after conviction, a defendant may have legal grounds for the judge to grant his or her motion for a new trial or for a judgment of acquittal despite the jury verdict. This motion may be successful if the defendant can show that evidence admitted at the trial should have been excluded for some legal reason or that in some other way the defendant's constitutional rights were violated.

If the motion for a new trial or for a judgment of acquittal is not granted (and most are not), the defendant may appeal the conviction on points of law. An appeal of a conviction is made to a court that has appellate jurisdiction over the trial court's decisions, which includes the judge's decisions regarding the inclusion or exclusion of evidence and other matters as well as the verdict. In effect, the appellate court looks at the actions of the trial court and decides whether any reversible errors were committed. Most cases are not reversed; most that are reversed are remanded for another trial, and a large percentage of defendants are again convicted on retrial.

Defendants may file writs as well. A **writ** is an order from a court for someone to do something or to give permission to do whatever has been requested. It is common for offenders to file a writ of habeas corpus, which literally means "you have the body." Frequently, this writ is filed by inmates who argue that they are being confined under conditions that violate their constitutional rights.

Defendants may also appeal their sentences, but when the legislature has given trial judges wide discretion in determining sentences, appellate courts rarely overturn those decisions. Usually, the appellate court shows deference to the judge who has heard and seen the evidence, evidence that is not seen and heard by appellate courts. If, however, the sentence constitutes cruel and unusual punishment, it violates the Eighth Amendment (see Appendix A) and is unconstitutional.

The U.S. Supreme Court

The highest court of appeals in the United States is the U.S. Supreme Court, an institution of great power that elicits considerable controversy. Although generally this Court has been held in high esteem in the United States,

The U.S. Supreme Court building in Washington, D.C., is the symbol of the country's civil and criminal justice systems.

in 2008, it received its first negative approval rating, with only 39 percent of respondents approving of the manner in which the justices were handling their jobs; 43 percent disapproved. In May 2007, 58 percent of respondents indicated approval of the Court.[158]

The U.S. Supreme Court has almost complete control over which cases it accepts. The Court does this by granting or denying a writ of **certiorari**. When the Court agrees to hear a case on appeal, it is said to have granted certiorari. Four of the nine justices who sit on the Court must vote in favor of the writ for it to be granted. In an average term, the Court hears fewer than 5 percent of the cases filed, and the number of cases it hears and decides has been declining. During its 2000–2001 term, the Court decided 85 cases. In its 2002–2003 term, the Court issued 79 opinions. In the term that ended in June 2004, the U.S. Supreme Court also decided 79 cases. During 2005–2006, the Court signed 69 decisions, and during 2006–2007, the justices decided 68 cases. In its 2008–2009 term, the Court handed down 74 signed opinions. During its 2009–10 term, the Court decided 81 cases. In previous years, the Court decided up to 150 or more cases.[159]

There are two reasons the U.S. Supreme Court limits the number of cases it hears and decides. First, because of time, the Court must limit cases (although with the same number of justices—nine—that does not explain the virtually 50 percent drop in recent years). The second reason the U.S. Supreme Court hears only some of the appealed cases is that the justices view their mission as deciding cases that have an impact beyond the immediate parties and on which lower federal courts have disagreed. For example, before the Court decided *Mistretta v. United States* (discussed earlier), 116 U.S. district court judges had ruled that the federal sentencing guidelines were constitutional, and 158 had ruled they were unconstitutional. Federal appellate courts that had ruled on the issue were divided.[160]

When the U.S. Supreme Court rules on an issue that has been in conflict among lower federal courts, its decision becomes the final court resolution of the issue unless or until it is overruled by a subsequent U.S. Supreme Court decision. Supreme Court decisions may also be nullified by subsequent statutes (provided those are not unconstitutional) or by constitutional amendment.

The principal function of the U.S. Supreme Court is to determine whether the litigants' *federal* constitutional or statutory rights have been violated. Controversial court decisions should be considered in the context of constitutional and statutory law and a changing society, with its concomitant need for settling conflicts. The law and the Constitution must be flexible enough to deal with different factual situations, which require adjudication as they arise.

The membership of the U.S. Supreme Court changed in recent years. With the death of Chief Justice William H. Rehnquist and the retirement of Sandra Day O'Connor, President Bush appointed two justices to the Court, including the new Chief Justice, for the 2006–2007 term. After his first nominee withdrew under pressure, the president appointed Samuel A. Alito Jr. to the position vacated by Justice O'Connor. He was confirmed and joined the Court along with John G. Roberts Jr., who was confirmed as Chief Justice.

In 2009, Justice David H. Souter retired, and President Barack Obama appointed the first Hispanic to the high Court: Justice Sonia Sotomayor, who took her seat in October of that year. At the end of the Court's 2009–10 term, Justice John Paul Stevens retired. President Obama's nominee for that seat, Elena Kagan, was confirmed. She began her tenure on the Court when its 2010–11 term opened the first Monday of October 2010. Kagan is the third woman on the Court and the fourth in history to serve in that capacity. Among other positions, Kagan served as legal advisor to President Clinton and as the dean of the Harvard College of Law. The other members of the U.S. Supreme Court are Antonin Scalia, Anthony M. Kennedy, Clarence Thomas, Ruth Bader Ginsburg, and Stephen G. Breyer.

Courts and Congestion

There is no question that most courts, including the U.S. Supreme Court and the lower federal appellate courts and trial courts, along with state courts at all levels, are overburdened. There are several reasons for this situation. One significant reason is the trend toward increasing the number of *federal* crimes. For example, the Violent Crime Control and Law Enforcement Act of 1994 increased fed-

eral jurisdiction over a number of crimes and increased penalties for others, especially those involving illegal drug trafficking.[161] Stalking, carjacking, hate crimes, and other relatively recent additions to criminal law have been included in federal as well as state codes.

We have already noted that significant increases in court cases have resulted from drug arrests, but there are other areas as well. Today, for example, immigration is another important focus of arrests and prosecutions, as it has been in the past. One example illustrates the impact of increased arrests and prosecutions on courts. Five years after the Clinton administration began a massive attempt to stop the flow of illegal drugs and illegal immigration from Mexico into the United States, the five federal judicial courts in the Southwest were handling twice to four times as many cases as the average in other federal districts throughout the country. Senior judges (semiretired judges) along with judges from as far away as Vermont were called in to hear cases.[162]

Shifting cases to state courts, however, also has problems because many of them are overcrowded. In 2000, Chief Justice Rehnquist emphasized that, in general, the state courts were more congested than the federal courts, with many of them facing budget cuts. He concluded that year that "it seems likely for the foreseeable future that a regime of fiscal austerity will predominate at the national and state levels."[163]

At the time, perhaps nobody realized how accurate the Chief Justice's predictions were, but the economic slowdown that began in 2008 led to cutbacks in courts as well as other public agencies and private businesses. For courts, cutbacks mean a slowing of the judicial process. One example is New York, which ended 2009 with its largest case backlog in history. Many of those were thought to be related to the recession: home foreclosures, family violence possibly because of job losses, bad debt issues, bankruptcies, and so on. One judge described the situation in that state as a "train wreck" and predicted the situation would get worse.[164]

In late 2009, an editorial in the *New York Times* quoted the chief justice of the Massachusetts Supreme Judicial Court as warning that, as the result of budget cuts, state courts, which handle 95 percent of all U.S. civil and criminal cases, were reaching the "tipping point of dysfunction." Many courts had already imposed hiring freezes or furloughs on state employees, including those who work in the courts, and some, such as New Hampshire, had suspended civil and criminal trials in some counties. According to the ABA, the brunt of cutbacks had the greatest negative impact on those who are most vulnerable: those in family and juvenile court cases, along with misdemeanors and small claims litigants. The editorial concluded: "But, at some point, slashing state court financing jeopardizes something beyond basic fairness, public safety and even the rule of law. It weakens democracy itself."[165]

Sonia Sotomayor (left) became an associate justice of the U.S. Supreme Court in October 2009, replacing Associate Justice David H. Souter, who resigned that year. In 2010, Justice John Paul Stevens retired and was replaced by Elena Kagan (right), who joined the Court in October of that year. The confirmation of these two justices gives the Court three women, the largest number ever to serve.

In an effort to cut its budget deficit, California began closing courts on the third Wednesday of each month, beginning in mid-September 2009 and continuing through July 2010, for an estimated savings of $84 million. By January 2010, California faced even greater budget shortfalls and looked for more ways to cut spending. Toward the end of 2009, more than 22 states were reporting budget shortfalls; agency and program cuts were already in force in some of them.[166]

Courts are also facing other issues that drain their staff time and exhaust their resources. The National Center for State Courts listed 10 trends that impact state courts. Among those 10 are emergency preparedness, the impact of an aging population, increased technology, problem-solving courts, budget challenges, privacy and public access to court records, and measuring court performance. Another is the impact that cultural diversity has on, for example, the need for court interpreters.[167]

It is probably common knowledge that most states have, in recent years, experienced severe budget cuts. In some states, budget cuts have resulted in delayed trials along with pay cuts, personnel reductions, and court congestion. Several suggestions have been made for alleviating this congestion. One is to fine attorneys for filing frivolous cases. Another is to increase the numbers of judges and other personnel. Still another is to create more courts. Reorganization of courts is another suggestion that some state systems have followed. Improving internal management of courts relieves some congestion.

For example, shifting judges from one court to another might ease congestion problems during the vacation of a judge in one court. But problems arise when judges are shifted to areas in which they have no experience—for example, from civil to criminal, or vice versa—and take on heavy caseloads quickly without time for much learning. Night courts and weekend courts have been used in some cities, particularly large cities with high caseloads (e.g., Miami), but such procedures take their toll on participants. Another means of relieving congestion is the use of computers and other technology to speed up court paperwork.

Alternative dispute resolution is one of the most efficient ways to ease court congestion. In less complicated cases, litigants may use **mediation** rather than court resolution. Mediation has been successful in many countries. Mediators may be laypersons with some training in dispute resolution but without the legal training of attorneys. In informal situations, such as within a neighborhood, many disputes may be resolved successfully without the formality and cost of a court trial.

A final suggestion for reducing congestion in our general criminal and civil courts is to add specialized courts, such as drug courts, mental health courts, and domestic violence courts, all discussed earlier in the chapter. These specialized courts enable us to focus on specific problem areas, but if they are actually oriented toward treatment rather than punishment, as we might hope, they will increase the costs of judicial administration.

Courts and Violence

Courts are no longer a safe place for the events that occur within them. Despite the increased security of most, if not all, state and federal courts, the events of March 2005 shocked the nation. In Atlanta, Superior Court Judge Rowland W. Barnes was shot and killed as he presided over a civil trial in the old Fulton County Courthouse. The court reporter, Julie Ann Brandau, was shot in the head and killed. The gunman, Brian Nichols, was a defendant in a criminal trial presided over by Judge Barnes. Nichols, who was charged with rape and other felonies, was being tried for the second time after his first trial ended with a hung jury. Two days previously, two shanks had been found in Nichols's shoes, and Judge Barnes had notified the defense and prosecution lawyers that they should be careful and that he, the judge, had suggested that security needed to increase.

Nichols, who was on his way to the courtroom where his second trial was to resume, overpowered his guard, Cynthia Hall, who was critically injured, and took her weapon. He went to the judge's chambers, where he overpowered another deputy, handcuffed him, and stole his gun. Nichols then went to the courtroom where Judge Barnes was presiding, shot and killed the judge and the court reporter, went to the parking garage, overpowered and pistol-whipped a reporter, and stole his car. Outside the courthouse, a third victim, Sergeant Hoyt Teasley, was shot in the abdomen and killed.

Initially, it was assumed that the suspect fled in the reporter's car; that car was subsequently located in the garage but not before one of the largest organized searches in Georgia history began. After Nichols fled the courthouse, he took public transportation to an apartment area, where he forced Inman Adam, 23, at gunpoint to let him into her apartment. Inside the apartment, Nichols was confronted by Adam's boyfriend, Shelton Warren, 26. Nichols hit Warren three times in the head and fled. Nichols then went three blocks to a home being built by David Wilhelm, an off-duty federal customs agent, and his wife. Wilhelm was shot and killed; his badge, gun, and truck were stolen.

That truck was later found in the parking lot of an apartment building, where Nichols forced a woman at gunpoint to admit him to her apartment, telling her that if she followed his orders, she would not be killed. The woman was able to get out of the apartment and went to the leasing office, where she dialed 911 and told police her story. Local, state, and federal law enforcement officers surrounded the area; Nichols surrendered peacefully, was handcuffed, and was taken into custody. He was convicted; the jury deadlocked on the death penalty; the judge sentenced him to consecutive life sentences without parole.[168]

Less than two weeks prior to the Atlanta shooting rampage, Judge Joan Humphrey Lefkow of the U.S. District Court in Chicago found her husband, Michael F. Lefkow, 64, and her mother, Donna Humphrey, 89, dead in the Lefkows's home, the victims of gunshot wounds. Judge Lefkow had been the target of death threats. White supremacist Matthew Hale was convicted of soliciting a person to murder the judge. He was sentenced to 40 years in prison, and in 2006, a federal court upheld his conviction and sentence. Hale targeted Judge Lefkow because of a decision she made in 2002 that ordered him to pay $200,000 for "violating an Oregon group's trademark on the name World Church of the Creator." The judge had been under federal protection, but after Hale's conviction, she and the U.S. marshals, who, among other duties, protect federal judges and justices, did not think it was necessary to continue that protection. A spokesperson for the U.S. marshals said: "It would be impossible to put round-the-clock security on the nation's 2,000 federal judges in 400 court facilities." During the previous 216 years, only three federal judges had been killed; no family members had been slain prior to the murders of the judge's husband and mother. Approximately 600 threats are made yearly against federal judges.[169] Hale was a suspect in the murders until Bart Ross, an unsuccessful plaintiff, who had spent a decade seeking monetary damages in a health-related claim, confessed in a note he left prior to committing suicide that he killed Lefkow's family while hunting for her.

These violent acts in Chicago and in Atlanta along with those in other courts have resulted in a reassessment of the security provided to local, state, and federal judges. In the final analysis, however, we cannot provide round-the-clock security to all judges, and all would not want that intensive surveillance. The need to protect judges must be balanced against the cost to society and the invasion of the privacy of judges and their families.

Summary

This chapter presented an overview of courts and their procedures. It began with a brief explanation of legal terms necessary to understand court functions. It examined the dual court system and the differences between trial and appellate courts before turning to an examination of four specialized courts: juvenile, domestic violence, drug, and mental health courts. The dynamics of each type were analyzed in the light of today's problems and issues, with highlights and excerpts from the U.S. Supreme Court's 2010 decision regarding life without parole for crimes committed as a juvenile.

The next section focused on the role of lawyers in criminal court systems, with a look first at the prosecution and then at the defense. Pretrial processes were discussed, with the focus on three controversial processes: pretrial release procedures, the granting or denying of bail, and plea bargaining. The trial of a criminal case was examined, with an emphasis on the right to a speedy trial and the role of the judge and jury in criminal trials.

Sentencing, one of the most hotly debated topics in criminal justice today, was presented in more detail. After a short look at the sentencing process, the discussion turned to current sentencing issues. There was a brief section on the issue of disparity and then some more detail on three strikes and you're out. Some of the practical problems with three-strikes legislation were noted along with the legal issues, including an exhibit featuring a recent U.S. Supreme Court case upholding three-strikes legislation. The disparity between convictions for crack compared to powder cocaine was underscored, with an emphasis on recent developments in the federal laws covering these crimes. A look at possible race and ethnic discrimination was followed by a discussion of gender issues in sentencing.

The control of sentence disparity was discussed in the context of sentencing guidelines, especially those in the federal system. Those guidelines are hotly contested, and the chapter noted the latest U.S. Supreme Court decisions regarding them.

In previous editions, capital punishment was scaled back at the request of reviewers. Today, however, capital punishment has again become one of the most important issues in sentencing. The chapter explored the most recent data, looked at the key legal issues regarding capital punishment, and considered the issue of deterrence. It noted recent U.S. Supreme Court decisions, such as those concerning the execution of mentally ill persons, persons who were juveniles when they committed capital murder, and the use of lethal injection. The future of capital punishment was discussed, noting that most countries no longer use this punishment method. The chapter noted that some

states have recently abolished the practice; others have declared a moratorium on its implementation.

Procedures for appealing convictions and sentences were noted. The U.S. Supreme Court, its method of operation, and some of the controversy surrounding it were discussed, along with the latest appointments to the Court. A discussion of court congestion and suggestions for reducing this problem was followed by an overview of courts and violence.

The importance of the court system cannot be overemphasized, for it is in the courts that the final determination is made of how many criminal justice problems are resolved. Once a person has committed an offense punishable by the state, even if the police's handling of the situation is above question and society has provided all the necessary resources for treatment in whatever setting that may take place, a positive resolution of the problem may be thwarted by the courts. The rights of due process guaranteed by the Constitution may become a farce in the hands of incompetent lawyers and judges. With long delays, trials can become meaningless or unfair. It is incumbent on lawyers, judges, probation officers, and all other functionaries of the courts, as well as society, to make the improvement of courts a primary goal in the war against crime.

Many of the topics discussed in this chapter underscore the importance of discretion in criminal justice systems. Prosecutors have wide discretion in deciding whether to bring charges, which charges to bring, if and when to drop charges, whether to plea bargain, and which sentences to recommend for convicted defendants. Juries exercise discretion in deciding whether defendants are innocent or guilty. Defense attorneys exercise discretion in determining trial strategy and whether to advise their clients to plea bargain. Judges exercise discretion in their supervision of pretrial and trial procedures and in sentencing, for it is obvious that a move toward determinate sentencing does not remove all discretion.

It is not wise to attempt to remove all discretion in criminal justice systems. The real questions are where the bounds of that discretion will lie and how discretion may be checked. The control of discretion, not its abolition, should be the issue. The legal profession should recognize and accept the challenge of successful control of judicial and prosecutorial discretion, especially as it relates to sentencing. Some of the problems of criminal justice systems, however, cannot be solved by the legal profession alone. Society must take responsibility for offering adequate legal services for all. The social structure should be appraised with the realization that criminal justice systems do not exist in isolation from the rest of society. Research must be supported, and the tendency to abandon philosophies, such as treatment, before they have been given a real trial should be reexamined. As this author concluded in an earlier publication:

> It is easier to put the offender out of sight than to examine the social structure for cracks. It is easier to punish than to treat. It is easier to abolish the entire system of discretionary sentencing by attacking the abuses than to correct those abuses and provide the resources needed for an adequate implementation of the philosophy of individualized sentencing. It is easier to attack the judges for "leniency" than to examine the need to decriminalize the criminal code or to provide sufficient and well-trained probation and parole officers or adequate treatment facilities. It is also easier to lose than to win the war against crime.[170]

Study Questions

1. Define *judicial review*, *jurisdiction* (concurrent, appellate, and exclusive), *stare decisis*, and *legal reasoning*.

2. Illustrate the meaning of *dual court system*.

3. Distinguish between appellant and appellee in the context of the appeals process.

4. Do we need a juvenile court? If not, why not? If so, why?

5. Should all rights of the adult criminal court be extended to juvenile courts?

6. Assess the current status of sentencing to life without parole a person who commits a serious but nonhomicide crime as a juvenile.

7. Explain why we have domestic violence courts, and relate your answer to Chapter 12's discussion of mandatory arrests of batterers.

8. Explain the purpose of drug courts, and relate your answer to Chapter 10's discussion of drug offenses.

9. Explain why we have special courts for mental health issues.

10. What is the prosecutor's duty in the criminal justice system?

11. Explain and critique the role of defense attorneys in U.S. criminal justice systems.

12. Analyze the meaning of the right to appointed assistance of counsel.

13. State the advantages and disadvantages of pretrial release, noting in particular the federal system.

14. Critique the bail system.

15. Evaluate the plea bargaining process.

16. In U.S. criminal justice systems, defendants have a right to a speedy trial. Explain.

17. Contrast the roles of judge and jury in criminal trials.

18. Define and evaluate *three-strikes legislation*. Define *truth in sentencing*.

19. Discuss the argument that drug laws discriminate against minorities, especially African Americans. Summarize the recent changes or proposed changes in legislation regarding drug laws.

20. Why do we have sentencing guidelines? Are they effective in reducing sentence disparity? What has the U.S. Supreme Court held regarding federal sentencing guidelines?

21. Give an overall assessment of the cost of capital punishment.

22. How should we compensate inmates who are released from prison, especially from death row, after years of serving a sentence for a crime they did not commit?

23. What is the role of the jury in determining sentencing in a capital case?

24. How would you define *mentally ill* for purposes of excluding those people from executions upon conviction of capital murder?

25. At what age should persons who murder be considered for capital punishment? Justify your answer with practical, social, and legal reasons.

26. Analyze the issue of whether capital punishment is a deterrent to murder.

27. What do you think is the future of capital punishment in the United States?

28. Evaluate the purpose and role of the U.S. Supreme Court.

Brief Essay Assignments

1. Examine the issue of court congestion historically and in terms of recent developments.

2. Discuss and critique the use of specialized courts, such as juvenile, domestic violence, drug, and mental health courts.

3. Critique the use of three-strikes legislation.

4. Discuss the meaning of *sentence disparity*, and illustrate with race, gender, and ethnicity.

5. Evaluate the use of federal sentencing guidelines, and discuss the implications of the recent U.S. Supreme Court decisions in this area.

6. Discuss the legal issues regarding capital punishment.

7. Analyze the problem of providing security for all judges and other court personnel.

Internet Activities

1. Using your Web browser, search for information on sentencing issues and drug policies related to crack cocaine. The Sentencing Project's website at http://www.sentencingproject.org, accessed 8 November 2010, is a good place to start. What is the sentencing policy? Explain the racial disparity in sentencing for crack/powder cocaine. Do you believe the sentencing differences between crack and powder cocaine are justified, even with recent changes? Why or why not? What are the overall impacts of this sentencing policy?

2. Access the Death Penalty Information Center at http://www.deathpenaltyinfo.org, accessed 8 November 2010, and look for your state. Does it have a death penalty? If so, when was it last used? What have been the causes of wrongful convictions? What information does the site provide concerning race and ethnicity and the death penalty? Juveniles and the death penalty? Deterrence and the death penalty?

Notes

1. Earl Warren, "Delay and Congestion in the Federal Courts," quoted in *Delay in Court*, ed. Hans Zeisel et al. (Boston: Little, Brown, 1959), p. xxi.
2. *Marbury v. Madison*, 5 U.S. 137 (1803).
3. "The Federal Judiciary: United States Courts of Appeal," U.S. Courts, http://www.uscourts.gov/FederalCourts/UnderstandingtheFederalCourts/CourtofAppeals.aspx, accessed 4 November 2010.
4. Howard N. Synder and Melissa Sickmund, Office of Juvenile *Justice and Delinquency Prevention, Juvenile Offenders and Victims: 2006 National Report*, hereafter referred to as OJJDP 2006 Report, http://www.ojjdp.gov/ojstatbb/nr2006/downloads/NR2006.pdf, accessed 6 November 2010.
5. *OJJDP 2006 Report*, pp. 67–68, 128, 132, 137, 139, 141–142.
6. *Crime in the United States: Uniform Crime Reports, 2009* (September 2010), http://www2.fbi.gov/ucr/cius2009/data/table_32.html; http://www2.fbi.gov/ucr/cius2009/arrests/index.html, both accessed 6 November 2010.
7. See USCS, Title 18, Section 5032 (2010).
8. *OJJDP 2006 Report*, p. 103.
9. *Kent v. United States*, 383 U.S. 541 (1966).
10. *In re Gault*, 387 U.S. 1 (1967).
11. American Bar Association, *Maryland: An Assessment of Access to Counsel and Quality of Representation in Delinquency*. The report is summarized in and the quotations in this chapter were taken from, "ABA Finds Right to Lawyer Is 'an Unfilled Promise,'" *Criminal Justice Newsletter* (17 November 2003), p. 2.
12. *In re Winship*, 397 U.S. 358 (1970).
13. *Breed v. Jones*, 421 U.S. 519 (1975).
14. *United States v. R.L.C.*, 503 U.S. 291 (1992).
15. *McKeiver v. Pennsylvania*, 403 U.S. 528 (1971).
16. *OJJDP 2006 Report*, pp. 110, 112.
17. "Judges' Group Criticizes Trend Toward Waiver to Adult Court," *Criminal Justice Newsletter* 25 (1 March 1994): 1.
18. Benjamin Steiner et al., "Legislative Waiver Reconsidered: General Deterrent Effects of Statutory Exclusion Laws Enacted Post-1979," *Justice Quarterly* 23, no. 1 (March 2006): 34–59.
19. *The Consequences Aren't Minor: The Impact of Trying Youth as Adults and Strategies for Reform*, Campaign for Youth and Justice (March 2007), pp. 1–16 http://www.campaignforyouthjustice.org/

key-research/national-reports.html#consequences, accessed 8 November 2010.
20. Quoted in "Adult System Worsens Juvenile Recidivism, Report Says," *Washington Post* (30 November 2007), p. 14.
21. *Hughes v. State*, 653 A.2d 241 (Del. 1994), *clarified, reh'g. denied*, 1995 Del. LEXIS 36 (Del. 1995).
22. Benjamin Steiner, "The Effects of Juvenile Transfer to Criminal Court on Incarceration Decisions," *Justice Quarterly* 26, no. 1 (March 2009): 77–106.
23. Daniel P. Mears, "Public Opinion and the Foundation of the Juvenile Court," *Criminology* 45, no. 1 (February 2007): 223–258.
24. See Carrie Pettus-Davis and Eric Garland, "Ban Juvenile Transfer to Adult Court in Homicide Cases: Brain Development and the Need for a Blended Sentence Approach," in *Contemporary Issues in Criminal Justice Policy*, ed. Natasha A. Frost et al. (Belmont, CA: Wadsworth, Cengage Learning, 2010), pp. 311–321. For a response, see in the same book: Barry C. Feld, "In Defense of Waiver and Youthfulness as a Mitigating Factor in Sentencing," pp. 321–326.
25. "Death in Prison Sentences for 13- and 14-Year Olds," Equal Justice Initiative (28 November 2007), http://www.eji.org/eji/childrenprison/deathinprison, accessed 8 November 2010.
26. "Lifers as Teenagers, Now Seeking Second Chance," *New York Times* (17 October 2007), p. 1.
27. *Graham v. Florida*, 130 S.Ct. 2011 (2010); *Sullivan v. Florida*, 130 S.Ct. 2059 (2010).
28. John S. Goldkamp et al., *The Role of Drug and Alcohol Abuse in Domestic Violence and in Its Treatment: Dade County's Domestic Violence Court Experiment*, Report to the National Institute of Justice (Philadelphia: Crime and Justice Research Institute, 1996).
29. *Domestic Violence Court: Evaluation Report for the San Diego County Domestic Violence Courts*, as cited in "Domestic Violence Courts Said to Reduce Recidivism," *Criminal Justice Newsletter* 31, no. 4 (19 December 2000): 4.
30. Lynette Feder and Laura Dugan, "A Test of the Efficacy of Court-Mandated Counseling for Domestic Violence Offenders: The Broward Experiment," *Justice Quarterly* 19, no. 2 (June 2002): 343–375; quotation is on p. 343.
31. Rebecca Emerson Dobash, "Domestic Violence: Arrest, Prosecution, and Reducing Violence," *Criminology and Public Policy* 2, no. 2 (March 2003): 313–318; quotation is on p. 317.
32. Angela R. Gover et al., "Combating Domestic Violence: Findings from an Evaluation of a Local Domestic Violence Court," *Criminology and Public Policy* 3, no. 1 (November 2003): 109–132; quotation is on p. 128.
33. Faith E. Lutze and Megan L. Symons, "The Evolution of Domestic Violence Policy Through Masculine Institutions: From Discipline to Protection to Collaborative Empowerment," *Criminology and Public Policy* 2, no. 2 (March 2003): 319–328; quotation is on p. 325.
34. Office of National Drug Control Policy, *Drug Treatment in the Criminal Justice System* (Washington, D.C.: U.S. Department of Justice, March 2001), p. 4.
35. U.S. Department of Justice, Office of Justice Programs, National Institute of Justice, *Drug Courts: The Second Decade* (June

2006), http://www.ncjrs.org/pdffiles1/nij/211081.pdf, accessed 8 November 2010. The enactment statute for drug courts in the federal system may be found in Sections 50001–50002 of the Violent Crime Control and Law Enforcement Act of 1994, Public Law 103–322 (13 September 1994).

36. "Courts' Drug Treatment System Is Found to Be Effective," *New York Times* (9 November 2003), p. 28.

37. "Ohio Report Demonstrates Positive Outcomes from Drug Courts," *Behavioral Health Accreditation and Accountability Alert* 7, no. 9 (1 September 2002), p. 2.

38. Denise C. Gottfredson et al., "Effectiveness of Drug Treatment Courts: Evidence from a Randomized Trial," *Criminology and Public Policy* 2, no. 2 (March 2003): 171–196, referring to the work of Mark A. R. Kleiman, "Controlling Drug Use and Crime with Testing, Sanctions, and Treatment," in *Drug Addiction and Drug Policy: The Struggle to Control Dependence*, ed. Philip Heyman and William N. Brownsberger (Cambridge, MA: Harvard University Press, 2001).

39. John S. Goldkamp, "The Impact of Drug Courts," *Criminology and Public Policy* 2, no. 2 (March 2003): 197–205; quotation is on p. 199.

40. Adele Harrell, "Judging Drug Courts: Balancing the Evidence," *Criminology and Public Policy* 2, no. 2 (March 2003): 207–212.

41. Executive Office of the President, Office of National Drug Control Policy, *Fiscal Year 2011: Congressional Budget Submission*, http://www.ondcp.gov/policy/Congress_budget_submission.pdf, accessed 8 November 2010.

42. Office of National Drug Control Policy, "Of Substance Blog: 20 Years of Healing: Drug Court Celebrates Anniversary," http://ofsubstance.gov/blogs/pushing_back/archive/2009/05/11/48376.aspx, accessed 8 November 2010.

43. Quoted in "Holder Sees Drug Courts as a Lifeline," The Sentencing Project (4 June 2010), http://www.sentencingproject.org, accessed 8 November 2010.

44. Doris J. James and Lauren E. Glaze, Bureau of Justice Statistics, *Mental Health Problems of Prison and Jail Inmates* (September 2006), p. 1, http://bjs.ojp.usdoj.gov/content/pub/pdf/mhppji.pdf, revised 14 December 2006, accessed 6 November 2010.

45. USCS, Title 42, Section 379611 (2010).

46. "For School Truants, Attendance Court Offers Tough Love," *New York Times* (28 April 2010), p. 20.

47. See Lauren O'Neill Shermer and Brian D. Johnson, "Criminal Prosecutions: Examining Prosecutorial Discretion and Charge Reductions in U.S. Federal District Courts," *Justice Quarterly* 27, no. 3 (June 2010): 394–430.

48. Rodney F. Kingsnorth and Randall C. MacIntosh, "Intimate Partner Violence: The Role of Suspect Gender in Prosecutorial Decision-Making," *Justice Quarterly* 24, no. 3 (September 2007): 460–491.

49. *ABA Standards for Criminal Justice: Prosecution Function and Defense Function*, 3d ed., Standard 3-1.2(c) (Chicago, IL: American Bar Association, 1993).

50. "Seligman, Other Former Duke Lacrosse Players Sue Nifong," *University Wire* (10 October 2007), n.p. "Duke Guy's Dramatic Comeback: Beat 'Rape' Smear," *New York Post* (25 April 2010), p. 24.

51. "Violent Central City Gang Faces Federal Charges," *Times-Picayune* (New Orleans) (7 August 2010), p. 1.

52. *Banks v. Dretke*, 540 U.S. 668 (2004).

53. Richard D. Hartley et al., "Prosecutorial Discretion: An Examination of Substantial Assistance Departures in Federal Crack-Cocaine and Powder-Cocaine Cases," *Justice Quarterly* 24, no.3 (September 2007): 382–407.

54. See ABA, *Standards for Criminal Justice*, 3d ed., Standard 4-1.2(b).

55. "Center for State Courts Finds Indigent Defenders Perform Well," *Criminal Justice Newsletter* 23 (15 May 1992): 4.

56. "Court Rules That Suit on Public Defender System Can Proceed," *New York Times* (7 May 2010), p. 18.

57. American Bar Association "ABA Ten Principles of a Public Defense Delivery System" (February 2002), p. 1, http://www.abanet.org/legalservices/downloads/sclaid/indigentdefense/tenprinciples booklet.pdf, accessed 7 November 2010.

58. "Court Rules That Suit on Public Defender System Can Proceed."

59. Steiner, "The Effects of Juvenile Transfer to Adult Courts," p. 102.

60. Thomas H. Cohen and Tracey Kyckelhahn, Bureau of Justice Statistics, *Felony Defendants in Large Urban Counties, 2006* (May 2010), pp. 1–12, http://bjs.ojp.usdoj.gov/content/pub/pdf/fdluc06.pdf, accessed 7 November 2010.

61. Thomas H. Cohen and Brian A. Reeves, Bureau of Justice Statistics, *Pretrial Release of Felony Defendants in State Courts* (November 2007), pp. 1–8, http://bjs.ojp.usdoj.gov/content/pub/pdf/prfdsc.pdf, accessed 7 November 2010.

62. *Stack v. Boyle,* 342 U.S. 1, 5 (1951).

63. District of Columbia Court Reform and Procedure Act of 1970, D.C. Code, Section 23-1321 et seq. (2010).

64. *United States v. Salerno*, 481 U.S. 739 (1987). The Bail Reform Act of 1984 is codified at USCS, Title 18, Chapter 207, Section 3142(e) (2010).

65. See, for example, Stewart J. D'Alessio and Lisa Stolzenberg, "Unemployment and Pretrial Incarceration: Does the State Use Imprisonment to Control Labor Surplus?" *American Sociological Review* 60 (June 1995): 350–359.

66. Stephen Demuth, "Racial and Ethnic Differences in Pretrial Release Decisions and Outcomes: A Comparison of Hispanic, Black, and White Felony Arrestees," *Criminology* 41, no. 3 (August 2003): 873–908; quotation is on p. 899.

67. See, for example, Darrell Steffensmeier and Stephen Demuth, "Ethnicity and Judges' Sentencing Decisions: Hispanic-Black-White Comparisons," *Criminology* 39, no. 1 (February 2001): 145–178.

68. *Santobello v. New York*, 404 U.S. 257, 260–261 (1971).

69. *Bordenkircher v. Hayes*, 434 U.S. 357 (1978).

70. *Brady v. United States,* 397 U.S. 742 (1970).

71. *Arizona v. Horning*, 761 P.2d 728 (Ariz.App. 1988).

72. See Federal Rule of Evidence 410 and Federal Rule of Criminal Procedure 11(c)(5)(f) (2010).

73. *United States v. Mezzanatto*, 513 U.S. 196 (1995).

74. Deirdre M. Bowen, "Calling Your Bluff: How Prosecutors and Defense Attorneys Adapt Plea Bargaining Strategies to Increased Formalization," *Justice Quarterly* 26, no. 1 (March 2009): 2–29.

75. *United States v. Blanco*, 861 F.2d 773 (2d Cir. 1988), *cert. denied*, 489 U.S. 1019 (1989).

76. *Doggett v. United States*, 505 U.S. 647 (1992).

77. For an analysis, see Stuart Nagel, "Decision Theory and Juror Decision-Making," in *The Trial Process*, ed. Bruce Dennis Sales (New York: Plenum, 1989), pp. 353–386.

78. *Duncan v. Louisiana*, 391 U.S. 145 (1968).

79. "Jurors Ignore, Misunderstand Instructions," *American Bar Association Journal* 81 (May 1995): 30–31.

80. Jason Krause, "Judge v. Jury," *American Bar Association Journal* 93 (June 2007): 46–49; quotations are on pp. 46, 47.

81. Bureau of Justice Statistics, *Probation and Parole 1982* (Washington, D.C.: U.S. Department of Justice, 1983), p. 2.

82. Cal Pen Code, Title 16, Section 667 (2010).

83. Franklin Zimring et al., *Three Strikes and You're Out in California* (New York: Oxford University Press, 2001), cited in *Criminal Justice Newsletter* 31, no. 12 (25 May 2001): 10; "California Prison System Struggling to Find Balance in Upheaval," *Corrections Professional* 10, no. 17 (27 May 2005): n.p.

84. "California Court System's Analysis of Three-Strikes Law," *Criminal Justice Newsletter* 20 (15 October 1996): 4.

85. "Retroactively, Panel Reduces Drug Sentences," *New York Times* (12 December 2007), p. 1; The Sentencing Project, "U.S. Sentencing Commission Decision Takes Effect Today," (3 March 2008), http://www.sentencingproject.org, accessed 9 March 2008.

86. The Fair Sentencing Act of 2010, P.L. 111-220 (2010).

87. Michael H. Tonry, "Racial Politics, Racial Disparities, and the War on Crime," *Crime and Delinquency* 40 (October 1994): 475, 483–488. See also Tonry, *Malign Neglect: Race, Crime, and Punishment in America* (New York: Oxford University Press, 1994).

88. See, for example, *United States v. Lattimore*, 974 F.2d 971 (8th Cir. 1992), *cert. denied*, 507 U.S. 1020 (1993).

89. *United States v. Armstrong*, 517 U.S. 446 (1996).

90. The Sentencing Project, "Racial Disparity," http://www.sentencing project.org/template/page.cfm?id=122, accessed 8 November 2010. The studies are The Human Rights Watch report, *Targeting Blacks: Drug Law Enforcement and Race in the United States*, http//www.hrw.org; and The Sentencing Project report, Ryan S. King, *Disparity by Geography: The War on Drugs in America's Cities* (May 2008), http://www.sentencingproject.org/doc/publications/dp_drugarrestreport.pdf, accessed 8 November 2010.

91. The Sentencing Project, "Sentencing Policy," http://www.sentenc ingproject.org/template/page.cfm?id=92, accessed 10 November 2010.

92. *McCleskey v. Kemp*, 481 U.S. 279 (1987).

93. John H. Kramer and Jeffrey T. Ulmer, "Sentencing Disparity and Departures from Guidelines," *Justice Quarterly* 13 (1996): 402–425.

94. Brian Daniel Johnson, "Racial and Ethnic Disparities in Sentencing Departures Across Modes of Conviction," *Criminology* 41, no. 2 (May 2003): 449–490.

95. "Fewer Blacks in Prison for Drugs, Sentencing Project Report Finds," *Criminal Justice Newsletter* (16 March 2009), p. 6.

96. See Otto Pollak, *The Criminality of Women* (Philadelphia: University of Pennsylvania Press, 1950).

97. Samantha Jeffries et al., "Pathways to Sex-Based Differentiation in Criminal Court Sentencing," *Criminology* 41, no. 2 (May 2003): 329–353, quotation is on p. 350. The reference is to the work of Kathleen Daly and Rebecca L. Bordt, "Sex Effect and Sentencing: An Analysis of the Statistical Literature," *Justice Quarterly* 12, no. 1 (1994): 142–175.

98. See, for example, Meda Chesney-Lind, "Girls in Jail," *Crime and Delinquency* 34 (1988): 150–168; and "Girls' Crime and Woman's Place: Toward a Feminist Model of Female Delinquency," *Crime and Delinquency* 35 (1989): 5–29.

99. Barbara A. Koons-Witt, "The Effect of Gender on the Decision to Incarcerate Before and After the Introduction of Sentencing Guidelines," *Criminology* 40, no. 2 (May 2002): 297–358.

100. *Women in the Criminal Justice System: Briefing Sheets*, The Sentencing Project (May 2007), http://www.sentencingproject.org/Admin/Documents/publications/womenincj_total.pdf, accessed 8 November 2010.

101. Ronald L. Akers and Christine S. Sellers, *Criminological Theories: Introduction, Evaluation, and Application*, 5th ed. (New York: Oxford University Press, 2009), p. 272.

102. See the Sentencing Reform Act of 1984 as amended, USCS, Title 18, Section 3551 et seq. and USCS, Title 28, Chapter 227, Sections 991–998 (2010).

103. *Mistretta v. United States*, 488 U.S. 361 (1989).

104. See "Sentencing Guidelines Reduce Disparities, Commission Says," *Criminal Justice Newsletter* 23 (3 February 1992): 3–4.

105. "Mandatory Minimum Sentences Hit," *American Bar Association Journal* 77 (December 1992): 36.

106. "Chorus of Judicial Critics Assail Sentencing Guides," *New York Times* (17 April 1992), p. 2.

107. "Justice Backs a Bar Plan to Ease Sentencing," *New York Times* (24 June 2004), p. 16.

108. "American Bar Assn. Delegates Pass Resolution Against Mandatory Minimum Sentencing Laws," *Minnesota Lawyer* (16 August 2004), n.p.

109. Amy L. Anderson and Cassia Spohn, "Lawlessness in the Federal Sentencing Process: A Test for Uniformity and Consistency in Sentencing Outcomes," *Justice Quarterly* 27, no. 3 (June 2010): 363–394; quotations are on pp. 389, 390. The reference to the federal judge is to Marvin Frankel, "Lawlessness in Sentencing," *University of Cincinnati Law Review* 42 (1972): 1–54.

110. *Blakely v. Washington*, 542 U.S. 296 (2004).

111. *United States v. Apprendi*, 530 U.S. 466 (2000).

112. *United States v. Booker*, 375 F.3d 508 (7th Cir. 2004), *aff'd., remanded*, 543 U.S. 220 (2005).

113. *United States v. Fanfan*, 2004 U.S. LEXIS 18593 (D.Me, 2004), *vacated, remanded*, 543 U.S. 220 (2005).

114. *United States v. Booker; United States v. Fanfan*, 543 U.S. 220 (2005).

115. *Rita v. United States*, 551 U.S. 338 (2007).

116. *Claiborne v. United States*, 551 U.S. 338 (2007).

117. *Cunningham v. California*, 549 U.S. 270 (2007). The relevant California statutes are 117 Cal Pen Code Sections 288.5(a) and 1170(b)(2007).

118. *Shepard v. United States*, 544 U.S. 13 (2005).

119. Richard S. Frase, "The *Apprendi-Blakely* Cases: Sentencing Reform Counter-Revolution?" *Criminology and Public Policy* 6, no. 3 (August 2007): 403–432; quotation is on p. 428.

120. Paul J. Hofer, "*United States v. Booker* as a Natural Experiment: Using Empirical Research to Inform the Federal Sentencing Policy Debate," *Criminology and Public Policy* 6, no. 3 (August 2007): 433–460.

121. Shawn D. Bushway and Anne Morrison Piehl, "Social Science Research and the Legal Threat to Presumptive Sentencing Guidelines," *Criminology and Public Policy* 6, no. 3 (August 2007): 461–482; quotation is on p. 461.

122. Kim Steven Hunt, "Reaction Essay: Standards of Evidence," *Criminology and Public Policy* 6, no. 3 (August 2007): 483–492.

123. Nicole Leeper Piquero, "What About Organizational Defendants? They're Affected as Well," *Criminology and Public Policy* 6, no. 3 (August 2007): 493–502; quotation is on p. 500.

124. *Furman v. Georgia*, 408 U.S. 238 (1972).

125. See Utah Code Ann., Section 77-18-5.5 (2010) (amended effective 3 May 2004).

126. "Financial Facts About the Death Penalty," Death Penalty Information Center, p. 4, citations omitted, http://www.deathpenaltyinfo.org/documents/FactSheet.pdf, accessed 22 December 2010.

127. See "Decision to Seek the Death Penalty in One Case Costs Georgia More than $3 Million," May 25, Death Penalty Information Center, http://www.deathpenaltyinfo.org/, accessed 7 November 2010.

128. See *State v. Young*, 172 P.3d 138 (N.M. 2007).

129. Editorial, *Los Angeles Times* (20 March 2009), p. 36. The New Mexico statute is N.M.Stat.Ann, Section 31–18–14 (2010).

130. See N.J. ALS, P.L. 2007, Chapter 204 (2007).

131. "Court Pressure in Arizona Leads to Settlements in Death Cases," Death Penalty Information Center, http://www.deathpenaltyinfo.org/court-pressure-arizona leads-settlements-death-cases, accessed 8 November 2010.

132. Justice for All Act of 2004, Pub. Law 108–405 (2008).

133. *Atkins v. Virginia*, 536 U.S. 304 (2002).

134. *Panetti v. Quarterman*, 552 U.S. 930 (2007).

135. *Pinholster v. Ayers*, 590 F.3d 651 (9th Cir. 2009), *cert. granted, mot. granted, Cullen v. Pinholster*, 130 S.Ct. 3410 (2010).

136. *Ring v. Arizona*, 536 U.S. 584 (2002).

137. *Schriro v. Summerlin*, 542 U.S. 348 (2004).

138. *Wiggins v. Smith*, 539 U.S. 510 (2003).

139. *Baze v. Rees*, 553 U.S. 35 (2008). The statute is KRS 431.220 (2009).

140. *Base v, Rees*, 553 U.S. 35 (2008), Justice Ginsburg dissenting.

141. "Why California Ok'd, Then Delayed First Execution In Years," *Christian Science Monitor* (30 September 2010), n.p. To examine the legal issues, see *Morales v. Tilton*, 465 F.Supp. 2d 972 (N.D. Cal. 2006); *Morales v. Brown*, 2010 U.S. Dist. LEXIS 103846 (N.D.Cal. 28 September 2010).

142. *State v. Kennedy*, 957 So.2d 757 (La. 2007), *rev'd., remanded, Kennedy v. Louisiana*, 554 U.S. 407 (2008). The previous case was *Coker v. Georgia*, 433 U.S. 584 (1977).

143. *Skinner v. Switzer*, 130 S.Ct. 3323 (24 May 2010). The civil action requested would be under Section 1983 of the USCS (2010). The lower court case is *Skinner v. State*, 956 S.W.2d 532 (Tex. Crim. App. 1997), *cert. denied*, 532 U.S. 1079 (1998).

144. Thorsten Sellin, "The Death Penalty," in *Capital Punishment*, ed. Sellin (New York: Harper & Row, 1967).

145. Richard O. Lempert, "Desert and Deterrence: An Assessment of the Moral Bases of the Case for Capital Punishment," *Michigan Law Review* 79 (May 1981): 1207.

146. Ibid., pp. 1205–1206.

147. Daniel Glaser and Max S. Zeigler, "Use of the Death Penalty v. Outrage at Murder," *Crime and Delinquency* 20 (October 1974): 337.

148. William C. Bailey, "Use of the Death Penalty v. Outrage at Murder: Some Additional Evidence and Considerations?" *Crime and Delinquency* 22 (January 1976): 37.

149. Daniel Glaser, "A Response to Bailey: More Evidence on Capital Punishment as Correlate of Tolerance for Murder," *Crime and Delinquency* 22 (January 1976): 43.

150. Lempert, "Desert and Deterrence," p. 1207. See also Isaac Ehrlich, "The Deterrent Effect of Capital Punishment: A Question of Life and Death," *American Economic Review* 65 (June 1975): 397–407. For other reactions to Ehrlich's work, see David C. Baldus and James W. L. Cole, "A Comparison of the Work of Thorsten Sellin and Isaac Ehrlich on the Deterrent Effect of Capital Punishment," *Yale Law Journal* 85 (December 1975): 170–186.

151. John Sorenson et al., "Capital Punishment and Deterrence: Examining the Effect of Executions on Murder in Texas," *Crime and Delinquency* 45 (1999): 481–493.

152. See William C. Bailey, "Deterrence, Brutalization, and the Death Penalty: Another Examination of Oklahoma's Return to Capital Punishment," *Criminology* 36 (1998): 711–733; Keith Harries and Derral Cheatwood, *The Geography of Execution: The Capital Punishment Quagmire in America* (Lanham, MD: Rowman & Littlefield, 1997).

153. Akers and Sellers, *Criminological Theories*, 5th ed., pp. 22–23.

154. *Roper v. Simmons*, 543 U.S. 551 (2005).

155. *Roper v. Simmons*, 543 U.S. 551 (2005).

156. Cited in Death Penalty Information Center, http://www.deathpenaltyinfo.org/documents/FactSheet.pdf, accessed 8 November 2010.

157. "ABA Study: States Death Penalty Systems Deeply Flawed," ABA News Release (29 October 2007), http://www.abanet.org/abanet/media/release/news_release.cfm?releaseid=209, accessed 8 November 2010.

158. "Supreme Court Gets First Negative Approval Rating," *ABA Journal*, http://www.abajournal.com/weekly/supreme_court_gets_first_negative_approval_rating, accessed 8 November 2010.

159. Information on the 2009–10 term secured from the public relations office of the U.S. Supreme Court (202-479-3211), accessed 8 November 2010. For information on previous years, see "Justices Opt for Fewer Cases, and Professors and Lawyers Ponder Why," *New York Times* (29 September 2009), p. 20.

160. *Mistretta v. United States*, 488 U.S. 361 (1989).

161. Violent Crime Control and Law Enforcement Act of 1994, Public Law 193-322 (13 September 1994).

162. "Expanded Border Policing Clogs the Courts and Jails," *New York Times* (1 July 2000), p. 7.

163. Ibid.

164. "The Recession Begins Flooding into Courtrooms," *New York Times* 28 (December 2009), p. 1.

165. "State Courts at the Tipping Point," *New York Times* (25 November 2009), p. 26.

166. "Budget Crisis Closes California Courts," *New York Times* (17 September 2009), p. 17; "Plan to Close California's Budget Deficit," *New York Times* (9 January 2010), p. 11; "California's Fiscal Health Continues to Deteriorate, Despite Many Deep Cuts," *New York Times* (1 November 2009), p. 22.

167. National Center for State Courts, *Ten Trends Impacting State Courts*, http://contentdm.ncsconline.org/cgi-bin/showfile.exe?CISOROOT=/ctadmin&CISOPTR=979, accessed 8 November 2008.

168. Summarized from various media sources.

169. "Man in Plot to Kill Judge Says Slayings Are 'Heinous,'" *New York Times* (4 March 2005), p. 11. The case is *United States v. Hale*, 448 F.3d 961 (7th Cir. 2006).

170. Sue Titus Reid, "A Rebuttal to the Attack on the Indeterminate Sentence," *Washington Law Review* 51 (July 1976): 606

PART FIVE

Social Reaction to Crime: Corrections

The final part of this text covers the ways society reacts to offenders after they have been processed through court systems. **Chapter 14** begins with an overview of the use of jails and prisons for punishment. It examines early U.S. penal facilities, distinguishes between jails and prisons, and addresses the problems of overcrowding. How inmates live in and adjust to prison is discussed, along with prison violence and ways of controlling violence and providing an orderly existence for inmates and officials. Attention is given to inmates' legal rights as well as to their health issues.

Overcrowding has led to a greater emphasis on alternatives to prison, and recidivism rates have encouraged more thought about preparing incarcerated offenders for reintegration into society. These and other issues are the basis for **Chapter 15's** analysis of community corrections. Two of the major topics are probation and parole, but attention is also given to the recent and controversial Megan's law and its implications. The chapter closes with an evaluation of community corrections.

CHAPTER 14

The Confinement of Offenders

Security is tight on California's death row cell block in the San Quentin State Prison. This aging prison near San Francisco occupies over 400 acres of waterfront property and is the focus of controversy. Some officials wanted to build a new death row to reduce overcrowding at San Quentin, but others argued for demolishing the structure, which was built before the Civil War and is costly to maintain.

KEY TERMS

deprivation model
hands-off doctrine
importation model
incarceration
jail
offenders
penitentiary
prison
prisonization
reformatory
transportation

INTRODUCTION

This chapter focuses on the evolution of prisons and jails for the purpose of punishment. It provides a historical background of prisons in Europe and their evolution within the United States, looks at current correctional populations, distinguishes between prisons and jails, examines private facilities, and goes inside the inmates' prison world. An analysis of the inmates' social world incorporates discussions of the prison socialization process and a look at the special problems of female inmates and their children. This is followed by a discussion of elderly, physically and mentally challenged, and finally, juvenile inmates. The section on prison violence discusses self-inflicted violence as well as violence against others, sexual violence, prison riots, and escapes. The role of correctional officers is analyzed. After briefly noting problems of maintaining control and order within the prison, the chapter presents an overview of inmates' legal rights, including health issues and the impact of the Americans with Disabilities Act on prisons.

The confinement of offenders as a method of punishment is a relatively recent development. In earlier times, offenders were punished through social or psychological methods, often by the victims or their families. Serious (and sometimes not so serious) offenders were subjected to corporal punishments, some of which were so brutal that death resulted. These punishments were abandoned, at least theoretically, in favor of **incarceration** as punishment.

The Emergence of Prisons for Punishment

The use of institutions for confining people against their will is ancient. It includes short-term detention facilities for the confinement of persons awaiting trial, sentencing, execution, **transportation** (deportation to other countries as punishment), whipping, or some other form of corporal punishment. But placing **offenders** in an institution for the purpose of punishment is a relatively modern development.[1]

The transition from corporal punishment to incarceration took place in the eighteenth century in many European countries. One of the more significant developments was that of prison hulks (ships used as prisons) in England. The American colonies had rebelled against England's transportation of criminals to the New World; the use of Australia as a penal colony had also run into difficulties. Crime rates were rising, leading to larger numbers of inmates. Therefore, England legalized the use of hulks, most of which were broken-down war vessels. By 1828, there were 4,000 prison hulks, which were characterized by overcrowding, inmates with contagious diseases, lack of work opportunities, unsanitary conditions, lack of ventilation, and corporal punishment. England used prison hulks until the middle of the century.

The prison reform movement in Europe provides a lengthy and fascinating area of study that goes beyond the scope of this text. But mention should be made of the great prison reformer John Howard (1726–1790), an Englishman to whom many give credit for the beginnings of the **penitentiary** system. Howard traveled throughout Europe and brought to the attention of the world the sordid conditions under which inmates were confined. In 1777, he published his classic book, *State of Prisons*, which was influential in prison reform in Europe and the United States.

U.S. Contributions to the Emergence of Prisons

Despite the existence of prisons in other countries before their emergence in the United States, the new country could claim one unique contribution, at least in theory: the substitution of prison for corporal punishment. Some claim that this idea originated in Europe. Others argue that the prison system began with the Newgate prison in Connecticut and, 20 years later, the Walnut Street Jail in Philadelphia.[2] But credit is usually given to two systems, the Auburn (New York) system and the Pennsylvania system, with the Pennsylvania system becoming known throughout the world as the embodiment of the new philosophy.

The Pennsylvania and Auburn Systems

The Pennsylvania system began in the eighteenth century, when the Quakers substituted incarceration for corporal punishment. Prison confinement was combined with hard labor rather than with the idleness characteristic of confinement in the English hulks.

The Walnut Street Jail, actually a prison, was typical of the institutions in the Pennsylvania system. It was remodeled to comply with the provisions of a 1790 statute that provided for the solitary confinement of offenders. This statute was the beginning of the modern prison system in the United States. It established the philosophy that was the basis of the Pennsylvania and the Auburn prison systems. Inmates worked an 8- to 10-hour day in their cells, and they were paid for their work. They received religious instruction. They were allowed to talk to each other only in the common rooms in the evenings. This plan with variations was followed in some other states.

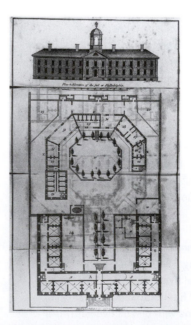

The early Pennsylvania prison known as the Walnut Street Jail was typical of confinement institutions that followed the requirements of a 1790 statute. Inmates spent most of their time in solitary confinement, eating and working in their cells.

By 1800, some problems in the Pennsylvania system had become obvious. Crowded facilities made work within individual cells impossible, and there was not enough productive work for the large number of inmates. The Walnut Street Jail eventually failed because of the lack of finances, shortage of personnel, and overcrowding, but it had gained recognition throughout the world. The jail has been called the "birthplace of the prison system, in its present meaning, not only in the United States but throughout the world."[3]

The failure of the Walnut Street Jail and other early American prisons led some critics to argue for a return to corporal punishment. But prison reformers were able to get Pennsylvania to enact a statute providing for solitary confinement without labor. The first prison, the Western Penitentiary, was opened in Pittsburgh in 1826, but idleness created problems. Subsequently, the law was changed to permit solitary confinement with inmates working in their cells. This set the stage for the Cherry Hill Prison (discussed next) and further development of the Pennsylvania prison system.

In 1829, Pennsylvania established a prison named for its location in a cherry orchard. The Cherry Hill Prison represented the first major attempt to implement the Pennsylvania system of inmate solitary confinement with work provided in their cells. To maintain this system without endangering the health of the inmates or permitting their escape, the architect designed a prison with seven wings, each connected to a central hub by covered passageways. The single cells had individual outdoor exercise yards. Inmates were not permitted to see one another even when taken to chapel. The chaplain spoke from the rotunda, with inmates remaining in their individual cells. The Pennsylvania prison architecture was not popular in the United States but became the model for most of Europe. The system that prevailed in the United States was the New York, or Auburn, plan.

In contrast to the Pennsylvania system, the Auburn plan permitted inmates to congregate but not to communicate. The system was much more economical than the Pennsylvania system. The architecture featured a fortress-like building with a series of tiers set in a hollow frame. Silence was enforced by having inmates eat face to back rather than face to face. They were required to stand with arms folded and eyes down so that they could not communicate with their hands; when walking, they maintained a lockstep with a downward gaze. They were further isolated through rules limiting their contact with the outside world. When they attended religious functions, the inmates sat in boothlike pews that prevented them from seeing anyone other than the speaker.

Auburn's warden, Captain Elam Lynds, believed in strict discipline. He took the position that reformation could not occur until the spirit of the inmate was broken. By 1821, Lynds was placing dangerous inmates in solitary confinement for long periods, a practice that led to mental illness and, in some cases, death. Many inmates pleaded to be permitted to work. A commission appointed to study the prison recommended abolishing solitary confinement and putting all inmates to work.

Both the Auburn and the Pennsylvania prison systems were based on the belief that inmates would corrupt one another if they were permitted to have contact. The Pennsylvania system isolated inmates physically; the Auburn system permitted congregation but enforced the silence rule. In the Pennsylvania system, the Quaker emphasis on religious training and time for reflection was emphasized; moreover, inmates were expected to read their Bibles and meditate. Corporal punishment was not permitted. The Auburn plan included corporal punishment. The two prison systems were also different in their architectural design. The Auburn plan was less expensive to build, but the Pennsylvania system was more economical to administer. Both systems were severe, although it has been argued that both were improvements over the cruel punishments that had existed in the United States and Europe.

Prison Expansion

In the late 1800s, prison overcrowding became a problem as prison populations increased rapidly. New prisons were built in the early 1900s, including Attica (New York) in 1931 and Stateville (Illinois) in 1925, both still in use today. Most of the prisons built in the early 1900s followed the Auburn architectural plan. Some educational and other programs were available for inmates, and some work was provided, but the work was based on institutional rather than inmate needs. Prison products were sold on the open market, a practice later prohibited by statute because of complaints from private industry. Attempts were made to segregate inmates by classifications, such as age, gender, and type of offense. Prison reformers argued that inmates should be treated as individuals and that communication was important. The silence system was abolished, and attempts were made to increase social activities. But by 1935, for most inmates, "the penitentiary system had again reverted to its original status: punishment and custody."[4]

The 1800s and early 1900s were characterized by an emphasis on probation and parole (discussed in Chapter 15). Of primary concern here is that the prison concept became a total institution for confinement with little, if any, emphasis on reformation. Other scholars have argued that even if prisons were initially intended to be humanitarian, they evolved as institutions for the political and social manipulation of certain classes of people.[5]

The Reformatory Era

Not all early prisons were penitentiaries. In the 1800s, some reformers recognized the need to separate children from adults and women from men and to classify offenders by the seriousness of their offenses. A meeting on 12 October 1870, conducted by penologist Enoch C. Wines, led to the emergence of the **reformatory** system, culminating in the establishment of the Elmira (New York) Reformatory in 1876. Elmira became the model for reformatories designed primarily for youthful offenders. Although Elmira was similar architecturally to Auburn, its programs placed a greater emphasis on education and vocational training. Indeterminate sentences with maximum terms, opportunity for parole, and classification of inmates according to conduct and productivity were Elmira's most significant achievements.

It was predicted that Elmira would dominate U.S. prison systems. Headed by Zebulon R. Brockway, who was proclaimed by some authorities as the "greatest warden America has ever produced," Elmira "changed the course of corrections by introducing 'scientific reform' and the 'new penology.'" But Elmira was also viewed as an institution that was instrumental in perpetuating sexism and racism and in repressing the lower classes.[6]

Thus, although there is disagreement on the place of Elmira in history, it does seem clear that what was designed to be a reformatory was, in fact, a prison.

Beginning in 1910, the reformatory system declined primarily because of the lack of trained personnel to conduct the education programs and carry on the classification systems adequately. Some of the techniques of management and discipline at the reformatories were characteristic of prisons. Brockway was accused of using "cruel, brutal, excessive and unusual punishment" to achieve his purpose of reforming inmates. A series of investigations led to recommendations for some changes, such as the improvement of medical care, reduction of overcrowding, and restriction of whipping, permitted only on the buttocks. Serious allegations against Brockway were dropped. He continued in power at Elmira until 1900, "and the Elmira experiment came to an end just as 'prison science' and the 'new penology' were taking hold across the country."[7] Reformatories continued, but many were really prisons, presenting only an illusion of reformation.

The Modern Era of American Prisons: An Overview

In discussing the modern era of American prisons, it is interesting to note that in the Preface to her brief text on prisons, criminologist Marilyn McShane emphasized that prison environments are dynamic and changing in terms of politics, law, demographics, and other factors. However, "there is no doubt that even though the architecture and technology changes and the demographics of the inmate population shift, there is great similarity between the first American prison and the institutions we encounter today."[8]

Despite McShane's observation, in the past few decades, significant attempts have been made to change the nature

of incarceration. Many of these attempts are related to the use of alternatives to incarceration, discussed in Chapter 15, but changes were also made in prisons. Despite the continued use of many of the fortresslike prisons built in the 1800s and early 1900s, some progressive designs were incorporated into the construction of new prisons. A greater emphasis was placed on rehabilitation combined with improved opportunities for education and vocational training. Treatment programs, at least in theory, were emphasized. Indeterminate sentences were instituted to fulfill the claim that inmates would not be released until they were reformed.

Despite these alleged changes, many authorities now recognize that most prison reform was illusory; few real changes occurred, and escapes and riots increased. As crime rates climbed, rehabilitation was declared a failure. As sentences were lengthened, inmate populations strained prison capacity. As prison conditions deteriorated, federal courts became active in the inmates' rights movement, which is discussed later in this chapter. Prisons have remained, but the serious conditions of today's institutions have led many to question the so-called reform era.

Institutions for the Confinement of Adult Offenders

Most adult offenders are confined in jails, prisons, or community-based facilities. In some jurisdictions, adults are detained in *lockups*, which are temporary holding facilities for short-term detention while suspects are awaiting court hearings. Most lockups are operated by police departments and located in police stations. They may be used to detain juveniles until their parents or other guardians take custody of them from police or they are placed in other facilities. Community-based facilities are discussed in Chapter 15 along with noninstitutional confinement, such as house arrest and electronic monitoring. Jails and prisons are the focus here. Before we look at these facilities individually, inmate populations in general are discussed.

Correctional Populations

The estimated number of inmates under state or federal control in the United States was 1,613,740 by the end of 2009. The states incarcerated 1,405,622 of those inmates; 208,119 were under federal control. Prison growth between 2008 and 2009 was 3,981, only 0.2 percent, representing the smallest increase in the decade and the "third consecutive year of slower growth." Figure 14.1 graphs the change and percent in the number of inmates between 2000 and 2009. Figure 14.2 graphs the percentage change between 2000 and 2009 by whether the inmates were under state or federal jurisdiction. Note that between 2008 and 2009, state inmate populations decreased (for the

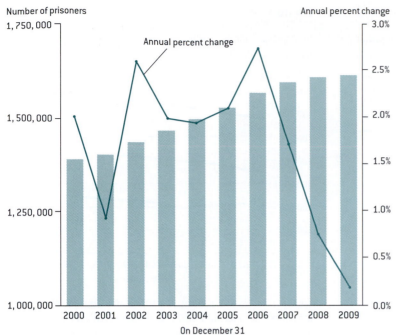

Figure 14.1

Prisoners Under State and Federal Jurisdiction at Yearend, 2000–2009

Source: Heather C. West and William J. Sabol, Bureau of Justice Statistics, *Prisoners in 2009* (December 2010), p. 1, http://bjs.usdoj .gov/content/pub/pdf/p09.pdf, accessed 24 December 2010.

third consecutive year) and federal inmate populations increased (by 3.4 percent) after a decrease between 2007 and 2008. Among the 24 states that experienced a decrease in inmates, Michigan had the largest decrease in numbers (down 3,260), followed by California (down 2,395). Rhode Island had the largest percentage decrease (9.2 percent), followed by Michigan (down 6.7 percent). Among the 26 states with increased inmate populations, Pennsylvania led in absolute numbers (up 2,214), followed by Florida (up 1,527). Alaska had the largest percentage increase (up 5.4 percent), followed by West Virginia (up 5.1 percent) and Vermont (up 4.9 percent). In 2009, men constituted 93 percent (a 0.3 percent increase) and women 7 percent (representing a 0.1 percent decline) of U.S. prisoners. Whites comprised approximately 34 percent of all inmates, with blacks constituting 38 percent and Hispanics 20 percent. Men were incarcerated at a rate of 14 times higher than that of women. In 2009, one in 1,987 white women and one in 1,356 Hispanic were incarcerated compared to one in 703 black women.[9]

Another measure of inmate populations is the rate (number of inmates per 100,000 U.S. residents) of imprisonment. Between 2008 and 2009, the imprisonment rate increased in the federal system but declined overall among states, with 28 states showing a decrease. Alaska led with the largest reported rate decrease and Louisiana reported the largest increase. Figure 14.3 graphs the changes in the number of state inmates and the state imprisonment rate between 1990 and 2009 and demonstrates the divergence between these two measures since 2000.

Inmate populations are also affected by changes in the emphasis on crimes for which sentences are imposed and for which inmates are released from prison. The Bureau

of Justice Statistics publishes analyses of the numbers of inmate populations by the categories of violent, property, drug, public order, and other crimes. In December 2010, the BJS published offense-specific data for the years 2000–2008 for state inmates. Table 14.1 presents those data. The table also indicates the specific crimes the BJS includes in

Figure 14.2

Percentage Change in Numbers of Prisoners Under State or Federal Jurisdiction, 2000–2009

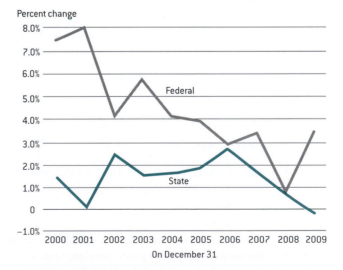

Source: Heather C. West and William J. Sabol, Bureau of Justice Statistics, *Prisoners in 2009* (December 2010), p. 1, http:// bjs.usdoj.gov/content/pub/pdf/p09.pdf, accessed 24 December 2010.

Figure 14.3

Number and Imprisonment Rate of Sentenced Prisoners Under State Jurisdiction, 1990–2009

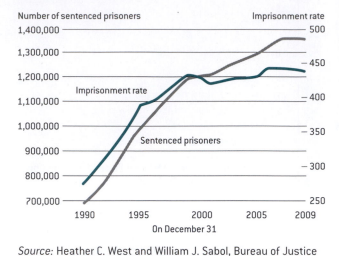

Source: Heather C. West and William J. Sabol, Bureau of Justice Statistics, *Prisoners in 2009* (December 2010), p. 3, http://bjs .usdoj.gov/content/pub/pdf/p09.pdf, accessed 24 December 2010.

Figure 14.4

Sentenced Prisoners Admitted into State Prison, by Type of Admission, 2000–2009

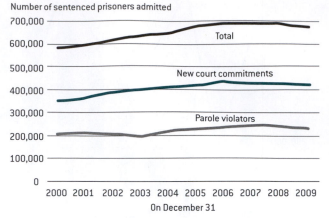

Source: Heather C. West and William J. Sabol, Bureau of Justice Statistics, *Prisoners in 2009* (December 2010), p. 5, http:// bjs.usdoj.gov/content/pub/pdf/p09.pdf, accessed 24 December 2010.

each category. As table 14.1 indicates, almost 60 percent of the increase in state inmates between 2000 and 2008 were inmates convicted of violent offenses, with public-order offenses in second place (33.6 percent). Approximately 12,400 fewer inmates were in prison for drug offenses in 2008 compared to 2000.

Finally with regard to state prison inmates, an important factor that influences prison populations is the reincarceration of paroled inmates after they violate the terms of their release. Parole is discussed in Chapter 15, but the impact of parole revocation is critical to an understanding of total prison populations. Figure 14.4 graphs the data on

Table 14.1

Estimated Number of Sentenced Prisoners Under State Jurisdiction, by Offense Category, 2000–2009

Offense category	2000	2008	Change, 2000–2008	Percent of total change
Total	1,206,200	1,365,400	159,200	100.0%
Violent[a]	620,000	715,400	95,400	59.9
Property[b]	246,000	251,800	5,800	3.6
Drug	263,800	251,400	−12,400	−7.8
Public-order[c]	72,400	125,900	53,500	33.6
Other/unspecified[d]	4,100	17,800	13,700	8.6

Note: Numbers were estimated and rounded to the nearest 100.

[a]Includes murder, nonnegligent manslaughter, manslaughter, rape, other sexual assault, robbery, assault, and other violent offenses.

[b]Includes burglary, larceny, motor vehicle theft, fraud, and other property crimes.

[c]Includes weapons, drunk driving, court offenses, commercialized vice, morals and decency offenses, liquor law violations, and other public-order offenses.

[d]Includes juvenile offenses and other unspecified offense categories.

Source: Heather C. West and William J. Sabol, Bureau of Justice Statistics, *Prisoners in 2009* (December 2010), p. 7, http://bjs.usdoj.gov/content/pub/pdf/p09.pdf, accessed 24 December 2010.

state prisoners in terms of whether they were admitted to prison as new commitments or as parole violators. Note that between 2008 and 2009 the number of parole violators decreased.

Jail populations have also shown growth changes over the years. The latest data, released by BJS in June 2010, concern the 2009 midyear jail population. Figure 14.5 graphs the number of inmates and the annual percentage change in jail populations between 2000 and 2009. The decline in jail populations between 2008 and 2009 was 2.3 percent. As Figure 14.5 reveals, jail populations slowed after 2005. The report on jail inmates in 2009 included data on juveniles held in adult jails, showing 5,847 held as adults and 1,373 held as juveniles at midyear 2009. In terms of characteristics, 87.8 percent of adult jail inmates were men and 12.2 percent were women; 42.5 percent were white, 39.2 percent were black/African American, and 16.2 percent were Hispanic/Latino. With regard to conviction status, 37.8 percent had been convicted.[10]

Overcrowding

Despite the slowing growth of inmates incarcerated in jails and prisons, many of the facilities are overcrowded. During the 1990s and thereafter, more prisons were built to accommodate the increasing number of inmates. This eased, but did not eliminate, jail and prison overcrowding, and some prison systems were (and in some cases, still are) under federal court orders to cut their populations. Here we focus on two systems and the issues of overcrowding.

California and New York Correctional Systems

California's correctional system serves as a prime example of significant prison population growth and costs over the past two decades. In previous discussions, we have noted that state's treatment programs. In 2005, California changed the name of its Department of Corrections to the Department of Corrections and Rehabilitation. The enabling statute, however, made it clear that despite the return to an emphasis on rehabilitation, the primary goal of the department remained security and the protection of California's people. Subsequently, the state's legislature commissioned a study of its correctional system by a panel of 16 highly qualified corrections experts, cochaired by the director of the Center for Evidence-Based Corrections at the University of California, Irvine. The commission's report contained the following information:

- Approximately 70 percent of released inmates are returned to prison within a year.
- The overcrowded prisons prevent the availability of programs for alcohol and drug addiction treatment, anger management, job training, and so on.
- The state could save between $561 million and $684 million a year if it followed all of the committee's recommendations.
- Of the $43,287 spent yearly on each inmate, 50 percent is for security, with only 5 percent for programs such as job training.
- The state has over 170,000 inmates in facilities designed for 100,000.[11]

In October 2006, before this report was issued, California's governor, Arnold Schwarzenegger, declared a state of emergency in the state's prison system due to overcrowding. Federal courts had given the state, under threat of being placed under federal receivership, until the spring of 2007 to devise an acceptable plan to solve the correctional

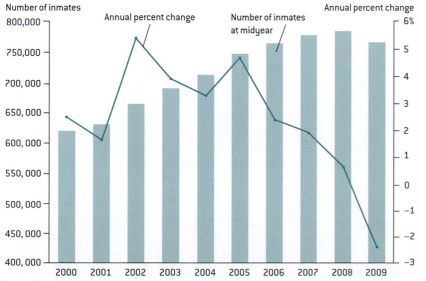

Figure 14.5

Inmates Confined in Local Jails at Midyear and Percentage Change in the Jail Population, 2000–2009

Source: Todd D. Minton, Bureau of Justice Statistics, *Jail Inmates at Midyear 2009—Statistical Tables* (June 2010), p. 1, http://bjs.ojp.usdoj.gov/content/pub/pdf/jim09st.pdf, accessed 11 November 2010.

system's problems of overcrowding and other issues. On 3 May 2007, the California legislature, along with Governor Schwarzenegger, agreed on a plan to expand correctional facilities.[12]

In the summer of 2007, however, two federal district court judges, in separate actions, held that California's reaction to federal court orders was inadequate. Their conclusions and recommendations were followed by the Ninth U.S. Circuit Court of Appeals. The two judges, Thelton Henderson of San Francisco and Lawrence Karlton of Sacramento, along with Judge Stephen Reinhardt of the federal appeals court constituted a panel with the power to determine whether the state's overcrowded prisons were making court-ordered improvements impossible and, if so, to impose a lid that would require the state to release inmates. The governor's argument that this was not necessary because the state's newly enacted law to build prisons would take care of the situation was rejected.[13]

In August 2009, federal judges gave California two years to reduce its prison population by 27 percent. In a long opinion, the judges described the crisis in that state, attributing to overcrowding the serious issues of unconstitutional conditions regarding medical care in general and mental health care in particular. A portion of that opinion is included here to emphasize the overcrowding in that state prison system. The state appealed to the U.S. Supreme Court to stay the opinion; that Court denied the request but stated, "In denying the stay, the Court takes note of the fact that the three-judge district court has indicated that its final order will not be implemented until this Court has had the opportunity to review the district court's decree."[14]

Coleman v. Schwarzenegger

"California's correctional system is in a tailspin," the state's independent oversight agency has reported. Tough-on-crime politics have increased the population of California's prisons dramatically while making necessary reforms impossible. As a result, the state's prisons have become places "of extreme peril to the safety of persons" they house, while contributing little to the safety of California's residents. California "spends more on corrections than most countries in the world," but the state "reaps fewer public safety benefits." Although California's existing prison system serves neither the public nor the inmates well, the state has for years been unable or unwilling to implement the reforms necessary to reverse its continuing deterioration. . . .

[The court addressed the issues of mental and physical health, which are discussed later in this chapter.]

California's inmates face a second everyday threat to their health and safety: the unprecedented overcrowding of California's prisons. Since reaching an all-time population record of more than 160,000 in October 2006, the state's adult prison institutions have operated at almost double their intended capacity. As Governor Schwarzenegger observed in declaring a prison state of emergency that continues to this day, this creates "conditions of extreme peril" that threaten "the health and safety of the men and women who work inside [severely overcrowded] prisons and the inmates housed in them. . . ." Thousands of prisoners are assigned to "bad beds," such as triple-bunked beds placed in gymnasiums or day rooms, and some institutions have populations approaching 300% of their intended capacity. In these overcrowded conditions, inmate-on-inmate violence is almost impossible to prevent, infectious diseases spread more easily, and lockdowns are sometimes the only means by which to maintain control. In short, California's prisons are bursting at the seams and are impossible to manage. . . .

Two federal lawsuits have brought the crisis in California's prisons to this three-judge court. Plaintiffs in the two lawsuits contend that a reduction in the prison population is necessary to bring the California prison system's medical and mental health care into constitutional compliance. In both *Plata v. Schwarzenegger* and *Coleman v. Schwarzenegger*, the federal courts initially issued narrow orders requiring California to develop and implement remedial plans to meet this objective. However, as the state time and again failed to meet its own remedial targets—let alone to achieve constitutional compliance—both courts were forced to adopt increasingly drastic remedies, culminating in the *Plata* court's 2005 appointment of a receiver to manage the prison medical system. Ultimately, by late 2006 it became apparent that the overcrowding in California's prisons rendered the efforts of the courts, the *Coleman* Special Master, and the *Plata* Receiver utterly insufficient. At the request of the *Plata* and *Coleman* courts, the Chief Judge of the United States Court of Appeals for the Ninth Circuit convened this three-judge court to consider the plaintiffs' request for a court-ordered reduction in the California prison population.

During the pendency of this proceeding, the outlook for California's prisons has only grown dimmer. The state is now in the throes of a fiscal crisis that renders it unable or unwilling to commit the necessary resources to fix the problems in its prisons. . . .

California has reduced spending on education, health care, the social safety net, and services for the needy, the blind, and children to the breaking point. Under these circumstances, we would be reluctant to direct the state to allocate additional funds to its prisons or to rehabilitative services at the expense of others to whom it has a legal and moral obligation.

Federal law makes any prisoner release order, including the population reduction order requested by plaintiffs, a "remedy of last resort," and imposes various conditions upon the issuance of such an order. . . . [T]hose conditions have been met here: (1) crowding is the primary cause of the state's failure to provide its inmates with constitutionally sufficient medical and mental health care; (2) no relief besides a prisoner release order can bring the California prison system into constitutional compliance; (3) an order requiring the state to reduce the population of its adult institutions to a lower percentage of their combined design capacity than presently exists—a population cap—is narrowly tailored to the constitutional violations identified by the *Plata* and *Coleman* courts, extends no further than necessary to remedy those violations, and is the least intrusive possible remedy; and (4) the state can comply with such an order with little or no impact on public safety and the operation of the criminal justice system. There are numerous means by which the state can reduce the prison population, from parole reform and the diversion of technical parole violators and low-risk offenders to sentencing reform and the expansion of good time credits and rehabilitative programming. There is no need for the state to release presently incarcerated inmates indiscriminately in order to comply with our order. Much of the relief can be achieved instead by reducing prison intake in a manner recommended by the state's own experts.

We recognize the gravity of the population reduction order we issue herein, and we do not intervene in matters of prison population lightly. Nonetheless, when federal court intervention becomes the only means by which to enforce rights guaranteed by the Constitution, federal courts are obligated to act. . . . California's prisoners have long been denied constitutionally adequate medical and mental health care, often with tragic consequences, and the overcrowding in California's prisons, which have become criminogenic, must be reduced if the prison system is to achieve constitutional compliance. California's prisoners, present and future, (and the state's population as a whole) can wait no longer.

The history of this case involves an agreement between the parties with regard to correcting the deficiencies in the prison system, specifically the medical care system, that allegedly violated the Eighth Amendment (see Appendix A) and the Americans with Disabilities Act.[15]

When the state did not comply with that agreement, the California Department of Corrections and Rehabilitation

(CDCR) was placed in receivership under the authority of a federal monitor.

California did not challenge the appointment of the monitor in 2006 but chose to do so three years after the monitor proposed the construction of 10,000 new prison beds at a cost of $6 billion. The monitor scaled his recommendation back to two hospitals, with space for 3,400 inmates, at a cost of $1.9 billion. On 30 April 2010, a panel of judges of the Ninth Circuit held that the district court was within its power to appoint the monitor, and California lost its appeal. The judges emphasized that three years after the state had agreed to make specific changes in its medical care system, not one prison had done so despite the fact that substandard medical care had resulted in the suicides of a "significant number" of inmates. The court held that federal law permits receiverships. The district court's finding that a receivership was the least restrictive alternative to eliminate the unconstitutional conditions in the state prison system was not in error, and the district court's order concerning construction was not appealable. Thus, the system remained under the control of a federal receiver.[16]

By the spring of 2010, when this decision was announced, California had experienced a third year of inmate population decline, but the state still had approximately 170,000 inmates, representing only a 0.4 percent *decrease* in 2009, but up from 76,000 in 1988. Between 2000 and 2010, the state's corrections budget doubled to approximately $8 billion, representing about 11 percent of the state's total budget. In early 2010, the state was opening prison doors because, in the words of the media, it was "driven to the financial brink." The state was attempting to reduce overcrowding (e.g., the state prison in Lancaster, California, was housing twice as many inmates as its capacity, with 150 of them bunked in the gymnasium) and to cut its recidivism rate of approximately two-thirds, the highest in the nation. The state senate voted unanimously to change the system enacted in 2009, permitting counties to release jail inmates early, a plan that was enacted to ease prison overcrowding. The state was sending to county jails many of the inmates who normally would have been sent to state prisons.[17]

In contrast to the California system is that of New York. By no means a model system and one with many problems, the New York prison system has at least had significant population declines within the past decade. In the fall of 2000, New York had approximately 59,300 prison inmates compared to 71,600 in 1999. This decrease was accomplished in several ways. One method was to reduce the penalties for minor, nonviolent drug offenses (see Chapter 10's discussion of the Rockefeller drug laws) and to reduce the number of parolees returned to prison for technical parole violations (see Chapter 15 for a discussion of parole). And the state's efforts to close prisons were under pressure from correctional officer unions and politicians from the districts in which the facilities are located. However, the state closed three prison camps and seven prison annexes for an estimated savings of $52 million over two years.[18] New York's 2011 budget calls for the closure of two minimum-security prisons and the minimum-security portion of a third prison and closing a medium-security prison. All of these facilities are for men.[19]

According to the BJS, New York experienced a prison population decline in 2009, extending its decline since 2000. As noted previously, 23 other states also experienced prison inmate population declines in 2009 as compared to 2008.[20]

Analysis of Overcrowding

In many states, prison populations are projected to grow significantly despite the recent retraction in growth rates in some jurisdictions. Costs will soar and have already jumped from $11 billion to approximately $50 billion in the past two decades, making corrections the "second fastest growing state budget category, behind only Medicaid."[21]

This occurred at a time when 42 states (in 2010) were experiencing serious budget shortfalls, with predictions that those shortfalls could reach a total of $103 billion by 2011.[22] In some of the states that experience growth, prison overcrowding will result.

The general effect of jail and prison overcrowding magnifies the negative aspects of confinement. Crowded conditions lead to greater contact among inmates, resulting in aggressive and at times violent behavior (including sexual assaults). Overcrowding may also induce stress in inmates *and* staff and lead to physical and mental problems. Another contributor to stress in prison is boredom. Most inmates do not have jobs and do not have access to educational or vocational programs. When facilities are overcrowded, the transportation of inmates to and from program sites becomes difficult. Many administrators assign inmates to more time in their cells rather than cope with moving large numbers around the facilities. The existing educational, recreational, and vocational programs, already limited, have long waiting lists. Administrators do not have funds to run enough programs to keep all inmates busy, and they cannot hire sufficient staff to manage large numbers of active inmates. Instead, inmates are expected to spend time in their cells or to do menial maintenance work, which does not prepare them for jobs after their release. A federal judge who was involved in the long-running prison condition lawsuit in Texas concluded that "overcrowding . . . exercises a malignant effect on all aspects of inmate life."[23]

Numerous solutions to jail and prison overcrowding have been suggested. Several states have enacted statutes granting their governors permission to declare an emergency when prison populations reach a specified level. At that point, inmates must be released to provide space for newly convicted offenders. This procedure has led to criticism when violent offenders are released, as has occurred in some states. Some jurisdictions contracted with other states to house their surplus inmates, but that is not a viable option in some cases; many jails and prisons are overcrowded, and budgets do not permit reasonable payments to the host states. Others are planning to change or have already changed local ordinances and state statutes to decrease penalties to reduce jail and prison populations. Some are seeking funds for renovation and expansion of existing facilities, and others are building new facilities. Still others have turned to community corrections and reinstituted parole release (see Chapter 15 for a discussion).

Although jails and prisons share some of the same problems, especially with regard to overcrowding, the two types of penal institutions do have some unique features.

Jails

The Latin root of the word **jail** is *cavea*, meaning "cavity," "cage," or "coop." It has been suggested that jails should be defined as public cages or coops. As Exhibit 14.1 discloses, jails are used for several purposes.

Ironically, although the jail is the oldest of American penal institutions, less is known about it than about any of the others. Except for an occasional scathing commentary, it has been tolerated but has received little attention. It was not until 1970 that some systematic data on jail populations became available. At that time, the first national jail census was conducted for the Law Enforcement Assistance Administration by the U.S. Bureau of the Census.

Jails can be traced far back into history. They made their debut "in the form of murky dungeons, abysmal pits, unscalable precipices, strong poles or trees, and suspended cages in which hapless inmates were kept."[24] Their main purpose was to detain people awaiting trial, transportation, corporal punishment, or the death penalty. The old jails were not escape-proof, and often, the persons in charge received additional fees for shackling inmates. Inmates were not separated according to any system of classification. Physical conditions were terrible, food was inadequate, and no treatment or rehabilitation programs existed.

The conditions in American jails worsened over the years. In 1923, Joseph Fishman, a federal prison inspector, investigator, and consultant, published *Crucible of Crime*, in which he described American jails, basing his descriptions and evaluations on visits to 1,500 jails. Fishman claimed that some of the convicted would ask for a year in prison in preference to six months in jail because of the horrible jail conditions. Most jails were overcrowded, and inmates did not have adequate food, medical care, or bathing facilities. Separate facilities were not provided for juveniles. Fishman's conclusion might be summarized by his definition of a *jail* as

EXHIBIT

14.1 — Purposes of Jails

- "Receive individuals pending arraignment and hold them awaiting trial, conviction, or sentencing;
- Readmit probation, parole, and bail-bond violators and absconders;
- Temporarily detain juveniles pending transfer to juvenile authorities;
- Hold mentally ill persons pending transfer to appropriate mental health facilities;
- Hold individuals for the military, for protective custody, for contempt, and for the courts as witnesses;
- Release inmates to the community upon completion of sentence;
- Transfer inmates to federal, state, or other authorities;
- House inmates for federal, state, or other authorities because of crowding of their facilities;
- Sometimes operate community-based programs as alternatives to incarceration."

Source: "Local Jail Inmates and Jail Facilities," Bureau of Justice Statistics (27 May 2010), http://bjs.ojp.usdoj.gov/index.cfm?ty=tp&tid=12, accessed 16 November 2010.

---

an unbelievably filthy institution in which are confined men and women serving sentences for misdemeanors and crimes, and men and women not under sentence who are simply awaiting trial. With few exceptions, having no segregation of the unconvicted from the convicted, the well from the diseased, the youngest and most impressionable from the most degraded and hardened. Usually swarming with bedbugs, roaches, lice, and other vermin; has an odor of disinfectant and filth which is appalling; supports in complete idleness thousands of ablebodied men and women, and generally affords ample time and opportunity to assure inmates a complete course in every kind of viciousness and crime. A melting pot in which the worst elements of the raw material in the criminal world are brought forth blended and turned out in absolute perfection.[25]

In 1931, the American jail was described by the National Commission on Law Observance and Enforcement as the "most notorious correctional institution in the world."[26] By the early 1980s, it was described by noted authorities as "the worst blight in American corrections"[27] and a place where "anyone not a criminal when he goes in, will be when he comes out."[28]

The typical jail in the United States is small and was built between 1880 and 1920. There has been little renovation of its physical facilities. It is located in a small town, often the county seat of a predominantly rural county. These small rural jails constitute the majority of jails but house only a minority of the jail population. Some are used infrequently, and usually, they are not crowded. Most inmates are confined in large urban jails, some of which are targets of court suits on jail conditions. Others are already under federal court orders to reduce populations or to change conditions found to be unconstitutional.

The fact that the typical jail is financed and administered locally involves the jail's administration in local politics. Historically, American jails have been under the direction and supervision of the sheriff, usually an elected official. Recently, some states have assumed control of their jails, but in most instances, the standards remain low, with few if any educational or rehabilitative programs.

Staffing local jails is a serious problem. The employees receive low pay, and some have little or no professional training. Jails have low budgets because local governments have less money to spend than state or federal governments; in many communities, jails have the lowest priority for local funds. Most jails are understaffed.

Many of the larger jails are overcrowded. In May 2010, severe crowding in Dallas County (Texas) jails resulted in a new staffing policy requiring the correctional officers to work two additional weekly shifts. They received overtime pay for only half of those shifts, with the rest accommodated by time off at other times. The county was facing a $60 million budget gap and could not pay more overtime. The Dallas County jails had "failed eight straight inspections, in part because of inadequate staffing."[29]

The absence of adequate supervision gives inmates little protection from sexual and other violent attacks, and the lack of staff increases the probability that inmates who attempt suicide will be successful. Exhibit 14.2 provides additional information on U.S. jails. Some of these issues are discussed later in the chapter, but a brief focus on the nation's largest jail system (Los Angeles County) and the largest single-cite jail (Cook County Jail in Chicago) are noted here.

The Los Angeles County jail system houses approximately 20,000 inmates on any given day. About 5,000 of those inmates are incarcerated in the Men's Central Jail, which is 50 years old. According to a national expert on correctional mental health, who completed a study of the Los Angeles jail system in 2009, about one-half of the detainees in the Men's Central Jail had some type of mental illness. They were housed at a total cost of over $50,000 per year at a daily rate of $140 per inmate. Inmates' mental health conditions were not always diagnosed (or diagnosed properly), and the mental health illnesses were

EXHIBIT **14.2**

U.S. Jails

The Justice Policy Institute, a public policy organization in Washington, D.C., which is dedicated to increasing community-based treatment rather than jail and prison incarceration of offenders, published an extensive analysis of U.S. jails. Among their findings are the following:

- "Jail populations have been increasing at higher rates than the prison population. . . .
- Ten percent of the people in jail on any given day are people who have been sentenced to *prison*, a result that may be occurring due to prison overcrowding. . . .
- A jail stay negatively impacts a person's health and mental health; jails do not have adequate facilities or programs to deal with these issues. . . .
- Sixty percent of the jail population suffers from a mental health disorder, compared to 10 percent of the general population. . . .
- People detained for immigration violations are increasingly held in jails. . . . [The number increased by 500 percent between 1995 and 2006.]
- More people are denied pretrial release and of those who are granted bail, fewer can afford to post it.
- Latino felony defendants receive the highest bail amounts set by the court. . . .
- In general, whites are more likely to be released than people of color. . . .
- The suicide rate in jails is almost 4 times that of the general population. . . .

- Jails are expensive for counties and localities. . . .
- Jail construction comes with hidden costs to taxpayers and citizens. . . .
- Jail lawsuits can reach millions of dollars—a bill that counties must pay. . . .
- Jails are harmful to the environment. . . .
- People incarcerated for nonviolent offenses make up the majority of people in jail. . . .
- Community supervision can be a more effective public safety strategy than incarceration. . . .
- Prison incarceration rates are more racially disparate than jail incarceration rates, but African Americans are still more than four times as likely as whites to be in jail. . . .
- People of color make up the largest percentage of the jail population incarcerated for drug offenses. . . .
- The steady increase in the use of jail for both convicted and unconvicted people has directed county money away from other county services that benefit all citizens and that may reduce the chance that someone commits a crime."

Source: Amanda Petteruti and Nastassia Walsh, *Jailing Communities: The Impact of Expansion and Effective Public Safety Strategies,* Justice Policy Institute (April 2008), pp. 2–28, http://www.justicepolicy.org/images/upload/08_04_REP_JailingCommunities_AC.pdf, accessed 11 November 2010.

exacerbated by idleness and massive overcrowding. These conditions also lead to violence, especially sexual assaults, as well as to the development of mental problems in otherwise reasonably healthy inmates.[30]

Despite these problems, in June 2010, a $74 million, modern, state-of-the-art jail in Los Angeles was empty of inmates. Due to budget constraints, the city did not have sufficient funds to hire correctional officers for the facility.[31]

Chicago's Cook County Jail, with an average daily population of more than 8,500, has a long history of problems, including understaffing. In May 2010, authorities announced sweeping changes in that jail. A recent federal inquiry exposed violence of inmates against each other, "unnecessary inmate deaths, unnecessary amputations, grossly inadequate medical jail and dental care as well as inmate beatings by prison guards." Many of the problems were attributed to a lack of adequate staffing. The agreement involves hiring 600 more correctional officers. Four monitors were to oversee that the jail officials were in compliance and would remain in place until they were in compliance for 18 months; violations would result in fines. The agreement still needed the approval of the judge.

The settlement with the Cook County Jail came as the result of a 2008 investigation by the U.S. Department of Justice, which concluded that the culture in that facility "led to systematic inmate beatings" and that available medical care was so inadequate that it led to inmate deaths.[32]

Prisons

In the United States, the *prison* was established for the long-term incarceration of offenders.

Prison Security Levels

Frequently, although the term *prison* is used synonymously with *maximum-security* institution, that is only one of several types of prisons. Historically, *maximum-security* prisons were the most secure facilities. Most are surrounded by high fences topped with razor wire and are watched by armed correctional officers in observation towers. The architecture of many of these prisons follows the Auburn plan, discussed earlier in this chapter, with large tiers of cell blocks made up of cells housing more than one offender. Theoretically, maximum-security prisons incarcerate only serious offenders or others who

In maximum-security prisons, inmates may be served their meals in their cells to avoid the additional security issues that exist when groups of inmates are interacting within the common areas of prisons.

might present a security risk. In reality, it is not uncommon to find less serious offenders in these facilities.

The second type of prison security level is the *medium-security* prison. This type is surrounded by fences topped with razor or barbed wire; armed correctional officers may or may not be present. Housing architecture, more varied than that of the maximum-security prison, may include individual rooms or dormitories rather than cells. Inmates have greater freedom of movement than those in maximum-security prisons, and theoretically, they are less serious offenders. Generally, *minimum-security* prisons do not have armed correctional officers; many do not have fences or bars. Inmates may be housed in individual rooms or dormitories.

Other types of facilities may also be available. Those listed in Exhibit 14.3, which describes the federal facilities, are illustrative.

Focus on Supermax Prisons

In recent years, some prisons, or designated wings within them, have become *maxi-maxi* or *supermax* institutions, housing the most dangerous inmates. Ohio built a supermax prison after a riot at the state's maximum-security prison. In 2005, when the U.S. Supreme Court decided a lawsuit from that prison, the Court upheld the concept of supermax prisons and emphasized that, despite the severity of the conditions in these prisons, some inmates must be confined in them for security reasons. The Court also held, however, that because of these severe conditions, inmates have a right to a due process hearing before they are classified as risks sufficient to be housed in supermax facilities. At the time of the lawsuit, 30 states were operating supermax prisons, and the federal government had two of them.[33]

The federal supermax prison in Florence, Colorado, is the most secure prison in the federal system. It is referred to as the Administrative Maximum (ADX) prison,

which is part of the Florence Federal Correctional Complex (FCC). Virtually all inmates are in solitary confinement in this prison (allowed out of their cells only one hour maximum a day). This prison houses such infamous inmates as Eric Rudolph (who pleaded guilty to terrorist attacks, including the 1996 bombings at the Atlanta Olympics); Theodore "Ted" Kaczynski, the so-called Unabomber, who used mail bombs to kill three people and injure 22 others over a 17-year period; Richard Reid, the shoe bomber whose plan to blow up an airline over the ocean was foiled; and approximately 40 convicted terrorists. This prison was suggested as a possible venue if the prison at Guantánamo Bay is closed, but the Colorado prison was already full and understaffed.[34]

On 21 June 2009, CBS's *60 Minutes* ran a documentary on the Florence prison; on that program, a former warden referred to the prison as "a clean version of hell."

The assumption behind the building of supermax or maxi-maxi prisons is that they are needed to protect staff and other inmates from the most dangerous inmates. A study of three maxi-maxi prisons questioned this assumption.

> Mixed support was found for the hypothesis that supermax increases staff safety; the implementation of a supermax had no effect on levels of inmate-on-staff assaults in Minnesota, temporarily increased staff injuries in Arizona, and reduced assaults against staff in Illinois.[35]

Issues with supermax prisons have been raised by human rights groups. The director of the American Civil Liberties Union's (ACLU) Institutionalized Persons Project in Illinois summarized his views of these prisons as follows:

> To build these supermaxes is one thing, but we've gone out of our way to torture these guys and deprive them of human contact in a way that cannot be justified.[36]

EXHIBIT

14.3

Prison Types and Descriptions

The federal Bureau of Prisons (BOP) publishes the following information about prison levels within the federal system.

"The Bureau operates institutions at five different security levels in order to confine offenders in an appropriate manner. Security levels are based on such features as the presence of external patrols, towers, security barriers, or detection devices; the type of housing within the institution; internal security features; and the staff-to-inmate ratio. Each facility is designated as either minimum, low, medium, high, or administrative. Institutions may undergo institution population changes to accommodate the agency's bed space capacity, security level, and population management needs.

Minimum Security

Minimum security institutions, also known as Federal Prison Camps (**FPCs**), have dormitory housing, a relatively low staff-to-inmate ratio, and limited or no perimeter fencing. These institutions are work- and program-oriented; and many are located adjacent to larger institutions or on military bases, where inmates help serve the labor needs of the larger institution or base.

Low Security

Low security Federal Correctional Institutions (**FCIs**) have double-fenced perimeters, mostly dormitory or cubicle housing, and strong work and program components. The staff-to-inmate ratio in these institutions is higher than in minimum security facilities.

Medium Security

Medium security **FCIs (and USPs designated to house medium security inmates)** have strengthened perimeters (often double fences with electronic detection systems), mostly cell-type housing, a wide variety of work and treatment programs, an even higher staff-to-inmate ratio than low security FCIs, and even greater internal controls.

High Security

High security institutions, also known as United States Penitentiaries (**USPs**), have highly-secured perimeters (featuring walls or reinforced fences), multiple- and single-occupant cell housing, the highest staff-to-inmate ratio, and close control of inmate movement.

Correctional Complexes

A number of BOP institutions belong to Federal Correctional Complexes (**FCCs**). At FCCs, institutions with different missions and security levels are located in close proximity to one another. FCCs increase efficiency through the sharing of services, enable staff to gain experience at institutions of many security levels, and enhance emergency preparedness by having additional resources within close proximity.

Administrative

Administrative facilities are institutions with special missions, such as the detention of pretrial offenders; the treatment of inmates with serious or chronic medical problems; or the containment of extremely dangerous, violent, or escape-prone inmates. Administrative facilities include Metropolitan Correctional Centers (**MCCs**), Metropolitan Detention Centers (**MDCs**), Federal Detention Centers (**FDCs**), and Federal Medical Centers (**FMCs**), as well as the Federal Transfer Center (**FTC**), the Medical Center for Federal Prisoners (**MCFP**), and the Administrative-Maximum (**ADX**) U.S. Penitentiary. Administrative facilities are capable of holding inmates in all security categories.

Satellite Camps

A number of BOP institutions have a small, minimum security camp adjacent to the main facility. These camps, often referred to as satellite camps, provide inmate labor to the main institution and to off-site work programs. FCI Memphis has a non-adjacent camp that serves similar needs.

Satellite Low Security

FCI Elkton and FCI Jesup each have a small, low security satellite facility adjacent to the main institution. FCI La Tuna has a low security facility affiliated with, but not adjacent to, the main institution."

Source: Federal Bureau of Prisons, "Prison Types and General Information," http://www.bop.gov/locations/institutions/index.jsp, accessed 11 November 2010.

Four of every five states have supermax prisons, and the cost is enormous. For example, at the time the U.S. Supreme Court heard the Ohio supermax prison case, the cost of incarcerating an inmate in that institution was $49,007 yearly compared to $34,167 for less secure facilities in that state.[37]

Some scholars reviewed the research literature, media accounts, and legislative reports on supermax prisons, visited prisons in three states, conducted focus groups and interviews, and conducted telephone interviews with correctional professionals in supermax institutions in eight other states and one federal supermax prison. They concluded that the following issues should be considered and evaluated regarding the use of supermax prisons.

- There is not enough evidence on supermax prisons to determine whether or not they are effective.
- Any general assessment of supermax prisons should take into account several unintended impacts, some of which are positive (improving the

quality of life of inmates and staff and improving the economy of the community) and some of which are negative (the opposite effect on quality of life).

- There exists little logic on how supermax prisons "are supposed to achieve specific goals."
- There are numerous barriers to the possible effectiveness of supermax prisons (such as methods for identifying the types of inmates these prisons are designed to incarcerate).
- There are moral, political, and fiscal issues that influence whether supermax prisons are a wise idea.[38]

Investigators who conducted a three-year study of Florida's supermax housing of inmates and its effects on recidivism came to the conclusion that such confinement might increase violent recidivism after the inmates were released. They also found no evidence of a "substantial specific deterrent effect of supermax incarceration."[39]

State and Federal Prisons

Prisons may also be differentiated as *state* or *federal*. All states have prison systems, although the systems vary in terms of security levels and other characteristics. Most states have all levels of security, but not all levels are available for female offenders because of their smaller numbers. States differ significantly in the amount of money spent per inmate (for comparative data, see Figure 15.5 in Chapter 15).

It was not until 1930 that the federal government established the Federal Bureau of Prisons (BOP). Prior to that time, long-term federal inmates were incarcerated in state prisons on a contract basis, and most short-term federal inmates were confined in local jails, also on a contract basis. The BOP "consists of 116 institutions, 6 regional offices, a Central Office (headquarters), 2 staff training centers, and 22 community corrections offices." The BOP employs more than 38,000 persons and is responsible for approximately 210,000 federal offenders. Approximately 82 percent of those offenders are incarcerated in BOP-operated facilities. The remainder are in private correctional facilities (discussed in the next section) or community-based facilities (discussed in Chapter 15) and local jails.[40] Exhibit 14.3 presented the types of institutions that are available in the federal system (see again Exhibit 14.3).

Private Jails and Prisons

The cost of jails and prisons has placed such a financial burden on the federal government and the states that many authorities are looking for innovative ways to finance construction, maintenance, or administration of facilities and care of inmates. Some states levy a fee on convicted persons; the rates are usually higher for serious than for minor offenses. In 1992, Congress approved legislation permitting the federal prison system to levy user fees on inmates. It was estimated at that time that

approximately 9 percent of new inmates would be able to pay their fees at least for their first year of incarceration and that $48 million might be raised in new revenue through these fees. In a 1995 case, the U.S. Court of Appeals for the Second Circuit held that this cost-of-imprisonment fine could be imposed even in cases in which normal fines based on sentencing guidelines are not imposed. Other circuit courts have not agreed on this approach, and the U.S. Supreme Court has not decided the issue.[41]

One of the disadvantages of the cost-of-imprisonment approach is that inmates may leave prison without funds and with debts; payment for room and board thus reduces their ability to support their families, pay for educational or other needs, and reintegrate into society when they are released.

A more common plan for financing jails and prisons is privatization. Under privatization, a profit-making company, with money from private investors, finances, builds, and owns the jail or prison or contracts to provide some service (e.g., food or medical care) within the institution. The facility may be leased to the government to operate, leaving the state (or federal) government with no responsibility for upkeep. In some cases, the private company manages the jail or prison; in others, the private company actually plans, finances, builds, and manages the facility. The Corrections Corporation of America (CCA) is the largest provider of correctional services to federal and state governments in the United States. In 2010, CCA had 17,000 employees in charge of 75,000 inmates in prisons of all security levels.

> CCA designs, builds, manages and operates correctional facilities and detention centers on behalf of the Federal Bureau of Prisons, Immigration and Customs Enforcement, the United States Marshals Service, nearly half of all states and nearly a dozen counties across the country.[42]

Forbes magazine named CCA as the best managed company among 21 other corporations in the services and supplies category of businesses.[43]

Privatization of jails and prisons is not a new practice in the United States. Private contracts for service within jails and prisons were common in earlier days, but it is the significant increase in prison and jail populations and the cost of maintaining them that has led to the current expanded use of privatization in the United States. States and the federal government may, in addition to contracting with private corporations to run the correctional facilities within their respective jurisdictions, contract with private corporations out of state to house their inmates. For example, Colorado contracted with CCA to house 240 of its offenders in a CCA facility in Oklahoma while Colorado expanded its own correctional facilities.[44] In 2009, the latest data available, a total of 129,336, or 8 percent of all inmates incarcerated as of the end of that year, were held in private facilities.[45]

There are problems with privatization of jails and prisons. In 2006, six Colorado prisons under private management were short of mandatory staff requirements and fined by the Colorado Department of Corrections. One of those prisons, the Crowley County Correctional Facility, was the scene of a riot in 2004, which focused on several problems, including staffing problems. The facility was managed by CCA.[46]

In 2005, it was reported that CCA, which had the only contract for prisons in Hawaii, was supervising other Hawaiian inmates in prisons located within the lower 48 states, mainly in Arizona, Oklahoma, and Mississippi. Several of these facilities had disturbances involving Hawaiian inmates. And although problems occur in government owned and operated facilities (as will be seen later), a national prison study found that privately operated prison facilities, compared to government operated ones, had 65 percent more inmate-on-inmate assaults and 49 percent more inmate-on-staff assaults.[47]

Other issues with privatization focus on the claims that this approach reduces both recidivism and costs. In 2010, a research organization studied the six prisons operated by private agencies (GEO Group and CCA) in Florida. It reported that the effectiveness in reducing recidivism through the education and rehabilitation programs managed by these two groups was a toss-up. It was impossible to discern whether they really were, as claimed, operating at a cost of 7 percent less than the state's Department of Corrections.[48]

A response to such criticisms came from the National Institute of Justice as follows:

> The original promise was that prison privatization would increase service quality. The premise was that the free market would introduce efficiency previously unknown in the Florida state adult correctional system. The resulting performance suggests that neither promise nor premise was correct. The research results are clear.[49]

A criminologist with Homeland Security Corporation argued that the research methods of the Florida study and the earlier studies that supported the premise of increased recidivism in private prisons are so different that the results are not comparable.

> The [Florida] study and the studies on which it is based directly and indirectly raise important intellectual and policy issues that deserve answers we simply cannot provide today. Passionate ideological rhetoric may well give rise to intensified commitment by the faithful. What criminology needs, however, is not more faith-based zealousness. What criminology needs is more well-conceptualized, well-executed research. And what policy makers need is research aimed at informing rather than at shaping public policy.[50]

Further evidence of Florida's problems with privatization were evident in May 2010 when a county jail, which had been under the supervision of CCA for 22 years, was taken back by the county and placed under the responsibility of the sheriff.[51]

Privatization of correctional facilities is not limited to the United States but is also typical of other countries. Some of the problems those countries have experienced were noted in a 2008 publication analyzing the 1997 riot in a public Australian prison that experienced competition from privatization. For cost-cutting reasons, the administration experimented with privatization in that the public agency had to compete to get the bid to build and manage the prison. The public agency won but "promised more than it could deliver," and within three weeks after the new prison opened, a riot occurred. The investigators reviewed the basic theories of prison riots, ranging from poor prison conditions to unstable and disorganized prison management, but they emphasized that public or private prisons can be well managed or poorly managed; they can have excellent or poor conditions. The issue is not public or private but the type of management and understanding of the inmate population. They concluded that, in the Australian prison, "external pressure bore down on internal prison life, disaffected the main players, and led to an institutional breakdown and, ultimately, to a riot."[52]

A response to that research emphasized that, traditionally, prison administrations have not been held accountable. In short, "many systems do not measure relevant dimensions of performance or outcomes . . . [and many systems do not have the capacity or authority] to act on any monitoring results that may exist." Prison systems operate "under exceptionally difficult circumstances," usually without sufficient funding for adequate staff and resources. They must respond to the public and to policy makers, who may place conflicting demands on them. Nevertheless, the systems must be held accountable.[53]

One final issue with regard to private prisons involves a threatened boycott of the state of Arizona in protest of its newly enacted immigration law, originally set to go into effect in mid-2010 (see the discussion in Chapter 12 concerning legal issues and, in particular, an injunction). For states, such as California, that contract with Arizona to house their inmates, a boycott could be difficult. Some of California's inmates under the control of CCA are housed in Arizona (4,100 in 2010; 6,100 expected in 2011), which California did to save money (estimated to be $105 million in 2010). It was not clear whether these contracts would be covered if a boycott was in effect.[54]

The Inmate's World

There are a variety of ways to deal with the stress created by prison life. Some inmates feel they must be active to survive the prison experience. Their activities may include watching television or listening to the radio or stereo, lifting weights or participating in other physical activities, cleaning cells, participating in prison education and other programs, scheming, or daydreaming. Some of these activities are becoming impossible, however, as some jurisdictions are cutting back or eliminating cable television along with prison educational and other programs. Inmates also spend their time in illegal activities, such as fighting, obtaining and using drugs, making alcoholic beverages, and so on.

Inmates must cope with the physical, social, and psychological problems that result from the worst punishment—the deprivation of liberty. In his classic study of male inmates, Gresham M. Sykes discussed the moral rejection by the community (which is a constant challenge to the inmate's self-concept) and the deprivation of goods and services in a society that values material possessions. There is also the deprivation of heterosexual relationships, and the resulting threat to the inmate's masculinity, and the deprivation of security in an inmate population that threatens his safety and sometimes his health and life.[55]

Everything the inmates do, including the showers they can take and the hours they can sleep, is regulated by the prison staff. Inmates have no autonomy and can show no initiative. They are forced to define themselves as weak, helpless, and dependent, which threatens their self-concepts. The prison system rarely, if ever, permits them to function as adults. They face the conflict that while the prison's isolated social system stresses adaptation to the inmate subculture, that same system, along with the correctional staff, stresses preparation for release.

Prisonization

In 1940, a classic study of the prison community was published by Donald Clemmer, who proposed the concept of **prisonization** to explain the formation of inmate sub-

cultures. He defined *prisonization* as "the taking on, in greater or lesser degree, of the folkways, mores, customs, and general culture of the penitentiary." When a new inmate enters prison, he or she begins the process of prisonization. This process is not the same for all inmates and may be affected by the inmate's personality, environment, and relationships outside prison; whether the inmate joins a primary group in prison; and the degree to which the inmate accepts the codes of prison life. Prisonization may also impact an inmate's adjustment after release.[56]

Clemmer's concept of prisonization was tested empirically by Stanton Wheeler in a study at the Washington State Reformatory. Although Wheeler's findings supported Clemmer's concept, Wheeler also found that the degree of prisonization varied according to the phase of an inmate's institutional career, developing along a U-shaped curve. Inmates tended to be more receptive to the values of the outside world during the first period of incarceration (measured at the end of the first six months) and the last period (the last six months before release) and less receptive during the middle, or prison career, period. In the last six months of incarceration, when inmates were anticipating their releases back into society, their main reference group shifted from the other inmates within the institution to the society outside. Wheeler concluded that Clemmer's concept of prisonization should be reformulated to include the variable of the career phase.[57]

Subsequent researchers have found some support for Wheeler's U-shaped curve of attitudes.[58] Others, comparing prisonization among male and female inmates, have questioned Wheeler's hypothesis. There is some evidence that although time spent in prison was significantly related to prisonization among female inmates, this was not true among male inmates. For men, variables such as age and attitudes toward law and the judicial system were significant. Among women, attitudes toward race and the police were significant.[59]

Social life in prison is limited, especially when inmates are confined to their cells. One technique inmates use to see more people is to hold a mirror outside the cell bars. In this photo, a Folsom Prison inmate in California uses his mirror to see the state lawmakers who visited the prison.

Prisonization Models

Most sociological analyses of the prisonization process and the emergence of a prison subculture have followed two models: the **deprivation model** and the **importation model**.

The *deprivation model* is illustrated by Gresham Sykes's position that the inmate subculture is the product of an attempt to adapt to the deprivations imposed by incarceration. Inmates have few alternatives to alleviate their deprivations (including loss of status) and degradation. They cannot escape psychologically or physically; they cannot eliminate the pains of imprisonment. Inmates have a choice of uniting with fellow captives in a spirit of mutual cooperation or withdrawing to seek only the satisfaction of their own needs. In either case, their behavior patterns are adaptations to the deprivations of their environment.

According to the deprivation model, the inmates' social system is functional in that it enables them to minimize the pains of imprisonment through cooperation. For example, the cooperation of inmates in exchanging favors removes the opportunity for some to exploit others and enables them to accept material deprivation more easily. In addition, available goods and services are distributed and shared willingly if the inmates have a cooperative social system. This system helps resolve the problem of personal security, alleviate the fear of further isolation, and restore the inmates' sense of self-respect and independence.[60]

The *importation model* was illustrated by the work of John Irwin and Donald R. Cressey, who maintained that too much emphasis had been placed on the impact of prison on inmates. They argued that the prison subculture is a combination of several types of subcultures that exist outside the prison and are imported by offenders when they enter.[61]

Scholars have found support for each of these models. It has been shown that, like the rest of us, inmates have a past, a present, and a future, and all are related to the prisonization process. New inmates face two social systems in prison: the formal organization (resocialization) and the inmate society (prisonization). Both compete for the inmate's allegiance. The goals of the formal organization are custody and confinement; the goal of inmates is freedom. Because these two social systems conflict, if one succeeds, the other must fail. The prison is not a closed system, and when explaining the inmate culture, we must examine the following factors: pre-prison experience, both criminal and noncriminal; expectations of staff and fellow inmates; quality of contacts with persons or groups outside the walls; post-prison expectations; and immediate adjustment problems. The greater the degree of similarity between pre-prison activities and prison subculture values and attitudes, the more receptive the inmate is to prisonization. Inmates from the lower social classes are more likely to become highly prisonized. Those who have the highest degree of contact with the outside world have the lowest degree of prisonization. Finally, those with a higher degree of prisonization are among those who have the bleakest post-prison expectations.[62]

A study of race relations in an eastern prison led its investigator to criticize the deprivation model, arguing that this model "diverts attention from interrelationships between the prison and the wider society . . . and hence away from issues such as racial violence." The two models should not be seen as opposites but as complementary. The form of inmate subculture that prevails depends on the degree of security and deprivation in the institution. In maximum-security prisons, we would expect the deprivation model to prevail, but in prisons with less security and fewer deprivations, the importation model is more likely to dominate. This research lends support to the importation model, but the investigator took the position that the model was incomplete.[63]

Other researchers have argued that the importation and deprivation models should be integrated, and both are important to explaining prisonization. The functional, or adaptation, model was supported only partially by research data from several countries and one U.S. jurisdiction. The data showed that "the inmate culture varies by whatever differences in organization environment there are from one institution to the next."[64]

This integrative approach has been summarized as follows:

> The existence of collective solutions in the inmate culture and social structure is based on the common problems of adjustment to the institution, while the content of those solutions and the tendency to become prisonized are imported from the larger society.[65]

Thus, it is not sufficient to argue that the importation or deprivation model alone explains the individual adaptations of inmates to prison or the development of an inmate subculture; rather, variables of each are important.

Prisonization and Violence

The deprivation model and two other models have been utilized to examine prison violence. Some scholars argue that deprivation or *relative* deprivation (changes in deprivation) may lead to violence. Others suggest there is no relationship between deprivation and collective violence. Some scholars take the position that it is not deprivation but *failed prison management*, such as inadequate security and poorly disciplined or inadequately trained officers, that is related to inmate problems and may result in collective violence. Another point of view suggests that internal problems are related to prison size. It is much more difficult to maintain order in a megaprison than in a small facility with a lower inmate-to-officer ratio. Finally, some scholars argue that prisons are not total institutions[66] and that both inmates and prison personnel are influenced by life outside prison. Thus, internal prison order may be influenced by external prison conditions.

An analysis of these various models in the context of data from 371 prisons led to the conclusion that the deprivation model was least useful in explaining collective violence. There was no evidence that prison order was affected negatively by prison conditions or that increased security led to disorder, and there was little evidence to suggest the existence of the society of captives referred to by Sykes in his earlier studies. Indeed, "there has been little that resembles a 'community' behind the walls for more than two decades." There is no single inmate subculture and no uniform code of behavior among today's inmates. Finally, prison programs—educational, vocational, recreational, and so on—are good management tools for keeping control. Poor prison management is a "major structural condition that fails to control, and may promote, individual acts of violence in prison."[67]

These studies on internal prison life reemphasize the need to look at the total social structure, not only of the prison but also of the pre-prison and post-prison experiences, to understand the effects of imprisonment on the inmate.

Female Inmates

Most of the studies of prisonization were conducted on male inmates, but the few studies of female inmates note some differences in their methods of coping with prison life. Only a small percentage of prison inmates are women, and historically, researchers did not study them. The research focus has changed in recent years, and the number of female inmates has increased twice as fast as males, although women continue to constitute only a small percentage of the total prison populations. Many of these women have been sexually abused and are substance abusers; approximately one of every three is in prison for a drug offense.[68]

In an analysis of female inmates, The Sentencing Project reported that 30 percent of female inmates are black, 16 percent are Hispanic, and 50 percent have not completed high school. Almost one-third of female inmates said they committed their current offenses to obtain drugs. Female inmates are more likely than male inmates to be diagnosed with mental illness or to be HIV positive.[69]

The increase in the number of women in jails and prisons has created several problems, and some states face placement issues. Several states proposed to build new prisons, and some transferred women to other facilities. In Colorado, the number of female prison inmates more than doubled between 1998 and 2004, and in 2006, the state was seeking bids for building a private prison for women.[70] However, by 2010, the female inmate population had declined sufficiently to permit the state to close the Colorado Women's Correctional Facility in Cañon City. The reduction in inmates resulted from several factors, including crime reduction, the reduction in recidivism, and the increased use of parole and diversion through drug courts. Colorado had projected a prison population of 29,443 by 2013; in March of 2010, that estimate was lowered by 9,000.[71]

Despite this encouraging news from Colorado, the fact is that, as already noted, the increase in female inmates has grown faster than that of male inmates, and many of the incarcerated women are in prison for drug offenses. The Institute on Women and Criminal Justice of the Women's Prison Association recommended alternative sentencing and more programs to prepare women to be self-sufficient and to combat substance abuse problems rather than incarcerating female offenders.[72]

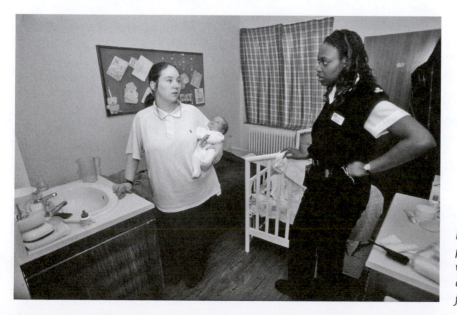

In some countries, female inmates are permitted to have their small children with them in prison. This inmate in London, England, is housed in a special unit for such arrangements.

The incarceration of parents, particularly women, causes enormous problems for children, especially young children. In 2007, 1.7 million children had at least one parent in prison (over 8 million had one parent in correctional supervision), and 70 percent of those children were persons of color. Approximately two-thirds of female state inmates have at least one child under age 5, and the children of nine of every ten incarcerated women are living with the inmate's parent or grandparent or a friend rather than with their fathers. Female inmates are five times more likely than male inmates to have their children placed in foster homes or put up for adoption. Many of the children of incarcerated parents are not permitted to visit their parents or live too far away to do so. Most incarcerated parents are held more than 100 miles from their families (43 percent of federal inmates are more than 500 miles away). Only about one-third of incarcerated mothers have ever spoken by phone with their children; one-half have never been visited in prison by their children.[73]

Additional information concerning inmate parents and their children is presented in Exhibit 14.4.

There are some encouraging efforts to reconnect incarcerated parents with their children. Many of these programs focus on the children of female inmates. Some prisons have special facilities where female inmates can visit with their children in a homelike atmosphere. These facilities may provide a kitchen as well as a play area. The emphasis in some programs is on helping mothers maintain and improve their relationships with their children while enhancing their own self-esteem by caring for their children, if only part time. Other programs help female inmates develop mothering skills along with vocational skills that will enable them to support their children after their release. Still others provide free bus service for children and their guardians to visit the prisons. Here are some examples.

For over 30 years, New York's maximum-security prison for women, the Bedford Hills Correctional Facility, has provided weekly summer camps for inmates' children, giving inmates who apply and are approved (the childrens' guardians must also approve) an opportunity to interact with each other.[74]

Two private charities in Kentucky take newborns and other babies for weekend visits with their mothers in prison. The director of Operation Open Arms in Louisville said, "These children didn't commit a crime, and shouldn't have to pay for it." The children may spend a day with their mothers, and parenting classes are provided. Some states provide live-in prison nursery programs, but Kentucky has rejected that approach. Officials believe that such programs help only a small percentage of incarcerated mothers and that the benefits have not been proven.[75]

Some prisons provide programs for fathers to meet with their children. Two organizations that sponsor these programs are Returning Hearts and Malachi Dads. The Louisiana State Penitentiary at Angola began a program in 2004 that permits children to visit their fathers, grandfathers, uncles, and cousins on the grounds rather than inside the "shack," as the inmates call the visiting quarters.

EXHIBIT 14.4 — Incarcerated Parents and Their Children

In February 2009, The Sentencing Project published a report on incarcerated parents and their children. This exhibit features some of the findings of that report.

- Between 1991 and 2007, the number of minor U.S. children who had at least one incarcerated parent increased by 82 percent. Incarcerated mothers increased by 122 percent, and incarcerated fathers increased by 79 percent.
- In 2007, only 1 in every 111 white children had a parent in prison. The figures were 1 in 15 for black children and 1 in 42 for Latino children.
- In 2007, one-half of all inmates had children.
- In 2004, 45 percent of federal inmates and 59 percent of state inmates had never been visited in prison by their child(ren).
- There is evidence that children of incarcerated parents suffer more if the mother rather than the father is incarcerated.
- Incarcerated parents are in danger of losing custody of their children as a result of the Adoption and Safe Families Act (ASFA) of 1997, which authorizes the termination of parental rights of a parent whose child has been in foster care for 15 of the last 22 months.
- The federal Personal Responsibility and Work Opportunity Reconciliation Act (PWRORA) enacted in 1996 imposes limitations on food stamps and cash assistance for persons who have been convicted of drug offenses, a limitation that negatively impacts inmates when they are released and wish to reestablish their homes and families.
- Aggression and declining school grades are among the many adverse effects that children suffer when a parent is incarcerated.

Source: The Sentencing Project, "Incarcerated Parents and Their Children: Trends 1991–2007" (February 2009), pp. 7–11, http://www.sentencingproject.org/doc/publications/inc_incarceratedparents.pdf, accessed 14 November 2010.

The prison has an all-day program of activities, such as amusement rides, balloon-twisting clowns, and horses along with hamburgers and hotdogs.[76]

Female inmates in other countries face many of the challenges and issues we have discussed. Global Focus 14.1 contains some of the recommendations of the Quaker United Nations office concerning the treatment of women and their children. Some of those recommendations, such as permitting female inmates to be supervised only by female correctional officers, will probably not pass constitutional muster in the United States.[77]

Elderly, Physically, and Mentally Challenged Inmates

As prison populations have increased in recent years, correctional institutions have encountered new problems. Today's facilities may house older inmates as well as those who are physically or mentally challenged. An increase in the number of older inmates can be expected as the normal result of incarcerating more people for longer periods of time along with the increasing percentage of the population over 50.

GLOBAL FOCUS

14.1

Women in Prison and Children of Imprisoned Mothers: Recent Developments in the United Nations Human Rights System

The Quaker United Nations office in Geneva, Switzerland, along with other Quaker international organizations made the following recommendations concerning female inmates and their children.

General

"States should ensure that female prisoners are adequately protected from violent and sexual assault, in particular by prohibiting the inappropriate use of male correctional staff and the mixing of genders in prison facilities.

States should take note of and implement the Concluding Observations and General Recommendations of the Human Rights Treaty Bodies by:

- reviewing their use of pre-trial detention;
- ensuring that prison staffing policies and practices conform with the requirement that female prisoners be supervised by female guards;
- ensuring that female and male prisoners are detained separately;
- establishing a procedure for addressing complaints by women of physical and sexual violence experienced in prison;
- ensuring that the best interests of the child are considered in decisions on detaining or imprisoning their parent and giving serious consideration to the social cost of the increasing use of custodial sentences as punishment for non-violent offences committed by women, and to consider alternative, non-custodial sentences for non-violent female offenders;
- guaranteeing that children living in prisons are protected from violence and enjoy the full extent of their rights; ensuring that children deprived of parental care through parental imprisonment are able to enjoy the full extent of their rights, including by maintaining a relationship with their imprisoned parent and include information regarding women's imprisonment and report on measures they have taken to decrease the rate of women's imprisonment." . . .

Protection from Violence

"States must ensure that female prisoners are adequately protected from violent and sexual assault, in particular by prohibiting the inappropriate use of male correctional staff and the mixing of genders in prison facilities.

States should ensure that women and girls in detention are protected from violence.

Measures to achieve this include:

- Drafting and implementation of policies and processes to prevent and investigate any physical, sexual or psychological violence whether committed by other prisoners or by prison staff and to hold to account those responsible.
- Dissemination of procedures for reporting violence committed by other prisoners or prison staff.
- Protection from intimidation and retaliation for those who report violence committed by other prisoners or prison staff.
- Training for prison staff that incorporates sensitisation to the vulnerability of women prisoners to abuse by other prisoners or prison staff and the policies and procedures for preventing and responding to abuse.
- Separation of male and female prisoners. . . .
- Separation of juvenile detainees from the adult prison population. . . .
- Supervision of women and girl prisoners only by women prison guards."

Source: Laurel Townhead, Quaker United Nations Office, *Women in Prison & Children of Imprisoned Mothers: Recent Developments in the United Nations Human Rights System* (Geneva, Switzerland, April 2006), http://www.quno.org/geneva/pdf/humanrights/women-in-prison/WiP-Recent-UN-developments-200603.pdf, pp. 18, 19, accessed 12 November 2010.

Inmate populations have been aging, and, according to a 2004 BJS report, the most significant increases between 1995 and 2003 were among inmates aged 45 to 54. This age group accounted for 46 percent of the total U.S. population growth during that time period.[78] Older persons have different needs in areas such as food and medical care. They are more likely to need frequent attention by doctors, which may result in higher medication and surgery costs. The National Commission on Correctional Health Care estimates that, on the average, it costs between $60,000 and $70,000 per year to incarcerate an elderly inmate compared to about $27,000 for younger inmates. In states that have a large retired population, such as Florida and Arizona, the financial burden of prison costs for the elderly may be particularly acute. Florida outranks all states in the percentage of its population (17.6 percent) that is 65 or older. The national average is 12.4 percent.[79]

In 2000, the Florida legislature enacted a law requiring an annual report on the status of the elderly inmate population (defined as 50 or older). Among other information, the report must contain specific findings and recommendations for implementation and "include an examination of promising geriatric policies, practices, and programs currently implemented in other correctional systems within the United States."[80]

In 2009, Florida had 16,000 inmates who were over age 50, representing approximately 15 percent of the state's total inmate population. These elderly inmates account for a significant portion of the $1.3 million per day that the state spends on health care in its $2.2 billion annual budget. In 2008–2009, elderly inmates accounted for 32 percent of the prescription medications dispensed to inmates and 42.3 percent of all hospital days. Forty-eight percent of Florida's elderly inmates had no prior prison commitments. The oldest male inmate was 84; the oldest female inmate was 71. The highest category of offenses among the elderly was drugs, followed by property crimes. Florida does not have separate prisons for the elderly but does have some separate units within its other prisons. It was predicted that by the year 2030, 50 percent of Florida's inmates would be elderly. On 4 April 2010, a bill creating the Elderly Rehabilitated Inmate Program died in the state's senate. This bill would have authorized the Parole Commission to approve early release for elderly inmates who had already served 25 years in prison and were otherwise qualified according to the terms of the legislation.[81]

New York, which had 74,100 inmates 55 or older in 2008, representing a 79 percent increase since 1999, estimated that it costs the state $150,809 a year to incarcerate and care for a gravely ill inmate.[82] According to one New York prison administrator, the inmate population in that state "is growing older, getting sicker, and staying longer." To accommodate this elderly and sick population of inmates, the state developed a special-needs facility, possibly the first in the nation. It specializes in treating inmates with dementia-related conditions such as Alzheimer's dis-

ease. The 30-bed facility opened in 2006. Corrections officials from other states have toured the facility, but some have reacted to the cost. New York's position is to pay now or later "because if you don't take care of these inmates in a dedicated unit like this, you'll pay a premium for their care in an outside healthcare facility." The staff are specially trained to understand the behavior of inmates with such cognitive problems. The behavior may at first appear problematic, requiring disciplinary action, but it really is simply a manifestation of the inmates' cognitive problems. One of the activities is that inmates are visited regularly by special-needs dogs, which are trained by other inmates in the New York correctional system.[83]

A geriatrician at the San Francisco Veterans Administration Medical Center, after conducting a study of elderly California female inmates age 55 or older, concluded: "Prison is not a safe place for vulnerable older people. . . . Prisons are not geared to the needs of older people." Approximately 69 percent of the elderly female inmates had difficulty in one or more of the following daily activities: standing in line, listening to orders, climbing into a top bunk, dropping to the floor rapidly when the alarm sounded, or walking to and from the dining hall. Within the previous year, 55 percent of the women had fallen; 16 percent needed assistance to perform at least one daily function. That percentage was twice the national average for nonincarcerated persons age 65 or older. Some of the difficulties the elderly face call for physical adjustments in facilities, such as grab bars on showers, but other issues, such as health care, are not so easily handled.[84]

Not all inmates with medical problems are elderly, and prisons are facing high costs of maintaining all physically challenged and medically ill inmates. These inmates were incarcerated in the past, but today, we are more cognizant of their special needs due to federal court orders (discussed later in this chapter) and the Americans with Disabilities Act (ADA) and related statutes. The ADA and its predecessor, the 1973 Rehabilitation Act, have been interpreted as applying to incarcerated persons in some situations.[85]

The extent of medical problems among inmates was noted in a December 2009 publication of the Bureau of Justice Statistics (BJS). The highlights of that study are reproduced in Exhibit 14.5. According to the BJS, male and female inmates were equally likely to report dental problems, but women were more likely to report medical problems, and women were one and one-half times more likely than men to report two or more current medical problems. Most of these inmates did report that they received a medical exam and/or medical treatment since they entered prison. The BJS has also reported the leading causes of death among inmates in state prisons. The top five are heart diseases, cancer, liver diseases, AIDS, and suicide. Heart diseases and cancer accounted for one-half of the deaths.[86]

This section looks in depth at two contagious diseases in prisons and jails: tuberculosis (TB) and AIDS. Both ex-

EXHIBIT

14.5 — Medical Problems of U.S. Inmates

The Bureau of Justice Statistics (BJS) reported the following highlight from its analysis of the medical problems of U.S. inmates.

- "An estimated 44% of state inmates and 39% of federal inmates reported a current medical problem other than a cold or virus.

- Arthritis (state 15%; federal 12%) and hypertension (state 14%; federal 13%) were the two most commonly reported medical problems.

- Among inmates who reported a medical problem, 70% of state and 76% of federal inmates reported seeing a medical professional because of the problem.

- More than 8 in 10 inmates in state and federal prisons reported receiving a medical exam or a blood test since admission. . . .

- More than a third (36%) of state inmates and nearly a quarter (24%) of federal inmates reported having an impairment.

- Learning was the most commonly reported impairment among state and federal inmates (23% and 13%, respectively).

- 16% of state inmates and 8% of federal inmates reported having multiple impairments."

Source: Laura Maruschak, "Medical Problems of Prisoners," Bureau of Justice Statistics (1 April 2008, page last revised 26 February 2010), http://bjs.ojp.usdoj.gov/index.cfm?ty=pbdetail&iid=1097, accessed 12 November 2010.

---

ist in U.S. facilities and in other countries, too, and both raise many questions. For example, one solution to prison overcrowding is to incarcerate two or more inmates per cell. That arrangement, however, increases the possibility of the spread of contagious diseases. Although AIDS requires more intimate contact, TB can be spread through the air, usually by coughing. Recognition of these problems led officials to close admission to the AIDS unit at the California Medical Facility at Vacaville in 1996 after an outbreak of TB at the prison. Twenty of the prison's AIDS inmates were diagnosed with TB. The weakened immune system of AIDS patients increases their susceptibility to TB.[87] Since 1996, other cases of TB have been diagnosed in U.S. jails and prisons. For example, in August 2007, an inmate who was detained briefly in two San Diego centers tested positive for TB, necessitating testing of everyone—more than 700 persons—who might have come into contact with him.[88]

AIDS is a special problem in jails and prisons for two reasons. First, the age group that is at the greatest risk, ages 20 to 39, is that into which most persons in the correctional system fall. Second, this population has a high rate of intravenous drug use, one critical method of transmitting the disease. Thus, many inmates as well as offenders on probation and parole are at high risk for AIDS or have already contracted the human immunodeficiency virus (HIV).[89]

It is essential that correctional institutions develop policies and practices concerning testing for HIV and AIDS as well as for protecting the community (and other offenders) from situations in which the virus may be contracted. But policy statements are only a beginning. Continued research on a cure must be accompanied by intensive education of the general public as well as by the targeted education of high-risk groups and AIDS testing to minimize the spread of the deadly disease.

In terms of data, BJS reported that at the end of 2008, state and federal prisons were housing 20,075 male inmates and 1,912 female inmates who were HIV positive or had AIDS. California, Missouri, and Florida, in that order, reported the largest increases in 2008. In 2007, 130 died from the virus or the disease.[90]

The Legal Aid Society of New York brought a class action on behalf of that state's 4–5,000 inmates with HIV or AIDS, challenging the lack of treatment for those inmates. The Society reported on its webpage that significant changes were made over the years of the case. The parties agreed to a settlement in 2007, and that was approved by the court. Part of the settlement included monitoring of compliance with the agreement. That process revealed appropriate changes, and monitoring was concluded in 2009. In 2010, the Society emphasized its intention to continue monitoring the needs of inmates with HIV or AIDS. However, it was hoped that "the reforms achieved by the settlement agreement are now well established."[91]

A final category of special-needs inmates is that of the mentally challenged. As noted in Chapter 13, over one-half of all inmates in U.S. jails and prisons have mental health problems. Mentally challenged inmates, compared to inmates without mental problems, are more likely to be incarcerated for a violent offense, to report past sexual abuse, to have been homeless during the year prior to their current arrests, to have used drugs in the month prior to arrest, to have served previous terms, and to have been injured in a fight since they were incarcerated. Mental health issues were reported more often among female than among male inmates.[92]

The importance of treating mentally challenged inmates was recognized at the federal level, as noted in the congressional findings reported in Exhibit 14.6, with reference to the Prison Rape Elimination Act (PREA). Prison rape is discussed later, but the PREA is mentioned here because of its findings concerning the mental health of inmates. Congress took steps to provide more treatment for mentally challenged inmates. The Mentally Ill Offender Treatment and Crime Reduction Act of 2004 was enacted to ensure that effective resources are available for mentally ill juvenile and adult offenders. The statute listed seven major congressional findings concerning the mentally challenged, including this important one:

> The majority of individuals with a mental illness or emotional disorder who are involved in the criminal or juvenile justice systems are responsive to medical and psychological interventions that integrate treatment, rehabilitation, and support services.[93]

It is to the advantage not only of inmates and their families but also to society that we capitalize on this receptiveness to treatment.

Juveniles in Corrections

Recent data on juveniles incarcerated in adult jails and prisons were reported earlier in this chapter. Media Focus 11.1 (see again Chapter 11) detailed some of the problems that are encountered in adult prisons when juveniles are incarcerated there. Other issues also exist. The most important may be that there is recent evidence that institutionalizing juveniles "seriously compromises multiple life domains in adulthood, especially for females." Investigators who studied the consequences of delinquent behavior and of institutionalizing juveniles reported, "Institutionalization is strongly predictive of precarious, premature, unstable, and unsatisfied conditions in multiple life domains but much less predictive of behavioral outcomes." A high level of delinquency during adolescence, however, is predictive of antisocial behavior during adulthood but "tends to have no direct effects on adversity in other life domains." Specifically, adults who were institutionalized during adolescence had more socioeconomic problems and more difficult transitions into adulthood. Compared to others, they had more instability in their work and romantic relationships. They were not as emotionally well adjusted and had trouble trusting others, even significant others. They more frequently engaged in antisocial behavior. The researchers also found gender differences in the specifics of the problems institutionalized teens had as adults. In particular, the women in the study, compared to the men, were more likely to be depressed as adults and to be dissatisfied with their relationships with their parents.[94]

Other issues arise when juvenile inmates are compared to incarcerated adults. Younger inmates are more impulsive and more difficult to manage. And in states such as Florida (which has the highest number of juveniles tried in criminal rather than juvenile courts), with the reduction in good-time credits that may be earned, juveniles have

less incentive to behave. Most of the juveniles incarcerated in adult facilities have records of violence or at least habitual offenses, and they present safety and security issues for the institutions in which they are incarcerated. In short, according to one national study, the incarceration of juveniles in adult prisons and jails "is a burgeoning issue in many correctional systems," and measures should be taken to minimize the impact of this situation. One measure that is essential is the careful classification of each juvenile to "ensure that youths are not improperly housed with adult inmates." Staff members who will work with the juveniles should be trained in their particular problems, and education and other programs should be adapted to the needs of young persons. Security staff should be adequately prepared to react to violent juveniles in a meaningful manner but without the massive display of force that might be appropriate with adult offenders.[95]

The authors of the national study found that, with regard to the juveniles housed in adult facilities, 21 percent were being held awaiting trial or after adjudication as juvenile offenders, and 75 percent had been sentenced as adults. Further,

- "In comparison with the adult prison population, a higher proportion of youth were black (55 percent of youthful inmates versus 48 percent of adult inmates) and were convicted of a crime against persons (57 percent of youth versus 44 percent of adult inmates).
- The vast majority of these youth are age 17 (79 percent) or age 16 (18 percent). . . .
- Health, education, and counseling programs were fairly standard, with little evidence of efforts to customize programs for youthful offenders."[96]

The combined problems of the mentally ill and juveniles should not be handled as some jurisdictions are attempting: by incarcerating mentally ill juveniles in juvenile correctional institutions (or adult jails) rather than in mental institutions. According to one juvenile court judge,

> It is a serious national problem. . . . In essence, we are criminalizing mental illness among young people who, through no fault of their own, have been abused or neglected by their parents, then bounce around the child dependency system, and finally, because they are untreated, their illness leads them to act out, sometimes violently, so we lock them up in the juvenile justice system.[97]

The incarceration of juvenile delinquents in juvenile facilities also has problems. Shortage of staff and a lack of resources, along with due process violations, characterize juvenile corrections. The first nationwide investigation of juvenile institutions, published in 1993, disclosed that 75 percent of juveniles were housed in institutions that violated at least one standard relating to living space; 47

14.6 The Prison Rape Elimination Act of 2003

In 2003, the U.S. Congress passed, and President George W. Bush signed, the Prison Rape Elimination Act (PREA), which was designed to eliminate this form of prison violence. This exhibit presents some of the major findings as well as the provisions of the new law. The purpose of the law is to "provide for the analysis of the incidence and effects of prison rape in federal, state, and local institutions and to provide information, resources, recommendations, and funding to protect individuals from prison rape."[1]

Section 15601. Findings

"Congress makes the following findings: . . .

(2) Insufficient research has been conducted and insufficient data reported on the extent of prison rape. . . . [The estimates were that over 1 million inmates were assaulted during the previous 20 years.]

(3) Inmates with mental illnesses are at increased risk of sexual victimization. America's jails and prisons house more mentally ill individuals than all of the Nation's psychiatric hospitals combined. As many as 16 percent of inmates in State prisons and jails and 7 percent of Federal inmates suffer from mental illness.

(4) Young first-time offenders are at increased risk of sexual victimization. Juveniles are 5 times more likely to be sexually assaulted in adult rather than juvenile facilities—often within the first 48 hours of incarceration.

(5) Most prison staff are not adequately trained or prepared to prevent, report, or treat inmate sexual assaults.

(6) Prison rape often goes unreported, and inmate victims often receive inadequate treatment for the severe physical and psychological effects of sexual assault—if they receive treatment at all.

(7) HIV and AIDS are major public health problems within America's correctional facilities. . . . Prison rape undermines the public health by contributing to the spread of these diseases, and often giving a potential death sentence to its victims.

(8) Prison rape endangers the public safety by making brutalized inmates more likely to commit crimes when they are released. . . .

(9) The frequently interracial character of prison sexual assaults significantly exacerbates interracial tensions. . . .

(10) Prison rape increases the level of homicides and other violence against inmates and staff, and the risk of insurrections and riots.

(11) Victims of prison rape suffer severe physical and psychological effects that hinder their ability to integrate into the community and maintain stable employment upon their release from prison. They are thus more likely to become homeless and/or require government assistance. . . .

(13) The high incidence of sexual assault within prisons involves actual and potential violations of the United States Constitution. . . .

(14) The high incidence of prison rape undermines the effectiveness and efficiency of United States Government expenditures through grant programs such as those dealing with health care; mental health care; disease prevention; crime prevention, investigation, and prosecution; prison construction, maintenance, and operation; race relations; poverty; unemployment and homelessness. The effectiveness and efficiency of these federally funded grant programs are compromised by the failure of State officials to adopt policies and procedures that reduce the incidence of prison rape.

Section 15602. Purposes

The purposes of this Act are to—

(1) establish a zero-tolerance standard for the incidence of prison rape in prisons in the United States;

(2) make the prevention of prison rape a top priority in each prison system;

(3) develop and implement national standards for the detention, prevention, reduction, and punishment of prison rape;

(4) increase the available data and information on the incidence of prison rape, consequently improving the management and administration of correctional facilities;

(5) standardize the definitions used for collecting data on the incidence of prison rape;

(6) increase the accountability of prison officials who fail to detect, prevent, reduce, and punish prison rape;

(7) protect the Eighth Amendment rights of Federal, State, and local prisoners;

(8) increase the efficiency and effectiveness of Federal expenditures through grant programs such as those dealing with health care; mental health care; disease prevention; crime prevention, investigation, and prosecution; prison construction, maintenance, and operation; race relations; poverty; unemployment; and homelessness; and

(9) reduce the costs that prison rape imposes on interstate commerce."

Along with many other provisions, the statute provides for the collection of data on prison rape, the reporting of such data, and the establishment of a Review Panel on Prison Rape within the U.S. Department of Justice.

---

1. The Prison Rape Elimination Act of 2003 is codified at USCS, Title 42, Sections 15601 et seq. (2010).

percent lived in overcrowded institutions, up from 36 percent in 1987. Overcrowding was described as a "pervasive and serious problem across the nation."[98]

The study, mandated by Congress in 1988, found that only 27 percent of juvenile facilities met security standards. Only 25 percent of juveniles were in facilities that met standards for controlling suicidal behavior, and 11,000 youths committed more than 17,000 suicidal acts in a year, although only 10 were completed in 1990. The study disclosed that between 1987 and 1991, the proportion of confined juveniles who were minorities increased from 53 percent to 63 percent, with Hispanics increasing from 13 percent to 17 percent and African Americans from 37 percent to 44 percent.[99]

There is also evidence of violence against institutionalized juveniles. In October 2007, seven correctional officers and a nurse were acquitted in the death of a 14-year-old boy in a Florida boot camp despite the fact that the defendants were caught on tape hitting and kicking the boy prior to his death. The official cause of death was listed as complications from sickle-cell traits, but the boy's parents and many others were skeptical of that conclusion. A second autopsy, ordered by the governor, listed suffocation as the cause of death. The death of Martin Lee Anderson led the state to overhaul its juvenile justice system. Anderson was in the facility for having violated probation for stealing his grandmother's car. In April 2010, federal officials announced that after an extensive investigation, they did not have sufficient evidence to charge the prison officials with violating Anderson's civil rights; the case was closed. In May 2010, a 21-year-old inmate was in critical condition in a medically induced coma after he said he could not complete the rigorous exercise required of him at a Florida lockup for young people. Florida's governor ordered an investigation into the facts of the case. It was reported that Samuel Joel Dread was taking medication and should not have been exercising in the heat (86 degrees). The results of the investigation into this case were not available at the time this manuscript went to press. Dread was serving a 10-year sentence for armed robbery.[100]

Juveniles are also subjected to sexual violence in adult jails and prisons as well as in juvenile correctional facilities. The BJS is mandated by the Prison Rape Elimination Act of 2003 to collect data yearly on sexual victimization in prisons. The BJS has several data collections. The June 2010 report included the reporting of data from the National Survey of Youth in Custody. Among other findings were the following:

- "An estimated 12% of youth in state juvenile facilities and large non-state facilities reported experiencing one or more incidents of sexual victimization . . . during the past 12 months. . . .
- About 2.6% of youth reported an incident involving another youth, and 10.3% reported an incident involving facility staff.

- About 4.3% of youth [experienced sexual acts after force or threat; approximately 6.4% were involved in such acts without threat or force].
- Approximately 95% of all youth reporting staff sexual misconduct said they had been victimized by female staff."[101]

Earlier discussions in this text focused on rehabilitation in general as well as with reference to juveniles. It is important to emphasize that some experts still support that philosophy. There is evidence that the public is willing to use tax funds to pay for the rehabilitation of young offenders, even in the form of early childhood intervention programs. As noted already, some jurisdictions have instituted a number of recent rehabilitative efforts, such as drug courts for juveniles.[102]

Long-time advocate of rehabilitation, criminologist Francis T. Cullen, stated, "The rationale for rehabilitation is thus persuasive because of a trinity of considerations: The public supports it, it works, and it is cost effective. . . . It is time to reaffirm rehabilitation."[103]

Finally, recall Chapter 13's discussion with regard to the 2010 holding by the U.S. Supreme Court that life without parole for a nonhomicide committed when one was a juvenile constitutes cruel and unusual punishment and thus is not permitted.

Prison and Jail Violence

One reaction to incarceration is violence, including violence against oneself. Jails and prisons house many violent or potentially violent individuals. It is not unreasonable to expect explosive and bloody behavior from them. In an analysis of state inmates, the BJS stated that one in ten reported being injured during a fight within prison. Female inmates and federal inmates were much less likely to be injured in fights than male state inmates. Inmates age 24 or younger were twice as likely as inmates older than 44 to be in fights. Inmates who had served six or more years were twice as likely as those who had served fewer than six years to be in fights. In terms of offenses, inmates incarcerated for drug offenses were least likely to be involved in fights; those whose current convictions were for violent crimes were twice as likely as property offenders to be injured.[104]

In focusing on jail inmates, the BJS reported that physical injuries resulting from fights during incarceration were highest for males, younger inmates, inmates with a physical or mental impairment, and inmates held on charges for violent crimes. Further, the chances that an inmate would be injured increased with time served.[105]

It is reasonable to assume that violence among inmates is underreported. Many inmates do not report incidents for fear of reprisals from other inmates or the staff. Administrators want to avoid the criticism that comes with the media reports of violence in their prisons. But some prison systems, faced with high violence rates, have taken extra security precautions, such as adding more correctional officers, conducting more searches, or instituting lockdown policies.

Self-Inflicted Violence

One type of jail and prison violence is inflicted by inmates upon themselves. Some injure themselves to gain attention. Others attempt suicide; some of those succeed, but many do not. The reasons for self-inflicted violence are varied. They have been linked to overcrowded institutions, extended periods of solitary confinement, and the psychological and physical consequences of being victimized by other inmates. Some inmates who are threatened with homosexual rape or other violence become depressed and desperate about their physical safety. Victims may lack the interpersonal skills and resources that would help fend off would-be aggressors. They may be socially isolated. Another factor contributing to their psychological state is the perception that the only options are fight or flight. Victims know that if they submit to violence, they are branded as weak, but if they seek help, they are called snitches or rats. Many of those who inflict violence upon themselves are young and without histories of drug addiction, past criminal records, or past prison sentences. Frequently, prison administrators segregate these inmates, although psychologists recommend human contact and communication as the best method for preventing self-inflicted violence.

The Death in Custody Reporting Act of 2000 requires the collection of data concerning inmate deaths in all local jails beginning in 2000 and in state prisons beginning in 2001. The BJS published its first analysis of such data in 2005, noting that jail suicides were three times as high as state prison suicides (where homicides are higher) and that jail suicides steadily declined between 1983 and 2002. Prison suicides fell between 1980 and 1990, at which time they stabilized. The data also show that suicides were twice as high among violent offenders compared to nonviolent offenders.[106]

Sexual Violence

Sexual attacks are one form of violence in prison. Many of the problems with sexual aggression in prison first occur when the inmate arrives at the prison or jail. Newly arrived male inmates may be attacked in dormitories or in cells by two or more established inmates. Earlier studies of male sexual aggression in prison found that sexual overtures might involve an actual sexual assault, other physical violence, insulting or threatening language, or propositions.[107] Violence can be precipitated by the aggressor or by the victim. In the first case, the aggressor plans to use violence to coerce his victim before the incident begins. In the second case, the victim reacts violently to sexual innuendo or a proposition perceived as threatening.[108]

The victim may refuse a sexual advance, and the aggressor may react violently to that refusal, interpreting it as an insult or a challenge to fight. Violence may also erupt when gay partners disagree. These arguments, similar to disagreements between heterosexual partners, may pertain to breakups, power, rejection, or pride. Another type of sexual violence in male prisons concerns arguments between two (or more) rivals over the sexual favors of a third. Regardless of the social arrangements, violence in the form of rape in prison does exist and has caught the attention of the U.S. Congress. Exhibit 14.6, presented earlier, contains a portion of the Prison Rape Elimination Act of 2003. Note that the findings include the increased vulnerability of mentally ill and juvenile inmates to prison rape.

Same-gender sexual relationships also occur among female inmates; although force may be used, in most cases the relationship between female inmates is consensual. It develops out of mutual interest, for the purpose of alleviating the depersonalization of the prison, and for gaining status. Women seem to be looking for love, interpersonal support, community, family, and social status.[109]

For female inmates, the relationship may take the place of the primary groups of their pre-prison lives. Some female inmates form partnerships not primarily for sexual purposes but to simulate the families they left behind or would like to create. For these women, the relationship with other women may not be sexual, as in the case of male inmates.[110]

For female inmates, however, sexual violations most often occur at the hands of correctional officers. Most jurisdictions prohibit sex between correctional officers and inmates even if they are allegedly consensual. Recent sex scandals have led to more extensive legislation and more intense enforcement of policies prohibiting sex between staff and inmates. For instance, an investigation in South Carolina resulted in the firing of 51 correctional officers and staff who were found to have behaved improperly toward inmates. Some were found guilty of having sex with inmates; others smuggled drugs into the prison or engaged in other illegal conduct. The investigation began after it was alleged that one or two officers had sexual relations with Susan Smith, who is serving a life sentence for driving a car into a lake with her two little boys strapped in the back seat, jumping out, and leaving the boys to drown. Houston Cagle, one of the officers found to have had sex with Smith, was sentenced to 10 years in prison, but that was suspended for a 90-day term.[111]

In August 2009, Hawaii announced that the 168 female inmates they had contracted to house at a privately run Kentucky prison would be removed because of allegations that correctional officers sexually abused female inmates. Hawaii had sent its inmates to Kentucky to save money, paying $58.46 a day for them to be housed in Kentucky facilities compared to $86 a day in Hawaii. Hawaii officials alleged that several Kentucky employees, including a chaplain, were having sex with inmates. Four of the five accused were convicted. In Kentucky, sex by a correctional officer with an inmate is a misdemeanor, unlike most jurisdictions, where it is a felony.[112]

As noted earlier, the Prison Rape Elimination Prevention Act (PREA) requires the annual collection of data regarding sexual misconduct in jails and prisons. The 2008–2009 report was published in August 2010. The report presents data from "167 state and federal prisons, 286 local jails, and 10 special correctional facilities . . . between October 2008 and December 2009, with a sample of 81,566 inmates ages 18 or older."[113]

The PREA requires the establishment of a national prison rape elimination panel. Following are selected highlights of the latest report in terms of the prevalence of sexual victimization in jails and prisons.

- "An estimated 4.4 percent of prison inmates and 3.1 percent of jail inmates reported experiencing one or more incidents of sexual victimization by another inmate or facility staff in the past 12 months or since admission to the facility, if less than 12 months. Nationwide, these percentages suggest that approximately 88,500 adults held in prison had been sexually victimized.

- About 1.2 percent of prison inmates and 1.5 percent of jail inmates reported an incident involving another inmate. An estimated 1.0 percent of prison inmates and 0.8 percent of jail inmates said they had nonconsensual sex with another inmate (the most serious type of acts), including unwilling manual stimulation and oral, anal, or vaginal penetration.

- About 2.8 percent of prison inmates and 2.0 percent of jail inmates reported having had sex or sexual contact with staff. At least half of the inmates who experienced staff sexual misconduct (1.8 percent in prison and 1.1 percent in jail) said that they willingly had sex or sexual contact with staff." . . .

- Most victims of staff sexual misconduct were males; most perpetrators were females. Among male victims of staff sexual misconduct, 69 percent of those in prison and 64 percent of those in jails reported sexual activity with female staff. An additional 16 percent of prison inmates and 18 percent of jail inmates reported sexual activity with both female and male staff.

- Among inmates who reported staff sexual misconduct, nearly 16 percent of male victims in prison and 30 percent of male victims in jail said they were victimized by staff within the first 24 hours, compared to 5 percent of female victims in prison and 4 percent of female victims in jail."[114]

A study of sexual assaults in California prisons revealed that an estimated 4 percent of inmates had been sexually assaulted and that transgender inmates were 13 times more vulnerable than other inmates, with 59 percent reporting some type of sexual abuse. Twenty percent of inmate victims reported sexual abuse between two and five times; 30 percent reported they were abused more than five times.[115]

Finally, the prosecution of prison rape cases is quite difficult. A member of the bipartisan National Prison Rape Elimination Commission stated that as she studied the issue, she realized that prosecuting such cases has little, if any, positive impact on a prosecutor's local image and may even weaken it in the local community "by making him or her appear to be soft on criminals." This is because most of the alleged perpetrators are correctional officers. Other reasons that prosecuting alleged prison rape cases is high risk for prosecutors are as follows: "unsympathetic victims, delayed reporting of incidents, a lack of physical evidence, poor investigations and conflicting testimony."[116]

Riots

The most brutal type of prison violence has occurred during riots, some of which have resulted in extensive property damage, injuries, and deaths. Although a few riots occurred early in the history of U.S. prisons, most riots are relatively recent. These riots differed from earlier ones in that, although they involved the usual complaints about food and conditions, they were more organized. They have also been brutal and destructive, as Exhibit 14.7 notes.

In the 1960s, along with the civil rights and antiwar groups on college and university campuses and elsewhere, inmates' rights groups developed and expanded. Inmates were viewed as normal persons except that they suffered from excessive discrimination and reduced opportunities. Civil rights groups focused on equalizing the legal rights and social circumstances of inmates as well as free persons.[117]

Riots during this time took a dramatic shift. Although inmates continued to demand improvements in medical care, food services, recreational opportunities, disciplinary proceedings, and educational programs, they also began to question the legitimacy of their incarceration. They claimed that they were political victims of unjust and corrupt systems, meaning that they were imprisoned for breaking laws enacted by political systems that reflected unequal distributions of power. They argued that the sole purpose of criminal justice systems was to protect the entrenched interests of the wealthy and powerful at the expense of the poor and the weak. Today, many inmates assert that their crimes are justifiable retaliations against a society that has denied them opportunities for social and economic gains. This denial of basic rights in prison, cruel and disproportionate punishment, racial prejudice, and other violations of the system make inmates one of America's deprived minorities. Political protests in prisons began when inmates, like workers and minorities who were not imprisoned, sought an effective

14.7   Selected Incidents of Prison Violence: 1980–2009

Chino, California, 2009

A riot thought to involve racial issues occurred on 8 August 2009, at the California Institute for Men in Chino. An estimated 249 inmates and 8 staffers were injured in violence that lasted about 11 hours. The overcrowded prison lost 1,300 beds in the destructive fire. The prison was redesigned, and the renovation cost was an estimated $5.2 million.[1]

Huntsville, Texas, 2007, 2001

In September 2007, two Texas inmates at the maximum-security prison in Huntsville killed a correctional officer in an escape attempt. The inmates overpowered Susan Canfield, who was on horseback watching the inmates as they worked in the fields. They took her gun, stole a truck, and ran over her as she tried to stop them. John Ray Falk, 40, was apprehended within an hour. He has been in prison since 1986, convicted of murder. Jerry Martin, 37, was serving 50 years for attempted murder. He was apprehended a few hours later. Both men had good disciplinary records in the prison and thus were permitted to work in the fields under minimum security.

Texas has one of the most secure prison systems in the country, but in December 2000, the so-called Texas Seven, led by death row inmate George Rivas, escaped and eluded authorities for over a month, killing a police officer before being apprehended in Colorado in late January 2001. One killed himself just prior to capture; the others were tried for capital murder, convicted, and sentenced to die. Falk and Martin were charged with capital murder, as killing a correctional officer falls within the Texas statute covering that crime.[2]

Crescent City, California, 2000

On the same day that a federal grand jury indicted two former correctional officers for beating inmates, one of whom died, approximately 200 minority inmates in the Pelican Bay Prison began fighting. During the fight, eight inmates were injured, one critically, and one inmate was killed. The Pelican Bay Prison houses the most violent inmates in California; at the time of the riot, the prison held 3,400 inmates in a facility designed to accommodate only 2,280. In a previous riot (in 1997), six inmates were killed at this institution.

Lucasville, Ohio, 1993

Eight correctional officers were taken hostage when inmates seized a wing of the Southern Ohio Correctional Facility, a state maximum-security prison in Lucasville. Inmates controlled the wing for 11 days. Ten people, including one correctional officer, died. Among the list of inmate complaints were the religious repression of Muslims and forced integration within cells. Inmates alleged that correctional officers had "blatantly killed innocent people in these jails and called it suicide."[3]

In March 1995, the leader of the riot was convicted of aggravated murder (killing another inmate and an officer) and kidnapping. In May 2003, James Were, 46, the last of the four inmates charged with the death of correctional Officer Robert Vallandingham, was convicted of kidnapping and murder.

Deer Lodge, Montana, 1991

Five inmates were beaten, tortured, and killed by other inmates in a siege that lasted over four hours at the Montana State Prison. Four of the victims were hanged. After seeing an inmate being beaten, prison officials stormed the facility and took control without resistance from the inmates.

Folsom, California, 1989

During one of the most violent periods of the Folsom Prison's history, one inmate was killed and 48 were wounded. Correctional officers were able to bring the violence, which began in the exercise yard, under control by firing 10 shots into the prison yard.

Moundsville, West Virginia, 1986

On 1 January 1986, inmates in the West Virginia Penitentiary, wielding homemade weapons, took correctional officers hostage and seized control of the prison. Sixteen hostages were taken. Inmates had control of the prison for 43 hours, during which time they brutalized, tortured, and then killed three inmates who they thought were snitches. One inmate, a convicted child molester and murderer, was dragged up and down the cell block for other inmates to abuse. Inmates, angered by restrictions on contact visits with family and friends and the cancellation of a Christmas open house, demanded changes in visiting regulations, better meals, control of the temperature in their cells, and improved medical facilities and living conditions. Other demands included a reduction in the inmate population, permission to wear long hair and mustaches or beards, and an opportunity to negotiate with the governor and director of corrections. The inmates demanded that they be treated like human beings rather than like trash or animals. The prison had been placed under court order in 1983 because of unconstitutional living conditions and overcrowding.

Santa Fe, New Mexico, 1980

On 2 February 1980, the worst prison riot in American history occurred at the state prison in Santa Fe. For 36 hours, inmates rioted, burned prison facilities, and tortured other inmates. At the end of the riot, 33 inmates were dead. The cost of replacing the penitentiary was estimated to be between $60 million and $70 million. Survivors reported that inmates were tortured with blowtorches and possibly acetylene torches. Some were decapitated, and others were slashed and beaten.

(continued)

The New Mexico riot occurred just three weeks after the completion of a special investigation of the prison. The report indicated that the prison was overcrowded, housing 1,200 persons in a facility designed for a maximum of 900. The prison was understaffed. The correctional officers were not trained properly, and their morale was low, partly because of their low salaries. The investigation was prompted by the December 1979 escape of 11 inmates. Management problems were evident in frequent turnover within the administration; for example, the prison was headed by five different wardens within a five-year span. The state director of corrections had resigned after the December escapes.

Before the New Mexico riot, three inmates had filed suit in federal court alleging that their constitutional rights were being violated in the areas of mail and visiting privileges, food, and treatment (both psychological and medical). They also alleged that overcrowding contributed to the increase in general violence as well as homosexual rape within the prison.

Source: Summarized by the author from media sources.
1. "Chino Prison Repairs Damage from Riot," *Los Angeles Times* (17 March 2010), p. 4.
2. "Prison Escapes: Myth and Mayhem," *Houston Chronicle* (1 October 2007), p. 1.
3. "Court OKs TB Tests for Ohio Prison That Had Riots," *Orlando Sentinel* (Florida) (22 June 1993), p. 6; "Second Hostage Is Freed Unhurt by Ohio Inmates," *New York Times* (17 April 1993), p. 6.

way of expressing their demands and achieving results from the political system.

Organized groups help inmates focus on the expansion of their constitutional rights, better communication between inmates and the outside world, development of meaningful work with fair wages, and restoration of their normal rights and privileges upon release. Inmates want to emphasize the poor prison conditions in the hope that community sympathy and support will lead to reform. It has worked in some instances, but it has not led to substantial prison reform in most cases. For example, the 1971 riot at New York's Attica Correctional Facility resulted in 43 deaths (32 inmates and 11 correctional employees). This riot was described by the investigating commission as "the bloodiest one-day encounter between Americans since the Civil War." After extensive investigation and considerable litigation, reforms were ordered. But in 1985, a federal court judge, hearing another case

on Attica, noted that after a peaceful inmate strike about prison conditions, the only thing changed was the flavor of ice cream available for purchase.[118]

Various reasons for prison violence have been cited, but one important factor that must be considered is the presence of gangs within institutions. Gangs have existed in prisons for years, but recently, the violence attributed to prison gangs has become a more serious problem, as has gang violence outside prisons, noted earlier in this text.

Escape

A final type of prison violence of great concern is that associated with the escape of an inmate, especially from maximum security. In 1988, seven inmates escaped from the nation's largest death row in Huntsville, Texas. They cut through the fence, moved to a roof, and dropped to the ground outside the prison. All but one surrendered

Prison riots may be quite destructive. One of the most costly, both in terms of property damage and human life, was the 1980 riot at the New Mexico State Penitentiary. The riot lasted 36 hours, resulting in the deaths of 33 inmates and damage of more than $60 million to the prison.

when correctional officers opened fire. Martin E. Gurule escaped, the first inmate to do so from that death row since 1934. His body was found six days later by two off-duty officers who were fishing. The cause of Gurule's death was drowning.[119]

Texas prison officials were not as successful in the case of the Texas Seven, who escaped from the Connally Unit, a maximum-security prison in South Texas, on 13 December 2000, as noted in Exhibit 14.7. Six were apprehended (the seventh killed himself as law enforcement authorities were closing in) but only after they had spent a month on the run and killed an Irving, Texas, police officer, Aubrey Hawkins, during a Christmas Eve robbery. The admitted leader of the escape, George Rivas, was the first to be tried. In November 2003, the last of the six living escapees was sentenced to death, setting a record since capital punishment was reinstated in 1976: six capital sentences for the murder of one person.[120]

Texas was in the national news again in December 2009 when Arcade Joseph Comeaux Jr. escaped while being transferred from one prison to another. Comeaux pulled a gun on the correctional officers in charge, handcuffed them to each other, and escaped in their van. He was captured eight days later, but his escape led to major changes in the Texas prison system security mandates. All correctional officers must now pass a yearly physical agility test, in-service training was enhanced, and academic standards for entry testing were imposed. Nine employees, including top prison administrators, were fired as a result of this escape.[121]

Control Within Prisons: The Role of Correctional Officers

In early prisons, wardens and correctional officers controlled inmates and kept prisons secure by separating inmates and by using force. Court interpretations of

constitutional rights have changed the methods that may be used for maintaining internal security, and in many ways, it is more difficult today as a result. For example, a contraband item in prisons is cell phones, which could be used to intimidate witnesses on the outside, smuggle drugs, continue with organized crime activities, plot escapes, and engage in other illegal acts. Most prisons have policies that forbid the use of cell phones, and in some states, possession of a cell phone by an inmate is a crime. But phones are smuggled into prisons by visitors and staff, as illustrated by a correctional officer, Dwayne Brewton, who was convicted of taking cell phones (and drugs) into a prison and selling them to inmates.[122]

Cell phones are only one example of problems within prisons. Internal control remains an issue in which correctional officers continue to play a crucial role, although as the previous paragraph emphasizes, they can be part of the problem rather than the solution. Correctional officers have the most extensive contact and perhaps the greatest impact on inmates, but we know very little about them because they have infrequently been the subject of intensive or systematic analyses.

In the past, correctional officers maintained control within prisons by manipulating inmate social systems. Select inmates were permitted greater freedom within the institution, given power over other inmates, and permitted some infractions of the rules. In exchange, these privileged inmates used their influence in the inmate social control system to get other inmates to behave. The system worked rather well, but federal judges have prohibited arrangements whereby inmates have control over jobs or privileges or are granted privileges by correctional officers. These restrictions reflect judicial awareness of the corruption that may occur when correctional officers and inmates are too cooperative.

There is evidence that correctional officers have used force, sometimes torture, as a control device, even recently.

In many prisons, especially those that are medium security, correctional officers do not carry weapons within the institution, although as here, they may stand guard with weapons in secure areas of the prison or outside. A guard tower is common, as illustrated by this photo from Joseph Harp Correction Center in Lexington, Oklahoma.

To illustrate, for years, inmates and correctional officers battled for control of the special disciplinary unit (referred to by inmates as the "House of Pain") within Rikers Island in New York. In 1998, it was alleged that the officers gave inmates "greeting beatings" when they arrived at the unit. These were a preview of severer disciplinary action.

As the result of the settlement of a lawsuit over the officers' behavior, legal documents supporting inmates' allegations were released. According to the court documents, between the opening of the disciplinary unit in 1988 and the settlement of the lawsuit brought by 15 inmates, correctional officers engaged in over 1,500 instances of force against inmates. Some of these acts caused severe injuries, and one resulted in death. A provision of the settlement was that two outside consultants would monitor the disciplinary unit for two years.[123]

A lawsuit filed in 2002 by inmates who claimed a pattern of abuse in New York City jails was settled in 2006. New York officials agreed to pay $2.2 million to the 22 inmate plaintiffs who were injured by correctional officers (one inmate lost his eye when he was kicked in the face). The city agreed that officers would not use any more force than necessary and that force would not be used as punishment. Video cameras would be available in all units, and supervisors would be notified (if reasonable) when force was required. Photographs must be taken after each use of force, officers must be trained in specific use of force techniques and policies, and so on.[124]

Policy changes were also made after an inmate-beating scandal in Pennsylvania in 2009. The "interview" of the inmate occurred in an area that had no cameras. According to a prison warden, "All interviews will be conducted in the presence of a camera. That's for our protection as well as the inmates." Four corrections officers were fired and two resigned after the investigation into the alleged beating of James Edwards, 27. Edwards, who had pleaded guilty in 2003 to attempted capital murder in Texas, was apprehended in Pennsylvania for violating the conditions of his release in Texas.[125]

The other side of the picture is that the lives of correctional officers are in danger in many institutions. In June 2007, in Salt Lake City, Utah, Curtis M. Allgier overpowered a correctional officer, stole the officer's gun, killed the officer, and then carjacked an SUV and escaped. He led police in a high-speed chase but bailed out at an Arby's restaurant, where he shot at an employee. The gun did not fire. A 59-year-old truck driver jumped over the counter and wrestled the gun away from Allgier. Allgier cut the driver with a knife, but he was not seriously injured. Police arrived and arrested Allgier. Allgier had been transported outside the prison by the officer to a medical facility for an MRI, and the test required that the metal restraints on his hands and feet be replaced with plastic ones.[126] In October 2007, the Utah Department of Corrections discontinued its policy of using inmates on road crews after two inmates tried

to escape and another two were reportedly intoxicated on several occasions.[127]

The job of a correctional officer is not an easy one, and recruiting qualified persons to serve in this capacity, especially in maximum-security prisons, is a challenge. Some of the hiring difficulties are discussed in Media Focus 14.1.

This discussion of correctional officers raises one of the problems of changing one aspect of a system without changing another. The recognition of inmates' rights, long overdue in the United States, was done without sufficient preparation of correctional officers and others who work with inmates on a daily basis. There is serious controversy over the resulting problems, and close attention must be given to inmates' rights. Although some people believe that inmates "get what they deserve," federal courts have ruled that prisons must maintain certain conditions to avoid violation of the Eighth Amendment ban against cruel and unusual punishment (see Appendix A).

Inmates' Legal Rights: An Overview

In 1872, a state court declared that the convicted felon "has as a consequence of his crime, not only forfeited his liberty, but all his personal rights except those which the law in its humanity accords to him. He is for the time being the slave of the state."[128] Under the rule of that case, prison officials could grant privileges to inmates as they deemed proper. Freedom of speech, freedom to worship in one's religious faith, visits from family and friends, incoming and outgoing mail, and all other important aspects of life inside prison could be regulated, even denied, by officials.

Historical Overview

The past several decades have been characterized by significant changes in the recognition of inmates' legal rights, as federal courts have abandoned their earlier **hands-off doctrine** toward prisons. In 1974, in *Wolff v. McDonnell*, the U.S. Supreme Court declared,

> But though his rights may be diminished by the needs and exigencies of the institutional environment, a prisoner is not wholly stripped of constitutional protections when he is imprisoned for crime. There is no iron curtain drawn between the Constitution and the prisons of this country.[129]

Prior to this decision, lower federal courts had begun hearing cases in which inmates alleged violations of their constitutional rights. Those and subsequent cases have covered virtually every area of life inside prison. The number of cases is immense. The law changes rapidly in this

14.1   The Crisis in Recruiting Correctional Officers

MEDIA FOCUS

A front-page article in the *New York Times* thrust into the national spotlight the problems of staffing prisons. The article, entitled "Desperate for Prison Guards, Some States Even Rob Cradles," focused on Kansas but also contained information about other states.[1]

In Kansas, the minimum age for correctional officers had recently been dropped from 21 to 19 solely because of the difficulty of recruiting candidates for the positions. Several reasons were cited for recruitment problems there and elsewhere: new prisons, low salaries in these positions and higher ones elsewhere, inmates who are serving longer sentences and thus have fewer incentives to cooperate, more violent inmates, and more inmates who are mentally ill or have drug problems. The result is a severe shortage of correctional officers throughout the country. One authority on prisons stated that if recruiters were honest, they would advertise like this: "Come to work with us. Have feces thrown at you. Be verbally abused every day."

Some systems lose more officers than they hire in a given year. Low salaries are an important factor. For example, in Oklahoma, one-fifth of correctional officer positions were vacant. The starting salary was below the poverty line for a family of four.

Another media account on hiring correctional officers was more upbeat, but it involved a new prison in the federal system that was apparently being used as a recruiting device. "Get your foot in the door as a correctional officer, and after that, opportunities abound" was the approach. The new prison in Forrest City, Arkansas, provided about 300 jobs, including jobs for teachers, medical personnel, drug treatment personnel, and food service personnel as well as correctional officers, whose starting salary was $34,000 annually. But the head of the state's corrections department was concerned that his lowest salaries, $22,193 annually, would not attract qualified applicants.[2]

In 2007, Alabama, which loses approximately 300 trained prison correctional officers a year, was only able to hire 73 new ones despite a massive ad campaign. A recent study reported that the state might need to hire 1,300 more officers.[3]

In 2004, the U.S. Department of Labor predicted that the demand for correctional officers would "grow faster than the average for all occupations through 2012." But turnover remains high, with one report showing that turnover was as high as 25 percent in some jurisdictions.[4]

The lack of job satisfaction was an even greater factor than low salaries contributing to the consideration of some correctional officers to leave their positions. Dissatisfaction with supervisors was another factor. The investigators in one study of a department of corrections (DOC) concluded the following:

> Previous generations felt that loyalty to an organization was expected and believe that younger generations lack that loyalty. However, it is not that their loyalties are lacking, they simply have a different value system. To retain younger employees, the department must determine what is important to them. DOCs can reward younger employees by making performance the primary level for controlling rewards, accelerating the timeliness of rewards and feedback, empowering first-line supervisors through modification of the current management structure, and including them in defining problems and developing creative solutions.[5]

1. Summarized from "Desperate for Prison Guards, Some States Even Rob Cradles," *New York Times* (21 April 2001), p. 1. This cite is the source for all information up to the second note.
2. "Federal Prison Hunting Recruits: Forrest City Lockup to Provide 300 Jobs, Not All as Guards," *Arkansas Democrat-Gazette* (8 July 2004), n.p.
3. "Increased Prison Hiring Fails Alabama's Needs," *Corrections Professional* 12, no. 14 (11 May 2007): n.p.
4. Rhonda J. Jones, "Correctional Officers: Support, Commitment, and Ethnicity," *Corrections Compendium* 32, no. 3 (1 May 2007): 1.
5. Ryan Crews and Gene Bonham Jr., "Strategies for Employee Retention in Corrections," *Corrections Compendium* 32, no. 3 (1 May 2007): 7.

area, and not all lower federal courts agree on how similar cases should be decided. Thus, in many areas of inmates' rights, there is conflict until the U.S. Supreme Court decides an issue. Although the Court has decided relatively few cases in this area, some general points may be made.

The U.S. Supreme Court looks at the *totality of circumstances* of a prison environment before deciding whether the alleged conditions violate inmates' constitutional rights. That is why the case law on this subject must be read carefully. In general, inmates have been granted the right to practice their religion, to engage in reasonable visits with family and friends, to visit with their attorneys, and to address the courts. They are entitled to a limited due process hearing in discipline cases and to be free of unreasonable searches and seizures. They must be provided reasonable medical care, be given a sufficient amount of nutritious food, and be fed and housed in sanitary conditions. They may not be physically abused by correctional officers or other prison officials. Theoretically, male and female inmates are entitled to equal protection, although they need not be given identical treatment and facilities. Inmates may not be transferred arbitrarily from one institution to another, but transfers may be made when necessary for security or other recognized penal goals. Inmate rights may be restricted when necessary for internal security.

The U.S. Supreme Court has held that the Eighth Amendment (see Appendix A) prohibition against cruel and unusual punishment applies to inmates. This has been interpreted to mean that inmates may not be subjected to corporal punishment such as whippings, but it does not preclude imposing solitary confinement or other deprivations on inmates under appropriate circumstances. Again, the totality of circumstances must be examined to determine whether an inmate's constitutional rights have been violated. The Supreme Court has held that, to be cruel and unusual, conditions "must . . . involve the wanton and unnecessary infliction of pain, [or] be grossly disproportionate to the severity of the crime warranting imprisonment."[130] The Eighth Amendment "must draw its meaning from the evolving standards of decency that mark the progress of a maturing society."[131]

Recent changes in inmates' rights may be illustrated by cases in three areas: physical restraint and discipline, the Americans with Disabilities Act, and general health issues.

Physical Restraint and Discipline

The U.S. Supreme Court has interpreted the cruel and unusual clause to mean that inmates may bring suits against prison officials who abuse them physically. *Hudson v. McMillian* involved an inmate, Hudson, who had an argument with a security officer, McMillian. McMillian and Woods, another security officer, handcuffed and shackled Hudson and took him to the administrative lockdown section of the prison. The other pertinent facts and the Supreme Court's analysis are in the following excerpt.[132]

Hudson v. McMillian

Hudson testified that on the way [to the administrative lockdown area] McMillian punched Hudson in the mouth, eyes, chest, and stomach while Woods held the inmate in place and kicked and punched him from behind. He further testified that Mezo, the supervisor on duty, watched the beating but merely told the officers "not to have too much fun." As a result of this episode, Hudson suffered minor bruises and swelling of his face, mouth, and lip. The blows also loosened Hudson's teeth and cracked his partial dental plate, rendering it unusable for several months. . . .

[We have previously held that] "the unnecessary and wanton infliction of pain . . . constitutes cruel and unusual punishment forbidden by the Eighth Amendment."

What is necessary to establish an "unnecessary and wanton infliction of pain," we said, varies according to the nature of the alleged constitutional violation. For example, the appropriate inquiry when an inmate alleges that prison officials failed to attend to serious medical needs is whether the officials exhibited "deliberate indifference.". . .

By contrast, officials confronted with a prison disturbance must balance the threat unrest poses to inmates, prison workers, administrators, and visitors against the harm inmates may suffer if guards use force. Despite the weight of these competing concerns, corrections officials must make their decisions "in haste, under pressure, and frequently without the luxury of a second chance." We accordingly concluded in [an earlier case] that application of the deliberate indifference standard is inappropriate when authorities use force to put down a prison disturbance. Instead, "the question whether the measure taken inflicted unnecessary and wanton pain and suffering" ultimately turns on "whether force was applied in a good-faith effort to maintain or restore discipline or maliciously and sadistically for the very purpose of causing harm.". . .

[W]e hold that whenever prison officials stand accused of using excessive physical force . . . the core judicial inquiry is . . . whether force was applied in a good-faith effort to maintain or restore discipline, or maliciously and sadistically to cause harm. . . .

Under [this] approach, the extent of injury suffered by an inmate is one factor that may suggest "whether the use of force could plausibly have been thought necessary" in a particular situation, "or instead evinced such wantonness with respect to the unjustified infliction of harm as is tantamount to a knowing willingness that it occur.". . .

When prison officials maliciously and sadistically use force to cause harm, contemporary standards of decency always are violated. This is true whether or not significant injury is evident. Otherwise, the Eighth Amendment would permit any physical punishment, no matter how diabolic or inhuman, inflicting less than some arbitrary quantity of injury. Such a result would have been as unacceptable to the drafters of the Eighth Amendment as it is today.

U.S. Supreme Court Associate Justice Clarence Thomas wrote a dissent in which he was joined by Associate Justice Antonin Scalia. They maintained that inmates should have to show *serious injuries* in their cruel and unusual punishment claims for physical abuse.

In 2002, the U.S. Supreme Court again visited the issue of disciplining inmates and held that chaining an inmate to a hitching post constitutes cruel and unusual punishment. In the following excerpt from *Hope v. Pelzer*, the Court explains the punishment. The decision involves technical issues beyond this discussion, but the cruel and unusual punishment issue is relevant here.[133]

Hope v. Pelzer

In 1995, Alabama was the only State that followed the practice of chaining inmates to one another in work squads. It was also the only State that handcuffed prisoners to "hitching posts" if they either refused to work or otherwise disrupted work squads. Hope was handcuffed to a hitching post on two occasions. On May 11, 1995, while Hope was working in a chain gang near an interstate highway, he got into an argument with another inmate. Both men were taken back to the Limestone prison and handcuffed to a hitching post. Hope was released two hours later, after the guard captain determined that the altercation had been caused by the other inmate. During his two hours on the post, Hope was offered drinking water and a bathroom break every 15 minutes, and his responses to these offers were recorded on an activity log. Because he was only slightly taller than the hitching post, his arms were above shoulder height and grew tired from being handcuffed so high. Whenever he tried moving his arms to improve his circulation, the handcuffs cut into his wrists, causing pain and discomfort. . . .

[T]he hitching post is a horizontal bar "made of sturdy, nonflexible material," placed between 45 and 57 inches from the ground. Inmates are handcuffed to the hitching post in a standing position and remain standing the entire time they are placed on the post. Most inmates are shackled to the hitching post with their two hands relatively close together and at face level.

On June 7, 1995, Hope was punished more severely. He took a nap during the morning bus ride to the chain gang's worksite, and when it arrived he was less than prompt in responding to an order to get off the bus. An exchange of vulgar remarks led to a wrestling match with a guard. Four other guards intervened, subdued Hope, handcuffed him, placed him in leg irons and transported him back to the prison where he was put on the hitching post. The guards made him take off his shirt, and he remained shirtless all day while the sun burned his skin. He remained attached to the post for approximately seven hours. During this 7-hour period, he was given water only once or twice and was given no bathroom breaks. At one point, a guard taunted Hope about his thirst. According to Hope's affidavit: "[The guard] first gave water to some dogs, then brought the water cooler closer to me, removed its lid, and kicked the cooler over, spilling the water onto the ground."

The use of the hitching post as alleged by Hope "unnecessarily and wantonly inflicted pain," and thus was a clear violation of the Eighth Amendment. . . . The obvious cruelty inherent in this practice should have provided respondents with some notice that their alleged conduct violated Hope's constitutional protection against cruel and unusual punishment. Hope was treated in a way antithetical to human dignity—he was hitched to a post for an extended period of time in a position that was painful, and under circumstances that were both degrading and dangerous. This wanton treatment was not done of necessity, but as punishment for prior conduct. . . . [T]he use of the hitching post under the circumstances alleged by Hope was unlawful.

Americans with Disabilities Act (ADA)

In the U.S. Supreme Court's continuing interpretation of the cruel and unusual punishment prohibition, it is clear that although inmates are not entitled to luxury, they are entitled to reasonable accommodations for their health and safety. In *Pennsylvania Department of Corrections v. Yeskey*, in a case brought by a state inmate, the Court held that Title II of the ADA applies to state prisons. Title II provides that "no qualified individual with a disability" may be denied the "benefits of the services, programs, or activities of a public entity," and according to the U.S. Supreme Court, state prisons "fall squarely within the statutory definition of 'public entity.'"[134]

The ADA also applies to incarcerated juveniles. In May and June 2004, the DOJ entered into settlement agreements with the Maryland Department of Juvenile Services, Youth Services International Inc., Correctional Services Corporation in Sarasota, Florida, and the District of Columbia Department of Corrections. As a result, juvenile and adult correctional facilities in these and all other jurisdictions are required to supply hearing aids and interpreters for hearing-impaired inmates so they can participate in educational and other programs within their facilities. Staff must be trained in ADA requirements, and inmates must be evaluated for their needs under the ADA. Visual alarms, text telephones, volume controls, and other devices to assist the hearing impaired may also be required.[135]

The ADA also applies to mentally challenged inmates. In 2003, a federal appeals court upheld the decision of an Oregon district judge who ruled that the rights of that state's mentally ill inmates were violated when they were kept in county jails for long periods before being transferred to the state hospital, the only place psychiatric care was provided for them.[136]

In 2007, the Florida legislature approved an emergency expenditure of almost $19 million to provide 373 additional psychiatric beds for mentally challenged inmates along with programs to support those inmates. The state approved moving mentally challenged inmates from county jails to these special facilities. This measure came after a state judge fined the former secretary of the Department of Children and Families $80,000 for holding mentally challenged inmates for too long in jails before transferring them to prisons, where they could receive treatment.[137]

A lawsuit filed by a nonprofit advocacy organization, Disability Advocates Inc., regarding the treatment of mentally challenged inmates in New York was settled. It resulted in changes such as the 2009 opening of what is billed as a first-in-the-nation facility for mentally ill inmates. The 100-bed Residential Mental Health Unit was opened at Marcy Correctional Facility in Oneida County, New York, in December 2009. The facility "will provide mental health and correctional rehabilitative services in a state-of-the-art correctional residential setting by affording participants the opportunity to develop skills that address their individual needs."[138]

General Health Issues

In addition to mental health issues, inmates have brought successful lawsuits with regard to general medical care. As a result, in 2006, California began an overhaul of its medical system, with the court-appointed receiver's first report to the court describing the pharmacy system as a "logistical train wreck." The overall medical system was found to be much worse than anticipated. It was described by the receiver in these words:

> Almost every necessary element of a working medical care system either does not exist, or functions in a state of abject disrepair, including but not limited to the following: medical records, pharmacy, information technology, peer review, training, chronic disease care and specialty services.[139]

The receiver began with the medical system in San Quentin, a system he described as "too troubled, too decrepit and too overcrowded for fixing." Nevertheless, "improvements with the delivering of medical care should be achieved through a carefully planned, timely and limited project."[140]

In September 2007, the receiver reported that at least 16 and possibly 66 inmate deaths in California prisons in 2006 were preventable, citing asthma as the number one cause of death. "These tragic deaths depict the very problem that the court ordered the state to solve years ago, and that the receiver must now take on." The receiver stated that it would take between five and ten years to bring the California system into constitutional compliance and perhaps that much longer to turn the system back over to the state. "It is clear that every aspect of the system contributes to its current problems and each area must be addressed."[141]

The receiver warned the California governor's cabinet that he intended to carry out his mission as provided by the court that appointed him the medical "czar" of the state with these stern words: "Every one of you is subject to being in contempt of court if you thwart my efforts or impede my progress." Apparently, the monitor was too dogmatic, however, and the federal judge removed him in January 2008.[142]

J. Clark Kelso was appointed as the new receiver. When the state asked to have him removed, the Ninth Circuit Court of Appeals in May 2010 upheld the lower federal court's refusal to dismiss him, upheld his plans for constructing new medical facilities, and refused to agree with the state's allegations that Kelso was spending too much money. Kelso and the state legislature and the governor battled over the state's budget for prison health care, all looking for cost-saving measures. The state spends more than $2 billion a year on inmate health care, and over one-fourth of that is for specialty health care, with 1,175 of those inmates accounting for $185 million a year. The cost for medical care for the last year of one inmate's life was $1 million. More attention is given to the California legal issues in Chapter 15.[143]

Among other problems with California's correctional medical system, a recent state audit revealed that at least $13 million in medications were wasted in 2009 because of inadequate record-keeping procedures or the fact that drugs were lost when inmates were transferred from one prison to another.[144]

A special focus of health care concerns issues regarding the health care needs of female inmates. In the mid-1990s, female inmates in the District of Columbia won legal concessions concerning such needs. A court held that using physical restraints on female inmates during the third trimester of pregnancy constituted cruel and unusual punishment. The court issued numerous orders concerning requirements for the health care needs of female inmates.[145]

More recently, female inmates in California won a stipulated agreement from correctional officials after filing a lawsuit concerning their special health care needs.[146] California also has several statutes designed to aid inmates during their pregnancies. First, the Pregnant and Parenting Women's Alternative Sentencing Program Act contains sentencing alternatives to prison for convicted pregnant women, provided they have not been convicted of violent or other serious acts, such as burglary.[147]

The California penal code contains a provision that pregnant inmates may receive the services of a physician of their choice to determine whether they are pregnant. For the examination, the warden must adopt "reasonable rules and regulations with regard to the conduct of examinations to effectuate this determination." If the inmate is pregnant, she is entitled to a determination of the services she needs to maintain her health and that of her fetus and to her choice of physicians for prenatal care. The inmate must pay for any services by a physician who is not provided by the institution. These provisions of the state statute must be posted in a place available to all female inmates.[148] Pregnant inmates must be provided adequate prenatal care, including a nutritious diet, a dental cleaning, necessary vitamins as recommended by a doctor, and education on childbirth and infant care.[149]

When a California inmate is transported to the hospital to give birth to her child, she must be taken in the "least restrictive way possible, consistent with the legitimate security needs of each inmate." Once the inmate is, in the judgment of the attending physician, in active labor, she "shall not be shackled by the wrists, ankles, or both, unless deemed necessary for the safety and security of the inmate, the staff, and the public."[150]

Most states do permit the shackling of pregnant inmates. Jurisdictions that retain such policies are being challenged. In 2009, the Eighth Circuit Court of Appeals decided *Nelson v. Correctional Medical Services*, the case of Shawanna Nelson, a 29-year-old nonviolent offender who was six months pregnant with her second child when she was incarcerated. When Nelson went into labor she was taken by Officer Patricia Turensky to a contracting civilian hospital. Nelson had difficulty walking to the van, had to stop twice, and said she was in too much pain to walk. Nelson was handcuffed, and when she and Turensky arrived at the hospital, Turensky shackled Nelson's legs to a wheelchair. After Nelson was in the bed, her ankles were shackled to opposite sides of the bed. "According to Nelson's testimony, the shackles prevented her from moving her legs, stretching, or changing positions." The attending nurse said she wished the shackles were not necessary. Nobody on the hospital staff asked for the restraints, and each time the nurse had to measure Nelson's dilation, she had to ask Turensky to remove the shackles. Apparently, before Nelson was taken to the delivery room, the doctor was successful in his request that the shackles be removed. At no time was there any evidence that Nelson was a flight risk. Her baby was born within minutes after she arrived in the delivery room. Nelson presented evidence "that the shackling caused her extreme mental anguish and pain, permanent hip injury, torn stomach muscles, and an umbilical hernia requiring surgical repair. She has also alleged damage to her sciatic nerve." Her orthopedist stated that as a result of the shackling, Nelson's hips were deformed. Nelson alleged that she cannot play with her children and has been advised not to have more children because of her injuries. "She is unable to sleep or bear weight on her left side or to sit or stand for extended periods."[151]

Nelson sued Officer Turensky and the director of the state's Department of Corrections, alleging that the officer failed to follow proper prison policies that required her to "balance any security concern against the medical needs of the patient." She alleged that the director "failed to ensure that appropriate policies for the treatment of pregnant inmates were implemented." The Eighth Circuit held that Nelson could sue Turensky but that the state's prison director had qualified immunity. The court cited the 2002 case of *Hope v. Pelzer*, excerpted earlier in this chapter, concerning hitching posts. In that case, the U.S. Supreme

Court held that although qualified immunity may protect government officials from liability under federal statutes, that is not the case if their conduct violated "clearly established statutory or constitutional rights of which a reasonable person would have known." The *Nelson* case involved a request for summary judgment on the basis of a qualified immunity. The Eighth Circuit held that Nelson should be permitted to bring her suit against Officer Turensky, a female correctional officer, but not against Director Norris of the Arkansas Department of Correction. To prevail at her trial, Nelson had to prove damages and that the treatment constituted cruel and unusual punishment in violation of her Eighth Amendment rights. She won, but the jury awarded her only the minimum, $1, in damages. The judge ruled that she was entitled to attorney fees as the prevailing party. However, the Prison Litigation Reform Act of 1966, discussed later, limits attorney fee awards to 150 percent of the plaintiff's damage award. The judge awarded the four attorneys $1.50, but she did award them reimbursement for expenses.[152]

In March 2010 (effective 10 June 2010), Washington State's governor signed into law a bill prohibiting restraints on female inmates who are in labor or postpartum recovery and limiting restraints during the third trimester of pregnancy. Restraints may be used in "extraordinary circumstances" (defined as the inmate's possible escape or endangerment of the inmate to herself, medical personnel, or other persons). In those cases, medical personnel must state in writing the reasons for the restraints and the type of restraints, which must be the least restrictive available.[153]

Analysis of Inmates' Legal Rights

In 1977, in *Bounds v. Smith*, the U.S. Supreme Court held that inmates have a right of access to courts, but the Court did not articulate the details of what that means. In 1996, the Court held that to file a claim under *Bounds v. Smith*, an inmate must show actual injury.[154]

Concern over frivolous lawsuits filed by inmates led Congress to pass a bill, the Prison Litigation Reform Act (PLRA), which was signed by President Bill Clinton in 1996 and revised portions of the Violent Crime Control and Law Enforcement Act of 1994 and other statutes. The PLRA places numerous restraints on inmate filings and has led to considerable litigation and criticism. One federal court alleged that the act had caused so much confusion that it could be concluded that when "Congress penned the Prison Litigation Reform Act . . . the watchdog must have been dead."[155]

What has been the result of recognizing inmates' legal rights? Clearly, there have been improvements in living conditions and changes in many prison rules and regulations. Prison systems have been forced into changes that should have occurred without the necessity of legal intervention. Those who complain about judicial intervention and allege that judges are making law might heed the words of Judge William Wayne Justice, speaking about his role in a Texas prison case. Admitting that his actions constituted judicial activism ("I was not a potted plant"), Judge Justice emphasized that the requirement to be an impartial judge does not mean a judge must be inactive. The judge's job is to "get the right answer" in each case. The judge continued:

> Due process of law does not require that all those who feel aggrieved be able to get what they want from a court. But it does require that when such a person comes to court with a potentially cognizable claim, he be given a chance to say what he wants.... The right to be heard, whether one's conditions be exalted or lowly, is a right the courts have a duty to vindicate.[156]

Recognition of inmates' rights has been opposed by some correctional officers and other prison officials who claim that it makes their jobs of maintaining security more difficult. Citizens have resented the costs involved. We are left with the basic problem of the conflict that exists between recognizing inmates' constitutional rights while giving prison officials the latitude they need to maintain security within the prison and protect society. Congress and state legislatures will continue to try to curb some rights; courts will continue to assess whether they go too far in doing so.

We are also left wondering what the full ramifications are of inmates' rights to access the courts. Thus far, they have not been granted the right to have the assistance of licensed attorneys, but the courts have recognized the services of jailhouse lawyers. These are inmates who assist other inmates in filing legal actions. Some of these jailhouse lawyers are excellent, as Media Focus 14.2 illustrates.

Many other issues with regard to prisons and jails could be noted, but clearly, some of the most important concern preparing inmates for their release and return to society, the focus of Chapter 15.

MEDIA FOCUS

14.2 Jailhouse Lawyers: The Death of the Greatest of Them All

In 2009, when Jerry Rosenberg died, major newspapers from all over the world carried his obituary. Rosenberg was the longest serving inmate in the New York system, having served 42 years when he died at age 72. Rosenberg was serving life for the murder of two police officers in the first double homicide of police in 35 years in that state. He and a friend were sentenced to death, but when he was only hours away from execution in 1965, the state's governor commuted the sentences to life in prison. Rosenberg maintained his innocence and fought for release. In the process, he earned two law degrees by correspondence, becoming the first inmate in New York history to do so. During his law studies, he took exams in 77 subjects and earned all As in such subjects as criminal procedure and constitutional law. He could not be admitted to the bar, but a brief he filed on behalf of another inmate, Carmine Galante, was influential in the decision of the U.S. Supreme Court to order Galante's release.

Rosenberg was one of the negotiators for the inmates during the Attica riots in September 1971, which resulted in the deaths of 11 prison employees and 32 inmates. When law enforcement officials stormed the prison, Rosenberg was shot in the knee and beaten. After the uprising ended, he was transferred to Sing Sing and put in charge of the law library.

Rosenberg's goals were to be released from prison and to be admitted to the bar. ("I've been making precedent all my life.") He did not achieve either despite the canny argument he made in his own defense: His heart stopped beating during surgery; thus, he had completed his life sentence.

Stephen Bello wrote a biography of Rosenberg, *Doing Life: The Extraordinary Saga of America's Greatest Jailhouse Lawyer*. The book was published in 1982 by St. Martin's Press. This book led to a television movie in 1986 starring Tony Danza.

Rosenberg was quoted as saying that anyone who plans to become a lawyer should "do some time in jail." He earned the respect of legal scholars and judges. One judge told Rosenberg's parents, "If your son had taken a different path in life . . . he might have become one of the greatest attorneys that ever lived."

Rosenberg was a problem child who was dismissed from Hebrew school when he was 7. He cut classes in his next school and spent most of his days on the rides at Coney Island. He was picked up by the police when he was 9, dropped out of school completely when he was 10, and was operating a racket by the time he was 12. He had a long arrest record as a teen, claimed he was beaten by police, and declared that he hated "everything that wears a badge—including the postman."

He joined the Army in 1956 but was given a dishonorable discharge 90 days later. He was sentenced to four years for robbery, and during that incarceration, he earned his high school equivalency degree. Famed defense attorney William Kunstler called Rosenberg "a very shrewd guy."

Source: Summarized from the following media sources: "Jerry Rosenberg: Inmate Became Noted Jailhouse Lawyer," *Boston Globe* (5 June 2009), p. 12; "Jerry Rosenberg, 72, Jailhouse Lawyer," *New York Times* (2 June 2009), p. 19; "Obituary of Jerry Rosenberg, Killer Who Escaped the Electric Chair by Hours to Become America's Most Successful 'Jailhouse Attorney,'" *Daily Telegraph* (London) (16 June 2009), p. 27.

Summary

This chapter focused on prisons and jails as institutions for confining offenders. Both European and American developments contributing to this evolution were discussed, followed by a look at the types of institutions for confining adults. Of particular importance today is the crush of numbers in these facilities. Overcrowding—its extent, its effects, its legal implications, and its potential solutions—was examined in general and in the context of two large states: California and New York. Jails and prisons were distinguished, and particular attention was given to supermax prisons. Privatization of prisons and jails was presented and analyzed.

The chapter examined the world of the prison inmate, beginning with the process of socialization in the prison subculture. The issue of whether inmates bring that subculture from the outside or whether it evolves as inmates attempt to adapt to the pains of imprisonment was analyzed.

Problems that have been created primarily by the increase in female inmates were noted. The question of what to do with the children who are abandoned while their mothers are in jails or prisons was raised. Along with the unique problems of female inmates, the chapter looked at those of elderly, physically challenged, and mentally challenged inmates before turning to the problems that occur when juveniles are incarcerated, especially when they are housed in adult prisons and jails.

Violence in prisons and jails is an aspect of prison life that receives considerable attention when riots occur, but little attention is given to the internal violence of inmates against each other or against themselves. The discussion of sexual attacks noted that this type of violence is common among male inmates. An account of the historical background of riots and the details and causes of more recent riots, followed by a brief discussion of escaping inmates, completed the discussion of violence.

Violence within prisons increases security and control problems. How are inmates controlled? Correctional officers cannot rely on former methods of control through the use of inmates who, for certain favors, would cooperate with officers in maintaining internal control. An overview of inmates' legal rights looked at those rights in general, and efforts to curb inmate lawsuits were noted.

It is important to recognize that the modern prison is an institution in transition. Prison populations have soared while budgets have been reduced, although some states have added sufficient prison and jail beds to create a surplus.

Prison administrators and correctional officers feel frustrated with their lack of control over prison populations. Other agencies determine how many inmates are sent to prison and when they are released. Many techniques used to accommodate large numbers of inmates are being challenged in the courts, and in some cases, they have been declared unacceptable. Overcrowding is a serious problem for which there are no easy and acceptable solutions.

Society has not yet made the choices that will be necessary to resolve the problems. Do we want prisons only to punish? Or do we want prisons to educate and train offenders to aid their reintegration into society? Are we going to continue to ignore the problems in prisons until riots, with their extensive destruction of property and human life, force us to look at our institutions? Are we willing to acknowledge that, as a society, we must punish criminals but must do so in a way that does not wreak havoc on society and on the inmates when they are released? Do we want to live in constant fear that our next-door neighbor or the person down the block is an ex-convict and that this offender's treatment in prison was so harsh that his or her cynicism and resentment are worse now than before imprisonment? Are we willing to decide to fund correctional systems that will give us back men and women who are less dangerous and better equipped to manage in the free world? It appears that "we must resign ourselves to spending more money on the people we hate most, or find creative, alternative ways to punish criminals who are not so dangerous that they have to be caged with their heads against toilets."[157]

Study Questions

1. What is meant by the phrase "the emergence of prisons as punishment"?

2. Identify John Howard, and note briefly his contributions to the history of prisons.

3. Describe and evaluate the Pennsylvania prison system, noting the place of the Walnut Street Jail and Cherry Hill Prison in that system.

4. Describe and evaluate the Auburn system.

5. Discuss the evolution of the reformatory system.

6. Evaluate early prison reform.

7. Distinguish among lockups, jails, and prisons.

8. Describe correctional populations. What accounts for the increase in recent years?

9. Evaluate early jails as a replacement for corporal punishment.

10. Describe briefly the administration and staffing of jails.

11. List and distinguish among prison security levels.

12. What are the effects of prison overcrowding?

13. Explain and evaluate privatization of prisons and jails.

14. Define *prisonization*, and discuss its impact on inmates' adjustment to prison life.

15. Contrast the deprivation, importation, and integrative models of adaptation to prison life.

16. Describe the problems resulting from the increase of female prison inmates.

17. What are the issues with regard to elderly, physically challenged, and mentally challenged inmates?

18. Should juveniles in adult facilities be given special attention?

19. Evaluate the causes of inmate deaths.

20. Describe briefly the problems corrections officers face in maintaining control within prisons.

21. Analyze the hands-off doctrine in prison settings.

22. Explain the major problems that exist in today's prisons with regard to health issues.

Brief Essay Assignments

1. Discuss the relationship between corporal punishment and imprisonment historically and in terms of the development of modern U.S. prison systems.

2. Evaluate the impact of the Auburn and Pennsylvania prison systems on modern U.S. prisons.

3. Compare early prison expansion with prison overcrowding today, especially with regard to the California and New York correctional systems.

4. Discuss prison violence from a historical point of view.

5. Evaluate recent congressional and U.S. Supreme Court efforts regarding prison litigation.

Internet Activities

1. Go to The Sentencing Project's website, http://www.sentenc ingproject.org/doc/publications/inc_prisonprivatization.pdf, and read the article, "Prison Privatization and the Use of Incarceration." What information does it contain about the cost and efficiency of private prisons? What policy issues are discussed? Also go to the Corrections Corporation of America (CCA) website, http://www.correctionscorp.com. The CCA is one of the many private businesses that operate prisons. What can you learn from this source about private prisons? Do you think prison privatization is a potential solution for jail and prison overcrowding? Why or why not? (sites accessed 14 November 2010).

2. Visit the website of the Center for AIDS Prevention Studies, http://www.caps.ucsf.edu. Under "Browse by," select the Prison link. What is the relationship between AIDS and other diseases in prison? What should the role of criminal law be with regard to the transmission of AIDS? (Site accessed 14 November 2010).

Notes

1. For a history of the development of prisons, see Harry Elmer Barnes, *The Story of Punishment: A Record of Man's Inhumanity to Man*, 2d rev. ed. (Montclair, NJ: Patterson Smith, 1972; originally published 1930). For a more recent, brief analysis, see Marilyn D. McShane, *Prisons in America* (New York: LFB Scholarly Publishing, 2008), pp. 19–56.

2. See Alexis M. Durham III, "Newgate of Connecticut: Origins and Early Days of an Early American Prison," *Justice Quarterly* 6 (March 1989): 89–116.

3. Karl Menninger, *The Crime of Punishment* (New York: Viking, 1968), p. 222.

4. Howard Gill, "State Prisons in America, 1787–1937," in *Penology*, ed. George C. Killinger and Paul F. Cromwell (St. Paul, MN: West, 1973), p. 53.

5. See Richard Quinney, *Criminology*, 2d ed. (Boston: Little, Brown, 1979).

6. See the discussion by Alexander W. Pisciotta, "Scientific Reform: The 'New Penology' at Elmira, 1876–1900," *Crime and Delinquency* 29 (October 1983): 613–630; quotation is on p. 613. But see also Pisciotta, *Benevolent Repressing* (New York: New York University Press, 1994), questioning the alleged humanitarian reforms of Elmira and other reformatories.

7. Pisciotta, "Scientific Reform," p. 626.

8. McShane, *Prisons in America*, Preface, p. xi.

9. Heather C. West and William J. Sabol, Bureau of Justice Statistics, *Prisoners in 2009* (December 2010), pp. 1, 2, 9, http://bjs.usdoj .gov/content/pub/pdf/p09.pdf, accessed 24 December 2010 and the source for the 2009 data on state and federal prison inmates included in this section.

10. Todd D. Minton, Bureau of Justice Statistics, "Jail Inmates at Midyear 2009—Statistical Tables," Bureau of Justice Statistics (June 2010), pp. 1, 9, 10. http://bjs.ojp.usdoj.gov/content/pub/pdf/ jim09st.pdf, accessed 11 November 2010.

11. Executive Summary, *Meeting the Challenges of Rehabilitation in California's Prison and Parole System: A Report from Governor Schwarzenegger's Rehabilitation Strike Team* (hereafter referred to as *Meeting the Challenges*). This report was chaired by Joan Petersilia and published in December 2007. It can be found online at http://www.cdcr.ca.gov/News/docs/GovRehabilitationStrikeTeam-Rpt_012308.pdf, accessed 11 November 2010.

12. "California Officials Agree on Prison Expansion Plan," *Criminal Justice Newsletter* (1 May 2007), p. 8; "California to Address Prison Overcrowding with Giant Building Program," *New York Times* (27 April 2007), p. 16.

13. "New Court to Address California Prison Crowding," *New York Times* (24 July 2007), p. 16; "Schwarzenegger's Stand on Inmates Rejected," *San Francisco Chronicle* (12 September 2007), p. 5B.

14. *Coleman v. Schwarzenegger*, 2009 U.S. Dist. LEXIS 67943 (E.D. Cal. 2009), footnotes and citations omitted, *stay denied, Schwarzenegger v. Coleman*, 130 S.Ct. 46 (2009).

15. Americans with Disabilities Act, USCS Title 42, Sections 12101–12213 (2010).

16. *Plata v. Schwarzenegger*, 603 F.3d 1088 (9th Cir. 30 April 2010). This case was one of four pending class actions concerning the provision of constitutionally inadequate medical care in California state prisons. The other three are *Coleman v. Schwarzenegger*, 2010 U.S. Dist. LEXIS 49510 (E.D.Cal. 14 April 2010) (mental health care, especially suicide issues); *Perez v. Cate*, 2009 U.S. Dist. LEXIS 18949 (N.D. Cal. 23 Feb. 2009) (dental care); *Armstrong v. Schwarzenegger*, 2009 U.S. Dist. LEXIS 91494 (N.D. Cal. 2009) (compliance with the Americans with Disabilities Act).

17. "State Lawmakers Move to Repeal Early-Release Law," *Los Angeles Times*, Home Edition (30 April 2010), p. 3; "Court Supports Prison Receiver," *Los Angeles Times* (1 May 2010), p. 4; "Justice Kennedy on Prisons," *New York Times*, Late Edition (16 February 2010), p. 26; "State's Prison Population Falls," *Los Angeles Times*, Home Edition (17 March 2010), p. 3; "California Loses Fight to End Prison Oversight," *San Jose Mercury News* (California) (30 April 2010), n.p.; "Driven to the Financial Brink, a State Opens the Prison Doors," *New York Times* (24 March 2010), p. 1.

18. "The High Cost of Empty Prisons," *New York Times*, Late Edition (12 October 2009), p. 23.

19. New York Department of Correctional Services Fact Sheets, http://www.docs.state.ny.us/FactSheets/index.html, accessed 11 November 2010.

20. West and Sabol, Bureau of Justice Statistics, *Prisoners in 2009*.

21. Adam Gelb, "Testimony on the Hill," (11 May 2010), Pew Center on the States, http://www.pewcenteronthestates.org/news_room_detail.aspx?id=58882, accessed 11 November 2010.

22. "Thinking Outside the Cell," *Daily News* (New York) (21 March 2010), p. 31.

23. *Ruiz v. Estelle*, 503 F.Supp. 1265 (S.D. Texas, 1980), *aff'd. in part, vacated in part, modified, in part, appeal dismissed in part*, 679 F.2d 1115 (5th Cir. 1983), *cert. denied*, 460 U.S. 1042 (1982).

24. Edith Elisabeth Flynn, "Jails and Criminal Justice," in *Prisoners in America*, ed. Lloyd E. Ohlin (Englewood Cliffs, NJ: Prentice Hall, 1973), p. 49.

25. Joseph F. Fishman, *Crucible of Crime: The Shocking Story of the American Jail* (New York: Cosmopolis, 1923), pp. 13–14.

26. National Commission on law Observance and Enforcement, *Report on Pena Institutions, Probation, and Parole* (Washington, D.C.: U.S. Government printing office, 1931, p. 273.

27. Daniel Fogel, quoted in "The Scandalous U.S. Jails," *Newsweek* (18 August 1980), p. 74.

28. Norman Carlson, quoted in "Crises and Cutbacks Stir Fresh Concerns on Nation's Prisons," *New York Times* (5 January 1982), p. 10B.

29. "Guards Told to Work 2 Extra Shifts a Week," *Dallas Morning News* (21 May 2010), p. 1B.

30. "ACLU Releases Expert's Report on Nightmarish Conditions at Men's Central Jail in Los Angeles" American Civil Liberties Union (14 April 2009), http://www.aclu.org/prison/, accessed 16 November 2010.

31. "$74M Jail Has It All Except Inmates," *Los Angeles Times* (24 June 2010), p. 12.

32. "Sweeping Deal to Improve Jail; Reforms to Address Decades of Woes Include Hiring 600 More Guards," *Chicago Sun Times* (14 May 2010), p. 11.

33. *Wilkinson v. Austin*, 545 U.S. 209 (2005).

34. Bruce Finley, "Supermax Too Full for Guantánamo Detainees," *Denver Post* (22 Mayy 2009), n.p.

35. Chad S. Briggs et al., "The Effect of Supermaximum Security Prisons on Aggregate Levels of Institutional Violence," *Criminology* 41, no. 4 (November 2003): 1341–1376, quotation is on p. 1341.

36. "New Prisons Reflect Society," *Orlando Sentinel* (Florida) (2 August 1998), p. 8.

37. *Wilkinson v. Austin*, 545 U.S. 209 (2005).

38. Daniel P. Mears and Jamie Watson, "Towards a Fair and Balanced Assessment of Supermax Prisons," *Justice Quarterly* 23, no. 2 (June 2006): 232–270; quotation is on p. 266.

39. Daniel P. Mears and William D. Bales, "Supermax Incarceration and Recidivism," *Criminology* 47, no. 4 (November 2009): 1131–1166; quotation is on p. 1154.

40. Federal Bureau of Prisons, "About the Bureau of Prisons," http://www.bop.gov/about/index.jsp, accessed 11 November 2010.

41. "Congress OKs Inmate Fees to Offset Costs of Prison," *Criminal Justice Newsletter* 23 (15 October 1992): 6. See *United States v. Sellers*, 42 F.3d 116 (2d Cir. 1994), *cert. denied*, 516 U.S. 826 (1995), referring to Section 5E1.2(a) of the federal sentencing guidelines.

42. Corrections Corporation of America, http://www.correctionscorp.com, accessed 11 November 2010.

43. "CCA Management Commended," *Corrections Professional* 12, no. 9 (26 January 2007): n.p.

44. "Colorado Inmates Go to Oklahoma," *Corrections Professional* 12, no. 9 (12 January 2007): n.p.

45. West and Sabol, Bureau of Justice Statistics, *Prisoners in 2009*, p. 9.

46. "Colorado Fines Private Prisons $131,000 for Staffing Shortages," *Corrections Professional* 12, no. 7 (15 December 2006): n.p.

47. "Riots Plague Prisons Housing Hawaiians," *Corrections Professional* 11, no. 5 (28 October 2005): n.p.

48. "Are the Savings There? Report Grades Florida's Privatized Prisons," *Tallahassee Democrat* (Florida) (19 April 2010), p. 9; William D. Bales, "Recidivism of Public and Private State Prison Inmates in Florida," *Criminology and Public Policy* 4, no. 1 (February 2005): 57–82.

49. Gerald Gaes, "Prison Privatization in Florida: Promise, Premise, and Performance," *Criminology and Public Policy* 4, no. 1 (February 2005): 83–88; quotation is on p. 83.

50. Charles W. Thomas, "Recidivism of Public and Private State Prison Inmates in Florida: Issues and Unanswered Questions," *Criminology and Public Policy* 4, no. 1 (February 2005): 89–100; quotation is on p. 97.

51. "The Sheriff Takes Over in August: But There's a Lot to Do to Ease the Transition from CCA," *St. Petersburg Times* (Florida) (23 May 2010), p. 1.

52. John Rynne et al., "Market Testing and Prison Riots: How Public-Sector Commercialization Contributed to a Prison Riot," *Criminology and Public Policy* 7, no. 1 (February 2008): 117–142; quotation is on p. 135.

53. Daniel P. Mears, "Accountability, Efficiency, and Effectiveness in Corrections: Shining a Light on the Black Box of Prison Systems," *Criminology and Public Policy* 7, no. 1 (February 2008): 143–152; quotations are on pp. 144 and 150.

54. "State Boycott of Arizona a Risky Move: Protest of Immigration Law Could Harm California Firms," *San Francisco Chronicle* (1 May 2010), p. 1.

55. Gresham M. Sykes, *The Society of Captives* (Princeton, NJ: Princeton University Press, 1958), pp. 63–83.

56. Donald Clemmer, *The Prison Community*, 1940 reprint ed. (New York: Holt, Rinehart & Winston, 1958), pp. 298–301.

57. Stanton Wheeler, "Socialization in Correctional Communities," *American Sociological Review* 26 (October 1961): 697–712.

58. See, for example, Peter G. Garabedian, "Social Roles and Processes of Socialization in the Prison Community," *Social Problems* 11 (Fall 1963): 139–152; Daniel Glaser, *The Effectiveness of a Prison and Parole System*, abridged ed. (Indianapolis, IN: Bobbs-Merrill, 1969).

59. Geoffrey P. Alpert et al., "A Comparative Look at Prisonization: Sex and Prison Culture," *Quarterly Journal of Corrections* 1 (Summer 1977): 29–34.

60. Gresham M. Sykes and Sheldon L. Messinger, "The Inmate Social System," in *Theoretical Studies in Social Organization of the Prison*, ed. Richard A. Cloward et al. (New York: Social Science Research Council, 1960), p. 17.

61. John Irwin and Donald R. Cressey, "Thieves, Convicts and the Inmate Culture," *Social Problems* 19 (Fall 1962): 142–155. For a discussion of the impact that traditional roles of women in our society have on the inmate culture, see Rose Giallombardo, *Society of Women: A Study of a Woman's Prison* (New York: Wiley, 1966).

62. Charles W. Thomas, "Prisonization or Resocialization: A Study of External Factors Associated with the Impact of Imprisonment," *Journal of Research in Crime and Delinquency* 10 (January 1975): 13–21.

63. Leo Carroll, "Race and Three Forms of Prisoner Power: Confrontation, Censoriousness, and the Corruption of Authority," in *Contemporary Corrections: Social Control and Conflict*, ed. C. Ronald Huff (Beverly Hills, CA: Sage, 1977), p. 40. See also Leo Carroll, *Hacks, Blacks, and Cons: Race Relations in a Maximum-Security Prison* (Lexington, MA: D. C. Heath, 1974).

64. Ronald L. Akers et al., "Prisonization in Five Countries: Type of Prison and Inmate Characteristics," *Criminology* 14 (February 1977): 538.

65. Charles W. Thomas, quoted in Akers et al., "Prisonization in Five Countries," p. 548.

66. See Keith Farrington, "The Modern Prison as Total Institution? Public Perception Versus Objective Reality," *Crime and Delinquency* 38 (January 1992): 6–26, rejecting the view that prisons are total institutions, a view developed earlier by Erving Goffman, *Asylums: Essays on the Social Situation of Mental Patients and Other Inmates* (Garden City, NY: Anchor, 1961).

67. Richard C. McCorkle et al., "The Roots of Prison Violence: A Test of the Deprivation, Management, and 'Not-So-Total' Institution Models," *Crime and Delinquency* 41 (July 1995): 317–331; quotations are on pp. 326–329.

68. The Sentencing Project, http://www.sentencingproject.org, accessed 11 November 2010.

69. The Sentencing Project, *Women in the Criminal Justice System* (May 2007), http://www.sentencingproject.org/doc/publications/womenincj_total.pdf, accessed 11 November 2010.

70. "Bids Sought for Private Prison," *Corrections Professional* 11, no. 11 (24 February 2006): n.p.

71. "Prison Trend Defies Times: Colorado's Inmate Numbers Are Projected to Fall," *Denver Post* (30 March 2010), p. 1.

72. "National Study Examines Rise in Female Inmate Populations," *Corrections Professional* 11, no. 18 (23 June 2006), n.p.

73. The Sentencing Project, "Women in the Criminal Justice System." See also Lauren E. Glaze and Laura M. Maruschak, Bureau of Justice Statistics, *Parents in Prison and Their Minor Children* (August 2008, last revised, 30 March 2010), http://bjs.ojp.usdoj.gov/content/pub/pdf/pptmc.pdf, accessed 11 November 2010.

74. "Having Summer Camp Behind a Prison's Fence," *New York Times* (22 August 2007), p. 19.

75. "Family Ties in Prison," *Courier-Journal* (Louisville, KY) (11 July 2009), p. 1.

76. "Fathers in Angola Get to Spend a Precious Day with Their Children," *Times-Picayune* (New Orleans) (10 September 2006), p. 1.

77. See, for example, *Johnson v. Phelan*, 69 F.3d 144 (7th Cir. 1995), *cert. denied*, 519 U.S. 1006 (1996).

78. Paige M. Harrison and Allen J. Beck, Bureau of Justice Statistics, *Prisoners in 2003* (November 2004), p. 8, http://bjs.ojp.gov/content/pub/pdf/p03.pdf, accessed 12 November 2010.

79. Jamie Shimkus, National Commission on Correctional Health Care, "The Graying of America's Prisons," http://www.ncchc.org/pubs/CC/aging_inmates.html, accessed 11 November 2010.

80. Fla. Stat. Ann., Chapter 944.8041 (2010).

81. "Measure Would Allow Some Older Inmates Out of Prison," *Gainesville Sun* (Florida), http://www.gainesville.com/article/20100323/ARTICLES/100329778, accessed 12 November 2010; "Elderly Inmates Costing Taxpayers Millions," WFTV Orlando (Florida), n.p. (18 November 2009), http://www.wftv.com/news/2165595/detail.html, n.p., accessed 12 November 2010. The bill was FL. S.B. 484 (2010).

82. "Law Has Little Impact on Compassionate Release for Ailing Inmates," *New York Times* (30 January 2010), p. 17.

83. "Spotlight July/August 2008—Prison Gray," (29 July 2008), http://www.docs.state.ny.us/NewsRoom/external_news/2008-07-09_Prison_Gray.pdf, accessed 18 June 2010.

84. "Study: U.S. Prisons Fall Short in Caring for Elderly Inmates," *Corrections Professional* 11, no. 14 (7 April 2006): n.p. See also Shimkus, "The Graying of America's Prisons."

85. *Bonner v. Lewis,* 857 F.2d 559 (9th Cir. 1988), *cert. denied sub nom.,* 498 U.S. 1074 (1991). The Americans with Disabilities Act of 1990 is Public Law 101–336, USCS, Title 42, Section 12101 et seq. (2010).

86. Laura Maruschak, "Medical Problems of Prisoners," Bureau of Justice Statistics (1 April 2008), http://bjs.ojp.usdoj.gov/index.cfm?ty=pbdetail&iid=1097, accessed 12 November 2010; Christopher J. Mumola, Bureau of Justice Statistics, *Medical Causes of Death in State Prisons, 2001–2004* (January 2007), http://bjs.ojp.usdoj.gov/content/pub/pdf/mcdsp04.pdf, accessed 12 November 2010.

87. "TB Outbreak at Vacaville Prison," *United Press International,* News Release (4 January 1996), BC Cycle.

88. "San Diego," *City News Service* (23 August 2007), p. 1.

89. For an analysis of the possibility of contracting HIV while in prison, see Christopher P. Krebs, "Inmate Factors Associated with HIV Transmission in Prison," *Criminology and Public Policy* 5, no. 1 (February 2006): 113–136, followed by two reaction essays: Kimberly R. Jacob Arriola, "Debunking the Myth of the Safe Haven: Toward a Better Understanding of Intraprison HIV Transmission," pp. 137–148; Curt G. Bechwith et al., "Addressing the HIV Epidemic Through Quality Correctional Healthcare," pp. 149–156.

90. Laura M. Maruschak, Bureau of Justice Statistics Bulletin, *HIV in Prisons, 2007–08* (December 2009, revised 28 January 2010), p. 1, http://bjs.ojp.usdoj.gov/content/pub/pdf/hivp08.pdf, accessed 12 November 2010.

91. *Inmates with HIV v. Goord,* 90 CV 252 (N.D.N.Y.), discussed by the Legal Aid Society of New York, http://www.legal-aid.org, accessed 12 November 2010.

92. Lauren E. Glaze and Doris J. James, Bureau of Justice Statistics, *Mental Health Problems of Prison and Jail Inmates* (6 September 2006), p. 1, http://bjs.ojp.usdoj.gov/index.cfm?ty=pbdetail&iid=789, accessed 12 November 2010.

93. Mentally Ill Offender Treatment and Crime Reduction Act of 2004, Public Law 108–414, 118 Stat. 2327 (2010).

94. Nadine Lanctôt et al., "Delinquent Behavior, Official Delinquency, and Gender: Consequences for Adulthood Functioning and Well-Being," *Criminology* 45, no. 1 (February 2007): 131–158; quotation is on pp. 131–132.

95. James Austin et al., Bureau of Justice Assistance, U.S. Department of Justice, *Juveniles in Adult Prisons and Jails: A National Assessment* (October 2000), p. 6, http://www.ncjrs.gov/pdffiles1/bja/182503.pdf, accessed 12 November 2010.

96. Ibid., pp. x–xi; quotation is on p. xi.

97. "Concern Rising over Use of Juvenile Prisons to 'Warehouse the Mentally Ill,'" *New York Times* (5 December 2000), p. 14.

98. "Crowding of Juvenile Facilities Is 'Pervasive,' Study Finds," *Criminal Justice Newsletter* 24 (15 April 1993): 4.

99. Dale G. Parent et al., *Conditions of Confinement: Juvenile Detention and Corrections Facilities. Research Summary* (Washington, D.C.: U.S. Department of Justice, February 1994), p. 1. This publication is a summary of the congressionally mandated study; it was prepared by Abt Associates, Inc., under a grant from the Office of Juvenile Justice and Delinquency, Office of Justice Programs, U.S. Department of Justice.

100. "8 Acquitted in Death of Boy, 14, in Florida," *New York Times* (13 October 2007), p. 8; "US Won't File Charges in Boot Camp Death," *Boston Globe* (17 April 2010), p. 2; "From Prison Yard to Coma," *St. Petersburg Times* (Florida) (27 May 2010), p. 1.

101. Bureau of Justice Statistics, Status Report, *Prison Rape Elimination Act of 2003: PREA Data Collection Activities, 2010* (June 2010), p. 2, http://bjs.ojp.usdoj.gov/content/pub/pdf/pdca10.pdf, accessed 12 November 2010.

102. Daniel S. Nagin et al., "Public Preferences for Rehabilitation Versus Incarceration of Juvenile Offenders: Evidence from a Contingent Valuation Survey," *Criminology and Public Policy* 5, no. 4 (November 2006): 627–652; in the same journal, Donna M. Bishop, "Public Opinion and Juvenile Justice Policy: Myths and Misconceptions," pp. 653–664.

103. Francis T. Cullen, "It's Time to Reaffirm Rehabilitation," *Criminology and Public Policy* 5, no. 4 (November 2006): 665–672; quotation is on p. 669.

104. Laura M. Maruschak and Allen J. Beck, Bureau of Justice Statistics, *Medical Problems of Inmates, 1997* (January 2001), http://bjs.ojp.usdoj.gov/content/pub/pdf/mpi97, accessed 12 November 2008.

105. Laura M. Maruschak, Bureau of Justice Statistics, *Medical Problems of Jail Inmates* (November 2006), pp. 4, 5, http://bjs.ojp.usdoj.gov/content/pub/pdf/mpji.pdf, accessed 12 November 2010.

106. Christopher J. Mumola, Bureau of Justice Statistics, *Suicide and Homicide in State Prisons and Local Jails* (August 2005), http://bjs.ojp.usdoj.gov/content/pub/pdf/shsplj.pdf, accessed 12 November 2010.

107. Daniel Lockwood, *Prison Sexual Violence* (New York: Elsevier, 1980), pp. 16–23.

108. Daniel Lockwood, "Reducing Prison Sexual Violence," in *The Pains of Imprisonment,* ed. Robert Johnson and Hans Toch (Beverly Hills, CA: Sage, 1982), pp. 257–265.

109. See David A. Ward and Gene G. Kassebaum, "Women in Prison," in *Correctional Institutions,* ed. Robert M. Carter et al. (Philadelphia: Lippincott, 1972), pp. 217–219.

110. See Giallombardo, *Society of Women*; David A. Ward and Gene G. Kassebaum, "Sexual Tensions in a Women's Prison," in *Crime*

and Justice: The Criminal in Confinement, ed. Leon Radzinowicz and Marvin E. Wolfgang (New York: Basic Books, 1971), pp. 146–155.

111. "Prison Vice Probe Over," *Greenville News* (South Carolina)(20 January 2003), p. 1.

112. "Hawaii to Remove Inmates over Sex Abuse Charges," *New York Times* (26 August 2009), p. 12.

113. Allen J. Beck and Paige M. Harrison, Bureau of Justice Statistics, *Sexual Victimization in Prisons and Jails Reported by Inmates, 2008–09* (26 August 2010), http://bjs.ojp.usdoj.gov/index .cfm?ty=pbdetail&iid=2312, accessed 12 November 2010.

114. Allen J. Beck et al., Bureau of Justice Statistics, *Sexual Victimization in Prisons and Jails Reported by Inmates, 2008–09* (August 2010), p. 5, http://bjs.usdoj.gov/content/pub/pdf/svpjri0809 .pdf, accessed 12 November 2010.

115. "Transgender Inmates Vulnerable to Sexual Assaults, Study Finds," *Criminal Justice Newsletter* (15 June 2007), p. 4, reporting on a study by the Center for Evidence-Based Corrections at the University of California, Irvine.

116. Mark Hansen, "Hunting Rapists Behind Bars: Sexual Assault Prosecution Is Nearly Impossible in Prison, Study Shows," *American Bar Association Journal* 95 (May 2009): 17–18.

117. John Irwin, *Prisons in Turmoil* (Boston: Little, Brown, 1980), pp. 94–98.

118. *Abdul Wali v. Coughlin*, 754 F.2d 1015 (2d Cir. 1985).

119. "Death Row Escapee Found Dead," *New York Times* (4 December 1998), p. 16.

120. "Texas 7 Sentences Set Precedent," *Dallas Morning News* (23 November 2003), p. 1B.

121. "Prison System Shaping Up, and That Includes Guards Physical Testing Mandated After Escapes, Smuggling Troubles Jailers," *Houston Chronicle* (18 April 2010), p. 1B.

122. "Inmates Use Smuggled Cell Phones to Maintain a Foot on the Outside," *New York Times* (21 June 2004), p. 1.

123. "In Disciplinary Unit, Rikers Island Guards Created a 'House of Pain' for Inmates," *New York Times* (16 August 1998), p. 34.

124. "New York City Accepts Limits on Use of Force Against Jail Inmates," *Criminal Justice Newsletter* (15 March 2006), p. 6.

125. "Prison Guards Accused of Inmate Beatings," *Pittsburgh Post-Gazette* (7 July 2009), p. 1B.

126. "Utah Man Describes Fight with Escapee," *Grand Rapids Press* (Michigan) (28 June 2007), p. 16.

127. "Prisoner Work Crews Reach End of the Road," *Desert Morning News* (Salt Lake City) (19 October 2007), n.p.

128. *Ruffin v. Commonwealth*, 62 Va. 790, 796 (1872).

129. *Wolff v. McDonnell*, 418 U.S. 539 (1974), *rev'd. in part, Bell v. Wolfish*, 441 U.S. 520 (1979).

130. *Rhodes v. Chapman*, 452 U.S. 337 (1981).

131. *Trop v. Dulles*, 356 U.S. 86 (1958).

132. *Hudson v. McMillian*, 503 U.S. 1 (1992).

133. *Hope v. Pelzer*, 536 U.S. 730 (2002), notes and citations omitted.

134. *Pennsylvania Department of Corrections v. Yeskey*, 524 U.S. 206 (1998), *summ. judgment granted*, 76 F.Supp. 2d 572 (M.D.Pa. 1999). The Americans with Disabilities Act (ADA) is codified at USCS, Title 42, Sections 12131-12165 (2010).

135. "Deaf Juveniles in Maryland Detention Facilities Get Access to Interpreters," *Corrections Professional* 9, no. 16 (10 May 2004): n.p.

136. *Oregon Advocacy Ctr. v. Mink*, 322 F.3d 1101 (9th Cir. 2003).

137. "Florida Adopts Plan for Mentally Ill Inmates," *New York Times* (11 January 2007), p. 23.

138 "DOCs, OMH Open Residential Mental Health Unit at Marcy Correctional Facility," New York Department of Correctional Services (15 December 2009), http://www.docs.state.ny.us/pressrel/2009/ MarcyRMHU.html, accessed 12 November 2010.

139. "Report: State Prison Health Care Woes Deeper Than Expected," *Inside Bay Area* (California) (6 July 2006), n.p.

140. "Troubled Medical System at San Quentin Faces Reform," *Marin Independent Journal* (California) (7 July 2006), n.p.

141. "Report Finds 'Tragic' Deaths in State Prisons," *Inside Bay Area* (California) (24 September 2007), n.p.

142. "Using Muscle to Improve Health Care for Prisoners," *New York Times*, Late Edition (27 August 2007), p. 12; "Prison Health Czar Shown the Door," *San Jose Mercury News* (California) (24 January 2008), p. 2.

143. "Huge Care Costs for Small Group of Sick Inmates," *San Francisco Chronicle* (19 May 2010), p. 1.

144. "Audit: California Wasted Millions on Drugs for Inmates," *San Jose Mercury News* (California) (15 April 2010), n.p.

145. *Women Prisoners of the District of Columbia Department of Corrections v. District of Columbia*, 899 F.Supp. 659 (D.D.C. 1995), *vacated, in part, remanded,* 93 F.3d 910 (D.C.Cir. 1996), *cert. denied*, 520 U.S. 1196 (1997).

146. The case is *Shumate v. Wilson*, filed in the U.S. District Court, Eastern District of California, in 1995.

147. Pregnant and Parenting Women's Alternative Sentencing Program Act, Cal Pen Code, Title 7, Section 1174 (2010).

148. Cal Pen Code, Section 3406 (2010).

149. Cal Pen Code, Section 3424 (2010).

150. Cal Pen Code, Section 5007.7 (2010).

151. *Nelson v. Correctional Medical Services*, 583 F.3d 522 (8th Cir. 2009).

152. *Nelson v. Correctional Medical Services*, 583 F.3d 522 (8th Cir. 2009); "1.50 Fee Awarded to Four Attorneys; Ex-Inmate Client Had Won $1 in Suit," *Arkansas Democrat-Gazette* (Little Rock) (16 September 2010), n.p.

153. RCW, Chapter 181, Hs. Bill 2747 (2010). A permanent code number had not been assigned to this statute in time for this publication.

154. *Bounds v. Smith*, 430 U.S. 817 (1977), *and overruled in part by Lewis v. Casey*, 518 U.S. 343 (1996).

155. Prison Litigation Reform Act of 1995, P.L. 104-134 (2010). For an example of litigation, see *Jones v. Bock*, 549 U.S. 199, *on re-*

mand, summ. judgment granted, Jones v. Michigan, 2010 U.S. Dist. LEXIS 25438 (E.D. Mich. 2010). For criticisms of the bill, see "Critics Call for Overhaul of Limits on Prison Lawsuits," *Criminal Justice Newsletter* (2 April 2007), p. 6.

156. William Wayne Justice, "The Origins of *Ruiz v. Estelle*," *Stanford Law Review* 43 (November 1990): 6, 12.

157. Richard Reeves, "High Price of Punishing Criminals," *Tulsa World* (Oklahoma) (27 June 1982), p. 13.

CHAPTER 15

Corrections in the Community

Returning to society after serving time in prison is a difficult transition for inmates, especially for those who have been incarcerated for a long time. Inmates need preparation and assistance with this transition, and halfway houses are utilized in some jurisdictions. In this photo, Bob Sauter serves dinner at the Aphesis House in Memphis, Tennessee. The facility is a halfway house to assist male offenders in their transition from prison back into society. The Greek word aphesis means "forgiveness."

CHAPTER OUTLINE

KEY TERMS

boot camps
community-based corrections
community work service
diversion
electronic monitoring
felony probation
furlough
global positioning systems
halfway house
house arrest
intensive probation supervision
Megan's Law
parole
parole board
parole officers
prerelease programs
probation
probation officer
reintegration
shock incarceration
work release

INTRODUCTION

This final chapter examines the practice of handling offenders within the community rather than within institutions. Many offenders are not sentenced to jail or prison, and most who are incarcerated return to society. If offenders and the community are not prepared for that event, we can expect many to return to a life of crime.

INTRODUCTION continued

Perhaps some will commit crimes no matter what we do, whereas others might be integrated successfully into the law-abiding society.

This chapter focuses on the methods for handling offenders within the community. After an overview of diversion, the chapter proceeds to a discussion of various types of community corrections before focusing on probation and parole, the major systems under which offenders are supervised within the community. Consideration is given to the problems faced when inmates are released from incarceration, including the recent emphasis on required community registration and other restrictions on released sex offenders. Where those are not considered sufficiently secure, civil commitment proceedings are proposed. The chapter closes with a discussion of the future of corrections.

Previous chapters traced the emergence of prisons and the changes in philosophies of punishment and imprisonment. Early reformers thought offenders should be incarcerated in total institutions. Their segregation from home and society was deemed necessary to remove the evil influences that had led to their criminal behavior. While incarcerated, offenders would have time to think and reflect on their behavior and become involved in religious services and other efforts at reformation.

Before long, prison reformers were declaring that incarceration in total institutions did not reduce the criminal activity of offenders after they were released and that it intensified the problems of those who served time. In 1777, reformer John Howard referred to prisons as "seats and seminaries of idleness and every vice." In prison, "by the greatest possible degree of misery, you produce the greatest possible degree of wickedness." In 1864, Jeremy Bentham (see again the discussion in Chapter 3) declared that most prisons "include every imaginable means of infecting both body and mind . . . [and that] an ordinary prison is a school in which wickedness is taught. . . . All the inmates raise themselves to the level of the worst." In 1890, the English prison system was described as "a manufactory of lunatics and criminals." In 1922, imprisonment was described as "a progressive weakening of the mental powers and of a deterioration of the character in a way which renders the prisoner less fit for useful social life, more predisposed to crime, and in consequence more liable to reconviction." These early declarations have been described as conclusions without evidence,[1] yet as noted in Chapter 14, empirical research has shown that modern prisons have also failed.

In 1973, the National Advisory Commission on Criminal Justice Standards and Goals called for an increased emphasis on probation, already the most frequently used form of sentencing.[2] During the 1970s, the goal of corrections appeared to be the reintegration of the offender into society. In the 1980s and 1990s, however, we moved away from a philosophy of rehabilitation and reintegration to one of retribution and just deserts. With that movement, rates of incarceration in total institutions increased to the point that many states were under court orders to reduce their prison and jail populations, as previous chapters noted.

The need for additional jails and prisons came at a time when construction and operating costs were soaring. As soon as most new, larger facilities were available, they were filled, and many jurisdictions did not have sufficient space to sentence offenders who would otherwise be incarcerated. Some resorted to a policy of releasing inmates early to make room for new and more serious offenders. Other systems diverted offenders to other agencies, such as alcohol and drug treatment programs; imposed fines, restitution, or community work sentences in place of a prison term; or placed offenders on probation. All of these procedures are controversial, but all have positive features that should be addressed. The use of sentencing alternatives to jail and prison is a sensitive issue, and selling the public on some of these programs is not easy.

There is some encouraging news, however. A 1995 study conducted by the American Correctional Association (ACA) noted that three of four Americans believed that using a balanced approach toward offenders is better than relying solely on incarceration. The ACA president stated: "The public's mood may not be as punitive as some politicians would have us believe." He emphasized that it is the position of corrections officials that punishment alone will not reduce crime. In the long run, crime can be reduced only through prevention and treatment. The president concluded that we "cannot afford not to pay for literacy programs, vocational training, and drug and alcohol treatment."[3]

The concern with the issues discussed in this chapter is illustrated by a bill introduced in the U.S. Senate in March 2010. The Prevention Resources for Eliminating Criminal Activity Using Tailored Interventions in Our Neighborhoods (PRECAUTION) Act of 2010 provides for a national commission of experts in law enforcement and crime prevention to sift through the scientific knowledge and draft proposals for Congress and the states. Although the future of this bill was uncertain as of this writing, its introduction and consideration by the U.S. Senate focused on the importance of social science research in crime prevention and challenged scholars to utilize this knowledge for practical reasons. The purposes of the bill are reproduced in Exhibit 15.1.

Community-based approaches are discussed further in this chapter after a brief look at the philosophy of diverting offenders from incarceration facilities.

Diversion

We have already noted that many jails and prisons are overcrowded. In 2009, more than 7.2 million adults in the United States were under some form of correctional control. Figure 15.1 graphs their distributions between 1980 and 2009 by the type of supervision. Figure 15.2 graphs characteristics of offenders under correctional control in 2007, and Map 15.1 shows the wide variance in correctional control by states in the year 2007. One solution to the overcrowding of jails and prisons is to divert some offenders from those facilities into other programs.

Technically, **diversion** is meant to funnel the offender away from criminal justice systems and into community programs that might be more beneficial than incarceration. Diversion is used most frequently in juvenile justice systems, where historically, offenders have been handled with less formality than is characteristic of adult criminal court systems. Diversion also refers to *pretrial diversion*, which includes the release of the accused pending trial.

Figure 15.1

Adult Correctional Populations, 1980–2009

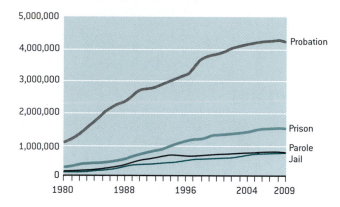

Source: Bureau of Justice Statistics, "Key Facts At a Glance," http://bjs.ojp.usdoj.gov/content/glance/corr2.cfm, accessed 26 December 2010.

In the late 1960s and throughout the 1970s, diversion was a popular concept. Many diversionary programs were developed. Most focused on juveniles, although some provided services for adults. Adult offenders with alcohol and drug problems were typical targets. Some of the evaluations of these programs concluded that instead of diversion, the programs were widening the net and capturing people who would not have been processed through criminal court systems before diversionary programs began.

Diversion is frequently used in cases involving substance abuse. Diversion into a treatment program may be

Figure 15.2

Characteristics of Offenders Under Correctional Control

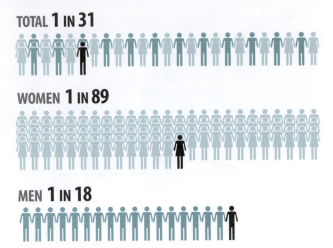

TOTAL 1 IN 31

WOMEN 1 IN 89

MEN 1 IN 18

WHITE 1 IN 45

HISPANIC 1 IN 27

BLACK 1 IN 11

Source: The Pew Center on the States, *One in 31: The Long Reach of American Corrections* (March 2009), p. 7, http://www .pewcenteronthestates.org/uploadedFiles/PSPP_1in31_report_FINAL_WEB_3-26-09.pdf, accessed 14 November 2010.

Map 15.1

Adults Under Correctional Control by States, 2007

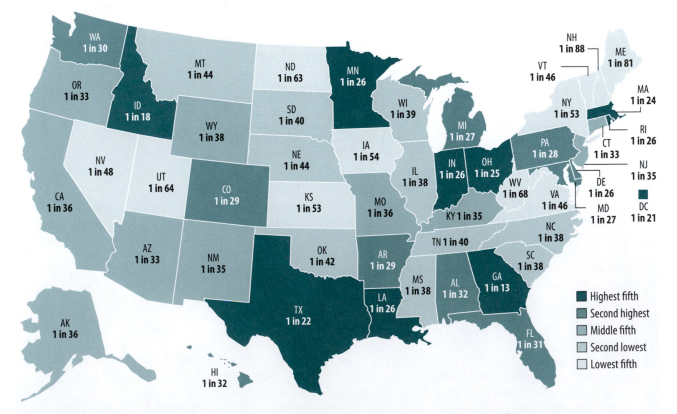

Source: The Pew Center on the States, *One in 31: The Long Reach of American Corrections* (March 2009), p. 7, http://www .pewcenteronthestates.org/uploadedFiles/PSPP_1in31_report_FINAL_WEB_3-26-09.pdf, accessed 14 November 2010.

a condition of pretrial release. This practice is employed in the federal system. Chapter 13 discussed the recent trend toward treatment rather than punishment of nonviolent first- and second-time substance abusers, often combined with the use of drug courts.

The success of some diversion programs for juveniles was illustrated by the release of a report by the Coalition for Juvenile Justice in Washington, D.C. This group named Chicago's Juvenile Detention Alternative Initiative (JDAI) as one program that was successful in diverting nonviolent juveniles from detention. The program reduced the county juvenile detention population by almost 40 percent between 1996 and 2003. It offers judges several alternatives to detention when they are assessing each individual delinquent. Programs include home surveillance and monitoring as well as community programs, such as evening reporting centers, which operate along with social service organizations to provide highly structured and monitored group activities for juveniles. Judges order the youths to attend the sessions, and transportation is provided for them. They are given an evening meal along with programs in recreation and education and development workshops.[4]

The JDAI was designed to ensure that all youths in criminal justice systems have an opportunity to become healthy, productive adults. The organization focuses on juveniles because, it states, they are too often detained unnecessarily, with a negative impact on themselves and on society. The JDAI claims that it has (1) lowered detention populations, (2) reduced juvenile delinquency at its sites, and (3) reduced racial disparities.[5]

A Chicago diversion program, Drug School, began in 1972. It diverts and educates low-level drug offenders who do not have a history of violence. Between 2001 and 2005, this program diverted approximately 4,000 defendants annually, for an estimated savings of approximately $2 million a year. Almost 90 percent of those diverted completed the program.[6]

Community Corrections: An Attempt at Reintegration

The focus on diversion has been accompanied by an emphasis on helping offenders who serve time to reintegrate into the community. **Reintegration** may be defined as "the process of preparing both the community and offender for the latter's return as a productive and accepted citizen. . . . The emphasis is on creating the circumstances around him [or her] that will enable him [or her] to lead a satisfying and law-abiding life."[7] Exhibit 15.2 presents information on a recently enacted law to improve reintegration: the Second Chance Act, which became law on 10 April 2008.

Rehabilitation is the primary goal of **community-based corrections**, and many jurisdictions recognize that in their

enabling statutes. Other goals may be listed: custody/supervision, punishment, restitution, reintegration, employment training, and reduction of prison populations. An example of a state statute authorizing community-based corrections is that of California, which states, in part:

> The Director of Corrections may enter into an agreement consistent with applicable law for a city, county, or city and county to construct and operate community corrections programs, restitution centers, halfway houses, work furlough programs, or other correctional programs authorized by state law.[8]

As noted earlier in the text, California changed the name of its Department of Corrections to the Department of Corrections and Rehabilitation and took other measures to indicate the state's commitment to the reintegration of inmates back into society as law-abiding citizens. As noted later in this chapter, the state has not achieved significant success in this goal.

The federal government also has community corrections, with its Bureau of Prisons (BOP) Web page stating that "Community corrections is an integral component of the Bureau's correctional programs." The BOP continues:

> Through the community corrections program, the BOP has developed agreements with state and local governments and contracts with privately-operated facilities for the confinement of federally adjudicated juveniles. . . . and with residential reentry centers (RRCs) . . . to provide assistance to inmates who are nearing release.[9]

When we talk about community-based corrections, we must distinguish these facilities and programs from those that may be located in the community but are not, strictly speaking, community based. The degree to which a correctional system is community based can be measured by the frequency, quality, and duration of community relationships; by the number of commitments to large state institutions; by the extent to which other community services are used; and by the degree of involvement by local groups and individuals.

Community correctional centers comprise a wide variety of programs, including both residential and nonresidential facilities. Criminal justice systems in the United States and in other countries have experimented with a variety of community-based correctional plans. In some states, such as California and Minnesota,[10] the state assists counties in developing community-based correctional facilities designed to reintegrate or to maintain the offender in the community. Numerous jurisdictions use several methods of community-based corrections.

EXHIBIT 15.2

Second Chance Act of 2007

On 10 April 2008, the Second Chance Act of 2007 became public law. The stated purposes of this statute are as follows:

"(1) to break the cycle of criminal recidivism, increase public safety, and help States, local units of government, and Indian Tribes, better address the growing population of criminal offenders who return to their communities and commit new crimes;

(2) to rebuild ties between offenders and their families, while the offenders are incarcerated and after reentry into the community, to promote stable families and communities;

(3) to encourage the development and support of, and to expand the availability of, evidence-based programs that enhance public safety and reduce recidivism, such as substance abuse treatment, alternatives to incarceration, and comprehensive reentry services;

(4) to protect the public and promote law-abiding conduct by providing necessary services to offenders, while the offenders are incarcerated and after reentry into the community, in a manner that does not confer luxuries or privileges upon such offenders;

(5) to assist offenders reentering the community from incarceration to establish a self-sustaining and law-abiding life by providing sufficient transitional services for as short of a period as practicable, not to exceed one year, unless a longer period is specifically determined to be necessary by a medical or other appropriate treatment professional; and

(6) to provide offenders in prisons, jails, or juvenile facilities with educational, literacy, vocational, and job placement services to facilitate reentry into the community."

Source: 110 Public Law 199 (2010).

Community Work Service, Fines, and Restitution

One approach to reintegrating offenders as well as compensating victims is to order offenders to perform community service, pay a fine to the state, or pay restitution to the victim. A *fine* is ordered by the judge and paid by the offender to the state (or county or other entity in which the judge presides). Fines are often used in combination with other punishments, such as probation.

Restitution is a method of reimbursement paid by the offender to the victim. It was approved by the U.S. Supreme Court in 1913 and has received the support of most crime commissions. Restitution is permitted in the federal system by the Victim and Witness Protection Act of 1982, which has been amended subsequently. The Violent Crime Control and Law Enforcement Act of 1994 provides for mandatory restitution for some federal crimes.[11]

Restitution and fines are used frequently in conjunction with **community work service** assignments. The assignments may be designed to benefit the victim or the community. The assignments often involve work in community or government agencies.

All of these approaches sound progressive and advantageous on the surface. They raise revenue, they permit compensation to victims, and they keep offenders working. But there are also problems. First, the programs require funding, and with cutbacks in correctional programming, some community corrections programs have been significantly reduced or eliminated. Second, victims may overestimate or underestimate their losses. Third, enforcement problems abound. Because offenders may steal to pay, supervision may be necessary—and that is expensive. Fourth, the community may react negatively to the presence of offenders working in their midst. Fifth, the cost of fines and restitution may mean that offenders cannot support their families. Finally, there are legal issues with regard to fines, restitution, and work service. Some of these issues have been resolved by the courts, but others have resulted in contradictory court decisions.

Halfway Houses

Sociological theories discussed earlier in the text emphasized the socialization problems characteristic of many offenders. They have not been able to integrate into their environments or bond with significant persons. For many of them, the transition from prison to release is difficult, especially if they have been incarcerated for a long time. Some jurisdictions place these offenders in a **halfway house** (also called a community correctional facility) prior to unconditional release. Programs and supervision within a halfway house assist offenders in adjusting to other people and in coping with their own problems. The halfway house may focus on a special problem, such as alcohol or drug treatment, and it may be used in lieu of incarceration rather than as a transition from incarceration to the free world. Halfway houses are also used for some high-risk offenders considered unsuitable for probation.

There are many studies of halfway houses, but most were conducted during the 1960s and 1970s, when the use of such facilities was extensive. Today, in some jurisdictions, halfway houses are available for the use of prison administrators who need to solve overcrowding conditions, but many of the facilities are underutilized, perhaps because officials view them as providing an easy way to do time. Additionally, it is difficult to predict which inmates are most suitable for the programs. Staffing, cost, liability, and other issues are involved.

The federal system has provisions for the use of halfway houses, generally during the last 120 to 180 days of an offender's sentence, but most federal inmates are not released from prison until they have completed their sentences. There are several reasons for this: (1) the release criteria are vaguely worded; (2) institutions differ widely in their use of the release policy; (3) in many cases, plans do not begin soon enough to place the inmates for the recommended time period or at all; and (4) some inmates scheduled for movement to halfway houses do not want to go, perhaps because of the more stringent release requirements, such as securing a job in advance.[12]

In 2003, the U.S. Department of Justice (DOJ) transferred 125 nonviolent federal inmates from halfway houses to prisons, representing a change in policy that occurred at the end of 2002. For approximately 20 years, the federal Bureau of Prisons assigned nonviolent criminals, such as white-collar offenders, to serve their terms in halfway houses rather than in prisons. But the DOJ's attorney general's office took the position that the BOP did not have the legal authority to do this even though a federal judge was always involved with the assignment. Federal law provides that after being sentenced to prison, the inmate shall be assigned by the BOP to a place of confinement. It is clear that the BOP may assign the federal offender to any federal penal facility, including those in other districts, but it may not take into consideration the financial or social status of inmates in making these decisions. The BOP may also transfer inmates from one institution to another although, as noted in Chapter 14, in some cases the inmate may be entitled to a hearing to challenge the proposed transfer. Federal law also provides that inmates serving more than a year but not a life sentence may, at the end of the first year of incarceration, receive up to 54 days of good-time credit for each year that they engage in exemplary behavior in accordance with prison regulations and policies. The federal code also provides that during the last 10 percent of their terms, not to exceed six months, inmates may serve out their time "under conditions that will afford the prisoner a reasonable opportunity to adjust to and prepare for the prisoner's re-entry into the community. The authority provided by this subsection may be used to place a prisoner in home confinement."[13]

The BOP has interpreted these statutes to permit the assignment of nonviolent offenders to halfway houses, and federal judges have done so. After the DOJ declared that this practice is illegal, several inmates sued, arguing that the DOJ policy subjected them to illegal *ex post facto* rules—that is, rules that did not exist when the inmates were convicted and incarcerated. The new policy was implemented in December 2002 with no announcement; there was just a directive to the BOP that the new policy was effective immediately. The new policy also tightened the time any inmate could spend in a halfway house prior to release. In March 2004, an inmate who challenged this latter part of DOJ's policy as unconstitutional won his case, as the court held that the policy violated the *ex post facto clause* of the U.S. Constitution. Some courts have agreed with this decision, but others have held that the clause is not violated by the interpretation.[14]

Shock Incarceration and Boot Camps

One solution to prison overcrowding (and other prison problems) has been **shock incarceration**, which takes different forms but is designed to incarcerate the offender for a brief period, followed by supervision within the community. The term is used synonymously with *shock probation*, which began in 1965 in Ohio, where judges were permitted to sentence offenders to brief periods of incarceration, followed by probation. The purpose of the Ohio program was to expose offenders to the shock of prison and to release them before they were negatively influenced by the prison experience. They were then placed on probation. The Ohio program was adopted in some form by other states, although it has been criticized as violating the main purpose of probation, which is to avoid the negative impact of prisons.

Shock probation differs from *shock incarceration* in that the former involves sending offenders to prison to be exposed to the general prison population and experience. In shock incarceration, however, the offenders were separated from the general prison population. Usually, they were placed in special facilities, often called **boot camps**. In the boot camp atmosphere, offenders participated in strongly regimented daily routines of physical exercise, work, and discipline that resemble military training. Many of the boot camp programs included rehabilitative measures, such as drug treatment and educational programs.

Early studies suggested that offenders who went through boot camp programs showed greater changes in social attitudes than those who went through regular probation and parole programs. However, they were just as likely to be returned to prison for committing other offenses after their release from the programs. Thus, the positive changes the boot camp offenders experienced might not be sufficient to enable them to "overcome the difficulties they face in returning to the home environment." In short, according to one authority, "there is no evidence . . . that shock incarceration will reduce recidivism or improve positive adjustment."[15]

It is also argued that the boot camp experience per se is not related to lower recidivism. Rather, boot campers who were engaged in aftercare programs had lower recidivist rates than those who were not in such programs (16 percent compared to 21 percent after one year; 22 percent compared to 33 percent after two years). Thus, some investigators concluded that research "has provided an important avenue for discussing recent major concerns about U.S. corrections and reentry. . . . [I]t is possible to develop programs that will have an impact on recidivism."[16]

This conclusion was confirmed by a study of Pennsylvania boot camps and aftercare,[17] leading one investigator to emphasize that we need to move to a correctional system based on care rather than militarism. We need to "move past defining offenders as the enemy and recognize them as important parts of our communities—important members who teeter on the edge of either producing more harm or in engaging in their own ethic of care."[18]

It is also argued that the military style characteristic of boot camps does not work even in the military today, and when this style is combined with rehabilitative goals, there are negative consequences. Among those are increased aggression against other offenders and staff, a "devaluation of women and so-called feminine traits (for example, sensitivity), and other negative effects of an unpredictable, authoritarian atmosphere."[19]

Many jurisdictions abolished their boot camp programs because of various problems. In 1997, the California Department of Corrections announced that it was making plans for an immediate phaseout of the only boot camp operated in its adult correctional system, located at San Quentin. The state legislature had approved the program for five years for experimental purposes but failed to renew that commitment in 1997. A study of the state's program found some measures of success, such as the placement of some graduates in jobs paying more than the minimum wage, but there were no significant signs of a reduction in recidivism. Nor was the program a cost-saving one. Although participants spent less time in prison than their nonboot camp cohorts, their incarceration costs were slightly more than those in prisons because of labor-intensive programs requiring more staff members and other resources.[20]

After experiencing problems with its boot camps, the state of Maryland closed all of them. Georgia began phasing out its programs after a study by the U.S. DOJ gave boot camps a negative evaluation.[21] Media Focus 15.1 provides more information on some of the recent problems in boot camps.

Day Reporting Centers

Another type of nonresidential supervision program and alternative to incarceration are day reporting centers (DRCs). The concept comes from a British system developed in the early 1970s. Since the early 1980s, the U.S. federal system has utilized a DRC concept through its community treatment centers. Offenders who have completed the program are permitted to report to the centers for treatment while living elsewhere. In 1986, Massachusetts and Connecticut began operating DRCs. These centers may be combined with monitoring systems (discussed later) and intensive supervision, housing assistance, education (especially in literacy), job training, and health and personal care. They vary widely in their clientele and in their programming and services.[22] Excerpts from a legal opinion that emphasized the reasons for day reporting systems are presented in Exhibit 15.3.

Unlike other community corrections services, which focus on the surveillance of offenders, DRCs provide services designed to assist offenders in establishing law-abiding lives in the community. Drug treatment and drug abuse education, assistance on how to locate a job, and training in life skills are examples of the types of services offered. Although reducing jail and prison overcrowding is a goal, the most important aim of these programs is to provide necessary assistance to offenders. Surveillance is important, but it is not a primary mission. The emphasis is on frequent contacts between offenders and the DRC staff.

Day reporting centers continue to gain support. But like many other programs and agencies, they, too, face budget cuts or even abolition. One recent article about DRCs in California, where approximately 40 percent of new prison admittees are felony probationers who commit new crimes while on probation, stated that they are used to reduce prison populations. In Los Angeles County, for example, where most probationers are seen about 10 or 15 minutes a month by their probation officers, offenders in DRCs are supervised more closely. They are required to attend sessions several times weekly, with six deputy probation officers supervising approximately 150 offenders in those sessions. They are provided counseling on mental health and drug abuse issues. They take classes for the high school equivalency test, and they attend classes on moral reasoning, life skills, and anger management. The cost per offender is approximately $7,000 a year compared to an estimated $45,000 in prison. The program began in late 2008 with state funds, but with budget cuts, it was in danger of being cut.[23]

Day reporting centers raise interesting legal issues. In 2008, the Illinois Supreme Court decided a case brought by a petitioner who argued that he should be given credit for time served for the 171-plus days he was under the sheriff's jurisdiction but living in a day reporting center. He based his claim on a 2005 case in which the state's supreme court held that a person in a day reporting center is "in custody." The lower appellate court agreed with the petitioner. The prosecutor appealed, and the state supreme court upheld the lower court.[24]

15.1   Boot Camps: The Media Reports

MEDIA FOCUS

In October 2007, various media covered the release of the Government Accountability Office's (GAO) report on boot camps, citing many examples of abuse, even deaths, and noting that most of those responsible were not punished. One headline read, "Report Recounts Horrors of Youth Boot Camps," and another declared, "GAO: Boot Camps Neglected Teens' Fatal Health Problems."[1]

The mother of Marvin Lee Anderson, 14, who died in one of Florida's boot camp programs, holds a picture of her young son at a press conference after the state's governor, Jeb Bush, signed into law a statute abolishing boot camps. Eight state boot camp employees were acquitted of criminal charges in Anderson's death, and federal prosecutors declined to bring federal civil rights charges.

Widespread media coverage was given to the report of the death of Marvin Lee Anderson, 14, in a Florida boot camp in January 2006. Eight state employees (seven correctional officers and a nurse) were acquitted by an all-white jury in the death of Anderson, who was black, and civil rights advocates and others pushed for federal charges in the case. The Anderson case resulted in a statute, the Marvin Lee Anderson Act, which eliminated boot camps in Florida. The camps were replaced with juvenile detention centers that focus on education.[2] In April 2010, federal prosecutors announced that they were closing the case, as they did not have sufficient evidence to charge

Charles Long II, former director of the Arizona boot camp in which 14-year-old Anthony Haynes died, was charged with child abuse, second-degree murder, and aggravated assault in connection with Haynes's death. In January 2005, Long was convicted of manslaughter and aggravated battery and was sentenced to six years in prison. He was released in February 2010.

the eight defendants with federal charges of violating Anderson's civil rights.[3]

Another case that attracted significant media attention was that of Tony Haynes, also 14, who died in 2001 while in residence in a boot camp in an Arizona desert. While the Arizona death was still under investigation, the media reported that, prior to his death, Haynes was beaten by correctional authorities and forced to eat dirt.[4]

When Haynes died, there were no medical personnel on hand at the camp, and one Arizona newspaper reported that before his death, the youth vomited dirt. Investigators said that they did not know whether the camp had adequate food and water for the youths, but the air temperature was 120 degrees the day they visited. Haynes's mother said that her son was in the camp because of behavioral problems (e.g., shoplifting and slashing the tires on his mother's car) but that he had started to control his anger before he died. Some parents supported the rigorous approach of the camp; others were critical.[5]

Investigators were told by some of the other youths at the Arizona camp that they, too, were abused by counselors: They were kicked, punched, forced to swallow mud, and handcuffed if they asked for food or water.[6] In February 2002, Charles Long II, age 56, the camp's director, was arrested on charges of second-degree murder and child abuse. One of the staffers, Troy A. Hutty, 29, was also charged in the

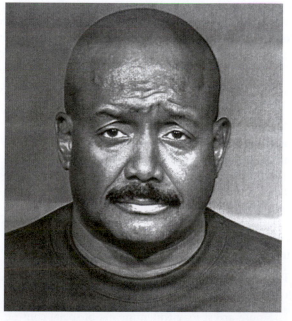

(Continued)

case. Hutty accepted a plea agreement. In exchange for his testimony against Long, Hutty pleaded guilty to negligent homicide, and the manslaughter charges against him were dropped.[7] In 2005, Long was convicted of manslaughter and aggravated battery. He was sentenced to six years in prison. He was released in February 2010.

---

1. "Report Recounts Horrors of Youth Boot Camps," *New York Times* (11 October 2007), p. 19; "GAO: Boot Camps Neglected Teens' Fatal Health Problems," *USA Today* (10 October 2007), p. 10.
2. Marvin Lee Anderson Act of 2006, 2006 Fl. ALS 62 (2009).

3. "U.S. Won't File Charges in Boot Camp Death," *Boston Globe* (17 April 2010), p. 2.
4. "States Pressed as 3 Boys Die at Boot Camps," *New York Times* (15 July 2001), p. 1.
5. "Desert Boot Camp Shut Down After Suspicious Death of Boy," *New York Times* (4 July 2001), p. 8.
6. "Accounts Put Darker Cloud over Camp," *New York Times* (5 July 2001), p. 13.
7. "Ex-Camp Worker Pleads Guilty," *Arizona Republic* (21 February 2002), p. 1B; "Judge Wants Camp-Death Trial to Start Soon," *Arizona Republic* (18 May 2004), p. 8B.

House Arrest

Prison overcrowding in the past two decades has led to another proposed solution—**house arrest**, with or without electronic surveillance or some other type of monitoring. Offenders, who are placed on probation in their own homes, must follow specified regulations, including restrictions on when they may leave the premises and for what purposes. *Home confinement*, as it is called in the federal system, was launched in 1986 as an experimental program, with electronic monitoring added a few years later.[25]

The advantages and disadvantages of house arrest were summarized in a Rand Corporation report after extensive study of the programs. The advantages include cost effectiveness; social benefits, such as permitting the offender to keep a job and to continue interacting with his or her family; flexibility, which permits adaptation of the plan to the individual needs of the offender and of the community; and implementation ease and timeliness. The author, Joan Petersilia, concluded:

> Because house arrest sentencing requires no new facilities and can use existing probation personnel, it is one of the easier programs to implement (particularly if no electronic monitoring devices are used). House arrest programs, for the most part, do not require legislative changes and can be set up by administrative decisions. The conditions of house arrest are usually easy to communicate, facilitating implementation.[26]

The disadvantages of house arrest were stated as follows:

1. House arrest may widen the net of social control.
2. House arrest may narrow the net of social control.

3. House arrest focuses primarily on offender surveillance.
4. House arrest is intrusive and possibly illegal.
5. Race and class bias may enter into participant selection.
6. House arrest may compromise public safety.[27]

That last disadvantage is of concern to many. Despite the widespread use and reported success of house arrest, the public reacts to the failures, many of which receive extensive media coverage. In addition, house arrest may be perceived as luxurious accommodation rather than as punishment.

An example of a house arrest or home detention program is that of Indianapolis and Marion County, Indiana. The program permits participants to leave home for their jobs, counseling and treatment appointments, educational classes, medical appointments, and religious services. Follow-up services are provided for offenders and their families involved in substance abuse treatment, mental health counseling, and other needs. All are monitored electronically; all are subject to random drug testing and must remain drug and alcohol free; all (except those who are indigent) are required to fund part of the costs ($75 initial fee plus $12 per day); and all must be employed if physically able.[28]

Electronic Monitoring (EM) and Global Positioning Systems (GPS)

Many participants in house arrest programs are required to wear electronic devices, which are attached to the offender's ankle or wrist and monitored by a probation officer or a telephone system. **Electronic monitoring** was introduced in 1964, but only recently has the practice gained widespread attention and use.

EXHIBIT

15.3   The Case for Day Care Reporting Centers and Other Sentencing Alternatives

In a case decided by the West Virginia Supreme Court in 2003, the Chief Justice wrote the following concurring opinion.

"This case involved a man who stole some very valuable hunting dogs and radio equipment, and for this crime he was sentenced to a year in jail. It was a rotten crime, although the offender apparently had no previous criminal record and it was not a crime of violence. I concur in the court's judgment and opinion because the sentence of incarceration was within the sentencing judge's discretion.

"However, I write separately because the sentence of incarceration in this case—although legally permissible—vividly illustrates the most important issue facing West Virginia's criminal justice system: our failure to use economical, non-incarceration, community-based sanctions for criminal misconduct.

"West Virginia taxpayers are being required to spend large amounts of money on putting people in prisons and jails, at a time when our state's budget is said to be in crisis. At the same time, new technology like electronic bracelets (even with satellite tracking) will allow us to monitor offenders and protect society at a fraction of the cost of incarceration. And instead of sitting in a $20,000-a-year cell at the taxpayers' expense, we can get our offenders out working, to clean our streets and parks; and paying restitution to their victims.

"The wasteful, unnecessary use of imprisonment is not limited to West Virginia. It is a national problem. In 1974, there were 1,819,000 U.S. adults who had at some time been incarcerated in a state or federal prison; that was 1.3 percent of our nation's population. Twenty-seven years later, in 2001, that number had more than doubled—to 5,618,000, or 2.7 percent.

"In 1974, 8.7 percent of black Americans had ever been in prison. In 2001, the number is 16.6 percent. If current incarceration rates remain unchanged, Bureau of Justice Statistics predict that one in three black males, one in six Hispanic males, and one in 17 white males will go to prison sometime during their lives.

"Put another way, at current rates, an astonishing 6.6 percent of all persons born in the United States in 2001 will go to state or federal prison during their lifetime; this is up from 5.2 percent in 1991, and from 1.9 percent in 1974.

"Are we a safer society than we were in 1974? I don't think so.

"These numbers are horrifying. They reflect our society's utterly failed reliance on imprisonment to try to deal with the problem of hard drugs, and politicians who are playing the knee-jerk politics of fear and vengeance.

"We who have worked daily in the criminal justice system know what is needed to deal with offenders effectively and economically, and it sure isn't more incarceration.

"We need more treatment programs for drug addicts, and more day reporting centers and community corrections centers.

"We need high-tech home confinement and offender monitoring systems, and we need a limited amount of secure imprisonment, with good in-house rehabilitation services, for the violent people who pose a true danger.

"We need to get rid of mandatory minimum sentences, because they clog our jails and prisons with offenders who don't need that level of security.

"The sentence in this case of a year in jail for a dog-stealer means that tens of thousands of dollars of taxpayer money will go to feed, clothe, house, and give medical care to a person who should be outside, on supervised probation, working, to pay his debt to society and to his victim. Multiply this offender's incarceration sentence by hundreds of other similar cases, and we can see why West Virginia is spending money that we need—for teachers and nurses and doctors and roads and bridges and schools—on wasteful, unnecessary imprisonment.

Source: State v. Watkins, 590 S.E.2d 670 (W.Va. 2003), Chief Justice Stracker, concurring.

Evaluation of EM and house arrest programs must consider all the programs involved. An earlier analysis of three programs in California disclosed, for example, that increasing surveillance did not result in significant decreases in crime. But when it was combined with counseling, employment, restitution, and community service, recidivism rates fell.[29] One analysis of offenders with drug problems revealed the difficulties of achieving success in treating these problems but suggested that the combination of drug treatment programs with electronic monitoring "may offer some help."[30]

Electronic bracelets may also be used to detect offenders who violate alcohol prohibitions while on bail. In June 2010, the judge doubled the bail for actress Lindsey Lohan, whose alcohol-monitoring bracelet recorded that she consumed alcohol in violation of the judge's orders.

An alternative to electronic monitoring is used in Florida, where 600 offenders are watched by a **global positioning system**, which uses satellites to track the location of offenders. For example, a GPS device can be programmed to inform an official when a sex offender approaches a schoolyard. The statute was passed after the abduction and murder of Jessica Lunsford (see page 577 of this chapter). The cost of monitoring, however, can be prohibitive for some state and local budgets.[31]

Most states now use some form of GPS tracking for persons accused or convicted of violating the criminal law. The system could also be used for tracking abducted persons, lost hikers, and other persons in trouble. A journal that focuses on terrorism described how the GPS systems work:

> Subjects under GPS tracking and monitoring wear a removable personal tracking unit (PTU) and a non-removable wireless ankle cuff. The ankle cuff is the size of a large wristwatch. The cuff communicates with the PTU to ensure that both items are always within a close and specific proximity of each other. If communication with the cuff is lost, the PTU assumes that the user has abandoned it and a violation is recorded. The PTU acquires its location from the Department of Defense's GPS satellites, and records this time and location into an Internet-based database system.
>
> This information is communicated back to probation, parole, bonding, and court officials. Using a web browser, authorities are able to look at a detailed map to determine where the person has been.[32]

With this system, the monitor can determine whether a person has violated the terms of his or her release and respond accordingly.

In June 2007, Illinois contracted with a private company to provide the state with GPS devices to be used initially on 100 high-risk sex offenders and, later, on 700 such offenders.[33] Likewise, in Wisconsin, sex offenders are monitored by GPS systems 24 hours a day for the rest of their lives. Both states require GPS monitoring by statute.[34]

One problem with EM and GPS monitoring is that they are expensive. A report on the use of ankle-bracelet monitoring in California estimated the cost to be $80 million annually ($65 million for GPS). More important is the more serious issue of whether they are effective. The California study concluded there was no evidence that society is any safer from monitored than from unmonitored offenders.[35]

Investigators who compared parolees who were released with EM with those released without EM concluded that "adding an EM component to parole supervision has no significant independent effect on the likelihood of a parolee's being recommitted to prison during the follow-up period or on the amount of time before recommitment to prison, after controlling for other relevant variables, including parole success likelihood and prior criminal history." These researchers also found that parolees with drug problems were more likely to return to prison than were those without such problems, which was consistent with other research findings. They did find, however, that the effect of EM differed among types of offenders. For example, whereas sex offenders are more likely than non-sex offenders to be returned to prison, EM did reduce the likelihood that this would occur.[36]

Probation

Most of the offenders in the United States who are under community supervision are on **probation**, a judicial determination that does not involve confinement but does include conditions imposed by a court. In both of these characteristics, it resembles the suspended sentence. The two are distinguished, however, by a third characteristic of probation—supervision, usually by a **probation officer**. The term *probation* also refers to the status of a person placed on probation, to the subsystem of the criminal justice system that handles this disposition of offenders, and to a process that involves the activities of the probation system: preparing reports, supervising probationers, and providing or obtaining services for them. The word *probation* comes from the Latin word *probare*, which means "to test" or "to prove."

History

Scholars do not agree on the origin of probation, but as they do with many other aspects of criminal justice systems, most trace it to English common law. Generally, U.S. probation is traced to a prosperous shoemaker in Boston, John Augustus, often called the "father of probation." As early as 1841, Augustus introduced into Boston courts the concept of friendly supervision in the community. From his own resources, Augustus paid the fines for many people who were jailed; he worked on rehabilitation as well as on release.[37]

In 1878, Massachusetts became the first state to enact a probation statute. By 1900, only five states had probation statutes, but the establishment of the juvenile court in 1899 in Chicago gave impetus to the probation movement. By 1915, 33 states had probation statutes, and by 1957, all states had them. The Probation Act of 1925 authorized probation in the federal system. Initially, federal probation was under the jurisdiction of the U.S. Department of Justice and delegated to the federal Bureau of Prisons. In 1940, jurisdiction over federal probation was transferred to the Administrative Office of U.S. Courts. The Speedy Trial Act of 1974 authorized the establishment of pre-trial services in 10 judicial districts, and those were expanded by the Pretrial Services Act of 1982. In 1978, the federal system began providing aftercare treatment for probationers who are drug dependent. In 1984, the Bail Reform Act was enacted. Among other provisions, this act gives judges the authority to consider a defendant's potential danger to the community in deciding whether to release the individual awaiting trial. The result was a significant increase in the number of suspects detained pending trial.[38]

Data

Recall Figure 15.1, which graphs the increases in correctional populations between 1980 and 2009. In 2009, the number of adults under community supervision (5,018,855, representing 1 of every 47 adults) decreased by 0.9 percent from 2008, the first decline since 1980. Most of that decrease (87 percent) was the result of a reduction in the number of adults on probation. That number dropped by 40,079 (0.9 percent) to a total of 4,203,967. Almost one-half of the decrease in U.S. probationers occurred in three states: Washington, California, and Florida.[39] Table 15.1 provides data on the characteristics of adults on probation in the United States at three time periods: 2000, 2008, and 2009.

The Probation Process

Technically, probation, which may be granted only by the court, is a form of sentencing. Often, however, it is considered a disposition in lieu of sentencing. In some cases, the court sentences a defendant to a term of incarceration but suspends that sentence for a specified period of time, during which the offender is on probation. If the terms of

Table 15.1

Characteristics of Adults on Probation, 2000, 2008–2009

Characteristics	2000	2008	2009
Total	100%	100%	100%
Sex			
Male	78%	76%	76%
Female	22	24	24
Race and Hispanic or Latino origin			
White[a]	54%	56%	55%
Black[a]	31	29	30
Hispanic or Latino	13	13	13
American Indian/Alaska Native[a]	1	1	1
Asian/Native Hawaiian/other Pacific Islander[a]	1	1	1
Two or more races[a]	. . .	1	—
Status of supervision			
Active	76%	71%	72%
Residential/other treatment program	. . .	1	1
Financial conditions remaining	. . .	1	1
Inactive	9	8	6
Absconder	9	8	8
Supervised out of jurisdiction	3	3	3
Warrant status	. . .	6	6
Other	3	2	2
Type of offense			
Felony	52%	49%	51%
Misdemeanor	46	48	47
Other infractions	2	2	2
Most serious offense			
Violent	. . .	19%	19%
Domestic violence	. . .	4	4
Sex offense	. . .	3	3
Other violent offense	. . .	12	13
Property	. . .	25	26
Drug	24	29	26
Public-order	24	17	18
DWI/DUI	18	14	15
Other traffic offense	6	4	4
Other[b]	52	10	10

Note: Each characteristic is based on probationers with a known status. Detail may not sum to total because of rounding.

—Less than 0.5%.

. . .Not available.

[a]Excludes persons of Hispanic or Latino origin.

[b]Includes violent and property offenses in 2000, because those data were not collected separately.

Source: Lauren E. Glaze and Thomas P. Bonczar, Bureau of Justice Statistics, *Probation and Parole in the United States, 2009* (December 2010), p. 26, http://bjs.ojp.usdoj.gov/content/pub/pdf/ppus09.pdf, accessed 26 December 2010.

probation are not violated, the sentence is not imposed, but if the offender violates probation, he or she may be incarcerated.

Because probation is a form of sentencing, which the U.S. Supreme Court considers a critical stage in criminal justice systems, the defendant is entitled to due process at the probation hearing. Under the U.S. Constitution, due process requires that a person not be deprived of life, liberty, or property without reasonable and lawful procedures (see Appendix A, Amendments V and XIV). This means that the judge may not be unreasonable, arbitrary, or capricious in the decision to grant or deny probation. The defendant is entitled to an attorney at this stage as well as when probation is revoked and the suspended sentence is imposed.[40]

Probation can be a cost-saving program for counties and states. In 2006, the New York City Independent Budget Office (IBO) announced the use of two programs providing intensive probation for youthful offenders. The youths were not perceived as risks to the community, but they needed more intensive probation supervision than usually provided. Such youths had been placed in one of two facilities located outside New York City at a cost of approximately $150,000 per child for 12 months. The distance made it difficult for the juveniles' families to visit, the recidivist rate was approximately 75 percent, and the cost was prohibitive. The two new programs, the Enhanced Supervision Program (ESP) and Esperanza, were less expensive ($5,900 and $15,000 per child, respectively) and had lower caseloads for probation supervision. They focused on family-based therapeutic services, crisis management, substance abuse therapy, home visits, community service requirements, and so on. Esperanza was more expensive because it is more intensive. The IBO pointed out that the city would obviously save money with these programs, but it would be a few years before researchers would know whether they cut the 75 percent recidivism rate of return within three years of release.[41]

Probation Supervision

Authorities do not agree on important supervision issues in probation, such as whether the size of a probation officer's caseload is related significantly to the success or failure of probation. But it is clear that traditional probation has problems. Supervision practices and probation conditions vary from jurisdiction to jurisdiction and often involve little supervision.

More recently, the concept of **intensive probation supervision (IPS)** has gained prominence and has focused on another purpose of probation—the diversion of defendants from incarceration. Diversion is seen as one way to attack the problem of prison overcrowding.

In addition to its purpose of diversion, IPS has the following characteristics. First, in many jurisdictions, probation caseloads are so high and probation is con-

sidered so ineffective, both in helping the offender and in protecting society, that judges may see IPS as the only alternative to the incarceration of convicted offenders. Second, despite the increased cost of IPS compared with traditional forms of probation, a difference that results from smaller caseloads, IPS is considerably less costly than incarceration. Third, IPS may have eliminated some of the negative public attitudes toward probation in that it can be viewed as more punitive because of the increased supervision.

There are problems, however. An earlier study of IPS in Texas disclosed the following:

> The IPS program did not alleviate prison crowding and may actually have increased it;
>
> The IPS program costs considerably more than most advocates have realized; [and]
>
> The IPS program was no more effective than routine parole in reducing offender recidivism, as measured by arrests and convictions.[42]

In a study of an IPS program designed for drug offenders, investigators reported that, compared with probationers without IPS, the IPS drug offender subjects had more supervision (an average of three hours a month compared with 20 minutes for the non-IPS probationers), but they had more technical violations. There was no significant difference between the two groups in the arrests for new crimes. It was suggested that more intensive supervision coupled with more treatment might produce better results, but it is not known how strict that supervision must be. Furthermore, the costs increase as supervision increases.[43]

Another point to consider with regard to probation may strike the reader as unreasonable: the use of probation to prevent murder. But a noted criminologist pointed out, "The concentration of homicide among offenders on community supervision makes these [probation and parole] agencies a prime focus for homicide prevention." It was estimated that in Philadelphia 70 percent of all murders "could involve victims or offenders under community supervision." By using modern sophisticated developments in both hardware (desktop supercomputers) and statistics, it is now possible to develop models that can be reasonably accurate in forecasting who is likely to commit murder. These models could be used in planning treatment programs for those under community supervision as well as in devising the degree of control that might be reasonable for the offenders.[44]

Probation Conditions

Regardless of the nature of probation supervision, most judges impose probation conditions. Usually, there are restrictions on travel, such as prohibitions against leaving the state or country without permission, and prohibitions against the use of alcohol (or if permitted to drink alcohol, prohibitions about going to bars) and illegal drugs. There are prohibitions concerning associating with questionable people and requirements to hold a job, attend counseling, or enter substance abuse or other treatment programs. When challenged, most probation conditions are upheld, but occasionally, appellate courts rule that the trial judge imposed a condition that is not permitted. A few examples illustrate the trend in rulings.

Courts have held that mandatory drug testing is a reasonable probation condition in some cases, such as that of the offender who admitted at sentencing that sometimes he smoked six marijuana cigarettes and drank 14 beers daily and that he had consumed 5 beers on the day he committed the burglary for which he was being sentenced. When he tested positive for cocaine, his probation was revoked. He appealed, arguing that mandatory drug testing was unreasonable. The Hawaii Supreme Court upheld the drug testing and ruled that state law provides for these tests and that they do not represent an unconstitutional invasion of privacy.[45]

A Pennsylvania court held that it was reasonable to require a female probationer to stay away from her boyfriend for two years. Under Pennsylvania law, a probationer may be required to "refrain from frequenting unlawful or disreputable places or consorting with disreputable persons." The probationer in question was convicted of assisting her boyfriend to avoid apprehension after he entered guilty pleas to numerous burglary counts but absconded before sentencing. The court reasoned that the probationer would have a better chance at rehabilitation if she had no contact with her boyfriend, who subsequently had become her fiancé.[46]

A federal court held that it was reasonable for a judge to order a probationer to get a paying job rather than become a missionary. The probationer had been ordered to pay restitution and fines after conviction of a series of religious scams.[47] A California state court held that it was permissible to require a probationer to attend nonspiritual programs aimed at assisting with substance abuse.[48]

The Wisconsin Supreme Court held that it was not unreasonable for a lower court to require as a condition of probation that a defendant who fathered nine children must agree not to father additional children unless he could prove that he could and would support them. The defendant had been convicted of intentionally refusing to pay child support, for which he could have been incarcerated. The U.S. Supreme Court declined to review the case.[49]

In another case which the U.S. Supreme Court declined to review, a lower appellate court did not approve a probation condition of a defendant who pleaded guilty to receiving more than 1,000 pictures of child pornography. The trial court had made as one condition of probation that the defendant could not access the Internet without his probation officer's approval. The appellate court held that the condition was too broad and must be modified to withstand constitutional scrutiny.[50]

Finally, as with medical parole, discussed later, medical probation may be granted to avoid incarcerating offenders who are very ill. Strict terms may be placed on that probation. For example, in 2008, a senior federal judge had serious reservations about sending an ill defendant to federal prison for possessing child pornography. He was placed on probation with one condition being that he not view child pornography. The judge was severely criticized for this decision even though the defendant was awaiting a kidney transplant. In May 2010, when Ralph Rausch was back in court on a charge of viewing child pornography, Judge John L. Kane said,

> You are slamming the door in the face of the people who are trying to help you, and I don't care how sick you are, there is no excuse for that—none. . . . You could have gone to prison and you would have been dead by now. You are a very sick man, and I am very concerned about that, but at the same time, you have to start putting forth some effort.

Judge Kane sent Rausch to a federal halfway house for 180 days and told him that if he violated the terms of his probation, he would be sent to federal prison no matter how sick he was. In 2009, Judge Kane testified before the U.S. Sentencing Commission, stating that there was no empirical evidence supporting the belief that severe prison terms will enable an offender who has been convicted of possessing child pornography to cease that behavior upon release from prison.[51]

Although probationers constitute the majority of offenders under community supervision, and some prison inmates are released without supervision, all need assistance in this transition.

Release from Incarceration

Most incarcerated offenders are released from jail or prison back into the community. Little if anything is done to prepare jail inmates for their return to society. Theoretically, jail inmates are incarcerated for brief times, although that is not always the case. But where prerelease programs do exist, they are usually for offenders who are released from prison. These individuals face many problems upon release. Most have limited or no financial resources. Many do not have employment, and some do not have residences or families to whom they may return. Most receive indifferent or hostile reactions from the community. Those who have been incarcerated for long periods of time have the additional problem of catching up on how contemporary society operates. Probably all encounter emotional problems in reacting to a new environment, and many feel depressed, estranged, lonely, and rejected.

Release from prison may also be a dangerous time for inmates. A recent study published in the *New England*

Journal of Medicine involved inmates released between 1999 and 2003 in Washington State. It reported that, during the first two years of release, these inmates, compared to people in the general population, were 12 times more likely to die of drug overdoses and 10 times more likely to be killed. One researcher said that despite the higher rates of smoking, mental health problems, chemical dependence, and risk taking of this group, that is probably a much higher death rate than one would reasonably expect.[52]

Criminologist Joan Petersilia published a book entitled *When Prisoners Come Home* in which she looked at some of the problems released inmates face. Three-fourths of them have a history of substance abuse; 40 percent have not graduated from high school or obtained a GED; one in six is mentally ill. A high percentage of these releasees (as high as two of every three) will be returned to prison either for committing a new crime or for breaking the terms of release. Petersilia emphasized that we cannot break this cycle without funding adequate programs to give releasees alternatives to prison. She suggested more educational, work, and rehabilitation opportunities. Discretionary parole policies should involve inmates in planning for release, and there should be better parole, including supervision and surveillance of those who are at highest risk. Service providers, releasees and their families, law enforcement officials, victim advocates, and neighborhood social service agencies should develop avenues for improving social control among releasees.[53]

Other changes that might assist offenders with reintegration are included in the Second Chance Act of 2007. The purposes of that statute, presented earlier in Exhibit 15.2, were based upon numerous congressional findings, including the fact that, according to recent studies, within three years of release from incarceration in state prisons, two-thirds of inmates may be expected to be re-arrested for a serious misdemeanor or a felony.[54]

Reentry: The Challenge

The obvious challenge is to determine which inmates to release and how to prepare them for that release. In recent years, significant attention has been given by researchers to the reentry process in an effort to determine what works and what does not work for the inmates and for society. In 1974, Robert Martinson published an article that gained attention for years. He asked the simple question, "What works?" and concluded that nothing does.[55] Twenty years later, Joan Petersilia, who conducted numerous studies on recidivism and other issues in criminology, reviewed the literature on what works in prisoner reentry. She concluded that we know a lot in theory, but practice and theory are "moving on independent tracks and the gulfs between them are still wide."[56]

Other scholars have examined specific programs, and they are not in agreement over what works. Consider, for

example, the analysis of a short-term reentry program in New York between February 2003 and February 2004. Project Greenlight, designed and evaluated after one year by the Vera Institute of Justice, involved three groups of men who returned to New York City after their release from prison. The groups were similar in race, age, criminal history, and level of education. One group (344) spent its final 60 days in a minimum-security institution engaging in eight weeks of daylong reentry training in such areas as substance abuse prevention, family counseling, and practical skills (e.g., managing time and a bank account, budgeting, and using public transportation). They also participated in programs designed to divert them from homeless shelters. The second group (278) was transferred to the same facility but participated in less intensive prerelease training. The third group (113) did not participate in any prerelease training programs. This last group had the lowest recidivist rate after one year of release, and the first group had the worst. Investigators referred to these results as "unexpected and puzzling." They stated that their analysis suggested

> some short-term, prison-based programs, especially attractive to states and criminal justice agencies because of the low cost and capability to handle large numbers of offenders, may be poorly situated to address the multiple needs of offenders as they return to the community, and may in fact, increase the probability of criminal behavior. These findings also suggest that correctional interventions need to pay attention to the treatment principles underlying successful interventions and not simply the components of programs known to work.[57]

Project Greenlight was based in part on a Canadian program entitled Reasoning and Rehabilitation (R&R) in which inmates are taught how to deal with impulsive behavior. A reviewer of that program and others suggested that a lack of follow through might have been an issue. As an example, the investigator noted that since most offenders are irresponsible and have difficulty dealing with basic obligations, "It defies logic to expect that increasing the dosage of ineffective treatments would improve their outcomes."[58]

Others concluded that Project Greenlight's failure was not surprising because the program did not follow all of the principles that we know to work, including those associated with R&R. In short, Project Greenlight demonstrated the problems with programs that are implemented with fiscal constraints and are terminated too quickly.[59]

Other research is more promising. Researchers who considered the question of whether a relationship exists between program integrity and program effectiveness analyzed data from 38 halfway houses with programs for parolees in Ohio. They reported an overall "fairly strong correlation between program integrity . . . and reductions in recidivism." These researchers emphasized that, in determining the effectiveness of a treatment program, one must consider program implementation, offender assessment, and program evaluation.[60] If program integrity is compromised by budgetary constraints, as is frequently the case, one can expect less impressive treatment results.

Criminologists have emphasized the importance of including reentry programs that assist inmates in managing violence, especially in domestic situations. No reentry program is complete "unless some attention is devoted to assisting prisoners and their families strengthen their relationships and develop the capacity to negotiate conflict and change."[61]

Another issue that must be considered in the evaluation of treatment programs is theory. (Recall that Chapters 3 through 6 of this text focus on theory.) In an analysis of reentry, one criminologist noted the significant amount of research on the subject that has been conducted since 2000. However, much of the research evaluating various programs is descriptive and not based on theory, which "complicates the interpretation of results." Those that are based on theory are based on "theories of the clinicians who are providing the service rather than persons who are specifically interested in reentry per se," which limits the application of the knowledge.[62]

Recognition of the importance of preparation for reentry has led a majority of states to provide various programs for inmates close to their release dates. Exhibit 15.4 describes the programs that are available in Texas.

Prerelease Programs: An Overview

There is wide variation in the types and availability of **prerelease programs** for reentry of inmates back into the community. Most, however, make some attempts to

---

EXHIBIT 15.4 Reentry into Society: A Look at Texas Rehabilitation Programs

The Community Justice Assistance Division (CJAD) of the Texas Department of Criminal Justice (TDCJ) offers the following programs to assist inmates in their reentry back into society from incarceration. The programs are offered by community supervision and corrections departments (CSCDs), are categorized as *Rehabilitation Programs*, and are described as follows:

- "*Adult Education Programs*—These programs assist adults under community supervision acquire to [sic] academic competencies for literacy skills, General Education Development (GED) certificates, and English as a Second Language.
- *Cognitive Programs*—These psycho-educational, nonacademic programs assist adults under community supervision acquire competencies in problem solving, anger management, understanding the impact of their behavior on others, changing thinking and changing behavior to noncriminal alternatives.
- *Vocational/Employment and Life Skills Training*—These educational, non-academic programs assist adults under community supervision acquire skills to obtain and keep employment and function at a higher level in daily life.
- *Substance Abuse Treatment Programs*—These programs include a continuum of care ranging from screening/assessment, outpatient, intensive outpatient and residential programs to treat those under community supervision with drug and/or alcohol problems.
- *Programs for the Mentally Impaired*—This new mental health initiative provides intensive case management, treatment referral and resource linkage to

either divert the mentally impaired offender from the criminal justice system, or to provide sufficient supportive services to minimize the risk of revocation.
- *Sex Offender Surveillance and Treatment*—This intensive supervision requires mandated registration and reporting, and also requires treatment by licensed therapists to reduce the risk of recidivism.
- *Restitution Programs*—Restitution is required of nearly every person under community supervision. The supervisee repays and restores society and/or the victim by monetary payment and/or community service work without pay. Hundreds of thousands of hours of community service are accomplished each year in Texas, restoring communities and contributing the equivalent of millions of dollars of service. In addition, each county collected court-ordered monetary restitution.
- *Batterers Intervention and Prevention Programs (BIPP)*—These are operated by nonprofit organizations that provide, on a local basis to batterers referred by the courts for treatment, treatment and educational services designed to help the batterers stop abusive behavior. TDCJ-CJAD works in collaboration with the Texas Council on Family Violence (TCFV) and has established minimum Guidelines for programs to receive funding."

Source: Texas Department of Criminal Justice, Community Justice Assistance Division, "Rehabilitation and Victim Services Programs," http://www.tdcj.state.tx.us/cjad/cjad-rehab.htm, accessed 14 November 2010.

deal with the two most immediate problems—money and jobs. Programs differ among institutions, ranging from information on etiquette and changing social mores to practical details on how to knot a tie and interview for a job. Some institutions offer training sessions to assist inmates in preparing for release; others offer halfway programs for a gradual reentry into society. Still others, such as Michigan, offer a mentoring program. The Michigan Prisoner ReEntry Initiative (MPRI) has as its mission creating better citizens while keeping the community safe. The MPRI claims to deliver "a seamless plan of services, support, and supervision from the time a prisoner enters prison through their return to a community." Mentoring is a crucial part of the MPRI system. Each releasee is paired with someone in the community to which he or she returns. The program, which began in 2005, claims a much lower rate of recidivism than usual (11.4 percent compared to 50 percent).[63]

In general, the purpose of a prerelease program is to train the offender in the ways of daily living: how to get a job, how to keep a job, how to relate to his or her family, and how to live in a world that may have changed significantly since the offender began the incarceration period. Prerelease programs may include educational and vocational programs, treatment programs, or life enrichment programs (in which offenders are taught how to control their emotions, make plans, and establish goals). Inmates are taught how to manage money, and they may participate in recreational and other leisure activities. Decision making and problem solving are also featured. Participants are made aware of and given access to databases, including those of state agencies, and they are instructed in employment and career issues. Ideally, they will have jobs before they are released from incarceration, and some states require that they have jobs before they are released on parole. But jobs for ex-felons are not easy to obtain, and this is an even more difficult problem with the high unemployment rates in the United States.

The Hiring Crisis

The employment picture is bleak for all ex-offenders, and many have not had adequate training before or during incarceration. Some jurisdictions are trying to alleviate the problems. For example, Ohio opened its first "work prison" in 1996. Nonviolent, minimum-security inmates live in a community facility while working in the community. They work for nonprofit groups, government agencies, and public schools at skills that will be useful when they are released.[64] Ohio also permits low-risk inmates to work outside the prisons, although that program was in jeopardy in May 2010, when two inmates who were working in the governor's mansion were under the influence of alcohol, presumed to have been obtained in that facility. The governor suspended the program during an investigation of the incident. The investigation was concluded in late June 2010. There was no evidence of how much liquor was consumed, and the prison director recommended that the prison work program be continued. The inmates were disciplined with 15 days of segregation.[65]

In 2004, Indiana began a program to provide jobs for inmates leaving prison. The Indiana Offender Reintegration Project is funded by the federal government. The program provides substance abuse treatment and assists inmates with housing, job training, and employment. The Department of Corrections and the state Family and Social Services Administration, along with faith-based groups, are partnered to achieve the goal of assisting inmates in adjusting to life outside prison and in not committing further crimes. Indiana officials were hoping to cut their prison populations and looking closely at treatment alternatives.[66]

America Works, a company that has placed welfare recipients in jobs for the past two decades, is now working on placing released offenders. The emphasis in this program is not on specific training (much of which can be learned on the job) but on teaching dedication and determination. In an intensive one-week seminar, participants learn appropriate dress for work; good work behavior, demeanor, and attitude; the importance of being prompt; and other work chores and habits that may be expected by potential employers. After a candidate is placed in a job, he or she is assigned a caseworker to assist with any issues that might arise. America Works is not a government program. It is a for-profit organization involved in job placement. In an analysis of the results of the program involving ex-offenders, Columbia University researchers concluded that "the cost–benefit ratio for this program to date is excellent. . . . If employment can be sustained and retention rates improved, the savings to the taxpayer become enormous."[67]

One critical issue with regard to hiring ex-offenders is that over 80 percent of U.S. employers require criminal background checks on potential employees. With modern technology making records easily available and a growing concern with legal liability, it is reasonable to assume that ex-offenders will have difficulty getting jobs.[68] This has led some researchers to propose that job applications no longer include "the box" that requires an applicant to indicate whether he or she has ever been arrested, charged, convicted, and so on.[69] Another issue is abolishing some or all lifetime bans on ex-felons. For example, in some jurisdictions, ex-felons are prohibited for life from many activities, such as foster parenting and adoption, financial support for education, and professional licensing in many areas.[70]

The U.S. Department of Justice (DOJ) sponsored a research project, the results of which may relax some problems related to hiring ex-felons. Criminologist Alfred Blumstein and other researchers at Carnegie Mellon University conducted the research, which examined the criminal history records of 88,000 persons who were arrested for the first time in New York State in 1980. They focused on persons who were 16 (considered an adult in that state), 18, and 20 and who were arrested for robbery, burglary, and aggravated assault. These subjects were compared to the risk of arrest of people of the same ages in the general population and to persons who had never been arrested. The goal was to determine at what point the risk of committing another crime for the offender population was no greater than the risk that the control populations might commit a crime. The researchers determined a "hazard rate," which is the probability over time that a person who has been arrested will remain clean. Their conclusion was that it takes about seven and one-half years for a person arrested for robbery at age 18 and four years for one arrested for aggravated assault at that age to achieve the same hazard rate as their counterparts in the general population. These preliminary results will be compared with studies in other places and with other populations. The research may provide employers with some reasonable time frame for deciding that it is no longer a risk to hire an ex-offender.[71]

Furlough and Work-Release Programs

In some jurisdictions, **work-release** programs and **furloughs** are utilized to prepare inmates for release. Although furloughs were introduced in 1918, the extensive use of them or of work release in the United States is recent, stemming from their provision in the federal system by the Prisoner Rehabilitation Act of 1965. Most of the programs in existence today were established by state laws after the 1965 federal law had been enacted.

A *furlough* is a brief absence from the institution, usually for a specified purpose other than work or study. Furloughs may be granted to allow inmates to visit sick relatives, attend family funerals, secure employment, obtain a driver's license, meet with future parole officers, arrange for housing, or visit family members. Furloughs may last from several hours to several days. Their main advantage is that offenders are placed in contact with their families and the outside world. They have a chance to make decisions on their own away from the closely monitored prison routine, and the community is given time to adjust to them.

In *work release*, the offender is permitted to leave the institution temporarily to work or to attend school. Inmates may participate in vocational study, take courses at an educational institution, or work at a job in the community. There may be statutory restrictions on eligibility for work release. For example, Minnesota provides that an inmate is eligible for work release only if she or he is regularly employed. Minnesota also has requirements concerning disposition of the work releasee's income, providing as follows:

> The earnings of an inmate may be collected by the sheriff, probation department, local social services agency or suitable person or agency designated by the court. From the earnings, the person or agency designated to collect them may pay:
>
> (1) the cost of the inmate's maintenance, both inside and outside the jail, but the charge for maintenance inside the jail may not exceed the legal daily allowance for board allowed the sheriff for ordinary inmates;
>
> (2) to the extent directed by the court, pay the support of dependents, if any;
>
> (3) court costs and fines; and
>
> (4) court-ordered restitution, if any. Any balance must be retained until the inmate's discharge and then paid to the inmate.[72]

An advantage of furloughs and work releases is that they give offenders an opportunity for closer contacts with their families. These ties may ease the problems of adjusting to society. In addition, work release enables offenders to provide financial support for their families and helps improve inmates' attitudes toward socially responsible work. Improvements in self-esteem, self-image, and self-respect are additional benefits to offenders. An advantage to society and to correctional systems is the lower cost of furloughs compared with incarceration. Further, inmates on work release may be required to reimburse the state for part of the cost of their incarceration. They pay taxes and may be required to contribute to victim restitution funds, as noted in the preceding Minnesota statute.

Offenders who are on work release may have problems in adjusting to the contrast between the community during the day and the institution at night. Indeed, on the one hand, it might be easier to make a complete break with the institution and attempt to readjust to society without having to return to prison. On the other hand, release during the day may eliminate or interrupt participation in some prison programs that benefit offenders. In addition, problems such as whether the offender is required to pay for room and board may arise over the use of money earned. Transportation is frequently a problem because many correctional institutions are not located in urban areas where inmates are most likely to find jobs.

A final problem with work release and furlough is the possibility that participants may commit additional crimes or escape from supervision.

Parole

One of the most controversial aspects of criminal justice systems is **parole**, which refers to the release of offenders from correctional facilities after they have served part of their sentences. It is distinguished from *unconditional release* in that conditions are imposed on the parolee's behavior, and usually, the parolee is placed under supervision. When offenders are released unconditionally from a correctional facility, the state (or federal) government does not have jurisdiction to supervise their behavior. Unconditional release *must* occur after the entire sentence has been served. Release may occur after a portion of the sentence has been served and the remainder waived because of good-time credits the inmate has accrued.

History

Authorities do not agree on the origin of parole. Some trace it to the English system of sending criminals to the American colonies. Criminals were pardoned by the English government after being sold to the highest bidder in America. The buyer became the master of the offender, whose new status was that of indentured servant. The system was similar to parole in that, to receive the change in status, an individual agreed to specific conditions similar to those imposed on parolees today.[73]

Others claim that the concept of conditioned liberty was first introduced in France around 1830. It was an intermediary step of freedom between prison confinement and complete freedom in the community. Still others trace the history of parole to the reform efforts of Captain Alexander Maconochie, who began the reformatory movement in 1840 in Australia, where he was in charge of the worst of England's penal colonies—Norfolk Island. Maconochie eliminated the definite sentence and instituted a system of marks that inmates could earn for good behavior and work. Marks were used to reduce the amount of time served in the prison colony. Maconochie evaluated his term at Norfolk in these words: "I found Norfolk Island a hell, but left it an orderly and well-regulated community." His work was not appreciated by the English, and he was recalled, but his reform efforts had a lasting effect in England and in America.[74]

Maconochie's system was taken to Ireland by Sir Walter Crofton, who added supervision to the early release program. In 1870, Crofton spoke to the American Prison Association, which adopted a "Declaration of Principles" that included parole release. The actual use of formal parole in the United States is traced to 1876 in the Elmira Reformatory in New York State.[75]

All states and the federal government eventually adopted parole systems. Parole was used extensively, although in recent years it has been questioned and, in some jurisdictions, has been restricted or abolished. More recently, some states have reinstituted parole to relieve jail and prison overcrowding.

Data

As indicated in Figure 15.1, introduced earlier, parole is used much less frequently than probation; however, parole has been a more frequent method of releasing inmates than is expiration of sentence. Discretionary release to parole declined significantly between 1980 (55 percent) and 2004 (22 percent), and the most frequent method of release from custody became mandatory release to parole. These percentages reflect statutory changes that eliminated or reduced possibilities for parole based on discretion in

favor of determinate sentences with mandatory release to parole supervision.[76]

The state parole population rose about 10 percent per year between 1980 and 1992, at which point the rise continued but at a slower pace, growing about 1.4 percent annually through 2005, when the adult parole population reached 780,616. In 2006, the adult parole population was 799,875, and in 2007, it was approximately 821,177 (some states were unable to produce data that year). The population increased by only 0.9 percent between 2007 and 2008, reaching a total of 828,169 adults on parole in that year. This figure represented 16 percent of the total U.S. adults under community supervision. Figure 15.3 graphs the changes in the parole population between 2007 and 2008 by jurisdiction, showing that most of the growth during that period was in the federal system. In 2008, drug offenders were the most common parolees (37 percent); violent offenders constituted 26 percent, and property offenders made up 23 percent. Most parolees (88 percent) in 2008 were men, 41 percent were white, 38 percent were black, and 19 percent were Hispanic. In 2009, the total U.S. parole population decreased from 824,834 to 819,308.[77]

Although these data reveal that a majority of those released from prison were minorities, that fact must be interpreted in light of the percentage sentenced. African Americans constituted 61 percent (58 percent male, 3 percent female) of the inmate population in 2008. African American men were six and one-half times more likely than any other group to be sentenced to prison despite the fact that their numbers decreased between 2000 and 2008 (due primarily to the decrease in drug sentences).[78]

Numerous researchers claim that race is a factor at every stage of decision making in the criminal justice system, and although approximately 95 percent of incarcerated offenders will be released at some time, it is not clear if race plays a role in whether an inmate is released on parole. It is true that blacks serve longer sentences before they are paroled and that they may be required to "go through more hoops" before that decision. But it is not clear whether this is due to legitimate factors (e.g., offense for which incarcerated, discipline while in prison, and so on) or to race. Researchers in an Alabama study, a state in which 61 percent of inmates are African American, concluded that race was not a factor either at the preliminary screening stage for parole or at parole release.[79]

An important issue with regard to parole is whether parolees are unsuccessful and, if so, returned to prison. The BJS calculates the *at-risk population*, "defined as the number of offenders under supervision at the start of the year (on January 1) plus all offenders who entered supervision during the year." Theoretically, all of these persons could be incarcerated; thus, they are "at risk." Figure 15.4 graphs the estimated percentage of the at-risk population who were returned to incarceration between 2000 and 2009.[80]

Figure 15.3

Change in the Parole Population

Source: Lauren E. Glaze and Thomas P. Bonczar, Bureau of Justice Statistics, *Probation and Parole in the United States, 2008* (December 2009), p. 8, http://bjs.ojp.usdoj.gov/content/pub/pdf/ppus08.pdf, accessed 14 November 2010.

*Includes an estimated decrease for Virginia. Virginia was excluded from the graph because the state could not provide data for the January 1, 2008 population.

The Parole System

The organization of parole is complex. It consists of two main divisions: the **parole board**, responsible for release decisions in most but not all jurisdictions, and **parole officers,** who supervise parolees. These divisions carry out the main functions of parole: releasing and placing inmates on parole, supervising parolees, and releasing parolees from supervision upon completion of their sentences or proof

that they are no longer a risk to the community. They also revoke parole when the parolees have violated parole conditions (although some of these processes also involve courts, as we will see).

The most important stage in the administration of parole is the parole hearing. Until recently, the legal requirements at this stage were unclear, and the nature of the hearing differed from state to state. Most allowed the inmate to

Figure 15.4

Estimated Percent of the At-Risk Parole Population Returned
to Incarceration, 2000–2009

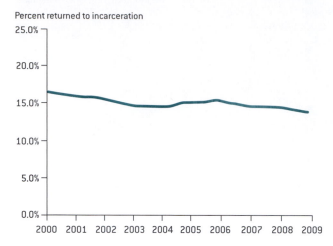

Percent returned to incarceration

Source: Lauren E. Glaze and Thomas P. Bonczar, Bureau of
Justice Statistics, *Probabtion and Parole in the United States,
2009* (December 2010), p. 6, http://bjs.ojp.usdoj.gov/content/
pub/pdf/ppus09.pdf, accessed 26 December 2010.

be present, but some refused an oral hearing. Some parole boards heard cases with all members present; others
divided into panels, with each panel hearing and deciding
different cases. Usually, the hearings were private, attended
only by the inmate (where permitted), board members, and
a representative of the institution in which the inmate was
incarcerated. Reports from family members, psychological
or other treatment personnel, or institutional staff members
might have been included. Some boards requested information concerning the inmate's plans upon release. Reasons
for denial of parole might or might not have been given to
the inmates.

Federal courts were divided over the requirements of
due process at the parole hearing. But in 1979, in *Greenholtz v. Inmates of Nebraska Penal and Correctional
Complex*, the U.S. Supreme Court held that due process
requirements were met by the Nebraska statute that allowed inmates, at the time of the first parole decision in
their cases, an opportunity to speak on their own behalf
and, in the case of parole denial, be given statements of
the reasons for those denials. The Court in *Greenholtz*
held that the Nebraska statute created an *expectation*
of parole that must be protected by due process. Thus,
although there is no *federal constitutional* due process
requirement, jurisdictions may create *statutory requirements* by the way in which their statutes are worded. Each
jurisdiction's due process requirements must be determined by examining that jurisdiction's statute. But even
if some elements of due process are required, it is not
required that a parole hearing involve all the elements
of due process required at a criminal trial. The parole

board is not required to specify the particular evidence
that influenced a denial.[81]

In *Board of Pardons v. Allen*, decided in 1987, the U.S.
Supreme Court reaffirmed its decision in *Greenholtz*, holding that Montana's statute created an expectation of parole
provided certain conditions are met by the inmate. If the inmate meets those conditions, parole must be granted. Once
again, it is the wording of the statute, not the possibility of
parole per se, that creates the expectation of liberty that
must be protected. The use of *shall* rather than *may* in a
statute creates this expectation.[82] In 1995, in *Sandin v. Conner*, the Court criticized *Greenholtz* but left it standing.[83]

Prior to these court cases, John Irwin emphasized the
problems that arbitrary decisions by parole boards could
create for inmates. In his classic book *The Felon*, Irwin
said that arbitrariness by parole boards created a sense of
injustice, which increased the inmate's loss of commitment to conventional society.[84]

Perhaps former U.S. Supreme Court Justice Hugo
Black best summarized the view of many inmates toward
the parole board:

> In the course of my reading—by no means confined
> to law—I have reviewed many of the world's reli
> gions. The tenets of many faiths hold the deity to be
> a trinity. Seemingly, the parole boards, by whatever
> names designated in the various states, have in too
> many instances sought to enlarge this to include
> themselves as members.[85]

The administrative and legal issues regarding parole supervision and parole conditions are similar in nature (although not always in degree) to those of probation and thus
are not discussed further, although some of the issues are
raised in the following discussion on the future of parole.

The Future of Parole

As the result of highly publicized crimes committed by offenders while on parole as well as the trend toward harsher
punishment, some jurisdictions abolished parole. When
parolees commit crimes, especially violent ones, society is
outraged, and such crimes may result in changes in the parole systems. After a parolee killed Police Officer Anthony
Mosomillo, age 36, in New York City in 1998, the state
enacted a statute that limits access to early release and imposes required supervision for all determinate sentences.
The new criminal statute provides, in part, as follows:

> In general, when a court imposes a determinate sen
> tence it shall in each case state not only the term
> of imprisonment, but also an additional period of
> post-release supervision.[86]

This law, which is part of Jenna's Law, was the result of
lobbying by the parents of Jenna Grieshaber, who was
killed by a parolee in her Albany apartment in 1997. The
New York State Division of Parole's explanation of Jenna's
Law is reproduced in Exhibit 15.5.

15.5 The Sentencing Reform Act of 1998 (New York): Jenna's Law

"The Sentencing Reform Act of 1998—also known as Jenna's Law—was passed by the Legislature and signed into law by Governor George Pataki in August 1998.

"The law establishes determinate sentences for first-time violent felony offenders and requires their incarceration for longer periods by mandating that they serve at least six-sevenths of their determinate sentences. By requiring that first-time violent felony offenders receive determinate sentences, the law eliminates discretionary release from prison. For class B, C and D violent felony offenses, the law increases the minimum sentence of imprisonment that a court can impose. To provide greater protection to the public, the law also specifies that all violent felony offenders must serve a period of post-release supervision and establishes guidelines for the administration of post-release supervision. The law also expands victim notification when persons convicted of violent felonies and other offenses are released, abscond or escape from prison, or are released to the supervision of the Division of Parole.

"The law adds a new section to the Penal Law [§70.45] that establishes the terms of post-release supervision and the methods for calculating the terms of post-release supervision.

- "A term of post-release supervision must be a part of every determinate sentence.
- "Violations of post-release supervision may result in reincarceration for a fixed term between six months and the unserved balance of the post-release supervision term, not to exceed five years." . . .

"The period of post-release supervision for all second-time violent felony offenders is five years."

Source: New York State Division of Parole, "The Sentencing Reform Act of 1998—Jenna's Law," https://www.parole.state.ny.us/legislation-jl.html, accessed 12 November 2010. Jenna's Law is codified at NY CLS Penal, Section 70.45 (2010).

What happens when parole as a method of release from prison is abolished? Most states with flat-term or determinate sentencing laws allow early release based on good-time credits earned in the institution. New York was the first state to permit inmates to accumulate days off for good behavior while incarcerated, and that state began the process in 1817.[87] However, if good-time credits are not available and parole is abolished, the most obvious result is an increase in time served in institutions. No longer can parole boards reduce acute overcrowding in prisons. Where good-time provisions remain, the control of sentence length has moved from the parole board to prison officials. Individual correctional officers make the initial decisions about inmate conduct and behavior and thus control inmates' good-time credits. Thus, abolition of parole may relocate, not remove, discretion.

Earlier chapters noted that discretion exists in all areas of criminal justice systems. The exercise of that discretion involves predictions. Police, judges, probation and parole officers, attorneys, and correctional personnel all make decisions according to such predictions. Our ability to predict accurately is limited, and it may not improve in the near future. But the point is that predictions are made, and discretion is exercised. Nevertheless, the movement to abolish parole has continued.

Others claim that the abolition of parole is a serious mistake. A report by the American Probation and Parole Association and the Association of Paroling Authorities International concluded: "The abolition of parole has been tried and has failed on a spectacular scale. . . . The absence of parole means that offenders simply walk out the door of prison at the end of a pre-determined period of time, no

questions asked."[88] The two organizations began a move toward convincing Americans that parole does not mean being soft on crime; rather, it is a necessary measure for the release and supervision of releasees. They noted that the public thinks parole means shorter sentences, but that is not necessarily the case. Sentences may be determined by the availability of prison space, and releasing inmates because of space shortage and without parole supervision may be dangerous. The report concluded that in all states that had abolished parole, "the alternative has resulted in shorter, definite sentences which automatically release offenders at the end of a set sentence."[89]

Nevertheless, parole failures are high in some jurisdictions, with some estimates that 42 percent of parolees are returned to prison, some for additional crimes but many for technical violations (see again Figure 15.4). There is reason to argue, however, that the problem is not parole but the lack of proper parole supervision and agreements. We must change the "contracts" that parolees have with their parole officers so that contracts reflect the research evidence

on how to increase motivation and promote behavioral change in resistant clients. At the center of the revised contract must be a system of "earned discharge" or accelerated release, whereby parolees have the ability to reduce the total length of their parole term by demonstrating arrest-free behavior and self-sufficiency.[90]

The parole system, it is argued, must focus on behavior change rather than simply surveillance and deterrence. The current approach is to detail for the parolee what he or she must do to avoid the serious consequences (e.g., return to prison). But it does not show the offender how to change behavior to accomplish the ultimate goal: release from parole. "A balance of rewards and sanctions is necessary to foster prosocial behavior and treatment participation." It is also important to provide sufficient incentives to encourage parolees to continue their involvements with treatment and other positive programs. It is suggested that we should reduce the amount of time that nonviolent offenders who pose little risk are on parole. It is recommended that all parolees be required to spend at least six months on parole under supervision because most who commit additional crimes will do so quickly after release. Recidivism rates are even lower after the first year and lower still for parolees who are working or participating in educational and substance abuse programs. Possibly, "A greater number of parolees might participate usefully in rehabilitation programs if they were convinced that the duration of their parole might be reduced appreciably."[91]

One final issue with regard to the future of parole is that for humane reasons, but perhaps, more important, due to prison overcrowding and the high cost of medical care, an increasing number of jurisdictions today are permitting medical parole. Individuals who are frail, who have life-threatening diseases or illnesses, or who for other reasons are near death may be released early on parole.

In California, which, as noted earlier, is facing serious budget issues as well as prison costs and overcrowding, approximately one-fourth of the $2.1 billion the state spent on health care for inmates in 2007–2008 was spent on health care beyond normal. For example, it cost $1 million to cover the medical care of a dying inmate during the last year of his life. Only 1,175 California inmates accounted for $185 million a year in specialty health care. Recall that California's prison medical care system is now under federal receivership. With the backing of the federal monitor, in June 2010, the state's senate passed a bill to permit the release of medical parolees from the state's prisons. The bill was referred to the Committee on Public Safety. In part, it provides as follows:

> This bill would provide that, except as specified, any prisoner who the chief medical officer determines, based on the results of medical evaluations, suffers from a significant and permanent condition, disease, or syndrome resulting in the prisoner being physically or cognitively debilitated or incapacitated shall be granted medical parole, if the Board of Parole Hearings determines that the conditions under which the prisoner would be released would not reasonably pose a threat to public safety. Those provisions would not apply to any prisoner sentenced to death or life in prison without possibility of parole or to any inmate who is serving a sentence for which parole pursuant to this bill is prohibited by any initiative statute.[92]

Parole is also used as a method of release in other countries, as illustrated by Global Focus 15.1, which provides brief information concerning the parole system in China.

Probation and Parole Revocation

Historically, the granting of parole and the revocation of probation or parole were conducted with little if any due process. Recent cases are examined here, but first, we need to consider the issue of searching and seizing offenders while they are in the community to determine whether they have violated probation or parole. Two cases are noted.

In 2001, the U.S. Supreme Court upheld the search of a probationer's apartment without a search warrant. According to the Court in *United States v. Knights*, police had reasonable suspicion that the probationer had committed arson and vandalism. A probationer has a reduced expectation of privacy, and thus, probable cause was not required for the search. As a condition of probation, the offender had signed a document agreeing that his personal effects, home, and person could be searched at any time with or without a search warrant. Police had observed items in the offender's truck as well as suspicious activities at the location of his apartment.[93]

In 2006, the U.S. Supreme Court upheld the California statute concerning searching parolees. That statute provides, in part, the following:

> Any inmate who is eligible for release on parole pursuant to this chapter shall agree in writing to be subject to search or seizure by a parole officer or other peace officer at any time of the day or night, with or without a search warrant and with or without cause.[94]

In *Samson v. California*, Justice Clarence Thomas, writing for the U.S. Supreme Court's majority of six, noted that California had more than 130,000 parolees as of 30 November 2005 and that 68 percent of adult parolees are returned to prison for violations (55 percent) or new offenses (13 percent). To require the state to have individualized suspicion to search any of those offenders would undermine the safety of the state. Citing the Court's previous case, *United States v. Knights*, discussed above, Justice Thomas stated that parolees' reasonable expectation of privacy is even more reduced than that of probationers. In *Samson*, a police officer searched the parolee without any reason other than the fact that he was a parolee. Illegal drugs were found, and the offender was arrested, charged, convicted, and sentenced to seven years in prison. Justice John Paul Stevens, in dissent, stated, in part, as follows:

> What the Court sanctions today is an unprecedented curtailment of liberty. Combining faulty syllogism

15.1 Western and Chinese Correctional Systems: A Comparison

A U.S. corrections journal recently carried a series of three articles comparing the Chinese corrections system with that of Western countries. This focus summarizes portions of two of those articles, both of which are based on a study by Wu Zongxian, director of the Institute of Crime and Corrections at Beijing Normal University. The professor visited more than 25 correctional facilities in the United States, Canada, and the United Kingdom. The selection begins with the journal's description of China.

China is a nation slightly smaller in area than the United States, with a population of around 1.3 billion people compared with America's population of about 300 million. The age and gender breakdowns between the two nations are fairly similar; the median age in the United States is only a couple of years higher than that of China. The life expectancy at birth in the United States is 77.8 years, and in China it is 72.6 years. The literacy rate of those over the age of 15 in the United States is 99 percent for both males and females. In China, the literacy rate is 95 percent for males and 87 percent for females.

"As of December 2003, China housed about 1.5 million inmates (excluding pretrial detainees) in about 704 prisons and 283 labor redemption camps. As for sentenced inmates only, China incarcerates about 118 per 100,000 people. That compares with 62 per 100,000 for Japan, 83 for Switzerland, 128 for the Netherlands and 107 for Canada."[1] The U.S. incarcerated 502 inmates per 100,000 population in 2009, down from 506 in 2007.[2]

Although on the outside, China appears to be very tough on crime, according to this study, the major focus within prison is rehabilitation. This is because "contemporary China holds that people can be changed, and the great majority of prisoners can be reformed."[3]

Parole

As noted in the text, in the United States, although jurisdictions vary, in general, parole is decided by a parole board, which may be elected or appointed. The state's governor may or may not have final decision-making power. In China, prison and other agency officials make recommendations, but the court makes all decisions concerning the granting or denying as well as revoking parole. Parole supervision is under the jurisdiction of the police in contrast to correctional or parole officers.[4]

Community Corrections

In China, community corrections programs are very limited. There are fines, public surveillance, deprivation of political rights, and confiscation of property, but the significant development of community corrections characteristic of the United States and some other Western countries has not yet occurred.[5]

1. "Chinese and Western Prisons—Similarities and Differences," *Corrections Compendium* 31, no. 6 (1 November 2006): 24 (3).
2. Heather C. West and William J. Sabol, Bureau of Justice Statistics, *Prisoners in 2009*, p. 1 (December 2010), http://bjs.ojp .usdoj.gov/content/pub/pdf/p08.pdf, accessed 26 December 2010.
3. "Chinese and Western Prisons—Similarities and Differences."
4. Ibid.
5. "Chinese and Western Prisons—Similarities and Differences, Part 3," *Corrections Compendium* 32, no. 2 (1 March 2007): 30 (3).

with circular reasoning, the Court concludes that parolees have no more legitimate an expectation of privacy in their persons than do prisoners. However superficially appealing that parity in treatment may seem, it runs roughshod over our precedent. It also rests on an intuition that fares poorly under scrutiny. And once one acknowledges that parolees do have legitimate expectations of privacy beyond those of prisoners, our Fourth Amendment jurisprudence does not permit the conclusion, reached by the Court here for the first time, that a search supported by neither individualized suspicion nor "special needs" is nonetheless "reasonable."[95]

The U.S. Supreme Court has, however, held that certain due process requirements must be observed at parole and probation revocation proceedings. In 1967, in *Mempa v. Rhay*, the Court ruled that a probationer is entitled to be represented by counsel (state-appointed counsel for indi-

gents) at a combined revocation and sentencing hearing because sentencing is a stage of the actual criminal proceeding "where substantial rights of a criminal accused may be affected."[96]

In 1972, the U.S. Supreme Court considered parole revocation. In *Morrissey v. Brewer*, the Court held that before parole may be revoked, the parolee is entitled to two hearings. The first is a hearing to determine whether there is probable cause to believe that the individual has violated parole terms. The second and more extensive hearing is to consider the evidence and determine whether parole should be revoked. In *Morrissey*, the U.S. Supreme Court stated that (1) the purpose of parole is rehabilitation; (2) until the rules are violated, an individual may remain on parole; (3) full due process rights used in criminal trials do not apply to parole revocation; (4) the termination of liberty by revocation results in "grievous loss," mandating some due process protection; (5) informal parole revocation hearings are proper; (6) parole should not be revoked unless the rules are violated; and (7) the requirements of due process will change with particular cases.[97]

The U.S. Supreme Court requires the following elements of due process at the parole revocation proceedings:

- Written notice of the alleged parole violations
- Disclosure to the parolee of the evidence of violation
- Opportunity to be heard in person and to present evidence as well as witnesses
- Right to confront and cross-examine adverse witnesses unless good cause can be shown for not allowing this confrontation
- Right to judgment by a detached and neutral hearing body
- Written statement of reasons for revoking parole as well as of the evidence used in arriving at that decision

The importance of fairness in parole revocation was emphasized by the U.S. Supreme Court in the following brief excerpt from the case.[98]

Morrissey v. Brewer

The parolee is not the only one who has a stake in his conditional liberty. Society has a stake in whatever may be the chance of restoring him to normal and useful life within the law. Society thus has an interest in not having parole revoked because of erroneous information or because of an erroneous evaluation of the need to revoke parole, given the breach of parole conditions. And society has a further interest in treating the parolee with basic fairness: fair treatment in parole revocations will enhance the chance of rehabilitation by avoiding reactions to arbitrariness.

In 1973, in *Gagnon v. Scarpelli*, the U.S. Supreme Court held that *Morrissey*'s minimum due process requirements apply to probation revocation hearings, but due process does not require the right to counsel at all revocation hearings. Whether counsel is required by due process should be determined on the basis of the facts of each case. Counsel is required when it is necessary for fundamental fairness. For example, an inmate who has serious communication problems might need counsel at revocation hearings for those hearings to be fair.[99]

In *Bearden v. Georgia*, the U.S. Supreme Court held that probation cannot be revoked because an indigent cannot pay a fine and restitution unless there is a determination that the probationer has not made a bona fide effort or that there were no adequate alternative methods of punishment.[100] In *Black v. Romano*, the Court held that generally, when a court revokes probation and a suspended prison sentence is imposed, the court is not required to indicate that it considered alternatives to prison. This case did not involve the indigency issue regarding failure to pay a fine and restitution as in the *Bearden* case.[101]

Even when U.S. Supreme Court guidelines are being followed, it is important to remember that probation or parole revocation is a serious matter. It is possible to grant fair hearings and still revoke probation or parole because of some minor infraction of the rules. For example, in some jurisdictions, any violation of parole conditions results in revocation and the return to prison. In deciding which actions are serious enough to warrant parole revocation, we should keep in mind the potentially harmful effects of incarceration as well as its cost. As budget problems continue to plague corrections systems and many prisons remain overcrowded, we must consider costs when deciding how to punish. Violent offenders are one issue, but violation of a minor parole condition, such as driving a car without the parole officer's permission, is quite another.

Before we turn to an assessment of community corrections, it is important to consider one additional factor: the recent requirement of community notification that sex offenders who have served time in a prison or correctional facility are being released to live in specific areas.

Focus on Sex Offenders

The safety and security of society are concerns any time an offender is released from incarceration, and this is particularly true when convicted sex offenders are released. Various methods try to maintain security when this occurs.

Registration and Related Laws

The most common restrictions placed on released sex offenders are that they must register with local law enforcement when they move into a community, change their addresses, phone numbers, or license plates, and so on. These requirements can be traced to the sexual assault and murder of a little girl by a paroled sex offender, who was her neighbor.

Megan's Law

Seven-year-old Megan Kanka was sexually assaulted and murdered on 29 July 1994. Megan had been enticed into the home of a neighbor who promised her a puppy. Neither Megan, her parents, nor local law enforcement officials knew that the neighbor, Jesse Timmendequas, had been convicted of previous sex offenses against young girls and that he lived with two other men, both of whom had been convicted of sex offenses. Knowledge of that information outraged local, state, and national officials and citizens. By 31 October 1994, New Jersey had enacted its Sexual Offender Registration Act. It requires a person who has completed a sentence for conviction of certain designated offenses to register if, at the time of sentencing, his or her conduct was found to be "characterized by a

On 17 May 1996, in the Oval Office of the White House, President Bill Clinton signed the federal Megan's Law, with Megan Kanka's mother, Maureen, and brother Jeremy, 7, looking, along with New Jersey's Representative Dick Zimmer and John Walsh, host of the television show America's Most Wanted. States followed with their own versions of Megan's Law, designed to require the registration of sex offenders who move into communities after they are released from prison. Other federal and state laws have been enacted subsequently.

pattern of repetitive and compulsive behavior." A second requirement involves notifying the community that the sex offender will be living in the neighborhood.[102]

Other jurisdictions followed New Jersey's lead, and by May 1996, 49 states had adopted a version of **Megan's Law.** As part of its 1994 crime bill, Congress urged states to establish programs requiring the registration of sexually violent persons, persons convicted of sexually violent offenses, and those convicted of offenses against minors.[103]

In January 2002, New Jersey began posting the names of moderate- to high-risk sex offenders online for the world to access, thus joining 30 states and the District of Columbia in this approach to notifying communities of sex offenders living among them. This action was made possible by New Jersey voters' overwhelming support of a constitutional amendment in November 2000 and the legislative enactment of laws in the spring of 2001. The lawmakers took considerable time in their formulation, hoping to avoid successful challenges to these provisions.[104]

In 2004, California began posting information about registered sex offenders online. California had required sex offenders to register since the 1950s, but the information was not available to the public unless individuals went to law enforcement agencies.[105]

In 2006, Congress enacted the Adam Walsh Child Protection and Safety Act.[106] It includes the Sex Offender Registration and Notification Act (SORNA), under which the federal government provides grants to assist states with registering sex offenders, provided the states follow the federal registration requirements. The SORNA also creates a new federal crime: failure to register as a sex offender when required to do so.[107]

The Adam Walsh Act was named after a 6-year-old child who was abducted from a Sears department store

and beheaded in 1981. It was not until December 2009 that law enforcement authorities concluded that Adam was killed by Ottis Toole, a serial killer who died in prison in 1996 after being convicted of other crimes. That conclusion has been challenged, in particular by a lawsuit filed in June 2010 in which the litigant, Willis Morgan, seeks copies of the files of the retired police officer on whose report that conclusion was allegedly based. According to Morgan, serial killer Jeffrey Dahmer was in the Sears store the day Adam was abducted.[108]

The Walsh Act was signed 25 years after the abduction of Walsh, whose father, John Walsh, became a victims' advocate who helped establish and now is in charge of the National Center for Missing and Exploited Children. He is also the anchor of the TV show America's Most Wanted.

Concern with Internet use by sexual predators led to an amendment to the Walsh Act. In 2008, the Keeping the Internet Devoid of Sexual Predators (KIDS) Act of 2008 was enacted. This law requires registered sex offenders to register their email and instant messenger addresses with the National Sex Offender Registry. The Department of Justice makes the information available to sites that could use it to block these predators from preying on children. The KIDS Act makes it a crime for Internet users to misrepresent their ages for the purpose of luring children into sexual conduct. The act also requires, at a minimum, GPS monitoring of sex offenders 24/7 upon release.[109]

Jessica's Law

In recent years, many jurisdictions have gone beyond registration requirements for sex offenders and enacted stricter laws in an attempt to restrain them. Some of these laws are patterned after that of Florida's Jessica Lunsford Act. In March 2005, the body of Jessica, age 9, who had been missing for three weeks, was found approximately

Jessica Lunsford, rape and murder victim, was 9 years old when she disappeared from her home in Homosassa, Florida, on 25 February 2005. After her body was discovered, her father began a campaign to change the statutes with regard to sex offenders. Among other requirements, Florida's Jessica Lunsford Act increases the amount of time sex offenders must spend in prison and enhances the registration and monitoring of those who are living in the community. Some other jurisdictions have enacted stricter sex offender laws based on Jessica's law.

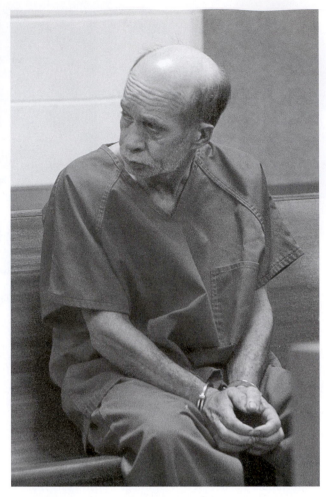

John E. Couey, shown here awaiting arraignment at the Citrus County Florida Detention Center on 22 March 2005, was convicted and sentenced to die for the death of Jessica Lunsford. Couey, a convicted sex offender, was required to register as a sex offender and give his address, but he failed to do so when he moved into the neighborhood in which Jessica lived with her father and his parents.

150 yards from the home in which she lived with her father and grandparents. John E. Couey, 46, a registered sex offender, was convicted of kidnapping and murdering Jessica and sentenced to death. Among other requirements, the Lunsford act increases sentences for convicted sex offenders and tightens reporting and monitoring requirements.[110]

The toughest sex offender law was enacted in California after 70 percent of the state's voters approved Proposition 83, which became effective 8 November 2006 and represents that state's Jessica's Law. Among other provisions, the Sexual Predator Punishment and Control Act (SPPCA) eliminates good-time credits for sex offenders, increases the mandatory minimum prison term, and requires sex offenders released on parole to wear GPS monitoring systems for life. The act permits categorizing released offenders as sexually violent predators subject to civil commitment on the basis of one, rather than two, crimes and makes it illegal for released offenders to live within 2,000 feet of any school or other place where children congregate regularly. It also contains provisions concerning the use of date rape drugs and providing child pornography.[111]

Analysis

The success of sex offender registration laws is based on several presumptions. First, it is presumed that if notification is provided, potential victims will read the notice and act accordingly. This is not always the case, especially when the sexual abuser is a family member or friend. Second, it is presumed that law enforcement officials will have accurate data for notification. Third, it is presumed that law enforcement officials will have the resources to perform all of the duties associated with community notification of sex offenders. Fourth, it is presumed that community notification will serve as a deterrent to registered sex offenders, who will not be inclined to commit a sex crime in their neighborhoods. This presumes that sex offenders will not travel to other areas where notification has not occurred. There is reason to question all of these presumptions.

To illustrate, California's attorney general's office posts on its Web page information concerning myths and facts about sex offenders. In short, most sex offenders (over 90 percent) know their victims, and almost 50 percent of the victims are family members. Most offenders and victims are of the same race. Most sexual offenders use enticement or deception rather than force to commit their crimes. Most of the victims are not found in schoolyards and playgrounds. Women as well as men are offenders. Most victims do not report the offense quickly.[112]

There are also problems with maintaining an accurate database of sex offenders. For example, an audit in California found "thousands of errors, inconsistencies, and out-of-date information," much of which put the public at risk. Specifically, among other problems, the report by the Bureau of State Audits disclosed that information had not been updated in a year for 23,000 of the 80,000 sex offenders required to register in California.[113]

Another issue is that the registration laws are too extensive, encompassing offenders who do not need to be covered. Although some jurisdictions have a provision for a hearing to enable an offender to be removed from the requirement, many do not. The case of Genarlow Wilson, discussed in Chapter 1, is one illustration of a problem. Had the Georgia legislature not acted, Wilson would have been required to register as a sex offender for life as the result of a consensual act in which he engaged at age 17 with a girl who was age 15.

Another example occurred in a prison setting in which female officers engaged in consensual relationships with male inmates. In the summer 2002, two female correctional officers were apprehended for engaging in sexual acts with male inmates at the supermax prison in Florence, Colorado. In May 2003, Christine Achenbach, 42, was sentenced to five years' probation and four months' home detention, fined $3,000, and required to register as a sex offender. The sentencing judge said that she did not believe this defendant fell within the intended purpose of the sex offender registration requirement, but "I must apply the law as it is written, not as I wish it were written." The judge even stated that she did not think the inmates felt victimized but, rather, probably enjoyed the sexual acts.[114] Although the reaction of an inmate to a sexual encounter with a correctional officer is not the point and any form of sexual activity between a superior and a subordinate may cause depression or other problems and is considered inappropriate, if not illegal, one might question the wisdom of requiring these defendants to register for life as sex offenders.

Still another issue is the presumption that requiring convicted sex offenders to register will make our communities safer. Several empirical studies have revealed

evidence that suggests there is no support for this belief. A study published in 2010 found no significant difference between the recidivist rate of sex offenders who failed to register and those who registered. The investigators concluded, "The punitive emphasis on registration enforcement may not be justified and might divert limited resources away from strategies that would better facilitate public protection from sexual violence."[115]

Another investigator looked at the available evidence concerning deterrence and sex offender registration requirements and noted some conflict. He concluded that the "totality of the evidence" indicates that such requirements are not effective and that "residency restrictions should be eliminated and replaced with more effective means of reducing sex offender recidivism."[116]

The failure of law regulating the conditions under which sex offenders may live in a community came under national criticism in 2009 when Jaycee Dugard was found 18 years after she was kidnapped at age 11, allegedly by Phillip and Nancy Garrido. In an article entitled "America's

Jaycee Lee Dugard was kidnapped in 1991 when she was 11 years old. In 2010, California authorities agreed to pay $20 million to Dugard and her two daughters for failure to apprehend Nancy and Phillip Garrido, the persons who allegedly kidnapped and raped Dugard and held her hostage in a facility in their backyard for 18 years. Phillip Garrido, a paroled rapist, is allegedly the father of Dugard's two children. The suspects were charged with 29 criminal counts and entered not guilty pleas.

Flawed Sex Offender Laws," Human Rights Watch used the Dugard case to emphasize that registration requirements do not guarantee the capture of high-risk offenders. The article pointed out that most sex crimes do not move through the criminal justice system, and approximately 87 percent of new sex crimes reported each year are allegedly committed by persons who do not have a record for such crimes. Human Rights Watch recommended that legislation be changed to require registration for only the high-risk offenders and, even there, for as long as they pose a significant risk to society. The conclusion was:

> Sex offender registration and community notification laws didn't cause Garrido's crimes, but they didn't help the police stop them, either. While Americans are starting to question the value of our extensive sex offender monitoring system, it remains to be seen whether these doubts will lead to real reform.[117]

Garrido, a convicted sex offender, complied with his obligations to register and report to local authorities for at least 10 years, even taking his victims with him on at least one occasion. Furthermore, his parole officer visited his home. Yet Dugard and her two teenage daughters, allegedly fathered by Garrido, were not discovered in Garrido's backyard until August of 2009. In July 2010, Dugard was awarded $20 million in a settlement for her lawsuit regarding the negligence in this case.

One scathing critique of sex registration laws came in the form of a January 2010 Recommendations Report by California's Sexual Offender Management Board (CASOMB). The CASOMB, a 15-member commission, was created by a bill signed into law by the state's governor on 20 September 2006 after near unanimous support. Its purpose is to serve as a resource for the legislature and for the governor.[118]

The CASOMB's 2010 Recommendations Report raised significant questions about California's statutes regarding sex offenders in the community. The report challenged the premise of Jessica's Law with regard to residence restrictions. "The hypothesis that sex offenders who live in close proximity to schools, parks and other places children congregate have an increased likelihood of sexually re-offending remains unsupported by research. . . . On the contrary, there is almost no correlation between sex offenders living near restricted areas and where they commit their offenses." The report noted that the law requires the state to send more sex offenders through mental health analysis to determine whether they should be civilly committed (discussed later). The monthly costs of that process had escalated from $161,000 prior to the passage of Jessica's Law to more than $1 million after the law was enacted. The report questioned the wisdom of GPS and noted its expense and the lack of evidence of its effectiveness. The report emphasized that California had 90,000 registered sex offenders, 68,000 of whom lived in communities; all

were required to register for life. The public has no way to distinguish the dangerousness of these offenders. "In this one-size-fits-all system of registration, law enforcement cannot concentrate its scarce resources on close supervision of the more dangerous offenders or on those who are at higher risk of committing another sex crime." The board recommended the following:

- "Not all California sex offenders need to register for life in order to safeguard the public and so a risk-based system of differentiated registration requirements should be created.
- Focusing resources on registering and monitoring moderate to high risk sex offenders makes a community safer than trying to monitor all offenders for life.
- A sex offender's risk of re-offense should be one factor in determining the length of time the person must register as a sex offender and whether to post the offender on the Internet. Other factors which should determine duration of registration and Internet posting include:
  Whether the sex offense was violent
  Whether the sex offense was against a child
  Whether the offender was convicted of a new sex offense or violent offense after the first sex offense conviction
  Whether the person was civilly committed as a sexually violent predator
- Monitoring of registered sex offenders once they are no longer under any form of formal community supervision is critical to public safety."[119]

The CASOMB also made extensive recommendations for improving law enforcement with regard to monitoring sex offenders.

Still another issue with regard to the many statutes regulating sex offenders who live in communities is the impact on minorities. Some researchers have found that these restrictions more negatively impact sex offenders in disadvantaged as compared with affluent neighborhoods and that sex offenders are more likely to live in the disadvantaged areas.[120]

Legal Challenges

There have been many legal challenges to sex offender registration and related laws. To mention a few, the New Jersey Supreme Court ruled that the state's Megan's Law had limitations with regard to juveniles. Although the original intent of the legislature was that the statute would apply to juveniles, the court ruled that this provision would conflict with the state's Code of Juvenile Justice. In July 2001, the court unanimously held that Megan's Law registration requirements "will end at the age of eighteen for offenders who committed a sex crime under the age of fourteen if they can show by clear and convincing evidence that they are not likely to commit another offense." The case on which this ruling was based involved a 17-year-old boy who, when he was 10, sexually molested an 8-year-old girl. The court was struggling to balance the purpose of Megan's Law—protection of the public—with that of the juvenile code—rehabilitation of the young.[121]

In another New Jersey Megan's Law case, a lower federal court ruled that the state's requirement that a registered sex offender's name can be released on the Internet does not violate the federal constitutional right to privacy. According to the Third Circuit Court of Appeals, ruling in *A.A. v. New Jersey*, "The state's compelling interest in preventing sex offenses substantially outweighs any interest the [sex offenders] may have in not having public—yet scattered—information [about their addresses] compiled [and made available]." In 2007, the U.S. Supreme Court refused to hear the case. The Third Circuit has ruled in several Megan's Law cases, upholding the registration requirements against challenges of double jeopardy, ex post facto, due process, equal protection, and vagueness.[122]

In 2003, the U.S. Supreme Court upheld Alaska's sex registration statute against an ex post facto claim. The Supreme Court also upheld the Connecticut statute in the face of a due process challenge. The Alaska case, *Smith v. Doe*, involved two fathers who were convicted of sexually molesting their own daughters. They argued that requiring them to register as sex offenders under the Alaska Megan's Law was unconstitutional because the law was passed after their respective convictions. Thus, applying it to them was ex post facto because the statute imposed additional punishment, which is not permitted. The U.S. Supreme Court did not agree and ruled that requiring a sex offender to register when moving into a neighborhood does not constitute punishment. The purpose of this requirement is to protect society, not to punish offenders.[123]

In the Connecticut case, *Connecticut Department of Public Safety v. Doe,* the U.S. Supreme Court held the fact that the state did not require a hearing on the issue of whether a sex offender is dangerous before requiring that offender to register was not a violation of due process. The statute did not, as the appellant claimed, deny him a liberty interest without due process because the registration requirement was based on a prior conviction, not on a prediction of current dangerousness.[124]

The widespread use of sex registration requirements and restrictions on living accommodations makes it virtually impossible for low-level offenders, who are not at risk to the community, to reenter the community and live law-abiding lives. For example, in September 2009, nine male sex offenders who were living in tents at a makeshift camp in Marietta, Georgia, were forced to move by order of state officials. The men had been directed to that area by their probation officers, who said it was a "site of last resort."[125] The 16,000 sex offenders living in Georgia communities

must observe the Georgia statute, which provides, in part, as follows:

> (B) No individual shall reside within 1,000 feet of any child care facility, church, school, or area where minors congregate. . . .
>
> (c) (1) No individual shall be employed by or volunteer at any child care facility, school, or church or by or at any business or entity that is located within 1,000 feet of a child care facility, a school, or a church.
>
> (2) No individual who is a sexually dangerous predator shall be employed by or volunteer at any business or entity that is located within 1,000 feet of an area where minors congregate.[126]

Such statutes regulating where sex offenders may live have been challenged. In 2007, two federal judges ruled that California's Jessica's Law prohibiting sex offenders from living within 2,000 feet of specified areas, where it can be expected that children congregate, could not be applied retroactively.[127] In 2009, the Kentucky Supreme Court held that state's law prohibiting sex offenders from living within 1,000 feet of a school, licensed day care center, or a public playground could not be applied retroactively. The state wanted to apply the statute to more than 5,500 sex offenders who were convicted before the law became effective in 2006. The state's attorney general said he would appeal.[128]

Another legal issue is whether Congress had the constitutional authority to create a *federal* crime of failing to comply with a state statute's provision that a sex offender must register. The issue was raised in a 2009 decision by the 11th Circuit Court of Appeals, which reversed a decision by a federal judge in Tampa, Florida. The federal judge, who acknowledged the "commendable" congressional goal of protecting society from sexual predators, concluded that "a worthy cause is not enough to transform a state concern (sex offender registration) into a federal crime." The case of *United States v. Powers* involved Robert Powers, who has an IQ of 68 and reads at a second-grade level. While living in South Carolina in 1995, Powers was convicted of a sex crime and required to register as a sex offender. In 2007, he moved to Florida and did not register as a sex offender as required by SORNA. He was arrested and indicted for the federal crime of failure to register as a sex offender. The 11th Circuit Court of Appeals reversed the lower court's decision that SORNA was unconstitutional under the Commerce clause of the U.S. Constitution and ordered the lower court to reinstate the indictment against Powers.[129]

In June 2010, however, the U.S. Supreme Court handed down its decision in *Carr v. United States*. This case differed from *Powers* in that the appellant in *Carr* traveled interstate prior to the effective date of SORNA. Carr was arrested, convicted, and sentenced to prison in Alabama but released on probation on 3 July 2004. He registered as a sex offender as required by Alabama law. Prior to the enactment of SORNA, Carr relocated to Indiana but did not register as required by Indiana law. He subsequently became involved in a fight, which brought him to the attention of Indiana law enforcement authorities. He was charged by federal prosecutors with violating SORNA. He challenged that charge on the grounds that it constituted an ex post facto (and thus illegal) application of SORNA. His challenged was rejected. He entered a guilty plea, reserving his right to appeal the legal issue, which he did. The U.S. Supreme Court did not decide the ex post facto issue, holding it was not necessary because the Court held that SORNA does not extend to travel prior to the effective date of the statute. Specifically, SORNA applies to a person who "is required to register under the Sex Offender Registration and Notification Act."[130]

Civil Commitment of Released Sex Offenders

Because registration requirements for released sex offenders may not be effective, some states provide for the civil commitment of sex offenders after they complete their prison terms. In 1997, the U.S. Supreme Court upheld the Kansas civil commitment statute in the case of Leroy Hendricks, who was convicted in 1984 of indecent liberties with two 13-year-old boys. After serving most of his 10-year sentence, Hendricks was scheduled for release from prison, but a jury determined that he was a sexual predator, and the judge found that he had a mental abnormality. He was involuntarily confined indefinitely under the Kansas Commitment of Sexually Violent Predators Act, which defines a *sexually violent predator* as "any person who has been convicted of or charged with a sexually violent offense and who suffers from a mental abnormality or personality disorder which makes the person likely to engage in the predatory acts of sexual violence." In a 5–4 decision, the U.S. Supreme Court upheld the commitment.[131]

According to a 2007 media report (no later report was available), Hendricks remained in a Kansas prison where, at age 72, he spent most of his time in a wheelchair or leaning on a cane because of various medical problems. The state of Kansas was paying approximately $185,000 a year to confine Hendricks, a cost of almost eight times that for the usual inmate.[132]

More recently, the U.S. Supreme Court decided a limited legal issue with regard to the civil commitment of sex offenders after they have completed their prison sentences. In May 2010, in *United States v. Comstock*, the Court considered whether Congress has the constitutional authority under Article I of the U.S. Constitution to authorize such civil commitments. At issue was the Adam Walsh Child Protection and Safety Act, mentioned earlier, which authorizes the civil commitment of federal sex offenders judged dangerous to society. The *Comstock* case did not involve state jurisdiction but focused only on the U.S. Constitution's delegation to Congress to enact statutes that are "necessary and proper for carrying into execution" the other powers delegated to Congress. The U.S. Supreme Court, by a vote of 7–2, ruled that Congress does have that power. The case was argued for the government by the U.S. Solicitor General Elena Kagan, who subsequently became President Obama's successful nominee to the U.S. Supreme Court to fill the seat held by retiring Justice John Paul Stevens.[133]

The Future of Corrections

This final section of the book considers some of the issues that our society must face now and in the future. Despite the slight decline in prison populations in some jurisdictions, the reduction of overcrowding in some prison systems, and the decline or leveling off of crime rates, we have not solved crime or incarceration problems. We begin this section with an evaluation of community corrections, focusing on return offenders.

An Evaluation of Community Corrections

Advocates of community corrections argue that, in addition to decreasing the populations of prisons and jails and saving money, community corrections aids in the rehabilitation of offenders. Most evaluations of community corrections, especially of probation and parole, involve a study of recidivism, which may include new law violations or violations of the terms of probation or parole or other programs.

Researchers do not agree on the meaning of the term *recidivism* or on how it should be measured. As a result, recidivism data vary. Early studies reported that as many as two-thirds of offenders released from prison became recidivists. These figures were questioned in the early 1960s in an extensive analysis of federal data by Daniel Glaser, who argued that the best way to study recidivism was to follow a cohort of offenders for a specified period after their release.[134] Earlier studies (especially those of juveniles) took that approach.[135]

More recent studies of recidivism have focused on **felony probation** and parole. Joan Petersilia conducted a study of felony probation for the National Institute of Justice. She found that nearly two-thirds of all convicted offenders were placed on probation, and of those offenders, two-thirds were re-arrested, 51 percent were convicted of a new crime, and 34 percent were given a jail or prison sentence. The recidivists committed the crimes of burglary, theft, and robbery. The study pointed out that certain variables were significantly related to recidivism:

- *Type of conviction crime.* Property offenders had the highest rates of recidivism.
- *Number of prior juvenile and adult convictions.* The greater the number, the higher the probability of recidivism.

- *Income at arrest.* Regardless of source or amount, the presence of income was associated with lower recidivism.
- *Household composition.* If the offender was living with spouse and/or children, recidivism was lower.[136]

Petersilia acknowledged that felony probation presents great risks, but she suggested that, rather than discard probation, we should extend the use of intensive probation supervision (IPS).[137] In fact, Petersilia noted in a subsequent publication that, although three-fourths of the correctional populations were in the community, only approximately one-tenth of the correction budgets was spent on supervision. Thus, most of those on probation and parole had inadequate supervision.[138]

These reports by Petersilia were published over 20 years ago. In recent years, this scholar has continued her analysis of recidivism and release and has been even more emphatic about the need for release under supervision. The next two sections look at her work and that of others in the state of California, already discussed as a problem state with regard to corrections. That discussion is followed by recent changes in a much smaller state, South Carolina.

Focus on California

California is selected for focus here because it is a large state with a big corrections problem, but it is also a state that has historically been a leader in corrections policies, especially rehabilitation. A 2010 report on the state's parole system stated it this way:

> Once a model of good correctional management and inmate programs, the system has been identified by experts as in need of reform at every level—operationally, economically, and programmatically. California now has the nation's largest prison population (about 167,000 prisoners), and while some other state prison populations have declined in recent years, California's continues to increase. Its prison expenditures are among the highest in the nation—per inmate, per staff, and as a share of the overall state budget. The average annual cost of housing a California prisoner in 2008–09 was $49,000, 1.9 times higher than the national average of about $26,000. . . . Based on current spending trends, California's prison budget will overtake spending on the State's universities in five years. No other large state spends as much to incarcerate compared with higher education funding.[139]

This text has already focused on some of California's correctional problems, noting the issues of overcrowding, the serious condition of the state medical prison system, which has led to federal oversight, and the state's budget shortfalls. None of these problems are new, and in 2007, California enacted a law, the Public Safety and Offender Rehabilitation Services Act of 2007, also referred to as As-

sembly Bill 900 (AB 900),[140] designed to reform the state's correctional system. When he signed this bill, Governor Arnold Schwarzenegger stated,

> Every bed that we add will include rehabilitation programs and in that critical few months before an inmate is released, our reentry facilities will focus intensely on job training and placement, on education, on anger management, substance abuse, and family counseling and housing placement.[141]

To make recommendations on the implementation of AB 900, the governor appointed two strike teams, one regarding rehabilitation and one to focus on the construction of correctional facilities (to add 53,000 beds to the system). Assembly Bill 900 provided for $7.7 billion to fund this two-prong approach to reforming the state's prison system. The rehabilitation strike team (RST), which is the focus here, was chaired by Joan Petersilia. It published a detailed report in which it concluded that California's high rates of adult recidivism were due to the state's shifting public opinion. In 1976, California instituted a policy of determinate sentences that was among the toughest in the nation. In 1994, it began the toughest three-strikes legislation. The report noted that between 1976 and 2007, California enacted 80 other laws aimed at getting tougher on crime, although in 2005, the Department of Corrections became the Department of Corrections and Rehabilitation, with a new mission statement: "To improve public safety through evidence-based crime prevention and recidivism reduction strategies." According to these researchers, the state had not achieved that mission and continued to release almost 50 percent of its inmates without any assignment to rehabilitation programs, "which might improve their behavior, or *any* job assignments, which might improve their life skills." The RST concluded that if the state followed all of its recommendations, it could save between $561 and $684 million per year. The RST developed four initiatives to bring rehabilitation back into the California correctional system:

- "The development of an Offender Accountability and Rehabilitation Plan (OARP) designed to assess inmates' needs at intake . . . and direct inmates to appropriate rehabilitation programs and services in prison and on parole;
- The identification of rehabilitation-oriented training curriculum for correctional and rehabilitation staff, and a method of delivering that curriculum via the California Community College Districts;
- The installment of a Prison to Employment Program designed to facilitate offenders' successful employment after release, . . .
- The implementation of parole reform anchored in the structural possibility of earned discharge or banked caseloads, and guided by a new risk assessment tool and a parole violation decision-making matrix."[142]

The RST recommended specific programming in the following major areas:

- Academic, vocational, and financial
- Alcohol and drugs
- Aggression, hostility, anger, and violence
- Criminal thinking, behaviors, and associations
- Family, marital, and social relationships
- Treatment for sex offenders

The RST concluded that if its recommendations were followed, the state could put the R for rehabilitation back into the California Department of Corrections and Rehabilitation. Otherwise, "We will just keep filling up the prison beds we have expanded."[143]

Only time and sophisticated research will reveal whether California is successful in its efforts to reform corrections, and as noted earlier, the prison health care system is still under a federal monitor. One good sign, however, was that a December 2009 report on the fourth initiative mentioned previously—implementing the use of the Parole Violation Decision Making Instrument (PVDMI), a new risk-assessment tool in the state's parole system—was found to be on schedule. Experts describe the PVDMI as the "next generation" of "decision matrices in corrections, due to its complexity and its electronic automation."[144]

Focus on South Carolina

The South Carolina Department of Corrections, a state agency with approximately 6,000 employees, has 23,000 inmates in 28 institutions. The department now faces a new challenge: complying with the state's comprehensive law signed by the governor on 2 June 2010, the Omnibus Crime Reduction and Sentencing Reform Act of 2010.[145] This bipartisan effort was reportedly supported by victims' rights advocates and criminal justice professionals and experts as well as Democrats and Republicans. The statute is designed to provide adequate housing for high-risk offenders without a state expenditure of $350 million for a new prison. The South Carolina Reduction of Recidivism Act of 2010, a part of the sentencing overhaul, focuses on assisting released inmates' transition back into communities and increases supervision over them. Twenty-two new crimes are added to the list of violent crimes, many with longer sentences. But the statute also provides incentives for probationers and parolees to participate in substance abuse programs and remain law abiding, thus saving the state money for further incarceration. New standards for parole and probation assessments became effective in January 2011. Probationers and parolees are able to earn good-time credits toward release, victim restitution amounts are increased, and the disparity between sentences for crack and powder cocaine was removed.[146]

It is unusual for a state to make such substantial changes in its penal and correctional laws. South Carolina deemed this necessary to reduce its correctional populations and

costs, which had escalated from $63 million a year in the mid-1980s to $394 million in 2010 despite the fact that the state is the second lowest in its daily per capita costs per inmate ($40). According to one state senator, it was a massive undertaking that was necessary to restructure a haphazard criminal justice system. The senator predicted that the new statute will "change people's lives. It will help offenders get back on their feet and make sure victims get compensated."[147] Ideally, that is correct, and at the same time, it will protect society.

South Carolina had already recognized the need for community correctional facilities to reduce prison populations, with a statute that states, in part, the need for the state to cooperate with local jurisdictions to establish "less costly facilities for housing state and local inmates in alternative sentencing programs."[148]

In the final analysis, cost may be the deciding factor for many states facing budget crises and having to decide whether to build more prisons or turn to community corrections for detaining nonviolent offenders (see Figure 15.5 for comparative national data).

Juvenile Justice

This text focuses primarily on adult criminals, adult courts, and correctional institutions, and space does not permit a thorough analysis of juvenile justice issues, which are normally covered in a separate course. The discussions throughout the text have noted, however, that the topic of juvenile crime cannot be avoided in the discussion of major crimes in this country. The violence among juveniles led many jurisdictions to enact legislation providing for transfer of these offenders to criminal courts. Convictions in those courts led to the incarceration of juveniles in adult facilities, with many resulting problems. The entire concept of the juvenile court and of detention and incarceration for the purpose of rehabilitation is being rethought by some. A consideration of the future of corrections must embrace an analysis of juvenile justice. Let's consider just a few of the issues raised in recent years.

The special needs of female inmates were addressed in Chapter 14, which noted, among other problems, the issue of child care. But little attention has been given to the special needs of incarcerated female juveniles. A report by the American Bar Association emphasized that females are the fastest-growing segment of juvenile offenders and that girls who are incarcerated are often placed in facilities that do not have adequate programs for their health, education, or vocational training. Some of those juvenile offenders have children, and the care of these children is an additional issue that must be faced.[149]

Mental health treatment of juveniles in custody is another issue. Too frequently, young, mentally ill offenders are not classified appropriately upon intake. Staff are not trained to recognize the signs of mental health problems as they develop during incarceration. According to the

Figure 15.5

State Daily Correctional Costs Per Offender, by Type of Facility

1 day in prison costs more than 10 days on parole or 22 days on probation.

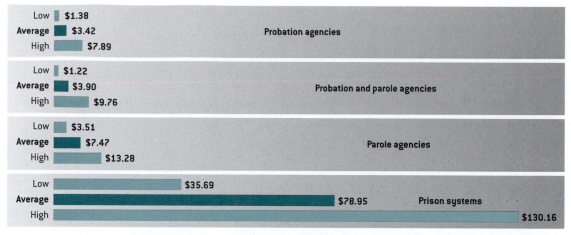

Source: The Pew Center on the States, *One in 31: The Long Reach of American Corrections* (March 2009), p. 13, http://www.pewcenteronthestates.org/uploadedFiles/PSPP_1in31_report_FINAL_WEB_3-26-09.pdf, accessed 27 December 2010.

Coalition for Juvenile Justice (CJJ), between 50 and 75 percent of juveniles in custody have mental health issues, but juvenile courts are ineffective in diagnosing and providing treatment for these youths.[150]

There is evidence, however, that some mental health programs are effective with juveniles, with a 25 percent lower rate of recidivism than juveniles without such treatment. The treatment should include the following:

- "Highly structured, intensive programs that focus on changing specific behavior
- Development of basic social and life skills
- Individual counseling that directly addresses behavior, attitudes, and perceptions
- Sensitivity to a youth's race, culture, gender and sexual orientation
- Strong aftercare services . . .
- Recognition that youth think and feel differently than adults, especially under stress"[151]

One method of treatment that educators have found successful with problem juveniles is art therapy. Prison art programs have been developed and evaluated. For example, the YouthARTS project in Atlanta, Georgia, provides literacy education, job training, and art instruction. Intensive training—with one instructor per student—is often utilized for first-time offenders between the ages of 14 and 16. The sponsors worked closely with personnel in the juvenile court system while planning the program. The evaluation of this program showed that all juveniles who participated improved in "art skills, cooperating with others, participation and communicating effectively with their peers."[152]

Other innovative programs designed for young offenders have also shown some success. The Special Options

Services (SOS) program in Brooklyn, New York, was designed to provide additional services for youths in the federal system. Its founder convinced judges that it would be wise to send some young offenders to this program for counseling, job training, social services, and housing. The program was viewed as an alternative to the harsh federal sentencing guidelines that would otherwise apply. One judge, who was faced with sending to prison a young offender for whom he thought prison would be harmful, was looking for a way to avoid the strict federal sentencing guidelines. Potential participants were interviewed by the program's director, who then filed a recommendation with the judge. The judge could inform the defendant that he or she would be sent to prison if this program was not completed.[153] Although the program has not been evaluated sufficiently, it shows promise for diversion from prison.

These and similar programs raise the issue of whether we should continue our march toward stricter punishments for juveniles, particularly those who commit violent crimes, and whether we should try them in adult criminal courts. Some jurisdictions are rethinking this movement toward the harsh treatment of juveniles, especially when it involves incarcerating juveniles in adult prisons. As noted in earlier discussions, the U.S. Supreme Court ruled that the death penalty or even life without parole for persons who committed a nonhomicide crime as a juvenile constitutes cruel and unusual punishment and thus is unconstitutional.

Some jurisdictions are rethinking their juvenile justice policies, and Missouri is often cited as a model. In 2007, a national report cited Missouri as having above average success with educating its juvenile offenders and reducing recidivism. The report was by the National Evaluation and Technical Assistance Center for the Education for Children and Youth Who Are Neglected, Delinquent, or At Risk (NDTAC). According to the report, of youths in detention, 91 percent in Missouri earned high school credits compared to 46 percent nationally, and 15 percent earned GED certificates compared to only 6 percent nationally. In Missouri, all youths who enter the correctional systems are carefully assessed to determine which programs they need; the emphasis is on rehabilitation, of which education is a major part.[154]

Missouri has spent almost 30 years working to improve its juvenile justice system. Among other provisions, a state supreme court rule adopted in 1990 specifies such matters as physical plants, stating they should be geographically close to those who will inhabit them, be built to maximize communication and interaction between juveniles and staff, be limited to 20 residents, and so on.[155] The system also provides care and services after release, including substance abuse treatment, therapy, and help with school issues.

In January 2007, a reporter in Ohio published an article in which the differences between the Ohio and Missouri systems were compared. It referred to the Missouri system as the "guiding light" for juvenile justice reform. Among other differences, the article cited the consistency in the Missouri system, with its emphasis on rehabilitation rather than punishment in all facilities. Ohio was described as an inconsistent system with some excellent facilities, while "others churn out youths worse off than when they came."[156]

In October 2007, a *New York Times* editorial cited the Missouri system as a correct model for juvenile justice. It concluded as follows:

> A law-and-order state, Missouri was working against its own nature when it embarked on this project about 25 years ago. But with favorable data piling up, and thousands of young lives saved, the state is now showing the way out of the juvenile justice crisis.[157]

The Missouri system emphasizes rehabilitation in small groups, little force, and constant therapeutic interventions. The facilities do not have barbed wire; the youths live in cottage-style dormitories, with a maximum of ten youths and two counselors per unit. The youths are trained to "talk down" a colleague who misbehaves. The recidivist rate is one of the lowest in the country. Other states use this system as a model.[158]

In 2009, ABC News featured the Missouri system on *Good Morning America*, stating that the system of "trading in the orange uniforms and cell blocks for therapists and dorm rooms" was successful. The program noted that according to the Annie E. Casey Foundation, a private charitable organization headquartered in Baltimore, Maryland,

and dedicated to the purpose of improving the future for America's disadvantaged children, only 10 percent of Missouri's juveniles, compared to as high as 40 percent in other states, go to adult prisons, and they are four times less likely to be assaulted by other inmates than in other juvenile detention programs.[159]

The opportunities to reduce juvenile delinquency were noted by criminologist Francis T. Cullen, who has conducted extensive research on rehabilitation:

> First, there is a growing body of evidence—now at the point of being virtually incontrovertible—that offender treatment programs that conform to the "principles of effective intervention" are capable of achieving meaningful reductions in recidivism among high-risk juveniles and adults. The corollary finding is that punishment-oriented programs are decidedly ineffective in undercutting reoffending. . . .
>
> Second, . . . there is also a growing body of evidence showing that rehabilitation programs . . . are cost effective.[160]

Other Issues

Numerous other issues discussed within this text must be considered with regard to the future of corrections. Better training of police along with more diverse and larger numbers of trained officers, more adequate training of lawyers and judges and more resources in criminal court systems, and revision of sentencing laws are only a few. Discrimination against persons because of race and ethnicity, gender, disability, homelessness, or age must be eliminated. But we must also consider the systems effect of changes. We cannot make significant changes in one part of the system without expecting changes in another. Thus, if we increase sentences, we will eventually have a shortage of prison space; if we reduce sentences, we may have a surplus of prison beds. The overall picture must be kept in view as changes are proposed. Most important, we must not become complacent with the recent leveling off of crime.

Evidence-Based Practices

Finally, it is important to emphasize the need for rigorous research, based on theory, to provide the basis for changes in correctional systems. Modern social scientists rely on *evidence-based practices* (EBP), with the term defined by the National Institute of Corrections (NIC) as "practices informed by the results of scientific research and shown to increase public safety and reduce recidivism." According to the NIC, EBP have had a "profound and positive impact on the corrections field." (Recall the discussion earlier in this chapter, noting the EBP is part of the new mission statement of California's correctional system.) The NIC also emphasized the importance of motivational interviewing (MI), which was first used in the addiction treatment field in the 1980s when it was recognized that the confrontational approach was not working. Treatment therapists began to "implement strategies that recognized and encouraged autonomy, self-determination and positive reinforcement." Success rates rose, and now MI is adapted to the corrections field, especially in probation and parole.

> The principle behind MI is that by listening to offenders and following up on the positive aspects of their speech and thinking, corrections professionals can help increase offenders' motivation to make positive changes in their lives that will reduce their likelihood of reoffending.[161]

Many, if not most, of the recent problems in corrections have occurred as the result of a lack of earlier attention to the systems approach (e.g., increase sentences; strain the system, especially the facilities). Now that budgets are an issue in most, if not all, jurisdictions, criminal justice professionals and politicians are forced to find alternatives to prison. We can only hope that in this process careful thought will be given to finding the best solutions to correctional problems.

State and federal budget shortfalls have changed the face of U.S. corrections. According to a 2009 report of the Vera Institute of Justice's Center on Sentencing and Corrections, which surveyed state reactions to the budget issue, at least 31 states were predicting budget shortfalls for 2011. The report found that in 26 states the trend toward increasing corrections budgets yearly had been reversed. But with states continuing to face budget cuts and "one in every 15 state general fund dollars now spent on corrections," state officials would need to look to corrections for further savings. The report warned that in cutting corrections budgets, however, states "must be careful to find cuts that will not compromise public safety."[162] To achieve that goal while maintaining corrections programs that are associated with rehabilitation will be the challenge.

Finally, a national commission to study the criminal justice system might aid the progress toward reform. Exhibit 15.6 reprints the brief findings proposed by a bill passed by the U.S. House of Representatives in 2010. The bill provides for the creation of a National Criminal Justice Commission analogous to the President's Commission on Law Enforcement and Administration of Justice established in 1965. The bill was on the Senate's calendar but had not passed as of this writing.

EXHIBIT 15.6 The National Criminal Justice Commission Act of 2010: A Bill

On 27 April 2010, a bill to create a National Criminal Justice Commission on crime prevention was introduced into the U.S. House and the U.S. Senate. The bill passed the House on 27 July 2010. On 5 August 2010, the House bill was placed on the Senate's calendar. Among other provisions are the following:

"Congress finds that—

(1) it is in the interest of the Nation to establish a commission to undertake a comprehensive review of the criminal justice system;
(2) there has not been a comprehensive study since the President's Commission on Law Enforcement and Administration of Justice was established in 1965;
(3) that commission, in a span of 18 months, produced a comprehensive report entitled: "The Challenge of Crime in a Free Society," which contained 200 specific recommendations on all aspects of the criminal justice system . . . and

(4) developments over the intervening 45 years require once again that Federal, State, tribal, and local governments, religious organizations, business groups, and individual citizens come together to review evidence and consider how to improve the criminal justice system."

A major focus of the act is to establish a commission known as the National Criminal Justice Commission, which "shall undertake a comprehensive review of the criminal justice system, encompassing current Federal, State, local, and tribal criminal justice policies and practices, and make reform recommendations for the President, Congress, State, local, and tribal governments."

Source: The National Criminal Justice Commission Act of 2010, 2010 H.R. 5143. The Senate bill is S. 3160 (2010).

Summary

This chapter focused on handling offenders within the community by putting them in community correctional facilities, placing them on probation without a prison term but with supervision, providing pre- and postrelease assistance, and releasing offenders early from prison on parole. It began with a brief discussion of the history of corrections before turning to the diversion of offenders from the correctional system.

The next major section of the chapter highlighted community-based corrections and the concept of the reintegration of offenders into the community after they have served time in prison. In response to claims that treatment in prison does not work and that incarceration is too expensive, community programs such as work service, fines, restitution, halfway houses, shock incarceration, boot camps, day reporting centers, house arrest, and electronic monitoring and the use of global positioning systems were proposed as potential solutions to both problems.

Four exhibits related information concerning congressional attempts at instituting programs aimed at reintegrating offenders into the community and proposing the establishment of a national commission to study and make recommendations concerning reforming the nation's justice systems. Media Focus 15.1 updated boot camps, focusing on recent events in Florida and Arizona. The impact of the courts on reintegration was illustrated in Exhibit 15.3, which reproduced a portion of a judicial opinion concerning the importance of day reporting centers and other sentencing alternatives. Information on electronic monitoring, house arrest, and GPS highlighted the significance of maintaining security when inmates are released into the community.

The section on probation began with an overview and then turned to a more intensive analysis of probation, including a look at its history, current data, the probation process, probation supervision, and probation conditions. Release from incarceration and preparation for release began with the challenge of reentry for inmates back into society and then looked at prerelease programs. Special attention was given to the problems of hiring ex-felons, suggesting changes in the current lifetime bans on hiring and other issues regarding ex-felons. Consideration was given to research on the probability that an ex-felon would not commit another crime after a certain period (i.e., the hazard rate). The advantages of and problems with furloughs and work release from incarceration were noted.

The next major section concerned parole, looking at its history, current data, the parole system, and the future of parole. The issue of racial disparity was raised, and legal issues with regard to granting parole were discussed. The problems that arise when a parole system is abolished were noted along with efforts to improve parole supervision. Special attention was given to the recent emphasis on medical parole, particularly in California.

Probation and parole revocation were considered together, as they involve similar legal issues. Major cases, especially those decided by the U.S. Supreme Court, were summarized as was that Court's analysis of searches and seizures of probationers and parolees.

Significant attention was given to the various statutory requirements for sex offenders who are released into the community. Megan's Law and Jessica's Law were noted and discussed in terms of their effectiveness in achieving their goals and the various legal issues they raise. Recent legal cases were discussed. Current events, such as the Jacyee Dugard case, were incorporated where relevant. That case illustrated the lack of effectiveness of the laws, a problem noted in an extensive analysis of the California sex offender registration and related statutes. A final section on sex offenders was devoted to an analysis of civil commitment proceedings for those still considered dangerous when they have completed their prison sentences.

This chapter closed with a look at the future of corrections beginning with an evaluation of community corrections. This section focused on California and South Carolina, representing large and small correctional systems, each with different problems and vastly different approaches to the solution of those problems. Another important major issue is juvenile justice, with juvenile corrections discussed in the context of the successful Missouri plan.

Although they may be necessary for many offenders, prisons have been declared failures. Clearly, we cannot continue increasing the incarceration rates without massive expense or the greater use of probation and parole. There are indications that despite their unpopularity, probation and parole will continue to be used for large numbers of offenders. It seems wise, therefore, to study the problems and attempt to improve both systems. The importance of evidence-based practices was emphasized.

The chapter ended by noting, once again, that federal and state budget shortfalls have forced changes that might not have occurred otherwise and citing experts who are optimistic about rehabilitation and reform. The chapter ended as it began, with a look at congressional attempts at change. Only time will tell whether the U.S. Congress (and state legislatures) will give serious consideration to the evidence-based research that criminologists and others have produced.

Study Questions

1. Suggest historical changes that may account for the recent increased emphasis on community corrections.

2. Explain and evaluate the practice of diversion.

3. Define *community-based corrections*, and cite examples.

4. What specific steps should be taken for the diversion of juvenile offenders?

5. Compare fines and restitution.

6. Explore the concept of community work service.

7. What should be the role of halfway houses in corrections?

8. Define *shock incarceration*, and explain the concept in the context of boot camps.

9. Discuss day reporting centers.

10. Explain and evaluate house arrest, electronic monitoring (EM), and global positioning systems (GPS).

11. Distinguish between probation and parole, and explore the history of each.

12. Explain the process of granting probation and parole.

13. Define and evaluate *intensive probation supervision* (IPS).

14. Comment on the most recent data on probation and parole.

15. What are the legal implications of probation conditions?

16. Why are prerelease programs important?

17. Distinguish between and evaluate furlough and work-release programs.

18. Explain the functions of parole boards and parole officers.

19. What are the legal issues regarding the granting of parole?

20. What do we know about parole supervision?

21. What should be the role of medical parole?

22. Should parole be abolished?

23. What are the legal issues concerning probation and parole revocation?

24. Explain Megan's Law and Jessica's Law, and evaluate their use.

25. Discuss whether sex offender registration laws are effective.

26. Are there any human rights issues involved in sex offender registration and related laws?

27. What are the legal issues regarding sex offender registration and related laws?

28. Should sex offenders be subject to civil commitment proceedings? What are the legal issues? Social issues?

29. Discuss the pros and cons of community corrections.

30. Contrast the California and South Carolina general approaches to corrections.

31. Should juveniles accused of serious crimes be handled in adult criminal courts? Detained or incarcerated in adult jails and prisons? Give reasons for your answers.

32. Would a national commission on criminal justice issues be helpful or just a political move?

Brief Essay Assignments

1. Discuss the impact of recent drug treatment programs such as diversion techniques. Refer to Chapters 10 and 12 to enhance your answer.

2. Evaluate the use of boot camps and discuss their future.

3. Explain what is meant by *global positioning systems* (GPS), and evaluate this approach in terms of these punishment philosophies: deterrence, reintegration, rehabilitation, retribution, and incapacitation.

4. Probation and parole are forms of leniency, are dangerous to society, and should be abolished. Discuss the pros and cons of this statement.

5. Analyze the ways in which U.S. criminal justice systems react to convicted sex offenders.

6. Evaluate the problems and attempted solutions in the California corrections system.

Internet Activities

1. Using your Web browser, look for articles on sex offender registration requirements. Start with http://www.MissingKids.com and check information on your home state. What can you find out about *Amber Alert*? What is the purpose of the National Center for Missing and Exploited Children? (site accessed 15 November 2010)

2. Go to the Bureau of Justice Statistics website at http://bjs.ojp.usdoj.gov/. What can you find out about reentry trends? What information does the BJS provide on probation and parole? (site accessed 15 November 2010)

3. Using your Web browser, see what you can find out about the use of global positioning systems to track offenders, especially sex offenders.

Notes

1. Gordon Hawkins, *The Prison: Policy and Practice* (Chicago: University of Chicago Press, 1976), pp. 56–59.
2. National Advisory Commission on Criminal Justice Standards and Goals, *A National Strategy to Reduce Crime* (Washington, D.C.: U.S. Government Printing Office, 1973).
3. "Public Supports Balance in Corrections, ACA Survey Shows," *Criminal Justice Newsletter* 26 (15 June 1995): 2.
4. "Keeping Youths Out of Detention Is Key Priority for Court," *Chicago Daily Law Bulletin* (3 February 2004), n.p.
5. "Results from the Juvenile Detention Alternatives Initiative," http://www.aecf.org/MajorInitiatives/JuvenileDetentionAlternativesInitiatives.aspx, accessed 14 November 2010.
6. "Criminal Justice System Overwhelmed with Drug Cases," *Chicago Lawyer* (January 2007), p. 10050.
7. Robert M. Carter et al., *Program Models: Community Correctional Centers* (Washington, D.C.: U.S. Government Printing Office, 1980), p. 3.

8. Cal Pen Code, Section 2910.6 (2010).

9. "Community Corrections," Bureau of Prisons, http://www.bop.gov/locations/, accessed 14 November 2010.

10. Minn. Stat., Section 401.01 et seq. (2009).

11. The federal restitution provisions are codified at USCS, Title 18, Section 3663 (2010). The early U.S. Supreme Court case is *Bradford v. United States*, 228 U.S. 446 (1913). The Violent Crime Control and Law Enforcement Act of 1994, Public Law 103–322 (13 September 1994), amended the victim restitution provisions of USCS, Title 18, Section 3663(a) (2010).

12. For an overview of the federal system, see the Web page of the federal Bureau of Prisons at http://www.bop.gov/, accessed 14 November 2010.

13. USCS, Title 18, Section 3621 (a) and (b) and 3624 (b) and (c) (2010).

14. The case holding that the policy is unconstitutional is *Schorr v. Menifee*, 2004 U.S. Dist. LEXIS 10758 (S.D.N.Y. 2004). For a case upholding the policy, see *Cohn v. Federal Bureau of Prisons*, 302 F.Supp.2d 267 (S.D.N.Y. 2004).

15. Doris Layton MacKenzie et al., "Characteristics Associated with Successful Adjustment in Supervision: A Comparison of Parolees, Probationers, Shock Participants, and Shock Dropouts," *Criminal Justice and Behavior* 19 (December 1992): 437–454; quotations are on pp. 439, 452.

16. Doris Layton MacKenzie, "Editorial Introduction: Aftercare Following a Correctional Bootcamp May Reduce Recidivism," *Criminology and Public Policy* 5, no. 2 (May 2006): 359–362; quotation is on p. 361. See also MacKenzie, "Evidence-Based Corrections: Identifying What Works," *Crime and Delinquency* 46 (2000): 456–471; MacKenzie, *What Works in Corrections: Reducing the Recidivism of Offenders and Delinquents* (Cambridge, UK: Cambridge University Press, 2006); MacKenzie et al., "Effects of Correctional Boot Camps on Offending," *Annals of the American Academy of Political and Social Sciences* 578 (2001): 126–143.

17. Megan Kurlychek and Cynthia Kempinen, "Beyond Boot Camp: The Impact of Aftercare on Offender Reentry," *Criminology and Public Policy* 5, no. 2 (May 2006): 363–388.

18. Faith E. Lutze, "Boot Camp Prisons and Corrections Policy: Moving from Militarism to an Ethic of Care," *Criminology and Public Policy* 5, no. 2 (May 2006): 389–399; quotation is on p. 396.

19. Merry Morash and Lila Rucker, "A Critical Look at the Idea of Boot Camp as a Correctional Reform," *Crime and Delinquency* 36 (April 1990): 204–222, quotation is on p. 218.

20. "Poor Evaluation Brings End to California's Boot Camp," *Criminal Justice Newsletter* 28 (1 August 1997): 1.

21. "Maryland Is Latest of States to Rethink Youth Boot Camps," *New York Times* (19 December 1999), p. 1. For a scholarly analysis of boot camps, see Faith E. Lutze and David C. Brody, "Mental Abuse as Cruel and Unusual Punishment: Do Boot Camp Prisons Violate the Eighth Amendment?" *Crime and Delinquency* 45 (April 1999): 242–255.

22. "Day Reporting Centers Growing as a New Intermediate Sanction," *Criminal Justice Newsletter* 22 (15 April 1991): 6.

23. "Yet Another Hurdle: An L.A. County Pilot Program That Gives Gangbangers the Tools They Need to Change Their Lives Is in Danger of Losing Its Funding," *Los Angeles Times* (4 June 2010), p. 1.

24. *State v. Campa*, 840 N.E. 2d 1157 (Illinois 2005) is the precedent case. The case on appeal was *People v. Beachem*, 871 N.E.2d 805 (Ill.1st Dist. 2007), *aff'd.*, 890 N.E.2d 515 (Illinois 2008).

25. See Federal Bureau of Prisons, http://www.bop.gov/, accessed 14 November June 2010.

26. Joan Petersilia, National Institute of Justice, *House Arrest* (Washington, D.C.: U.S. Department of Justice, 1988), p. 2.

27. Ibid., pp. 3–4.

28. Marion County Community Corrections, http://www.indy.gov/eGov/County/Corrections/Services/Detention/Pages/hoe.aspx, accessed 14 November 2010.

29. For an analysis of the effects of treatment on recidivism, see D. A. Andrews et al., "Does Correctional Treatment Work? A Clinically Relevant and Psychologically Informed Meta-Analysis," *Criminology* 28 (August 1990): 369–404.

30. Annette Jolin and Brian Stipak, "Drug Treatment and Electronically Monitored Home Confinement: An Evaluation of a Community-Based Sentencing Option," *Crime and Delinquency* 38 (April 1992): 158–171; quotation is on p. 168.

31. Florida's Jessica Lunsford Act is codified at Fla. Stat., Section 948.06 et seq. (2010).

32. "GPS Tracking Is the Wave of the Future for Law Enforcement Authorities," *Journal of Counterterrorism and Homeland Security International* 9, no. 1 (2003 Winter): n.p.

33. *Corrections Today* 69, no. 3 (1 June 2007): 77.

34. See, for example, Wis. Stat., Section 301.48 (2010).

35. Recommendations Report of California's Sexual Offender Management Board, as reported in "Another Girl Dies, Another Law Will Pass," *Los Angeles Times* (14 March 2010), p. 35.

36. Mary A. Finn and Suzanne Muirhead-Steves, "The Effectiveness of Electronic Monitoring with Violent Male Parolees," *Justice Quarterly* 19, no. 2 (June 2002): 293–312; quotation is on p. 307.

37. Harry Elmer Barnes and Negley K. Teeters, *New Horizons in Criminology*, 3d ed. (Englewood Cliffs, NJ: Prentice-Hall, 1959), p. 554.

38. Administrative Offices of U.S. Courts, "Beginnings of Probation and Pretrial Services," http://www.uscourts.gov/FederalCourts/ProbationPretrialServices/History.aspx, accessed 14 November 2010.

39. Lauren E. Glaze and Thomas P. Bonczar, Bureau of Justice Statistics, *Probation and Parole in the United States, 2009* (December 2010), pp. 1, 2, http://bjs.ojp.usdoj.gov/content/pub/pdf/ppus09.pdf, accessed 26 December 2010.

40. *Mempa v. Rhay*, 389 U.S. 128 (1967).

41. "Juvenile Intensive Probation Said to Save New York City Money," *Criminal Justice Newsletter* (17 July 2006), p. 4. See also http://www.esperanzany.org, accessed 14 November 2010.

42. Susan Turner and Joan Petersilia, "Focusing on High-Risk Parolees: An Experiment to Reduce Commitments to the Texas Department of Corrections," *Journal of Research in Crime and Delinquency* 29 (February 1992): 34–61; quotation is on p. 57.

43. Susan Turner et al., "Evaluating Intensive Supervision Probation/Parole (ISP) for Drug Offenders," *Crime and Delinquency* 38 (October 1992): 539–556.

44. Lawrence W. Sherman, "Use Probation to Prevent Murder," *Criminology and Public Policy* 6, no. 4 (November 2007): 843–850; quotation is on p. 844.

45. *State v. Morris*, 806 P.2d 407 (Hawaii 1991).

46. *Commonwealth v. Koren*, 646 A.2d 1205 (Pa.Super. 1994).

47. *United States v. Myers,* 864 F.Supp. 794 (N.D.Ill. 1994).

48. *O'Connor v. California*, 855 F.Supp. 303 (C.D.Cal. 1994).

49. *State v. Oakley,* 629 N.W.2d 200 (Wis. 2001), *cert. denied*, *Oakley v. Wisconsin*, 537 U.S. 813 (2002).

50. *United States v. Sofsky*, 287 F.3d 122 (2d Cir. 2002), *cert. denied*, *Sofsky v. United States*, 537 U.S. 1167 (2003).

51. "Sex Offender Back Before Annoyed Judge," *Denver Post* (14 May 2010), p. 1B.

52. Ingrid Binswanger, *New England Journal of Medicine* (January 2007), referred to in "Life After Prison Can Be Deadly, a Study Finds," *New York Times* (11 January 2007), p. 23.

53. Joan Petersilia, *When Prisoners Come Home* (New York: Oxford University Press, 2003).

54. Second Chance Act of 2007, 110 Public Law 199(b)(3)(2010).

55. Robert Martinson, "What Works? Questions and Answers About Prison Reform," *Public Interest* 35 (1974): 22–35.

56. Joan Petersilia, "What Works in Prisoner Reentry? Reviewing and Questioning the Evidence," *Federal Probation* 68 (2004): 4–8; quotation is on p. 8.

57. James A. Wilson and Robert C. Davis, "Good Intentions Meet Hard Realities: An Evaluation of the Project Greenlight Reentry Program," *Criminology and Public Policy* 5, no. 2 (May 2006): 303–338; quotation is on pp. 303–304.

58. Douglas B. Marlowe, "When 'What Works' Never Did: Dodging the 'Scarlet M' in Correctional Rehabilitation," *Criminology and Public Policy* 5, no. 2 (May 2006): 339–346; quotation is on p. 344.

59. Edward E. Rhine et al., "Implementation: The Bane of Effective Correctional Programs," *Criminology and Public Policy* 5, no. 2 (May 2006): 345–358.

60. Christopher T. Lowenkamp et al., "Does Correctional Program Quality Really Matter? The Impact of Adhering to the Principles of Effective Intervention," *Criminology and Public Policy* 5, no. 3 (August 2006): 575–594; quotation is on p. 588.

61. William Oliver, "Prisoner Reentry Planning and Programming Must Address Family Reunification, Relationship Conflict, and Domestic Violence," in *Contemporary Issues in Criminal Justice Policy: Policy Proposals from the American Society of Criminology Conference,* ed. Natasha A. Frost et al. (Belmont, CA: Cengage, 2010), pp. 389–396; quotation is on p. 394. See also two other articles in this book concerning the same issue: Joanne Belknap, "The Multi-Pronged Potential Effects of Implementing Domestic Violence Programs in Men's Prisons and Reentry Programming," pp. 397–400; Johnna Christian, "The Importance of Family Reunification in the Prisoner Reentry Process," pp. 401–406.

62. James P. Lynch, "Prisoner Reentry: Beyond Program Evaluation," *Criminology and Public Policy* 5, no. 2 (May 2006): 401–412; quotations are on p. 405.

63. "Creating Safer Neighborhoods and Better Citizens: State Program Aims To Keep Parolees Out of Prison," *Muskegon Chronicle* (Michigan) (9 February 2010), n.p., http://www.michpri.com/index.php?page=home, accessed 14 November 2010.

64. "State to Build First 'Work Prison' at Lima," *Columbus Dispatch* (Ohio) (16 February 1996), p. 4B.

65. "Ohio Work Program in Jeopardy After Inmates Found Drinking," CorrectionsOne (28 May 2010), http://www.correctionsone.com, accessed 14 November 2010; "Inmate Program May Get Reprieve," *Columbus Dispatch* (Ohio) (30 June 2010), p. 1.

66. "Prison Population Control," *Indianapolis Star* (Indiana) (4 April 2004), p. 2B.

67. William B. Eimicke and Steven Cohen, Manhattan Institute for Policy Research, *America Works' Criminal Justice Program: Providing Second Chances Through Work,* Civic Bulletin no. 29 (November 2002), http://www.manhattan-institute.org/html/cb_29.htm, accessed 14 November 2010.

68. For a series of scholarly articles on criminal background checks, see *Criminology and Public Policy* 7, no. 3 (August 2008): Christopher Uggen, "Editorial Introduction: The Effect of Criminal Background Checks on Hiring Ex-Offenders," pp. 367–370; Michael A. Stoll and Shawn D. Bushway, "The Effect of Criminal Background Checks on Hiring Ex-Offenders," pp. 371–404; Richard Freeman, "Policy Essay: Incarceration, Criminal Background Checks, and Employment in a Low(er) Crime Society," pp. 405–412; Bruce Western, "Policy Essay: Criminal Background Checks and Employment Among Workers with Criminal Records," pp. 413–418.

69. See, for example, Jessica S. Henry and James B. Jacobs, "Ban the Box to Promote Ex-Offender Employment," *Criminology and Public Policy* 6, no. 4 (November 2007): 755–762.

70. For a discussion, see Shawn D. Bushway and Gary Sweeten, "Abolish Lifetime Bans for Ex-Felons," *Criminology and Public Policy* 6, no. 4 (November 2007): 697–706.

71. Alfred Blumstein and Kiminori Nakamura, "Redemption in the Presence of Widespread Criminal Background Checks," *Criminology* 47, no. 2 (May 2009): 327–360.

72. *State v. Bachmann,* 521 N.W.2d 886 (Minn.Ct.App. 1994). The statute is Minn. Stat. 631.425 (2009). The provisions for payments from earnings are from Subdivision 5 of this statute.

73. Howard Gill, "The Origins of Parole," in *Corrections in the Community: Alternatives to Imprisonment*, ed. George C. Killinger and Paul F. Cromwell Jr. (St. Paul, MN: West, 1974), p. 400.

74. Barnes and Teeters, eds., *New Horizons in Criminology*, 3d ed., pp. 417–422.

75. Ibid., pp. 423, 425.

76. Lauren E. Glaze and Thomas P. Bonczar, Bureau of Justice Statistics, *Probation and Parole in the United States, 2005* (November 2006, revised 18 January 2007), p. 8, http://bjs.ojp.usdoj.gov/content/pub/pdf/ppus05.pdf; Glaze and Bonczar, *Probation and Parole in the United States, 2009*, p. 4, both accessed 26 December 2010.

77. Glaze and Bonczar, *Probation and Parole in the United States, 2008*, pp. 8, 9.

78. William J. Sabol et al., Bureau of Justice Statistics, *Prisoners in 2008* (December 2009, revised 1 April 2010), p. 9, http://bjs.ojp.usdoj.gov/content/pub/pdf/p08.pdf, accessed 14 November 2010.

79. Kathryn D. Morgan and Brent Smith, "The Impact of Race on Parole Decision-Making," *Justice Quarterly* 25, no. 2 (June 2008):

411–435. See this article for a review of the literature on the impact of race on parole decisionmaking.

80. Morgan and Smith, "The Impact of Race on Parole Decision-Making," p. 9.

81. *Greenholtz v. Inmates of Nebraska Penal and Correctional Complex*, 442 U.S. 1 (1979).

82. *Board of Pardons v. Allen*, 482 U.S. 369 (1987).

83. *Sandin v. Conner*, 515 U.S. 472 (1995).

84. John Irwin, *The Felon* (Englewood Cliffs, NJ: Prentice-Hall, 1970), p. 173.

85. Quoted in Jessica Mitford, *Kind and Usual Punishment: The Prison Business* (New York: Knopf, 1973), p. 216.

86. NY CLS Penal, Section 70.45 (2010).

87. New York State Division of Parole, "History of Parole in New York State," http://www.parole.state.ny.us/introhistory.html, accessed 14 November 2010.

88. "Parole Groups Launch Campaign to Curb Abolition Efforts," *Criminal Justice Newsletter* 26 (3 April 1995): 5.

89. Ibid.

90. Joan Petersilia, "Employ Behavioral Contracting for 'Earned Discharge' Parole," *Criminology and Public Policy* 6, no. 4 (November 2007): 807–814; quotation is on p. 808.

91. Ibid., pp. 810, 811.

92. 2009 Bill Tracking CA S.B. 1399 (2010).

93. *United States v. Knights*, 534 U.S. 112 (2001).

94. Cal Pen Code, Section 3067(a) (2010).

95. *Samson v. California*, 547 U.S. 843 (2006). The quotation is from the dissenting opinion of Justice John Paul Stevens.

96. *Mempa v. Rhay*, 389 U.S. 128 (1967).

97. *Morrissey v. Brewer*, 408 U.S. 471 (1972).

98. *Morrissey v. Brewer*, 408 U.S. 471, 484 (1972).

99. *Gagnon v. Scarpelli*, 411 U.S. 778 (1973).

100. *Bearden v. Georgia*, 461 U.S. 660 (1983).

101. *Black v. Romano*, 471 U.S. 606 (1985).

102. The New Jersey Sexual Offender Registration Act (Megan's Law) is codified at N.J.Stat., Section 2C:7-1 et seq. (2010).

103. The 1994 statute, the Jacob Wetterling Crimes Against Children and Sexually Violent Offender Act, is codified at USCS, Title 42, Section 14071 (2010).

104. "Sex Offender Registry: Challenge Likely," *New Jersey Lawyer* (30 July 2001), p. 5.

105. For a summary, see *California's Megan's Law*, California Department of Justice's Violent Crime Information Center (July 2000), http://ag.ca.gov/megan/pdf/ca_megans.pdf, accessed 15 November 2010.

106. The Adam Walsh Child Protection and Safety Act is codified at USCS, Title 18, Section 4248 (2010).

107. The registration requirements of the Sex Offender Registration and Notification Act (SORNA) are codified at USCS, Title 42, Section 16913 (2010). The federal crime of failure to register as a sex offender is codified at USCS, Title 18, Section 2250(1)(2)(A) (2010). For a scholarly analysis of these and related sections, see Robin Morse, "Note: Federalism Challenges to the Adam Walsh Act," *Boston University Law Review* 89 (December 2009): 1753.

108. "Witness in Adam Walsh Case Seeks Report," *Orlando Sentinel* (Florida) (4 June 2010), p. 9B.

109. "Rep. Pomeroy Testifies on His Bill to Keep Kids Safe from Sex Offenders on Internet," *US Fed News* (17 October 2007), n.p. Keeping the Internet Devoid of Sexual Predators (KIDS) Act of 2008, P.L. 110–400, 42 USCS 1690 (2010).

110. "More and More States Pass Laws to Strengthen Sex Crime Penalties," *Criminal Justice Newsletter* (1 March 2007), p. 3. The Florida statute, the Jessica Lunsford Act, is codified at Fla. Stat., Section 948.06 et seq. (2010).

111. California's Jessica's law is codified at Cal Pen Code, Section 3003.5 et seq. (2010).

112. Office of the Attorney General of California, "California Megan's Law: Facts About Sex Offenders," http://www.meganslaw.ca.gov/facts.aspx?lang=ENGLISH, accessed 15 November 2010.

113. *California Law Enforcement and Correctional Agencies: With Increased Efforts, They Could Improve the Accuracy and Completeness of Public Information on Sex Offenders,* Report no. 2003-105 (August 2003), http://www.bsa.ca.gov/pdfs/sr2005/2003-105.pdf, accessed 15 November 2010.

114. "Official Gets Probation for Inmate Sex," *Denver Post* (16 May 2003), p. 4B.

115. Jill Levenson et al., "Failure to Register as a Sex Offender: Is It Associated with Recidivism?" *Justice Quarterly* 27, no. 3 (June 2010): 305–331; quotation is on p. 306.

116. Jeffrey T. Walker, "Eliminate Residency Restrictions for Sex Offenders," *Criminology and Public Policy* 6, no. 4 (November 2007): 863–870; quotation is on p. 866.

117. "America's Flawed Sex Offender Laws," Human Rights Watch, http://www.hrw.org/en/news/2009/09/05/americas-flawed-sex-offender-laws, accessed 15 November 2010.

118. Assembly Bill 1015, Chapter 335, Statutes of 2006.

119. California Sex Offender Management Board (CASOMB), California Department of Mental Health, Recommendations Report (January 2010), p. 51, http://www.casomb.org, accessed 15 November 2010.

120. See Lorine A. Hughes and Keri B. Burchfield, "Sex Offender Residence Restrictions in Chicago: An Environmental Injustice?" *Justice Quarterly* 25, no. 4 (December 2008): 647–673; Hughes and Colleen Kadleck, "Sex Offender Community Notification and Community Stratification," *Justice Quarterly* 25, no. 3 (September 2008): 469–495. See also Michelle L. Meloy et al., "Making Sense Out of Nonsense: The Deconstruction of State-Level Sex Offender Residence Restrictions," *American Journal of Criminal Justice* (Fall 2008): 209–222.

121. *In re Registrant J.G.*, 777 A.2d 891 (N.J. 2001).

122. *A.A. v. New Jersey*, 341 F.3d 206 (3d Cir. 2003), *cert. denied*, 549 U.S. 1181 (2007).

123. *Smith v. Doe*, 538 U.S. 84 (2003).

124. *Connecticut Department of Public Safety v. Doe*, 538 U.S. 1 (2003).

125. "Georgia Closes Camp of Sex Offenders," *New York Times* (30 September 2009), p. 19.

126. O.C.G.A., Section 42-1-15 (2010).

127. See, for example, *Doe v. Schwarzenegger*, 476 F.Supp.2d 1178 (E.D. Cal. 2007).

128. *Commonwealth ex rel Conway*, 300 S.W.3d 152 (Ky. 2009).

129. *United States v. Powers*, 544 F.Supp.2d 1331 (M.D.Fla. 2008), *vacated and remanded, United States v. Powers*, 562 F.3d 1342 (11th Cir. 2009).

130. *Carr v. United States*, 130 S.Ct. 2229 (2010). The Court was quoting from USCS, Section 2250(1) (2010).

131. Commitment of Sexually Violent Predators, K.S.A., Section 59-29a01 (2009). The case is *Kansas v. Hendricks*, 521 U.S. 346 (1997).

132. "Doubts Rise as States Hold Sex Offenders After Prison," *New York Times* (4 March 2007), p. 1.

133. The case is *United States v. Comstock*, 130 S.Ct. 1949 (2010).

134. Daniel Glaser, *The Effectiveness of a Prison and Parole System* (Indianapolis, IN: Bobbs-Merrill, 1964).

135. See, for example, Marvin E. Wolfgang et al., *Delinquency in a Birth Cohort* (Chicago: University of Chicago Press, 1972); Wolfgang et al., *From Boy to Man: From Delinquency to Crime* (Chicago: University of Chicago Press, 1987).

136. Joan Petersilia, *Probation and Felony Offenders*, Research in Brief, National Institute of Justice (Washington, D.C.: U.S. Department of Justice, March 1985), p. 4.

137. Joan Petersilia, "Rand's Research: A Closer Look," *Corrections Today* 47 (June 1985): 37.

138. Joan Petersilia, "A Crime Control Rationale for Reinvesting in Community Corrections," in *Community Corrections: Probation, Parole, and Intermediate Sanctions*, ed. Petersilia (New York: Oxford University Press, 1988), p. 23.

139. Amy Murphy and Susan Turner, University of California, Irvine, Center for Evidence-Based Corrections, *Parole Violation Decision-Making Instrument (PVDMI) Process Evaluation* (December 2009, revised February 2010), p. 1, http://ucicorrections.seweb.uci.edu/Sites/ucicorrections.seweb.uci.edu/files/PVDMI.pdf, accessed 15 November 2010.

140. Public Safety and Offender Rehabilitation Services Act of 2007, California Advanced Legislative Service, Chapter 7, Assembly Bill 900 (2010).

141. Executive Summary, *Meeting the Challenges of Rehabilitation in California's Prison and Parole System: A Report from Governor Schwarzenegger's Rehabilitation Strike Team* (hereafter referred to as *Meeting the Challenges*). This report was chaired by Joan Petersilia and published in December 2007. It can be found on line at http://www.cdcr.ca.gov/News/docs/GovRehabilitation StrikeTeamRpt_012308.pdf, accessed 15 November 2010.

142. Ibid., p. 11.

143. Ibid.

144. Murphy and Turner, *Parole Violation Decision-Making*, p. 45.

145. Omnibus Crime Reduction and Sentencing Reform Act of 2010, 2010 S.C. Acts 273.

146. "New Law Changes Criminal Sentencing," *Post and Courier* (Charleston, SC) (3 June 2010), n.p.

147. Ibid. The statute is the South Carolina Reduction of Recidivism Act of 2010, 2010 S.C. Acts 151.

148. S.C. Code Ann, Section 2-48-10 (2009).

149. "Correctional Educators Must Meet the Needs of the Rising Female Prison Population," *Correctional Educational Bulletin* 4 (30 July 2001), p. 1.

150. Coalition for Juvenile Justice, "Unaddressed Mental Health Needs," http://www.juvjustice.org/position_4.html, accessed 15 November 2010.

151. "Teachers Must Handle Mental Health Students with Care," *Correctional Educational Bulletin* 4 (30 July 2001): 1.

152. "YouthARTS Project Uses Creativity to Help Juvenile Offenders Avoid Delinquency," *Correctional Educational Bulletin* 4 (2 July 2001): 1.

153. "Young Offenders Routed to New Federal Program," *New York Law Journal* (18 June 2001), p. 1.

154. "Success of Blunt's Administration's Division of Youth Services Highlighted in National Report," *US States News* (27 July 2007), n.p.

155. Missouri Rules of Practice and Procedure in Juvenile Courts, Rule 111.03 (2007).

156. "Two Approaches to Juvenile Justice," *Plain Dealer* (Cleveland) (21 January 2007), p. 7.

157. "The Right Model for Juvenile Justice," *New York Times* (28 October 2007), Section 4, p. 11.

158. "Missouri System Treats Juvenile Offenders with Lighter Hand," *New York Times* (26 March 2009), http://www.nytimes.com/2009/03/27/us/27juvenile.html, accessed 15 November 2010.

159. "Missouri's New Take on Juvenile Justice," ABC News, *Good Morning America* (8 September 2009).

160. Francis T. Cullen, "It's Time to Reaffirm Rehabilitation," *Criminology and Public Policy* 5, no. 4 (November 2006): 665–672; quotation is on pp. 668, 669. See also Peter R. Jones and Brian R. Wyant, "Target Juvenile Needs To Reduce Delinquency," *Criminology and Public Policy* 6, no. 4 (November 2007): 763–772.

161. Scott Walters et al., *Motivating Offenders to Change: A Guide for Probation and Parole*, National Institute of Corrections (June 2007), p. vii, http://www.nicic.org/downloads/PDF/Library/022253.pdf, accessed 15 November 2010.

162. Christine S. Scott-Hayward, Vera Institute of Justice, *The Fiscal Crisis in Corrections: Rethinking Policies and Practices* (July 2009), p. 3, http://www.pewcenteronthestates.org/uploaded Files/Vera_state_budgets.pdf?n=5515, accessed 15 November 2010.

APPENDIX A

Amendments to the Constitution of the United States of America

Amendment I

Congress shall make no law respecting an establishment of religion, or prohibiting the free exercise thereof; or abridging the freedom of speech, or of the press; or the right of the people peaceably to assemble, and to petition the Government for a redress of grievances.

Amendment II

A well regulated Militia, being necessary to the security of a free State, the right of the people to keep and bear Arms, shall not be infringed.

Amendment III

No Soldier shall, in time of peace be quartered in any house, without the consent of the Owner, nor in time of war, but in a manner to be prescribed by law.

Amendment IV

The right of the people to be secure in their persons, houses, papers, and effects, against unreasonable searches and seizures, shall not be violated, and no Warrants shall issue, but upon probable cause, supported by Oath or affirmation, and particularly describing the place to be searched, and the persons or things to be seized.

Amendment V

No person shall be held to answer for a capital, or otherwise infamous crime, unless on a presentment or indictment of a Grand Jury, except in cases arising in the land or naval forces, or in the Militia, when in actual service in time of War or public danger; nor shall any person be subject for the same offence to be twice put in jeopardy of life or limb, nor shall be compelled in any criminal case to be a witness against himself, nor be deprived of life, liberty, or property, without due process of law; nor shall private property be taken for public use without just compensation.

Amendment VI

In all criminal prosecutions, the accused shall enjoy the right to a speedy and public trial, by an impartial jury of the State and district wherein the crime shall have been committed; which district shall have been previously ascertained by law, and to be informed of the nature and cause of the accusation; to be confronted with the witnesses against him; to have compulsory process for obtaining witnesses in his favor, and to have the assistance of counsel for his defence.

Amendment VII

In Suits at common law, where the value in controversy shall exceed twenty dollars, the right of trial by jury shall be preserved, and no fact tried by a jury shall be otherwise re-examined in any Court of the United States, than according to the rules of the common law.

Amendment VIII

Excessive bail shall not be required, nor excessive fines imposed, nor cruel and unusual punishments inflicted.

Amendment IX

The enumeration in the Constitution of certain rights shall not be construed to deny or disparage others retained by the people.

Amendment X

The powers not delegated to the United States by the Constitution, nor prohibited by it to the States, are reserved to the States respectively, or to the people.

Amendment XI

The Judicial power of the United States shall not be construed to extend to any suit in law or equity, commenced or prosecuted against one of the United States by Citizens of another State, or by Citizens or Subjects of any Foreign State.

Amendment XII

The Electors shall meet in their respective states, and vote by ballot for President and Vice President, one of whom, at least, shall not be an inhabitant of the same state with themselves; they shall name in their ballots the person voted for as President, and in distinct ballots the person voted for as Vice-President, and they shall make distinct lists of all persons voted for as President, and of all persons voted for as Vice-President, and of the number of votes for each, which lists they shall sign and certify, and transmit sealed to the seat of the government of the United States, directed to the President of the Senate;—The President of the Senate shall, in the presence of the Senate and House of Representatives, open all the certificates and the votes shall then be counted;—The person having the greatest number of votes for President, shall be the President, if such number be a majority of the whole number of Electors appointed; and if no person have such majority, then from the persons having the highest numbers not exceeding three on the list of those voted for as President, the House of Representatives shall choose immediately, by ballot, the President. But in choosing the President, the votes shall be taken by states, the representation from each state having one vote; a quorum for this purpose shall consist of a member or members from two-thirds of the states, and a majority of all the states shall be necessary to a choice. [And if the House of Representatives shall not choose a President whenever the right of choice shall devolve upon them, before the fourth day of March next following, then the Vice-President shall act as President, as in the case of the death or other constitutional disability of the President—] The person having the greatest number of votes as Vice-President, shall be the Vice-President, if such number be a majority of the whole number of Electors appointed, and if no person have a majority, then from the two highest numbers on the list, the Senate shall choose the Vice-President; a quorum for the purpose shall consist of two-thirds of the whole number of Senators, and a majority of the whole number shall be necessary to a choice. But no person constitutionally ineligible to the of-fice of President shall be eligible to that of Vice-President of the United States.

Amendment XIII

Section 1. Neither slavery nor involuntary servitude, except as a punishment for crime whereof the party shall have been duly convicted, shall exist within the United States, or any place subject to their jurisdiction.

Section 2. Congress shall have power to enforce this article by appropriate legislation.

Amendment XIV

Section 1. All persons born or naturalized in the United States and subject to the jurisdiction thereof, are citizens of the United States and of the State wherein they reside. No State shall make or enforce any law which shall abridge the privileges or immunities of citizens of the United States; nor shall any State deprive any person of life, liberty, or property, without due process of law; nor deny to any person within its jurisdiction the equal protection of the laws.

Section 2. Representatives shall be apportioned among the several States according to their respective numbers, counting the whole number of persons in each State, excluding Indians not taxed. But when thc right to vote at any election for the choice of electors for President and Vice President of the United States, Representatives in Congress, the Executive and Judicial officers of a State, or the members of the Legislature thereof, is denied to any of the male inhabitants of such State, being twenty-one years of age, and citizens of the United States, or in any way abridged, except for participation in rebellion, or other crime, the basis of representation therein shall be reduced in the proportion which the number of such male citizens shall bear to the whole number of male citizens twenty-one years of age in such State.

Section 3. No person shall be a Senator or Representative in Congress, or elector of President and Vice President, or hold any office, civil or military, under the United States, or under any State, who, having previously taken an oath, as a member of Congress, or as an officer of the United States, or as a member of any State legislature, or as an executive or judicial officer of any State, to support the Constitution of the United States, shall have engaged in insurrection or rebellion against the same, or given aid or comfort to the enemies thereof. But Congress may by a vote of two-thirds of each House, remove such disability.

Section 4. The validity of the public debt of the United States, authorized by law, including debts incurred for payment of pensions and bounties for services in suppressing insurrection or rebellion, shall not be questioned. But neither the United States nor any State shall assume or pay any debt or obligation incurred in aid of insurrection or rebellion against the United States, or any claim for the loss or emancipation of any slave; but all such debts, obligations and claims shall be held illegal and void.

Section 5. The Congress shall have power to enforce, by appropriate legislation, the provisions of this article.

Amendment XV

Section 1. The right of citizens of the United States to vote shall not be denied or abridged by the United States or by any State on account of race, color, or previous condition of servitude.

Section 2. The Congress shall have power to enforce this article by appropriate legislation.

Amendment XVI

The Congress shall have power to lay and collect taxes on incomes, from whatever source derived, without apportionment among the several States, and without regard to any census or enumeration.

Amendment XVII

The Senate of the United States shall be composed of two Senators from each State, elected by the people thereof, for six years; and each Senator shall have one vote. The electors in each State shall have the qualifications requisite for electors of the most numerous branch of the State legislatures.

When vacancies happen in the representation of any State in the Senate, the executive authority of such State shall issue writs of election to fill such vacancies: *Provided*, That the legislature of any State may empower the executive thereof to make temporary appointments until the people fill the vacancies by election as the legislature may direct.

This amendment shall not be so construed as to affect the election or term of any Senator chosen before it becomes valid as part of the Constitution.

Amendment XVIII

Section 1. After one year from the ratification of this article the manufacture, sale, or transportation of intoxicating liquors within, the importation thereof into, or the exportation thereof from the United States and all territory subject to the jurisdiction thereof for beverage purposes is hereby prohibited.

Section 2. The Congress and the several States shall have concurrent power to enforce this article by appropriate legislation.

Section 3. This article shall be inoperative unless it shall have been ratified as an amendment to the Constitution

by the legislatures of the several States, as provided in the Constitution, within seven years from the date of the submission hereof to the States by the Congress.

Amendment XIX

The right of citizens of the United States to vote shall not be denied or abridged by the United States or by any State on account of sex.

Congress shall have power to enforce this article by appropriate legislation.

Amendment XX

Section 1. The terms of the President and Vice President shall end at noon on the 20th day of January, and the terms of Senators and Representatives at noon on the 3d day of January, of the years in which such terms would have ended if this article had not been ratified; and the terms of their successors shall then begin.

Section 2. The Congress shall assemble at least once in every year, and such meeting shall begin at noon on the 3d day of January, unless they shall by law appoint a different day.

Section 3. If, at the time fixed for the beginning of the term of the President, the President elect shall have died, the Vice President elect shall become President. If a President shall not have been chosen before the time fixed for the beginning of his term, or if the President elect shall have failed to qualify, then the Vice President elect shall act as President until a President shall have qualified; and the Congress may by law provide for the case wherein neither a President elect nor a Vice President elect shall have qualified, declaring who shall then act as President, or the manner in which one who is to act shall be selected, and such person shall act accordingly until a President or Vice President shall have qualified.

Section 4. The Congress may by law provide for the case of the death of any of the persons from whom the House of Representatives may choose a President whenever the right of choice shall have devolved upon them, and for the case of the death of any of the persons from whom the Senate may choose a Vice President whenever the right of choice shall have devolved upon them.

Section 5. Sections 1 and 2 shall take effect on the 15th day of October following the ratification of this article.

Section 6. This article shall be inoperative unless it shall have been ratified as an amendment to the Constitution by the legislatures of three-fourths of the several States within seven years from the date of its submission.

Amendment XXI

Section 1. The eighteenth article of amendment to the Constitution of the United States is hereby repealed.

Section 2. The transportation or importation into any State, Territory, or possession of the United States for delivery or use therein of intoxicating liquors, in violation of the laws thereof, is hereby prohibited.

Section 3. This article shall be inoperative unless it shall have been ratified as an amendment to the Constitution by conventions in the several States, as provided in the Constitution, within seven years from the date of the submission hereof to the States by the Congress.

Amendment XXII

Section 1. No person shall be elected to the office of the President more than twice, and no person who has held the office of President, or acted as President, for more than two years of a term to which some other person was elected President shall be elected to the office of the President more than once. But this Article shall not apply to any person holding the office of President when this Article was proposed by the Congress, and shall not prevent any person who may be holding the office of President, or acting as President, during the term within which this Article becomes operative from holding the office of President or acting as President during the remainder of such term.

Section 2. This article shall be inoperative unless it shall have been ratified as an amendment to the Constitution by the legislatures of three-fourths of the several States within seven years from the date of its submission to the States by the Congress.

Amendment XXIII

Section 1. The District constituting the seat of Government of the United States shall appoint in such manner as the Congress may direct:

A number of electors of President and Vice President equal to the whole number of Senators and Representatives in Congress to which the District would be entitled if it were a State, but in no event more than the least populous State; they shall be in addition to those appointed by the States, but they shall be considered, for the purposes of the election of President and Vice President, to be electors appointed by a State; and they shall meet in the District and perform such duties as provided by the twelfth article of amendment.

Section 2. The Congress shall have power to enforce this article by appropriate legislation.

Amendment XXIV

Section 1. The right of citizens of the United States to vote in any primary or other election for President or Vice President, for electors for President or Vice President, or for Senator or Representative in Congress, shall not be denied or abridged by the United States or any State by reason of failure to pay any poll tax or other tax.

Section 2. The Congress shall have power to enforce this article by appropriate legislation.

Amendment XXV

Section 1. In case of the removal of the President from office or of his death or resignation, the Vice President shall become President.

Section 2. Whenever there is a vacancy in the office of the Vice President, the President shall nominate a Vice President who shall take office upon confirmation by a majority vote of both Houses of Congress.

Section 3. Whenever the President transmits to the President pro tempore of the Senate and the Speaker of the House of Representatives his written declaration that he is unable to discharge the powers and duties of his office, and until he transmits to them a written declaration to the contrary, such powers and duties shall be discharged by the Vice President as Acting President.

Section 4. Whenever the Vice President and a majority of either the principal officers of the executive departments or of such other body as Congress may by law provide, transmit to the President pro tempore of the Senate and the Speaker of the House of Representatives their written declaration that the President is unable to discharge the powers and duties of his office, the Vice President shall immediately assume the powers and duties of the office as Acting President.

Thereafter, when the President transmits to the President pro tempore of the Senate and the Speaker of the House of Representatives his written declaration that no inability exists, he shall resume the powers and duties of his office unless the Vice President and a majority of either the principal officers of the executive department or of such other body as Congress may by law provide, transmit within four days to the President pro tempore of the Senate and the Speaker of the House of Representatives their written declaration that the President is unable to discharge the powers and duties of his office. Thereupon Congress shall decide the issue, assembling within forty-eight hours for that purpose if not in session. If the Congress, within twenty-one days after receipt of the latter written declaration, or, if Congress is not in session, within twenty-one days after Congress is required to assemble, determines by two-thirds vote of both Houses that the President is unable to discharge the powers and duties of his office, the Vice President shall continue to discharge the same as Acting President; otherwise, the President shall resume the powers and duties of his office.

Amendment XXVI

Section 1. The right of citizens of the United States, who are eighteen years of age or older; to vote shall not be denied or abridged by the United States or by any State on account of age.

Section 2. The Congress shall have power to enforce this article by appropriate legislation.

Amendment XXVII

No law, varying the compensation for the services of the Senators and Representatives, shall take effect, until an election of Representatives shall have intervened.

APPENDIX B

How to Read a Court Citation

Pugh v. Locke, 406 F.Supp. 318 (M.D.Ala. 1976), *aff'd., remanded sub nom.*, *Newman v. Alabama*, 559 F.2d 283 (5th Cir. 1977), *reh'g. denied*, 564 F.2d 97 (5th Cir. 1977), and *rev'd. in part sub nom.*, 438 U.S. 781 (1978) [numerous later proceedings omitted from this citation], and *cert. denied*, *Newman v. Alabama*, 438 U.S. 915 (1978).

This case has a number of citations, which is not common among all cases but is common among those involving unconstitutional conditions in prisons and jails. The case is used here because it illustrates so many elements of case citations. As noted, other citations to later proceedings were not included in this discussion.

Original Citation

[*Pugh v. Locke*][1] [406][2] [F.Supp.][3] [318][4] [M.D.Ala.][5] [1976][6]

1. Name of original case.
2. Volume number of reporter in which that case is published.
3. Name of reporter; see "Abbreviations for Commonly Used Reporters," later in this appendix.
4. Page on which the decision begins in the reporter.
5. Abbreviation of the court that decided the case.
6. Year decided.

Additional Case History

[*aff'd., remanded sub nom.*][7] [*Newman v. Alabama*][8] [559][9] [F.2d][10] [283][11] [(5th Cir. 1977)][12] [*reh'g. denied*][13] [564 F.2d 97][14] [(5th Cir. 1977)],[15] *and rev'd. in part sub nom.*[16] [438 U.S. 781][17] [(1978)],[18] [*and cert. denied, Newman v. Alabama*, 438 U.S. 915 (1978)][19]

7. Lower court decision was affirmed and remanded (sent back for further proceedings) under a different name. The appellate court told the lower court that it agreed with part of its decision but that some aspect of the decision needed to be reconsidered.

8. Name under which the case was affirmed and remanded.
9. Volume number of the reporter in which this appellate decision is published.
10. Abbreviated name of reporter (Federal Reporter Second Series).
11. Page number on which the opinion begins.
12. Court deciding this appellate opinion (the Fifth Circuit) and the year decision was handed down.
13. Another hearing was denied.
14. Volume number, reporter, and page number for the citation of the rehearing denial.
15. Name of the court (Fifth Circuit) denying the rehearing and year of its decision.
16. Decision was reversed in part under another name.
17. That decision is recorded in volume 438 of the U.S. Reports, beginning on page 781. The decision was made by the U.S. Supreme Court; only its decisions appear in this reporter.
18. That decision was made in 1978.
19. The U.S. Supreme Court denied *certiorari* in 1978, and that decision is recorded in volume 438 of the U.S. Reports, beginning on p. 915.

Abbreviations for Commonly Used Reporters for Court Cases

Decisions of the U.S. Supreme Court

S.Ct.: Supreme Court Reporter
U.S.: United States Reports

Decisions from Other Courts: A Selected List

A., A.2d: Atlantic Reporter, Atlantic Reporter Second Series
Cal.Rptr: California Reporter

F.2d: Federal Reporter Second Series

F.3d: Federal Reporter Third Series

F.Supp: Federal Supplement

N.Y.S.2d: New York Supplement Second Series

N.W., N.W.2d: North Western Reporter, North Western Reporter Second Series

N.E., N.E.2d: North Eastern Reporter, North Eastern Reporter Second Series

P., P.2d: Pacific Reporter, Pacific Reporter Second Series

S.E., S.E.2d: South Eastern Reporter, South Eastern Reporter Second Series

Definitions

Aff'd. Affirmed. The appellate court agrees with the decision of the lower court.

Aff'd. sub nom. Affirmed under a different name. The case at the appellate level has a different name from that of the trial court level.

Aff'd. per curium. Affirmed by the courts. The opinion is written by "the court" instead of by one of the judges or justices; a decision is affirmed, but no written opinion is issued.

Cert. denied. Certiorari denied. The U.S. Supreme Court (or some other appellate court) refuses to hear and decide the case.

Concurring opinion. An opinion agreeing with the court's decision, but offering different reasons.

Dismissed. The court is dismissing the case from legal proceedings, thus refusing to give further consideration to any of its issues.

Dissenting opinion. An opinion disagreeing with the reasoning and result of the majority opinion.

Later proceeding. Any number of issues could be decided in a subsequent proceeding.

Reh'g. denied. Rehearing denied. The court refuses to rehear the case.

Remanded. The appellate court is sending a case back to the lower court for further action.

Rev'd. Reversed, overthrown, set aside, made void. The appellate court reverses the decision of the lower court.

Rev'd. and remanded. Reversed and remanded. The appellate court reverses the decision and sends the case back for further action.

Vacated. Abandoned, set aside, made void. The appellate court sets aside the decision of the lower court.

GLOSSARY

administrative law Rules, regulations, and enforcements made by agencies to which power has been delegated by state legislatures or the U.S. Congress. Administrative agencies investigate and decide cases concerning potential violations of these rules; their decisions can, in some cases, be appealed to courts.

adolescent limiteds Adolescents whose antisocial behavior peaks during adolescence and then declines. They constitute the majority of antisocial adolescents and are strongly influenced by their peers. *See also* **life-course persisters**.

adversary system One of two primary systems for settling disputes in court. The accused is presumed to be innocent. A defense attorney and a prosecuting attorney attempt to convince a judge or a jury of their respective versions of a case. *See also* **inquisitory system**.

age-graded theory A theory referring to age-graded, informal social controls such as the bonding that occurs within the family and schools, with peers, and in later life, with marriage and jobs.

aggravated assault Technically, an **assault** is a threat to commit an immediate, offensive, and unauthorized touching, which is a **battery**. But often, the term *assault* refers to the actual battery. In that case, an *aggravated assault* involves an assault or a battery intended to cause serious injury or death and often includes the use of a deadly weapon; in contrast, a *simple assault* does not involve any aggravating conditions, such as the use of a weapon.

anomie A state of normlessness in society that may be caused by decreased homogeneity and that provides a setting conducive to crimes and other antisocial acts.

anticipatory search warrant A warrant that is issued for a search at a particular place at a particular time *in the future*. It is based on evidence of a *triggering* event that gives probable cause to believe that the evidence, contraband, or fugitive will be at that place at that future time.

antitrust laws State and federal statutes designed to protect trade and commerce from unlawful restraints, such as price fixing, price discrimination, and monopolies.

appeal A step in a judicial proceeding in which a higher court is asked to review a lower court's decision.

appellant The losing party in a lower court who appeals to a higher court for review of the decision.

appellee The winning party in a lower court who argues on appeal that the lower court's decision should not be reversed.

arraignment In criminal law, the stage in criminal justice systems when the defendant appears before the court, hears the charges, is given instructions on his or her legal rights, and may enter a plea.

arrest The act of depriving persons of their liberty; taking suspects into custody for the purpose of formally charging them with a crime.

arson The willful and malicious burning of the property of another with or without the intent to defraud. Burning one's own property with the intent to defraud is included in the statutes of some, but not all, jurisdictions.

asportation The act of moving things or people from one place to another; it is a required element for the crime of larceny-theft.

assault *See* **aggravated assault**.

attempt crimes Crimes in which the offender engages in some effort to commit a crime but does not carry through with it. Planning is not sufficient; some step must be taken toward committing the criminal act, and a criminal intent must be proved.

attention-deficit hyperactivity disorder (ADHD) The most commonly diagnosed psychiatric condition among U.S. children today, affecting approximately 3 percent of them. Difficult to diagnose and more common among boys than girls, ADHD is manifested by inattentiveness, difficulty stifling inconvenient impulses, and daydreaming, as well as by not finishing projects, repeatedly making careless mistakes, switching haphazardly from one activity to another, and having problems obeying instructions. These and other behaviors inhibit school, work, and social relationships.

Baby Moses laws Recently enacted laws, named after the biblical baby, that are designed to protect from prosecution mothers (or fathers) who abandon their newborn children in ways that will protect those infants, such as leaving them at designated safe places.

bail The release of a defendant from custody pending a legal proceeding, such as a trial. *See also* **bail bond**.

bail bond A legal document stating the terms under which a defendant is granted release from jail prior to a legal proceeding, such as a trial. The bail bond may or may not be secured with money or property pledged by the defendant or others. Technically, if the defendant does not appear at the time and place designated in the document, the court may require the forfeiture of any money or property used to secure the bail bond.

battered person syndrome A syndrome arising from a cycle of abuse by a special person, usually a parent, a spouse, or an intimate partner, that leads the battered person to perceive that violence against the offender is the only way to end the abuse. If the battered person kills the alleged batterer, some jurisdictions will admit evidence of the battered person syndrome as a defense to that killing.

battery *See* **aggravated assault**.

behavior genetics The study of the effects of genetic and environmental influences on the characteristics of humans and other animals.

behavior theory A theory based on the belief that all behavior is learned and can be unlearned. It is the basis for behavior modification, one approach used for changing behavior in both institutional and noninstitutional settings.

biocriminology The introduction of biological variables into the study of criminology.

blackmail The unlawful demand for money or property by threatening bodily harm or exposure of information that is disgraceful or criminal. *See also* **extortion**.

booking The process of recording an arrest officially by entering the suspect's name, offense charged, place, time, arresting officer, and reason for arrest; it is usually done at a police station by the arresting officer.

boot camps Correctional facilities designed to detain offenders, primarily juveniles or young adults, for short periods, such as six months; they usually include a regimented daily routine of physical exercise, work, and discipline, resembling military training. Most of the programs include rehabilitative measures such as drug treatment and educational courses. Because of recent problems, including the deaths of some inmates, many jurisdictions have stopped using this form of incarceration.

bootlegging The illegal production, use, or sale of alcoholic beverages. *See also* **Prohibition**.

bribery The offering or receiving of money, goods, services, information, or anything else of value for the purpose of influencing public officials to act in a particular way.

burden of proof In a legal case, the duty of proving a disputed fact. For example, in a criminal case, the prosecution has the burden of proving the defendant's guilt beyond a reasonable doubt. The prosecution must prove every element of the crime charged.

Bureau of Justice Statistics (BJS) An agency established by Congress to furnish an objective, independent, and competent source of crime data to the government. Agency researchers analyze data and issue reports on the amount and characteristics of crime as measured by surveys of a sample of the general population, who are asked questions about crime victimization.

burglary Under the common law, breaking into and entering the dwelling of another in the nighttime with the intent to commit a felony therein. Most modern statutes do not limit the crime to the nighttime or to a dwelling and may not even require the element of breaking. Rather, they include any unauthorized entry into an enclosed structure for the purpose of committing a felony therein.

CAN-SPAM Act A federal statute containing, among other provisions, measures for the elimination of unwanted spam on computers and directing the Federal Trade Commission (FTC) to adopt a rule requiring a warning on spam that is sexually explicit. The FTC did that, and the provision carries civil as well as criminal penalties, with the latter including a possible prison sentence and a large fine.

capital punishment The imposition of the death penalty for an offender convicted of a capital offense.

career criminals Persons who commit a variety of offenses over an extended period of time or offenders who specialize in particular types of crime, for example, burglary.

carjacking Auto theft by force or threat of force.

case law The aggregate of reported judicial decisions, which are legally binding interpretations of statutes, constitutions, previous court decisions, and rules.

castration The removal of the testes in the male or the ovaries in the female; in earlier times, it was used as a punishment for male rape offenders. In recent times, some courts have ordered chemical castration of sex offenders. This process involves using female hormones to alter the male's chemical balance to reduce his sex drive and potency.

causation The assumption of a relationship between two phenomena in which the occurrence of the former brings about changes in the latter. In criminal law, causation is the element of a crime that requires the existence of a causal relationship between the offender's conduct and the particular harmful consequences.

certiorari Literally, *certiorari* means "to be informed of." Technically, a **writ** of certiorari is requested by a party objecting to a lower court's decision on some point of law. If the higher court agrees to hear the appeal, it issues a writ of certiorari, ordering the lower court to certify the record and send it to the appellate court for review. If the appellate court denies the writ, the decision of the lower court stands.

charge The formal allegation that a suspect has committed a specific offense; it also refers to instructions on matters of law given by a judge to the jury.

child abuse Physical, emotional, or psychological abuse of children, including sexual abuse and the use of children in pornography.

civil law That part of the law concerned with the rules and enforcement of private or civil rights as distinguished from criminal law. In a civil suit, an individual who has been harmed seeks personal compensation in court rather than criminal punishment through prosecution; the standard of proof and the rules of evidence differ from those of the criminal court.

classical theorists Eighteenth-century writers and philosophers who argued that the punishment should fit the crime because people are rational and choose pleasure over pain. Sufficient punishment would deter criminal behavior, but any punishment beyond that would be excessive. The popularization of this school of thought led to the abolition of the death penalty and of torture in some countries and generally to more humane treatment of criminals.

cognitive development theory A psychological theory of behavior based on the belief that people organize their thoughts into rules and laws and that the way those thoughts are organized results in either criminal or non-criminal behavior. This organization of thoughts is called *moral reasoning*, and when applied to law, *legal reasoning*.

cohort The total universe of people defined by an event or events or by certain characteristics. For example, all students living in Minneapolis in 2005 and enrolled in the eighth grade constitute a cohort. This cohort might be interviewed or given questionnaires to gather data on delinquent behavior. At specified intervals, for example, every five years in the future, the cohort might be tested again to discover the existence of delinquent behavior.

community-based corrections An approach to punishment that stresses the reintegration of the offender into the community through the use of local facilities. As an alternative to incarceration, the offender may be placed in the community on probation or, in conjunction with imprisonment, in programs such as parole, furlough, work release, foster homes, or halfway houses.

community service A type of punishment in which the offender is assigned to community service or work projects; also called **community work service**. Sometimes it is combined with **restitution** or **probation**.

community work service *See* **community service**.

computer crime A crime that involves the use of a computer.

concentric circle An ecological theory that divides cities into zones based on environmental and other characteristics and measures the relationship between those zones and the crime and delinquency rates within them.

conceptual absorption The process of taking concepts from one criminological theory and integrating them into other theories that have overlapping concepts.

conceptual fusion An integrated theory approach that involves linking together propositions of various theories that are somewhat different but are also similar enough to be combined, or fused.

conflict In contrast to the **consensus** approach, the conflict approach views values, norms, and laws as creating dissension and conflict. Conflict thinkers do not agree on the nature or the source of the conflict, nor do they agree on what to call this perspective. The *pluralistic* approach sees conflict emerging from multiple sources, and the *critical* approach assumes that the conflict reflects the political power of the society's elite groups. Also called *Marxist approach*, *new conflict approach*, *new criminology*, *materialist criminology*, *critical criminology*, *radical criminology*, or *socialist criminology*.

consensus An explanation of the evolution of law that considers law to be the formalized views and values of the people, arising from the aggregate of social values and developing through social interaction. Criminal law is viewed as a reflection of societal values broader than the values of special interest groups and individuals.

conspiracy An agreement with another to work together for the purpose of committing an unlawful act, or agreement to use unlawful means to commit an act that would otherwise be lawful. It is not necessary to commit the unlawful act; the crime of conspiracy involves the *agreement* to commit the unlawful act.

constable In medieval England, a police officer who presided over a **hundred** in the **frankpledge** system. Today, the term refers to a municipal court officer whose duties include keeping the peace, executing court papers, transporting inmates, and maintaining the custody of juries.

constitutional approach An approach to explaining criminal behavior that assumes behavior is influenced by a person's structure or physical characteristics.

constructive possession   A legal doctrine referring to the condition of having the power to control an item along with the intent to do so.

containment theory   An explanation of criminal behavior that focuses on two insulating factors: (1) the individual's favorable **self-concept** (definition of self) and commitment to long-range legitimate goals and (2) the pressure of the external social structure against criminal activity.

contempt   A legal action imposed on a person who has violated a court order, such as the refusal to abide by a judge's order to behave properly in court. Contempt may be civil or criminal.

control balance desirability   A method of classifying deviant acts that involves the extent to which the actor will gain long-term control and the extent to which the act can be done indirectly by the actor.

control balance theory   A concept referring to the ratio between how much a person needs to control behavior and how much that person is able to control behavior. It includes the processes of both inhibiting and motivating deviant behavior.

control theory   An explanation of criminal behavior that focuses on the control mechanisms, techniques, and strategies for regulating human behavior, leading to conformity or obedience to society's rules. It argues that deviance results when social controls are weakened or break down so that individuals are not motivated to conform to them.

conversion   In law, the process of exercising ownership of the property or goods of another without permission.

corporal punishment   The infliction of punishment on the physical body.

corporate crime   An intentional act (or omission of an act when there is a legal duty to act) that violates criminal statutory or case law and that is committed by individuals in a corporate organization for the benefit of the corporation.

counterfeiting   Forging, copying, or imitating without authority and with the intent to defraud. The crime involves an offense against property as well as an **obstruction of justice**. The object of counterfeiting may be coins, paper money, or anything else of value (e.g., stamps). *See also* **forgery**.

crime   An intentional act or omission of an act that violates criminal statutory or case law and for which the government provides punishment.

Crime Classification System (CCS)   A collection of crime data based on the severity of crimes and the effect of the crimes on victims.

crime control model   A criminal justice model that places great emphasis on controlling crime; this goal is considered more important than the due process rights of defendants, which may be sacrificed for rigorous crime control. *See also* **due process model**.

crime rate   In the *Uniform Crime Reports*, the number of offenses recorded per 100,000 population.

crimes known to the police   The record of serious offenses for which the police find evidence that the alleged crimes occurred.

criminal justice systems   The agencies responsible for enforcing criminal laws, including legislatures, police, courts, and corrections. Their decisions pertain to the prevention, detection, and investigation of crimes; the apprehension, accusation, detention, and trial of suspects; and the conviction, sentencing, incarceration, or official community supervision of adjudicated adult or juvenile defendants.

criminal law   State and federal penal statutes, the violation of which may subject the accused person to government prosecution and result in the imposition of fines, incarceration, community service, and other penalties. In general, criminal laws encompass those wrongs considered serious enough to threaten the welfare of society. In some jurisdictions (but not the federal), case law may also constitute criminal law.

criminology   The scientific study of crime, criminals, criminal behavior, and efforts to regulate crime.

critical criminology   *See* **radical criminology**.

cruel and unusual punishment   Punishment prohibited by the Eighth Amendment to the U.S. Constitution. The interpretation rests with the courts. Some examples are excessive lengths or conditions in sentences and the death penalty for rape but not murder.

culpability   Blameworthy or at fault. In criminal law, unless there is a case of **strict liability**, to be legally culpable of a crime, one must act purposely, knowingly, recklessly, *or* negligently. Different crimes may require different kinds of culpability to establish guilt.

culture conflict theory   An analysis of crime resting on a clash of two or more conduct norms, which are accepted partially and lead to contradictory standards and opposing loyalties. *Primary conflict* refers to the clash of conduct norms between two different cultures; *secondary conflict* refers to the clash of conduct norms between groups within a single culture.

cumulative disadvantage   The accumulation of structural disadvantages that occurs when one is labeled delinquent or criminal, resulting in a decrease of structural advantages. For example, labeling a teen a delinquent results in a "snowball" effect, reducing the opportunities that person will have for future legitimate opportunities.

custom   The usual way of behaving or acting in situations; habit. This may relate to the individual, group, or community.

cybercrime A type of computer crime that involves the Internet.

cyberphobia An irrational fear of the Internet or of working with computers.

cyberstalking Stalking someone by use of a computer. *See also* **stalking**.

date rape *See* **rape**.

defendant In criminal law, the party charged with a crime and against whom a criminal proceeding is pending or has commenced.

defense A legal response by the defendant. It may consist of presenting evidence or only of a denial of the factual allegations of the prosecution (or in a civil case, the plaintiff). A defense that offers new factual allegations in an effort to negate the charges is an *affirmative defense*.

defense attorney The attorney who represents the accused in legal proceedings and whose main function is to protect that individual's rights.

deferred prosecution Under deferred prosecution, the defendant must acknowledge the accused criminal act, and if the judge accepts the agreement between the defense and the prosecution, prosecution will be deferred for a specified time. If, during that period, the defendant is found guilty of another crime, the admission can be used against him or her in a prosecution of the crime for which prosecution was deferred.

demonology The belief that persons are possessed by spirits that cause crime and other evil behavior and that this behavior can be eliminated only when the spirits are eliminated.

Department of Homeland Security (DHS) A cabinet-level department created after the 9/11 terrorist attacks. Its creation constituted the most extensive federal government reorganization in 50 years; it combines 22 federal agencies and constitutes the third-largest federal agency.

deprivation model A model of **prisonization** based on the belief that the prison subculture arises from inmates' adaptations to the severe physical and psychological losses imposed by incarceration.

desistance Ceasing or stopping; it refers to the ending of delinquent or criminal activity during the span of one's life.

determinate sentence A sentence whose length is determined by the legislature or legally binding sentencing guidelines, precluding adjustment by any judicial or correctional authorities.

determinism A doctrine holding that one's options, decisions, and actions are decided by inherited or environmental factors.

deterrence A justification for punishment based on the prevention or discouragement of crime through fear or danger, as by punishing offenders to serve as examples to potential criminals or by incarcerating offenders to prevent them from committing further criminal acts.

developmental and life-course (DLC) theory A theoretical approach that attempts to explain how offending and antisocial behavior develop through one's life span, along with the risk factors at various ages and the effect that life events have on the course of development.

differential association A person's associations that differ from those of other persons; a theory of crime causation resting on the belief that criminal behavior is learned through associations with criminal behavior and attitudes. A person who engages in criminal behavior can be differentiated by the quality or quantity of his or her learning through associations with those who define criminal activity favorably and by the relative isolation from lawful social norms.

differential association-reinforcement A crime-causation theory based on the belief that criminal behavior is learned through associations with criminal behaviors and attitudes combined with a learning theory of operant conditioning. Criminal behavior is learned through associations and is continued or discontinued as a result of the positive or negative reinforcement received.

differential opportunity A crime-causation theory that attempts to combine the concepts of anomie and differential association by analyzing both the legitimate and the illegitimate opportunity structures available to individuals. Criminal behavior is possible because the environment has models of crime as well as opportunities to interact with those models.

discretion In criminal justice systems, the authority to make decisions and choose among options according to one's own judgment rather than according to specific legal rules and facts. Discretionary decision making may result in positive actions tailored to individual circumstances or in the inconsistent or discriminatory handling of offenders, such as basing decisions on gender, race, ethnicity, or other extralegal variables.

disintegrative shaming The process of shaming a person and including no attempt to reintegrate that individual into society. In contrast, *see* **reintegrative shaming**.

diversion A practice that removes offenders from criminal justice systems and channels them into other agencies, such as social welfare. The term also describes the handling of juveniles in a system separate from adult criminal justice systems and the sentencing of offenders to community-based correctional facilities rather than to prison.

doing gender Acting in masculine or feminine ways to verify one's gender; these acts are influenced by social structure and the constraints within that structure. *See also* **structured action theory**.

domestic violence Violence within the family or other close associations and including violence against spouses, lovers, house mates, children, and parents. *See also* **intimate partner violence (IPV)**.

drug A product used in diagnosing, curing, mitigating, treating, or preventing diseases in humans or other animals.

drug abuse The chronic or periodic misuse of alcohol or other drugs. Drug abuse is considered detrimental to society as well as to the individual abuser. It may occur even if the substance has been prescribed by the individual's physician.

drug paraphernalia An item, product, or material that can be used to violate the controlled substance statutes of a particular jurisdiction.

drug trafficking Trading in illegal drugs.

dual court system The separate judicial structure of various levels of courts within each state in addition to the national structure of federal courts. The origin of the laws violated dictates which court—state or federal—is an appropriate forum for the case. Most state systems consist of trial courts, appellate courts, and a state supreme court that governs the interpretation of state laws. The federal system includes district trial courts, circuit appellate courts, and the U.S. Supreme Court. Trial courts hear factual evidence, and the issues are decided by a judge or jury. Appellate court judges and justices review lower court decisions and determine questions of law.

dualistic fallacy In criminological studies, the assumption that a population has two mutually exclusive subclasses, such as criminals and noncriminals.

due process A fundamental constitutional or statutory concept that a person should not be deprived of life, liberty, or property without reasonable and lawful procedures; it also refers to the interpretation of the specifics required.

due process model A criminal justice model that emphasizes defendants' rights. The individual constitutional rights of the accused take priority in this approach. For example, a confession that is obtained in violation of the defendant's rights must be excluded at the trial. *See also* **crime control model**.

ecological school In criminology, a school of thought that studies the quantitative relationship between geographical phenomena and crime.

elder abuse The mistreatment of elderly persons by family members or other persons; it may include such acts as withholding food, stealing savings and Social Security checks, verbal abuse, and threats to send an elderly person to a nursing home.

electronic monitoring (EM) The use of electronic devices to keep track of the location of a person, such as one released on parole or placed on probation; it is often used on registered sex offenders.

embezzlement Obtaining rightful possession of property with the owner's consent and subsequently wrongfully depriving the owner of that property.

enterprise liability The process of holding an entire business enterprise legally liable for an act or event; also called *corporate liability*.

equal protection The constitutional principle that guarantees all people equal treatment in U.S. criminal justice systems regardless of factors such as age, race or ethnicity, religion, disability, or gender.

exclusionary rule The rule developed by the U.S. Supreme Court that excludes from a criminal trial any evidence seized in violation of the Fourth Amendment, which provides, in part, that "the right of the people to be secure in their persons, houses, papers, and effects, against unreasonable searches and seizures, shall not be violated."

ex post facto method In research, the method of studying an event after the fact. An ex post facto law is one that provides punishment for an act that was not defined as a crime when the act was committed or to a law that increases the penalty for a crime committed prior to the enactment of the statute.

extortion Obtaining property from another by wrongful use of actual or threatened force, fear, or violence or the corrupt taking of a fee by a public officer, under color of his or her office, when that fee is not due. *See also* **blackmail**.

extradition The process by which an accused is removed from one jurisdiction (usually a state or country) and taken to another for purposes of proceeding with legal actions, such as a trial.

false imprisonment The unlawful and knowing restraint of a person against his or her wishes so as to deny freedom. *See also* **kidnapping**.

false pretense Representation as being true of some fact or circumstance that is not true and that causes the other party to transfer title of the property to the offender.

felony A serious type of offense, such as murder, armed robbery, or rape, punishable for a year or longer in prison or a more serious penalty, such as capital punishment.

felony murder The doctrine used to hold a defendant liable for murder when a death occurs during the commission of another felony, such as armed robbery, kidnapping, or arson, even if that defendant did not engage in an act that led directly to the victim's death.

felony probation The placement on probation of an offender convicted of a felony.

feminist theory A theoretical approach that focuses on women's interests and perspectives, along with social justice and equality, in an attempt to explain crime and criminal behavior.

fence In criminology and criminal law, a person who disposes of stolen goods.

fetal abuse Abusing a fetus; in some jurisdictions, any resulting injury may lead to legal culpability. Some jurisdictions provide that killing a fetus is grounds for a murder charge.

fine A type of punishment in which the offender is ordered to pay a sum of money to the state in lieu of or in addition to other forms of punishment.

forcible rape *See* **rape**.

forensic psychiatry A branch of psychiatry that is concerned with disorders of the mind as they relate to legal issues. It is not limited to a study of the criminal mind but includes issues in civil as well as criminal law.

forfeit In law, the relinquishment of property or rights as a result of legal actions; may apply to civil as well as criminal law.

forfeiture The process of taking from an accused items, such as money, a boat, a car, and so on, thought to be associated with illegal acts, such as drug trafficking. The property may be taken by the government and held until the case is decided; upon a conviction, it may be retained by the government and sold or disposed of in some other way.

forgery Falsely making or altering, with the intent to defraud, a negotiable and legally enforceable instrument, such as a check. *See also* **counterfeiting**

frankpledge Mutual pledge system in medieval English law in which 10 families, constituting a **tithing**, were responsible for the acts of all other members. Ten tithings constituted a **hundred**, which was under the charge of a **constable**, who can be considered the first police officer. Hundreds were later combined to form **shires**, similar to counties, over which a **sheriff** had jurisdiction.

fraud Falsely representing a fact, either by conduct or by words or writing, to induce a person to rely on the misrepresentation and surrender something of value.

free will The belief that human behavior is controlled by one's choice; the behavior is purposive and based on **hedonism**, the pleasure–pain principle that human beings choose actions that give pleasure and avoid those that bring pain. The accompanying punishment philosophy advocates sanctions severe enough to cause people to choose to avoid criminal acts that incur those punishments.

furlough An authorized, temporary leave from a prison or other place of incarceration or detention by an inmate for the purpose of attending a funeral, visiting his or her family, or attempting to secure a job.

general deterrence The philosophy of punishment resting on the belief that punishment in an individual case inhibits others from committing the same offense.

general strain theory (GST) According to Robert Agnew, a much broader theory than traditional **strain theory**. GST includes additional strains (beyond the social structure), such as the inability to achieve goals due to one's own inadequacies; the gap between one's expectations and achievements, which may result in resentment, even anger, as well as disappointment; and the person's impression that there is a difference between the actual outcome and what the outcome should be.

global positioning system (GPS) In criminal justice systems, the use of satellites to track the location of offenders.

good faith exception An exception to the **exclusionary rule** in criminal court proceedings, which provides that even if the police seized evidence illegally, the evidence may be used in court if the police had a good faith belief that the evidence was related to the crime and to the suspect under investigation.

good-time credit The credit resulting in a reduction of prison time; it is awarded for satisfactory behavior in prison.

graft In criminal law, obtaining money, position, or other gain through illegal or dishonest means, especially through one's position as a public official, a politician, or a businessperson.

grand jury A group of citizens convened by legal authority to conduct secret investigations of evidence, evaluate accusations against suspects for trial, or issue indictments when appropriate.

grand larceny A felony involving the theft of property or money over a specified amount or value, in contrast to **petit larceny** (often a misdemeanor), which involves smaller amounts or values. The values for each type of crime may differ among jurisdictions.

guilty but mentally ill An alternative to the insanity defense; it permits finding that the defendant was mentally ill but not insane at the time he or she committed the crime charged. The defendant is guilty and may be punished, but generally, the jurisdictions that have this defense require that the defendant receive psychiatric treatment while confined.

habeas corpus A written court order to bring the petitioner before the court to determine whether his or her custody and confinement are lawful under constitutional due process of law.

halfway house A prerelease center used to help an inmate in changing from prison life to community life, or a facility that focuses on special adjustment problems of offenders, such as a substance abuse treatment center. The term also refers to a residential facility used as an alternative to prison for high-risk offenders considered unsuitable for probation.

hands-off doctrine A doctrine embraced by federal courts to justify nonintervention in the administration of correctional facilities; it has been abandoned recently but only when federal constitutional rights are at issue.

harmful error An error in legal proceedings that is considered to have resulted in actions so detrimental that some relief, such as a new trial, must be granted. It may also be called *reversible error* and is in contrast to a *harmless error*, which is a mistake that is not considered serious enough to warrant remedial action.

hate crimes Crimes committed against persons because of specified characteristics, such as gender, race, age, religion, ethnicity, disability, or sexual orientation. Statutes differ in their inclusion of these characteristics. Some statutes designate the crimes that serve as predicates for hate crimes, such as murder, rape, intimidation, arson, and so on.

hedonism The belief that people choose pleasure and avoid pain. In law, its proponents advocate clearly written laws and certainty of punishment without any departure from the prescribed penalties. *See also* **free will**.

home-invasion robbery A robbery that occurs when a person enters a dwelling for the purpose of committing a robbery and engages in a robbery of the occupant.

homicide A general term that includes all killings, some of which are deemed justifiable or excusable, whereas others might constitute the crime of manslaughter or murder.

house arrest A sentence, usually combined with probation, that permits the offender to remain at home under restrictions. In some cases, electronic monitoring of the offender's activities is combined with house arrest.

hundred *See* **frankpledge**.

identity theft The stealing of an individual's Social Security number or other important information about his or her identity and using that information to commit crimes, such as removing funds from the victim's bank account.

immunity (criminal) The exemption from criminal liability for acts that would otherwise be criminal.

importation model A model of **prisonization** based on the assumption that the inmate **subculture** arises not only from internal prison experiences but also from external patterns of behavior that inmates bring to the prison.

incapacitation A punishment theory and a sentencing goal, generally implemented by incarcerating an offender to prevent him or her from committing any other crimes. In earlier times, incapacitation involved such measures as removing the hands of thieves or castrating rapists.

incarceration Confinement in a jail, a prison, or another penal facility as a form of punishment for a criminal act.

incest Sexual relations between members of the immediate family who are too closely related to marry legally, such as between siblings, a parent and child, or a grandparent and grandchild.

indeterminate sentence A sentence whose length is determined not by the legislature or the court but by professionals at the institution or by parole boards, which decide when an offender is ready to return to society. The sentence imposed by the judge may range from one day to life.

index offenses Serious crimes as formerly designated by the FBI's *Uniform Crime Reports*, including murder and nonnegligent manslaughter, forcible rape, robbery, aggravated assault, burglary, larceny-theft, motor vehicle theft, and arson. In June 2004, the FBI discontinued publishing data according to this category because of the misrepresentation of overall crime that can be caused by a very high (or low) volume or rate of crime of only one of these serious crimes in a jurisdiction.

indictment The grand jury's written accusation charging the named suspect with a criminal offense. The grand jury may refuse to return an indictment if jurors do not believe the evidence warrants one.

individual (or specific) deterrence A punishment philosophy based on the belief that punishing an offender for criminal acts will keep that person from reoffending. *See also* **general deterrence**.

inevitable discovery exception An exception to the exclusionary rule in criminal court proceedings. It provides that illegally seized evidence is admissible if police would have found it later by legal methods.

information The most common formal document used to charge a person with an offense. Prosecutors, acting on evidence from police or citizens (or secured on their own), file this document with the court, and it is tested at the preliminary hearing. Unlike the indictment, filing an information does not require participation by the grand jury.

initial appearance The defendant's first appearance before a magistrate; this process must take place quickly if the accused has been detained in jail (or any other holding facility) after arrest. At the initial appearance, the magistrate decides whether **probable cause** exists to detain the suspect and, if so, tells the suspect of the charges and of his or her constitutional rights, including the right to an attorney.

inquisitory system A system in which the accused is presumed to be guilty and must prove his or her innocence. *See also* **adversary system**.

insanity defense A defense that enables the defendant to be found not guilty because he or she does not have the mental capacity required to assess legal responsibility for criminal behavior.

insider information Information known to corporate officers (or others) before it is available to the public. *See also* **insider trading**.

insider trading Type of transaction that exists when officers, directors, and stockholders who own more than 10 percent of a corporation's stock that is listed on a national exchange buy and sell corporate shares based on **insider information**. Federal law requires that such transactions be reported monthly to the Securities and Exchange Commission.

institutional anomie theory (IAT) A theory that goes beyond traditional anomie theory and maintains that eliminating social-structural obstacles to achieving goals will not reduce crime rates significantly. The theory assumes that the desire to succeed economically is so strong in America that all the country's social institutions have lost their ability to control behavior. The more we have, the more we want.

instrumental Marxism A school of thought in Marxist criminology which takes the position that the state is the instrument used by those in power to control those they dominate. Instrumental Marxists view the law, the state, and the ruling class as one, which enables the ruling class to take advantage of other classes by determining the nature and enforcement of law.

integrated cognitive antisocial potential (ICAP) theory A theory that integrates concepts from strain, control, learning, labeling, and rational choice theories. The key concept of ICAP is *antisocial potential* (AP), which refers to a person's potential to engage in antisocial acts. It assumes that cognitive thinking and decision-making processes, both of which take into account the availability of victims and the actor's opportunities, are influential in translating the potential to be antisocial into antisocial behavior. Antisocial potential may be either short-term or long-term.

integrated systems theory (IST) A theory based on integrating academic disciplines as well as concepts and propositions into a theory to explain all deviant behavior.

intensive probation supervision (IPS) The close supervision of probationers by probation officers who have smaller than average caseloads.

intent In the legal sense, the design, determination, or purpose with which a person uses a particular means to effect a certain result; it shows the presence of will in the act that consummates a crime.

interactional theory A theory that the behavior of adolescents is based on their interactions with other people and institutions.

INTERPOL An international police organization that was established for the purpose of cooperation among nations in common policing problems.

intimate partner violence (IPV) Violence toward a current or former spouse but could also include romantic friends of either gender, which is often referred to as *courtship violence*.

involuntary manslaughter *See* **manslaughter**.

Irangate The illegal exchange of arms for U.S. hostages in Iran in the 1980s. *See also* **Watergate**.

jail A locally administered confinement facility used to detain persons awaiting a trial or those serving short sentences, usually one year or less.

judge A judicial officer elected or appointed to preside over a court of law. Judges are the neutral and final arbiters of law and have primary responsibility for all court activities, ranging from monitoring the attorneys and instructing the jury to deciding cases (in those tried without a jury) and sentencing those found guilty.

judicial review A court's power to determine whether legislative and executive acts and the decisions of lower courts infringe on the rights guaranteed by state constitutions or the U.S. Constitution.

jurisdiction The lawful right to exercise official authority, whether executive, judicial, or legislative; the territory of authority within which such power may be exercised. For the police, it refers to the geographical boundaries of power; for the courts, it refers to the power to hear and decide cases.

jury In a criminal case, sworn persons who hear the evidence at trial, determine certain facts, and render a verdict of guilty or not guilty. In some jurisdictions, juries recommend or determine sentences.

jury nullification The power of juries to ignore the evidence in a trial and acquit even in the face of strong evidence of guilt.

just deserts The philosophy that an individual who commits a crime deserves to suffer for it; also called **retribution**.

justice model A philosophy holding that justice is achieved when offenders receive punishments based on what is deserved by their offenses as written in the law; the crime determines the punishment. In sentencing, this model presumes that prison should be used only as a last resort. Determinate (or flat-time) sentences are set for each offense. **Parole** is abolished, and early release can be achieved only through **good-time credits**.

juvenile delinquent A person under legal age (the maximum age varies among the states from 16 to 21, but 18 is the most common) whom a juvenile court has determined to be incorrigible or in violation of a criminal statute.

kidnapping Restricting the freedom of a victim against his or her will and removing the victim from one place to another. Kidnapping is **false imprisonment** with aggravating circumstances, such as a ransom, torture, sexual abuse, extortion, prostitution, or pornography.

labeling theory An attempt to explain deviance as a social process by which some people who commit deviant acts come to be known as deviants and others do not. Deviance is seen as a consequence of society's decision to apply that term to a person, and deviant behavior is behavior that society labels deviant.

larceny-theft Taking personal property without the owner's consent and with the intent to deprive the owner of it permanently. Historically, **petit larceny** involved small amounts, with imprisonment as punishment, and **grand larceny** involved larger amounts and the death penalty. Most modern theft statutes abolish the common law distinctions, and U.S. courts have ruled that the death penalty may not be imposed for larceny-theft.

learning theory A theory based on the assumption that although human aggression may be influenced by physiological characteristics, the activation of those characteristics depends on learning and is subject to the person's control. Social learning determines whether aggressive behavior occurs and, if so, the nature of that behavior.

left realist theorists In criminology, theorists who react against conservative, right-wing as well as left-wing theorists. They advocate reducing the emphasis on the crimes of the power elite and facing the realism of street crimes as well.

legal duty An obligation to another that is imposed by law, such as the duty of a parent to go to the aid of his or her child or the duty taken on by contract by a day care center to protect its clients/children.

lesser included offense A crime less serious than the one with which a defendant is being charged. A lesser included offense has some but not all of the elements of the greater offense and no elements not included in that crime.

life course The paths through which a person travels during a life span. *See also* **trajectories; developmental and life-course (DLC) theory**.

life-course persisters Those few adolescent antisocials who had social problems as children, began delinquent behavior early, and continued it. These adolescents are thought to have a neuropsychological deficit. They have low self-control, have exhibited difficult temperaments during childhood, may be impulsive, and may demonstrate hyperactivity. They may be expected to continue offending into adulthood. Unlike adolescent limiteds, life-course persisters are not strongly influenced by their peers. *See also* **adolescent limiteds**.

loan sharking Lending money at very high interest rates and later using extortionate means to force the borrower to repay the loan.

Mafia A secret organization with a strict hierarchical structure that is thought to be involved in smuggling, racketeering, drug trafficking, and other illegal activities worldwide. The Mafia infiltrates legal as well as illegal businesses.

magistrate A lower judicial officer in the state or federal court system.

mala in se Acts that most people believe are morally wrong in themselves, such as rape, murder, or robbery.

mala prohibita Acts that are wrong because they are prohibited by legislation, such as possessing small amounts of marijuana, although they may not be recognized by most people as morally wrong.

manslaughter The unlawful killing of a human being by a person who lacks malice in the act; a killing under mitigating circumstances of adequate provocation or diminished capacity, which reduces the offense from murder to manslaughter. Manslaughter may be **involuntary** (or **nonnegligent**), the result of recklessness while committing an unlawful act such as driving while intoxicated, or **voluntary**, an intentional killing committed in the heat of passion.

marital rape *See* **rape**.

mediation The structured act of attempting to settle claims between parties outside the courtroom to reduce the backlog of cases in the court systems.

Megan's Law A law requiring the registration of convicted sex offenders when they move into a community. Some jurisdictions require sex offenders to notify neighbors; others require only that law enforcement authorities be notified. The initial laws were named after Megan Kanka, who was raped and murdered by a neighbor who was a released sex offender living with two other such offenders.

mens rea Criminal intent; the guilty or wrongful state of mind of the defendant at the time he or she committed a criminal act.

Miranda warning The rule from *Miranda v. Arizona* which mandates that before persons in custody are interrogated, they must be told of their right to remain silent, that anything they say can and will be used as evidence against them, and that they have a right to an attorney, who will be appointed if they cannot afford to retain one.

misdemeanor An offense less serious than a felony and generally having a penalty of short-term incarceration in a local facility, a fine, probation, community service, and so on.

modernism An approach, characteristic of the twentieth century, that takes the position that facts can be determined by use of the objective, scientific method.

money laundering Hiding the existence, illegal use, or illegal source of income and making it appear that the income was obtained legally.

murder The unlawful and unjustified killing of another human being (or a fetus in some jurisdictions) with malice aforethought. Categories of murder include a killing with the intent to kill, a killing with the intent to do great bodily harm, a killing in willful disregard of the strong likelihood that death or great injury would result, or a killing committed during the commission of another felony. Murder may also be categorized in terms of seriousness by degrees, such as first-degree murder and so on.

National Crime Victimization Survey (NCVS) The victimization data collected and published annually by the Bureau of Justice Statistics (BJS).

National Criminal History Improvement Program (NCHIP) A federal program that provides grants to assist states in improving their crime record systems.

National Incident-Based Reporting System (NIBRS) A method of collecting crime data that views crimes as involving numerous elements. Twenty-two crimes are categorized in this system.

National Youth Survey (NYS) A program for gathering crime data by interviewing adolescents over a five-year period. The program has been structured to overcome many of the criticisms of other self-report studies.

neoclassical school Eighteenth-century writers and philosophers who argued that situations or circumstances that made it impossible to exercise free will were reasons to exempt the accused from conviction.

nonnegligent manslaughter *See* **manslaughter**.

obstruction of justice Interference with the orderly processes of civil and criminal courts, such as refusing to produce evidence, intimidating witnesses, and bribing judges. If the crime is committed by judicial and other public officials, it might constitute **official misconduct in office**.

offenders Persons who are convicted of criminal offenses.

official misconduct in office Any willful, unlawful behavior by public officials in the course of their official duties. The misconduct may be a failure to act, a wrongful act, or an act that the actor had a right to do but that was performed improperly.

organized crime The highly structured association of people who work together to make large profits through illegal and legal means while utilizing graft and corruption in the criminal justice arena to protect their activities from criminal prosecution.

pardon An act by a state governor or the president of the United States that exempts an individual from punishment for a crime he or she committed and removes the legal consequences of the conviction. Pardons may be absolute or conditional, individual or granted to a group or class of offenders, or full or partial, in which case the pardon remits only part of the punishment or removes some of the legal disabilities resulting from conviction.

parens patriae Literally, "parent of the country"; the doctrine from English common law that was the basis for allowing the state to take over the guardianship of a child. In the United States, the doctrine forms the basis for the juvenile court's jurisdiction. It presumes that the state acts in the best interests of the child.

parental kidnapping Kidnapping a child by a parent who does not have the legal authority to take the child at that time and place.

parole The continued custody and supervision in the community by federal or state authorities after an offender is released from an institution before expiration of the sentenced term. Parolees who violate parole conditions may be returned to the institution.

parole board A panel that decides how much of a sentence offenders serve in the institution and whether they are ready to return to society with continued supervision in the community.

parole officers The government employees responsible for counseling and supervising inmates released on parole and living in the community.

peacekeeping In criminological theory, the transforming of power plays and other violent relations into safe, balanced, and trustworthy relationships.

penitentiary A state or federal prison or place of punishment for the confinement of offenders convicted of serious crimes and sentenced for a term of a year or longer.

peremptory challenge A challenge by prosecution or defense attorneys to excuse a potential juror from the jury panel. No reason is required. Each side is entitled to a specified number of peremptory challenges.

perjury False statements made willingly and knowingly under oath in a judicial proceeding.

petit larceny *See* **grand larceny**.

phishing A way Internet scammers lure people into their nets. They go fishing for information by sending to a potential victim an email or a pop-up message that appears to be from a company with which the target normally does business. The message states that the target needs to update or verify personal information and directs the individual to a website that appears to be, but is not, legitimate. The purpose is to trick the target into disclosing confidential information, which can then be used to commit a crime, such as **identity theft**, against the potential victim.

phrenology A theory of behavior based on the belief that the exterior of the skull corresponds to the interior and to the brain's conformation; phrenologists claim that a propensity toward certain types of behavior may be discovered by examining the bumps on the head.

plea bargaining Negotiations between the prosecution and the defense concerning the nature and number of charges against the defendant, the plea the defendant might enter, punishment that might be recommended, or other issues associated with the trial. The prosecution may agree to some concessions in exchange for a plea or for the defendant's cooperation in providing evidence against other suspects.

police Local, state, and federal law enforcement officials within the department of government that maintains and enforces law and order throughout a geographical area.

positivist school Early writers and philosophers who advocated that the study of crime should emphasize the individual and the scientific treatment of the criminal, not the postconviction punishment. Adherents believed that the punishment should fit the criminal, not the crime.

posse A group of private citizens called to assist in law enforcement.

postmodernism An approach that goes beyond **modernism** and looks closely at the full meaning of language, which may be used by those in power to define crime in a way that imposes their own values upon others.

postpartum depression (PPD) syndrome A medical disorder experienced by some women following childbirth.

posttraumatic stress disorder (PTSD) A disorder in which stress is experienced by people who have suffered severe trauma, such as war trauma, rape, or some other type of abuse. Symptoms include nightmares, feel-ings of guilt, disorientation, and reliving the traumatic event(s).

power-control theory A theory that blends social control and feminist theories and is built on the Marxist tradition.

preliminary hearing A court proceeding before a judge; its purpose is to determine whether there is probable cause to believe that the defendant committed a crime and should be held for trial.

prerelease programs Institutional programs that assist inmates in adjusting to life after release from incarceration. The programs cover subjects such as money management, job interviewing, and basic social skills.

presumptive sentencing A method for determining punishment in which the legislature sets a standard sentence in the statute, but the judge may vary that sentence if the case has mitigating or aggravating circumstances.

preventive detention The practice of holding the accused in jail before trial to ensure that he or she does not commit further crimes and is present at trial.

prison A state or federal custodial facility for the confinement of offenders serving long terms, usually a year or more.

prisonization The process by which a prison inmate assimilates the customs, norms, values, and culture of prison life.

proactive The response to criminal behavior in which the police detect crimes actively and seek offenders instead of relying on citizens' reports of crimes.

probable cause An evidentiary standard; a set of facts and circumstances that justifies a reasonably intelligent and prudent person's belief that an accused person has committed a specific crime.

probation A judicial determination in which the offender is allowed to remain in the community, usually under supervision. The term also refers to the component of the criminal justice system that administers all phases of probation.

probation officer The official who is responsible for preparing presentence reports, supervising offenders placed on probation, and helping them integrate into society as lawful citizens.

Prohibition The period in U.S. history (1919–1933) during which it was illegal for anyone to make, sell, or buy alcoholic beverages.

property crimes Those serious crimes not directed toward the person but rather at his or her personal or real property. The four serious property crimes as categorized by the FBI are burglary, larceny-theft, motor vehicle theft, and arson.

prosecuting attorney A government official whose duty is to initiate and maintain criminal proceedings on behalf of the government against persons accused of committing crimes.

psychiatry A field of medicine that specializes in the understanding, diagnosis, treatment, and prevention of mental problems and diseases.

psychoanalysis A special branch of psychiatry based on the theories of Sigmund Freud and employing a particular personality theory and method of treatment; the approach concentrates on the individual case study and focuses on the relationship between the unconscious and the conscious aspects of personality.

public defender An attorney whose function is to represent defendants who cannot afford to retain private counsel.

punishment Any of a series of impositions (e.g., a fine, probation, work service, incarceration) imposed by the authority of law upon a person who has been determined to be a criminal offender.

racial profiling The reaction by law enforcement officers to potential suspects based solely on their race or ethnicity.

Racketeer Influenced and Corrupt Organizations (RICO) An act passed by Congress in 1970 to combat organized crime, but it has also been applied beyond that specific area of criminal activity.

racketeering An organized conspiracy to attempt or to commit extortion or coercion by the use of force or threats.

radical criminology An approach to the study of crime and criminals that explores and verifies the connection between economic reality and social phenomena; most radical theorists express a desire to change situations for the betterment of suppressed classes. *See also* **conflict**.

rape Unlawful sexual intercourse (limited to female victims in some jurisdictions); it is called **forcible rape** if committed against the victim's will by the use of threats or force. **Date rape** is forced sexual acts that occur during a social occasion. The alleged victim may have agreed to some intimacy but not to the acts defined in that jurisdiction as constituting the elements of forcible rape. **Marital rape** occurs when the victim of forcible rape is the spouse of the alleged offender. *Rape by instrumentation*, a relatively new legal concept, refers to any forced intrusion of the male penis or any object into any part of another person's body that could be interpreted as done for the purpose of sexual arousal or gratification or as an act of violence. **Statutory rape** is illegal sexual contact with a minor, who is presumed by law to be too young to consent.

rape shield A type of statute aimed at the protection of evidence in a sexual assault, or rape trial, prohibiting the introduction of evidence of the alleged victim's past sexual experiences. It is assumed that such evidence is not only embarrassing to the alleged victim, who as a result may not wish to report the attack, but is also prejudicial to the case and is not relevant. Evidence relevant to the trial, such as evidence that might exonerate the defendant, may be considered an exception to the rape shield statute and thus be admissible.

reactive The response to criminal behavior in which police rely on notification by alleged victims or others that a crime has been committed instead of taking active measures to detect crimes and identify offenders.

recidivism The relapse into further violations of the law by released suspects or inmates or into noncriminal violations of conditions by probationers and parolees.

reflective appraisal A person's perceptions of how others view him or her.

reformatory A correctional facility that is less secure than a prison or penitentiary and that, at least in theory, has as its primary goal the **rehabilitation** of offenders.

rehabilitation The rationale for the reformation of offenders based on the premise that human behavior is the result of antecedent causes that may be discovered by objective analysis and that permit the scientific control of human behavior. The focus is on treatment, not punishment, of the offender.

reintegration A philosophy of punishment that focuses on returning the offender to the community so that education, employment, and family ties may be restored.

reintegrative shaming A process in which attempts are made to reintegrate the offender into the community by taking measures to remove a deviant label. In contrast, *see* **disintegrative shaming**.

restitution A type of punishment in which the offender must reimburse the victim financially or with services. Restitution may be required in lieu of or in addition to a fine or other punishment or as a condition of probation.

restorative justice An approach that provides both adults and juveniles with a wide range of programs designed to restore crime victims and the community—that is, to provide justice for them.

retribution A punishment theory that contends an offender should be punished for the crime committed because he or she deserves it.

RICO *See* **Racketeer Influenced and Corrupt Organizations Act**.

robbery Taking personal property from the possession of another against his or her will by the use of force or fear.

routine activity approach An approach explaining crime by means of three elements: (1) likely offenders (people who are motivated to commit crimes), (2) suitable targets (presence of things that are valuable and that can be transported fairly easily), and (3) absence of capable guardians (people who can prevent the criminal activity).

sanctions A penalty or punishment imposed to gain compliance or obedience to the law. In terms of **social control**, informal sanctions may include a parental stare, a frown, or the extreme of social ostracism. Formal sanctions would be those specified in substantive law.

Sarbanes-Oxley (SOX) Act of 2002 Legislation enacted for the purpose of preventing corporate financial mismanagement and fraud. SOX applies only to publicly held companies. The act provides protection for employees who report fraud. It established an oversight board for corporations. The constitutionality of that board was challenged and upheld with the exception of the provision for the dismissal of board members.

search warrant A court-issued writ authorizing an officer to search a designated person, property, object, or place.

securities Stocks, bonds, notes, and other documents that are representative of a share in a company or a debt of a company.

selective incapacitation The selection of certain offenders, usually the most serious, for incarceration.

self-concept The image one has of oneself, including an assessment of strengths and weaknesses; a self-image. *See also* **containment theory**.

self-control theory A theoretical approach in criminology that focuses on self-control as the explanation of behavior, with self-control referring to one's ability to refrain from engaging in certain acts that cause harm and violate norms.

self-derogation theory A theory proposing that young people become involved in drug use, delinquent or criminal behavior, or other deviant behaviors because they have low self-esteem, or self-derogation.

self-report data (SRD) The method of collecting data by asking people to give information about their prior involvement in crime; it is based on selected samples of the total population or a subset such as juveniles or incarcerated criminals. Data may be obtained in several ways, such as by anonymous questionnaires or by interviews.

sentence The decision of the judge or jury, according to statutory law, fixing the punishment for an offender after conviction.

sentence disparity The variations and inequities that result when defendants convicted of the same crime receive different sentences; it may also refer to varying legislative sentences from state to state.

sentencing The postconviction stage in the criminal justice system that includes all those decisions the court makes with regard to the official handling of a person who pleads guilty or is convicted of a crime.

sequential integration A process by which scientists examine the distinct but complementary aspects of various theories in an effort to reach a broader explanation.

shaming Forms of social disapproval intended to create, or have the effect of creating, remorse in the target and/or result in the condemnation of that person by others who are aware of the shaming efforts.

sheriff In medieval England, a shire-reeve (later pronounced "sheriff"), who was the director, appointed by the king, of a shire. Today, the term refers to a county's chief law enforcement officer, usually elected by popular vote, who may perform varied functions in addition to law enforcement, such as collecting county taxes, supervising some government activities, and serving as the county coroner in some jurisdictions.

shires *See* **frankpledge**.

shock incarceration The incarceration of a person for a brief period prior to release on probation or other type of supervision.

shoplifting The illegal removal of merchandise from stores by customers or persons posing as customers.

singular theory assessment Evaluating one individual theory and the tests of that theory's propositions.

social capital Life-sustaining, positive relations with other people and institutions, which increase the bonding of those individuals with society by intimidating them from committing crimes against others.

social contract The philosophy that for greater protection, people voluntarily surrender their rights to protect themselves to the government, which must govern by the consent of the people.

social control Mechanisms through which conformity or compliance may be achieved in society. Informal social control may be achieved through socialization while formal social control relies upon **sanctions** provided by law.

social support Social integration within group relationships in which individuals provide social, emotional, and material support for each other.

sociobiology The application of the principles of biology to the study of social behavior.

stalking Defined in the National Violence Against Women Survey as "a course of conduct directed at a specific person that involves repeated visual or physical proximity, nonconsensual communication, or verbal, written or implied threats, or a combination thereof, that would cause a reasonable person fear." The term *re-*

peated means two or more times. Stalking is not limited to female victims.

stare decisis Literally, "let the decision stand." The doctrine that courts will abide by or adhere to their previous rulings when deciding cases with substantially the same facts.

status offenses A class of crime that does not consist of proscribed action or inaction but of the personal condition or characteristic of the accused—for example, being a vagrant. In juvenile law, it may refer to a variety of acts that would not be considered criminal if committed by an adult. Examples are being insubordinate or truant.

status quo Literally, "the state in which." The existing or current state of affairs.

statutory law The law created or defined in a written enactment by the legislative body, in contrast to **case law**, which is decided by courts.

statutory rape *See* **rape**.

Stockholm syndrome An incongruous feeling of empathy by hostages toward the hostage takers and a displacement of frustration and aggression on the part of the victims against the authorities.

strain theory A theory of social disorganization, anomie, and subculture that focuses on negative social structures and relationships that prevent individuals from achieving their goals. *See also* **general strain theory**.

strict liability Holding a person (or a corporation) legally liable for an action of that person or another even though the actor may not have intended to engage in inappropriate or illegal action.

structural Marxism A Marxist position that although law may be explained by capitalism, it does not always reflect the interests of the ruling class. Structural Marxists look for the underlying forces that shape law, and those forces may create a conflict between capitalism in general and any particular capitalist.

structured action theory A theory that distinguishes characteristics designating *sex* (e.g., hair, clothing) from those designating *gender* (e.g., the ways of acting that verify sex). So persons do *masculinity* or *femininity*, which means they act in ways to verify their sex. Masculinity and femininity are not static structures; we "do" them in specific situations, which are influenced by social structure and the constraints within that structure. *See also* **doing gender**.

subculture An identifiable segment of society or group having specific patterns of behavior, folkways, and mores that set that group apart from the others within a culture or society.

syndicate A group of persons who organize for the purpose of carrying out matters (usually, financial) of mutual interest; syndicates are not illegal by definition but are often associated with illegal activities such as organized crime.

terrorism Violent acts or the use of the threat of violence to create fear, alarm, dread, or coercion, usually against governments.

theoretical integration The process of identifying the common concepts in two or more theories and integrating them to produce a theory that is superior to any of the individual theories. *See also* **conceptual absorption**.

theory Part of an explanation; an attempt to relate two or more factors in ways that can be tested. If properly constructed and tested, a theory can be supported or shown to be incorrect or at least questioned. Thus, a theory is more than an assumption. It involves efforts to test the reality of thoughts or explanations about how factors (e.g., gender) are related to phenomena (e.g., criminal behavior).

theory competition The process of comparing two or more theories on the basis of their scope of crime coverage and the empirical support for the theories.

three strikes and you're out Legislation enacted in most states and in the federal government in recent years and designed to impose long sentences on persons who are convicted of a third serious crime.

tithing *See* **frankpledge**.

trajectories Long-term patterns of behavior or lines of development—such as marriage, career, or parenthood—that consist of **transitions**, which are short-term events, such as a first job or even a first marriage.

transitions Short-term events, such as a first job or even a first marriage. *See also* **trajectories** and **turning points**.

transportation The historical practice of deporting criminals to other countries as punishment.

Transportation Security Administration (TSA) A federal agency created by the Aviation and Transportation Security Act (ATSA) enacted two months after the 9/11 terrorist attacks and subsequently amended. The TSA was developed to take over the security screening functions for all commercial flights in the United States.

trial In criminal law, the formal fact-finding process in court in which the evidence in a case is presented and examined and a decision is made by the judge or jury about whether the defendant is guilty, beyond a reasonable doubt, of criminal charges.

truth in sentencing A concept requiring that actual time served by offenders be closer to the time allocated for the sentence. Many jurisdictions are establishing 80 to 85 percent as their goal, meaning that offenders may not be released for any reason until they have served the required percentage of their sentences.

turning points The changes in life courses generated by the relationships between **trajectories** and **transitions**. *See also* **developmental and life-course (DLC) theory** and **life-course persisters**.

under color of law Pertaining to inappropriate or illegal action taken by government employees (e.g., law enforcement officers) while acting under the authority of their government positions.

Uniform Crime Reports **(UCR)** The official government source of national crime data collected, compiled, and published annually by the Federal Bureau of Investigation.

USA Patriot Act A law enacted after the 9/11 terrorist attacks and subsequently amended; its full name is the Uniting and Strengthening America by Providing Appropriate Tools Required to Intercept and Obstruct Terrorism Act of 2001. It was designed primarily to provide tools for combating terrorism.

utilitarianism The philosophy that makes the happiness of the individual or society the main goal and the criterion for determining what is morally good and right. In politics, it means that the greatest happiness of the greatest number is the sole end and criterion of all public action.

venue The location of a trial; defendants who think they cannot get a fair trial in the jurisdiction in which the alleged crime occurred may petition the court for a change of venue, which is granted or denied at the discretion of the court, generally after hearing arguments from the defense and the prosecution.

vicarious liability Placing legal culpability on one person (or corporation) for the action of another. An example would be holding the owner of a bar responsible for an employee who sold liquor to an intoxicated person who then drove a car and caused an accident that injured or killed another person.

victim compensation programs Plans for assisting crime victims in making social, emotional, and economic adjustments.

victimology The academic discipline that studies the nature and causes of victimization as well as programs for assisting victims and preventing victimization.

victim precipitation A concept proposing that an alleged crime victim "asked for it" by, for example, being in a questionable place such as a bar, hitchhiking on a highway, having a questionable reputation, or wearing provocative clothing. The implication is that the crime would not have been committed had the alleged victim not behaved in a questionable way.

victims' compensation legislation Legislation that provides financial and other types of assistance to crime victims.

violent crimes Crimes against the person (as contrasted to crimes against property). The four *serious* violent crimes as defined by the FBI in its *Uniform Crime Reports* are murder and nonnegligent manslaughter, forcible rape, robbery, and aggravated assault.

voir dire "To speak the truth"; the process of questioning prospective jurors to determine their qualifications and desirability for serving on a jury.

voluntary manslaughter *See* **manslaughter**.

watch system A system of policing that existed in early England and in colonial America. Bellmen walked throughout the city on a regular basis ringing bells and providing police services. Later, they were replaced by a permanent watch of citizens and still later by paid constables.

Watergate A political scandal connected with the Republican White House during the 1972 presidential election campaign. It involved a break-in at the Democratic national headquarters at the Watergate building in Washington, D.C., and eventually led to the resignation of President Richard M. Nixon, the first U.S. president to resign in disgrace. Although Nixon was pardoned by his successor, President Gerald Ford, some of his associates served prison sentences for their roles in the scandal.

white-collar crime Violations of the law by persons with high socioeconomic status; usually, the term refers to corporate or individual crimes in connection with businesses or occupations regarded as a legitimate part of society.

work release An authorized absence from a jail, prison, or other penal facility that allows the inmate to hold a job or attend school but that requires him or her to return to the institution during nonworking hours.

writ An order from a court mandating that specific action be taken or giving someone permission to do whatever has been requested.

year-and-a-day rule A common law rule requiring that for a murder charge, death must occur within one year and one day from the time the crime was committed. Today, many jurisdictions have abandoned that rule, although they may still impose some restrictions, such as three years and a day.

CASE INDEX

NAME INDEX

GENERAL INDEX

A

ABA. *See* American Bar Association
Abuse of a child. *See* Child abuse
Abuse, homicide by, 203
Academy of Criminal Justice Sciences (ACJS), 16
ACLU. *See* American Civil Liberties Union
Act, as an element of crime, 8
ADA. *See* Americans with Disabilities Act
Adam Walsh Child Protection and Safety Act, 577, 578, 582
Adaptation, modes of, anomie and, 111
Adelphia Communications Corporation, 292
ADHD. *See* Attention-deficit hyperactivity disorder, crimes and
Administrative law
  business-related crimes and, 280, 281, 282, 307
  correctional facilities and, 518
  crime processed by, 24
  criminal law compared to, 8–9
  critical criminology and, 131
  defined, 8–9
  differential association theory and, 280–281
  environmental crimes and, 294
  immigration and, 307
  prison release and, 56–57
  shaming and, 172
  workplace violations and, 298, 299–300
Adolescent limiteds, developmental theory and, 179
Adoption and Safe Families Act (ASFA) of 1997
Adoption studies, crime and, 70, 75–77, 90
Adversary system, 360–365, 466, 469
Aerial surveillance, 377
Affirmative duty, to act, 8
Age. *See also* Age-graded theory; Elderly; Juveniles; and individual theories (e.g., Cultural transmission)
  arrests and, 31, 459
  arson and, 257
  bail release and, 470
  business-related crimes and, 284
  career criminals and, 172, 177, 268, 272
  child abuse and, 218
  control balance theory and, 181
  crime rates and, 172
  defense of, 52
  discrimination and, 586
  domestic violence and, 25
  fear of crime and, 222, 231
  gender and, 31, 32–33, 137, 433
  IPV and, 215, 217
  learning theory and, 161, 178
  offenders and, 31
  offending onset and, 177
  physical abuse in prison and, 530
  police use of force and, 431
  prosecutorial abuse and, 457
  recidivism and, 269
  self-control theory and, 168
  shoplifting and, 252
  stolen property and, 259
  television and, 157
  victimization and, 33–34
  violence and, 31

Age-graded theory, 177–179, 185
Agema Thermovision 210, 377
Aggravated assault, 204, 211–212, 215
Aggravating and mitigating circumstances, 25, 461–462, 488
Agriprocessors slaughterhouse case, 301
AIDS, 320, 423, 425–426, 523, 526–527, 529
Air pollution, 134
Akers's social learning theory, 161–162, 163
Alabama, University of, shooting at, 202, 299–300
Alaska pipeline, 295
Alcohol. *See also* Driving while intoxicated; Drug abuse; Fetal alcohol syndrome; Substance abuse
  abuse of, 319, 320
  binge drinking, 323
  bootlegging, 328
  college students and, 319, 320, 323, 324
  genetics, alcoholism, and, 77
  laws regarding, 15, 328
  Prohibition, 15, 328, 340
  vehicle fatalities and, 320
  Volstead Act, 340, 380
  workplace and, 298–300, 319
America Works, 568
American Bar Association, 460, 481–482, 490, 492, 584
American Civil Liberties Union (ACLU), 438, 517
American colonies, prisons and, 506–508
American Correctional Association (ACA), 552
American Institute of Criminal Law and Criminology, 15
American Law Institute, 226
American Probation and Parole Association, 573
American Psychiatric Association, 80, 87
American Revolution, 403
American Social Health Association, 316
American Society of Criminology (ASC), 16, 57, 106, 176, 177, 184, 186, 187, 189, 408, 432
American Sociological Association, 280
Americans with Disabilities Act (ADA), 133, 513, 526, 538, 539–540
Anger management training, 584
Angola (LA) prison, 524
Animal abuse, crime and, 74, 103–104, 257
Animal and Plant Health Inspection Service, 407
Anomie/strain theories, 109–114, 115, 137–138, 141
  adaptation, modes of, 111
  classic approach, 109–111, 115
  contemporary approaches, 111–114, 115
  control balance theory and, 181
  differential opportunity theory and, 119
  Durkheim and, 109–110, 115
  female offenders and, 137–138, 141
  general strain theory (GST), 112–114, 115
  homicide and, 110
  institutional anomie theory (IAT), 112, 115
  integrated/strain control perspective, 181–182, 185
  juvenile delinquency and, 182
  learning theory and, 161
  Merton and, 110–111, 115
  modes of adaptation, 111
  murder explained by, 205
  policing and, 436
  race and ethnicity and, 167

social support explanation, 114, 115
social disorganization, crime, and, 182
suicide and, 110
Anti-Car Theft Act of 1992, 255
Anti-Drug Abuse Act of 1988, 328
Anti-Racketeering Act of 1934, 344
Anticipatory search warrant, 370
Antisocial behavior theory, 182, 185
Antisocial personality disorder (APD), 87, 183–184
Antiterrorism and Effective Death Penalty Act of 1996, 229
Antitrust violations, 293–294
Anxiety disorder, 84
Aphesis House, 550
Appeals, 11, 229, 368, 369, 385, 455, 456, 491–492
Appellant, 456
Appellee, 456
Architecture, in prisons, 507, 516–517
Arellano Felix cartel, 338
Arizona
  boot camps and, 559–560
  immigration policies and, 408
Armed Career Criminal Act (ACCA), 483
Arraignment, 368, 369
Arrest. *See also* Policing; Search and seizure
  age and, 31, 51, 459
  crimes cleared by, 22, 24, 246, 247, 253
  data on, 24, 30, 33, 459
  domestic violence and, 25, 218, 433–434
  drug offenses and, 31, 319, 423
  gender and, 31, 32–33, 137, 433
  juveniles and, 31, 51, 459
  mandatory, 36, 188, 218, 433–434, 463, 467–468
  probable cause for, 426, 428
  race and ethnicity and, 31–32, 394
  rape victims and, 36
  social control theory and, 169
  sociology of, 428–429
  as stage in criminal justice system, 368
  vehicle stops and, 372
  violent crimes and, 30, 33
  zero tolerance policy and, 418
Arson, 246, 256–257, 295
ASA. *See* American Sociological Association
ASC. *See* American Society of Criminology
Asportation, 210, 219, 223
Assault, 211, 459. *See also* Aggravated assault
Assembly Bill 900 (CA), 583
Association of Paroling Authorities International, 573
Atavism, 71
Athletes, crime victimization and, 213, 214
Atlanta Olympics, 517
Atlanta Police Department (APD), 435–436
Attachment, AP theory and, 183
Attempt crimes, 247
Attendance courts, 465
Attention-deficit hyperactivity disorder (ADHD), crime and, 82–83, 90, 320, 462, 534, 542
Attica Prison (NY), 507, 534, 542
Attorneys, U.S., 282
Auburn prison system, 506–507, 516, 542
Authoritative parenting, 168
Auto Accident Insurance Fraud Initiative, 302

Control theory, 162–179. *See also* Integrated theories
 age-graded theory, 177–179, 189
 bonding theory, 164–167, 169, 172, 176, 177
 business crimes and, 283, 284
 containment theory, 163–164, 169
 defined, 162
 family social structure and, 124
 Gottfredson and Hirchi's self-control theory, 167–170
 Reiss and Nye's theory, 162–163, 169
 self-control theory, 167–170
 self-derogation theory and, 180–181, 185
 socialization and, 162
Conviction rates, television influence on, 157
Convictions, social control theory and, 169
Cook County Jail (Chicago), 516
COPS. *See* Community-Oriented Policing Services
Corporal punishment, 475, 538. *See also* Cruel and
  Unusual Punishment
 of children, 212, 214, 217, 219
 defined, 475
 flogging, 49
 historically, 48–49, 506
 Iraq, in 347
 in jails and prisons, 347, 506, 507, 514, 538
 mental health and, 85
 of women, 214, 217
 violent crime and, 212, 214
Corporate crime, 285, 296. *See also* Business-related
  crime; White-collar crime
 critical criminology and, 130
 defined, 281
 deterrence and, 307–308
 fraud, 302
 gender and, 138
 media and, 282, 299
 punishment of offenders, 63
 white-collar crime distinguished from, 281–282
Correctional officers, 535–536, 537
 brutality by, 172, 516, 533, 536
 corruption of, 535
 discretion of, 366
 job satisfaction and, 534
 recruiting of, 537
 salaries of, 537
 sexual victimizations by, 530, 531, 532
 training of, 534
Correctional Services Corporation, 539
Corrections Corporation of America, 519, 520
Corruption. *See also* Bribery
 correctional officers and, 535
 organized crime and, 335
 political, 112
 police and, 434–436
 public officials, drugs and, 335, 392
Cost, of crime
 budget cuts, 492–493
 California corrections, 51, 510, 513, 540, 583
 campus security, 410
 capital punishment, 456, 485–486, 488
 computer crime and, 262–263, 264, 266
 community corrections, 552, 558, 560–564, 566,
  568–69, 575, 576, 580, 582–586
 day reporting centers and, 558, 561
 defense systems, 469, 470
 drug abuse and, 187, 324–325, 329
 drug courts and, 464
 drug offenders, 325
 drug testing, 335
 drug treatment and, 334, 555
 drug trafficking, 336, 337, 338
 electronic monitoring, 560–562
 elderly inmates and medical care, 526
 embezzlement, of, 259
 federal monitors and, 438, 512–513, 516
 GPS and, 561–562
 health care, in prisons, 540–541
 health care fraud, 302
 house arrest and, 560
 identity theft, 260
 incarceration, of, 585
 intensive probation supervison (IPS), 564
 jails, of, 516
 larceny-theft, 251

mental treatment in jails and prisons, 515–516
motor vehicle theft, 253
organized crime, 339
parole and, 576
policing and, 409–411
prisons and, 513, 514, 518, 519, 526, 535, 556, 557
private security and, 409, 410, 411, 510
probation, 564
riots, 533, 535
securities crimes, 288–289, 291–292
sentencing reform in South Carolina, reduced
  by, 584
shoplifting, 253
special courts and, 188
supermax prisons, 518
trials, 456
victims' compensation programs and, 388
war on drugs and, 329
Counsel, right to, 370, 382–385
 capital punishment and, 485–486, 490
 cost of, 469–470
 effective assistance of, 383–385, 469, 486
 juveniles and, 460
 parole revocation and, 575
Counterfeiting, 258
Court systems, 453–501. *See also* all phases of courts
  (e.g., Judges; Sentencing)
 attendance court, 465
 budget cuts, 492–493
 congestion and, 492–493
 defense, 52, 468–470
 domestic violence, 217, 456, 461–465, 493, 498
 drug, 334–335, 456, 463–465
 dual systems, 455–456
 juvenile, 456–461, 462–463
 lawyers, role in, 465, 467–470
 mental health, 456, 465, 466
 overcrowding and, 365
 overview of, 455–456
 pretrial processes, 470–473
 procedures of, 455
 prosecution, role in, 465, 467–468
 special, 188
 structure, jurisdiction, and function of, 457
 trial and appellate, 456–457
 violence in, 494
Courtship violence. *See* Intimate partner violence
Crack cocaine. *See* Cocaine
Credit card theft, 258. *See also* Identity theft
Crime. *See also* categories of crime (e.g., Violent
  crimes), and individual crimes (e.g., Murder)
 act, as an element of, 8
 concept of, 6–10
 criminal law violation required for, 7–8
 data. *See* Crime data, measurement and impact of
 definitional issues, 6–10, 52, 54, 167, 203
 failure to act, as a basis for, 8, 205, 303
 intent requirement for, 8
 measurement of, 20–43
 morality and, 11–15
 property. *See* Property crimes
 reporting of. *See* Crime data, reporting of
 substance abuse and, 88, 321–327
 violent. *See* Violence and violent crimes
Crime Classification System (CCS), 28
Crime control model, 361
Crime data, measurement and impact of, 20–43.
  See also individual crimes (e.g., Murder), and
  categories (e.g., Violent crime
 age and, 25
 agencies contributing to, 23
 analysis of, 37–38
 Bureau of Justice Statistics (BJS) and, 23–24
 cleared by arrest, 22, 24, 246, 247, 253
 climate and, 25
 coding of and lesser included offenses, 25
 Crime Classification System and, 28
 ecology and, 185
 education and, 26
 employment and, 186
 errors in interpretation of, 39–40
 family structure and, 25
 function of, 22
 gender and, 135, 158, 185

intelligence and, 73, 78, 83, 87–88, 91, 183, 208
 juvenile arrests and, 459
 marital status and, 186
 media and. *See* Media
 methods of counting, 24
 misuse of, 22, 23
 mobility and, 25
 NCHIP and, 28
 NCVS and 22, 26
 NIBRS and, 26
 offenders, characteristics of, 30–33
 overview of, 28–30
 political uses of, 37–38
 population density and, 25
 public policy and, 22
 race and ethnicity and, 27, 31–32, 34–35, 186
 reporting of. *See* Crime data, reporting of
 self-report data (SRD), 26–27
 social status and, 25, 186
 sources of, 22–28
 substance abuse and, 27, 321–327
 trends in, 22, 29–30
 types, studies of, 202–203. *See also* individual
  types (e.g. Murder)
 UCR and, 22, 24–26, 29–30
 victims, characteristics of, 33–36
Crime data, reporting of, 22, 25, 206–209, 413
 carjacking, 255
 compstat, 423
 domestic violence and, 214
 elder abuse and, 222
 hate crimes and, 225
 incest and, 221
 intimate personal violence (IPV) and, 25, 206–207,
  208–209, 213, 214, 217
 police procedures and, 25, 413
 race and ethnicity and, 25, 27
 rape and, 207–209, 413, 532
 sex crimes and, 207–209, 213, 392
 shoplifting and, 251, 252
 stalking and, 225
 statutory rape and, 121, 205, 220–221, 298
Crime rates, 9, 23, 158, 172
Crime Victims' Rights statute, 390
Crimes Against Children Research Center, New
  Hampshire, 220
Crimes cleared by arrest, 22, 24, 246, 247
Crimes known to the police, 24, 37
Criminal History Improvement Program, National
  (NCHIP), 28
Criminal justice systems, 357–399 *See also* individual
  components (e.g., Courts); and individual
  stages (e.g., Bail)
 adversary system, 360–365, 466, 469
 assessment of, 393–395
 concepts of, 360–367
 congestion in, 492–493
 costs of. *See* costs
 crime control model of, 361
 critical criminology and, 131
 defendants rights and, 370–388
 discretion in, 365–367
 due process and, 360–361
 equal protection, 360, 361
 gender and, 217, 250, 395–396
 health care issues, 438, 508, 512, 514, 515, 516,
  526–527, 532, 540–542
 stages in the system, 367–370,
 substance abuse, impact on, 327
 systems effect in, 15, 52, 62, 63, 108, 188, 365,
  477–478, 586
 terrorism, issues regarding, 395–396
 victims in. *See* Victims
 victims' rights and, 388–390
 witness participation in, 366, 388, 389, 392. *See
  also* Testimony
 wrongful convictions, 358, 359, 361, 362, 363,
  366, 388, 389, 392, 469
Criminal law
 administrative law compared to, 8–9
 business control and, 307
 civil law compared to, 9
 defined, 8
 elements of, 6–10

social structure and, 126, 212
terrorism. *See* Terrorism
trends in, 30
victimizations reported, 30
youth, factors associated with, 31, 105
Violent Crime Control and Law Enforcement Act, 214
Violent Crime Control and Law Enforcement Act of
  1994, 117, 214, 339, 421, 463, 492, 556
Virginia Tech shootings, 198, 409
Virginia, University of, lacrosse student murder, 409
Virtual child pornography, 236–237
Visitation, in prisons, 524, 525
Vitamins, behavior and, 81
Vocational programs, in prisons, 57, 523, 524, 556, 568
Voir dire, 385, 387
Volstead Act, 340, 380
Voluntary manslaughter, 205
Von Maur department store killings, 368, 409

W

Waivers,
  of constitutional rights, 379
  judicial, 460
  of juveniles to adult courts, 460, 461
Wales, policing in, 404–405
Wall Street. *See* Securities and investment crimes
Walnut Street Jail, 506–507
War, control and, 132
War on drugs, 327–330
Wardens, 57, 508
Warrantless searches, 371
Washington State, pregnant inmates and, 541
Washington State, statutory rape defined in, 220
Watch system, 403
Watchman style, of policing, 436
Watergate, 304

Weapons
  aggravated assault and, 211–212
  carjacking and, 254
  disability, victimization and, 36
  domestic violence and, 215
  gangs and, 117
  gun control legislation, 232–233
  race and ethnicity, victimization and, 34
  robbery and, 210
  school violence and, 120
  used in crime, 25
  violent crime and, 231–234
Wellcome Trust, 82
West Virginia Penitentiary, 533
Western Penitentiary, 507
Whistle-blower claims, 293, 406
White-collar crime. *See also* Business-related crime;
    Corporate crimes
  administrative law, and, 280, 281, 282, 307
  anomie theory and, 112
  conflict perspective and, 127
  crime data and, 186
  critical criminology and, 130
  defined, 280–281
  differential association theory and, 280–281
  left realism and, 132–133
  organized crime, compared to, 345
  sentences and, 308
  social class and, 280–282
  street crime compared to, 132–133
  theories and, 283–285
  victims of, 280, 281, 284, 285, 289, 294, 296, 298,
    300, 303, 307, 308
White-Collar Crime Program (FBI), 302
White House Office of Combating Terrorism, 229
White House, 226, 229
Witchcraft, 85
Witness Protection Program, 339, 348

Witnesses, to crime, 33, 366, 388, 389, 392
Women's liberation theory, 135–141
  anomie and, 112
  critique of, 136–137, 141
  economic marginalization hypothesis, 136, 141
  opportunity theory, 135–136, 141
  power-control theory, 136, 141
Women's Prison Association, 480
Work gang, in prison, 33
Work health and safety rules, 134
Work prisons, 568
Work service, community, 556
Work, life events and, 177
Workplace, substance abuse in, 319
Workplace violations, 130, 134, 298–300
World Health Organization, 81
WorldCom, 292
World Trade Center, 7, 226
Worldwide Cyber Security Summit, 266
Writ, 491
Wrongful convictions, 358, 359, 361, 362, 363, 366,
    388, 389, 392, 469
Wrongful death, 10, 296

X

Xanax, 320, 408, 409
Xe Services, 411–412

Y

Year-and-a-day rule, 204
Youth Services International Inc., 539
Youth ARTS, 585

Z

Zero tolerance policy, 418–419, 529

PHOTO CREDITS